PENNSYLVANIA

GENEALOGIES;

CHIEFLY

SCOTCH-IRISH AND GERMAN.

By
WILLIAM HENRY EGLE, M. D., M. A.

JANAWAY PUBLISHING, INC.
2013

Notice

In many older books, foxing (or discoloration) occurs and, in some instances, print lightens with wear and age. Reprinted books, such as this, often duplicate these flaws, notwithstanding efforts to reduce or eliminate them. The pages of this reprint have been digitally enhanced and, where possible, the flaws eliminated in order to provide clarity of content and a pleasant reading experience.

Copyright © 1896, William Henry Egle

Originally Published:
1896

Reprinted by:

Janaway Publishing, Inc.
732 Kelsey Ct.
Santa Maria, California 93454
(805) 925-1038
www.janawaygenealogy.com

2013

ISBN: 978-1-59641-303-0

Made in the United States of America

PREFATORY.

In the prefatory note to the first edition, published in 1886, the author said :

"This volume is the author's contribution to the Genealogy of his native State. It is the result of years of conscientious labor in this neglected field of our State History, and comprises only a portion of the material which he has gathered. On the reception of this volume, with its limited edition, will depend, in a measure, whether another volume shall follow."

Owing to the demand for this initial volume while in the course of preparation for a second series of "Pennsylvania Genealogies," it has been deemed proper to re-print the same. Corrections and additions have been made, which will add greatly to the permanency of the volume. In due time another series relating to representative Pennsylvania families will appear. Grateful acknowledgements are due to a number of kind friends for their hearty co-operation in this revision.

To
HON. JOHN BLAIR LINN,
of Bellefonte,
In Remembrance of Fraternal Labor
in the
Harvest Fields of History,
These Pennsylvania Family Records
are Sincerely Inscribed.

TABLE OF CONTENTS.

AINSWORTH AND ANDREWS,	1-6
ALLEN OF HANOVER,	7-14
ALRICKS FAMILY,	15-26
ANDERSON OF DONEGAL,	27-36
AWL OF PAXTANG,	37-46
AYRES FAMILY,	47-61
BARNETT FAMILY,	62-77
BEATTY FAMILY,	78-97
BOAS FAMILY,	98-106
BOMBERGER FAMILY,	107-112
BOYD OF DERRY,	113-119
BUCHER FAMILY,	120-142
COWDEN OF PAXTANG,	143-147
CRAIN OF HANOVER,	148-155
DIXON OF DIXON'S FORD,	156-158
THE FAMILY OF EGLE,	159-186
ELDER OF PAXTANG,	187-213
ESPY OF DERRY,	214-227
FERGUSON OF HANOVER,	228-231
FLEMING FAMILY,	232-245
FAMILY OF FORSTER,	246-263
FULTON OF PAXTANG,	264-268
GALBRAITH OF DONEGAL,	269-288
GREGG AND CURTIN,	288-302
GREENAWALT OF LEBANON,	303-314
HAMILTON FAMILY,	315-333
HAY OR HAYS FAMILY,	334-340
KELLER OF LANCASTER,	341-349
KENDIG OF SWATARA,	350-356
FAMILY OF KUNKEL,	357-366
LINN OF LURGAN,	367-382
LYON OF JUNIATA,	383-407
MACLAY OF LURGAN,	408-439
McCORMICK FAMILY	440-487

Table of Contents.

McNair of Derry,	488–491
McNair of Hanover,	492–494
Müller and Lobingier,	495–504
Murray of Harris' Ferry,	505–525
Murray of Swatara,	526–540
Neville and Craig,	541–555
Orth of Lebanon,	556–578
Parker and Denny,	579–604
Roan of Derry,	605–610
Family of Robinson,	611–626
Rutherford of Paxtang,	627–644
Stewart of Drumore,	645–667
Swan Family,	668–673
Thomas of Heidelberg,	674–693
Wallace of Hanover,	694–702
Wallace and Weir,	703–707
Wallace and Hoge,	708–718
Wiestling Family,	719–732
Wiggins and Simonton,	733–739
Wilson of the Irish Settlement,	740–755
Wyeth Family,	756–764
Genealogical Notes.—Byers Family,	765–767
Eagley Family,	767–768
Gray of Paxtang,	768–771
Gross Family,	771–773
Index to Surnames,	775–

AINSWORTH AND ANDREWS.

[Abbreviations—b., born ; d., died ; d. s. p.. died without issue : m., married; s., son ; dau. daughter.]

I. SAMUEL AINSWORTH[1] settled in Hanover township, Lancaster county, Pa., about 1736. His name appears upon the first assessment list (1751) of that township. In that for 1756 it is noted that his son was taken captive by the Indians, and that he had fled from his farm. Little is known of him save that his wife was MARGARET YOUNG, daughter of John Young and Margery Stewart, of Hanover, ancestors of all of the name. We have, however, the record of but one of his children, although the names of two :

2.   i. *John*, b. 1740 ; m. Margaret Mayes.
     ii. *Lazarus*, d. March, 1777 ; m. Margaret ———— ; no issue—leaving his estate to his brother John.

II. JOHN AINSWORTH,[2] (Samuel,[1]) b. 1740, in Hanover township, Lancaster county, Pa.; d. August 14, 1812, in Hanover township, and there buried ; m. in 1764, MARGARET MAYES, dau. of James Mayes ; b. 1744 ; d. September 13, 1828. They had issue :

3.   i. *Samuel*, b. November 11, 1765 ; m. Margaret McEwen.
     ii. *Nancy* [Agnes], b. January 8, 1767 ; m. William Allen. (*see Allen record.*)
4.   iii. *James*, b. February 5, 1770 ; m. Lydia Crain.
5.   iv. *John*, b. June 30, 1772 ; m. Mary Stewart.
6.   v. *Elizabeth*, b August 26, 1774 ; m. Hugh Andrews.
     vi. *Margaret*, b. November 24, 1777 ; m. Thomas Brown.
     vii. *Sally*. b. November 18, 1780 ; m. James Todd.
     viii. *Jean*, b. July 2, 1784 ; m. John Snodgrass.
     ix. *Matthew*, b. February 1, 1787 ;. d. s. p.

III. SAMUEL AINSWORTH,[3] (John,[2] Samuel,[1]) b. November 11, 1765, in Hanover ; d. February, 1798, in Philadelphia. He was brought up on his father's farm in Hanover, receiving a year's education in Philadelphia in addition to that acquired in the schools in the neighborhood. After the organization of the county he became quite prominent, and twice elected to the Legislature. He died while in attendance on this body. Mr. Ainsworth m., May 10, 1792, by Rev. James Snodgrass, MARGARET McEWEN, dau. of Richard McEwen, b. 1770, in Hanover; d. October 29, 1867, near Lancaster, Ohio. They had issue:

7.   *i. John*, b. Feb. 15, 1793; Sarah Hulings.
8.   *ii. Jane-Eliza*, b. Oct. 29, 1794; m. David Ewing.
9. *iii. Richard-McEwen*, b. 1796; m. Emily Hollister.

IV. JAMES AINSWORTH,³ (John,² Samuel,¹) b. Feb. 5, 1770, in Hanover; d. in 1803; m. LYDIA CRAIN, b. 1770, dau. of George Crain, of Hanover. They had issue:

    i. John, d. in Franklin, Warren county, O.; m. Sarah (Vail) Jenkins, and had *Sarah* and *Elizabeth*.
   ii. George-Crain, d. in Fairfield, O.; m. Matilda Cox, and had *Sarah* and *Lydia*.
  iii. Samuel, m. Mercy Searles, and had *Enos, Mary, Samuel*, and *Nancy-Jane*.
  iv. Nancy, b. Nov. 11, 1803; m. Nov. 29, 1825, James Lucas, b. July 4, 1798, and had issue (surname Lucas) *Mary-Jane, Lydia-Ann, Margaret, Caroline*, and *Miranda*.
   v. James, m. and left two sons residing in Van Wert county, O.
  vi. Joseph, m. Mary Beetle, and left issue.
 vii. Martha, d. s. p.
viii. Margaret, m. Nathan Anderson, and left issue.
  ix. William, d. in the army, at Pittsburgh Landing; m. Susan Mitten, and left issue.
   x. Elizabeth, m. Henry Van Riper, of Van Wert county, O. and had issue.

V. JOHN AINSWORTH,³ (John,² Samuel,¹) b. June 30, 1777, in Hanover; removed to Ohio about 1803, and after some years returned to Pennsylvania, residing two or three years near New Market, York county. He then went back to Ohio, settling in Montgomery county. He died Dec. 11, 1827, and was buried at Bath, Greene county, O. He m. MARY STEWART; she subsequently m. Hugh Wilson, removed to Crawfordsville, Ind., where she died.

VI. ELIZABETH AINSWORTH,³ (John,² Samuel,¹) b. August 26, 1774; d. September 1, 1850, in Dayton, O.; was twice married; first, Sept. 10, 1799, HUGH ANDREWS, b. August 31, 1764. in Hanover township Lancaster, now Dauphin, county, Pa.; d. May, 1811, in Dayton, O.; son of James Andrews and Jean Strain.* Hugh Andrews was twice married; first, on the 25th of December, 1789, Ann Speer, d. May 25, 1799, without issue. The children of Elizabeth Ainsworth and Hugh Andrews were (surname Andrews):

10. *i. Nancy-Spear*, b. Oct. 1, 1800; m. David Shaw.
11. *ii. Samuel-Ainsworth*, b. Jan. 28, 1802; m. Margaret Ramsey.
12. *iii. James*, b. Nov. 26, 1805; m. Mary-Cornelia Van Cleve.
13. *iv. Eliza*, b. Dec. 17, 1807; m. Alexander Stephen.
14. *v. Hugh*, b. Sept. 2, 1810; m. Phœbe Cook.

Mrs. Elizabeth Ainsworth Andrews, m. 2dly, April 22, 1813, JAMES GUTHRIE, b. August 19, 1784; d. August 3, 1860, and had issue (surname Guthrie):

vi. Abelard, b. March 9, 1814; m. Nancy Brown.
vii. Eloise, b. June 19, 1817; m. Jacob Light.
viii. Margaret, b. May 19, 1819; m. Isaac Strohm.

VII. JOHN AINSWORTH,⁴ (Samuel,³ John,² Samuel,¹) b. February 15, 1793, in Hanover; d. February 15, 1860, in Sidney, O.; bur. at Piqua; m., February 24, 1820, SARAH HULINGS, b. September 29, 1798; d. May 3, 1839. They had issue:

---

*JOHN ANDREWS, a native of Londonderry, Ireland, came to Pennsylvania in 1737, and located on the Manada, in Hanover township, Lancaster county. His name appears on the first assessment for the "East End of Hanover." Among his children were *Robert, John*, and *James*. Robert Andrews d. Sept., 1762, leaving a wife, Agnes, and children, *John, Robert, Margaret, Arthur, Mary, Humphrey, Moses*, and *Agnes*. James Andrews, son of John, d. December, 1785. He married, March 8, 1761, Jean Strain, daughter of John Strain, of Hanover. They had issue:

i. *John*, b. 1762.
ii. *Hugh*, b. August 31, 1764; m. 1st, Ann Speer; 2d, Elizabeth Ainsworth.
iii. *Elizabeth*, m. Robert Thompson, of Franklin county, Pa.

 i. Eliza-Mary, b. March 24, 1821; m. April 15, 1841, James Black, b. September 22, 1814, in Perry county, Pa., and had issue.

 ii. Samuel-Hulings, b. April 5, 1824; d. August 26, 1829.

 iii. John-Mayes, b. September 30, 1826; m. Elizabeth L. Swingley, and had issue.

 iv. Dr. Richard-McEwen, b. April 5, 1829; m. June 17, 1858, Rebecca-Anna Neal, of Sidney, O., and had issue.

 v. Ephraims-Huling, b. August 13, 1832; m. Jane Gaston Anderson, and had issue.

 vi. Manassah-Newton, b. March 23, 1835; m. Miss Hamil, of Leavenworth, Kansas.

 vii. David-Ewing, b. June 17, 1837; entered the army as lieutenant; promoted captain; killed at Spottsylvania C. H., May 12, 1864.

VIII. JANE ELIZA AINSWORTH,[4] (Samuel,[3] John,[2] Samuel,[1]) b. October 25, 1794, in Hanover; d. near Lancaster, O.; m. January 9, 1810, DAVID EWING, b. October 20, 1784; d. December 30, 1844; was for a number of years judge of the courts. They had one son, *David*.

IX. RICHARD McEWEN AINSWORTH,[4] (Samuel,[3] John,[2] Samuel,[1]) b. 1796, in Hanover township; d. March 14, 1847, in Fairview, O.; m. EMILY HOLLISTER; and had *Juliet*, m. Joseph C. Kincaid, of Lancaster, O. The widow of Mr. Ainsworth subsequently married a Mr. Rogers, of Circleville, O.

X. NANCY SPEER ANDREWS,[4] (Elizabeth,[3] John,[2] Samuel,[1]) b. October 1, 1800; m. July 29, 1819, DAVID SHAW, and had issue (surname Shaw):

 i. Charles-Green, b. May 20, 1820: m. June, 1850, Sallie Carr, and had *Charles-Green* and *Frank*.

 ii. George-Wilson, b. November 19, 1822; m. November, 1852, Mary dau. of James Perrine, and had *Ella, Nancy-Andrews, Julia-Daret, James-Perrine*, and *George*.

 iii. Elizabeth-Mary, b. May 10, 1832; m. June 10, 1853, Jonathan Richards, of Chicago, Ill., and had (surname Richards) *Charles* and *Anna*.

 iv. Eleanora, b. August 21, 1844; m. Charles S. Hunt, of Chicago, Ill., and had (surname Hunt) *Jennie* and *Lizzie*.

 v. Theodore-Andrews, b. November 20, 1836; m. Sallie Van Doren, and had issue.

 vi. Edwin-Clinton, b. September 10, 1842; m. Alice Winters.

XI. SAMUEL AINSWORTH ANDREWS,[4] (Elizabeth,[3] John,[2] Samuel,[1]) b. January 28, 1802; m. February 3, 1831, MARGARET RAMSEY, and had issue (surname Andrews):

    i. Mary-Eliza, b. February 19, 1832; m. October 18, 1849, Rev. Patterson Reece, d. January 23, 1855, and had (surname Reece) *Patterson-Andrews*.
    ii. Hugh, b. March 16, 1834; a lawyer of Jonesboro', Illinois.
    iii. James-Ramsey, b. May 25, 1836; m. Alice Hagenbach.
    iv. John, b. December 15, 1837.
    v. Elizabeth-Agnes, b. March 9, 1840; m. Rev. James T. Pollock.
    vi. George-Washington, b. February 22, 1842; a lawyer of Murfreesboro', Illinois.
    vii. Sarah-Ellen, b. January 14, 1844.
    viii. Anna-Isabella, b. August 8, 1846.
    ix. William-Chalmers, b. August 13, 1850; d. August 17, 1866.
    x. Margaret-Effie, b. August 25, 1852.

XII. JAMES ANDREWS,[4] (Elizabeth,[3] John,[2] Samuel,[1]) b. November 26, 1805; m. November 20, 1827, MARY CORNELIA VAN CLEVE, b. December 2, 1807. They had issue (surname Andrews):

    i. Benjamin-Van-Cleve, b. September 5, 1828; m. Samantha Bucher.
    ii. America, b. April 8, 1835.
    iii. Franklin-Morrow, b. August 22, 1838; m. Mary Eloisa Price.
    iv. John-Van-Cleve, b. May 5, 1842.
    v. Samuel-Dover, b. October 11, 1844.
    vi. Laura-N., b. April 8, 1849.

XIII. ELIZA ANDREWS,[4] (Elizabeth,[3] John,[2] Samuel,[1]) b. December 17, 1807; d. February 4, 1860, at Xenia, Ohio; m. ALEXANDER STEPHEN. They had issue (surname Stephen):

    i. Elizabeth-Ann, m. —— Loomis.
    ii. Nancy-Jane, m. —— Williams.
    iii. Hugh-Andrews, m. Artemisia ——.
    iv. Eloise-Margaret, m. Luther Haines.
    v. Charles-Alexander, m. Mary Lester.
    vi. John-Ainsworth, m. Harriet Galbraith.
    vii. Martha-Isabella, m. —— Dunn.
    viii. George-Washington.
    ix. Eleanora.

XIV. HUGH ANDREWS,[4] (Elizabeth,[3] John,[2] Samuel,[1]) b. September 2, 1810; d. March, 1862; m., January 18. 1831, PHŒBE COOK, b. March, 1810. They had issue (surname Andrews):

 i. Angelina, b. Jan. 7, 1833; m. Jan. 18, 1855, Levi Kirby.
 ii. Abraham, b. July 12, 1835; m. Dec. 30, 1855, Jane Pearson.
 iii. Samuel, b. Jan. 10, 1841; m. ―――― Hollingshead.
 iv. Elenora, b. May 7, 1846; m. John Cochran.
 v. Joseph-Wilbur, b. Dec. 4, 1848.
 vi. Eliza, b. Oct. 11, 1851.

ALLEN OF HANOVER.

I. WILLIAM ALLEN,[1] b. in Scotland; left his native country on account of religious persecutions, and settled in the Province of Ulster, Ireland. Whether he came to America cannot now be determined. He had, among other children, two sons:

  2.   *i. William*, b. February, 1709; m. Elizabeth ———.
  3.   *ii. Joseph.*

II. WILLIAM ALLEN,[2] (William,[1]) b. February, 1709, in county Antrim, Ireland; d. December 26, 1784. He came to America about 1730, and settled in Hanover township, Lancaster, now Dauphin county, Pa. His name appears on all the early Provincial tax lists, and in 1777 took the oath of allegiance. His w fe, ELIZABETH, b. March, 1705; d. May 3, 1800. They had issue, all b. in Hanover:

    i. John.
    ii. Sarah, m. James Dixon.
    iii. Jean, m. John Sawyer.
    iv. Elizabeth, m. Samuel Mann.
    v. Mary, m. John Snodgrass.
  4. *vi. Samuel*, m. Rebecca Smith.
  5. *vii. William*, b. 1744; m. Rebecca Green.

III. JOSEPH ALLEN,[2] (William,[1]) arrived in the Province of Pennsylvania about the year of his brother's coming (1730) and died soon after in Philadelphia; m. in Ireland, and had issue:

  6.   *i. Joseph*, m. Jane Riddle.
    ii. Thomas (see *Penn'a Archives, 3d. ser., vol. i., pp. 349, 418.*)

IV. SAMUEL ALLEN,[3] (William,[2] William,[1]) b. in the county Antrim, Ireland, and died prior to 1788; m. by Rev. John Roan, of Derry church, REBECCA SMITH. Samuel Allen's name appears on the petition against the division of Hanover township, February, 1769, and also on the Provincial assessment lists. They had issue, all born in Hanover:

i. Mary, b. September 9, 1765 ; d. March 10, 1806 ; m. Captain John Barnett. (*see Barnett record.*)

7. *ii. William,* b. May 16, 1767 ; m. Nancy Ainsworth.

iii. Robert, b. July 14, 1769.

iv. Elizabeth, b. July 20, 1771 ; m. October, 1792, by Rev. J. Snodgrass, David Strain, and had (surname Strain) *William, James,* and a *daughter,* who married Samuel Hiser.

v. David, b. 1773 ; m. —— Price, of Barren county, Kentucky, where he lived and died.

vi. Samuel, b. 1776.

V. WILLIAM ALLEN,[3] (William,[2] William,[1]) b. 1744 ; d. October 16, 1794. He was a lieutenant in Colonel Green's battalion, Revolutionary army, and was wounded in the arm at the battle of White Plains, and taken prisoner. He was accidently killed at a cider press, and buried in old Hanover churchyard. Colonel Allen, m., in 1780, REBECCA GREEN, daughter of Colonel Timothy Green. After his death his children were sent to school at Lititz and Philadelphia. Mrs. Allen remained a widow some years, and then married Moses Barnett. She died July 30, 1837. Colonel Allen's children were :

i. Elizabeth, (1st,) b. 1781 ; d. 1786.

ii. Effy, b. October 19, 1783 ; d. January 25, 1811 ; m. February 16, 1804, by Rev. James Snodgrass, Robert Rogers, and had (surname Rogers) *Rebecca,* b. May 1, 1805, m. Thomas Mitchell McCormick ; *Andrew,* b. 1806, d. 1845 ; *William-Allen,* b. 1809, d. 1855 ; was judge of the courts at Springfield, O.; and *Robert-Henderson,* b. June 25, 1811.

iii. William, b. 1785 ; d. in Philadelphia, by accidental poisoning.

iv. Elizabeth, (2d,) b. April 16, 1789; bap. July 26, 1789 ; m.. March 13, 1813, Joseph Barnett, of Hanover. (*see Barnett record.*)

v. Timothy-Green, b. June, 1791 ; bap. July 11, 1791. In the war of 1812, he and his cousin, Joseph Barnett, enlisted in the Chambersburg Union Volunteers, Captain McClintock. He was taken ill on the march to Buffalo, New York, and died at an inn, seven miles from that town, on the 12th of December, 1812. In 1867, Isaac Moorhead, of Erie, had his remains removed to Pennsylvania and placed beside those of his mother.

Allen of Hanover.

VI. JOSEPH ALLEN³ (Joseph,² William¹) was brought to this country when a boy by his father, who died in Philadelphia. Settled on the Manada, in Hanover township, and d. March 24, 1817. Joseph Allen signed the petition against the division of Hanover township in 1769. His name is on the Provincial assessment lists. He was a contributor and a member of old Hanover church, where he and his wife were buried. He m. JANE RIDDLE, daughter of James and Janett Riddle, of Hanover, b. 1729, d. January 6, 1804. They had issue:

8. i *James*, m. Elizabeth Painter.
    ii. *Jane*, d. in infancy.
9. iii. *Joseph*, b. Jan. 25, 1768 ; m. Eleanor McEwen.
    iv *Margaret*, m. Mar. 25, 1790, by Rev. J. Snodgrass, Charles Brown ; settled in Warren county, Ohio, about 1800, and had issue (surname Brown):

    1. *James*, m. Jane Crain.
    2. *William*, m. Martha McVeagh.
    3. *Joseph*, m. Lucinda Corbett, of Pa.
    4. *Jane*, m. Joseph Barnett.
    5. *Mary*.
    6. *Martha*, m. Wm. Crain.
    7. *Agnes*, m. Horatio Claypool.

10. v. *John*, m. Hannah Sawyer.
11. vi. *Robert*, m. Nancy McNamara.
    vii. *Tristram*, d. July 8, 1817 ; buried at Hanover church.

VII. WILLIAM ALLEN,³ (Samuel,² William,¹) b. in Hanover, May 16, 1767 ; d. Nov. 14, 1844 ; m. March 18, 1790, by Rev. J. Snodgrass, NANCY AINSWORTH, daughter of John Ainsworth and Margaret Mayes, b. Jan. 8, 1767 ; d. Jan. 2, 1845. Their children, all born in Hanover, were :

12. i. *Samuel*, b. 1791 ; m. Eleanor Brown.
    ii. *Margaret*, b. 1794 ; m. John Mahargue; lived and died in Halifax, Dauphin county, Pa.
    iii. *Rebecca*, b. July 24, 1796 ; m. Dec. 15, 1816, by Rev. J. Snodgrass, David Espy. (*see Espy record*.)
    iv. *Nancy*, b. August 10, 1799 ; m. Samuel Todd.
    v. *Mary*, (Polly,) b. 1802 ; d. in Hanover, July 4, 1822.
    vi. *Sally*, b. 1803 ; m. George W. Dumars ; d. Sept. 15, 1869, near Tivoli, Peoria county, Ill.
    vii. *William*, b. March 1, 1809 ; m. Mary Albright.

VIII. JAMES ALLEN,⁴ (Joseph,³ Joseph,² William,¹) m. ELIZABETH PAINTER, who died in 1818. They had issue, all born in Hanover:

    i. Joseph, moved to Illinois in 1829.
    ii. John, d. near Linglestown in 1878.
    iii Thomas, moved to Iowa.
    iv. James, moved to Iowa.
    v Mary, d. at 14 years of age.
    vi. Jane, d. at 24 years of age.
    vii. Eleanor, moved to Iowa.

IX. JOSEPH ALLEN,⁴ (Joseph,³ Joseph,² William,¹) b. in Hanover, Jan. 25, 1768; d. Oct. 1, 1839; m. May 6, 1794, by Rev. James Snodgrass, ELEANOR McEWEN, b. Sept. 12, 1769; d. Feb. 1, 1834; both buried in Hanover grave-yard. Major Joseph Allen was a prominent citizen of Hanover township, and a contributor and a member of old Hanover church from 1795 until his death. Their children, all born in Hanover, were:

    i. Jane (1st), b. July 22, 1795; d. May 3, 1803.
    ii. John, b. March 5, 1797; merchant in Harrisburg, and moved thence to Springfield, Ill.; m. Mary Ramsey, and d. 1874, leaving three sons and three daughters.
14. *iii. Joseph*, b. Nov. 10, 1798; m. Mary Krider.
    iv. Eleanor, b. Sept. 27, 1800; d. Sept., 1873; m. James B. Oliver, of West Newton, Westmoreland county, Pa.
15. *v. Robert*, b. May 7, 1803; m. Eleanor Bucher.
    vi. Mary Elizabeth (1st), b. Nov. 5, 1805; died in infancy.
    vii. Margaret, b. June 24, 1809; d. 1881, in Blair county, Pa.
    viii. Jane (2d), b. July 27, 1812.
16. *ix. Mary-Elizabeth* (2d), b. Oct. 6, 1814.

X. JOHN ALLEN,⁴ (Joseph,³ Joseph,² William,¹) b. in Hanover township, August, 1769; m. Feb., 1800, HANNAH SAWYER, b. Feb., 1775, of Derry township in now Dauphin county, Pa., who died 1819, and buried in Hanover graveyard. John Allen moved to Franklin, Warren county, Ohio, about 1823, and d. August 27, 1839. From thence the family moved to Covington, Fountain county, Indiana, where many of his descendants now reside. They had issue, all born in Hanover township, Dauphin county, Pa.:

i. Jane, b. 1801; d. Aug. 27, 1812.
   ii. Nancy, b. April 16, 1802; d. Nov. 21, 1871; m. Christian S· Vickers, who d. 1886; they had (surname Vickers) *Allen-S., Joseph-A.*, and *William-E.*
   iii. Margaret, b. Augt. 11, 1804; d. April 12, 1849; m. Feb. 26, 1829, John B. Crain, who d. 1880; had issue, 5 sons and 4 daughters.
   iv. Sarah, b. Feb. 6, 1809; d. May 12, 1882; m. Aug. 21, 1832, William V. Du Bois, b. Dec. 6, 1811, d. April 5, 1885; they had (surname Du Bois) *Hannah-J., Denice, Sarah E., Willampy, Joseph-A., William-Treon, M.-Maria, Nancy M., John-T., Emma-*E., and *Walter-S.*
   v. John, b. May, 1811; d. March 11, 1874; m. 1836, Sarah Pressler, b. in Centre county, Pa., June 15, 1815, d. April 27, 1883; they had issue, eleven children.
   vi. Joseph, b. July 24, 1814; d. Feb. 17, 1877; m. Nov., 1841, Mary J McFadden, of Richmond, Ind., who d. Aug. 13, 1863; they had issue, all born in Covington, Indiana:

       1. *John*, b. Sept. 16, 1843; d. in infancy.
17.   2. *James-L.*, b. May 24, 1845.
       3. *Viola*, b. Feb. 29, 1848.
       4. *Joseph*, b. Sept. 2, 1850; d. in infancy.
       5. *Mack*, b. July 18, 1853; d. young.
       6. *Lenora*, b. July 19, 1859; d. in infancy.
       7. *Frank*, b. April 6, 1861.

   vii. Hannah, b. Feb. 16, 1815; d. Dec. 15, 1801; m. March 18, 1832, Jeremiah C. Ludlow, b. April 28, 1811, d. Aug. 20, 1870; they had issue, ten children

XI. ROBERT ALLEN,[4] (Joseph,[3] Joseph,[2] William,[1]) m. NANCY MCNAMARA, and in 1822 moved from Hanover to Frankstown, on the Juniata, where he died in 1830. They had issue:

   i. Anna–Jane, d. in Frankstown, 1832.
   ii. Margaret, d. in Hollidaysburg, 1878.
   iii. Sarah, d. in Altoona, 1874.
   iv. Joseph, d. in Ohio.
   v. Robert, lives in Hastings-on-Hudson.

XII. SAMUEL ALLEN,[5] (William,[4] Samuel,[3] William,[2] William,[1]) b. in Hanover in 1791; bap. Feb. 3, 1792; d. Jan. 23, 1863, in Three Rivers, Mich.; m. 1822, ELEANOR BROWN, who d. Nov. 23, 1859. They had issue:

i. Nancy-Jane, b. 1823 ; m. Elias R. Millman of Three Rivers, Mich.
ii. Mary, b. 1825 ; m. Joseph W. Marshall of Bellefonte, Pa.
iii. William, b. 1827 ; m. Sally McKee of Vincennes, Ind., and had *William-Archibald, Anna-Mary, Ella*, and *Samuel-Brown*
iv. Samuel-Brown, b. 1830; m. Elizabeth Smith, of Franklin county, Ohio, and had *Nellie, Rumney*, and *William-Smith*.
v. Sally-Margaret, b. 1832.

XIII. WILLIAM ALLEN,[5] (William,[4] Samuel,[3] William,[2] William,[1]) b. March 1, 1809 ; m. MARY ALBRIGHT, and d. in Hanover, 1880. They had issue :

i. William.
ii Mary-Jane.
iii. Rebecca-Emerson.
iv. John-Marshall.

XIV. JOSEPH ALLEN,[5] (Joseph,[4] Joseph,[3] Joseph,[2] William,[1]) born in Hanover, November 10, 1798 ; d. in Washington county, Iowa, November 23, 1869; m. MARY KRIDER, of Selinsgrove, Snyder county, Pennsylvania, who was b. in 1808, and d. January 18, 1879. They moved to then Iowa Territory, near Burlington, November 10, 1841. They had issue :

i. Ellen-M., b. February 5, 1837 ; m. September 20, 1863, J. B. Goble, of Cass county, Michigan.
ii. Mary-E., b. November 20, 1838 ; d. early.
iii. Robert, b. December 4, 1840; d. February 6, 1862, in the War of the Rebellion.
iv. John-G., b. September 29, 1844 ; d. May 20, 1863, in the War of the Rebellion.
v. Joseph, b. March 4, 1846 ; m., July 3, 1877, Eva Craig, and lives near Riverside, Washington county, Iowa.
vi. Mary-C., b. February 26, 1850 ; m. March 5, 1876, D. W. Ott, of Riverside, Washington county, Iowa.

XV. ROBERT ALLEN ;[5] (Joseph,[4] Joseph,[3] Joseph,[2] William,[1]) b. in Hanover, May 7, 1803 ; d. July 29, 1872, and is buried in Laurel Hill Cemetery, Philadelphia ; m. January 21, 1830, ELEANOR BUCHER, daughter of Jacob Bucher, of Harrisburg, Pa., (*see Bucher record.*) Robert Allen commenced merchandising in Harrisburg, but changed his residence to Philadelphia in 1828, where he became a wholesale merchant and manufacturer. He was prominent in politics and in the church, and held numerous public and responsible positions, as bank director, railroad director, and commissioner of the old Richmond district before consolidation in 1854. They had one daughter, *Susan-Bucher*, b. May 21, 1832 ; d. June 9, 1889, and buried in Laurel Hill Cemetery.

XVI. MARY ELIZABETH ALLEN,[5] (Joseph,[4] Joseph,[3] Joseph,[2] William,[1]) b. Oct. 6, 1814, in Hanover Township, Dauphin co., Pa., m. Oct. 27, 1842, by Rev. James Snodgrass, the Rev. ADIE K. BELL ; b. Dec. 9, 1815 ; d. Aug. 25, 1888. Mr. Bell was a son of Edward Bell, Esq., one of the oldest and most noted pioneer settlers of Tuckahoe Valley, Blair county, and Mary A. Martin, his wife. He was educated at Washington College, Washington, Pa., entered the Baptist ministry and filled successive charges at Hollidaysburg, Logans Valley, Lewisburg, Allegheny City, and died during his large charge at Altoona, 1882–88. Buried at Lewisburg, Pa. They had issue (surname Bell):

    i. Mary, b. in Hollidaysburg; m. Rev. Aaron Wilson, of Rochester, Pa.
    ii. Robert-Allen, d. in early youth.
    iii. Ellen-Allen, b., Feb'y 15, 1848, in Logans Valley, Pa.; m. Calvin Roller, M. D., of Hollidaysburg, Pa.
    iv. Martin, b. Sept. 30, 1849, in Logans Valley, Pa.; educated at the University at Lewisburg, Pa.; admitted to the Blair county bar May, 1873, and on November 7, 1893, was elected President Judge of the 24th Judicial District, Blair county, Pa. Residence, Hollidaysburg. Judge Bell m. May 21, 1877, Irene Lemon, daughter of Robert M. Lemon and his wife, Eliza Blair, both of Hollidaysburg. They had issue :

        1. *Eliza-Blair.*
        2. *Elizabeth-Allen.*
        3. *Roberta-F.*
        4. *Adie-Kyle.*
        5. *Martin.*

    v. David, d. in infancy.

XVII. JAMES L. ALLEN,[6] (Joseph,[5] John,[4] Joseph,[3] Joseph,[2]

William,[1]) b. May 24, 1845, in Covington, Indiana ; m., November 7, 1866, LOURISSA CAMPBELL, daughter of Abram Campbell, of Fountain county, Indiana, Clerk of the Circuit and Common Pleas Courts of Fountain county, to which he was elected consecutive terms. They had issue :

  i. H.-Grace, b. Dec. 26, 1868 ; m. Granville Adkins.
  ii. Alvis, d. in infancy.
  iii. Wilbur, b. Sept. 22, 1872 ; d. Oct. 13, 1879.
  iv. Helen, b. Nov. 15, 1874.
  v. James-L., b. Feb'y 13, 1878.
  vi. Ethel, b. April 1, 1879 : d. in infancy.
  viii. Russell, b. Feb'y 22, 1881.

ALRICKS FAMILY.

On the 19th of December, 1656, JACOB ALRICKS, whose father is supposed to have been Claes Alricks, born *circa* 1603, at Groeningen, Holland, was appointed by the Burgomasters and Council of the city of Amsterdam, Governor of that city's colony on the Delaware. He sailed from the Texel on the 25th of the same month, in the ship *Printz Maurits*, and reached the American coast on the 8th of March following. The vessel was wrecked on Long Island, but, fortunately, every man was saved, as well as their baggage, the vessel being merely stranded. He, subsequently, through the kindness of some natives, reached Manhattan Island (New York). On the 16th of April, he sailed in the ship *Bever* from the harbor of New Amsterdam, and arrived at Fort New Amstel, on the Delaware, five days after. He at once assumed command, and sent forward, by the first opportunity, a full report of the condition of the Dutch Colony on the Delaware. His position was far from an easy one. Not only the Swedes, who had been the first settlers, and whose conquest had been made by the Dutch under Stuveysant, Governor of all the New Netherlands, but the English, as also the Maryland colonists, gave him considerable concern. Besides, the Dutch themselves were more or less dissatisfied on account of the failure of the crops for several years in succession, and this operated in retarding emigration. By direction of the commissioners, he made treaties with the Indians for lands, prepared a map of the country, and employed his utmost exertions to promote trade on the Delaware. On the 30th of December, 1659, aged fifty-six years, Governor Jacob Alricks died at New Amstel. His papers and property were sequestrated by his successor, Governor D'Hinayossa, but Governor-General Stuveysant ordered their release "on pain of disgrace;" bearing testimony that he was "a man of discreet character." Mr. Alricks' wife died January 6, 1658; and both were buried in old Drawyer's church-yard, near Odessa, New Castle county, Delaware. There was no issue.

I. PIETER ALRICKS, a nephew of Jacob Alricks, and whose father is supposed to have been also named Pieter, was sent, in 1658, by the Dutch Government, with instructions for New Netherlands, and, more than probable, with the intention of remaining in the new country. In March, 1659, we find him carrying on trade in the "Hore-Kihl." In January, 1660, D'Hinayossa appointed him commander there. On the 6th of September, 1664, New Amsterdam was captured by the English, and Governor-General Stuveysant expelled. Thirteen days after, Sir Robert Carr appeared on the Delaware, and in a fortnight thereafter took the Dutch forts. The estate of Pieter Alricks was confiscated; but some years afterward the Dutch again obtained possession not only of the banks of the Delaware, but also of Fort Amsterdam, now New York city, and held possession until the English Governor, Andross, arrived, and then the annals inform us: "Nov. 10, 1674, Fort Amsterdam, New York, was this day surrendered to Governor Andross, and all the magistrates in office at the time of the Dutch coming here to be reinstated for the Delaware river, except Pieter Alricks, he having proffered himself to the Dutch at their first coming of his own motion, and acted very violent as their chief officer ever since." Commissary Alricks subsequently swore fidelity to the English, and continued his trade on the South river. In August, 1672, he was appointed bailiff for New Castle, on the Delaware; in October, 1677, commissioned one of its justices, and re-commissioned June 7, 1680, being one of the justices in commission when the Proprietary Government was formed. He was a member of the first Assembly of the Province, 1682 and 1683, and from 1685 to 1689 served as one of the Provincial Councillors. In 1685, William Penn bought out the title of the Indians in a large body of land lying between Philadelphia and Wilmington, extending back from the Delaware river as far as a man "can ride in two days with a horse." The first witness to this Indian deed is Pieter Alricks. He was commissioned one of the justices of the peace for the Lower Counties, April 13, 1690, and again May 2, 1693. On the 2d of September, 1690, he was also appointed a judge of the Provincial Court, serving until 1693. Pieter Alricks died in 1697, aged about sixty-five years. His children according to his will were:

  i. Sigfridus; nothing known.
  ii. Hermanus; d. in 1707, leaving a wife Mary.
  iii. Jacobus; m. and among other children, had *Peter·Sigfridus,* who m. Susanna Stidham and left a large family.
2. *iv. Wessels,* (or Weselius;) m. and left issue.

II. WESSELS, or WESELIUS ALRICKS,³ (Pieter,² Pieter,¹) b. circa 1670, in New Castle county, Delaware; d. there circa 1730. He was very prominent in the affairs of New Castle county, and was sheriff in 1700; he subsequently removed to Philadelphia, and held several important offices under the Proprietary. He m. and left at least four children.

  i. Peter.
  ii. Sigfridus.
  iii. Murtha.
3. *iv. Hermanus,* b. *circ* 1715; m. Ann West.

III. HERMANUS ALRICKS,⁴ (Wessels,³ Pieter,² Pieter,¹) b. about 1715 in Philadelphia; d. December 14, 1772, in Carlisle, Cumberland county. He resided some years in his native city, but afterwards settled in Cumberland county. He was chosen the first member of the General Assembly from that county, and was commissioned prothonotary, etc., of Cumberland, and also a justice of the peace. Until his death he was a man of mark and influence in the valley west of the Susquehanna. Hermanus Alricks was twice married, for we find by the Administration book F, p. 322, Philadelphia, that letters of administration were granted to Hermanus Alricks, of Cumberland county, on the estate of Sarah Alricks, June 19, 1750, he being designated as her husband. There was probably no issue. He m. secondly, ANN WEST, b. 1733, at Clover Hill, near Sligo, Ireland; d. November 21, 1791, in Donegal township, Lancaster county, and is buried in the old church graveyard there. She was the daughter of Francis West, Sen. They had issue:

Pennsylvania Genealogies.

   i. William, b. 1758.
4. *ii. Ann*, b. October 7, 1760 ; m. Alexander Boggs.
   iii. Hermanus, b. 1762 ; d. 1840 ; settled in Baltimore, Md.; m. Jane Parks, d. 1844 ; and they had issue : *Margaret, Ann, Francis-West, Jane-A., Harriet-Parks.* and *Thomas-Parks.*
   iv. West, b. 1765.
5. *v. James*, b. December 2, 1769 ; m. Martha Hamilton.

  Mrs. Alricks subsequently married Col. Alexander Lowrey* of Donegal, and by him there was issue (surname Lowrey):

   i. Fannie, b. Feb. 1, 1775 ; m. Samuel Evans.

---

  *ALEXANDER LOWREY, the son of Lazarus Lowrey, was born in the north of Ireland, in December, 1725. His parents, with several elder children, came to America in 1729, and settled in Donegal township, Lancaster county, Pennsylvania. His father became an Indian trader, which occupation Alexander entered about 1748, in partnership with Joseph Simon of the town of Lancaster, the fur trade with the Indians being at that period quite lucrative. The connection with Mr. Simon, continuing for forty years, was finally closed and settled without a word of difference between them, with large gains resulting, over many and severe losses from Indian depredations on their trains and trading posts. Mr. Lowrey was, from the first, outspoken and ardent for separation from the mother-country. In July, 1774, he was placed on the Committee of Correspondence for Lancaster, and was a member of the Provincial Conference held in Philadelphia on the 15th of that month ; and of that convened in Carpenters' Hall, 18th of June, 1776 ; and of the Convention of the 15th of July following. He was chosen to the Assembly in 1775, and, with the exception of two or three years, served as a member of that body almost uninterruptly until 1789. In May, 1777, he was appointed one of the commissioners to procure blankets for the army. In 1776 he commanded the Third Battalion of the Lancaster County Associators, and was in active service in the Jerseys during that year. As senior colonel, he commanded the Lancaster county militia at the battle of the Brandywine. At the close of the Revolution, Colonel Lowrey retired to his fine farm adjoining Marietta. Under the Constitution of 1789-90, he was commissioned by Governor Mifflin justice of the peace, an office he held until his death, which occurred on the 31st of January, 1805. His remains lie interred in Donegal church graveyard. Colonel Lowrey was a remarkable man in many respects, and his life an eventful one, whether considered in his long career in the Indian trade, a patriot of the Revolution, or the many years in which he gave his time and means to the service of his country. He

IV. ANN ALRICKS,⁵ (Hermanus,⁴ Wessels,³ Pieter,² Pieter,¹) b. October 7, 1760, in Cumberland county, Penn'a; d. September 20, 1847, in Donegal township, Lancaster county, Penn'a;

---

was greatly beloved by his neighbors, and during his long life, shared with his associate and friend, Colonel Galbraith, the confidence and leadership accorded to both in public, church and local affairs. Col. Lowrey was thrice married:

1st, September 26, 1752, MARY WATERS, b. 1732; d. 1767; and there was issue (surname Lowrey):

    i. Alexander, b. April 21, 1756; settled near Frankstown, Penna.; m. and left issue.

    ii. Elizabeth, b. October 31, 1757; m. Daniel Elliott of Cumberland county, who subsequently removed to St. Clair township, Allegheny county, Penna., where he deceased in 1794, his wife dying several years prior; and they had (surname Elliott): *John, West, Mary*, m. James Hamilton, of Middletown, and *William*.

    iii. Mary, b. May 21, 1761; m. 1st, John Hays; 2d, Joseph West; went to Allegheny county, Penna., where they lived and died.

    iv. Lazarus, b. January 27, 1764; m. Miss Holliday, daughter of Capt. John Holliday, and, with his brother Alexander, settled in what is now Blair county, Penna.

    v. Margaret, b. September, 1765; d. June 24, 1818; m. August, 1784, George Plumer, b. December 5, 1762, at Fort Pitt; d. June 8, 1843, near West Newton, Westmoreland county, Penna.; served in the Legislature from 1812 to 1818; represented the Westmoreland district in the Seventeenth, Eighteenth and Ninteenth Congresses. Their children were (surname Plumer): *Jonathan*, d. unm.; *Alexander*, m. Susan Robinson; *John-Campbell, Lazarus-Lowrey, Mary, Nancy, Sarah, William, Elizabeth* and *Rebecca*.

Col. Lowrey m. 2d, in 1774, ANN (WEST) ALRICKS, widow of Hermanus Alricks, and had issue:

    vi. Fanny, b. Feb. 1, 1775; m. Samuel Evans, of Chester county, Penna., b. 1758; d. April 21, 1805, at Col. Lowrey's homestead in Donegal; son of Evan Evans and Margaret Nevin; and had *Alexander, Evan-Reese, Ann, Margaret, Jane-H.*, and *Elizabeth*. Mr. Evans had served in the Legislature, and was also an associate judge of Chester county.

Col. Lowrey m. 3d, in 1793, Mrs. SARAH COCHRAN, of York Springs.

m. ALEXANDER BOGGS, b. October 7, 1755, in Donegal township, Lancaster county, Penn'a; d. March 30, 1839: and with his wife are interred in Old Donegal church graveyard. They had issue:

> *i. Andrew*, m. 1810, Eliza Cook, daughter of David Cook; removed to Hagerstown, Maryland.
> *ii. Francis*, m. 1818, Maria Jefferis.
> *iii. Hermanus*, m. Margaret Parks; removed to Baltimore, Maryland.
> *iv. Ann*, b. 1790; d. 1864.
> *v. Jane*, b. 1794; d. 1860.
> *vi. John.*
> *vii.* William.
> *viii. James-Alricks*, b. 1802; d. August 18, 1824.

V. JAMES ALRICKS,[5] (Hermanus,[4] Wessels,[3] Pieter,[2] Pieter,[1]) b. December 2, 1769, at Carlisle, Penn'a; d. October 28, 1833, at Harrisburg, Pa. He received a good education in the schools of the day, and was brought up to a mercantile life. In 1791-92, he was engaged in business in May Town, Lancaster county, and in 1814 he removed with his family from Lost Creek Valley to Harrisburg. He was a man of extensive reading, passionately fond of books, and he regarded an honest man, of fine education and refined manners, as the most remarkable object on the face of the earth. After his father's death, he was raised on a farm in Donegal, Lancaster county, and used to say that at that period no one could get an education for want of teachers. While lamenting his own lack of education, he was remarkably well acquainted with history, ancient and modern, and with geography. He was likewise quite familiar with the writings of Shakespeare, Goldsmith, Burns, Campbell, etc. While living in the prime of life on the Juniata, he was delighted to meet and converse with such men as the Rev. Matthew Brown, the first Dr. Watson, of Bedford, Judge Jonathan Walker, (the father of Robert J. Walker,) William R. Smith, etc. On March 10, 1821, he was appointed clerk of the orphans' court and quarter sessions, serving until January 17, 1824. He subsequently served as one of the magistrates of the borough. Mr. Alricks,

m. July 21, 1796, at Harrisburg, by Rev. N. R. Snowden, MARTHA HAMILTON, b. August 5, 1776 ; d. March 16, 1830 ; daughter of John Hamilton and Margaret Alexander. They had issue :

    i. Ann-West, b. 1799; d. August, 1828 ; m. Samuel Thompson, of Juniata county, Penn'a ; no issue.
    ii. Margaret, d. September 19, 1856.
6. *iii. Hermanus*, b. August 22, 1803 ; m. Mary Elder Kerr.
7. *iv. Hamilton*, b. June 1, 1806 ; m. Caroline Jacobs Bull.
8. *v. Jane*, b. 1808 ; m. Ovid Frazer Johnson.
    vi. Frances-E., d. July 19, 1875.
    vii. Catharine-Allen, d. s. p.

VI. HERMANUS ALRICKS,[6] (James,[5] Hermanus,[4] Wessels,[3] Pieter,[2] Pieter,[1]) b. August 22, 1803, at Oakland Mills, Lost Creek Valley, now Juniata county, Penn'a; d. January 28, 1874, at Harrisburg, Penn'a. His father removed to Harrisburg in 1814, and there the son grew to man's estate, thereafter one of the most respected citizens, receiving his education in the Harrisburg Academy. He read law in the office of Thomas Elder, Esq., and was admitted to the Dauphin county bar. He quickly obtained a lucrative business before the courts, became one of the prominent men at the bar, and at his death the oldest practitioner in Dauphin county. He was averse to holding office. The only one of prominence held by him was that of deputy attorney-general in 1829. He frequently served his fellow-citizens in municipal office, was a popular man with them, and his counsel sought upon all questions of importance. In addressing a jury, his manner was quiet, his statement clearly presented, and argument logical. His rule was to undertake no cause unless his client was able to demonstrate the justness of his case. His early training in the practice of the orphans' and register's courts soon gave him a lucrative business in that branch of his profession, where clear, concise expositions are of far more weight than the stirring eloquence of the quarter sessions. He was an excellent, precise, real-estate lawyer. No one was a better reference upon questions of town or county history. His personal acquaintance was extensive, and his taste ran in acquiring the family traditions of the earliest settlers. His fund of information was at the service of his friends, always pleasantly and accurately retold, with the authority for each fact or anecdote, and he abounded with many curious and fascinating ones. His presence was imposing, quite six feet in stature, large frame, erect, and neatly clad, quite "like a lawyer of the olden time." Mr. Alricks m., in 1831, MARY ELDER KERR, b. May 5, 1809; d. March 30, 1857, at Harrisburg; daughter of Rev. William Kerr,* of Donegal, and his wife, Mary Wilson. They had issue:

    i. James, d. s. p.
    ii. Mary-Wilson, m. James McCormick, jr. (*See McCormick record.*)
    iii. Jane, d. s. p.
    iv. William-Kerr; cashier of the Dauphin Deposit Bank at Harrisburg.
    v. Hamilton; a civil engineer; m. Mary Barr.
    vi. Herman, d. s. p.
    vii. Clara-Bull.
    viii. Martha-Orth.
    ix. Rosanna-Hamilton, d. s. p.

---

*The Rev. William Kerr was born in Bart township, Lancaster county, Penn'a, October 13, 1776. His father dying early, he was left to the tender care of a pious mother. After some years spent in the schools of the neighborhood, he was sent to Jefferson College, Cannonsburg, where he was graduated. For some years thereafter, he was principal of an academy at Wilmington, Delaware. He subsequently placed himself under the care of the Presbytery of New Castle, and was shortly after ordained by that body. He preached in Harrisburg about the years 1805-6, and upon the resignation of the Rev. Mr. McFarquhar was sent to supply the pulpit of the Old Donegal church. In the fall of 1808, the congregation at Columbia made application to Mr. Kerr for part of his time It was not, however, until the year following that he assented to give them a portion of his ministerial labors. He continued to be the stated supply there until the first Sunday in January, 1814, when he preached his farewell sermon. Mr. Kerr also preached at Marietta in addition to his charge at Donegal. He died at that town on the 22d of September, 1821, aged forty-five years, and is interred in Old Donegal church graveyard. The Rev. Mr. Kerr married Mary Elder, daughter of James Wilson and Mary Elder, of Derry. b. 1788; d. February 22, 1850, at Harrisburg, and their children were *Mary-E.*, m. Hermanus Alricks, of Harrisburg; *William M., J.-Wallace, James-Wilson* and *Martha*, m. Dr. Edward L. Orth, of Harrisburg. As a minister, there were few who stood higher in the estimation of his brethren in the Presbytery than the Rev. William Kerr.

VII. HAMILTON ALRICKS,[6] (James,[5] Hermanus,[4] Wessels,[3] Pieter,[2] Pieter,[1]) b. June 1, 1806, at Oakland Mills, in Lost Creek valley, now Juniata county, Pa.; d. July 16, 1893, at Harrisburg, Pa. He was educated at the Harrisburg Academy at such a period as those who passed through it, from 1816 until 1826, know that the whole land was stricken with poverty, and collegiate education out of the question. Indeed, out of the thirty students of the classics at the academy, and among them the son of Governor Findlay, but one is remembered who went, or could afford to go, to college. With such an education as the school could afford, and the study of history on top of it, Hamilton Alricks commenced reading law with Samuel Douglas, Esq., afterward Attorney-General, and was admitted to practice in 1828. During his professional career of half a century, Mr. Alricks has been engaged, at every term of the court, in the trial of many of the most important civil and criminal cases, and in numerous cases in the Supreme Court, as the reports will show from 2d Watts to the last volume of Outerbridge. In the outset of his practice, he was engaged as counsel by Mr. Gest, in the case of Gest *vs.* Espy, 2d Watts, 266, after Thomas Elder, Esq., a senior member of the bar, had abandoned the case, upon a verdict being found for defendant. Mr. Alricks removed the case to the Supreme Court, where he succeeded in reversing the judgment. On one occasion, in arguing a case in the Supreme Court, and while reading an authority, he was abruptly interrupted by Judge Huston, saying, "That is not the law." "But," said Mr. Alricks, "I am citing from the opinion of the court." Judge Huston sharply responded: "I don't care; no judge ever declared such to be the law." To which Mr. Alricks further replied: "I have been reading the opinion of the court delivered by your Honor." "Then, said the judge, "the reporter took me down wrong; let me see the book." After examining it for some time, the judge closed it with the remark, "After all, I don't think this authority has any application to the case in hearing." Proceedings were commenced before the Legislature of Pennsylvania, about the year 1845, and testimony taken for the purpose of framing articles of impeachment against the Hon. William N. Irvine, judge of the York and Adams judicial district, and the only counsel of the respondent was Mr. Alricks, who conducted the defense with such skill and ability that the committee refused to report articles. The then State Treasurer and Auditor General on several occasions selected Mr. Alricks to argue cases on the part of the Commonwealth involving questions of Constitutional law. His argument before the Supreme Court of the United States, in Butler *et al.*, late Canal Commissioners of Pennsylvania, *vs.* the Commonwealth of Pennsylvania, 10th Howard, United States Supreme Court Reports, 402, was not only well received by the profession as a sound exposition of the law as to what constitutes a contract within the meaning of the Tenth Section of the First Article of the Constitution of the United States, prohibiting a State from passing any law impairing the obligation of contracts, but also an able definition of the power of the Legislature to create and abolish offices, to impose taxes, etc.; and will remain a lasting memorial of his research, industry, and ability as a lawyer. He was one year a member of the Legislature; was a member of the Chicago Convention in 1864, which nominated General McClellan for President, and the series of resolutions drawn up and offered in the convention by him abounded in patriotic sentiments, evincing marked ability. He was a member of the Constitutional Convention for the revision of the Constitution of the State, in 1872-3, that held its sessions first in Harrisburg and subsequently in Philadelphia, and acted on the committees on Cities and Charters, and on Religious and Charitable Corporations and Societies. Mr. Alricks married, December 28, 1837, CAROLINE BULL, daughter of Rev. Levi Bull, D. D., of Chester county, Pa., a son of Colonel Thomas Bull, of Revotionary fame. She was born August 3, 1811; d. February 28, 1885, at Harrisburg, Pa. They had issue:

    i. Annie-Bull, b. October 6, 1838; d. April 26, 1888; m. June 8, 1864, Benjamin Law Forster. (*see Forster record.*)
    ii. Martha, b. May 24, 1840; d. January 10, 1866.
    iii. Caroline-Jacobs, d. s. p.
    iv. Levi-Bull, b. October 15, 1843; m. first, October 1, 1872, Anna Henderson; d. August 1, 1880; daughter of John

G. Henderson, and had *John-Hamilton;* m. secondly, Emily Shevelle Fisher, daughter of Hon. Robert J. Fisher, of York, Pa.

v. Eliza-Jane, b. September 19, 1846; d. September 28, 1849.

VIII. JANE ALRICKS,[6] (James,[5] Hermanus,[4] Wessels,[3] Pieter,[2] Pieter,[1]) b. 1808 at Oakland Mills, in Lost Creek Valley, now Juniata county, Pa.; d. December 21, 1891, at Harrisburg; m. OVID FRAZER JOHNSON, b. in the year 1807, in the Valley of Wyoming, near the town of Wilkes-Barre; d. February, 1854, in Washington, D. C. He was descended from some of the early settlers of that historic locality. His paternal grandfather, the Rev. Jacob Johnson, was a superior linguist and man of rich education and culture; a graduate of Yale College, he took his degree as early as 1740, with distinguished honor. In 1778, he was called from his home in Connecticut to reside in Wilkes-Barre. After that terrible event, the massacre of Wyoming, he assisted Col. Dennison with his advice and influence, in protecting the inhabitants that remained, and the original articles of capitulation were in the proper handwriting of Mr. Johnson. In quite a lengthy biography written of him in the year 1836, by the historian of Wyoming, Charles Miner, appears this : '' When the Revolutionary war broke out, Mr. Johnson took his stand early and firmly in behalf of freedom. And through the whole contest he rendered the utmost service in his power, which, from his learning, talents, and the respect he commanded, was very considerable. A son born while the animated discussions preceding the Revolution were going on, and the elder Pitt was thundering his anathemas against ministers for their tyrannous conduct to the Colonies, Mr. Johnson named Jehoiada Pitt. . . Jehoiada is sometime since deceased, but a son of his with hereditary genius is winning his way to enviable distinction.'' The latter is the subject of this sketch. At the close of his early education, in which he had as school and class-mates many who afterwards rose to positions of eminence and distinction, he commenced the study of the law with John N. Conyngham, of Wilkes-Barre, afterwards Judge Conyngham. He was duly admitted to the bar and entered into the practice of the law at that place. In 1833, he removed to Harrisburg, and there married. In 1839, at the early age of thirty-two years, his talent secured for him the appointment as attorney general of Pennsylvania. In 1842, his term of office having expired, he was re-appointed and served through a second term until 1845. As an orator, Mr. Johnson was brilliant; as a lawyer, he had superior abilities, and somewhat of a wide-known reputation, being frequently employed to try cases in different States of the Union. It may be here remarked that, in addition to Mr. Johnson's legal ability, he had a high reputation as a political writer. He was the author of the celebrated "Governor's Letters," published during the administration of Governor Ritner, and which purported to give the ludicrous side to the political characters then figuring in the politics of the State. Jane Alricks and Ovid Frazer Johnson had issue (surname Johnson):

    i. *Fanny-Alricks*, b. Sept. 2, 1836; m. Hon. Samuel T. Shugert, of Bellefonte.
    ii. *Hannah-Ianthe*, b. Sept. 31, 1837.
    iii. *Martha-Alricks*.
    iv. *Ovid-Frazer*, b. February 10, 1842; a lawyer, now practicing his profession in Philadelphia.

ANDERSON OF DONEGAL.

I. JAMES ANDERSON,[1] b. November 17, 1678, in Scotland; was educated at Edinburgh, under the care of Principal Stirling. He was ordained by Irvine Presbytery, November 17, 1708, with a view to his settlement in Virginia. He sailed March 6, 1709, and arrived in the Rappahannock on the 22d of April following; but the condition of affairs not being favorable for introducing any other religion than that of the established Church of England in that Colony, he came northward, and was received by the Presbytery September 20 following. He settled at New Castle, where he was installed pastor in 1713. In 1714, out of regard for the desolate condition of the people in Kent county, he was directed to supply them monthly on a Sabbath, and also to spend a Sabbath at Cedar Creek, in Sussex. In 1716, receiving a call from the first church organization of New York city, he went there and labored with his accustomed zeal and energy; but his strict Presbyterianism and rigid Scottish habits and doctrines were distasteful to the people, and his charge, consequently, did not prove to be happy or comfortable, and he desired a removal. He was called, September 24, 1726, to Donegal, on the Susquehanna, and accepted. He was installed the last Wednesday in August, 1727. In September, 1729, he gave every fifth Sabbath to the people on Swatara, and joined the congregation of Derry, thus becoming the first settled pastor over that church, until the call to Rev. William Bertram, in 1732. He died July 16, 1740. In the language of Presbytery, "he was high in esteem for circumspection, diligence, and faithfulness as a Christian minister." His name and fame are associated with the early history of the Presbyterian church in America. He was a man of talent, learning, and piety, a graceful and popular preacher—a leader among men. Mr. Anderson was twice married; m., first, February, 1713, Mistress SUIT GAR-

LAND, dau. of Sylvester Garland, of the head of Apoquinimy, Delaware, who d. December 24, 1736, and lies buried in Donegal churchyard, where a large flat stone marks the resting-place of herself and her distinguished husband. From a mutilated leaf in the Rev. James Anderson's Bible, (Imprint "Edinburgh, A. D. 1676,") on which was recorded the family registry, is copied the following imperfect list of births and deaths. In his will he names only James, Susannah and Thomas, but refers to *all* his children. He left a large estate, including most of the land upon which Marietta now stands, a valuable ferry-right called "Anderson's Ferry," land on the opposite side of the river, together with several slaves:

2.   i. *Garland*, b. Nov. 21, 1714; m. Jane Chevalier.
3.   ii. *Ann*, b. July 24, 1716, in New Castle; m. John Stewart.
     iii. [. . .], b. Feb. 17, 1717-8, in New York.
     iv. [. . .], b. Feb. 23, 1718-9, in New York.
4.   v. *James*, b. May 14, 1721; m. Ruth Bayley.
     vi. [a son], b. Dec. 18, 1722, in New York.
     vii. *John*, b. Jan. 13, 1724-5, in New York.
     viii. *Susannah*, b. Oct. 4, 1725-6, in New York.
     ix. [a son], b. March —.
     x. [.], b. July —.
     xi. *Thomas*.

The Rev. James Anderson m., secondly, December 27, 1737, REBECCA CRAWFORD, of Donegal. After his death the Widow Anderson married Joshua Baker, whose daughter, Mary Baker, became the wife of the Rev. John Elder, of Paxtang. Several of his children appear to have died young, and none of his descendants remain in Lancaster county.

II. GARLAND ANDERSON,[2] (James,[1]) b. November 21, 1714, in New Castle, Del.; m. JANE CHEVALIER, daughter of Peter Chevalier, of Philadelphia, whither he removed, and died young. He administered on his father's estate, in conjunction with his stepmother, Rebecca Anderson, (who renounced as executrix.) He left a daughter, *Elizabeth*, of whom it is recorded that she was "a woman of great excellence.' License to marry issued January 6, 1768, to Samuel Breeze and Elizabeth Anderson (*Penn'a Archives, 2d ser., v*). They lived in New York. The Rev. E. Hazzard Snowden, of the Presbyterian church of Kingston, Pa., is a descendant of this branch.

III. ANN ANDERSON,[2] (James,[1]) b. in New Castle, Del., July 24, 1716; m. JOHN STEWART, son of George Stewart, the progenitor of the Stewart family of Donegal township, Lancaster county, Pa.; a landed proprietor, and a member of the General Assembly. John Stewart d. Oct. 1749. They had issue (surname Stewart):

    i. George, b. Nov. 10, 1736; moved to the Tuscarora Valley, then Cumberland, now Juniata county, where he d. Aug. 13, 1787. He took an active and prominent part in the Revolutionary war, in which he was a lieut. col. He m. Margaret Harris, of an honorable Scottish family, b. Jan. 11, 1737; d. April 15, 1815, and had nine children. Among them were:

        1. *John*, m. Margaret Harris, daughter of John Harris, founder of the town of Mifflin. and Jean Harris, and had among others:

            a. *James-Harris*, M. D., m. Jane A. Fuller, from whom descends the *Rev. Robert Stewart*, D. D., of the United Presbyterian church, late missionary to Sialkot, India; present residence, Bellevue, Allegheny co., Pa.

            b. *Ann-Bryson*, m. Joseph Kelly, M. D., of Tuscarora Valley, from whom descends the *Rev. Joseph Clarke Kelly*, of the Presbyterian church, of Williamsburg, Pa., m. Mary G. Weber.

        2. *Thomas-Harris*, b. Feb. 5, 1767; d. Feb'y 25, 1831; settled in Alexandria, Huntingdon co., Pa.; m. Nov. 5, 1795, Anne Gemmill; and had issue, among others:

            a. *Eliza*, b. Nov. 2, 1799; m. May 1, 1821, Rev. James Thompson, from whom descends (surname Thompson) Ann, William and Jane.

            b. *John Gemmill*, m. Sarah Steinman, from whom descends the Rev. T. Calvin Stewart, of the Presbyterian church, of South Easton, Pa., who married Sallie D. Ward.

            c. *Anna-Maria*, b. Aug. 1, 1814,; m. first, May 9, 1837, John H. Woolverton, from whom descends (surname Woolverton) Anna Margaret and William H., of New York city Mrs. Woolverton m. secondly, William Kinsloe, of Alexandria, Pa.

    d. *Zechariah-Gemmill*, from whom descends Francis Laird Stewart an author of some repute; Thomas, an M. D. of great ability, and the Rev. Robert L., theological professor, Lincoln University, Oxford, Pa.

  ii. Suit, m. Sept. 21, 1758, Matthew Harris, b. Jan. 12, 1735; d. Dec. 9, 1819.

  iii. Jean, who m. Stewart Roan, of Donegal.

ANN ANDERSON STEWART, m. secondly JOHN ALLISON, of Lancaster county, and had issue (surname Allison):

  iv. James.
  v. Anna, who m. first, Thomas Anderson, (*see IV*;) m. secondly, Samuel Cook; m. thirdly, Joseph Vance.
  vi. William.
  vii. Robert.

IV. JAMES ANDERSON,[2] (James,[1]) b. May 14, 1721, in New York; bap. May 28, 1721; d. June 1, 1790, on his patrimonial estate, at Anderson's Ferry, Lancaster county, Pa.; bur. at Donegal church; he was a member of the Assembly from 1777 to 1780 inclusive, and took the oath of allegiance July 2, 1777; was twice married; first, March 5, 1741, RUTH BAYLEY, b. in 1722; d. January 2, 1784; daughter of Thomas and Mary Bayley. They had issue:

5.   *i. James*, b. December 26, 1741; m. Jean Tate.
  ii. Mary, b. April 6, 1744; d. July 14, 1749.
  iii. Suit, b. February 22, 1746; d. May 24, 1747.
  iv. Anna, b. November 23, 1748; d. at an early age.
  v. Susannah, b. May 7, 1751; d. June 13, 1777; m. William Kelly, and had issue (surname Kelly) *Elizabeth, Ruth* (first,) *John*, and *Ruth* (second).
  vi. Thomas, b. June 13, 1753; d. November 11, 1778; m. November 30, 1774, Anna Allison, of Donegal; had one child, *Ruth*, b. November 26, 1775; d. March 10, 1785.
  vii. Mary, b. April 18, 1756; d. October 16, 1757.
  viii. [. .], b. June 13, 1758; died in infancy.

James Anderson m., secondly, MARGARET TATE, the widow of the Rev. Joseph Tate, of the Donegal Presbytery. She d.

Anderson of Donegal. 31

May 13, 1801. The Rev. Joseph Tate left surviving him numerous children, who were settled principally in Virginia.

V. JAMES ANDERSON,³ (James,² James,¹) b. December 26, 1741; bap. January 31, 1742; d. December 13, 1799; served in the war of the Revolution and was at Valley Forge; he was a captain in the 4th battalion of Lancaster county militia and took the oath of allegiance July 26, 1777; was twice married; m. first, April 3, 1766, JEAN TATE, b. February 22, 1751; d. February 7, 1777; daughter of the Rev. Joseph and Margaret Tate. They had issue :

6.   i. *James*, b. October 18, 1767 ; m. Mary Bayley.
    ii. *Margaret*, b. December 4, 1769 ; d. June 3, 1800 ; m. November 10, 1791, Nathaniel Weakley.
   iii. *Joseph-Tate*, b. June 6, 1771.
    iv. *Ruth*, b. November 4, 1773 ; m. April 6, 1794, Thomas Williamson, of Cumberland county, Pa.

James Anderson m., secondly, February 19, 1778, by Rev. John Elder, MARGARET CHAMBERS, of Cumberland county; b. June 22, 1757. They had issue :

7.   v. *Thomas*, b. Jan. 28, 1779 ; m. Mary Addams.
    vi. *Jean*, b. Oct. 4, 1780.
8. vii. *John*, b. Jan. 4, 1783 ; m. Margaret McAllen.
   viii. *Mary*, (Polly,) b. Jan. 1, 1785 ; d. Sept. 6, 1804 ; bur. at Silvers Spring, Cumberland county.
    ix. *William*, b. March 6, 1787 ; d. July 20, 1838.
     x. *Michael-Simpson*, b. August 13, 1789.
9. xi. *Chambers*, b. Nov. 1, 1791 ; m. Ellen T. Peeples.
   xii. *Garland*, b. Dec. 14, 1793 ; d. April 27, 1846.
  xiii. *Elizabeth*, b. March 8, 1796 ; d. October 7, 1807 ; bur. at Silvers Spring church.
   xiv. *Eleanor*, b. February 6, 1799 ; m. Robert Dunlap Kincaid.

After the death of her husband, the Widow Anderson moved to Fannetsburg, Franklin county, Pa., where she died March 28, 1836.

VI. JAMES ANDERSON,⁴ (James,³ James,² James,¹) b. October 18, 1767; d. June 7, 1815; bur. at York, Pa. He was a man of enterprise and progress—laid out the town of Marietta, in Lancaster county, on his patrimonial estate; run the ferry at the same place, known as Anderson's Ferry, and constructed, at great expense, a road leading to York, whither he removed. He was overtaken by reverses, the result of circumstances beyond his control, and thus the estate, which had descended through three generations, passed from the family. He was twice married; m., first, December 31, 1795, MARY BAYLEY, daughter of John Bayley, who d. January 31, 1797. They had issue:

  i. *Mary-Bayley*, b. Jan. 12, 1797; d. at Baltimore, Sept. 6, 1832; m., Nov., 1824, David B. Prince, b. Nov. 22, 1790, in Cumberland, Maine; d. March 30, 1876, in York; was principal of the York Academy from 1819 to 1866. They had issue (surname Prince):
   1. *David-Oaks*, b. Nov. 18, 1826.
   2. *James-Anderson*, b. Dec. 7, 1828; d. March 15, 1856.
   3. *Mary-Elizabeth*, b. Feb. 6, 1831.

James Anderson m., secondly, in Carlisle, March 22, 1798, MARY McQUEEN, a granddaughter of Rev. Joseph Tate, b. July 7, 1781; d. February 4, 1845, in York, Pa. They had issue:

  ii. *James*, b. Dec. 12, 1798; d. Jan. 12, 1839; unm.; an attorney-at-law, York, Pa.
10. iii. *Joseph-Tate*, b. Aug. 19, 1800; m. Jane McMordie.
  iv. [a dau.], b. September 9, 1802; d. in infancy.
  v. *Margaret*, b. September 9, 1804; d. May 14, 1854.
  vi. *Jane*, b. August 25, 1806; d. December, 1808.
  vii. *Benjamin*, b. July 6, 1808; d. August 12, 1844.
  viii. *Eliza-Ann*, b. February 4, 1810; d. May 1, 1824.
  ix. *David*, b. June 12, 1812; moved to Los Angelos, California; d. March 24, 1876.
  x. *Sarah-Jane*, b. September 4, 1814; d. May 21, 1865.

VII. THOMAS ANDERSON,[4] (James,[3] James,[2] James,[1]) farmer, b. January 28, 1779, at Anderson's Ferry, (now Marietta); bap. Feb 2, 1779; settled on a farm, about the year 1800, in Silvers Spring township, Cumberland county, Pennsylvania. (James Anderson, his father, and Rev. Samuel Waugh made an exchange of farms, which new farm was bequeathed to this son Thomas, and is now a very valuable property, owned and occupied by his descendants,) d. December 29, 1850. He m., April 15, 1811, MARY ADDAMS, b. 1787; d. March 8, 1840;

Anderson of Donegal. 33

daughter of Abraham Addams, of Cumberland county ; both buried in Silvers Spring church-yard. They had issue:

11.   *i. James*, b. March 7, 1812 ; m. Mary Elizabeth Ayres.
     ii. Abram-Addams, b. January 25, 1815 ; d. December 29, 1841.
     iii. Elizabeth-Addams, b. June 24, 1819 ; m. June 2, 1842, John Slaughter, of Ohio.

VIII. JOHN ANDERSON,[4] (James,[3] James,[2] James,[1]) b. January 4, 1783 ; d. March 5, 1863, in Minneapolis Minnesota ; m., April 27, 1821, MARGARET MCALLEN ; they had issue :

12.   *i. Drusilla*, b. February 10, 1822 ; m., 1st., Abner Perkins ; m., 2d., Alexander McCormick.
13.   *ii. Margaret-Geddes*, b. August 19, 1824 ; m. David Edwards.
14.   *iii. James-Garland-McAllen*, b. July 8, 1827 ; m. Margaretta J. Kennedy.

IX. CHAMBERS ANDERSON,[4] (James,[3] James,[2] James,[1]) b. November 1, 1791, on his father's farm, in Silvers Spring township, Cumberland county ; bap. by the Rev'd Samuel Waugh, of Silvers Spring church ; removed to Chester, Illinois, where he d. December 28, 1858 ; m. February 15, 1837, ELLEN T. PEEPLES, of Fannetsburg, Franklin county, Pennsylvania ; b. April 22, 1813 ; d. December 21, 1882 ; both buried at Chester, Illinois. They had issue :

15.   *i. Adolphus-Albert*, b. November 29, 1837 ; m. Eunice Elizabeth Jones.
     ii. Thomas-Chambers, b. at Fannetsburg ; killed May 9, 1862, in the great Rebellion, at the battle of Farmington, Mississippi.
     iii. William-Curtis-Peeples, b. April 10, 1843, at Chester, Illinois ; d. August 25, 1867.
     iv. Mary-Frances, b. January 15, 1846 ; m. John M. Wright.
     v. Seth-Allen, b. February 13, 1852 ; d. January 30, 1854.
     vi. Joshua-Tate, b. November 29, 1856 ; d. January 7, 1891.

X. JOSEPH-TATE ANDERSON,[5] (James,[4] James,[3] James, James,[1]) b. August 19, 1800, at Marietta, Lancaster county, Pa.; d. Jan. 17, 1854; m. first, March 25, 1835, JANE MCMORDIE, daughter of Rev. Robert McMordie, a chaplain in the

Pennsylvania Line in the Revolution (*vide Penna. Archives*); d. March 28, 1837. They had issue:
  16. *i. JamesMcMordie*, b. July 15, 1836; m. Elizabeth P. Barker.

Joseph-Tate Anderson m. secondly, April 15, 1847, CORNELIA S. ROCK; d. Jan., 1885, in Philadelphia. They had issue:

    ii. Mary-Susan, b. March 14, 1848.
    iii. Joseph-Tate, b. July 19, 1851; d. June 19, 1886; buried at Marietta, Pa.

XI. JAMES ANDERSON,[5] (Thomas,[4] James,[3] James,[2] James,[1]) b. March 7, 1812; d. Dec. 15, 1882, in the house in which he was born, on his patrimonial estate. He was a farmer by profession and influential in his political associations; represented Cumberland county in the Pennsylvania Legislature of 1856 and '57. A director of the Carlisle Bank. His undeviating integrity and practical wisdom caused him to be sought after in counsel and in private and public trusts. He m. June 20, 1843, MARY ELIZABETH AYRES, daughter of William Ayres, Esq., of Harrisburg, (*see Ayres record*.) They had issue:

    i. Mary-Elizabeth, b. April 18, 1844; d. April 15, 1870; buried at Silvers Spring church; m. June 6, 1867, Dr. Richard M. Crain, of Hogestown, Cumberland county; born Oct., 1844; d. at Muscogee, Indian Territory. Jan. 18, 1886. (*see Crain record*); and had issue (surname Crain):
        1. *Elizabeth-Whitehill*, b. July 10, 1868.
        2. *Anderson*, b. Feb. 7, 1870; m. June 1, 1893, Mary C. Swartz, of Mechanicsburg, Pa.
    ii. Eleanor-Allen, b. June 14, 1845.
    iii. Thomas, b. Jan. 4, 1847; m. Sept. 14, 1887, Elizabeth Shelly, of Mechanicsburg, Pa.
    iv. Althea, b. May 20, 1849; m. Dec. 23, 1873, John Chambers Parker, of Cumberland county, Pa., b. March 21, 1848; (*see Parker family*); and had issue (surname Parker):
        1. *Mary-Anderson*, b. July 30, 1876; d. in infancy.
        2. *Sara-Chambers*, b. December 19, 1877.
        3. *Eleanor-Anderson*, b. February 1, 1882.
    v. William-Ayres, b. March 1, 1852; d. March 3, 1856.
    vi. Susan-Ayres, b. December 19, 1853; d. January 29, 1888.
    vii. JennyAyres, b. August 4, 1856.

XII. DRUSILLA ANDERSON,[5] (John,[4] James,[3] James,[2] James,[1]) b. Feb. 10, 1822; was married twice; m. first, Sept. 14, 1846, ABNER PERKINS, b. Oct. 10, 1821; d. Sept. 14, 1853. They had issue (surname Perkins):

  i. *Sarah-Margaret*, b. Aug. 8, 1847; m. Dec. 24, 1872, William E. Clark, b. May 6, 1841; d. Aug. 11, 1883; and had issue (surname Clark):
      1. *Mabel-Drusilla*, b. Sept. 22, 1874.
      2. *James-W.*, b. June 8, 1877.
      3. *Florence-Jennie*, b. Sept. 25, 1881.
  ii. *Mary-Isabella*, died in infancy.
  iii. *Edward-Lucas*, died in infancy.

Drusilla Anderson (Perkins) m. secondly, Nov. 28, 1858, Alexander McCormick, of Lockhaven, Pa., b. Nov. 25, 1817; d. Jan. 14, 1877. They had issue (surname McCormick):

  iv. *Agnes-A.*, b. July 4, 1860, at Minneapolis, Minn.

XIII. MARGARET–GEDDES ANDERSON,[5] (John,[4] James,[3] James,[2] James,[1]) b. Aug. 19, 1824; d. Oct. 15, 1894, buried in Lakewood cemetery, Minneapolis; m. Nov. 12, 1846, DAVID EDWARDS, b. Franklin county, Pa., March 19, 1816; d. Sept. 11, 1890; residence, Minneapolis. They had issue (surname Edwards):

  i. *Drusilla-Elizabeth*, b. Feb. 8, 1847; m. Jan. 29, 1874, A. A. Page; and had issue (surname Page): *Lulu*, *Albert-A.*, *Sarah-J.*, and *Roy*.
  ii. *Catharine*, b. June 1, 1849.
  iii. *Sarah-Isabella*, b. July 12, 1851.
  iv. *Mary-Ellen*, b. Feb. 8, 1854; d. May 9, 1855.
  v. *David-Anderson*, b. March 23, 1856.
  vi. *William-Alexander*, b. May 9, 1859.
  vii. *John-Walter*, b. May 21, 1862.
  viii. *Margaret-McAllen*, b. Feb. 4, 1864; m. Nov. 16, 1892, Marshall P. Blackburn, of Blackburn, Me.; and had issue (surname Blackburn).
      1. Marshall P., Jr., b. Sept. 15, 1893.

XIV. JAMES–GARLAND–MCALLEN ANDERSON,[5] (John,, James,[3] James,[2] James,[1]) b. July 8, 1827; d. Oct. 21, 1862, at

Chester, Ill.; was a graduate of Dickinson College; m. MARGARETTA J. KENNEDY, of Chester, Ill. They had issue;

    i. John-Kennedy, b. August 14, 1854; d. Jan. 7, 1855.
    ii. Hettie-Margaret, b. Oct. 31, 1856; d. Dec. 26, 1857.
    iii. Francis-Chambers, b. March 12, 1859; m. May 19, 1883, Georgie-Hyse-McKeig; now living in Louisville, Ky. and had issue:
        1. *Chambers*, b. July 10, 1886.

XV. ADOLPHUS–ALBERT ANDERSON,[5] (Chambers,[4] James,[3] James,[2] James,[1]) b. Nov. 29, 1837, in Fannetsburg, Franklin county, Pa.; taken to Chester, Ill., in 1841; d. May 17, 1888; m. Feb. 8, 1865, EUNICE ELIZABETH JONES, of Chester. They had issue:

    i. Ellen-Elizabeth, b. Nov. 23, 1865.
    ii. Eunice-Ruth, b. April 27, 1868.
    iii. Mabel-Dean, b. April 30, 1870.
    iv. Albert-Clark, b. June 2, 1872.
    v. Eloise, b. Feb. 7, 1881.

XVI. JAMES MCMORDIE ANDERSON,[6] (Joseph-Tate,[5] James,[4] James,[3] James,[2] James,[1]) b. July 15, 1836, at Marietta, Lancaster county, Pa.; m. July 6, 1860, ELIZABETH P. BARKER; now residing at Daisey, Leavenworth county, Kansas. They had issue:

    i. Jennie-Elizabeth, b. May 28, 1861.
    ii. Nellie-Boyd, b. Oct. 23, 1865.
    iii. Maggie, b. Oct. 21, 1873.

AWL OF PAXTANG.

I. JACOB AWL, b. August 6, 1727, in the north of Ireland; d. September 26, 1793, in Paxtang township, Dauphin county, Pa. The name should properly be spelled AULD, and the first settler wrote it AUL, which the descendants have changed into Awl. He learned the trade of a tanner. Was a man of means when he came to America, and settled, at an early date, in Paxtang, near his relative, John Harris, of Harris' Ferry, where he took up a large tract of land, which he improved, erected a tannery, and on which he lived to the time of his death. He became a prominent personage in Paxtang, was an ensign and lieutenant in Colonel John Elder's battalion of rangers in the frontier wars from 1756 to 1764, and at the outset of the war for independence, aided, by his counsel and his purse, in organizing the associated battalions of Lancaster county, which did such effective service in the Revolution. When the new county of Dauphin was erected, Mr. Awl was appointed one of the commissioners in the act relating thereto, and John Harris afterwards appointed him one of the trustees or commissioners for the public grounds ceded by him, at the laying out of the town of Harrisburg, for public uses. He was a representative man, influential and potential in the county, yet preferred domestic retirement to the struggle for office, and when he was offered the nomination for representative in the General Assembly, he positively declined. Over his grave, in the burial ground of old Paxtang church, is a stone with this inscription:

Sacred to the memory
of
JACOB AWL
Who departed this life Sept. 26th 1793
Aged 66 years 1 month and 20 Days
This stone is placed over his remains by
his relict and children as a testimony of
their Regard for his many virtues.

*Is he perhaps your Guardian Angel still
O widow, children, live as you would obey his will
So shall you join him on that happy shore
Where death or grief will visit you no more.*

Jacob Awl m., July 26, 1759, by Rev. John Elder, SARAH STURGEON; b. September 1, 1739; d. June, 1809, in Paxtang, and with her husband there buried. She was the daughter of Jeremiah Sturgeon, one of the first settlers. They had issue:

    i. *James*, b. May 10, 1760; d. s. p.
    ii. *Elizabeth*, b. November 18, 1761; d. 1850, at Harrisburg; m. John Elder, b. August 3, 1759; d. April 27, 1811; son of Rev. John Elder; (*see Elder record.*)
2.   iii. *Sarah*, b. February 24, 1764; m. Timothy Green, Jr.
    iv. *Samuel*, b. July 1, 1766; d. in early life in Philadelphia.
    v. *Margaret*, b. September 8, 1768.
3.   vi. *Jacob*, b. March 26, 1770; m. [Sarah] Stroh.
4.   vii. *Samuel*, b. March 5, 1773; m. Mary Maclay.
5.   viii. *Jane*, b. September 25, 1774; m. Thomas Gregg.
    ix. *Rachel*, b. March 17, 1778.
    x. *Agnes*, b. June 17, 1780.
    xi. *Thomas*, b. October 13, 1782.
    xii. *James*, b. August 17, 1784; first, m. Rebecca Elder; daughter of Rev. John Elder; (*see Elder record*); and they had issue:
      1. *Joshua-Elder.*
      2. *Sarah*, m. May, 1821, —— Lusk.

II. SARAH AWL,² (Jacob,¹) b. February 24, 1764, in Paxtang township, Lancaster, now Dauphin county, Pa.; d. about 1835, in Chillicothe, O.; m. February 25, 1783, by Rev. John Elder, TIMOTHY GREEN, JR.,* b. September 7, 1765, in Han-

---

* TIMOTHY GREEN, son of Robert Green, was born about 1733, on the "Monoday," Hanover township, Lancaster, now Dauphin county, Pa.; d. February 27, 1812, at Dauphin Pa., and is buried in the old graveyard there. His father, of Scotch ancestry, came from the north of Ireland about 1725, locating near the Kittochtinny mountains on Manada creek. The first record we have of the son is subsequent to Braddock's defeat, when the frontier settlers were threatened with extermination by the marauding savages. Timothy Green assisted in organizing a company, and for at least seven years was chiefly in active service in protecting the settlers from the fury of the blood-thirsty Indians. In the Bouquet expedition he commanded a company of Provincial troops. For his service at this time, the

over township, now Dauphin county, Pa.; d. in 1820, at Chillicothe, O., where he was among the earliest settlers. We have the following account of that wedding :

"On the morning of the wedding, the party accompanying Mr. Green came riding ' down the lane ' to Mr. Awl's house, all in the style of the day. The groom wore his hat with three black plumes, long stockings, knee-breeches, buckles, &c. It was a gay affair for those days. On the Sunday following, all went to the Rev. Mr. Elder's church. Jenny Awl, sister of

---

Proprietaries granted him large tracts of land in Buffalo valley and on Bald Eagle creek. At the outset of the Revolution, Captain Green became an earnest advocate for independence, and the Hanover resolutions of June 4, 1774, passed unanimously by the meeting of which he was chairman, show that he was intensely patriotic. He was one of the Committee of Safety of the Province, which met November 22, 1774, in Lancaster, and issued hand-bills to the import that "agreeable to the resolves and recommendations of the American Continental Congress, that the freeholders and others qualified to vote for representatives in Assembly choose, by ballot, sixty persons for a Committee of Observation, to observe the conduct of all persons towards the actions of the General Congress ; the committee, when elected, to divide the country into districts and appoint members of the committee to superintend each district, and any six so appointed to be a quorum, etc." Election was held on Thursday, 15th December, 1774, and, among others, Timothy Green was elected from Hanover. This body of men were in correspondence with Joseph Reed, Charles Thompson, George Clymer, John Benezet, Samuel Meredith, Thomas Mifflin, etc., of Philadelphia, and others. They met at Lancaster again, April 27, 1775, when notice was taken of General Gage's attack upon the inhabitants of Massachusetts Bay, and a general meeting called for the 1st of May, at Lancaster. Upon the erection of the county of Dauphin, Colonel Green was the oldest justice of the peace in commission, and, under the Constitution of 1776, he was presiding justice of the courts. He continued therein until, under the Constitution of 1790, which required the presiding judge "to be learned in the law," Judge Atlee was appointed. After his retirement, Judge Green returned to his quiet farm at the mouth of Stony creek, where he had erected a mill and other improvements. He was thrice married : m. first, in 1760, EFFY FINNEY ROBINSON, daughter of James and Jean Finney, and widow of Thomas Robinson. She d. December 28, 1765, and is buried in old Hanover church graveyard. They had issue :

 i. *Joseph*, b. March 29, 1761.

the bride, it seems, was one of the singers for tune raising on that occasion. She had made her debut, having sent to Philadelphia for a handsome pair of stays, which she wore that day; but caused some stir by fainting, and having to be carried out."

They had issue (surname Green):

    i. Jacob-Awl; was a successful merchant of Lancaster, O., a member of the Ohio Legislature, and a prominent citizen of that State; m. and left issue.

    ii. Timothy-Awl, m. and left issue.

    iii. William-Awl, m. and left issue.

    ii. Rebecca, b. 1763; d. July 30, 1837; m. Colonel William Allen. (*see Allen record.*)

    iii. Timothy, b. September 7, 1765; m. Sarah Awl.

Colonel Green m. secondly, in 1771, JEAN EDMUNDSTON; d. February 18, 1774; interred in Hanover church graveyard. They had issue:

    iv. Rosanna, b. July 2, 1772; d. December 30, 1820; m. Robert Sterret, son of David Sterret and Rachel Innis. The Sterrets were early settlers in Donegal township, from which locality the family has spread over the State. The father of Robert Sterret settled in Hanover about 1741, but subsequently removed to the old homestead in Donegal. The Sterrets however, became allied to many of the Hanover families, and the history of this family would elucidate much of the history of the others. Robert Sterret and Rosanna Green removed to the Kishacoquillas valley, where some of their descendants yet reside. They had a large family, seven sons and six daughters.

Colonel Green m., thirdly, in 1775, MARY INNES, daughter of Brice Innes and Elizabeth Graham of Hanover. She survived her husband twenty years. They had issue:

    v. Innes, b. March 25, 1776; d. August 4, 1839; m. Rebecca Murray; (*see Murray of Swatara.*)

    vi. Elizabeth, b. December 17, 1779; m., January 10, 1805, by Rev. N. R. Snowden, John Lytle, b. 1772; d. 1808; son of Joseph Lytle and Sarah Morrison, of Lytle's Ferry, on the Susquehanna.

    vii. Richard, b. January 10, 1789; d. May, 1852; unm.

    viii. Mary, b. October 24, 1792; d. November 14, 1857.

Awl of Paxtang. 41

iv. *Joseph-Awl*, m. and left issue ; owned extensive paper mills at Lancaster, O., and was largely engaged in business operations.

v. *Effie*, d. unm., at the age of forty years.

III. JACOB AWL,[2] (Jacob,[1]) b. March 26, 1770, in Paxtang township, Lancaster county, Pa.; d. January, 1792, was a young man of considerable promise, and lived on a farm adjoining his father. He m. in 1791, [SARAH] STROH, daughter of Michael Stroh. They had issue:

i. *Jacob-Michael*, b. February 24, 1792 ; d. September 5, 1849, at Harrisburg, Pa. ; was long a leading member of the Methodist church ; at the time of his death the *Democratic Union* said he was "a gentleman of the purest piety and strictest integrity in all his intercourse with his fellow men; while the *Keystone* stated that "no man enjoyed in a higher degree the confidence and respect of the community"—that "his life had been a continual exemplification of what the walk and conversation of a Christian should be." Mr. Awl served as a soldier in the war of 1812-14. He m. April 27, 1824, Fanny Horning, b. February 17, 1803 ; d. July 12, 1869, at Harrisburg ; and they had issue :

1. *Ann-Mary*, b. October 14, 1826 ; d. December 8, 1836.
2. *Elizabeth*, b. November 1, 1828 ; d. September 30, 1830.
3. *Sarah*, b. September 12, 1830 ; d. April 17, 1835.
4. *John-Wesley*, b. Nov. 21, 1832 ; d. March 2, 1894, unm.; he was educated at Dickinson College, read law with F. K. Boas, Esq., and admitted to the bar in 1856 ; during the war for the Union he entered the service in 1862 as captain in the 127th regt., P. V.; upon the organization of the 201st regt., P. V. he was commissioned lieutenant-colonel ; in May, 1865, was appointed commandant of the "Soldier's Rest" at Alexandria, Virginia ; mustered out with his regiment June 21, 1865 ; upon the organization of the National Guard of Penn'a, he was adjutant of the Fifth Division, and subsequently adjutant of the Third Brigade; as an attorney he was careful, methodical and trustworthy ; as a military officer he was highly re-

5. *Francis-Asbury*, b. April 8, 1837 ; resides at Harrisburg; at the beginning of the Civil War in 1861 served in the three months' service as adjutant of the 11th regt. P. V. ; in 1862 raised for the nine months' service company A of the 127th regt., P. V., and participated in the Fredericksburg campaign ; in 1864 he assisted in organizing the 201st regt , P. V., of which he was commissioned colonel and served in that capacity until mustered out at the close of the war ; he was a clerk in the Harrisburg National Bank prior to the war ; subsequently cashier of the banking house of Jay Cooke & Co., in New York, for a period of seven years ; was a trustee for twelve years of the Pennsylvania State Lunatic Hospital, and secretary of the Board ; and from 1891 to 1895 deputy superintendent of banking. Col. Awl, m. June 5, 1872, Mary Elizabeth Thompson, b. August 9, 1847 in New York city ; and they had issue :

    a. *Jay-Wesley*, b. May 19, 1873.

    b. *Fruncis-Asbury*, b. August 13, 1876.

6. *Jacob-McKendree*, b. February 25, 1840 ; d. August 29, 1850.
7. *Fannie-Horning*, b. May 8, 1842.
8. *Martha-Ann*, b. April 27, 1844 ; d. July 19, 1849.
9. *Stephen-George*, b. June 9, 1848 d. December, 31, 1848.

IV. SAMUEL AWL,² (Jacob,¹) b. March 5, 1773, in Paxtang township, then Lancaster county, Pa.; d. July 1, 1842, in Augusta township, Northumberland county, Pa. In the early part of his life was engaged in the mercantile business in Harrisburg, but about 1800 removed to a farm in Augusta township, Northumberland county, one mile east of Sunbury, where he resided during life ; served as commissioner of the county, was a justice of the peace, and filled other offices of trust ; he was a prominent member of the masonic fraternity, and during the anti-masonic crusade, one of the few who kept up old Lodge No. 22, at Sunbury. Mr. Awl, m., April 27, 1795, MARY MACLAY; b. March 9, 1776, at Harris' Ferry; d.

August 13, 1823; daughter of Hon. William Maclay and Mary McClure Harris. They had issue:

 i. William-Maclay, b. May 24, 1799, in Harrisburg, Pa.; d. November 19, 1876, in Columbus, O. He studied medicine and graduated at Jefferson College, Philadelphia. At first located near Lancaster, Ohio., in 1825; but shortly after removed to Somerset, in that State. In 1833, he went to Columbus, and was appointed physician at the State prison. While acting in that capacity, the lamentable condition of the few insane persons there confined for want of a better asylum, first awoke in him a desire to ameliorate their condition. Out of this sympathy came his suggestion, in 1835, for the organization of the Ohio Medical Association, through which grew all, save one, of the benevolent institutions of that State. Upon the incorporation of the Ohio Lunatic Asylum in 1837, he was appointed, first, a director, and afterwards superintendent. He occupied the position for twelve years, resigning in 1850. In 1844, at the meeting of the American Medical Association, Dr. Awl first proposed the education of feeble-minded persons. Governor Todd, in 1862, appointed him superintendent of the State Capitol, which office he held six years. In his declining years, he served as physician to the Ohio Institution for the Blind, which he had been largely instrumental in organizing. He was alike useful, distinguished and respected in the church. He was a member of the First Presbyterian church of Columbus, and chosen an elder in 1856, in which office he served to the day of his death with distinguished devotion and fidelity. Dr. Awl m. January 28, 1830, Rebecca Loughey, of Circleville, O., and had *Mary-Harris, John, Woodward, Maggie* and *Jennie*.

 ii. Mary-Harris, b. September 1, 1802; d. November 29, 1870; m. William C. Gearhart, of Rush township, Northumberland county, Pa., and they had issue (surname Gearhart): *Maclay, Mary-Ann, Washington* and *Charles*.

 iii. Charles-Maclay, b. January 5, 1804; d. s. p.

 iv. Eleanor-Maclay, b. November 22, 1806; a widow, residing in Sunbury, Pa.; m. Ezra Grosman, many years engaged in the printing business in New York city; their only child, *John-Ira*, was wounded in the first battle of Bull Run, and died soon after.

 v. Charles-Samuel, b. August 1, 1808; removed early in life to Peoria county, Ill., where he engaged in farming;

was a justice of the peace several years, up to the time of his death ; m. Lucy Duncan, of New Berlin, Pa., and they had *Ellen, George, Harriet, Lucy, William, Samuel* and *Robert-Harris.*

vi. *George-Washington,* b. July 27, 1810 ; d. September 4, 1829, in Augusta township, Northumberland county, Pa.

vii. *Sarah-Irwin,* b. June 1, 1812 ; resides in Sunbury, Pa.; m. Hon. George C. Welker, of Sunbury, and they had issue(surname Welker)*Amelia-E., Annie-M., William I., Rachael, J.-Cares, Sarah-A. Eliza, George-J.* and *Mary.*

viii. *Hester-Hall,* b. August 16, 1814; resides in Sunbury, Pa.; m. William Brindel, a nephew of Governor Ritner, and they had issue (surname Brindel) *Rebecca, Dyson, Ezra, Jane* and *Ann.*

ix. *Elizabeth-Jane,* b. November 28, 1816 ; m. Daniel Rohrbach, and they had issue (surname Rohrbach) *Ellen, Harris, Elmira, Clara, Elizabeth* and *Jerome.*

x. *Robert-Harris,* b. December 27, 1819 ; studied medicine and graduated from Pennsylvania Medical College, Philadelphia, in 1842 ; practiced medicine at Gratztown and Halifax, in Pennsylvania, and afterwards at Columbus, O., where for three years he was an assistant physician in the State Lunatic Asylum, resigning on account of ill-health ; he returned to Sunbury in 1841, where he again resumed practice, and now resides ; was elected treasurer of Northumberland county in 1863. Dr. Awl was twice married ; m. first, Eliza Bower, who deceased shortly after ; m. secondly, November 21, 1849, Rebecca Pursel, and their children are *William-Maclay. Ellen-E.* and *Mary-Pursel.*

V. JANE AWL,[2] (Jacob,[1]) b. September 25, 1774, in Paxtang ; d. May, 1832, in Chillicothe, O.; was twice m.; first, to THOMAS GREGG, b. about 1770 ; d. in 1805, at Chillicothe, O.; was several years a prominent merchant in Harrisburg, Pa., where he married the daughter of Jacob Awl ; subsequently removed to the "Far West," in that day the State of Ohio—at Chillicothe, where he lived and died. They had issue (surname Gregg) :

i. *Sarah-Sturgeon,* d. in Chillicothe, O., December, 1830 ; m. William Steele, son of Rev. Robert Steele, of Pittsburgh, and had issue (surname Steele) *Jane, Isabel,* m. Joseph R. Porter, and *Frederick-R.*

6.   ii. *Margaret-Ferguson*, m. first, William D. Clarie ; second, William D. Skerrett.
   iii. *Robert-Nathan-Awl*, d. at the age of twenty-three, unm.

Mrs. Jane Awl Gregg, m. secondly, Hon. ARCHIBALD MACLEAN. No issue.

VI. MARGARET FERGUSON GREGG,[3] (Jane,[2] Jacob,[1]) b. January 2, 1799, in Harrisburg ; d. August 24, 1864, in Cincinnati, O.; was twice married : first, in 1817, WILLIAM D. CLARIE, of Philadelphia ; d. 1822. They had issue (surname Clarie):

   i. *Jane-Mary*, b. May 11, 1820, in Chillicothe, O.; m. Lewis French, b. January 24, 1814, in Troy, O.; son of Asa French and Sarah Benham ; graduated from Denison University in 1840 ; was an educator ten years ; graduated from the Law School of the Cincinnati University in 1853, and was in the active practice of his profession until 1882, since which time, occasionally, in the higher courts of his own State and of the United States ; their only son, *Morris-Stroud French*, b. September 28, 1856, in Cincinnati, O.; educated in the public schools and University of Cincinnati ; a two years' course in medicine in the medical college at Cincinnati, graduating from Jefferson Medical College in 1876 ; is in the active practice of his profession at Philadelphia, where he now holds the office of police surgeon ; he m., in 1877, Fannie Boyd, only daughter of Thomas A. and Susan W. Boyd, and they have *Susan-Whitmore*.

Mrs. Clarie, m. secondly, April 7, 1825, WILLIAM HENRY SKERRETT, of Philadelphia, b. February 4, 1792 ; d. July 17, 1864, at Cincinnati, O.; son of Joseph Skerrett* and Mary Eva Humbert. They had issue (surname Skerrett) :

   i. *Ann*, b. December 27, 1825 ; d. s. p.
   ii. *Mary-Ann*, m. Morris Robeson Stroud, of Philadelphia.
   iii. *Elizabeth*.

---

*JOSEPH SKERRETT, b. September 17, 1752; d. June 11, 1804 ; m., June 20, 1776, by Rev. Henry Muhlenberg, MARY EVA HUMBERT, d. in 1812 ; both of Philadelphia. They had issue :

   i. *Eliza*, b. March 19, 1777.
   ii. *Margaret*, b. February 2, 1779 ; m. George Tryon.

    iv. *Joseph-Salathiel*, captain in United States Navy ; m. Maggie Love Taylor, daughter of Captain Algernon Sidney-Taylor, United States Marine Corps.
    v. *William-Henry*, m. Ella-Virginia-Delemere Browne, daughter of John M. Browne, of California.
    vi. *Margaret-Maria-Denning*, d. December 14, 1879 ; m. Benjamin Evans, of Cincinnati, O.

---

  iii. *Mary*, b. January 15, 1781 ; d. January 23, 1857.
  iv. *Joseph-Warner*, b. December 24, 1782 ; d. s. p.
  v. *James*, b. December 18, 1784 ; m. Jane Armatt.
  vi. *George-Adam*, b. March 22, 1787 ; d. June 27, 1862 ; m. Ann Pancoast.
  vii. *Kitty*, (twin) b. March 22, 1787 ; d. 1812 ; m. John Parham.
  viii. *William-Henry*, b. February 4, 1792 ; d. July 17, 1864 ; m. Mrs. Margaret Ferguson Gregg Clarie.
  ix. *David-Christie*, b. August 6, 1796 ; m. Fannie Bailey.

AYRES FAMILY.*

I. SAMUEL AYRES, of the county Antrim, Province of Ulster, Ireland, born of Scottish Covenanter ancestors, arrived in Philadelphia, with his wife and daughters, in 1745. The voyage across the ocean was protracted, causing much suffering for want of water. His wife was MARGARET RICHMOND, of same county, who died in Philadelphia in 1746. He then moved to the Scotch-Irish settlement at Deep Run, Bucks county, Pa., where he died in 1747. They had issue, all born in Ireland:

2.   i. *William*, b. 1720; m. Mary Kean.
     ii. *John*, d. young.
     iii. *Mary*, m. John Kean, of Philadelphia, and d. soon after marriage, s. p. John Kean m. secondly Mary Dunlop. (*see Hamilton record.*)
3.   iv. *Elizabeth*, b. 1731; m. Anthony McNeill.
     v. *Margaret*, m. John Moore, and left one daughter, Elizabeth, who m. Joseph Featherbee. They had a son and daughter, *Margaret*, who m. Richard Streeper.

II. WILLIAM AYRES,² (Samuel,¹) b. in 1720, in the county Antrim, Ireland, came to the Province of Pennsylvania previous to 1745, in advance of his father's family and settled in the country contiguous to the Pennepack, then Philadelphia county, Pa. In the year 1773, William Ayres with all his family, excepting Samuel and Charles, who remained in the old locality, moved to the West, then in Paxtang township, Lancaster county, now Middle Paxtang, Danphin county, Pa., and purchased land on the east side of Peter's mountain, where the turnpike crosses, three miles above Dauphin. The com-

---

*The name " Ayres," with its synonyms Ayers, Ayre, Eyre, &c., is not uncommon; commentators differ as to its origin. Lower, in "Family names," London, 1860, derives it from "Hæres," an heir. Whilst Ferguson, in his "Name System," derives it from old Saxon "Hari," warrior.

mon road terminated at that point, and when supervisor of roads in 1781, he constructed the first road *across* the mountain. In the map of purchase from the Indians, only twenty-four years previously (1749), the country west of the mountain is entitled "Saint Anthony's wilderness." He was several times elected to township offices. Although nearly sixty years old, we find him doing Revolutionary service in Captain Richard Manning's Company of the 4th Battalion of Lancaster county, Colonel James Burd, March 13, 1776 (*see Penna. Archives*). In the winter of 1784–5, he was accidently drowned in Fishing creek, near old Fort Hunter, his wife having died previously, and both were buried in the old graveyard above Dauphin, where sleep all the oldest residents of that section of the county. William Ayres m. MARY KEAN, daughter of Charles Kean,* of the same locality. They had issue, all born in Philadelphia county, now Moreland township, Montgomery county, Pennsylvania:

4.   i. *Samuel*, b. March 28, 1749; m. Deborah Yerkes.
5.   ii. *Charles*, b. 1750; m. Esther Yerkes.
6.   iii. *John*, b. February 9, 1752; m. Mary Montgomery.
     iv. *Margaret*, b. October 9, 1754; d. December 24, 1823; m. William Forster; (*see Forster record.*)
     v. *Esther*, (Hettie,) b. 1755; d. March 2, 1830; m. March 31, 1782, by Rev. John Elder, James Reed, of one of the oldest families of Paxtang township, and located on Scull's map of 1759, and for whom Reed township, Dauphin county, was named. Their children (surname Reed) were *John; Deborah; Elizabeth*, m. her cousin, Judge McNeil, of Montgomery county; *William*, b. July 9, 1789; d. November 6, 1864; m. first, Elizabeth Steele; m. secondly, Clara Hatfield; he was a highly esteemed and prominent man in his township; and *Mary*, m. Thomas McConnell.

III. ELIZABETH AYRES,² (Samuel,¹) b. 1731; d. Dec. 28, 1818; m. 1752, Anthony McNeill, a fellow passenger from the north of Ireland, who arrived in the province in 1745, and settled in Moreland township, now Montgomery county, Pa.; b.

---

* *Charles Kean* d. September 5, 1747, aged forty-six. His tombstone bears nearly the earliest date in Abington graveyard.

Ayres Family. 49

1723; d. February 27, 1791. Both buried in Abington church cemetery. They had issue (surname McNeill):

   i. Samuel, b. Aug. 29, 1753; d. May 8, 1817. He was a volunteer in Capt. Longstreth's co. in the War of the Revolution, and wounded in the battle of Princeton; subsequently appointed brigade quartermaster in Gen. Hand's brigade, of Gen. Sullivan's expedition against the New York Indians, in 1779. His journal of the expedition is printed in vol. xv. of Penn'a Archives. Major McNeill m. May 25, 1780, Mary Palmer, dau. of John Palmer and Mary Lukens, and sister of Geo. Palmer, deputy surveyor of Northampton co., and of the Penn family estates; b. July 11, 1752; d. July 11, 1810. They had issue:

     1. *Palmer*, b. Oct. 4, 1781; d. Dec. 15, 1809.
     2. *Elizabeth*, b. Sept. 12, 1783; d. March 24, 1854, unm.
     3. *Sarah*, b. Dec. 29, 1786: d. in Philadelphia, Jan'y 16, 1882, aged 96 years. This venerable lady seemed to be the connecting link between the present generation and the kindred who had crossed the ocean nearly a century and a half before—whom she had seen and whom she had known. She m. Joseph Heaton, of Philadelphia, and had (surname Heaton):

       a. *Maud-Hayes*, b. 1807; d. 1872; m. David Hunter, M. D., Tamaqua.
       b. *Reuben-Ayres*, b. June 21, 1813; d. July 14, 1893; m. Mary Carter, of Penzance, Cornwall, England, b. Jan'y 17, 1819. They had issue, all born in Tamaqua, Schuylkill co., Pa.:

         1. *Samuel-McNeill*, b. Nov. 2, 1838.
         2. *Elizabeth-Ayres*, b. Oct. 15, 1840; m. W. F. Donaldson, of Phila.
         3. *William-Henry*, b. March 22, 1843.
         4. *Robert-Carter*, b. March 1, 1846.
         5. *Sarah-Jane*, b. Jan'y 2, 1849.
         6. *Edmund-Hunter*, b. April 18, 1851; m. Jeannette Dales Marr, of Milton.
         7. *George-Washington*, b. Nov. 24, 1853.
         8. *Reuben-Augustus*, b. May 12, 1856.
         9. *Mary-Alice-Maud*, b. Aug. 16, 1859.
         10. *James-Arthur*, b. May 23, 1861.

   ii. Hiram, b. Oct. 6, 1763; a country gentleman; he was appointed, Nov. 28, 1817, by Gov. Snyder, an associate judge for Montgomery county, which honorable position he held until his death, April 22, 1837. Judge McNeill m. his cousin Elizabeth Reed, dau. of James Reed and Esther Ayres, both of Dauphin county; b. Sept. 11, 1787; d. Jan'y 7, 1836; both buried in Abington cemetery. They had issue :

    1. *Esther-Ayres*, b. July 2, 1818; d. May 6, 1859; buried in Abington cemetery; m. Feb. 5, 1839, David Shelmire, of Montgomery county, and had issue (surname Shelmire) *Mary-Elizabeth*, b. Dec. 25, 1839; d. in infancy, and *Jacob*, b. Oct. 24, 1841.
    2. *Samuel-Ayres*, b. Oct. 2, 1823: d. in infancy.
    3. *Elizabeth*, b. July 7, 1824; d. June 14, 1892; m. William Edge, of Downingtown, Penn'a, d. April 1, 1892.

  iii. *Margaret*, b. April 10, 1766; d. Sept. 2, 1797; m. Jesse Kirk.
  iv. *Mary*, b. Jan'y 16, 1767; d. Dec. 21, 1856; unm.

IV. SAMUEL AYRES,[3] (William,[2] Samuel,[1]) b. March 28, 1749; became a prominent citizen, a substantial farmer, and an elder in the Presbyterian church at Abington; license to marry issued December 12, 1772, (Penn'a Arch., 2d ser., vol. v.,) and January 17, 1773, m. DEBORAH YERKES, eldest daughter of Silas Yerkes and his wife, Hannah Durgan, of Welsh descent, and Baptists in religion, whose ancestors arrived at an early period from Holland, whither they had fled from their fatherland on account of religious persecution, and settled in that part of Montgomery county called "North Wales" to this day. Samuel Ayres d. October 26, 1804, and his wife d. February 11, 1826; both buried in the cemetery of Abington church, a stronghold of Presbyterianism founded in 1709. They had issue;

    i. *Silas*, b. June 15, 1774; d. November 13, 1795.
7. *ii.* *William*, b. December 23, 1776; m. Mary Shelmire.
    iii. *Esther*, (Hetty,) b. September 15, 1781; m. November 20, 1800. John Carr, of Montgomery county, Pa; had nine children. *Eliza*, third child, m. John Shelmire; residence, Huntingdon valley, Montgomery county, Pa.
8. *iv.* *Elizabeth*, b. February 25, 1791; m. James Comly.
9. *v.* *Hiram*, b. August 13, 1795; m. Mary Ann Ralston.

V. CHARLES AYRES,[3] (William,[2] Samuel,[1]) b. 1750; d. 1806, in Montgomery county, Pa.; a Revolutionary soldier; m. ESTHER YERKES, b. 1755; d. 1809; sister of his brother Samuel's wife. Had one child, *Mary;* b. January 10, 1780; d. July 24, 1869; buried in the Baptist cemetery at Davisville, Bucks county; she m. Dec. 31, 1804, Jonathan Yerkes, of Moreland township, Montgomery county, Pa., son of George and Rebecca Yerkes. Had issue (surname Yerkes):

    i. *Eliza-Bowen*, b. August 3. 1805; d. Dec. 25, 1864.
    ii. *Edward-Ayres*, b. March 20, 1808.
    iii. *Israel-Hallowell*, b. April 22, 1814.
    iv. *Charles-Ayres*, b. June 7, 1816.
    v. *George-Leach*, b. May 4, 1821.

VI. JOHN AYRES,[3] (William,[2] Samuel,[1]) b. February 9, 1752. At the age of twenty-one years, accompanied his father and family in their movement to Paxtang township, Lancaster, now Dauphin county, Pa.; subsequently became the owner of the homestead there established, and added thereto a certain tract of land called "Ayresburg." In 1775, on the first call for volunteers for the Revolutionary army, he enlisted in Captain Matthew Smith's company of riflemen, formed in Lancaster county, and detailed on the expedition against Quebec under Arnold, but whilst the army lay before Boston, he took sick and was invalided. On the 13th March, 1776, he again enlisted in Captain Manning's company, 4th Battalion of Lancaster county, commanded by Colonel James Burd. His father and several of his connections belonged to the same company. The *Oracle of Dauphin*, in announcing his death, August 17, 1825, remarks that "he was the last of the Revolutionary patriots in his neighborhood." John Ayres was twice married; m. first, in 1781, MARY MONTGOMERY, daughter of General William Montgomery, of Mahoning, now Danville, Pa., who died at the age of twenty-three years, without issue. He m. secondly, in 1786, JANE LYTLE, eldest daughter of Joseph Lytle, of Lytle's Ferry, in Upper Paxtang township, Dauphin county, Pa. Jane Lytle was born near Anderson's Ferry, March 1, 1767; d. in Harrisburg, Pa., May 7, 1831. The old burying-ground, one mile above Dauphin, contains the remains of this branch of the Ayres family. They had issue, all born in Middle Paxtang township, Dauphin county, Pa.:

      i. Sarah-Ellen, b. March 9, 1787; d. August 17, 1864; unm.
10. *ii. William*, b. December 14, 1788; m. Mary Elizabeth Bucher.
      iii. Mary, b. December 17, 1790; d. September 17, 1868; unm.
      iv. Margaret, b. February 25, 1793; d. December 23, 1867; m. James Forster; (*see Forster record.*)
      v. John-Lytle, b. June 7, 1795; d. August 10, 1857; unm.
      vi. Matilda, b. June 7, 1797; d. July 2, 1872; buried at Dauphin; m. April 30, 1826, William Armstrong, a descendant of Robert Armstrong, the earliest settler and first landholder about Halifax, in Dauphin county, receiving his deeds, 1764, from the Penns, and giving name to Armstrong creek and Armstrong valley; b. October 7, 1801; d. at the homestead in Millersburg July 31, 1878. Had issue (surname Armstrong):

          1. *Jane Elizabeth*, b. October 6, 1827; m. October 9, 1854, B. Frank Horning, of Phoenixville, and had (surname Horning):

              a. James Oscar, b. August 3, 1855.
              b. Charles, b. March 12, 1858.
              c. Lewis, b. March 17, 1861.

          2. *John Ayres*, b. October 31, 1830; d. young.
          3. *Charles*, b February 22, 1837; d. in infancy.
          4. *William Ayres*, b. December 12, 1837.

      vii. Eliza-Jane, b. January 17, 1806; d. August 2, 1830; unm.

VII. WILLIAM AYRES,[4] (Samuel,[3] William,[2] Samuel,[1]) former, of Huntingdon Valley, Moreland township, Montgomery county, Pa., b. December 23, 1776; d. December 14, 1854; m., January 22, 1801, MARY SHELMIRE of the same locality, who was b. February 24, 1776; d. August 30, 1846; both buried in Abington churchyard. They had issue:

      i. Charles, b. December 24, 1801; d. December 7, 1887; unm.
      ii. Deborah, b. March 21, 1803; d. July 10, 1854; m., December 14, 1825, David Shipps; had 10 children; among others William Ayres Shipps, of Philadelphia.
      iii. Samuel, b. September 20, 1805; d. June 24, 1866; m., January 15, 1829, Emily W. Sheetz, and had:

          1. *Catharine S.*, b. October 3, 1829.

Ayres Family. 53

2. *William S*, b. February 16, 1831; m., December 28, 1858, Sarah B. Blake, of Indianapolis, Ind., and had Margaret, b. February 16, 1862; d. November 21, 1887; m. O. C. Robinson, M. D.
3. *Mary-Anna*, b. September 5, 1838; m., April 30, 1863, Edwin Rodney Rose, b. March 4, 1885, in New Hope, Bucks county, Pa.; and had issue (surname Rose) *Emily*, b. May 15, 1864.

iv. Rachel, b. November 8, 1816; d. March 22, 1893, s. p.; m. William Horner Hart, b. April 28, 1818, in Warminster, Bucks county, Pa.

VIII. ELIZABETH AYRES,[4] (Samuel,[3] William,[2] Samuel,[1]) b. February 25, 1791, in Montgomery county, Pa.; d. August 25, 1863. Her name and memory have been perpetuated in "Bethayres," an important station on the North Pennsylvania railroad. She m., in 1812, JAMES COMLY, a descendant of Henry Comly and Joan Tyler, who came to Philadelphia with William Penn in 1682. He was a prominent man in his county, a member of the Legislature, and a justice of the peace. They lived at the "Manor House" in Moreland township, Montgomery county. They had issue (surname Comly):

i. Franklin-Ayres, b March 12, 1813; d. at his residence, "Valley Green," near Fort Washington, Pa., April 23, 1887; buried in Abington cemetery. Mr. Comly was thirty years president of the North Pennsylvania railroad, and a prominent man in financial circles of Philadelphia. Unm.

ii. Sarah-Willett, b October 29, 1814; d. at her residence in Germantown, April 11, 1887; m , April 6, 1839, William Lawrence Paxson, son of Joshua and Mary Willett Paxson; b. February 29, 1808; d. June 12, 1878. Both buried at Abington; and had issue (surname Paxson):

1. *Franklin-Comly*, b. November 16, 1839.
2. *Eliza-Ayres*, b. June 11, 1842; m. Jacob C. Paxson, and had issue.
3. *Ann-Willett*, b. May 12, 1848; m. Samuel H. Dickey, and had issue.
4. *William-Henry*, b. September 9, 1851.

iii. Joshua, b. April 7, 1819; d. November 20, 1887, at his residence in Chestnut Hill, Philadelphia; m., September 12, 1848, Catharine, daughter of Jacob Peters and Elizabeth Rex, and had:

1. *Elizabeth*, b. September 13, 1849; m., June 29, 1871, Winfield Scott Purviance, son of Samuel H. Purviance and Caroline Irwin, attorney-at-law, Allegheny City, Pa.; and had issue (surname Purviance): *Samuel-H.*, *Catharine-C.*, *Wynne* and *Evelyn*.

iv. *Samuel-Willett*, b. December 17, 1820; d. May 25, 1884, in San Francisco; he was major of the 20th Cavalry in the War of the Rebellion; m. Julia E. Peters; both buried at St. Thomas church, White Marsh; and had issue:
  1. *Emma*, m., 1872, William F. Trexler.
  2. *James.*
  3. *Franklin-Ayres.*

IX. HIRAM AYRES,[4] (Samuel,[3] William,[2] Samuel,[1]) b. in Huntingdon Valley, Montgomery county, Pa., August 13, 1795; d. October 17, 1870. Moved to Philadelphia in 1828. December 14, 1848, appointed by Governor Wm. F. Johnston, "Bark Inspector" for the city and county of Philadelphia, and held this office until February 12, 1852. Elected one of the Commissioners of the old Spring Garden District previous to the "consolidation" in 1854. An elder in the Presbyterian church. He was a man of exemplary character, learning and ability. Mr. Ayres m., first, May 22, 1817, MARY ANN RALSTON, of Philadelphia; b. in 1796; d. July 11, 1864; both buried at Abington church. They had issue:

i. *George-Ralston*, b. in Montgomery county, Pa., March 20, 1818; d. July 16, 1881; m., December 23, 1852, Ellen Weatherly, daughter of David Weatherly, of Philadelphia; b. November 17, 1826; d. May 20, 1880; both buried in Woodland cemetery; and had issue:
  1. *Mary*, d. early.
  2. *Henry*, b. August 6, 1856, in Philadelphia; manufacturer; m., November 2, 1885, Lizzie W. Hicks; and had issue:
    a. Edward-Clifford, b. September 24, 1886.
    b. Wayne-Egbert, b. August 11, 1889.
  3. *Isabella-R.*
  4. *Ellen-Ralston.*

11. ii. *William*, b. March 27, 1820; m., first, Elizabeth DeArmand Chambers; second, Ellen L. Wolf.

Hiram Ayres m., secondly, January 12, 1865, in Holmesburg, Philadelphia county, ELIZABETH NEVILLE, daughter of Charles and Elizabeth Neville, of Somerset county, New Jersey, who survived her husband, and d. May 2, 1873 ; buried in the old Pennepack church cemetery, near Bustleton.

X. WILLIAM AYRES,[4] (John,[3] William,[2] Samuel,[1]) b. December 14, 1788, at the homestead in Middle Paxtang township, Dauphin county, Pa.; d., May 26, 1856, in Harrisburg, Pa. William Ayres quit the farm to enter upon more congenial pursuits. First, a justice of the peace by commission, Dec. 13, 1819, from Governor Findlay, and afterwards in 1824 by Governor Shultz ; appointed, in 1824, by Governor Hiester, major of the 16th regiment Pennsylvania militia. Becoming a citizen of Harrisburg, he was admitted to the bar of Dauphin county April 7, 1826. Elected to the Pennsylvania Legislature for the years 1833, '34, and '35, he became prominent in the political party to which he was attached, and one of the most eloquent and persistent advocates for the establishment of the free-school system of Pennsylvania. In 1839, elected to the councils of the borough, he projected the water works, which were constructed and completed in 1841, mainly through his individual efforts. In 1841, he was elected a director of the United States Bank, at Philadelphia. In 1850, he organized the Harrisburg gas company, and, as first president, constructed the works, which have been a success from the beginning. In 1853, on the solicitation of citizens of Huntingdon, he became the president of the Huntingdon and Broad Top railroad ; put the road under contract, and in course of construction, which insured its early completion. In 1854 he projected and organized the Harrisburg and Hamburg railroad company, and was engaged in this improvement, as president, with engineers in the field, at the time of his death. Possessing public confidence, he was the recipient of many honorable and responsible trusts. He was a man of large *physique*— impressive and handsome appearance—popular manners, with untiring energy and ambition, and unselfish to a fault. His life was a useful one, and his works live after him. William

56   *Pennsylvania Genealogies.*

Ayres m., May 16, 1817, MARY ELIZABETH BUCHER, b. April 23, 1795, in Harrisburg, Pa.; d. July 31, 1847 (*see Bucher record*); with her husband buried in the Harrisburg cemetery. They had issue :

12.   *i. Bucher*, b. February 3, 1818; m. Jane Alice Lyon.
    ii. John, b. September 16, 1819 ; d. September 17, 1821 ; buried in old Dauphin graveyard.
    iii. Mary-Elizabeth, b. June 8, 1821 ; m., June 20, 1843, James Anderson. (*see Anderson record.*)
13.   *iv. William*, b. March 8, 1823 ; m. Ellen Criswell.
    v. Susan-Bucher, b. October 6, 1826; d. August 7, 1861; m., December 11, 1856, Andrew J. Jones, of Harrisburg, son of Robert T. Jones and Margaret Williamson, who emigrated to America in 1806, and settled in Bainbridge, Lancaster co., Pa. Andrew was b. in County Donegal, Ireland, in 1803, and was well educated. He became a successful merchant in Harrisburg. Was appointed postmaster by President Taylor, which position he held four years ; d. Jan. 18, 1867 ; buried with his wife, Susan B. Ayres, and her children, in the Harrisburg Cemetery. Mr. Jones m., first, Mary Ann Jones, and had John Cameron and Samuel T.: m., secondly, Susan B. Ayres and had (surname Jones):
      1. *Mary-Ellen*, b. Oct. 9, 1857; d. April 16, 1862.
      2. *Andrew-J.*, b. Oct. 5, 1859 ; d. May 26, 1860.
      3. *Susan-Ayres*, b. June 8, 1861 ; d. Jan. 17, 1864.
    Mr. Jones m.. thirdly, Sarah A. Buckman, of Burlington, N. J.
14.   *vi. George-Bucher*, b. Feb. 12, 1829 ; m. Mary R. Smith.
    vii. Eliza-Jane, b. Jan. 10, 1831 ; d. May 10, 1879 ; m. Sept. 28, 1852, by the Rev. Dr. Wm. R. Dewitt, Samuel Lytle Addams, of Cumberland co., Pa.; b. Jan. 19, 1821; d. May 22, 1881, and both buried in the Shippensburg cemetery. Mr. Addams was a successful farmer, and the son of Samuel Addams, b. 1774; d., 1823 ; and Elizabeth Harkness, his wife, b. 1784, d. 1833 ; and grandson of Abraham Addams, of Cumberland county. They had issue (surname Addams):
      1. *William-Ayres*, b. May 12, 1853 ; banker ; m. by Rev. W. A. McCarrell, Dec. 31, 1884, Alice J. Lawton, b. Jan. 12, 1857 ; d. Nov. 30, 1888; daughter of Robert J. and Elouisa Lawton, of Shippensburg.
      2. *Mary* (twin), b. May 12, 1853 ; m. March 6, 1879, David T. Holland, Shippensburg, merchant.
15.   *viii. John*, b. Feb. 27, 1835 ; m. Matilda Scott.

XI. WILLIAM AYRES,[5] (Hiram,[4] Samuel,[3] William,[2] Samuel,[1]) b. March 27, 1820, in Moreland township, Montgomery county, Pa.; d. September 10, 1881, in Philadelphia; by occupation a merchant and manufacturer, he was eminently successful; elected, November 29, 1851, by the commissioners of the old Spring Garden District, a director of the Pennsylvania Railroad Company, a high and honorable position, which he retained until February 6, 1854; m., first, ELIZABETH DEARMAND CHAMBERS, daughter of John Chambers, of Philadelphia; d. March 4, 1873; both buried in Woodland cemetery. They had issue, all b. in Philadelphia:

16.   *i. George-Ralston*, b. June 25, 1846; m. Laura Hayes.
17.   *ii. John-Chambers*, b. October 22, 1848; m. Mary C. Beach.
     iii. William-Montgomery, b. May 8, 1851; merchant and manufacturer, and prominent in business and political circles of Philadelphia; m. Sarah, daughter of Benjamin T. Stauffer, of Manheim, Pa.
18.   *iv. Louis-Harlow*, b. March 2, 1855; m. Anna T. Cox.
     v. Mary-Ralston, m. James Edwin Huston, of Philadelphia.

William Ayres m., secondly, March 10, 1874, ELLEN LOUISE WOLF, of Philadelphia, who d. Dec. 27, 1890.

XII. BUCHER AYRES,[5] (William,[4] John,[3] William,[2] Samuel,[1]) b. Feb. 3, 1818, in Harrisburg, Pa.; baptized by Rev. N. R. Snowden; educated in the schools of the city and at Dickinson College, Carlisle; commenced civil engineering on State works; entered the service of the Pennsylvania Railroad Co. on the opening September 1, 1849; appointed Superintendent of the Memphis and Charleston Railroad, residence, Memphis, in 1854, and continued until 1861, when he removed to Centre county, Pa., and in 1872 removed to Philadelphia. Appointed by Daniel Webster, Secretary of State, to his Department, Washington city, and detailed as Secretary to the Commissioners from Maine and Massachusetts in the negotiation of the Webster–Ashburton Treaty of 1842. Appointed August 19, 1848, Aid de Camp, with the rank of Lieut. Colonel, by Governor Wm. F. Johnston; m. April 11, 1854, by Rev. Daniel L. Hughes, of Spruce Creek Presbyterian church, JANE ALICE

Lyon, daughter of John Lyon, of Pennsylvania Furnace, Huntingdon co. (*see Lyon record.*) They had issue :

- *i. Cleonie*, b. Sept. 25, 1855, in Memphis, Tenn.; m. Jan'y 5, 1887, J. Bucher Ayres. (*See XX.*)
- *ii. Annie-Lyon*, b. Feb'y 1, 1857, in Memphis ; d. April 1, 1875, in Philadelphia ; bur. in Mount Vernon cemetery.
- *iii. Lyonel*, b. Sept. 4, 1858, in Memphis; civil engineer ; residence, Duluth, Minn.
- *v. Jane-Lyon*, b. May 24, 1862, in Centre co., Pa. D. A. R.
- *iv. Mary-Bucher*, b. November 20, 1860, in Centre co., Pa. D. A. R.
- *vi. Bucher*, b. Nov. 18, 1869, in Centre co., Pa.; machinery ; m. Oct. 12, 1892, by Rev. Charles H. Richards, May Thatcher Harlan, daughter of G. Passmore Harlan and Ellen B. Entriken, of Philadelphia, and b. Augt. 29, 1870. They have issue : *Dorothy Harlan*, b. Augt. 25, 1894, at Swarthmore, Pa.

XIII. WILLIAM AYRES,[5] (William,[4] John,[3] William,[2] Samuel,[1]) b. March 8, 1823, in Harrisburg, Pa.; commenced merchandising with his uncle, Hon. John C. Bucher, and removing to Philadelphia, entered the wholesale trade; he was appointed by Gov. Wm. F. Johnston an Aid de Camp, with the rank of Lieut. Colonel ; whilst in Major General Wm. F. Smith's Division of the Army of the Potomac, in the Rebellion, Col. Ayres was captured on Bull Run battlefield, and confined in Libby prison, Richmond, Va.; he was released April, 1862, under a *Parole d'honneur*. Col. Ayres m. first, Oct. 16, 1864, ELLEN CRISWELL, daughter of the Hon. James Criswell, of Mifflin county, (*see Criswell Family*), b. Augt. 17, 1821 ; d. Decr. 8, 1863 ; buried at McVeytown, Pa. They had issue :

- 19. *i. Mary Elizabeth*, b. Oct. 4, 1847, in McVeytown.
- *ii. James-Criswell*, b. March 16, 1849 ; d. July 17, 1851.
- *iii. Charles-Criswell*, b. Nov. 27, 1852.
- 20. *iv. Jacob-Bucher*, b in Philadelphia May 16, 1856.
- *v. John-Vance-Criswell*, b. in Phila. June 7, 1859; d. Oct. 21, 1875 ; buried in Mount Vernon cemetery.

Col. Ayres m. secondly, Jan'y 5, 1865, CATHARINE F. WATSON, of Prince Edwards' Island, and had issue :

- *vi. William-Watson*, b. in Phila., Nov. 24, 1867 ; Dr. Watson graduated at the National Medical school of the Col-

Ayres Family. 59

umbian University, Washington city, March 20, 1890; residence and practice in same city.

Col. Ayres m. thirdly, Sept. 7, 1876, Mrs. KATE W. BOTTORFF *nee* WILLIAMS, of Carlisle, Pa.

XIV. GEORGE BUCHER AYRES,⁵ (William,⁴ John,³ William,² Samuel,¹) b. February 12, 1829, in Harrisburg, Pa.; an artist, and author of a work on painting; resides in Philadelphia; m. October 10, 1867, MARY ROBBINS SMITH, b. March 29, 1838 ; d. February 1, 1878; daughter of Spencer C. Smith, of Bloomsbury, Hunterdon county, New Jersey. They had issue :

 i. Edith-Lyon, b. February 5, 1875.
 ii. Annie-Smith, b. September 15, 1876.

XV. JOHN AYRES,⁵ (William,⁴ John,³ William,² Samuel,¹) b. February 27, 1834, in Harrisburg, Pa.; d. in Reynoldsville, Pa., Jan'y 13, 1890 ; a master mechanic on the Allegheny Valley Railroad ; m. October 27, 1858, MATILDA, daughter of Frederick Scott and Ann Eliza Herman, of Harrisburg, Pa.; b. July 14, 1836. They had issue:

 i. Susan-Bucher, b. November 12, 1862.
 ii. Marylile, b. Jan'y 1, 1865: m. at home, in Reynoldsville, Pa., June 21, 1892, William H. Snyder, of Renovo, Pa.; and had issue (surname Snyder), *Helen-Ayres*, b. August 28, 1893.
 iii. William-Frederick, b. January 20, 1867.
 iv. Roberta, b. April 11, 1869.
 v. George-Bucher, b. May 14, 1871.
 vi. Charles-Scott, b. November 28, 1874.
 vii. Jane Allen, b. Nov. 22, 1877.

XVI. GEORGE RALSTON AYRES,⁶ (William,⁵ Hiram,⁴ Samuel,³ William,² Samuel,¹) b. June 25, 1846 ; manufacturer; d. at his residence in Germantown December 9, 1890; a prominent and one of the most public spirited of citizens advocating improvement to streets, etc.; m. March 7, 1867, LAURA HAYES, daughter of Robert Hayes, of Philadelphia. They had issue :

 i. William-Graham, b. February 18, 1868 ; merchant ; m. Oct. 15, 1890, Maria Jennie Saurman, b. Feb'y 26, 1868; have

Laura-Rebecca-Ayres, b. Oct. 2, 1891 ; residence, Philadelphia.
ii. *George-Ralston*, b. January 10, 1871 ; manufacturer ; m. Oct. 30, 1894, Flora Adele Moore, b. July 22, 1873 ; residence, Philadelphia.
iii. *Albert-Hayes*, b. August 14, 1873 ; d. March 25, 1882 ; buried in Laurel Hill cemetery, Philadelphia.
iv. *Elizabeth-DeArmand*, b. November 23, 1874 ; d. April 30, 1875 ; buried in Laurel Hill cemetery, Philadelphia.
v. *Helen*, b. August 8, 1879.
vi. *Walter-Chambers*, b. December 16, 1880.

XVII. JOHN CHAMBERS AYRES,[6] (William,[5] Hiram,[4] Samuel,[3] William,[2] Samuel,[1]) b. October 22, 1848 ; d. March 22, 1883 ; buried in Laurel Hill cemetery ; m. October 9, 1873, MARY C. BEACH, of Wilkes-Barre, Pa. They had issue :

i. *Charles-Sturdevant*, b. February 18, 1876.
ii. *Robert-Cox*, b. February 16, 1879.
iii. *Lucy*, b. March 11, 1880 ; d. August 18, 1880.
iv. *Mary-Kathleen*, b. August 21, 1882.

XVIII. LOUIS HARLOW AYRES,[6] (William,[5] Hiram,[4] Samuel,[3] William,[2] Samuel,[1]) b. March 2, 1855. Mr. Ayres is one of the proprietors of a large manufacturing house, a bank director and a director of the Philadelphia Bourse, and prominent in business as well as in social circles ; m. April 19, 1877, ANNA T. COX, daughter of Stephen Cox, of Philadelphia. They had issue :

i. *Elizabeth-Cox*, b. February 28, 1878.
ii. *Marion-Kent*, b. January 3, 1884.

XIX. MARY ELIZABETH AYRES,[6] (William,[5] William,[4] John,[3] William,[2] Samuel,[1]) b. in Philadelphia, October 4, 1847; m. April 30, 1866, James Victor Mazurie, b. in Philadelphia, Nov. 23, 1838 ; d. March 23, 1890 ; buried in Mount Peace cemetery, Philadelphia. He was the son of James Victor Mazurie and Sarah Lesher, and grandson of Jean Jacques Patient Mazurie ; b. Sept. 11, 1764, in Bretagne, France, merchant and a contemporary of Stephen Girard, who m. 1810, Caroline Parmentier, born in Paris. They had issue (surname Mazurie) :

1. *Henry-Roumfort*, b. Feb'y 14, 1867, in Philadelphia.
2. *William-Ayres*, b. Feb'y 1, 1870, in Warren, Pa.
3. *Ellen-Criswell*, b. Sept. 25, 1873, in Philadelphia.
4. *James-Victor*, b. Dec. 11, 1875, in Philadelphia.
5. *Mary-Bucher*, b. Nov. 16, 1877, in Philadelphia.

XX. JACOB BUCHER AYRES,[6] (William,[5] William,[4] John,[3] William,[2] Samuel,[1]) b. in Philadelphia, May 16, 1856; m. January 5, 1887, by Rev. Loyal Y. Graham, D. D., his cousin, Cleonie, daughter of Bucher Ayres and Jane Alice Lyon, of Philadelphia, iron manufacturer, McKeesport, Pa. Residence, Dravosburg, Allegheny co., Pa. They had issue :

   i. *Cleon*, b. April 4, 1888 ; d. Aug. 11, 1888.
  ii. *Alice-Lyon*, b. Dec. 19, 1891.

BARNETT FAMILY.

I. JOHN BARNETT,[1] b. 1678, in the neighborhood of Londonderry, Ireland. In company with his brother William Barnett, emigrated with his family to Pennsylvania prior to 1730, locating in Hanover township, then Lancaster county, being among the earliest settlers in that township. He died in September, 1734, his will being probated at Lancaster on the first day of October following. John Barnett left a wife, JENNETT, and the following children, all born in county Derry, Ireland:

  i. *Robert*, b. 1701; m. and removed to Virginia.
  ii. *James*, b. 1703; m. and went to Virginia with his brother; from them most of the names in the South have sprung.
3. iii. *John*, b. 1705; m. Margaret Roan.
  iv. *Joseph*, b. 1708.
  v. *Mary*, b. 1710.
  vi. *Jennett*, b. 1713; d. in 1787; unm.
  vii. *Jean*, b. 1715: m. Moses Swan; (*see Swan record.*)

II. WILLIAM BARNETT, brother of the foregoing, b. in Londonderry, Ireland, came to America with his brother John; he died in February, 1762, leaving a wife, MARGARET, and children, beside other daughters:

  i. *Joseph*.
  ii. *Sarah*.

III. JOHN BARNETT,[2] (John,[1]) b. 1705, in County Derry, Ireland; d. in January, 1785, in Paxtang township, Lancaster, now Dauphin county, Pa.; came to America with his father, having previously married MARGARET ROAN; b. 1710, in Greenshaw, Ireland; d. January, 1790, in Paxtang. They had issue:

4. i. *William*, b. 1729; m. Rebecca ———.
  ii. [*a son*], whose wife was Agnes, and had *Joseph*.
5. iii. *Samuel*, b. 1733; m. Martha ———.

Barnett Family.

6.   *iv. Joseph,* b. 1726 ; m. Elizabeth Graham.
       v. Sarah, b. 1737 ; m. ——— Curry.
7   *vi. Ann,* b. 1739 ; m. James Johnston.
       vii. Margaret, b. 1741 ; m. William Patterson, and had *John* and *Andrew.*
      viii. Andrew, b. 1743.
      ix. John, b. 1745.
      x. Jennett, b. 1747 ; d. March, 1788 ; unm.

IV. WILLIAM BARNETT,³ (John,² John,¹) b. 1729 ; d. in September, 1764, in Hanover, leaving a wife, REBECCA, and issue as follows :

    i. John, b. 1754 ; d. September 2, 1797 ; m. Jean Crain ; b. December 22, 1762 ; d. May 9, 1830.
    ii. William, b. 1756.
    iii. Mary, b. 1758.
    iv. Rebecca, b. 1760.
    v. Isabel, b. 1762.
    vi. Jehn, b. 1763.

V. SAMUEL BARNETT,³ (John,² John,¹) b. 1733, in County Derry, Ireland ; d. August, 1758 ; was twice married ; second wife, MARTHA, survived her husband. There was probably issue by both :

    i. Samuel, b. 1746 ; d. s. p.
8.   *ii. Elizabeth,* b. 1748 ; m. William Moorhead.
    iii. Martha, b. 1750 ; d. s. p.
9.   *iv. John,* b. 1753 ; m. Rachel Crosby.
    v. Sarah, b. 1755.
    vi. Rebecca, b. 1757.

VI. JOSEPH BARNETT,³ (John,² John,¹) b. 1726, in County Derry, Ireland. He married in 1749, ELIZABETH GRAHAM. Concerning him and his family, we have these incidents of pioneer life in 1757, communicated in a letter by the late Samuel Barnett, of Springfield, O. " Mr. Barnett's son William, with a son of Mr. Mackey, a neighbor, of Hanover, were taken prisoners by a band of prowling Indians. The parents of the boys tried in vain to raise a party to pursue the savages, and rescue the captives, but could obtain no assistance. Mr. Barnett and Mr. Mackey, however, armed with rifles, mounted their horses and went in pursuit. They came up to the Indians, several in number, between Hugh Grimes' (Graham's) farm and Beaver creek, likely, not more than three-fourths of a mile from Hugh Grimes, immediately in the neighborhood of where Thomas Bell, Squire Wilson, and grandfather Allen lived. They fired on the Indians, who returned it briskly. Mr. Barnett and Mr. Mackey were near together. Mackey in putting down the bullet in his rifle observed that he run down the bullett hard to kill dead. By this time the savages were close on them, and just as Mackey presented his gun a bullet passed through his arm, and his rifle fell to the ground. At this moment an Indian near by picked up his gun and shot Mackey dead. By this time Mr. Barnett had received a shot in his arm and one in the shoulder. This bullet he carried with him to the grave. So Mr. Barnett retreated. By this time he reached a little east of where Mr. Grimes lived, and between his house and Robert Elder's, he got faint from loss of blood, when he dismounted and hid himself in a field of buckwheat. I give the names of Grimes and Elder, as they occupied these farms in my day. Grandfather Barnett resided east of these farms. His horse ran home, and the neighborhood turned out. As they passed along the road Mr. Barnett got out of his hiding and resting place. He had but little use of his arm the rest of his days. I will continue the history of the captive boys. The Indians had left their encampment before they were sighted by the party who went in pursuit. They passed up Beaver creek toward the mountain, then through an orchard once owned by Andrew Kerr, afterwards Samuel Finney. The Indians told the boys to take plenty of apples as they were the last they would get for a length of time. They then took to the mountain, and this was the last of the boys. Tedious days, nights, and years passed away. For nearly seven years a kind Providence, who hears and answers the prayers of his children, watched over the boys. It appears the Indians had their cabins on or near the head waters of the Allegheny river, on a branch called something like Miskelitas. At length an Indian trader discovered the party who held William Barnett and Mackey. They, with the boys, had been several times across what is now the State of Ohio to Detroit. This Indian trader was employed by Grandfather Barnett to procure William, for which he was to give the trader an elegant horse. * * * * It was with some difficulty the traders got him away, William not being very willing to leave at first, and the squaw who had him to part with him. At last he succeeded, and was returning with him. Mr. Barnett went to Carlisle, on his way to meet them, and stopped at the same tavern which his son had reached the early part of the evening. The boy was tired traveling, and had retired. When this became known Mr. Barnett desired to see him, but the landlord at first objected ; but a fond father, who had not beheld his son for seven years, who had been the subject of anxious thoughts and prayers, now answered, could not be put off until the morrow. The son awakened from his sleep knew his father and embraced him. As may be readily supposed there was great rejoicing in Hanover, not only in the houses of the Barnetts, but all through the country, at the return of the captive. Young Mackey was sold to a Frenchman at Detroit, afterwards taken to England, and at the outset of the war of the Revolution came over with the British troops, and subsequently reached his home in old Hanover. His mother was yet living ; but she insisted that her son was killed by the Indians, and would not own him. He assured her that he was her boy ; when, at length, she told him that if he was her son he had a scar on his leg from a cut, that she would know. This was shown her, when she acknowledged that he was her long-lost child." There is extant an extended account of this thrilling episode in frontier life ; but Mr. Barnett's simple story differs little in detail thereof. Joseph Barnett, d. November, 1808, in Allegheny county, Pa., and was buried in Lebanon churchyard, ten miles from Pittsburgh. His wife, Elizabeth, d. a few years subsequent and was interred in old Hanover graveyard. They had issue:

10.   i. *William*, b. 1750 ; m. Mary Eshercombe.
11.   ii. *John*, b. August 29, 1752 ; m. Mary McEwen.
12.   iii. *Joseph*, b. 1760 ; m. Sarah Dickson.
13.   iv. *James*, b. 1762 ; m. Mary Allen.
14.   v. *Thomas*, b. 1758 ; m. Jane Finney.
15.   vi. *Elizabeth*, b. 1761; m. Samuel Sherer.
16.   vii. *Moses*, b. November 24, 1764 ; m. Martha Snodgrass.

VII. ANN BARNETT,³ (John,² John,¹) b., about 1735, in Hanover township, Dauphin county, Pa., m., first, JAMES JOHNSTON, who was killed by the Indians in 1755. They had issue (surname Johnston):

    i. Joseph.
    ii. Margaret.
    iii. Jane.

Mrs. Johnston, m., secondly, WILLIAM MCILHENNY. They had issue (surname McIlhenny):

    i. Thomas,
    ii. Agnes.
    iii. Mary.
    iv. Elizabeth.
    v. Ann.

VIII. ELIZABETH BARNETT,⁴ (Samuel,³ John,² John,¹) b. 1748; m. WILLIAM MOORHEAD. They had issue (surname Moorhead):

    i. Josiah.
    ii. Samuel, was grandfather of Rev. George Hill, D. D., of Blairsville, Pa., Rev. J. D. Moorhead, of Beaver Falls, Pa., and Rev. W. W. Moorhead, of Greensburg, Pa.
    iii. Rev. William, m. Jane, daughter of Rev. Dr. McMillan.
    iv. James.
    v. Martha, m. —— Hamilton.
    vi. Nancy, m. —— Craig.
    vii. Elizabeth, m. —— Gibson.
    viii. Esther, m. —— Gibson.
    ix. Rebecca, m. —— Wilson.
    x. Sarah, m. [John] McMillan.
    xi. Rachel, m. —— Pollock.
    xii. Lydia, m. —— Marquis; their son was Rev. D. C. Marqus, D. D., of St. Louis, Mo.

IX. JOHN BARNETT,⁴ (Samuel,³ John,² John,¹) b. 1755, in Hanover township, Dauphin County, Pa.; d. July 7, 1825, in Derry township, Westmoreland county, Pa.; served in the war of the Revolution; removed to Westmoreland county, Pa., in 1784; served as Justice of the peace from 1808 until his death; m. RACHEL CROSBY, of Fagg's Manor; b. 1758; d. April 28, 1833. They had issue:

i. Samuel, m. Rebecca McClure.
17. *ii. William*, m., first, Jane Wallace ; second, Mrs. Johnston.
18. *iii. John*, b. September 19, 1795 ; m. Nancy Morrison.
    iv. Elizabeth, m. William Hughes.
    v. Martha, m. Isaac Taylor.
    vi. Rachel, m. John Laird.

X. WILLIAM BARNETT,⁴ (Joseph,³ John,² John,¹) b. 1750. At the age of seven he was taken captive by the Indians, as previously noted. His harsh treatment by the savages impaired his health. He subsequently married MARY ESHERCOMBE, of Philadelphia, by whom he had one daughter, *Mary*, b. May 11, 1782, who married a Mr. Franks, of New York, and whose descendants now reside in that city. Mr. Barnett died about the close of the Revolution.

XI. JOHN BARNETT,⁴ (Joseph,³ John,² John,¹) b. August 18, 1752, in Hanover township. He was a farmer by occupation. At the outset of the Revolution he was appointed a lieutenant in the Hanover battalion of Associators, commanded by Colonel Timothy Green. He served with distinction at Long Island, August 27, 1776, and through the campaign of 1777 was in constant active service. During the remainder of the war, he was in command of a volunteer company, which was formed for the protection of the frontiers from the encroachments of the Tories and their allies, the savage Indians of New York. The sword which he carried through the war is now in the possession of William Barnett, of Dayton, Ohio. Major Barnett died May 12, 1823. He married, April 29, 1784, MARY MCEWEN, of Hanover, a very estimable lady. She was born September 9, 1762; died March 10, 1806, and is interred by the side of her husband. They had issue:

   i. Mary, b. June 2, 1785; d. July 7, 1840; m., December 16, 1819, Frederick Hatton, b. May, 1774; d. June 3, 1835.
   ii. Eleanor, b. 1787 ; d. 1822 ; m., February, 17, 1807, David Johnson, and had issue (surname Johnson):
      1. *John*, b. Dec. 2, 1807 ; d. Nov. 27, 1828.
      2. *David*, b. 1809 ; d. s. p.
      3. *Mary*, b. 1811; d. July 27, 1863 ; m. Harlan Morrison Hollingsworth.
      4. *Isabella*, b. 1813 ; resides in Dayton, O.

5. *William*, b. 1815; d. April 5, 1849.
6. *Elizabeth*, b. 1819; resides in Dayton, O.
7. *Joseph-Barnett*, b. May, 1821; d. July 1, 1842.

iii. Joseph, b. Oct. 1, 1789; d. Jan. 2, 1858, at Dayton, O.; m. first, April 8. 1813, Elizabeth Allen, b. April 16, 1794; d. Oct. 16, 1837, s. p.; m. secondly, April 9, 1839, Jane Rogers, b. Feb. 27, 1813; no issue. Joseph Barnett and his brother, James S., were contractors on the Pennsylvania canal, and subsequently partners in the great Sligo Iron Works, at Pittsburgh, firm of Barnett, Shorb & Co. Joseph, in the war of 1812, was in service on the Niagara frontier. He represented Montgomery county, Ohio, two terms in the Senate of that State.

iv. John-McEwen, b Sept. 7, 1791; d. July 11, 1846; m. first, Sept. 7, 1815, Jane Sherer, b. Feb. 22, 1792; d. August 30, 1829; and had issue:

1. *Elizabeth-Sherer*, b. March 14, 1817; d. February 23, 1831.
2. *Mary-Jane*, b. March 7, 1820.
3. *John-Joseph*, b. July 2, 1822; d. May 21, 1853.
4. *Eleanor*, b. September 15, 1824; d. September 18, 1827.
5. *Emily*, b. February 14, 1827; d. November 2, 1858.

Mr. Barnett, m. secondly, January 3, 1832, Julia Barnett, b. August 23, 1797; d. January 1, 1882, daughter of John Barnett. They had issue:

6. *William-Apollos*, b. Nov. 28, 1832; resides at Springfield, O.; m. June 14, 1859, Laura Theresa-Easton, b. June 24, 1834; d. May 15, 1881; and had issue:
   a. *Mary-Easton*, b. July 4, 1860.
   b. *Harry*, b. April 19, 1863; d. July 18, 1863.
   c. *Elizabeth-Johnson*, b. August 4, 1864.
   d. *William-Warren*, b. August 6, 1865.
   e. *Joseph-Guy*, b. November 26, 1871; d. July 27. 1872.
   f. *John-McGuffey*, b. October 28, 1874.

7. *Juliet-Paulina*, b. February 5, 1834.
8. *Margaret*, b. June 28, 1835; d. July 21, 1835.
9. *Samuel-Smith*, b. August 16, 1836; d. February 21, 1838.

v. William, b. September 22, 1793; d. March 31, 1831; m. December 11, 1817, Ann, daughter of Hugh Graham

Barnett Family. 69

and Mary Wallace, and had *William*. At his death she m. Colonel Jacob Wonderly, of Montgomery county, Ohio.

vi. Elizabeth, b. October 15, 1795 ; d. September 7, 1862.

vii. James-Snodgrass, b. November 25, 1798 ; d. about 1836 ; m. Hannah Thaw daughter of the late John Thaw, who went to Pittsburgh at an early day. She was a sister of William Thaw, of the Pennsylvania railroad. When a widow, in 1845, she married Reverend William Martin, of Philadelphia ; went there to reside, and died about 1865.

viii. Margaret, b. December 7, 1800 ; d June 24, 1844.

ix. Jean, b. August 22, 1803 ; d. May 23, 1804.

XII. JOSEPH BARNETT,[4] (Joseph,[3] John,[2] John,[1]) b. 1760 ; m. SARAH DICKSON of Chambersburg. He died at Pittsburgh, June 3, 1812, at the residence of his daughter, Mrs. McClure. They had issue :

19. *i. Joseph*, b. August 27, 1784 ; m. Mary Boyd.

ii. Polly, b. 1786 ; m. John Hume ; settled in the Genesee country, N.Y., but subsequently removed to near Indianapolis, Ind., and was appointed one of the first associate judges there.

iii. Sarah, b. 1788 ; m. Andrew McClure ; resided at Pittsburgh, and had issue (surname McClure) : *William* and *Alexander*.

iv. Richard, b. 1790 ; removed to and died in Missouri.

XIII. JAMES BARNETT,[4] (Joseph,[3] John,[2] John,[1]) b. 1762; d. May 1, 1805 ; m. MARY ALLEN, daughter of Samuel Allen ; b. 1762 ; d. August 13, 1813 ; both buried in Hanover church graveyard. They had issue :

20. *i. Joseph*, b. June 1, 1787 ; m. Sarah Harrison.
21. *ii. Samuel*, b. September 30, 1790 ; m. Mary Mitchell.
22. *iii. James*, b. June 11, 1796 ; m. Louisa Shira.

iv. John, b. August 30, 1798 ; d. May 1, 1818, in Lebanon, Pa.

v. Allen, b. 1799 ; d. September 19, 1859 ; m. February 19, 1826, —— Shaffer ; resided in Clark county, Ind., and had issue.

vi. Thomas, b. December 5, 1800 ; d January 20, 1866, in St. Louis.

vii. William, b. March, 5, 1803 ; d. June 13, 1828, in Warren county, Ohio.

viii. Mary, b. 1805; d. August 18, 1877; unm.
ix. Moses, b. 1807; d. s. p.

XIV. THOMAS BARNETT,⁴ (Joseph,³ John,² John,¹) b. November 13, 1761; d. March 28, 1836; m. April 27, 1790, JANE FINNEY, daughter of Samuel Finney; b. December 22, 1769; d. May 9, 1830. They had issue:

  i. *Mary,* b. November 29, 1791; d. 1848; m. Thomas Snodgrass, son of John; d. 1855. One of their daughters m. Wilson Todd, son of John Todd, of Warren county, O.
  ii. *William,* b. May 31, 1793; d. September 6, 1828; m. Mary Hummel, b. 1798; d. February 19, 1829, and had *Thomas, Josiah,* and *Harriet,* (b. 1829; d. 1881;) m. Joseph Barnett.
  iii. *Thomas,* b. January 14, 1795; d. March 13, 1858; unm.
  iv. *Susanna,* b. October 12, 1796; d. March 7. 1862; unm.
  v. *Joseph-Sherer,* b. April 17, 1798; removed to Southern Missouri, then to Arkansas, where he d. in 1858; m. and had *Carrie J.*, m. D. W. Percy; and *Marion.*
  vi. *Samuel-Finney,* b. December 19, 1799; d. s. p.
  vii. *Jane,* b. May 29, 1801; m. Henry Lutz; both deceased.
  viii. *Elizabeth,* b. June 5, 1803; d. s. p.
  xi. *Eliza-Sherer,* b. October 17, 1804; m. James B. Robinson; both deceased; and had issue (surname Robinson), *Jane, Elizabeth, Margaret,* and *Marshall.*
  x. *Sarah,* b. March 13, 1806; m. Robert Stewart. (*see Stewart record*)
  xi. *Margaret,* b. November 28, 1807; m. James A. Elder of Elder's Ridge. (*see Elder record.*)
  xii. *Nancy-Rebecca,* b. June 27, 1809; d. 1829; unm.
  xiii. *John,* b December 12, 1811; d. 1878; unm.

XV. ELIZABETH BARNETT,⁴ (Joseph,³ John,² John,)¹ b. 1761; d. September 21, 1816; m. SAMUEL SHERER,* son of

---

*Among the earliest of the Scotch-Irish emigrants was Samuel Sherer. He came from near Londonderry, Ireland, to the Province of Pennsylvania in the autumn of 1734, and located in Paxtang township, Lancaster, now Dauphin county. He was a man of means, was well educated, and became quite prominent in the Scotch-Irish settlement. His son, Joseph Sherer, was about four years old when his parents came to America. He secured a fair English education and was brought up to the life of a frontiersman, that of a farmer. During the French and Indian war, he served as a non-commissioned

Joseph Sherer of Paxtang, b. 1755; d. December 26, 1821, and are interred in Paxtang churchyard. They had issue (surname Sherer):

 i. Mary, b. September 29, 1782; d. October 21, 1807; m. November 17, 1803, James Stewart.
 ii. Joseph, b. September 6, 1785; d. March 5, 1825, near Hummelstown, Pa.; m. Mary Snodgrass. She died in Clark county, O. Their daughter *Mary* m. a Mr. Heymer, who removed to Clark county, Ohio.
 iii. Margaret, b. September 8, 1787; d. July 17, 1822; unm.
 iv. Martha-Montgomery, b. November 3, 1789; d. January 30, 1824; m. John Graham and removed to Ohio, and afterwards to Kentucky.
 v. Jane, b. February 22, 1792; d. 1829; m. John Barnett, and removed to Ohio.
 vi. Elizabeth, b. July 19, 1794; d. February 26, 1860, in Canfield, Ohio; m. March 2, 1820, Robert Elder (miller). (*see Elder record.*)

---

officer, and was in active service as a scout or ranger on the frontiers. When the thunders of the Revolution reverberated along the valley of the Susquehanna, with all his Scotch-Irish and German neighbors, he entered into the contest for liberty. In 1775 and 1776, he was in command of one of the companies of Colonel James Burd's battalion of Associators, a roll of which is to be found in the recent history of Dauphin county. Colonel Burd's farm at Tinian joined the Sherer homestead, and the two patriots were intimate friends. Captain Sherer was a member of the Committee of Observation for the county of Lancaster, and was chosen by the vote of the people a member of the first Constitutional Convention of the State of Pennsylvania, which met at Philadelphia, on the 15th of July, 1776. While in attendance on this representative body of the Revolutionary era, he took ill, returned home, and died on the 1st or 2d of December following. His remains were interred in the burial ground of old Paxtang church, of which he was a consistent member. Captain Sherer m., first, February 6, 1759, Mary McClure; subsequently m. Mary McCracken, of Northumberland county, Pa., and had issue:

 i. Mary, m. Samuel Cochran.
 ii. Samuel, b. 1755; m. Elizabeth Barnett.
 iii. John.
 iv. Jean.
 v. Richard.
 vi Joseph.
 vii. William.
 viii. Catharine.

vii. Sarah, b. March 14, 1797 ; d. November 25, 1836 ; m. June 8, 1824, Robert R. Elder. (*see Elder record.*)

viii. Juliana, b. May 23, 1799 ; d. March 7, 1879, m. December 8, 1825, David Elder, of Indiana county, Pa. (*see Elder record.*)

ix. Eleanor-W., b. 1803 ; d. April 2, 1837 ; m. March 12, 1826, Joshua Elder. (*see Elder record.*)

x. Samuel-B., b. 1805 ; d. September 6, 1866, in St. Louis ; m. in 1827, Mary Oves, of Harrisburg.

XVI. MOSES BARNETT,⁴ (Joseph,³ John,² John,¹) b. November 24, 1764 ; d. November 19, 1848 ; resided on a tract of land, deeded to him by his father, called "Barnett's Conquest," in the "Forks of Beaver Creek;" was twice married ; m., first, MARTHA SNODGRASS, daughter of William Snodgrass, b. 1773 ; d. June 1, 1802. They had issue :

i. Richard, b. November 23, 1792 : d. November 8, 1868 ; m. first, Martha Merriman ; 2dly, Eliza Dunn ; no issue.

ii. Ann, b. January 29, 1794 ; d. 1823 ; m., June, 1813, Samuel Johnson ; d. August 27, 1854, and had issue.

iii. Molly, b. September 14, 1795 ; d. April 13, 1877.

iv. Matilda, b. May 27, 1797 ; m. George Moorhead.

v. Margaret, b. March 8, 1799 ; d. 1843 ; m. Fannie Morton, and had issue.

vi. Martha, b. February 14, 1801 ; d. 1803.

Moses Barnett m., secondly, March 27, 1805, REBECCA [GREEN] ALLEN, b. 1763 ; d. July 27, 1837 (*see Allen record*). They had issue :

23. *vii. Rebecca*, b. February 19, 1806 ; m. Thomas Moorhead.

viii. Moses, b. April, 1808.

XVII. WILLIAM BARNETT,⁵ (John,⁴ Samuel,³ John,² John,¹) b. about 1793 ; was twice married : m., first, JANE WALLACE. They had issue :

i. Peter-W.
ii. Samuel.
iii. William.
iv. James.
v. Jane, m. James Patterson.
vi. Rachel, m. John Shields.
vii. Joseph-Craig.

William Barnett, m., secondly, Mrs. JOHNSTON ; d. s. p.

Barnett Family.

XVIII. JOHN BARNETT,[5] (John,[4] Samuel,[3] John,[2] John,[1]) b. October 19, 1795, in Westmoreland county, Pa.; m. February 7, 1822, NANCY MORRISON, b. March 9, 1799; d. May 27, 1876. They had issue:

    i. Jane-Elizabeth, b. October 12, 1822; d. s. p.
    ii. Rachel, b. June 27, 1824; d. April 6, 1854; m. June 12, 1849, Rev. W. M. Donaldson, and bad issue (surname Donaldson), *Sarah, John-B.,* and *Alexander-M.*
    iii. John-Morrison, b. May 20, 1826; m. Martha R. Elder, daughter of James Elder, of Elder's Ridge, and had *James-Elder, Mary-Agnes,* and *Maggie-Bright.*
    iv. Martha-Jane, b. March 26, 1828; m. October 14, 1845, Thomas C. Pollock, of Ligonier valley, and had issue (surname Pollock), *Agnes-Morrison,* m. Rev. S. S. Gilson, *Elizabeth-Herron,* m. Robert J. Smith, *Mary-Emma,* m. Albert Shupe, *Annie-Rachel, Martha-Jane,* m. H. F. Stark, *Jesse-Irvin, John-Barnett, Kate-Mabel,* and *Thomas-Cathcart.*
    v. Elizabeth-Irvin, b. June 25, 1830; d. May 27, 1839.
    vi. Nancy, b. July 16. 1833, m. Rev. James Sherer Elder. (*see Elder record.*)
    vii. Mary, b. January 27, 1837; m. Thomas Barnett Elder. (*see Elder record.*)
    viii. James-Wilson, b. May 27, 1839, was in the United States army nearly five years; m. Sophronia C. Gore, and had *John-Irvin, Ella-Amanda, Nannie-Elder,* and *Mary-Olin.*

XIX. JOSEPH BARNETT,[5] (Joseph,[4] Joseph,[3] John,[2] John,[1]) b. August 27, 1784, in Hanover township; d. June 23, 1833; removed to Fayette county, Pa., and m. MARY BOYD, of that locality, b. 1786; d. May 16, 1856. They had issue:

    i. William-Boyd, b. February 5, 1810; d. 1874, in California.
    ii. Hamilton, b. June 3, 1811; d. about 1870; m. Ann Clokey.
    iii. Clarissa, b. April 27, 1814.
    iv. Edwin, b. September 13, 1816; d. in infancy.
    v. Joseph, b. May 14, 1823; m., first, Sarah Stewart, of Montgomery county, Ohio; d. June 2, 1861; and they had issue, *Joseph, John, Anna,* and *William;* he m. secondly, Harriet Barnett, of Blair county, Pa.; d. April 21, 1881; s. p.

XX. JOSEPH BARNETT,[5] (James,[4] Joseph,[3] John,[2] John,[1]) b. June 1, 1787, in Hanover; d. Jan. 1, 1870, in Warren county, Ohio; m. April 29, 1817, SARAH HARRISON, sister of General John Harrison, of Hanover; b. 1789; d. December 12, 1834. They had issue:

 i. Sarah-Jane, b. November 10, 1823 ; m. March 15, 1855, William Silvers; d. June 7, 1824 ; and had issue (surname Silvers), *Joseph-Barnett, Myra, Annie,* and *Sallie.*
 ii. James-Allen, b. August 11, 1827 ; d. March 2 1893 ; m. October 15, 1856, Sarah E. Barker, and they had issue : *Mary-Virginia,* and *Joseph-Samuel.*

XXI. SAMUEL BARNETT,[5] (James,[4] Joseph,[3] John[2], John,[1]) b. September 30, 1790, in Hanover; d. June 10, 1869, in Clark county, Ohio. Mr. Barnett was, in many respects, a remarkable man. At the age of seventy-seven, near the close of a long life of industry, his memory was most excellent, and to him are we indebted for what is here given relative to the Barnetts—as also what is in our possession concerning the Allens, Sawyers, and other Hanover families. It is to be regretted that the information that he could have given as to the olden time was not taken down by some faithful chronicler, and thus preserved unto us. He removed to Ohio in 1817, locating in Warren county. He subsequently removed to Butler county, and, in 1841, to Springfield, Ohio, where he spent the remainder of his days. Mr. Barnett m., first, August 22, 1815, MARY MITCHELL ; b. January 16, 1790, in Hanover ; d. May 17, 1851, in Springfield, Ohio. They had issue:

 i. James, b. June 17, 1816 ; d. October 18, 1884, at Emporia, Kansas ; he graduated from Miami University in 1839, and studied for the ministry ; licensed by the first Presbytery of Ohio in 1842, and for nearly two years preached on the then western frontiers. In 1844 he was sent as a missionary, in company with his brother-in-law Dr. Paulding, to Asia Minor. In 1854 he was transferred to Cairo, Egypt, to begin a mission, which proved to be one of the most prosperous in the world. After an absence of seventeen years, he returned to America, married Margaret Lees Duff, daughter of Rev. Jackson Duff, of Wood county, Ohio. In the fall of 1865 he returned to his work in Egypt, where he labored for eight years more when he returned to the United States for the benefit of his shattered health·

For several years he did home missionary work in Kansas. His children were:
  1. *Lulu-Lees*, b. July 4, 1867 ; d. March 9, 1891.
  2. *James-Duff*, b. October 25, 1870.
  3. *Samuel-Jackson*, b. December 14, 1873.
  4. *Mary-Paulding*, b. April 4, 1875.
  5 *Isabella-Cantley*, b. September 17, 1877.
  6. *Lily-May-Winifred*, b. May 15, 1879.

ii. *Susannah-Wilson*, b. December 13, 1817; d. March 7, 1873: m. William Carothers.

iii. *David-Mitchell*, b. April 1, 1819 ; d. February 21, 1872; m. first, Mary Isabella Graybill ; m. secondly, Sarah Elizabeth Kane.

iv. *Mary*, b September 27, 1820 ; d. November 28, 1890 ; m. Dr. Joseph Gardner Paulding, of Mason, Warren county, Ohio ; b. September 13, 1813 ; d. April 30, 1875. Accompanied the Rev. James Barnett as missionary to Turkey and to Egypt. They left a large family of children.

v. *William-Allen*, b. October 8, 1822 ; m. Sarah-Belle Grove ; b. October 11, 1831 ; and they had issue.

vi. *Levi*, b. August 30, 1824 ; d. June 26, 1891 ; m. Eliza Sturgeon ; b. September 9, 1826, dau. of Allen Sturgeon; and they had *Mary-Elizabeth* and *Sarah-Martha*.

vii. *Nancy-Allen*, b. June 8, 1826 ; m. Rev. Samuel Wallace, of Piqua, Ohio, b. January 23, 1816 ; d. August 26, 1869 ; and had issue (surname Wallace) :
  1. *Margaret-J.*, b. June 1, 1846 ; m. John M. Riddle.
  2. *James-Paulding*, b. August 5, 1849 ; d. March 11, 1894 ; m. Laura E. Garvey.

viii. *Sarah*, b. January 28, 1828 ; m. Dr. John B. Hunt, b. June 5, 1822 ; d. December 23, 1891 ; and left issue.

ix. *George-Washington*, b. May 24, 1829 ; m. Sarah Ann Bain, d. January 10, 1827.

x. *Samuel*, b. October 4, 1831 ; m. Mary Campbell, b. October 26, 1831 ; d. January 13, 1885 ; and left issue.

Mr. Barnett, m. secondly, October 13, 1858, ANN J. TORRENCE (*nee* Ann J. Stewart), dau. of James Stewart and Jane Elder, of Paxtang.

XXII. JAMES BARNETT,[5] (James,[4] Joseph,[3] John,[2] John,[1]) b. 1792; d. 1861; m. LOUISA SHIRA, of Louisville, Ky., but a native of Hummelstown, Dauphin county, Pa. They had issue:

  i. *Henry-C.*

ii. *Jacob.*
  iii. *James-W.*
  iv. *Diana,* d. s. p.

The sons are all sugar planters in Louisiana.

XXIII. REBECCA BARNETT,[5] (Moses,[4] Joseph,[3] John,[2] John,[1]) b., February 19, 1806, in Hanover township, Dauphin county, Pa.; d., February 22, 1867, in Erie county Pa.; m., March 29, 1827, THOMAS MOORHEAD, b. Sept. 1, 1803; d. August 5, 1859.* They had issue (surname Moorhead):

> i. *Isaac,* b., January 28, 1828, at Erie, Pa.; d. June 4, 1881, at Eaton Rapids, Mich. Mr. Moorhead received a good academic education. Entered mercantile pursuits for a few years, but relinquished the same owing to his delicate constitution, and accepted the appointment of conductor on the Lake Shore railway, a position he filled acceptably almost twenty-eight years, with the exception of several winters, when, obtaining leave of absence, he served as transcribing clerk of the House of Representatives at Harrisburg. In the early part of the year 1880 he was appointed postmaster at Erie. Accommodating, attentive and polite, the appointment was an exceedingly popular one. The relinquishment of an active railroad life for the humdrum cares of official position, no doubt, was the primary cause of the disease of which Mr. Moorhead died, at Eaton Rapids, Mich., whither he had gone for the restoration of his health. In historic research he was deeply interested, and the citizens of Erie are indebted to him for many pleasant reminiscences of their city, over the signature of "John Ashbough." He wrote for the Centennial year a historical review of Erie county, and was the au-

---

*The great-grandson of Thomas Moorhead, a native of county Donegal, Ireland, who settled in Donegal, Penn'a, in 1732. His wife was Christine Robinson, sister of Andrew Robinson. Robert, second in descent, m. Margaret Boal, and had issue among others :

> i. Captain *John-B.*, b. January 3, 1774 ; d. May 15, 1854; buried in Derry graveyard ; m. Ann Snodgrass ; b. 1779 ; d. December 14, 1848.
> ii. *Jane,* b. October 7, 1776 : d. June, 1864 ; m. February 11, 1800, Jeremiah Sturgeon.
> iii. *Thomas,* m., March 17, 1792, Ann Clark, and had issue, *Robert, John, Thomas* and *Sarah.*

thor of the Erie county sketch in Egle's History of Pennsylvania, which contains the best and most lucid account of Perry's battle on Lake Erie extant. In the performance of a great duty, he prepared a genealogy of his own and allied families, and few, in our State, possessed as full knowledge as he of the French occupation in western Pennsylvania. He had made this subject one of study and research, and it was confidently expected that, in due time, the results of his investigation would have been given to us. Mr. Moorhead, m., September 6, 1853, Caroline Hoskinson, daughter of William and Eleanor Hoskinson, of Erie, and had *Ruth*, m. Fred. Metcalf, and *Maxwell-Wood*.

ii. *Emily* b. March 30, 1830; m. March 19, 1868, Calvin Leet, b. November 19, 1819.
iii. *Rebecca-Jane*, b. 1832; d. May 27, 1834.
iv. *Timothy-Green-Allen*, b. 1834; d. May 5, 1836.
v. *Clarissa*, b. March 10, 1837.
vi. *William Wilberforce*, b. August 6, 1839; d. December 30, 1873; m. April 28, 1864, Mary Yale.
vii. *Anna*, b. December 1, 1841; m. May 21, 1863, Charles Derrickson, of Meadville, Penna.
viii. *Elizabeth*, b. November 20, 1844; m. January 30, 1868, Charles Warren Stone, b. June 29, 1843, at Groton, Mass.; fitted for college at Lawrence Academy, Groton, and graduated from Williams College in 1863; admitted to the bar in 1867; was school superintendent of Warren county, Penna.; elected a member of the Legislature in 1870 and 1871; member of the State Senate in 1877 and 1878; elected Lieutenant Governor in 1878; appointed Secretary of the Commonwealth under Governor Beaver in January 1887, which office he resigned to take his seat in the Fifty-first Congress made vacant by the death of Mr. Watson, elected to the Fifty-second and Fifty-third Congresses.

BEATTY FAMILY.

I. JAMES BEATTY,[2] son of JOHN BEATTY,[1] b., about 1670, in Ayrshire, Scotland, emigrated to Ireland shortly after the battle of the Boyne, in 1690, when occurred that large influx of Scotch families into the northern counties of the Green Isle, in company with his brother John. The latter settled in county Antrim, and was the father of the Rev. Charles Beatty. James located in the county Down, at what is now called Ballykeel-Ednagonnel, in the parish of Hillsborough. He was the head of a large family, having nineteen children by three wives. He died in Ballykeel-Ednagonnel, in 1745. We have the Christian name of only one of his wives—AGNES, who was the mother of at least *William*, *John*, *Agnes* and *Alexander*. The names of the children which have come down to us are:

    i. James.
    ii. Robert.
    iii. George.
    iv. Thomas.
    v. Richard.
    vi. Alexander.
2. *vii. William*, m. Mary McKee.
    viii. Agnes.
3. *ix. John*, m. Jane Swan.

II. WILLIAM BEATTY,[3] (James,[2] John,[1]) b. about 1718; d. in February, 1784, at Ballykeel-Ednagonnel. "Buried in Anahilt glebe. The grave is covered with a flat tombstone, and with the exception of the name, nothing can be traced, owing to the wear and tear of the weather and the continual friction of passing feet. The central portion of the stone has been worn perfectly smooth."—(*Letter of Miss M. Beatty*, 1878.) William Beatty m., in 1741, MARY McKEE, b., about 1820, at McKee's Dam, Clogher, county Down, Ireland; d. about 1796, and buried in Anahilt churchyard, Ballykeel-Ednagonnel. They had issue:

Beatty Family.

4. *i. George*, b. 1743 ; m. Mary Blackburn.
5. *ii. James*, b. 1746 ; m. Alice Ann Irwin.
7. *iii. Agnes*, b. 1751 ; m. Robert Finlay.
    iv. Jane, b. 1752 ; d. 1777 ; unm.
7. *v. Mary*, b 1758 ; m. James Nelson.

III. JOHN BEATTY,³ (James,² John,¹) b. about 1722; d. about 1765, at Ballykeel-Ednagonnel, county Down, Ireland; m. JANE SWAN, b. about 1727 ; d. about 1817, at Ballykeel-Ednagounel. They had issue:

8. *i. Agnes.* b 1757 ; m. William Dawson.
9. *ii. William,* b. 1759 ; m. Elizabeth Rutherford.
10. *iii. James.* b. 1761 ; m. Jane Nelson.
    v. John, b. 1763 ; d. 1771.

IV. GEORGE BEATTY,⁴ (William,³ James,² John,¹) b., 1743, at Ballykeel-Ednagonnel ; d., 1815, at Ballykeel-Ednagonnel, and there buried; m., in April, 1771, by Rev. Robert McClure, MARY BLACKBURN, b., about 1749, at Ballylinlagh, county Down, Ireland ; d. in the city of London, England. They had issue :

    i. Charlotte, b. January, 1772 ; d. in America ; m. William Beatty ; they had two children when they emigrated to the United States.
11. *ii. Ann,* b. April, 1773 ; m. Robert McCloy.
12. *iii. Steward,* b. 1775 ; m. Mary Wilson.
13. *iv. George,* b. 1777 ; m Jane Beatty.

V. JAMES BEATTY,⁴ (William,³ James,² John,¹) b. 1746, in the townland of Ballykeel-Ednagonnel, parish of Hillsborough, county Down, Ireland; d. December 1, 1794, at Harrisburg, Pa. From the family record, in the possession of his descendants, we have this entry: "That my children may know the place of their nativity, I, James Beatty, was born in the Kingdom of Ireland, and County of Down, Parish of Hillsborough, and Townland of Ballykeel-Ednagonnel, in the year of our Lord 1746, and came to America in the year 1784. My wife, Ally Ann Irwin, was born in said kingdom, county and parish, and Townland of Tillynore, within two miles of Hillsborough, three of Lisburn, three miles of Dromore, and six miles of Bally-nahinch, and ten of Belfast, which last place we sailed from the 27th of June, 1784." In the fall of this year, he settled at Harrisburg, Pa., and thus became one of its first inhabitants. He subsequently was the purchaser of a number of lots in the town, some of which remain in possession of his descendants. He was quite prominent in his adopted home, and held several official positions under the borough charter. He was buried in the Presbyterian graveyard, of which church he held membership. In personal appearance, Captain Beatty was about five feet eight inches, thickset, florid complexion, dark hair and blue eyes. He was an active and energetic business man, and his death was a great loss to the young town. James Beatty m., in 1768, at Tullynore, ALICE ANN IRWIN, b. 1750, in the townland of Tullynore, parish of Hillsborough, county Down, Ireland, daughter of Gawin Irwin and Mary Brereton; d. June, 1805, at Harrisburg, Pa., and there buried. They had issue, all b. in Ireland:

   i. Mary-Brereton, b. July 14, 1769; m. Patrick Murray. (*see Murray record.*)
14. *ii. Nancy*, b. May 2, 1771; m. Samuel Hill.
15. *iii. Gawin-Irwin*, b. September 18, 1773; m. Letitia Greer.
   iv. William (1st,) b. 1774; d. s. p.
16. *v. Rebecca*, b. December 4, 1775; m. Daniel Houseman.
17. *vi. Alice-Ann*, b. February 12, 1777; m. John Downey.
   vii. William, (2d,) b. June 30, 1778; d. September 8, 1790, at Harrisburg, Pa.
   viii. Sarah, b. October 6, 1779; d. August 4, 1861, unm., at Ashland, O.
18. *ix. George-Washington*, b. January 4, 1781; m., first, Eliza White; secondly, Sarah Shrom; thirdly, Catharine Shrom.

VI. AGNES BEATTY,[4] (William,[3] James,[2] John,[1]) b. 1751, at Ballykeel-Ednagonnel, county Down, Ireland; d. 1844; m., in 1772, by Rev. Robert McClure, ROBERT FINLAY, b. 1746; d. August 15, 1803. They had issue (surname Finlay):

19. *i. Elizabeth*, b. 1774; m. William Haliday.
20. *ii. William*, b. 1776; m. Mary McKee.
21. *iii. David* (twin), b. 1776; m. Agnes McKee.
   iv. James, b. 1780; emigrated to America, and died there in 1872.

Beatty Family.

  v. Robert, b. 1784 ; d. 1811 ; unm.
22. *vi. George*, b. 1786 ; m Mary Frazer.
  vii. Matthew, b. 1790 ; d. 1845 ; unm.
23. *viii. Wilson* (twin), b. 1790 ; m. Mary Greer.
24. *ix. Agnes*, b. 1795 ; m. David McKee.

VII. MARY BEATTY,[4] (William,[3] James,[2] John,[1]) b. 1758 ; d., July 13, 1847, at Ballykeel-Ednagonnel, county Down, Ireland ; m., in 1781, by Rev. Robert McClure, JAMES NELSON, b. 1769 ; d. December 19, 1829. There was no issue. In Anahilt glebe is a large tombstone with this inscription :

Erected | *To the memory of* JAMES | NELSON *who departed this* | *life 19th Dec. 1829 aged 69 years* | *Also, his wife* MARY *who* | *died 13th July 1847 aged* | *89 years.*

VIII. AGNES BEATTY,[4] (John,[3] James,[2] John,[1]) b. 1757 ; in county Down, Ireland ; d. there about 1780 ; m. WILLIAM DAWSON ; he lived and died in the townland of Rathvarneth, county Down, Ireland. They had issue (surname Dawson):

  i. John, d. s. p.
  ii. William, m. Catharine Gibson ; d. s. p.

IX. WILLIAM BEATTY,[4] (John,[3] James,[2] John,[1]) b. 1759 ; d., 1844, in county Down, Ireland ; m., in 1784, ELIZABETH RUTHERFORD, b. 1758 ; d., October 23, 1830, in county Down, Ireland. They had issue :

25. *i. James*, b. March 17, 1780 ; m. Dorothy Jefferson.
26. *ii. William*, b. May 21, 1782 ; m. Mary McCormick.
  iii. John (1st), b. October 9, 1784 ; d. s. p.
27. *iv. John (2d)*, b. July 29, 1786 ; m. Jane Hanna.
  v. Adam, b. November 23, 1778 ; d. 1813 ; unm.
28. *vi. Martin*, b. February 19, 1790 ; m. Eliza Matthews.
29. *vii. Thomas*, b. March 16, 1794 ; m. Margaret Chambers.
  viii. Jane, b. August 13, 1797 ; m. Samuel Beatty.
  ix. Richard, b. 1804 ; d. 1828 ; unm.

X. JAMES BEATTY,[4] (John,[3] James,[2] John,[1]) b., 1761, in county Down, Ireland ; d. 1843 ; m., in 1780, JANE NELSON ; b. 1755 ; d., January 17, 1839, in county Down, Ireland. They had issue :

  i. John, b. 1781 ; d. 1783.

30.   *ii. Ellen*, b. 1783 ; m. James McKee.
31.   *iii. Jane*, b. 1785 ; m. William Carothers.
      iv. Jane, b. 1788 ; d. 1861 : m., in 1826, Dorothy Ben, b. 1805 ; and had *James*, b. 1826.
32.   *v. William*, b. 1790 ; m. Eliza Carson.
      vi. Eliza, b. 1793 ; d. 1797.
33.   *vii. James*, b. March 26, 1795 ; m. Mary Ann McCloy.
34.   *viii. Samuel*, b. 1797 ; m. Jane Beatty.
      ix. David, b. 1800 ; d. 1804.

XI. ANN BEATTY,[5] (George,[4] William,[3] James,[2] John,[1]) b. 1773, in Ballykeel-Ednagonnel, county Down, Ireland ; d. 1803 ; m., 1793, by Rev. Robert McClure, ROBERT MCCLOY ; b., 1760, in Londonderry, Ireland ; d., 1854, in Belfast, Ireland ; son of William and Susannah McCloy. They had issue, all b. at Carrickfergus, Ireland, (surname McCloy):

    i. Susannah, b. 1795 ; d. 1869 : m. Samuel Hogg.
    ii. George, b. 1798 ; emigrated to America ; m. Esther McComb.
    iii. Mary-Ann, b. 1800 ; m. James Beatty. (*xxxiii.*)
    iv. William, b. 1802 ; d. in Barbadoes, West Indies.

XII. STEWARD BEATTY,[5] (George,[4] William,[3] James,[2] John,[1]) b., 1775, in Ballykeel-Ednagonnel, county Down, Ireland ; d. 1853 ; m., in 1815, by Rev. William Wright, minister of Anahilt, MARY WILSON, b. 1793 ; d. June 1, 1879, at Birmingham, England. They had issue :

    i. Mary-Ann, b. 1816 ; d. 1853 ; m. Robert Beatty.
    ii. Rebecca, b. 1818 ; d. 1871 ; m. Samuel Bingham.
    iii. Charlotte, b. 1820 ; d. 1853, unm.
    iv. Phebe, b. 1822 : m. James Kemp, of Birmingham, England.
    v. George, b. 1824 ; m. Sarah Cordner.
    vi. Agnes, b. 1828 ; m. George Scott.
    vii. Steward, b. 1830 ; d. 1849, unm.

XIII. GEORGE BEATTY,[5] (George,[4] William,[3] James,[2] John,[1]) b., 1777, in Ballykeel-Ednagonnel, county Down, Ireland ; d. 1847 ; m., in 1812, JANE BEATTY,[6] (William,[5] James,[4] John,[3] James,[2] John,[1]) b. 1820. They had issue :

    i. William, b. 1843 ; m. Eliza Jane Cargin.
    ii. George, b. 1844.
    iii. James, b. 1846 ; resides at Hillsborough, county Down, Ireland.
    iv. Margaret, (twin) b. 1816 ; m. John McKee.

Beatty Family. 83

XIV. NANCY BEATTY,[5] (James,[4] William,[3] James[2], John,[1]) b. May 2, 1771, at Ballykeel-Ednagonnel, county Down, Ireland; d. May 7, 1839, at Steubenville, O.; m., at Harrisburg, Pa., February 5, 1790, by Rev. John Elder, SAMUEL HILL, b. about 1765, in England, son of Arundel and Charlotte Hill. His ancestors belonged to one of the representative families of that country. He received a good English and classical education, and learned the trade of clock and watchmaker in London. He came to Pennsylvania about 1785, and shortly afterward established himself in business at Harrisburg, Pa. He was a skilled and ingenious workman. He was quite prominent in the early affairs of the new town, and was among the first to jump into the water to tear down the obnoxious mill-dam in the Paxtang creek, in 1795. He was a volunteer in Captain Reitzell's company on the expedition westward in 1794; and twice visited England on matters connected with his father's estate, then considered quite an undertaking; and what particularly distinguished his last visit was his reception by his fellow-citizens of Harrisburg on his return, which was an ovation, showing what a strong hold he had upon his friends in America. He died very suddenly, while sitting in his chair on Monday evening, November 6, 1809, aged forty-four years, and the *Oracle of Dauphin* speaks of his loss to the community as "irreparable." They had issue (surname Hill):

35.   *i. Arundel,* b. December 5, 1791; m. Hettie Shields.
     ii. George, b. April 1, 1793; d. at Harrisburg, s. p.
     iii. Charlotte, b. September 25, 1795; d. January 25, 1809, at Harrisburg.
36.   *iv. Anna,* b. December 19, 1798; m. William Kilgore.
     v. Samuel-Truxton, b. March 15, 1800; went to Bogota, South America, and there m. an English lady; d. on voyage to England, leaving two children.
     vi. Rebecca, b. December 19, 1802; d. s. p. at Harrisburg.
     vii. Sarah, b. 1805; d. s. p.
37.   *ix. Mary,* b. January 8, 1808; m. Joseph G. Davidson.

XV. GAWIN-IRWIN BEATTY,[5] (James,[4] William,[3] James,[2] John,[1]) b. September 13, 1773, at Ballykeel-Ednagonnel, county Down, Ireland; d. December 14, 1843, at Harrisburg, Pa.; m., May, 1799, by Reverend Nathaniel Snowden, LETITIA

GREER, daughter of James and Anna Greer, b. 1778; d. April, 1838, at Harrisburg, and there buried. They had issue:

38.   i. *Isabella*, b. February 26, 1800;. m. Christian Charles Fechtig.
39.   ii. *James*, b. September 16, 1802; m., first, Jane Ann McMullin; second, Judith Towles.
      iii. *Mary*, b. 1804; d. 1828: m. Bartis Crangle, b. 1799; d. 1830; and had *James-Beatty*, m. Dortai Emilie Kuhne, and *Isabella-Fechtig*, m. George F. Gilmore.

XVI. REBECCA BEATTY,[5] (James,[4] William,[3] James,[2] John,[1]) b. December 4, 1775, at Ballykeel-Ednagonnel, county Down, Ireland; d. 1819, at Harrisburg, Pa.; m., December 12, 1809, by Rev. James Buchanan, DANIEL HOUSEMAN, son of Frederick Houseman, b. 1774, at York, Pa.; d. 1818, at Harrisburg. They had issue (surname Houseman):

      i. *Frederick*, b. November 2, 1812; bap. March 4, 1813, by Reverend Philip Gloninger, of Harrisburg.
40.   ii. *James-Downey*, b. September 17, 1817; m. Emily Watson.

XVII. ALICE ANN BEATTY,[5] (James,[4] William,[3] James,[2] John,[1]) b. February 12, 1777, at Ballykeel-Ednagonnel, county Down, Ireland; d. May 14, 1841, in Orange township, Ashland county, O.; m., June 5, 1798, by Reverend N. Snowden, JOHN DOWNEY, b., in 1765, at Germantown, Pa. He was a son of Captain John Downey and Sarah, his wife. The elder Downey was an officer of the Revolution, under General Lacey, and was inhumanly massacred at the battle of the Crooked Billet. The son received a classical education in the old academy at Germantown, and, in 1793, located at Harrisburg, where he opened a Latin and grammar school. At this period, in a letter to Governor Thomas Mifflin, he proposed a "Plan of Education," remarkably foreshadowing the present common-school system, and which has placed him in the front rank of early American educators. He was for many years a justice of the peace, and served as town-clerk for a long time. He was the first cashier of the Harrisburg bank, largely instrumental in securing the erection of the bridge over the Susquehanna, and one of the corporators of the Harrisburg and Middletown

Turnpike company; was a member of the Legislature in 1817-18, and filled other positions of honor and profit. He died at Harrisburg, on the 21st of July, 1827, and the *Oracle* speaks of him as "a useful magistrate and a pious man." He wrote much for the press, and a series of articles published in the *Dauphin Guardian*, entitled "Simon Easy Papers," were from his pen, sparkling with wit. They are worth a permanent setting, as a valuable contribution to literature. Their daughter, Ellen Downey, b. 1811, at Harrisburg; d. 1869, at Springfield, O.; m., April 5, 1831, Hon. Daniel Kilgore, of Steubenville, O., and had issue.

XVIII. GEORGE BEATTY,[5] (James,[4] William,[3] James,[2] John,[1]) b. January 4, 1781, at Ballykeel-Ednagonnel, county Down, Ireland. He received a good early education in the Latin-school of John Downey, and learned the watch and clock-making with his brother-in-law, Samuel Hill, whose clocks are more or less celebrated to this day. In 1808, Mr. Beatty established himself in business, which he continued uninterruptedly for upwards of forty years. He was an ingenious mechanician, and constructed several clocks of peculiar and rare invention. In 1814 he was orderly-sergeant of Captain Thomas Walker's company, the Harrisburg Volunteers, which marched to the defense of the city of Baltimore. Mr. Beatty in early life took a prominent part in local affairs, and, as a consequence, was frequently solicited to become a candidate for office, but he almost invariably declined. He, nevertheless, served a term as director of the poor, and also as county auditor. He was elected a burgess of the borough, and was a member of the town-council several years, and, while serving in the latter capacity, was one of the prime movers in the efforts to supply the borough with water. Had his suggestions, however, been carried out, the water-works and reservoir would have been located above the present city limits. Mr. Beatty retired from a successful business life about 1850. He died at Harrisburg, on the 10th of March, 1862, aged eighty-one years, and is interred in the Harrisburg cemetery. He was an active, enterprising, and upright Christian gentleman. Mr. Beatty was thrice married; m. first, May 18, 1815, by Reverend George

Lochman, D. D., ELIZA WHITE, daughter of William White, b. January 20, 1797; d. September 10, 1817. They had issue:

   i. Margaret, b. February 18, 1816; d. December 3, 1837; m. Reverend Allen John, and had *George-Beatty*

Mr. Beatty, m. secondly, November 22, 1820, by Reverend George Lochman, D. D., SARAH SMITH SHROM, daughter of Casper Shrom* and Catharine Van Gundy, b. January 15, 1796, at York, Pa.; d. August 25, 1828. They had issue:

   ii. Eliza-White, b. August 11, 1823; d. November 24, 1832.
   iii. Mary-Ann-Jefferson, b. September 15, 1824; m. Immanuel Meister Kelker.

Mr. Beatty m. thirdly, September 21, 1830, by Rev. Eliphalet Reed, CATHARINE SHROM, b. December 26, 1807, at York, Pa.; d. August 11, 1891, at Harrisburg, Pa. They had issue:

---

* CASPER SHROM, b. May 29, 1768; d. November 23, 1844, at Harrisburg; son of Jacob Shrom and Christiana Smith; m. March 5, 1789, CATHARINE VAN GUNDY, b. December 13, 1767; d. April 21, 1855, at Harrisburg; daughter of Captain Joseph Van Gundy, of the army of the Revolution. They had issue (surname Shrom):

   i. Henry, (first,) b. February 9, 1790; d. July 4, 1801.
   ii. Jacob, b. February 22, 1792; d. June 18, 1855, at Harrisburg, Pa.; unm.
   iii. Mary, b. December 15, 1793; d. May 5, 1879, at Harrisburg; m. Andrew Findley Laird, b. November 5, 1789; d. September 13, 1832, at Columbia, Pa.; son of John Laird and Sarah Ann Findley. They had issue (surname Laird): *John-Findley*, b. July 4, 1811; d. s. p.; *Sarah-Ann-Findley*, b. October 16, 1812; m. Samuel Shoch Bigler; *Catharine-Shrom*, b. February 4, 1815; d. June 12, 1866; m. Thomas Robinson; *Harriet-Smith*, b. February 5, 1818; d. October 2, 1871; Doctor *John-Wesley*, b. March 4, 1824; and *George-Beatty*, b. October 17, 1826; d. October 27, 1856; unm.
   iv. Sarah-Smith, b. January 15, 1796; m. George Beatty. (see Beatty record.)
   v. Catharine, (first,) b. February, 1798; d. August, 1802.
   vi. Henry, (second,) b. April 24, 1801; d. May 31, 1822, at Williamsport, Pa.; unm.
   vii. Elizabeth, b. January, 1804; d. August, 1807.
   viii. Catharine, (second,) b. December 26, 1807; m. George Beatty. (see Beatty record.)

41. iv. *Sarah-Shrom*, b. October 2, 1831; m. Reverend Beverly Roberts Waugh.
  v. *Eliza-White*, b. January 5, 1833; m. William Henry Egle, M. D. (*see Egle record.*)
  vi. *Margaretta*, b. December 25, 1837; d. December 9, 1841.
  vii. *George-Washington-Irwin*, b. May 11, 1840; m. June 5, 1873, Eliza Watson Anderson, b. June 25, 1848.
  viii. *Catharine-Shrom*, b. March 27, 1842.
  ix. *Henry-Jacob*, b. April 2, 1847.

XIX. ELIZABETH FINLAY,[5] (Agnes,[4] William,[3] James,[2] John,[1]) b. in 1774, in county Down, Ireland; m. WILLIAM HALIDAY; emigrated to America and both died there. They had issue (surname Haliday):

  i. *Agnes.*
  ii. *William.*
  iii. *David.*
  iv. *Barbara.*
  v. *Maria.*
  vi. *Armstrong.*
  vii. *Eliza.*
  viii *Ann-Jane.*
  ix. *Robert.*

XX. WILLIAM FINLAY,[5] (Agnes,[4] William,[3] James,[2] John,[1]) b. 1776, in Ballykeel-Ednagonnel; d. 1856; m. MARY McKEE, b. 1779; d. March 7, 1849. They had issue (surname Finlay):

  i. *Robert*, b. 1808; d. 1856; unm.
  ii. *Agnes*, b. 1810; m. Doctor Hood; emigrated to Australia.
  iii. *Eliza*, b. 1812; m. Robert Bell.
  iv. *Mary*, b. 1816; d. 1842; unm.
  v. *Margaret*, b. 1817; m. Ralph Walsh; emigrated to America.
  vi. *John*, b. 1819; d. 1845; unm.
  vii. *Rebecca*, b. 1821; d. 1864; m. Alexander Brownlee.

XXI. DAVID FINLAY,[5] (Agnes,[4] William,[3] James,[2] John,[1]) b. 1778, in county Down, Ireland; d. in 1853; m. in 1812, AGNES McKEE, b. June 2, 1795; d. September 6, 1872. They had issue (surname Finlay):

  i. *John*, b. 1813; m. Christiana Brownlee.
  ii. *Robert*, b. 1815; d. 1854.
  iii. *David*, b. 1817; d. 1844.

 iv. George, b. 1820; d. 1848.
 v. Agnes, b. 1822; d. 1850.
 vi. Mary, b. 1826; d. 1846.
 vii. Eliza, b. 1834; resides in Belfast, Ireland.

XXII. GEORGE FINLAY,⁵ M. D., (Agnes,⁴ William,³ James,² John,¹) b. 1786, in county Down, Ireland; d. 1854, at Strangford; m. MARY FRAZER, b. September 26, 1798; d. September, 1877, at Strangford, county Down, Ireland. They had issue (surname Finlay):

 i. Dr. *Robert* d. November, 1850, at Strangford.
 ii. Eliza, b. October 28, 1828; d. November 21, 1876, in Pointz-pass; m. Rev. Thomas Irvine, of Pointz-pass, and had issue (surname Irvine) Dr. *George-Edward*, Dr. *Robert-Finlay, Mary-Louisa, Lizzie-Ann*, and *Caroline-Emma.*
 iii. Dr. *George*, b. 1831; d. 1852, at Strangford.
 iv. Mary, b. 1833; d. March, 1854, at Strangford.

XXIII. WILSON FINLAY,⁵ (Agnes,⁴ William,³ James,² John,¹) b. 1790, in county Down, Ireland; d. 1856; m. in 1842, MARY GREER, daughter of Thomas Greer, of Carnreagh, county Down, Ireland. They had issue (surname Finlay):

 i. Robert, b. 1843; d. 1863; m., and left one son.
 ii. Agnes. b. 1845; d. 1867; m. 1865, Alexander Brownlee; left one daughter.
 iii. James, b. 1847.
 iv. Thomas, b. 1849; resides at Belfast, Ireland.
 v. John, b. 1851.
 vi. Margaret, b. 1852.

XXIV. AGNES FINLAY,⁵ (Agnes,⁴ William,³ James,² John,¹) b. 1795, in county Down, Ireland; d. 1872; m., 1815, DAVID MCKEE, b. 1788; d. 1850. They had issue (surname McKee):

 i. John, b. 1816; m. Alice Brownlee.
 ii. Agnes, b. 1817; d. 1841.
 iii. Mary, b. 1819; d. 1844.
 iv. Margaret, b. 1822; d. 1844.
 v. Robert, b. 1827; d. 1834.
 vi. Sarah, b. 1830; m. John Gibson.

XXV. JAMES BEATTY,⁵ (William,⁴ John,³ James,² John,¹) b. March 17, 1780, in county Down, Ireland; d. 1832; m., 1809,

Beatty Family.

DOROTHY JEFFERSON, b. 1792; d. April 17, 1875. They had issue:

    i. William, b. 1810; d. 1862; m. Sarah Gibson, b. 1816.
    ii. Pearse, b. 1812; d. 1828.
    iii. Eliza, b. 1817.
    iv. Margaret, b. 1819.
    v. Adam, b. 1821.
    vi. Martin, b. 1828; m. Mary Finlay.

XXVI. WILLIAM BEATTY,[5] (William,[4] John,[3] James,[2] John,[1]) b. May 21, 1782, in county Down, Ireland; d. 1842; m., 1818, MARY MCCORMICK, b. August 16, 1784; d. 1837. They had issue:

    i. Mary, b. 1819; m. William Cowan.
    ii. Eliza, b. 1821; d. 1871; m. Samuel Carothers.
    iii. Margaret, b. 1823; m. James Taylor.
    iv. Letitia, b. 1826; m. Thomas Young.

XXVII. JOHN BEATTY,[5] (William,[4] John,[3] James,[2] John,[1]) b. July 29, 1786, in county Down, Ireland; d. December, 21, 1828; m. in 1820, JANE HANNA, b. 1783, in Hillsborough, county Down, Ireland; d. 1867, in Hollywood, county Down, Ireland, and buried in Belfast. They had issue:

    i. Eliza, b. 1821; m. Dr. William Mawhiney.

XXVIII. MARTIN BEATTY,[5] (William,[4] John,[3] James,[2] John,[1]) b. February 19, 1790, in county Down, Ireland; d. 1839; m., 1831, ELIZA MATTHEWS, b. 1802; d. June 26, 1861. They had issue:

    i. John, b. 1832; m. Mary Moorhead.
    ii. Eliza, b. 1834; resides at Ballycrune.
    iii. Alice-Ann, b. 1836; m. John Anderson.
    iv. William, b. 1838; m. Fanny Wallace.

XXIX. THOMAS BEATTY,[5] (William,[4] John,[3] James,[2] John,[1]) b. March 16, 1794, in county Down, Ireland; d. 1849; m., in 1820, MARGARET CHAMBERS, b. 1788; d. November 12, 1866. They had issue:

    i. Joseph, b. 1821; emigrated to America.
    ii. William, b. 1822; emigrated to America in 1849.

iii. Eliza, b. 1824; d. 1859; m. William Coburn.
iv. Samuel, b. 1826.
v. Mary-Ann, b. 1829; d. November 17, 1878.

XXX. ELLEN BEATTY,[5] (James,[4] John,[3] James,[2] John,[1]) b. 1783, in county Down Ireland; d. 1816; m., 1804, JAMES McKEE, elder brother of David McKee (xxiv); emigrated to America in 1817. They had issue (surname McKee):

i. Mary, b. 1805.
ii. Agnes, b. 1807.
iii. Thomas, b. 1808.
iv. John, b. 1809.
v. James, b. 1811.

XXXI. JANE BEATTY,[5] (James,[4] John,[3] James,[2] John,[1]) b. 1785, in county Down, Ireland; d. 1872; m. 1809, WILLIAM CAROTHERS, b. September 17, 1777; d. February 18, 1857. They had issue (surname Carothers):

i. James, b. 1810.
ii. John, b. 1811; d. 1814.
iii. William, b. 1813; d. 1876
iv. Margaret, b. 1815; d. 1834.

XXXII. WILLIAM BEATTY,[5] (James,[4] John,[3] James,[2] John,[1]) b. 1790. in county Down, Ireland; d. 1872; m. 1811, ELIZA CARSON, b. 1792; d. August 20, 1867. They had issue:

i. George, b 1815; m. Bella Eden.
ii. James, b. 1816; d. 1840.
iii. Robert, b. 1819; emigrated to America; m. Mary-Ann Beatty.
iv. Jane, b. 1820; m. George Beatty. (see xiii.)
v. Margaret-Ann, b. 1822; m. John Todd.
vi. William, b. 1823; d. 1859; m Mary Moore.
vii. John, b 1825; d. 1859.
viii. Eliza, b 1826; d. 1851.
ix. Samuel, b. 1828; emigrated to America.
x. Nelson, b. 1830; m. Mary Bell.
xi. Ellen, b. 1832; d. 1868; m. John Kennedy.

XXXIII. JAMES BEATTY,[5] (James,[4] John,[3] James,[2] John,[1]) b. March 26, 1795, in county Down, Ireland; d. October 18, 1873; m. October 10, 1827, MARY ANN McCLOY,[6] (Ann,[5]

Beatty Family.

George,⁴ William,³ James,² John,¹) (xi.) b. 1800; d. November 24, 1884, at Ballykeel-Ednagonnel. They had issue:

 i. John, b. April 4, 1828; m. Jane McCauley, of Ballycrune, county Down, Ireland.
 ii. James, b. November 4, 1829.
 iii. Mary, b. December 26, 1831; d. July 14, 1881; m. William Coburn, d. April 1, 1884; left one daughter.
 iv. Robert, b. May 4, 1834; d. May 5, 1859.
 v. Ann, b. November 12, 1836.
 vi. Jane, (twin,) b. November 12, 1836.
 vii. Margaret, b. May 18, 1840; d. November 14, 1891, near Hillsborough, Ireland; to her we were indebted for much of the genealogical data herewith given.

XXXIV. SAMUEL BEATTY,⁵ (James,⁴ John,³ James,² John,¹) b. 1797, in county Down, Ireland; d. 1836; m. in 1826, JANE BEATTY,⁵ (William,⁴ John,³ James,² John,¹) b. August 13, 1797, in county Down, Ireland; d. 1832. They had issue:

 i. Elizabeth, b. 1827.
 ii. Richard, b. 1828; m. Eliza Watson.
 iii. Jane, b 1830
 iv. Samuel, b. 1832; d. s. p.

XXXV. ARUNDEL HILL,⁶ (Nancy,⁵ James,⁴ William,³ James,² John,¹) b. December 5, 1791, at Harrisburg, Pa.; d. April 5, 1848, at Steubenville, O.; was twice married; m. first, at Steubenville, O., May 29, 1823, by Rev. Thomas Hunt, HETTIE SHIELDS; d. March 12, 1829, at Steubenville. They had issue (surname Hill):

 i. Mary-Ann, b. March 27, 1824; d. July 11, 1825.
 ii. Mary, b. June 20, 1826; d. September 17, 1827.
 iii. Samuel, b. June 29, 1828; d. December 19, 1828

Mr. Hill m. secondly, at Steubenville, O., August 31, 1830, by Rev. Elisha Swift, MARGARET SEMPLE, daughter of John M. Semple, and his wife, Margaret Whiteside, b. 1806; d. August 20, 1864. They had issue (surname Hill):

 iv. Mary-Jane, b. August 2, 1831; d June 26, 1833.
 v. Margaretta, b. December 22, 1833; m James Hunter.
 vi. Mary, b. June 8, 1836; d. June, 1840.
 vii. Alice-Ann-Downey, b. Nov. 24, 1837; d. August 29, 1839.

viii. Martha-Semple, b. August 9, 1840; m. September 21, 1865, Rudolphus B Zoll; b. May 6, 1826; and had (surname Zoll) *Hettie-Hill Annie-Hill*, and *George-Arundel*.

ix. Ann-Elizabeth-Hair, b. September 15, 1842; m. September 15, 1868, Frank B. Aldrich, b March 15, 1843; and had (surname Aldrich) *Frank-Edward* and *Ella-Marguretta*.

x. Hettie-Sabrah-Marsh, b. February 17, 1844; m. April 13, 1869, Caleb Newton Wells, b February 3, 1843; and had (surname Wells) *Birdie, May*, and *Sherman*

xi. Sarah-Beatty, b. July 11, 1847; d. August 20, 1847.

XXXVI. ANNA HILL,⁶ (Nancy,⁵ James,⁴ William,³ James,² John,¹) b. December 19, 1798, at Harrisburg, Pa.; d. October 8, 1872, at Steubenville, O.; m., at Steubenville, O., September 16, 1824, by Rev. Charles C. Beatty, D.D., WILLIAM KILGORE, b. July 18, 1796, near King's creek, Virginia; d. January 1, 1877, at Steubenville, O. Mr. Kilgore located at Steubenville in 1815, where he subsequently established himself in mercantile business. In 1854, he erected the Jefferson Iron Mills in that city, and was for many years president of the Jefferson National Bank. He was an enterprising and prominent business man. The children of Anna Hill and William Kilgore were (surname Kilgore):

i. Nancy-Ann, b. January 6, 1826; d. January 19, 1878, at Philadelphia; m. William Sinclair, b. 1824, in Ireland; and they had (surname Sinclair) *Ann-Eliza*, d. s. p., *William-Kilgore, Charles Ricketson*, d. s. p., *Mary-Alice, George-Marshall*, and *Eleanor-Kilgore*.

ii. Daniel, b. August 3, 1827; m. August, 1858, Emily Mossgrove.

iii. Mary, b. June, 1829; d. s. p.

iv. Eleanor, b. 1831; d. s. p.

v. John-Downey, b. March 18, 1833; m. Sarah P. James, and has issue.

vi. William, b. 1837; d. August 11. 1845.

XXXVII. MARY HILL,⁶ (Nancy,⁵ James,⁴ William,³ James,² John,¹) b. January 8, 1808, in Harrisburg, Pa.; d. 1887, at Steubenville, O.; m. March 20, 1832, by Rev. Charles C. Beatty, D. D., JOSEPH GORDON DAVIDSON, b. September 19, 1801, in Washington county, Pa.; d. April 2, 1883, at Steubenville, O.; son of Joseph Davidson and his wife, Jane Gordon. They had issue (surname Davidson):

i. Anna Elizabeth, b. June 17, 1833 ; d. February 25, 1836.
ii. Mary-Jane, b. October 15, 1835 ; d. March 13, 1880.
iii. Joseph-Hill, b. March 26, 1888 ; d. June 22, 1839.
iv. Ellen-Kilgore, b. September 20, 1840.
v. Josephine, b. January 17, 1845 ; d. October 18, 1865.
vi. Annie, b. February 17, 1848 ; d. March 4, 1851.
vii. William-Kilgore, b. October 23, 1851.
viii. George-Beatty, b. May 6, 1855 ; d., March 7, 1880, at Poughkeepsie, N. Y., where he was studying for the ministry. A young man of rich promise and rare mental endowment.

XXXVIII. ISABELLA BEATTY,⁶ (Gawin-Irwin,⁵ James,⁴ William,³ James,² John,¹) b. February 26, 1800, at Harrisburg, Pa.; d. August 20, 1870, at Galveston, Texas ; m. November 28, 1819, at Chambersburg, Pa., by Reverend Caleb Reynolds, CHRISTIAN CHARLES FECHTIG, b. February 6, 1794, in Washington county, Md.; d. September 7, 1835, at Williamsport, Md.; son of Christian Fechtig and his wife, Susan Folk. They had issue (surname Fechtig):

43. *i. James-Irwin.* b. September 30, 1820 ; m. Catharine Jane Emmert.
   ii. Christian-Charles, b. August 23, 1822 ; d. August 28, 1846 ; m. Sarah Ann Carver, b. March 9, 1825, and they had *Christian-Charles.*
   iii. Louis Randolph, b. January 12, 1825 ; m. Mary Ann Oden, b December 5, 1825, and they had *William-Christian, Jacob-Louis,* and *Mary-Louisa.*
   iv. George-Frederick, b. August 21, 1827 ; d. 1883, at Baltimore, Md.; m. Mary Elizabeth Berger, b. June 18, 1835 ; no issue.
   v. Christian, b. 1829 ; assassinated in Brenham, Washington county, Texas, in 1864.
   vi. Letitia-Ann, b. March 29, 1834, at Williamsport, Md.; d. May 23, 1869, at Galveston, Texas ; m. Henry Baldwin, b. July 25, 1835, at Brookfield, Conn.; d. at Galveston, Texas ; and they had (surname Baldwin) *Isabella-Tamer, Cora-Estella, Katie-Flynn,* and *Henry-Smith.*

XXXIX. JAMES BEATTY,⁶ (Gawin-Irwin,⁵ James,⁴ William,³ James,² John,¹) b. September 16, 1802, at Harrisburg, Pa.; a physician ; d. March 6, 1887, at Miltonvale, Kansas ; was twice married; first, May 2, 1833, in Mason county, Va., by Reverend Benjamin Smethers, JANE ANN MCMULLIN, b. in Mason county, Va.; d. in Buffalo, Putnam county, Va.; dau. of Joseph and Jane McMullin. They had issue:

    i. George-Frederick, b. May 5, 1834, in Buffalo, Putnam county, Va.; m. Mary Posey, b. March 18, 1840, in Henderson county, Ky; dau. of William Thornton Posey and Eliza J. Dixon.

    ii. Gawin-Irwin, b. October 16, 1835, in Buffalo, Putnam county, Va.; m. Susan Rudy. dau. of John and Margaret Rudy, of Henderson, Ky., and had *Ann* and *Sarah*.

Dr. James Beatty m., secondly, May 19, 1857, at Henderson, Ky., by Reverend D. H. Deacon, JUDITH TOWLES, dau. of Captain Henry Dixon, and widow of Judge Thomas T. Towles. They had issue:

    iii. Fannie-Dixon, b. March 16, 1858; m. Ira F. Ball.

XL. JAMES DOWNEY HOUSEMAN,[6] (Rebecca,[5] James,[4] William,[3] James,[2] John,[1]) b. September 17, 1817, in Cumberland county, Pa., resides at Paris, Texas; m., December 23, 1846, at St. Louis, Mo., by Reverend William S. Potts, M. D., EMILY WATSON, b. November 17, 1824, at Newbern, N. C., dau. of Thomas Watson and his wife, Sarah Hannis. They had issue (surname Houseman):

    i. Elizabeth-Hannis, b. October 25, 1847; d. December 28, 1857.

    ii. Alice-Downey, b. November 26, 1849; m. William F. Fisher, of Paris, Texas.

    iii. James-Downey, b. February 8. 1851; m. Lillie Powell O'Neal, b. January 24, 1855, dau of James O'Neal and Rachel Powell, and had *Lillie-Emily*, d. s. p.

    iv. Emily, b. December 1, 1853; d. April 3, 1857.

    v. Ellen-Kilgore, b. August 18, 1860.

XLI. SARAH SHROM BEATTY,[6] (George,[5] James,[4] William,[3] James,[2] John,[1]) b. October 2, 1831, at Harrisburg, Pa., and there resides; m., August 25, 1853, at Harrisburg, by Rev. John F. Mesick, D. D., Rev. BEVERLY ROBERTS WAUGH, b. July 28, 1824, at Liberty, Md.; son of Right Rev. Beverly

Waugh,* of the Methodist Episcopal Church, and his wife Catharine Bushby. He received a thorough English and classical education, and entered Dickinson College, where he graduated. His *alma mater* subsequently conferred upon him the degree of A. M. Mr. Waugh was licensed to preach by the Baltimore Conference; but accepted the position of Professor of Mathematics and English Literature in the Baltimore Female College, an institution then in the full tide of success. In 1853, the trustees of the Pennsylvania Female College at Harrisburg secured him as principal of that institution, in which position he labored faithfully and successfully to the day of his death. It was not alone in the capacity of teacher that Mr. Waugh devoted his energies and talents; but his labors were varied, incessant, faithful, in season and out of season,

---

*BEVERLY WAUGH, b. October 25, 1789, in Fairfax county, Va.; d. February 9, 1858, in the city of Baltimore, Md. He was the son of James Waugh and Henrietta Turley, and received a good classical education. In his twentieth year he was admitted to trial as a traveling minister in the Methodist Episcopal Church, and, in 1810, had charge of the Greenbrier circuit, Virginia. In 1811, he was ordained a deacon, and in 1813, an elder, and stationed in Baltimore. From that period until 1828, he was in active pastoral life. That year he was elected assistant book-agent, head-quarters in New York city, and in 1832, the principal in that work. In 1836, he was chosen a bishop of the church, and in 1852, became the senior officer of the Methodist Episcopal Church. In 1857, he presided over six conferences scattered from the Atlantic seaboard to Michigan and Indiana, besides aiding his colleagues in three or four others. During his term of episcopal service, his toil and peril, fatigue and suffering, were very great; but always without complaint. He was a faithful Soldier of the Cross, and universally loved and respected. He was a man of God—a consistent Christian, a devoted minister and scrupulous in the performance of every known duty. Bishop Waugh m., April 21, 1812, in the city of Washington, by Rev. Nicholas Snethen, CATHARINE BRUCE BUSHBY, b. September 4, 1791, in Fairfax county, Va.; d. March 23, 1865, in the city of Baltimore; daughter of William Bushby and Mary (Haight) Manning. They had issue (surname Waugh):

    i. *James-Beverly*, b. January 5, 1813; d. December 9, 1850; m. Mary Elizabeth Darke Manning and had *Mary-Virginia*, d. s. p., and *Henrietta*.

for the good of humanity. His devoted Christian life-work ended on the 24th of March, 1861, in his thirty-seventh year. There was issue (surname Waugh):

    i. Eliza-Beverlina, b. November 21, 1855, at Harrisburg; baptized December 18, 1855, by Rev. Beverly Waugh, D. D.; m. Charles Augustus Kunkel. (*see Kunkel record.*)
    ii. Beverly-Roberts, b. October 15, 1861; baptized December 1, 1861, by Rev. Francis Hodgson, D. D., of the Methodist Episcopal Church; d. March 9, 1863.

XLII. MARGARETTA HILL,[7] (Arundel,[6] Nancy,[5] James,[4] William,[3] James,[2] John,[1]) b. December 22, 1835, at Steubenville, O.; resides at Bynumsville, Mo.; was twice married; first, April 10, 1855, at Steubenville, O., by Rev. William P. Breed, JAMES HUNTER, b. February 1, 1831, at Steubenville, O.; d. June 24, 1868, at West Quincy, Mo.; son of Samuel D. Hunter, and his wife Mary Ann Buell. They had issue (surname Hunter):

    i. Charles-Cole, b. January 6, 1856.
    ii. Mary-Davidson, b. August 24, 1857.
    iii. Ella-Margaretta, b. August 24, 1862.
    iv. Willie-Arundel, b. July 25, 1866.

Margaretta Hill Hunter, m., secondly, February 17, 1872, in Macon county, Mo., by Rev. John W. Scott, EMERY BISSEL DOWNER, b. June 8, 1824, in Jefferson county, N. Y., son of Avery Downer and Electa Mitchell.

XLIII. JAMES IRWIN FECHTIG,[7] (Isabella,[6] Gawin-Irwin,[5]

---

    ii. Eliza, b. August 10, 1815; d. November 12, 1822.
    iii. William-Bushby, b. September 3, 1817; d. May 18, 1877; m. Caroline M. Kettlehume, and had four children, all d. s. p.
    iv. Alexander-Townsend. b. December 22, 1819; d. unm.
    v. Henrietta-Maria, b. September 11, 1821; d. June 17, 1845.
    vi. Beverly-Roberts, b. July 28, 1824; d. March 24, 1861; m. Sarah Shrom Beatty.
    vii. John-Wesley, b. October 5, 1827; d. 1880; m. Margaret A. Disney, and left issue.
    viii. Catharine Virginia, b. January 9, 1830; m. Charles M. Cullen, a lawyer of Georgetown, Del., and had issue.

James,[4] William,[3] James,[2] John,[1]) b. September 30, 1820, in Hagerstown, Md.; d. August 31, 1860; m. May 7, 1846, at Hagerstown, Md., by Rev. David Steele, CATHARINE JANE EMMERT, b. April 8, 1826, in Meadville, Washington county, Md., daughter of Michael Emmert and Addie Myers. They had issue (surname Fechtig):

 i. Alice-Ann, b. April 11, 1847; d. December 1, 1848.
 ii. Clara-Jane, b. August 18, 1848; m. Allen Yingling, b. October 31, 1841, and they had (surname Yingling) *Katie, Harvey-Allen, Margaret* and *Walter.*
 iii. Michael-Emmert, b. November 17, 1850.
 iv. Isabella-Beatty, b. December 6, 1851; d. April 13, 1854.
 v. Millard-Fillmore, b. March 14, 1856.
 vi. Annie-Amelia, b. June 20, 1858; d. May, 1860.

BOAS FAMILY.

I. WILLIAM BOAS,[2] son of Frederick Boas,[1] was born in 1739, in the Canton of Zurich, not far from the city of Berne, Switzerland. He was of the Reformed faith, as "all his fathers were," some of his ancestors being distinguished ministers in the church of Zwingli. William passed through a regular course of scientific and theological training at the University of Halle, after which he, in 1770, came to America under the auspices of the congregations at Berne, but not with the necessary credentials from the Fathers of the Reformed church in Holland, from whom that denomination in this country received its authority. In the Cötal minutes of the Reformed church for the year 1771, mention is made of the fact that he "had been joyfully expected from Europe for several years; that he had now arrived, but that Cötus felt disappointed because he brought no testimonials with him; that they declined, on that account, receiving him." However, the congregation at Reading, Pa., earnestly petitioned Cötus that he might be given them as their pastor, because they had been so long destitute. The Fathers in Holland were very tenacious of their rights, and warned Cötus against acknowledging the Reverend Boas a member, but had the consideration, in 1773, to say: "As Pennsylvania is a free country, we cannot drive him away from his congregation," by whom he was dearly loved. He labored faithfully in the Master's vineyard, and Cötus, in a letter to the Fathers, under date of May, 1777, bestowed the highest praise upon Rev. Mr. Boas, stating "that his congregation in Reading is in a most flourishing condition, through his industry and zeal; that he is at this time a learned and expert laborer in the kingdom of Christ; that he is beloved, not only in Reading, but by all the members of Cötus." About the year 1781, he resigned the charge of the Reading church, to which he had been a faithful pastor for ten years. He afterward appears to have had charge of the same congregation at Reading, for in the record-books of the church in Cocalico, Lancaster county, Pa., we find that "the Rev. Mr. Boas, of the Reading congregation, on the 15th of September, 1786, preached the funeral sermon of Reverend John Waldschmid, from Psalm lxxiii. 23, 24." During the Revolution, when every able-bodied man (save those having conscientious scruples) was enlisted in the patriotic cause, the Rev. Mr. Boas served a tour as chaplain to one of the associated battalions of Berks county, namely, that in and around Philadelphia in the summer of 1777. He did not cease his pastoral work until late in life, but was the same devout and earnest minister of the New Testament. He was a good, earnest preacher, had a remarkably strong voice, and nothing could move him from the path of duty. Full of years he d. November 28, 1814, at Reading, Pa., and is there buried. He married [SUSANNA] EPPLER. They had issue :

  i. John; was a hatter by trade, and d. in Reading, Pa.; m. —— Herbein, and had, among others, *John* and *Daniel.*

  ii. William; removed to Allentown, Pa., where he succeeded Charles Deshler—whose daughter he had married—in merchandising. He was register and recorder of Lehigh county, and held other offices of honor. Of his children, we have the names of Dr. *Charles*, d. s. p.; *William, Henry-Jacob,* and *Mary-Ann.*

  iii. Susanna; m. [Samuel] Wanner, of Kutztown, Berks county, Pa., and had, (surname Wanner), *William, Samuel, Catharine. Maria,* d. s. p., and *Harriet.*

  iv. Daniel; was also a hatter ; d. in Reading ; m., and had, among others, *William, Augustus, Franklin G., Jacob,* a minister of the Gospel ; *Obediah* and *Jeremiah.*

2. *v. Jacob,* b. 1779 ; m. Sarah Dick.

  vi. Catharine; m. Frederick Rapp, and had, among others, (surname Rapp) *William, Anna,* and *Susan-Boas.*

3. *vii. Frederick,* b. July 3, 1785 ; m. Elizabeth Krause.

  viii. Barbara; m. Jacob Levan, a coppersmith, residing in Kutztown, and had (surname Levan) *Hester,* m. Mr. Bunstine, *Elmina,* and *Juliann.*

II. JACOB BOAS,[2] (William,[2] Frederick,[1]) b. 1779, at Reading, Pa.; d. October 8, 1815, at Harrisburg, Pa. He learned, at first, the trade of tinsmith, but subsequently entered mercantile life, removing to Harrisburg, Pa., in 1805, where he established himself in business. He served as a member of the borough council, and was appointed and commissioned by Governor Snyder, February 6, 1809, prothonotary and clerk of the courts of quarter sessions—an office he held at the time of his death. He was a man of sterling integrity, and prominent and influential in the affairs of the community in which he lived. Mr. Boas m., April 20, 1802, at Reading Pa., SARAH DICK, b. September 2, 1781, in Reading, Pa.; d. October 23, 1859, in Reading, Pa.; dau. of Jacob Dick. They had issue :

4.   i. *William-Dick*, b. September 6, 1803 ; m. Martha Smith Ingram.
5.   ii. *Jacob-Dick*, b. October 5, 1806 ; m., first, Elizabeth Seiler ; second, Emeline Yeakel Krause.
       iii. *John-Philip*, b. July 12, 1809 ; d. in New Jersey ; m. Miss Stem, and left several children.
6.   iv. *Augustus-Frederick*, b. March 1, 1813 ; m. Emma Elizabeth Boyer.
7.   v. *Daniel-Dick*, b. February 19, 1816 ; m. Margaret Bates.

III. FREDERICK BOAS,[3] (William,[2] Frederick,[1]) b. July 3, 1785, at Reading, Pa.; d. June 13, 1817, at Philadelphia, Pa. He learned the trade of coppersmith and tin-plate worker at Reading, Pa., but commenced business for himself at Reading. He removed to Harrisburg, Pa., in 1811, where he carried on his trade successfully. He was an enterprising citizen, and, although quiet and unobtrusive, a representative man in the community. He m., May 17, 1811, ELIZABETH KRAUSE, b. September 23, 1796, in Lebanon, Pa.; d. April 23, 1847, in Harrisburg, Pa.; dau. of David Krause and Regina Orth. They had issue:

8.   i. *Elmina-Elizabeth*, b. July 7, 1813 ; m. William Jennings.
9.   ii. *Frederick-Krause*, b. April 5, 1815 ; m. Sarah C. Nolen.

IV. WILLIAM DICK BOAS,[4] (Jacob,[3] William,[2] Frederick,[1]) b. September 6, 1803, in Reading, Pa. ; d. May 20, 1889, at Harrisburg, Pa. ; learned the art of printing with George Getz, of Reading, on the *Berks and Schuylkill Journal*, and afterward worked at his profession in Philadelphia, Allentown, and Harrisburg. In 1837, he purchased an interest in the *Reporter* office, at Harrisburg, in partnership, first, with Samuel D. Patterson, and then with William F. Copeland, retiring in 1842. During this period, he was printer of the journals and bills of the House and Senate. He was cashier and clerk in the State Treasury Department during the administrations of Bickel, Bailey, Magraw, and McGrath, about nine years in all; was a clerk in the Surveyor General's office, and four years prothonotary of the county of Dauphin. From 1866 to 1868, he was one of the publishers of the *Patriot*. Mr. Boas m. March, 1828, MARTHA SMITH INGRAM, b. November 30, 1808; d. August 23, 1850, in Harrisburg, Pa. They had issue:

 i. Jacob-Dick, b. November 10, 1830; d. December 8, 1840.
 ii. Margaret-Ingram.
 iii. Emma-Elizabeth.

V. JACOB DICK BOAS,[4] (Jacob,[3] William,[2] Frederick,[1]) b. October 5, 1806, in Harrisburg, Pa.; d. there March 28, 1887. After his father's death, went to live with his uncle, Jacob Levan, at Kutztown, where he remained until his fifteenth year, when he went to learn the trade of hatter. He subsequently worked as a journeymen until 1831, when he established himself in business at Allentown, Pa. A year or two after, he was chosen a member of the borough council, and, in 1840, elected treasurer of the county of Lehigh. He represented the district in the State Senate during the years 1847, 1848, and 1849. In 1850, he removed to Harrisburg, where he established himself in the jewelry business, in which he was succeeded by his son. With Mr. Forster he was afterwards engaged in the forwarding business until his election as sheriff of Dauphin county in 1860. In 1868, he was appointed United States gauger in the Internal Revenue Department of the Government, resigning upon being elected Mayor of the city of Harrisburg, in 1873, which office he held one term. Mr. Boas m. in 1831, ELIZABETH SEILER, b. April 12, 1807; d. August 26, 1850, in Harrisburg, Pa.; daughter of Christian Seiler. They had issue:

i. Sarah-Elizabeth, m. Jacob Horter Smith, of Philadelphia, and had (surname Smith) *Bessie, Sallie, and Edith.*
ii. Charles-Augustus, b. 1835; d. 1886; m. Mary A. Reel, and had *Charles-Ross* and *Sarah-Reel.*

Jacob D. Boas m., secondly, Mrs. EMELINE YEAKLE KRAUSE; d. November, 1873, in Harrisburg, Pa.; s. p.

VI. AUGUSTUS FREDERICK BOAS,⁴ (Jacob,³ William,² Fredrick,¹) b. March 1, 1813, in Harrisburg, Pa.; d. Oct. 22, 1894 at Reading, Pa. He studied law at Allentown with Charles Davis a leading lawyer there, and was admitted to the Lehigh county bar, February 1, 1836; it is not known if he ever practiced his profession, for shortly after, on returning to Reading, he became a clerk in the Berks County Bank. In 1855, he was largely interested in the lumber trade, and subsequently the banking business. During the Rebellion, he sold for the Government about fifteen million dollars' worth of bonds. Mr. Boas m. EMMA ELIZABETH BOYER, daughter of Jacob K. Boyer, of Reading. They had issue :

i. Sarah-Jane, d. s. p.
ii. Edward-Payson, m. and resides in Reading, Pa.
iii. Martha-Jane, m. William S. Manus; resides at Thurlow, near Philadelphia, Pa.
iv. Emma-Elizabeth, m. William A. Sober, a lawyer, at Sunbury, Pa.
v. Catharine-M.

VII. DANIEL DICK BOAS,⁴ (Jacob,³ William,² Frederick,¹) b. February 19, 1816, in Harrisburg, Pa.; d. May 9, 1878, in Harrisburg, Pa., and there buried. Received the limited education afforded by the public schools prior to the establishment of the common-school system. In 1843, was appointed a clerk in the Harrisburg post-office, a position he held until the year 1845, when he went into business with O. Bellman, and subsequently established himself in the lumber trade, in which he was successfully engaged at the time of his death. He was a public-spirited and enterprising citizen, and his life was a useful one. He was church-warden and treasurer of St. Stephen's Episcopal church, Harrisburg—a marble tablet and memorial window within that edifice bear testimony to his services and virtues. Mr. Boas m. MARGARET BATES; b. August 1, 1819; d, May 20, 1889, at Harrisburg. They had issue :

    i. Sarah-Tyler, m. John Wister, iron manufacturer, of Duncannon, Pa., and had issue (surname Wister) *Jane-Boas-*d. s. p., *Elizabeth, Sarah-Logan* and *Margaret.*
    ii. William-Stuart; d. 1894, unm.
    iii. Jane-Eliza, m. Joseph Wood, and had issue (surname Wood) *William-Boas, Cooper* and *Margaretta.*
    iv. Henry-Daniel, m. Susanna Espy, and had *Mary-Espy* and *Sarah-Wister.*
    v. Helen-Margaret; m. John W. Reily.

VIII. ELMINA ELIZABETH BOAS,[4] (Frederick,[3] William,[2] Frederick,[1]) b. July 7, 1813, in Harrisburg, Pa.; d. October 10, 1884, in Harrisburg, Pa.; m. WILLIAM JENNINGS, b. September 23, 1807, in Juniata valley, Pa.; d. October 6, 1875, in Harrisburg, Pa., and there buried; son of William Jennings, who raised a company for the war of 1812-14, but who died suddenly before the company left home; he went to Harrisburg, Pa., about the year 1823, to learn blacksmithing, subsequently establishing a foundry, which he successfully carried on until near the close of his life. He was an enterprising citizen, active and influential in the public affairs of the municipality from 1830 to 1850, and in the church, of which he and his wife were consistent members, (the first Methodist,) prominent and zealous. They had issue (surname Jennings):

    i. Elmer-Frederick. b. May, 1833; d. December 22, 1876.
10. *ii. William-Wesley*, b. July 22, 1838; m. Emma Van Horn.
    iii. Elizabeth-M., b. September 3, 1843; m. B. Frank Scheffer October 15, 1867, of Harrisburg, and had issue (surname Scheffer), *Theodore-William* and *Nellie-Boas.*
    iv. Elmina-Regina, b. January 8, 1845; d. August 17, 1846.
    v. Mary-Emma, b. September 26, 1847; d. January 16, 1857.
    vi. Fannie-Boas, b. March 9, 1854; d. December 23, 1869.

IX. FREDERICK KRAUSE BOAS,[4] (Frederick,[3] William,[2] Frederick,[1]) b. April 5, 1815, in Harrisburg, Pa.; d. February 15, 1891. In 1825 he went into the printing office of Messrs. Krause & Cameron to learn that art, where he continued three years. In 1829 and 1830 he was a mercantile clerk, and afterward went one year to school. The latter part of 1831 he was again in mercantile life, in which he remained until August, 1832, when he entered the post-office at Harrisburg, under James Peacock. In the meantime he studied law under his uncle, David Krause, and was admitted to the Dauphin county bar, August 22, 1837. He opened his law office in 1838, but remained connected with the post-office department until 1843, assisting in the accounts, etc. In that year he entered into law partnership with David Krause, under the firm name of Krause & Boas. In 1845 Mr. Krause was appointed presiding judge of the Montgomery county district, from which time Mr. Boas continued the practice of his profession ; he was appointed by Governor Porter aid on his staff, with the rank of colonel, which he held from 1839 to 1845 ; was school director from 1839 to 1848, being treasurer of the board from 1840 to 1842, and also served in the borough council six years, from 1847 to 1853. Colonel Boas m., February 6, 1871, SARAH CATHARINE NOLEN, dau. of William and Maria H. Nolen, of Harrisburg, Pa.; no issue.

X. WILLIAM WESLEY JENNINGS,[5] (Elmina-Elizabeth,[4] Frederick,[3] William,[2] Frederick,[1]) b. July 22, 1838, in Harrisburg, Pa.; d. February 28, 1894. He attended the public schools of Harrisburg until his fifteenth year, when he commenced to learn the trade of iron-molder in his father's foundry. From 1860 to 1875 he was engaged in the iron business. During the war of the Rebellion he raised the One Hundred and Twenty-seventh Regiment, Pennsylvania Volunteers, a nine months' regiment, and was in the battles of Fredericksburg and Chancellorsville. (For a history of the regiment, see History of Dauphin county, Pa., p. 202.) Shortly after being mustered out of service, the Gettysburg campaign opened, and Colonel Jennings was placed in command of the Twenty-sixth Regiment, Pennsylvania Militia. The following account concerning it we have from Jacobs' " Battle of Gettysburg:" " The Twenty-sixth regiment arrived at Gettysburg on Friday the 26th of June, and by order of Major Haller, although contrary to the earnest remonstrances of Jennings, colonel of the regiment, was sent forward at 10.30 a. m., on the Chambersburg turnpike.

This was a suicidal movement of a handful chiefly of inexperienced men, in the face of a large body of experienced troops. The rebels afterwards laughed at the folly of the order. But, advancing to the distance of about three miles westward, our little band encamped and threw out their pickets. At about 3 p. m., the rebels in force made their appearance, and captured nearly all their pickets, forty in number. Colonel Jennings, who had on several occasions shown himself to be an officer as skillful as he is cool and brave, seeing the trap into which he had been led, immediately, upon sight of the enemy, divided the regiment into three squads, in order to deceive them with the appearance of a large body of infantry. The deception proved so far successful that the rebels did not press them, fearing that a direct attack might prove more serious than a mere skirmish. Jennings' command, however, hastily retreated eastward over the fields and by country roads, occasionally skirmishing with the enemy's cavalry, which was sent in pursuit of them; and after losing one hundred and twenty men of their number near Hunterstown, and zigzagging very frequently, being often within hearing distance of their pursuers, they reached Harrisburg on Sunday the 27th of June, much fatigued, having marched fifty-four out of sixty continuous hours. Too much praise cannot be awarded Colonel Jennings for the skillful manner in which he conducted this retreat and saved the regiment from capture." From 1863 to 1866, Colonel Jennings served as sheriff of the county of Dauphin, and again from 1876 to 1879. At the breaking out of the railroad riots in July, 1877, Colonel Jennings was absent from home, but, hastening to the State capital, he at once assumed control, organized the citizens, and restored peace to the city, seriously threatened with mob violence. His example was favorably commented upon at the time, not only by the newspaper press in general, but by the Governor of the State in his annual message, and was deserving of all praise. Upon the death of Mr. Calder, president of the First National Bank of Harrisburg, in 1880, he was elected to that position, in which he continued until his decease, and also president of the Commonwealth Guarantee Trust and Safe Deposit Company. In 1884, he was chosen a director of the Cumberland Valley Railroad Company. Colonel Jennings m., December 17, 1861, EMMA VAN HORN, b. November 26, 1842. They had issue (surname Jennings):

    i. Frederick-Boas, b. November 13, 1862; d. February 28, 1870.
    ii. Mary, b. September 7, 1864.
    iii. William, b. August 18, 1868; m., October 13, 1892; Jean Belle West, dau. of Rev. William A. West, and have issue:
        1. *Dorothy*, b. December 2, 1893.
    iv. Fannie, b. January 7, 1870.
    v. Harry, b. March 31, 1872.

BOMBERGER FAMILY.

I. CHRISTIAN BOMBERGER,[1] and Maria, his wife, emigrated from Eshelbrun, Baden, Germany, and arrived in Pennsylvania on the 12th day of May, 1722. He took up and settled upon a tract of land in Warwick township, Lancaster county, a portion of which remains in the possession of his descendants to this day. The original patent bears date May 22, 1734, and included 548 acres in the survey. This patent is now in the hands of reverend Christian Bomberger, a preacher of the Mennonite church. The first Christian died prior to 1750, and left, among other children:

2.   *i. John*, b. 1703; m. Mary Bausman.
3.   *ii. Christian;* m. and had issue.

II. JOHN BOMBERGER,[2] (Christian,[1]) b. about 1703; m. MARY BAUSMAN. They had issue, all b. in Warwick township, Lancaster county:

    i. Michael, b. 1737; m. and settled in Maryland.
4   *ii. John*, b. January 31, 1739; m. Catharine Flora.
5   *iii. Christian*, b. 1740; m. Elizabeth Dussinger.
    iv. Joseph, b. 1742; m. and had *Peter*, who settled in Canada.
    v. Jacob, b. 1744. He received the rudiments of a German education at Lititz, and was brought up on his father's farm. During the Provincial era, he served as an officer in the Second battalion of the Pennsylvania troops, under General Forbes and Colonel Bouquet. During the Revolution, he was some time in service, but turning his attention to religion, he began to study such theological works as were within his reach. After the peace of 1783, he went into the Western country, and for many years missionated among the Indians in the Northwest. During the war of 1812–14, well advanced in life, he returned to Pennsylvania, and remained with his friends. He died near Harrisburg, Pa., on the 4th of August, 1829, at the age of eighty-five, and was buried in Shearer's burying-ground. The

labors of Mr. Bomberger, for many years, were of that self-sacrificing spirit and devotedness which proved that others there were beside the zealous Jesuit and the faithful Moravian whose religious fervor and Christ-like example stand out as shining lights in the galaxy of the followers of the doctrines and teachings of Jesus of Nazareth.

III. CHRISTIAN BOMBERGER,² (Christian,¹) m. and had issue, among others:

6. i. *John*, m. Maria Reist.
    ii. *Christian*.
    iii. *Jacob*, d. s. p.
    iv. *Joseph;* m. Miss Erb; settled near Manheim, Lancaster county, Pa., and they had *Christian, Joseph,* and *John.* The latter m. and had *Elias, John, Martin, David* and *Christian*.

IV. JOHN BOMBERGER,³ (John,² Christian,¹) b., January 31, 1739, in Warwick township, Lancaster county, Pa.; d., May 6, 1798, near Middletown, Pa.; m. CATHARINE FLORA. They had issue:

   i. *Elizabeth;* m. Michael Rodenberger; removed to Centre county, Pa.
7. ii. *John*, b. April 11, 1768; m., first, Rachel Blattenberger; secondly, Elizabeth (Cauffman) Heppich.
   iii. *Joseph*, b. 1772; d. March 20, 1814; unm.
8. iv. *Jacob*, b. July 25, 1775; m. Sophia Ettley.
   v. *Michael*, d. s. p.
   vi. *George;* m. and removed to Lancaster, Ohio.
   vii. *Jonas;* m. and removed to Centre or Clearfield county, Pa., and had one daughter, *Sophia*.

V. CHRISTIAN BOMBERGER,³ (John,² Christian,¹) b., about 1740, in Lancaster county, Pa.; m., first, ELIZABETH DUSSINGER; m. secondly, JULIA DUSSINGER; and there was issue, among others:

   i. *Joseph;* m. and had two sons, one of whom, *Elias*, removed to Virginia.
   ii. *David*; m. and left issue—*Isaac* and Doctor *Christian*, both of whom left families.
   iii. *Moses*, d. s. p.
   iv. *Peter*, d. s. p.

v. Samuel; m. and settled in Canada.
vi. Christian; m. and settled in Canada.
vii. John, d. s. p.

VI. JOHN BOMBERGER,³ (Christian,² Christian,¹) ; m. MARIA REIST. They had issue :

i. *Christian;* m. and settled in Lebanon county, Pa.
ii. *John;* m. and had, among others, *Christian* and *Jacob.*
iii. *Jacob:* m. and had *Henry.*
iv. *Joseph.*
v. *Abraham;* m. Veronica ———, and located in Dauphin county, Pa.
vi. *Daniel.*
vii. *Peter;* m. and located in Conestoga township, Lancaster county, Pa.

VII. JOHN BOMBERGER,⁴ (John,³ John,² Christian,¹) b. April 11, 1763; d. September 2, 1847, in Middletown, Pa.; m. first, RACHEL BLATTENBERGER, b. August 5, 1771 ; d. August 19, 1814. They had issue :

i. *Catharine,* b. December 22, 1796 ; d. May 19, 1829 ; m., November 7, 1822, Isaac Simcox, and had (surname Simcox) *Rachel,* m. Samuel McElfatrick ; and *Abraham.*

9. ii. *Magdalena,* b. September 16, 1799 ; m. James Ringland.
iii. *John;* killed by a runaway horse ; s. p.
iv. *Eliza,* b. February 24, 1802 ; d. June 8, 1888 ; m. Jacob Albert, and had (surname Albert) *John* and *Elizabeth.*
v. *Christiana,* b. November 22, 1810 ; d. February 7, 1870 ; m. Henry Schreiner, and had, among others, (surname Schreiner) *Mary,* m. Henry A. Etter ; *James-R.,* d. s. p. ; *Ann,* m. Eckert Sheaffer ; *Henry-J.,* and *Lavinia* m. John D. Myers

John Bomberger m. secondly, Mrs. ELIZABETH (CAUFFMAN) HEPPICH, b. July 19, 1784; d. January 31, 1857. They had issue :

vi. *Jacob-Cauffman,* b. December 16, 1817, at Middletown, Pa. His education was received in the schools of the town, which, at that period, was quite limited. His early life was passed in merchandising, and subsequently in the business of banking. During the sessions of the Pennsylvania State Senate for 1851 and 1852, he served as assistant clerk of that body ; the year following, upon

Pennsylvania Genealogies.

the establishment of the Mechanics Bank, at Harrisburg, Pa., as cashier of that institution. Mr. Bomberger subsequently became its sole owner, and through his energy, financial tact, and ability, it has become one of the most successful banking-houses in Pennsylvania. For many years Mr. Bomberger held the position of one of the trustees of the State Lunatic Hospital, at Harrisburg, under the appointment of the Governor. Few men are held in higher esteem for integrity, and in the community where he is among its leading citizens, he has its respect and confidence.

 vii. Rachel; m. Samuel Kunkel. (*see Kunkel record.*)

VIII. JACOB BOMBERGER,[4] (John,[3] John,[2] Christian,[1]) b. July 25, 1775, in Dauphin county, Pa.; d. August 21, 1842, at Middletown, Pa.; m. SOPHIA ETTELE, b. March 6, 1778; d. December 11, 1839, in Middletown, Pa. They had issue:

  i. Elizabeth, d. in 1866; m. Jacob Erb; removed to Centre county, Pa.; and left issue.
  ii. John, b. February 14, 1806; d. April 5, 1852; m. Elizabeth Parthemore, b. February 2, 1809; d. January 31, 1865; and removed to Ohio, leaving issue.
10. *iii. Mary,* m. Jacob Rife.
  iv. William, b. May 6, 1813; m. Sarah Parthemore; resided in Fairview township, York county, Pa., and had issue.
  v. Joseph-H., d. in 1845; was a minister of the "Church of God."
  vi. Catharine, m. David Motter, and had issue; resided in Washington township, Dauphin county, Pa.

IX. MAGDALENA BOMBERGER,[5] (John,[4] John,[3] John,[2] Christian,[1]) b. September 16, 1799, in Middletown, Pa.; m. JAMES RINGLAND, b. December 5, 1795, in Chester county, Pa. His father was a native of county Down, Ireland, and came to America in 1793; he d. at Lancaster, Pa., m. 1842. James Ringland settled at Middletown, Pa., about 1821, where he entered mercantile life, subsequently establishing himself in business, which he successfully carried on. They had issue (surname Ringland):

11. *i. John,* b. January 9, 1825; m. Margaret E. Smith.
  ii. James, d. April, 1855.
  iii. Eliza-Jane, m. Samuel L. Yetter, of Middletown, Pa.
  iv. Mary-M , m. Benjamin F. Kendig.

X. MARY BOMBERGER,[6] (Jacob,[4] John,[3] John,[2] Christian,[1]) b. in Middletown, Pa.; m. August 12, 1828, JACOB RIFE, b. March 2, 1805, in Londonderry townsnip, Dauphin county, Pa.; son of Henry Rife and Susan Shelly; he was educated in the schools of the time, and worked on a farm until he went to learn the tanning trade with William King, of Middletown; afterwards carried on the business for himself, several years, at what is known as the Keystone tannery, at the same time conducting a small farm, now within the limits of that borough. They had issue (surname Rife):

- i. *Susan*, m. Lewis P. Brady
- ii. *Sophia*, m. Enoch Matlack.
- iii. *Henry-Jacob.*
- iv. *Mary*, m. William C. Ross, of Iowa.
- v. *Joseph-B.*
- vi. *Margaret-Shelley*, m. David C. Kolp, of Iowa, and had issue.
- vii. *Clara-Lauman.*
- viii. *John-Winebrenner*, b. August 14, 1846; was educated in the common schools and Crittenden's Commercial College, from which latter he graduated in 1862; he learned tanning with his father, and when the latter retired from active business he and his brother Jacob took charge of the Keystone steam tannery, where they are extensively engaged in the manufacture of leather; served in the One Hundred and Forty-fourth regiment, Pennsylvania Volunteers; was elected a member of the Fiftieth and Fifty-first Congresses.
- ix. *Jacob-Flake*, b. September 29, 1848; was educated in the public schools and at the Pennsylvania College, Gettysburg; he learned the tanning trade with his father, and is now associated with his brother, above-named, in the business.
- x. *William-Bomberger.*

XI. JOHN RINGLAND,[6] (Magdalena,[5] John,[4] John,[3] John,[2] Christian,[1]) b. January 9, 1825, in Middletown, Pa., where he now resides. He was educated in the common schools of Middletown. At the age of fifteen he entered the *Examiner and Herald* office, at Lancaster, to learn the art of printing, with R. White Middleton, who afterwards sold the office and removed to Carlisle, where he purchased the *Carlisle Herald*, John accompanying him, as also back again to Lancaster, when he sold.

out the *Herald* and purchased the *Lancaster Union*. Here he remained until 1845. In 1846, Mr. Ringland commenced the study of medicine with Dr. Benjamin J. Wiestling, of Middletown, and graduated from the medical department of the University of Pennsylvania in 1850. He located at Portsmouth, now Middletown, where he entered upon the practice of medicine; but was subsequently compelled to relinquish it, owing to impaired hearing. In the fall of 1852, he engaged in the lumber business at New Cumberland, in which he continued until the spring of 1855, when he returned to Middletown, and established himself in the drug business. In 1860, he was elected recorder of deeds and clerk of the orphans' court of Dauphin county, and re-elected in 1863. While in Portsmouth, in 1850, a post-office was established there, and Dr. Ringland appointed postmaster. He has served as justice of the peace, was census enumerator in 1870, and filled various borough offices. Dr. Ringland married, in 1850, MARGARET E. SMITH, daughter of Henry Smith, of Middletown. They had issue (surname Ringland):

 i. James-Henry.
 ii. Robert-Wiestling, d. s. p.
 iii. John-Augustus.
 iv. Kate-Shelly, d. s. p.
 v. Mary-Jane; m. M. L. Emminger.
 vi. Louisa-Bomberger.
 vii. Harry-Smith, d. s. p.
 viii. Margaret-Smith, d. s. p.
 ix. Anna-Laura.
 x. Edwin-Shott, d. s. p.
 xi. Edith-Matilda, d. s. p.
 xii. Almeda-Kunkel.

BOYD OF DERRY.

I. WILLIAM BOYD,[1] a native of county Antrim, Province of Ulster, Ireland, emigrated to Pennsylvania prior to 1730, settling in Derry township. He had a large family of children, of whom we have the following:

  i. Robert, b. 1705, who took up several tracts of land in Derry township; m. and had *Elizabeth, Catharine* and *Mary*.
  ii. Alexander, b. 1707; m. and had *Alexander, Robert, William* and *Margaret*.
  iii. Jennett, b. 1710; d. October 17, 1757; m. John McCosh; d. November, 1754. At his death he left considerable of an estate, which his widow disposed of as follows: To her brothers, William, John, Alexander and Robert Boyd; her niece, Margaret, daughter of John Boyd; to Alexander, Robert, William and Margaret, children of Alexander Boyd; to Benjamin, Joseph and William, children of William Boyd; niece Catharine Boyd, who, we presume, was a daughter of William Boyd; to her sister-in-law, Jean Boyd; to her nieces, Elizabeth, Catharine and Mary, daughters, we suppose, of Robert Boyd; to Rev. John Roan; and "the sum of twenty shillings to Derry congregation."
2. *iv. William*, b. 1712; m. and left issue.
  v. John, b. 1715; m. and had *Margaret*.

II. WILLIAM BOYD,[2] (William,[1]) b. 1712, in county Antrim, Ireland; d. prior to 1760, in Derry township, Lancaster county, Pa.; m. and had among others the following issue:

3. *i. William*, b. 1733; m. Jennett Brisben.
4. *ii. Benjamin*, b. 1738; m. Jennett Elliott.
5. *iii. Joseph*, b. 1740; m. Elizabeth Wallace.
  iv. Catharine, b. 1743.

III. WILLIAM BOYD,[3] (William,[2] William,[1]) b. about 1733 in Derry township, then Lancaster county, Pennsylvania. He was brought up as a farmer, became quite prominent in Provincial days, and was an officer during the French and Indian war, and the struggle for independence. He belonged to the Paxtang Boys, whose zeal in defense of their firesides compelled them to destroy the murdering savages of Conestoga. During the latter part of his life, he served in the commission of a justice of the peace. He was one of the charter members of Lodge 21, at Paxtang, and its second Master. In his will, he left a legacy to the lodge's-charity fund. Mr. Boyd died May 17, 1808, and is buried in Derry church graveyard. He m. JENNETT BRISBEN. They had issue:

  i. James, b. 1759.
6. *ii. John*, b. 1761 ; m. Mary Williams.
  iii. Jennett, b. 1763 ; m. —— Moore.
  iv. Mary, b. 1765 ; m. —— Strawbridge.
  v. Margaret, b. 1767; m. William Williams.
  vi. William, b. 1769 ; d. December, 1807 ; m. and left issue.

IV. BENJAMIN BOYD,³ (William,² William,¹) b. 1738 ; d. May 8, 1803 ; m. December 31, 1761, by Reverend John Roan, JENNETT ELLIOTT, b. 1737 ; d. November 21, 1820; and, with her husband, lie buried in old Derry church graveyard. They had issue :

  i. Margaret, b. October 12, 1763; d. September, 1826 ; m. James Wilson.
  ii. Mary, b. October 6, 1765 ; d. February 18, 1814 ; m. William Frazer, b. 1763 ; d. January 19, 1816.
  iii. William, b. August 20, 1767 ; d. September 19, 1803 ; m. Mary Orr.
  iv. Jean, b. June 13, 1770 ; d. October 26, 1826 ; m. September 8, 1791, John Craig.
  v. Eleanor, b. August 20, 1772 ; d. January 5, 1810 ; m. James Rogers, of Hanover.
  vi. Rachel, b. December 24, 1774 ; d. ; m. William Hamilton, of Derry.
  vii. Esther, b. April 23, 1779 ; d. unm.
  viii. Elizabeth, (twin) b. April 23, 1779 ; m. Moses Wilson, of Hanover.

V. JOSEPH BOYD,³ (William,² William,¹) b. 1740 ; d. September 20, 1781, in Londonderry township, Dauphin county, Pennsylvania ; m. in 1766, by Reverend John Elder, ELIZABETH WALLACE, daughter of Robert Wallace, b. 1746; d.

April 13, 1802, in Londonderry township, Dauphin county, Pennsylvania; both buried in old Derry church graveyard. They had issue:

7. i. *Mary*, b. 1768; m. William Baird.
    ii. *Margaret*, b. 1770; m. William McDonald, of Dickinson township, Cumberland county, Pennsylvania.
    iii. *Elizabeth*, b. 1772; d. October 15, 1805.
    iv. *Ann*, b. 1774.
8. v. *William*, b. 1776; m. Martha Cowden.
    vi. *Jean*, b. 1778.
    vii. *Isabel*, b. 1780; d. December 1, 1789.

VI. JOHN BOYD,[4] (William,[3] William,[2] William,[1]) b. about 1761, in Derry township, Lancaster county, Pa.; d. April 6, 1799, at Harrisburg, Pa. He was one of the first settlers in the new town, locating there in 1785—the year it was laid out—and became quite prominent and influential. He m., the year previous, MARY WILLIAMS, dau. of George Williams, b. 1761, in Paxtang township; d. September 25, 1844, at Harrisburg, and there buried. They had issue:

   i. *Mary*, b. July 21, 1785; d. s. p.
   ii. *William*, b. November 12, 1786; d. July 1, 1805, at Baltimore, Md.
   iii. *George*, b. July 17, 1788; d. inf.
   iv. *Elizabeth*, (twin,) b. July 17, 1788.
9. v. *James-Rutherford*, b October 13, 1790; m. first, Margaret Emerson; second, Eliza Keller; third, Eliza Sloan Baird.
   vii. *John-Brisben*, b. June 27, 1793; d. June 12, 1804.
10. viii. *George-Williams*, b. November 12, 1796; m. Elizabeth S. Mish.

After the death of John Boyd, his widow m. STACY POTTS, concerning whom, as he was a man of mark, we have this information: Thomas Potts, the ancestor of Stacy Potts, was a Quaker, who emigrated from England with his wife and children, in company with Mahlon Stacy and his family, in the ship "Shield," and landed at Burlington, N. J., in the winter of 1678, she being the first ship that went so far up the Delaware. Stacy was a leading man in the Society of Friends and in the government of West Jersey. At Trenton, 1731, Stacy Potts was born. He received a good education, and learned the trade of a tanner, a business which he successfully carried on at least up to the time of the Revolution. Mr. Potts seems to have been a very enterprising and public-spirited citizen. In 1776, besides owning a tannery, he built the steel-works on Front street, Trenton, and after the close of the Revolution was largely interested in the erection of a paper-mill in the same locality. This was prior to the publication of Collins' Bible. In December, 1788, it was advertised by its proprietors, Stacy Potts and John Reynolds, as "now nearly completed." About this period Stacy Potts removed to Harrisburg, Pa. It is difficult to divine what were his motives in leaving his native town, where he was very popular, and with his ample competency, to settle in the then new town on the Susquehanna. His second marriage may, perchance, have had somewhat to do with his removal from Trenton. Going to Harrisburg, he made large purchases of land, and whether it was due to this fact, or his agreeable manner, Stacy Potts became quite prominent ; was chosen to the Legislature in 1791 and in 1792. During the mill-dam troubles of 1794-95, Mr. Potts was quite active, and was one of the committee of citizens who were willing to take upon themselves all responsibility accruing by the destruction of the obnoxious dam. He served as burgess of the borough, and was a member of the Town Council. From 1799 to 1803 he again represented Dauphin county in the State Legislature. About the year 1805, he returned to Trenton ; subsequently became mayor of that city, an office he held for several years. He died in that city April 28, 1816, in his eighty-fifth year. Mr. Potts was thrice married. We have no knowledge as to his first wife. He married, secondly, Miss Gardiner, of Philadelphia, a Presbyterian lady of superior intelligence. She died at Harrisburg in 1799. His third wife was Mrs. Mary Boyd. Upon the death of Mr. Potts, his widow removed to Harrisburg, where she resided with her son, George W. Boyd, until her death in 1844.

VII. MARY BOYD,[4] (Joseph,[3] William,[2] William,[1]) b. 1768, in Derry township, Lancaster county, Pa.; d. 1866, in West Hanover township, Dauphin county, Pa.; m. WILLIAM BAIRD. They had issue, (surname Baird):

i. James, b. 1794.
11. *ii. Joseph-Boyd*, b. October, 1796 ; m. Mary Todd.
iii. William, b. 1798; m. —— McNair.
iv. Elizabeth, b. 1800.
v. John, b. 1802.
v. Wallace, b. 1804; d. September 2, 1858; m. Martha Todd.

VIII. WILLIAM BOYD,[4] (Joseph,[3] William[2] William,[1]) b. 1776 ; removed to, and died in Cumberland county, Pa.; m. June 4, 1807, MARTHA COWDEN, daughter of James and Mary Cowden. They had issue.

i. Elizabeth, m. —— Dallas.
ii. James, m. McMurray.
iii. Joseph.
iv. Matthew.
v. William
vi. Edward.
vii. Martha.
viii. Mary.

IX. JAMES RUTHERFORD BOYD,[5] (John,[4] William,[3] William,[2] William,[1]) b. October 13, 1790, at Harrisburg, Pa.; d. December 29, 1865. He learned the trade of cabinet-making, at Trenton, New Jersey, and for many years successfully carried on that business. He served as third sergeant in Captain Richard M. Crain's company, the Harrisburg Artillerists, in the war of 1814, and for a long time was a member of the borough council. Mr. Boyd was thrice married; m., first, MARGARET EMERSON; d. May 24, 1824. They had issue:

i. Mary, d. —— : m. Dr. William S. Cresap. d ——; had issue (surname Cresap) *Mary, Boyd, Nade*, and *William*.
ii. John-R., b. December 26, 1815; d. March 26, 1862; m. Caroline E. Truman, and had *Annie, Truman, Margaret, Albert, Peter*, and *Caroline*, d. s. p.
iii. Sarah-Ann, b. March 29, 1818 ; d. October 8, 1854 ; m. John B. Bratton, and had *Laura*, and *Edward*.

Mr. Boyd m., secondly, ELIZA KELLER; b. June 12, 1803 ; d. February 27, 1828; daughter of John Peter Keller and Catharine Shaeffer, (*see Keller record.*) They had issue:

iv. Peter-Keller, b. 1826; m. Caroline E. Barnitz ; resides at Harrisburg, Pa.

Mr. Boyd m., thirdly, February 3, 1831, by Rev. William R. DeWitt, ELIZA SLOAN BAIRD, b. Dec. 21, 1800; d. February 5, 1886; daughter of Robert Sloan and Sarah McCormick. They had issue:

 v. Robert-Sloan, d. 1884.
 vi. Isabella-McCormick, b. October 4, 1833; d. February 10, 1850.
 vii. George-William, m. Nettie Hershey.
 viii Eliza-Potts, m. James Murphy; reside in Philadelphia.
 ix. Maria; d. at Harrisburg, Pa.
 x. James-Alexander, m. Dessie Spahr; b. September 28, 1847; d February 13, 1870.

X. GEORGE WILLIAMS BOYD,[5] (John,[4] William,[3] William,[2] William,[1]) b. November 12, 1796, in Harrisburg, Pa.; d. August 31, 1863. He was a chair-maker, and carried on the business many years at Harrisburg. Was also a member of the council of that borough, and a man of influence in the community. He m. October 31, 1822, by Rev. William R. DeWitt, D. D., ELIZABETH S. MISH, b. November 23, 1802; d. March 26, 1849, in Harrisburg, Pa., and, with her husband, there buried. They had issue:

12. *i. John-Brisben,* m. Elizabeth J. Carson.
 ii. Jacob-Mish, m.
 iii Elizabeth, m. William S. Rowson, civil engineer; reside at Perth Amboy, New Jersey, and had issue (surname Rowson) *Mary* and *William.*
 iv. Mary-Ellen, m. John B. Bratton, of Carlisle, Pa., and had issue (surname Bratton) *Mary, Bessie, John-Brisben,* and *Georgie.*
 v. Catharine-Mish.
 vi. Caroline-Virginia, m. John H. Tennent, of Alabama; reside in New York city.
 vii. George-Williams, b. December 21, 1836; d. January 6, 1867; served in the quartermaster's department during the Rebellion.

XI. JOSEPH BOYD BAIRD,[5] (Mary,[4] Joseph,[3] William,[2] William,[1]) b. October, 1796; removed to Franklin county, Pa., where he died; m. October 7, 1834, MARY TODD, b. November 1, 1805, in Hanover township, Dauphin county, Pa. In 1880, was residing in Franklin, Warren county, Ohio. They had issue (surname Baird):

Boyd of Derry.

    i. Martha-Ann, b. February 8, 1836 ; m. October 12, 1854, John Smith ; reside in Taylorsville, Christian county, Illinois.
    ii. Harriet-Jemima, b. May 12. 1838.
    iii. Caroline-Todd, b. May 14, 1841 ; m. January 11, 1866, Manlius T. Leachman ; reside in Christian county, Illinois.
    iv. Francina.

XII. JOHN BRISBEN BOYD,[6] (George-Williams,[5] John,[4] William,[3] William,[2] William,[1]) b. September 4, 1824, in Harrisburg, Pa., where he resides; m., in 1849, ELIZABETH J. CARSON ; b. in Harrisburg, Pa.; daughter of William M. Carson and Sarah Kunkel. They had issue :

    i. Emma-Louise, m. William H. Henderson, and had *Anna.*
    ii. Elizabeth-Carson, m. Mordaunt L. Harrington.

BUCHER FAMILY.

I. CLAUS BUCHER,[1] born in Neukirch, in the Canton of Schaffhausen, Switzerland, Anno Domini 1524, heads the family record. This record, beginning about the dawn of the Reformation, in the land of its source, is inscribed on an antiquated sheet of paper, in the German language, with the coat of arms* emblazoned thereon. There is also a copy of the family record from Schafthausen, certified by the seal of the United States consul at Basle. Claus Bucher m., April 6, 1545, DOROTHEA ZELLER. They had issue:

2.   i. *John*, b. February 13, 1547; m. Elizabeth Lutzen.
   ii. *George*, b. October 27, 1548; m. August 31, 1572, Christiana Muller, and had *Dorothea*, who m. Adam Diller, of Andelfing; *John* and *Elizabeth*.
   iii. *Anna*, b. April 7, 1550.
   iv. *Elizabeth*, b. May 5, 1554.
   v. *Nicholas*, (Claus), b. April 2, 1559.
   vi. *Margaretta*, b. May 7, 1565; m. May 15, 1596, George Botts.
   vii. *Agnes*, b. November 27, 1569.

II. JOHN BUCHER,[2] (Claus,[1]) b. February 13, 1547; m. October 18, 1572, ELIZABETH LUTZEN, of Ellenhausen. They had issue:

   i. *Anna*, b. July 17, 1573; m. first, May 5, 1594, Jacob Veith; m. second, in 1607, George Yunker, of Wickenshine.
   ii. *Barbara*, b. August 9, 1578; m. Conrad Mosher.
   iii. *Martin*, b. July 18, 1580; m. November 13, 1605, Agatha Kohrbaus, of Barrington, and had *Martin*, *Casper*, b. October 24, 1609, and *Catharine*; m. second, Anna Ulmer, and had *John*, who m. October 25, 1642, Dorothea Blank.

Coat of Arms.—Shield, azure, and centre argent, on which is a beech tree, eradicated, vert, on which hang's a hunter's horn, stringed, or. *Crest.*—The tree and horn as on the shield.

3. iv. *John*, b. January 20, 1583 ; m. Barbara Ryschacker.
    v. *Stephen*, b. January 30, 1584.
    vi *Catharine*, b. February 16, 1589.

III. JOHN BUCHER,[3] (John,[2] Claus,[1]) b. January 20, 1583 ; m. November 15, 1604, BARBARA RYSCHACKER, of Freithaler. They had issue :

    i. *Anna*, b. September 8, 1605.
    ii. *Verina*, b. July 13, 1614.
    iii. *Barbara*, b. August 10, 1615.
4. iv. *John*, b. December 4, 1619 ; m. Maria Burtin.
    v. *Elizabeth*, b. April 14, 1622.

IV. JOHN BUCHER,[4] (John,[3] John,[2] Claus,[1]) b. December 4, 1619 ; d. July 4, 1675 ; *Landschreiber* (clerk of the courts) in Neukirch, in the Canton of Schaffhausen, from 1642 to 1648 ; m. May 20, 1644, MARIA BURTIN. They had issue :

    i. *Catharine*, b. August 1, 1645; m. John Kolbmar, M. D.
    ii. *Dorothea*, b. May 31, 1650 ; m. Jeremiah Oswald.
5. iii. *John*, b. 1652 ; m. Maria Bellar.
6. iv. *Henry*, b. 1654 ; m. Barbara Biggler.
7. v. *John-Conrad*, b. 1656 ; m. Margaretta Mentrengern.
8. vi. *John-Jacob*, b. 1658 ; m. Elizabeth Steiner.

V. JOHN BUCHER,[5] (John,[4] John,[3] John,[2] Claus,[1]) b. 1652 ; clerk of the courts, 1683 ; *Vogt*, (magistrate,) April 15, 1696; *Oberlandtmeister*, (superintendent of woods and forests,) April 14, 1702 ; *Zumftmeister*, (master of a corporation or guild,) July 1, 1703 ; *Obervogt über Lohn*, (master of loans,) August 24, 1705 ; m. MARIA BELLAR. They had issue :

    i. *John*, b. May 2, 1676.
    ii. *Henry*, b. January 10, 1678.
    iii. *Anna-Maria*, b. April 16, 1679 ; m. J. Fogle.
    iv. *Margaretta*, b. September 7, 1680.
    v. *Barbara*, b. June 24, 1683.
    vi. *Ferdinand*, (first), b. August 12, 1685 ; died in infancy.
    vii. *Ferdinand*, (second,) b. April 7, 1691.

VI. HENRY BUCHER,[5] (John,[4] John,[3] John,[2] Claus,[1]) b. 1654; *Hauptman über eine stadt comp.*, (chief burgess ;) *Wagemeister in der Oberzee waag*, (weighmaster,) Oberzee, July 2, 1683 ; m. BARBARA BIGGLER. They had issue :

i. Maria, b. July 19, 1672; m. William Moorbach.
ii. Veronica, (first,) b. May 20, 1674.
iii. Casper, b. February 1, 1677.
iv. John, (first,) b. June 2, 1679.
v. John, (second,) b. July 7, 1680.
vi. Henry, b. July 30, 1682 ; d. July 8, 1753 ; goldschmidt; m. August 22, 1706, Catharine Veith, and had *Barbara, Henry, John, Conrad, Catharine, John-Casper*, b. June 6, 1720, and *John-George*.
vii. Veronica, (second,) b. July 24, 1686.

VII. JOHN CONRAD BUCHER,⁵ (John,⁴ John,³ John,² Claus,¹) b. 1656; d. August 30, 1739 ; m. MARGARETTA MENTRENGERN. They had issue :

i. Margaret, b. June 22, 1690.
ii. John, (first,) b. May 30, 1691.
iii. Magdalena, b. May 16, 1693.
iv. Barbara, b. December 19, 1695 ; m. 1715, Sebastin Niewiler, of Englisshausen.
v. Elizabeth, b. April 15, 1698 ; m. J. Conrad Swenck.
vi. Dorothy, b. June 14, 1700 ; m. George Shultze.
vii. John, (second,) b. April 4, 1703; goldschmidt; m., first; Elizabeth Veith ; m., second, Elizabeth Stabin.
viii. Catharine, b. July 9, 1706.
ix. Ursula, b. August 9, 1713.

VIII. JOHN JACOB BUCHER,⁵ (John,⁴ John,³ John,² Claus,¹) b. 1658 ; d. July 28, 1707; May 16, 1687, *Grosswaibel*, (an officer of the court;) m. November 5, 1685, ELIZABETH STEINER. They had issue :

i. Maria, b. April 30. 1691.
ii. John, b. July 9, 1692.
iii. Emanuel, (first,) b. February 3, 1695.
iv. Elizabeth, (first,) b. July 5, 1696.
v. Emanuel, (second,) b. August 1, 1697.
9. *vi. John-Jacob*, b. January 1, 1699 ; m. Dorothea Burgauer.
vii. Emanuel, (third,) b. June 30, 1700.
viii. John-Henry, b. May 24, 1702.
ix. Bernhart, b. June 1, 1704.
x. Elizabeth, (second,) b. June 15, 1706.

IX. JOHN JACOB BUCHER,⁵ LL. D., (John-Jacob,⁵ John,⁴

Bucher Family.   123

John,³ John,² Claus,¹) b. January 1, 1699 ; d. in 1788 ; *Landvogt im Neukirch*, (Governor of Neukirch ;)* m. December 13, 1725, DOROTHEA BURGAUER. They had issue:

    i. Anna-Maria, (first,) b. November 2, 1726.
    ii. John-Jacob, b. August 9, 1728.
10. *iii. John-Conrad*, b. June 10, 1730; m. Mary Magdalena Hoch.
    iv. Mary-Elizabeth, b. May 16, 1732; d. March 26, 1826; m. first, Doctor Ott; m. secondly, the Hon. John Conrad Pyre; d. February 22, 1812.
    v. Anna-Maria, (second,) b. August 19, 1734.
    vi. John, b. August 26, 1737.

X. JOHN CONRAD BUCHER⁷ (John-Jacob,⁶ John-Jacob,⁵ John,⁴ John,³ John,² Claus,¹) b. June 10, 1730, in Neukirch, Canton of Schafthausen, Switzerland. Educated for the ministry of the German Reformed Church at the Universities of Marburg and St. Gall. Arrived in the Province of Pennsylvania, November 1, 1755. The French and Indian war being in progress he entered the Provincial army, and was commissioned ensign April 1, 1758, and stationed at Fort Louther, Carlisle. Served in Forbes' great expedition against Fort Duquesne in the summer and autumn of 1758. April 19, 1760, he was promoted to a lieutenancy, and July 12, 1764, commissioned as adjutant, and promoted to a captaincy on the 31st of the same month. His several commissions on parchment are in custody of his descendants in Harrisburg, Pa. He served in Bouquet's expeditions against the Indians in 1763 and 1764; they fought the battle of Bushy Run, August 5, 1763, the greatest battle on record between the whites and Indians (*Penn'a Arch. sec. series, vol. 2*). As remuneration to the officers for their services, the Proprietaries appropriated twenty-four thousand acres of land to be distributed among them according to rank, of which Captain Bucher drew six hundred and sixteen acres in Buffalo valley, now Union county, and five hundred and forty acres on the north side of Bald Eagle, in-

---

*His seal of office is in the possession of the family of his great-grandson, the late George Horter Bucher, of Cumberland co., Pa.

cluding mouth of Marsh creek, in Centre county. This is known as the *Officers' survey*. Peace with the French and Indians having been secured, he resigned his commission in 1765, and thenceforward devoted his time and labors to the ministry, servingwith zeal and self-abnegation the churches at Falling Spring (Chambersburg), Shippensburg, Carlisle, Hummelstown, etc., etc., until the year 1768, when he accepted the *call* to the German Reformed Church at Lebanon, then Lancaster county, whither he removed his family in 1769. Here he remained, officiating statedly and serving the several congregations in, then, Lancaster and Cumberland counties, until his death, actually dying " in harness," August 15, 1780, and was buried in the graveyard of the church of which he was pastor. An ancient-looking sandstone, inscription in German, in which language he usually preached, marks the spot. He took the oath of allegiance to the State of Penn'a June 10, 1778. The Rev. Bucher m. February 26, 1760, at Carlisle, by the Rev. George Duffield, MARIA MAGDALENA HOCH, daughter of George Hoch, one of the very earliest citizens of York, Pa., (and of his wife who was of the Lefevre family— French Huguenots;) b. February 2, 1742; d. at Alexandria, Pa., March 11, 1819. They had issue:

11.   *i. John-Jacob*, b. January 1, 1764; m. Susannah Margaret Hortter.
     ii. John-George, b. October 4, 1766, at Carlisle, Pa.; d. March, 1843, at Lebanon, Pa.; m. Hannah ———; d. s. p.
     iii. Anna-Dorothea, b. July 1, 1769, in Lebanon; d. September 3, 1770.
     iv. Eleanora-Dorothea, b. April 23, 1772, in Lebanon; d. October 18, 1772.
     v. Maria-Elizabeth, b. April 8, 1773, in Lebanon; d. April, 1791.
12.   *vi. John-Conrad*, b. June 18, 1775; m. Hannah Mytinger.

XI. JOHN JACOB BUCHER,[8] (John-Conrad,[7] John-Jacob,[6] John-Jacob,[5] John,[4] John,[3] John,[2] Claus,[1]) b. January 1, 1764, in Carlisle, Pa. In 1790, located in Harrisburg as a hatter and furrier; in 1796, elected coroner of Dauphin county; in 1798, appointed justice of the peace by Governor Mifflin; and represented Dauphin county in the Pennsylvania Legislature sitting at Lancaster, nine successive terms from 1803. In 1810 he was appointed by Governor Snyder one of the Commissioners for the erection of the public buildings at Harrisburg. In 1818 appointed by Governor Findlay an associate judge for the county of Dauphin, filling the office, honorably, until his death, October 16, 1827. Endowed with great wisdom and sagacity, and of unimpeachable integrity and honesty, he was called upon to fill many public and private trusts of honor and responsibility. His remains now lie in the Harrisburg cemetery. Judge Bucher m. March 27, 1792, SUSANNA MARGARET HORTTER, one of the five daughters of John Valentine Hortter, of Spires, Bavaria, who settled in Harrisburg in 1785. She was born in Germantown September 24, 1774; d. in Harrisburg, December 30, 1838. She was three years old when the battle of Germantown was fought, October 4, 1777, and remembered the experience of the family who were confined in the cellar of their residence, which was on the route of the battle. They had issue, all born in Harrisburg:

13.   *i. John-Conrad*, b. December 28, 1792; m. Ellen Isett.
      ii. Mary-Elizabeth, b. April 23, 1795; m. first, John Swift, of New York, who d. February 24, 1813, and had *John*, d. in infancy; m. secondly, William Ayres. (*see Ayres record.*)
14.   *iii. George-Horter*, b. June 15, 1797; m. first, Rebecca Pool; m. secondly, Hannah Hough.
      iv. Maria Magdalena, b. January 27, 1800; d. April 27, 1801.
15.   *v. Maria*. b. March 4, 1802; m. Joseph Lawrence.
      vi. Eleanor, b. August 15, 1804; d. April 15, 1884; m. Robert Allen. (*see Allen of Hanover.*)
      vii. Jacob, b. March 26, 1807; drowned in the Susquehanna river, July 21, 1809
16.   *viii. Susan-Dorothea*, b. August 22, 1810; m. first, David M. Johnson; secondly, Robert Bryson.

XII. JOHN CONRAD BUCHER,[8] (John-Conrad,[7] John-Jacob,[6] John-Jacob,[5] John,[4] John,[3] John,[2] Claus,[1]) b. in Lebanon, Pa., June 18, 1775; d. October 21, 1852; merchant in Alexandria, Huntingdon county, Pa.; postmaster from 1812 to 1815; represented Huntingdon county in the State Legislature 1815 to 1818; county commissioner, 1825 to 1828; m. December 10, 1799, HANNAH MYTINGER, daughter of Captain Jacob Mytinger,

126   *Pennsylvania Genealogies.*

of the Revolutionary army, and member of the Society of the Cincinnati. She d. August 15, 1863; both buried in Alexandria cemetery. They had issue, all b. in Alexandria:

17.   *i. Maria,* b. May 3, 1801; m. John Porter.
18.   *ii. Ann-Dorothy,* b. October 22, 1803; m. Charles Porter.
    iii. Elizabeth, b. June 30, 1806; d. February 20, 1869; unm.
19.   *iv. Susanna,* b. November 17, 1808; m. Daniel Houtz.
20.   *v. Hannah,* b. May 17, 1811; m. William Swoope, M. D.,
21.   *vi. Caroline,* b. May 8, 1814; m. John Hatfield.
    vii. John-Jacob, M. D., b. March 25, 1817; d. May, 1845, s. p.;
        m. Ann Thompson, dau. of Reverend James Thompson, of Alexandria, Pa.
22.   *viii. George-Conrad,* b. November 15, 1821; m. Susan Scott.

XIII. JOHN CONRAD BUCHER,[9] (John-Jacob,[8] John-Conrad,[7] John-Jacob,[6] John-Jacob,[5] John,[4] John,[3] John,[2] Claus,[1]) b. December 28, 1792; d., suddenly, October 26, 1851. In early life was engaged in merchandising; in 1830, elected to represent Dauphin and Lebanon counties in the twenty-second Congress of the United States; appointed by Governor Porter, in 1839, an associate judge of the courts of Dauphin county, which office he held for twelve years. He was a man of enlarged views and of public spirit, unsullied reputation and unimpeachable integrity, engaged in all the public enterprises of his day, and held various positions of honor and responsibility. Many years a school director and president of the board of education of his native city, Harrisburg. A member and an officer of the German Reformed congregation at home, he was one of the leading laymen in the ecclesiastical councils of the church; treasurer of one of its boards and of its theological seminary. Judge Bucher m., January 17, 1820, ELLEN ISETT, daughter of Jacob Isett, of Huntingdon county, Pa.; b. September 10, 1797; d. March 6, 1881; both buried in Harrisburg cemetery, of which he was one of the founders. They had issue, all b. in Harrisburg:

    i. Maria-Elizabeth, b. May 8, 1821; d. April 18, 1824.
23.   *ii. John-Conrad,* b. April 14, 1827; m. Isabella M. Jacoby.
    iii. Susan, b. November 24, 1829; m., June 4, 1867, Alexander Ray, esquire, of Washington city, who d. July, 1878.
    iv. Ellen (twin); d. January 25, 1877, in Harrisburg.
24.   *v. Eliza-Isett,* b. June 5, 1834: m. Richard H. Hummel.

XIV. GEORGE HORTER BUCHER,[9] (John-Jacob,[8] John-Conrad,[7] John-Jacob,[6] John-Jacob,[5] John,[4] John,[3] John,[2] Claus,[1]) b. June 15, 1797. He was educated in the Latin schools of the borough and in the Harrisburg academy. In early life he was engaged in merchandising. In 1836, he removed to Cumberland county, Pa., locating near Hogestown. He soon became one of the men of mark of the valley, and quite prominent in public affairs. He represented Cumberland county in the State Senate during the years 1863, '64, and '65. After that period he led a retired life at Mechanicsburg, honored and respected by his fellow-citizens; and died there, of paralysis, on Thanksgiving Day, November, 27, 1884, in his eighty-eighth year, and his remains were interred in Chestnut Hill cemetery. Mr. Bucher was twice married; m., first, October 15, 1822, REBECCA POOL, of Harrisburg, who d. June 19, 1829, s. p.; m., secondly, May 19, 1831, HANNAH HOUGH, b. April 15, 1811; dau. of Joseph Hough,* of Bainbridge, Lancaster county, Pa. They had issue:

    i. Mary-Hough, b. in Harrisburg, March 9, 1832; m. Abram H. Musselman, ironmaster, of Marietta, Pa.; b. November 30, 1831; d. February 14, 1877, and had issue (surname Musselman):
        1. *Anna-Bertha,* b. in 1856.
        2. *George-Bucher,* b. 1859; d. 1887, in Colorado.
        3. *Charles-H.,* b. 1862.
        4. *Ellen-Bucher,* b. 1864; m. Kline Montgomery, of Philadelphia, and had issue (surname Montgomery) *Mary.*
        5. *Henry-Peter,* b. 1866.
    ii. Rebecca, b. in Harrisburg, May 20, 1834; m., September 9, 1854, George W. Scott, manufacturer, of Decatur, Geor-

---

*JOSEPH HOUGH was a descendant of Richard Hough, of Mackelsfield, Chester, England, who arrived in the province August, 1683, and settled in Lower Makefield, Bucks county. He married Mary Ann, daughter of John Clows, the same year. He represented Bucks county in the General Assembly, and was drowned in 1705 on his way down the Delaware river to take his seat, in Philadelphia. When William Penn heard of it he wrote to James Logan "I lament the loss of Honest Richard Hough, such men must needs be wanted." The family is of Roman-French descent and of great antiquity.—*Davis' History of Bucks County.*

gia. Colonel Scott, b. in Alexandria, Pa., was son of the Hon. John Scott, who represented the district in the 21st Congress; and had issue (surname Scott):
1. *George-Bucher*, m. Bettie Winn.
2. *Annie-Irwin*, m. Thomas Cooper.
3. *Mary-Hough*, m. Charles Murphy Candler.
4. *Nellie-Bucher*, m. Milton Candler, and d. in 1873.
5. *Bettie Hough*.

iii. *George*, b. September 6, 1835; d. March 8, 1837.
iv. *Susan-Dorothea*, b. April 8, 1837; d. November 24, 1838.
25. v. *Robert-Allen*, b. February 18, 1840; m. Mary Young.
vi. *Ellen*, b. December 24, 1841; m., November 29, 1883, George Mytinger Cresswell, of Petersburg, Huntingdon county, Pa., who was appointed April 26, 1893, by Governor Pattison, Associate Judge for the county of Huntingdon.
vii. *Anna-Caroline*, b. October 11, 1843.
viii. *Clara-Maria*, b. November 10, 1846; m., first, September 19, 1867, Alfred M. Scott, of Alexandria, Huntingdon county. Pa.; d. September 21, 1876, in Savannah, Georgia, of yellow fever; and had issue (surname Scott): *Ralph-B.*, *Carrie*, and *Irwin*; m., secondly, September 11, 1884, L. Mallard Cassels, of Decatur, Ga.
ix. *Hannah-Cordelia*, b. March 24, 1849.
x. *John-George*, b. March 23, 1851; m. Elizabeth Addams Smallwood, of New Jersey.
xi. *Joseph Hough*, b. July 27, 1857; d. April 8, 1860.

XV. MARIA BUCHER,[9] (John-Jacob,[8] John-Conrad,[7] John-Jacob,[6] John-Jacob,[5] John,[4] John,[3] John,[2] Claus,[1]) b. March 4, 1802, in Harrisburg, Pa.; d. April 19, 1861; bur. in the cemetery at Harrisburg; m. September 4, 1823, JOSEPH LAWRENCE, b. in 1788, in Adams county, Pa.; d. April 17, 1842, in the city of Washington; bur. in the Congressional burying-ground. His father, John Lawrence, of English birth, emigrated to America at an early day, and settled near Hunterstown, Adams county, Pa. There he married Sarah Moffitt, by whom he had ten children. John Lawrence died about 1789, and three years afterward his widow removed with her family to Washington county, Pa., and settled on a farm lying upon the headwaters of Pigeon creek. Of the sons of John Lawrence, John settled at Beaver, Pa., twice represented the county in the Legislature, subsequently removing to Delaware county, Ohio, where he died. Samuel followed his brother to Beaver county, and located upon a farm. He was nine years prothonotary of the county, and twice elected to the State Assembly. He died about 1828. Joseph Lawrence, the youngest of the family, remained in Washington county, becoming a farmer and a man of mark ; in 1818 was elected to the Legislature, and served continuously until 1826, being Speaker of the House during the sessions of 1820 and 1822. From 1825 to 1829, he was a member of Congress ; in 1834 and 1835, returned to the Legislature, and in 1836 elected State Treasurer. He was re-elected to Congress in 1840, and died during his term. Several years after her husband's death the Widow Lawrence moved with all her family to Harrisburg. Mr. Lawrence had previously married in 1812, Rebecca Van Eman, and their children were *Joseph*, m. Eliza Horner and settled in Ohio ; *Samuel*, died young ; *George-Van Eman*,* and *Sarah*, m. Ard Moore, and settled in Carthage, Mo. Maria Bucher and Joseph Lawrence had issue (surname Lawrence), all b. in Washington county, Pa.:

---

*GEORGE VAN EMAN LAWRENCE, b. November 13, 1818, in Washington county, Pa. Educated as a farmer he entered the political arena in 1843 and for over fifty years has been identified with national and State politics ; a representative in Congress, in the State Senate of which he was Speaker, and the House of Representatives, several terms in each, and a delegate to the Constitutional Convention of 1873. At the same time Mr. Lawrence has always taken an active part in all enterprises and improvements ; is a bank director and a director of the P. V. & C. R. R. Residence, Monongahela City. He m. first, ELIZABETH WELSH, December 26, 1839, daughter of William Welsh, of Washington county, b. 1820 ; d. March 26, 1855, and had issue :

    i. Mary-Virginia, b. January 5, 1850.
    ii. Joseph, d. young.

He m. secondly, January 8, 1857, MARY REED, daughter of Rev. John Reed, of Indiana co., Pa, b. 1830. They had issue :

    iii. George-Reed, b. March 7, 1858 ; d. November 10, 1891 ; educated at Lafayette College ; studied law in Philadelphia and settled in Pittsburgh ; m., November 6, 1889, Margaret Shaw, daughter of Dr. Shaw, of Pittsburgh.
    iv. Carrie-Belle, b. January 7, 1866 ; m. June 9, 1887, C. B. Wood, M. D., of Monongahela City, and have issue (surname Wood) *Lawrence*, b. August 20, 1888.

26. i. *John-Jacob*, b. March 7, 1827 ; m Annie E Watson.
 ii. *James-Kennedy*, b. January 14, 1830; d. July 29, 1888, in Reynoldsville, Pa. ; appointed by General Cameron, Secretary of War, captain in the army of the U. S. in the war of the Rebellion, and promoted major ; resigned to enter into mercantile pursuits ; m. first, Mary Somerville, of Elk county, Pa., and had issue : *Charles-Kennedy*, b. May 19, 1856, who m. Elizabeth Wolf, of Calicoon, N. Y. and *Julia-Maria*, b. August 15, 1857, who m. August 27, 1881, Alexander C. Riston, of Reynoldsville, b. September 3, 1852, and have *Paul*. Major Lawrence m. secondly, August, 1867, Eleanor Isett, daughter of John Isett and Mary Bell, of Spruce Creek Station, Pa.
 iii. *William-Caldwell-Anderson*, b. May 18, 1832 ; d. April 21, 1860, in Harrisburg, Pa.; was educated at Washington College, where he graduated in 1850 ; came to Harrisburg, and began the study of law with John C. Kunkel. He was admitted to the Dauphin county bar August 31, 1853, and entered upon the practice of his profession at Harrisburg, as law partner of Mr. Kunkel. He was elected to the Legislature in 1857, 1858 and 1859, and was Speaker of the House of Representatives, sessions of 1859 and 1860. Mr. Lawrence was remarkable for genius of a rare order, and his success at the bar and in public life at the commencement of his career gave promise of a future of extraordinary brilliancy, frustrated by his early death
 iv. *Samuel-Moffitt*, b December 14, 1835, in Washington county, Pa.; d. October 17, 1864, in Warren, Pa.; buried in the cemetery at Harrisburg, Pa. His father's death occurring when he was six years old, his mother removed, two years later, to Harrisburg, her former home, where she continued to reside during the remainder of her life, and there Samuel received his principal education, although attending Jefferson College for a time. From boyhood he was a remarkable student, and had a perfect hunger for knowledge. At an early age he adopted the profession of civil engineering, and was engaged in the survey of the Huntingdon and Broad Top railroad, and afterwards on the Sunbury and Erie, (now Philadelphia and Erie,) and continued on it until its completion in 1864. He was perfectly familiar with every part of the road, and had traveled it all on foot from Sunbury to Erie. He was one of the four original contractors who built the Oil Creek railroad, and was

chief engineer of it. He was also engaged in the survey of the Warren and Franklin railroad at the time of his death. He was nominated by the Republican party in the counties of Clearfield, McKean, Jefferson and Elk for the Legislature, and represented them in the term of 1860-61, thus spending this winter in Harrisburg, his old home. Not having a taste for politics, he declined further nomination. The last three or four years of his life he resided at Warren. Mr. Lawrence m. April 4, 1864, Hanna Green, daughter of Hon. John Green, of Germantown; d. s. p.

v. *Susan-Mary*, b. October 19, 1838; m. April 8, 1869, Myron Sanford, of Erie, Pa. He was the son of Giles Sanford and Laura Goodwin, and a direct descendant of John Sanford, Governor of Rhode Island in 1655. Mr. Sanford was a banker, and one of Erie's prominent citizens; d. November 26, 1886. They had *Henry-Lawrence*, b. May 16, 1870, who d. January 22, 1889, at Riverside, California; buried in Erie.

XVI. SUSAN DOROTHY BUCHER,[9] (John-Jacob,[8] John-Conrad,[7] John-Jacob,[6] John-Jacob,[5] John,[4] John,[3] John,[2] Claus,[1]) b. August 22, 1810; m. first, June 17, 1830, DAVID M. JOHNSON, of Beaver county, b. in 1804; d. March 23, 1836. He was the son of David Johnson, of Irish descent, whose ancestral family included the distinguished Sir William Johnson, Superintendent-General of Indian Affairs in North America, under the British Crown. David Johnson left Philadelphia about 1788 for Washington county, where he became conspicuous in connection with the learned institutions of the period, and removing to Beaver in 1803, on the judicial organization of the county, became prominent as the first prothonotary, register and recorder, as a learned teacher and as one of the original elders of the Presbyterian church, where he d. in 1837, aged 90 years. They had issue (surname Johnson):

i. *Anna-Catharine*, b. April 8, 1831; m. Oct. 13, 1853, William Bryson Irwin, of Cumberland co., Pa., b. November 15, 1829; d. August 13, 1890; buried at Silvers Spring. He was a son of Matthew Irwin and Priscilla Bryson, daughter of William Bryson and Jane Harkness, all of Cumberland county. William B. Irwin represented his county in the Legislature of 1860-61, and commissioned by successive governors a notary public, office in Harrisburg. They had issue (surname Irwin):

1. *Allen*, b. July 15, 1854; artist, resides in Florida.
2. *James*, b. October 22, 1856; d. September 26, 1866.

ii. *John-Bucher*, b. January 26, 1833, in Harrisburg, Pa. He was educated in the public schools of the town and in Captain Partridge's military school, but completed his education at Washington College, Pa., where he graduated in the class of 1852. He adopted civil engineering as his profession, and until 1861 was engaged in several of the public improvements in this State. At the breaking out of the Rebellion he entered the Eleventh Pennsylvania regiment, Colonel Jarrett, and was appointed captain of a company from Pittston. On May 14, 1861, he was appointed by the Secretary of War, General Cameron, first lieutenant in the Sixth Cavalry of the regular army, and was subsequently made brevet-major and lieutenant-colonel for meritorious service. He became captain by regular promotion February 3, 1875. He served on the staff of General Hancock at Baltimore, and at New Orleans, and was afterwards assigned to several stations in Texas. In April, 1870, he was obliged to leave Texas on account of failing health, and returned to his home at Harrisburg, where he died June 24, 1871.

Mrs. Johnson m. secondly, June 8, 1841, ROBERT BRYSON, b. March 15, 1801; son of William Bryson and Jane Harkness, daughter of a Revolutionary Patriot. Mr. Bryson was a well-known and prominent citizen of Cumberland county; in early life a prosperous and progressive farmer, and in 1861 was appointed by Gov. Curtin an associate judge. He removed to Harrisburg in 1865, where he died October 4, 1887. Buried in Silvers Spring churchyard, of which church he had been a trustee 50 years. Mrs. Bryson d. May 8, 1891. Silvers Spring the burial place of all the family. They had issue (surname Bryson):

iii. *William-Harkness*, b. March 14, 1842.
iv. *George-Bucher*, b. September 27, 1844; d. May 23, 1891.
v. *Robert*, b. October 30, 1846; d. August 16, 1880.
vi. *James-McCormick*, b. December 14, 1848; d. March 13, 1851.
vii. *Eleanor*, b. March 9, 1851.
27. viii. *Susan-Bucher*, b. July 9, 1854; m. Henry J. Maris.

Bucher Family. 133

XVII. MARIA BUCHER,⁹ (John-Conrad,⁸ John-Conrad,⁷ John-Jacob,⁶ John-Jacob,⁵ John,⁴ John,³ John,² Claus,¹) b. May 3, 1801; d. January 17, 1892; m, March 13, 1821, JOHN PORTER, merchant of Alexandria, Pa., b. September 9, 1797; d. March 24, 1881. Both interred in the Alexandria cemetery. Mr. Porter [son of Thomas Porter, who came from Donaghedy, county Down, Ireland, in 1790, and settled in Centre county; m. in 1796, Jane Montgomery, and d. September 22, 1801] was the most prominent man of the vicinage, and represented his county in the Legislature of 1831-32. He was a noted churchman of the Presbyterian denomi ation, an elder for many years, and superintendent of a Sabbath-school for half a century. In him were exemplified all the qualities and virtues of the Christian gentleman. They had issue (surname Porter):

28.   i. *Thomas-Conrad*, b. January 22, 1822; m. Susan Kunkel.
    ii. *Mary-Elizabeth*, m. May 13, 1845, Samuel Milliken, of Lewistown, Pa.; b. February 22, 1819; d. December 25, 1894; and had issue (surname Milliken):
       1. *James-Foster*, b. July 19, 1847; m. Frances Caldwell, of Hollidaysburg.
       2. *Allan-Creswell*, b. January 13, 1849; m. Alice B. Bennett, of Pittsburgh; dau. of James I. Bennett.
       3. *Rose-Gemmill*, b. January 3, 1858.
       4. *Anna-Porter*, b. May 11, 1860; m. Bushrod W. Perry, of Baltimore: and had (surname Perry) *Mary-Allan* and *Alice-Claire*.
    iii. *George-Bucher*, m. Sarah W. Lyon. (*see Lyon record.*)
29.   iv. *Clara-Jane*, m. Samuel T. Charlton, M. D.
    v. *Anna-Caroline*, m. George W. Lyon. (*see Lyon record*).
    vi. *John-Montgomery*, m. November 18, 1869, Rebecca Moore, of Alexandria, Pa., b. November, 18, 1846; d. August 1, 1876.
    vii. *Howard*, m. June 7, 1864, Kathleen Banks, daughter of Hon. Thaddeus Banks, of Hollidaysburg, d. Mar. 16, 1895.
30.   viii. *Eleanor*, m. Augustus S. Landis.

XVIII. ANN DOROTHY BUCHER,⁹ (John-Conrad,⁸ John-Conrad,⁷ John-Jacob,⁶ John-Jacob,⁵ John,⁴ John,³ John,² Claus,¹) b. October 22, 1803; d. April 19, 1879; m. March 3, 1824, CHARLES PORTER, merchant of Alexandria, and son of Thomas

Porter (*see* XVII.,) born March 3, 1779 ; d. in 1877 ; interred with his wife in Alexandria cemetery. They had issue (surname Porter):

    i. Caroline-Elizabeth, b. July 30, 1826 ; m. May 7, 1851, Joshua Stevenson, b. in Newry, county Down, Ireland, who d. September 26, 1857 ; and had issue (surname Stevenson):
        1. *Charles-Porter*, b. February 10, 1853 ; m. Louise Grace Wade, of Pittsburgh.
        2. *Sarah-Grace*, b. November 24, 1855.
    ii. John-Bucher, b. December 17, 1828; m. Mary A. Hopkins and had six children.
    iii. Jane-Montgomery, b. January 27, 1832 ; m. Rev. Hugh H. Harvey from Bainbridge, Ireland, now pastor of a Presbyterian congregation, Hartstown, Crawford co., Pa.
    iv. Alfred, b. January 17, 1835, merchant of Alexandria, Pa.; m. January 26, 1869, Salome Walker, and had *Sallie-Stewart*, b. November 15, 1870, and *Helen-Salome*, d. April 28, 1888.
    v. Calvin, b. February 7, 1837 ; a physician, Alexandria, Pa.
    vi. Hannah-Mary, b. December 20, 1845.

XIX. SUSANNAH BUCHER,[9] (John-Conrad,[8] John-Conrad,[7] John-Jacob,[6] John-Jacob,[5] John,[4] John,[3] John,[2] Claus,[1]) b. November 17, 1808 ; d. February 14, 1878 ; m. July 21, 1829, DANIEL HOUTZ, b. April 15, 1807, in Lebanon, Pa.; d. September 20, 1873, in Alexandria, Huntingdon county, Pa.; son of Christian Houtz and his wife, Anna Elizabeth Zellers ; received an academic education, studied medicine with Doctor James Charlton, and graduated from Jefferson Medical College in 1832 ; located at Alexandria, where he practiced his profession until near the close of life ; represented his county in the Legislature of 1857-8 ; both buried in Alexandria Presbyterian cemetery. They had issue, all born in Alexandria, Pa. (surname Houtz):

    i. Hannah-Elizabeth, b. August 24, 1830 ; m. August 20, 1860, George Mytinger Brisbin, coal operator in Clearfield region and banker, and an elder in the Presbyterian church ; b. June 29, 1826 ; son of Samuel Brisbin and Catharine Mytinger, and a grandson of Captain John Brisbin, and Captain John Jacob Mytinger, a member of the "Society of the Cincinnati," both Revolutionary veterans ; and had issue, (surname Brisbin):

Bucher Family. 135

1. *George-Houtz*, b. September 17, 1861 ; d. March 8, 1872.
2. *Susan-Bucher*, b. December 17, 1864 ; m. Roberts Lowrio. (*see Lyon family*).
3. *Mary*, b. July 1, 1873 ; d. in infancy.

ii. John-Bucher, b. November 30, 1832 ; d. April 30, 1836.

iii. George-McClellan, b. September 24, 1835 ; graduated at Jefferson College, Canonsburg ; studied law with Hon. John Scott, of Huntingdon ; admitted to the bar April 13, 1857 ; located at Lock Haven until failure of health compelled him to relinquish the practice of his profession ; d. June 9, 1861, in Alexandria, Pa.

iv. Eliza-Bucher, b. June 27, 1838 ; m. Daniel Good, M. D., of Osceola, and had, among others (surname Good). *George-M. H.*, *Elizabeth-R.*, *David-D.*, and *Clara-Houtz*.

v. Clara-Porter, b. April 16, 1841 ; m., October 26, 1865, Harry J. McAteer, representative in the Pennsylvania Legislature 1870–71, and Senator from the Huntingdon district, 1885–88 ; residence, Alexandria, Pa.; appointed, 1894, Assistant Naval Officer for the Port of Philadelphia ; and had issue (surname McAteer), *Dorothy-Bucher*, b. May 4, 1882.

XX. HANNAH BUCHER,[9] (John-Conrad,[8] John-Conrad,[7] John-Jacob,[6] John-Jacob,[5] John,[4] John,[3] John,[2] Claus,[1]) b. May 17, 1811 ; d. July 10, 1884 ; m., June 10, 1830, WILLIAM SWOOPE, M. D., of Huntingdon, Pa., who was b. October 19, 1804, and d. January 13, 1861 ; both buried in Alexandria cemetery. Dr. Swoope was the son of Peter Swoope (1763–1839), and Elizabeth Snyder (1768–1851), who settled in Huntingdon before 1790. They had issue (surname Swoope):

31. *i. Henry-Bucher*, b. July 17, 1831 ; m. Susanna P. Irvin.
ii. Caroline-Elizabeth, b. August 28, 1833.
iii. Granville-Pattison, b. October 6, 1835 ; served through the war of the Rebellion in the Fifth regiment Pennsylvania Reserves, promoted to a captaincy for gallant conduct at the battle of Gettysburg ; d. at Alexandria, June 9, 1869.
iv. William-Conrad, b. August 10, 1838 ; d. April 21, 1874.
v. Hannah-Mary, b. May 19, 1841; m., September 14, 1876, William W. Brisbin (*see* XIX.), who d. June 2, 1879 ; family residence, Alexandria, Pa.
vi. George-Howard, b. September 9, 1843 ; d. March 5, 1844.
vii. John-Porter, b. January 9, 1845.

viii. Clara, b. September 1, 1847 ; m. September 21, 1871, George S. Ballantyne, M. D., who d. July, 1891, at Huntingdon, and had issue (surname Ballantyne), *George-S.*

ix. George-Edwards, b. December 2, 1850 ; d. July 1, 1873, at Pittsburgh.

XXI. CAROLINE BUCHER,[9] (John-Conrad,[8] John-Conrad,[7] John-Jacob,[6] John-Jacob,[5] John,[4] John,[3] John,[2] Claus,[1]) b. May 8, 1814 ; d. September 19, 1884 ; m., January 5, 1841, JOHN HATFIELD, iron manufacturer, b. May 1, 1816 ; d. February 3, 1843. He was son of Samuel Hatfield and Katharine Kepler, an old and prominent Chester county family. His works and residence was near Alexandria on the Juniata. They had issue (surname Hatfield) :

i. Charles-Porter, b. October 15, 1841; merchant, Alexandria; m., December 14, 1870, Ellen Cryder, daughter of George Cryder of Delaware, Ohio, b. October 5, 1843 ; d. November 9, 1889, and buried in Alexandria cemetery ; and had issue :

1. *Walter-Bucher*, b. November 11, 1871 ; d. August 14, 1872.
2. *Caroline*, b. October 6, 1873 ; d. November 12, 1898.
3. *Rebecca*, b. August 21, 1876.

XXII. GEORGE CONRAD BUCHER,[9] (John-Conrad,[8] John-Conrad,[7] John-Jacob,[6] John-Jacob,[5] John,[4] John,[3] John,[2] Claus,[1]) b. November 15, 1821, merchant of Alexandria ; d. February 3, 1868 ; m. December 9, 1845, SUSAN SCOTT ; d. April 16, 1887 ; daughter of the Hon. John Scott, who represented the district in the 21st Congress. They had issue :

i. John-Conrad, b. January 12, 1847 ; seedsman and florist of Atlanta, Ga.; m. December 20, 1880, Marian C. Bidwell; b. February 10, 1859, in Binghampton, N. Y.; daughter of Oliver B. Bidwell and Augusta Header; and had issue :

1. *Irene-Marian*, b. July 26, 1883, at Decatur, Ga.

ii. Hannah-Mytinger, b. January 15, 1850.

iii. Annie-Irwin, b. March 2, 1852; m. Dec. 12, 1872, John N. Hatfield.

32. *iv. Eliza*, b. July 27, 1854 ; m. John Phillips.

v. Mary, b. October 10, 1857.

vi. George-Scott, b. February 18, 1859 ; m. August 26, 1884, Rose Douglass, of Altoona ; reside at Grand Rapids, Mich.

Bucher Family.

vii. Susan-Scott, b. January 15, 1863; m. George Phillips, of Alexandria.
viii. Caroline, b. December 31, 1865; m. October 23, 1889, Everet C. Bidwell; b. November 7, 1857, in Binghampton, N. Y.; residence, Decatur, Ga.; and had issue (surname Bidwell):
   1. *Agnes-Irwin,* b. October 19, 1890.
   2. *Everet-Oliver,* b. July 18, 1892.
ix. Alfred-Scott, b. March 10, 1867; m. March, 1892; Ethel Butt, b. February 17, 1879, at Atlanta, Ga.; daughter of Jesse Butt and Rebecca Burke, of Atlanta, and have issue:
   1. *George-Conrad-Bucher,* b. January 21, 1893.

XXIII. JOHN CONRAD BUCHER,[10] (John-Conrad,[9] John-Jacob,[8] John-Conrad,[7] John-Jacob,[6] John-Jacob,[5] John,[4] John,[3] John,[2] Claus,[1]) b. in Harrisburg, Pa., April 14, 1827; d. in Clinton, Iowa, March 12, 1870; merchant; m. October 3, 1853, ISABELLA M. JACOBY, b. September 15, 1832, dau. of Samuel Jacoby, of Montgomery county, Pa. They had issue, all born in Clinton, Iowa:

   i. John-Conrad, (first,) b. January 8, 1855; d. in infancy.
   ii. Susan, b. August 15, 1856; m. February 14, 1878, George Gilbert Bauder, of Clinton, Iowa.
   iii. Eleanor, b. February 1, 1859; m., May 10, 1881, Edgar Marshall Robison, of Dubuque, Iowa.
   iv. John-Conrad, (second,) b. April 12, 1861; d. May 1, 1870.
   v. George-Horter, b. September 15, 1865; d. in infancy.

XXIV. ROBERT ALLEN BUCHER,[10] (George-H.,[9] John-Jacob,[8] John-Conrad,[7] John-Jacob,[6] John-Jacob,[5] John,[4] John,[3] John,[2] Claus,[1]) b. February 18, 1840; m. December 1, 1870, MARY YOUNG, b. December 27, 1840; dau. of Dr. Robert G. Young, of Mechanicsburg, Cumberland county, Pa. They had issue, all born in Mechanicsburg:

   i. Annetta-Culbertson, b. April 27, 1873.
   ii. George-Hough, b. July 11, 1874.
   iii. Mary-Roberta, b. July 13, 1878.

XXV. ELIZA ISETT BUCHER,[10] (John-Conrad,[9] John-Jacob,[8] John-Conrad,[7] John-Jacob,[6] John-Jacob,[5] John,[4] John,[3] John,[2] Claus,[1]) b. June 8, 1834; m. September 18, 1855, by Rev. Daniel Gans, RICHARD HENRY HUMMEL, b. 1826; d. October

6, 1880; son of the Hon. Valentine Hummel, of Harrisburg; [b. February 7, 1787; d. September 4, 1870.] A very prominent man and a representative in the Legislature 1822–23 and 1840; appionted by Gov. Shultze November 12, 1827, an associate judge for the county of Dauphin, and was at the time of his death president of the Harrisburg National bank; his wife, Elizabeth Walborn, died October 25, 1867. RICHARD HENRY HUMMEL succeeded to his father's general business operations in real estate and the lumber trade. They had issue (surname Hummel) all born in Harrisburg.

 i. *Eleanor-Bucher*, b. June 23, 1856; d. March 24, 1858.
 ii. *Elizabeth-Bucher*, b. December 24, 1857; d. May 3, 1892; m. October 11, 1879, I. L. Fendrich, of Columbia, Pa., and had issue (surname Fendrich):
  1. *Eleanor-R.*, b. July 8, 1880; d. in infancy.
  2. *Eliza-Hummel*, b. February 13, 1882.
  3. *Helen-Ray*, b. July 25, 1883.
 iii. *Valentine*, b. May 4, 1859; m. December 17, 1885, by Rev. Francis Lobdell, D. D., in New York City, Mary E. Ross; dau. of Andrew Ross, of Cumberland Co., Pa.; and had issue:
  1. *Andrew-Ross*, b. September 11, 1887.
  2. *Valentine-Lorne*, b. January 31, 1889.
  3. *Haly*, b. October 30, 1891; d. in infancy.
 iv. *Richard-Henry*, b. September 9, 1860.
 v. *John-Bucher*, b. February 4, 1864; d. July 18, 1887.

XXVI. JOHN JACOB LAWRENCE,[10] (Maria-Bucher,[9] John-Jacob,[8] John-Conrad,[7] John-Jacob,[6] John-Jacob,[5] John,[4] John,[3] John,[2] Claus,[1]) b. March 7, 1827; began professional life as superintendent of the Huntingdon and Broad Top Railroad, and on the call of President Lincoln for trooops in 1862, resigned; enlisted a company of one hundred men by whom he was elected captain, and went into the War of the Rebellion, and on the organization of the 125th regiment of Pennsylvania, was elected major; was wounded at the second Bull Run battle and at Chancellorsville. After leaving the army Major Lawrence was appointed a superintendent on the Philadelphia and Erie Railway, afterwards became general superintendent of the Pittsburgh and Erie R. R., and finally general superintendent of the Allegheny Valley R. R., from which he resigned to enter into commercial business in Pittsburg. He resided

Bucher Family. 139

in Allegheny City, where he died March 27, 1893; interred in the Harrisburg cemetery. Major Lawrence m., May 16, 1854, ANNA ELIZABETH WATSON, daughter of General David Correy Watson, a well known and very prominent citizen of Northumberland county, a descendant of John Watson, founder of Watsontown (b. November 26, 1804; d. at his home, near McEwensvlile, June 23, 1873. Gen. Watson m. Margaret Wilson, b. 1810; d. 1873; thus becoming allied with the Pollock, Montgomery and Sample families, of the West Branch of the Susquehanna.) They had issue (surname Lawrence):

 i. Ellen, b. in Harrisburg, April 23, 1855; d. January 4, 1859.
 ii. Joseph, b. in Huntingdon, February 1, 1857; d. December 30, 1858; both buried in Harrisburg cemetery.
 iii. William-Watson, b. April 22, 1859; manufacturer, Pittsburgh, Pa.
 iv. Maria-Theresa, b. March 31, 1861; m. December 10, 1891, William Robert Turner, b. April 8, 1860, in Rochester, England; a clergyman of the Protestant Episcopal church; residence, Baltimore.
 v. Anna-Margaret, b. January 1, 1864.
 vi. John-Jacob, b. October 5, 1865; manufacturer, Pittsburgh, Pa.; m. in Cincinnati, O., October 19, 1892, Clara Louise, daughter of Hugh Alexander Andrews and Laura Clarissa Van Dyke, and have issue:
  1. *Louise*, b. October 11, 1893.
 vii. Susan-Mary, b. January 17, 1868.

XXVII. SUSAN BUCHER BRYSON,[10] (Susan-Dorothea Bucher,[9] John-Jacob,[8] John-Conrad,[7] John-Jacob,[6] John-Jacob,[5] John,[4] John,[3] John,[2] Claus),[1] b. July 9, 1854; m. April 14, 1880, HENRY J. MARIS, of Philadelphia, son of John McIlvaine Maris and Sarah Louise Wainwright, a direct descendant of George Maris, of Grafton Flyford, county of Worcester, England, and Alice, his wife (d. 1699), who, with their six children, emigrated to the Province in 1683, and settled in Springfield township, Delaware county, Pa. He was one of the justices of Chester county, a member of the General Assembly and of the Provincial Council, and a minister of the Society of Friends; he purchased the "Home," direct, from William Penn, which remains in the family to the present day. George Maris was b. 1632; d. 1705. Henry J. Maris, b. June 18, 1850, is a graduate of the University of Pennsylvania, and

140 *Pennsylvania Genealogies.*

in business a merchant, manufacturer, and importer. They have issue (surname Maris), all b. in Philadelphia :

 i. Dorothy-Wainwright, b. April 30, 1883.
 ii. Henry-McIlvaine, b. January 13, 1889.
 iii. Louis-Bryson, b. March 11, 1894.

XXVIII. THOMAS CONRAD PORTER, D.D., LL.D.,[10] (Maria Bucher,[9] John-Conrad,[8] John-Conrad,[7] John-Jacob,[6] John-Jacob,[5] John,[4] John,[3] John,[2] Claus,[1]) graduated at Lafayette College in 1840, and after passing through the full course of Princeton Theological Seminary, was licensed to preach by the Presbytery of Huntingdon, Pa., May, 1844. After serving churches in Georgia, and in Reading, Pa., he was appointed in 1849, Professor of Natural Sciences in Marshall College, Mercersburg, and after removal and consolidation with Franklin College at Lancaster, he was elected to the same *chair*, which he resigned in 1866 to accept the *chair* in Lafayette College, which he has now filled for over a quarter of a century. In 1865 he received the degree of D.D. from Rutgers College, and the degree of LL.D. from Franklin-Marshall College in 1880. Beyond official duties Dr. Porter has delivered a great many sermons, lectures and addresses—has done much scientific work, especially in Botany—has contributed to the Reviews—has made many translations, being familiar with several modern languages, and has published several volumes. He is a thorough theologian and has the art of wise exposition—with a charming voice he is persuasive and demonstrative in delivery, and always holds attention. Dr. Porter m., December 24, 1850, SUSAN KUNKEL. (*See Kunkel record.*) They had issue (surname Porter):

 i. Mary; m. P. V. D. Conway, of Fredericksburg, Va.; d. August 18, 1893.
 ii. John, educated at Lafayette college, studied law in Harrisburg, and music in Leipsic and Milan, and d. June 5, 1887, in Oveido, Spain, d. s. p.
 iii. Catharine-Kunkel, m. Rev. Samuel A. Martin, President of Wilson Female College, Chambersburg, Pa.

XXIX. CLARA JANE PORTER,[10] (Maria-Bucher,[9] John-Conrad,[8] John-Conrad,[7] John-Jacob,[6] John-Jacob,[5] John,[4] John,[3] John,[2] Claus,[1]) b. September, 1828; d. July 24, 1893; m.

December 20, 1855, SAMUEL TEMPLETON CHARLTON, M.D., son of James Charlton, B.A., M.D., of Alexandria, Pa., and Nancy Templeton; was b. in New Berlin, Snyder county, Pa., July 25, 1825; d. November 9, 1886, at Harrisburg. Both interred in Alexandria cemetery. Dr. Charlton graduated from the Medical College of New York City; was house surgeon to Bellevue Hospital one year and demonstrator of anatomy two years, associated with Drs. Mott and Bedford, famous physicians of New York City. Dr. Charlton finally established himself in Harrisburg, Pa., where he attained celebrity and died at the height of his usefulness. They had issue (surname Charlton), all born in Harrisburg:

> *i. Paul*, attorney-at-law, Omaha, Nebraska, b. November 2, 1856; m. November 24, 1887, Elizabeth Patton Denniston, b. in Chicago May 15, 1859, daughter of John Denniston, of Hollidaysburg, and Maria Milliken; and had issue, all born in Omaha:
> > 1. *Porter*, b. September 21, 1888.
> > 2. *Robert*, b. March 14, 1890.
> > 3. *Denniston*, b. December 31, 1892.
>
> *ii. John Porter*, civil engineer; m. June 7, 1894, Caroline Maria Bayley, daughter of Wm. C. Bayley, of Hollidaysburg, and have issue: Twins, b. February 22, 1895, in Dravosburg, Pa.
>
> *iii. Annie-Claire*, m. October 4, 1894, John Van Wicheren Reynders, of the Steelton Iron Works, Pa.

XXX. ELEANOR PORTER,[10] (Maria Bucher[9], John-Conrad,[8] John-Conrad,[7] John-Jacob,[6] John-Jacob,[5] John,[4] John,[3] John,[2] Claus[1]), b. June 5, 1843; m. November 23, 1865, AUGUSTUS S. LANDIS, Attorney-at-Law, Hollidaysburg, Pa., b. June 4, 1834, in Pennington, N. J. He was the son of Joseph A. Landis, M.D., who died November 20, 1886, and of Maria Letitia Holcombe, who died August 27, 1891. Judge Landis graduated at Washington-Jefferson College in 1853, read law with the Hon. Samuel Calvin, and was admitted to the Blair county bar April 28, 1857. He has held numerous local offices, and was elected to the Pennsylvania Constitutional Convention of 1873-4 in which he took an active part. On the 31st of December, 1892, was appointed by Governor Robert E. Pattison, President Judge of the Twenty-fourth Judicial District. They had issue, (surname Landis), all b. in Hollidaysburg.

i. Maria-Porter, b. August 18, 1866; m. October 15, 1891, by Rev. D. H. Barrow, Samuel Porcher, Civil Engineer P. R.R., and have issue (surname Porcher):
   1. *Eleanor-Landis*, b. February 24, 1894.
ii. Letitia-Holcombe, b. September 9, 1870.
iii. Helen-Montgomery, b. October 31, 1878.

XXXI. HENRY BUCHER SWOOPE,[10] (Hannah Bucher,[9] John-Conrad,[8] John-Conrad,[7] John-Jacob,[6] John-Jacob,[5] John,[4] John,[3] John,[2] Claus[1]), b. July 17, 1831; educated in the schools of his native place; studied law with the Hon. John Scott; admitted to the bar April 14, 1853. In 1854 established himself in Clearfield, Pa., where he rapidly attained a high position in his profession, with a lucrative practice. Being a leader in the Republican party he supported General Grant for the Presidency, by whom he was appointed District Attorney for the Western District of Pennsylvania. He was re-appointed for a full term in 1874, but d. February 16, 1874; buried in Clearfield. Mr. Swoope was a man of marked ability and genius—a poet—a bold and brilliant orator, and one of the brightest ornaments of the bar. He m. September 6, 1855, SUSANNA PATTON IRVIN, b. August 31, 1835, dau. of William Irvin and Jane Patton of Clearfield, Pa. They had issue (surname Swoope).

i. Roland-Davis, b. August 26, 1856; attorney-at-law, Curwensville, Pa.; m. Cora Arnold.
ii. William-Irvin, b. October 3, 1862; attorney-at-law, Clearfield, Pa.; a graduate of Harvard Law School.
iii. Jane-Irvin, b. December 25, 1865; m. December 25, 1885, F. P. Van Valkenburgh, attorney-at-law, Millwaukee, Wis.

XXXII. ELIZA BUCHER,[10] (George-Conrad,[9] John-Conrad,[8] John-Conrad,[7] John-Jacob,[6] John-Jacob,[5] John,[4] John,[3] John,[2] Claus,[1]) b. July 27, 1854; m. March 21, 1878, JOHN PHILLIPS, b. August 3, 1854, merchant and manufacturer, son of William Phillips and Susan Moore, all of Alexandria, Pa. They had issue (surname Phillips):

i. Walter, b. July 23, 1879.
ii. Susan-Scott, b. September 21, 1880.
iii. George-Irwin, b. December 9, 1882.
iv. Marion-Bucher, b. May 9, 1888.
v. John, b. November 20, 1889.
vi. Eliza-Bucher, b. December 17, 1891.

COWDEN OF PAXTANG.

I. MATTHEW COWDEN,² son of William Cowden,¹ b. about 1707, in the north of Ireland; d. July, 1773, in Paxtang township, then Lancaster county, Pa. He came to America prior to 1729, and took up a tract of land in Paxtang, upon which he resided until his death. He m., in 1730, MARTHA JOHNSON, who survived her husband several years; both buried in Paxtang Church graveyard. They had issue:

    i. *William*, b. January 11, 1731; was a soldier of the Revolution; was at Yorktown, and died of camp fever while in the service, February, 1782.
2.   ii. *Margaret*, b. 1733; m. John Gilchrist.
3.   iii. *John*, b. 1735; m. Mary ———.
4.   iv. *James*, b. June 16, 1737; m. Mary Crouch.
    v. *Mary*, b. December 10, 1739; d. July 5, 1809; m. David Wray, b. 1728; d. April 3, 1805; both buried in Derry Church graveyard.
    vi. *Elizabeth*, b. 1741; m. Robert Keys.
    vii. *Rebecca*, b. 1743.
    viii. *Benjamin*, b. 1745; m. and removed to South Carolina prior to the Revolution, where he was killed by the Tories.

II. MARGARET COWDEN,³ (Matthew,² William,¹) b. about 1733; m. JOHN GILCHRIST, son of John Gilchrist.* They had issue (surname Gilchrist):

    i. *Martha*, m. October 14, 1778, John Bell.
    ii. *Matthew*, m. November 13, 1781, Elizabeth Crouch.

III. JOHN COWDEN,³ (Matthew,² William,¹) b. 1735, in Paxtang; d. August, 1776, in Cumberland county, Pa.; m. MARY ———. The family afterward removed to "Crooked Creek Settlement," in Westmoreland county, Pa. They had issue:

---

*JOHN GILCHRIST, senior, a native of Londonderry, Ireland, came, with his family, to America, in 1730, locating in Paxtang township, Lancaster (now Dauphin) county, Pa.; where he died in February, 1745-6, leaving a wife and children—*James; John*, m. Margaret Cowden; *Elizabeth;* and *Robert*, m. Sarah Ellis.

ii. *Joseph.*
iii. *Matthew.*
iv. *William.*
v. *Esther.*
vi. *Margaret.*
vii. *Jane.*

IV. JAMES COWDEN,³ (Matthew,² William,¹) b. June 16, 1737, in Paxtang township, Lancaster, now Dauphin, county, Pa.; d. October 10, 1810, in Paxtang. He was brought up on his father's farm, enjoying, however, the advantages of that early education of those pioneer times, which, among the Scotch-Irish settlers, was remarkably comprehensive and ample. Apart from this, he was well-grounded in the tenets of the Westminster Confession, which among our pious ancestry formed a part of the instruction given to all. Until the thunders of the Revolution rolled toward the Susquehanna, Mr. Cowden remained on the paternal acres, busily engaged in farming. At the outset, he was a strong advocate for active defensive measures, and in favor of independence. He was one of the leading spirits at the meeting at Middletown, June 9, 1774, of which Colonel James Burd was chairman, and whose action, in conjunction with those of Hanover, nerved the people of Lancaster in their patriotic resolves. Suiting the action to the word, Mr. Cowden and the young men of his neighborhood took measures toward raising a battalion of associators, of which Colonel James Burd was in command, and a company of which was intrusted to Captain Cowden. His company, although not belonging to the Pennsylvania Line, was, nevertheless, in several campaigns, and did faithful service at Fort Washington, in the Jerseys, at Brandywine and Germantown, and in the war on the Northern and Western frontiers, defending them from the attack of the savage Indian and treacherous Tory. At the close of the war, Captain Cowden returned to his farm. Under the Constitution of 1790, he was appointed the justice of the peace for the district of Lower Paxtang, April 10, 1793, which he held up to the time he was commissioned by Governor Thomas Mifflin one of the associate judges of the county of Dauphin, on the 2d of October, 1795, an office he filled acceptably and creditably. In 1809, he was chosen Presidential elector, and was an ardent supporter of Madison. Judge Cowden m. March 20, 1777, by Reverend John Elder, MARY CROUCH, b. 1757, in Virginia ; d. October 14, 1848, in Paxtang township, Dauphin county, Pa., and bur. in Paxtang Church graveyard ; dau. of James and Hannah Crouch.* They had issue :

---

*JAMES CROUCH was b. about 1728, in Virginia. The Crouches were an old family, who emigrated at an early day from England, and settled in King and Queen county, near the court house. James Crouch received a good education, came to Pennsylvania prior to 1757, purchasing about three thousand acres of land in York county, where the town of Wrightsville now stands, on which he settled for a few years, but which he subsequently sold, and removed to then Paxtang township, Lancaster county, Pa., where he bought one thousand acres of land. He was a soldier of Quebec, being a sergeant of Captain Matthew Smith's company of Paxtang volunteers. On his release from captivity, he became an officer of the associators, and subsequently paymaster of the battalion. He served during the whole of the Revolutionary war with honor and distinction. He died at his residence, Walnut Hill, near Highspire, Pa., on the 24th of May, 1794, aged sixty-six years. Colonel Crouch m. September 22, 1757, Hannah Brown, b. 1727 ; d. May 24, 1787. Their children were : *Edward; Mary*, m. Colonel James Cowden; *Elizabeth*, m. Matthew Gilchrist, removed to Washington county, Pa.; and *Hannah*, m. Roan McClure.

EDWARD CROUCH, son of Colonel James Crouch, was b. at Walnut Hill, in Paxtang, November 9, 1764. He was a merchant by occupation. At the age of seventeen, he enlisted in the army of the Revolution, and commanded a company in the Whiskey Insurrection, in 1794. He served as a member of the House of Representatives from 1804 to 1806, and was a Presidential elector in 1813. Governor Snyder appointed him one of the associate judges of the county of Dauphin, April 16, 1813, but he resigned upon his election to the Thirteenth United States Congress. He d. on the 2d of February, 1827, and is buried in Paxtang graveyard, "In private life he was an able and an honest man," wrote one of his contemporaries, and the record of his life shows him to have been a gentleman of uprightness of character, and as honorable as he was influential. Mr. Crouch m., first, Margaret Potter, b. 1775 ; d. February 7, 1797 ; dau. of General James Potter, of the Revolution. Their only daughter, *Mary*, b. October 23, 1791 ; d. October 27, 1846 ; m. Benjamin Jordan, who succeeded to the estate of Walnut Hill. He m., secondly, Rachel Bailey, b. April 16, 1782 ; d. March 2, 1857.

i. Hannah, b. 1778, in Paxtang township, Lancaster county Pa.; d. May 31, 1850; m. November 16, 1819, John Cochran, b. 1773; d. November 16, 1845; bur. in Paxtang Church graveyard ; son of James Cochran.
ii. Martha, b. 1780; m. June 4, 1837, William Boyd. (*see Boyd record.*)
iii. Margaret, b. 1782; d. August 19, 1818; unm.
iv. Elizabeth, b. March 27, 1784; d. October 17, 1857; m. William Gillmor. (*see Wallace of Hanover.*)
5. *v. Matthew-Benjamin,* b. June 24, 1786; m. Mary Wallace.
vi. James.
vii. Mary, m. May 30, 1821, Joseph Jordan.

V. MATTHEW BENJAMIN COWDEN,[4] (James,[3] Matthew,[2] William,[1]) b. June 24, 1786, in Paxtang township, Dauphin county, Pa.; d. January 15, 1862; was an associate judge of Dauphin county, a gentleman of sterling integrity, and of marked influence in the community; m. MARY WALLACE, b. 1788; d. May 26, 1844, and, with her husband, buried in the graveyard of old Paxtang church ; dau. of James Wallace and Sarah Elder (*see Wallace Record*). They had issue:

i. James, b. 1815 ; d. July 21, 1877 ; m. Anna M. Chambers, d. June 28, 1882, in Columbia, Pa.; with her husband, bur. in Harrisburg, Pa. They had: *Matthew-A., Anna, Sarah,* and *William-Chambers,* d. April 13, 1888.
ii. John-Wallace, b. August 29, 1817, in Lower Paxtang township, Dauphin county, Pa.; was brought up as a farmer, but as he grew to mature years his attention was turned to surveying, and he came to Harrisburg, where his latter days were passed as a practical surveyor, and where he died on the 22d of July, 1872; "he was," writes a contemporary, "an unobtrusive, modest and estimable citizen, successful in his business, trustworthy in all the relations of life, and a sincere and earnest Christian." Mr. Cowden m. Mary E. Hatton, daughter of Frederick Hatton and Mary Barnett, of Lower Paxtang. They had issue : *Margaret; Frederick-Hatton; Mary,* d. s. p.; *Sarah,* m. H. H. Cummings; *Matthew-Benjamin,* city surveyor of Harrisburg; *Ellen; Elizabeth,* m. Matthew Beck ; *Josephine;* and *William-Kerr.*
iii. Sarah; resides in Harrisburg.
iv. William-Kerr, b. January 5, 1822, in Lower Paxtang township, Dauphin county, Pa.; d. July 17, 1888. He was brought up a farmer, receiving such facilities of educa-

tion as the schools of the township afforded prior to the adoption of the common school system. He continued the occupation of a farmer until 1868, when he removed to Harrisburg, and engaged in the coal and lumber business, subsequently establishing a plaining-mill. For a decade of years, he was one of the inspectors of the Dauphin county prison. Mr. Cowden m. Elizabeth M. Elder, daughter of Joshua Elder and Mary C. Gillmor (see *Elder record*), and had issue, among others: *Mary-Wallace, Helen-Gillmor, John-Edward* and *Anna-Chambers*.

v. Mary, m. David R. Elder. (see *Elder record*.)
vi. Edward, d. s. p.
vii. Margaret, d. July 7, 1822, in inf.

CRAIN OF HANOVER.

I. WILLIAM CRAIN,[1] and JEAN, his wife, natives of county Down, Province of Ulster, Ireland, came to America in 1732, and located on the Manada, a branch of the Swatara creek, in, now, Hanover township, Dauphin county, Pa. William Crain, b. 1704; d. in 1780; his wife Jean, b. 1795; d. February 15, 1754, and are buried in old Hanover Church graveyard. They had issue, among others:

    i. Ambrose, b. 1734; received a good English education, and was brought up a farmer. At the outset of the Revolution, he enlisted as a private in Captain John Marshal's company, March 25, 1776, and was promoted quartermaster sergeant, Colonel Samuel Miles' battalion of the Pennsylvania Line, July 15, 1776. At the expiration of his term of service, he returned home, and was on subsequent duty during the inroads of the British, Tories, and their Indian allies, in the closing years of the war for independence. Captain Crain removed to Loudoun county, in the Valley of Virginia, in 1793 or 1794, and died there.

2.   *ii. George*, b. 1739; m. and had issue.
3.   *iii. Joseph*, b. 1741; m. Mary Moore.
    iv. William, b. 1742; d. January 8, 1802; was a private in Captain William Brown's company of Lancaster county associators in 1776; m. Ann Espy, b. 1739; d. December 12, 1802.
4.   *v. Richard*, b. 1745; m. and left issue.

II. GEORGE CRAIN,[2] (William,[1]) b. 1739; d. May 12, 1796; was twice married; m., first, in 1760, JEAN STURGEON. They had issue:

5.   *i. George*, b. 1761; m. Martha Ritchey.
6.   *ii. William*, b. 1763; m. Mary Sawyer.
    iii. Jean, b. 1765; m. Andrew Robinson. (*see Robinson of Derry.*)
    iv. James, b. 1767; m. Margaret McClure.
    v. Lydia, b 1770; m. James Ainsworth. (*see Ainsworth and Andrews.*)
    vi. Jeremiah, b. 1772; m. November 3, 1803, Anna Cochran.

George Crain, m., secondly, January 22, 1778, by Rev. John Elder; but we have no information as to her name. There was no issue.

III. JOSEPH CRAIN,² (William,¹) b. 1741; d. February, 1789; in the struggle for independence he served as first lieutenant in Col. Green's battalion of Lancaster county associators in service in the Jerseys, August, 1776; captain in the sixth battalion in 1777, and in the ninth battalion, Lancaster county militia, in 1780. He m. about 1764, MARY MOORE, b. 1744; d. April 8, 1789; daughter of Andrew and Sarah Moore.* They had issue:

  i. Andrew, b. 1765; m. December 20, 1790, Jean Strain; resided in Hanover township, Dauphin county, in 1792.
  ii. Jean, b. December, 1767; d. May 9, 1830; m. John Barnett. (*see Barnett record.*)
  iii. George, b. 1769; d. November, 1824.
  iv. William, b. 1771.
  v. Sarah, b. 1773; m. William Knox.
  vi. Joseph, b. 1775.
7. *vii. Richard-Moore*, b. 1777; m. Elizabeth Whitehill.
  viii. Mary, b. 1779.
8. *ix. John*, b. 1781; m. and left issue.
  x. Nancy, b. 1783; m. Isaac Harrison, Jr.

IV. RICHARD CRAIN,² (William,¹) b. about 1745, in Hanover township, Lancaster, now Dauphin county, Pa.; d. prior to 1790, in Middleton township, Cumberland county, Pa.; he located west of the Susquehanna previous to the Revolution, and during the struggle for independence was an officer in one of the associated battalions; was at the battle of Long Island under Colonel Frederick Watts, and captured there, but

---

*ANDREW MOORE, of Derry township, Lancaster county, Pa., d. October, 1767. His children were:

  i. Elizabeth, m. James Forster. (*see Forster record.*)
  ii. Agnes, m. —— Craig.
  iii. Mary, m. Joseph Crain.
  iv. John, m. Agnes Forster, and had *William, Sarah*, and *Agnes*.
  v. William, m. June 1, 1761, Margaret Wright, and had *Andrew*.

paroled soon after on account of wounds received in the engagement. We have no knowledge to whom he was married. He left issue:

    i. Espy, d. in October, 1804, in Middleton township, Cumberland county, Pa.; it is stated that he was a man of good education, and taught school a number of years.
    ii. Elizabeth.
    iii. William.
    iv. George.
    v. Mary, m. James Hamilton.
    vi. Jane, m. Joseph Vanhorn, d. prior to 1804, and they had issue (surname Vanhorn): *Espy* and *Mary.*
    vii. Ann, m. Matthew Dill.
    viii. Richard.

V. GEORGE CRAIN,³ (George,² William,¹) b. 1761; d. prior to 1800; m. MARTHA RITCHEY. Mrs. Martha Crain, subsequently, in 1803, m. Major ROBERT BOAL; they afterwards removed to Ohio. The children of George and Martha Crain were:

    i. Joseph, b. July 1, 1789.
    ii. Andrew-Lee, b. December, 1791.
    iii. Martha, b. 1793.
    iv. Frances, b. 1795.

VI. WILLIAM CRAIN,³ (George,² William,¹) b. 1763; d. January 8, 1802; m. June 24, 1788, MARY SAWYER, daughter of William and Jane Sawyer, b. in 1767; d. about 1820. They had among others:

    i. Mary, b. May, 1789.
    ii. William-Sawyer, b. October, 1791.

VII. RICHARD MOORE CRAIN,³ (Joseph,² William,¹) b. in November, 1777, in Hanover township, Lancaster county, Pa.; d. Friday, September 17, 1852, in Harrisburg, Pa. He received a fair education, and was brought up on his father's farm. He became quite prominent in public affairs the first decade of this century, and during the incumbency of General Andrew Porter as surveyor general of Pennsylvania, Mr. Crain received the appointment of deputy secretary of the Land Office, a position he acceptably filled through all the changes of administration for forty years, until the advent of

Governor Ritner, when he was displaced. He then retired to his farm in Cumberland county, from which district he was sent a delegate to the Constitutional Convention of 1837, in which he was a leading spirit. During the war of 1812-14, he commanded a company of volunteers from Harrisburg, and was subsequently commissioned colonel of the Pennsylvania militia. Colonel Crain m., in 1802, ELIZABETH WHITEHILL, b. 1771; d. October 2, 1848; daughter of Robert Whitehill* and Eleanor Read. They had issue:

9.   *i. Dr. Joseph*, b. December 25, 1808; m. first, Rebecca Gibson Wills; secondly, Ellen Chambers.

       ii. Eleanor, b. July 18, 1805; m. Dr. William Wilson Rutherford. (*see Rutherford record.*)

       iii. Elizabeth, b. March 18, 1809; m. Leopold N. Wikoff, b. August 30, 1800, in Philadelphia; d. October 30, 1874, in Harrisburg, Pa.

       iv. Agnes, b. November 24, 1810; d. unm. in Harrisburg, Pa.

10.   *v. Mary-Adeline*, b. May 1, 1817; m. first, Dr. Joseph Junkin; secondly, Dr. Alexander T. Dean; thirdly, Isaac Van Horn.

---

* ROBERT WHITEHILL, son of James and Rachel Whitehill, was born July 24, 1738, in the Pequea settlement, Lancaster county, Pa. He was educated at the school of Rev. Francis Alison. In the spring of 1771, he removed to Cumberland county, locating on a farm two miles west of Harrisburg. He was a member of the County Committee of 1774-5; of the Convention of July 15, 1776; of the Assembly, 1776-8; Council of Safety from October to December, 1777; member of the Supreme Executive Council, December 28, 1779, to November 30, 1781; of the Assembly, 1784-7; under the Constitution of 1790, member of the House of Representatives from 1797 to 1801, and of the Senate from 1801 to 1804. During his term as Senator, he was Speaker of that body, and presided at the celebrated impeachment of the judges of the Supreme Court of Pennsylvania. In 1805 he was elected to Congress, and continued to be a member thereof until his death, which occurred at his residence on the 7th of April, 1813. His remains are interred at Silvers Spring Presbyterian graveyard. Mr. Whitehill m. in 1765, ELEANOR READ, daughter of Adam and Mary Read, of Hanover in Lancaster county, Pa., b. March 11, 1734; d. July 15, 1785.

VIII. JOHN CRAIN,³ (Joseph,² William,¹) b. circa 1781, in Hanover township, Lancaster county, Pa. Settled in Ohio. He was twice married; m. first, LYDIA REEDER. They had issue:

 i. Milton, m. —— Donovan; and had issue: *John, William, Elizabeth*, and *Samilda*.
 ii. Jacob, m. and left one child.
 iii. John, m. Anna Bacon, and had issue:
  1. *Bacon;* resided in Springfield, Ohio.
  2. *Mary.*
  3. *Charles.*
  4. *Edward*: resided in Philadelphia.
 iv. Richard, m. —— Morton, and had issue:
  1. *Cornelia*, m. George Hatch.
 v. Jackson, m. Susan Miller, and they had issue, *John, Charles,* and *Charity*.

John Crain, m. secondly, NANCY MULHOLLAND, daughter of Jonathan Mulholland. They had issue:

 vi. Lydia, m. in 1841, William S. Reyburn, of Ohio; reside in Philadelphia, where Mr. Reyburn has been quite prominent in public affairs; and had issue (surname Reyburn):
  1. *John-Edgar*, b. February 7, 1845, in Clark county, Ohio.; admitted to Philadelphia bar in 1870; member of Pennsylvania House of Representatives 1871, 1874, 1875 and 1876; of the State Senate 1876 to 1890, of which body he was president pro. tem. in 1883; elected to the Fiftieth, Fifty-first, Fifty-second and Fifty-third Congresses. Mr. Reyburn m., in 1880, Margaret Crozier, daughter of Judge Crozier, of Kansas; and they had issue: *William* and *Eleanor.*
  2. *Ellen*, d. s. p.; m. 1878, Dr. William Greer.
 vii. Mary, m. Orlando Serviss, of Carlisle, O.; and had issue (surname Serviss) *Elizabeth*, and *Rena*.
 viii. James, m. Nancy Wilson; resided in Cairo, Ill.; and had issue, *Ridle, Festal, Claude,* and *Choral*.
 ix. Nancy, m. John Keifer, of Kansas, who d. in 1892; and had issue (surname Keifer) *Frank, James, Edwin, Elizabeth, Emily,* and *Bertill*.
 x. Jonathan; settled in Cairo, Ill.: m. Margaret ——, of St. Louis; and had issue, *Edward, Ella, Rena, Mary, Emma, William,* and *Henry*.

IX. JOSEPH CRAIN,[4] (Richard-Moore,[3] Joseph,[2] William,[1]) b. December 25, 1803, at Lancaster, Pa.; d. April 18, 1876, in Hoguestown, Pa. He was educated at Dickinson College, and graduated from Jefferson Medical College in 1826. He settled first at Harrisburg, where he practiced his profession several years, when in 1842 he located permanently at Hoguestown, Cumberland county, where he became well known as a skillful practitioner. He was a member of old Silvers Spring Church, where his remains lie buried. Dr. Crain was twice married. He m. first, in 1831, REBECCA GIBSON WILLS, b. January 23, 1811; d. September 16, 1850; daughter of Alexander Wills and Isabella Wallace (*see Wallace of Hanover*). They had issue:

 i. Isabella-Wallace, b. December 21, 1832; d. December 12, 1834.
 ii. Elizabeth-Whitehill, b. November 29, 1834; m. April 21, 1853, James Orr, of New Bloomfield, Perry county, Pa.; b. August 9, 1818; and they had issue (surname Orr):
  1. *Rebecca*, b. August 5, 1855; m. William Henry Sponsler, of New Bloomfield, Pa., and they had issue (surname Sponsler):
   a. William, b. October 14, 1877.
  2. *William*, b. November 27, 1858; m. 1882, Jane Shuler, of New Bloomfield, Pa.; and had issue (surname Orr):
   a. Marmaduke, b. 1883.
  3. *Eleanor-Rutherford*, b. September 22, 1860; d. August 13, 1861.
  4. *Joseph*, b. June 15, 1862.
  5. *James-Stanley*, b. October 13, 1867.
 iii. Caroline-Jane, b. January, 1837; d. November 23, 1837.
 iv. Agnes-Caroline, b. October 20, 1844; d. July 17, 1890; m. September 3, 1861, Marmaduke Burrough Taylor, b. August 17, 1835; d. January 15, 1890; second son of Othniel Hart Taylor and Evelina Burrough; was educated at the Protestant Episcopal Academy, Philadelphia, and at Rutger's College, graduating from the National Law School at Poughkeepsie, N. Y., in 1856; settled at Camden, N. J., where he became quite prominent in his profession; took a warm interest in many of the business enterprises of that city, and the municipality as well as the church found in him an earnest worker. He was a descendant of one of the oldest

families of New Jersey, his ancestor, John Fenwick, having established an English colony on the Delaware river in 1675, and was the first Governor of New Jersey. Mr. and Mrs. Taylor had issue (surname Taylor):
  1. *Clarence-Wills*, b. July 11, 1862; was educated at the P. E. Academy, Philadelphia, and University of Pennsylvania, graduating in 1884; is engaged in active business enterprises in Camden, N. J.
  2. *Eveline-Constance*, b. December 5, 1865; d. 1870.
  3. *Annie*, b. September 3, 1871; m. November 2, 1893, Rev. Robert Atkinson Mayo, of Holy Trinity Memorial Chapel, Philadelphia.
v. *Richard-Moore* (M. D.), b. October 20, 1844; d. 1886; m. first Mary Anderson; and had issue:
  1. *Elizabeth.*
  2. *Anderson.*
Mr. Crain m. secondly Anna Neil, of North Carolina; and had issue: *Agnes*, b. 1879; *Richard* and *Alexander* (twins):
vi. *Alexander-Wills*, b. March 10, 1847; resides in Oklahoma; m. December 26, 1880, Lucy Brown; and they had issue:
  1. *Anna-M.-Brown*, b. November 30, 1881.
  2. *Allen-Wills*, b. September 23, 1883.
  3. *Ambrose-Marmaduke*, b. January 10, 1886.
vii. *Whitehill*, b. September 11, 1850; d. September 3, 1856.

Dr. Joseph Crain, m. secondly, October 11, 1853, ELLEN J. CHAMBERS. They had issue:

viii. *Talbot-Chambers*, b. May 20, 1855; m., first, in 1878, Ellen Totten, and they had issue *Joseph*; m. secondly, in October, 1893, Miss Davis, of Mechanicsburg, Pa.

X. MARY-ADELINE,[4] (Richard-Moore,[3] Joseph,[2] William[1]), b. May 1, 1817, at Harrisburg, Pa.; d. March 3, 1881, at Camden, N. J.; was thrice married; m. first Dr. JOSEPH JUNKIN, of Cumberland county, Pa.; no issue. She m. secondly ALEXANDER TRACY DEAN, who d. November 4, 1844, at Harrisburg, Pa. They had issue (surname Dean).

  i. *Jennie*, m. William S. Bishop, M. D.; appointed assistant surgeon U. S. Navy April 11, 1843; promoted passed assistant surgeon May 11, 1845; surgeon on retired list March 27, 1866; d. December 28, 1868.
  ii. *Richard-Crain*, b. May 26, 1836; graduated from Jefferson Medical College: appointed assistant surgeon U. S. Navy April 17, 1856; promoted passed assistant surgeon

March 25, 1861; surgeon August 1, 1861; medical inspector June 8, 1873; medical director June 10, 1880. He m. in 1858, Anna Mulford, dau. of Dr. Isaac S. Mulford, of Camden, N. J.; and had issue (surname Dean):
1. *Emma*, m. Arthur Ainley; reside in New York.
2. *Alexander-Tracy*, appointed from Pennsylvania second lieutenant in Twenty-fifth Regiment U. S. Infantry November 26, 1880; transferred to Fourth Cavalry February 13, 1882; m. Miss Todd, of Florida.

Mrs. Dean m. thirdly, Isaac Van Horn, of Camden, N. J. They had issue (surname Van Horn).

iii. Francis-Crain, m. Harriet Simmons and had issue (surname Van Horn), *Eva* and *Dora*, all residing in Paris, France.

DIXON OF DIXON'S FORD.

I. JAMES DIXON,[1] a native of the north of Ireland, of Scotch descent, emigrated to America about 1735. In 1738 he took up a tract of four hundred acres of land on the Swatara in the county of Lancaster, Province of Pennsylvania, at what was named and known for a century as Dixon's ford. This ford is directly back of the town of Palmyra, in Lebanon county, leading into Hanover township, and upon Smith's map of the county of Dauphin, in Pennsylvania, published in 1816, it is so marked. "A few years ago," wrote the late Hermanus Alricks, Esq., in 1873, "bridge viewers located a bridge a short distance above the fording where the banks of the creek were high, on land of Mr. Loudermilch, and now it is called Loudermilch's bridge or ford." In 1765 James Dixon obtained possession of the Graham tract on Bow creek. We have no record of his death, but presume it was prior to the Revolution. Of his family, we have the record of one—JOHN DIXON,[2] b. about 1724, in Ireland; d. in December, 1780, in Hanover. It is stated that the loss of his eldest son, Robert, who had been killed at Quebec, and the non-return of another favored child, who had "gone to the war," hastened his death, through grief. The father had been an officer during the Indian wars, and served in several civil positions of honor. His wife, ARABELLA, died in the autumn of 1775. They had quite a large family, and the authority just quoted states that he had heard his old Scotch-Irish friends say that the Dixons belonged to the best blood of the Revolution. John Dixon and wife, Arabella, had issue:

 i. Robert, b. 1749; was sergeant in Captain Matthew Smith's company of Paxtang, Colonel William Thompson's battalion of riflemen, in June, 1775; and fell at Quebec, December 31, 1775, "the first martyr of the Revolution," wrote William Darby.

 ii. Isabella, b. 1751; d. May 10, 1824, at Harrisburg; m. James McCormick, who removed to the White Deer valley about 1774. Mr. McCormick enlisting in the patriot army, his wife and children fled from the valley in 1778, owing to the incursions of the Indians on the West Branch. Mr. McCormick never returned from the war, and she remained among her friends at Dixon's ford. They had *Hugh*, m. Esther Barbara Kumbel, of New York city, (see *McCormick record*,) and *Sarah*, m. Robert Sloan, of Hanover.

 iii. *Richard*, b. 1753 ; d. February, 1848 ; served as a private in Captain Matthew Smith's company in 1775 ; but subsequently enlisted for the war, serving until its close ; was promoted to quartermaster-sergeant in the Continental Line ;* m. Elizabeth ———, and had *Anna*, and *Maria*, who m. and went West.

 iv. *James*, b. 1756 ; d. September 19, 1782 ; m. Sarah Allen, of Hanover, daughter of William and Elizabeth Allen, and had *Allen*. James Dixon and his wife are buried in old Hanover churchyard.

2. v. *Sankey*, b. 1759 ; m. Anna Cochran.

 vi. *Mary*, b. 1761 ; m. James Breden, and had *Anabella ;* they removed, in 1786, to Western Pennsylvania, and it is thought died there.

 vii. *Anna*, b. 1763 ; m. first, Samuel Carson, and had *Samuel* and *Robert ;* secondly, Duncan Campbell. Mrs. Carson, with her husband, removed in 1786, to Washington county, Pa., where Mrs. Carson shortly after died. Nothing is known of their descendants.

---

* Robert Strain, a native of Hanover, and until his removal to Ohio, about the commencement of the present century, a member of Rev. Snodgrass' church, under date of "Dayton, Ohio, November 24, 1835," gives this record of Richard Dixon :

"*A statement of facts with regard to the services of Richard Dixon in the War of the Revolution.*

"Richard Dixon, of Lancaster county, Pa., enlisted in Lancaster, Pa., in the early part of the year 1775, under Matthew Smith, a captain, and remained under Captain Smith until his term of enlistment was ended. He then enlisted for and during the war, and said Dixon was promoted to the rank of quartermaster-sergeant or sergeant-major. I am very distinct in my recollection of Richard Dixon. When he first enlisted I made a shot-pouch for him, and stamped on the cover the motto of 'Liberty or death !' The whole of the four brothers of the Dixon family were in the service until the war was ended, and were of the truest kind of Whigs and Patriots.

ROBERT STRAIN."

viii. John; nothing is known of him; he went into the Revolution, and his father, at the date of writing his will, (1780,) in making a bequest to him, provided for him "if he ever returns." He probably died in battle.

ix. Anabella, m. James Gibson.

II. SANKEY DIXON,[3] (John,[2] James,[1]) b. 1759, in Londonderry township, Lancaster, now Dauphin county, Pa.; d. November 11, 1814, at Knoxville, Tenn. He entered the army of the Revolution in June, 1775, and served until the close of the war for Independence, holding the rank of ensign and lieutenant in the Pennsylvania Line; was wounded at Brandywine and Yorktown; settled, in 1786, in the Buffalo valley, where he married; the following year removed to Rockbridge county, Virginia; in the spring of 1800 emigrated to East Tennessee, near Knoxville; m. in 1787, ANNA COCHRAN, b. August 16, 1763, in Lancaster, now Dauphin county, Pa.; d. April 12, 1857, at Winchester, Tenn., daughter of George Cochran and Anna Henry. They had issue :

i. John, b. August 14, 1789; d. April 1, 1791, in Rockbridge county, Va.

ii. Matthew-Lyle, b. January 24, 1792, in Rockbridge county, Va.; d. September 30, 1836, at Talladega, Ala.; received a good education and studied medicine; served as surgeon's mate during the war of 1812-14, and afterwards located at Talladega, where he practiced his profession, lived and died, honored and respected.

iii. Robert, b. April 18, 1794; d. October 28, 1834, near Selma, Ala.; became a minister in the Cumberland Presbyterian Church.

iv. Nancy-Henry, b. January 17, 1796; d. May 12, 1848, at Louisville, Ky.; m. Charles G. Nimmo, of Winchester, Tenn.; and had issue, (surname Nimmo,) *Hiram, Samuel, Elizabeth,* and *Joseph Warren.*

v. Isabella, b. October 19, 1801; d. December 4, 1801.

vi. Mary-Roan, b. December 3, 1804; d. in 1837, at Shelbyville, Tenn.; m. James H. Martin, and had issue, surname Martin,) *William-H., Jane,* and *John.*

vii. Margaret, b. April 21, 1807; d. June 3, 1850, in Winchester, Va.; m. in 1830, M. W. Robinson, of Winchester, and had issue, (surname Robinson,) *Rachel-A.,* m. James R. Mankin; *Elizabeth-White, Samuel, Isabella-White, William-Darby, Sarah-Sloan, Henry-Clay,* and *Mary.*

THE FAMILY OF EGLÉ.

[The family of EGLE, or EGLI, belonged to the ancient German tribe of Langobards (Longbeards), which settled in the northern part of Italy in the fourth or fifth century. The ancestor of the Swiss Egli's emigrated from the Canton Tessino to St. Gall, about the twelfth century. This ancestor had five sons, three of whom settled in the department of the Loire, in France, subsequently, upon the revocation of the Edict of Nantes, removing to the Canton of Zurich, where they became followers of the Swiss reformer, Zwingli, whilst the other two remained in the Canton of St. Gall. A branch of the latter, somewhat later, emigrated to the Canton of Lucerne. The St. Gall and Lucerne families adhered to the Roman Catholic faith, but a friendly relation with the Zurich branch was constantly maintained. It is more than probable that some one of the same family reached England at an early period, for we find that in the seventh year of the reign of Edward I. (A. D. 1278), "Wilelmus Egle et Custancia uxor," had holdings in the Hundred of Northstowe, county of Cambridge. The English family of Eagle is different in its origin. The orthography of the name is somewhat perplexing, from the fact that Egle is that adopted by the Zurich branch, while that of Egly by those of St. Gall. Although the first settlers in America wrote their name Egle, there are changes in different sections of the Union, chiefly due to ignorance or carelessness. The New York and Central Pennsylvania families write it correctly, *Egle;* those in Ohio, Illinois and Arkansas, *Eagle;* while in the Southern States it is *Egley* or *Eagley*, and in California, *Ekel*, all having the same origin—descendants of Marcus Egle. In the genealogy which is herewith presented, we have given the uniform spelling EGLE. *Arms*—1 & 2, de sable un leon d'or ; 2 & 3, d'argent a l'emauche de trois pisces de gules. *Crest—* Le leon entre un vel coupé à dexter l'argent sur gules a sinister d'or sur sable. *Motto—*" Tien la Foy."]

I. MARCUS EGLE,[1] the first of the name in Pennsylvania, was born about the year 1690, in the Canton of Zurich, Switzerland, not far from the city of Berne, from whence he and his family emigrated to America prior to 1740. He took up a tract of land in Cocalico township, Lancaster county, Pa., where he died in September, 1767, leaving a wife, ELIZABETH, and five children. We have the names of only four:

2.   i. *John,* b. 1723 ; m. Rosina Dick.
3.   ii. *Caspar,* b. October 16, 1725 ; m. first, Elizabeth Mentges secondly, Catharine Bintling.
4.   iii. *Adam,* b. 1730; m. and left issue.
      iv. *Susannah,* m. Colonel Philip Cole, who, prior to the Revolution, settled in Buffalo Valley, Pa., and owned the tract of land upon which the town of Hartleton, Union county, is located. He was quite prominent during the early part of the war for independence, but in the "Great Runaway," left the valley, and was residing after the war at York, Penn'a; subsequently it is thought removing to Baltimore, Md. Nothing further is known.

II. JOHN EGLE,² (Marcus,¹) b. 1723, in the Canton of Zurich, Switzerland; d. April, 1796, in Reading, Pa. He seems to have been a person of means ; was a storekeeper at New Providence, Philadelphia (subsequently Montgomery) county, Pa., from 1750 to 1763, afterwards, in 1772, residing in Alsace township, Berks county, and, at the time of his death, at Reading. His will, which was probated May 6, 1796, makes Reverend William Boas executor, the witnesses being John Spyker and Jacob Dick. His wife, ROSINA [DICK], died prior. They had issue :

   i. *Joseph,* b. 1753 ; m. and left issue, but nothing further known.
  ii. *John,* b. 1755, in Providence township, Philadelphia (now Montgomery) county, Pa., removed to Harrisburg prior to 1804, for on the 8th of November that year he and his wife gave a deed for a lot of ground in that borough to their sons *Samuel,* and *Marcus* ; nothing further known.
 iii. *Jacob,* b. 1757.
  iv. *Catharine,* b. 1763 ; m., first, Robert Copeland ; secondly, William Lauer ; nothing further known.

III. CASPAR EGLE,² (Marcus,¹) b. October 16, 1725, in the Canton of Zurich, Switzerland ; d. September 3, 1804, in Harrisburg, Pa. He was brought up on his father's farm, a winegrower ; received a good education, and with the other members of his family, came to America prior to 1740. His father, as before stated, located in Cocalico township, Lancaster county, Pa., but the son settled in Alsace township, Berks county. He was naturalized in October, 1762, as appears by the *Penn-*

sylvania Archives. In 1770, he was engaged in merchandising at Reading, while in 1774 he established a brewery at Lancaster. He took the oath of allegiance August 24, 1777. He remained at Lancaster until 1794, when he and his wife removed to Harrisburg, Pa., where they both died at the residence of his son, Valentine. Caspar Egle was twice married. By first wife, ELIZABETH MENTGES,* b. circ. 1730 ; d. January 3, 1760. They had issue :

  5.   *i.* *Valentine*, b. October 27, 1756; m. Elizabeth Thomas.
  6.   *ii.* *Jacob*, b. December 12, 1758; m. Catharine Backenstose.

Caspar Egle m., secondly, in 1763, CATHARINE BÏNTLING, b. about 1738, in Switzerland ; d. 1811, at Harrisburg, Pa. They had issue :

  7.   *iii.* *John*, b. September 20, 1764 ; m. Catharine Spencer.
       iv. *Christian*, b. July 6, 1766 ; bap. August 17, 1766.
       v. *Catharine*, b. March 21, 1768 ; bap. April 16, 1768.
       vi. *Anna-Maria*, b. March 22, 1770 ; bap. March 28, 1770.
       vii. *George-Frederick*, b. October 6, 1773 ; bap. December 7, 1773; d. April, 1816, in Harrisburg, Pa.; unm.
       viii. *Philip*, b. April 9, 1775 ; was captain of a merchant vessel, and d. prior to 1830, in the city of Baltimore ; unm.
  8.   *ix.* *William*, b. March 6, 1777 ; m. Sarah Thorn.
       x. *Mary*, b. January 5, 1780; m. Moses Guest. They settled in Ohio. He was the author of a work, published in Cincinnati, Ohio, in 1823 : "Poems on several Occasions ; To which are annexed Extracts from a journal kept by the author during a journey from New Brunswick, N. J., to Montreal and Quebec." They left descendants.

---

*ELIZABETH MENTGES, was the daughter of Francis Mentges, sen., a Huguenot, b. in Switzerland, city of Berne. There were two other children, both younger, who came to Pennsylvania ; *Katharine*, d. unm.; and *Francis*, b. 1740 ; d. circa, 1800. The latter married but left no issue. Francis Mentges was appointed from Lancaster county a lieutenant in Col. Atlee's Musketry Battalion, March 20, 1776, and on the 22d, adjutant. He was promoted to major of Eleventh Regiment Pennsylvania Line, October 25, 1776, to rank from October 7, 1776 ; promoted lieutenant-colonel Fifth Pennsylvania October 9, 1778 ; and retired January 1, 1783. Col. Mentges was the first inspector-general of the U. S. army; and one of the original members of the Pennsylvania Society of the Cincinnati.

IV. ADAM EGLE,² (Marcus,¹) b. about 1726, in the Canton of Zurich, Switzerland ; d. about 1779, in Lancaster, Pa.; was wagon-master of Colonel William Thompson's battalion in the army of the Revolution. He married in Lancaster county, and had, among others, children :

      i. John, b. 1750 ; d. 1826 ; m. and removed to Rowan county, N. C.; and had, among others, *David*, and *John*.
9.   *ii.* George, b. 1752 ; m. [Mary] Heilig.
10. *iii.* Philip, b. 1758; m. Hannah Long.

V. VALENTINE EGLE,³ (Caspar,² Marcus,¹) b. October 27, 1756, in Bern township, Berks county, Pa.; d. November 23, 1820, at Harrisburg, Pa. At the age of nineteen, he enlisted in the war for independence, and served for a time in the First Regiment of the Pennsylvania Line of the Revolution; and subsequently was lieutenant in Eighth Battalion Lancaster county militia. He learned the trade of a hatter, and settled in Harrisburg, Pa., where he established himself in business and was a gentleman universally respected and esteemed. He died suddenly from nervous shock and over-exertion, caused by the complete destruction of his property by fire a few months prior. He m., in 1796, by Rev. Anthony Hautz, pastor of Frieden's Kirche, in Cumberland county, Pa., ELIZABETH THOMAS, b. May 2, 1772, in Londonderry township, Lancaster, now Lebanon county, Pa.; d. August 5, 1867, at Harrisburg, Pa. She was the daughter of Martin Thomas and Ursula Müller. Said a contemporary, at the time of her decease : "During her long and eventful life she was highly esteemed by all who knew her. She was an eye-witness of many interesting scenes, not only in frontier times, at a period when the red man was occasionally to be seen revisiting his old hunting grounds, but during the struggle for liberty—the war of the Revolution." She was indeed a remarkable woman, and the incidents of her life were such as few persons have experienced. To her the writer of this record is indebted much, for she was to him more than a mother. She was faithful and loving to him in his orphanage, and her memory is respected and honored as few mothers could be. She was a devoted Christian, and her good deeds are the heritage of her descendants. Valentine Egle and his wife, Elizabeth Thomas, had issue, all born at Harrisburg, Pa.:

11.   i. *John*, b. February 7, 1798; m. Elizabeth von Treupel.
      ii. *Sarah*, b. December 25, 1801; baptized November 29, 1814; d. March 30, 1870; m. William Bomgardner, and left issue.
      iii. *William*, b. May 2, 1803; baptized November 29, 1814; d. June, 1839; unm.
      iv. *Thomas*, b. December 18, 1808; baptized November 29, 1814; d. May, 1838; m. Nancy McCallum, and had *Andrew-J.*, d. s. p., and *Adelaide*.
12.   v. *Mary-Ann*, b. December 22, 1811; m. Francis John Smith,
      vi. *Valentine*, b. August 26, 1813; baptized November 29, 1814; d. November 4, 1893; unm.
      vii. *Hiram*, b. August 20, 1817; m. November 14, 1851, by Rev. Charles A. Hay, D. D., Margaret-Elizabeth Myers, b. July 20, 1821, in Mount Joy township, Lancaster county, Pa.; d. July 13, 1886, at Harrisburg, Pa.; daughter of George Myers and Margaret Elizabeth Bishop; no issue.

VI. JACOB EGLE,[3] (Caspar,[2] Marcus,[1]) b. December 12, 1758, in Alsace township, Berks county, Pa.; d. September 6, 1796, in Lebanon county, Pa.; m. about 1785, CATHARINE BACKENSTOSE, b. about 1765, in Berks county, Pa.; d. May 3, 1847, near Decatur, Macon county, Ill.; dau. of John Backenstose. They had issue:

13.   i. *John*, b. March 19, 1788; m. Elizabeth Morrett.
      ii. *Sarah*, b. March 15, 1795, in Womelsdorf, Berks county, Pa.; d. circa, 1881, in Lebanon county, Pa.; m. Jonathan Barlett, b. April 9, 1804; d. April 24, 1874, in Lebanon county, Pa.; son of Elias Barlett and Rebecca Winter; and they had issue (surname Barlett):
         1. *Reuben*, resides at Jonestown, Pa.
         2. *Lavinia*, m. Henry Wagner.
         3. *Nathan*, resides at Wadsworth, O.
         4. *Adam*, resides at Wadsworth, O.

VII. JOHN EGLE,[3] (Caspar,[2] Marcus,[1]) b. September 20, 1764, in Alsace township, Berks county, Pa.; d. January 10, 1838, in Licking county, Ohio. He learned the trade of hatter in Philadelphia, and about the year 1796, accompanied his brother, William Egle, to the Genesee country, N. Y., where he purchased land in Livingston county. Becoming dissatisfied, he returned to Pennsylvania, and settled near Alexandria, Huntingdon county, where he married. In 1825 he removed to Licking county, Ohio, where he resided until his death. He m., in 1802, CATHARINE SPENCER, b. August 2, 1785; d. June 28, 1861; daughter of John Spencer and Mary Holihan; her remains, with those of her husband, rest in Spencer's graveyard, four miles north of the city of Newark, Ohio. They had issue, all save Elizabeth, born in Huntingdon county, Pa.:

 i. Mary, b. August 17, 1803; d. s. p.
 ii. John, b. January 4, 1805; resided near Carthage, Illinois, until, in 1854, the second great rush was made for California, when he set out for the gold regions, but died on the way in Utah; m. Susan Whitlock, and they had issue, among others:
  1. *Jane*, m. John Nichols, of St. Louis.
  2. *William.*
  3. *Elizabeth*, m., and had issue.
  4. *John*, m., and had *Catharine;* resided near Quincy, Ill.
  5. *Thomas-Jefferson;* studied medicine in St. Louis.
  6. *Cassandana.*
  7. *Valentine.*
  8. *Rufus.*
 iii. William, b. April 19, 1807; d. 1863, in St. Louis, Mo.; unm.
 iv. Robert, b. June 8, 1809; d. September 10, 1837, in Brighton, Ohio; unm.
 v. Mary, b. August 27, 1811; d. s. p.
14. *vi. Valentine*, b. October 17, 1813; m. Mary Louisa Hines.
 vii. George, b. June 15, 1816; d. s. p.
 viii. Emily-Holihan, b. June 15, 1817; d. February 11, 1883, in St. Louis, Mo.; was twice married; first, January 10, 1838, in Columbus, Ohio, by Reverend Reed, William Reily, of Columbus, Ohio. They had no issue as far as we can learn. Mrs. Reily, m., secondly, August 14, 1841, at Columbus, Ohio, by Reverend John Eager, Daniel Emerson, b. January 5, 1812, in Vermont; d. in 1870, at Salem, Ill.; son of John Emerson and Elizabeth Patterson, and had issue (surname Emerson):
  1. *William-Styles*, b. February 26, 1839, in Columbus, Ohio; resides in the city of St. Louis, Mo.
 ix. Margaret, b. Dec. 30, 1819; d. 1849; m. —— Patterson.
 x. Hiram, b. March 4, 1822; resides near Newark, Ohio; m. July 1, 1849, near Newark, Ohio, by Reverend John B. Fry, Rebecca Glover, b. June 28, 1824, in Hardy county, Va.; daughter of Alfred Glover and Jane Finch; and had issue, all born near Newark, Ohio:

1. *David-Emerson*, b. April 14, 1850.
2. *Milton-Lorenzo*, b. October 28, 1851; m. November 12, 1878, Clara L. Bowlby.
3. *Jennie*, b. August 9, 1856.
4. *Francis-Elmer*, b. October 18, 1864.

xi. David, b. April 22, 1824; resides near Carlyle, Ill.; m. February 18, 1858, in Newark, Ohio, by Reverend William Robinson, Susan Cornelia Martin, b. November 2, 1835, in Newark, Ohio; daughter of William Martin and Margaret Wilson; and had issue:
1. *William-Renic-Seymour*, b. April 20, 1859; d. May 13, 1878, near Carlyle, Ill.
2. *Kaddie-May*, b. June 1, 1863.
3. *Tig*, b. February 6, 1870.

xii. Elizabeth, b. October 31, 1827; m. James Patheal; reside at Salem, Ill.

VIII. WILLIAM EGLE,[3] (Caspar,[2] Marcus,[1]) b. March 6, 1775, at Lancaster, Pa.; d, November 28, 1847, at Groveland, Livingston county, N. Y.; an early settler in the "Genesee country;" m. September 5, 1804, SARAH THORN, b. December 10, 1785, at Newtown, Bucks county, Pa.; d. May 11, 1869, at Groveland, N. Y.; daughter of Lerein Thorn. They had issue:

15. *i.* Mary, b. December 24, 1805; m. William Bodine.
     ii. Valentine, b. June 28, 1808; d. at Farmington, Mich.; m., first, September, 24, 1834, Sarah Sage; d. at Farmington, Mich., and had *Malissa*, d. s. p., *Sarah-Ann, Joseph-Warren*, and *Effie;* no information as to second marriage.
16. *iii.* George, b. December 25, 1811; m. Almira Lycetta Wright.
17. *iv.* William-Henry, b. October 18, 1814; m. first, Rosanna Keith Bennett; secondly, Synthia Webb.
18. *v.* James, b. September 18, 1815; m. Emeline Bird.

IX. GEORGE EGLE,[2] (Adam,[2] Marcus,[1]) b. 1752, in Lancaster county, Pa., removed to Rowan county, N. C., where he died about 1820; m. [MARY] HEILIG, of Germantown, Pa.; d. about 1825, in Cabarras county, N. C. They had issue, among others:

i. Mary, b. 1776.
ii. Margaret, b. 1778.
19. *iii.* George, b. 1780; m. Mary Haldeman.

X. PHILIP EGLE,[3] (Adam,[2] Marcus,[1]) b. 1758, in Lancaster county, Pa.; d. 1822, in Rowan county, N. C. He served several tours in the Lancaster county battalions of associators and militia. At the close of the struggle for independence he removed with probably all of his father's family to Rowan county, N. C. He m. HANNAH LONG, d. 1832, in Maury county, Tenn. They had issue: [This entire family write their surname Eagle.]

20.   *i. Joseph*, b. 1785 ; m. Sena Furr.
    ii. James, m. and raised a large family ; descendants chiefly in North Carolina.
    iii. John, m.; descendants reside in North Carolina.
    iv. Samuel, removed to Tennessee about 1831 ; m. and left issue :
        1. *Sandy*, d. 1848, in Tennessee ; m. Eliza Furlow, and had *Joseph*.
    v. Philip, emigrated from North Carolina to Maury county, Tenn., in 1831; m. Betsy Long, and they had issue, *Alexander*, d. 1889, unm.
    vi. Esther, m. Frank Bane, of Maury county, Tenn.; and had issue (surname Bane):
        1. *Harriet*, m. Tom Shoat, and left issue ; d. in 1860.
        2. *Ann*, d. 1889 ; m. Samuel Cox, and left issue.
        3. *Frances-M.*, m. Lou Stephenson ; they removed to Arkansas in 1870, and thence to Hill county, Texas, and left issue.
    vii. David, d. 1873 ; resided in Tennessee, until about 1850, when he removed to Prairie county, Ark.; he m. Betsy Long Eagle, his brother Philip's widow, d. 1855, and had issue :
        1. *Philip*, resides in Lonoke county, Ark.
        2. *Joseph*, m. Sallie Calahan, and had several daughters.
        3. *John*, d. 1878 ; m. —— Driscol, and left issue.
        4. *James*, b. 1836 ; k. in battle of Pea Ridge, Ark., March 7, 1862, C. S. A.
        5. *Nancy*, b. 1840 ; d. 1862.
        6. *Frances*, m. Joseph Kirkpatrick.
    viii. Elizabeth, m. Simeon Lutz, and had issue (surname Lutz), *Sophia*, and *Henry*.

XI. JOHN EGLE,[4] (Valentine,[3] Caspar,[2] Marcus,[1]) b. February 7, 1798, in Harrisburg, Pa.; bap. November 29, 1814, by Reverend George Lochman, D. D.; d. June 5, 1834, at

The Family of Egle.

Harrisburg, Pa.; m. December 13, 1829, in Harrisburg, Pa., ELIZABETH VON TREUPEL,* b. December 21, 1810, in Schuylkill township, Montgomery county, Pa.; bap. April 12, 1811, by Reverend Beverly Waugh ; d. September 10, 1841, in Harrisburg, Pa. They had issue, all b. at Harrisburg, Pa.:

21.   i. *William-Henry*, b. September 17, 1830; m. Eliza-White Beatty.
22. ii. *George-Boyd*, b. December 21, 1831 ; m. Martha Kerr.

XII. MARY ANN EGLE,⁴ (Valentine,³ Caspar,² Marcus,¹) b. December 22, 1811, in Harrisburg, Pa.; bap. November 29, 1814, by Reverend George Lochman, D. D.; d. May 29, 1837, in Plymouth, Luzerne county, Pa., and there buried; m. FRANCIS JOHN SMITH, b. June 3, 1809, at Stratford, Conn.; d. October 19, 1865, on Put-in-Bay Island, Ohio; bur. at Four Corners, Ohio. He was the son of John Smith and Frances Halliburton, and a man of intelligence, energy, and enterprise. They had issue (surname Smith):

23.   i. *Welding-Egle*, b. March 6, 1833 ; m. Charlotte Ashton.
24. ii. *Wayman-French*, b. March 31, 1836 ; m. Susan Fox.

XIII. JOHN EGLE,⁴ (Jacob,³ Caspar,² Marcus,¹) b. March 19, 1788, in Womelsdorf, Berks county, Pa.; d. February 6, 1863, near Decatur, Ill. For many years he was engaged in the mercantile business in Pennsylvania, and was a leading contractor during the period of internal improvements in that State. He afterwards, in 1837, removed to a tract of land near Decatur, Ill., where he engaged in farming. He m., October

---

*She was the daughter of John von Treupel, b. December 12, 1782, in Haigerseelbach, Nassau, Germany ; d. September 13, 1832, in Harrisburg, Pa.; son of John Conrad von Treupel, magistrate of Haigerseelbach, and Christina Thielmann, of Oberossbach, Germany. He married in Haigerseelbach, December 15, 1803, by the Reverend Ph. Cl. Schmidt, Elizabeth Catharine Yüng, b. March 16, 1783, in Haigerseelbach, Nassau, Germany ; d. February 11, 1860, in Harrisburg, Pa.; dau. of John Adam Yung, schoolmaster, of Haigerseelbach, and Elizabeth Kring, of Obersdorf, in Siegen, Germany. They emigrated to America in 1805, and took up their residence in Montgomery county, Pa., where all their children were born. He was a soldier of the war of 1812-14, and in active service on the Delaware during that contest.

25, 1812, ELIZABETH MORRETT, b. November 13, 1791, near Lebanon, Pa.; d. March 15, 1879, near Decatur, Ill.; daughter of Mathias Morrett and Barbara Orth. (*see Orth record.*) They had issue, all born in Lebanon county, Pa.:

    i. Jeremiah-Morrett, b. December 19, 1818; d. April 14, 1859, near San Francisco, Cal.; was twice married; m., first, Ann Thompson, d. near Springfield, Ill., and had *John-Joseph*; *Henry*; and *William*, d. 1881, m. daughter of John Kline, of Macon county, Ill., and left five children. He m., secondly, Sarah M——, and left four children.

25. *ii. Sarah-Morrett*, b. January 30, 1815; m. Robert Henry Jones.

    iii. Rosanna-Morrett, b. August 8, 1817; m., first, George Rausb, d. at Napierville, Ill., and had issue (surname Raush), *John*; *Margaret*, m., first, Mr. Sheldon, secondly, Mr. Vogelsang; *James-J.*; *Sarah*, m. Charles Williams; and *Luther*. She m., secondly, John Baughman; resides in Macon county, Ill.

    iv. Mary-Ann, b. April 10, 1820; d. March 19, 1854, in Macon county, Ill.; m. October 18, 1842, Michael Elson, and had three children, d. s. p.

    v. Elmira, b. February 10, 1823; d. May 24, 1862, in Macon county, Ill.; m. March 14, 1854, Herman Mears, and had issue (surname Mears), two children, d. s. p., and *Mary*, m. Robert Huddlestone.

    vi. Rebecca, b. May 8, 1824; d. February 6, 1864, at Boody, Ill.; m. Frederick Nintker, and had issue (surname Nintker): *John*; *Elizabeth*; *Mary*; *Amanda*, deceased, m. Mr. Fisher; *Minnie*, and a daughter, m., residing in Kansas.

XIV. VALENTINE EGLE,[4] (John,[3] Caspar,[2] Marcus,[1]) b. October 17, 1813, in Alexandria, Huntingdon county, Pa.; resided near Hunt's Station, Knox county, Ohio; m. in Columbus, Ohio, September, 1837, MARIA LOUISA HINES, b. June 11, 1815, in Franklin county, Pa.; daughter of Jeremiah Hines and Elizabeth, daughter of Captain Michael Baymiller, of the army of the Revolution. They had issue:

    i. John, b. February 7, 1840, in Franklin county, Ohio; m. October 18, 1861, Martha Ann McDonald, b. October, 1840, in Knox county, Ohio; d. October 18, 1876; daughter of William McDonald; and had issue, all b. in Knoxville, Ohio.

        1. *Mary-Bell*, b. July 28, 1862; d. September 8, 1864.

The Family of Egle. 169

2. *Maria-Zerena*, b. April 4, 1864; d. December 28, 1865.
3. *Edward*, b. September 7, 1868; d. Sept. 15, 1868.
4. *Orlendo-Benton*, b. September 20, 1869.
5. *Martha-Adelia*, b. November 20, 1871.
6. *Matilda-Maude*, b. January 15, 1875.

ii. *William-Spencer*, b. September 18, 1842, in McDonough, Ill.; m. December, 1869, Martha Ann Smith, b. August 14, 1850, in Knox county, Ohio, daughter of Henry D. Smith and Elizabeth McVeagh; and had issue, all b. in Licking county, Ohio.

1. *Ella-Mabel*, b. December 1, 1870.
2. *Charles-Oran*, b. June 12, 1873.
3. *Daisy-Dell*, b. June 11, 1875.
4. *Bessie*, b. August 14, 1877; d. September 20, 1877.

iii. *Mary-Virginia*, b. October 3, 1844, in McDonough county, Illinois.

iv. *Hiram-Hines*, b. December 12, 1846; m. in Knox county, Ohio, Anna Elizabeth Lowe, b. January 1, 1850, in Johnstown, Licking county, Ohio; daughter of David Rowe and Scottie Kidner.

v. *Catharine-May*, b. March 18, 1849, in Licking county, Ohio.

vi. *Margaret-Louisa*, b. June 18, 1851, in Licking county, Ohio.

XV. MARY EGLE,[4] (William,[3] Caspar,[2] Marcus,[1]) b. December 24, 1805, in Groveland, N. Y.; d. May 28, 1865, in Pine Run, Genesee county, Mich., and there buried; m. November 17, 1825, in Groveland, N. Y., by Rev. Silas Pratt, WILLIAM BODINE, b. July 11, 1803, in Pennsylvania; d. April 13, 1868, in Pine Run, Genesee county, Mich., They had issue, all born at Groveland, N. Y., (surname Bodine):

i. *Catharine*, b. September 25, 1826; m. May 8, 1847, by Rev. John C. Wright, John H. Francisco, b. 1828, at White Hall, Washington county, N. Y.; son of Robert Francisco.

ii. *Oscar-Fitzler*, b. December 1, 1828.

iii. *Mortimer-Charles*, b. April 10, 1831; member of the Twenty-third Regiment Michigan Volunteers, and d. in service, November 12, 1862, at Lebanon, Ky.

iv. *Sarah-Jane*, b. August 2, 1836.

v. *Oakley*, b. September 5, 1839; m. September 18, 1865, Barbara Celeste Devoe, b. 1848, in Otsego county, N. Y.; daughter of Philip and Eliza Ann Devoe, and had *Flora-Ada*, d. s. p., and *Daisy-May*.

vi. *Ellen-Eugenie*, b. September 17, 1842.

vii. *Charlotte-Russell*, b. May 31, 1846.

XVI. GEORGE EGLE,[4] (William,[3] Caspar,[2] Marcus,[1]) b. December 25, 1811, in Groveland, N. Y.; d. in 1882, near Otisville, Genesee county, Mich.; m. January 1, 1835, at Perez, N. Y., by Rev. Samuel Gridley, ELMIRA LYCETTA WRIGHT, b. in Scipio, Genoa county, N. Y. Her parents were Edmund Wright, b. in 1760, in county Tyrone, Ireland; d. June 6, 1849; m. Sarah Fields, b. in 1786, at Trenton, N. J.; d. January 24, 1839, at Perez, N. Y. George Egle had issue:

 i. Sarah-Jane, b. September 25, 1835, in York Centre, N. Y.; m. first, December 20, 1855, John Waters Webber; d. in Holly, Oakland county, Mich.; son of Edward Freeman Webber, and had, (surname Webber,) *John-Waters*, and *Harriet-Louisa*. Mrs. Webber m. secondly, October 27, 1867, Lyman Witter Spalding, b. January 18, 1814, in Monroe county, N. Y.; son of Ephraim Spalding and Lydia Stephens.

 ii. Edmund-Wright, b. July 29, 1837, in Perez, N. Y.; enlisted in Company K, First Michigan Cavalry, in 1861, and was killed at the battle of Cold Harbor, Va., June 1, 1864, at 10 a. m., and buried on the field where he fell, under an apple tree—grave marked on the tree—name and age.

 iii. Mary, b. July 4, 1839, in Mount Morris, N. Y.; m. January 1, 1856, Frank Lemuel Palmer, b. October 11, 1845, in Boston, Mass.; son of William Palmer and Mary Ridgway; served in the civil war, in Company A, First Michigan Regiment.

 iv. Helen-Louisa, b. November 4, 1841, in Mount Morris, N. Y.; m. September 20, 1861, George Ives, b. in Newtown, Pa., and had (surname Ives), *Frank, Minnie, May*, and *George-Edward*.

 v. William-Henry, b. March 23, 1843, in Groveland, N. Y.; m. May 18, 1875, Agnes Ralph Simons, b. May 8, 1853, in Sterling county, Canada West; daughter of Timothy Potter Simons and Maria Jane Goodrich.

 vi. Adelaide-Victoria, b. January 18, 1845, in Grand Blanche, Genesee county, Mich.; m. July 4, 1866, Robert Alexander, b. November 24, 1843, in Flint, Mich, and had, (surname Alexander), *Ida*, d. s. p., and *Robert-Edez*.

 vii. Betsy-Ann, b. April 18, 1849, in Flint, Mich.; m. October 19, 1873, Donald Ferguson, b. in Glasgow, Scotland.

 viii. John-Jefferson, b. July 6, 1851, in Buston, Genesee county, Mich.

ix. Harriet-Lycetta, b. January 9, 1853, in Flint, Mich.; m. December 4, 1870, William W. Alexander, b. January 26, 1851, in Flint, Mich., and had (surname Alexander), *Julia-Almira, Mary-Ermina,* and *Arthur-Eugene.*

x. Margaret-Ermina, b. August 6, 1856, in Flint, Mich.

xi. George-Clinton, b. January 12, 1859, in Davidson Centre, Genesee county, Mich.

XVII. WILLIAM HENRY EGLE,[4] (William,[3] Caspar,[2] Marcus,[1]) b. October 18, 1814, in Groveland, N. Y.; d. August, 1853, in Burns, Allegheny county, N. Y.; m. first, July 4, 1839, in Groveland, by Rev. Mr. Brown, ROSANNAH KEITH BENNETT, b. 1818, near Newtown, Bucks county, Pa.; d. September 25, 1849, in Burns, N. Y.; daughter of George Bennett and Martha Torbert. They had issue:

26.   *i. Aramanda,* b. April 15, 1842; m. Charles V. Craven.
27.   *ii. Alburtis,* b. March 31, 1843; m. Lydia McNair.

William H. Egle, m., secondly, July 4, 1850, by Rev. Mr. Brown, SYNTHIA WEBB, d. in Burns, N. Y.; daughter of William and Sarah Webb. They had issue:

iii. Frank, b. October 9, 1851; d. March 25, 1864.

XVIII. JAMES EGLE,[4] (William,[3] Caspar,[2] Marcus,[1]) b. September 18, 1815, in Groveland, Livingston county, N. Y.; d. January 11, 1863; m. May 8, 1845, in Groveland, EMELINE BIRD, b. in Hackettstown, N. J.; d. April 4, 1872, in Groveland, N. Y., and with her husband there buried. They had issue, all born in Groveland, N. Y.:

i. William-Henry, b. November 1, 1846; m. April 29, 1875, by Rev. J. B. Countryman, Mary Smock, b. March 9, 1855, in Groveland, N. Y.; daughter of Isaac and Hannah Smock, and had *Charles,* d. s. p, *James,* and a daughter.

ii. Mary, b. February 25, 1848; resides in Groveland, N. Y.

iii. Elizabeth, b. October 15, 1849; m. October 12, 1876, by Rev. David Conway, George Bennett, b. January, 1852, in Groveland, N. Y.; son of Samuel and Mary Bennett; and had three boys.

iv. James-Orlendo, b. March 11, 1851; resides in Groveland, N.Y.

v. Lerein-Thorn, b. April 8, 1853; resides in Groveland, N. Y.

XIX. GEORGE EGLE,[4] (George,[3] Adam,[2] Marcus,[1]) b. 1780, in Lancaster county, Pa.; removed with his parents to Rowan

172   *Pennsylvania Genealogies.*

county, N. C.; d. in Newton county, Mo.; m. MARY HALDEMAN, b. 1782, in Lancaster county, Pa.; d. in 1864, in Newton county, Mo. They had issue:
    i. Leah, b. 1802; resides in Newton county, Mo.
    ii. Mary, b. 1804; d. 1878.
    iii. Elizabeth, b. 1806; resides in Cabarras county, N. C.
    iv. Solomon, b. 1808; d. 1878.
    v. John, b. 1810; d. 1870.
28. *vi. George-Adam,* b. December 25, 1815; m. Nancy Shandy..
    vii. Sophia, b. 1817; resides in Newton county, Mo.
    viii. Moses, b. 1819; resides in Newton county, Mo.

XX. JOSEPH EGLE,[4] (Philip,[3] Adam,[2] Marcus,[1]) b. 1785, in Rowan county, N. C.; d. in 1842 in Pulaski county, Ark. He removed to Maury county, Tenn., in 1829; and in 1841 to Pulaski county, Ark. He m. in 1811, SENA FURR, b. 1789, in Cabarras county, N. C.; d. 1862, in Prairie county, Ark.; daughter of Henry Furr. They had issue.
29. *i. James.* b. March 24, 1813; m. Charity Swaim.
    ii. Maria, b. 1815; d. 1892; m. in 1834, Thomas Furlow; d. 1894; and had issue (surname Furlow):
        1. *Sarah,* b. 1835; m. —— Brewer.
        2. *Ivy,* b. 1837; m. first, —— Allen, and had issue, (surname Allen), *Anna;* m. secondly, in 1889, ——.
        3. *Doll,* b. 1842; m. —— Brewer, and had issue.
        4. *Thomas-J.,* m. first, —— Carroll; m. secondly Mrs. Apple; reside in Lonoke county, Ark.
        5. *Elizabeth,* m. and had issue.
    iii. Philip, b. 1817; d. 1842; m. Sallie Swaim, and had *Henry.*
    iv. Henry, (twin), b. 1817; d. 1886; m. first, Louisa Dunardy, and had issue:
        1. *Rosannah;* m. first, in 1866, Monroe Glover, and had issue; m. secondly, Loster.
        2. *Elizabeth,* m.
    Henry, m. secondly, —— Derabery; and had issue:
        3. *James,* d. 1892; m. —— Felton, and left issue.
        4. *Alexander,* m. —— Parker; and had issue.
        5. *William,* m. Mrs. Loug.
    v. Elizabeth, d. circ. 1854; m. in 1842, James Dunawdry; and had issue, (surname Dunawdry):
        1. *Mary,* (Polly), b. 1843.
        2. *James-D.,* b. 1845; m. Elizabeth McNealy.

The Family of Egle.   173

    3. *William*, b. 1847; removed to Texas in 1888; m. and had issue.
    4. *Elizabeth*, m. ——— Seaman; d. 1870.
  vi. *Joseph*, d. 1847, in San Antonio, Texas; a soldier.
  vii. *John*, d. 1855; m. 1843, Byaline Dismukis; d. 1894; and had issue:
    1. *Mary*, b. 1852; m. Joe Deaton.
    2. *John*, b. 1855; m. in 1857, Mrs. Dye.
  viii. *George-A.*, d. 1874; m, Sarena Swaim; and had issue.
    1. *William*, b. 1852; d. 1874.
    2. *John-B.*, b. 1854; m. Mattie Walters, and had issue.
    3. *Francis*, m. E. H. Halloday.
    4. *Joseph*, m. ——— Brown, and had issue.
    5. *Charity*, m. Goodrum Swaim, and had issue.
    6. *James*, resides in Lonoke county, Ark.
    7. *Pettus*, resides in Lonoke county, Ark.
  ix. *Rosannah*, d. 1861; m. 1847, William Swaim, and had issue, (surname Swaim):
    1. *Martha*, m. Sam. Austin, and had issue.
    2. *Joseph*, m. Elizabeth King, and had issue.
    3. *William*, m. first, Ella Boyd; m. secondly, ——— Boyd, and have issue.
    4. *Goodrum*, d. 1892; m. Charity Eagle.
    5. *Margaret*, m. Philmore Cook.
  x. *Daniel*, b. 1833; d. 1875, in Lonoke county, Ark.; m. Elizabeth Hicks, and had issue, among others:
    1. *Albert*, d.
    2. *Elizabeth*, m. ——— Foster.
    3. *Charles*.
  xi. *David*, b. December 25, 1834; d. 1877 in Lonoke county, Ark.; m. in 1858, Louisa Ferguson, and had issue:
    1. *Antone*, b. 1859; m. ——— Bransford.
    2. *Rosannah*, b. 1862; m. John Wright, and had issue
    3. *Miles*.
    4. *John*.
    5. *Jinnie*, m. first, L. Wright; secondly, ———
    6. *David*.
    7. *Bertha*.
    8. *Ada*.

XXI. WILLIAM HENRY EGLE,[5] (John,[4] Valentine,[3] Caspar,[2] Marcus,[1]) b. September 17, 1830, in Harrisburg, Pa., where he now resides. His father dying when he was four years of age, he went to his paternal grandmother's, to whom he was indebted for his careful training during childhood and youth. He was educated in the public and private schools of Harrisburg, and at the Harrisburg Military Institute. In 1848 he was tendered the appointment of midshipman in the United States Navy, but declined the honor. At the close of his school life he spent three years in the office of the *Pennsylvania Telegraph*, during most of which time he was foreman of the establishment. Subsequently he had charge of the State Printing Office. In 1853, having been a frequent correspondent to the monthly magazines, he undertook the editorship of the *Literary Companion* (which was discontinued at the end of six months), editing at the same time the *Daily Times*, afterwards merged into one of the other newspaper ventures of Harrisburg. In 1854 he began the study of medicine with Charles C. Bombaugh, M. D., of Harrisburg. During this period he was also assistant teacher in the Boys' school, of the then North ward, afterward becoming mailing clerk in the postoffice. In the fall of 1857 he resigned this position and entered the Medical Department of the University of Pennsylvania, from which institution he was graduated in March, 1859. The same year established himself at Harrisburg, and was in the practice of his profession there, when in 1862, after the battles of Chantilly and the second Bull Run he went to Washington in response to a telegram from General Russell, of Pennsylvania, to assist in the care of the wounded. In September of that year he was commissioned assistant surgeon of the Ninety-sixth Regiment, Pennsylvania Volunteers, and in the summer of 1863, surgeon in the Forty-seventh Regiment, Pennsylvania Volunteer Militia. At the close of service with the latter command, he resumed his profession, but afterwards accepted the appointment of surgeon of Volunteers by President Lincoln, and was ordered to Camp Nelson, Kentucky, to examine the colored regiments then being raised in that State. He was subsequently detailed with the cavalry battalions under Cols. James Brisbin and James F. Wade, thence ordered to the Department of the James under General Butler, as surgeon of the 116th U. S. C. I., subsequently assigned to the Twenty-fourth Army Corps as executive medical officer during the Appomattox campaign. Upon the return from that duty he was ordered to Texas with General Jackson's

Division, Twenty-fifth Army Corps, as chief medical officer. In December, 1865, he resigned the service and returned home, partly resuming the practice of his profession. For a period of four years he served, by appointment of the President, on the board of medical examiners for pensions ; and for twenty years was annually appointed physician to the Dauphin county prison, which position he resigned in March, 1887, when Governor Beaver appointed him State Librarian, the Senate promptly confirming the nomination. So well has he administered this office that Governor Pattison re-commissioned him in 1891, and again in March, 1894. The present effectiveness of the Pennsylvania State Library, now in the front rank of the large libraries of America, largely due to Dr. Egle's management, has been greatly appreciated by students at large. Upon the organization of the National Guard in 1870, Dr. Egle was appointed Surgeon-in-Chief of the Fifth Division with the rank of Lieutenant-Colonel, and subsequently in the consolidation of the commands, transferred to Surgeon of the Eighth Regiment. In 1885 he was commissioned Surgeon-in-Chief of the Third Brigade, which military position he now holds, being the senior medical officer of the National Guard of Pennsylvania. Acquiring an early taste for historical research, during relaxation from professional duties, when he returned from the army, in 1866, he commenced the preparation of his " History of Pennsylvania," published in 1876, of which twelve thousand copies were sold, when a second edition was issued in 1883. Principally among his other historical publications are : Historical Register, 2 vols., (1883-4); History of the County of Dauphin, (1883); History of the County of Lebanon, (1883) ; Centennial—County of Dauphin and City of Harrisburg, (1886); Pennsylvania Genealogies—Scotch-Irish and German, (1886) ; Harrisburg-on-the Susquehanna, (1892); Historical Register, 2 vols., (1883-4); Notes and Queries, Historical, Biographical and Genealogical, first and second series, 2 vols., (1878-82); Reprint, 2 vols., (1894-95); third series, 2 vols., (1887-91); fourth series, 2 vols., (1891-95). He was co-editor of the "Pennsylvania Archives," second series, vols. I to XII; editor of the same series, vols. XIII to XIX; and also of the third series now passing through the press. Lafayette College in 1878, conferred upon Dr. Egle the honorary degree of M. A., appreciative of his services in American history. He is a member of the American Historical Association, and has been honored by election as corresponding member of the principal historical societies of the United States, as well as of several learned societies in France and England. He was one of the founders and the first presiding officer of the Pennsylvania-German Society, and by virtue of service as an officer in the War of the Union, a member of the "Military Order of the Loyal Legion," and also a member of the Grand Army of the Republic. He is likewise a member of the Society of Colonial Wars, of the Sons of the Revolution, and of that of the War of 1812-14. In addition he preserves his membership in the Dauphin County Medical Society, and is an active member of the "Association of Military Surgeons of the United States." He resides at Harrisburg, Pa. Doctor Egle, m. July 24, 1860, at Harrisburg, Pa., by the Reverend Daniel Gans, D. D., of the Reformed church, ELIZA WHITE BEATTY, b. January 5, 1833, at Harrisburg, Pa., daughter of George Beatty and his wife Catharine Shrom. (*see Beatty record.*) They had issue, all born at Harrisburg, Pa.:

 i. *Beverly-Waugh*, b. Thursday, May 2, 1861; bap. Sunday, December 1, 1861, by Reverend Francis Hodgson, D. D., of the Methodist Episcopal church; d. Wednesday, June 21, 1882, at Chicago, Ill.; bur. Monday, June 26, 1882, at Harrisburg, Pa. Beverly, at the age of six years, was sent to the school of Miss Sabina Kelker, subsequently the select school of Professor L. H. Gause, and finally to the Harrisburg Academy under the care of Professor Jacob F. Seiler, A. M., continuing there until his eighteenth year. Expressing a wish to study medicine, special courses were given him in chemistry and *materia medica*, and in the early part of September, 1880, he was sent to Chicago to the care of his relative, Professor S. J. Jones, M. D., of the Chicago Medical College, an advanced medical institution in the West, where the advantages afforded him for pursuing his studies were unsurpassed. Remaining there, with the exception of a few weeks' visit to his home in the spring of 1881, he realized the necessity of the highest education in the profession he had selected for his life-work.

and became a devoted student. His hospital and clinical experience lifted him, as it were, into the front rank of his class, while fellow-students and professors alike admired his mental achievements and his courteous manners. He was the acknowledged leader of the senior class, and a bright future was seemingly before him of position, and honor, and usefulness in the profession. Although completely absorbed in his studies, he was not unmindful of other duties devolving upon him, and his rare social qualities gained him many friends in the city of Chicago. He never swerved in the performance of his mission, and a few weeks before his death he remained by the bedside of a young man near his own age, dying of diphtheria, when others had fled the room. About the 1st of June he complained of a small boil on his left upper lip. Little attention, however, was paid to it, save to lessen the swelling of the face, yet alarming cerebral symptoms soon set in, and, notwithstanding the best medical skill in the country, he breathed his last at 11.30, p. m., on Wednesday, June 21—St. Aloysius' day—1882. And thus, in the opening years of manhood, with prospects as brilliant as any could possibly desire, he passed from out the circle of loving hearts to the blessed realizations of the life eternal. He was a noble boy, intelligent, manly, upright, loving and dutiful, and it need not be wondered at that his sudden departure from this earthly life caused wounds which time can never fully heal.

ii. *Sarah-Beatty*, b. Friday, July 13, 1866; bap. Saturday, February 9, 1867, by Rev. B. B. Leacock, D. D., Rector of St. Stephen's Episcopal Church, Harrisburg, Pa. She m., November 22, 1893, at St. Stephen's Church, Harrisburg, by Rev. Thomas B. Angell, Rector, Robert John Holmes; reside at Altoona, Pa.; and had issue (surname Holmes):

    1. *William-Henry-Egle*, b. November 8, 1894; baptized Sunday, April 7, 1895, by Rev. A. S. Woodle, Rector of St. Luke's Episcopal Church, Altoona, Penna.

iii. *Catharine-Irwin*, b. Tuesday, January 19, 1869; bap. Tuesday, March 14, 1871, by Rev. Robert J. Keeling, D. D., Rector of St. Stephen's Episcopal Church, Harrisburg, Pa.

178 *Pennsylvania Genealogies.*

XXII. GEORGE BOYD EGLE,[5] (John,[4] Valentine,[3] Caspar,[2] Marcus,[1]), b. December 21, 1831, in Harrisburg, Pa.; served in the three months service at the outbreak of the civil war; in 1868 removed to West Virginia, near Martinsburg, where he now resides; m. August 29, 1852, by Rev. William McFadden, MARTHA KAUFFMAN KERR, b. December 25, 1834, in York county, Pa.; d. December 1, 1879, near Martinsburg, W. Va.; buried at Harrisburg, Pa.; daughter of James Kerr and Jane Atkinson. They had issue:

- i. *Mary-Elizabeth*, b. August 11, 1853, in Harrisburg, Pa.; d. August 7, 1874, near Martinsburg, W. Va.; buried at Harrisburg, Pa.
- ii. *Lavinia*, b. February 14, 1855; d. July 12, 1856.
- iii. *Lucinda*, b. January 6, 1857; d. February 3, 1857.
- iv. *William-Henry*, b. October 30, 1858; d. December 3, 1891, at McKeesport, Pa., buried at Harrisburg; m. Nettie Dallas Sigler, of McKeesport, Pa., and had *Hiram*.
- v. *Martha*, b. January 10, 1861; m. Jacob Strine of Martinsburg, W. Va.; and had issue.
- vi. *Margaret-Mary*, b. January 2, 1862; d. February 6, 1864.
- vii. *Hiram*, b. December 5, 1864; d. December 10, 1865.
- viii. *Virginia*, b. February 5, 1874; d. September 13, 1878, near Martinsburg, W. Va.; buried at Harrisburg, Pa.
- ix. *Margaret*, b. May 23, 1875.

XXIII. WELDING EGLE SMITH,[5] (Mary-Ann,[4] Valentine,[3] Caspar,[2] Marcus,[1]) b. March 6, 1833, in Plymouth, Luzerne county, Pa.; m. April 13, 1857, in Huron county, Ohio, CHARLOTTE ASHTON, b. September 19, 1837, in Lyme, Huron county, Ohio; daughter of Thomas Ashton * and Mary Edgar. They had issue, all b. in Four Corners, save the last four, who were born in Monroeville, (surname Smith):

- i. *Shelden-Egle*, b. August 16, 1858; m. June 1, 1889, Bessie Brown, b. March 27, 1865, at Plymouth, England.
- ii. *Allison-Halliburton*, b. January 18, 1861.
- iii. *Francis-Draper*, b. April 26, 1862; resides near McCook, Neb.

---

* THOMAS ASHTON was b. in 1810, in Prescott, Lancastershire, England; came to America in 1831; d. June 2, 1879, in Huron county, Ohio; m. MARY EDGAR, b. in 1815, in Somersetshire, England, coming to America in 1832. Mrs. Ashton resides near Monroeville, Huron county, Ohio.

iv. Walter-Ashton, b. February 16, 1864 ; m. May 10, 1893, Julia Etta McGrew, b. January 31, 1868, in Shelby co., Ill.; reside at Oberlin, Kan.

v. Hiram-Egle, b. February 21, 1866 ; m., June 14, 1894, Harriet G. Fish, b. March 28, 1871, at Monroeville, O.; reside at Galion, O.

vi. Charles-L., b. April 2, 1868.

vii. Evelyn-Charlotte, b. September 4, 1870.

viii. Mable-M., b. July 27, 1872 ; d. February 5, 1884, at Monroeville, Ohio.

ix. Lottie-Nine, b. August 6, 1877 ; d. February 9, 1884, at Monroeville, Ohio.

XXIV. WAYMAN FRENCH SMITH,[5] (Mary-Ann,[4] Valentine,[3] Caspar,[2] Marcus,[1]) b. March 31, 1836, in Plymouth, Luzerne county, Pa.; resides in Monroeville, Ohio ; m. May 19, 1863, SUSAN FOX. They had issue (surname Smith) :

i. Mary-Ann, b. July 24, 1864 ; d. February 3, 1881.

ii. Welding-M., b. January 9, 1866.

iii. Wilson-B., b. July 5, 1868 ; d. July 15, 1869.

iv. Wayman-H., b. May 11, 1870.

v. Lucy, b. August 19, 1872.

vi. Fannie-L., b. April 20, 1875.

vii. George-W., b. July 5, 1880.

viii. Ida-May, b. October 6, 1883.

XXV. SARAH MORRETT EGLE,[5] (John,[4] Jacob,[3] Caspar,[2] Marcus,[1]) b. January 30, 1815, in Myerstown, Lebanon county, Pa.; d. May 15, 1895, at Chicago, Ill.; bur. at Bainbridge, Pa.; m. October, 1833, in Sunbury, Pa., by Reverend John Peter Schindel, ROBERT HENRY JONES, b. March 22, 1803, in county Donegal, Ireland ; d. April 29, 1863, in Bainbridge, Pa. His father, Robert Jones, b. March 28, 1772, in Donegal, Ireland ; d. September 22, 1840, in Bainbridge, Pa.; came to America, landing at Philadelphia on the 12th of June, 1806, and was in active mercantile life for a period of twenty-five years. He m. April 20, 1792, Margaret Williamson, b. June 5, 1772, in county Monaghan, Ireland ; d. March 30, 1844, in Bainbridge, Pa. Their son Robert Henry Jones, received a good education, studied medicine with Doctor David Watson, of Donegal, and graduated from the medical department of the University of Pennsylvania in 1830. He commenced the practice of his profession at Bainbridge, in which he continued, very successfully, up to the time of his death. For many years there was no physician in the neighborhood, and his labors were very arduous. Apart from his professional duties, he became interested in various business operations; was a contractor on the old Philadelphia and Columbia railroad, and assisted in laying out the village of Bainbridge. Doctor Jones was highly respected and honored in the community in which he resided, and his memory remains green with many who honored him with the title of "the good doctor." Doctor Jones and his wife, Sarah Morrett Egle, had issue, all b. in Bainbridge, Pa., (surname Jones):

   i. Amanda-Egle, b. August 29, 1834; d. January 8, 1889.
   ii. Samuel-Jeremiah, b. March 22, 1836. He received a good preliminary education, and, in 1853, entered Dickinson College, from which institution he graduated with distinguished honors in 1857. After his graduation, he commenced the study of medicine under his father, and, in 1858, matriculated in the medical department of the University of Pennsylvania, taking his degree as M. D. from that institution in 1860. In the same year, he entered the United States Navy as assistant surgeon, was attached to the United States steamer Minnesota—the flag-ship of the Atlantic squadron—which participated in the battle with the Merrimac, upon which steamer he remained for two years, except when absent as Admiral Goldsborough's staff surgeon at the battle of Roanoke Island, and Admiral Rowan's staff surgeon at the battle of Newbern, when he was promoted to the grade of surgeon. Doctor Jones was United States examining surgeon for the appointment of volunteer medical officers during 1863 and 1864, with his head-quarters at Chicago. He was one of the youngest surgeons ever appointed in the United States Navy, being not yet twenty-eight years of age when he received his promotion. When relieved from duty in Chicago, in 1864, he was ordered to New Orleans as surgeon-in-chief of the United States naval hospital at that place, during an epidemic of yellow fever, and as medical purveyor of Admiral Farragut's (blockading) squadron. After the close of the war, he was transferred to the naval hospital at Pensacola, Florida, as surgeon of that hospital, and surgeon of the navy yard at Pensacola. He was also the surgeon of the sloop-of-war Portsmouth, at New Orleans, and of the frigate Sabine, the practice ship for naval apprentices on the

Atlantic coast. He continued in the naval service until 1868, when he resigned. In that year he was chosen as a delegate from the American Medical Association to the European Medical Associations, which held meettings at Oxford, Heidelberg, and Dresden. The late Professor Samuel D. Gross, with Dr. Goodman, of Philadelphia, and Doctor Baker, of New York, were his associates. He was also, at the same time, commissioned by Governor Geary, of Pennsylvania, to investigate and report upon sanitary matters abroad, in the interest of that State. Upon his return from Europe, he located at Chicago, and commenced a general practice, and was appointed president of the Chicago board of examining surgeons for United States pensions. In 1870, he was appointed professor of ophthalmology and otology in the Chicago Medical College, a chair which had just been established. His studies had been, partly by the natural trend of his mind and partly by circumstances, directed to diseases of the eye and ear, and the call to this chair in the Chicago Medical College determined his life-work. He has held this chair ever since, and after establishing the eye and ear department of St. Luke's Hospital, was appointed attending surgeon of that department, and has held the post for sixteen years. He also established the eye and ear department of Mercy Hospital and of the South Side Dispensary, and was their attending surgeon for ten years. He was also connected, as attending surgeon, with the Illinois Charitable Eye and Ear Infirmary, a State institution, located in Chicago. In 1880, Doctor Jones was elected permanent secretary of the Illinois State Medical Society, to succeed Doctor N. S. Davis, who had held the position for twenty years. He is an active member of that society, of the American Medical Association, American Academy of Medicine, the American Ophthalmological and Otological societies, and has been thrice a member of the International Medical Congress; and to these bodies, and to the *American Journal of Medical Sciences*, and other medical journals, his contributions to the literature of his profession have been chiefly made. A partial list of some of his valuable monographs, in which are condensed the knowledge and discoveries of centuries, and his own addition to that knowledge and those discoveries in his favorite branch of study, are herewith given: "The Present State of Ophthalmology," was delivered before the Illinois Medical Association, in May. 1879. "The

Present State of Otology," "A Report on Otology," "Iritis: some of Its Dangers," and "Affections of the Lachyrmal Apparatus," were also delivered before the Illinois Medical Society. "Strabismus: Its Nature and Effect," was contributed to the Chicago *Medical Gazette*, of January 5, 1880. "On the Introduction of Liquids into the Eustachian Tube and Middle Ear," was delivered before the American Medical Association, at New York, in June, 1880, and "Modifications of the Methods of Treating Chronic non-Suppurative Inflammation of the Eustachian Tube and Middle Ear," was delivered before the International Medical Congress, in 1876. In 1884, his *alma mater*, Dickinson College, at its one hundred and first annual commencement, conferred upon him the degree of Doctor of Laws, in recognition of his valuable services in medical and surgical science.

 iii. Georgianna, b. May 22, 1838; d. June 18, 1846.
 iv. William-Henry-Harrison, b. October 16, 1840; d. March 16, 1841.
 v. Robert-Henry, b. July 30, 1843; d. December 8, 1848.
 vi. Sarah-Williamson, b. May 10, 1848; d. August 19, 1859.

XXVI. ARAMANDA EGLE,[5] (William-Henry,[4] William,[3] Caspar,[2] Marcus,[1]) b. April 15, 1842, at Groveland, N. Y.; m. December 20, 1865, near Newtown, Bucks county, Pa., by Rev. J. M. Milliken, CHARLES VANARTSDALE CRAVEN, b. March 16, 1837, at Hatboro', Pa., son of John Craven and Elizabeth Hart; reside near Newtown, Bucks county, Pa. They had issue (surname Craven):

 i. John-Burroughs, b. November 7, 1866.
 ii. Frank-Bennett, b. July 26, 1869.
 iii. George-Washington, b. October 7, 1873.
 iv. Bessie-Wynkoop, b. December 9, 1875.

XXVII. ALBURTIS EGLE,[5] (William-Henry,[4] William,[3] Caspar,[2] Marcus,[1]) b. March 31, 1843, at Groveland, N. Y.; m. November 25, 1868, at Addisville, Bucks county, Pa., by Reverend Hugh L. Craven, LYDIA McNAIR, b. March 3, 1847, at Addisville, Bucks county, Pa., dau. of James S. McNair and Eliza Crull; reside near Newtown, Pa. They had issue:

 i. James-McNair, b. December 23, 1870; d. August 6, 1871.
 ii. Charles-Wilson, b. May 27, 1872.
 iii. George-Newman, b. December 6, 1875.
 iv. Rosannah, b. May 12, 1879.
 v. Alice-Vanartsdale, b. October 23, 1883.

The Family of Egle. 183

XXIII. GEORGE ADAM EGLE,[5] (George,[4] George,[3] Adam,[2] Marcus,[1]) b. December 25, 1815, in Cabarras county, N. C.; resides in Iredell county, N. C.; m. in 1834, in Cabarras county, N. C., NANCY SHANDY, b. February 5, 1814, in Davidson county, N. C., dau. of Sidney Shandy and Harriet Grouf. They had issue:

 i. *Daniel-Alexander*, b. May 31, 1835; d. 1863; m. June 19, 1859, Martha M. Weems, of Mo., and had *Sterling-Price*, and *Nancy-Virginia*.

 ii. *Peyton-Wesley*, b. January 14, 1838; m. August 15, 1867, Caroline Lazenby, and had *George-Adam*, and *Jane*; reside in Iredell county, N. C.

 iii. *Julia-A.*, b. October 4, 1839; d. October 16, 1859.

 iv. *Edwin-D.*, b. May 17, 1842; d. November 17, 1844.

 v. *Lydia-Ludemia*, b. February 26, 1844; m. D. L. Dry, and had issue (surname Dry): *Leroy Whitfield*, *William-Alfred*, *John-Wesley*, *Henry-Lueco*, *Fanny-Julia*, *Viola-Eveoxia*, *Linny-Clara*, and *Nannie Elizabeth*; reside in Iredell county, N. C.

 vi. *William-Sidney*, b. April 24, 1846; m. March 12, 1867, Mary Elizabeth Barnsley, and had *William-Barnsley*, *Sarah-Elizabeth*, *George*, and *Zebulon-Vance*; reside in Iredell county, N. C.

 vii. *Nancy-Jane*, b. August 2, 1848; d. April 26, 1877; m. August 24, 1863, Thomas Melmoth Beard, and had issue (surname Beard): *Mary-Etta*, *Washington-Henry*, *John-Franklin*, and *James-Albert*.

 viii. *George Washington*, b. September 13, 1850; resides in Ellis county, Texas.

 ix *Harriet-Josephine*, b. October 21, 1852; m. July 26, 1871, Joseph Stanhope Martin, and had issue (surname Martin): *George-Alexander*, *Charles-Leroy*, *William-Theophilus*, and *Lilly* and *Julia* (twins); reside in Iredell county, N. C.

 x. *John-Franklin-C.*, b. November 18, 1854; resides in Iredell county, N. C.

 xi. *James-Albert*, b. February 21, 1857; resides in Ellis county, Texas.

 xii. *Wilburn-W.*, b. March 5, 1879; d. October 14, 1859.

XXIX. JAMES EGLE,[5] (Joseph,[4] Philip,[3] Adam,[2] Marcus,[1]) b. March 24, 1813, in Rowan county, N. C.; d. October 3, 1863, in Austin, Texas. He removed to Maury county, Tenn., in 1829, and in 1839 to Pulaski county, Ark. He m. in 1834

184   *Pennsylvania Genealogies.*

CHARITY SWAIM, d. June 6, 1881, in Lonoke county, Ark. They had issue :

i. *William-H.*, b. May 5, 1835, in Maury county, Tenn.; is one of the wealthiest merchants and planters in his county; represented Lonoke county in the State Legislature of 1893 and 1895 ; m. in February 1858, Malinda A. Robinson ; d. 1882 ; and had issue :
   1. *James*, b. February, 1859 ; d. September, 1872.
   2. *Rosannah*, b. July 14, 1861 ; m. Pat. H. Wheat ; and had issue.
   3. *Joseph-P.*, b. September 27, 1862 ; m. Minnie Sanders, and had issue.
   4. *Madela-M.*, b. August 4, 1864 ; m. Robert Dougherty, and had issue.
   5. *Robert-E.-Lee*, b. April 2, 1866.
   6. *Mary-U.*, b. September 8, 1868 ; d. inf.
   7. *Laura-V.*, b. April 28, 1870 ; d. July 15, 1888.
   8. *William-R.*, b. September 25, 1872 ; d. May 25, 1873.
   9. *George-R.*, b. January 8, 1876 ; d. October 13, 1889.
   10. *Pat.*, b. July 17, 1878.
   11. *Charley*, b. July 21, 1880 ; d. October 15, 1880.
   12. *Lynn-K.*, b. February 9, 1882.
William H. Egle m., secondly, October 29, 1884, Ada Monroe, of Lonoke county, Ark., and had issue :
   13. *Bessie*, b. October 29, 1885.
   14. *Mamie*, b. July 8, 1887 ; d. September 18, 1891.
   15. *Lillian*, b. November 28, 1889.
   16. *W.-H.*

ii. *James-P.*, b. August 10, 1837, in Maury county, Tenn.; in 1839 went with his father to Pulaski county, Ark. At the outbreak of the Civil War in 1861 he enlisted in the Fifth Arkansas regiment in the State service, but shortly after was transferred to the Second Arkansas mounted rifleman, C. S. A. In the autumn following he was elected second lieutenant and in the spring of 1862 captain of his company. In 1863 he was promoted to major of the regiment. By direction of the Confederate Congress, early in 1865, Reynolds' brigade of Arkansas troops to which his command was attached, was consolidated into one regiment, the First regiment of Arkansas mounted riflemen, dismounted, of which he was commissioned lieutenant colonel. He participated in the battles of Hominy Creek, Elk Horn, Farmersville, Richmond, Ky., Murfreesboro', Chickamauga, Dug Gap, and in all the conflicts from Dalton to and including Peach Tree Creek in front of Atlanta, where he was wounded. He was also in the battles of Franklin, Nashville and Bentonsville, N. C., and many others of less importance. He was made a prisoner at the battle of Murfreesboro', and for several months was in Camp Chase and Fort Delaware prisons. On his return to Arkansas in 1865 he found his home had been broken up by the ravages of war: but with his indomitable energy built himself a cabin, and in a few years found himself comfortably fixed, and prominent among the successful farmers of Arkansas. In 1870 he was ordained to the ministry by the Missionary Baptist church, and for fourteen years was president of the Arkansas Baptist State convention and chairman of its Executive Board. In 1872 Col. Eagle was elected to the State Legislature, and in the called session of 1874 was chosen by that body a member of the board to adjust the claims growing out of the Brooks-Baxter war. He was a member of the convention which framed the present constitution of Arkansas, and represented his county in the Legislature in 1877 and 1885, in the last session being chosen speaker. In 1888 he was nominated for Governor and elected by a good majority; and in 1890 renominated and elected for the second term. Governor Eagle resides at Little Rock. He m. January 3, 1882, Mary Kavanaugh Oldham, of Madison county, Kentucky.

 iii. *Rosannah*, b. March 10, 1840; d. 1880; m. first, in 1859, James A. Winfred; and had issue (surname Winfred): *Booker*, and *Louisa*; m. secondly, in 1868, E. E. Sullivan, and had issue (surname Sullivan): *Annie*; m. thirdly, 1877, G. B. Long, and had issue (surname Long), *Robert*, and *Joseph*.

 iv. *Joseph*, b. March 15, 1843; k. in battle of Murfreesboro, Tenn., C. S. A.

 v. *George-L*., b. January 1, 1845; d. August, 1848.

 vi. *Robert-J*., b. July 17, 1847; d. September, 1874, in Lonoke county, Ark.; m. first, Victoria Robinson; m. secondly, Sou Fletcher; no children

 vii. *Mary-J*., b. April 12, 1850; m. William Jones, and had issue, among others, (surname Jones): *Jacob-B.*, *William-H.*, *Rosannah*, and *Charity-P*.

 viii. *Martha-A*., b. March 15, 1852; m. first, in 1868, S. A. Young; d. 1879, s. p.; m. secondly, T. S. Boyd, and had issue (surname Boyd):

  1. *Robert-S*., b. July 16, 1873.

2. *Charity-Prudence*, (twin) b. July 16, 1773.
3. *William*, b. November 18, 1875.
4. *James-P.*, b. December 3, 1882 ; d. inf.
5. *Mattie-L.*, b. August 18, 1886.
6. *Sallie-F.*, b. December 31, 1888.
7. *Eagle*, b. September 26, 1892.

ix. *John*, b. January 11, 1854 ; d. March, 1856.
x. *Sallie-A.*, b. November 30, 1857 ; m. in 1878, Allen J. Mewer; resides in Lonoke county, Ark.

ELDER OF PAXTANG.

I. ROBERT ELDER,[1] b. about 1679 in Scotland, emigrated from Lough Neagh, county Antrim, Ireland, where he had previously settled, to America about 1730, locating in Paxtang township, then Lancaster, now Dauphin county, Pa., on a tract of land near the first ridge of the Kittochtinny mountains, five miles north of Harrisburg. He died the 28th of July, 1746, in Paxtang, and is buried in the old church graveyard. He married, in 1703, ELEANOR ———, b. in 1684; d. October 25, 1742. They had issue:

- 2.   i. *Robert*, b. 1704 ; m. and had issue.
- 3.   ii. *John*, b. January 26, 1706; m. 1st, Mary Baker ; 2d, Mary Simpson.
- 4.   iii. *Thomas*, b. 1708 ; m. Mary Patterson, dau. of William Patterson, of Paxtang.
- 5.   iv. *David*, b. 1710 ; m. Hannah Anderson.
-     v. *James*, b. 1712 ; settled in Fannett township, Cumberland (now Franklin) county, Pa.
-     vi. *Ann*, b. 1713 ; m. [John] Anderson, of Octoraro. We have no further information of this the perchance only sister of Reverend John Elder.

II. ROBERT ELDER,[2] (Robert,[1]) b. in 1704, in Scotland ; m. and had issue :

-     i. *John*, b. 1730; d. December, 1756, in Hanover, probably unm.
- 6.   ii. *Robert*, b. 1732 ; m. Mary Taylor.
- 7.   iii. *Samuel*, b. 1734 ; m. Mary Robinson.
-     iv. *Isabel*, b. 1736 ; m. Adam Breaden, concerning whom we have no record.
-     v. *David*, b. 1738 ; m. and removed, late in life, to Ohio, where he died. He had, among other children, *Joshua* and *Robert*.
-     vi. *Elizabeth*, b. 1740.

III. JOHN ELDER,[2] (Robert,[1]) b. January 26, 1706, in the city of Edinburgh, Scotland ; d. July 17, 1792, in Paxtang township, Dauphin county, Pa. He received a classical education, and graduated from the University at Edinburgh. He subsequently studied divinity, and in 1732, was licensed to preach the gospel. Four or five years later, the son followed the footsteps of his parents and friends, and came to America. Coming as a regularly licensed minister, he was received by New Castle Presbytery, having brought credentials to that body, afterward to Donegal Presbytery, on the 5th of October, 1737. Paxtang congregation having separated from that of Derry in 1735, and Rev. Mr. Bertram adhering to the latter, left that of Paxtang vacant, and they were unanimous in giving Rev. John Elder a call. This he accepted on the 12th of April, 1738, and on the 22d of November following he was ordained and installed, the Rev. Samuel Black presiding. The early years of Mr. Elder's ministry were not those of ease; for in the second year the Whitfield excitement took a wide spread over the Presbyterian Church. He preached against this religious *furore*, or the "great revival," as it was termed, and for this he was accused to the Presbytery of propagating "false doctrine." That body cleared him, however, in December, 1740; "but a separation was made," says Webster, "and the conjunct Presbyters answered the supplications sent to them the next summer, by sending Campbell and Rowland to those who forsook him. He signed the protest. His support being reduced, he took charge of the 'Old Side' portion of the Derry congregation." Following closely upon these ecclesiastical troubles came the French and Indian war. Associations were formed throughout the Province of Pennsylvania for the defense of the frontiers, and the congregations of Mr. Elder were prompt to embody themselves. Their minister became their leader—their captain—and they were trained as scouts. He superintended the discipline of his men, and his mounted rangers became widely known as the "Paxtang Boys." During two summers, at least, every man who attended Paxtang church carried his rifle with him, and their minister took his. Subsequently, he was advanced to the dignity of colonel by the Provincial authorities, the date of his commission being July 11, 1763. He had command of the block-houses and stockades from Easton to the Susquehanna. The Governor, in tendering this appointment, expressly stated that nothing more would be expected of him than the general oversight. "His justification," says Webster, "lies in the crisis of affairs . . . Bay at York, Steele at Conecocheague, and Griffith at New Castle, with Burton and Thompson, the church missionaries, at Carlisle, headed companies, and were actively engaged." During the latter part of the summer of 1763, many murders were committed in Paxtang, culminating in the destruction of the Indians on Conestoga Manor and at Lancaster. Although the men composing the company of Paxtang men who exterminated the murderous savages referred to belonged to his obedient and faithful rangers, it has never been proved that the Rev. Mr. Elder had previous knowledge of the plot formed, although the Quaker pamphleteers of the day charged him with aiding and abetting the destruction of the Indians. When the deed was done, and the Quaker authorities were determined to proceed to extreme lengths with the participants, and denounced the frontiersmen as "riotous and murderous Irish Presbyterians," he took sides with the border inhabitants, and sought to condone the deed. His letters published in connection with the history of that transaction prove him to have been a man judicious, firm and decided. During the controversy which ensued, he was the author of one of the pamphlets: "Letter from a Gentleman in one of the Black Counties to a Friend in Philadelphia." He was relieved from his command by the Governor of the Province, who directed that Major Asher Clayton take charge of the military establishment. Peace, however, was restored —not only in civil affairs, but in the church. The union of the synods brought the Rev. John Elder into the same Presbytery with Messrs. John Roan, Robert Smith, and George Duffield, they being at first in a minority, but rapidly settling the vacancies with New Side men. By the leave of synod, the Rev. Mr. Elder joined the Second Philadelphia Presbytery May 19, 1768, and on the formation of the General Assembly, became a member of Carlisle Presbytery. At the time the British army overran New Jersey, driving before them the fragments of our discouraged, naked, and half-starved troops, and without any previous arrangement, the Rev. Mr. Elder went on Sunday, as usual, to Paxtang church. The hour arrived for church-service, when, instead of a sermon, he began a short and hasty prayer to the Throne of Grace; then called upon the patriotism of all effective men present, and exhorted them to aid in support of liberty's cause and the defense of the country. In less than thirty minutes a company of volunteers was formed. Colonel Robert Elder, the parson's eldest son, was chosen captain. They marched next day, though in winter. His son John, at sixteen years, was among the first. His son Joshua, sub-lieutenant of Lancaster county, could not quit the service he was employed in, but sent a substitute. Until his death, for a period of fifty-six years, he continued the faithful minister of the congregations over which he had been placed in the prime of his youthful vigor, passing the age not generally allotted to man—that of fourscore and six years. His death was deeply lamented far and wide. Not one of all those who had welcomed him to his early field of labor survived him. Charles Miner, the historian of Wyoming, gives this opinion of Rev. John Elder: "I am greatly struck with the evidences of learning, talent, and spirit displayed by him. He was, beyond doubt, *the most* extraordinary man of Eastern Pennsylvania. I hope some one may draw up a full memoir of his life, and a narrative, well digested, of his times . . . He was a very extraordinary man, of most extensive influence, full of activity and enterprise, learned, pious, and a ready writer. I take him to have been of the old Cameronian blood. Had his lot been cast in New England, he would have been a leader of the Puritans." He had, with one who well remembered the old minister, "a good and very handsome face. His features were regular—no one prominent—good complexion, with blue eyes . . . He was a portly, long, straight man, over six feet in height, large frame and body, with rather heavy legs . . He did not talk broad Scotch, but spoke much as we do now, yet grammatically." His remains quietly repose amid the scenes of his earthly labors, in the burying-ground of old Paxtang church, by the side of those who loved and revered him. Over his dust a marble slab bears the inscription dictated by his friend and neighbor, William Maclay, first

Elder of Paxtang. 191

United States Senator from Pennsylvania. The Rev. Mr. Elder was twice married; m., first, in 1740, MARY BAKER, b. 1715, in county Antrim, Ireland; d. June 12, 1749, in Paxtang; dau. of Joshua Baker, of Lancaster, Pa. They had issue :

8.   *i. Robert*, b. Friday, June 11, 1742; m. Mary J. Thompson.
9.   *ii. Joshua*, b. March 9, 1744-5; m., 1st, Mary McAllister; 2d, Sarah McAllister.
    iii. Eleanor, b. December 3, 1749; m. John Hays.
    iv. Grizel, b. May 2, 1749; d. September 18, 1769.

Mr. Elder m., secondly, November 5, 1751, MARY SIMPSON, dau. of Thomas and Sarah Simpson, of Paxtang; b. 1732, in Paxtang; d. October 3, 1786, at 6 a. m., and had issue :

    v. Sarah, b. October 19, 1752; d. February 14, 1822; m. James Wallace, (*see Robert Wallace record*).
10. *vi. Ann*, b. October 8, 1754; m. Andrew Stephen.
11. *vii. John*, b. August 3, 1757; m. Elizabeth Awl.
    viii. Mary, b. January 12, 1760; m. James Wilson, (*see Wilson record*).
    ix. Jane, b. May 21, 1762; d. August 6, 1763.
12. *x. James*, b. Friday June 15, 1764; m. Lucinda Wallace.
13. *xi. Thomas*, b. January 30, 1767; m., 1st, Catharine Cox; 2d, Elizabeth Shippen Jones.
14. *xii. David*, b. May 7, 1769; m. Jane Galbraith.
15. *xiii. Samuel*, b. February 27, 1772; m. Margaret Espy.
16. *xiv. Michael*, b. Aug 9, 1773 : m. Nancy NcKinney.
    xv. Rebecca, b. March 1, 1775; m. James Awl, (*see Awl record*).

IV. THOMAS ELDER,[2] (Robert,[1]) b. 1708; d. July, 1752; m. MARY PATTERSON, dau. of William Patterson. They had issue :

    i. John.
    ii. Rachel.
    iii. Robert.

V. DAVID ELDER,[2] (Robert,[1]) b. 1710; d. 1753; m. in 1730, HANNAH ANDERSON, of Donegal; d. about 1811, in Westmoreland county. They had issue :

17. *i. Robert*, b. 1751; m. Mary Whiteside,

VI. ROBERT ELDER,[3] (Robert,[2] Robert,[1]) b. 1734, in Hanover township, then Lancaster county, Pa.; was twice married. His first wife's name was COLE, and they had one son,

Joseph. After his death he removed to Maryland, afterwards returning to his old home near Harris' Ferry. About 1786, he went to Indiana county, Pa., where he died in 1790. His second wife was MARY TAYLOR, who d. April 15, 1813. They had issue :

18. i. *James,* b. 1763, in Penn'a ; m. Martha Robinson.
19. ii. *David,* b. October 16, 1764, in Maryland ; m. Ann Nesbit.
20. iii. *Robert,* b. 1767 : m. Mary Smith.
21. iv. *Anne,* b. 1770 ; m. Archibald Marshall.

VII. SAMUEL ELDER,[3] (Robert,[2] Robert,[1]) b. about 1734 ; removed to Maryland prior to the Revolution, where he died ; m. MARY ROBINSON, of Hanover township, Lancaster, (now Dauphin) county, Pa. They had issue :

    i. *Samuel,* b. 1758 ; m. Mary―――, b. 1759 ; d. October 21, 1830, and had issue :
        1. *Joseph-Robinson,* b. 1801 ; d. November 16, 1825.
        2. *Samuel,* accidentally drowned, s. p.
    ii. *John,* d. prior to 1823 ; m. Esther McKinley, b. 1763 ; d. July 24, 1823, and had issue :
        1. *John,* b. March 25, 1784.
        2. *Mary,* b. March 29, 1785 ; d. April 10, 1857 ; m. James Harwood, and had issue (surname Harwood): *James, Mary,* d. s. p.; *Margaret,* d. s. p., and *Henry.*
        3. *James,* b. March 26, 1787, d. s. p.
        4. *Margaret,* b. August 9, 1789 ; m. Henry White, of Baltimore, and had (surname White): *William,* b. 1815.
        5. *John,* (first,) b. September 19, 1792,
        6. *McKinley,* b. October 21, 1791.
        7. *Stephen,* b. April 11, 1794.
        8. *Samuel,* b. November 9, 1795 ; d. March 8, 1866 ; unm.; a flour merchant in Baltimore, Md.
        9. *Elizabeth,* b. January 14, 1798.
        10. *James,* b. July 26, 1802 ; d. November, 1860 ; m. August 8, 1848, Deborah D. Keene, of Nashua, N. H., and had issue, *Samuel-J.,* counsellor-at-law, Boston, Mass.
        11. *John* (second), b. July 30, 1804.

VIII. ROBERT ELDER,[3] (John,[2] Robert,[1]) was b. June 11, 1742, in Paxtang ; d. September 29, 1818. He was educated at the academy in Chester county, and was destined by his father for the ministry. His inclinations, and the breaking out of the French and Indian war, when the boy enlisted with his father as a ranger on the frontiers, determined otherwise. With his Scotch-Irish neighbors, he entered heartily into the contest for independence, and throughout the war of the Revolution was in the field or engaged in organizing the associators, of which he was colonel, succeeding Colonel Burd in the command of the companies raised in Paxtang. At the close of the conflict, he continued his occupation of farming, avoiding public office, preferring the quiet of domestic life. Colonel Elder m. MARY J. THOMPSON, of Derry; b. October 19, 1750; d. August 18, 1813. They left issue.

IX. JOSHUA ELDER,[3] (John,[2] Robert,[1]) b. March 9, 1744–5, in Paxtang township, then Lancaster county, Pa.; d. December 5, 1820, and is interred in Paxtang church graveyard. He was a farmer by occupation ; served in the Provincial forces during the French and Indian war; one of the sub-lieutenants of the county of Lancaster during the Revolution, and a justice of the peace. Under the Constitution of 1790, he was appointed, by Governor Mifflin, one of the associate judges of the county of Dauphin. Governor McKean, a warm personal friend, commissioned him prothonotary January 5, 1800, which position he filled nine years ; was afterwards chosen chief burgess of the borough of Harrisburg, in 1810. Joshua Elder was twice married; m., first, September 15, 1773, by the Rev. John Elder, MARY MCALLISTER, b. 1753 ; d. November 21, 1782 ; m., secondly, on May 23, 1783, by the Rev. John Elder, SARAH MCALLISTER, b. 1762; d. December 6, 1807. By neither marriage did Judge Elder leave any issue, and his estate was devised to a large number of relatives.

X. ANN ELDER,[3] (John,[2] Robert,[1]) b. October 8, 1754 ; d. August 10, 1814; m. September 23, 1779, by Rev. John Elder, ANDREW STEPHEN [Steen], b. 1753; d. December 3, 1800; both bur. in Paxtang graveyard. They had issue (surname Stephen):

    i. Robert-Elder.
    ii. Ann, b. 1785 ; d. April 20, 1800; bur. in Paxtang graveyard.

iii. Andrew, b. May 30, 1791; d. January 12, 1832 ; bur. in Paxtang Church graveyard.
iv. John, a physician, who practiced near Halifax, Pa.

XI. JOHN ELDER,³ (John,² Robert,¹) b. August 3, 1757 ;
d. April 27, 1811, in Paxtang. He was educated under Joseph
Hutchinson, a celebrated teacher in his day, and gave special
attention to land-surveying. He was a farmer. At the commencement of the Revolution, although a youth of eighteen,
he was enrolled among the associators, and was an ensign in
Colonel Burd's battalion. On the 18th of April, 1780, he was
appointed deputy surveyor, and for several years filled that
position. He was elected sheriff of the county of Dauphin in
1794, serving from the 19th of November, that year, until October 17, 1787. Like the majority of persons who have filled
that responsible office in this locality, he came out of it the
poorer. Captain Elder m. December 16, 1778, ELIZABETH
AWL, b. November 18, 1781 ; d. about 1850, at the residence
of her son-in-law, General John Forster. They had issue:

i. Mary, b. 1779 ; m. John Forster, (see *Forster record*.)
ii. Jacob, b. 1783 ; d October, 1816 ; received a thorough English and classical education, learned the art of printing
at Lancaster, and in 1802, commenced the publication
of the *Dauphin Guardian*, one of the most influential
newspapers published in the early days of Harrisburg,
as it was the first Democratic English newspaper there.
In 1815, he prepared and published "A History of the
Late War," and was the author of a preliminary work
on the history of the United States. Under his arduous
literary labors, Mr. Elder's health failed him, and he
died at the early age of thirty-three years. He never
married. His entire life was an active and busy one,
and he exerted a great influence in the times he lived.
iii. John, m. October 17, 1826, Mrs. Mary Thompson, dau. of
John McCammon, of Middletown.
iv. Robert.
v. Joshua.
vi. Sally-Ann.
vii. Eliza-Awl, m. Henry Alward.

XII. JAMES ELDER,³ (John,² Robert,¹) b. June 15, 1764 ;
d. January 14, 1827 ; m. December, 1801, LUCINDA WALLACE,
of Virginia ; b. May 28, 1781 ; d. July 26, 1826 ; removed to

Clarkesville, Tenn. After the death of James Elder, his widow m., in February, 1829, James B. Reynolds, of Tennessee. They had issue :

 i. *Joshua*, b. January 31, 1803 ; m. and left issue.

XIII. THOMAS ELDER.³ (John,² Robert,¹) b. January 30, 1767 ; d. April 29, 1853, in Harrisburg, Pa. He received a good English and classical education, especially under Joseph Hutchinson, a celebrated teacher in his day. He subsequently attended the academy at Philadelphia, where he graduated. Studied law with General John A. Hanna, and was admitted to the Dauphin county bar at the August term, 1791. He at once began the practice of a profession in which he became distinguished, and which he followed with great success for upward of forty years, and "was eminent as a safe and sagacious counselor, a laborious and indefatigable lawyer." During the Whiskey Insurrection, he volunteered as a private in Captain Dentzel's company, which marched westward, preferring the ranks to that of a commissioned office, which his company offered him. He subsequently held the office of lieutenant colonel of the militia, and was frequently designated by the title of colonel. As a citizen in the early years of the borough of Harrisburg, Mr. Elder possessed public spirit and enterprise in advance of his contemporaries generally. He was the prominent and leading spirit in organizing a company to erect the Harrisburg bridge, the first constructed over the Susquehanna, and for many years the longest in the Union. Upon the permanent organization, he was unanimously elected the president, which office he held by annual re-election of the directors, until his resignation in June, 1846. He was chosen president of the Harrisburg Bank in June, 1816, which office he held until his death. Governor Hiester appointed him Attorney General of the Commonwealth, a position he filled with marked ability from December 20, 1820, to December 18, 1823, but he ever after positively refused to accept office, although he took deep and active interest for many years in the political affairs of the State and Nation. He was blessed with a physical constitution which enabled him to accomplish an extraordinary amount of labor without diminishing the elasticity of his spirits or the vigor of his mind. He lived to the advanced age of over eighty-six years. Mr. Elder was twice married ; m., first, March 23, 1799, CATHARINE COX, d. June 12, 1810 ; dau. of Colonel Cornelius Cox, of Estherton, Pa. They had issue :

 i. George-Washington, d. s. p.

 ii. Mary-R., m. June 13, 1816, Amos Ellmaker, b. February 2, 1787, in New Holland, Lancaster county, Pa.; d. November 18, 1851, in Lancaster, Pa ; son of Nathaniel Ellmaker. He graduated at Yale College, and after completing his law studies at the celebrated law school under Judge Reeves, at Litchfield, Conn., he came to Harrisburg, and continued his studies under Thomas Elder, and was subsequently admitted to the bar at the December term, 1808. He was commissioned deputy attorney general for the county of Dauphin, January 13, 1809, serving until 1812, and represented Dauphin county in the Legislature from 1812 to 1814. He was appointed, by Governor Snyder, president judge of that judicial district, July 3, 1815. In 1814, he accompanied the volunteers to Baltimore, as an aid to General Forster. On the 30th of December, 1816, he resigned to accept the position of Attorney General of the State, serving to 1819. In June, 1821, he removed to Lancaster, resuming the practice of his profession. He was the anti-Masonic candidate for Vice-President of the United States in 1832. "Mr. Ellmaker," says Mr. Harris, in his "Reminiscences," "was reported to be a good lawyer, and his addresses to the jury, when at the bar, were clear, distinct, and argumentative." As a gentleman, he possessed, in an eminent degree, those characteristics which distinguish men of rare endowment. He was well-informed, and of a lively social disposition, and in all the relations and positions of life was a model worthy of imitation. They had issue (surname Ellmaker) :

  1. *Nathaniel*, a lawyer at Lancaster, Pa.; m. October 1, 1844, Cecilia M. Hager.

  2. *Franklin*, d. s. p.

  3. *Catharine-Cox*, d. s. p.

  4. *Elizabeth-Elder*, d. s. p.

  5. *Thomas*, resides at Lancaster, Pa.

  6. *Levi*, m. January 13, 1859, Elizabeth Carson, and had *Mary-Elder*, d. s. p.; *Elizabeth-Elder, Susan-Carson*, and *Amos*, d. s. p.

Elder of Paxtang. 197

Thomas Elder m., secondly, May 30, 1813, ELIZABETH SHIPPEN JONES, b. December 13, 1787, in Burlington, N. J.; d. October 31, 1871, in Harrisburg, Pa.; dau. of Robert Strettell Jones and Ann Shippen. They had issue:

    iii. Ann-Shippen, b. October 19, 1814; d. March 5, 1818.
    iv. Catharine-Jones, b. July 20, 1816; m. Samuel Bethel Boude, b. January 1, 1806; d. June 26, 1880; son of Captain Thomas Boude of the Revolution; and had issue (surname Boude.)
        1. *Elizabeth-Shippen*, b. September 8, 1836; m. Jasper Green.
        2. *Emily-Alice*, b. December 23, 1838.
        3. *Helen-Mary*, b. August 10, 1843; m. Edward Hudson Worrall.
        4. *Thomas-Elder*, b. January 24, 1847; d. Feb. 29, 1852.
        5. *Charles-Henry*, b. June 22, 1849; d. May 20, 1893; accidentally killed; m. Eleanor P. Beatty, and had issue:
            a. Mary-Scott-Clendenin, b. January 20, 1873.
            b. Philip-Bethel, b. October 16, 1875.
        6. *Samuel-Bethel*, b. November 22, 1854.
22. *v. Thomas*, b. June 28, 1818; m Margaretta Wilson.
    vi. John, b. May 27, 1820; d. April 27, 1867, near Atlanta, Ga.
    vii. Sarah-Wallace, b. January 13, 1822; d. December 19, 1832.
    viii. Elizabeth-Shippen, b. October 6, 1824; d. Dec. 19, 1832.
23. *ix. James-Shippen*, b. April 29, 1826; m. Mary Carpenter.

XIV. DAVID ELDER,[3] (John,[2] Robert,[1]) b. May 7, 1769, in Paxtang; d. May 22, 1809; m. JEAN GALBRAITH, b. 1772; d. January 13, 1842; dau. of Colonel Bertram Galbraith, (*see Galbraith record*). They had issue:

    i. Mary, m., 1st, Doctor Henry B. Dorrance, d. October 1, 1828, and bur. at Paxtang; m., 2d, Judge David Scott, of Wilks-Barre, Pa.
    ii. Ann, d. unm.
    iii. Elizabeth-Galbraith, b. March 17, 1806; m. Robert R. Elder. (*see Elder record*, xxx.)
    iv. Robert, b. 1806; d. 1854; m. in 1830 Hannah Deitrick, and had issue:
        1. *Mary-Simpson*, b. 1832; d. 1871; m. in 1860 Walter G. Sterling; b. November 24, 1821, at Black Walnut, near Meshoppen, Pa.; d. April 12, 1889, at Wilkes-Barre, Pa. He was the son of Daniel and Rachel Sterling; in 1835 entered the office of George M. Hollenbach; in 1849 went to California

where he remained two years, returning to Wilkes-Barre; in connection with Mr. Hollenbach established a private bank; subsequently assisted in organizing the Second National bank and became its vice-president; was secretary and treasurer of the Wilkes-Barre Bridge company, and associated himself in every progressive movement which entered into the business of the city of Wilkes-Barre. They had issue (surname Sterling):

 a. *Mary-Scott*, b. 1861.
 b. *Emily*, b. 1862; d. in inf.
 c. *Florence*, b. 1864; d. in inf.
2. *Jane-Galbraith*, b. 1834; d. 1894; m. in 1867, John MacFarland, of Mount Joy, Pa.
3. *David*, b. 1838.
4. *Ann-Elizabeth*, b. 1843; m. in 1868, Samuel Bickle, of Millersburg, Pa.
5. *Robert*, b. 1851.
6. *Emma*. b. 1853; m. in 1872, Walter G. Sterling (named above), and had issue (surname Sterling)
 a. *Margaret*, b. 1873.
 b. *Walter-Carl*, b. 1876.
 c. *Knight*, b. 1877.
 d. *Paul*, b. 1879.
 e. *Leila*, b. 1881.

XV. SAMUEL ELDER,[3] (John,[2] Robert,[1]) b. February 27, 1772: d. September 26, 1815, in Harrisburg, Pa. He was educated at the schools of Joseph Hutchinson and Joseph Allen, and followed farming in his early years. He was a soldier in the expedition westward in 1794, and held a position in the military establishment of 1798. He filled the office of sheriff of Dauphin county from October 23, 1800, to October 21, 1803, which, as in the case of his brother John, financially crippled him. Mr. Elder died at Harrisburg on the 26th of September, 1815, aged forty-three years. In paying brief tributes to his memory, the newspapers of the day speak in the warmest terms of his faithfulness as a public officer, his prominence as a citizen, and the upright character of his entire life, passing away in the vigor of his manhood. Mr. Elder m., March 7, 1793, MARGARET ESPY, b. February 27, 1772; d. September 4, 1851; dau. of Josiah Espy and Anne Kirkpatrick. They had issue:

Elder of Paxtang. 199

24.   *i. Ann-Espy,* b. February 25, 1794 ; m. Alexander M. Piper.
25.   *ii. John,* b. 1796 ; m. Jane Henderson Ritchey.
26.   *iii. Mary-S.,* b. 1798 ; m., 1st, Adams Campbell; 2d, William Line.
       iv. Josiah, b. 1801 ; d. October 80, 1844.
27.   *v. Sarah-McAllister,* b. September 16, 1803 ; m. William H. Doll.

XVI. MICHAEL ELDER,³ (John,² Robert,¹) b. August 9, 1773 ; d. September 25, 1850, at Columbia, Pa.; was twice married ; m. first, June 4, 1795, NANCY MCKINNEY, of Middletown. They had issue :

   i. Myra, m. Christian Haldeman.
   ii. Preston-Billings, b. February 6, 1810; d. January 6, 1840, in Columbia; m. in 1834, Henrietta E. V. Claiborne ; was cashier of the Columbia Bank and Bridge company, at the same time editor of the *Spy;* was a brilliant writer of prose and verse, a volume of which was published after his death.

Michael Elder m., secondly, April 5, 1827, CHARLOTTE GIBERSON. They had issue :

   iii. William, d. s. p.

XVII. ROBERT ELDER,³ (David,² Robert,¹) b. in 1751, in Paxtang township; d. October, 1837, in Derry township, Westmoreland county, Penn'a. At the close of the War of the Revolution, Robert Elder accompanied his mother to Westmoreland county, where they settled, He had previously married MARY WHITESIDE, a daughter of Thomas Whiteside, an early English settler in Lancaster county, most of whose descendants reside in Ohio and Illinois. Mary Whiteside Elder d. in February, 1823. They had issue :

28.   *i. Hannah,* b. 1779 ; m. James Richards.
29.   *ii. Thomas,* b. 1781 ; m. Mary McConnell.

XVIII. JAMES ELDER,⁴ (Robert,³ Robert,² Robert,¹) b. 1763, in Dauphin county ; removed to Indiana county, Pa., in 1786, where he d. April 13, 1813 ; m. December 25, 1792, MARTHA ROBINSON, daughter of Robert Robinson, b. 1772 ; d. May 27, 1812. They had issue :

30.   *i. Robert R.,* b. October 8, 1793 ; m. Sarah Snerer.
31.   *ii. David,* b. August 22, 1795 ; m. Juliana Sherer.

32.   iii. *John*, b. October 2, 1797 ; m. Elizabeth McKee.
33.   iv. *Polly*, b. October 22, 1799 ; m. Samuel Russell.
34.   v. *Joshua*, b. January 18, 1802 ; m. Eleanor Sherer.
35.   vi. *James*, b. February 18, 1804 ; m. Margaret Barnett.
36.   vii. *Rachel*, b. December 18, 1806 ; m. Rev. Jesse Smith.
37.   viii. *Thomas*, b. March 1, 1810 ; m. Elizabeth Coleman.

XIX. DAVID ELDER,[4] (Robert,[3] Robert,[2] Robert,[1]) b. October 28, 1764, in Maryland ; d. January 8, 1834, in Fontaine county, Ind.; m., June 3, 1790, ANN NESBIT, b. December 27, 1771, in Lancaster county, Pa.; d. July 22, 1854, in Clark county, Ohio. They had issue :

38.   i. *Robert*, b. May 28, 1791 ; m. Elizabeth Sherer.
  ii. *Sarah*, b. May 23, 1793 ; d. July 16, 1835, in Ohio ; m. in 1816, Robert Johnson.
  iii. *Mary*, b. April 21, 1795 ; d. August 18, 1796.
  iv. *John-Nesbit*, b. March 23, 1797 ; resided in Fontaine county, Ind., in 1850.
  v. *Ann*, b. March 18, 1799 ; m. in 1820, Abram Brewer, and had issue.
  vi. *James*, b. July 7, 1800 ; d. December 9, 1837 ; m. in 1830, Susan Noble, and left issue.
  vii. *Polly-Taylor*, b. October 31, 1802 ; d. August 17, 1819.
  viii. *Nancy*, b. December 25, 1804 ; m. Robert Elder, son of Robert Elder and Ann Ingram.
  ix. *Joshua-David*, b. February 18, 1807 ; d. October 30, 1836, in Pittsburgh, Pa.; m. in 1825, Eliza Murray, who d. at Lewisburg, Pa., and had issue : *Glorvina*, m. James C. McClure, of Northumberland county, and *Andrew*.
39.   x. *Eliza-Moorhead*, b. February 14, 1809 ; m. Jacob Tice.
  xi. *Martha-Robinson*, b. May 19, 1811 ; m. James A. White ; reside in Vermillion county, Ind.

XX. ROBERT ELDER,[4] (Robert,[3] Robert,[2] Robert,[1]) b. 1767 ; d. April 12, 1813, at Elder's Ridge, Pa.; m. MARY SMITH ; d. December, 1857. They had issue :

  i. *Margaret*, b. 1796 ; d. June 7, 1837 ; m. in 1820, William Ewing, of Indiana county ; d. August 31, 1844 ; and had issue (surname Ewing): *John, Joshua, Robert*, Rev. *James-A.*, and *William*.
  ii. *Joshua*, b. 1798 ; d. November 11, 1825, unm., at Harrisburg, Pa.
  iii. *Mary*, [*Polly*,] b. 1800 ; m. John Laird ; and they had issue (surname Laird): *Zachariah, Maria, Judith, Margaret*, and *Robert-Elder*.

iv. Ann, b. 1802 ; d. 1816.
v. John, b. 1804 ; d. 1823.
vi. Hannah, b. 1807 ; d. 1832 ; unm.
vii. Robert, b. December 23, 1809 ; m. March 20, 1834, Nancy Douglass ; and they had issue :
1. *Maria-J.*, m. Rev. Thomas R. Elder.
2. *John-Douglass*, k. in the army in Tennessee.
3. *Robert-T.*
4. *Cordelia*, m. and had issue.
5. *Julia-M.*, m. and had issue.
6. *Lydia-A.*
7. *Josephine.*
8. *Agnes-V.*
9. *Lizzie-E.*

XXI. ANNIE ELDER,[4] (Robert,[3] Robert,[2] Robert,[1]) d. in Indiana county, Pa.; m. ARCHIBALD MARSHALL. They had issue (surname Marshall:

i. Anne, m. James Mowry.
ii. Polly, m. Alexander Templeton.

XXII. THOMAS ELDER,[4] (Thomas,[3] John,[2] Robert,[1]) b. June 28, 1818, in Harrisburg, Pa.; d. April 29, 1855, in Waverly, Mo.; m., May 7, 1850, MARGARETTA WILSON, daughter of Thomas Low Wilson and Julianna Margaretta Bender. They had issue :

i. Thomas, b. February 21, 1851 ; d. s. p.
ii. Wilson, b. January 13, 1853.

XXIII. JAMES-SHIPPEN ELDER,[4] (Thomas,[3] John,[2] Robert,[1]) b. April 29, 1824, in Harrisburg, Pa.; enlisted in the Cameron Guards in the war with Mexico ; appointed second lieutenant Eleventh infantry, July 24, 1847 ; disbanded August 17, 1848 ; at the breaking out of the Rebellion, appointed captain Eleventh infantry, May 14, 1861, remaining in the service until January 6, 1864. Captain Elder m. MARY CARPENTER, daughter of Israel and Catharine Carpenter. They had issue:

i. Robert-James, b. November 14, 1850 ; m. Annie Nesbit, d. April 3, 1872, s. p., dau. of William and Martha Nesbit.
ii. Thomas, b. February 18, 1852 ; d. July 1, 1852.
iii. William-Smedley, b. July 25, 1854 ; resides in Wellington, Mo.
iv. Joshua, b. March 23, 1857 ; m. Emma-Jane Schroover, and they had *James-Henry*, *Mary-Elizabeth*, and *John-Thomas*.

 v. Thomas-Brown, b. February 19, 1859; resides in Elderton, Mo.
 vi. John-James, b. March 4, 1861.
 vii. Charles-McIntire, b. June 18, 1866.

XXIV. ANN ESPY ELDER,⁴ (Samuel,³ John,² Robert,¹) b. February 25, 1794; d. June 3, 1886, in Carlisle, Pa.; m. in 1816, ALEXANDER M. PIPER, b. in 1786, in Bedford, Pa.; d. March 17, 1868, in Carlisle, Pa. They had issue, all born in Harrisburg, Pa., (surname Piper):

 i. John, b. 1817; d. 1825.
 ii. Samuel, b. 1819; d. 1843; m., 1842, Lucinda Wall, of Philadelphia, and left one daughter.
 iii. William, b. 1821; d. in infancy.
 iv. Margaret-Elder, b. 1823; m. May 1, 1845, Erkuries Beatty, b. May 6, 1817, in Columbia, Pa.; d. March 8, 1880, in Carlisle, Pa.; son of William Pitt Beatty, and grandson of Rev. Charles Beatty, the first Presbyterian missionary west of the Allegheny mountains; Erkuries learned the profession of printing and commenced the publication of the Columbia *Spy;* in 1843 removed to Carlisle, Pa., where, for a period of fourteen years, he conducted the *Herald* establishment; during the Rebellion he entered the volunteer service as second lieutenant in the Seventh regiment, Pennsylvania Reserves; appointed ordnance officer of McCall's division, participated in the seven days' battles on the Peninsula, in June, 1862, and was severely wounded at New Market × Roads; he subsequently re-entered the service, and mustered out with his regiment in June, 1864. Mr. and Mrs. Beatty had issue (surname Beatty):
  1. *William-Pitt,* b. February 18, 1846.
  2. *Alexander-Piper,* b. January 12, 1848.
  3. *Annie-Elder,* b. August 14, 1849; d. July 8, 1852.
  4. *Fannie,* b. October 13, 1852; d. in infancy.
  5. *Helen-Ansley,* b. December 15, 1853.
  6. *George,* b. December 30, 1855; d. January 2, 1856.
 v. William-Kirkpatrick, b. 1825.
 vi. Alexander, b. 1828; graduated from West Point; commissioned brevet second lieutenant, third artillery, July 1, 1851; second lieutenant, December 12, 1851; first lieutenant, January 31, 1855; appointed captain of the Eighteenth infantry, May 14, 1861, but declined, and commissioned captain Third artillery same day; for gallant and meritorious service during the campaign in

Northern Virginia, commissioned brevet major August 30, 1862; appointed colonel Tenth New York artillery, January 7, 1863; for gallant and meritorious service in the siege of Petersburg, Va., appointed brevet lieutenant colonel, June 15, 1864; mustered out of volunteer service, July 6, 1865; commissioned major Fourth artillery, December 20, 1875, and subsequently lieutenant colonel of First artillery. Colonel Piper m., in 1870, Adelaide Cozzens, of West Point, N. Y.

vii. *James-Wilson*, b. 1832; left civil life for the army upon the breaking out of the war for the Union, and continued in the service until his death, October 30, 1876, in consequence of wounds received in front of Richmond; m. in 1863, Sarah B. Ross, of Fort Hamilton, Long Island, and had *Alexander-R.*, second lieutenant U. S. A., and *Vandyke*.

viii. *Annie*, b. 1834; d. young.

ix. *Mary-Campbell*, b. 1836; d. 1875; m. John J. White, of Loudoun county, Va.; had three sons and two daughters, now living with their father at Atlanta, Ga.

x. *Annie-Elder*, b. September 23, 1842; m. May 19, 1863, Aglb Ricketts, b. October 12, 1834, at Rohrsburg, Columbia county, Pa., son of Elijah Green Ricketts, an early settler in the county; was educated at Wyoming Seminary, taught school several years, afterwards graduating from Dickinson College, Carlisle; then entered the law office of William G. Hurley, at Bloomsburg, admitted to the Columbia county bar in 1856, and on January 6, 1857, was admitted to the bar of Luzerne county, where he has been in continual practice since. They had issue (surname Ricketts):

1. *Miriam*, b. May 3, 1864; m. Harry Harkness Stoek.
2. *Alexander*, b. October 29, 1866; a lawyer at Wilkes-Barre.
3. *John*, b. November 18, 1870.
4. *Annie-Piper*, b. March 30, 1873.
5. *Margaretta-Beatty*, b. February 19, 1877.

XXV. JOHN ELDER,[4] (Samuel,[3] John,[2] Robert,[1]) b. September 2, 1796, in Dauphin county, Pa.; d. November 3, 1857, in Sacramento city, California; in 1833, removed to Indianapolis, Ind., where he followed his profession of architect successfully, being for many years the prominent one of Indiana. Evidences of his talent remain in many public buildings throughout the State; notably the Hospital for the Insane, at

Indianapolis; In 1850, he went to California, where he died of typhoid fever, at the age of sixty-one years. He m., March 2, 1820, near Harrisburg, Pa., by Rev. James R. Sharon, JANE HENDERSON RITCHEY, b. May 20, 1800, in Dauphin county, Pa.; she was a woman possessed of rare ease and grace of manner, and the honored center of her household; only daughter of John and Margaret Ritchey. John Ritchey was a prominent and wealthy member of the community in which he lived, honored and esteemed by all; Margaret, his wife, a cultured, refined woman, of strong christian character, was devoted throughout her life to the promotion of the cause of Christ. They had issue:

    i. John-Ritchey, b. December 7, 1820, in Dauphin county, Pa. At the time of his birth, there were present in the house three grandmothers, (Elder, Ritchey, and Ritchey No. 2,) and two great-grandfathers, (Espy and Ferguson,) showing he comes of a long-lived race. When he was thirteen years old, his parents removed to Indianapolis, where his boyhood was spent; was educated at Dickinson College, Carlisle, Pa., from whence he entered the publishing house of Robert Craighead, New York city; in 1848, returned to Indianapolis, and has since been identified with the public interests of that city; in 1849 became editor and publisher of *The Locomotive*, a popular weekly paper, which he conducted until 1860, when, with John H. Harkness, purchased the Indianapolis *Daily Sentinel*, which they published until 1866; he was for some years president of the Water Works Company, at the same time holding the honorable position of president of the Board of City Schools; later treasurer of the Indianapolis, Decatur and Springfield railroad. Since 1882 has been engaged in the construction of the Mississippi, Terre au Bœuf and Lake railroad of Louisiana, running into New Orleans, and is president of the road. Mr. Elder was twice married; m. first, December 19, 1848, at Indianapolis, Ind., by Rev. W. Myers, Julia Ann Ohr, who d. April 9, 1853, and had issue:

        1. *Henry-David*, b. December 31, 1850; d. March 6, 1853.

        2. *Julia-Ohr*, b. March 31, 1853; d. October 21, 1854.

    Mr. Elder m., secondly, October 19, 1854, by Rev. C. P. Wing, Amelia Ann Line, dau. of Judge William Line, of Carlisle, Pa.; and had issue:

Elder of Paxtang. 205

    3. *William-Line*, b. July 81, 1855.
    4. *Mary-Jane*, b. May 15, 1858.
    5. *John-Henry*, b. November 19, 1860 ; d. Aug. 16, 1861.
    6. *Edward-Clinton*, b. August 15, 1863.
ii. *Samuel-Piper*, b. October 25, 1822, near Harrisburg, Pa.; d. October 3, 1857, at Bradford, Iowa ; for a number of years was a dry goods merchant in Chicago, Ill.; m. in 1850, in Rockford, Ill., Helen Holmes, d. 1882, in Nashua, Iowa ; and had issue :

    1. *Jane-Henderson*, b. February 24, 1853, in Rockford, Ill.; m., at Bradford, Iowa, December 1, 1871, J. D. Knapp ; and had issue (surname Knapp) : *Willis-Adelbert*, b. September 1, 1872, at Nashua, Iowa.
    2. *Frances-Mary*, b. August 11, 1855, in Monroe, Wis.; m. October 23, 1879, at Nashua, Iowa, to La Fayette Lamberson ; and had issue (surname Lamberson): *Flora-Sarah*, b. November 17, 1880, at West Union, Iowa.

iii. *Margaretta*, b. October 25, 1824 ; d. August 15, 1825.
iv. *Alexander-James*, b. January 17, 1827, in Harrisburg, Pa.; in 1833 removed with his parents to Indianapolis, and was educated at the University in that city ; he entered the printing office of John D. Defrees, where he learned his trade ; in 1849 went to California, where he remained for fifteen years, with the exception of two years spent in Chili, South America ; while in California he spent a number of years in the mines, and for four years was State Printer at Sacramento ; returned to the East and engaged in the wholesale mercantile business in Chicago ; in 1872 removed to Boulder Valley, Montana, where he now resides, and occupies the position of Circuit Judge, and is prominently connected with school interests of the territory ; m., August 31, 1879, Rilla Preston ; no issue.
v. *David-Ritchey*, b. June 25, 1830, in Harrisburg, Pa.; d. March 19, 1850, of congestion of the brain, caused by over-exertion while preparing to enter the ministry.
vi. *Adaline*, b. March 16, 1834, in Indianapolis, Ind.; m. March 29, 1854, at Rockford, Ill., by Rev. Mr. Goodwin, John Addison Bradshaw, who was born near Staunton, Va., and removed with his parents to Indianapolis, where he has since resided ; no issue.
vii. *Ann-Mary*, b. July 10, 1836, at Indianapolis, Ind.; m. November 12, 1856, William Moore Guilford ; b. November 26, 1832, in Lebanon, Pa., son of Simeon Guilford

and Catharine E. Doll; received a classical education at the Lebanon Academy, and at the age of sixteen commenced the study of medicine with Professor Henry Childs, of Berkshire Medical College, Pittsfield, Mass.; in 1849 attended a course of lectures in that institution, and also the lectures of the College of Physicians and Surgeons of New York city; then returned to Lebanon, entered the office of Dr. John W. Gloninger as a student, subsequently attending two full courses of lectures in the Medical Department of the University of Pennsylvania, from which he graduated in April, 1852: the winter of 1852-3 he spent in the hospitals of Philadelphia, and in November of the latter year entered upon the practice of his profession at Lebanon, where he has continued to reside; for fifteen successive years was appointed by the directors of the poor physician to the county hospital, was one of the examining surgeons for the Ninety-third Regiment of Pennsylvania Volunteers before it was mustered into service during the late war, second lieutenant of the Lebanon county cavalry company during the emergency in 1863, and subsequently examining pension surgeon for the Government; was one of the directors of the Lebanon National Bank, one of the founders and directors of the Farmers' and Mechanics' Bank, and a director of the Lebanon Manufacturing Company; and their children living are (surname Guilford): *Jane-Ritchey*, *William-Moore*, *Paul*, *Adaline-Elder*, and *Arthur-Bryant*.

viii. *Thomas-Josiah*, b. November 25, 1838, at Indianapolis, Ind.; was a Union soldier in the Rebellion; shortly after the close of the war went to California, where he remained until his death, February 26, 1870, near Tuolumme City, Stanislaus county, in that State.

ix. *Margaretta-Sarah*, b. July 21, 1842, at Indianapolis, Ind.

XXVI. MARY S. ELDER,[4] (Samuel,[3] John,[2] Robert,[1]) b. 1798; d. April 17, 1882, at Carlisle, Pa.; was twice married; m., first, April 19, 1827, at Harrisburg, Pa., by Rev. William R. DeWitt, ADAMS CAMPBELL, d. January 25, 1840; buried in Donegal Church graveyard, Lancaster county, Pa. They had issue, (surname Campbell):

i. *William-Kirkpatrick*, b. March 17, 1828; m., 1874, Mrs. Rebecca Sordis, of Cumberland county, Pa.; no issue.

ii. *Samuel-Elder*, b. November 18, 1830; d. September 12, 1835.

iii. *Margaret-Myra-Elder*, b. January 15, 1833; m., May 31,

Elder of Paxtang. 207

1857, John W. Duvall, of Prince George county, Maryland; and they had issue (surname Duvall):
  1. *William-Benjamin*, b. May 29, 1859.
  2. *Anna-Mary*, b. February 6, 1861.
  3. *Martha-Rebecca*, b. November 12, 1862.
  4. *Margaret-Elder*, b. January 21, 1867.

iv. *Anna-Martha*, b. October 15, 1835; m , December 16, 1858, Samuel Coyle, d. August 23, 1879; no issue.

v. *Sarah-Jane*, b. August 19, 1838; d. March 22, 1841.

Mary S. Campbell, m., secondly, July 10, 1845, by Rev. T. V. Moore, William R. Line, of Carlisle, Pa.; no issue.

XXVII. SARAH McALLISTER ELDER,[4] (Samuel,[3] John,[2] Robert,[1]) b. September 16, 1803; d. May 26, 1895, at Harrisburg, Pa.; m., April 13, 1824, by Rev. William R. DeWitt, D. D., WILLIAM H. DOLL; b. 1796, in Harrisburg; d. August 16, 1852, in Harrisburg, Pa.; son of Joseph Doll, silversmith. They had issue, besides three children died in infancy, (surname Doll):

  i. *Samuel-Elder*, b. 1828; d. 1853, in Callao, Peru.
  ii. *Ann-Espy*, b. 1830; d. 1847.
  iii. *Esther-Mary*, b. 1832; m., 1862, James Martin Bradshaw, of Indianapolis, Ind.; was captain and acting quartermaster in the Rebellion; and had issue (surname Bradshaw):
    1. *Charles-Bailey*, b. January 28, 1864; d. December 12, 1866.
    2. *John-Edward*, b. December 2, 1869.
  iv. *Catharine-Elizabeth*, b. 1834; m., first, in 1858, John Whitehill Reily, d. March 20, 1860; eldest son of Dr. Luther Reily; and they had issue (surname Reily): *Rebecca-Elizabeth* and *John-Whitehill;* m., secondly, Dr. William Hall Harris, and had issue (surname Harris): *Sarah-Esther*, m. Lucius S. Bigelow.
  v. *Emma-Harriet*, b. 1836; m., in 1856, Charles Lukens Bailey, b. March 9, 1821, in Chester county, Pa.; son of Joseph Bailey and Martha Lukens. He obtained his early education at the Westtown school, Chester county. In 1838 he began to clerk for his father at Coatesville, where he became thoroughly conversant with the details of the iron business carried on at that place. He removed with his parents to Berks county, where he continued his clerkship for five years, and from 1849 to 1852 was a partner with his father in the Pine Iron

Works. In August of the latter year, Mr. Bailey removed to Harrisburg, Pa., and founded the old Central Iron Works. Here he continued business until 1859, when he became interested in the nail-works at Fairview, Cumberland county, rebuilt the works, and carried them on successfully until 1866, when he retired from the firm, and in connection with his brother, Dr. George Bailey, founded and erected the Chesapeake Nail-Works in Harrisburg, now carried on under the firm name of Charles L. Bailey & Co. In 1869, Mr. Bailey removed to Pottstown, and until 1875 was the treasurer and general manager of the Pottstown Iron Company, manufacturing nails, boiler-plate and pig-iron. Closing out his interests there, he returned to Harrisburg, and in 1877-78 erected the Central Iron-Works contiguous to the Chesapeake Nail-Works, of which he is president. He is one of the directors of the Harrisburg National Bank, and in 1880 was appointed by Governor Hoyt a trustee of the Pennsylvania Insane Asylum He was elected a member of the select council of the city of Harrisburg in 1877, was a member of the State Legislature in 1879, and in 1881 was again elected a member of the select council of the city. They had issue (surname Bailey):

1. *Joseph*, d. s. p.
2. *William-Elder*, a graduate of Yale, class 1882; m. Miss Alger, dau. of Gen. Alger, of Detroit, Mich.
3. *Edward*, a graduate of Yale Scientific Course, 1881; m. Elizabeth H. Reily.
4. *Charles-Lukens*, m. Mary F. Seiler.
5. *Morris-Patterson*, d. s. p.
6. *James-Bradshaw*.
7. *Emma-Doll*; m. Robert E. Speer.
8. *Henry-Bent*, d. s. p.

vi. *Henry-Clay*, b. 1838; m., 1874, in Salt Lake City, Utah, Catharine Geisey, of Lancaster, O., and had *Howard*, *Gilbert*, *Henry*, and *Esther*; reside in Denver, Col.

vii. *Sarah-Elder*, b. 1844; m., 1869, Gilbert Martin McCauley, of Ashland, O ; served during the late war in the quartermaster's department of the army; is now engaged in the iron manufacture in Harrisburg, Pa.

XXVIII. HANNAH ELDER,[4] (Robert,[3] David,[2] Robert,[1]) b. in 1779, in Lancaster county; d. in September, 1855, in Indiana county, Pa.; m., in 1809, JAMES RICHARDS, who died in April, 1833, in Indiana county, Pa. Mr. Richards, in conjunction with his brother Alexander, introduced the first machine for carding wool in Western Pennsylvania. They established a small factory opposite Saltsburg, on the Kiskiminetas, which, owing to the discovery of salt wells in the neighborhood, they sold about 1815, and erected works for the manufacture of salt on Crooked creek, in Armstrong county. They had issue (surname Richards):

 i. Mary, m. James Smith, of Erie county.
 ii. Martha, d. unm.
 iii. Eliza, m. Samuel Holmes; they were cousins-germaine, being grandchildren of Thomas Whiteside.
 iv. James, d. in Erie county in 1880, leaving a large family.
 v. Robert, d. in 1857; his widow resides in Saltsburg, Pa.
 vi. Lucinda, m. Thomas Richards, a distant relative.

XXIX. THOMAS ELDER,[4] (Robert,[3] David,[2] Robert,[1]) b. in 1781, in Lancaster county; m. MARY MCCONNELL. They had issue :

 i. Eliza, m. John Cannon, and had a son, *Calvin,* and three daughters.
 ii. Thomas, m., and resides in Armstrong county, Pa.
 iii. John, who resides in the old homestead.

XXX. ROBERT ROBINSON ELDER,[5] (James,[4] Robert,[3] Robert,[2] Robert,[1]) b. October 8, 1793; d. April 5, 1858, near Harrisburg, Pa.; was twice married; m., first, SARAH SHERER, b. 1798, d. November 25, 1836. They had issue :

 i. James, b. August 18, 1826; d. January 12, 1877, in Harrisburg, Pa.; m., March 2, 1854, Rebecca Orth Whitehill, b. August 14, 1828; d. February 17, 1890; dau. of John Whitehill, and they had *Catharine-Orth, Robert-R., Martha-K., Edward,* and *Ida.*
 ii. Robert, b. May 2, 1830; d. March 8, 1861.
 iii. Martha, m. Samuel Hemphill Wallace, and had *Samuel.*
 iv. Sarah, m. John Montgomery Forster, (*see Forster record*).

Robert R. Elder m., secondly, May, 1840, ELIZABETH GALBRAITH ELDER, b. March 17, 1806; d. February 16, 1862. They had issue :

 v. Scott, m. and resides in California.
 vi. Thomas, m. Tacie Elizabeth Jarrett; reside at Dayton, O.; and had issue :
  1. *Mary-Moore,* b. November 13, 1872.

2. *Florence*, b. October 24, 1875 ; d. March 10, 1878.
3. *William-Woolston*, b. May 7, 1879 ; d. January 5, 1881.
4. *Robert-Jarrett*, b. Feb. 24, 1884.
5. *Elsie-Jennette*, b. April 3, 1887.
6. *Helen-Tacie*, b. December 28, 1889.

XXXI. DAVID ELDER,⁵ (James,⁴ Robert,³ Robert,² Robert,¹) b. August 22, 1795, in Maryland ; d. April 5, 1879, at Elder's Ridge ; m. JULIANNA SHERER. They had issue :

    i. *James-Sherer*, a Presbyterian minister at Clarion, Pa.; m. December 22, 1858, Nancy Barnett, dau. of John Barnett and Nancy Morrison, of Westmoreland county, Pa.; and had issue : *John-Barnett, James-M.,* and *David-Judson,* d. s. p.
    ii. *Sarah-E.*, m., 1860, S. Judson Craighead, b. December 5, 1834 ; and had issue (surname Craighead) : *David-Elder, George-V., Julia-Eliza, James-R.-E., Sarah-Maria, Emeline-M.,* and *Nannie-Judson.*

XXXII. JOHN ELDER,⁵ (James,⁴ Robert,³ Robert,² Robert,¹) b. October 2, 1797 ; d. at Elder's Ridge, April 4, 1870 ; m. ELIZABETH McKEE. They had issue :

    i. *Elizabeth*, m. Robert Bills.
    ii. *Martha-J.*, d.; m. Alexander Thompson.
    iii. Rev. *Thomas-R.*, d.; m. Maria J. Elder.
    iv. *Caroline.*
    v. *J.-McKee*, d. unm.

XXXIII. POLLY ELDER,⁵ (James,⁴ Robert,³ Robert,² Robert,¹) b. October 22, 1799; resides at Clarksburg, Pa.; m. SAMUEL RUSSELL, of Westmoreland county. They had issue, (surname Russell):

    i. *William*, d. s. p.
    ii. *Rachel*, d. s. p.
    iii. *Dorcas*, m.
    iv. *Martha*, resides at Clarksburg, Pa.
    v. *Polly*, d. unm.
    vi. *Samuel*, d. s. p.

XXXIV. JOSHUA ELDER,⁵ (James,⁴ Robert,³ Robert,² Robert,¹) b. January 13, 1802 ; d. August 25, 1883 ; was thrice married; m. first, March 12, 1829, ELEANOR SHERER, b. 1802 ; d. April 2, 1837. They had issue :

    i. *Joshua-Reed.*

ii. David-Robinson, m., February 18, 1858, Mary E. Cowden; and had issue:
1. *Joshua-Wallace*, b. February 25, 1861.
2. *William-Cowden*, b. April 20, 1864.
3. *Eleanor-Sherer*, b. December 21, 1870.

iii. John, m., October 29, 1863, Mary J. Rutherford; and had issue:
1. *Herbert*, b. October 14, 1864; m.
2. *Charles*, b. August 2, 1866.
3. *John-Park*, b. January 1, 1872; d. s. p.
4. *Eliza-Rutherford*, b. February 5, 1874; d. s. p.
5. *Jannet-Sherer*, b. August 20, 1875.

Mr. Elder m., secondly, January 1, 1839, MARY C. GILMOR, d. February 26, 1844. They had issue:

iv. Elizabeth M., m. William Kerr Cowden, (*see Cowden record*).

Mr. Elder m., thirdly, December 4, 1845, NANCY BROWN. They had issue:

v. Margaret, m. John Quincy Adams Rutherford.
vi. Matthew-Brown.
vii. Eleanor-Sherer, m. Francis W. Rutherford.
viii Matilda.
ix. Mary-A., d. s. p.

XXXV. JAMES ELDER,[5] (James,[4] Robert,[3] Robert,[2] Robert,[1]) b. February 18, 1804; d. February 5, 1877, at Elder's Ridge; m. MARGARET BARNETT, daughter of Thomas Barnett. They had issue:

i. Martha-Robinson, m. Rev. J. M. Barnett.
ii. Thomas-Barnett, m. Mary Barnett, dau. of John Barnett and Nancy Morrison; and had issue: *Nettie. Wilson-Barnett, Margaret, May,* and *John*.

XXXVI. RACHEL ELDER,[5] (James,[4] Robert,[3] Robert,[2] Robert,[1]) b. December 18, 1806; d. February, 1840, in Jefferson county, Pa.; m. April, 1829, Rev. Jesse Smith. They had issue (surname Smith):

i. Sybil-M., d. unm.

XXXVII. THOMAS ELDER,[5] (James,[4] Robert,[3] Robert,[2] Robert,[1]) b. May 1, 1810; resides at Elder's Ridge; was thrice married; m., first, ELIZABETH COLEMAN. They had issue:

i. Sarah, m.; resides at Blairsville, Pa.
ii. Robert, d. s. p.

Thomas Elder, m., secondly, JANE COOK. They had issue:
  iii. Maggie, m. Rev. Moorhead.

Thomas Elder m., thirdly, MARTHA CALDWELL.

XXXVIII. ROBERT ELDER,[5] (David,[4] Robert,[3] Robert,[2] Robert,[1]) b. May 29, 1791 ; d. October 19, 1827 ; m. March 2, 1820, ELIZABETH SHERER, daughter of Samuel and Elizabeth Sherer, b. 1795; d. February 26, 1860; both interred in Paxtang churchyard. They had issue :

  i. Annie, m. John Ferguson, of Lawrence county, Pa.
  ii. Joshua-Nesbit, d. January 7, 1874, at Helena, Ark.; was twice married; first, Sophia Patton; second, Sarah Summers; no issue.
  iii. Samuel-Sherer, d. April 6, 1885, aged 58 years, at Fortress Monroe, Va.; entered the United States army in 1853 as a private; appointed second lieutenant First Artillery March 23, 1861; promoted first lieutenant May 14, 1861 ; brevet captain September 17, 1862; captain First Artillery August 1, 1863; brevet major February 20, 1864, and brevet lieutenant colonel May 15, 1864; m. Elizabeth Garland, of Henderson, Ky; d. November 19, 1890, at Cincinnati, Ohio; both buried in Paxtang graveyard.
  iv. Elizabeth-J., m. Rev. William G. March.

XXXIX. ELIZA MOORHEAD ELDER,[5] (David,[4] Robert,[3] Robert,[2] Robert,[1]) b. February 17, 1809, in Indiana county, Penna.; d. November 15, 1890, in Covington, Ind. She m., July 25, 1826, JACOB TICE, b. May 18, 1798, in Middlesex county, N. J.; d. February 5, 1886, in Covington, Ind. They had issue (surname Tice), all b. in Covington, Ind., save the oldest, who was b. in Hamilton county, Ohio :

  i. Catharine, b. April 30, 1827 ; m., in 1844, Alexander Gordon.
  ii. Joshua-David, b. September 28, 1830 : d. November 25, 1830.
  iii. John-Rappelyea, b. August 15, 1832 ; d. October 20, 1889, in Jackson county, Oregon.
  iv. Ann-Amelia, b. August 28, 1837 ; d. February 23, 1866 ; s. p.
  v. Frederic-Randolph, b. March 26, 1841 ; reside at Frankfort, Ind.
  vi. Margaret-Duncan, b. February 10, 1843 ; d. March 4, 1843.
  vii. Eliza-Elder, b. July 12, 1844 ; m., May 31, 1865, Thomas F. Davidson, b. February 17, 1839; d. May 19, 1892, in Crawfordsville, Ind.; studied law and was admitted to the bar in 1861; in 1870 he was elected judge of one of

the county circuit courts of Indiana, and re-elected in 1876 ; he was the author of several admirable law text books, the principal one being " Davidson's Overruled Cases ;" a contemporary spoke of him as " one of the most popular judges who ever sat on the bench in Indiana ;" the attorneys and the people alike loved him for his justice, his fearlessness and his impartiality ; he left one child (surname Davidson):

1. *Annie-Mary*, m. Prof. M. B. Thomas, of Wabash College.

ESPY OF DERRY.

I. GEORGE ESPY,² son of JOSIAH ESPY,¹ d. in March, 1761, in Derry township, Lancaster county, Pa., where he was a settler as early as 1729, an emigrant from the north of Ireland. He m. in Ireland, JEAN TAYLOR. They had issue:

    i. *John*, b. 1716; m. and had a daughter *Jean*.
2.   ii. *Josiah*, b. 1718; m. Elizabeth [Crain.]
    iii. *William*, b. 1720; d. in August, 1761, leaving his estate, which was considerable, to his brothers and sisters.
3.   iv. *Mary*, b. 1722; m. John Woods.
    v. *Jean*, b. 1725.
    vi. *Elizabeth*, (twin,) b. 1725; m. James Forster, (see *Forster record*).
4.   vii. *James*, b. 1727; m. and left issue.
5.   viii. *David*, b. 1730; m. Jane Woods.
    ix. *George*, b. 1732; m. and had, among others, *Thomas*, who d. in 1808, leaving a wife, Anna, and children, *William, James, Robert, Margaret*, m. —— Wilson, and *Rachel*, m. —— Bell.
    x. *Anna*, b. 1736; m. William Crain, (see *Crain record*).

II. JOSIAH ESPY,³ (George,² Josiah,¹) b. 1718, in the north of Ireland; d. 1762, in Hanover township, Lancaster county, Pa., leaving a wife, ELIZABETH [CRAIN,] and issue as follows; it may be possible that Josiah Espy was twice married—his first wife's name being PRISCILLA.

6.   i. *Josiah*, b. March 10, 1742; m. Anne Kirkpatrick.
    ii. *Susanna*, b. 1743; m. John Patton.
7.   iii. *Mary*, b. 1745; m. James McClure.
    iv. *Martha*, b. 1747; m. Captain Lazarus Stewart,
8.   v. *George*, b. 1749; m. Mary Stewart.
    vi. *John*, b. 1751; d. s. p.
    vii. *Priscilla*, b. 1753.
    viii. *Robert*, b. 1755.
    ix. *Samuel*, b. 1757.

Mrs. Elizabeth Espy subsequently married Robert Ewing, who d. in 1787, s. p.

Espy of Derry. 215

III. MARY ESPY,³ (George,² Josiah,¹) b. 1722, in the north of Ireland; m. JOHN WOODS.* The latter died in Hanover, then Lancaster county, Pa., in December, 1769, leaving issue (surname Woods):

    i. George, b. 1740.
    ii. Andrew, b. 1742.
    iii. John, b. 1745.
    iv. William, b. 1747.
    v. Samuel, b. 1749.
    vi. Martha, (twin,) b. 1749.
    vii. Sarah, b. 1751; m. William Clark.
    viii. Anna, b. 1753; m. James Montgomery.
    ix. Margaret, b. 1755.
    x. Jennett, b. 1758.
    xi. Mary, (twin,) b. 1758.
    xii. Elizabeth, b. 1760.

IV. JAMES ESPY,³ (George,² Josiah,¹) b. about 1727, in the north of Ireland; was a small child when his father emigrated to America and settled on the Swatara; about 1760, accompanied his brother David to what is now Bedford county, and shortly after to Westmoreland county, Pa.; subsequently emigrating to Kentucky, where he lived and died. He had twelve children— the names of a portion we glean from Josiah Espy's "Tour in Ohio, Kentucky, and Indiana Territory, in 1805."

    i. George, remained in Pennsylvania.
    ii. Thomas; in 1805, resided on the Little Miami, seventeen miles above Columbus, O., having a wife, and children as follows: *Mary,* m. John Kibby, *Anna, Josiah, William, Betsy, Nancy, Sally, Thomas,* and *James.*
9. *iii. Josiah,* b. 1771; m. Maria Moore Murdock.
    iv. David, resided a short distance from his brother Thomas;

---

*JOHN WOODS was the second son of Andrew and Sarah Woods, of Hanover. Andrew Woods died in August, 1756, and left issue (surname Woods).

    i. Andrew, d. 1761, leaving a wife Jean, (*see Ferguson record*).
    ii. John, m. Mary Espy.
    iii. Margaret.
    iv. Jennett, m. John Calhoun.
    v. Agnes, m. Neal McAllister.
    vi. Sarah, m. Andrew Cochran.
    vii. Martha, m. James McClenaghan.

m. Dorcas Keene, and had *Mary*, m. John Westcott, *Eliza*, m. Rev. David Powell, *James*, and *Eunice*.

v. Hugh, resided "at Springville, a little town in Clarke's grant, in the Indiana territory."

vi. Martha, resided on the Little Miami, about forty-five miles from its mouth ; m. James Mitchell, and had issue (surname Mitchell) : *Margaret, David, Eliza, Anna, Maria,* and *James-Espy.*

vii. Anna, resided at Mount Sterling, Kentucky ; m. Joseph Simpson, and had issue (surname Simpson): *Eliza, Jane, Maria, Martha-Mitchell,* and *James-Wilkinson.*

viii. Mary, m. Joseph Stevenson, and left issue.

ix. James, b. May 9, 1786, in Westmoreland county, Pa. His father removed to the State of Kentucky when James was in his fourth year. His thirst for knowledge was from his childhood insatiable, and his means being limited, he began, while yet in his teens, teaching during a portion of each year, to pay for the instruction received in the Transylvania University, Lexington, where he graduated at the age of twenty-one. The following year he was invited to Cumberland, Md., to take charge of a classical academy at that place, then newly endowed by the Legislature. His zeal for instructing the young was such that he soon made it a well-known institution, to which students came from every part of the country. In the meantime he studied law, went to Bedford, Pa., and was admitted to the bar there, subsequently going to Xenia, Ohio, whither his father had previously removed, where he practiced law four years. His profession did not seem to accord with the literary and scientific tendencies of his mind, and he accepted, in 1817, a call to the classical department of the Franklin Institute, Philadelphia, and that city became his home for twenty years. During this period he published several pamphlets reviewing and rejecting the theories of storms and currents which prevailed, and these attracted the attention of the scientists of America. Professor Espy, having formed his own theory, brought it practically to the test of many storms. In 1841 he published his great work, "The Philosophy of Storms." Prior to its publication in this form, the new theory had caused a sensation in the principal cities of England and France, and Professor Espy was invited to visit Europe and compare his results with those which had been reached by Redfield, Forbes, Pouillet, Fournet, and others. He accordingly visited

Europe, and in September, 1840, the British Association appointed a day to entertain the professor's statement which was made in the presence of Professor Forbes, Mr. Redfield, Sir John Herschel, Sir David Brewster, and other eminent naturalists. The discussion which followed was one of the most interesting ever reported in the journals of the association. In the Academy of Sciences at Paris, the interest was equally great, and a committee, consisting of Arago and Pouillet, was appointed to report upon Espy's observations and theory. They were satisfied of the importance of the theory at once, and so reported. It was in the debate which took place in the Academy at this time that Arago said, "France has its Cuvier, England its Newton, America its Espy." On his return from this satisfactory visit, Professor Espy was appointed corresponding member of the Smithsonian Institution. In 1843 he was employed by the War Department, in the Washington Observatory, to prosecute his investigations and collate the reports from the different observers throughout the country. Several quarto volumes of this matter were published by the department. The remainder of his life was spent at the National capital, although his vacation days were enjoyed at Harrisburg, amid the society of endeared friends. On the 17th of January, 1860, while on a visit to Cincinnati, Professor Espy was stricken with paralysis, from which he died on the 24th of the same month. His remains rest in the Espy burial lot in the Harrisburg cemetery. He married, at the age of thirty-seven, MARGARET POLLARD, of Cumberland, Maryland, born September 28, 1795, whose maiden name, for some fancied reason, he assumed, and was ever afterward known as James Pollard Espy. She died May 30, 1850, and is buried by the side of her husband at Harrisburg, Pennsylvania. They left no issue.

V. DAVID ESPY,[3] (George,[2] Josiah,[1]) b. about 1730, in Derry township, Lancaster county, Pa.; d. June 13, 1795, in Bedford, Pa. Studied law, and early in life, removed to the county of Bedford, where he became quite prominent in public affairs. At the outset of the Revolution he entered heartily into the contest; was a deputy to the Provincial Conference held at Carpenter's Hall, Philadelphia, June 18, 1775; member of the Council of Safety, July 23, 1776, serving until

March, 1777, and also colonel of battalion of associators; was appointed prothonotary of the county of Bedford, December 18, 1778; one of the justices of that county, December 18, 1778; and, under the Constitution of 1789-90, prothonotary, register, etc., from December 23, 1790, to June 13, 1795, the date of his death. He filled other positions of honor and usefulness—was one of the original trustees of Dickinson College, and a member of the General Assembly of the State. The provincial records contain numerous references to him and his actions. Colonel Espy married JANE WOODS, of Bedford, b. 1735; d. 1813; sister of George Woods, a man of mark in that section during and subsequent to the Revolution. They had issue:

  i. Captain *David*, d. unm. in Bedford
  ii. Mary, b. 1779; d. 1815; m. 1807, Dr. John Anderson, of Bedford, and left issue, (see *Lyon record*).
  iii. George, b. 1781; d. 1855.

VI. JOSIAH ESPY,[4] (Josiah,[3] George,[2] Josiah,[1]) b. March 10, 1742; d. July 22, 1813; m. July 8, 1769, by Rev. John Roan, ANNE KIRKPATRICK, b. January 11, 1750; d. May 31, 1842; daughter of William and Margaret Kirkpatrick;* both buried in Paxtang church graveyard. They had issue:

  i. Margaret, b. November 8, 1771; d. September 4, 1851; m. Samuel Elder, (see *Elder Record*).
10. *ii. Priscilla*, (twin,) b. November 8, 1771; m. Robert McClure.
  iii. Josiah, b. 1774; d. April 13, 1811, in Bloom township, Northumberland county, Penna.
11. *iv. William*, b. June 2, 1776; m. Susanna Gray.
12. *v. James Snodgrass*, b. July 18, 1788; m. 1st, Mary Huling; 2d, Mary H. Pollard.

---

*WILLIAM KIRKPATRICK, of Paxtang, died in September, 1760, leaving a wife, MARGARET, and children as follows:
  i. John, m. Jane, daughter of John Wilkins.
  ii. William, was a merchant in Lancaster, and died there.
  iii. Anne, m. Josiah Espy.
  iv. Sarah, b. March 27, 1726; d. February 25, 1826; m. Captain Samuel Kearsley, of the Revolution.

Margaret Kirkpatrick, b. 1726; d. November 3, 1802, and is buried in Paxtang church graveyard.

Espy of Derry.

vi. John Elder, b. October 12, 1790; d. April 26, 1831; unm.; was a physician of ability—studied with Dr. Whiteside, subsequently entering into partnership with him in the practice of his profession at Harrisburg, Pa.

13. vii. *David*, b. June 11, 1792; m. Rebecca Allen.

VII. MARY ESPY,[4] (Josiah,[3] George,[2] Josiah,[1]) b. 1745, in Hanover township, then in Lancaster county, Pa.; d. 1818, in what is now Columbia county, Pa.; m. JAMES MCCLURE, b. 1733, in Paxtang township, then in Lancaster county, Pa.; d. November 14, 1805, at McClure's Fort, now Columbia county, Pa. He removed in 1769 to the "Wyoming settlement," and settled upon the west bank of the North Branch of the Susquehanna river, about one mile above the mouth of Fishing creek, where he built a log house, surrounded by a stockade, which was known as McClure's Fort. He was a member of the Committee of Safety during the Revolution, and a man of prominence during that illustrious era. Of his children we have little knowledge. One of his daughters became the wife of the somewhat famous Major Moses Van Campen. A son, James McClure, who died upon the old homestead on October 4, 1850, was the youngest child, and the first one of white parents born in that section of Pennsylvania.

VIII. GEORGE ESPY,[4] (Josiah,[3] George,[2] Josiah,[1]) b. 1749, in Hanover township, Lancaster, now Dauphin, county, Pa.; d. April, 1814, in Luzerne county, Pa. His father, in March, 1775, conveyed to him a tract of land granted him by the Proprietaries in then Northumberland county, Pa., to which he moved the same year. The tract of land was situated not far from the present borough of Nanticoke, upon which he built a log house. He was commissioned May 31, 1800, a justice of the peace for the district consisting of the townships of Hanover and Wilkes-Barré, which office he held at the time of his death; was a mason by trade, and built by contract the old stone jail which was situated on East Market street, Wilkes-Barré. George Espy married MARY STEWART, who died about the year 1820, daughter of John Stewart. They had issue, among others:

i. *Ann*, b. April 5, 1777; m. Ambrose Tilly; d. in Hanover, Luzerne county, s. p.

14.   ii. *John*, b. July 26, 1779 ; m. Lovina Inman.
     iii. *Mary*, [*Polly*,] b. November 29, 1781 ; m. Thomas Bennett ; resided in Nanticoke, and both died there and had issue (surname Bennett):
         1. *Allen.*
         2. *Samuel*, d. s. p.
         3. *Mary-Ann*, m. in 1829, Alden I. Bennett, third son of Isaac Bennett; studied medicine with Gaius Halsey, M. D., and located at Nanticoke, Pa., in 1825, being the first physician of that borough ; in 1831 removed to Bolivar, Ohio ; was a member of the constitutional convention of that State in 1851 ; in 1853 located at Beloit, Wisconsin ; was a State Senator, and d. there in 1862. Two of his sons, *Thomas* and *Phineas*, served during the late civil war as lieutenants of Wisconsin regiments ; subsequently Thomas Bennet became chief clerk, and then Quartermaster under General Sherman, of the military division of Mississippi ; he married Jennie Ewing, dau. of Hon. James Ewing, of Ohio.
     iv. *George*, b. December 19, 1784 ; shortly after his marriage went to the then far West, and is supposed to have been killed by the Indians ; m. Elizabeth Eicke, and had issue :
         1. *Sarah-Ann*, b. May 9, 1814 ; d. May 27, 1877 ; m. 1838, Joseph Tyson Preston, of Philadelphia ; collonel State militia; a merchant and coal operator at Plymouth ; and they had issue (surname Preston):
             a. *Edwin-Ruthven*, b. Sept. 23, 1839 ; d. Oct. 17, 1876 ; m. Mary McCormick, and had *Virginia*, m. Dr. H. L. Whitney, of Plymouth.
             b. *George-Espy*, b. 1840 ; d. August 22, 1882, unm., civil engineer.
             c. *Gertrude*, b. 1842 ; m. Frank Turner ; educated at West Point; merchant and coal operator, Plymouth.
             d. *Marion-Wallace*, b. April 27, 1844 ; m. December 5, 1866, Stephen Buckingham Vaughan, of Kingston, and had issue (surname Vaughan):
                 Fanny-Buckingham, b. July 29, 1868; d. February 22, 1872.
                 Marion-Matilda, m. November 12, 1889, Fred. Hurlbut Payne, and had (surname Payne) *Eugene*, *Robert*, and *Dorothy-Marion.*
                 John-Bennett.
                 Gertrude-Turner.

IX. JOSIAH ESPY,[4] (James,[3] George,[2] Josiah,[1]), b. about 1771, Bedford, Pa.; d. in 1847, in Columbus, Ohio. When his father removed to Kentucky, Josiah remained with his uncle, David, who was, at the time, prothonotary of Bedford county, which gave him some social and educational advantages he would not otherwise have had. In 1791 he received an appointment as clerk in the War Department at Philadelphia, where he remained several years, returning to Bedford and took a prominent part in politics, and was elected to the State Legislature. In 1805 he visited Ohio, of which tour he preserved a brief journal, which has been published in the "Ohio Valley Historical Series." Later in life he located permanently in Columbus, Ohio; in 1826 was elected cashier of the Franklin Bank at that place, and continued to fill that position until the final winding up of the bank, upon the expiration of its charter in 1843. Mr. Espy married, in 1812, MARIA MOORE MURDOCK, daughter of Judge Murdock, of Cumberland, Maryland. At the date of his marriage he adopted the family name of his wife, and ever after signed his name Josiah M. Espy. They had ten children, five of whom died in youth; those living are:

 i. Henry-P., m.; a banker, resides in Urbana, O.
 ii. Lavinia-M., resides in Columbus, Ohio; m., in 1839, James T. Morehead, b. May 24, 1797, near Shepherdsville, Bullitt county, Kentucky. Was educated at Transylvania University, and studied law under Judge H. P. Brodnax, of the circuit court of Kentucky, and Hon. John J. Crittenden. In the spring of 1816 he began the practice of law at Bowling Green, and was elected to the State Legislature in 1828, serving until 1830. In 1832 he was elected Lieutenant Governor of Kentucky, and, in 1834, upon the death of Governor Breathitt, succeeded that gentleman in the executive office. He served another term in the Legislature, and, in 1841, was elected to the United States Senate for the full term of six years. Upon his retirement from that body he located at Covington, where he died.
 iii. James, m.; a banker, resides in Cincinnati, Ohio.
 iv. Isabel, m. Dr. Francis Carter, Dean of Starling Medical College, Columbus, Ohio.
 v. Ellen-Graham, m. first, Col. James C. McCoy, chief of staff to General Sherman; secondly, Judge T. W. Bartley, of Washington, D. C.

X. PRISCILLA ESPY,⁵ (Josiah,⁴ Josiah,³ George,² Josiah,¹) b. December 8, 1771, in Paxtang; d. September 29, 1845; m. ROBERT MCCLURE, b. December 18, 1763; d. July 21, 1839, in Paxtang; son of William McClure and Margaret Wright; both buried in old Paxtang church graveyard. They had issue (surname McClure):

    i. *William*, b. Feb. 1, 1795; d. Aug. 16, 1852; m. and left issue.
    ii. *Ann*, b. 1797.
    iii. *Robert-Wright*, b. 1800; d. September 26, 1865.
    iv. *Priscilla-Jane*.
    v. *Josiah-Espy*, removed to Franklin county, Pa.; m. and left issue.
    vi. *Margaret*.
    vii. *Rebecca*, m. May 27, 1834, Matthew Brown.

XI. WILLIAM ESPY,⁵ (Josiah,⁴ Josiah,³ George,² Josiah,¹) b. June 2, 1776; d. July 28, 1850, in Harrisburg, Pa.; m. June 2, 1807, by Rev. James R. Sharon, SUSANNA GRAY, b. June 18, 1782; d. July 10, 1854; daughter of Joseph Gray and Elizabeth Forster; both buried in Paxtang church graveyard. They had issue:

    i. *Elizabeth-Gray*, b. 1808; bap. July 24, 1808; resides at Harrisburg, Pa.; m. December 29, 1859, Samuel W. Sharp, of Cumberland county, Pa.; b. March 27, 1822; d. December 6, 1877, s. p.
    ii. *Josiah*, b. 1810; bap. June 24, 1810; d. August 12, 1891; m. Mary McKeehan daughter of Samuel McKeehan; resides in Harrisburg, Pa.; and had issue:
        1. *William*, b. April 19, 1844; d. September 10, 1852.
        2. *Samuel-McKeehan*, b. April 14, 1847; d. December 19, 1849.
        3. *James-G.*, b. September 12, 1849; d. Sept. 22, 1852.
        4. *Susanna*, b November 1, 1852; m. Harry D. Boas, (*see Boas record*).
        5. *Helen*, b. July 21, 1857.
    iii. *Ann*, b. August 3, 1812; m. Abner Rutherford, (*see Rutherford record*).

XII. JAMES SNODGRASS ESPY,⁵ (Josiah,⁴ Josiah,³ George,² Josiah,¹) b. July 18, 1788; d. September 21, 1872, in Harrisburg, Pa.; was a merchant, and a prominent citizen; m. first, March 30, 1817, at Isle Benvenue, MARY HULING, daughter of Thomas Huling. They had issue:

Espy of Derry.

i. *Thomas-Huling*, b. December 30, 1817; studied medicine with Dr. W. W. Rutherford; graduated at Jefferson Medical College; m. January 1, 1845, Elizabeth M. Wilson, and had twelve children; reside at Lampasas, Texas.
ii. *Anna-Elizabeth*, b. January 1, 1820; d. June 15, 1854; m. January 1, 1838, Hugh H. Stockton, and had issue (surname Stockton):
   1. *James-Espy*, d. s. p.
   2. *Mary-Pollard*, m. Captain Dean Monahan, U. S. A., and had (surname Monahan) *Dean-Stockton, Anna*, and *Henry*, d. s. p
   3. *Hugh*, d. s. p.
   4. *William*, d. s. p.
   5. *Henry-T.*, Lieut. U. S. N.; m. Kathleen Onslow, of Cornwall, England, and had *Reginald-Wallace-Ledgerwood, Hugh-Cyril-Onslow*, and *Kathleen-Gwendolin-Violet*.
iii. *Mary*, b. December 22, 1823; d. 1832.

James S. Espy, m. secondly, March 10, 1825, MARY H. POLLARD, b. December 15, 1802; resides at Harrisburg, Pa. They had issue:
   iv. *Margaret-Pollard*, b. December 20, 1825; d. Nov. 26, 1847.
   v. *James-Pollard*, b. 1827; d. February 26, 1880.
   vi. *Louisa*, b. September 20, 1829; d. September 27, 1846.
   vii. *William-Kirkpatrick*, b. 1831; d. March 4, 1868, at Clouterville, Louisiana; graduated in medicine, and was in active practice at the time of his death; m. Rectina St. Croix Cockfield; and had *Mary*.
   viii. *Eliza-Lawrence*, m. November 8, 1853, William Sergeant, b. 1829, in Philadelphia, Pa., son of Hon. John Sergeant; graduated from Princeton College in 1847; studied law under Benjamin Gerhard, and admitted to the Philadelphia bar in 1850; he held a prominent position at the bar, and was for a time a representative in the State Legislature; on the breaking out of the rebellion was commissioned captain of the Twelfth infantry U. S. A.; afterwards colonel of the Two Hundred and Tenth regiment Pennsylvania volunteers; on the 31st of March, 1865, was wounded in his thigh by a ball, while resisting an attack of the enemy on the White Oak road, near the Boynton plank-road, in front of Petersburg, Va., from which he died on board of the hospital boat, while on his way home, April 11, 1865; he was a gentleman of marked ability, and a gallant officer. They had issue (surname Sergeant):

1. *Mary.*
2. *Margaretta,* m. November 27, 1878, Alexander James Dallas Dixon.
3. *Louisa,* m. John C. Kunkel, jr.
4. *John,* d. s. p.
5. *Sarah-Haly.*
6. *Eliza,* m. Oct. 15, 1884, William Heyward Meyers.

XIII. DAVID ESPY,[5] (Josiah,[4] Josiah,[3] George,[2] Josiah,[1]) b. June 11, 1792; d. April 21, 1840, in Paxtang; m. December 17, 1816, REBECCA ALLEN, b. July 24, 1796; d. 1872. They had issue:

    i. Josiah, b. September 29, 1817; m. Mary ———.
    ii. William-Kirkpatrick, b. October 9, 1819; m. Martha Sturgeon; reside near Groveland, Tazewell county, Illinois.
    iii. Anna-Maria, b. May 11, 1822; m. March 1, 1849, James Todd.
    iv. David, b. September 8, 1826; m. August 19, 1851, Ann Catharine Jackson.
    v. John-Alexander, b. July 26, 1829; m. Martha Fry.
    vi. Susanna-Margaret, b. February 1, 1833; m. Dr. Marvin S. Carr.

XIV. JOHN ESPY,[5] (George,[4] Josiah,[3] George,[2] Josiah,[1]) b. 1779, in Hanover township, then Lancaster, now Dauphin, county, Pennsylvania; d. March 25, 1848, in Hanover township, Luzerne county, Pennsylvania. A contemporary newspaper states that he "was a man of honorable feelings, hospitable, and generally beloved." He m. April 5, 1809, LOVINA INMAN, b. 1787; d. 1876, in Luzerne county, Pa.; daughter of Colonel Edward Inman, of the Revolution. They had issue:

15.   *i. James,* b. 1811; m. Mary A. Miller.
16.   *ii. Fannie,* b. March 21, 1813; m. Abram Line.
    iii. Lovina, b. 1820; m. Peter Miller, and had issue (surname Miller), *John,* and *Winfield,* who reside at Irving Mills, Michigan.
    iv. Mary, b. 1822; d. November 29, 1889; m. April 10, 1845, John R. Line, b. March 25, 1825; d. November 22, 1890.
    v. Priscilla, b. 1827; m. Levi M. Miller, and had issue (surname Miller), *Edward, Dollie, Ida, Otis, Mary, Oscar, Wallace,* and *Paul;* reside in Des Moines county, Iowa.

XV. JAMES ESPY,[6] (John,[5] George,[4] Josiah,[3] George,[2] Josiah,[1]) b. 1811, in Nanticoke, Luzerne county, Pa.; d. 1872, at Rummerfield Creek, Bradford county, Pa., whither he removed in 1863. He married in 1841, MARY A. MILLER, b. December 26, 1818; d. February 15, 1878, in Wilkes-Barré, Pa.; daughter of Barnett Miller and Mary DeWitt. Barnett Miller was the son of Andrew and Christina Miller, of Harmony, New Jersey; and Mary DeWitt the daughter of Peter DeWitt and Hannah Hill, emigrants from France. Barnett Miller and his wife removed about, 1830, to Hanover township, Luzerne county, Pa., where they died. James Espy and his wife, Mary A. Miller, had issue, all born in Hanover township, Luzerne county, Pa.:

> *i. John*, b. September 21, 1842; went West in 1860, and located at Burlington, Iowa; when the War of the Rebellion began, in April, 1861, he enlisted in Company E, First Iowa Volunteer Infantry, a three month's regiment; the command was hurried into service, and sent to Missouri, where it formed a part of the gallant little army of General Nathaniel Lyon, which did so much to save that State to the Union; he participated in the engagement at Dug Springs, and in the memorable battle of Wilson's Creek, Mo.; shortly after the regiment was mustered out of service. Returning to Iowa, Mr. Espy met with a serious accident, which prevented him from re-entering the service, by having his left hand crushed in the machinery of a sorghum mill. He then went to his native State and entered the Academy, and subsequently the Albany Law School, from which he graduated in 1866; admitted to the Luzerne county bar, April 20, 1868. In 1871, he was commissioned an aid-de-camp with the rank of major in the National Guard of Pennsylvania, and was in active military service during the Scranton riots the same year, the railroad riots of 1877, and the Hazleton riots of 1878; from 1871 to 1877 he was a member of the banking house of J. B. Wood & Co., at Wilkes-Barre, which was dissolved upon the death of Mr. Wood. In 1879 Major Espy located at St. Paul, since which period he has taken a very active part in the business affairs of that prosperous city, where he now resides. He m. March 23, 1868, Martha M. Wood, b. March 12, 1843; dau. of John B. Wood and Sarah Gore; and had issue:
>> 1. *John-B.-Wood*, b. January 23, 1869.
>> 2. *Lila-Wood*, b. June 22, 1872; graduated M. Sc., Univ. of Minn.

3. *Maude-M.*, b. February 11, 1875.
4. *Olin*, b. July 29, 1877.

ii. *Theodore-Frelinghuysen*, b. November 5, 1844; resides in Towanda, Pa.; m. February 25, 1873, Mary Catharine Schoonover, b. March 8, 1844, in Stillwater, Sussex county, N. J.; and had issue:
 1. *Mary-Lines*, b. November 27, 1873.
 2. *Bertha-Blanche*, b. July 14, 1874.
 3. *Carrie-Louisa*, b. December 16, 1876.

iii. *Barnett-Miller*, b. May 16, 1846; is a lawyer by profession, of Wilkes-Barre, Pa., and secretary and treasurer of the Wilkes-Barre Water company; m. September 23, 1873, Caroline Wood, b. 1847, daughter of Abraham Wood and Caroline Bowers; and had issue:
 1. *Blanche-Wood*, b January 18, 1880.
 2. *Ridgway-Bowers*, b. September 2, 1881.
 3. *Bruce-Miller*, b. December 1, 1886.
 4 *Charles-Wood*, b. August 20, 1891.

iv. *Frank*, b. December 9, 1848; m. Effie F. Harding, b. November 2, 1851, of Herrick Centre, Bradford county, Pa., where they reside, and had issue:
 1. *James-Byron*, b. January 26, 1873.

v. *Edward-Inman*, b. July 23, 1852; m. July 25, 1880, Fanny Maltby, of Marshalltown, Iowa; reside in Chicago, Ill.; and had issue, *Ralph-Edward*, and *Harold-Maltby*.

vi. *Minnie-M.*, b. October 29, 1859; m. Charles R. Wood, b. October 11, 1854, and had issue (surname Wood):
 1. *Stanley V.*, b. July 27, 1887.
 2. *Christine*, b. August 1, 1890.

XVI. FANNIE ESPY,[6] (John,[5] George,[4] Josiah,[3] George,[2] Josiah,[1]) b. March 21, 1813, in Nanticoke, Luzerne county, Pa.; d. November 1, 1881; m. ABRAM LINE, b. November 28, 1811. They had issue (surname Line):

i. *Frances-V.*, b. May, 1838; m., first, William H. Lueder, d. 1862; and had issue (surname Lueder):
 1. *Fanny*, b. April 10, 1862; m. October 28, 1884, Frank Garringer, b. March, 1857.

Mrs. Frances V. Leuder, m., secondly, 1869, Dr. A. A. Lape, b. 1842; d. December 7, 1884; and had issue (surname Lape):
 2. *Vienna*, b. January 10, 1871.
 3. *Mary*, b. August 27, 1874.

ii. *Lovina*, b. October 5, 1839; m., 1864, W. S. Smythe, and had issue (surname Smythe), *Genevieve*, and *Winfield*.

Espy of Derry. 227

iii. *Annette-C.*, b. September 27, 1842 ; m. October 12, 1864, C.
D. Wells, b. May 6, 1839 ; reside at Wilkes-Barre, Pa.;
and had issue (surname Wells):
1. *Edith*, b. January 7, 1869.
iv. *Augusta-M.*, b. June 7, 1844; m. October 12, 1865, C. W.
Hollenback, and had issue, *Camilla* ; reside in Kingston
township, Luzerne county, Pa.
v. *Edward-Espy*, b. January 29, 1850 ; m. Rosa Moyer, and
had issue, *Camilla*.

FERGUSON OF HANOVER.

I. WILLIAM FERGUSON[1] and his wife MARGARET, natives of the north of Ireland, emigrated to America about 1740, and settled in Hanover township, then Lancaster county, Pa. William Ferguson d. about 1755, his wife a few years later. They had, among others, the following children:

    i. James, b. 1720; d. in April, 1750, in Paxtang, leaving a wife, and children *Francis* and *Margaret*.
2. *ii. Samuel*, b. 1723; m. and had issue.
3. *iii. David*, b. 1725; m. and had issue.
    iv. Margaret, b. 1727; m. and left issue.

II. SAMUEL FERGUSON,[2] (William,[1]) b. 1723; d. September, 1785; m. MARY ———. They had issue:

    i. Elizabeth, b. 1757; d. October 4, 1792; m. Samuel Graham.
    ii. Agnes.
    iii. Margaret, m. James Taggart.
    iv. Mary, m. David Ramsey, b. 1745; d. September 18, 1787.
    v. Robert.
    vi. Samuel.
    vii. William.
    viii. Thomas.

III. DAVID FERGUSON,[2] (William,[1]) b. about 1725, in the north of Ireland; d. July, 1775, in Hanover township, Lancaster, now Dauphin county, Pa.; came to Pennsylvania with his father about 1740, and located in the Swatara region; was twice married; the name of his first wife is not known; by her there was issue:

    i. William, b. 1757; m. Sarah Woods.
    ii. John, b. 1759; d. 1813; his wife Sarah b. 1760; d. August 5 1823; buried in old Hanover Church graveyard.
4. *iii. Elizabeth*, b. 1761; m. Henry Graham.

David Ferguson, m. secondly, in 1763, JEAN WOODS, widow of Andrew Woods,* of Hanover. After the death of Mr. Fer-

---

* I. ANDREW WOODS, an emigrant from the north of Ireland, came to Pennsylvania prior to 1740. He died in Hanover township, then

guson, his widow married the third time, becoming the wife of Thomas George, of Upper Paxtang township, now Dauphin county, Pa. They had issue:

 5. iv. *David*, b. May 10, 1764; m. Jane (Henderson) Rogers.
 6. v. *Andrew Woods*, b. 1766; m. Hester Graham.
   vi. *Thomas*, b. 1768; never married; was a graduate of the University of Pennsylvania; studied theology—licensed to preach, but never entered the ministry.

IV. ELIZABETH FERGUSON,³ (David,² William,¹) b. 1761, in Hanover township, then Lancaster county, Pa.; d. 1805, in Northumberland county, Pa.; m. June 24, 1788, HENRY GRAHAM, b. 1760, in Hanover township, then Lancaster county, Pa., d. in 1836, son of John Graham; removed about 1804, to Northumberland county, Pa., near Warrior Run church, six miles from Milton. They had issue (surname Graham):

  i. *John*, b. April 17, 1789; d. July 14, 1849, in Adams county, Ohio. Mr. Graham was educated at the Philadelphia academy under Drs. Wylie and Gray, and studied theology at the seminary in New York. In the spring of 1819 he was licensed by the Monongahela Presbytery, and on the 30th of August, 1820, was ordained by the same body. He was pastor of Cross Roads and Wash-

---

Lancaster county, in August, 1756, leaving a wife, Sarah, and the following issue (surname Woods):

 2. i. *Andrew*, m. Jean ———.
   ii. *John*, m. Mary Espy, (*see Espy record*).
   iii. *Margaret*, m. ——— Patton.
   iv. *Jennett*, m. John Calhoun.
   v. *Agnes*, m. Neal McAllister.
   vi. *Sarah*, m. Andrew Cochran.
   vii. *Martha*, m. James McClenaghan.

II. ANDREW WOODS, (Andrew,) b. in Hanover township, then Lancaster county, Pa.; d. prior to 1761, leaving a wife, JEAN, who afterwards became the wife of David Ferguson, and issue (surname Woods):

  i. *Matthew*, b. 1758; d. September 13, 1784, in Hanover township; was licensed to preach by the Presbytery of Carlisle in 1780; called to Hanover congregation July 20, 1781, accepted it, and was ordained and installed pastor thereof on the 19th of June, 1782. He left a wife, and issue—*Andrew*, and a posthumous child.
  ii. *Sarah*, m. William Ferguson.
  iii. *Agnes*.

ington, Washington county, Pa., from August 30, 1820, to October 8, 1829, during a portion of which period, from 1823 to 1828, he filled the position of professor of languages in Washington college. From 1830 to 1834 he was the stated minister of the congregations of Sycamore and Hopkinsville, Warren county, Ohio; of Greenfield and Fall Creek, Ohio, from 1834 to 1839. From 1839 to 1840 he was principal of the academy at Chilicothe, Ohio, which position he resigned to accept a call to the churches of West Union and West Fork, Adams county, Ohio, in 1841, in which field he ministered until his death. Columbia college conferred upon him the degree of doctor of divinity. He was an able teacher and a faithful and conscientious minister of the gospel. A sermon by him, published in the second volume of the "Pulpit of the Associate Reformed Church," shows his deep theological learning.

ii. James, b. 1791; d. 1861, unm.
iii. David-E., b. 1793; d. in Illinois; m. Elizabeth Foster.
iv. Matthew-Woods, b. 1795; d. 1870, near Freeport, Illinois: m. Martha Shannon.
v. Henry.
vi. Jane, b. 1797; d. 1867, near Warrior Run, Northumberland county, Pa.; m. William McGuire; and they had issue (surname McGuire): *David, Henry, William,* d. s. p., Dr. *John, Matthew-Woods*, k. at the second battle of Bull Run, *Jane* and *Ellen.*
7. *vii. Eleanor*, b. 1799; m. Robert Finney.
viii. Elizabeth, m. Joseph Philips.

V. DAVID FERGUSON,³ (David,² William,¹) b., May 10, 1764, in Hanover township, Lancaster, now Dauphin, county, Pa.; d. March 20, 1848, in Hanover; was a member of the Pennsylvania Legislature, 1811–14; m., February 13, 1787, JEAN (HENDERSON) ROGERS, b. 1753, in Bucks county, Pa.; d. November 18, 1824, in Hanover township, Dauphin county, Pa., daughter of Robert Henderson, of Bucks county, and widow of Robert Rogers; by her first husband she had *Robert*, *Frances* m. John Harrison, and *Margaret* m. John Ritchey. They had issue:

i. Jean, b. December 27, 1787; d. January 2, 1819; m. John Graham, (see *Wallace of Hanover*).
ii. Elizabeth, b. November 12, 1789; m. John Stinson.
iii. David, b. April 14, 1791; d. August, 1793.

  iv. Andrew, b. May 5, 1793 ; d. August 29, 1804.
  v. Agnes, b. March 14, 1795 ; d. July 20, 1848 ; m. Thomas McNair, (*see McNair record*).
  vi. David, b. January 16, 1797 ; d. October 24, 1822, near Shippensburg, Pa., and buried in Middle Spring Church graveyard; was preparing for the ministry at the time of his death.

VI. ANDREW WOODS FERGUSON,³ (David,² William,¹) b. 1766 in Hanover township, Dauphin county, Pa.; removed to near Jersey Shore, Lycoming connty, Pa., where he died; m. HESTER GRAHAM, of Cumberland county, Pa. They had issue:

  i. Jane, m. Andrew McKinney.
  ii. Ruth, m. Matthew McKinney.
  iii. Elizabeth, d. s. p.
  iv. Priscilla, m. —— Brown.
  v. Nellie, m. —— Brown, his second wife.
  vi. Sallie, m. —— Hunt.
  vii. Rebecca, m. Samuel Deyarmond, of Warrior Run, Northumberland county, Pa., and left issue.
  viii. James.
  ix. Matthew-Woods.
  x. David, d. s. p.

VII. ELEANOR GRAHAM,⁴ (Elizabeth,³ David,² William,¹) b. 1799, in Hanover township, Dauphin county, Pa.; d. September, 1881, near Warrior Run, Penna.; m. ROBERT FINNEY, of Union county, Pa.; b. 1794 ; d. 1870. They had issue (surname Finney):

  i. Eliza, d. 1880 ; m. O. P. Peiper.
  ii. Jane-Graham, m. James R. Caldwell, of Lawrenceville, N. J.
  iii. Spencer-L.-F., a minister of the Gospel, m. Isabella Matthews, of New York.
  iv. Mary-Agnes, d. 1870 ; m. J. Edward Hackenburg, a lawyer of Philadelphia.
  v. Henry-Graham, a minister of the Gospel; m. Sallie Gardner.
  vi. Eleanor-Graham, m. William Matthews, of Rye, N. Y.
  vii. Hadassa, resides near Winchester, Va.
  viii. Robert-Bines, resides near Winchester, Va.

FLEMING FAMILY.

I. ROBERT FLEMING,[1] a native of Argylesshire, Scotland, where he was born in 1716, with his wife emigrated to America in 1746, and settled near Flemington, Chester county, Pa. In 1760 he removed to Cecil county, Md., thence to the West Branch of the Susquehanna, near the mouth of Bald Eagle creek, from which he and his family were driven by the Indians in the "Great Runaway." Until the close of the Revolution they located in Hanover township, then Lancaster, now Dauphin county, Pa., when, about 1784, they removed to Western Pennsylvania, and settled on Harmon's creek, in Washington county, where Mr. Fleming died on the 3d of April, 1802. Robert Fleming married, about 1745, in the province of Ulster, Ireland, JANE JACKSON, b. 1719; died June 16, 1803. They had issue:

   i. [a son,] b. 1746; died at sea.
   ii. Jesse, b. 1748; d. s. p.
2. *iii. John,* b. 1752; m. Mary Jackson.
3. *iv. Robert,* b. June 6, 1756; m. Margaret Wright.
4. *v. James,* b. 1758; m. Jane Glen.
5. *vi. Samuel,* b. October 30, 1761; m. Sarah Becket.
6. *vii. Mary,* b. February 15, 1767; m. Alexander McConnell.

II. JOHN FLEMING,[2] (Robert,[1]) b. 1752, in Chester county, Pa.; d. December 15, 1800, in Montgomery county, N. Y. In 1774, he married MARY JACKSON, b. about 1756, in Orange county, N. Y.; d. December 5, 1816; eldest daughter of John Jackson (1730–1820) and Elsie Armstrong, of Pine Creek, Lycoming county, Pa. At the time his father's family abandoned the Big Island, he sought protection at Fort Hunter, where he remained until, in 1790, he removed to the "Military Tract"—lands lying between Cayuga and Seneca Lakes—in the State of New York. Here he and his wife resided until their death. They had issue:

   i. Jesse, b. 1777; d. April 20, 1795, in Romulus, N. Y.
7. *ii. John,* b. February 6, 1780; m. Susannah Harton.
8. *iii. Robert,* b. November 26, 1781; m. Lettice Smith.

Fleming Family. 233

9.   iv. *Mary*, b. June 20, 1784; m. Samuel McMath.
10.   v. *James*, b. January 28, 1787; m. Martha Wade.
11.   vi. *Elsie*, b. July 21, 1791; m. Josiah Jacobus.
12.   vii. *Samuel*, b. December 5, 1793; m. Phebe Wade.

III. ROBERT FLEMING,[2] (Robert,[1]) b. June 6, 1756, in Chester county, Pa.; d. February 4, 1817. When his parents removed to Western Pennsylvania, Robert remained in Dauphin county; purchased land in Hanover township, on which he resided during his lifetime. On the 6th of February, 1783, he married MARGARET, daughter of John Wright. He was one of the founders of the Harrisburg Bank, and instrumental in the erection of the Harrisburg bridge. He was an officer in the volunteer force of 1812, and filled acceptably various local offices. He was an elder in the old Hanover Church during the ministration of Rev. James Snodgrass. MARGARET WRIGHT, b. 1754; d. December 12, 1843. They left no issue.

IV. JAMES FLEMING,[2] (Robert,[1]) b. 1758, in Chester county, Penna.; d. February 1, 1830, in Washington county, Penna.; accompanied his father's family during their frequent changes, and finally about 1781, to a farm on Harmon's creek, Hanover township, Washington county, Penna. He married, October 5, 1797, JANE GLEN, d. March 1, 1841. They had issue:

13.   i. *John*, b. October 27, 1799; m. Elizabeth McClurg.
    ii. *Martha*, b. February 26, 1801; d. April 1, 1841; m. October 17, 1831, James Patterson.
    iii. *Robert*, b. August 23, 1802; d. July 8, 1824.
14.   iv. *David-S.*, b. August 16, 1804; m. Martha Steele.
15.   v. *James*, b. August 5, 1806; m. Catharine B. Parks.
16.   vi. *Samuel*, b. June 20, 1811; m. Rebecca McCombs.

V. SAMUEL FLEMING,[2] (Robert,[1]) b. October 30, 1761, in Cecil county, Md.; d. August 3, 1851, in Harrisburg, Dauphin county, Penna. Removed with his father's family to Western Pennsylvania, where he served as justice of the peace and surveyor for Washington county; was captain of a ranging company on the frontiers to protect them from the Indian marauders from the Ohio; was one of the local committee to treat with the insurgents during the Whiskey Insurrection. In 1812 he removed to West Hanover township, Dauphin county, where he resided until a few years before his death. Mr. Fleming m.

234   *Pennsylvania Genealogies.*

September 24, 1789, SARAH BECKET, b. 1771; d. January 21, 1831, in Hanover township, Dauphin county, Penna. They had issue:
- i. *Robert*, b. August 3, 1790; d. February, 1793.
- 17. ii. *Mary*, b. July 17, 1792; m. James Newell.
- 18. iii. *Jane*, b. May 22, 1794; m. Robert Gilchrist.
- iv. *Samuel-Becket*, b. July 31, 1797, in Hanover township, Washington county, Pa.; d. January 19, 1855, at Mt. Vernon, O.; buried in old Hanover churchyard; was a farmer and merchant,—a man of upright character and stern integrity; m. in 1833, Mary Cathcart, of Dauphin county, Pa.; d. 1836; and they had two sons, one died young. *Samuel-Wright*, d. October 19, 1848, aged fourteen years.
- v. *Margaret*, b. October 17, 1799; d. February 13, 1802.
- vi. *Eliza*, b. October 23, 1801; d. February 14, 1828; m. William Smith, and had (surname Smith) *Sarah-Jane*, m. Mr. Merriman, a planter in Louisiana.
- 19. vii. *Robert-Jackson*, b. November 16, 1803; m. Sarah Ann Poor.
- viii. *John*, b. 1805; d. s. p.
- ix. *Sarah*, b. October 1, 1807; d. July 18, 1828
- 20. x. *James*, b. June 25, 1810; m. Jennette Street.
- 21. xi. *David*, b. July 17, 1812; m. Susan Mowry.
- xii. *Margaret-Wright*, b. July 14, 1815; d. March 30, 1857.

VI. MARY FLEMING,[2] (Robert,[1]) b. February 15, 1767, in Cecil county, Md.; d. July 3, 1849, in Hanover township, Washington county, Penna.; m. May 7, 1791, ALEXANDER MCCONNELL, b. 1769; d. October 24, 1839. They had issue (surname McConnell):
- i. *John*, b. March 11, 1792; d. s. p.
- 22. ii. *Robert*, b. December 5, 1794; m. Edith Hamlin.
- 23. iii. *James*, b. October 27, 1796; d. May 29, 1852; m. Nancy Shipley.
- 24. iv. *Elizabeth*, b. April 9, 1798; m. Samuel McCarrell.
- v. *Alexander*, b. October 16, 1804; d. August 30, 1829, while a member of senior class in Washington College, Pa.

VII. JOHN FLEMING,[3] (John,[2] Robert,[1]) b. February 6, 1780, at Pine Creek, Lycoming county, Penna.; d. May 8, 1863, near Albion, Michigan. Settled upon a part of his father's farm in Romulus, Seneca county, N. Y., where he resided about forty years. Was a captain of infantry in the war of 1812. In 1844 removed to Michigan, where he settled on a farm. He m., March 4, 1802, SUSANNAH HARTON, b. 1785; d. February 28, 1860. They had issue:

i. *Polly*, b. April 3, 1803; d. s. p.
ii. *Hannah*, b. January 25, 1805; m. John Gilliland; and had issue.
iii. *Mary-Ann*, b. January 14, 1807; d. May 7, 1848; m. Silas H. More; d. June 23, 1852; and left issue.
iv. *Elsie*, b. January 2, 1809; d. February 22, 1844; m. Jesse Gardner; and left issue.
v. *Eusebia*, b. November 26, 1811; m. Hiram H. Slauson; and left issue.
vi. *Susan-M.*, b. March 7, 1814; m. Jeptha H. Wade, the artist, b. August 11, 1811, at Romulus, N. Y.
vii. *Abigail*, b. August 2, 1816; d. November 17, 1852, at Havana, N. Y.; m. Rev. Morrison Huggins, b. 1816; d. February 15, 1859, at Rockford, Ill.; and left issue.
viii. *Newell*, b. September 16, 1818; m. Mary M. VanDwyn; and had issue.
ix. *John-Mark*, b. February 20, 1821; m. Maria Belcher; and had issue.
x. *Cornelia-Elizabeth*, b. February 10, 1823; m. Ralph Giddings; and had issue.
xi. *Amanda-Watson*, b. April 12, 1825: m Orlando M. Barnes; and had issue.
xii. *William*, b. August 1, 1827; m. Elizabeth Janette Leonard; and had issue.
xiii. *James*, b. May 3, 1831; m. Sarah R. Soule; and had issue.

VIII. ROBERT FLEMING,[3] (John,[2] Robert,[1]) b. November 26, 1781, in Hanover township, Dauphin county, Penna.; d. February 3, 1858, at Romulus, N. Y.; m., first, January 15, 1806, LETTICE SMITH, b. 1789; d. March 4, 1826. They had issue:

i. *John-S.*, b June 26, 1807; m. Elizabeth Ayres.
ii. *Charles-Mosher*, b. October 31, 1809; m. Peninah Amesbury, d. August 1, 1838.
iii. *Jervis*, b. January 28, 1812; m. Amanda Crane.
iv. *Robert*, b. April 23, 1814; d. October 10, 1838; m. Juliet Smith.
v. Rev. *Samuel*, b. May 9, 1816; m. Juliet Fleming, d. January 25, 1862.
vi. *Asa*, b. November 16, 1818; m., first, Julian Smith, d. 1848; secondly, Mary A. Gilbert.
vii. *Sarah*, b. February 12, 1821; m. William Rogers, d. October 2, 1862.
viii. *Lettice*, b. August 27, 1824; m. James H. Gage.

Robert Fleming m., secondly, December 7, 1826, Mrs. Arazina Leddick.

236 *Pennsylvania Genealogies.*

IX. MARY FLEMING,[3] (John,[2] Robert,[1]) b. June 20, 1784, in Hanover township, Dauphin county, Penna.; d. November 20, 1860, at Niles, Mich.; m., May 24, 1805, SAMUEL McMATH; b. 1782; d. September 16, 1826, near Ypsilanti, Mich. They had issue (surname McMath):

    i. Archy, b. May 13, 1806; m. Elizabeth Kimmel.
    ii. Fleming, b. January 14, 1806; m. Eliza Prudden.
    iii. Roxanna, b. September 26, 1809; m. Orrin Derby, d. June 14, 1855, at San Francisco.
    iv. Mabel, b. June 13, 1811; d. April 14, 1839, at Berrian, Mich.; m. Uzal Williams.
    v. Samuel-K., b. March 23, 1813; m. Caroline Stuart.
    vi. Rev. *Robert*, b. February 15, 1815; m. Betsy Caroline Huggins.
    vii. Mary, b. August 2, 1817; d. January 14, 1850, at Niles, Mich.; m. Albert Percels.
    viii. Elsie, b. July 21, 1819; d. June 5, 1849, near Niles, Mich.; m. William Brewer.
    ix. William-E.-B., b. July 22, 1821; d. January 23, 1824.
    x. John-Watson, b. June 3, 1824; m. Ella Royse.

X. JAMES FLEMING,[3] (John,[2] Robert,[1]) b. January 28, 1787, at Pine Creek, Lycoming county, Penna.; d. 1870, at Rome, Lenawee county, Mich.; m. MARTHA WADE, of Romulus, N. Y. They had issue:

    i. Jeptha-Wade, b. November 13, 1808; m. Lucy Eldridge.
    ii. Jesse, b. May 14, 1811; m. Susan McConnell.
    iii. Jane, b June 12, 1812; d. July 26, 1843, at Laporte, Ind.; m. William K. Parker.
    iv. Josiah-Jacobus, b. August 6, 1814; d. 1855, at Marengo, Mich.; m. Clarissa Horner.
    v. John, b. October 6, 1816; d. July 21, 1856, at Warsaw, Mich.; m. Nancy Shuart.
    vi. Charles, b. October 30, 1818; m. Jane Shuart.
    vii. Miranda, b. February 28, 1821; d. August 9, 1822.
    viii. Lettice-S., b. January 11, 1823; m. Selek W. Chase.
    ix. Martha, b. February 17, 1825; m. Wilson Matthews.
    x. Sarah-Eliza, b. July 11, 1828; m. Thomas McConnell.
    xi. William-Allen, b. February 21, 1832; m. Angeline Stevens.

XI. ELSIE FLEMING,[3] (John,[2] Robert,[1]) b. July 21, 1791, at Romulus, N. Y.; d. April 10, 1816; m. January 2, 1810, JOSIAH JACOBUS, d. at Lodi, Michigan, aged eighty-five years. They had issue (surname Jacobus):

Fleming Family.

    i. Mary, b. October 17, 1818, at Romulus, N. Y.; m., November 19, 1835, Calvin Townsend, and they had issue (surname Townsend):
        1. *Edward-Calvin*, b. 1836.
        2. *Julius-L.*, b. March 7, 1888.

XII. SAMUEL FLEMING,³ (John,² Robert,¹) b. December 5, 1793, at Romulus, N. Y.; d. December 5, 1858, in Lenawee county, Michigan; m. PHEBE WADE. They had issue:

    i. Mary, b. November 19, 1816.
    ii. Martha, b. January 28, 1819; m. W. H. Clark.
    iii. Clarissa, b. September 15, 1821; m. Jesse Gardner.
    iv. Sarah, b. January 4, 1824; d. July 27, 1854; m. Thomas Older.
    v. Franklin-B., b. May 29, 1826; m. Louise Stoddard.
    vi. Jesse-L., b. March 3, 1829; m. Mary H. More.
    vii. Jeptha, b. July 27, 1831; m. Nancy Bust.
    viii. Rebecca-Louise, b. June 12, 1833; m. Dr. Luman S. Stevens.

XIII. JOHN FLEMING,³ (James,² Robert,¹) b. October 27, 1799, in Washington county, Pa.; m. December 24, 1835, ELIZA MCCLURG. They had issue.

    i. James, b. December 11, 1836; m. April 17, 1858, Margaret Ralston.
    ii. Joseph-M., b. April 25, 1839; m. January 27, 1860, Isabel Mercer.
    iii. Mary-Jane, b. Aug 18, 1841.
    iv. Martha-E., b. February 24, 1844; m. July 30, 1864, Alexander Ingraham.
    v. Sarah-A., b. February 19, 1846; d. 1852.
    vi. John C., b. February 7, 1848.
    vii. Robert A., b. September 12, 1849.
    viii. Rachel-A., b. May 18, 1852.
    ix. David-H., b. April 15, 1855.

XIV. DAVID S. FLEMING,³ (James,² Robert,¹) b. August 16, 1804; m, August 29, 1841, MARTHA STEELE. They had issue:

    i. Thomas-Steele, b. May 31, 1842.
    ii. Jane-Glen, b. October 9, 1844.
    iii. James-Samuel, b. August 7, 1846.
    iv. Robert, b. August 30, 1849.
    v. Rachel-Amanda, b. April 27, 1852.
    vi. Martha-Ann, b. May 21, 1856.
    vii. David-Wilson, b. March 17, 1859.

XV. JAMES FLEMING,³ (James,² Robert,¹) b. August 5, 1806, in Washington county, Pa., graduated from Washington College, Pa., in 1833, and was for two years principal of an academy in Baltimore county, Md.; licensed as a minister June 26, 1839, and installed pastor of West Union Presbyterian Church, Marshall county, Va., where he continued seventeen years; in 1858 was installed pastor of the Presbyterian Church, Washington Pa. Rev. James Fleming m. October 31, 1829, CATHARINE B. PARKS. They had issue:

  i. David-Brainerd, b. July 22, 1840, in West Union, Va.; served in the army three years, and afterwards studied for the ministry.
  ii. Martha-Jane, b. November 13, 1842; m., February 13, 1868, James F. Craighead.
  iii. James-Calvin, b. May 31, 1844.
  iv. Mary-Isabella, b. January 26, 1846; m., November 27, 1867, Martin G. Parks, of Nesponsit, Ill.
  v. John-Samuel, b. November 7, 1847.
  vi. Louise-Amanda, b. September 28, 1850.
  vii. Harriet-Newell, b. June 18, 1853.
  viii. William-Henry, b. September 17, 1856.
  iv. Alfred-Paul, b. May 31, 1859.
  x. Henry-B., December 20, 1861.

XVI. SAMUEL FLEMING,³ (James,² Robert,¹) b. June 20, 1811; resides in Armstrong county, Pa.; m., July 4, 1839, REBECCA McCOMBS. They had issue:

  i. James-Robert, b. May 29, 1840; d. October 1, 1864, in the army.
  ii. David-McCombs, b. June 1, 1841.
  iii. John-Anderson, b. April 10, 1843; killed in battle May 3, 1865.
  iv. Kosciusko-Glen, b. September 2, 1844; wounded in the shoulder in front of Petersburg, Va., which has disabled him for life.
  v. William-Kinney, b. February 13, 1845.
  vi. Samuel-Byers, b. September 19, 1848.
  vii. Elizabeth, b. May 1, 1851.
  viii. Irene-Margaret, b. February 24, 1853.
  ix. Vinet-Jane (twin), b. February 24, 1853.
  x. Stockton-McConnell, b. August 5, 1865.

XVII. MARY FLEMING,³ (Samuel,² Robert,¹) b. July 17, 1792, in Hanover, Washington county, Pa.; d. April 15, 1850, near Mt. Vernon, O.; m. June, 1811, JAMES NEWELL, b. 1782; d. December 9, 1848, near Mt. Vernon, O. They had issue (surname Newell):

   i. Margaret, b. August 1, 1812; m., May 29, 1834, Elias Murphy; resided near Newton, Iowa; and had issue (surname Murphy):

      1. *Mary-Ellen*, b. July 1835; m. George Blackman, and had issue (surname Blackman), *Clarence, Franklin*, and *George*.
      2. *Hannah-Jane*, b. May 8, 1837; m , July 10, 1863, Mr. Cox, of Tennessee.
      3. *Sarah-Newell*, b. March 15, 1840.
      4. *James-F* , b. September 25, 1842; d. August 23, 1844.
      5. *Eliza-Olive*, b. December 12, 1844.
      6. *Lewis-Mordello*, b. February 21, 1846.
      7. *Almeda*, b. May 31, 1850.
      8. *Martha-Luelle*, b. January 8, 1856.

   ii. Samuel-Fleming, b. June 10, 1814; m., December, 1838, Julia Ann Tugard; and had issue (surname Newell):

      1. *Harriet-Ann*, b. December 15, 1839 , m. Simon Galulia, of Newton, Iowa; and had issue (surname Galulia), *Harry, Franklin, Malcolm*, and *Murray*.
      2. *Mary-Adeline*, b. December 11, 1845.
      3. *Jackson-Fleming;* mortally wounded at Vicksburg, February, 1863.
      4. *Margaret-Ellen*, b. May, 1854.
      5. *Ellsworth-Loire*.

   iii. Sarah, b. July 4, 1816; d. April 3, 1849; m., March 20, 1845, Caleb Hipsley; and had issue (surname Hipsley):

      1. *Jonathan*, b. July 6, 1846.

   iv. Jane, b September 20, 1818; m., May 15, 1851, Peter Loire; reside near Mt. Vernon, O.

   v. Eliza-Ann, b. December 25, 1821.

   vi. Hugh, b. December 25, 1821; an attorney at Newton, Iowa; m. December 25, 1851, Lucinda Lee; and had issue (surname Lee), *Oneda-Ida-Irene, Duane*, and *Lunet*.

   vii. James-Scott; an attorney-at-law; m., August, 1854, Amanda Cook, and had issue (surname Newell), *Emma*, d. s. p.

XVIII. JANE FLEMING,[3] (Samuel,[2] Robert,[1]) b. May 22, 1794, in Hanover, Washington county, Pa.; d. November 30, 1843, in Knox county, Ohio; m. March 12, 1816, ROBERT GILCHRIST. In 1822 removed to Knox county, Ohio; thence in 1875 to Vernon Springs, Howard county, Iowa. They had issue (surname Gilchrist):

    i. James, b. December 29, 1816; accidentally killed April 6, 1831, in Knox county, Ohio.

    ii. Samuel-Fleming, b. August 21, 1819; educated in Kenyon College, Ohio, and Washington College, Pa.; studied law in Mt. Vernon, Ohio; was a member of the Ohio Legislature in 1849–50; afterwards probate judge of Knox county, Ohio; in 1855, removed to Howard county, Iowa, and thence to San Francisco, California; m. December 25, 1848, Mary-Ann Blackman; and had issue (surname Gilchrist):

        1. *Francis-Marion*, b. October 10, 1844.
        2. *Inez-Augusta*, b. August 10, 1847.
        3. *William Murray*, b. July 19, 1849.
        4. *John Halder*, b. August 21, 1851.
        5. *Frederick*, d. in infancy.

    iii. Robert Jackson, b. February 5, 1822; d. October 12, 1822.

    iv. Robert-Scott, b. August 5, 1823, in Knox county, Ohio; educated at Kenyon College, Ohio; studied medicine, and graduated from Cleveland Medical College in 1853; located at DeGraff, Ohio; m. first, August 31, 1852, Philena H. Brooks, of Columbus, Ohio; d. November 18, 1854, and had issue, *Mary*, d. s. p.; m. secondly, May 15, 1856, Annie M. Brooks, of DeGraff, Ohio; and had issue, *Fay-H.*

    v. Elizabeth, b. September 12, 1826; d. March 2, 1845.

    vi. Sarah-Jane, b. September 12, 1830; d. August 20, 1845.

    vii. Mary-E., b. July 6, 1836; m., August 4, 1855, in Granville, Ohio, Rev. A. Nichols, of the M. E. Church, and had issue (surname Nichols) *Jamas, Inez, William,* and *Gura.*

XIX. ROBERT JACKSON FLEMING,[3] (Samuel,[2] Robert,[1]) b. November 16, 1803, in Hanover township, Washington county, Pa.; d. December 2, 1874, at Harrisburg, Pa. He received an academical education, and while yet a young man became a teacher and lecturer on English grammar and on music, and took a trip to the then West, lecturing on his favorite topic. In 1834 he established the coach-making business on an extensive scale at Harrisburg, Pa., and continued it with success until his entire establishment was destroyed by fire June 15, 1865. He did not resume it. He built at his shop the first eight-wheel passenger car which ran on the Pennsylvania railroad between Columbia and Philadelphia, also the first on the Williamsport and Elmira railroad, taking it up the canal on a flat boat. He was appointed notary public in 1861, and held the office until his death, for years doing the business of the Harrisburg National Bank in this official capacity. He was deservedly honored in his adopted city as an upright and enterprising citizen, a man of intelligence and high moral character, and in the Presbyterian Church, of which he was a life-long member, he was one of its elders for twenty years. Mr. Fleming married, June 5, 1845, at McConnellsville, Morgan county, Ohio, SARAH ANN POOR, b. January 30, 1814, at York Haven, Pa.; dau. of Charles Merrill Poor and Elizabeth (Karg) Roberts; died in Harrisburg, Pa., at the residence of her son, Samuel W. Fleming, January 7, 1892. They had issue:

 i. Sarah-Elizabeth, b. January 25, 1847; d. July 18, 1850.
 ii. Mary-Frances, b. February 27, 1848; d. January 28, 1852.
 iii. Samuel-Wilson, b. December 11, 1849; has been engaged in the book and stationery business since graduating at Lafayette College in 1875; was a member of the Common Council of Harrisburg for five years; serving one year as president of that body; elected by Councils in 1856 to fill the unexpired term of the mayor, who died in office; m. October 7, 1875, Mary Malvina Sausser, b. March 4, 1852, in Massillion, Ohio; dau. of Benjamin F. Sausser and Lucetta Dangler; and had issue:

  1. *Lucetta*, b. December 16, 1876; d. March 30, 1881.
  2. *Robert-Jackson*, b. February 3, 1878; d. October 17, 1878.
  3. *Elizabeth*, b. August 7, 1879; d. June 30, 1880.
  4. *Mary*, b. November 22, 1880.
  5. *Margaret*, b. October 30, 1882.
  6. *Alice*, b. March 2, 1884; d. October 16, 1886.
  7. *Samuel-Wilson*, b. July 7, 1885.
  8. *Charles-Sausser*, b. August 4, 1887; d. May 25, 1888.

XX. JAMES FLEMING,[3] (Samuel,[2] Robert,[1]) b. June 25, 1810, in Hanover township, Washington county, Pa.; d. January 30, 1875, in Harrisburg, Pa. In 1812 his parents removed to Hanover township, Dauphin county, Pa., where his early years were passed. His boyhood was marked by a laudable ambition to excel in his studies, and the influence of his mother in this direction had its good effect, not only during his youth, but throughout his life. Thrown upon his own resources, at the age of eighteen, he resolved to educate himself by alternately acting as teacher and pupil, and pursued this course for seven years, thereby becoming conversant with the higher mathematics, the ancient languages, and French. Much of his time was passed in the States of Kentucky and Ohio. About 1835 he commenced the study of medicine, and graduated at Jefferson Medical College, Philadelphia, in March, 1838. For four years he practiced his profession, but finding the duties too arduous for his slender constitution, his attention was drawn to the science of dental surgery, then comparatively in its infancy. Observing the necessity for good operators in this field, he went to Philadelphia and acquired a thorough knowledge of that specialty. Returning to Harrisburg, he met with deserved and well-marked success. During the remainder of his life he was a frequent contributor to both medical and dental journals, and occasionally to the newspaper press. He was a member of the Pennsylvania Association of Dental Surgeons and of the American Society, and one of the original advocates of the establishment of a dental college at Philadelphia, in which he was subsequently tendered a professorship, but declined. He was twice the recipient of the honorary degree of Doctor of Dental Surgery. He was a director of the Harrisburg National Bank, president of the board of school-directors, and an elder of the First Presbyterian church there. Dr. Fleming married, June, 1852, JENNETTE STREET, daughter of Col. Thaddeus Street and Martha Davenport Reynolds, of Cheshire, Conn., a lineal descendant of Rev. John Davenport, the founder of New Haven. Her maternal grandmother, Martha Davenport, was a descendant of Oliver Wolcott, a signer of the Declaration of Independence. She resides in Germantown, Pa. They had issue:

>   i. *Helen-Street*, b. June 2, 1853; m., November 10, 1881, Daniel Pastorious Bruner, of Columbia, Pa., a lawyer and civil engineer.
>   ii. *James-Lewis*, b. February 28, 1856; d. June 8, 1858.
>   iii. *William-Reynolds*, b. May 9, 1862.

XXI. DAVID FLEMING,[3] (Samuel,[2] Robert,[1]) b. July 17, 1812, in Hanover township, Washington county, Pa.; d. at Harrisburg, Pa., January 14, 1890. He received his education in the public schools of the day, and in the Harrisburg Academy, alternating later in life by teaching the classics and higher mathematics. In 1838 he began the editing of a newspaper at Harrisburg, at the same time reporting the proceedings of the Legislature for several of the Philadelphia journals. In 1839 he commenced the study of the law with William McClure, admitted to the Dauphin county bar at the November term, 1841, and was in active practice at the courts until his decease. From 1843 he practiced in the Supreme Court of the State. In 1847 he was elected chief clerk of the House of Representatives, and served during the session. In 1854 he was elected district attorney. In 1863 elected to the State Senate, and was Speaker of that body at the closing session of the term. In the various business enterprises of the city of Harrisburg he took a prominent part, and was largely interested in a number of them. Mr. Fleming married, January 1, 1852, SUSAN MOWRY, daughter of Charles Mowry* and Mary Richmond. They had issue:

> i. *Charles-Mowry*, b. March 9, 1853; d. March, 1883; a graduate of Princeton, studied law with his father, and was admitted to the bar September 1, 1877; naturally gifted, he was entering upon a career of usefulness, when he was stricken down by disease.

---

*CHARLES MOWRY was born in Litchfield, Providence county, R. I., in 1777. He received a classical education, and came to Pennsylvania about 1800, and engaged in teaching. In 1808 he began the publication of the *Temperate Zone*, at Downingtown, Chester county. This was subsequently changed to the *American Republican*, and Mr. Mowry continued its publication until 1821, when he came to Harrisburg in the interest of William Findlay, who was a candidate for Governor of Pennsylvania for a second term, and became editor of the *Pennsylvania Intelligencer*, previously the *Harrisburg Republican*. This paper he eventually disposed of to Gen. Simon Cameron, who had been associated with him as co-partner in its management, in order that he might assume the duties of Canal Commissioner, to which he had been appointed by Governor Shulze. During his career as editor, he acquired considerable celebrity as a political writer, and exercised a marked influence upon the policy of his party. He died at Harrisburg, July 29, 1838. He married, March 31, 1812, MARY RICHMOND, daughter of George Richmond, of Sadsbury township, Chester county. She died March 28, 1862, aged seventy-six years. They had six children—three sons, since deceased, and three daughters—*Mary*, m. Samuel D. Young, d. January 1, 1885; *Susan*, m. David Fleming; and *Jane*, unm.

ii. *Sara*, b. April 15, 1855; graduated at Vassar College; m., June 5, 1890, Joshua W. Sharpe, a lawyer; reside at Chambersburg, Pa.
iii. *David*, b. May 4, 1857; graduated at Princeton College, N. J.; m., October 16, 1884, Mary Curwen, dau. of Dr. John Curwen; and had issue:
  1. *Martha-Elmer*, b. March 6, 1889.
  2. *David*, b. April 21, 1892.
iv. *George-Richmond*, b. September 19, 1860; graduated at Princeton College, N. J.; m., October 9, 1890, Eliza McCormick Robinson, dau. of Rev. Thomas H. Robinson, D. D.; and had issue:
  1. *Anna-Margaretta*, b. July 30, 1891.
  2. *Susan-Mowry*, b. 1895.

XXII. ROBERT MCCONNELL,³ (Mary,² Robert,¹) b. December 5, 1794; m., June 13, 1825, EDITH HAMLIN. They had issue (surname McConnell):

i. *Fleming*, b. July 14, 1826; m., December 27, 1858, Elizabeth M. Donald.
ii. *Alexander*, b. November 1, 1828; m., October 23, 1856.
iii. *Robert-Simpson*, b. May 25, 1831.

XXIII. JAMES MCCONNELL,³ (Mary,² Robert,¹) b. October 27, 1796; d. May 28, 1852; m. NANCY SHIPLEY. They had issue (surname McConnell):

i. *John*, b. 1821; m. Margery Steele, and had issue: *James-A.*, *John-C.*, *Rachel-A.*, *Nancy-C.*, and *Thomas-N.*
ii. *Henrietta*, b. January 10, 1823; m., November 2, 1850, Nathaniel Gillespie; and had issue (surname Gillespie):
  1. *Emma-Virginia*, b. September 1, 1852.
  2. *Ella-Amanda*, b. November 2, 1853.
  3. *Clara-Bell*, b. November 19, 1854; d. September 14, 1856.
  4. *Maggie Jane*, b. December 20, 1855.
  5. *Adaliza-Clarissa*, b. January 12, 1857.
  6. *Mary-Mabel*, b. September 29, 1859.
  7. *Laura-Etta*, b. December 16, 1860.
  8. *William-McConnell*, b. February 22, 1862.
  9. *James-Anderson*, b. February 26, 1863.
  10. *John-Orlando*, b. May 27, 1864.
  11. *Sarah-Eva*, b. August 6, 1865.
iii. *Martha-Ann*, m. Nelson Maxwell, and had issue (surname Maxwell) *Nancy-Ann*, *Sarah-Jane*, and *Joseph*.
iv. *Rachel*, m. September 30, 1857, Brown McKay; and had issue.
v. *Mary-Elizabeth*, m. John Steele; and had issue.

vi. Sarah, m. William Reed, and had issue (surname Reed).
Alexander, James-Clement, John-Willis, and William-H.-Franklin.
vii. Jane, m. John Ryenearson.
viii. Nancy-Adaline, d. s. p.
ix. Robert-A., d. in hospital at Gallatin, Tennesse, in 1865.

XXIV. ELIZABTEH McCONNELL,[2] (Mary,[2] Robert,[1]) b. April 9, 1798; d.; m. June 6, 1816, SAMUEL McCARRELL, b. March 1, 1788, in York county, Pa.; d. June, 1881, in Hanover township, Washington county, Pa. They had issue (surname McCarrell):

    i. Alexander, b. September 22, 1817; d. May, 1881; graduated from Washington College, Pa., in 1841; licensed by Washington Presbytery April 17, 1844; pastor of the Presbyterian church, Claysville, and was commissioner to the general assembly of his church at St. Louis, in 1851, and at Newark, N. J., in 1864; m., January 22, 1842, Martha McClain, and had issue (surname McCarrell):

        1. *Samuel-John-Milton*, b. October 19, 1842; graduated from Washington College, Pa., 1864; studied law with David Fleming, at Harrisburg, Pa., and admitted to the bar in 1866; elected district attorney for Dauphin county, Pa., 1880, and re-elected in 1883; elected State Senator from the Dauphin county district for the full term of four years commencing January, 1893; m. Rebecca Wallace, and had issue:

            a. Wallace-Alexander, b. November 26, 1876; d. December 16, 1880.

            b. Samuel-John-McClain, b. December 7, 1881.

        2. *William-Alexander*, b. August 20, 1846.

        3. *Joseph-James*, b. July 9, 1849.

        4. *Thomas-Calvin*, b. September 29, 1856.

        5. *Elizabeth-Mary*, b. July 28, 1862.

    ii. Louise-Jane, b. December 25, 1819.

    iii. Mary-Elizabeth, b. October 28, 1822; d. September 12, 1826.

    iv. Samuel-Milton, b. July 22, 1825; d. September 24, 1851; a physician.

    v. Mary-Eleanor, b. November 6, 1830; graduated from Female College, Washington, Pa.; d. November, 1858.

    vi. James-Fleming, b. October 26, 1832; a physician; residing at Eldersville, Washington county, Pa.; m., November 16, 1865, Jennie E. Hayes; and had issue:

        1. *John-Milton*, b. August 17, 1866.

    vii. Lysander-Thomas, b. July 22, 1840.

    viii. Elizabeth-Alvira, b. December 17, 1842.

FAMILY OF FORSTER.

I. JOHN FORSTER,[1] a native of county Antrim, Ireland, of Scotch parentage, emigrated to America prior to 1722, and located in Paxtang township, Lancaster, now Dauphin, county, Penna.; he was twice married, dying prior to 1749. By his first wife, ELIZABETH CHAMBERS, a daughter of Arthur Chambers, dying in the Province of Pennsylvania, there was issue:

    i. *Thomas*, b. 1696; d. July 25, 1772. He came to America with his father's family, and was among the first who took up land in what is now Dauphin county, Penna. He was a gentleman of means, had received a good education, and was for many years one of the Provincial magistrates. He was removed late in life, on account of his refusal to oust some squatters on Proprietary lands. He was a prominent personage, on the then frontiers of the Province, in civil affairs. During the Indian troubles he greatly assisted in preparing for the defense of the border settlements, and his name appears frequently in the voluminous correspondence preserved in the archives of the State. He died in Paxtang, aged seventy-six years, and is buried in the old church graveyard. Mr. Forster was never married; the principal part of his estate went to his brother, John, and nephew, Thomas Forster, the latter named for him.

    ii. *Arthur*, b. 1705; d. unm.

    iii. *Agnes*, b. 1708, m. John Moore, son of Andrew Moore, of Derry.

    iv. *William*, b. 1710; m. Rachel Kelly, daughter of Patrick and Rachel Kelly, of Londonderry township, then Lancaster county, Pa.; and had *James*, m. Elizabeth Espy.

    v. *Elizabeth*, b. 1713; m. Jacob Ellis, of Hanover; descendants removed to Virginia; their daughter, *Sarah*, m. Robert Gilchrist.

    vi. *Margaret*, b. 1720; m. John Graham, d. 1764.

2.   vii. *John*, b. 1725; m. Catharine Dickey.

By his second wife, Sarah, there was issue:

3.   viii. *James*, b. 1728; m. Elizabeth Moore.

    ix. *Isabel*, b. 1731.

4.   x. *Stephen*, b. 1733; m. Mary Chambers.

Family of Forster. 247

II. JOHN FORSTER,² (John,¹) b. 1725, in Paxtang township, Lancaster county, Pa.; d. September, 1789, in Paxtang township, Dauphin county, Pa.; was a private in Capt. William Bell's company of the Fourth Battalion of Lancaster county associators in service in the Jerseys during the summer of 1776; m. CATHARINE DICKEY, b. 1738, in Chester county, Pa.; d. November 23, 1804, in Paxtang township, Dauphin county, Pa., daughter of Moses and Agnes Dickey. They had issue:

5.   *i. Thomas*, b. May 16, 1762; m. Sarah Pettit Montgomery.
6.   *ii. Dorcas*, b. 1764; m. William Bell.
    iii. Mary, b. 1767; d. August 2, 1810, s. p.; m. Cornelius Cox.
    iv. Agnes, m. George Nelson.
7.   *v. John*, b. September 17, 1777; m. first, Mary Elder; second, Margaret S. Law.
    vi. Elizabeth, m. William R. Hanna; no issue.
8.   *vii. Margaret*, m. first, John McFarland; secondly, Thomas Stewart.

III. JAMES FORSTER,² (John,¹) b. 1728, in Paxtang township, Lancaster, now Dauphin county, Pa., d. in Londonderry township; was a Revolutionary soldier in the Jersey campaign of 1776, Col. Burd's battalion of Lancaster county associators; m. ELIZABETH MOORE, daughter of Andrew Moore, of Derry. They had issue:

    i. Andrew.
    ii. Mary, d. March 15, 1796; m. James Cavet, removed to Westmoreland county, Penna.; and had (surname Cavet), *James-Forster*, and *Mary.*
    iii. Sarah, m. David Patton.
    iv. Elizabeth, m. James Kelly, Esq.
    v. Catharine, m. Andrew Moore.
    vi. David, m. and removed to Rowan county, N. C.; had *John*, and other children.
9.   *vii. William*, b. 1757; m. Margaret Ayres.
    viii. Josiah.

IV. STEPHEN FORSTER,² (John,¹) b. 1733, in Paxtang township, Lancaster, now Dauphin county, Penna; d. February, 1792, in Turbut township, Northumberland county, Penna; m. MARY CHAMBERS, daughter of John and Margaret Chambers, of Paxtang. They had issue:

    i. Chambers.
    ii. Stephen.
    iii. Thomas.

V. THOMAS FORSTER,³ (John,² John,¹) b. May 16, 1762, in Paxtang township, Lancaster, now Dauphin county, Pa.; d. June 29, 1836, at Erie, Pa. He received a good education, and was brought up as a surveyor. In the Revolutionary struggle he was a private in Capt. John Reed's company in the summer of 1776, in active service during the Jersey campaign of that year. In 1794, during the so-called Whiskey Insurrection, he served as colonel of one of the volunteer regiments on that expedition. He was one of the associate judges of Dauphin county, appointed October 26, 1793, by Governor Mifflin, resigning December 3, 1798, having been elected one of the representatives of the State Legislature that year. At the close of 1799 or early in 1800, as the agent of the Harrisburg and Presque Isle Land company, he permanently removed to Erie. In the affairs incident to the early settlement of that town and the organization of that county, he took a prominent part. He was one of the first street commissioners of the town, president of the Erie and Waterford Turnpike company, one of the directors of the first library company and its librarian, and captain of the first military company formed at Erie, and which in 1812, was in service at Buffalo, Capt. Forster being promoted brigade inspector. In 1823 he was appointed by Governor Shulze one of the commissioners to explore the route for the Erie extension of the Pennsylvania canal, and in 1827 was chairman of the meeting organizing St. Paul's Episcopal church. In 1799 he was appointed by President Adams collector of the port at Erie, and successively commissioned by Presidents Jefferson, Madison, J. Q. Adams, and Jackson, filling the office until his death. Col. Forster m. October 5, 1786, SARAH PETTIT MONTGOMERY, b. July, 1766, at Georgetown, Kent county, Md.; d. July 27, 1808, at Erie, Pa.; daughter of Rev. Joseph Montgomery,* and Elizabeth Reed. They had issue:

---

*JOSEPH MONTGOMERY, son of John and Martha Montgomery emigrants from Ireland, was born September 23, 1733, (O. S.,) in Paxtang township, then Lancaster, now Dauphin county, Pa. He was educated at the College of New Jersey, from which he graduated in 1755, and was afterwards appointed master of the grammar school connected with the college. In 1760 the College of Philadelphia and Yale College conferred upon him the Master's degree. About this

Family of Forster. 249

  i. Elizabeth-Rachel, b. July 25, 1787, in Paxtang; d. 1852 at Syracuse, N. Y.; m. Major James E. Herron, d. ln 1860 or 1862 at Syracuse, N. Y.; no surviving issue.
10. *ii. John-Montgomery*, b. June 21, 1789; m. Jennette Wright.
  iii. Catharine-Ann, b. June 10, 1791, in Paxtang; d. December 17, 1839, at Erie, Pa.; m. first, February 6, 1816, Richard T. Timberlake, purser U. S. N.; d. October 2, 1816; m., secondly, James Armstrong Bailey, captain U. S. A., and had (surname Bailey,) *Theodore*, d. s. p.; and *Sarah* m. Mr. Rathbone, of Elmira, N. Y.
  iv. Mary-Theodosia, b. August 16, 1793, at Harrisburg, Pa.; d. 1820; m. Col. John Harris, who died at Washington a few years ago, commandant of the marine corps; no issue.
  v. Joseph-Montgomery, b. March 21, 1795; d. s. p.
11. *vi. Thomas*, b. September 13, 1796; m. Juliet Bell.
  vii. Sarah, b. November 24, 1797, at Harrisburg; d. 1879 in Erie county, Pa.; m. ―――― Roberts; no issue.
  viii. Eleanor-Reed, b. August 20, 1799; d. August 5, 1801.
  ix. Samuel-Laird, b. August 8, 1801, at Erie. Pa., where he d. in 1860; m. Jane H. Benedict; and had issue.
12. *x. Hannah-Wickersham*, b. January 31, 1804; m. Edwin Vose Sumner.
13. *xi. Margaret-Wallace*, b. September 10, 1806; m. George W. Wright.

---

time he was licensed to preach by the Presbytery of Philadelphia, and soon after, by request, entered the bounds of the Presbytery of Lewes, from which he was transferred to that of New Castle, accepting a call from the congregations at Georgetown, over which he was settled from 1767 to 1769. He was installed pastor of the congregations at Christiana Bridge and New Castle, Delaware, on the 16th of August, 1769, remaining there until the autumn of 1777, when he resigned, having been commissioned chaplain of Col. Smallwood's (Maryland) regiment of the Continental Line. During the war his home was with his relatives in Paxtang. On the 23d of November, 1780, he was chosen by the General Assembly of Pennsylvania one of its delegates in Congress, and re-elected the following year. He was elected a member of the Assembly of the State in 1782, serving during that session. He was chosen by that body, February 25, 1783, one of the commissioners to settle the difficulty between the State and the Connecticut settlers at Wyoming. When the new county of Dauphin was erected, the Supreme Executive Council appointed him recorder of deeds and register of wills for the county, which office he held from March 11, 1785, to October 14, 1794, the date of his death. "Mr. Montgomery filled conspicuous and honorable positions in church

VI. DORCAS FORSTER,³ (John,² John,¹) b. 1764, in Lower Paxtang township, Lancaster, now Dauphin county, Penna.; d. April 10, 1826, at Erie, Penna.; she m. WILLIAM BELL, b. 1744, in Lower Paxtang township, Lancaster county, Penna.; d. September, 1813, at Erie, Pa.; son of William Bell. He was captain of a company in the Lancaster County battalion of associators, commanded by Col. James Burd, in 1776, and in active service in the Jerseys during that year, as also in the years 1777 and 1778. Mr. Bell was an ardent patriot, and influential in public affairs. They had issue (surname Bell):

  i. Catharine, m. William McDonald ; family went South.
  ii. Lucinda, m. Jonathan Baird ; no record.
14. *iii. Jane*, m. Samuel Hays.

---

and State in the most trying period of the early history of the country. In the church he was the friend and associate of men like Witherspoon, Rogers, and Spencer, and his bold utterances in the cause of independence stamp him as a man of no ordinary courage and decision. * * * He enjoyed to an unusual degree the respect and confidence of the men of his generation." The Rev. Mr. Montgomery was twice married ; m., first, in 1765, ELIZABETH REED, d. March, 1769, daughter of Andrew and Sarah Reed, of Trenton, N. J., and had issue :

  i. Sarah-Pettit, b. July, 1766 ; m. Thomas Forster.
  ii. Elizabeth, b July 17, 1768 ; d. October 12, 1814, in Harrisburg, Pa., m. Samuel Laird, b. at Carlisle, Pa., 15th February, 1769, son of Samuel Laird (1732-1806) and Mary Young, (1741-1833,) daughter of James Young. His father was for many years one of the provincial magistrates of Cumberland county, and, under the Constitution of 1776, one of the justices of the courts. Mr. Laird received a classical education, studied law at Carlisle, and was admitted to the Dauphin county bar at the September term, 1792. He located at Harrisburg, and soon secured a large and successful practice. In the early years of the borough he took an active part in its local affairs, and was a prominent actor in the first decade of its history. He died at Harrisburg, Pa., January 15, 1815.

Mr. Montgomery m., secondly, July 11, 1770, RACHEL (RUSH) BOYCE, b. 1741, in Byberry ; d. July 28, 1798, in Harrisburg, Pa.; widow of Angus Boyce, and daughter of Thomas and Rachel Rush : and had issue :

  iii. John, b. December 23, 1771 ; probably d. s. p.

Family of Forster.

   iv. John, m. Matilda Reed ; and had issue : *William-Edwin,* m., and had *Mary* and *Jessie.*
   v. Elizabeth, m. James Tewksbury, Master in U. S. Navy; d. September 1, 1843, and they had issue (surname Tewksbury):
      1. *Elizabeth,* m. ———— Williams, of Philadelphia.
      2. *Mary.*
      3. *Josephine,* m. Stephen Law, of New York ; and had issue (surname Law): *James-Tewksbury.*
      4. *James,* m. Helen Reed, and had *Kate* and *Elizabeth.*
   vi. Sarah, m. Robert Heron ; went South.
   vii. Juliet, m. Thomas Forster, Jr. (*see* XI.)
   viii. William, d. unm.
   ix. Maria-Dorcas, m. Peter King Rockwell, of California, and left issue.

VII. JOHN FORSTER,[3] (John,[2] John,[1]) b. September 17, 1777, in Paxtang, Lancaster, now Dauphin county, Pa.; d. May 28, 1863, at Harrisburg, Pa.; he received a good education and was at Princeton when a call was made by President Washington for volunteers to march to Western Pennsylvania to put down the so-called " Whiskey Insurrection " of 1794, and was on that expedition as an aid to General Murray. He subsequently read law with General Hanna, but never applied for admission, turning his attention to mercantile pursuits, in which he was very successful. During the military era of the government prior to the war of 1812 he was colonel of State militia, and in 1814, when the troops from Pennsylvania marched to the defense of the beleaguered city of Baltimore, he was placed in command of a brigade of volunteers. For his gallant services in that campaign the thanks of the general commanding were tendered in special orders. He served in the State Senate from 1814 to 1818. General Forster was cashier of the Harrisburg Bank for a period of at least sixteen years, established the Bank of Lewistown, and in 1837 was cashier of the Exchange Bank of Pittsburgh. He subsequently became president of the Branch Bank at Hollidaysburg, but in a few years retired from all business pursuits and returned to his home at Harrisburg. General Forster was faithful, honest and upright in all his business connections, and a good financier. He was twice married; m., first, September 25, 1798,

MARY ELDER, b. 1779; d. December 18, 1831, at Harrisburg, Pa.; dau. of John Elder and Elizabeth Awl, (*see Elder Record*). They had issue:

 i. John-Elder, b 1799; d. May 15, 1879, at Washington city, D. C.; m. Elizabeth Culbertson Law; d. January 26, 1889; dau. of Benjamin Law, of Mifflin county, Pa.; and had issue:

  1. *John-Theodore*, b. March 24, 1834; m., November 20, 1862, Annie Elizabeth McMicken, b. November 29, 1836.
  2. *Henry-Kirkland*.
  3. *William-Law*, d. August 25, 1881; m., first, Euphemia North; and had issue, *Mary* and *Lewis;* m., secondly, Frances Welles; and had issue, *William-H., John-W., Carrie*, and *Francis-R.*
  4. *James-Henry-Stuart*; d. January 7, 1878; d. s. p.
  5. *Thomas*, d. March 28, 1868.
  6. *Rebecca-Lusk*, b. April 3, 1845; m. Alfred Foot, major U. S. A.; d. September 1, 1869; and had issue (surname Foot):
   a. Samuel-Alfred, b. October 24, 1866.
  7. *Mary-Elder*, d. July 4, 1881; s. p.; m. Prescott Hosmer.
  8. *Eliza-Heron*, b. June 19, 1850; m., November 12, 1873, Charles C. Duncanson, b. September 30, 1845.
  9. *Annie-Cowden*, b. September 19, 1853; m. Thomas Humphries Young, b. September 1, 1845; and had issue (surname Young):
   a. Mary-Elizabeth, b. September 27, 1874.
   b. Jane-Randolph, b. May 16, 1876.
   c. Charles-Duncanson, b. May 19, 1878.
  10. *Wilson-Rutherford*, m. Alice B. Weizgarver; and had *Jessie*.

 ii. Catharine, b. 1802; d. February 8, 1872; m. Henry Antes, b. December 4, 1784; d. January 8, 1860, at Harrisburg, Pa.; son of Philip Antes and his wife Susanna, dau. of Charles Williams, of Paxtang; was in mercantile life many years at Harrisburg; was a soldier of the war of 1812-14; clerk in the Land Department of the State; and frequently a member of the borough council of Harrisburg; and had issue (surname Antes):

  1. *John Forster*, m. and resides in Missouri.
  2. *Henry-P.*
  3. *Emory*, d. s. p.
  4. *Mary-Forster*, m. M. R. Simons; and had issue (surname Simons), *Antes-Marcus*, and *Marcus-Antes*.

5. *Lucy*, m. Signor Muzio.
6. *Josephine*, d. s. p.
7. *Elizabeth*, d. s. p.

iii. *Mary*, d. s. p.
iv. *Joshua-Elder*, b. 1800 ; d. July 30, 1864 ; m., August 11, 1832, Elizabeth Lewis Alder, eldest daughter of Joshua William Alder ; and had issue :
   1. *Joshua-Alder*, b. May 27, 1833.
   2. *Oscar-Elder*, b. December 22, 1834.
   3. *Charles*, b. June 23, 1836.
   4. *John-Adams*, b. November 1, 1838; d. October 18, 1841.
   5. *Frank-Emlin*, b. June 9, 1845 ; m., March 29, 1894, Louise Wistar, youngest dau. of Hon. James Lowrie, of Wellsboro', Pa.

v. Rev. *Thomas*, b. November 15, 1812 ; d. February 17, 1889 ; m., February 9, 1848, Eliza Rich Hall ; b. July 8, 1822 ; dau. of Dr. Ebenezer Hall ; and had issue :
   1. *Mary-Elizabeth*, b. November 3, 1848.
   2. *Thomas-Hall*, b. January 7, 1852; m. January 17, 1879, Mary Estella Brehler ; d. January 6, 1894; and had issue :
      a. *Frank-Spencer*, b. January 13, 1880.
      b. *Grace-Mary*, b. March 23, 1882.
      c. *Burton*, b. January 1, 1894.
   3. *John-Ebenezer*, b. September 15, 1855.
   4. *George-Chalmers*, b. February 9, 1858 ; m. Jennie Moon ; and had issue :
      a. *Thomas-Chalmers*, b. October 31, 1891.

vi. *Theodore*, d. January 9, 1883, in St. Louis, Mo.; was twice married; m., first, Mary Bryan, daughter of Judge Bryan, of Geneseo, N. Y.; and had issue :
   1. *Bryan*, b. April 6, 1852, at Selma, Mo., d. July 20, 1883 ; m., May 6, 1874, Jennie T. Cole ; b. April 2, 1852 ; dau. of Capt. George Cole, of Potosi, Mo.; and had issue :
      a. *Theodore*, b. October 29, 1875.
      b. *Katharine-Peers*, b. September 29, 1877.
      c. *George-Cole*, b. January 7, 1880.
      d. *Bryan*, b. December 25, 1881.

He m., secondly, April 14, 1875, Virginia Hamilton, second dau. of Hon. Alexander Hamilton, of St. Louis, Mo., and Julia A. Keen, his wife, who was a dau. of Reynold Keen and Nancy Lawrence ; Alexander Hamilton was a son of Hugh and Sarah Hamilton, of Philadelphia, who entered upon his professional career when quite young,

in the west, and it was said of him that he brought his code of practice with him—attaining high rank as a lawyer and judge in Missouri. No issue.
 vii. *Washington,* d. unm.
 viii. *William-M.,* b. August 8, 1820 ; d. September 25, 1893 ; m. Rachel Elvira Whitely, b. June 1, 1828, in Baltimore county, Maryland ; d. April 25, 1891, at Lancaster, Pa.

Gen. Forster m., secondly, July 9, 1833, MARGARET SNODGRASS LAW; b. March 6, 1804; d. December 9, 1891 ; daughter of Benjamin Law, of Mifflin county, Pa., and widow of Rev. James H. Stuart,* a Presbyterian minister of the Kishacoquillas valley. They had issue :

 ix. *Benjamin-Law,* b. August 29, 1834 ; educated at Harrisburg Academy, Hartsville, Bucknell University, and at Yale College; studied law under Herman Alricks, and was admitted to the Dauphin county bar January 22, 1858. Mr. Forster m., June 8, 1864, Annie Bull Alricks, b. in 1838 ; d. April 26, 1888 ; and had issue :
  1. *Caroline-Alricks,* b. June 20, 1865 ; m. December 29, 1891, William Rollison Duncan, of Wilmington, Del.; and had issue (surname Duncan):
   a. *Margery-Alricks,* b. October 30, 1892.
   b. *Hamilton-Alricks,* b. May 12, 1895.
  2. *John-Douglass,* b. October 12, 1866 ; a civil engineer ; educated in Harrisburg Academy and Lehigh University ; has been employed on the Clinch Valley extension and Norfolk & Western railroad, Pennsylvania railroad, and on the Second Corps Inter-Continental Railway on surveys from Quito, Ecuador, to Cusco, Peru, South America.
 x. *Orsan-Douglass,* b. January 21, 1843 ; d. November 30, 1865 ; unm.; entered the military service as first sergeant mounted artillery in 1862 ; afterward commissioned assistant surgeon, Twelfth Pennsylvania Cavalry.
 xi. *Margaret-Snodgrass,* b. May 6, 1844 ; m., January 18, 1866, Edwin Vose Sumner, b. August 16, 1835, at Carlisle Barracks, Pa.; in April, 1861, offered his services as first sergeant of the Clay Guards, of Washington, D. C.; appointed August 5, 1861, at large, second lieutenant First Cavalry ; promoted first lieutenant November 12, 1861, and captain September 23, 1863 ; served in the de-

---

*They had one son, Dr. James H. Stuart, assistant surgeon U. S. N., who was lost on the "Porpoise," which went down in the China Sea in 1854.

fenses of Washington, 1861–62, and in the Manasses and Peninsular campaign as an aide-de-camp to Brig. Gen. George Stoneman; participated in the closing operations of the Maryland campaign; was appointed an additional aide-de camp with the rank of major to date from May 19, 1863, serving until September, when he joined his regiment, and during winter of 1863–64, was on the line of the Rapidan until after the battle of the Wilderness; was wounded at the battle of Todd's Tavern; returned to duty in July, 1864; appointed colonel of the First New York Mounted Rifles to date from September 8, 1864, and served with the army of the James until the close of the war, and mustered out of volunteer service November 29, 1865; was made a brevet major to date from March 13, 1865, for gallant and meritorious services, and a brevet brigadier general of volunteers in April, 1866; joined his company on the Pacific coast and served in the Modoc, Nez Perces, and Bannock wars; promoted major of the Fifth Cavalry to date from March 4, 1879; lieutenant colonel Eighth Cavalry April 15, 1894, now colonel Seventh Cavalry; and had issue (surname Sumner):

  1. *Margaret-Forster*, b. March 5, 1867; m., December 14, 1887, John Miller Carson, Jr., first lieutenant Fifth Cavalry, U. S. A.; and had issue (surname Carson):
      a. *Margaret Sumner*, b. January 14, 1890.
  2. *Hannah*, b. July 7, 1876.
  3. *Edwin-Vose*, b. October 7, 1884.
xii. *Ellen-Rutherford*, b. November 19, 1846; m. George Conway Bent, b. July 11, 1844; and had issue (surname Bent):
  1. *Elizabeth-Conway*, b. May 21, 1874.
xiii. *Mary-Elizabeth*, b. May 23, 1850; m., September 2, 1875, James Edward Cann, b. May 15, 1846, in Nova Scotia; appointed from Pennsylvania assistant paymaster U. S. N., July 14, 1870; promoted to first assistant October 22, 1878; was paymaster 1895; and had issue (surname Cann):
  1. *Barry-Bingay*, b. September 3, 1876.

VIII. MARGARET FORSTER,[3] (John,[2] John,[1]) b. circa, 1780, in Paxtang township, Lancaster, now Dauphin county, Pa.; d. January 16, 1835, in Mill Creek township, Erie county, Pa. She was twice married. She m., first, JOHN MCFARLAND, b. 1777; d. circa, 1802. They had issue (surname McFarland):

i. Catharine, b. July 25, 1798, in Lycoming county, Pa.; m. David Love.

ii. John, b. February 13, 1800; d. September 2, 1881; m., first, Salome Atkinson, d. September 18, 1842, and had issue, *Thomas, John, Archibald, William, Margaret, George*, and *Georgiana*. He m., secondly, May 17, 1843, Augusta Atkinson, and had issue, *Salome, Malcolm, Sarah-Atkinson*, and *Frank-Monroe*.

iii. Thomas.

Mrs. McFarland m. secondly, THOMAS STEWART, b. 1778; d. March 6, 1838, at Meadville, Pa. They had issue (surname Stewart):

iv. Eleanor.

v. Archibald-Forster, b. December 25, 1805, at Erie, Pa.; d. August 27, 1867, at Meadville, Pa.; m., November 3, 1842, Rebecca Reynolds; and had issue:
  1. *Edward-Reynolds*.
  2. *Margaret-Forster*, m. Hon. John H. Derby, of Sandy Hill, Washington county, N. Y.; and had issue (surname Derby): *Archibald-Stewart, Anna-Louise,* and *John H.*
  3. *Mary-Catharine*.
  4. *Maria-Reynolds*, m. Hon. William B. Rundle, of Denver, Col., and had issue (surname Rundle): *William-B., Mary-Stewart*, and *Alice-P.*
  5. *Archibald-Forster*, m., at Meadville, Pa., Elizabeth Johnson; and had issue: *Louise, Henry-C.*, and *Norman-M.*
  6. *George-Runyon*.
  7. *Juliet*.

vi. Eliza, m. Joseph Kelsey.

vii. William, d. s. p.

viii. James, m. Elizabeth Stevens.

ix. Charles-Wallace, m., June 22, 1837, Juliet Bell Baird, dau. of Jonathan and Lucinda Baird; and had issue:
  1. *Thomas-Baird*, b. May 25, 1838; d. April 22, 1841.
  2. *Lucy-Catharine*, b. April 30, 1840; d. August 4, 1885; m. Robert Taylor Shank; and had issue (surname Shank): *Robert-Taylor*, and *Charles-Wallace*.
  3. *Thomas-Heron-Barber*, b. February 25, 1842; d. October 6, 1860.
  4. *Edward-Ellis*, b. June 28, 1845; d. March 3, 1872.
  5. *Rebecca-Reynolds*, b. November 14, 1847; d. April 17, 1867.

Family of Forster. 257

6. *Eliza-Bell*, b. October 2, 1849 ; d. November 20, 1879.
7. *Georgiana*, b. February 5, 1852 ; d. August 31, 1858.
8. *Charles-Wallace*, b. June 2, 1854; d. February 28, 1892 ; m. Mary Josephine Houser ; and had issue : *Marion-West, Juliet-Bell, Adelaide-Lucy,* and *George-Wallace.*
9. *Alfred-Clark*, b. March 29, 1856 ; d. Sept. 21, 1856.
10. *Joseph-Kelsey*, b. September 7, 1857 ; resides at Warren, Pa.
11. *Carrie-Benton*, b. January 8, 1860 ; m., October 14, 1890, Dudley Bemus ; and had issue (surname Bemus): *Marion-Prendergast.*
12. *Jennie-Forster*, b. February 14, 1865 ; d. July 19, 1865.

IX. WILLIAM FORSTER,[3] (James,[2] John,[1]) b. about 1757, in Londonderry township, Lancaster, now Dauphin county, Pa.; d. in 1789 in Upper Paxtang township, Dauphin county, Pa.; he was a Revolutionary soldier in the Jersey campaign of 1776, in Col. Burd's regiment of Lancaster county associators ; m., November 1, 1780, by Rev. John Elder, MARGARET AYRES, b. October 9, 1754; d. December 24, 1823 ; daughter of William Ayres and Mary Kean. They had issue :

    i. Mary, b. September 8, 1781 ; m., April, 1800, James Kirk.
    ii. William. b. March 21, 1784 ; d. July, 1829 ; m. Martha Cochran.
14. *iii. James*, b. August 25, 1787 ; m. Margaret Ayres.

Margaret Ayres Forster, m., secondly, Reuben Lockhart, of Middle Paxtang township, Dauphin county, Pa.; no issue.

X. JOHN MONTGOMERY FORSTER,[4] (Thomas,[3] John,[2] John,[1]) b. June 21, 1789, in Paxtang; d. September 21, 1858, at Harrisburg, Pa. He passed his youth partly at Harrisburg and partly at Erie, where his father removed about 1799. He studied law with his uncle, Samuel Laird, at Harrisburg, and was admitted to the bar of Dauphin county at May term, 1814. He marched with the volunteers from this section of the State to Baltimore, in 1814, and was elected or appointed brigade major of the brigade commanded by his uncle, General John Forster. After his return, he practiced law at Harrisburg, and was Deputy Attorney General for the counties of Dauphin and Lebanon, under the administration of Governor Hiester, Thomas Elder being Attorney General. Upon the occasion of

General Lafayette's visit to Harrisburg, he commanded the military. He was president of the Branch Bank of Pennsylvania, at Harrisburg, until it was discontinued. He represented this judicial district in the first Board of Revenue Commissioners, convened in 1844, to equalize taxation between the several counties of the State, and was elected secretary of the board at the session of 1847 and 1850. In 1846 he was commissioned by Governor Shunk as president judge of the counties of Chester and Delaware, and served for several months in this capacity. Major Forster m. JENNETTE WRIGHT, b. 1790, in Paterson, New Jersey; d. July 30, 1880, at Harrisburg, Penna., daughter of John Wright and Rose Chambers. They had issue:

    i. Thomas, b. December 21, 1819; d. January 31, 1858, at Harrisburg.

    ii. James, b. 1823, at Harrisburg; d. February 1, 1879, in New York city.

    iii. Weidman, b. September 4, 1825; d. May 27, 1894, at Mercersburg, Pa.; volunteered in the Cameron Guards to serve in Mexico December, 1846; appointed second lieutenant Eleventh U. S. Infantry, April 9, 1847; promoted to first lieutenant December 4, 1847; disbanded August 15, 1848; m. Mary Carroll; and had issue: *Carroll*, and *Margaret*.

    iv. John-Montgomery, studied law with his father, and admitted to the Dauphin county bar, April 24, 1850; in 1873 appointed Insurance Commissioner of Pennsylvania, serving six terms, retiring in 1891; m. Sarah Elder; and had issue:

        1. *Robert-Elder*, m., September, 1892, Ella List; and had issue, *John-Montgomery*.

        2. *Jennette*.

XI. THOMAS FORSTER,⁴ (Thomas,³ John,² John,¹) b. September 13, 1796, at Harrisburg, Penna.; d. October 17, 1864, at Westfield, N. Y. He m. JULIET M. BELL, b. October 12, 1802, at Erie, Pa.; d. February 4, 1866, at Houghton, Mich., dau. of Hon. William Bell. They had issue, b. at Erie, Penna.:

    i. John-Harris, b. May 29, 1822; d. June 15, 1894, at Houghton, Michigan; m. Martha Mullet.

    ii. Sarah-Pettit, b. July 16, 1824; unm.

    iii. Anna-M., b. October 7, 1826; d. March 26, 1893; unm.

iv. William-Thomas, b. November 10, 1828; m. Abby Griswold, and had issue :
    1. *William-Bell*, b. August 30, 1858; resides at Tacoma, Wash.
    2. *Thomas-Griswold*, b. June 11, 1860.
v. Theodore-Maurice, b. March 27, 1831.
vi. Edwin-Sumner, b. April 9, 1833, at Dunkirk, N. Y.; m. Mary E. Hays, of Erie, Pa.; and had issue :
    1. *William-Hays*, b. January 28, 1872.

XII. HANNAH WICKERSHAM FORSTER,[4] (Thomas,[3] John,[2] John,[1]) b. January 31, 1804, at Erie, Pa.; d. December 9, 1880, at Charlottesville, Va.; m., March 31, 1822, EDWIN VOSE SUMNER, b. January 30, 1797, at Boston, Mass.; d. March 21, 1863, at Syracuse, N. Y., son of Elisha Sumner. He was educated at the Milton (Mass.) Academy, and entered the army in 1819 as second lieutenant of infantry. In 1833 was promoted captain of the Second Dragoons and in active service on the Western frontiers, where he distinguished himself as an Indian fighter. In 1838 he was placed in command of the School of Cavalry at Carlisle Barracks, Pa. In 1846 was promoted major, and in the Mexican war led the cavalry charge at Cerro Gordo, commanded the reserves at Contreras and Churubusco, and at the head of the cavalry at Molino del Rey, checked the advance of 5,000 Mexican lancers. In 1850–51 he was Governor of New Mexico. In 1855 promoted colonel of the First Cavalry and made a successful expedition against the Cheyennes. In March, 1861, he was promoted brigadier general, and in 1862 was in command of the First Corps Army of the Potomac. The same year he was appointed a major general for gallant services before Richmond, and led the Second Corps at the battle of Antietam, where he was wounded; and at Fredericksburg commanded one of the three grand divisions of Burnside's army. At his own request, in 1863, he was relieved, and being ordered to the Department of the Missouri, he was on his way thither when he died. They had issue (surname Sumner):
    i. Nancy, b. February 12, 1823, at Sackett's Harbor, N. Y.; m., at Fort Atkinson, J. Leonidas Jenkins, U. S. A.; d. October 18, 1847, in Mexico.
    ii. Margaret-Forster, b. June 30, 1828, at Mackinac, Mich.; m.,

at Carlisle, Pa., September 2, 1848, Eugene E. McLean, b. March 5, 1821, at Washington, D. C.; graduated from West Point, in 1842; rose to be captain assistant quartermaster, August 29, 1855; resigned April 25, 1861, and entered the Confederate service, as colonel; after the war a civil engineer.

 iii. Sarah-Montgomery, b. December 15, 1831, at Sackett's Harbor, N. Y.; m., May 14, 1850, William Walter Teall, b. April 23, 1818, at Manlius, Onondaga county, N. Y.; reside at Syracuse, N. Y.; and had issue (surname Teall):

  1. *Oliver-Sumner*, b. January 23, 1852; m., November 28, 1882, Florence Sanford Wolcott Bissel; and had issue:

   a. Doris-Wolcott-Bissell, b. September 20, 1889.

  2. *Elizabeth-Heron*, b. April 7, 1854; m., June 7, 1876, John Bradford McIntyre; and had issue (surname McIntyre):

   a. Elizabeth-Heron-Teall, b. March 24, 1877.
   b. Bradford, b. March 18, 1880.
   c. Elizabeth-McDonald, b. July 23, 1885.
   d. John-Bradford, b. February 23, 1890.

  3. *Annah-Sumner*, b. May 20, 1859; m., October 31, 1883, Charles Herbert Halcomb; and had issue (surname Halcomb):

   a. Hannah-Mary, b. August 31, 1884.
   b. Charles-Herbert, b. March 19, 1886.
   c. Edith, b. May 27, 1889.
   d. Muriel (twin), b. May 27, 1889.
   e. William-Sumner-Teall, b. March 12, 1893.

  4. *Margaret-McLean*, b. February 25, 1863; m., December 10, 1884, Charles George Kidd.

  5. *Edwin-Sumner*, b. January 16, 1867; d. June 13, 1869.

  6. *William-Sumner*, b. March 26, 1870.

 iv. Mary-Heron, b. 1833; m. Armistead Lindsay Long, b. September 3, 1827, in Campbell county, Va.; d. April 29, 1891; graduated from U. S. military academy July 1, 1850; assigned to the Second Artillery and promoted first lieutenant July 1, 1854; resigned June 10, 1861, and entered the Confederate service as major; was promoted colonel and secretary to Gen. Robert E. Lee in April, 1862, and brigadier general of artillery in September, 1863, taking part in all of Gen. Lee's campaigns; author of "Memoirs of Gen. Lee;" and had issue (surname Long):

  1. *Virginia-Sumner*, m. Robert G. Brown, first lieutenant, Fourth Cavalry, U. S. A.

    2. *Sumner*; d. unm.
    3. *Eugene-McLean*; a civil engineer.
  v. Edwin-Vose, b. August 16, 1835; m. Margaret Snodgrass Forster, (see VII).
  vi. Samuel-S., entered the U. S. A. in 1861; at present lieutenant colonel Sixth Cavalry; m. Fredericka Bennett.

XIII. MARGARET WALLACE FORSTER,[4] (Thomas,[3] John,[2] John,[1]) b. September 10, 1806, at Erie, Pa.; lost in wreck of steamer "Brother Jonathan" on voyage from San Francisco, to Portland, Oregon, July 30, 1865; m. GEORGE WRIGHT, b. 1803, in Vermont; graduated from West Point in 1822; promoted adjutant, January, 1831–6; captain, October 30, 1836; brevet major for meritorious conduct in the Florida war, March 15, 1842; brevet lieutenant colonel for gallantry at Contreras and Churubusco, Mexico, August 20, 1847; and brevet colonel for gallantry in command of the storming-party at Molino del Rey, September 8, 1847, in which he was wounded; major Fourth Infantry, January 1, 1848; colonel Ninth Infantry, March 3, 1855; greatly distinguished in campaigns against the Indians of Washington Territory, 1856 and 1858; brigadier general of volunteers, September 28, 1861, and commanded the Department of the Pacific from October, 1861, to July, 1864, and the district of California, 1864, to the time of his loss on board the "Brother Jonathan," July 30, 1865. They had issue (surname Wright):

  i. Thomas Forster, b. in Missouri; educated at West Point; served as artillery officer to General Walker in the Nicaragua expedition; colonel of a California regiment during the Rebellion; appointed to United States army by President Lincoln; and was killed in action April 26, 1872, in the Lava Beds in the Modoc war.
  ii. John-Montgomery, resides at Louisville, Ky.; educated at West Point, and served on the staff of Gen. Buell; was adjutant general of that State; was marshall of the Supreme Court of the United States.
  iii. Eliza, m. Captain Wesley Owens, U. S. A., d. August 11, 1867; and had issue (surname Owens):
    1. *Margaret-Wright*.
    2. *Frank*; second lieutenant, Eighth Infantry, U. S. A.

XIV. JANE BELL,[4] (Dorcas,[3] John,[2] John,[1]) m. SAMUEL

HAYS, d. in Erie, Pa.; he was an early settler at Erie and quite prominent in public affairs. They had issue (surname Hays):

    i. William Bell, m. Caroline C. Kellog ; and had issue :
        1. *Mary-E.*, m. Edwin Sumner Forster.
        2. *Anna-C.*, m. Rinaldo R. Clemens ; and had issue (surname Clemens) : *John-Hays*, and *Hays-Hutchinson.*
    ii. John-Walker, m. Sarah Jackson, and had issue :
        1. *Ida*, m. Henry Clay McCormick ; and had issue (surname McCormick): *Nellie*, and *John-Hays.*
        2. *Sarah*, m. Hon. Henry Clay Bubb ; and had issue (surname Bubb): *John Hays, Harry-Burrows, Hugh-Jackson*, and *Charles*
    iii. Jane, m., first, George Kellog ; and had issue (surname Kellog):
        1. *Catharine-W.*, m. Edward A. Reynolds, of Meadville, Pa ; and had issue (surname Reynolds): *Effie, Mary, Catharine, Anna, Jane, Louise, Charles, Edward, George, Arthur*, and *Frank.*
        2. *Jane*, m. Dr. Thomas B. Lashells, of Meadville, Pa.; and had issue (surname Lashells):
            a. Dr. Edward-J., m. Margaret Watson.
        3. *Samuel Hays*, m. and had *Frank*, and *Lula.*
    Mrs. Jane Hays Kellog, m , secondly, Samuel Torbut, and had issue (surname Torbut):
        4. *Josephine*, d. s. p.
    iv. Catharine, m. Samuel Law ; and had issue (surname Law):
        1. *Samuel.*
        2. *Stephen*, m. Ella Kimball ; and had *Catharine*, and *Frank.*
        3. *Catharine*, m. Hon. Pearson Church, of Meadville, Pa.; and had issue (surname Church): *Alice*, and *Ethel.*
    v. Maria, m. John Law ; and had issue (surname Law): *William*, and *Josephine.*

XV. JAMES FORSTER,[4] (William,[3] James,[2] John,[1]) b. August 25, 1787, in Middle Paxtang, Dauphin county, Pa.; d. October 4, 1840; m., April 6, 1812, his cousin, MARGARET AYRES, dau. of John Ayres and Jane Lytle, b. February 25, 1793 ; d. December 23, 1867; both buried in the old Dauphin graveyard, (*see Ayres family*). They had issue :

    i. Matilda, b. December 9, 1818 : d. March 24, 1829.

Family of Forster. 263

 ii. *Eliza*, b. September 21, 1815; d. July 17, 1890, at Lock Haven, s. p.; m., April 14, 1869, Samuel F. Sigmund, of Clinton county, d. February 1, 1883.
 iii. *Maria*, b. December 1, 1817; d. January 11, 1893, unm.
 iv. *Eleanor*, b. January 22, 1819; d. April 4, 1832.
 v. *William*, b. January 21, 1821; d. May 24, 1862, s. p.; m., February 24, 1858, Sarah M. Irwin, of Dauphin.
 vi. *Jane*, b. August 20, 1823; d. April 29, 1835.
 vii. *Margaret*, b. October 29, 1825; d. June 22, 1878; m., June 10, 1845, John Bickel Till, b. in Reading, August 10, 1825; d. in Dauphin, Jan. 13, 1851; and had issue (surname Till):
  1. *George-Bickel*, b. March 4, 1846; d. Dec. 28, 1887.
  2. *James-Forster*, b. August 15, 1848; m. Nancy Artemisia Hall; and had issue (surname Till), all b. at Lock Haven, Pa.:
   a. *Jesse-Hall*, b. November 23, 1870.
   b. *Edwin-Welsh*, b. May 1, 1872; m. Ida Jane Strasser.
   c. *John-Simpson*, b. February 16, 1874; m. Catharine Helena Bently.
   d. *Mary-Elizabeth*, b. January 6, 1876.
   e. *William-Forster*, b. June 18, 1879.
  3. *Elizabeth-S.*, b. December 9, 1850; m.
 viii. *James*, b. August 31, 1828; d. in inf.
 ix. *John-Ayres*, b. November 17, 1830; m. March 17, 1864, Mary Jane Waream, of Lewistown, Pa.; and had issue.
 x. *Mary-Malvina*, b. November 26, 1834; m., June 12, 1870, Montgomery Bousch, of Williamsport, Pa.

FULTON OF PAXTANG.

I. RICHARD FULTON,[1] b. in 1706, in Londonderry, Ireland; d. November, 1774, in Paxtang township, Lancaster, now Dauphin county, Pa. He came to America in 1722, in company with some relatives, and was among the earliest settlers in Paxtang. His farm was situated on the bank of the Susquehanna river, just below Harrisburg, a portion of it being now included in the limits of that city. His will was probated at Lancaster, November 11, 1774, of which his sons-in-law, Moses Wallace and Hugh Wilson, were the executors. The inventory of the estate, made by them on the 6th of December following, gives the value of his plantation, £1,200, and that of his farming implements, etc., £340 6s. 6d., making a total of £1,540 6s. 6d. Richard Fulton married, in December, 1744, ISABEL MCCHESNEY, or, as often written in early records, Chesney, the Mc being omitted. She was the daughter of William McChesney; was born in 1714, and died April, 1779, in Paxtang, and, with her husband, buried in the old church graveyard there. They had issue:

  i. William, b. 1746; under certain conditions, his father left him, by his will, three hundred pounds. We have no further record of him.
  ii. Jean, b. 1748; d. May, 1786; m. Moses Wallace, (see *Robert Wallace record*).
2. *iii. Richard*, b. February 20, 1750; m. Mary Willson.
3. *iv. Isabel*, b. 1753; m. Hugh Wilson.
  v. Grizzle, b. 1755; m. Alexander Wilson, (see *Wilson record*).
  vi. Joseph, b. 1759; d. January 28, 1787; m. January 25, 1780, by Rev. John Elder, Elizabeth ———; and they had Richard.

II. RICHARD FULTON,[2] (Richard,[1]) b. February 20, 1750, in Paxtang township, Dauphin county, Pa.; d. 1806; m. MARY WILLSON, b. 1760; d. November 23, 1815; daughter of Hugh Willson and Margaret McKnight, and, with her husband, interred in Paxtang churchyard. They had issue:

4. *i. Isabel*, b. October 9, 1793; m. John Buffington.

Fulton of Paxtang.

    ii. John-William, b. July, 1795.
    iii. Richard, b. August 4, 1797; d. February 28, 1851 ; m. Mary Ann Boal ; no issue.
    iv. Hayes, b. October 2, 1799 ; d. s. p.
    v. Mary-Willson, b. August 26, 1801 ; m. James Kelton, Esq., of Chester county, Penna; no issue.

III. ISABEL FULTON,² (Richard,¹) b. 1753, in Paxtang township, Lancaster county, Pa.; d. 1796, in Derry township, Dauphin county, Pa.; m. April 30, 1772, by Rev. John Elder, HUGH WILSON, b. September 24, 1743 ; d. April 20, 1796, in Derry township, Dauphin county, Pa.; buried in Derry church graveyard. They had issue (surname Wilson):

5.   *i. Isabel*, b. March 9, 1773 ; m. Henry Fulton.
    ii. Jean, b. 1775 ; d. 1823 ; m. William McTeer, d. 1801 ; and had issue (surname McTeer): *William, James, Alice*, m. William Ross, and *Jane*.
    iii. Richard, b. 1777 ; d. January, 1809.
    iv. Hugh, b. April 23, 1780 ; d. March 31, 1810 ; buried in Derry church graveyard.

IV. ISABEL FULTON,³ (Richard,² Richard,¹) b. October 9, 1793, in Paxtang township, Dauphin county, Pa.; d. February 12, 1826, in Harrisburg, Pa., and there buried; m., January 9, 1816, by Rev. James Buchanan, JOHN BUFFINGTON, b. 1786 ; d. January 23, 1856, at Harrisburg, Pa.; son of Thomas Buffington and Elizabeth, his wife. They had issue (surname Buffington):

6.   *i. Mary-Hayes*, b. November 3, 1816 ; m. Dr. John H. Fager.
7.   *ii. Thomas-Wilson*, b. December 9, 1819 ; m. Elizabeth Sydney Chayne.
8.   *iii. Elizabeth-S.*, b. May 21, 1822 ; m. James Clark.
9.   *iv. Isabella-Fulton*, b. November 20, 1824 ; m. A. Fleming Slaymaker.

V. ISABEL WILSON,³ (Isabel,² Richard,¹) b. March 9, 1773 ; d. August 1, 1832, in Harrisburg, Pa.; m., 1788, HENRY FULTON, b. 1768, in Cecil county, Md.; d. 1824, at Jeffersonville, Ind.; was related to the first Richard Fulton, was a merchant, and resided at Harrisburg, Pa. They had issue (surname Fulton):

    i. Jane-Ann, b. August 11, 1789 ; m. Neville B. Craig, (*see Neville and Craig*).

10. ii. *Jefferson-Wilson*, b. 1791 ; m. Susan Thompson.
iii. *Hugh*, b. 1798 ; d. s. p.
iv. *Robert-Galt* (twin), b. 1793; d. October 24, 1824, at New Orleans, La.
v. *George-Washington*, b. 1795; d. December 12, 1818, at Henderson, Ky.

VI. MARY HAYES BUFFINGTON,[4] (Isabel,[3] Richard,[2] Richard,[1]) b. November 3, 1816, in Harrisburg, Pa.; d. there December 4, 1893; m., March 29, 1836, by Rev. Mr. Gerry, JOHN HENRY FAGER, b. March 31, 1806, at Harrisburg, Pa.; d., August 18, 1872, in Harrisburg, Pa., and there buried. He received careful training and a good education ; read medicine with Dr. Martin Luther, one of the more prominent of the early physicians at Harrisburg, and attended medical lectures at the University of Pennsylvania. In 1829, he began the practice of his profession at Harrisburg, which he continued until his death, a period of forty-three years. In 1840, his attention being called to homœopathy, the Doctor commenced the study of that theory, and afterwards adopted it in his practice. He was quite a successful physician, and enjoyed the confidence of the community. Apart from his professional life, Dr. Fager was a valued citizen. For thirty-three years he was a member of the school-board, during most of which period he was secretary or treasurer; for several terms a member of the borough council, and for fifty years an active worker in the Sunday-school of the First Lutheran church. He had been previously married to Eliza Jones, b. 1810, d. October 17, 1834, daughter of James and Mary Jones, and had *Albert-J.*, who served as first lieutenant Company B, One Hundred and Twenty-seventh Regiment, Pennsylvania Volunteers, and now an alderman of the city of Harrisburg. Mary Hayes Buffington and John H. Fager had issue, all born in Harrisburg, Pa. (surname Fager):

i. *Sarah-Cleckner*, d. s. p.
ii. *John-Buffington*, d. s. p.
iii. *Charles-Buffington*, b. 1841; was educated in the public schools of Harrisburg, read medicine with his father, graduated from the University of Pennsylvania in 1864, and commenced the practice of his profession at Harrisbur ; was a medical cadet in the United States army in 1862, and contract assistant surgeon in 1864; vaccine

physician of Harrisburg, 1866-67, and one of the founders of the Homœpathic Medical Society of Dauphin county in 1866; m., in 1865, Susan A. Hummel, daughter of Valentine Hummel, of Harrisburg, and had issue (surname Fager):

    1. *Valentine-Hummel*, b. December 17, 1866; a physician; m., April 5, 1895, Elizabeth Uhler.
    2. *Charles-Buffington*, b. September 4, 1869.
    3. *John-Henry*, b. October 26, 1877.

v. Ella-Elizabeth.
vi. Bella-Fulton.
vii. Annie-Mary, m., April 19, 1894, Samuel Kunkel.
viii. John-Henry, a physician, m., April 29, 1880, Alice Westbrook, and had issue (surname Fager):
    1. *Lucy*, b. June 26, 1881.
    2. *Paul*, b. June 22, 1884.

VII. THOMAS WILSON BUFFINGTON,[4] (Isabel,[3] Richard,[2] Richard,[1]) b. December 9, 1819; d. January 10, 1895; was for many years ticket-agent for the Philadelphia and Reading Railroad company at Harrisburg. He m., October 8, 1843, by Rev. A. Atwood, ELIZABETH SYDNEY CHAYNE. They had issue (suaname Buffington):

    i. Elizabeth-Chayne, d. s. p.
    ii. John-Buffington, d. s. p.
    iii. Mary-Keltin, d. s. p.
    iv. Henry-Augustus, m. Nettie Thomas, and had issue:
        1. *Robert-Thomas*, b. December 8, 1886.
    v. William-Urie.
    vi. Maria-Mytinger, d. s. p.

VIII. ELIZABETH S. BUFFINGTON,[4] (Isabel,[3] Richard,[2] Richard,[1]) b. May 21, 1822; m., October 23, 1845, JAMES CLARK, b. February 9, 1818, in Dauphin county, Pa.; d. March 23, 1851, in Huntingdon, Pa. He learned printing in Harrisburg with his elder brother, Samuel H. Clark. In August, 1845, he removed to Huntingdon, Pa., and became the editor of the *Journal,* continuing as such until his death. Governor Johnston appointed him, January 11, 1849, an aid-de-camp on his staff, with the rank of lieutenant colonel. As a political journalist, Mr. Clark had few equals in the State. He left issue (surname Clark):

    i. Isabel Fulton, d. s. p.

ii. Mary-Martin, m. Rev. J. Spangler Kieffer, a minister of the Reformed Church, residing at Hagerstown, Md., and had issue (surname Kieffer): *Elizabeth-Buffington, John-Brainard, James-Clark, Eleanor-Spangler, Henri-Grandlenard, Paul,* and *Richard-Fulton.*

iii. Sydney-Buffington, m. William N. Knisely, and had issue (surname Knisely): *Elizabeth-Clark.*

IX. ISABELLA FULTON BUFFINGTON,[4] (Isabel,[3] Richard,[2] Richard,[1]) b. November 20, 1824; d. May 21, 1885, at the Gap Lancaster county, Pa. She was a woman much loved and respected, and a consistent member of the Presbyterian church at Bellevue; m., September 5, 1850, A. FLEMING SLAYMAKER, b. March 7, 1823. They had issue (surname Slaymaker):

    i. Sophia-Elizabeth, b. June 13, 1851; m., November 26, 1872, Dr. David F. Unger, b. September 28, 1843, and had issue (surname Unger):
        1. *John-Buffington*, b January 19, 1874.
        2. *Frederick-Fleming*, b. February 14, 1876.
        3. *Henry-Slaymaker*, b. November 9, 1877.
        4. *Oswald-Josephus*, b. January 22, 1879.
        5. *Isabel-Fulton*, b. August 7, 1883.
    ii. Thomas-Buffington, b. January 26, 1853; d. January 13, 1857.
    iii. Rebecca-Cochran, b. March 2, 1858.
    iv. Henry-Fleming, b. August 28, 1863.

X. JEFFERSON WILSON FULTON,[4] (Isabel[3] [*Wilson*], Isabel,[2] Richard,[1]) b. 1791, in Harrisburg, Pa.; d. December 23, 1826, in Allegheny city, Pa.; was twice married; m., first, SUSAN THOMPSON, of Jeffersonville, Ind., d. December 8, 1825. They had issue:

    i. Susan-Thompson, d. 1879; m. Augustus F. Washington, of Pittsburg; and had issue (surname Washington): *Herbert*, and *Elizabeth.*

Mr. Fulton m., secondly, ANN DECATUR LEE, of Maysville, Ky. No issue:

GALBRAITH OF DONEGAL.

I. The family of Galbraith is of the remotest antiquity—the name being derived from the Celtic. It was in the parish of Baldunoch, county Stirling, that the Galbraiths of Baldunoch, chiefs of the name, had their residence. In Frazer's statistical account of the inhabitants of the Isle of Gigha, the following occurs: "The majority of them are of the names of Galbraith and McNeill, the former reckoned the more ancient. The Galbraiths in the Gaelic language are called Breatannieh, that is Britons, or the children of the Briton, and were once reckoned a great name in Scotland according to the following lines translated from the Gaelic:

"Galbraiths from the Red Tower,
Noblest of Scottish surnames."

The first of the name of whom we have any mention is JOHN GALBRAITH,[1] who was the father of the following. He probably died before the emigration of his sons from Ireland to America:

2.   i. *James*, b. 1666; m. Rebecca Chambers.
       ii. *John*, m. and left issue, but further than this fact we have no knowledge. After his arrival in America he remained several years in Philadelphia. Some of his children settled west of the Susquehanna, in now York or Adams county, and their descendants emigrated to Kentucky.

II. JAMES GALBRAITH,[2] son of John Galbraith,[1] of Scotch parentage, was born, in 1666, in the north of Ireland, from whence he emigrated about the year 1718, settling in Conestoga, afterwards Donegal township, then Chester county, Province of Penna. He was one of the founders of old Derry church, a man of prominence, and the head of a remarkable family. He died August 23, 1744, and is buried in the old graveyard at Derry. His wife was REBECCA CHAMBERS, daughter of Arthur Chambers. Of his children, we have the following:

Pennsylvania Genealogies.

3.   *i. John*, b. 1690; m. Janet ———.
4.   *ii. Andrew*, b. 1692; m. and left issue.
5.   *iii. James*, b. 1703; m. Elizabeth Bertram.
 iv. Eleanor, m. February 27, 1735, Patrick McKinley, and had issue (surname McKinley): *John, Joseph*, and *Janet*.
 v. Isabel, m. October 21, 1735, Alexander [McMillan].
 vi. Rebecca, d. in 1748; m. ——— Stewart, and had issue (surname Stewart): *Charles, Robert, William, Frances*, and *Margaret*.

III. JOHN GALBRAITH,³ (James,² John,¹) b. about 1690, in Ireland; d. October, 1753, in Donegal township, Lancaster county, Pa.; settled along Donegal Meeting-House run, about one and three-fourths miles below his brother, Andrew, in 1718; was a miller by trade, and built a grist and saw-mill in 1721, at the run along the "great road," which, very likely branched from the Paxtang and Conestoga road some miles east of Mount Joy, and extended through the Scotch-Irish settlement to the Conoy Indian town; he also kept an "ordinary;" was elected sheriff of the county of Lancaster in 1731; and was a member of the first jury drawn in that county. He married JANET ———, b. about 1693, and they had issue:

 i. John, b. circa, 1714; d. 1768; was a celebrated Indian trader and a man of mark on the frontiers. He m. Dorcas [Smith], and they had issue among others:
  1. *Elizabeth*, m. Robert Spear.
  2. *Mary*, m. ——— Cook.
  3. *Janet*, m. James Work.
  4. *Barbara*, m. ——— Allison.
  5. *Isabella*, d. prior to her father; m., 1764, Capt. William Patterson, and had one child, *Galbraith* Patterson.
6.   *ii. Robert*, b. 1716; m. Rebecca ———.
 iii. Elizabeth.
 iv. Margaret.
 v. Rebecca.
 vi. Eleanor.

IV. ANDREW GALBRAITH,³ (James,² John,¹) b. about 1692, in the North of Ireland; came to America with his father, and settled along the run which has its source at Donegal meeting house, now Lancaster county, Pa., in the year 1718. Upon the organization of the county of Lancaster, he was appointed the first coroner, afterwards, in 1730, one of the justices of the

Court of Common Pleas and Quarter Sessions, a position he held six years. In 1732 he and his neighbor, John Wright, were candidates for the General Assembly. At that time none but freeholders were allowed to vote, and the only polling place was the town of Lancaster, where all voters were obliged to go. Mr. Galbraith took no active part in the canvass himself, but his wife mounted her favorite mare, Nelly, and rode out through the Scotch-Irish settlement, and persuaded them to go with her to the county town. She appeared at the court-house leading a procession of mounted men, whom she halted and addressed. The effect was that her husband was triumphantly elected. After his first election he seems to have had no opposition. He took out a patent for two hundred and twelve and one half acres, May 2, 1737; and was one of the first ruling elders of old Donegal church; appointed a justice of the peace in 1730, a position he held until 1747, when he removed west of the Susquehanna; he served several years in the Provincial Assembly, and was one of the most prominent of the pioneer settlers—a safe and trustworthy officer. After the year 1746, when he disposed of his farm, very little is recorded concerning him. Of his children we have only the following:

7. *i. John*, b. 1717; m. Jennett McCullough.
   ii. Arthur, on the 22d of September, 1766, took up two hundred and fifty acres of land on Shaver's creek.
   iii. Robert, d. prior to 1768; m. and left *Ann*, aged sixteen years.

V. JAMES GALBRAITH,[3] (James,[2] John,[1]) b. 1703, in the north of Ireland; d. June 11, 1786, in East Pennsboro' township, Cumberland county, Pa.; buried in Derry church graveyard. He took up a tract in now Derry township, Dauphin county, on Spring creek not far from the church glebe, the warrant therefor being granted him the 13th of March, 1737. He became a man of note on the frontiers, and the early provincial records of Pennsylvania contain frequent reference to him; was elected sheriff of the county in October, 1742; for many years was one of the justices for the county of Lancaster, and served as an officer during the Indian wars of 1755–1763. Towards the Revolutionary period he removed to Cumberland county. He married, April 6, 1734, in Christ church, Philadelphia, ELIZABETH BERTRAM, b. 1718, in Newcastle-on-Tyne; d. February 2, 1799, in East Pennsboro' township, Cumberland county, Pa.; daughter of Rev. William Bertram;* she was a woman of rare accomplishments and excellence; buried in Derry churchyard. They had issue:

  i. William, b. 1736; nothing further is known of him.
8. *ii. Bertram*, b. September 24, 1738; m., first, Ann Scott; secondly, Henrietta Huling.
  iii. Robert, b. 1740; d. January, 1804, in Huntingdon county, Pa.; was commissioned president judge of the county, November 23, 1787.
  iv. Dorcas, b. 1744; m. John Buchanan; and had issue (surname Buchanan): *James-Galbraith.*
  v. Thomas, b. 1746.
9. *vi. John*, b. 1748; m., and left issue.
10. *vii. Andrew*, b. 1750; m. Barbara ———.
11. *viii. Elizabeth*, b. 1758; m. Charles Torrance.

VI. ROBERT GALBRAITH,[4] (John,[3] James,[2] John,[1]) b. about 1716, in the north of Ireland; d. March 8, 1748, in Donegal township, Lancaster county, Pa.; m. REBECCA ———. They had issue:

12. *i. John*, b. 1739; m. Mary McCormick.
13. *ii. Rebecca*, b. 1742; m. Ephraim Blaine.

Mrs. Rebecca Galbraith, subsequently married Captain John Byers, son of David Byers, of Donegal; who afterwards removed to Cumberland county, Pa.; he was an officer in the French and Indian wars, and a man of prominence in provincial days.

---

*WILLIAM BERTRAM was born, February 2, 1674, in the city of Edinburg, Scotland. He received his education in the university of his native place, studied for the ministry, and was licensed by the Presbytery of Bangor, Ireland, who gave him " ample testimonials of his ordination, ministerial qualifications, and regular Christian conversation." He married about 1706, Jane Gillespie, the widow of Angus McClain, and their children were, *John*, first, second and third, who d. in infancy; *Phebe*, d. at age of seventeen, and *Elizabeth*, m. James Galbraith. During one of those periodical political excitements in the British Isles, the son disappeared, and his parents, under the impression he had come to America, determined, if possible, to ascertain his whereabouts, and came to Pennsylvania about the year 1730. Failing in their search, they decided to remain in this

VII. JOHN GALBRAITH,⁴ (Andrew,³ James,² John,¹) b. about 1717, in Donegal township, Lancaster county, Pa.; d. January 20, 1757, in Cumberland county, Pa., and was buried in Silvers Spring churchyard; m., April 23, 1742, JENNETT MC-CULLOUGH. They had issue:

14.   *i. James*, b. 1743, m. Martha McClellan.
      ii. Jennett, b. 1745.
      iii. Sarah, b. 1747.
15.   *iv. Robert*, b. 1748; m. Mary ———.

VIII. BERTRAM GALBRAITH,⁴ (James,³ James,² John,¹) b. September 24, 1738, in Derry township, Lancaster, now Dauphin county, Pa.; d. March 9, 1804, in Cumberland county, Pa., while on a visit to his brother, Andrew; buried in Donegal church graveyard. He received the best education the schools of that day afforded, and studied surveying, a profession he followed many years. During the French and Indian wars, Colonel Galbraith served as an officer in a company of rangers formed for the protection of the frontiers. From 1760 to 1775, acting in his professional capacity, he surveyed the greater portion of the lands located in the present counties

country, and the following year we find the Rev. Mr. Bertram unanimously received by Donegal Presbytery, which he joined. At the same time George Renick presented him an invitation to settle at Paxtang and Derry, which he accepted. He was installed November 17, 1732, at the meeting-house on Swatara. The congregations then appointed representatives, who executed to Bertram the right and title to the "Indian town tract," situated in Hanover township, on the north side of the Swatara, containing three hundred and fifty acres. On the settlement of Rev. Bertram the congregation in Swatara took the name of Derry, and the upper congregation, on Spring creek, was styled Paxtang. In 1735, Mr. Bertram complained of the "intolerable burden" he was under with the two congregations, and September 13, 1736, he was released from the care of Paxtang. The Rev. William Bertram died on the 2d of May, 1746, aged seventy-two, and his remains are interred in Derry church graveyard, his wife dying prior thereto. He was a faithful minister of the gospel. It may be stated that, through his marriage with Miss Gillespie, his descendants became heirs to a handsome estate in Edinburg. Efforts were made to secure this, but the difficulties inherent upon proving descent, we presume, have been the means of keeping the rightful parties from enjoying this patrimony.

of Dauphin, Perry, and Juniata. He was a member of the provincial convention of January 23, 1775; delegate to the provincial conference of June 18, 1776, and member of the Constitutional convention of July 15, 1776. During that year was elected colonel of one of the Lancaster battalions of associators, and on duty in the Jerseys during the greater portion of that year, serving also as a member of the Assembly 1776–1777. On June 3, 1777, he was appointed county lieutenant; November 8, one of the commissioners to collect clothing for the army; and December 16, appointed by the Assembly to take subscriptions for the Continental loan. He acted as one of the commissioners which met at New Haven, Conn., November 22, 1777, to regulate the prices of commodities in the States. After four years of excessive and exhaustive labor, Colonel Galbraith was compelled to resign the office of county lieutenant, but remained in service as an officer of the militia until the restoration of peace. In 1789, he was appointed one of the commissioners to view the Juniata and Susquehanna, and mark the places where locks or canals were necessary to render these streams navigable. He was appointed deputy surveyor November 4, 1791, and, while acting as such, took up large tracts in Lykens Valley, but, dying before patents were issued to him, his heirs lost them all in the numberless litigations which ensued. Colonel Galbraith was twice married; m., first, March 30, 1759, ANN SCOTT, b. December 26, 1741; d. June 29, 1793; daughter of Josiah Scott, of Donegal. They had issue :

  i. Josiah, m. and had two sons, one of whom, *Bertram*, m. his cousin, Mary, and settled in Milton, Pa.; they also had two sons; Josiah's family, except Bertram's son, William, went to the West at an early day, and there is no record of any, save that the younger son was engaged in the Indian war in Minnesota in 1862.

  ii. Samuel-Scott, studied medicine; assisted in laying out the town of Bainbridge; was twice married; m., first, Margaret ———; b. 1772; d. April 29, 1801, s. p.; he m., secondly, Juliet Buchanan, b. 1774; d. April 1, 1813; dau. of John Buchanan and Dorcas Galbraith (*see* v.); and had issue :

    1. *Julietta*, b. April 1, 1803; m., Sept 28, 1820, ——— Leeper; and had issue (surname Leeper):

Galbraith of Donegal. 275

  a. William-Edward, b. November 23, 1822; d. February 8, 1828.
  b. Elizabeth-Heron, b. August 16, 1825.
  c. Bertram Galbraith, b. May 30, 1827; d. November 16, 1870, at Carson's Landing, Miss.; m. Hannah Elizabeth McCarrell.
  d. Edward-Shippen, b. November 21, 1830; d. May, 1868, at Louisville, Ky.
  e. Joseph-McCarrell, b. June 6, 1835; m. Mary Garrison Decker.
  f. Juliet-Abby, b. September 8, 1839; m. David Kuhn, of Norwalk, O.
 2. *Bertram,* a physician; m., first, Miss Riegart, of Lancaster; m., secondly, Miss Lehman, of same place.
 3. *James.*

16. *iii. Elizabeth,* m. Dr. Lecky Murray.
 iv. Mary, d. s. p.
 v. Henrietta, d. prior to 1804; m. David Cook, and had issue (surname Cook): *Bertram,* d. s. p , and *Mary-Ann,* m. Henry Carpenter, who left issue (surname Carpenter): *James Cook, Dr. Henry, Maria-Louisa,* and *Isaac-A.*
 vi. Jean, b. 1772; d. January 13, 1842; m. David Elder, (*see Elder record*).
 vii. Ann, m. Thomas Bayley; b. January 6, 1762; d. February 9, 1807; son of John Bayley, of Donegal; no issue.
 viii. James, m., April 6, 1810, Rosetta Work, daughter of Joseph Work, of Donegal; they lived on the island in the Susquehanna, opposite the village of Bainbridge; there was issue:
  1. *Sarah-Work,* d. unm.
  2. *Julia,* d. unm.
  3. *Mary,* m. her cousin, Bertram Galbraith, of Milton, Pa.
  4. *Annetta,* m. a physician; no issue.
  5. *Work,* went to Ohio when a lad, and d. there at the age of twenty-one.
 ix. William-Bertram, b. October 19, 1779; d. November 24, 1835; m. Sarah Hays, b. December 11, 1774; d. July 11, 1839; daughter of John and Eleanor Elder Hays.

Colonel Galbraith m., secondly, February 15, 1798, HENRIETTA HULING, of Isle Benvenue. They had issue:
 x. Sarah, m. Samuel Morris, of Philadelphia; and had issue (surname Morris): *Henrietta, Elizabeth, Sarah, Samuel,* and *Richard.*
17. *xi. Bertram-Gillespie,* b. May 9, 1804; m. Eliza Fager Bell.

After Colonel Galbraith's death, his widow married George Green, of Easton, Pa. They had issue (surname Green): *Charles*, d. unm.; *George*, of Princeton, N. J., and *Henrietta*, of Easton, Pa.

IX. JOHN GALBRAITH,[4] (James,[3] James,[2] John,[1]) b. about 1748; served in the War of the Revolution; was taken prisoner at the battle of Long Island, and suffered great hardships while in captivity; after the close of the war, he resided some time in Huntingdon county, from whence he removed to Butler county, Pa., about 1798, and where he remained until his death. Of his children, we have the following:

  i. Alexander, m. and left issue in Butler county, Pa.
  ii. James, became a physician of prominence.
18. *iii. John*, b. 1794; m. Amy Ayres.

X. ANDREW GALBRAITH,[4] (James,[3] James,[2] John,[1]) b. about 1750, in Derry township, Lancaster county, Pa.; d. March 7, 1806, in East Pennsboro' township, Cumberland county, Pa.; commissioned major of the Cumberland County battalion of foot, September 10, 1776; and in active service. He m., in 1780, BARBARA ———, b. in Donegal township, Lancaster county, Pa.; d. November 7, 1832. They had issue:

  i. Jean, b. 1780; d. 1863; m., in 1799, John Matthew Miller; and had issue (surname Miller):
    1. *Andrew*, b. September 18, 1801; d. September 30, 1874; was a judge of the U. S. courts thirty-five years.
    2. *Catharine*, m. Daniel M. Smyser.
    3. *Jane*, m. James Cooper, U. S. Senator.
    4. *Elizabeth*, m. Godlove S. Orth.
  ii. James, b. 1782; d. 1803.
  iii. Elizabeth, b. 1784; d. April 18, 1818; m. Dr. Thomas Kelso; and had issue (surname Kelso): *Mary*, m. Isaac Cruse, and *Charles*.
19. *iv. Julianna*, b. 1786; m. William McNeill Irvine.
  v. Mary [Molly], b. 1788; d. 1861; m. Michael Ege; and had issue (surname Ege): *Michael*, and *Henrietta*, m. Frederick Watts, of Carlisle.
20. *vi. Sarah-W. [Sally]*, b. January 25, 1791; m. John Bannister Gibson.
  vii. Barbara, b. 1793; d. 1871; m. Charles P. Gordon; and had issue (surname Gordon): *Andrew*, *Mary*, m. ——— Flournoy, *Virginia*, m. Dr. Abercrombie, and *Sarah*, m. ——— Wilkins.

viii. Andrew, b. 1795 ; d. 1798.
ix. Dorcas, b. 1798 ; d. February 23, 1808.
x. Ann, b. 1801 ; d. 1858 ; m., August 29, 1826, Charles Hall, b. 1796 ; d. 1835 ; and had issue (surname Hall):
  1. *George-D.*
  2. *Charles-Galbraith.*
  3. *Anna-B.*, m. Capt. James S. Colwell ; k. at Antietam ; and had issue (surname Colwell): *John*, Lieut. U. S. N.; *James, Mary-Hall,* and *Anna.*
  4. *John-Bannister.*
  5. *Mary*, m. Dr. Stevens G. Cowdrey, U. S. A.

XI. ELIZABETH GALBRAITH,[4] (James,[3] James,[2] John,[1]) b. 1758, in Derry township, Lancaster county, Pa.; d. May 24, 1829, in Baltimore, Md. She was a remarkably handsome woman, distinguished for her charm and grace of manner, and in her early years was the leader of society in her adopted home; and yet withal a consistent Christian and of great charity. She m., in 1777, CHARLES TORRANCE, b. 1745, in the parish of Clogher, county Tyrone, Ireland; d. July 23, 1822, in the city of Baltimore, and with his wife buried in the family vault in Westminster Presbyterian churchyard, that city. He came to America prior to the commencement of the struggle for independence. He resided at first in the city of Philadelphia and about 1780 removed to Baltimore, where for many years he was a distinguished merchant. At his death he left a large estate. They left issue (surname Torrance):

  i. *Elizabeth*, b. July 11, 1778; d. November 7, 1848 ; m., December 19, 1799, Alexander Mitchell, b. December 20, 1776; d. November 20, 1859; and had issue (surname Mitchell):
    1. *Eliza-Maitland.*
    2. *Charles-Jeffrey.*
    3. *Alexander.*
    4. *Stephen-Walker.*
    5. *Jane-Ann.*
    6. *Margaretta.*
    7. *William-Maitland.*
    8. *George-Torrance.*
    9. *Maria-Chamberlain.*
    10. *Edmund.*
    11. *Laura.*
    12. *Patrick-Henry.*

    ii. James, b. July 26, 1780 : d. inf.
    iii. Ann, b. February 28, 1782; d. January 28, 1850; m., 1805, Andrew Clopper, b. September 18, 1771; d. June 28, 1824; and had issue (surname Clopper):
        1. *Elizabeth.*
        2. *Cornelius.*
        3. *Charles-Torrance.*
        4. *Benjamin-May.*
        5. *Rachel.*
        6. *Ann.*
        7. *Andrew.*
        8. *George-Washington.*
        9. *Amelia.*
        10. *William-Lorman.*
    iv. Dorcas, b. November 24, 1783; d. December 2, 1848 ; unm.
    v. Mary, b. October 16, 1785; d. January 14, 1865; unm.
    vi. Charles, b. April 20, 1788; d. September 22, 1847 ; unm.
    vii. George, b. January 9, 1790; d. November 27, 1848 ; m., June 30, 1829, Eleanor Fulford, dau. of William Fulford, Esq., and Mary Frances Patterson, b. 1812 ; d. April 26, 1876; and had issue :
        1. *Elizabeth-Galbraith,* m. Charles Galbraith Hall, and had issue (surname Hall):
            a. Anna-Galbraith.
            b. George-Duffield.
            c. Charles-Galbraith, Jr.
            d. Elizabeth-G.
        2. *William-Henry.*
        3. *Mary-Frances.*
        4. *Eleanor-Fulford,* m. James A. Conner.
        5. *Georgiana.*
        6. *Louisa-Victoria,* m. John S. Moody.
        7. *Georgiana, 2d.*
    viii. Harriet, b. May 24, 1791; d. inf.
    ix. James, b. May 11, 1793 ; d. unm.
    x. John, b. November 24, 1794 ; d. March 14, 1832; m., June 19, 1830, Rebecca Abbott; and had issue :
        1. *Charles-A.,* b. March 10, 1831; d. February 24, 1879 ; unm.
    xi. Louisa, b. May 15, 1797; d. May 5, 1878 ; unm.

XII. JOHN GALBRAITH,[5] (Robert,[4] John,[3] James,[2] John,[1]) b. about 1739, in Donegal township, Lancaster county, Pa.; d. prior to 1803, in East Pennsboro' township, Cumberland county, Pa.; served in the Revolutionary war, and was taken prisoner at the battle of Long Island ; m. MARY McCORMICK. They had issue :

    i. Thomas.
    ii. James-McCormick.
    iii. John, m. and left issue.
    iv. Elizabeth, m. Patrick Hays.
    v. Dorcas.
    vi. Robert, d. March, 1787 ; m. and left issue:
        1. *Samuel*, m., February 27, 1789, Mary Decker.
        2. *James.*
        3. *John.*
        4. *William.*
        5. *Elizabeth.*
        6. *Mary.*
    vii. Agnes.
    viii. Mary.
    ix. William-Bertram.

XIII. REBECCA GALBRAITH,[5] (Robert,[4] John,[3] James,[2] John,[1]) b. 1747, in Donegal township, Lancaster county, Pa.; d. about 1780, in Middleton township, Cumberland county, Pa.; m., June 26, 1765, EPHRAIM BLAINE, b. May 26, 1741, in the north of Ireland ; d. February 16, 1804, in Middleton township, Cumberland county, Pa.; son of James and Elizabeth Blaine. The elder Blaine, born of Scotch ancestry, came with his family from the north of Ireland, in the vicinity of Londonderry, to America prior to 1745, and settled in Toboyne township, Cumberland county, Pa. He took up a large tract of land on the south side of the Juniata river, as did each of his children a few years later. He became an influential man on the then frontiers of the Province, and was quite prominent in affairs during the French and Indian wars, as well towards the close of his life in the struggle for independence. He died at his residence in Toboyne township, in July, 1792, well advanced in years, leaving a wife, Elizabeth, and nine children. The eldest of these was Ephraim, who received a classical education at the school of the Rev. Dr. Alison, in Chester county, and was recommended by him for an ensigncy in the provincial service as being "a gentleman of good family." He was appointed commissary sergeant, and, during the Bouquet expedition to the westward in 1763, was connected with the Second

Provincial Regiment. From 1771 to 1773 he served as sheriff of Cumberland county. At the outset of the Revolutionary struggle he entered heartily into the contest and assisted in raising a battalion of associators, of which he was commissioned lieutenant colonel, holding the position until his appointment, by the Supreme Executive Council, as county lieutenant of Cumberland, April 5, 1777. This office he resigned in August following, when he entered the commissary department in the Continental establishment. He was commissioned commissary general of purchases, February 19, 1778, a position he held over three years, including one of the most trying periods of the war—the cantonment at Valley Forge. He was a man of large fortune, and the record shows that, during that long and severe winter, with the aid of personal friends, he made an advance of $600,000 for the use of the patriot army. Millions of dollars passed through his hands without a suspicion of his purity and disinterestedness. Owing to his personal sacrifices, however, Col. Blaine's estate became impaired, although his fortune remained ample. While in the service he enjoyed the confidence of Washington and his fellow officers. It was at his home that the first president remained during his week's stay at Carlisle when on the so-called Whiskey Insurrection of 1794. Subsequently Col. Blaine retired to his farm in Middleton township, Cumberland county, where he closed his eminently patriotic and honorable career in his sixty-third year. He was twice married—his second wife being Sarah E. Duncan, widow of John Duncan, of Carlisle, and daughter of Col. Samuel Postlethwaite, and they had one son, *Ephraim*, who d. s. p. By first wife, Rebecca Galbraith, there was issue six children, of whom we have only the following (surname Blaine):

 i. *James*, d. 1832; m., first, Jean ———; secondly, Margaret Lyon, (*see Lyon record*).
 ii. *Robert*, d. January, 1826; m. Anna Susanna Metzgar, and had issue (surname Blaine):
  1. *Rebecca*, m. Rev. Jeremiah Chamberlain, D. D.
  2. *Anna-Susanna*, m. Samuel Alexander.
  3. *Ephraim-Metzgar*.
  4. *Eleanor*, b. 1789; d. January 9, 1839; m., first, Dr. Levi Wheaton, b. September 6, 1796; d. September 24, 1824, and had issue (surname Wheaton):

Ellen-Blaine, d. s. p., and *Mary-Blaine*, d. s. p.; m., secondly, John Hays, b. 1794; d. April 29, 1854, and had issue (surname Hays): *Robert*, d. s. p., *John*, m. Jenny Smead, and *Mary-Blaine*, m. Richard Mullikin.

  5. *Mary*.
  6. *James*, d. s. p.
 iii. David, d. December, 1804; m. Isabel Hill, and had issue, among others (surname Blaine):
  1. *Robert*, m. and had *John*, *David*, and *William*.
  2. *Ephraim*.

XIV. JAMES GALBRAITH,[5] (John,[4] Andrew,[3] James,[2] John,[1]) b. about 1741; d. prior to 1790; was county lieutenant of Cumberland county in 1777; a soldier of the Pennsylvania Line in the Revolution; in 1783, resided in "Washington borough, near Carlisle;" m. MARTHA MCCLELLAN, daughter of John McClellan,* of Donegal. They had issue:

 i. John.
 ii. Rebecca, m. July 18, 1793, David Herron.

XV. ROBERT GALBRAITH,[5] (John,[4] Andrew,[3] James,[2] John,[1]) b. about 1748, in Cumberland county, Pa.; d. in 1795, in Allen township, Cumberland county, Pa.; m. MARY ———. They had issue:

 i. Nancy [Agnes], m. James Pollock.
 ii. Elizabeth, m. Benjamin Hunt.
 iii. Mary, m. William Wray.
 iv. James.
 v. Jane, m. Joseph Williams.
21. *vi. Robert*, b. 1782; m. Mary White.
 vii. John, b. 1784.

XVI. ELIZABETH GALBRAITH,[5] (Bertram,[4] James,[3] James,[2] John,[1]) b. 1760, in Donegal township, Lancaster county, Pa.; d. July 25, 1845, near Washingtonville, Montour county, Pa.; m., August 9, 1779, LECKY MURRAY, b. 1750, in county Tyrone, Ireland; d. prior to October, 1815, in Lancaster, Pa.; son of Ed-

---

*JOHN MCCLELLAN had sons, *William-George*, d. a prisoner of war in New York, Colonel *James*, d. at Mercersburg, and Dr. *John*, d. at Greencastle. His daughters were *Martha*, m. James Galbraith, and others, who married, respectively, John Holliday, William Holliday, Captain John Blair, of Blair county, and Samuel Culbertson, Mr. McDowell, and Mr. Ramsey, of Franklin county, Pa.

ward Murray. He graduated in medicine, and came to America prior to the struggle for independence. In 1776 he was commissioned surgeon of the Fifth cattalion, Lancaster county associators, and was the surgeon in charge of the British prisoners at Lancaster during the years 1777 to 1779. He continued in the active practice of his profession until his death, which occurred suddenly while preparing to make a visit to Ireland. They had issue (surname Murray):

 i. *James-Galbraith*, b. February 20, 1781; emigrated to Kentucky about the close of the century and engaged in mercantile pursuits at Frankfort; m. Catharine Winebrenner, widow of M. N. Schneider, whose parents emigrated from Maryland at an early day; and left issue.

 ii. *Edward*, b. December 28, 1782; d. August 9, 1789.

 iii. *Ann-Scott*, b. October 23, 1784; d. unm.

 iv. *Bertram Galbraith*, b. January 7, 1787; d. August 28, 1862, at Locust Hill; m. Evaline Galbraith, b. 1805; d. September 9, 1883; daughter of Josiah Galbraith.

 v. *Arthur*, b. August 17, 1789; d. September 2, 1789.

 vi. *Samuel-Scott*, b. October 21, 1790; d. September 15, 1849; removed to Washington county, Md.; m. Sophia Davis.

 vii. *Josiah-Scott*, b. December 29, 1792; d. July 16, 1877, near Washingtonville, Pa.

 viii. *William*, b. November 21, 1796; d. August 6, 1802.

 ix. *Lecky-Caldwell*, b. April 15, 1799; practiced medicine in Washington county, Pa.; and died there.

 x. *Elizabeth-Jane*, b. November 12, 1803: d. 1884; m. ——— Morris.

 xi. *Caroline*, b. November 13, 1806; d. November, 1808.

XVII. BERTRAM GILLESPIE GALBRAITH,[5] (Bertram,[4] James,[3] James,[2] John,[1]) b. May 9, 1804, at Bainbridge, Lancaster county, Pa.; d. April 30, 1848, at Bainbridge; m., February 23, 1832, ELIZA FAGER BELL, the youngest daughter of John Bell and Elizabeth Consor, of Middle Paxtang township, Dauphin county, Pa. John Bell was the only child of William Bell and his wife, Catharine Park, of Scotch-Irish birth, and who came to America on the same vessel which conveyed John and Charles Wesley, the founders of Methodism. Mrs. Galbraith, for a period of twenty years, was postmistress at Bainbridge, resigning only by reason of her advanced years; being left a widow with a large family, she felt the necessity of bringing into action all her energies and business qualifications to the better support of her children. All her six sons were in the civil war and did faithful service. They had issue:

    i. William-Bell, b. October 15, 1833, in Harrisburg, Pa.; m. Elizabeth Lane, of Mount Joy, Pa.; and had *Frank-Lane*.

    ii. James-Carpenter, b. July 9, 1835, in Harrisburg, Pa.; d. July 18, 1872, unm., in Bainbridge, Pa.

    iii. John-Fager, b. July 23, 1837, in Bainbridge, Pa.; m. Henrietta Hoff, of Bainbridge, and had *Eliza, Laura, William, Catharine, John*,[1] d. s. p., *Henry, Robert*, and *John*.[2]

    iv. Jefferson Green, b. July 28, 1839, in Marietta, Pa.; m. Mary Filbert, of Bainbridge, Pa., and had *Emily, Charles, Mary*, d. s. p., *Wildey*, d. s. p., and *Annie Filbert*.

    v. Franklin-Grush, b. March 7, 1842, in Marietta, Pa.; m. Annie N. Meyer, of Harrisburg, Pa., (deceased), and had *Nettie Elizabeth*, and *Annie Meyer*, d. s. p..

    vi. Bertram-Gillespie, b. September 7, 1845; in Bainbridge, Pa.; m. Miriam Reese, of Mount Joy, Pa.; and had issue: *Miriam, Helen*, and *Aurelia*.

XVIII. JOHN GALBRAITH,[5] (John,[4] James,[3] James,[2] John,[1]) b. 1794, in Huntingdon county, Pa.; d. June 15, 1860, in Erie, Pa. His father removing to Butler county, Pa., towards the close of the century, he was brought up on the farm. When a young man he commenced teaching school, and later on began the study of law in the office of Gen. William Ayres, of Butler, and was admitted to the bar at the age of twenty-three. He shortly after removed to Franklin, Venango county, Pa., where he rose rapidly both in his profession and in popular esteem. His first official position was as a member of Assembly, to which he was elected three times. He was elected to Congress as a Democrat in 1832, 1834, and 1838. In 1837 he removed to Erie, where he resided until his death. On retiring from Congress in 1840, he practiced law until the fall of 1851, when he was elected president judge for Erie, Crawford, and Warren counties. His death occurred before the expiration of his term of office. Judge Galbraith was one of the foremost men in promoting the various public enterprises that gave the first strong impulse to Erie county. He was the pioneer in projecting the railroad from Erie to the Ohio State line, and aided greatly in reviving the long dormant proposed railroad from Erie to Sunbury, now the Philadelphia and Erie railroad. One of his favorite ideas, the establishment of a prison for youthful offenders exclusively, has been adopted by the State in the institution at Huntingdon and elsewhere. Judge Galbraith married in May, 1822, AMY AYRES, daughter of Rev. Robert Ayres, an Episcopalian minister, long a resident of Brownsville, Fayette county, Pa., and a brother of Gen. William Ayres. Mrs. Galbraith died March 2, 1868, in the city of Philadelphia. They had issue :

22.   *i. William-Ayres*, b. May 9, 1823 ; m. Fanny Davenport.
     ii. Elizabeth-Ann, m. William S. Lane, of Erie, now a practicing lawyer of Philadelphia.

XIX. JULIANNA GALBRAITH,[5] (Andrew,[4] James,[3] James,[2] John,[1]) b. about 1786, in Cumberland county, Pa.; d. January 13, 1862, in Philadelphia, at the residence of her son, William Callender Irvine ; buried in Laurel Hill cemetery ; m. July 26, 1808, WILLIAM McNEILL IRVINE, b. about 1778, in Carlisle, Pa.; d. September 25, 1854, in Harrisburg, Pa., and there buried. He was the second son of Gen. William Irvine, of the Revolution, and Anne Callender, daughter of Capt. Robert Callender, of Middlesex, Cumberland county, Pa. He was educated at Dickinson College, where he graduated ; subsequently studied law with Judge Thomas Duncan, and was admitted to the Cumberland county bar in 1802. He afterwards located at Harrisburg, and was admitted to the Dauphin county bar at an adjourned court March, 1807. He entered the United States army as captain May 3, 1808, in the regiment of light artillery, and was stationed several years at New Orleans. He left the army, by resignation, about 1811 or 1812, and resumed the practice of law at Sunbury. In July, 1813, he was acting Adjutant General of Pennsylvania, which duties he performed until his appointment by the President of the United States as colonel of the Forty-second regiment, United States infantry, August 4, 1813. At the close of the war he resigned, and located at Harrisburg, and was appointed deputy attorney general for the counties of Dauphin and Northumberland ; subsequently commissioned by Gov. Snyder, September

14, 1814, escheator general of the State, which position he filled until the abolishment of the office. From 1819 to 1821 he was Adjutant General of Pennsylvania, and had previously, 1818-19, represented the county of Dauphin in the State Legislature, and to him is due the credit of originating the bill authorizing and directing the erection of the capitol building at Harrisburg. From about the year 1826 to 1850, he resided at Gettysburg. In 1847, Gov. Shunk appointed him law judge for the York and Adams district on the expiration of Judge Durkee's term, but he resigned shortly after, owing to some difficulty with the members of the bar and efforts made to impeach him. Col. Irvine was a brilliant pleader, but not a lawyer, and hence his failure in the judicial station to which he had been elevated. He returned to Harrisburg, where he resumed the practice of the law for awhile, and subsequently died there. He was an excellent military officer, a gentleman of fine personal appearance, tall and commanding, of good conversational powers, a delightful companion, and for a period of thirty years was quite prominent and influential in public affairs. They left issue (surname Irvine):

 i. Andrew-Galbraith, a physician of prominence in Warren county, Pa., and died a few years since.
 ii. William-Callender, formerly in the quartermaster's department, United States army; now resides in Philadelphia.

XX. SARAH W. GALBRAITH,[6] (Andrew,[4] James,[3] James,[2] Robert,[1]) b. January 25, 1791; d. May 2, 1853, in Carlisle, Pa.; m. in 1810, JOHN BANNISTER GIBSON, b. November 8, 1780, in Shearman's Valley, now Perry county, Pa.; d. May 2, 1853, in the city of Philadelphia; buried in Carlisle, Pa. He was of Scotch-Irish descent, and the son of Colonel George Gibson, who fell in the defeat of St. Clair, on the 4th of November, 1791. He entered Dickinson College, graduated therefrom, and entered the law office of his kinsman, Thomas Duncan. He was admitted to the Cumberland county bar at the March term, 1803. In 1810 he was elected to the Pennsylvania Legislature, and in 1812, appointed president judge for the Eleventh judicial district, composed of the counties of

Tioga, Bradford, Susquehanna, and Luzerne. Upon the death of Judge Brackenridge, in 1816, Governor Snyder appointed Judge Gibson associate judge of the Supreme Court of Pennsylvania. Under the act of Assembly of April 8, 1826, the number of Supreme Court judges was increased from three to five. The year following, Chief Justice Tilghman died, when Judge Gibson succeeded him. In 1838, at the date of the adoption of the then new Constitution of the State, he resigned his office, but was immediately re-appointed by Governor Ritner. In 1851, when the judiciary became elective, his seat became vacant. He, however, was re-elected an associate justice, and discharged the high functions of that office until his death. No greater encomium can be passed upon him than is inscribed upon the marble shaft which marks the place of his repose—from the pen of that late eminent jurist, Jeremiah S. Black. They had issue (surname Gibson):

  i. Margaretta, b. 1813; d. December 15, 1893; m. Col. Charles McClure, and left issue.
  ii. Annie, m. Milnor Roberts, civil engineer, and left issue.
  iii. Sarah, m. Gen. Richard Anderson, U. S. A., and had issue.
  iv. John-Bannister, b. 1822; d. 1856, unm.
  v. George, colonel U. S. A.; m. Fannie Hunt.

XXI. ROBERT GALBRAITH,[6] (Robert,[5] John,[4] Andrew,[3] James,[2] John,[1]) b. 1782, in the Cumberland Valley; d. in 1826, in Butler county, Pa. When a young man he removed to Butler county, Pa., where he purchased a considerable tract of land. He m. MARY WHITE. They had issue:

  i. Samuel, d. s. p.
  ii. William, m., and left issue:
    1. *Mary*, m. Thomas Watson.
    2. *Anne*, m. William McClung.
    3. *Robert*, d. on the old homestead; m. Isabel ———; and left issue:
      a. Caroline, m. Dr. J. C. McKee.
      b. Mary, m. R. B. Ivory, of Pittsburgh.
      c. Belle.
      d. Henry.
      e. James-M., member of Butler county bar.
  iii. Mary, m. John Ralston; and left issue.
  iv. Robert, d. s. p.
  v. Joseph.
23. *vi. Elizabeth*, b. 1808; m. William McCain.

XXII. WILLIAM AYRES GALBRAITH,[6] (John,[5] John,[4] James,[3] James,[2] Robert,[1]) b. May 9, 1823, in Franklin county, Pa. He was educated at Allegheny College, Meadville, and at the academy in Erie, upon his father's removal to that town in 1837. He studied law with his father, being admitted to the bar May 9, 1844, on his twenty-first birthday. In September of the same year he entered Dane Law School, Harvard University, of which Judge Joseph Story and Prof. Simon Greenleaf were the instructors, and there graduated in 1845. Returning to Erie, he began the practice of law. In 1846 he was appointed by Judge Kane, then Attorney General of the State, deputy attorney general for Erie county, in which office he continued until 1850. Taking an active part in politics, he was a delegate to the Democratic State Convention of 1846, and of several succeeding ones. He was a delegate to the National Convention at Charleston in 1860, and at Chicago in 1864. In 1876 he was elected president judge of Erie county, as a People's candidate, although the Republican party ticket had about 2,600 majority. His term of office expired in 1887. Judge Galbraith m., May 25, 1846, FANNY DAVENPORT, daughter of Captain William Davenport, of Erie. They had issue:

    i. Fanny, m. Dr. Arnold P. Gilmore.
    ii. John-W.
    iii. Davenport.

XXIII. ELIZABETH GALBRAITH,[7] (Robert,[6] Robert,[5] John,[4] Andrew,[3] James,[2] John,[1]) b. 1803, in Butler county, Pa.; d. 1889, in Freeport, Armstrong county, Pa. She was a woman of remarkable force of character, especially notable for her strong will and her religious fervor. She m., in 1825, WILLIAM MCCAIN, who was one of the California pioneers of the early "fifties," and subsequently a manufacturer and farmer of Armstrong county. They had issue (surname McCain):

    i. Robert, b. 1829, at Slatelick, Armstrong county, Pa.; d. 1894, in Freeport, Pa.; m., in 1854, Elizabeth Griffin Rockefeller; and left issue:
        1. *George-Nox*, b. 1856; a prominent newspaper correspondent and reporter, residing in Philadelphia; m., 1879, Mary Virginia Overholt.
        2. *Margaret-Rockefeller*, b. 1858; m. W. B. F Brown.

 ii. George-Nox, b. 1831; d. 1867, in California; m. Elizabeth Hooker.
 iii. Rebecca, d. s. p.
 iv. William-G., m. Nancy Roland.
 v. Malinda, m., in 1859, John H. Shoop.
 vi. Joseph, d. s. p.
 vii. James Harvey, m., 1879, Charlotte Turner.
 viii. Laurette-J.
 ix. Samuel, d. s. p.

GREGG AND CURTIN.

Hon. ANDREW GREGG, who served as member and Senator in the councils of the nation from 1791 to 1813, left unfinished a sketch of family history which he commenced preparing in his old age, for "my own satisfaction," as he expresses it, "than for any other reason," which is interesting enough to excite a general regret that he did not complete it. He says:

My parents were both natives of Ireland. My father, whose name was Andrew, was born within the liberties of Londonderry, where the family resided. His father's name was John, and there my knowledge of ancestry in that line stops. I never heard him say from whom his father had descended, but believe, from information derived through other channels, that they were a Scotch family, which migrated to Ireland soon after the accession of William and Mary to the British throne.

My grandfather had three sons, John, David, and Andrew, and one daughter named Rachel. John remained in Ireland engaged in the business of trading, and became wealthy. He had a son called Andrew, who came to this country on business of his father's while I was at the academy in Newark (Delaware), where he called to see me, but I unfortunately happened to be away, and we never met. He returned to Ireland, and on his father's death succeeded him in the management of his business.

David and my father and their sister Rachel all married in Ireland, and all came to this country in the same vessel. They landed at Boston, and traveled into New Hampshire, where David settled and raised a large family, some of whose descendants occupy the very spot where he made his first establishment. I have received letters from three young men, who trace their origin back to that root, and who, I would presume, judging from their letters, are men of considerable promise. One of them, a full namesake of mine, is living as a trader in the northern part of the State of New York or at Montreal. Another, I think, is a clergyman, settled near Salem, Mass., where his father resides, pursuing the business of a chemist. The third became a lawyer, and is now settled at Indianapolis.

I will here just mention two anecdotes calculated to show that family relationship is often discovered by family likeness in branches far removed from the original stock. While in Congress, in 1793 or '94, Mr. Forster, a member of that body from the State of New Hampshire, asked me if I had any relations in that State. On answering in the affirmative, he said he had been led to make the inquiry struck with the imposing likeness betwixt me and Colonel Gregg, who had been the opposing candidate to him at the late election.

On my first introduction to Governor Clinton, when he became Vice President, he asked me whether I was a native of Pennsylvania. I told him I was. He then said there is so striking a resemblance betwixt you and a young man named James Gregg, who was a lieutenant in my brigade during the Revolution, that when I saw you my first impression was that you must be his brother. He was of a New England family then settled in the State of New York. He then related the story, often published in the newspapers, of that officer having been shot, scalped, and left for dead by the Indians, and rescued by a detachment sent by the commanding officer of the garrison,* where he had been stationed, and directed to the place where he lay, by his dog.

My father and Solomon Walker, the husband of their sister, Rachel, not pleased with the prospect of a settlement in New Hampshire, returned to Boston, and shipped for Philadelphia, but landed at Newcastle. I do not recollect the particular year of their arrival, but it was during the administration of Sir William Keith, and most probably in the autumn of 1732.† The winter immediately succeeding their landing they spent at a furnace, belonging to Keith, on Christiana creek, near the town of Newark in the State of Delaware. In

---

*Fort Schuyler, N. Y., Dr. Lossing relates the story in 1st vol. Field Book of the Revolution, page 252.

† *Quære*, 1726 ?

the following spring they moved up the country and commenced their settlement at a place called Chestnut Level, near the southern bounds of Lancaster county. In making their location they were both unfortunate, my father doubly so. Not being qualified to judge of land by superficial appearance, their attention was arrested by the flourishing growth of young chestnut timber with which that district was covered, and they concluded that land which produced such thrifty timber was just what they were in pursuit of. In proceeding onwards, the fine fertile valleys of Pequea and Conestoga lay before them, and a five pound warrant, followed up by settlement, would have insured them four hundred acres of land, which, at the present time, would sell from $50 to $100 per acre. In addition to the injudicious selection made by my father, a warrant had issued for it to William Meteer, of a date anterior to his settlement. He continued to reside on it until 1748, when, to avoid a law suit, he sold his claim to his adversary.

During the residence of my father at Chestnut Level, his wife died, leaving him with six children. He became the husband of my mother in somewhat less than two years after the death of his first wife. My mother's maiden name was Jane Scott. Her father, William Scott, lived in the county of Armagh, Ireland, whence he emigrated and settled at Chestnut Level. His family, at the time of his arrival, consisted of himself, wife, two sons, Moses and Thomas, and four daughters, Elizabeth, Margery, Jane, my mother, and Fanny. Moses settled and lived until his death near Newark, Delaware. He was a respectable man, and possessed good standing both in church and State. He raised a large family, the majority of them sons.

Thomas, with his family, migrated to the western part of Virginia. I never heard anything further of them. Elizabeth married David Montgomery; they settled and died near the Rock-fish gap in Virginia. I remember having seen them once on a visit at my father's, and some time after, two of their sons and a daughter paid us a visit. The young men, I well recollect, had a genteel appearance, and the daughter was accounted a beauty, and was nick-named the "Morning Star," on account of the effulgence of her complexion.

Margery was married to Hugh Caldwell. They lived and died in Lancaster county, near McCall's ferry. They had three sons and two daughters. The eldest son, Matthew, was killed at the battle of Long Island; their second son, Samuel, was drowned in the Susquehanna, at McCall's ferry, in a manly attempt to save some of the passengers of a sinking boat. He was in the store when the flat went down, and being a good swimmer, he plunged in and brought one person to the shore, but in the second attempt he failed, some of the drowning persons got hold of him, and all sank together.

Fanny, the youngest sister, was married to Andrew Baxter, who owned a valuable property in Lancaster county, which he imprudently sold, and moved to North Carolina, and there was inhumanly murdered by the Tories during the Revolutionary War. The family, I believe, is extinct, except one son, who lives in Georgia.

My father having sold his claim in Chestnut Level, set out some time in the year 1748 in quest of another residence. He traveled up the Susquehanna river to Swatara creek, and was nearly purchasing two plantations on the south side of the creek where the turnpike road now crosses it. Eighty pounds Pennsylvania currency was the price. He crossed the river where Harrisburg now stands, and traveled up Cumberland Valley. He met a certain Robert Amon, of Chester county, from whom he purchased a warrant for three hundred acres of land, including an improvement on the north side of the Conedoguinet. Here terminated his expeditionary survey. He returned home and made the necessary arrangements for the removal of his family to his new purchase.

On the settlement in Chestnut Level becoming sufficiently numerous, they formed a Presbyterian congregation, built a meeting-house, and invited Rev. Mr. Thom to become their pastor. He accepted their call, and on organizing a session, my father was elected a member of it, and continued so until his removal. Mr. Thom's certificate of this circumstance is somewhere among my papers.

When very young, I have noticed an old-fashioned sword and espontoon laying up stairs among other lumber. I recollect my mother saying that her grandfather had worn the sword in King William's army, at the battle of Boyne, and my father saying he carried the espontoon.

Mr. Gregg's manuscript ends abruptly, but from it, and other data in our possession, we have the following record of the family:

I. JOHN GREGG,¹ of Bally-arnat, near Londonderry, Ireland, was the son of DAVID GREGG,¹ a native of Ayreshire, Scotland. The son was possibly born in Caledonia, and with his father's family migrated to Ireland during the great influx. David Gregg was within the walls of Londonderry during the great siege, 1688–89; and was a captain in Cromwell's army. The children of John Gregg were:

    i. John, probably lived and died at Bally-arnat, Ireland. His son, *William*, emigrated to America, and settled in Paxtang township, Lancaster county, Pa., where he died in July, 1744; by his will he left his estate to his uncle, Andrew Gregg, then in America, to his father, and to his sister, Elizabeth Lang, of Bally-negallah, near Londonderry, Ireland.

    ii. David, came to America in 1722, and settled in Londonderry, New Hampshire; he married, in 1713, Mary Evans, of Londonderry, Ireland, and their descendants have not only been numerous, but many of them quite prominent in public affairs.

    iii. Rachel, m. Solomon Walker; they settled in the Cumberland valley.

2.   *iv. Andrew*, m. and left issue.

II. ANDREW GREGG,³ (John,² David,¹) b. about 1710; d. November 18, 1789; removed, in 1750, to a farm two miles north-westwardly of Carlisle, Pa., adjoining the glebe farm of Meeting-House Spring, which was within sight of his dwelling; was twice married; name of first wife unknown; by her there was issue:

3.   *i. John*, m. and left issue.
    ii. James, served in the army of the Revolution.
    iii. Rachel.
    iv. Margaret.
    v. Jean.
    vi. Elizabeth.

Andrew Gregg m., secondly, JEAN SCOTT, b. 1725; d. September 30, 1783, near Carlisle, Cumberland county, Pa.; daughter of William Scott, of Chestnut Level, Lancaster county, Pa. They had issue:

4.   *vii. Andrew*, b. July 10, 1755; m. Martha Potter.
      viii. Matthew, was a wagon-master in the army of the Revolution from January 9, 1778, to August 14, 1780.

III. JOHN GREGG,[4] (Andrew,[3] John,[2] David,[1]) served in the army of the Revolution; m., and had, among other children:

      i. Elizabeth; d. October 11, 1801, in Bellefonte, Pa.; m. George McKee.
5.   *ii. Margery*, b. 1776; m. Roland Curtin.

IV. ANDREW GREGG,[4] (Andrew,[3] John,[2] David,[1]) b. June 10, 1755, near Carlisle, Pa.; d. May 30, 1835, at Bellefonte, Pa. Andrew Gregg received his early education at Rev. John Steel's Latin School in Carlisle, and completed his education at Newark, Del.; while at the latter place he served several tours in the militia of the Revolution. In 1799 he accepted the tutorship in the college (now university) at Philadelphia, under Drs. Smith and Ewing, where he remained until his removal to Middletown, Pa., where he was engaged for four years in the mercantile business. On his marriage he removed to Lewistown, which was then, 1787, being laid out by General Potter and Major Montgomery, and in 1789 he removed to Penn's Valley, Centre county, two miles east of the "Old Fort." His public services commenced November 8, 1791, as a member of the House of Representatives of the United States, where he remained sixteen years, and in 1807 was chosen United States Senator, which exalted station he occupied until the 3d day of March, 1813. In 1814, he removed to Bellefonte, in order the better to educate his family, and was elected first president of the "Centre Bank." On the 19th of December, 1820, Mr. Gregg was appointed Secretary of the Commonwealth, by Governor Hiester, and on the 15th of May, 1823, nominated for Governor, in opposition to Mr. Shulze. Mr. Gregg had strong party predelictions, but was remarkable for independence, always acting according to the convictions of his conscience, though they differed sometimes from the views of his party associates. He was, while in office, the representative of the interests of his constituents, not of their limited views of subjects of moment. He was an elegant classical scholar, and had acquired extensive general information which large experience and deep reflection had molded to practical purposes. He was a man of vigorous constitution, preserved intact by a life of temperate habits and industry until he reached the age of four score years. Andrew Gregg m., January 29, 1787, MARTHA POTTER, b. April 10, 1769; d. August 20, 1815, daughter of General James Potter of the Revolution. They had issue:

    i. Mary, b. November 2, 1788; d. January 9, 1826; m. William McLanahan, of Antrim township, Franklin county, Pa.; and had issue (surname McLanahan):
        1. *Andrew*, b. August 13, 1807; d. near Greencastle, Pa., on the old homestead, February 26, 1891.
        2. *James-X.*, b. 1809; d. 1864; represented his district in the Senate of Pennsylvania from 1842 to 1844, and in the United States Congress from 1849 to 1853; left one son, *James-X.*, of New York city.
        3. *Isabella*, m. Dr. J. P. Hiester, of Franklin county, Pa.
        4. *Mary*, m. Dr. Richards, of Chambersburg, Pa.
    ii. Jean, b. February 17, 1791; m. Roland Curtin, (*see* v).
    iii. Martha, b. June 7, 1793; d. December 31, 1829; m. Dr. Constans Curtin, b. 1785; d. April 10, 1842; was a native of Ireland and came to America in 1806; completed his professional studies under Dr. Benjamin Rush, of Philadelphia, and located in Bellefonte, Pa., in 1810; was an accomplished and skillful physician, whilst his hospitality and generosity endeared him to a numerous circle of friends and acquaintances.
    iv. Eliza, b. June 2, 1795; d. December 22, 1882; m. David Mitchell, of Bellefonte, Pa.; b. November 28, 1790; d. March 27, 1873; served in Captain Record's company from Centre county, in the war of 1812; and had issue (surname Mitchell):
        1. *Margery*, m. John D. Leib, of Bellefonte.
        2. *Julia*, m. Rev. J. S. McMurray, of Tyrone, Pa.
6.   *v. Julianna*, b. June 26, 1797; m. Gen. James Irvin.
7.   *vi. Andrew*, b. November 30, 1799; m. Margaret Irvin.
    vii. James-P., b. April 28, 1802; d. September 8, 1845, in Virginia; m. Eliza Wilson.

8. *viii. Matthew-Duncan*, b. April 5, 1804 ; m. Ellen McMurtrie.
   ix. Sarah, b. January 23, 1807 ; d. March 28, 1836 ; m. Henry Kinney, b. ——— ; d. ——— ; and had issue (surname Kinney):
   1. *Andrew-Gregg.*
   2. *Martha*, m. John Brotherline.
   3. *Sarah-I.*, m. Dr. James P. Wilson, (*see Hugh Wilson record*).
   x. Margery, b. September 14, 1811 ; resides in Lewisburg, Pa.; m. Rev. Charles Tucker, now deceased, of the Baptist church ; and had issue (surname Tucker):
   1. *Andrew-Gregg*, Lieut. Co. E., 142d Regt., Pa. Vols., killed in battle of Gettysburg, July 1, 1863.
   2. *Augusta*, m. Rev. J. R. Loomis, LL. D., of Lewisburg, Pa.

V. MARGERY GREGG,[5] (John,[4] Andrew,[3] John,[2] David,[1]) b. 1776 ; d. January 15, 1813, in Bellefonte, Pa.; m. November 25, 1800, ROLAND CURTIN, b. 1764, in Ireland ; was educated in Paris, where he narrowly escaped the guillotine during the Reign of Terror; came to America, and located first at Phillipsburg, Centre county, Pa., then at Milesburg, where he became a merchant ; was coroner of Centre county in 1803, and elected sheriff in October, 1806; in 1810, with Moses Boggs, erected a forge at Eagle Works, Centre county, of which he became sole owner in 1815, and in 1818 built Eagle furnace ; in 1825, purchased the Antes grist and saw-mills near Curtin station, and in 1830, erected the rolling-mill there ; was prominently identified with all the public improvements made within the county; shortly before his death he removed to Bellefonte. They had issue (surname Curtin):

   i. Austin, b. August 26, 1801 ; d. July 27, 1871.
   ii. James, b. September 18, 1806 ; d. January 5, 1873.
   iii. Roland, b. September 2, 1808; d. August 15, 1875 ; m., June 17, 1834, Eliza Irvin, daughter of John Irvin ; and had issue (surname Curtin): Gen. *John-I.*, Col. of 45th Pa., Capt. *Austin*, Co. D, 45th Pa., *Andrew-G., Jr.*, and *William*, of Bellefonte.
9. *iv. John*, b. September 24, 1810 ; m. Julia Barnhart.

Roland Curtin, m., secondly, in 1814, JEAN GREGG, b. February 17, 1791; d. March 14, 1854, in Bellefonte, Pa., daughter of Andrew Gregg (*see* IV). They had issue (surname Curtin):

10.   *i. Andrew-Gregg*, b. April 23, 1815; m. Catharine I. Wilson.
      ii. Constans, b. March 8, 1817 ; iron-master, residing at Roland, Centre county ; unm.
11. *iii. Martha-M.*, b. August 29, 1819 ; m. Dr. William Irvin.
      iv. Ellen-Honora; m. William H. Allen, M.D., LL. D., b. March 22, 1808, in Augusta, Maine ; graduated at Bowdoin College ; professor of chemistry and of natural philosophy at Dickinson College, Carlisle, from 1836 to 1848 ; in January, 1850, he became president of Girard College ; resigned in December, 1862, and became president of State College, in Centre county ; in 1867, he was re-called to Girard College ; d. August 29, 1882, in Philadelphia. Mrs. Allen is also dead, and their only daughter, *Honora*, m. Henry Sheldon. now deceased, of Philadelphia. She resides in Philadelphia, and has one son, *Allen* Sheldon.
      v. Margery, b. December 23, 1823 ; m. Thomas R. Reynolds, of Bellefonte, and had issue (surname Reynolds): *William-F.*, and *Jennie*, m. James Pierepont
      vi. Nancy-J., b. May 4, 1828 ; m. Dr. Clark, of Philadelphia.
      vii. Julia, b. October 3, 1831 ; resides in Philadelphia.

VI. JULIANNA GREGG,[5] (Andrew,[4] Andrew,[3] John,[2] David,[1]) b. June 26, 1797 ; d. July 4, 1856 ; m., September, 24, 1822, JAMES IRVIN, b. February 18, 1800, at Linden Hall, Centre county, Pa.; d. November 26, 1762, at Hecla, Centre county, Pa.; son of John Irvin and Ann Watson. General James Irvin was many years a leading iron-master of Centre county, interested in Centre furnace, Mill Creek, Mercer Iron Works, Monroe, Washington, Martha, Julian, Hecla, and Hopewell. He was elected to Congress in 1840, and took a large part in the passage of the tariff act of 1842 ; he was re-elected in 1842, and served until March 3, 1845. In 1847, General Irvin was nominated by the Whig party for Governor, but was defeated by Francis R. Shunk, and after the campaign resumed business with his accustomed energy. He was one of the best business men of Centre county ; kind hearted and benevolent, he saved many a fireside from sheriff's sale. He donated a farm of two hundred acres to the State College, and gave it large contributions of money. In 1851, he was appointed naval store-keeper at Philadelphia navy-yard. He left no issue.

VII. ANDREW GREGG,[6] (Andrew,[4] Andrew,[3] John,[2] David,[1]) b. November 30, 1799; d. May 15, 1869. He was a prominent iron-master in Centre county, and an active business man, and represented the district composed of the counties of Lycoming, Clinton, and Centre, in the State Senate from 1856 to 1861; died at Milesburg, Pa. He m., December 2, 1824, MARGARET IRVIN, b. October 11, 1803; d. December 20, 1890; daughter of John Irvin and Ann Watson. They had issue:

    i. John-Irvin, b. July 19, 1826; educated at Boalsburg and Mifflinburg; volunteered as private in the Mexican war, and was appointed lieutenant in 11th infantry, U. S. A.; promoted captain September 5, 1847; honorably discharged August 15, 1848, when he engaged in the iron business in Centre county; June 21, 1861, entered service again as captain of Co. E, 5th Penn'a reserves, and promoted, in U. S. service, captain of 6th cavalry; in November, 1862, commissioned colonel of 16th Penn'a cavalry, continuing in service during the war; he was finally promoted brevet major general of volunteers at the close of hostilities for distinguished services during the war; after the war, he was sent to Lynchburg, Va., and put in command of that part of Virginia; afterwards, inspector general of freedmen in Louisiana; under the establishment of July 28, 1868, he became colonel of 8th U. S. cavalry, performing many arduous duties in Arizona and New Mexico; was wounded several times in service, and was placed on the retired list in October, 1878; d. December, 1891; m., first, Clarissa H. Everhart; secondly, Harriet C. Marr; resides in Lewisburg, Pa.

  ii. Martha, d. 1852; m. Dr. John B. Mitchell; both dead.

 iii. Anne.

 iv. Andrew, m. Mary J. Smith, dau. of Col. John Smith, of Clinton county, Pa.; reside in Centre Hall, Pa., and had issue: *Anne-Mary, James, Andrew*, and *John-Irvin*.

  v. James-P.; was first lieut., Co. D., 45th Pa. Vols.; killed in battle at Poplar Spring church, on Peeble's farm, Va., September 30, 1864.

 vi. Julia.

vii. Susan.

viii. Margaret.

VIII. MATTHEW DUNCAN GREGG,[5] (Andrew,[4] Andrew,[3] John,[2] David,[1]) b. April 5, 1804; d. July 27, 1845; m. ELLEN

McMurtrie, b. January 3, 1802; d. August 17, 1847; daughter of David McMurtrie and his wife, Martha Elliott. They had issue:

    i. Martha, m. Richard R. Bryan; d. 1851.
    ii. Andrew, b. ———; d. 1851.
12. *iii. David-McMurtrie*, b. April 10, 1833; m. Ellen F. Sheaff.
    iv. Mary, m. E. Dorsey Green.
    v. Ellen.
    vi. George.
    vii. Henry-H.; was major Thirteenth Pennsylvania cavalry; m. Rose Mitchell.
    viii. Thomas-J.; was lieutenant Sixth Pennsylvania cavalry, and captain Second U. S. cavalry; m. Elizabeth McKnight.

IX. John Curtin,[6] (Margery,[5] John,[4] Andrew,[3] John,[2] David,[1]) b. September 24, 1810, in Centre county, Pa.; resides in Bellefonte, Pa.; m., January 3, 1837, Julia Barnhart, b. March 14, 1811; daughter of Colonel Henry Barnhart. They had issue (surname Curtin):

    i. Margery-Irvin, m. General John I. Curtin, of Bellefonte, Pa.
    ii. James-B., m. Jane Holden; reside in Roland, Pa.
    iii. Sarah-C., m. J. F. Larimer, M.D.
    iv. Harry R., m. Eliza McMinn; reside in Roland, Pa.
    v. John-G., m. Stella Lowden; reside in Philadelphia.

X. Andrew Gregg Curtin,[6] (Margery,[5] John,[4] Andrew,[3] John,[2] David,[1]) b. April 23, 1815, in Bellefonte, Pa.; and d. there October 7, 1894. Educated under Dr. Kirkpatrick, at Milton; he studied law at Carlisle and Bellefonte, and was admitted to the bar in April, 1837. In 1840, took an active part in politics in the Harrison campaign, and in 1844 canvassed the State for Henry Clay. On the 17th of January, 1855, he was appointed Secretary of the Commonwealth by Governor Pollock, and in virtue of his office became Superintendent of the Public Schools. His superintendence has one great landmark, the institution of normal schools. In 1860, he was elected Governor of Pennsylvania. His administration of that office during the war gave him renown throughout the country, and added historic grandeur to the annals of his native Commonwealth. His foresight caused the organization of the Pennsylvania Reserves, and contributed largely to save our National Government, imperilled by the disaster of Bull Run. His ever enduring record, however, in connection with the war, was the establishment of orphans' schools for the children of those who fell in the service of their country. In 1869 he was appointed by President Grant Minister to Russia, and served creditably in that position until August, 1872, when he returned home. He was chosen a delegate-at-large to the State Constitutional Convention of 1873, and represented the Twentieth Pennsylvania district in the Forty-seventh, Forty-eighth, and Forty-ninth Congresses. In that body he was chairman of the Foreign Affairs Committee. His last term in Congress expired in 1887, when he retired from public life. He was a man of broad culture, extensive reading and thorough familiarity with affairs. Next to Lincoln, Governor Curtin was emphatically the greatest representative man in the nation during the war for the Union, and at his death, the sensation produced was cosmopolitan. Governor Curtin, m., May 30, 1844, CATHARINE IRVINE WILSON, b. January 17, 1821, (*see Wilson Irish-Settlement record*). They had issue (surname Curtin):

    i. Martha-Wilson, b. March 7, 1845 ; m., June 8, 1870, George F. Harris, M.D., son of William Harris, Esq., (1799-1865), of Bellefonte ; and had issue (surname Harris):
      1. *Catharine-Curtin*, b. March 28, 1871.
      2. *Adeline-F.*, b. December 15, 1877.
    ii. Jane-Gregg, b. January 17, 1847; d. November 22, 1893 ; m., May 20, 1869, William H. Sage, of Ithaca, N. Y.; and had issue (surname Sage):
      1. *Henry-W.*, b. April 7, 1872.
      2. *Andrew-Gregg-Curtin*, b. June 3, 1873.
      3. *Dewitt-L.*, b. February 3, 1879.
    iii. Martha-Irvine, b. March 19, 1849 ; m., January 23, 1873, Commander Kidder Randolph Breeze, U. S. N., d. September 13, 1881, at Newport, R. I.; and had issue (surname Breeze):
      1. *Andrew-Gregg-Curtin*, b. December 5, 1873.
      2. *Randolph*, b. January 27, 1876.
      3. *Elizabeth-Malbone*, b. November 4, 1877.
      4. *Jane-Curtin*, b. April 24, 1881.
    iv. William-Wilson, b. March 27, 1851 ; m., October 21, 1875, Harriet F. Harding, of Wilkes-Barre, Pa.; reside in Philadelphia ; and had issue :
      1. *Marion-Harding*, b. May 20, 1878.
      2. *Catharine Irvine*, b. February 6, 1884.

v. Catharine-Wilson, b. May 2, 1859; m., May 2, 1888, Dewitt Burnett, of Syracuse, N. Y.; and had issue (surname Burnett):
1. *Catharine-M.*, b. February 25, 1889.
2. *Margaret-B.*, b. March 2, 1890.

XI. MARTHA M. CURTIN,[6] (Margery,[5] John,[4] Andrew,[3] John,[2] David,[1]) b. August 29, 1819; d. August 6, 1880, in Lancaster, Pa.; m. in 1836, WILLIAM IRVIN, b. November 15, 1805, at Linden Hall, Centre county, Pa.; d. September 9, 1865, at Amoy, China; educated at Dickinson College, Carlisle, Pa.; pursued his medical studies at Jefferson College, Philadelphia, graduating in a class with Dr. Pancoast and others; located in practice at Bellefonte, afterwards removing to Milesburg Iron Works, where he entered into business partnership. In 1862, he relinquished the iron business, and accepted a clerkship in the second comptroller's office in the U. S. Treasury, Washington city. In 1864, was appointed consul to Amoy, where he died the following year of Asiatic cholera. They had issue (surname Irvin):

i. Roland-Curtin, of Bellefonte, Pa.

XII. DAVID MCMURTRIE GREGG,[6] (Matthew-Duncan,[5] Andrew,[4] Andrew,[3] John,[2] David,[1]) b. April 10, 1833; educated at Milnwood Academy, Huntingdon county, and at the University at Lewisburg. He entered the U. S. Military Academy at West Point in 1851, graduated in July, 1855, and appointed second lieutenant of Dragoons, after which he served on the frontiers in the notable Spokane expedition of 1858. Was promoted first lieutenant of Dragoons March 21, 1861; promoted captain of the Sixth Cavalry May 14, 1861, and on January 24, 1862, appointed colonel of the Eighth Pennsylvania Cavalry. He served in the campaign on the Peninsula and covered the movement from Harrison's Landing to Yorktown in August, 1862. He was promoted brigadier general, U. S. Volunteers, November 29, 1862, continuing with the Army of the Potomac and participating in the actions and battles in which it was engaged, frequently having command of all the cavalry of that department. At Gettysburg his command won a decisive victory known as the "Battle of Rummel's Farm." His important services in this decisive battle of the war are recognized by the principal authorities relating to that struggle. From March 26 to April 6, 1864, General Gregg commanded the cavalry corps of the Army of the Potomac, and the second cavalry division from April 6, 1864, to February, 1865, on the Richmond campaign. In several of the long lists of cavalry fights in which he was engaged, General Gregg was in chief command. August 1, 1864, he was made brevet major general, U. S. Volunteers, "for meritorious and distinguished conduct throughout the campaign, especially for reconnaissance on the Charlestown road." He resigned the service February 3, 1865, and General Sheridan, who succeeded him, speaks in his book in the highest terms of General Gregg and of his regret that he should have left the service. In 1874 President Grant appointed him U. S. Consul to Prague. He subsequently resigned and returned to Pennsylvania. In November, 1891, he was elected Auditor General of Pennsylvania for the period of three years. He is commander of the Pennsylvania Commandery of the Military Order of the Loyal Legion and a member of the Grand Army of the Republic. General Gregg married, October 6, 1862, ELLEN F. SHEAFF, a descendant of Governor Joseph Hiester and Frederick A. Muhlenberg. They had issue:

 i. George-Sheaff, b. March 9, 1867.
 ii. David McMurtrie, b. October 3, 1869.

GREENAWALT OF LEBANON.

I. PHILIP LORENTZ GREENAWALT,[1] b. June 10, 1725, in Hasslock, in Boehl, Germany; baptized June 22, 1725, the sponsors being Philip Lorentz Reehm and his wife; d. February 28, 1802, in Lebanon, Pa. His ancestors were of the best known families of his native place. He received a good German and classical education, and came to America in 1749, on the ship "Phœnix," John Mason, master, from Rotterdam, arriving in Philadelphia on the 15th of September. He at first located in Cocalico township, Lancaster county, where he took up one hundred acres of land, February 28, 1754, subsequently removing to Lebanon township. At the outset of the Revolution, he entered heartily into the struggle, and during the entire war was more or less in active service. Upon the organization of the associated battalions, he was commissioned colonel of the first battalion of Lancaster county. He was with Washington, during the Jersey campaign of 1776, at Trenton and Princeton. His battalion was at Brandywine and Germantown, and the conduct of Colonel Greenawalt during the former engagement received the commendation of the commander-in-chief for efficiency and gallantry, especially in the protection of the Continental supplies. He was appointed, May 6, 1778, one of the agents for forfeited estates. At the close of the war he retired to his farm, and, like many more of the brave officers of that struggle for independence, poorer in purse, but conscious of having done his duty to his country. The Assembly of the State appointed him one of the commissioners to take subscriptions for the Continental loan, December 16, 1777, and, during the darkest hour of the struggle, he did effective service in collecting blankets, food, and forage for the half-starved and half-clad army at Valley Forge, and for most of which he was never recompensed. But such was the fate of many who sacrificed their fortunes on the altar of liberty. Colonel Greenawalt reached a good old age, honored, loved and respected by his

304   *Pennsylvania Genealogies.*

neighbors and fellow-citizens. He was twice married; first, to the widow UHLAND, of Muddy Creek, who died the same year; secondly, in 1755, MARIA MARGARET FOESER, b. May 10, 1735; d. May 10, 1806, at Lebanon, and with her husband there buried. They had issue:

2.   i. *John-Philip,* b. June 17, 1756; m. Catharine Shaffner.
3.   ii. *Christian,* b. December 14, 1758; m. Elizabeth Kelker.
4.   iii. *John,* b. October, 1760; m. Regina ———.
      iv. *Elizabeth,* b. March 1, 1763; d. August 24, 1820; m. Henry Kelker.
5.   v. *Margaret,* b. July 17, 1765; m. Philip Stoehr.
6.   vi. *Matthias,* b. October 17, 1767; m. Anna Barbara Hetrick.
      vii. *Jacob,* b. February 14, 1770; d. November 11, 1824, at Hummelstown, Dauphin county, Pa.; m. Elizabeth ———, b. 1769; d. May 26, 1849; buried in Lutheran graveyard, Hummelstown, Pa.; left no descendants.
7.   viii. *Catharine,* b. July 20, 1772; m. John Jacob Zinn.
      ix. *Michael,* b. January 21, 1775; d. s. p.
8.   x. *Leonard* (twin),b. January 21, 1775; m. Catharine Pool.
      xi. *Maria-Magdalena;* d. s. p.

II. JOHN PHILIP GREENAWALT,[2] (Philip-Lorentz,[1]) b. June 17, 1756, near Ephrata, Cocalico township, Pa.; sponsors at baptism, John Weaver and wife; d. July 18, 1834, at Lebanon, Pa.; appointed one of the commissioners in the act erecting the county of Lebanon; m., April 17, 1782, CATHARINE SHAFFNER, b. March 17, 1760; d. January 25, 1850, at Lebanon, Pa.; dau. of Jacob and Elizabeth Shaffner. They had issue:

      i. *John-Philip,* b. May 2, 1783; d. January 25, 1785.
9.   ii. *Jacob,* b. December 6, 1784; m. Catharine Krause.
      iii. *Catharine,* b. April 27, 1786.
      iv. *John-Philip,* b. September 29, 1788; d. June 20, 1834.
      v. *Matthias,* b. September 9, 1790; d. unm.
      vi. *David,* b. November 19, 1792.
      vii. *John,* b. April 17, 1795; m. Ann Brown, and had *Henry* and *Philip.*
      viii. *Elizabeth,* b. April 17, 1795; d. August 4, 1856, in Lebanon, Pa.; m. Daniel Frantz, b. August 18, 1792; d. December 12, 1839; and had issue (surname Frantz): *Uriah, Theodore,* m. Susan Gutelius, *Daniel, Charles,* and *Lydia.*
      ix. *Charles,* b. August 3, 1797; d. September 18, 1880; m. Mary Ann Shaffner, b. March 7, 1805; d. September 14, 1867; and had issue: *Anna-Elizabeth, Catharine, Charles, Philip, Calvin, Alfred, Eliza-Jane, Mary-Ann,* and *Emma.*

x. *Lydia*, b. June 22, 1799 ; m. Benjamin Stees ; and had issue (surname Stees): *Charles, Alfred, Clinton, Washington, Matthias, Philip, Catharine*, and *Mary*.

III. CHRISTIAN GREENAWALT,[2] (Philip-Lorentz,[1]) b. December 14, 1758, in Cocalico township, Lancaster county, Pa.; d. February 3, 1796, in Harrisburg, Pa.; m. ELIZABETH KELKER, b. April 1, 1766, near Lebanon, Pa.; d. July 30, 1825, in Harrisburg, Pa., and with her husband there buried; daughter of Anthony Kelker and Mary Magdalena Meister. They had issue :

10. i. *Catharine*, b. 1790 : m. John Brooks.
11. ii. *Cassandra*, b. December 9, 1794 ; m. George Ackerman.
12. iii. *Margaret*, b. 1796 ; m. Samuel Swartz.

Elizabeth Kelker Greenawalt, subsequently, October 29, 1799, married John Gillum, tanner, of Harrisburg, who d. January 2, 1804, leaving two children, *Jesse* and *Rachel*, both under fourteen years of age, but whether by this or a previous marriage is not known.

IV. JOHN GREENAWALT,[2] (Philip-Lorentz,[1]) b. October 11, 1760, in Lebanon township, Lancaster, now Lebanon county, Pa.; d. November, 1823, in Lebanon, Pa.; m. REGINA ———. They had issue :

i. *Jacob*. m., October 1, 1816, Margaret Sweeny.
ii. *Philip*.
iii. *Elizabeth*, m. ——— Lemmon.
iv. *Mary*, m. [Henry] Poorman.
v. *Margaret*, m. ——— Mannon.
vi. *Sarah*, m. [John] Shatzer.
vii. *Catharine*, b. September 22, 1786 ; d. September 7, 1861 ; m. Daniel Miller, b. May 19, 1781 ; d. June 23, 1859.

V. MARGARET GREENAWALT,[2] (Philip-Lorentz,[1]) b. July 17, 1765, in Lebanon township ; d. ——— ; m. PHILIP STOEHR, son of Henry and Barbara Stoehr. They had issue (surname Stoehr):

i. *Philip*.
ii. *John*.
iii. *Jacob*.
iv. *Catharine*, m. ——— Kissel.
v. *Mary*, m. ——— Grossman.
vi. *William*.
vii. *Margaret*, m. [Samuel] Carper.

VI. MATTHIAS GREENAWALT,² (Philip-Lorentz,¹) b. October 17, 1767; d. November 2, 1808, in Lebanon, Pa.; m. ANNA BARBARA HETRICK; b. March 3, 1776; d. May, 1842, in Lebanon, Pa. They had issue:

    i. Samuel.
    ii. David, d. 1876, in South Bend, Ind.; unm.
    iii. William, resides in Plymouth, Ind.; m. Sarah Haart.
    iv. Philip, d. s. p.
    v. Rosanna, m. John George; d. prior to 1822; and had issue (surname George): *William, Ann, Charles, Edward, David,* and *Rebecca.*

VII. CATHARINE GREENAWALT,² (Philip-Lorentz,¹) b. July 20, 1772, in Lebanon township, Lancaster, now Lebanon county, Pa.; d. September 1, 1823, in Harrisburg, Pa.; m. JOHN JACOB ZINN, b. April 9, 1761; d. June 1, 1832, in Harrisburg, Pa. They had issue (surname Zinn):

13.   *i. Elizabeth,* b. April 8, 1793; m. David S. Forney.
    ii. John, b. 1806; d. August 26, 1868; m. Catharine Culp, and issue:
       1. *Elizabeth,* m. Dr. John A. Stehley, and had issue.
       2. *Catharine,* m. David Hummel, and had issue.
14.   *iii. George,* b. April 6, 1810; m. Anna Margaretta Miller.

VIII. LEONARD GREENAWALT,² (Philip-Lorentz,¹) b. January 21, 1775, in Lebanon township, Lancaster, now Lebanon county, Pa.; d. January 30, 1855, in Lebanon, Pa.; was a tanner by occupation; was elected county treasurer in 1836; m., November 2, 1796, CATHARINE POOL, b. January 14, 1780, in New Hanover township, now Montgomery county, Pa.; d. December 18, 1850, in Lebanon, Pa.; dau. of John Pool and Mary Barbara Rotharmel.* They had issue:

    i. Sarah, b. December 27, 1797; d. February 4, 1859; m. Michael Fichthorn, b. January 4, 1788; d. September 14, 1863, and had issue (surname Fichthorn):
       1. *Augustus,* m. Eliza Stover; and had issue: *Amanda, Barbara, Mary, Sallie, Alcott, Frank,* and *Augustus.*

---

* JOHN POOL m., August 16, 1770, in Pottsgrove, Pa., Mary Barbara Rotharmel, b. April 1, 1751, in New Hanover township, Philadelphia, now Montgomery county, Pa.; baptized by Rev. Henry Muhlenberg, of Falkner Swamp church; daughter of Daniel and Elizabeth Rotharmel.

2. *Catharine*, m. Charles Moore ; and had issue (surname Moore): *Emma-Clarissa.*
15. ii. *Josiah*, b. September 11, 1799; m. Mary Laub.
    iii. *George*, b. 1801 ; d. in New Orleans, La.; m. Catharine Hauer ; no issue.
    iv. *Maria-Barbara*, b. 1803.
    v. *Samuel*, b. 1805 ; d. 1863 ; m. Maria Zimmerman ; d. 1869 ; and had issue :
        1. *Leonard-Thomas-Calvin*, d. July 31, 1871.

IX. JACOB GREENAWALT,[3] (John-Philip,[2] Philip-Lorentz,[1]) b. December 6, 1784, in Lebanon, Pa.; d. May 13, 1854, in Harrisburg, Pa.; learned the trade of a tanner, and in 1810 went to Harrisburg, Pa., where he became an extensive leather manufacturer ; was a man of energy and enterprise, and quite prominent in the early years of his adopted home ; m. CATHARINE KRAUSE, b. March 20, 1789 ; d. June 3, 1864, in Harrisburg ; daughter of John Krause. They had issue :

   i. *Louisa-C.*, b. July 29, 1809 ; d. 1882 ; m. Philip Fisher, of Lebanon ; d. 1882.
   ii. *Elizabeth*, b. March 21, 1811 ; resides in Harrisburg, Pa.
   iii. *Theophilus-P.*, b. March 3, 1815 ; d. December 31, 1860.
   iv. *Camilla*, d. s. p.
   v. *Theodore-D.*, served in the army as paymaster ; resides in Harrisburg, Pa.
16. vi. *Regina-Camilla*, b. August 10, 1823 ; m. William Calder.
   vii. *Jacob*, m. Julia Peifer.
   viii. *Jeremiah-Krause*, b. 1830 ; m., September 18, 1858, Anna L. Wolfersberger ; d. April 8, 1895 ; and had issue :
        1. *William*, b. 1859 ; died in infancy.
        2. *Edwin-J.*, b. July 1, 1861.
        3. *Regina-Calder*, b. November 12, 1863.
        4. *Jeremiah Krause*, b. December 2, 1865

X. CATHARINE GREENAWALT,[3] (Christian,[2] Philip-Lorentz,[1]) b. 1790, in Harrisburg, Pa.; d. August 30, 1859 ; m. JOHN BROOKS, b. March 18, 1778, at Carlisle, Pa.; d. December 6, 1845, in Harrisburg, Pa.; son of John Brooks * and Sarah

---

*JOHN BROOKS, b. 1727, near Enniskillen, county Fermanagh, Ireland ; d. December 7, 1803, at Elizabethtown, Lancaster county, Pa., buried at Harrisburg, Pa. His parents were descendants of what is known in Ireland as "Cromwellians," a people who have ever proved the most loyal subjects of England, and the history of British arms is their patrimony. At the age of twenty-seven years we

Pardon; he was educated in the schools of Paxtang, and at the age of eighteen went to Lancaster to learn the trade of a gunsmith; completing his apprenticeship, he returned to Harrisburg where he established himself in business; he marched with his fellow-citizens to the defence of Baltimore, in the war of 1812–14; prior to the era of public improvement he erected a warehouse on the Susquehanna at Harrisburg, and was the factor for the Messrs. Coleman and others, pioneers in the iron industries of the State; he served as a justice of the peace, and was burgess and assistant burgess of the borough of Harrisburg several terms; was a member and trustee of the Presbyterian church, and a man of influence and strict integrity. They had issue (surname Brooks):

---

find him in His Majesty's service in the Enniskillen regiment of foot, as sergeant, served with that command in North America; disabled by a wound in the left hand, June 8, 1767, and honorably discharged therefor. Left Montreal and went to Newburyport, in the Massachusetts colony, where he resided until the breaking out of the Revolutionary war. In 1775 he removed to Carlisle, Pa., and on the 9th of January, 1776, he was commissioned second lieutenant in the Pennsylvania Line. During the occupancy of York by Congress in 1778, he was appointed, by General Gates, town major with rank of captain, and acting commissary of supplies. At the close of the war he was at Elizabethtown, Lancaster county, Pa., where he remained a brief period, subsequently returning to Carlisle. About 1784, he removed to Paxtang near Harris' Ferry, where he purchased land, and where he lived the remainder of his days. The *Oracle of Dauphin*, alluding to his death, says: "On Thursday his remains were brought to this place, and deposited by the side of his late consort, a daughter, and three grandchildren; Major Brooks was an old Revolutionary character, and for many years a peaceful and respectable inhabitant of this borough, as well as a distinguished member of the lodge of Free and Accepted Masons of this place." He was made a Mason in the year 1755, in Lodge 213, Registry of Ireland, was Master of Lodge 205, in the Enniskillen regiment, and, at the home of his adoption, of lodge 21, at Harrisburg. Major Brooks married, January, 1767, in the city of Montreal, and Province of Quebec, by Rev. D. Chabrand De Lisle, chaplain to Montreal, SARAH PARDON, d. April 9, 1789, in Harrisburg, Pa.; daughter of Thomas Pardon, of Norwich, county Norfolk, England; and had issue:

    i. Rebecca, b. January 17, 1768, at Newburyport, Mass.; d. July 18, 1793; m., April 20, 1786, at Harrisburg, Pa., James Brooks, of Cumberland county, Pa., and whose descendants removed to Virginia and Tennessee.

i. Thomas, d. in infancy.
ii. Sarah-Elizabeth, d. July 5, 1887, at Bellevue, Pa.
iii. Mary-Catharine, d. January 29, 1893, at Bellevue, Pa.
iv. Rebecca, b. March 20, 1815, at Harrisburg, Pa.; d. February 5, 1875, in Philadelphia; buried in Laurel Hill cemetery; m., at Carlisle, Pa., Gen. Horatio Hubbell, a member of the Philadelphia bar, an author of some prominence, and the projector of the Atlantic cable; and they had issue (surname Hubbell):
   1. *Frederick-Brooks*, b. July 21, 1842, in Harrisburg, Pa.; studied law, and was admitted to Philadelphia bar; resides in Pittsburgh, Pa.; m., 1880, Ella Sherman Hubbell, of Canandaigua, N. Y., and had issue (surname Hubbell):
      a. Stewart-Brooks, b. June 2, 1884.
   2. *Rebecca*, b., in Harrisburg, November 23, 1847; d. February 1, 1860.
   3. *Julia*, b. June 14, 1855, in Philadelphia; d. February 4, 1860.
v. De Witt-Clinton, d. January 14, 1859; a lawyer at the Dauphin county bar; was a clerk to the Pennsylvania Legislature, and author of "Brooks' Manual."
vi. Julia-Pardon, m., 1864, Boyle Irwin McClure, second son of William Denny McClure, of Allegheny county, Pa.; reside in Bellevue, near Pittsburgh, Pa.; and had issue (surname McClure):

---

ii. Elizabeth, b. April 20, 1770; d. October 6, 1772, at Newburyport, Mass.
iii. Nicholas, b. August 7, 1772, at Newburyport, Mass.; d. September 17, 1777, at Carlisle, Pa.
iv. Elizabeth, b. June 2, 1775, at Carlisle, Pa.; m. Thomas Blocher; resided near Waynesboro', Franklin county, Pa.; left a large family.
v. John, b. March 18, 1778, at Carlisle, Pa.
vi. Thomas, b. August 6, 1780, at Carlisle, Pa.; d. December 7, 1807, at Harrisburg, Pa.; was a clock and watchmaker; m. Martha Ramsey; daughter of John Ramsey, of Carlisle; and had issue:
   1. *Clarissa*, m. Henry S. Baugher, president of Pennsylvania College, Gettysburg; and left issue.
   2. *John Ramsey*, d. 1860; learned merchandising; was purser's clerk in the U. S. Navy during the Mexican war; settled at Pensacola, Florida; became a member of the State Senate; m. a lady from Strasburg, Germany, and left one son.

1. *John-Brooks*, b. September 27, 1865.
2. *William-Irwin*, b. September 28, 1867.

XI. CASSANDRA GREENAWALT,[3] (Christian,[2] Philip-Lorentz,[1]) b. December 9, 1794, in Harrisburg, Pa.; baptized March 19, 1795, by Rev. Henry Müller; d. October 15, 1873, in Harrisburg, Pa.; m. GEORGE ACKERMAN; d. at Harrisburg, Pa. They had issue (surname Ackerman):

    i. Ann-Elizabeth, b. July 10, 1821; resides in Harrisburg, Pa., m., November 19, 1839, by Rev. John H. Smaltz, William Weidler, b. 1819, at Lancaster, Pa.; d. July 31, 1845, at Harrisburg; and had issue (surname Weidler):
        1. *George*, b. January 19, 1841.
        2. *William-Frederick*, b. February 21, 1846; d. October 10, 1846.

XII. MARGARET GREENAWALT,[3] (Christian,[2] Philip-Lorentz,[1]) b. in 1796, in Harrisburg; d. March 28, 1839; m. SAMUEL SWARTZ, b. November 30, 1786; d. August 7, 1842, in Harrisburg, Pa., and with his wife there buried. He was the son of Ludwig Swartz, and born in Berks county, Pa., from whence his father removed, about 1789, to York county. The latter was a substantial farmer. They had issue (surname Swartz):

    i. Frederick-Kelker, b. March 21, 1819; many years a lumber merchant; served as member of the council of the city of Harrisburg, Pa., where he resides; m., October 15, 1851, Catharine Z. Hoffer, b. January 18, 1828, at Carlisle, Pa.; d. November 4, 1887; and had issue (surname Swartz):
        1. *Samuel-M.*, b. September 4, 1852; d. May 22, 1887.
        2. *Mary-Kepner*, d. August 11, 1855.
        3. *Frederick-Kelker*.
        4. *Catharine-Elizabeth*, m. J. McReiley; and have issue.
        5. *Margaretta-G.*
        6. *Georgiana*, d. July 20, 1869.
    ii. Elizabeth-Maria, b. January 9, 1821; d. July 16, 1821.
    iii. George W., b. January 17, 1822; d. April 25, 1885, in Harrisburg, Pa.; m. Emma L. Dietrick, and had issue (surname Swartz):
        1. *Benjamin*.
        2. *Franklin*.
    iv. Margaret Eleanora, b. February 11, 1825; d. Dec. 5, 1825.

v. Samuel-Christian, b. October 20, 1827 ; d. July 28, 1828.
vi. Juliana, b. July 31, 1834; d. September 13, 1834.

XIII. ELIZABETH ZINN,³ (Catharine,² Philip-Lorentz,¹) b. April 9, 1793, in Lebanon, Pa.; d. March 21, 1816 ; buried in Harrisburg, Pa.; m. David Shriver Forney, b. November 4, 1787; d. December 25, 1839, in Carlisle, Pa.; and had issue (surname Forney):

> *i. John-Zinn*, b. October 26, 1812 ; d. March 4, 1859, unm., in Liberia, while American consul there ; was a surgeon in the Mexican war.
> *ii. Catharine*, b. October 1, 1815, in Harrisburg, Pa.; m., March 20, 1834, Daniel Zacharias ; a prominent minister of the Reformed Church ; was pastor of the congregation at Frederick city, Md., forty years, and there closed his life's labors ; they had issue, all born in Frederick, Md. (surname Zacharias):
>> 1. *Granville*, d. 1875, in Colorado.
>> 2. *John-Forney*, resides in Cumberland, Md.
>> 3. *Elizabeth-Turbot*, b. June 14, 1840 ; m., May 22, 1866, Thomas Justus Dunott, b. May 29, 1831, in Philadelphia ; d. May 19, 1893 ; son of Dr. Justus Dunott and Sidney Paul Lancaster. Dr. Dunott graduated from the medical department of the University of Pennsylvania ; located in 1870 at Harrisburg, Pa., where he became prominent in his profession ; he was one of the surgeons to the City Hospital, and a member of the County, State and National Medical Associations ; and had issue (surname Dunott):
>>> a. *Justus*, b. June 5, 1867, in Frederick, Md.
>>> b. *Daniel-Zacharias*, b. February 11, 1870, in Frederick, Md.; a physician.
>>> c. *Catharine-Forney*, b. June 13, 1872, in Frederick, Md.
>>> d. *Sydney-Paul-Lancaster*, b. April 3, 1874, in Harrisburg, Pa.
>> 4. *Jane*, resides in Baltimore, Md.
>> 5. *Laurence-Brengel*, of New York city.
>> 6. *Merle-Herbine*, d. s. p.
>> 7. *George-Merle*, a minister in the Reformed Church.
>> 8. *Edwin-Daniel*, of Cumberland, Md.
>> 9. *William*, of New York city.

XIV. GEORGE ZINN,³ (Catharine,² Philip-Lorentz,¹) b. April 6, 1810, in Harrisburg, Pa.; d. January 21, 1878, in Harrisburg, and there buried; received a fair English education, and learned the trade of a tanner with his father, who had established a large business, and to which the son eventually succeeded and successfully carried on for over thirty years; served in several local offices, and, in whatever trusts confided, was faithful; m., April 19, 1836, ANNA· MARGARETTA MILLER, daughter of John Jacob Miller and Elizabeth Beader; resides in Harrisburg, Pa. They had issue (surname Zinn):

 i. Mary, b. 1837; m., December 20, 1864, William Henry Eckels, b. February 11, 1831, paymaster U. S. Army, retired, 1894; and had issue (surname Eckels):
  1. *Charles-Burd*, b. January 1, 1866.
  2. *Harry*, b. April 1, 1873.
  3. *George-Zinn*, b. January 22, 1875.
  4. *Mary*, b. May 2, 1881.
 ii. John, m., September 9, 1875, Alice M. Wickersham, daughter of Cadwalader Wickersham; and had issue (surname Zinn):
  1. *Maurice-C.*, b. 1879.
 iii. George, m., June 22, 1876, Nannie R. Rogers, of Wilmington, Del.; and had issue (surname Zinn):
  1. *May-R.*, b. 1879; d. 1892, in London.
  2. *George*, b. 1883.
 iv. Amy, d. February 10, 1888; m., October 28, 1869, George Hamilton Smith; and had issue (surname Smith):
  1. *Fanny-Miller*, b. August 25, 1870.
  2. *Edgar-Zinn*, b. May 11, 1880.
 v. Catharine, d. s. p.
 vi. Charles, d. s. p.
 vii. Margey, m., March 22, 1883, J. Ross Swartz, b. January 26, 1857, in McVeytown, Pa.; graduated from Hahnemann Medical College, Philadelphia, in March, 1879; reside in Harrisburg, Pa.; and had issue (surname Swartz):
  1. *Matilda*, b. September 1, 1888; d. February 10, 1889.

XV. JOSIAH GREENAWALT,[3] (Leonard,[2] Philip-Lorentz,[1]) b. September 11, 1799; d. March 7, 1865, in Lebanon, Pa.; was in early life a merchant, but afterwards associated as partner with his father in the tanning business; m., August 22, 1821, by Rev. Philip Pauli, of Reading, MARY LAUB, b. June 24, 1800; d. October 31, 1880; daughter of Michael and Mary Laub, of Berks county, Pa. They had issue:

 i. Dr. John, b. September 11, 1822; d. August 24, 1866; m. Sallie Mason, of Cincinnati, Ohio, and had issue.

ii. Wilhelmina-M., b. February 16, 1825; d. August 25, 1877; unm.

iii. Lorenzo-Leonard, b. January 6, 1827, at Lebanon, Pa.; was educated in the schools of the town and at the old Lebanon Academy; learned tanning and leather-dressing, the former of which occupations he followed many years; made two trips across the plains to the Pacific coast—one in 1852, when the undertaking was a hazardous one, the other in 1871; during the war for the Union he was captain of company E, 127th regiment, Pennsylvania Volunteers, subsequently in the 26th regiment, Pennsylvania militia, as major; and participated in the battles of Fredericksburg, Chancellorsville, and Gettysburg; was assistant burgess of Lebanon borough, and, in 1884–5, a mail agent in the Government employ. Major Greenawalt m., September 15, 1881, Anna Gorgas, b. in Stillwater, Minn.; daughter of Colonel Adam Gorgas.

iv. Josiah, b. September 11, 1828.

v. Catharine, b. December 3, 1831.

XVI. REGINA CAMILLA GREENAWALT,[4] (Jacob,[3] John-Philip,[2] Philip-Lorentz,[1]) b. August 10, 1823, in Harrisburg, Pa., and there resides; m., May 4, 1848, WILLIAM CALDER, b. July 31, 1821; d. July 19, 1880, in Harrisburg, Pa.; son of William Calder (1788–1861) and Mary Kirkwood (1790–1858). With only a limited education, he was inducted into the business of his father at an early age. When only sixteen he was placed in charge of the Philadelphia packet from Columbia to Pittsburgh. In 1851 he assumed the entire management of his father's affairs, and in 1857 undertook the completion of the Lebanon Valley railroad, employed six hundred men, finished the road and paid his men in full. In 1858, he became a member of the well-known banking firm of Cameron, Calder & Co., which afterwards became the first National Bank of Harrisburg, of which Mr. Calder was chosen president. The same year he was elected a director of the Northern Central railway, and was active in preserving Pennsylvania's interests in that corporation. At the breaking out of the Rebellion he rendered the government important service through his large knowledge in the purchase of horses, and supplied the government with no less than forty-two thousand horses and sixty-seven thousand mules, establishing the price ($125 and $117.50) so low as to effect a very great saving to the Government in this department. Mr. Calder was always foremost in the promotion of industrial enterprises. He was one of the founders of the Harrisburg Car Works, the Lochiel Rolling Mills, the Harrisburg Cotton Mills, Foundry and Machine Works, the Fire-Brick Works, the Pennsylvania Steel Works, etc. In 1873 he was appointed by Governor Hartranft a trustee of the Pennsylvania State Lunatic Hospital, and reappointed in 1876. In 1876 he was appointed by the same Governor a member of the commission to devise a plan for the government of cities, and in 1880, just prior to his death, was elected a director of the Pennsylvania Institution for the Deaf and Dumb. For many years he ably officiated in the management of city affairs through its councils, and his social qualities gathered about him a host of warm personal friends. He was among the founders of the Harrisburg Hospital and the Grace Methodist Episcopal church, of which he was an attendant. He was formerly a Whig, latterly a Republican, and influential in local and State politics, and one of the Presidential electors in 1876. They had issue (surname Calder):

 i. Edmund-Kirkwood, b. June 21, 1849; d. December 31, 1862.
 ii. William-Jacob, b. October 1, 1853; m. Jessie Remington, daughter of Eliphalet Remington, of Ilion, N. Y.; and had issue (surname Calder):
  1. *Helen.*
  2. *Ethel-Kirkwood.*
 iii. Catharine-Krause, b. July 27, 1857; d. s. p., at Baltimore, Md.; bur. at Harrisburg; m. William Robert Turner, of Kent, England, an Episcopalian minister.
 iv. Theodore-Greenawalt, b. December 2, 1860.
 v. Regina, b. July 27, 1862; m. Ehrman B. Mitchell; and had issue (surname Mitchell), *Ehrman-B.*
 vi. Mary-Kirkwood, b. April 10, 1865.

THE FAMILY OF HAMILTON.

[The original record of John Hamilton (1702-1755) commences with the words, "Colerain, 1612." About this time, county Colerain became "Derry," and the city of "Londonderry," in what is known in the State papers as "the settlement of Ulster," in Ireland. Thus the ancestry of this family obtained a portion of the 150,000 acres granted, in 1609, to the English and Scots of Colerain, when England determined to reclaim the north of Ireland by allotting forfeited lands to "servitors." Prior to 1617 these, generally Scots gentry became owners of the soil. Mrs. Judge McLean, born Sarah Bella Chambers Ludlow, of Cincinnati, who married, first, Hon. Jeptha D. Garrard, of Kentucky; secondly, Hon. John McLean, of Ohio, Postmaster General and Justice of the Supreme Court of the United States, thus writes of her maternal ancestry: "The maiden name of my grandmother Chambers was Catharine Hamilton. She was the daughter of John Hamilton and Isabella Potter. The coat-of-arms and records of John Hamilton's descent were carefully preserved by the family of my grandfather, General Chambers, for many years after his marriage to Catharine Hamilton, as a cherished relic; but in the infancy of the American Republic, and the essential and consistent training of the distinguished patriot and his accomplished wife, the children were taught to abhor aristocracy or anything like it, the proofs of these honors became playthings, and eventually disappeared." The American history of this family will be learned in what follows. It is not necessary to repeat details of the connection with its Scotch and Irish ancestry.]

I. JAMES HAMILTON,[1] b. 1670; d. 1716; and KATHARINE, his wife, emigrated from Lanarkshire, Scotland, to the "free lands of Ulster," in Ireland, where he became "a considerable land-holder." An only child was born to them on the banks of the Foyle.

II. JOHN HAMILTON,[2] (James,[1]) b. January, 1702, "in Colerain," Ireland; d. June 5, 1755, and is buried at New London Cross-roads, Chester county, Pa. By will, he left a farm to his daughter, Katharine, and a farm and mill to his son, John, in then Cumberland, now Perry and Juniata counties, Pa. He was a respectable and intelligent man, of means and standing. He resided on a farm in Chester county, Pa., which he purchased in 1742, a short time after his arrival in this country. At the period of his second marriage he was a well-established farmer and miller. The family have preserved no account of the personal appearance of John Hamilton, as he died when his only son John was a lad of six years of age, and his daughter Katharine a young girl of fifteen; but it has been told by her to her children, that he "was stoutly built, of handsome stature, florid complexion, and a Presbyterian." His will is dated May 31, 1755, and is recorded in Chester county. He m., first, January 6, 1735, by the Rev. Baptist Boyd, of Aghalow, ISABELLA POTTER, b. 1710; d. Friday, September 25, 1741, on shipboard, and buried at New Castle, September 26, 1741. She was sister of John Potter, who emigrated with John Hamilton to America "on the ship Donegal, arriving at New Castle, on the Delaware, Friday, September 25, 1741." Mr. Potter was the first sheriff of Cumberland county, and the ancestor of Major General James Potter of the Revolution. They had issue:

    i. James, b. Friday, November 27, 1736, d. s. p.
    ii. Katharine, b. Monday, December 18, 1738; d. January 14, 1820; m. Gen. James Chambers, of the Revolution.
    iii. John, b. Tuesday, September 30, 1740; d. Sunday, October 17, 1741, and is buried "at Archibald Beard's, in Mill Creek Hundred, New Castle county, Del."

John Hamilton m., secondly, in January, 1748, by Rev. Francis Alison, D.D., of New London, Chester county, Pa., JANE ALLEN,* b. 1715; d. February 4, 1791, and is buried at Harrisburg. She was the daughter of Robert and Mary

---

*The looking-glass, a wedding present from Captain Thomas Allen, R. N., to his sister Jane, is in the possession of her descendant, A. Boyd Hamilton, at Harrisburg; as also a silhoutte taken in old age.

Allen, granddaughter of Captain Thomas Allen, of "His Majesty's ship Quaker, on the Chesapeake bay in 1684, and commander in the Virginia waters." She was a woman of unusual force of character, and educated with great care. They had issue:

3.   iv. *John*, b. June 17, 1749; m. Margaret Alexander.

Mrs. Hamilton married, a second time, JOHN MITCHELL, an Irish gentleman, who died many years before her. By this marriage there was no issue.

III. JOHN HAMILTON,[3] (John,[2] James,[1]) b. June 17, 1749, in New London, Chester county, Pa; d. August 28, 1793, at Harrisburg, Pa. Under the will of his father he inherited a "plantation and fulling-mill, bought of James Long, on Shearman creek, in Cumberland county," (Perry county). He was educated principally in the celebrated academy of Rev. Mr. Alison, Chester county. When upon a visit to his patrimony in the Juniata region, he was attracted to the superior excellence of a tract of land called "Fermanagh," now in Juniata county. He purchased it. On the Shearman's creek farm Hugh Alexander was his adjoining neighbor; he became attached to his daughter, and at twenty-three years of age he married her; established himself at "Fermanagh," and erected a large stone mansion. This house is standing. It has been occupied by himself, his son John, and a grandson, Hugh Hamilton. He became, by successful industry, and in right of his mother, Jane Allen Hamilton, of great fortune for his day. The inventory of personal property at his death, in 1793, makes his effects in money, £7,500. At that moment he had active enterprises of various kinds in full operation—at Lost creek, at Fermanagh, in Shearman's valley, and at Harrisburg. He was one of the original lot-holders at Harrisburg. One of his largest houses was that at the south-east corner of the Market square; another on his lot, Front street and Raspberry alley. In 1792 he employed at his warehouse and stores, on what is now Mulberry street, between Second and Third streets, "as many as fifteen mules, and a far greater number of horses, upon which he sent nails and salt and other merchandise to Pittsburgh." Sending nails to Pittsburgh at this date would be reversing the usual course of trade. He was one of the last of those in the interior who held slaves, a half dozen in all. All but one continued in the family until the death of his widow, not as slaves, but as free laborers on the farms. Mr. Hamilton was a sergeant in Captain Gibson's company, Col. Wilson's battalion of Cumberland county associators in 1776; captain of a company in Colonel Samuel Lyon's battalion in August, 1777; and also captain in Colonel Buchanan's battalion in 1778, and was out in two campaigns, 1776 and 1781. In the family records of the McAlisters, of Lost Creek, Juniata, one of whom married a granddaughter of Captain Hamilton, we have the following narrative : "The American army, December, 1776, shattered, disheartened and decreasing daily, were making precipitate retreat across Jersey into Pennsylvania, before the victorious army of Howe and Cornwallis. In this gloomy hour a meeting of the people was called at the farm of Mr. William Sharon within a couple of miles of Mr. Hugh McAlister's, near the present town of Mexico, to consult and devise measures to reinforce Washington and the army. All the neighbors below the Narrows met. John Hamilton, of Fermanagh, was made chairman. It was unanimously agreed to raise a company of mounted men. All were young men, with younger families, but they did not hesitate. They agreed to march. Hamilton pledged himself to start immediately, then McAlister and Sharon. The former was chosen captain, the latter lieutenants, and in two days they were off, more than eighty strong, riding the first day to the mouth of the Swatara, over snow many inches in depth. They reached camp, on the Pennsylvania side, below Trenton, the day after the Hessians were captured." None but men with their whole hearts in the cause would have made such a dreary march in a most inclement winter, unless thoroughly in earnest. This was the sentiment that actuated all the frontier settlers. In 1793 Harrisburg was scourged by a pestilence resembling yellow fever, an epidemic that then prevailed at Philadelphia, Baltimore and New York. One of its victims was Mr. Hamilton. He m., in December, 1772, MARGARET ALEXANDER, b. March 17, 1754, in Shearman's Valley, Cumberland, now Perry county,

Pa.; d. August 22, 1835, at "Fermanagh," Juniata county, Pa.; daughter of Hugh Alexander and Martha Edmeston. They had issue :*

4.   i. *Jean*, b. June 1, 1774, m. John Kean.
    ii. *Murtha*, b. August 5, 1776; d. March 16, 1830; m. James Alricks, (see *Alricks record*).
    iii. [*A son*] b. February 1, 1781; d. March, 1781.
5.   iv. *John*, b. September 10, 1782; m. Francisca Blair Edmeston.
6.   v. *Hugh*, b. June 30, 1785; m. Rosanna Boyd.
    vi. *Mary*, b. December 30, 1787; d. in infancy.
7.   vii. *Margaret*, b. August 12, 1789; m. Moses Maclean.
8.   viii. *Katharine-Allen*, b. November 13, 1792; m. Jacob Spangler·

Mrs. Margaret (Alexander) Hamilton, m., secondly, in 1795, ANDREW MITCHEL, b. November 1, 1754, in Dublin, Ireland; d. December 21, 1825, in Harrisburg, Pa. He served as an officer in the War of the Revolution, having arrived in America in 1774. After the war taught school. He was an accomplished scholar, highly esteemed in social and public life; was cautious and methodical in his business, and precise in training pupils, his own and his numerous step-children. They had issue (surname Mitchel):

    i. *Jane-Alexander*, b. July 17, 1799; d. February 3, 1876; m., November 29, 1819, Dr. Thomas Whiteside, b. October 31, 1790; a son of John Whiteside and Mary Elton; and had issue (surname Whiteside):

---

* In a Bible presented to Martha Edmeston Alexander, mother of Margaret Hamilton, in 1732, we have the following:

"*Record of John and Margaret (Alexander) Hamilton, 1772.*"

"Jean Hamilton, daughter of John Hamilton, was born on the first day of June 1774 on Juniata.

"Martha Hamilton, was born on the fifth day of August, 1776 in Paxton.

"The first Boy was born Feb. 1 1781—on Juniata, died in March.

"John Hamilton was born September the 10th day 1782 at nine o'clock in the morning—at Fermanagh.

"Hugh Hamilton was Born the 30th day of June 1785 at two o'clock in the morning—at Fermanagh.

"Mary Hamilton born the 30th of Dec. 1787—Died at Harrisburg.

"Margaret Hamilton was born the 11th day of August, at four o'clock in the morning, 1789—at Harrisburg.

"Kitty Allen Hamilton was born the 13th day of November at four o'clock in the afternoon 1792—in Paxton."

1. *Margaret-Mitchel*, m. Dr. A. C. Stees, of Union county, Pa.; and had issue (surname Stees):
   a. *Marion*.
   b. *Jane-Whiteside*, m. Captain Joseph R. Orwig; and had issue (surname Orwig): *Margaret-Mitchel, Mary-Gilbert, Clara-Beaver, Joseph-Ralph, Louisa-Hayes,* and *Reuben-George*.
   c. *Thomas-Whiteside*.
   d. *Clarence*, m. Elizabeth Bowers, of Orrstown, Franklin county, Pa.; no issue.
   e. *John-Irvine*, m. Anna Armstrong; and had *Harry-Armstrong*.
   f. *Herman-Alricks*, m. Minnie Sheldon, of Beverly, N. J.
   g. *Abraham-Cypher*.
2. *Philip-Syng-Physick*, m. Mary E. Simpson; and had issue: *Amelia, Jane, William,* and *Elder*.
3. *Mary-Elton*, m. William B. Brandon, of Adams county, Pa.; and had issue (surname Brandon): *Jane-Whiteside, Katharine-Hamilton, Ellen,* and *Martha*.
4. *Jane-Gordon*, m. Leigh R. Baugher, of Adams county, Pa.; and had issue (surname Baugher): *Mary-Whiteside, Thomas-Brooks,* and *Henry-Lewis*.

IV. JEAN HAMILTON,[4] (John,[3] John,[2] James,[1]) b. June 1, 1774; d. March 20, 1847, at Harrisburg, Pa.; m., December 10, 1789, by Rev. Mr. Hoge, of Carlisle, JOHN KEAN, b. October 3, 1762, in Philadelphia; d. December 9, 1818, in Harrisburg, Pa.; son of John Kean [1728–1801] and Mary Dunlop [1728–1819]. His father removed to what is now Dauphin county, Pa., in 1775. In 1780, he entered the Revolutionary service, and was with the army until after the capitulation of Yorktown. Upon his discharge he was placed with James Clunie, a merchant at Hummelstown, second sheriff of Dauphin county, at a salary of one hundred dollars a year and boarding. In this period he taught himself conveyancing and surveying. In 1785 he located at Harrisburg, in partnership with Mr. Clunie. In 1788 he was one of the members of the famous "Harrisburg Conference." He was one of the managers of the first library company, established in 1787, and the same year elected a commissioner of the county; one of the trustees of the Harrisburg Academy, 1788; treasurer of the Presbyterian congregation in 1790; chosen captain of the first volunteer company upon the resignation of General Hanna, and president of the first fire company, and in 1792 appointed an associate judge. In 1796 Mr. Kean purchased, with John Elder, Jr., New Market forge, about three miles from Palmyra, and removed thence. Was elected to the State Senate, and re-elected in 1798, serving until 1802. In 1805 he was appointed by Governor McKean register general, serving for three years. He removed to Philadelphia in 1810, was a merchant there, returned to Harrisburg in 1813, was again appointed justice of the peace by Governor Snyder, which office he filled until his death. Judge Kean married in 1786 MARY WHITEHILL, daughter of Robert Whitehill, of Cumberland county. By her he had one daughter, *Eleanor*, who m., first, March 24, 1808, William Patton, M. D., son of Thomas Patton and Eleanor Fleming, b. in 1775, in Derry township, Lancaster, now Dauphin county, Pa.; d. March 30, 1816. Mrs. Patton m., secondly, Christian Spayd, and left descendants. By his second wife, Jean Hamilton, there was issue (surname Kean):

ii. *John*, b. January 21, 1795, d. s. p.
iii. *Louisa*, b. August, 1799; d. October 26, 1885, at Harrisburg, Pa.; m. General Samuel Power, of Beaver, d. July 3, 1836; and left one daughter, d. s. p.
iv. *Margaret-Hamilton*, b. February 17, 1806; d. October 11, 1855; unm.
v. *Jane-Duffield*, b. January 2, 1809; d. October 27, 1885; unm.

V. JOHN HAMILTON,[4] (John,[3] John,[2] James,[1]) b. September 10, 1782, at Fermanagh, Juniata county, Pa.; d. June 2, 1851, at Fermanagh, and is buried at Mifflintown. He received a careful education at Harrisburg, and was sent to Dickinson College, where he graduated. The estate of "Fermanagh" coming to him by inheritance, he resided on the ancestral farm until his death. Mr. Hamilton m., by Rev. Francis Hyndman, February 14, 1805, FRANCESCA BLAIR EDMESTON, b. in Chester county, Pa.; d. March 6, 1818, at Fermanagh; daughter of Dr. Samuel Edmeston and Martha Blair.* They had issue:

---

*MARTHA BLAIR was a daughter of Rev. Samuel Blair, D.D. Dr. Edmeston was a son of David, and grandson of David and Margaret Edmeston, who came to Maryland in 1647. Mrs. Edmeston was a granddaughter of Lawrence Van Hook, a judge under the Dutch rule in New York.

i. Samuel-Edmeston, b. November 14, 1805 ; d. December 18, 1847 ; m. Sarah Hawk, and had *Francesca-Blair,* m. Jacob Godshal, *John-Andrew, Mary, Sarah-Hawk,* d. s. p., and *Margaret,* m. Wellington Smith.

ii. John-Andrew, b. June 27, 1807; d. February 22, 1840, s. p.

iii. Hugh-Alexander, b. October 30, 1808 ; d. s. p.

iv. Margaret-Mitchel, b. October 27, 1810; d. July 22, 1838; m. John Alexander; no issue.

v. Martha-Edmeston, b. March 16, 1812; d. July 25, 1833, s. p.

vi. Thomas-Allen, b. August 17, 1813; d. October 28, 1820, s. p.

vii. Francesca-Blair, b. May 16, 1815 ; m., first, Hon. Amos Gustine ; secondly, Dr. James Frow ; no issue.

9. *viii. Hugh,* b. October 16, 1816 ; m., first, Sarah Gettys McDowell ; secondly, Sarah Ann Kloss.

ix. Van-Hook, b. March 4, 1818 : d. September 3, 1848, s. p.

VI. HUGH HAMILTON,[4] (John,[3] John,[2] James,[1]) b. June 30, 1785, at Fermanagh, Juniata county, Pa.; d. September 3, 1836, at Harrisburg, Pa. He received a careful preparatory education at Harrisburg, and with his brother John was sent to Dickinson College, where he graduated. He studied law under Thomas Elder, and was admitted to the Dauphin county bar in 1805. At the time of his admission to the bar Judge Henry had ordered the prothonotary to issue commissions on parchment. Accordingly the descendants of the young lawyer have his commission " on parchment," issued 21st of June, 1805, signed by "Joshua Elder, Pro'thy, by order of the Court," with the seal of the county attached. In 1808, Mr. Hamilton edited and published *The Times,* at Lancaster, and upon the removal of the seat of government to Harrisburg, with William Gillmor, *The Harrisburg Chronicle,* the leading and influential newspaper at the State capital for twenty years. The *Chronicle* was the first paper in Pennsylvania which gave full and systematic legislative reports. Mr. Hamilton was a vigorous and polished writer, and his editorials and letters models of elegant composition, and much of it has been preserved. For a quarter of a century he wielded considerable political influence through his newswaper. He was an active and enterprising citizen, twice chief burgess of Harrisburg, frequently a member of its council, and highly esteemed in social intercourse. Mr. Hamilton m., January 6, 1807, by Rev. James Snodgrass, of Hanover church, ROSANNA BOYD, b. December

1, 1786, at Harrisburg, Pa.; d. April 17, 1872, at Harrisburg, and there buried; daughter of Adam Boyd and Jeanette Mac-Farlane.* They had issue:

---

*Adam Boyd, son of John Boyd and Elizabeth Young, was a native of Northampton county, Pa., born in 1746. His ancestors were of that sturdy and fearless race, who, after winning religious liberty at home, braved the perils of the ocean and a life in the wilds of America, that they might establish civil and religious freedom in the New World. The ancestor of this family was Adam Boyd, an officer of the rank of captain in the army sent by Charles I. to Ireland, on the roll of Scottish division June 5, 1649. As was usual in Scotland, one of the sons, Adam (2) went into the Church; his son Adam (3) was also a Presbyterian clergyman. Early in 1714, his son John (4) and a younger brother, Rev. Adam Boyd, left their native land, Scotland, arriving at Philadelphia in the summer of that year. John m., the year following, Jane Craig, daughter of Thomas Craig, and subsequently became (1728) one of the first emigrants to the "Irish Settlement," now in Northampton county. His son John, born in Philadelphia in 1716, m., in 1744, Elizabeth, daughter of Sir William Young, "an Ulster baronet. Their eldest son was Adam Boyd, the subject of this sketch. He learned the trade of a carpenter, and was following that avocation when the War of the Revolution called to arms. When the State of Pennsylvania had formed its little navy for the protection of the ports of Delaware, in 1776, Adam Boyd received his first commission. In 1777 he was honorably discharged. He at once entered the army proper, holding the same rank therein. He was at the battles of Brandywine and Germantown, with two of his brothers, one of whom, John, was killed in the latter engagement. Subsequently, Lieut. Boyd acted as "master of wagons," with the rank of captain, and as such remained with the army until the surrender of Yorktown. Passing Harris Ferry, in the spring of 1782, to the home of his mother, near Newville, Mr. Boyd was struck with the immense advantages offered by the location of the proposed town. He subsequently purchased of the proprietor a lot on the corner of Second and Mulberry streets. In 1784 he became a permanent resident. Under the first charter of Harrisburg in 1791 he was chosen a burgess. In 1792 he was elected treasurer of the county, and held the office until 1806, when he declined a re-election. In 1809 Mr. Boyd was elected a director of the poor, and during his term of office the county poorhouse and mill were erected under his direction. He d. on the 14th of May, 1814; was interred in the Presbyterian graveyard, of which he was an elder. In private trusts Mr. Boyd was frequently employed. His correspondence and accounts are precise and methodical, particularly the care with which he managed the estate of the younger William Maclay.

10.   *i. Adam-Boyd,* b. September 17, 1808; m., first, Catharine Louisa Naudain ; secondly, Isabella Moore Hays.
      ii. Alexander, b. October 4, 1810 ; d. June 5, 1873, unm.
11.   *iii. John,* b. October 21, 1815 ; m. Amanda Jane Thomason.
     iv. Thomas-Allen, b. February 14, 1818 ; d. December 14, 1874. He received a good education, and learned the trade of a printer in his father's office, at which he worked until he received the appointment of an assistant engineer on the State Canals, under Col. James Worrall, but soon abandoned both avocations, in order to join a brother in a business, which they successfully prosecuted until his death. He served as a member of the city councils of Harrisburg a longer continuous period than any other citizen has ever done, being elected for about twenty years in succession, generally without serious opposition, although many epochs of great public excitement intervened to produce fierce and close political contests. His neighbors never failed to ascertain his political opinions, yet, whether voting for or against him, they rejoiced to know that he was their representative and the leader of the municipal legislature. In the language of a contemporary, "Mr. Hamilton, in his intercourse with his fellow citizens, was courteous to all, liberal to the poor, positive in opinion, methodical in business, reticent, deliberate, but prompt in judgment." His integrity was never impeached in public or private transactions. He died, unmarried, at Harrisburg, in the same house in which he was born.
     v. Margaret, b. February 2, 1820 ; d. April 27, 1876 ; m. Hon. Hugh Nelson McAlister, of Bellefonte, Pa.; no issue.
    vi. Andrew-Mitchel, b. April 9, 1822; d. May 16, 1827.

In person he was five feet eight inches in height, a stout, healthy, florid man, dark brown hair and eyes. At fifty years of age he had no gray hairs. He is rated on the "Mill Purchase" at £23 2s., being the fourth highest assessment upon that curious record. Mr. Boyd m., 1784, Jeannette Macfarlane, b. June 23, 1764 ; d. December 4, 1790, buried at Harrisburg ; daughter of Patrick Macfarlane and Rosanna Howard, (b. 1735.) Patrick Macfarlane, b. 1727, son of James Macfarlane and Jeannette Buchanan, daughter of Robert Buchanan ; James, b. in Scotland, December 24, 1695, came to America in 1717 ; m., in 1724, in Pequea, now Lancaster county, and d. October 31, 1770, buried at Meeting House Spring, near Carlisle. The only descendent of Adam Boyd and Jeannette was Rosanna Boyd, who m. Hugh Hamilton.

vii. William, b. February 10, 1824; an attorney residing in Bellefonte, Pa.; was in active service in the war of the Union.

viii. Catharine-Jane, b. June 30, 1826; d. November 11, 1826.

ix. Hugh, b. August 9, 1828; d. January 28, 1830.

VII. MARGARET HAMILTON,[4] (John,[3] John,[2] James,[1]) b. August 12, 1789, at Harrisburg, Pa.; d. November 18, 1814, at Harrisburg, and their buried; m., April 18, 1809, MOSES MACLEAN, b. 1785, in Adams county, Pa.; d. November 15, 1831, at Huntingdon, Pa. His grandfather, Archibald Maclean, born on the west coast of Scotland, in 1716, came to America, and had sons, Moses, William, Samuel, John, James, and Alexander. The father, Moses Maclean, was an active and prominent official in that part of then York county, both before, during, and after the Revolution. The son, Moses, chose the legal profession. After completing his studies, in 1807, he removed to Harrisburg, where he could have risen to a commanding position, if his diversified and unusual ability had been directed to a close attention to his profession. He represented Dauphin county in the Pennsylvania House of Representatives. He was well educated, possessed of pure literary taste; was a wit and a poet. In person heavily built, of good stature, and captivating address. In one of the best known of his poetical effusions, the standard hymn commencing, "Come, mourning souls, rejoice, be glad," the closing verse is an appeal so prophetic as to appear exactly fitted to his future—long after it was penned:

> "Should persecution's eager shaft,
> Pursue us while we live,
> JESUS, Benevolent, Divine,
> Oh, teach us to '*Forgive.*'"

They had issue (surname Maclean):

i. Sarah, b. April 16, 1811: m. Dr. William Elder, b. 1806; d. April 5, 1885; and had issue (surname Elder):

1. *Jessie*, b. October 7, 1835; m. June 15, 1863, Luther Ringwalt; and have issue.

ii. Margaret, b. April 3, 1813; d. July 21, 1876; buried at Harrisburg, Pa.

iii. Katharine-Hamilton, b. October 26, 1814; d. Oct. 8, 1889.

VIII. KATHARINE ALLEN HAMILTON,[4] (John,[3] John,[2] James,[1]) b. November 13, 1792, at Harrisburg, Pa.; d. June 12, 1873, at Harrisburg, Pa.; m., May 23, 1820, by Rev. Wm. R. DeWitt, JACOB SPANGLER, b. 1768, in York county, Pa.; d. 1843, at York, Pa., and with his wife there buried; son of Rudolph Spangler and Dorothea Dinkle. General Spangler learned the trade of a watchmaker; was, when a very young man, postmaster at York; county surveyor and county commissioner; a representative in Congress, 1816; Surveyor General of Pennsylvania, 1817 to 1820, under Governor Findlay, and again, 1823 to 1829, under Governor Shulze, and was a brigadier general of the Pennsylvania militia. They had issue (surname Spangler):

    i. Margaret-Dorothea, m. Hon. Stokes L. Roberts, of Bucks county, who d. February 21, 1884, and is buried at Doylestown, Bucks county, Pa.; no issue.

    ii. Jacob-Rudolph, d. March 2, 1882; m., May 18, 1847, Frances R. Elliott, b. April 12, 1828, daughter of Com. Jesse Duncan Elliott, U. S. N., and Frances Carr Vaughn; and had issue (surname Spangler):

        1. *Elliott*, b. May 5, 1848; m., February 20, 1870, Sarah Householder; and had issue:

            a. John-H., b. November 3, 1875.

            b. Jesse-E., b. May 27, 1882.

            c. Erwin-D., b. October 7, 1884.

        2. *Harry-Allen*, b. May 12, 1849; m., October 27, 1869; d. 1870, leaving a daughter, *Catharine Allen*, b. August, 1870.

        3. *Frances-Elliott*, b. July 16, 1850; m., May 3, 1870, George Shultz; and had issue (surname Shultz):

            a. Blanche, b. November 6, 1871.

            b. Valeria-E, b. December 16, 1879.

        4. *Jacob-R.*, b. October 25, 1852; m., and had issue.

        5. *Washington*, b. March 17, 1855; m., and had issue.

        6. *Ellen-Duncan*, b. December 16, 1856.

    iii. Jane-Martha, b. 1825; d. 1854; m. John Henry Small, of York; and had issue (surname Small):

        1. *Henry*, m.; resides at Leipsic, Germany.

    iv. Rosanna-Hamilton, d. s. p.

    v. Susan-Elizabeth, m. William Radcliffe DeWitt, M.D., of Harrisburg, (*see Maclay record*).

    vi. Frances, d. s. p.

The Family of Hamilton.   327

IX. HUGH HAMILTON,⁵ (John,⁴ John,³ John,² James,¹) b. October 16, 1816; d. July 22, 1894, at Fermanagh, Juniata county, Pa.; resided upon the farm his ancestor purchased in 1770; was a successful farmer and esteemed citizen of Juniata county. He m., September 10, 1840, first, SARAH GETTYS MCDOWELL, b. 1815, in Chester county, Pa.; d. September 17, 1847. They had issue :

 i. Mary-Mitchell, b. August 19, 1841 ; m. Ezra Parker, (*see Parker and Denny*).
 ii. John, b. February 19, 1843 ; served through the Civil War, now connected with the State College of Pennsylvania; m. Elizabeth M. Thompson, daughter of Moses Thompson, of Centre Furnace, Centre county, Pa.; and had issue :
  1. *Mary*, d. s. p.
  2. *Annie-Thompson.*
  3. *John-McDowell*, d. s. p.

Mr. Hamilton m., secondly, SARAH ANN KLOSS, of Juniata county, Pa. They had issue :

 iii. Susan-Alice, m. John Andrew Hamilton.
 iv. Martha-Ann, m. Milton Frazer ; reside in Akron, O.
 v. Emma-Jane, unm.
 vi. Ossian-Kloss, unm.
 vii. Rosanna, m. James W. Goodhart, of Lewistown, Pa.
 viii. Francesca-Blair, m.,* January 4, 1894, William Steele Turner, of Chester county, Pa.
 ix. Sarah-Ellen, m. Hugh P. Von Buskirk, of Greenspring, O.
 x. Hugh.

X. ADAM BOYD HAMILTON,⁵ (Hugh,⁴ John,³ John,² James,¹) b. September 18, 1808, in Harrisburg, Pa., where he now resides. His school training was under private tutors, and at the Harrisburg Academy. He learned the trade of printer in his father's establishment, the *Harrisburg Chronicle*. During this training he remembers two of the journeymen of the office, who, afterwards were Chief Justices of the Supreme Court of Pennsylvania, Messrs. Lewis and Thompson, as well as many others who became men of political and social eminence. As he rose to manhood, he was appointed in the engineer corps of the Juniata division of the State works, under DeWitt Clinton, Jr., as chief. The partner of his father having died, he returned to Harrisburg, and became part owner of the *Chronicle*. He was chosen when scarcely of voting age, one of the printers to the Legislature. After spending a couple of years in the South, he returned to Harrisburg, and was appointed to a position at Washington city; resigned, taking control of the *Pennsylvania Reporter* at Harrisburg; subsequently unanimously chosen assistant clerk of the Senate, resigning that, and becoming joint partner in the *Pennsylvanian*, at Philadelphia, with Mifflin Parry, Joseph Neal, J. W. Forney, and S. D. Patterson. At the termination of this partnership, he became printer to both houses of Congress, and at the repeal of the contract law, returned to Harrisburg, and for the following nine years was State printer. He has held a number of public positions: that of school director for twelve years; president of the select council; one of the commissioners of 1860, and of a subsequent one in 1870, to make a plot of the city of Harrisburg; president of the State Agricultural Society, and of the Dauphin County Society; a trustee of the Harrisburg Academy; secretary of the board of managers of the Harrisburg Hospital from the first meeting on the subject, in 1872; president of the board of trustees of Derry Presbyterian church, and president of the Dauphin County Historical Society since its formation. Mr. Hamilton m., in ·Philadelphia, December 18, 1845, by Rev. Thomas Brainard, CATHARINE LOUISA NAUDAIN, b. April 11, 1823, in New Castle county, Del.; d. September 11, 1883, in Harrisburg, Pa., and there buried; daughter of Dr. Arnold Naudain* and Mary Schee. On the death

---

* The family record of Hon. Arnold Naudain is interesting. Briefly stated, it is as follows:

Elias Naudain, b. 1657; d. 1694; m. Gahel Arnaud, 1676. Had Elias Naudain, b. 1686; d. 1752; m., in Philadelphia, Lydia Le Roux, 1715, daughter of Pierre Le Roux. Both Naudain and Le Roux were natives of La Tremblade, Saintonge, France. The former received his "denization" in England, November 17, 1681. Both were "naturalized" in London, March 8, 1682.

Arnold Naudain, b. 1728; m. Catharine Alfree, 1751—both died August 6, 1796.

Andrew Naudain, b. 1758; d. 1819; m. Rebecka Snow, b. 1770; d. 1813.

Arnold Naudain, b. 1790; d. 1872; m. in 1810, Mary Schee, b. 1787; d. 1860; daughter of Hermanus Schee and Mary Naudain.

of Mrs. Hamilton, one who knew her well, writes : " It is no eulogy, but the testimony of all who knew her, that few excelled her in those womanly traits of character and gentle at-

---

Dr. Naudain's first public service was in the war of 1812, when he was surgeon of the Delaware regiment. In 1822 he was nominated for Congress; his opponent was Louis McLane, who was elected. In 1824 and 1828, the political race between these distinguished gentlemen was run again, and with the same result. At each contest the vote was nearly equal. In 1825, Dr. Naudain was elected to the Legislature, a member from New Castle county, sitting with his brother, Elias, who represented Kent county. The former was chosen Speaker, serving with great acceptability. In 1828, he was commissioned a judge of the Court of Common Pleas, by Governor Charles Polk, the bench consisting of Thomas Clayton, Arnold Naudain, and Jacob Stout. In 1829, Louis McLane resigned his seat as United States Senator, and in January, 1830, Dr. Naudain was appointed; taking his seat the day he entered the forty-first year of his age. In 1832, while occupying this eminent position, he was nominated for Governor, although earnestly protesting "against a step so impolitic." In 1833, he was again chosen United States Senator. He fully appreciated this mark of high confidence, but his private business was suffering. After deliberate consideration he decided to resign his public position, and resume his professional avocation. He resigned June 17, 1836. In 1841, he again entered public life as a collector of the Port of Wilmington, and superintendent of the Light-houses on the Delaware. He resided in Philadelphia for some years, but in 1857 returned to his native State. Dr. Naudain m., in 1810, Mary Schee, b. 1787 ; d. 1860. They had issue (surname Naudain):

  i. James Schee, b. September 24, 1811 ; m., September 4, 1832, Ann Elizabeth Blackiston ; d. May 23, 1844, and had six children.

  ii. Andrew-Snow, b. February 20, 1813 ; d. March 8, 1895 ; m., March 7, 1833, Mary Pennel Corbit; and had two daughters.

  iii. Rebecka-Ann, b. February 22, 1815 ; m., April 20, 1837, Hugh Alexander ; d. November 14, 1883 ; and had eight children.

  iv. Mary-Hambly, b. October 11, 1817 ; m., March 19, 1845, William Newell Hamilton ; and had three children.

  v. Elizabeth-Riddle, b. September 29, 1820 ; m. February 9, 1842, James Edward Ellis ; and had six children.

  vi. Catharine-Louisa, b. April 11, 1823 ; m. *as above*.

  vii. Lydia-Frazer, b. May 29, 1825 ; m. September 14, 1847, Clayton Augustus Cowgill, d. in Florida, November 17, 1871 ; and had three children.

  viii. Caroline-Amelia, b. October 27, 1827 ; d. April 14, 1848, s. p.

tractions of manner and person that are fitted to charm and hold the hearts of friends. Under the discipline of suffering and the training of the Divine Saviour, her Christian life took on a serene and patient, a gentle and tender aspect, that betokened its heavenly origin. They had issue:

12. i. *Howard*, b. May 18, 1847; m. Ella Maria Harbert.
13. ii. *Hugh* (twin), b. May 18, 1847; m. Florence Wallace.
     iii. *Boyd*, b. June 6, 1849, in Philadelphia; d. March 13, 1854, at Harrisburg.
     iv. *Mary-Schee-Naudain*, b. July 24, 1854; d. March 3, 1856, at Harrisburg.
     v. *Naudain*, b. February 9, 1857, at Harrisburg, Pa.

Mr. A. Boyd Hamilton, m., secondly, May 29, 1888, ISABELLA MOORE HAYS, b. April 21, 1837, dau. of Samuel Wallace Hays, and his wife Margaret Rebecca Moore, (*see Hays record*).

XI. JOHN HAMILTON,[5] (Hugh,[4] John,[3] John,[2] James,[1]) b. October 21, 1815, at Harrisburg, Pa.; went to Texas at an early period, and yet resides there. He was an officer in the war for Texas independence in 1841, serving in Col. Nail's battalion, and for his services received a large tract of land in Jasper county, on the Angelina river, near its junction with the Neuces. In the war between Mexico and the United States he was an officer in Captain Veatch's company, Col. Bell's regiment. During the Civil War was conscripted into the C. S. A., but was not in service. Mr. Hamilton m., August 1, 1844, near Zavalla, Texas, AMANDA JANE THOMASON, b. February 4, 1830; d. April 26, 1867; daughter of Moses Kelley Thomason and Thyrza Ann Campbell.* They had issue:

---

*THYRZA ANNE CAMPBELL was a daughter of Dr. Duncan Campbell, of Flemingsburg, Ky. He was born at Edinburgh, Scotland, in 1764, closely related to the family of Argyle-Campbell, brother of George W. Campbell, United States Senator from Tenn., Secretary of the Treasury, and ambassador to Russia. Dr. Duncan Campbell married Ann Washburn, a native of Virginia and of English ancestry; and had issue (surname Campbell):

   i. *Argyle*, a prominent lawyer of Mississippi; d. prior to 1860.
   ii. *Archibald*, a lawyer residing in Alabama.

The Family of Hamilton.

i. *Rosanna-Catharine*, b. September 25, 1845; m. August 31, 1865, Lanier W. Ludlow; and had issue (surname Ludlow):
  1. *John-Lanier*, b. September 7, 1866.
  2. *Alexander-Franklin*, b. January 31, 1869.
  3. *Thomas-Riley*, b. October 8, 1870.
  4. *Josephine-Octavia*, b. November 25, 1872.
  5. *Charlotte-Amanda*, b. June 11, 1877.
  6. *Nancy-Mahala*, b. April 23, 1880.
  7. *Robert-Clinton*, b. April 21, 1882.
  8. *Rosanna-M.*
  9. *Catharine-E.*

ii. *Ann-Elizabeth*, b. May 31, 1847; d. February 24, 1888; m., December 23, 1868, William Byerly; and had issue (surname Byerly):
  1. *Adam-Boyd*, b. September 30, 1869.
  2. *Hugh-Alexander*, b. June 5, 1872.
  3. *James-William*, b. May 15, 1875.
  4. *Amanda-Caroline*, b. July 24, 1879.
  5. *Margaret-Penelope*, b. January 25, 1882.
  6. *John-Hamilton*, b. September 29, 1884.

iii. *Hugh-Moses*, b. September 26, 1849; d. June 25, 1880.

iv. *Margaret-Frances*, b. April 10, 1851; m., December 3, 1873, Wallace Ferguson; d. March 31, 1882; and had issue (surname Ferguson):
  1. *Emily-Jane*, b. December 13, 1874.
  2. *Argyle-Hamilton*, b. April 10, 1877.
  3. *Margaret-Ann*, b. December 26, 1880.

v. *Amanda-Jane*, b. April 18, 1853; m., May 16, 1873, John Wallace Williams; and had issue (surname Williams):
  1. *Sarah-Catharine*, b. July 31, 1874; d. s. p.
  2. *Henry-Lewis-Duncan*, b. May 31, 1875.
  3. *Amanda-Angeline*, b. March 8, 1880.
  4. *James-Kelly*, b. August 24, 1883.

vi. *John-Boyd*, b. June 16, 1855; m., October 14, 1876, Elizabeth Nicholas; d. May 13, 1884; and had issue:
  1. *Allen-Boyd*, b. August 27, 1881.
  2. *Elizabeth*, d. 1884.

---

iii. *Eliza*, m. David Hubbard, member of Congress from Alabama.

iv. *Cynthia*, m., first, Alexander Kerr, a merchant; second, Colonel Davis, a planter of Mississippi.

v. *Thyrza-Ann*, m. Moses K. Thomason, a merchant.

vi. *Mahala*, m. Andrew Smythe, of Alabama, father of George W. Smythe, member of Congress from Texas.

John B. Hamilton, m., secondly, Mary E. Williams; and had issue:
    3. *Anne,* d. inf.
    4. *Benjamin,* d. inf.
    5. *Daniel-A.*
    6. *Amanda-Jane.*
    7. *John-Sullivan.*
vii. *Alexander-Duncan,* b. June 5, 1857; m., January 22, 1887, Callie Hart, of the family of Hon. Thomas Hart Benton, of Missouri; and had issue:
    1. *Beaver Alricks,* b. December 13, 1887.
    2. *Golden-A.,* b. 1889; d. inf.
    3. *Thomas-Benton,* b. September 13, 1891.
viii. *Thyrza-Mahala,* b. September 26, 1860; m. J. M. Graham.
ix. *William-Allen,* b. August 24, 1863; m., July, 1889, Maud Pratt; d. May 6, 1892; and had issue:
    1. *Hugh-Hamilton,* d. s. p.
x. *Argyle-Campbell,* b. February 4, 1867, d. s. p.

XII. HOWARD HAMILTON,⁶ (Adam-Boyd,⁵ Hugh,⁴ John,³ John,² James,¹) b. Tuesday, May 18, 1847, in Philadelphia, Pa.; d. July 2, 1887; bur. in Philadelphia. He m., September 23, 1875, by Rev. Dr. Parker, ELLA MARIA HARBERT, b. August 29, 1851; daughter of Samuel C. Harbert.* They had issue:

    i. *Samuel-Harbert,* b. July 11, 1877, at Overbrook, Philadelphia.
    ii. *Charles-Naudain,* b. February 25, 1883; d. July 26, 1883.

XIII. HUGH HAMILTON,⁶ (Adam Boyd,⁵ Hugh,⁴ John,³ John,² James,¹) b. Tuesday, May 18, 1847, in Philadelphia; is a practicing physician at Harrisburg, Pa.; m., first, at Pittsburgh, February 25, 1875, by Rev. John K. McKallip, FLOR-

---

*SAMUEL CLOKE HARBERT, son of Zebedee Harbert and Sarah Cloke, whose ancestors settled in Maryland prior to 1700. Colonel Harbert entered the army from New Jersey, and at the close of the Civil War held the rank and position of a paymaster. His term of service was from the beginning to the end of the war. Mrs. Harbert descends from Thomas Lloyd, whose descent is known as early as 1515—Deputy Governor of Pennsylvania in 1684—through Rachel Lloyd Preston, whose daughter Hannah m. Samuel Carpenter, 1711, whose son Preston m. Hannah Smith, 1742, &c., (*see record by Charles Perrin Smith, of Trenton, N. J.*).

ENCE WALLACE, b. February 4, 1843; d. March 25, 1880, buried at Harrisburg, daughter of Rev. Dr. Benjamin John Wallace (*see Maclay record*), and Sarah Cochran, daughter of George Cochran (of Richard), Pittsburgh. They had issue:

  i. Adam-Boyd, b. December 5, 1875.
  ii. Benjamin-Wallace, b. November 20, 1877.
  iii. Louisa-Naudain, b. October 13, 1879; d. April 11, 1880; buried at Harrisburg.

Dr. Hamilton, m., secondly, November 17, 1885, ISABELLA CASS HAMILTON, b. October 28, 1849, dau. of Hon. William Hamilton and Louisa Slaymaker, of Lancaster county, Pa. Her paternal ancestors came to America in 1719, and purchased land in Leacock in 1742, yet remaining in the family.

HAY OR HAYS FAMILY.

I. WILLIAM HAYS,[1] a native of Scotland, left that country during the religious persecutions, and settled in the county Tyrone, north of Ireland. He was at the siege of Derry, and endured its trials until relief came, being absent from his family twenty-two months. His wife and two small children were of the number of those who had been "driven to the wall," having been forced to walk with her little ones twenty English miles—the only food, a little oatmeal secreted about her person. A piece of horse hide, purchased during the siege just before relief came for a guinea, was preserved. Of two of their children we have record:

    i. Martha, m. John Wallace, (see *Wallace and Weir record*).
2. *ii. James*, who m.; and left issue.

II. JAMES HAYS,[2] (William,[1]) b. at Derg Bridge, county Tyrone, Ireland; married, and had a large family, most of whose descendants came to America "between the Peace and 1789." William and Dickey Hays located at "Bald Ridge," in, then, Northumberland county; James; (Rev.) Joseph, of county Down, another son, father of Matthew, of Triana town, Madison county, Alabama; William, of Wythe Court House, Virginia; Rebecca Hay-Leitch; Sarah Hay-McCormick, of Pittsburgh, Pa., and Elizabeth, who remained in Ireland, with John, whose line is here given:

3. *i. John*, b. about 1740; m. Eleanor Leach.

III. JOHN HAYS,[3] (James,[2] William,[1]) b. about 1740, emigrated to America in 1789, arriving in Philadelphia in September of that year. After remaining the following winter at Maytown, Lancaster county, Pa., he purchased a farm at the head of Yellow Breeches creek, on the Walnut Bottom road, Cumberland county, Pa. He resided there ten or twelve years, but was unable to obtain a proper title for his property, and his first payment of £500 was lost. He afterwards purchased three hundred acres in Path Valley, Franklin county, Pa., where some of his descendants yet reside. He died in 1814. Mr. Hays married ELEANOR LEACH, a native of the north of Ireland, who died in 1826, in Path Valley. They had issue:

    i. Margaret, b. March 16, 1767; d. December 15, 1884, in Philadelphia, Pa.; m. John Gibson, of Ardstraw, county Tyrone, Ireland; in 1791, first accounting clerk in the auditor's office of the U. S. Treasury at Philadelphia; and had issue (surname Gibson):
        1. *John.*
        2. *Andrew.*
        3. *Jane.*

    ii. Frances, b. August 24, 1768; d. January 9, 1851, in Cumberland county, Pa.; m. Robert Patterson, and had issue (surname Patterson):
        1. *Eliza.*
        2. *Eleanor.*

    iii. James, b. January 4, 1770; went south; m. there, and died at Germantown, Hyde county, N. C.; and left issue:
        1. *Sidney-Smith.*
        2. *William-Gibson.*

4.   *iv. John*, b. October 14, 1771; m. Martha Wallace.

    v. Elizabeth, b. November 29, 1773; d. December 5, 1779.

    vi. William, b. October 17, 1775; d. May 1, 1864; resided on the old homestead in Path Valley, where he died.

    vii. Dickey, b. March 15, 1777; m. [Margaret] Lindsey, and had *John*, and *Margaret*.

    viii. Jennett, b. December 12, 1778, d. s. p.

    ix. Elizabeth, b. 1782; d. January 21, 1872, at the old homestead, unm.

    x. Eleanor, b. 1785; d. February 12, 1877, in Path Valley, Franklin county, Pa.; m. William Gamble; and had issue (surname Gamble):
        1. *Mary.*
        2. *Margaret.*
        3. *John.*
        4. *Eliza.*
        5. *Samuel.*
        6. *Sarah.*
        7. *Eleanor.*
        8. *Susan.*
        9. *William.*
        10. *Martha.*

    xi. Sarah, b. 1787; d. December 15, 1860; m. John Little; and had issue (surname Little):
        1. *William-Hays.*

2. *Eliza.*
3. *Mary.*
4. *James.*
5. *Eleanor.*
6. *Tirzah.*
7. *John.*
8. *Thomas.*

xii. Jane, b. July 2, 1789; d. April 20, 1864 : unm.

IV. JOHN HAYS,⁴ (John,³ James,² William,¹) b. October 14, 1771, in county Tyrone, Ireland ; d. June 15, 1811, at Somerset, Pa.; m., December, 1797, MARTHA WALLACE, b. April 23, 1773, in Allen township, Cumberland county, Pa.; d. September 25, 1843, at Harrisburg, Pa.; dau. of Samuel Wallace and Margaret Patton. They had issue :

5.   *i. Samuel-Wallace,* b. October 30, 1799 ; m. Margaret Moore.
6.   *ii. John-Leach,* b. December 28, 1801 ; m., first, Jane Gibson, d. 1853 ; and had *Margaret;* secondly, Margaret Camblin.
7.   *iii. William-Patton,* b. February 3, 1804 ; m. Rosanna Keller.
    iv. Margaret, b. March 27, 1806, at Somerset, Pa.; d. November 29, 1892, at Harrisburg, Pa.
    v. Eleanor, b. September 16, 1807 ; d. November, 1808.
8.   *vi. Joseph-Caldwell,* b. July 4, 1810 ; m. Anna M. Betts.

V. SAMUEL WALLACE HAYS,⁵ (John,⁴ John,³ James,² William,¹) b. October 30, 1790, at Newville, Cumberland county, Pa.; d. May 18, 1855, at Harrisburg, Pa. He received the education so freely given by the Scotch-Irish to their children. He came to Harrisburg in 1821, where he resided until 1825, when he went to Philadelphia, returning to the former place in 1828, which from that period became his permanent home. Mr. Hays then began business, which he successfully carried on until a few years prior to his death. He was an earnest, laborious worker in his church (Presbyterian), of which he was one of the ruling elders from 1840 to his decease. For a period of twenty-seven years he was superintendent of the first infant Sunday-school, which he organized in 1828, in Harrisburg, and only relinquished its care when failing health compelled him to give up his charge. The Rev. Dr. Robinson bears this testimony of him : " I remember him as a quiet, modest man and patient sufferer. The little I knew of him endeared him to me. . . . He was a warm friend and lover of the young, kind and genial in his intercourse with them, and an admirable teacher." Mr. Hays m., September 2, 1834, MARGARET REBECCA MOORE, b. August 7, 1806; d. February 8, 1851, at Harrisburg, Pa.; dau. of Archibald Moore and Rebecca Junkin, of Locust Grove, Mifflin county, Pa. They had issue :

    i. Isabella-Moore, b. April 21, 1837; m., May 29, 1888, Adam Boyd Hamilton.

VI. JOHN LEACH HAYS,[5] (John,[4] John,[3] James,[2] William,[1]) b. December 28, 1801, at Fannettsburg, Franklin county, Pa.; d. July 2, 1892, at Mt. Jackson, Lawrence county, Pa. Resided for several years in Philadelphia, removing to Mt. Jackson in 1842, where he was engaged in mercantile business. He was postmaster from 1845 for ten years. In 1859 he was commissioned a justice of the peace, which he held until almost the close of his long life. Mr. Hays m., September 17, 1835, Jane Gibson; d. November 29, 1853, dau. of John Gibson, of Philadelphia. They had issue :

    i. Margaret-Gibson, b. June 16, 1837 ; d. inf.
    ii. John-Gibson, b. March 13, 1838 ; d. inf.
    iii. Margaret-Gibson, (second), b. May 24, 1839 ; d. October 12, 1847.

Mr. Hays m., secondly, April 14, 1858, MARGARET CAMBLIN, b. April 23, 1826, at Mt. Jackson, Pa.

VII. WILLIAM PATTON HAYS,[5] (John,[4] John,[3] James,[2] William,[1]) b. February 3, 1804, at Somerset, Pa.; d. March 5, 1844, at Harrisburg, Pa.; m. ROSANNA KELLER, b. June 8, 1812; d. August 29, 1848, at Washington city, D. C.; dau. of Michael Keller and Margaret Schaeffer. They had issue:

    i. Anna-Margaret, b. August 26, 1832 ; d. February 14, 1892.
    ii. John-Keller, b. February 17, 1834 ; d. April 13, 1837.
    iii. William-Wallace, b. October 23, 1836 ; d. March 31, 1870, at Harrisburg, Pa. He received his preparatory education in the public schools and Harrisburg Academy ; entered the sophomore class of Jefferson College, Canonsburg, in 1853, graduating in 1856. He then went to Texas, where he remained two years, teaching in Victoria and Goliad. After returning North, he began

the study of law with Robert A. Lamberton, Esq., and was admitted to the Dauphin county bar December 6, 1859. He began the practice of his profession at Harrisburg, continuing until his appointment by Governor Curtin, in 1861, as chief clerk in the office of the Secretary of the Commonwealth. On May 1, 1866, he was appointed Deputy Secretary of the Commonwealth, discharging the duties of that office until the close of Governor Curtin's administration. He then resumed his profession of the law, and in connection with it served as clerk to the Board of Claims from January to June 1, 1868. In October following, having been nominated by the Republicans of the city of Harrisburg, he was elected mayor thereof, the duties of which office he entered upon January 11, 1869. His health, however, soon began to fail him, and he died while in office, in his thirty-fourth year. "Mr. Hays was a truly Christian gentleman, he thought more of right than he did of life. His nature was of that intensity which inspires men to die for the truth, while his convictions on all subjects relating to the ordinary and extraordinary affairs of life, here and hereafter, were governed by the strongest principles of religion and justice." Mr. Hays m., March 5, 1861, Mary Straughan Day, b. September 13, 1837; dau. of Dr. Stephen F. Day and Eliza Floyd Straughan, of Wooster, O.; and had issue:

1. *William*, b. September 10, 1862; d. inf.
2. *Jessie-Wallace*, b. August 8, 1864; d. July 11, 1866.
3. *Mary-Winifred*, b. September 20, 1865; m., October 10, 1889, Rev. John McCoy; b. October 20, 1861; son of Finley McCoy and Jane Carson; and had issue (surname McCoy): *Robert-Carson*.
4. *Martha-Wallace*, b. August 5, 1869.

VIII. JOSEPH CALDWELL HAYS,[5] (John,[4] John,[3] James,[2] William,[1]) b. July 4, 1810, at Somerset, Pa.; d. November 3, 1891, at Meadville, Pa. He received his early education at the Harrisburg Academy, and learned the profession of printer, and became editor and part proprietor of the *Expositor* at Carlisle. In 1836, removed to Meadville, Pa., and began the publication of the *Statesman*. Early in 1841 Mr. Hays was appointed postmaster at Meadville, but removed by President Tyler. In 1848 he established the *Crawford Journal*, which he successfully carried on until 1864. In 1859 he was elected treasurer of Crawford county, and was a delegate to the convention at Chicago which nominated Mr. Lincoln. In 1861 he was appointed by the President postmaster at Meadville and held that position until 1883. No man in the community was held in higher esteem. Mr. Hays m., April 17, 1838, ANNA MARIA BETTS, b. October 13, 1808; d. February 20, 1892; dau. of Ebenezer Betts and Sarah Gregory, of Meadville. They had issue:

    i. *John-Betts*, b. March 12, 1839; graduated from Allegheny College in 1858; admitted to the bar in 1861, and the same year entered the army as second lieutenant Nineteenth U. S. Infantry. He served in the Peninsular, Maryland, and Fredericksburg campaigns; promoted first lieutenant in 1862, and in 1863 was transferred with his company (H of First battalion, Nineteenth infantry) to the army of the Cumberland while at Murfreesboro, Tenn. In June of the same year detached under orders of the Secretary of War as commissary of musters, first division Reserve army corps. He served on staffs of Generals Baird, Steedman, and Thomas; took part in the operations of the Fourteenth and Reserve army corps in the Chattanooga campaign of 1863. His name appears in reports of the battle of Chickamauga, of Major General Rosecrans, commanding army of the Cumberland, and of Major General Gordon, commanding reserve corps, as "among those most conspicuous for efficiency and bravery, and deserving special mention." He served in the operations about Nashville; was promoted April, 1864, to captain Nineteenth U. S. Infantry; and in March, 1865, for "faithful and meritorious service," brevetted major U. S. A. He resigned from the army September 1, 1865. From 1866 to 1869 he was U. S. Assessor of Internal Revenue for Twentieth District of Pennsylvania. Major Hays m., May 24, 1863, Fannie Mead, dau. of Alexander J. Mead and granddaughter of David Mead, founder of the city of Meadville, where they reside; and had issue:

      1. *Joseph-Mead*, b. April 16, 1866.
      2. *Fannie-Mead*, b. August 13, 1868; m. January 15, 1890, David G. Baillie, of the New York *World*; and have issue (surname Baillie):
          a. Hugh, b. October 23, 1890.
          b. John Hays, b. May 12, 1894.
      3. *Anna-Louise*, b. July 20, 1870; d. January 13, 1871.
      4. *Marion-Mead*, b. February 20, 1876.

ii. *Samuel*, b. February 10, 1841 ; d. inf.
iii. *Frederick-William*, b. March 17, 1842; graduated from Allegheny College in 1861; studied law and was admitted to practice at the Crawford county bar in September, 1870; in April, 1871, commenced the practice of law in Venango county; held the office of solicitor for the municipality of Oil City from 1874 to 1884; was a member of the House of Representatives sessions of 1889-1892; m., June 12, 1873, Elizabeth Ida Lashells, b. November 26, 1850; daughter of George Edward Lashells and Eliza Baskin; and had issue :
  1. *Bessie*, b. June 13, 1875 ; d. March 19, 1881.
  2. *John-Lashells*, b. May 24, 1878.
iv. *Anna-Elizabeth*, b. December 2, 1844 ; m., October 20, 1868, David Compton Dunn, son of Renselaer K. and Rebecca E. Dunn ; and had issue (surname Dunn):
  1. *William-Compton*, b. December 7, 1869 ; m. May 1, 1893, Emma D. Brown.
  2. *Anna*, b. May 18, 1871.
  3. *Ellen*, b. May 31, 1873.
  4. *Wallace-Hays*, b. July 10, 1876.
  5. *Ruth*, b. June 27, 1885.
v. *Joseph*, b. May 22, 1847 ; d. January 13, 1854.
vi. *Wilson-Dick*, b. August 23, 1849 ; m. July 7, 1831, Ida M. Stewart; b. October 31, 1846, at Mt. Jackson, daughter of William and Hannah Stewart ; and have issue :
  1. *Frederick-Wallace*, b. July 24, 1882.

KELLER OF LANCASTER.

I. JOHANN PETER KELLER,[1] a native of Germany, emigrated to America prior to 1760, and settled in Lancaster county, Pa., where he died; his wife ANNA MARIA, b. in Germany, died in the town of Lancaster, on the 6th of January, 1782. They had two children born in Germany:

  2.   *i. Carl-Andrew*, b. July 14, 1750; m. Barbara Judith Bigler.
      ii. Johann-Adam; nothing further is known of him.

II. CARL ANDREW KELLER,[2] (John-Peter,[1]) b. July 14, 1750, in Germany; d. February 21, 1803, at Lancaster, Pa.; m., April, 1774, at Lancaster, BARBARA JUDITH BIGLER, b. August 9, 1755; d. August 15, 1831, at Lancaster, Pa. They had issue:

  3.   *i. John-Peter*, b. September 28, 1776; m., first, Catharine Schaeffer; secondly, Mrs. Rachel Cochran.
  4.   *ii. Adam*, b. December 7, 1784; m. Elizabeth Schaeffer.
  5.   *iii. John*, m. Susanna Nye.
  6.   *iv. Andrew*, m. —— Stahl.
  7.   *v. Jacob*, m., first, —— ——; secondly, Catharine Heisely.
  8.   *vi. Sophia*, m., first, David Kauffman; secondly, Samuel Kling.
  9.   *vii. Anna-Maria*, m. William Kurtz.
 10. *viii. Rev. Benjamin*, m., first, Eliza Craver Schaeffer; secondly, Maria Stroup.
      ix. Jeremiah, d. s. p.
 11. *x. Michael*, b. June 17, 1790; m., first, Margaret Schaeffer; secondly, Barbara Margaret Schaeffer.

III. JOHN PETER KELLER,[3] (Carl-Andrew,[2] Johann-Peter,[1]) b. September 28, 1776, in Lancaster, Pa.; d. October 1, 1850, at Harrisburg, Pa.; learned the trade of a brass-founder, located at Harrisburg in 1796. In 1801 he established himself in business as brass-founder and rope-maker, which proved successful, and afterwards in general merchandising. He was a member of the borough council almost continuously from 1810 to 1824, and was quite prominent and influential in the public affairs of his day. He was identified with nearly all the early enterprises of the town, such as the Harrisburg Bridge Company, Harrisburg and Middletown Turnpike Company, and at his death was the last survivor of the original board of directors of the Harrisburg Bank. He was a gentleman of thrift, industry, and indomitable energy, upright, honest, and respected by his fellow-citizens. He was no less decided and influential as a Christian, being one of the founders of the Lutheran church in Harrisburg. Was twice married; first, CATHARINE SCHAEFFER, b. November 6, 1774; d. October 1, 1859, at Harrisburg. They had issue:

  i. Frederick, b. February, 1796; d. 1797.
  ii. George, b. 1798; d. 1800.
  iii. Rev. *Emanuel*, b. September 30, 1801; d. April 11, 1837, at Mechanicsburg, Pa.; buried in Trindle Spring Church graveyard; he was educated in the schools and academy of Harrisburg, and pursued his classical studies under the direction of his uncle, the Rev. Benjamin Keller. He subsequently entered Dickinson College, where he remained two years, when he began the study of theology with the Rev. Dr. Lochman, of Harrisburg. In 1826 he was licensed by the Lutheran Synod of Pennsylvania, and the same year began his ministerial labors at Manchester, Md. Thence he removed to Mechanicsburg, Pa., where he continued in the pastorate until a short period before his death, his enfeebled health obliging him to resign his charge. The Rev. Mr. Keller married, April 14, 1825, Sabina Selzer, and had *Ann-Victoria*, and other children.
  iv. Eliza, b. June 12, 1803; m. James R. Boyd, (*see Boyd record*).
12. *v. Maria*, b. February 17, 1805; m. Lewis Plitt.
  vi. Catharine, b. November 4, 1806; d. November 15, 1836; m. James Gilliard; and had issue (surname Gilliard): *John-Peter*.
13. *vii. John-Peter*, b. February 25, 1808; m. Lydia Kunkel.
  viii. Sophia, b. May 20, 1810; d. August 24, 1840, at Harrisburg; m. Thomas Montgomery.
  ix. William-C., b. January 24, 1812, at Harrisburg; m. Camilla Lochman, and had *Charles*, d. s. p., and *Annie*, m. N. R. Miller, d. November 27, 1892.
  x. Frederick-George, b. September 14, 1814; d. at the age of sixteen years, having become blind.
  xi. Benjamin, b. April 6, 1816, d. s. p.
  xii. Peter-Charles, b. April 16, 1817, at Harrisburg; d. December 30, 1875, at Quincy, Ill.; engaged early in life in the

mercantile business at Harrisburg, Pa., subsequently removing to Philadelphia, where he remained until 1847; at that time he went West and located in Quincy, Ill., where he became quite prominent, enjoying the confidence and respect of the people of that city; m. Eliza Wells; and had *Elvey,* m. Robert Lockwood, *Levi,* and *Lemuel.*

 xiii. Charles-Andrew, b. July 26, 1819; d. October 21, 1871, at Harrisburg; m. first, Matilda Calder; and had *William-C.,* m. ——— Patterson, and had *Olie;* m. secondly, Rachel Compton; and had *Charles-C.,* m. and had *Charles-Compton.*

Mr. Keller married, secondly, Mrs. RACHEL COCHRAN, widow of William Cochran, formerly sheriff of Dauphin county, who survived him thirteen years.

IV. ADAM KELLER,³ (Carl-Andrew,² Johann-Peter,¹) b. December 7, 1784, at Lancaster, Pa.; d. January 30, 1863; m. ELIZABETH SCHAEFFER, b. June 15, 1786; d. January 30, 1854; she was a cousin of John Peter Keller's wife. They had issue:

 i. Barbara, m. William Frick; and had Rev. *William-Keller,* m. Louisa Klump, who had *William, Lillian, Norman,* and *Raymond.*

14. *ii. John-Andrew,* m. Harriet Tressler.

 iii. Adam, d. October 6, 1813.
 iv. Benjamin, d. at the age of nineteen years.
 v. Emanuel, m. Harriet Sharpe; and had *Julia, John,* and *Mary.*
 vi. Elizabeth, d. s. p.
 vii. Sophia, m. Frederick William Beates; and had issue (surname Beates): *William-Adam, Anna-Maria, Edward-Keller, Elizabeth-Caroline,* d. s. p., *James-Frederick, Louisa-Catharine,* and *Emily-Sophia,* d. s. p.
 viii. Anna-Maria.
 ix. Adam-Schaeffer, m., first, Mary ———; m., secondly, Mary Elizabeth Snyder; and had *Adam,* and *Elizabeth,* both deceased.
 x. Louisa, d. s. p.
 xi. Margaretta. m. William E. Heinitsh; and had issue (surname Heinitsh): *Sigmund-William, Charles-Luther,* d., *Lizzie-Keller,* d., *Walter-Augustus, William-Edward,* d., *Margie-Keller, John-Frederick,* and *Louisa-Keller,* d.
 xii. Louisa, d. unm.
 xiii. Samuel, d. s p.

V. JOHN KELLER,[3] (Carl-Andrew,[2] Johann-Peter,[1]) b. in Lancaster, Pa.; d. at Harrisburg in 1816; m. SUSANNA NYE, b. March 6, 1777; d. February 7, 1855, at Easton, Pa., daughter of Johannes and Maria Magdalena Nye, of Lancaster. They had issue:

    i. *Henry*, d. at Easton, Pa.; had five children.
    ii. *Andrew*, d. at Easton, Pa.
    iii. *Barbara-Ann*, b. 1807, at Reading; m. Charles A. Snyder; and had seven children surnamed Snyder.
    iv. *John*, b. at Reading; drowned at Harrisburg.
    v. *Susan*, b. at Harrisburg; d. at Easton; m. —— Abel.

VI. ANDREW KELLER,[3] (Carl-Andrew,[2] Johann Peter,[1]) b. in Lancaster, Pa., where he died; m. —— STAHL. They had issue:

    i. *George*, m. Catharine Strine; and had *Mary*, m. Mr. Fordney; *Andrew*, d. s. p.; *Adam*, d. s. p.; *George*, m. Miss Vondersmith; and *Kate*, m. Harry Diller.
    ii. *Maria*, m. Charles Demuth; and had issue (surname Demuth): *Annie*, m. Peter Regenaus; *Josephine*, m. William E. Kreider; *Emma*, m. Dr. William Tabret; *Caroline*, d. s. p.; *Amelia*, m. Oliver Sturges; *Maria*, m. Albert M. Zahm; and *William*, d. unm.

VII. JACOB KELLER,[3] (Carl-Andrew,[2] Johann-Peter,[1]), b. in Lancaster, Pa.; d. at Frederick, Md.; was twice married; by first wife there was issue:

    i. *Sophia*, m. Rev. Harper.
    ii. *Elizabeth*, m. Rev. James Harkley.

Jacob Keller m., secondly, CATHARINE HEISELY, b. April 22, 1797; d. at Frederick, Md.; daughter of Frederick Heisely and Catharine Juliana Hoff. They had issue:

    iii. *Charles*, m. Miss Hunt.
    iv. *Frederick*.
    v. *Benjamin*.
    vi. *Caroline*, m. Henry Handshue.
    vii. *Jacob*.
    viii. *Muhlenberg*.

VIII. SOPHIA KELLER,[3] (Carl-Andrew,[2] Johann-Peter,[1]) b. in Lancaster, Pa.; was twice married; first to DAVID KAUFFMAN. They had issue (surname Kauffman):

    i. *Rosanna*, m. Samuel Brumbaugh, and had issue (surname Brumbaugh):

Keller of Lancaster. 345

1. *Wilhelmina*, m. Spencer Barrett.
2. *Mary*, m. John Thomas, and had issue (surname Thomas): *Elvin*, and *William*.
3. *Samuel*.
4. *Emma*, m. George J. Bolton, and had issue (surname Bolton): *Jennie-E.*, *Rosa*, *George-J.*, *Monroe-K.*, and *Emma-Gertrude*.
5. *Jennie*.

ii. *William*, m. Ann McClone; had *William*.
iii. *David*.
iv. *Benjamin*, m. and had nine children.
v. *Sophia*, d. s. p.

Mrs. Kauffman m., secondly, SAMUEL KLING. They had issue (surname Kling):

vi. *Susanna-B.*, m. John D. Miller; and had issue (surname Miller):
1. *Samuel-Carroll*, m. Henrietta Zahm Killough.
2. *Eugene-Jasper*, m. Nellie Schram.
3. *Ella-Frances*, m. George Albright.

vii. *Eliza-K.*, resides at Harrisburg, Pa.; m. Joseph Jackson; d. October 18, 1858.
viii. *Mary*, m. William Halfman; and had issue (surname Halfman): *George*, and *Frank*, and seven others.
ix. *Henrietta*, m. William M. Buchanan; and had issue (surname Buchanan): *John Chambers*, *Martha-Weir*, *Anna-Eliza*, *Augusta*, and *David*.
x. *Lydia*, d. s. p.
xi. *Louisa*, m. Jesse I. Kays; had nine children.

IX. ANNA MARIA KELLER,[3] (Carl-Andrew,[2] Johann-Peter,[1]) b. in Lancaster, Pa.; m. WILLIAM KURTZ. They had issue, besides several died in infancy (surname Kurtz):

i. *William*, m. Ellen McCue; and had *Mary-Ann*, *Margaretta*, and three sons.
ii. *George*, m. Mary Vandivender.
iii. *Goehring*, m. Sarah Bowman; and had issue.
iv. *Anthony*, m., first, Susan Kauffman, no issue; secondly, Miss Holzworth; and had *Wesley*, m Ann Bunn, *Martin-Anthony*, *Frank*, m. Miss Hubley, *Susan*, *Annie*, *Keller*, and a son who died at Pittsburgh.
v. *Israel*, m. Caroline Oswald.
vi. Rev. *Michael;* was twice married, and had *Sarah-Ann*, *Emma*, d. s. p., *Thomas*, *William*, *M.-Olin*, *Alexander*, and *Edwin*, d. s. p.

    vii. Harriet, m. Andrew Porter; and had issue (surname Porter): *Mary, Charles, Nellie*, and *Scott*.
    viii. Sarah, m. Simon Young; and had issue (surname Young): *Emma, Eliza, Mary, Henrietta, Sarah, William*, and *Baker*.
    ix. Sophia, m. —— Seibert; and had issue (surname Seibert): *Edward, William, John, Emma, Ann*, and *Mary*.
    x. Maria, m., first, Mr. Mansfield; secondly, Mr. Rossiter; and had issue.

X. REV. BENJAMIN KELLER,³ D. D., (Carl-Andrew,² Johann-Peter,¹), was twice married; m., first, CATHARINE ELIZA (CRAVER) SCHAEFFER, widow of Rev. Frederick Schaeffer, D. D. They had issue:

    i. Mary-Ann-Barbara, d. s. p.
    ii. Rev. *Frederick-Augustus-Muhlenberg*, b. April 28, 1819. at Carlisle, Pa.; d. March 18, 1864, in Reading, Pa.; educated at Pennsylvania College, Gettysburg, from which he graduated in 1838; studied theology, and licensed to preach in 1840; founded St. James Lutheran church at Reading, serving it until his death; during the war for the Union he was in service; m., in 1848, Susan Hunter, and had issue, *Charles-H.*, and *Sarah*.

15. *iii. Anna-Cecilia*, m. Herman Haupt.
    iv. Mary-Elizabeth, m. Charles C. Norton; and had issue (surname Norton): *William-Benjamin*, d. s. p., and *Ann-Cecilia*, m. John Henry Hensel; Mr. Norton had by a former wife, *Charles D.*, m. Maggie S. Brown, and left *Mary-Ada*.
    v. Frederick-Emanuel, d. s. p.

16. *vi. Louisa-Caroline*, m. Lewis Haupt.
    vii. Peter-Paul, b. October 25, 1830; d. April 29, 1880; m., September, 1857, Emma Hassal; and had *Joseph-Henry, Pierre-Paul*, and *Paul-Hassal*.
    viii. Paul-Peter (twin), b. October 25, 1830; m., May 15, 1855, Cornelia M. Morris, of Philadelphia; and had *Jane-Morris*, d. s. p.
    ix. Catharine-Eliza, m. Henry W. Knauff; and had issue (surname Knauff): *Sarah-Emily* and *Muhlenberg-Keller*.

Rev. Benjamin Keller, D. D., m., secondly, MARIA STROUP; no issue.

XI. MICHAEL KELLER,³ (Carl-Andrew,² Johann-Peter,¹) b. June 24, 1790, in Lancaster, Pa.; d. August 21, 1861, in

Washington, D. C.; was twice married; first, MARGARET SCHAEFFER, who was a sister of John Peter Keller's wife. They had issue :

    i. Rosannah, b. June 8, 1812; d. August 29, 1848 ; m. William P. Hays, (*see Hays record*).

17. *ii. Harriet*, b. September 9, 1814 ; m. Samuel D. Finckle.

    iii. George-F., b. December 11, 1816 ; d. May 16, 1855, and had *Michael*, d. s. p., *Ann*, d. s. p., *Samuel, John*, and *Anna*.

    iv. Caroline, b. December 29, 1818 ; m. Samuel Berlin ; and had issue (surname Berlin): *Emma*.

    v. Mary-Ann, d. s. p.

Michael Keller m., secondly, BARBARA MARGARET SCHAEFFER, and they had issue :

    vi. Luther, d. s. p.

    vii. Louisa, d. s. p.

    viii. Margaret, b. October 20, 1827 ; m. Noble D. Larner ; and had issue (surname Larner): *Harry, John, Charles*, and *Philip*.

    ix. Adaline, d. s. p.

    x. Philip, b. July 1, 1831 ; m. Sarah M. Davy, and had *Ella, Robert*, and *Gertrude*.

    xi. Cecelia, d. unm.

    xii. Ann-Mary, m. John P. Stone ; and had issue (surname Stone): *John*, d. s. p.

XII. MARIA KELLER,[4] (John-Peter,[3] Carl-Andrew,[2] Johann-Peter,[1]) b. February 17, 1805, at Harrisburg; m. LEWIS PLITT. They had issue (surname Plitt):

    i. Rev. *John Keller*, m. Mary Horner ; and had issue (surname Plitt): *Horner, Charles, Maria*, and *George*.

    ii. Catharine, m. Albert Hummel ; and had issue (surname Hummel): *Mary*, d. s. p., *Annie, Kate*, m. Edward J. Stackpole, *Susan, Emma*, m. Rev. M. Ross Fishburn, *George*, d. s. p., and *Albert*.

    iii. Ann-Sophia, m. George Sadtler ; and had issue (surname Sadtler): *Howard, Florence*, and *Sophia*.

    iv. George, m. Susan Redsecker.

XIII. JOHN PETER KELLER,[4] (John-Peter,[3] Carl-Andrew,[2] Johann-Peter,[1]) b. February 25, 1808, at Harrisburg, Pa.; d. December 13, 1837; m. May 6, 1830, LYDIA KUNKEL, b. November 9, 1811 ; d. February 9, 1866, (*see Kunkel record*). They had issue:

    i. John-Peter, b. February 20, 1831 ; educated in the public schools and Harrisburg Academy ; studied dentistry with Dr. J. C. Stouch; resides in Harrisburg, Pa.; m.. June 21, 1861, Emeline Hannah Croll, daughter of John Croll and Eliza Lauman, of Middletown, Pa.; and had issue: *John-Peter, Croll, Helen-Lydia, Christian-Kunkel,* and *William-Lauman.*

    ii. *Christian-Kunkel,* b. October 1, 1832; educated in public schools of Harrisburg and Pennsylvania College; by profession, a druggist, residing in Harrisburg.

    iii. *Ann-Ellen,* d. s. p.

    iv. *Emily-Clarissa,* d. s. p.

XIV. JOHN ANDREW KELLER,[4] (Adam,[3] Carl-Andrew,[2] Johann-Peter,[1]) m. HARRIET TRESSLER; both lived and died in Lancaster, Pa. They had issue:

    i. *Samuel,* d. s. p.

    ii. *Benjamin-Schaeffer,* m. Miss Leiby; all deceased.

    iii. *William-Augustus,* m. Mary Smith, and had *Paul, William,* d. s. p., *Maggie,* d. s. p., *Lillian,* and *Harry.*

    iv. *Clara,* d. unm.

    v. *John-Adam,* m. Annie Garrigan.

    vi. *Lizzie,* m. John Frederick Sener, and had *Frank,* and *Rosa.*

    vii. *Kate,* d. unm.

    viii. *Harriet-Maria.*

    ix. *Ella,* m. David Early; and had issue (surname Early): *Leah, Harriet, Lizzie, Benjamin,* and *Frederick.*

    x. *Emanuel,* d. s. p.

    xi. *Charles-Buchter,* m. Harriet Leech; had two children.

XV. ANNA CECELIA KELLER,[4] (Rev. Benjamin,[3] Carl-Andrew,[2] Johann-Peter,[1]) m. HERMAN HAUPT; was a celebrated civil engineer on the Pennsylvania railroad during its original construction. They had issue (surname Haupt):

    i. *John-Stenger,* d. s. p.

    ii. *Jacob-Benjamin,* m. Mary E. Ziegler; and had issue (surname Haupt): *Charles-Ziegler, Edward, Katie,* and *Ann-Cecelia.*

    iii. *Louis-Muhlenberg,* m. Belle C. Cromwell.

    iv. *Mary-Cecilia.*

    v. *Ella-Catharine,* m. Frank Chapman; and had issue (surname Chapman): *Herman, Lucy-Lord,* and *Marion-Norton.*

    vi. *Herman.*

    vii. *Adelaide,* d. s. p.

    viii. *Charles Edgar,* m. Mary Griffiths.

    ix. *Frank-Spangler.*

    x. *Alexander-James-Derbyshire.*

    xi. *Grace-Hermania,* d. s. p.

XVI. LOUISA-CAROLINE KELLER,[4] (Rev. Benjamin,[3] Carl-Andrew,[2] Johann-Peter,[1]) m. LEWIS HAUPT, by profession a civil engineer; resides in the city of Philadelphia. They had issue (surname Haupt):

    i. (A son,) d. in infancy.
    ii. Rev. Charles-Elvin. m. Mary M. Geissinger; and had issue, Charles-Elvin, and David-Gearald.
    iii. Henry-Eugene, m. Mellie H. Witte.
    iv. William-Keller.
    v. (A son,) d. in infancy.
    vi. Fannie-Gertrude.
    vii. Mary-Louisa, m. Richard Cannarow.

XVII. HARRIET KELLER,[4] (Michael,[3] Carl-Andrew,[2] Johann-Peter,[1]) b. September 9, 1814, at Harrisburg, Pa.; m., in 1832, Rev. SAMUEL D. FINCKLE, D. D., b. February 11, 1811; d. February 13, 1873, in Washington, D. C.; a minister of the Lutheran church; had charge of the congregation at Middletown, Pa., and for upwards of twenty years pastor of the German Evangelical Lutheran Church of Washington city; for many years occupied an honorable and responsible position in the Government while serving his congregation; his life was one of incessant labor and usefulness in church and State. They had issue (surname Finckle):

    i. Caroline.
    ii. George.
    iii. Louisa.
    iv. Annie, deceased.
    v. Rev. Samuel-G., b. February 22, 1845, in Cumberland, Md.
    vi. William.
    vii. Luther.
    viii. Ruth, deceased.
    ix. Lillie, deceased.
    x. Frank.
    xi. Henrietta, d. s. p.
    xii. Ezra, d. s. p.

KENDIG OF SWATARA.

I. MARTIN KENDIG,[1] a descendant of one of the earliest Swiss settlers in Lancaster county, Pa., located on the Seneca lake, near Waterloo, N. Y., at the close of the Revolution, where he died; he m. MARY BRENNEMAN. They had issue:

2.   *i. John*, b. October 4, 1770; m. Elizabeth Hil!.
3.   *ii. Martin*, b. 1772; m. Leah Baer.
4.   *iv. Joseph*, b. 1774; m. and had issue.
      v. Daniel, b. 1777; d. s. p.
5.   *iii. Elizabeth*, b. 1778; m. William Crabb.
      vi. Christian, d. s. p.
6.   *vii. Mary*, b. 1783; m. Richard Larrobee.
      viii. Nancy, b. 1785; m. William Peacock.

II. JOHN KENDIG,[2] (Martin,[1]) b. October 4, 1770; d. October 12, 1831, at Middletown, Pa.; m. ELIZABETH HILL, b. September 17, 1770; d. March 20, 1845, at Middletown. They had issue:

7.   *i. Martin*, b. December 31, 1797; m., first, Rebecca McFarland; secondly, Sarah Seabaugh; thirdly, Mrs. Rachel Croll.
8.   *ii. Sarah*, b. 1800; m. George Allen.
9.   *iii. Daniel*, m., first, Susan Shelly; secondly, Sarah Rutherford.

III. MARTIN KENDIG,[2] (Martin,[1]) b. about 1772; m. LEAH BAER. They had issue:

   i. John.
   ii. Matilda, m. Richard P. Hunt.
   iii. Ann-Eliza, m. Samuel Birdsall, of New York City; and had issue (surname Birdsall): *Cornelia*, m. Joseph W. Runck.
   iv. Daniel-Waterloo, m. Mary Southwick.
   v. Susan, m. John Townsend.
   vi. Lucretia, m., first, Sexton Mount, of Illinois; secondly, James Wilson; thirdly, William Perrine, of New York.
   vii. Samuel-Washington, m. Elizabeth Carson.

IV. JOSEPH KENDIG,[2] (Martin,[1]) b. about 1774; m. and had issue:

i. Mary, m. David Barrett.
  ii. Catharine, m. —— McCook.

V. ELIZABETH KENDIG,² (Martin¹,) b. September 19, 1778; d. August 6, 1863; m., March 17, 1800, at Sunbury, Pa., WILLIAM CRABB, b. 1744, in county Clare, Ireland; d. April 12, 1812, in Middletown, Pa. He came to America prior to the Revolution, and with him a brother, Thomas Crabb, who settled in Maryland, and was the father of Commodore Thomas Crabb, of Princeton, N. J. William Crabb was a prominent man in his day, and filled several important official positions, among which was that of collector of the United States or direct tax in 1803. Mr. Crabb had been previously married; his first wife, Jane, dying, December 29, 1794. Some of the children mentioned were probably by this marriage. They had issue (surname Crabb):

 i. Horace, was an officer of the U. S. Navy.
 ii. Henry-S., b. March 21, 1803; d. August 1, 1866; m. Elizabeth Duane, b. April 21, 1801; d. May 4, 1870; daughter of Col. William Duane, of Philadelphia; and had *William*.
 iii. Mary, b. 1808; d. May 24, 1862; m. John Houser, b. 1801; d. October 22, 1860; in connection with his brother, Jacob, entered mercantile life; subsequently, for many years, was a justice of the peace, and clerk to borough council; and had issue (surname Houser):

  1. *Elizabeth*, resides at Elwyn, Pa.
  2. *Louisa*, d. s. p.
  3. *Alice*, m., September 8, 1868, Alfred E. Eyster, b. August 28, 1828, at Harrisburg, Pa.; son of Jacob Eyster,* and Mary Middlecoff; graduated from

---

*JACOB EYSTER, eldest son of George Eyster and Margaret Slagle, was born three miles west of Hanover, in what is now Adams county, Pa., June 8, 1782. He was a descendant of John Jacob Eyster, a native of the kingdom of Würtemberg, Germany, who emigrated to America between 1717 and 1727. Christian Eyster, the great-grandfather of the subject of this sketch, was born in Germany in 1710. The family settled first at Oley, in Berks county; from thence Christian removed, in 1736, to York county. The eldest son of Christian was Elias, born in 1734, who lived until almost a centenarian. His eldest son, George, born June 6, 1757, was a farmer and tanner; a soldier of the Revolution, captured at Fort Washington, and confined for some time on board the British prison-ships. He married, in 1780, Margaret,

Pennsylvania College, Gettysburg, in 1849; read medicine with Dr. George Dock, subsequently in the drug business; taught in the public schools of Harrisburg until 1862, when he was made chief clerk in the provost marshal's office, Fourteenth district; in 1865 detailed to take charge of the records of the office in Western Pennsylvania; resigned in September; engaged with the publishing house of E. H. Butler & Co.; and had issue (surname Eyster):

    a. *Bertha-Mary*, b. August 19, 1869.

4. *Daniel*, resides at Lancaster, Pa.; m. Susan Sponsler; and had issue (surname Houser): *Mabel, Elizabeth, Ralph, Reah*, and *Nellie*.

iv. *George-W.*, b. December 17, 1807, at Middletown, Pa.; d. October 17, 1878, at Harrisburg, Pa. After passing through the usual course of education, at the age of seventeen he entered the printing office of Simon Cameron, at Harrisburg, where he acquired the knowledge of the art preservative. In 1835 he started the Demo-

---

daughter of Jacob Slagle, and sister of Colonel Henry Slagle, of the Revolution. About 1783, they removed to near Hunterstown, within five miles of Gettysburg, where their son Jacob passed his youth and early manhood. When first enrolled among the militia of Adams county, he was appointed first sergeant, rose to captain, and then major, and, in 1814, appointed by Governor Snyder brigadier general Second brigade, Fifth division, Pennsylvania militia. During the invasion of Maryland by the British that year, he was employed by the Secretary of War (Armstrong) and the Governor of Pennsylvania in distributing and forwarding arms and supplies to the militia who were called into service. In 1811 he removed to Gettysburg and engaged in mercantile pursuits. In 1818 he was a candidate for the House of Representatives; defeated by sixty-two votes, while the remainder of the Democratic ticket fell from three hundred to fourteen hundred behind. The year following (1819), he was nominated State Senator for an unexpired term, elected, and subsequently for a full term. Previous to the nomination of Governor Shulze, General Eyster was spoken of as a gubernatorial candidate. In 1822 he removed to Harrisburg, and, in 1824, he resigned his seat in the Senate, and was appointed Deputy Surveyor General, an office he retained for fifteen years. He afterwards became cashier of a bank at Hagerstown, Md., but after a year's absence, returned to Harrisburg, where he passed the remainder of his life. He died there on the 24th of March, 1858. He married, in 1810, Mary Middlecoff, of Adams county, who died at Harrisburg, March 24, 1867, at the age of seventy-five years.

cratic *State Journal*, which he edited with ability. In 1843 he was editor of *The Commonwealth*, which had but a brief existence, and, in the same year, *The Argus*, in connection with Valentine Best, who was proprietor of the paper. In 1845-6, he was engaged as a clerk in in one of the departments at Washington city. In 1850 he removed to Janesville, Wis., where he resided several years, and of which town he was appointed postmaster. In 1852 he returned to Harrisburg, and at once took a position on the *Patriot*, which he edited with much vigor. In 1874 he was appointed a clerk in the Harrisburg postoffice, which he held up to the time of his death. As a journalist, he ranked with the ablest writers of his day. His fund of knowledge was large ; a natural student, he read extensively, and retained the valuable portions of what he read, so that his acquaintance with the English classics, which, with the political history of his own country, made him a valuable attache of the editorial staff with which he was associated. Mr. Crabb m. Elizabeth M. Mitchell, of Caledonia county, N. Y., who d. December 21, 1875, at Harrisburg, Pa.; and had issue (surname Crabb) :

    1. *George-W.*; entered the army as private, company I, 2d regiment, Pennsylvania volunteers, April 20, 1861 ; discharged July 2, 1861 ; appointed by the president, second lieutenant, 5th artillery, May 14, 1861 ; promoted brevet first lieutenant, September 17, 1862, for gallant and meritorious service in the battle of Antietam : promoted second lieutenant, 5th artillery, February 22, 1865 ; brevet captain, April 2, 1865, for gallant and meritorious service during the siege of Petersburg, Va.; m., and had issue.

    2. *Ella*, resides at Chattanooga, Tenn.

    3. *Louisa*, a teacher at Harrisburg, Pa.

    4. *Anna*, resides at Harrisburg, Pa.

    5. *Harry P.*, b. 1843; d. February 26, 1865.

v. H.-Louisa, b. 1810 ; d. December 7, 1846; m. George Myers Lauman, son of William Lauman and Elizabeth Myers ; and had issue (surname Lauman):

    1. *Ella-Virginia*, m., first, Dr. Hiester, of Reading, Pa.; and had issue (surname Hiester): *Anna*, m. Dr. McCherry ; and *Edwardine*; m., secondly, —— Keim, of Reading, Pa.

2. *Edwardine-Hubley*, d. January 19, 1871 ; m. Beverly Randolph Keim, b. November 13, 1847 ; and had issue (surname Keim): *Florence*, b. August 3, 1864.
3. *George-Somerfield*, d. s. p.
4. *Simon-Cameron*, d. s. p.

VI. MARY KENDIG,[2] (Martin,[1]) b. about 1783 ; m. RICHARD LARROBEE. They had issue (surname Larrobee) :

   i. Mary-Ann.
   ii. Henry, m. Jane Lester ; and had issue (surname Larrobee): *Richard*, m. Rachel Taylor ; and *David-W.*, m. Julia Welsh.
   iii. Ann-Eliza.
   iv. Martin.

VII. MARTIN KENDIG,[3] (John,[2] Martin,[1]) b. December 31, 1797, in Sunbury, Northumberland county, Pa.; d. August 28, 1850, near Middletown, Pa. After receiving a fair education, he learned the trade of saddle and harness-making at Harrisburg, and, upon attaining his majority, established the business at Middletown, carrying on, with his brother, Daniel, the lumber trade. Subsequently, in company with the latter, and Judge Murray, erected a large saw-mill at the mouth of the Swatara, and established an extensive business. He served as one of the auditors of the county from 1826 to 1828, and represented Dauphin county in the Legislature from 1837 to 1839. Mr. Kendig was an enterprising citizen, and a gentleman of probity and worth, highly esteemed in the community, and influential in public affairs. He was thrice married ; m., first, June 15, 1820, REBECCA MCFARLAND, of Lower Paxtang township, Dauphin county, Pa.; b. June 28, 1800 ; d. April 1, 1831. They had issue :

   i. Rev. Daniel, b. September, 1824 ; chaplain in U. S. army ; stationed at posts of Fort Steilacoom, Washington Territory, and the Presidio, San Francisco, from December 18, 1859, to May 27, 1867 ; post chaplain, April 3, 1867 ; on retired list U. S. A., 1891.
   ii. Walter-Henry, b. June 3, 1830 ; was educated in the public schools of Middletown, and learned merchandising ; became a railroad contractor, and at present engaged in the lumber business; was appointed by President Lincoln postmaster at Middletown, and removed by President Johnson ; m., December 25, 1856, Jane E. McMurtrie,

dau. of William McMurtrie, of Huntingdon, Pa.; and had issue: *Martin*, d. May 3, 1894; and *Edith-M.*

Mr. Kendig m., secondly, SARAH SEBAUGH, b. August 24, 1808; d. March 4, 1842; daughter of Conrad Sebaugh, of Middletown. They had issue:

iii. John-Allen, d. November, 1855; unm.
iv. James, d. November, 1891, s. p.; m. Maria Wilhelm.
v. Rebecca, m. Samuel Landis, of Middletown, Pa.
vi. William, m. Emma Nixon; and had issue: *Walter, George, Robert*, and *Faleda.*
vii. Elizabeth, m. Van Buren Beane, and had issue (surname Beane): *Horace, Alice, Hattie*, and *Cora*; reside in Iowa.

Mr. Kendig m., thirdly, September 1, 1842, Mrs. RACHEL (SHELLY) CROLL, widow of Abner Croll; d. November, 1875; no surviving issue.

VIII. SARAH KENDIG,[3] (John,[2] Martin,[1]) b. 1800; d. March 1, 1859, at Middletown; m. GEORGE ALLEN, b. September 8, 1800; d. February 14, 1848. They had issue (surname Allen):

i. Edward-A., d. 1894; m. Frances Rice, and had *George, James, Mary*, and *Charles.*
ii. Charles, m. Mary Rice, and had *Alvin.*
iii. Lot, d. in Buffalo, N. Y.; m. Augusta Bastedo.

IX. DANIEL KENDIG,[3] (John,[2] Martin,[1]) b. March 16, 1802, at Sunbury, Pa.; d. December 31, 1876, at Middletown, Pa. He went to Middletown when quite young, and was apprenticed to his brother Martin to learn saddlery, subsequently entering into partnership in the lumber trade, then the great business of that town. In 1862, he was appointed assessor of internal revenue for the district, which he had held until removed by President Johnson. He was at one time a candidate for sheriff, but defeated; was an elder in the Presbyterian church, and a gentleman of high integrity. He died at Middletown, December 31, 1876, and buried in the cemetery there. Mr. Kendig was twice married—first to SUSAN SHELLY, b. 1810; d. March, 1837. They had issue:

i. Annie-E.
ii. Benjamin, m. Margaret Ringland, and had *Marion*, d. s. p., and *Frank.*
iii. Frank, resides in Illinois.

iv. Louisa, dec'd ; m. William D. Hendrickson ; and had issue surname Hendrickson): *Alice, Annie,* and *William.*

Daniel Kendig m. secondly, SARAH RUTHERFORD. They had issue:

v. Clara, m. Van Camp Coolbaugh.
vi. Susan, m. A. Jackson Foster ; d. January 20, 1895, leaving six children.
vii. Mary, m. Joseph Fackler.
viii. Charles, m. Myra Hinny.
ix. John, m. Mary Jaeger.

FAMILY OF KUNKEL.

I. CHRISTIAN KUNKEL,[2] son of John-Christian Kunkel,[1] b. July 10, 1757, in the Palatinate, Germany; d. September 8, 1823, in Harrisburg, Pa. His father arrived in Pennsylvania September 23, 1766, subsequently locating at or near York. Christian was brought up to mercantile pursuits. In the War of the Revolution he was commissioned an ensign in Col. Slagle's battalion of associators, and was in active service during the campaign around Philadelphia in 1777 and 1778. In 1786, in company with his brother-in-law, George Hoyer, he located at Harrisburg. There he at once entered into business, which, with his indomitable energy and industry, proved highly successful. He was one of the prime movers and contributed toward the organization of the first German church in Harrisburg. He was burgess of the borough in 1796, and frequently a member of the council. He was elected, in 1809, one of the directors of the branch bank of Philadelphia at Harrisburg, and the same year appointed by Governor Snyder one of the commissioners for erecting a bridge over the Susquehanna, and was interested in other enterprises. His life was an active and busy one. Mr. Kunkel was twice married; m., first, on May 4, 1779, at York, Pa., CATHARINE HOYER, b. October, 31, 1758, in the Palatinate, Germany; d. August 27, 1796, at Harrisburg, Pa. They had issue:

2.   i. *George*, b. December 15, 1784; m. Catharine Ziegler.
     ii. *John*, b. April 22, 1788.
3.   iii. *Susannah*, b. May 31, 1790; m. David Hummel.
     iv. *Mary*, b. June 19, 1792; d. s. p.
4.   v. *Jacob*, b. April 23, 1794; m. Rebecca Stine.

Christian Kunkel m., secondly, May 25, 1797, ANNA MARIA ELIZABETH WELSHOFER, b. December 1, 1773, in York county, Pa.; d. July 24, 1862, at Harrisburg, Pa. They had issue:

5.   vi. *Elizabeth*, b. May 9, 1798; m. John Charles Barnitz.
6.   vii. *Benjamin*, b. August 12, 1801; m. Magdalena Gross.

7. viii. *Catharine*, b. December 22, 1803 ; m. Joseph Ross.
8. ix. *Sarah*, b. December 6, 1805 ; m., first, William Carson ; secondly, James Gilliard.
   x. *Magdalena*, b. May 26, 1809 ; d. s. p.
   xi. *Lydia*, b. November 9, 1811 ; d. February 10, 1866 ; m. John Peter Keller, (see *Keller record*).
9. xii. Rev. *Christian-Frederick*, b. September 12, 1814 ; m. Amanda M. Wilhelm.
10. xiii. *Samuel*, b. May 26, 1817 ; m. Rachel Bomberger.

II. GEORGE KUNKEL,³ (Christian,² John-Christian,¹) b. December 15, 1784, in York, Pa.; d. July 29, 1850, in Harrisburg, Pa.; was a prosperous merchant at Harrisburg for many years ; m., November 20, 1814, CATHARINE ZIEGLER, b. January 21, 1797; d. July 3, 1833, at Harrisburg, Pa., daughter of George Ziegler. They had issue:

11. i. *John-Christian*, b. September 18, 1816 ; m. Elizabeth Crain Rutherford.
12. ii. *George-Ziegler*, b. 1820 ; m. Isabella Herr.
    iii. *Elizabeth*, b. March 1, 1828 ; d. June 18, 1882; m., November 18, 1841, Daniel W. Gross, (see *Gross record*).
    iv. *Susan*, m. Prof. Thomas C. Porter, (see *Bucher record*).
    v. *Catharine*, m., July 10, 1866, George H. Small, cashier of First National Bank of Harrisburg, Pa., from its organization until September, 1885 ; and had issue (surname Small):
       1. *John-Kunkel;* professor of botany, Columbia College, New York.
    vi. *Sarah*, m. John Wiggins Simonton, (see *Wiggins and Simonton record*).

III. SUSANNAH KUNKEL,³ (Christian,² John-Christian,¹) b. May 31, 1790 ; d. January 1, 1851, in Harrisburg, Pa., and there buried ; m., October 13, 1807, DAVID HUMMEL, b. September 8, 1784, at Hummelstown, Pa.; d. June 30, 1860, at Harrisburg, Pa. He learned the trade of a saddler, and afterwards established himself in business in Harrisburg. He was quite prominent in public affairs ; was deputy sheriff under Melchior Rahm ; served as treasurer of the county of Dauphin from 1821 to 1824, and county commissioner from 1839 to 1841. They had issue (surname Hummel):

   i. *Catharine*, m. Philip W. Seibert.
   ii. *David*, m. Sarah Bombaugh, and had *Charles-B.*, killed at

Fredericksburg, at the age of twenty-two years; and *Catharine*, m. Augustus L. Chayne.
- iii. *Christian*, d. s. p.
- iv. *Mary*, m. Alexander W. Watson.
- v. *Elizabeth*, m. William R. Gorgas.
- vi. *George*, resides in Mechanicsburg, Pa.
- vii. *Albert*, d. July 27, 1885, aged fifty-nine years.
- viii. *Susan*, m. James L. Reily.
- ix. *Annie*, m. Eli H. Coover, M D., of Harrisburg, Pa.
- x. *Emma*.

IV. JACOB KUNKEL,³ (Christian,² John-Christian,¹) b. April 23, 1794, at Harrisburg, Pa.; d. February 23, 1835, at Greencastle, Franklin county, Pa.; m. REBECCA STINE, daughter of Daniel and Elizabeth Stine, b. February 7, 1799; d. October 23, 1865, at Harrisburg, Pa., and with her husband there buried. They had issue:

- i. *Christian*.
- ii. *Andrew-Jackson*, d. July 15, 1856.
- iii. *Elizabeth-W.*, m. James Myers.
- iv. *Harriet-Stine*, m. Anthony King, b. March 27, 1821; d. September 17, 1884; for many years a prominent merchant at Harrisburg, Pa.; and had issue (surname King):
    1. *Rebecca-Stine*, b. 1849; d. February 21, 1895; unm.
    2. *George-Kunkel*.
    3. *Lucy*, m. George F. Ross; and had issue (surname Ross): *Walter*, and *Frank*.
    4. *Lillie-M.*, d. September 29, 1881.
    5. *Hallie-C.*, d. May 31, 1873.
    6. *Mary*, m. Frank S. Keet.
    7. *Caroline*, m. Gordon H. Mullen, of Philadelphia.
- v. *Jacob*, m. Mary Evans.
- vi. *George*, b. 1823, in Greencastle; d. January 25, 1885, at Baltimore, Md.; learned printing in Philadelphia; in 1844 he appeared on the stage as a vocalist, and was considered one of the ablest delineators of negro minstrelsy; in the character of "Uncle Tom," he became widely celebrated both in this country and England: while his rendition of "The Old Sexton," remains unsurpassed; in person he was nearly six feet tall, with a fine expressive face; he m., in 1864, Ada Proctor, of Baltimore, and they had issue *Mamie*, and *George*.

V. ELIZABETH KUNKEL,³ (Christian,² John-Christian,¹) b. May 9, 1798, in Harrisburg, Pa.; d. January 19, 1880, in Harrisburg, Pa.; m., October 17, 1820, JOHN CHARLES BARNITZ, b. February 26, 1795, in York, Pa.; d. January 31, 1872, in Harrisburg, Pa.; son of George Barnitz (1770-1844) and Maria Catharine Spangler, (1769-1824). His ancestors were early settlers in York, and among the more prominent in the business and political affairs of that section. John C. was educated in the schools of York; learned the occupation of a brewer, and, in 1831, removed with his family to Harrisburg, Pa., where he built a brewery and which he managed for a long period; was an active and energetic citizen, and, in the First Lutheran church, with which he was connected many years, filled responsible positions, and was organist until the burning of the First church building, at Harrisburg, and also of the German Lutheran church there. They had issue (surname Barnitz):

 i. Frederick-Augustus, b. September 4, 1821, in York, Pa.; educated at Pennsylvania College, Gettysburg; licensed to preach in 1844; served as pastor of the congregation at Jersey Shore 1845 to 1849; Bloody Run (Bedford county) 1849 to 1852; Smicksburg, Pa., 1852 to 1855; Lairdsville, Pa., 1855 to 1861; and Ashland, Pa., 1861 to 1863; when, owing to impaired health, retired from the ministry; was twice married; m., first, March 9, 1846, Sarah J. Babb, of Jersey Shore. Pa.; d. July 23, 1864; no issue; m., secondly, November 13, 1866, Dora Reimsnyder, of Hummelstown, Pa.; and had issue (surname Barnitz): *Margaret-Jane*.

 ii. George-Cantler, b. October 4, 1825; m., December 8, 1850, Henrietta Loucks; and had issue (surname Barnitz):
  1. *Clara-Elizabeth*, b. Oct. 11, 1851; d. March 3, 1874.
  2. *John-Charles*, b. June 18, 1854; m., October 21, 1879, Annie Evans, of Elmira, N. Y.; and had issue (surname Barnitz):
   a. Clara-Elizabeth, b. June 17, 1885, in Washington, D. C.
  3. *Cassandra-Susan*, b. September 12, 1856; m., August 23, 1881, by Rev. A. H. Studebaker, Harry A. Nunemacher; and had issue (surname Nunemacher):
   a. George-Barnitz, b. July 17, 1883, in Round Rock, Texas.
   b. Mabel-E., b. Mar. 26, 1885, in Harrisburg, Pa.
  4. *Henrietta-Loucks*, b. September 15, 1862.

 iii. Jerome-Theophilus, b. September 30, 1830; m., October 19,

Family of Kunkel.

1852, Mary Henrietta Denning, dau. of James Denning and Caroline Burnett; and had issue (surname Barnitz):

1. *James*, b. November 19, 1853 ; m., 1879, Mary Bushman, of Pittsburgh, Pa.; and had issue (surname Barnitz):
    a. *John-Shoemaker*, b. 1882, in Pittsburgh, Pa.
    b. *Jerome-Denning*, b. 1884, in Akron, Ohio.
2. *Elizabeth-Kunkel*, b. September 30, 1855; m., October 19, 1875, John R. Shoemaker.
3. *Charles Henry*, b. August 12, 1857 ; m., November 19, 1884, Clara Elizabeth Vance.
4. *George Plitt*, b. June 25, 1859.
5. *Mary-Caroline*, b. June 27, 1861.
6. *Alice-Boyd*, b. May 23, 1872.
7. *LaTrobe-Maurer*, b. November 4, 1874.

iv. *Caroline*, m. Peter Keller Boyd, (*see Boyd of Derry*).
v. *Margaret-Jane*, resides in Harrisburg, Pa.

VI. BENJAMIN KUNKEL,[3] (Christian,[2] John-Christian,[1]) b. August 12, 1801, in Harrisburg, Pa.; d. September 22, 1888, in Philadelphia; m., September 17, 1827, MAGDALENA GROSS, b. September 15, 1810, in Middletown, Pa.; d. July 29, 1892, in Philadelphia. They had issue:

i. *Christian-H.*, b. October 1, 1828 ; m. Louisa Smith, dau. of Henry Smith, of Middletown, Pa.
ii. *George-Gross*, b. June 27, 1830 ; d. February 28, 1876 ; m., April 9, 1867, Elizabeth Reel, dau. of Jacob Reel, of Harrisburg, Pa.; and had issue.
iii. *Lovenia*, b. February 21, 1832 ; d. September, 1832.
iv. *Mary-Elizabeth*, b. March 14, 1834 ; d. December 12, 1887 ; m. Edward J. Lauman, son of William Lauman, of Middletown, Pa.
v. *Benjamin-S.*, b. June 20, 1836; m., May 15, 1862, Almeda C. Zollinger, dau. of Elias Zollinger, of Harrisburg, Pa.
vi. *Adaline*, b. June 24, 1838 ; d. May 9, 1870 ; m. Henry J. Rife, son of Jacob Rife, of Middletown, Pa.
vii. *Samuel-Augustus*, b. April 11, 1841 ; d. July 8, 1870 ; m., February 18, 1854, Mary E. Reel, dau. of John Reel, of Harrisburg, Pa.; and had *John-A.*, d. s. p.
viii. *Edwin-F.*, b. March 15, 1843.
ix. *William-F.*, b. July 20, 1846 ; m. Mary Roumfort, dau. of Charles E. Roumfort, of Harrisburg, Pa.
x. *Charles-H.*, b. November 23, 1849.

VII. CATHARINE KUNKEL,[3] (Christian,[2] John-Christian,[1]) b. December 22, 1803, at Harrisburg, Pa.; resides in Middletown, Pa.; m., September 19, 1822, by Rev. George Lochman, D. D., JOSEPH ROSS, b. July 14, 1798, at Elizabethtown, Pa.; d. January 26, 1863, at Middletown, Pa. At a proper age he went to Harrisburg, Pa., to learn the mercantile business. Afterwards he engaged in said occupation in that place, and then moved to Middletown, where he continued keeping store till near the close of his life. In the year 1824 he became acquainted with Rev. John Winebrenner, who visited Middletown to preach the Gospel, and under him became converted. At the first opportunity he identified himself with the Church of God, being one of the original members of that denomination in Middletown, where he continued to be among its most active workers until his death. His name appears as a ruling elder in the journal of the Fourth Annual Eldership, held at Middletown, December 25, 1833. He was licensed to preach at the Seventh Annual Eldership which convened at Churchtown, Cumberland county, November 5, 1836. At the time of his death he was a member of the board of publication, and treasurer of the General Eldership as well as treasurer of the East Pennsylvania Eldership. He traveled and labored in the ministry, at protracted and other meetings, "without money and without price," and was an eminently successful revival preacher. His liberality and benevolence were all well known at home, and in all the churches. His warmth of heart and affection made him beloved by all his acquaintances. He was a strict disciplinarian, and a great lover of order. Besides, he carried his religion into his business, being scrupulously truthful and honest in all his dealings, loving justice and hating sin in every form. He was devotedly attached to the doctrines of the Church of God, fearlessly defended them, and worked actively to establish them. They had issue (surname Ross):

 i. Christian-Kunkel, b. November 6, 1823; m., July 24, 1862, by Rev. Mr. Sewalt, Anuie Lewis, of Brookfield, Mass.
 ii. Joseph, b. November 11, 1825; m., March 19, 1849, by Rev. Abraham Swartz, Mary Bowman, of Cumberland county, Pa.
 iii. William-Carson, b. April 15, 1828; m., March 9, 1858, by Rev. Abraham Swartz, Mary A. Rife, of Middletown.

Family of Kunkel. 363

  iv. *Henry-A.*, b. August 15, 1830; m., June 22, 1871, by Rev. George F. Stelling, at Vernal Bank, Chester county, Pa., Mary A. Hartman.
  v. *John-J.*, b. August 20, 1832; m., December 25, 1860, by Rev. Benjamin Hunt, Lavinia A. Bunn, of Schellsburg, Pa.
  vi. *Harriet-Ann*, b. October 2, 1834; m., October 30, 1862, by Rev. D. A. L. Laverty, W. H. Beane, M. D., of Hagerstown, Md.
  vii. *George-F.*, b. April 17, 1837.
  viii. *Catherine-E.*, b. August 11, 1839.
  ix. *James-Mackey*, b. October 4, 1841; m., October 15, 1878, at Magnolia, Delaware, by Rev. Thomas Terry, Emma Terry.

VIII. SARAH KUNKEL,[3] (Christian,[2] John-Christian,[1]) b. December 6, 1805, at Harrisburg, Pa.; d. 1887 in Washington, D. C.; was twice married; m., first, WILLIAM M. CARSON, b. December 10, 1796; d. March 3, 1833. They had issue (surname Carson):

  i. *Elizabeth*, m. J. Brisben Boyd, (see *Boyd of Derry*).
  ii. *William-G.*, b. May 17, 1830; d. January 22, 1831.
  iii. *Mary-E.*, b. January 8, 1832; d. September 14, 1832.

Mrs. Sarah-Kunkel Carson m., secondly, JAMES GILLIARD, b. September 21, 1808; d. April 5, 1850; buried at Harrisburg, Pa. They had issue (surname Gilliard):

  iv. *Margaret*, m., October 18, 1864, George W. Parsons; and had issue (surname Parsons): *Jessie, Harriet, James, Robert, Lillie*, and *Hile*.
  v. *Sarah.*
  vi. *Mary.*
  vii. *Carrie*, m. Gilbert B. Towles, of Washington city; and had issue (surname Towles): *Alice, Bessie, Lucius-Lehman*, d. s. p., *Caroline*, and *Therett*.
  viii. *Emma*, b. March 4, 1849; d. October 22, 1849.

IX. Rev. CHRISTIAN-FREDERICK KUNKEL,[3] (Christian,[2] John-Christian,[1]) b. September 12, 1814, at Harrisburg, Pa.; d. September 16, 1865; m. AMANDA M. WILHELM, b. April 17, 1824. They had issue:

  i. *Charles-Henry*, b. April 2, 1842; resides in Greencastle, Pa.; m., May, 1870, Harriet Redsecker; and had *William*, d. s. p., and *Charles-E.*
  ii. *William-F.*, b. August 6, 1844.

364   *Pennsylvania Genealogies.*

    iii. Annie-Elizabeth, b. July 12, 1846; m., February 8, 1882, Charles C. Hackett.
    iv. Mosheim-Sidney, b. December 12, 1848.
    v. James-B., b. December 2, 1852; d. May 24, 1853.
    vi. Amanda-B., b. August 1, 1854; m., November 24, 1880, P. S. Wilhelm; and had *Samuel*.

X. SAMUEL KUNKEL,³ (Christian,² John-Christian,¹) b. May 26, 1817, in Harrisburg, Pa.; d. March 23, 1892, at Shippensburg, Pa.; m., in 1842, RACHEL BOMBERGER, b. February 26, 1821, at Middletown, Pa., (*see Bomberger record*). They had issue:

    i. George-Jacob, b. April 28, 1843; an attorney-at-law, Harrisburg, Pa.
    ii. John-Christian, b. July 26, 1845; d. April 17, 1887, at Shippensburg, Pa.
    iii. Charles-Augustus, b. June 10, 1847; resides at Harrisburg, Pa.; m., January 13, 1881, by Rev. C. W. Buoy, in Grace M. E. church, Harrisburg, Eliza Beverlina Waugh, b. November 21, 1855, (*see Beatty record*); and had issue :
        1. *Beverly-Waugh*, b. October 27, 1881.
        2. *Rachel*, b. October 17, 1882.
    iv. Anna-Elizabeth, b. November 26, 1848; m. William S. Montgomery; and had issue (surname Montgomery): *John-Kunkel*, d. May 5, 1893, and *Rachel-May*.
    v. Samuel, b. August 28, 1850; m. Annie Mary Fager.
    vi. Lydia-Josephine, b. May 8, 1852; d. April 4, 1854.
    vii. Ada-Serene, b. February 9, 1854; m., October 9, 1878, Rev. Isaac Martin Motter, b. January 19, 1852, at Emmitsburg, Md.; and had issue (surname Motter):
        1. *Samuel-Lewis*, b. August 21, 1879.
        2. *Guy-Kunkel*, b. December 9, 1880.
        3. *Mary*, b. January 28, 1883; d. February 11, 1883.
        4. *John-Christian*, b. December 28, 1883.
    viii. Lilly-May, b. March 11, 1856; m., August 15, 1889, Alf. A. Aughenbaugh, of Pittsburgh.
    ix. Rachel, b. September 2, 1858; d. May 5, 1884.

XI. JOHN CHRISTIAN KUNKEL,⁴ (George,³ Christian,² John-Christian,¹) b. September 18, 1816, in Harrisburg, Pa.; d. October 14, 1870, in Harrisburg, Pa.; he received a liberal scientific and classical education in the schools at Gettysburg and at Jefferson College, Canonsburg, at which latter institution he graduated. After leaving college he entered Carlisle law school under Judge Read, subsequently reading law with

James McCormick, and admitted to the Dauphin county bar. After his admission to the bar, he remained several years in the office with Mr. McCormick. He rapidly gained a large practice and a reputation which few members of the bar enjoy. He also became active in politics, and, in the earnest and exciting campaign of 1844, when the young men of the nation had made Henry Clay, then in the zenith of his career, their standard-bearer, the best talent and the most brilliant eloquence that ever graced the American rostrum was called into requisition. Amid all the magnificent display and power of logic, that of the young orator of Pennsylvania, as Mr. Kunkel was recognized, was conspicuous as well for force of argument as for grace of delivery. The same year he was elected to the Legislature, re-elected in 1845, and again in 1850. In 1851 he was elected to the State Senate, and was chosen speaker of that body at the close of the first session of his term. As a legislator Mr. Kunkel was prominent for the wisdom of his counsel as well as for the power of his eloquence. His services at the capital added greatly to his already wide reputation as a pure statesman and accomplished scholar. In 1854 and again in 1856 he was elected to the United States Congress. During the four years he spent in Washington city, he was regarded throughout the country as one of the ablest statesmen at the National capital. In 1858 he retired from public life, and gave his exclusive attention to the practice of his profession, varying the course of his life by occasionally helping a friend in a political canvass, and, wherever he went he was always the favorite of the people. In 1868 he was stricken down with paralysis, and never fully regained his health, dying as previously stated. Perchance, the loss of no member of the Dauphin county bar was so severely felt as that of Mr. Kunkel, if we are to judge of the glowing, sincere, and fraternal tributes paid to his memory by his brethren in the profession at the time of his death. Mr. Kunkel m., October 20, 1857, ELIZABETH CRAIN RUTHERFORD, daughter of Dr. William Wilson Rutherford and Eleanor Crain ; she resides at Harrisburg, Pa. They had issue :

  i. John, b. September 22, 1858; m. Louisa Sergeant.

  ii. William-Rutherford, b. March 30, 1861 ; d. Dec. 30, 1864.
  iii. Sarah-Eleanor, b. September 27, 1866 ; d. June 11, 1871.
 XII. GEORGE ZIEGLER KUNKEL,[4] (George,[3] Christian,[2] John-Christian,[1]) b. 1820, in Harrisburg, Pa.; a banker ; resides at Harrisburg, Pa.; m., December 28, 1852, ISABELLA HERR, daughter of Daniel Herr and Sarah Gilbert. They had issue :

  i. Mary, d. s. p.
  ii. George; educated at the Harrisburg Academy, and graduated from Franklin and Marshall College in 1876 ; studied law with Hon. John W. Simonton, and admitted to the Dauphin county bar in 1878. In 1885 he was elected district attorney, and re-elected in 1888. He was elected a member of the General Assembly in 1892 and again in 1894 ; and has won a prominent place among the legislators of the State. Mr. Kunkel m., November 11, 1891, Mae Minster ; and they had issue :
   1. *George*, b. March 10, 1893.
   2. *William-Minster*, b. July 31, 1894.
  iii. Daniel-Herr, b. 1857 ; d. April 21, 1880.
  iv. Sarah-B., d. inf.
  v. William A., d. inf.
  vi. A.·Catharine.
  vii. Paul-Augustus, graduated from Franklin and Marshall College ; studied law, and was admitted to the bar October 9, 1888 ; m., November 23, 1893, Mary Isabella King ; and had issue :
   1. *Arthur-King*, b. September 14, 1894.
  viii. Caroline-Beecher, m. September 25, 1890, Christian Gingerich Nissley ; and had issue (surname Nissley) :
   1. *Isabel*, b. June 23, 1891.
   2. *Anna-Ober*, b. July 24, 1894.

LINN OF LURGAN.

I. WILLIAM LINN,[1] the ancestor, emigrated from the north of Ireland, in 1732, and settled in Chester county. According to family tradition, his wife died in Ireland, and he brought with him an only son, William. They remained in Chester county but a few years, when, following the tide of emigration, they settled upon the frontiers of the Purchase of October, 1736, near what is now known as Roxbury, in Franklin county. The names of William Linn, senior, and William Linn, junior, appear on the assessment list of Lurgan township, Cumberland county, for the year 1751, one year after the erection of Cumberland county (1750). Here the ancestor died, having nearly reached the one hundredth year of his age. His father fought on the side of "The Orange" at Boyne, July 1, 1690, and was said to have been in Captain Hugh Wilson's company, the first Irish officer who crossed the river. Hugh Wilson's son went to the "Irish Settlement;" the Greggs came to Chester county the same year the Linns came —the descendants of these three soldiers of Boyne-water became kindred in 1869, when William H. Sage, of Ithaca, N. Y., was married to Jennie, daughter of Hon. Andrew Gregg Curtin, (*see Gregg and Curtin record*).

II. WILLIAM LINN,[2] Jr., (William,[1]) b. in 1722, in Ireland, was an officer in Middle Spring church. In June, 1755, he was in Philadelphia with his wagon, and was pressed into service, with his team, to haul supplies to General Braddock's army, and was at the noted defeat. He died April 16, 1812, and is buried in the graveyard attached to Middle Spring church. William Linn m., first, SUSANNA TRIMBLE; according to tradition, she died in Shippensburg, in November, 1755, where, in consequence of an Indian raid, the frontier inhabitants had gathered. They had issue, all born in Lurgan township :

3.   i. *William*, b. February 27, 1752; m., first, Rebecca Blair.
4.   ii. *John*, b. April 2, 1754; m. Ann Fleming.

William Linn² m., secondly, JANE MCCORMICK. They had issue:

5. iii. *James*, b. October 17, 1761; m. Griselda Patterson.
    iv. *Susanna*, b. 1765; m. Charles Maclay, (see *Maclay of Lurgan*).
    v. *Nancy*, b. 1768.
    vi. *Jane*, b. 1770; m., December 18, 1800, Abraham Smith, removed to Urbana, Ohio. Abraham Smith was one of the survivors of the massacre at Crooked-Billet, now Hatboro', Montgomery county, May 1, 1778, where his captain, Charles Maclay, the elder, was killed.
    vii. *Isaiah*, b. 1772; d., unm., April 20, 1809, in Union county, Pa.; bur. in Buffalo Cross-Roads Presbyterian churchyard.
    viii. *Charles*, d., unm., December, 1813.
    ix. *George*, d., unm., July. 1808.
6. x. *David*, b. May 28, 1776; m. Margery Coulter.

III. WILLIAM LINN,³ (William,² William,¹) b. February 27, 1752; graduated at Princeton, N. J., class 1772; studied theology under Rev. Robert Cooper, D. D.; appointed chaplain of Fifth and Sixth Pennsylvania battalions, February 15, 1776; pastor at Big Spring, now Newville, Cumberland county, until 1784; president of Washington College, Maryland, 1784–1785; pastor of Collegiate Dutch church, N. Y., 1786–1808; and first chaplain of the House of Representatives, U. S., May 1, 1789. His published works are " Sermons, Historical and Characteristical," N. Y., 1791; "Signs of the Times," N. Y., 1794; " A Funeral Eulogy on General Washington, delivered February 22, 1800, before the New York Society of the Cincinnati ;" " Sermon on the Death of General Alexander Hamilton," &c. Shortly before his death, Dr. Linn was elected president of Union College, Schenectady, but was never inaugurated. He died in Albany, N. Y., January 8, 1808. Dr. Linn m., first, January 10, 1774, REBECCA BLAIR, daughter of Rev. John Blair, vice-president of College of New Jersey, at Princeton, 1767–1768. They had issue:

7. i. *Elizabeth*, b. 1775; m. Charles Brockden Brown.
    ii. *John-Blair*, b. March 14, 1777, in Shippensburg, Pa.; graduated from Columbia College, N. Y., in 1795; read law under Alexander Hamilton; abandoned that profession for the ministry, and licensed 1798; installed co-pastor of First Presbyterian church of Philadelphia, 1799. Dr.

Linn's published writings are "The Powers of Genius," a poem, second edition, published 1802; "Valerian," a poem, published in 1805, after his death, with a sketch of his life, by Charles Brockden Brown, his brother-in-law. Dr. Linn, m., in 1799, Esther Bailey, daughter of Col. John Bailey, of Poughkeepsie, N. Y. They had one son, *John-Blair*, who died in 1858. Dr. Linn died August 30, 1804. His widow married John R. Bleeker, of Albany, and Mary, her daughter by Mr. Bleeker, became the wife of Hon. Horatio Seymour, of Utica, N. Y.

iii. Susan, b. October 30, 1778; d. May 5, 1824, in Ithaca, N. Y.; m., October 19, 1810, Simeon DeWitt, b. December 26, 1756; d. December 3, 1834; Surveyor General U. S. until July 13, 1796, and afterwards Surveyor General of N. Y.; Mrs. Dewitt was the author of a novel, entitled "Justinea," among the early publications of the Harpers; and of a poem entitled "The Pleasures of Religion;" and had issue (surname DeWitt):

1. *Susan-Linn*, b. September 3, 1811; d. April 1, 1849, at Milwaukee, Wis.; m., May 28, 1836, Hon. Levi Hubbell, b. at Ballston, N. Y., April 15, 1808; graduated at Union College; Adjutant General of N. Y., 1833–1836; member of Legislature, 1841; removed to Milwaukee, 1844; circuit judge, 1848; re-elected, 1851; circuit judge and associate justice Supreme Court until 1853; U. S. district attorney of Wisconsin, 1871–1875; d. December 8, 1876, in Milwaukee. (*See vol. viii, Wisconsin Hist. Collections, page 453*); and had issue (surname Hubbell):

    a. *Simeon-D.*, b. February 23, 1837; resides in Lompoc, Santa Barbara county, California.

    b. *Richard-Walter*, b. 1839; now judge in Oconto, Wis.

2. *William-Linn*, b. January 13, 1817; resides in Ithaca, N. Y.

3. *Mary-Linn*, b. February 23, 1819; d. March 20, 1871, at Ithaca.

iv. Rebecca, d. 1825; m., February 5, 1808, William Keese, Esq., attorney-at-law, New York city; b. December 7, 1780; d. March 19, 1819; son of John and Rhoda Keese; and had issue (surname Keese):

1. Rev. *William-Linn*, rector of the Episcopal church at New Haven, Conn., and died there; m. Mary Drake; their sons, *James-Drake, Hobart*, and

Lawrence, all young men of promise, died in early manhood. James D. was a lawyer; Hobart a physician.

2. *John*, b. November 24, 1805; d. May 30, 1856; was the John Keese of most excellent book-selling memory, an extraordinary man in the humorous handling of books and of an audience, &c. (See Keese-ana, by E. A. Duyckinck, Maga. of Am. Hist. vol. i, (1877), page 497; also *ibid.*, 734, Keese-ana continued by his son, Wm. L. Keese; see, also, "John Keese, Wit, Litterateur, and Macænas, by Henry Morford, June and July numbers, New Monthly Magazine, N. Y., 1880, accompanied by portrait.) John Keese m., July, 1832, Elizabeth Willetts, still living, and had issue (surname Keese):

   a. Jonathan-L., b. August 8, 1833; d. in U. S. service, May 9, 1861.

   b. William-L., b. February 25, 1835; m., October 2, 1864, Helen K. Thorne; and had issue (surname Keese): *E.-Willetts*, b. July 2, 1865, and *William-Lawrence*, b. July 4, 1872.

   c. Charlotte W., b. November 5, 1839; m. John A. Sherer; and had issue (surname Sherer): *John-K.*

   d. Charles-Hoffman, b. July 26, 1842; m. Emily Scriven.

   e. John, b. March 20, 1844.

   f. Mary-W., b. November 5, 1845; m. William Fitzhugh.

   g. Benton, b. May 5, 1854.

3. *Theodore*, of Port Chester, N. Y.

v. Mary, d. unm., at Ithaca, N. Y., January 29, 1870.

8. *vi. William*, b. August 30, 1790; m. Mary A. Biers.

viii. Sarah-Livingston, b. May 28, 1793; d. August 24, 1840, in Bethlehem, Pa.; m., May 7, 1817, John W. Peters, of Philadelphia, b. May 19, 1789; d. July 21, 1830; and had issue (surname Peters):

  1. *Frances-C.*, b. March 1, 1818; m. James R. Speed, of Caroline, Tompkins county, N. Y., (Mr. Speed was killed by stroke of lightning May 5, 1854,) and had issue (surname Speed):

    a. Mary-C., b. February 3, 1839; m., July 11,- 1862, Walter M. Boyer; she died in Win

field, Kansas, January 23, 1879, leaving issue
(surname Boyer): *R.-Speed*, and *Fannie-S*.
  b. *Richard*, b. February 25, 1841; d. October 10,
    1882; served in the war of Rebellion.
  c. *Robert-G.-H.*, b. July 5, 1845; m., October 29,
    1872; and had issue: *Robert, Bessie, Mary*,
    and *Reno*.
  d. *Henry-L.*, b. May 4, 1847; m., January 1, 1872:
    and had issue: *Maud*, and *James-R.*
  e. *Jesse-H.*, b. April 23, 1849; m., Henry A.
    Graham, December 17, 1878; and had issue
    (surname Graham): *Samuel-H.*, and *Fannie-S*.
  f. *Sallie-Peters*, b. March 29. 1851, of Slaterville,
    N. Y.
  g. *James-R.*, b. Nov. 9, 1854; d. April 3, 1855.
2. *John-Jordan*, of Ithaca, N. Y., b. August 7, 1825;
  m., May 15, 1848, Mary Snow, b. August 3, 1828,
  and had issue (surname Peters):
    a. *Sarah-L.*, b. March 19, 1850; m., October 2,
      1867, J. Hathaway Clark, b. July, 1847; d.
      February 7, 1883; and had issue (surname
      Clarke): *Herbert-H.*, b. July 25, 1870; *Mary-P.*, b. September 23, 1873; and *Harriet-G.*,
      b. July 13, 1879; d. 1880.
    b. *Harriet-L.*, b. May 26, 1853; m. George Doty;
      and had issue (surname Doty): *Floyd*, and
      Jay.
    c. *Richard-S.*, b. Mar. 7, 1856; d. Aug. 25, 1862.
    d. *Henry-Linn*, b. July 17, 1859.
3. *Mary-L.*, b. March 31, 1828, of Ithaca, N. Y.; m., in
  1875, William Coryell, M. D.; d. Aug. 30, 1880.

William Linn, D. D., had, by his second wife, CATHARINE
MOORE, widow of Dr. Moore, of New York:

  viii. James-Henry, b. February 15, 1798; attorney-at-law of Albany, N. Y.; d. in 1837; unm.

William Linn, D. D., had, by his third wife, *née* HELEN HANSON, d. in Schenectady, in 1846:

9. *ix. Archibald-L.*, b. October 5, 1802; m. Mary TenEyck McClellan.

IV. JOHN LINN,[3] (William,[2] William,[1]) b. April 2, 1754;
removed from Lurgan to Buffalo Valley, now Union county,
Pa., in 1775; d. March 18, 1809; buried in Presbyterian church

yard, Buffalo Cross-roads; m., November 7, 1780, ANN FLEMING, b. September 6, 1761; d. September 4, 1841; daughter of John and Ann Fleming, of Cumberland county. They had issue:

 i. Susanna, b. February 6, 1783; removed to Sugar Creek, Venango county, Pa., d. February 22, 1831; m., March 27, 1804, William Thompson, b. June 7, 1777; d. April 1, 1828, at Sugar Creek; son of Captain James Thompson of Buffalo Valley; and had issue (surname Thompson):

  1. *James*, b. October 11, 1805; d. January 21, 1833. On the morning of that day he was making fire in a stove in his store, in Franklin, Pa., and by mistake used a powder keg, in which there were a few pounds of caked powder, and was killed by the explosion.

  2. *Ann*, b. May 6, 1808; d. 1849; m., May 12, 1831, John B. McCalmont, b. September 7, 1806; d. at Altoona, Ill., February 24, 1884; and had issue (surname McCalmont): *W. R.*, d. 1853, *Susan-E.*, *Sarah A.*, and *Henry*.

  3. *John-L.*, b. May 28, 1810; d. September 9, 1846, in Cooperstown, Venango county, Pa.; m., October 9, 1833, Sarah Snyder, d. December 23, 1880; and had issue (surname Thompson) *Susan*, *Philetus*, *James*, d. 1874, and *John*.

  4. *Susan*, m. —— Bailey; resides in Union City, Erie county, Pa.

  5. *William*, b. May 12, 1812; d. November 16, 1888, at New Brighton, Pa.; m., August 4, 1831, Mary A. Foster; and had issue (surname Thompson): *Samuel*, *John*, *William*, and *Mrs. George Frederick*, all of New Brighton, Pa.

  6. *Elizabeth*, b. June 6, 1818; resides in Tuscola, Ill.; m., November 3, 1835, James Murray; d. January 6, 1877; and had issue (surname Murray): *Alfred*, a soldier of 1861–5, of Portsmouth, O.; *Charity-A.*, m. —— Murphey, of Tuscola, Ill.; *Edgar-T.*, killed by an explosion on Oil Creek, June 19, 1867; *Richard-H.*, *Wilson-L.*, and *James-L.*, of Sidney, Ill.

 ii. Ann, b. April 5, 1787; d. October 13, 1873, at Greencastle, Ind.; m. Andrew McBeth, b. September 10, 1777; d. July 3, 1854; son of John McBeth, of Haines township, Centre county, Pa.; and had issue (surname McBeth):

  1. *Elizabeth-A.*, b. March 24, 1818; d. December 20,

1850; m., January 28, 1840, William H. Coates,
d. March 21, 1859; and had issue (surname
Coates):
- a. *Elizabeth-A.*, b. December 11, 1850; d. December 6, 1871; m. David H. Stevenson, January 5, 1871; and had issue (surname Stevenson): *Elizabeth-S.*, b. Nov. 21, 1871.
2. *John-A.-H*, b. November 5, 1821; d. October 12, 1854, near New Hope, Brown county, Ohio.
3. *Jane-P.*, b. August 19, 1823; d. August 22, 1891, at Greencastle, Ind.; m. W. H. Coates above. Mrs. Coates is founder of Coates College, Terre Haute, Ind., the only college in the State devoted exclusively to the education of young women; she has provided means to purchase good grounds, and, in addition to annual donations, will make it the legatee of her estate.

iii. *William*, b. November 3, 1793; d. October 26, 1834, in Miami county, Ohio; m., October 14, 1824, Jane Morrow, b. March, 1802; d. March 15, 1848; and had issue:
1. *Matilda*, b. August 5, 1827; d. May 18, 1849; m. John Bobo.
2. *William-M.*, b. November 22, 1831; m., March 31, 1852, Maria Reed; she d. January 28, 1854; and had issue: *John-W.*, b. January 21, 1854; reside near Piqua, Ohio.

10.   iv. *John*, b. January 8, 1797, m. Mary F. Chamberlin.
v. *Margaret*, b. December 27, 1799; d. February 7, 1873, at Sugar Creek, Venango county; m., May 13, 1823, Joseph McCalmont, b. November 23, 1798; d. April 22, 1874; and had issue (surname McCalmont):
1. *Jemima-L.*, b. November 22, 1824; d. August 23, 1858; m., December 8, 1846, Andrew Johnston, of Huntingdon, Pa.; d. February 17, 1885, aged 83 years; and had issue (surname Johnston): *A.-P.-W.*, of Harrisburg, *Catharine*, of Greenville, Pa., *Jemima-L.*, m. W. A. Crawford, Cooperstown, Venango county, Pa., and *Joseph-M.*, Nebraska.
2. *Emily-A.*, b. August 1, 1827; m., November 26, 1864, Samuel Cooper, of Webster City, Iowa; and had issue (surname Cooper): *Ida-B.*, *John-McC.*, *Edwin*, *William*, and *Charles*.
3. *Sarah-J.*, b. July 14, 1831; m., December 16, 1852, T. W. Brown, d. June 27, 1886, near Greenville, Mercer county; and had issue (surname Brown):
- a. *George-H.*, b. December 6, 1856.

    b. *Charles-McC.*, b. October 27, 1876.
  4. *James-F. L.*, b. December 29, 1833; resides in Venango county.
  5. *Murray-L.*, b. August 14, 1836; m., October 4, 1864, Catharine Kochler; and had issue: *Anne, Charles,* and *John,* all of Sugar Creek.
  6. *Margaret-E.*, b. November 9, 1841; m., September 27, 1860, Charles Kochler ; and had issue (surname Kochler): *Penelope, Margaret, Sarah-L., Catharine-W.,* all of Unatilla county, Oregon.
  7. *John-L.*, b. September 4, 1843; m. Martha Beggs; and had issue: *Amy-L., Warren-A.,* and *Sarah-B.,* all of Sugar Creek, Pa.
11. vi. *James-F.*, b. December 6, 1802; m. Margaret I. Wilson.
  vii. *Jemima,* b. April 30, 1806; d. unm. April 17, 1873, at Sugar Creek.

V. JAMES LINN,[3] (William,[2] William,[1]) b. October 17, 1761; d. in Lurgan, May 28, 1835; served in the militia under Gen. Armstrong at Germantown; ordained a ruling elder of church at Middle Spring, September 22, 1822; m., February 3, 1786, GRISELDA PATTERSON, b. June 8, 1759; d. August 1, 1839. They had issue:

12. i. *William,* b. 1787; m. Mary Galbraith.
  ii. *Mary,* b. November 7, 1790; d. March 9, 1854, at Burgettstown, Pa.; m., December 20, 1814, Robert Patterson, b. October 8, 1784; d. January 9, 1861, son of Josiah Patterson; and had issue (surname Patterson):
    1. *Jane,* b. October 16, 1815; d. May 12, 1845; m., first, September 29, 1835, J. Watson Allen; and had issue (surname Allen): *Robert-P.*, of Powesheik, Iowa, m. Anna Cleaver; m., secondly, in 1842, James Ewing; and had issue (surname Ewing): *Jane,* b. March 3, 1845, m. L. B. Sisson.
    2. *Eliza,* b. March 17, 1818; d. June 15, 1841.
    3. *Sarah-Smith,* b. August 5, 1820; m. James Ewing, *(ante)* ; d. April 28, 1841.
    4. *James-L.*, of Burgettstown, b. November 12, 1824; m. Sarah A. Linn, of William (XI); and had issue (surname Patterson):
      a. *Mary L.*, b. February 6, 1855.
      b. *Addie-J.*, b. January 27, 1857.
      c. *Elizabeth,* b. February 20, 1861.
      d. *Anna-G.*, b. November 25, 1862.
      e. *James-F.,* b. April 20, 1865.

Linn of Lurgan.

5. *Mary*, b. October 17, 1829 ; m., March 15, 1859, Rev. James T. Frederick, D. D., of Burgettstown, d. July 2, 1886 ; and had issue (surname Frederick):
    a. Sarah-E., b. December 31, 1859 ; m., November 18, 1883, Rev. Samuel F. Marks, of Fort Wayne, Ind.
    b. William-J., b. March 6, 1865.
    c. John-D., b. September 10. 1869.
    d. David-P., b. January 16, 1872.

iii. *Jane*, b. 1793 ; d. July 9, 1860; m., May 11, 1826, James Rodgers, of Shippensburg ; d. September 10, 1831 ; and had issue (surname Rodgers):
    1. Rev. *James-L.*, b. May 5, 1827 ; m. Hetty B. Cochran, of Eliza (*postea* IV).
    2. Hon. *A.-Denny*, b. April 17, 1830 ; of Columbus, Ohio.

iv. *Eliza*, b. 1799 ; d. September, 1856 ; m. Robert Cochran, innkeeper at Shippensburg ; d. at Springfield, Ohio, April 28, 1873, aged eighty-nine years ; and had issue (surname Cochran):
    1. *James-L.*, d. s. p.
    2. *Hetty-B.*, b. 1830 ; d. January 5, 1887 ; m. Rev. J. L. Rodgers, above.
    3. *David.*
    4. *Andrew-Patterson-L.*, of Springfield, Ohio.

v. *Andrew-P.*, b. 1800 ; d. July 5, 1841 ; a physician ; m. ——— Walker.

VI. DAVID LINN,[3] (William,[2] William,[1]) b. May 28, 1776 ; d. July 26, 1848 ; removed from Lurgan to now Kelly township, Union county; served in the war of 1812, at Black Rock ; m., June 10, 1800, MARGERY COULTER, b. December 24, 1780 d. November 19, 1865. They had issue :

i. *Franklin-F.*, b. April 13, 1801 ; d. November 27, 1846 ; unm.
ii. *William-T.*, of Buffalo Cross-roads ; b. June 5, 1811 ; m. Catharine Robinson, b. 1807 ; d. September 18, 1889.
iii. *Margaret*, b. November 19, 1825 ; m., August 10, 1848, Rev. Ephraim Kieffer, who died at Carlisle, Pa., May 11, 1871 ; and had issue (surname Kieffer):
    1. Rev. *William-T.-L.*, of Mercersburg, Pa.; b. September 8, 1850 ; m., June 24, 1879, Elizabeth Miles, of Carlisle ; and had issue (surname Kieffer):
        a. William-M., b. August 13, 1882.
        b. Thompson-L., b. May 19, 1884 ; d. July 9, 1885.

2. *Mary-C.*, b. June 29, 1854; m. November 9, 1882, Phineas T. Ball, of Churchville, Maryland; and had issue (surname Ball): *Margaret-L.*
3. *Emma-B.*, b. March 26, 1859; m., November 6, 1884, W. B. Donehower, of Lewisburg, Pa.
4. *Catharine-L.*, b. June 17, 1861.
5. *Anna-M.*, b. April 3, 1864.
6. *Stephen-E.*, b. August 16, 1868.

VII. ELIZABETH LINN,[4] (William,[3] William,[2] William,[1]) b. 1775; d. July 31, 1834, at Philadelphia, Pa.; she was a woman of taste and literary acquirements. She m., November, 1804, CHARLES BROCKDEN BROWN, b. January 17, 1771; d. February 19, 1810. He was of Quaker lineage. His middle name was derived from his uncle, the skillful conveyancer and great scrivener of provincial days. He received a liberal education under Robert Proud, the historian, and at the age of sixteen already formed plans of extensive literary work. He was apprenticed to Alexander Wilcox, an eminent lawyer, but occupied himself with literary instead of legal studies. In 1796, he removed to the city of New York, where he devoted himself to letters with great eagerness to become conspicuous as a writer. In 1798, appeared his first novel, "Wieland," a powerful and original romance, and in 1799, "Osmond, or The Second Witness." At this time he had begun no less than five novels, two of which, "Arthur Merwyn" and "Edgar Huntley," were soon published. In "Arthur Merwyn" the ravages of the yellow fever, which the author had witnessed in New York in 1798, and Philadelphia in 1793, are painted with terrific truth. These were followed by others of more or less note. He published a number of political pamphlets, and edited with ability the *American Register*. He was a man of romantic temper, extensive attainments, and great industry. He was the first in America who ventured to pursue literature as a profession. To him his country is indebted for the high literary standard he gave it. His life and correspondence, edited by William Dunlap, in two volumes, was published in 1815. They had issue (surname Brown):

 i. *William-Linn*, b. September, 1805; resides in Philadelphia; m., October 10, 1836, Emily G. Burling, daughter of Samuel Burling, of New York city; and had issue:

1. *Virginia-P.*, d., Philadelphia.
2. *Laura-L.*, d. in infancy.
3. *Emily-B.*, d., Philadelphia.
4. *Eugene-A.*, d., leaving issue, one daughter, *Emily-B.*, of Philadelphia.
5. *William-Linn*, Jr., of Philadelphia.

ii. Charles-Brockden (twin), b. September, 1805 ; d. 1875, in the South.
iii. Eugene-L., b. 1807 ; d. 1824 ; m. and had issue, *Emily-B.*
iv. Mary-C., b. 1809 ; d. 1829.

VIII. WILLIAM LINN,[4] Esq., (William,[3] William,[2] William,[1]) b. August 31, 1790; d. January 14, 1867, at Ithaca, N. Y.; was a lawyer, and author of "A Life of Thomas Jefferson," Ithaca, 1834, and of the celebrated "Rohrbach Papers;" m. MARY A. BIERS, d. July 25, 1848, aged fifty. They had issue:

i. Susan-L., b. July 12, 1819; d. July 11, 1885 ; m., in 1840, Henry W. Sage, Esq., of Ithaca, b. January 31, 1814; founder of Sage College, Cornell University ; she was one of the founders of the Brooklyn (N. Y.) School for Training Nurses, and liberally endowed the female department of Cornell University. On Saturday, July 11, 1885, while returning with her husband and Miss Kate Linn from a visit of mercy at Slaterville, near Ithaca, she was, about half past six p. m., thrown from her carriage and instantly killed ; her former pastor, Henry Ward Beecher, said of her in his address at her funeral, "her soul had entered into the very spirit of the Gospel of Jesus Christ; to her virtues were joined all the graces which education could give, with great hopefulness, and that rare gift, the illumination of humor, which, together formed a wondrous combination of Christian character. She was a most noble, Christian woman, who, once known, can never be forgotten." They had issue (surname Sage):

1. *Dean*, m. Sarah Manning.
2. *William-H.*, m., May 20, 1869, Jennie Curtin, daughter of Hon. A. G. Curtin, of Bellefonte (*see Gregg and Curtin record*); and had issue (surname Sage):
   a. *Catharine-C.*, b. July 2, 1870.
   b. *Henry-W.*, Jr., b. 1872.
   c. *Andrew-Gregg-Curtin*, b. June 8, 1873.
   d. *De Witt*.

ii. De Witt, drowned near Staten Island, N. Y., May 28, 1872.
iii. Kate, residing in Ithaca, 1885.

IX. ARCHIBALD LAIDLIE LINN,⁴ (William,³ William,² William,¹) b. October 5, 1802; d. October 10, 1857, at Schenectady, N. Y.; graduated at Union College, Schenectady, 1820; twice mayor of Schenectady, N. Y.; member of Twenty-seventh Congress, 1841–43; of New York House of Representatives, 1844; and county judge; m., January 31, 1826, MARY TEN EYCK MCCLELLAND, b. November 8, 1808; living at Schenectady. They had issue:

  i. *William*, b. November 14, 1826; d. January 4, 1844.
  ii. *Peter-Van-R.*, b. October 20, 1828.
  iii. Rev. *John-Blair*, of Corsicana, Texas; b. December 5, 1830; m., October 20, 1857, Miss Morgan, d. October 11, 1892.
  iv. *Charles-F.*, b. October 19, 1833; d. June 5, 1861.
  v. *Mary-H.*, b. October 9, 1835; m., July 6, 1871, James Hastings, of Lisha's Kill, Albany county, N. Y.
  vi. *Archibald-L.*, b. April 3, 1839; d. in hospital at New Orleans, September 13, 1864; sergeant of company B, Second New York Veteran cavalry.
  vii. *Helen-L.*, b. December 30, 1843.
  viii. *Jennette*, b. June 26, 1845; d. May 21, 1861.

X. JOHN LINN,⁵ (John,⁴ William,² William,¹) b. January 8, 1797; d. April 9, 1891, at Mount Vernon, Knox county, Ohio; m., April 28, 1825, MARY F. CHAMBERLIN, b. September 29, 1804; d. April 3, 1865; daughter of Colonel William Chamberlin, of Kelly township, Union county, Pa. They had issue:

  i. *William Lawrence*, b. January 16, 1826; residence, Greenfield P. O., Iowa; m., May 26, 1853, Rachel A. Robertson, who d. April 16, 1870; and had issue: *R.-G.*, m. Dema Stewart; *Mary-A.*, m. —— Smith; *William-E.*, *Flora-E.*, *Anna-L.*, and *H.-Wayne.*
  ii. *John-F.*, b. September 29, 1827; resides at Greenfield P. O., Iowa.
  iii. *Mary-E.*, b. August 8, 1829; m., January 1, 1857, James Patterson, of Mount Vernon, O.; and had issue (surname Patterson): *Dora-M.*, m. J. W. McDonald, of Hampton, Iowa; *Elwyn-L.*, and *Otto-A.*
  iv. *Robert-H.*, b. April 7, 1832; m., May 27, 1857, Anna J. Pollock, b. 1834; d. February 6, 1894; and had issue:
    1. *Ida-M.*, b. December 1, 1858; m., November 30, 1882, M. J. Pusey, of Winfield, Iowa.
    2. *Renna-M.*, b. June 19, 1860; d. August 10, 1877.

v. *Ann-E.*, b. November 14, 1834 ; m., February 1, 1860, N. R. Ebersole ; d. near Tama, Iowa, October 10, 1867.

vi. *Susan-M.*, b. February 8, 1888 ; d. October 25, 1875 ; m., J. L. Serviss, of Marshall county, Iowa.

vii. *Catharine-J.*, b. May 12, 1840 ; m., July 4, 1861, John Pollock ; residing at Morning Sun, Louisa county, Iowa.

XI. JAMES F. LINN,⁵ (John,⁴ William,² William,¹) b. December 6, 1802 ; d. October 8, 1869 ; practitioner at law, in Lewisburg, Pa., 1826–1869 ; and specially prominent as an abolitionist, and as an advocate of temperance ; m., July 20, 1826, MARGARET I. WILSON, b. October 12, 1804 ; d. June 22, 1868 ; dau. of Hugh Wilson and Catharine Irvine, (*see Hugh Wilson record*). They had issue :

    i. *Mary-L.*, b. July 12, 1827 ; living at Mercersburg, Pa.; m., November 14, 1848, Rev. Henry Harbaugh, D. D., b. October 28, 1817 ; died while professor in the Theological Seminary of the German Reformed Church at Mercersburg, December 28, 1867 ; author of "The Sainted Dead," "Heavenly Recognition," "Fathers of the German Reformed Church," and editor of *The Mercersburg Review;* and had issue (surname Harbaugh):

        1. *Wilson-L.*, b. July 25, 1851, druggist, Mercersburg ; m., May 24, 1876, Rosanna McNaughton, b. 1852 ; d. March 24, 1894, at Ardmore, Pa.; and had issue : *Henry*, and *Duncan-J*.

        2. *Margaret-A.*, b. May 20, 1855 ; teacher at Radnor, Pa.

        3. *H.-Lange*, b. October 24, 1857 ; m., September 19, 1889, Rose McMahon.

        4. *J.-F.-Linn*, b. April 29, 1860 ; attorney-at-law, Chambersburg, Pa.; m., August 16, 1887, Paulina F. Kimmell.

        5. *M.-Louisa*, b. December 19, 1862.

        6. *John-A.*, b. February 8, 1867.

    ii. *Wilson-I.*, b. September 9, 1829 ; d. November 27, 1893 ; m., February 27, 1849, Elizabeth Brown, b. September 16, 1827 ; d. March 19, 1887, at Berwyn, Chester county, Pa.; and had issue :

        1. *Edwin-B.*, b. June 1, 1850 ; m., November 20, 1878, Elizabeth Siney ; and had issue : *Wilson-I.*, and *John-Siney*.

        2. *James-F.*, b. February 14, 1852 ; resides at Flourtown, Montgomery county, Pa.

        3. *Anna-B.*, b. October 21, 1855 ; d. April 17, 1882 ;

m., December 25, 1877, N. B. Sterner; and had issue (surname Sterner): *Emma-S.*
4. *Margaret-W.*, b. October 10, 1857.
5. *Mary-B.*, b. June 28, 1860.
6. *Merrill R.*, b. April 12, 1862; m., December 25, 1889, Catherine Comerer.
7. *Frank-S.*, b. February 19, 1864; m. Emma Keeley.
8. *Charles-E.*, b. October 6, 1866.

13. *iii. John-Blair*, m., first, Julia J. Pollock; second, Mary E. D. Wilson.
iv. J.-Merrill, b. October 17, 1833; an attorney-at law; resides at Lewisburg, Pa.; m., December 26, 1867, Mary E. Billmeyer, dau. of Philip Billmeyer; and had issue:
1. *Philip-B.*, b. May 25, 1869.
v. Oliver-D., b. January 3, 1836; d. May 12, 1840.
vi. Anne-C., b., July 31, 1839; m., May 9, 1878, Dr. John S. Angle, of Spread Eagle, Chester county, Pa.; and had issue (surname Angle):
1. *Laura L.*, b. April 9, 1879.
vii. Laura-S., b. March 11, 1845; d. October 9, 1871; m., December 22, 1864, Dr. John S. Angle; and had issue (surname Angle):
1. *Linn*, b. April 29, 1867; m. —— Schofield.
2. *Nora*, b. November 1, 1869; m., April 18, 1894, William S. Tash, of Camden, N. J.

XII. WILLIAM LINN,[6] (James,[5] William,[2] William,[1]) b. 1787; d. in Lurgan township, April 5, 1873; elder in Presbyterian church of Middle Spring; served in war of 1812, in defense of Baltimore; m., September 28, 1819, MARY GALBRAITH, b. December 14, 1796; d. April 3, 1867. They had issue:

i. James, b. July 30, 1820; m., November, 1846, Jane E. Coffee; d. July 25, 1885, in Lurgan township; and had issue: *James-McC., William-A.*, and *Mary*.
ii. Mary-G., b. April 2, 1822; m. Hayes Culbertson; resides at Princeton, Iowa; and had issue (surname Culbertson): *William-Linn, Stephen, Augustus, Mary, Robert, Harry, Elizabeth*, and *James*.
iii. Griselda, b. July 22, 1824; m., December 31, 1844, David G. Duncan, of Newville, Pa., b. February 14, 1817; and had issue (surname Duncan):
1. *William-Linn*, b. December 5, 1845; m., first, December 19, 1866, Arabella Davidson; secondly, September 21, 1876, Bell Tritt.

2. *Mary-Galbraith*, b. March 18, 1848.
3. *Samuel-A.*, b. June 23, 1851.
4. *Emma-J.*, b. March 5, 1854; m., December 1, 1875, John D. Mains.
5. *David-Galbraith*, b. January 19, 1856.
6. *John-K.*, b. July 14, 1858.
7. *Elizabeth-A.*, b. October 22, 1860.
8. *Sarah-P.*, b. February 7, 1863.
9. *Theressa-A.*, b. February 6, 1865; d. October 5, 1867.
10. *James-M.*, b. February 5, 1867.
11. *Flora-G.*, b. April 2, 1869.
12. *Eva*, b. August 20, 1873.

iv. *Elizabeth-S.*, b. June 23, 1826; d. March 19, 1884, in Shippensburg, Pa.; m., June 24, 1844, J. Anderson Kelso, d. prisoner of war on Belle Island, near Richmond, Va., November 1, 1863; and had issue (surname Kelso):
  1. Rev. *Alexander-P.*, b. October 4, 1845; missionary at Saharunpur, North India; m., October 12, 1870, in India, Louisa M. Bolton, daughter of an English officer.
  2. *Mary-J.*, b. July 12, 1847; d. November 22, 1850.
  3. *William-Linn*, b. July 30, 1849; m., first, April 7, 1870, Martha Thompson; secondly, 1881, Emma Sutherland; resides at Putnam, Ill.
  4. *Letitia-C.*, b. September 7, 1851; resides at Shippensburg.
  5. *Robert-G.*, b. November 4, 1853; m., October 25, 1883, Jane Lawrence, of Shippensburg.
  6. *Sarah-A.*, b. July 9, 1857.
  7. *James P.*, of Burgettstown, Pa., b. October 2, 1860; m., April 16, 1884, Belle M. Henricle.

v. *Sarah-A.*, b. November 7, 1830; m., April 20, 1854, James L. Patterson, of Burgettstown, son of Robert Patterson and Mary Linn, (*see* v).

vi. *William-A.-P.*, b. June 27, 1839; resides at Burgettstown P. O., Pa.; m., October 7, 1862, Elizabeth Proudfit, and had issue:
  1. *John-P.*, b. September 11, 1863.
  2. *William-B.*, b. June 28, 1867.
  3. *James-P.*, b. February 24, 1870.
  4. *Robert-F.*, b. June 26, 1872.
  5. *Edmund-L.*, b. June 3, 1874; d. 1882.

XIII. JOHN BLAIR LINN,[5] (James F.,[4] John,[3] William,[2] William,[1]) b. October 15, 1831, at Lewisburg, Pa. He was educated at Franklin and Marshall College, and studied the profession of law; served in the Rebellion; removed to Centre county in 1871; during the administration of Governor Hartranft, he was Deputy Secretary of the Commonwealth from 1873 to 1878, and Secretary of the Commonwealth, 1878–1879. In 1877 he published "Annals of Buffalo Valley," and edited, in connection with William H. Egle, M. D., Pennsylvania Archives, second series, 12 vols., 1874–1880; and, in 1883, History of Centre and Clinton counties; resides in Bellefonte, Pa.; engaged in his profession. Mr. Linn was twice married; m., first, October 22, 1857, JULIA J. POLLOCK, b. February 2, 1831; d. July 19, 1862; daughter of F. W. Pollock, of Milton, Pa. They had issue:

  i. Sarah-P.-G., b. April 9, 1859.
  ii. Bessie-W., b. September 13, 1860.

Mr. Linn m., secondly, November 21, 1867, MARY E. D. WILSON, daughter of Hunter and Mary Benner Wilson. They had issue:

  iii. Mary-Hunter, b. July 26, 1869.
  iv. Henry-W.-Sage, b. January 18, 1873, at Bellefonte, Pa.

LYON OF JUNIATA.

I. JOHN LYON,[1] son of William Lyon,* with his family, emigrated from Enniskillen, county Fermanagh, Province of Ulster, Ireland, to the Province of Pennsylvania, in the year 1763, and settled in Cumberland county, now Milford township, Juniata county, about two miles west of Mifflintown. The warrant for his tract of land, two hundred and seventy-three acres is dated September 18, 1766. In 1773 the Proprietaries grant to John Lyon *et al.* twenty acres of land for the use of the Presbyterian church of Tuscarora, where he is buried; d. in 1780; he m., in Ireland, MARGARET ARMSTRONG, sister of Colonel John Armstrong, one of the prominent and patriotic Pennsylvanians of Provincial and Revolutionary times; was a woman of bright intellect, remarkable intelligence, and a fine conversationalist; d. about 1793, and also buried in Tuscarora. They had issue, all born in Ireland:

3.   i. *William*, b. March 17, 1729; m Alice Armstrong.
4.   ii. *James*, m. ―― Martin.
5.   iii. *Samuel*, m. Eleanor Blaine.
6.   iv. *John*, m. Mary Harris.
    v. *Mary*, b. 1748; m. Benjamin Lyon, (*see* VIII).
    vi. *Frances*, b. 1752; d. May 4, 1839; m. William Graham, b. 1753; d. April 4, 1813; both buried in Tuscarora cemetery; and left descendants.
7.   vii. *Margaret Alice*, m. Thomas Anderson, in Ireland.
    viii. *Agnes*. d. unm.

II. JAMES LYON,[1] the younger brother of John Lyon, who heads this record, never emigrated to America, but his three sons came over with the family of John Lyon, their uncle, in 1763. Neither he nor his wife are believed to have been living at the date of the emigration. His sons were:

---

*REBECCA LYON, sister of John and James Lyon, also came to Pennsylvania. She married Colonel John Armstrong.

Arms of the Lyon Family of Pennsylvania—Arg. a Lion rampant az. *Crest*—A Lion's head erased ppr.

    i. William, who espoused the British cause in the Revolutionary war, settled in Canada, and became estranged from the family.

    ii. Robert, enlisted in the Revolutionary service; promoted from sergeant of the Twelfth Pennsylvania to a lieutenancy in the Sixth Pennsylvania regiment, Continental line, February, 1777; was taken prisoner by the British and held captive in Canada; after the war settled in Northumberland, Pa., where he died, August 19, 1823, aged seventy-seven years.

8.   *iii. Benjamin*, b. 1752; m. Mary Lyon.

III. WILLIAM LYON,² (John,¹) preceded his father and family to the Province, having arrived about 1750, and attained the position of assistant surveyor to his uncle, John Armstrong, deputy surveyor and justice of the peace of Cumberland county, a well educated man, who had arrived from Ireland in 1748. Together, they laid out the town of Carlisle, by order of the Proprietaries, in 1751, and the seat of justice was then permanently established there. William Lyon entered the Provincial military service for the defense of the frontier against the French and Indians, and as first lieutenant of the Pennsylvania regiment, appointed December 6, 1757, participated in Forbes' great expedition against Fort DuQuesne, in 1758; resigned March, 1759; appointed a magistrate in 1764, by Governor John Penn, then in Carlisle, dispatching Colonel Bouquet on his second expedition. On the opening of the Revolution and the suppression of the Provincial authority, he was appointed, by the "Supreme Executive Council," a member of the "Committee of Safety," October 16, 1776; prothonotary for Cumberland county, March 12, 1777; clerk of the orphans' court, February 9, 1779; and register and recorder, February 13, 1779; he was re-appointed, by Governor Mifflin, register of wills, September 4, 1790, and prothonotary, register, and recorder, and clerk of the orphans' court, August 17, 1791; he was also re-appointed, by Governor McKean, January 29, 1800, prothonotary and clerk of the courts, and continued prothonotary by proclamation in 1802 and 1805; he was appointed, by the "Supreme Executive Council," to receive subscriptions for Cumberland county, for a loan of twenty million dollars, authorized by Congress June 29, 1779. William Lyon, b.

March 17, 1729, in Ireland; d. in Carlisle, Pa., February 7, 1809; m., first, in 1756, ALICE ARMSTRONG, daughter of his uncle, Colonel John Armstrong, of Carlisle, Pa. They had issue :

9.   *i. James*, b. October, 1757; m. Sallie Eyre.

He married, secondly, 1768, ANN FLEMING, of Carlisle, Pa. They had issue:

    ii. Margaret, [Peggy,] b. May 9, 1770; m., in Carlisle, July 25, 1793, the Rev. David Denny, of Chambersburg, Pa.

    iii. John, b. October 13, 1771; m. Priscilla Coulter, of Greensburg, Pa. He was a prominent member of the bar at Uniontown, Pa., and appointed by act of the Legislature of Pennsylvania, March 31, 1806, in conjunction with Cadwallader Evans, commissioner on the Nicholson lands.

    iv. William, b. June 17, 1773; went South and died in early life at St. Francisville, La., where he is buried.

10.   *v. Samuel*, b. January 20, 1775; m. Betty Brown.

    vi. Mary, b. August 20, 1776; d. 1832; unm.

    vii. Alexander-Parker, b. August 4, 1778; d. 1808; unm.; lawyer in Carlisle.

    viii. Nancy, b. August 16, 1780; d. 1800; unm.

11.   *ix. Alice-Armstrong*, b. September 25, 1781; m. George Chambers.

12.   *x. George-Armstrong*, b. April 11, 1784; m. Anna G. Savage.

IV. JAMES LYON,² (John,¹) arrived in the Province of Pennsylvania, landing in Philadelphia in 1763, and, about 1766, located on land in Cumberland county, now in Granville township, Mifflin county, and near the site of old Fort Granville, which was captured by the French and Indians in 1756. The tract embraced all the broad plateau on the south bank of the Juniata river and the mountain side (known as Anderson station, Pennsylvania railroad). He was assessor for Cumberland county in 1777; died and buried on his own domain in the family burial-ground. He m., in Ireland, [ELIZABETH] MARTIN. They had issue:

    i. John, b in Ireland; settled in Butler county, and left descendants; was in the Revolutionary service, and lived on a farm on the north side of the Juniata river, in Mifflin county, until he went westward.

    ii. Margaret [Peggy], b. in Philadelphia, three days after the family arrived, in 1763; d. June 8, 1847; m., in 1783, John Oliver, b. in Derrybeg, county Derry, Ireland, in 1750; d. 1843, and both buried in McVeytown cemetery. John Oliver came over in the ship "Sophia," in 1770; became a citizen of Cumberland, now Mifflin county, and taught school in the neighborhood, his future wife being one of his pupils; he became a prominent man, and was appointed an associate judge for Mifflin county by Governor Mifflin; his residence was in Oliver township (named after him), on the Juniata, six miles west of Lewistown; and had issue (surname Oliver):

1. *James*, m. —— Cunningham; d. s. p.
2. *Rachel*, m. John Campbell, of Mifflin county; and had five children.
3. *Elizabeth*, m. Joseph Campbell, brother of John; and had eight children.
4. *Nancy* [Agnes], m. Samuel Campbell, brother of John and Joseph; had ten children.
5. *Margaret* [Peggy], m. Rev. Lochrane; d. s. p.
6. *Polly*, d. in 1871; unm.
7. *Jane*, m. John Campbell, of Centre county, cousin to John, Joseph, and Samuel; and had six children.
8. *Margery*, d. in 1882; unm.
9. *John*, m. Esther Strode, of Mifflin county; and had two children.
10. *George*, m. Margaret Jackson; and had three children.
11. *Sydney*, m. George A. Lyon, (see XXVI).
12. *Andrew*, m. —— Edwards; d. s. p.

13. iii. *William*, b. January 31, 1765; m. Rebecca Graham.
  iv. *Elizabeth*, lived to the age of eighty-eight years; m. John McVey, after whom the town of McVeytown, Mifflin county, was named; moved to Zanesville, O.
14. v. *Isabella*, b. August 14, 1770; m. John Patterson, merchant.
15. vi. *Nancy* (twin), b. Aug. 14, 1770: m. John Patterson, Esq.
  vii. *Mary*, b. May 6, 1774; d. February 24, 1861; m. Robert Forsythe, of Mifflin county, Pa.; and had eight children.
16. viii. *James*, b. February 11, 1786; m. Elizabeth Lyon.

V. SAMUEL LYON,² (John,¹) settled on land adjoining his father's tract, and inherited one half of his father's farm, in Cumberland, now Juniata, county, Pa.; became a deputy surveyor under his uncle, Col. John Armstrong; appointed, May 22, 1770, by Provincial authority, a magistrate for Milford township; re-appointed justice of the peace, June 19, 1777, by the "Supreme Executive Council," who made all appointments previous to the formation of the State Constitution of 1790. July 31, 1777, commissioned colonel of the Fourth battalion of Cumberland county militia; again commissioned May 14, 1778. April 3, 1780, Col. Lyon was appointed commissioner of purchases for the Revolutionary army for the county of Cumberland, and July 7, 1780, assistant commissioner of purchases, and the Council ordered his "*quota* of whiskey at 500 gallons per month." Before 1785, he changed his residence to Carlisle. November 9, 1789, appointed deputy surveyor for Cumberland county, and re-appointed, November 3, 1791. He m. ELEANOR BLAINE, b. 1750; d. April 9, 1795; sister of Col. Ephraim Blaine. They had issue:

 i. Margaret [Peggy], b. March 26, 1772; m., in Carlisle, January 16, 1795, her cousin, James Blaine, son of Col. Ephraim Blaine, and had *Ephraim-Lyon*, who married Maria Gillespie, of Washington county, Pa., and had *James-Gillespie*, author and statesman. The other children of Margaret Blaine were *Jane*, m. William Semple, of Washington, Pa.; *Ellen*, m. Major John H. Ewing,* a prominent citizen of Washington, Pa.; *Anna-Lyon*, m. Rev. D. Mason; *William, Samuel, James*, m. Miss DeVillemont; and *Mary*.

 ii. Isabella, b. February 14, 1774; m., first, in Carlisle, April 12, 1798, William Hoge, of Washington, Pa.; m., secondly, Alexander Reed, of same place; d. s. p.

---

*The Hon. John H. Ewing was born in Fayette county, Pa., October 5, 1796; died at his home in Washington, Washington county, Pa., June 9, 1887, in his ninety-first year. He graduated at Washington College in 1814; studied law under Thomas McGiffin, with whom he temporarily entered into partnership. Was admitted to the Washington bar in 1818. He was a member of the Senate and House of Representatives of Pennsylvania from 1835 to 1846, and was elected to the Twenty-ninth Congress, during which period he became the personal friend of the great men of the nation—Clay, Webster, Calhoun and their compeers. He served as a trustee of Washington College over half a century, also as a trustee of the Female Seminary since its foundation. A public spirited man, he was at the head of every enterprise and project which might benefit his town and county. Major Ewing and Ellen Blaine had issue: the Rev. *William E., George, John, Samuel, Margaret*, who m. Dr. Hollock, of Pittsburgh, *Elizabeth*, m. Rev. William Speer, and *Mary*, m. Professor Woods.

  iii. John, b. February 1, 1776 ; d. 1814, unm.; an attorney-at-law, Bedford, Pa.
  iv. Nancy, b. April 27, 1778; d. June 22, 1867, at Washington, Pa.; unm.
17. *v. Rebecca*, b November 2, 1785 ; m. James M. Russell.
18. *vi. Samuel*, b. January 19, 1791 ; m. Nancy Campbell.

 VI. JOHN LYON,[2] (John,[1]) came into possession of one half of the homestead, Samuel coming into possession of the other half, in Milford township, by the will of his father, dated December 13, 1779, after his death in 1780. Resided thereon until June 1, 1797, when he conveyed it to Stephen Dougleman, who conveyed it to the Sterrett family ; its present owners being Hon. James P. Sterrett and his brother Dr. John P. Sterrett. John Lyon then removed to Butler county, and d. about 1820. He m. MARY HARRIS, daughter of Capt. Thomas Harris. They had issue:

  i. Thomas-Harris.
  ii. William.
  iii. John.
  iv. James.
  v. Margaret.
  vi. Mary.
  vii. Catharine.
  viii. Nancy.

 VII. MARGARET ALICE LYON,[2] (John,[1]) m. THOMAS ANDERSON, who came to America in 1766. They had been previously married, and probably came from the home of the Lyon family in Ireland. They had four children, of whom we have the names of (surname Anderson):

  i. Robert, d. in infancy.
  ii. Rebecca, d. in infancy.
  iii. John, b. 1770, in Bedford, Pa.; d. in 1839; studied medicine at Carlisle, and entered upon the practice of his profession in 1796, in which he became very successful; for years he was the president of the Allegheny Bank at Bedford, and also president of the Chambersburg and Bedford turnpike company ; besides being actively engaged in other enterprises ; m., in 1804, Mary Espy, b. 1779; d. 1815, (*see Espy record*); and had issue (surname Anderson):
   1. *George-Woods*, b. June 27, 1805 ; d. June 20, 1879 ; studied medicine with Dr. Watson, and gradu-

ated from the University of Pennsylvania; m. Caroline Morsell, of Prince George's county, Md., who died in 1860.
2. *Espy-Lyon*, m. Louisa Watson.
3. *Ann-Jane*, d. in infancy.
4. *Mary.*
5. *Elizabeth.*

VIII. BENJAMIN LYON,[2] (James,[1]) b in Enniskillen, county Fermanagh, Ireland, in 1752; and emigrated with the family of his uncle, John Lyon, in 1763, finally settling in Milford township, Cumberland county, now Juniata, where he was assessed as a single freeman in 1775. He enlisted in the Revolutionary cause and was in Captain Hendrick's company of riflemen from Cumberland county in the expedition against Quebec, commanded by General Arnold. It is an interesting fact that Benjamin Lyon's Bible was found one hundred years afterwards in the Du Plante family, in the parish of St. Franscois on the Chaudiere river, Canada, down which the expedition passed. (*See* Henry's Narrative, Pennsylvania Archives, second series, vol. xv.) Returning, he participated in the battle of Long Island, August 27, 1776; was recommended by General Hand to General Washington for promotion, and appointed lieutenant, September 25, 1776. His regiment was engaged in the battles of Brandywine, Germantown, *et alios*. Promoted to first lieutenant, July 16, 1777, and to a captaincy, December 8, 1778. The hardships of the service affected his health, and, as a consequence, his resignation ensued in May, 1779, when he returned to Milford township. (*See* Pennsylvania Archives, second series, "Pennsylvania in the Revolution.") He removed about four years after his marriage to Northumberland, Pa., and returned to Tuscarora valley about the year 1800, where he remained till his wife's death, in 1811, when he went to reside with his daughter, Elizabeth, in Shirleysburg, Huntingdon county, Pa., where he died in 1826. Advanced in years, he appeared as a man above medium height, rather full in the face, with florid complexion, blunt in manner, and plain in speech. By act of March 14, 1818, he received an annuity from the State on account of his Revolutionary services. He m., in 1780, his cousin, MARY LYON, b. April, 1748, daughter of John Lyon;

she d. October 9, 1811, and buried in Tuscarora. They had issue:

    i. Elizabeth [Betsy], b. in Tuscarora valley, December 15, 1780; d. January 21, 1849; buried at Green Hill Presbyterian church, Fulton county, Pa.; m. James Lyon, her cousin, (*see* XVI).

19. *ii. John*, b. August 11, 1782; m. Jane Maclay.
20. *iii. James*, b. April 12, 1787; m. Ann Forman.
    iv. Margaret, d. at Pennsylvania Furnace, 1818, aged 25 years; buried in Bellefonte cemetery.

IX. JAMES LYON,[3] (William,[2] John,[1]) b. October, 1757; d. November 21, 1811; m., July 25, 1793, SALLIE EYRE, of Northampton county, Va., where he was a practicing physician. They had issue:

    i. William, d. unm.
    ii. Margaret, m. William Taylor, lawyer, Norfolk, Va.; and had issue (surname Taylor): *Sallie, William, Robert,* and *Archibald.*

X. SAMUEL LYON,[3] (William,[2] John,[1]) b. January 20, 1775; merchant, Baltimore, Md.; m., March, 1800, BETTY BROWN, of Wilmington, Del.; and had issue:

21. *i. William*, m., first, Miss Reynolds; secondly, Miss Mulholland.
22. *ii.* Rev. *George-Armstrong*, m. Mary Sterrett.
    iii. Jacob, lived in Clarion county, and died there.
    iv. John; resided in Clarion county, Pa.; deceased.
    v. Rachel, m. Hugh Campbell, M. D., Uniontown, Pa.; and had issue (surname Campbell): *Susan*, who m. an Allison; Rev. *Samuel*, Rev. *William*, Judge *Edward, Benjamin*, who m. Mary Hitner, *Sarah-Louise*, and *Hugh-Francis.*

XI. ALICE ARMSTRONG LYON,[3] (William,[2] John,[1]) b. September 25, 1781; d. 1848; m., in Carlisle, March 6, 1810, GEORGE CHAMBERS, of Chambersburg, Pa. They had issue (surname Chambers):

    i. Sally-Ann, d. unm.
    ii. Margaretta, d. unm.
    iii. George, d. unm.
    iv. Benjamin, m. Eleanor Thomas; and had issue (surname Chambers): *George, Mary, Benjamin, Annie, Emma, Oliver,* and *Bertha.*

v. William, m. Emeline Kennedy, and had issue (surname Chambers): *Alice, Margaretta, Ellen*, and *Carrie*.

XII. GEORGE ARMSTRONG LYON,[3] (William,[2] John,[1]) b. in Carlisle, Pa., April 11, 1784; d. January 6, 1855; an attorney-at-law, president of the Carlisle Bank, and a prominent and influential citizen of his native place; m., June 14, 1815, ANNA G. SAVAGE, daughter of Thomas Lyttleton Savage, of Northampton county, Va., where she was b. February 10, 1797; d. in Atlantic City, August 25, 1876, and buried in Carlisle, Pa. They had issue, all born in Carlisle, in the house in which their father was born and died:

        i. Virginia-T., b. July 31, 1817; d. 1866; unm.
23.   *ii. William*, b. August 3, 1819; m. Augusta Baldwin.
        iii. John (Reverend), b. July 26, 1821; unm; licensed to preach the Gospel October 4, 1843, by St. Louis presbytery.
        iv. Susan-Ellen, b. May 24, 1823; d. October 27, 1852; m. J. W. Burbridge, of New Orleans.
        v. Mary-Elizabeth. b. March 25, 1825; d. May 25, 1838.
        vi. Anna-Margaret, m. James B. Lyon, (*see* XXX).
24.   *vii. Alexander-Parker*, b. June 29, 1829; m. Eliza T. Denniston.
        viii. Thomas-Lyttleton, b. April 29, 1832; d. March 29, 1883; m., first, Mrs. A. Marks; m., secondly, Beulah Clark.
25.   *ix. Alice-Chambers*, b. April 13, 1836; m. Thomas C. Lazear.

XIII. WILLIAM LYON,[3] (James,[2] John,[1]) b. January 31, 1765, in Carlisle, during the temporary residence of his parents; buried on the farm on which he lived and died; m. REBECCA GRAHAM. They had issue:

        i. William Graham, b. March 7, 1799; d. April 11, 1816.
        ii. Ann Eliza, b. January 7, 1801; d. October 10, 1811.
26.   *iii. George-Armstrong*, b. Dec. 12, 1803; m. Jessie Alexander.
        iv. Rebecca-Armstrong, b. August 21, 1806; d. June 11, 1831; m. Stuart Turbett, of Tuscarora Valley; d. s. p.
        v. Amanda, b. August 31, 1808; d. in childhood.
        vi. John-R., b. August 19, 1810; d. in childhood.
        vii. James, m. Mary Holmes, of Pittsburgh; had two daughters: *Ann-Eliza*, and *Sarah*.

XIV. ISABELLA LYON,[3] (James,[2] John,[1]) b. August 14, 1770, at the homestead, west of Lewistown, on the Juniata river; d. June 28, 1858; buried at Tuscarora church; m., June 20, 1793, JOHN PATTERSON, merchant, b. October 2, 1763, the eldest of six children of John Patterson, one of six brothers, coming from Ireland in 1750, and settled in Bucks county, on the Delaware, on adjoining farms; the father being dead, the family sold the homestead, and in 1791 John commenced merchandising in Tuscarora Valley, in the vicinity of Academia, there being no store nearer than Carlisle; d. October 9, 1836. They had issue (surname Patterson):

    i. *James*, b. March 14, 1794; d. December 8, 1823; unm.
    ii. *Sarah*, b. June 1, 1795; d. May 9, 1835; m. Wm. C. Kelly.
    iii. *Margaret*, b. January 15, 1797; d. June 4, 1863; m., January 8, 1822, Robert Sterrett.
    iv. *William-Hart*, b. January 1, 1799; d. August 3, 1858; m. Mary Ann Wilson.
    v. *Robert*, b. March 20, 1801; d. March 7, 1873; m., first, Jane Wilson; m., secondly, Lucinda Blaine.
    vi. *Elizabeth*, b. May 1, 1803; d. April 9, 1839; unm.
    vii. *Andrew*, b. February 2, 1805; d. August 13, 1884; m., first, Ann Eliza Walker; m., secondly, Mrs. Mary Brazee.
    viii. *Mary-L.*, b. Jan. 10, 1807; d. 1871; m. Robert Patterson.
    ix. *John*, b. March 26, 1809; m., October 6, 1836, Ellen VanDyke, of Mercersburg, Pa.; residence, Peru Mills, Juniata county, Pa. Mr. Patterson is the only survivor of the twenty children of the Patterson connection.
    x. *Isabella*, b. January 16, 1811; d. April 5, 1837; unmarried.
    xi. *Jane*, b. April 30, 1813; d. May 25, 1837.

XV. NANCY LYON,³ (James,² John,¹) twin sister of Isabella (*see* XIV), b. August 14, 1770; d. April 16, 1855; buried at the Presbyterian church in Tuscarora; m. JOHN PATTERSON, Esquire, b. in Bucks county, Pa., October 6, 1772; d. October 10, 1843; first cousin and brother-in-law of John Patterson, merchant, (*see* XIV). He was son of Alexander Patterson, whose father, with six sons, came from Ireland about 1750, and settled in Bucks county; three of the sons moved to the Cumberland Valley, and two to Tuscarora; Alexander locating himself on a farm two miles distant from the Presbyterian church, now Academia, where he lived and died. John Patterson came into possession of the farm, and it is now owned by the fourth generation of the name. They had issue (surname Patterson):

    i. *Alexander*, b 1795; d. March 15, 1869; m., first, Elizabeth Hackett; secondly, Polly Sterrett, sister of Robert Sterrett, (*see* XIV).

ii. James, b. May 1, 1797; d. March 27, 1869; m. Jane Kelly, sister of W. C. Kelly; had eight children.
iii. Andrew, b. March, 1799; d. November, 1883; m. Elizabeth Fisher.
iv. Elizabeth, b. 1801; d. March 6, 1870; m. Moses Kelly.
v. Phebe, b. 1802; d. April, 1884; m. William McClure.
vi. Rachel, d. 1862; m. James McClure.
vii. John, b. November, 1807; d. March 19, 1877; m. Jane Graham, grand-daughter of William Graham.
viii. William-Lyon, b. April 11, 1809; d. August 24, 1846; m. Mary Neely.
ix. Robert, b. 1812; d. March 13, 1830.

XVI. JAMES LYON,³ (James,² John,¹) b. on his father's plantation in Mifflin county, February 14, 1786; d. March 20, 1872; buried in Green Hill cemetery, Fulton county, Pa.; m. April 12, 1808, ELIZABETH LYON, his cousin, (*see* VIII). Resided at Shirleysburg, Huntingdon county, and, finally, at West Dublin, Fulton county, where he died. They had issue :

    i. Margaret-Oliver, b. June 7, 1810; d. March, 1863; m., in 1832, D. C. Ross, who d. January 6, 1895; and left issue.
27. *ii. John-William*, b. December, 1811; m. Catharine V. Ross.
    iii. Benjamin-Alexander, b. May 25, 1818; unm.; postmaster at West Dublin, Fulton county, Pa.; appointed in President Lincoln's administration.
28. *iv. James-Graham*, b. October 3, 1820; m. Margaret Roberts.

XVII. REBECCA LYON,³ (Samuel,² John,¹) b. November 2, 1785; m., February 6, 1812, JAMES MCPHERSON RUSSELL, b. November 10, 1786, in York, Pa.; d. December 14, 1870, in Bedford, Pa.; son of Alexander Russell and Mary McPherson. He read law with James Riddle, of Chambersburg, and was admitted to the Franklin county bar November 10, 1807. The year following, he settled in Bedford, Pa.; and soon acquired a large practice. He held a number of civil offices, was trustee of the Bedford Academy, treasurer of the Chambersburg and Bedford Turnpike company during its construction, and chief burgess of the borough. He was a member of the constitutional convention of 1837–8, and served as a member of the Twenty-seventh Congress. They had issue (surname Russell):

i. *Alexander-Lyon*, b. November 29, 1812, in Bedford, Pa.; d. in 1885, at Montevideo, South America; he was educated in the schools and academy of Bedford, and at Washington College, Pa.; studied law under his father, and was admitted to the Bedford county bar August 28, 1834, but never practiced his profession; was appointed August 7, 1846, by Governor Johnston, Deputy Secretary of the Commonwealth, and January 25, 1850, Secretary of the Commonwealth; on January 9, 1862, was appointed by Governor Curtin, Adjutant General, and held the office until October 11, 1867; was re-appointed by Governor Geary, January 8, 1870, and continued in office until May 17, 1873; in 1879 was appointed by President Hayes, Consul at Montevideo, Uruguay, South America; was twice married: first, Miss King; secondly, Elizabeth Fisher.

ii. *Samuel-Lyon*, b. July 30, 1816; educated at Washington College, Washington, Pa.; studied law with his father, and was admitted to the Bedford county bar November 29, 1837; served as a member of the Thirty-third Congress, and was a member of the constitutional convention of 1873.

iii. *John-Lyon*, m. Elizabeth Ogden.

iv. *William-Hoge*.

v. *Algernon-Sydney*.

vi. *Ann-Lyon*, m. James King, M. D.; and had issue: *Annie*, and *Effie*.

vii. *Ellen-Blaine*, m. Rev. Robert Milligan.

viii. *Mary-McPherson*, m. Frederick Benedict.

ix. *James*; d. s. p.

XVIII. SAMUEL LYON,[3] (Samuel,[2] John,[1]) b. January 19, 1791; m. NANCY CAMPBELL, daughter of Parker Campbell, a distinguished lawyer of Washington, Pa., (*see Parker family*); residence, principally in Western Pennsylvania. They had issue:

i. *Parker-Campbell*, resided at Richmond, Va., where his widow and children still live; a very successful business man.

ii. *Ellen*, m. Rev. Nichols, of Mobile, Ala.

XIX. JOHN LYON,[3] (Benjamin,[2] James,[1]) b. in Tuscarora Valley, now Juniata county, Pa., August 11, 1782; d. in Allegheny City, January 25, 1868, and buried in the Allegheny cemetery. He was head of the well-known firm of Lyon,

Shorb & Co., among the earliest and most extensive iron manufacturers in Pennsylvania, with works in Huntingdon, Centre, Blair, Clarion, and Allegheny counties; principal office at Pittsburgh ; principal residence, Pennsylvania Furnace. Mr. Lyon entered into the business in 1813, and the history of the rise and progress of iron manufacturing in Western Pennsylvania would be the history of his business life. He was a man of large physique and vigorous constitution, erect in carriage, dignified and courteous in manner, positive in character and fearless in speech, terse and concise in language, with a well cultivated mind, hospitable and generous. His business abilities were of a high order, and his life was a success ; m., first, in Harrisburg, Pa., April 29, 1808, by Rev. Mr. Sharon, JANE MACLAY, b. 1782 ; d. April 30, 1809, youngest daughter of the Hon. William Maclay and Mary McClure Harris (*see Maclay record*); buried in Paxtang graveyard. They had issue :

    i. *William-Maclay*, b. April 30, 1809, in Harrisburg, Pa.; member of the firm of Lyon, Shorb & Co , Pittsburgh; d. July 3, 1889 ; bur. in Allegheny cemetery. Early in life Mr. Lyon became a member of the firm of which his father was the head, and soon gave evidence of business abilities of a high order. In the application of new methods and new principles in the manufacture of iron he was ever in the lead. He was largely endowed by nature, intellectually and physically. To not a few was he counsellor, friend, and benefactor; his extreme diffidence caused him to avoid opportunities for distinction; though in the promotion of public enterprises and whatever might inure to the benefit of Pittsburgh, the city of his residence, no man excelled him. His sudden death was publicly lamented.

John Lyon m., secondly, September 7, 1814, ANN (NANCY) PATTON, daughter of General John Patton, of Centre county, Pa., a Revolutionary officer ; she died May, 1817, aged twenty-six years ; buried in Bellefonte cemetery. They had issue :

29.   ii. *John-Patton*, b. June 5, 1815 ; m. Westanna S. Elliott.

John Lyon m., thirdly, July 20, 1820, MARGARET A. STEWART, dau. of Samuel Stewart, of Hanover township, Dauphin county, Pa. (*see Stewart record*), b. April 8, 1796; d. May 26, 1835 ; buried in the First Presbyterian churchyard, Pittsburgh. They had issue :

30. iii. *James-Benjamin*, b. April 21, 1821 ; m. Anna M. Lyon.
31. iv. *Samuel-Stewart*, b. November 11, 1822 ; m. Ann Valentine.
32. v. *Mary-A.*, b. December 24, 1824 ; m. J. Roberts Lowrie.
33. vi. *George-W.*, b. November 7, 1826 ; m. Anna C. Porter.
     vii. *Jane-Alice*, b. March 24, 1829 ; m. Bucher Ayres, (*see Ayres record.*)
34. viii. *Margaret-Elizabeth* (twin), b. March 24, 1829 ; m. Rev. Robert Hamill, D. D.
35. ix. *Sarah-Walker*, b. April 28, 1831 ; m. George Bucher Porter.
36. x. *Thomas-Stewart*, b. May 15, 1833 ; m. Hannah J. Wright.
     xi. *Emma*, b. in Pittsburgh, April 4, 1835 ; d. in inf.

John Lyon m., fourthly, in 1838, ANN PARR HUBLEY, daughter of Joseph Hubley, attorney-at-law, Lancaster, Pa., and an officer of the Revolutionary army. She was grand-daughter of Michael Hubley and Rosina Strumpf (both from Germany), a magistrate and a signer of a treaty with the Six Nations of Indians, made at Lancaster, July, 1748. She was b. October 21, 1788 ; and d. in Bellefonte, Pa., November 13, 1884 ; buried in Bellefonte cemetery. This distinguished lady enjoyed extraordinary and uninterrupted good health during her long life of over ninety-six years; survived her husband sixteen years.

XX. JAMES LYON,[3] (Benjamin,[2] James,[1]) b. April 12, 1787, at Northumberland, Pa.; d. August 28, 1851 ; merchant, and, in 1818, postmaster of Oswego, N. Y.; m., April 25, 1811, ANN FORMAN, of Rhinebeck, N. Y. They had issue :

   i. *Joseph-Benjamin*, b. March 3, 1812, at Onondago, N. Y. ; d. November 9, 1872, at Cleveland, Ohio ; m. Ann Terry, of Geddes, N. Y.
37. ii. *John-Edward*, b. June 18, 1813 ; m. Catharine M. Tracy.
     iii. *Mary-Elizabeth*, b. December 24, 1814, at Oswego, N. Y.; d. February 25, 1889 ; m., first, Theodore Morgan ; and had issue (surname Morgan): *James-Lyon*, killed in the war of the Rebellion ; Mrs. Morgan m., secondly, Charles Whittlesey, of Cleveland, Ohio.
38. iv. *James-H.*, b. April 6, 1817 ; m. Ann Maloney.
     v. *Margaret*, b. August 29, 1822, at Oswego, N. Y.; m., September 21, 1843, George W. Noxon, of Syracuse, N. Y.; and had issue (surname Noxon): *George, Mary*, and *Margaret*.
     vi. *Joshua-Forman*, b. June 6, 1830, at Oswego, N. Y.; d. April 12, 1856 ; unm.

XXI. WILLIAM LYON,[4] (Samuel,[3] William,[2] John,[1]) attorney-at-law, Bedford, Pa.; m., first, Miss REYNOLDS; m., secondly, Miss MULHOLLAND. They had issue, among others:
  i. *William.*
  ii. *Samuel,* attorney-at-law, Blairsville, Pa.
  iii. *Mary,* m. Gen. Duchat; residence, Chicago, Ill.
  iv. *George-Mulholland,* unm.; Chicago, Ill.
  v. *Mary.*
  vi. *[A dau.],* m. Edmund Burke.

XXII. Rev. GEORGE ARMSTRONG LYON,[4] D. D., (Samuel,[3] William,[2] John,[1]) of Erie, Pa.; b. March 3, 1806; d. March 24, 1871; m., 1829, MARY STERRETT, of Carlisle; she d. 1871. They had issue:
  i. *Margaret,* b. 1830; m. John W. Douglass, attorney-at-law, Washington city.
  ii. *Alexander-McDonald,* b. 1835; m., first, Anna Lowry; m., secondly, Maria Crolby; and had two children.
  iii. *George-Armstrong,* b. 1837; m. Rose Vincent; and had two children.
  iv. *Wilber,* b. 1841; m., first, Hattie Cadwell; m., secondly, Maria Derrickson; and had two children.

XXIII. Rev. WILLIAM LYON,[4] (George-Armstrong,[3] William,[2] John,[1]) b. August 3, 1819; d. June, 1862; m., July, 1846, AUGUSTA BALDWIN. They had issue:
  i. *George-Armstrong,* b. July 6, 1847; m. Alice Thaw, of Richmond, Va.
  ii. *John-Lyttleton,* b. August 18, 1849; m., 1893, Jennie Gerrett, of New York.
  iii. *Henry-Webb,* b. June, 1852.
  iv. *Lucy-Baldwin,* b. August, 1854; m. S. P. Townsend, of Baltimore, Md.
  v. *Anna-Grace,* b. June, 1859.
  vi. *William-Lyttleton,* b. September, 1860.

XXIV. ALEXANDER PARKER LYON,[4] (George-Armstrong,[3] William,[2] John,[1]) b. June 29, 1829; d. December 17, 1861, in Pittsburgh; m., May 10, 1855, ELIZA T. DENNISTON, of Pittsburgh. They had issue:
  i. *Catharine-Thaw,* b. May 6, 1856; m. Albert D. Fell, banker, of Philadelphia; and had issue (surname Fell):
    1. *Andrew-Fleming,* b. September 12, 1880.
  ii. *Charles-Lyttleton,* b. January 26, 1858; m., February 5, 1885, Annie Reed, of Pittsburgh.

iii. Alexander-Parker, b. December 27, 1859 ; d. March 8, 1892 ; m., December 7, 1882, Mary Suydam, of Pittsburgh ; and had issue : *Emma, Copeland, Alexander-Parker*, and *Katharine-T.-Denniston.*

iv. John-Denniston, b. January, 1861 ; banker, Pittsburgh.

XXV. ALICE CHAMBERS LYON,[4] (George-Armstrong,[3] William,[2] John,[1]) b. April 13, 1836; m., June 13, 1861, THOMAS C. LAZEAR, attorney-at-law, Pittsburgh. They had issue (surname Lazear):

    i. Anna-Lyon, b. March 29, 1862 ; m., March 26, 1886, Charles P. Orr ; and had issue (surname Orr):
      1. *Alice-Lazear*, b. September 2, 1891.
    ii. Jesse-Thomas, b. February 17, 1866 ; m., November 11, 1890, Christine L. McKelvy ; and have
      1. *Jane-Ralston*, b. July 30, 1891.
    iii. Lyttleton-Lyon, b. December 21, 1867 ; doctor of medicine.

XXVI. GEORGE ARMSTRONG LYON,[4] (William,[3] James,[2] John,[1]) b. on his father's estate, in Mifflin county, Pa., December 12, 1803 ; d. in Kishacoquillas Valley, October 23, 1873 ; m., first, November 11, 1830, JESSIE ALEXANDER, of Mifflin county ; b. January 17, 1806 ; who d. May 12, 1835. They had issue :

    i. Rebecca-Armstrong, b. November 18, 1831 ; m., first, James McAlister, of Juniata county, Pa., who d. July 25, 1876 ; m., secondly, January 16, 1879, David Wilson, Ph. D., of Port Royal, Juniata county, Pa. Professor Wilson was born in Lancaster county in 1813. Upon acquiring the printer's art, he entered Jefferson College and graduated with first honors, in 1837 ; after a year in teaching and study, he became, October, 1839, principal of the Tuscarora Academy, at Academia, a then recently incorporated institution of learning, which soon attained a high position through the influence of his scholarship and executive ability. In 1859, Dr. Wilson accepted the professorship of mathematics—subsequently changed to the chair of *belle-lettres*—iu the Pennsylvania State Agricultural College, Centre county, under the presidency of Dr. Pugh. This was the most popular and flourishing period in the life of this institution, and the only time in its existence when its halls were filled with students. After four and a half years, Professor Wilson returned to the home of his choice, at Port Royal, wnich he had previously established, where his years were passed in the education of youth in his "Airy View Academy," and in scientific farming; he was recently re-elected to the executive committee of the State Board of Agriculture, of which he was long a member. For more than forty years Dr. Wilson was a ruling elder in the Valley churches and a frequent delegate to Presbytery and the General Assembly of the Presbyterian Church. An association of his former students have erected a monument to his memory; he d. April 19, 1890; buried in Church Hill cemetery, Port Royal. Prof. Wilson m., first, Jane McCullogh, dau. of General McCullogh; and had issue.

   ii. James-Alexander, b. April 8, 1833; m. Orlie A. Mitchelson, of Galesburg, Ill.; and had issue: *Albert-Chase, James-Park*, and *Eugene*; resides at Wymore, Gage county, Nebraska.

George A. Lyon m., secondly, October 31, 1836, SIDNEY J. OLIVER, daughter of Judge John Oliver, of Oliver township, Mifflin county, Pa.; b. December, 1802; d. July 7, 1887, buried with her husband in West Kishacoquillas cemetery. They had issue:

   iii. Mary-M., b. March 23, 1840.

XXVII. JOHN WILLIAM LYON,[4] (James,[3] James,[2] John,[1]) b. December, 1811; d. February 27, 1845; farmer, Fulton county, Pa.; m., December, 1838, CATHARINE V. ROSS, of Shirleysburg, Pa.; d. January 1, 1885. They had issue:

   i. Elizabeth, b. October 10, 1839; m. George Chestnut, of Fulton county, Pa.
   ii. Margaret, b. May. 1841; d. March, 1890; m. J. W. Patterson, of Academia, Juniata county, Pa.; who d. March, 1893, accidentally; both buried in Bedford cemetery.
   iii. James-Graham, b. February, 1843; m., June, 1878, Mary Buchanan, of Chester county.
   iv. John, b. January, 1845; m., December, 1880, Mary Ensley, of Fulton county, Pa., and had issue: *Catharine, William*, and *Edward;* reside in Baltimore.

XXVIII. JAMES GRAHAM LYON,[4] (James,[3] James,[2] John,[1]) b. at Peru Mills, Juniata county, Pa., October 3, 1820; farmer, West Dublin, Fulton county, Pa.; m., June 27, 1857, MARGARET ROBERTS, of Somerset, Pa. They had issue:

   i. Mary-Ida, b. May 10, 1858; d. February 14, 1864.

ii. *Ettie-Elizabeth*, b. October 10, 1859; m., January 16, 1886,
J. Harvey Gilliland, merchant of Watsontown, Pa.; and
had issue (surname Gilliland):
   1. *Arthur-Peebles*, b. December 13, 1886.
   2. *James-Lyon*, b. April 10, 1888.
   3. *Margaret-Jane*, d. in infancy.
   4. *Edna*, b. April 16, 1891.
iii. *James-Elmer*, b. February 2, 1869.

XXIX. JOHN PATTON LYON,[4] (John,[3] Benjamin,[2] James,[1]) iron manufacturer, Sligo, Clarion county, Pa.; lieutenant colonel and aid-de-camp to Governor William F. Johnston; b. in Centre county, Pa., June 5, 1815; d. November 26, 1886; buried in Allegheny cemetery; m., February 11, 1840, WEST-ANNA S. ELLIOTT, b. March 7, 1821, daughter of Rev. David Elliott, D. D., for many years senior professor in the Western Theological Seminary, of Allegheny city, Pa. They had issue:

    i. *John-Edward*, b. November 10, 1841; d. in inf.
39. ii. *David-Elliott*, b. December 26, 1843; m. Ettie M. Smith.
    iii. *Anna-Ellen*, b. October 13, 1845; d. in inf.
40. iv. *Fanny-Grant*, m. February 22, 1870, George B. Logan.
    v. *Alice-Patton*, b. March 17, 1849; D. A. R.
    vi. *John-Patton*, b. December 24, 1852; d. in inf.
    vii. *Edward-West*, b. January 10, 1858, in Clarion county, Pa.; m., August 15, 1882, Minnie M. Reinhart, daughter of H. W. Reinhart, of Thomasville, N. C.; and had issue:
       1. *Marjorie-Minor*, b. September 25, 1883.
       2. *Frances-Logan*, b. January 7, 1886.
    viii. *Marian-Bella*; D. A. R.

XXX. JAMES BENJAMIN LYON,[4] (John,[3] Benjamin,[2] James,[1]) glass manufacturer, Pittsburgh, Pa.; b. at Pennsylvania Furnace, Huntingdon county, April 21, 1821; m., in Carlisle, by Rev. M. R. Johnson, October 3, 1850, ANNA M. LYON, daughter of George Armstrong Lyon, Esq., (*see* XII). They had issue:

    i. *Ellen-D.*, b. April 5, 1852; D. A. R.
    ii. *John-Glamis*, b. July 20, 1855; manufacturer, New York; m. Adelina C. Langworthy, of Westerly, R. I.; and had issue:
       1. *James-Benjamin*, b. October 3, 1883.
       2. *Prescott-Langworthy*, b. July 25, 1888.
       3. *Lowell-Thayer*, b. May 3, 1892.

Lyon of Juniata. 401

  iii. *Magaret-Stewart*, b. May 19, 1858 ; D. A. R. ; m., May 30, 1895, J. Ernest Yalden, of New York.
  iv. *James-Benjamin*, b. October 9, 1860.
  v. *George-Alexander*, b. March 22, 1863.
  vi. *Mary-Lowrie*, b. March 15, 1866 ; D. A. R.; m., December 11, 1890, Augustus P. Murdoch, of Oswego, New York; and had issue (surname Murdoch):
    1. *Annie-Lyon*, b. October 17, 1891.
  vii. *Thomas-Lyttleton*, b. February 17, 1869.

XXXI. SAMUEL STEWART LYON,⁴ (John,³ Benjamin,² James,¹) a citizen of Bellefonte, Pa.; elected chief burgess in 1877 ; b. at Pennsylvania Furnace, November 11, 1822 ; m., October 16, 1855, ANN VALENTINE, daughter of Abraham Valentine ; b. May 19, 1829, at Logan Furnace, Centre county, Pa.; d. April 5, 1885. They had issue :

  i. *John-Stewart*, b. in Centre county, Pa., January 4, 1857; m., April 2, 1885, Margaret McKnight, of Pittsburgh ; and had issue :
    1. *Samuel-Stewart.*
    2. *Margaret-Acheson.*
    3. *Frances.*
    4. *Ann-Valentine.*
    5. *Catharine-Spear.*
  ii. *Ann-Valentine*, b. in Bellefonte, Pa., April 1, 1858.
  iii. *Abraham-Valentine*, d. in infancy.
41. iv. *Clara-Valentine*, b. March 14, 1861 ; m. William J. Nicolls.
42. v. *Mary-Lowrie*, b. September 19, 1863 ; m. Ellis L. Orvis.
  vi. *Rebecca-Pugh*, b. January 23, 1872.

XXXII. MARY A. LYON,⁴ (John,³ Benjamin,² James,¹) b. at Coleraine Forges, Huntingdon county, Pa., December 24, 1824; d. March 7, 1863, and buried in the Warrior's Mark cemetery; m., February 15, 1848, at Pennsylvania Furnace, by Rev. Robert Hamill, J. ROBERTS LOWRIE,* attorney-at-law, Warrior's Mark, Huntingdon county, Pa.; b. in Butler county, Pa., February 17, 1823 ; d. December 10, 1885. Edu-

---

* He was the son of the Hon. Walter Lowrie, born in Edinburgh, Scotland, December 10, 1784, coming to America with his parents in 1791, and served in the Pennsylvania State Legislature several terms, and in the United States Senate from 1819 to 1825 ; was secretary of the Senate from 1825 to 1836, and, the last twenty years of his life, secretary of the Presbyterian Board of Foreign Missions ; died in New York, on January 1, 1868.

cated at Jefferson College; having studied law was admitted to the Blair county bar 1846, and settled to practice in Hollidaysburg; afterwards removed to Warrior's Mark as the land agent of the iron firm of Lyon, Shorb & Co. They had issue (surname Lowrie):

 i. Sarah-Roberts, b. December 29, 1854.
 ii. William-Lyon, b. November 18, 1859; M. D., graduated in his academic studies 1879; graduated from the Medical Department of the University of Pennsylvania in 1883, and in 1886 established himself in practice in Tyrone, Pa.; m., January 5, 1887, Bertha G., dau. of Rev. H. G. Finney; and had issue: *Mary-Lyon*, and *Sarah-Finney*.
 iii. Roberts, b. November 3, 1861; attorney-at-law; m., April 24, 1889, Susan Bucher Brisbin, (*see Bucher family*).

Mr. Lowrie m., secondly, in 1867, Matilda N. Nassua, of Lawrenceville, N. J.

XXXIII. GEORGE W. LYON,⁴ (John,³ Benjamin,² James,¹) b. at Coleraine Forges, Huntingdon county, Pa., November 7, 1826; iron manufacturer; residence, Pennsylvania Furnace; m., June 25, 1863, by Rev. Thomas C. Porter, D. D., ANNA C. PORTER, b. 1830, daughter of John Porter, of Alexandria, Pa., (*see Bucher record*). They had issue:

 i. Clare-Charlton, d. in 1865, in infancy.
 ii. George-Porter, d. in 1870, in infancy.
 iii. John-Porter, b. July 29, 1872.

XXXIV. MARGARET ELIZABETH LYON,⁴ (John,³ Benjamin,² James,¹) b. Centre Hall, Penn's Valley, Centre county, Pa., March 24, 1829; d. at Oak Hall, same county, October 12, 1867; buried in the cemetery of the Spring Creek Presbyterian church; m., October 15, 1851, at Pennsylvania Furnace, by Rev. Daniel L. Hughes, Rev. ROBERT HAMILL, D. D.; b. in Norristown, Pa., April 21, 1816; son of Robert Hamill, b. 1759; d. 1838; who came from county Antrim, Ireland, in 1798. He was the founder of the First Presbyterian church, at Norristown, and its first elder; m., Isabella, dau. of Andrew Todd and Hannah Bowyer, of Trappe, Montgomery county, Pa., b. 1784; d. 1850. Dr. Hamill graduated from Jefferson College 1839, and from Princeton Theological Seminary 1845. After having served as active pastor the same charge in Centre county, Pa., for forty-five years was retired as pastor emeritus. They had issue (surname Hamill), all b. in Centre county, Pa.:

    i. *John-Lyon*, b. July 21, 1852; m., June 8, 1881, Mary J. C. Faries, dau. of Robert Faries, of Williamsport, Pa.; eminent as a civil engineer on the Pennsylvania State works at an early day ; and had issue :
      1. *Margaret-Lyon*, b. November 14, 1882.
      2. *Mary-Faries*, b. August 13, 1885.

    ii. *Robert-H.*, b. May 24, 1855 ; pursued his academic studies at Lafayette College, and graduated from the Medical Department of the University of Pennsylvania, 1878. Dr. Hamill pursues a general practice in Philadelphia, and is obstetrician to the Philadelphia Maternity Hospital, and gynæcologist to the Howard Hospital; m., October 14, 1891, Fanny Maria, dau. of Charles L. Lincoln and Olivia Brewster, of Hartford, Conn., b. November 11, 1861 ; and had issue :
      1. *Robert-Lincoln*, b. November 23, 1892.
      2. *Francis-Lincoln*, b. August 29, 1894.

    iii. *Mary-Lyon*, b. March 6, 1858 ; m., June 7, 1893, Henry Wilson Armstrong, b. in Horncastle, Lincolnshire, England, March 9, 1856 ; reside in Bayard, Grant county, W. Va.

    iv. *James-Lyon*, b. January 11, 1861 ; graduate of Pennsylvania State College, and of the Law Department, University of Michigan; established practice at Welch, McDowell county, W. Va.

    v. *Samuel-McClintock*, b. November 3, 1864 ; pursued his academic course at Princeton College, and graduated from the Medical Department of the University of Pennsylvania in 1888; established practice in Philadelphia; m., April 17, 1895, by Rev. Robert Hamill, D. D., Eliza Clarke Kennedy, b. October 3, 1866 ; dau. of Elias Davidson Kennedy and Agnes Shields Clarke, all of Philadelphia.

    vi. *Margaret-Isabel*, b. September 28, 1867.

XXXV. SARAH WALKER LYON,[4] (John,[3] Benjamin,[2] James,[1]) b. Centre Hall, Penn's Valley, Centre county, Pa., April 28, 1831; d. at her residence, "The Cedars," on Spruce Creek, Huntingdon county, Pa., May 15, 1860; buried in the Alexdria Presbyterian cemetery; m., at Pennsylvania Furnace, by Rev. Robert Hamill, December 23, 1852, GEORGE BUCHER

PORTER, b. March 13, 1826, of Alexandria, Pa.; merchant, Tyrone, Blair county, Pa. (*see Bucher family*). They had issue (surname Porter):

    i. Maria-Bucher, b. in Alexandria, Pa., October 17, 1853; m., at the "Cedars," near Graysville, Huntingdon county, Pa., by Rev. J. C. Barr, February 24, 1881, Adolphus M. La Porte, mining engineer, Tyrone, b. September 16, 1844; son of the Hon. John La Porte, an associate judge of Huntingdon county; Mr. La Porte went into the war of the Rebellion at the age of seventeen, enlisting in the One Hundred and Twenty-fifth regiment, Pennsylvania Volunteers, in 1862, and participated in the principal battles, coming through unscathed; appointed by Governor Pattison on the Antietam battlefield commission, 1894.

    ii. John-Lyon, b. at Curlsville, Clarion county, Pa., September 15, 1857; machinist, Tyrone; m. November 25, 1880, by Rev. J. C. Barr, Caroline, dau. of William Phillips, of Alexandria, Pa., b. January 27, 1859, and had issue:
        1. *Susan-Phillips*, d. July 17, 1887.

    iii. William-Lyon, b. at the "Cedars," May 1, 1860; m., October 23, 1884, by Rev. J. C. Kelly, Elizabeth McCartney, dau. of Robert B. Brown, of Meadville, Pa., b. August 3, 1862; d. in York, Pa., May 9, 1893, bur. in Alexandria, Pa.; and had issue:
        1. *George-Lyon*, b. November 29, 1885, at Pennsylvania Furnace.
        2. *Margaret-Culbertson*, b. June 9, 1887, in Kansas.
        3. *Hugh-Frederick*, b. August 24, 1891, in York, Pa.

XXXVI. THOMAS STEWART LYON,[4] (John,[3] Benjamin,[2] James,[1]) b. at Huntingdon Furnace, Huntingdon county, Pa., March 15, 1833; m., September 14, 1865, HANNAH J. WRIGHT, b. August 17, 1847, daughter of Ezra Wright, of Rensselaer, Indiana. Resides at Topeka, Kansas. They had issue:

    i. Miriam, b. November 12, 1866, on Spruce Creek, Huntingdon county, Pa.; m. February 5, 1886, William Dwight Church, of Germantown, chemist; and have issue (surname Church):
        1. *Elizabeth-Stewart*, b. March 19, 1887.
        2. *William-Lyon*, b. May 7, 1889; both in Topeka, Kansas.

    ii. Margaret-Hamill, b. February 12, 1872; d. in infancy.

    iii. William-Maclay, b. March 16, 1874, in Pittsburgh, Pa.

XXXVII. JOHN EDWARD LYON,⁴ (James,³ Benjamin,² James,¹) b. June 18, 1813, at Onondaga, N. Y.; d. January 20, 1894; m., September 6, 1836, CATHARINE M. TRACY, of Utica, N. Y. Residence, Oswego (N. Y.) Flouring Mills. They had issue:

    i. *Catharine-Tracy*, b. September 14, 1838; d. July 28, 1871; m. June 12, 1862, John G. Kellogg ; and had issue (surname Kellogg):
        1. *Edward-Russell*, b. April 22, 1864; m. Sarah M. Burtis.
        2. *Lansing-Otterson*, b. September 11, 1865.
        3. *Karl*, b. August 8, 1867.
    ii. *James*, b. August 2, 1841; m., November 17, 1864, Annie Rodman Pardee, who d. June 6, 1886 ; and had issue :
        1. *Tracy*, b. September 13, 1865; mechanical engineer, St. Paul, Minn.; m., July 3, 1889, Frances de Saussure Gilbert, of Gilbertsville, N. Y.; and have issue:
            a. *Annie-Pardee*, b. May 11, 1890.
            b. *Robert-Gilbert*, b. February 13, 1892.
            c. *Laura-Parsons*, b. June 30, 1894.
        2. *Laura*, b. February 13, 1868 ; m., April 22, 1892, Edwin Parsons (3d), of New York; d. April 6, 1893.
        3. *Kate-Kellogg*, b. November 16, 1869.
        4. *Annie-Pardee*, b. July 19, 1872.
        5. *Edward-Lansing*, b. June 10, 1880.
    iii. *Gardiner-Tracy*, b. December 9, 1847.
    iv. *Annie*, b. April 10, 1851.

XXXVIII. JAMES H. LYON,⁴ (James,³ Benjamin,² James,¹) b. April 6, 1817 ; resides in Chicago, Ill.; m., February 23, 1846, ANN MALONEY. They had issue:

    i. *Mary*, m. F. Richie, Chicago, Ill.
    ii. *Kate*.

XXXIX. DAVID ELLIOTT LYON,⁵ (John-Patton,⁴ John,³ Benjamin,² James,¹) b. December 26, 1843, at Pennsylvania Furnace. Captain D. E. Lyon entered the military service in the Rebellion as first lieutenant of Company H, One Hundred and Fifty-fifth regiment, Pennsylvania volunteers, and, having been promoted, commanded his company in the battles of Chancellorsville and Gettysburg. Captain Lyon was born in the iron manufacturing firm of Lyon, Shorb & Co., Pittsburgh, and has naturally fallen into the same line of business, in which he is eminently successful. Resides in Allegheny city, Pa. He m., June 23, 1868, ETTIE M. SMITH, daughter of Daniel Smith, of Brookville, Jefferson county, Pa. They had issue:

 i. Alice-Patton-West, b. November 13, 1870, at Sligo, Clarion county, Pa.; m., November 29, 1892, Charles A. Morris, of Tyrone, Pa.; and had issue (surname Morris):
  1. *Mary-Elizabeth,* b. May 27, 1894.
 ii. Westanna-Elliott, b. November 17, 1874.

XL. FANNY GRANT LYON,[5] (John-Patton,[4] John,[3] Benjamin,[2] James,[1]) b. September 21, 1847, at Sligo, Clarion county, Pa.; m., February 22, 1870, GEORGE BRYAN LOGAN, b. December 21, 1845, in Allegheny city; wholesale hardware merchant and importer, Pittsburgh; an elder in the Presbyterian church, and a director in various institutions of that city; son of John T. Logan (1809–1871) and Henrietta S. Bryan, b. in Harrisburg, July 5, 1814. Mr. Logan is a grandson of George Bryan (1766–1838) who was appointed by Governor Snyder, in 1809, Auditor General of Pennsylvania; and great-grandson of George Bryan, of Scotch-Irish descent, b. in Dublin, 1731; d. in Philadelphia, 1791, a prominent citizen of Pennsylvania in Revolutionary days; he was naval officer of the port of Philadelphia in 1776; elected vice-president Supreme Executive Council, 1777, and acting president, 1778; one of the Pennsylvania commissioners who established the boundary line between Pennsylvania and Virginia, 1779; elected an associate justice of the Supreme Court of Pennsylvania, 1780, serving until his death; he was particularly noted as the originator, author, and chief promoter of the act of 1780 "for the gradual abolition of slavery in Pennsylvania." They had issue (surname Logan):

 i. David-Elliott, b. January 22, 1871; d. in infancy.
 ii. John-Thomas, b. July 2, 1872; d. November 13, 1886.
 iii. Patton-Lyon, b. April 30, 1874; a graduate of Washington and Jefferson College.
 iv. Archibald-Hodge, b. June 25, 1877.
 v. Alice-Lyon, b. June 24, 1879.
 vi. Henrietta-Bryan, b. April 17, 1881.
 vii. Frances-Elliott, b. October 11, 1884; d. in infancy.
 viii. George-Bryan, b. January 27, 1892.

XLI. CLARA VALENTINE LYON,[5] (Samuel-Stewart,[4] John,[3] Benjamin,[2] James,[1]) b. March 14, 1861, in Nittany Valley, Centre county, Pa.; m., January 2, 1882, in Bellefonte, WILLIAM JASPER NICOLLS, b. April 23, 1854, in Camden, N. J.; civil and mining engineer, the author of several railroad treaties; in 1878 was elected a member of the American Society of Civil Engineers, and in 1885 a member of the American Society of Mining Engineers; resides at Philadelphia. Mr. Nicolls is the second son of Jasper Nicolls, civil engineer, who was the second son of Lieut. Col. William Dann Nicolls, R. A., b. in Exeter, England, June 24, 1824, and m., September 19, 1848, Ellen, eldest dau. of Dr. Baillie, of Kilkenny College and rector of Clondevaddock, county Donegal, Ireland. The family trace their descent in an unbroken line to the present day from John Nicolls, of Arran, born in the reign of James V., of Scotland, A. D. 1540.* They had issue (surname Nicolls):

    i. Clara-Lyon, b. Sunday, November 16, 1884.
    ii. Mary-Eleanor, b. Sunday, September 22, 1889; d. April 18, 1895, buried in Woodland cemetery, Philadelphia.

XLII. MARY LOWRIE LYON,[5] (Samuel-Stewart,[4] John,[3] Benjamin,[2] James,[1]) b. September 19, 1863, in Centre county, Pa.; m., December 25, 1884, ELLIS LEWIS ORVIS, b. at Lock Haven, November 16, 1857; attorney-at-law, Bellefonte, Pa., and son of the Hon. John Holden Orvis, an eminent lawyer and jurist, of Puritan descent, b. in Tioga county, Pa., February 24, 1835; d. at his home in Bellefonte, November 6, 1893, and Caroline Elizabeth Atwood, b. October 14, 1833, in Salona, Clinton county, Pa. Mr. Ellis L. Orvis is learned in the law, has traveled extensively, and having been trained in a practical school is well qualified as the successor of his father. They had issue (surname Orvis):

    i. Anne Valentine-Lyon, b. February 5, 1886.
    ii. Caroline-Elizabeth, b. March 24, 1890.

---

*The family arms were confirmed in 1858, as follows:
Arms, Sa. Three Pheons, Argent. *Crest*, A Pheon. *Motto*, Fide et Industria.

MACLAY OF LURGAN.

I. CHARLES MACLAY[1] by his first marriage had three sons. The name of his wife has not come down to us. By a second wife, JEAN HAMILTON, he had one son, who was the ancestor of the name in America. By the first wife there was issue:

    i. Owen, was an officer in the army of James II.; followed the fortunes of that royal personage; remained a bachelor, and died in France.
    ii. Charles, an officer in the same army; was killed in a duel with a French officer in Dublin.
    iii. Henry, also an officer in the royal army; and fell in the battle of the Boyne, 1690.

By the marriage with Jean Hamilton there was issue:

2.   *iv. John*, who married and had issue:

It is stated that Owen Maclay, returning from France, desired to take his nephew, Charles, to that country and educate him. His father, however, would not consent without a guarantee that the boy would be brought up in the Protestant faith. This the uncle refused, returned to France, and dying left his estate to strangers, probably to the Roman Church.

II. JOHN MACLAY,[2] (Charles,[1]) b. circa, 1680; m., and had issue:

  3.   *i. Charles*, b. 1710; m. Eleanor Query.
      ii. Eleanor, b. 1719; m. a Mr. Johnson, and remained in Ireland.
  4.   *iii. John*, b. 1721; m. Elizabeth McDonald.

III. CHARLES MACLAY,[3] (John,[2] Charles,[1]) b. 1710, in county Antrim, Ireland; "sailed for America on the 30th day of May, 1734;" located in New Garden township, Chester county; but in 1742 settled in Hopwell township, Lancaster county, now Lurgan township, Franklin county, Pa. He died in September, 1753. Charles Maclay married, in 1733, ELEANOR QUERY, daughter of William Query, of county Antrim, Ireland. The latter came to America about 1740, settled in Path Valley, but subsequently removed to North Carolina. Eleanor Query Maclay was born in county Antrim, Ireland, in 1714, and died in Lurgan township, Franklin county, Pa., July 27, 1789. Charles Maclay and his wife are both interred at Middle Spring church graveyard. They had issue:

5.   *i. John*, b. May 10, 1734 ; m. Jean Dickson.
6.   *ii. William*, b. July 20, 1737 ; m. Mary Harris.
7.   *iii. Charles*, b. August 8, 1739 ; m. Mary Templeton.
8.   *iv. Samuel*, b. January 7, 1741 ; m. Elizabeth Plunket.
    v. Eleanor, b. September 20, 1750 ; m. John Maclay.

IV. JOHN MACLAY,[3] (John,[2] Charles,[1]) b. circa 1721, in county Antrim, Ireland; came with his brother Charles to America in 1734; located in Chester county, and subsequently removed to Lurgan township, Franklin county, where he died in April, 1779; buried in Middle Spring graveyard; he m. ELIZABETH McDONALD, who is buried by the side of her husband. They had issue:

9.   *i. John*, b. 1746 ; m. Eleanor Maclay.
    ii. Charles, b. 1748; recruited a company of militia, in the winter of 1777-8, of one hundred men, all six feet in height. At the battle of Crooked Billet, on the 4th of May, 1778, he was killed with most of his company, who refused to surrender. The killed and wounded were gathered by the enemy, thrown into a heap, covered with straw and fired. Thus perished some of the bravest spirits of the Cumberland Valley.
    iii. Elizabeth, b. 1750; m. Col. Samuel Culbertson, "of the Row." Their descendants include Rev. James Culbertson, of Zanesville, Ohio; Mrs. John Rea, the widow of General Rea, who was a member of Congress from Pennsylvania for several sessions, and Rev. S. C. McCune, of Iowa; John Culbertson m. Margaret Greer; whose son, Thomas Greer Culbertson, resides at Wheeling, W. Va.
    iv. Samuel, b. 1752; d. unm.
    v. Eleanor, b. 1755 ; d. young.
    vi. Martha, m. John Irwin.

V. JOHN MACLAY,[4] (Charles,[3] John,[2] Charles,[1]) was b. May 10, 1734, in Ireland, just twenty days prior to the sailing of his parents for America; d. October 17, 1804, in Lurgan township, Franklin county, Pa. He built the first mill on the Conedoguinet creek, and put up a substantial log house of hewn timber, strongly dove-tailed together, fortifying the doors and windows by heavy bolts for the repulsion of Indian aggressions. This house is yet standing, and is now occupied by the fourth John Maclay, a lineal descendant of the builder. He was appointed a Provincial magistrate in 1760, and was a member of the Provincial Conference, held at Carpenter's Hall, Philadelphia, June 18, 1776, and afterward served as a member of the Pennsylvania Assembly for several terms. His ability is attested to us by the fact that he, one of the settlers in the far western part, was chosen by the people of Cumberland county to represent both his immediate neighbors and the people of the vastly more thickly populated eastern portion of the county in that conference which declared that they, on behalf of the people of Pennsylvania, were " willing to concur in a vote of Congress declaring the United Colonies free and independent States." His bearing on this occasion probably had much to do with his election afterward to the Assembly. As were all the Scotch-Irish settlers, Mr. Maclay was deeply religious and manifested his great interest in the affairs of the church by officiating for a long time as a ruling elder in Dr. Cooper's church, at Middle Spring. Mr. Maclay married, December 17, 1755, JEAN DICKSON, daughter of David Dickson* and Catharine Greenlee; she was b. in Ireland, December 20, 1734, and was brought to America by her parents in 1741; she d. April 3, 1812, in Lurgan township, Franklin county, Pa. They had issue, all born in Lurgan township:

      i. *Nancy*, b. 1754; d. 1761.
10. ii. *Charles*, b. May 23, 1757; m. Susanna Linn.
11. iii. *Catharine*, b. July 28, 1760; m. William Irwin.
12. iv. *David*, b. November 20, 1762; m., first, Eleanor Maclay; secondly, Eleanor Herron.
13. v. *William*, b. March 22, 1765; m. Peggy Culbertson.
14. vi. *Samuel*, b. November 16, 1767; m. Margaret Snodgrass.
15. vii. *Eleanor*, b. February 5, 1769; m. David McKnight.
      viii. *Jane*, b. September 7, 1774; d. July 9, 1799; unm.
16. ix. *John*, b. November 9, 1776; m. Hannah Reynolds.

---

* David Dickson was a native of Ireland, b. December 15, 1705; d. in Lurgan township, Franklin county, Pa., October 18, 1784. His wife, Ketrain [Catharine] Greenlee, was born in Ireland, January 1, 1711; d. December 28, 1798.

VI. WILLIAM MACLAY,[4] (Charles,[3] John,[2] Charles,[1]) b. July 20, 1737, in New Garden township, Chester county, Pa.; d. Monday, April 16, 1804, at Harrisburg, Pa.; buried in Paxtang church graveyard. In 1742 his father removed to now Lurgan township, Franklin county, where his boyhood days were spent upon the paternal farm. When the French and Indian war broke out, he was at Rev. John Blair's classical school, in Chester county, and, desiring to enter the service of the Province, his tutor gave him a recommendation " as a judicious young man and a scholar," which secured him the appointment of ensign in the Pennsylvania battalion ; he was promoted lieutenant in the Third battalion, Lieutenant Colonel Hugh Mercer, May 7, 1758. Accompanied General Forbes' expedition that year, and especially distinguished himself at the battle of Loyalhanna. In Bouquet's expedition of 1763, he was in the fight of Bushy Run ; while in the subsequent campaign of that gallant officer, he was stationed, with the great portion of the Second Pennsylvania, on the line of the stockade forts on the route to Fort Pitt as lieutenant commanding the company. For these services he participated in the Provincial grant of land to the officers connected therewith, located on the West Branch of the Susquehanna, and most of which he assisted in surveying. He studied law, and was admitted to the York county bar, April 28, 1760, but it is doubtful if he ever practiced his profession at that court, the continued Indian war, and his subsequent duties as surveyor, engrossing his entire time, although, from a letter of John Penn's, it would seem that he was afterwards admitted to the Cumberland county bar, and had acted for the prothonotary of that county. At the close of the French and Indian war, he visited England, and had an interview with Thomas Penn, one of the Proprietaries, relative to the surveys in the middle and northern parts of the Province, and was the assistant of Surveyor Lukens on the frontiers. In 1772 he laid out the town of Sunbury, and erected for himself a stone house, which was standing a few years since. Upon the organization of the county of Northumberland, he was appointed prothonotary and clerk of the courts. He also acted as the representative of the Penn family, and took a prominent part in the so-called Pennamite war. In writing to the secretary of the Province, in April, 1773, he says, "If hell is justly considered as the rendezvous of rascals, we cannot entertain a doubt of Wioming being the place;" but, much as he was prejudiced against the Connecticut settlers, he foresaw the future value of the land in that valley, and advised Penn not to sell his reservation there. At the outset of the Revolution, although an officer of the Proprietary government, William Maclay took a prominent and active part in favor of independence, not only assisting in equipping and forwarding troops to the Continental army, but marched with the associators, participating in the battles of Trenton and Princeton. During the Revolution he held the position of assistant commissary of purchases. In 1781 he was elected to the Assembly, and from that time forward he filled the various offices of member of the Supreme Executive Council, judge of the Courts of Common Pleas, deputy surveyor, and one of the commissioners for carrying into effect the act respecting the navigation of the Susquehanna river. About this period he visited England in the interest of the Penn family. In January, 1789, he was elected to the United States Senate, taking his seat there as the first Senator from Pennsylvania. He drew the short term, and his position terminated March 3, 1791, his colleague, Robert Morris, securing the long term. His election to this body raised him upon a higher plane of political activity, but contact with the Federal chiefs of the Senate only strengthened his political convictions, which, formed by long intercourse with the people of Middle Pennsylvania, were intensely democratic. He began to differ with the opinions of President Washington very early in the session; he did not approve of the state and ceremony attendant upon the intercourse of the President with Congress,—he flatly objected to the presence of the President in the Senate while business was being transacted, and in the Senate boldly spoke against his policy in the immediate presence of President Washington. The New England historians, Hildreth and Goodrich, repute Thomas Jefferson as the "efficient promoter at the beginning and father and founder of the Democratic party." Contemporary records, however, show beyond the shadow of a doubt that this responsibility or honor, in whatever light it may be regarded, cannot be shifted from the shoulders or taken from the laurels of Pennsylvania statesmanship. Before Mr. Jefferson's return from Europe, William Maclay assumed an independent position, and in his short career of two years in the Senate propounded ideas and gathered about him elements to form the opposition which developed with the meeting of Congress at Philadelphia, on the 24th of October, 1791, in a division of the people into two great parties, the Federalists and Democrats, when, for the first time, appeared an open and organized opposition to the administration. The funding of the public debt, chartering the United States Bank, and other measures championed necessarily by the administration, whose duty it was to put the wheels of government in motion, engendered opposition. Mr. Maclay, to use his own language, "no one else presenting himself," fearlessly took the initiative, and with his blunt common sense (for he was not much of a speaker) and Democratic ideas, took issue with the ablest advocate of the administration. Notwithstanding the prestige of General Washington, and the ability of the defenders of the administration on the floor of the Senate, such was the tact and resolution of Mr. Maclay, that when, after his short service, he was retired from the Senate and succeeded by James Ross, a pronounced Federalist, their impress was left in the distinctive lines of an opposition party, a party which, taking advantage of the warm feeling of our people towards the French upon the occasion of Jay's treaty with Great Britain, in 1794, and of the unpopularity of the alien and sedition laws, passed under the administration of President John Adams, in 1798, compassed the final overthrow of the Federal party in 1800. While in the Senate, Mr. Maclay preserved notes of its discussions, both in open and secret sessions, with observations upon the social customs of the first statesmen of the Republic, which have been published and edited by George Washington Harris. Upon his retirement, he resided permanently on his farm adjoining Harrisburg, where he erected the stone mansion for many years occupied by the Harrisburg Academy. In the year 1795 he was elected a member of the Pennsylvania House of Representatives, and again elected in 1803. He was a presidential elector in 1796, and, from 1801 to 1803, one of the associate judges of the county of Dauphin. Mr. Harris, who edited his journal, gives us this summary of Mr. Maclay's character: "He was a man of strict integrity, of positive opinions, having implicit confidence in his own honesty and judgment; he was inclined to be suspicious of the integrity of others whose sentiments or action in matters of importance differed from his own, and the journal, to which reference has been made, is evidence of the strength of his intellect." "In personal appearance Mr. Maclay is said to have been six feet three inches in height, and stout and muscular; his complexion was light, and his hair, in middle age, appears to have been brown, and was worn tied behind or clubbed." Mr. Maclay m., April 11, 1769, MARY MCCLURE HARRIS, daughter of John Harris, the founder of Harrisburg, and Elizabeth McClure, his wife, b. April 13, 1750, at Harris' Ferry; d. April 20, 1809, at Harburg, and buried in Paxtang church graveyard. They had issue : *

      i. *John-Harris*, b. February 5, 1770 ; d. s. p.
      ii. *Eliza*, b. February 16, 1772 ; d. April 19, 1794 ; unm.; buried in Paxtang churchyard.
17.   iii. *Eleanor*, b. January 17, 1774 ; m. William Wallace.
      iv. *Mary*, b. March 19, 1776 ; d. August 13, 1823 ; m. Samuel Awl, (see *Awl of Paxtang*).
18.   v. *Esther*, b September 19, 1778 ; m. Dr. Henry Hall.
19.   vi. *Sarah*, b. January 5, 1781 ; m. John Irwin.
20.   vii. *Jean*, b. March 19, 1783 ; m. John Lyon.
      viii. *William*, b. 1784 ; d. 1785.
      ix. *William*, (2d) b. May 5, 1787 ; d. Monday, March 22, 1813, at Harrisburg ; unm.

---

*From "memoranda" in the handwriting of William Maclay, recently furnished us, we have the following, which differs slightly from that given in our record.

WILLIAM MACLAY & MARY his wife were married the 11th April 1769 — Eleventh April Anno Dom: one thousand seven hundred & sixty nine—in Paxtang.

John Maclay (their eldest) was born the fifth of February Anno Dom: one thousand seven hundred & seventy—5th Feby 1770—on Juniata.

Elizabeth Maclay was born the Sixteenth of Feby Anno Dom: one

VII. CHARLES MACLAY,[4] (Charles,[3] John,[2] Charles,[1]) b. August 8, 1739, in New Garden township, Chester county, Pa.; d. October 30, 1834, in Lurgan township, Franklin county, Pa. He lived a long and peaceful life not far from the old homestead. He married, August 23, 1763, MARY TEMPLETON, b. about 1742; d. December 12, 1812. They left no issue.

VIII. SAMUEL MACLAY,[4] (Charles,[3] John,[2] Charles,[1]) b. June 7, 1741, in Lurgan township, Franklin county, Pa.; was educated at the classical school of the Rev. Dr. Alison, and became assistant to his brother William, while surveying the officers' tracts in Buffalo Valley. He subsequently took up a large quantity of land and settled there. At the outset of the Revolution he was chosen lieutenant colonel of the Northumberland county associators, and was in active service. In 1792 he was appointed an associate judge of Northumberland county, which he resigned December 17, 1795, having been elected member of Congress for the session of 1795-6. In 1797 he was elected to the State Senate, of which body he was chosen Speaker, December 2, 1801, and again December 7, 1802. On the 14th of December following, he was elected United States Senator, and, being Speaker, signed his own certificate. In January, 1803, he presided at the impeachment trial of Judge Addison, and continued acting as Speaker

---

thousand seven hundred & Seventy Two—In Paxtang. Died 29th April 1794. Buried in Paxtang Grave yard.

Eleanor Maclay was born the seventeenth of Jany Anno Dom: one thousand seven hundred & seventy Four—at Fort Augusta.

Mary Maclay was born the nineteenth of March Anno Dom: one thousand seven hundred & seventy-six—in Sunbury.

Esther Maclay was born the nineteenth of Septem^r Anno Dom: one thousand seven hundred and seventy Eight—In Paxtang.

Sarah Maclay, born fifth of Jany Anno Dom: one thousand seven hundred & Eighty one—In Sunbury.

Jane Maclay born the nineteenth of March Anno Dom: one thousand seven hundred & Eighty three—In Paxtang.

William Maclay, born the fifth of May Anno Dom: one thousand seven hundred eighty-seven—In Sunbury.

As to our Three dear departed Babes, Faith, Hope, and Charity, too, must conspire to place them in celestial mansions; and their names of course will be found in the Registry of Heaven.

(against the protest of the opposition, however, after March 3) until March 16, when he resigned that position, and on the 2d of September, that of State Senator. Owing to ill-health, he resigned his seat in the United States Senate on the 4th of January, 1809. Mr. Maclay was very popular in his manners, a good scholar, an efficient writer, and was one of Pennsylvania's ablest statesmen. He died at his residence in Buffalo Valley Octobe r5, 1811, and is buried on the farm. He married, in 1773, ELIZABETH PLUNKET, b. 1755; d. 1823; daughter of Dr. William Plunket, the first presiding justice of Northumberland county (1772), and noted in the annals of the State for the part he took in the Pennamite war. Dr. Plunket's wife was a daughter of John Harris, Sr., of Paxtang. They had issue:

21. i. *William-Plunket*, b. August 23, 1774; m., first, Sallie Brown; secondly, Jane Holmes.
 ii. *Eleanor*, b. October 4, 1777; m. David Maclay.
 iii. *Charles*, b. 1779; d. in 1807, unm., while on a visit to Wayne county, N. Y.
 iv. *Esther*, b. 1782; d. 1807, in Wayne county, N. Y.; unm.
 v. *Jane-E.*, b. 1786; d. January, 1848; m. Dr. Joseph Henderson, b. 1791, at Shippensburg, Pa. He studied medicine, and attended a course of lectures in the winter of 1812–13 at the University of Pennsylvania. In the spring of 1813 he received and accepted the appointment of first lieutenant in the army—opened a recruiting office in Philadelphia, subsequently joining the army at Sackett's Harbor. He was present at the battles of Chippewa, Lundy's Lane, and the other operations connected with the army on the northern frontier, and was wounded in the breast by an explosion at Fort Niagara. He received a captain's commission, and towards the close of the war was breveted a major. When peace was declared, he resigned, graduated in medicine, and began the practice of his profession at Brown's Mills, Mifflin county. In 1832 and 1834 he was elected to Congress. After his marriage with Miss Maclay, he removed to Kishacoquillas Valley, where he remained until her death; in 1850, locating at Lewistown, where he married Margaret Isenberg. By his former wife there was no issue; by the latter, *James-L.*, *Joseph*, and *William-B.* Dr. Henderson died at Lewistown, Pa., December 25, 1863.

22.   vi. *John*, b. 1789 ; m. Annie Dale.
23. vii. *Samuel*, b. 1792 ; m., first, Margaret Johnston ; secondly, Elizabeth Johnston.
     viii. *David*, b. 1797 ; d. 1818 ; m. Isabella Patterson, daughter of Galbraith Patterson ; d. 1861.
24.   ix. *Robert-Plunket*, b. April 18, 1799 ; m. Margaret C. Lashells.

IX. JOHN MACLAY,[4] (John,[3] John,[2] Charles,[1]) b. 1748, in Lurgan township, Franklin county, Pa.; d. 1800 ; was a magistrate ; an elder in the Middle Spring church ; m., in 1770, his cousin, ELEANOR MACLAY, daughter of Charles Maclay and Eleanor Query, b. September 20, 1750 ; d. November 4, 1816. Mr. and Mrs. Maclay are interred at Middle Spring graveyard. They had issue :

   i. *Samuel*, b. 1772 ; d. 1816, in Boston.
  ii. *Elizabeth*, b. 1773 ; m. William Reynolds ; and left issue.
 iii. *Charles*, b. 1775 ; d. 1809 ; m., and left issue.
  iv. *Mary*, b. 1777 ; m., first, David Edgar, of Baltimore ; secondly, John Clendenin.
   v. *Eleanor*, b. 1780 ; m. Jacob Smith. John M. Smith, Esq., of Peoria, Ill., was their son.
  vi. *Robert*, of Concord, b. 1782 ; d. July 1, 1850 ; m. Arabella Irwin ; had five sons in the ministry, *John, Charles, Alexander, William*, and *Robert-S.*, the latter formerly of the Chinese, and later of the Japan mission.
 vii. *Jane*, b. 1785 ; d. unm.
viii. *Catharine*, b. 1787 ; d. unm.
  ix. *John-M.*, b. 1789 ; d. 1823 ; was a member of Captain Samuel Gordon's Waynesboro' company, and fought heroically in the battles of Chippewa, July 5, 1814, and Lundy's Lane, July 25, 1814, in which latter contest he was severely wounded, having been hit by musket balls in the head and legs. Notwithstanding this, he refused to be carried from the field, but continued to cheer on his comrades and to load and fire his rifle for the country which he loved so well, throughout the long engagement. After his return home he was elected, in November of 1820, sheriff of Franklin county, and held that office until his death, in June, 1823. A portrait of him is in the possession of the Miss Reynolds, of Shippensburg, Pa.
   x. *William*, b. 1791 ; d. 1824, unm.

X. CHARLES MACLAY,[5] (John,[4] Charles,[3] John,[2] Charles,[1]) was b. in Lurgan township, Franklin county, Pa., on the 23d

of May, 1757; removed, about 1790, to Urbana, Ohio, and d.
there, January 4, 1815; he m., June 18, 1788, SUSANNA LINN,
b. 1765; d. August 10, 1847, at Urbana, Ohio; daughter of
William Linn and Jane McCormick, (*see Linn of Lurgan*).
They had issue :

    i. John, b. 1789; d. inf.
    ii. William, b. 1792; d. 1817.
   iii. Charles, b. March 12, 1795; d. January 24, 1844; m., September 10, 1835, Sarah Ann Sidesinger, d. January, 1883; and had issue :
      1. *Charles-Linn*, b. 1836; d. inf.
      2. *Mary-Susannah*, b. January 15, 1838; m. John S. Kirkwood, of West Liberty, Ohio.
      3. *Charles-Milton*, b. February 24, 1844, in Champaign county, Ohio ; served in an Ohio regiment during the civil war; resides in Washington, D. C.; m., in 1872, Alphonson Mayee.
   iv. John, b. September 13, 1799; d. June 9, 1862, in Tazewell county, Ill.; m. Jane Thompson, of Washington county, Pa.; and had issue :
      1. *Susannah*, b. 1824; d. inf.
      2. *Charles*, b. 1825; d. 1849; s. p.
      3. *Sarah-Jane*, b. October 8, 1827; d. February 26, 1850; m. Thomas Campbell, d. 1857.
      4. *William-Ordway*, b. August 30, 1830; d. June 21, 1869; m. Catharine Kearney, b. 1832; d. October 18, 1871; and left issue: *Charles*, *Edith*, and *Frank*.
      5. *Ebenezer-Wills*, b. June 15, 1832; d. March 8, 1873, in Illinois; m. Rebecca Campbell; no issue.
      6. *Samuel*, b. July 28, 1834; served three years in the Seventeenth regiment, Illinois Volunteers, and disabled in battle; elected two terms as sheriff of Lancaster county, Neb.; resides at Lincoln; m. Sarah Lamb, and have issue.
      7. *Mary Eliza*, b. August 28, 1836; d December 14, 1870, at Beatrice, Neb.; m., in 1860, L. P. Brown, and had two children.
      8. *Matilda-Maria*, b. November 3, 1840; m., March 3, 1873, L. P. Brown, and had one child.
      9. *John-Hoge*, b. October 5, 1843; served in the war of the Rebellion; resides at Lincoln, Neb.; m. Tryphena M Wickivere.
     10. *Milton-Sacket*, b. December 1, 1845.
     11. *Harriet*, b. August 6, 1848; m George S. Warren.
   v. Elijah, b. 1802; d. 1877; unm.

vi. Jane, b. July 5, 1806; d. August 9, 1844; m., June 21, 1832, James Nichols; and they had issue (surname Nichols):
1. *Thomas-L.*, b. June 14, 1833; m. Sarah Foust; and had issue:
   a. *Margaret*, b. February 29, 1866.
   b. *Mary*, b. Feb. 19, 1870; d. March 27, 1889.
2. *Margery-S.*, b. January 5, 1836; m. Joseph Williamson.
3. *Lavinia*, b. September 7, 1837; d. February 1, 1881.
4. *Virginia-Octavia*, b. May 22, 1840; d. April 28, 1874; m. Joseph Williamson; and had issue.
5. *James-Henry*, b. July 21, 1844; m. Francena Mead.

vii. James-Linn, b. 1809; d. 1886.

XI. CATHARINE MACLAY,[5] (John,[4] Charles,[3] John,[2] Charles,[1]) was b. in Lurgan township, Franklin county, Pa., July 28, 1760; d. July 19, 1837; she m., December 28, 1783, WILLIAM IRWIN, d. March 12, 1828. They removed to Lexington, Ky., in 1784. They had issue (surname Irwin):

i. John, d. 1856; paid a visit to Franklin county while a commissioner to the General Synod of the Presbyterian Church in 1833, and again in 1837.

ii. Stephenson, d. June 21, 1825.

XII. DAVID MACLAY,[5] (John,[4] Charles,[3] John,[2] Charles,[1]) was b. in Lurgan township, Franklin county, Pa., November 20, 1762; d. February 9, 1839. He was a man of fine literary attainments, and found more pleasure in the perusal of his well-selected library, and in his home and family than in the political caldron of that period. At the very earnest demand of his fellow-citizens, however, he served two terms, from 1812 to 1814, in the Assembly or Legislature of this State, but beyond this he never could be induced to accept office. He was twice married; m., first, September 8, 1795, ELEANOR MACLAY, daughter of Samuel Maclay and Elizabeth Plunket, (*see* VIII), b. October 4, 1777; d. April, 1802. They had issue:

i. Samuel, b. 1797; d. s. p.
ii. Jane, b. 1799; d. s. p.
iii. Betty, b. 1801; d. s. p.

David Maclay m., secondly, October 2, 1806, ELEANOR HERRON, daughter of John Herron, and sister of Rev. Francis Herron, of Pittsburgh, b. June 1, 1784; d. February 23, 1825. They had issue:

  iv. John-Herron, b. July 14, 1807; d. ———, 1871; m. Margaret Hemphill; and had issue:
    1. *Jane-Ellen*, b. 1837; d. April 23, 1882; m. Thomas Sharpe; no issue.
    2. *James-Hemphill*, b. June 12, 1839; served in the war of the Rebellion in the Fourth Pennsylvania Light Artillery; m. Annie Morgan Fickes, of Pittsburgh, and had eleven children.
  v. David, b. November 27, 1808; served two terms in the Legislature from Franklin county.
  vi. Jane-Eleanor, b. 1810; d. 1866; m., first, John McGinley, son of Dr. McGinley, of Adams county; m., secondly, Judge Joseph Pomeroy, of Juniata county.
  vii. Charles-Templeton, b. September 13, 1812; d. August 7, 1888; graduated from Jefferson Medical College in 1839, and settled at Green Village, Franklin county, and became eminent in his profession; he m., first, Mary Ann Frazer, and had six children; m., secondly, a sister of Hon. Thaddeus M. Mahon.
  viii. Francis-Herron, b. June 22, 1815; removed to Rolla, Mo.; m. Sarah Cox, and have issue.
  ix. James-Herron, b. May 16, 1818; d. August 26, 1845, at Albany, Ill., unm.
  x. Mary-Eleanor, b. 1822; d. July 14, 1854; m. Samuel Elder McCune, d. 1859; and had issue (surname McCune): Dr. *David-Maclay*, *Theodore*, and *James-Albert*.

XIII. WILLIAM MACLAY,[5] (John,[4] Charles,[3] John,[2] Charles,[1]) was b. in Lurgan township, Franklin county, Pa., March 22, 1765; was a member of Assembly in 1807 and 1808, as also a member of the Fourteenth and Fifteenth Congresses; he was subsequently appointed one of the associate judges of the court; he d. on the 4th of January, 1825, and was buried at the lower graveyard, near Fannettsburg, the Rev. Dr. McGinley officiating, he being for many years an elder in his congregation. Mr. Maclay was a large muscular man, six feet two inches in height, but very pleasant and affable. He m., December 22, 1789, by Rev. John Craighead, of Rocky Spring, MARGARET CULBERTSON, b. 1773; d. May 4, 1834; daughter of Alexander Culbertson. They had issue:

  i. Mary-Sharp, b. November 26, 1790; d. September 11, 1850; m. John King, of Chambersburg.
25. *ii. John*, b. December 1, 1792; m. Jane Findlay.

iii. *Jane*, b. October 31, 1794 ; d. 1822, in Georgia ; m. Gen. Samuel Dunn, who was a member of the Pennsylvania Legislature 1820-1.
iv. *Eliza-Culbertson*, b. October 16, 1796 ; d. February 20, 1856 ; m., first, John Dunn ; secondly, John Graham.
v. *Catharine-Irwin*, b. February 2, 1799 ; d. December 22, 1873, in Williamsport ; m. Dr. John Geddes, of Newville.
vi. *Alexander*, b. November 12, 1801 ; d. 1877 ; m. Mary McNaughton, of Pittsburgh.
vii. *William*, b. March 12, 1803 ; d. February 20, 1849 ; m. Mary Palmer, of Bedford county, Pa.
viii. *Margaretta*, b. March 31, 1805 ; d. Aug. 29, 1844 ; m. James W. Burbridge, of Pittsburgh.
ix. *James-Ross*, b. June 4, 1807 ; d. April 27, 1840 ; unm.
x. *Charles-Samuel*, b. May 30, 1809 ; d. May 28, 1828, at Fannettsburg.
xi. *Nancy-Eleanor*, b. June 25, 1812 ; living in 1886 ; m., 1836, Cyrus D. Culbertson, d. 1870.
xii. *David-Irwin*, b. September 26, 1814 ; d. December, 1839, at Carrick, Franklin county, Pa. ; unm.

XIV. SAMUEL MACLAY,[5] (John,[4] Charles,[3] John,[2] Charles,[1]) b. November 16, 1767, in Lurgan township, Franklin county, Pa.; d. February 5, 1843 ; m. MARGARET SNODGRASS, d. August 1, 1871 ; dau. of Thomas Snodgrass. They had issue :

i. *Mary-Jane*, b. 1813 ; m. George Ewing.
ii. *John-Enoch*, b. December 24, 1815 ; unm.
iii. *Ellen*, b. 1818 ; m. William Smith.
iv. *Charles-Henry*, b. January 16, 1820.
v. *Elizabeth*, b. 1822 ; d. inf.
vi. *Thomas-James*, b. November 22, 1824 ; m. Annie E. Fassett ; and had six children.
vii. *Robert-Snodgrass*, b. November 25, 1825 ; d. April 24, 1881 ; m. Catharine E. Willis ; and left issue.
viii. *Samuel-Dickson*, b. December 17, 1829 ; served in the war of the Rebellion ; m. Martha Jenkins, of Doylestown, Pa.; and had issue.

XV. ELEANOR MACLAY,[5] (John,[4] Charles,[3] John,[2] Charles,[1]) b. February 5, 1769, in Lurgan township, Franklin county, Pa.; d. September 5, 1833 ; m., November 18, 1770, DAVID MCKNIGHT, son of John and Mary McKnight, of Middleton township, Cumberland county. They resided near Shippensburg until 1812, when they removed to Ohio. At the death of their mother, the sons went to eastern Tennessee, where descendants now reside. They had issue (surname McKnight):

 i. John.
 ii. David.
 iii. Elisha.
 iv. Ebenezer-Findlay.
 v. Eleanor.
 vi. Charles-Maclay.
 vii. Jean.

XVI. JOHN MACLAY,[5] (John,[4] Charles,[3] John,[2] Charles,[1]) b. November 9, 1776; d. December 22, 1852, while on a visit to his son-in-law, Rev. Dr. Brownson, at Washington, Pa.; resided for many years on the old homestead, whence he removed to Shippensburg, and represented Cumberland county in the Legislature several terms; he m., October 8, 1808, HANNAH REYNOLDS. They had issue:

 i. Hannah-Jane. b. 1810; d. July 24, 1851; m. Prof. William Marvel Nevin, of Franklin and Marshall College, at Lancaster, one of the most thoroughly educated men in Pennsylvania; and had issue (surname Nevin): five children, only one of whom reached maturity:
  1. *Martha-Ellen,* m. J. B. Kremer, of Carlisle.
 ii. Abigail-Catharine, b. 1812; d. July 31, 1850; m. Benjamin Sterrett, of Cincinnati, O.; and left issue.
 iii. Sarah-Ellen, b. 1814; d. April 14, 1853; m. Rev. James Irwin Brownson, D. D,; and had issue (surname Brownson):
  1. *Sarah-Smith,* b. 1844; m. Henry R. Whitehill, a lawyer; reside in Montana.
  2. *John-Maclay,* b. October 10, 1845; graduated from Washington and Jefferson College; resides at Pittsburgh; m. Mary Conrad.
  3. *Elliot-Creigh,* b. 1847; d. 1849.
  4. *Ellen-Maclay,* b. 1849.
  5. *Mary Reynolds,* b. 1852; d. 1853.
 iv. Livia-Eliza, b. 1816; m. Alexander Plumer.
 v. John-Reynolds, b. 1819; d. young.
 vi. Margaret-Reynolds, b. 1821; d. young.
 vii. Charles-Benjamin, b. April 23, 1824; graduated from Franklin and Marshall College; studied theology, and licensed by Carlisle Presbytery in 1846; subsequently studied medicine, and became professor in the Cincinnati College of medicine and surgery; m. Louisa Irwin; and had issue.

viii. Mary (twin), b. April 28, 1824; d. young.
ix. William-John, b. 1828; d. young.

XVII. ELEANOR MACLAY,[5] (William,[4] Charles,[3] John,[2] Charles,[1]) b. January, 17, 1774, at Harris' Ferry; d. January 2, 1823, at Harrisburg, Pa.; m., 1806, by Rev. Nathaniel Snowden, WILLIAM WALLACE, b. October, 1768, in Hanover township, Dauphin county, Pa.; d. Tuesday, May 28, 1816, and with his wife buried in Paxtang church graveyard. He was the eldest son of Benjamin Wallace and Elizabeth Culbertson; received a classical education; graduated at Dickinson College; studied law at Harrisburg under Galbraith Patterson, and was admitted to the bar at the June term, 1792. He became interested in the Harrisburg and Presqu' Isle Land Company, and, about 1800, removed to Erie, in the affairs of which place and in the organization of the county he took an active and leading part. About 1810 he returned to Harrisburg and partly resumed his profession. Besides being a member of the bar he was a partner of his brother-in-law, John Lyon, at Pennsylvania Furnace. He was nominated by the Federalists for Congress in 1813, but defeated. He was elected the first president of the old Harrisburg Bank and was burgess of the borough at his death. He was a polite, urbane man, of slight frame and precise address. Mr. Wallace had previously married, in 1803, Rachel Forrest, daughter of Dr. Andrew Forrest, of Harrisburg, who died at Erie in 1804. Eleanor Maclay and William Wallace had issue (surname Wallace):

26. *i. Mary-Elizabeth*, b. May 7, 1867; m. Rev. William R. DeWitt, D. D.
    ii. William-Maclay, b. August 15, 1808; d. June 26, 1877, at Erie; unm.; a physician of prominence.
27. *iii.* Rev. *Benjamin-John*, b. June 10, 1810; m. Sarah Cochran.
28. *iv. Irwin-Maclay*, b. October 10, 1813; m. Elizabeth Reed.

XVIII. ESTHER HARRIS MACLAY,[5] (William,[4] Charles,[3] John,[2] Charles,[1]) b. September 19, 1778, in Sunbury, Pa.; d. September 6, 1819, in Harrisburg, Pa.; m., April 26, 1800, by Rev. Mr. Snowden, HENRY HALL, b. October 18, 1775, in Cecil county, Md.; d. May 25, 1808, in Harrisburg, Pa.; son of Elihu Hall and Catharine Orrick. His ancestor, Richard Hall, of Mount Welcome, was one of the earliest settlers at the head of the Elk. Henry studied medicine and located at Harrisburg, Pa., in 1794, where, as was usual with early physicians, he kept an "apothecary shop." He was quite a successful practitioner, but died early. They had issue (surname Hall):

29.
    i. *William-Maclay*, b. February 16, 1801 ; m. Ellen Campbell Williams.
    ii. *Mary-Elizabeth*, b. April 21, 1802; d. 1884 ; m. George Washington Harris.

30.
    iii. *Catharine-Julia*, b. August 14, 1804; m. Garrick Mallery.
    iv. *Henrietta*, b. 1807; d. s. p.

XIX. SALLIE MACLAY,[5] (William,[4] Charles,[3] John,[2] Charles,[1]) b. January 5, 1781 ; d. Nov. 16, 1832; m., March 10, 1804, by Rev. N. Snowden, Major JOHN IRWIN; d. November 16, 1832, at Long Hollow, Mifflin county, Pa. They had issue (surname Irwin):

    i. *Mary-Maclay*, m., first, Edmund Burke Patterson ; secondly, Rev. Samuel Bryson.
    ii. *Henrietta*, m. Samuel Purviance ; and had issue (surname Purviance): *Sarah, Mary, Howard, John*, and *Ann*.
    iii. *Jane*, m. Robert McClelland ; and had issue (surname McClelland): *Sarah, Mary*, and *Howard*.
    iv. *George*, m. Ann Bryson; and had *E.-Howard*; reside at Lodi, Wis.
    v. *William-Maclay*, d. at Lewistown ; m. Mary Edmeston ; and had *Henrietta*.
    vi. *Ellen*, m. Dr. Caleb Brinton, of West Chester; and had issue (surname Brinton): *Sarah, Mary, Caleb*, Dr. *William*, and *George*.
    vii. *Ann*, m. Dr. Horatio Worrall; and had issue (surname Worrall): *Charles*, and *John*.

XX. JEAN MACLAY,[5] (William,[4] Charles,[3] John,[2] Charles,[1]) b. March 19, 1783 ; d. April 30, 1809 ; m. April 28, 1808, by Rev. Mr. Sharon, JOHN LYON. They had issue (surname Lyon):

    i. *William-Maclay*, b. April 30, 1809, (*see Lyon record*).

XXI. WILLIAM PLUNKET MACLAY,[5] (Samuel,[4] Charles,[3] John,[2] Charles,[1]) b. August 23, 1774, in Buffalo Valley ; d. September 2, 1842, in Milroy, Mifflin county, Pa. In the year 1808 he was appointed by Governor S. Snyder prothonotary of Mifflin county, which office he held until elected to

Congress in 1814, to fill a vacancy occasioned by the resignation of Thomas Burnside, appointed judge of the Court of Common Pleas. Mr. Maclay was subsequently elected to Congress for two full terms, 1816 and 1818; he was a member of the constitutional convention of 1837–8, and declined signing the document framed at that time, on account of its prohibition of the colored vote. He was twice married; m., first, December, 1802, SALLIE BROWN, daughter of Judge William Brown, of Mifflin county; d. January 2, 1810, aged twenty-six years. They had issue :

 i. Dr. *Samuel*, b. October 5, 1803; m., first, Margaret Baxter; d. July 3. 1863; m., secondly, November 22, 1864, Mrs. Harriet Gwin (*nee* Patton); and had issue:
  1. *Sallie-Brown*, b. September 7, 1865.
  2. *Nannie-Patton*, b. May 7, 1867; d. Dec. 1, 1872.
  3. *Ellen-Margaret*, b. August 20, 1868.
 ii. *William-Brown*, b. April 5, 1805; d. March 29, 1853; m. Eleanor Lashells, and had issue :
  1. *Sarah-Jane*, d. s. p.
  2. *Mary-Brown*, d. s. p.
  3. *Elizabeth*.
  4. *Ralph-L.*, b. 1836; d. January, 1866; captain in Forty-ninth regiment, Pennsylvania Volunteers.
  5. *Isabella Plunket*, m. A. A. McDonald, of Covington, Virginia.
  6. *Ellen*, d. 1861.
 iii. *Charles John*, b. January 12, 1807; d. December, 1828; unm.

William Plunket Maclay m., secondly, in 1812, JANE HOLMES, of Carlisle. They had issue :

 iv. *Holmes*, b. 1818; was a member of Pennsylvania Legislature in 1864; m. Isabella Plunket Richardson, and had issue: *Mary-Holmes, William-Plunket,* and *Ella-Richardson*.
 v. *David*, b. 1819; was a member of the Pennsylvania Senate, 1872 to 1875; m., in 1846, Elizabeth Richardson, and had issue :
  1. *Jane-Holmes*, m. S. Clever; reside in Dakota.
  2. *Mary-Porter*, m. Daniel Curll, of Clarion, Pa.
  3. *William-Plunket*, resides in Montana.
  4. *Margaret*, resides in Montana.
  5. *Elizabeth*, m. and resides in Dakota.
  6. *Samuel*, of Montana.
  7. *Sallie-Brown*, of Clarion, Pa.

8. *David*, of Montana.
9. *Harriet-Patton*, of Clarion, Pa.
10. *Anna*, of Clarion, Pa.
vi. *Robert-Plunket*, b. 1821; d. April 20, 1881; m. Martha Barr, and had issue:
    1. *William-Barr*, resides in Mifflin county, Pa.
    2. *Jennie-Landrum*, resides in Mifflin county, Pa.
vii. *Joseph Henderson*, b. 1824; was a member of the Legislature from 1878 to 1882; m. his cousin, Mary Maclay, daughter of Robert P. Maclay, deceased, having issue, *Margaret-Lashells*.

XXII. JOHN MACLAY,[5] (Samuel,[4] Charles,[3] John,[2] Charles,[1]) b. 1789; d. June 25, 1855; m., February 11, 1812, ANNIE DALE, sister of Hon. James Dale, of Union county, Pa. They had issue:

i. *Samuel*, d. in Buffalo Valley.
ii. *Charles*, d. in Illinois.
iii. *William-Plunket*, d. s. p.
iv. *Elizabeth*, m., first, —— Armstrong; secondly, Dr. Alexander, and had issue.
v. *Anne*, d. July 6, 1835.

XXIII. SAMUEL MACLAY,[5] (Samuel,[4] Charles,[3] John,[2] Charles,[1]) b. 1792; d. February 17, 1836; m., first, MARGARET JOHNSTON, daughter of Rev. James Johnston. They had issue:

i. Dr. *Samuel*, b. 1814; d. 1851, in Cincinnati, O.
ii. *James-Johnston*, b. 1815; d. 1848, unm., in Cincinnati, O.
iii. *William-John*, d. in infancy.

Mr. Maclay m., secondly, ELIZABETH JOHNSTON, sister of his first wife. They had issue:

iv. *Robert-Plunket*, b. 1818; graduated at West Point; appointed brevet second lieutenant, Sixth Infantry, July 1, 1840; second lieutenant, Eighth Infantry, October 1, 1840; first lieutenant, December 31, 1845; captain, January 22, 1849; resigned, December 31, 1860; resides in Waterloo, La.
v. *Charles*, m. Miss Cox, of Franklin county, Pa., and had issue:
    1. *Elizabeth*, widow, residing in Washington city; m M. H. Candee.
    2. *Nora*, d. May, 1885.
vi. *David*, studied medicine in Missouri.
vii. *John*, d. in North Carolina, during the war.

viii. *Margaret*, m. Thomas S. Briscoe, and had issue (surname Briscoe): *Bessie, Fannie*, and *Samuel-Maclay*.
ix. *Elizabeth*, d. in 1884, in Galesburgb, Ill.
x. *Jane*, a widow, at St. Mary's Indian school, Minnesota; m. Robert C. Johnston.

XXIV. ROBERT PLUNKET MACLAY,[5] (Samuel,[4] Charles,[3] John,[2] Charles,[1]) b. April 19, 1799, in Buffalo Valley, now Union county, Pa.; d. August 16, 1884, in Kishacoquillas Valley, Brown township, Mifflin county, Pa. His father died when the son was in his twelfth year. The latter was sent, however, to an academy at Bedford, Pa., where he pursued a course of study for some time, and then returned to his mother's home, in Buffalo Valley. In 1833, he was elected to the Legislature from Union county, and served one term; and January 6, 1836, he was appointed by Governor Ritner prothonotary of Union county, serving until 1839, when he entered the Senate of Pennsylvania, serving until 1843. In 1844, Mr. Maclay removed to Clarion county, and was afterwards appointed associate judge of that county by Gov. Johnston. In 1854 he went to Missouri where he remained about three years engaged in the construction of the Iron Mountain railroad. In 1857 he returned to Clarion county, and in 1864, after the decease of his brother-in-law, Dr. Joseph Henderson, he went to reside in Kisacoquillas Valley, with his sons and grandsons, where he remained until his death. Judge Maclay was a very tall, well-proportioned man, with an intellectual cast of countenance, a nobly-shaped head, of commanding presence, standing straight as an arrow, he always attracted attention, while his amiable and genial disposition and social qualities endeared him to his many friends. He had wonderful conversational powers, a great memory, well stored with the traditionary history of our State and anecdotes of its prominent citizens and politicians. His last visit of any consequence from home was on the occasion of the reunion of the surviving members of the Pennsylvania Legislature in 1875, when he and his old friend, John Williamson, of Huntingdon, emerged from their retirement to delight their admiring juniors for a while with their old-time tales, *repartee*, and humor. Judge Maclay was a firm believer in revelation, and had great veneration, as he himself said, "For the plan of salvation as given in the four Gospels; magnificently beautiful in its simplicity." At the foot of Chestnut mountain, with company and associations that suited him, dispensing a liberal hospitality, enjoying good health until the spring of 1884, the judge passed a serene old age, and died sincerely regretted by all who ever had the pleasure of his acquaintance. Mr. Maclay m., May 6, 1825, by Rev. John Dreisbach, MARGARET C. LASHELLS, b. about 1801; d. May 6, 1845, a neice of John Lashells, Esq., a noted lawyer of New Berlin, Pa., and daughter of Ralph Lashells, of Gettysburg, Pa. They had issue:

    i. *Samuel-Ralph*, b. August 11, 1826; m.. and left issue.
    ii. *George-Lashells*, b. July 28, 1828; d. October 27, 1853; unm.
    iii. *Charles-Maclay*, b. August 31, 1831; d. November 25, 1865; m., and left issue.
    iv. *Mary-Elizabeth*, b. 1834; m. Joseph Henderson Maclay.
    v. *William-Plunket*, b. May 4, 1841; unm.

XXV. JOHN MACLAY,[6] (William,[5] John,[4] Charles,[3] John,[2] Charles,[1]) b. December 1, 1792, in Lurgan township, Franklin county, Pa.; died April 22, 1854, in St. Louis, Mo. Mr. Maclay was twice married; m., first, May 6, 1819, JANE FINDLAY, of Chambersburg; d. April 27, 1827; daughter of Col. John Findlay. They had issue:

31.   *i.* *William-Irwin*, b. March 27, 1820; m. Sarah Stackhouse.
    ii. *John-Findlay*, b. February 18, 1822; d. December 13, 1822.
    iii. [*A son,*] b. September 24, 1823; d. September 30, 1823.
    iv. *Nancy-Jane*, b. March 12, 1825; d. May 27, 1827.

Mr. Maclay m., secondly, September 18, 1832, ANNA MARIA GLEIM, of Pittsburgh; d. October 18, 1868; daughter of Christian Gleim. They had issue:

    v. *Annie-Maria*, b. January 1, 1834; m. Fisk Gore.
    vi. *John-King*, b. June 29, 1835; d. September 4, 1836.
    vii. *Martha Gleim*, b. December 18, 1836; d. May 21, 1854.
    viii. *James-Brown*, b. November 7, 1838; d. February 21, 1872.
    ix. *John-Gleim*, b. July 10, 1840.
    x. *Cyrus-Culbertson*, b. September 7, 1842; m. Laura Miller.
    xi. *Edgar-Gleim*, b. August 26, 1844; m. Blanche Murphy.
    xii. *Charles-Gleim*, b. September 2, 1846; d. May, 1847.
    xiii. *Ellen-Brown*, b. July 11, 1849; d. August 28, 1849.

XXVI. MARY ELIZABETH WALLACE,[6] (Eleanor,[5] William,[4] Charles,[3] John,[2] Charles,[1]) b. May 7, 1807; d. October 16, 1881, at Harrisburg, Pa.; m., March 15, 1825, by Rev. Dr. Duffield, Rev. WILLIAM RADCLIFFE DEWITT, b. February 25, 1792, at Paulding's Manor, Duchess county, N. Y.; d. December 23, 1867, at Harrisburg, Pa.; son of John DeWitt and Katharine Van Vliet. His ancestors were among the first immigrants from Holland to New Netherlands, in 1623. His early years were spent in commercial pursuits, but, about 1810, he turned his attention to the sacred ministry. He studied with Dr. Alexander Proudfit, of Salem, N. Y., and entered Washington Academy. The war of 1812 interrupting his studies, he volunteered in the regiment of Colonel Rice, and was in service at Lake Champlain at the time of McDonough's victory, September 11, 1814. After the close of the war, in 1815, he entered Nassau Hall, Princeton, as a sophomore, but subsequently entered the senior class of Union College, Schenectady, where he graduated with distinction, completing his theological studies under Rev. Dr. John M. Mason, of New York. He was licensed to preach by the Presbytery of New York April 23, 1818. In the fall of that year he went to Harrisburg by invitation, and was called to the pastorate of the Presbyterian church, October 5, 1818. He was received by the Presbytery of Carlisle April 13, 1819, but not ordained until the 26th of October, of that year. Dr. DeWitt received the degree of A. M. in course from Union College, and in 1838 the University of Pennsylvania conferred on him the title of Doctor of Divinity. From 1854 to 1860 he held the office of State Librarian, appointed by Governors Bigler and Pollock. In 1854 he felt the necessity of taking a colleague—Rev. T. H. Robinson, D. D., the recent minister. Dr. DeWitt was twice married, his first wife being JULIA A. WOODHULL, daughter of Rev. Nathan Woodhull, of Newton, L. I. During a ministry of nearly fifty years in Harrisburg, Dr. DeWitt enjoyed the confidence of all his ministerial brethren. In the community he was greatly appreciated and respected by all classes. As a theologian he had few equals in the ministry, and, although firm and decided in his views, he was liberal and catholic in spirit. His published writings were limited to twelve or thirteen pamphlets, the most popular of which was a small volume entitled "Her Price above Rubies." He preached many powerful discourses, a volume of which should certainly be preserved in permanent form. They had issue (surname DeWitt):

    i. William-Radcliffe, b. December 5, 1826; d. at Palatka, Fla.; was educated under the direction of his father and the Rev. Benjamin J. Wallace, both men of rare scholarly attainments; Princeton College conferred upon him the degree of A. M., and in 1852 he graduated in medicine at Philadelphia; appointed assistant physician of the State Lunatic Hospital at Harrisburg, and, while serving in this capacity, visited, in 1855, the various hospitals of England, France, Germany, and Belgium; in 1859, resigned, having been appointed by the President physician and surgeon in the United States Hospital at Honolulu, Sandwich Islands; in 1862, returned to this country, and was appointed an acting assistant surgeon at the Georgetown College Hospital; in 1864 commissioned by President Lincoln surgeon-in-chief, First division, Fifth corps of the army of the Potomac, serving until the close of the war for the Union; in November, 1867, mustered out of service; resumed the practice of his profession in Harrisburg several years; afterwards, on account of his health, removing to Florida, near Palatka; he m., November 4, 1865, at York, Pa., Susan E. Spangler, (*see Hamilton record*); and they had issue (surname DeWitt):

        1. *William-Radcliffe*, b. November 22, 1867.
        2. *John-Hamilton*, b. June 14, 1870; d. Dec. 15, 1871.

  ii. Julia, b. November 5, 1828; resides at Carlisle, Pa.
  iii. Eleanor-Wallace, b. August 21, 1830; d. in infancy.
  iv. Kate-Van Vliet, b. May 21, 1833; m., October 3, 1861, George Edwards Sterry, of New York city; and had issue (surname Sterry):

        1. *William DeWitt*, b. July 7, 1862.
        2. *George-Edwards*, b. March 14, 1864.
        3. *John-DeWitt*, b. November 25, 1865.
        4. *Edward-Augustus*, b. June, 1867; d. March, 1868.
        5. *James-Weaver*, b. December 24, 1869.
        6. *Wallace-Maclay*, b. December 25, 1872.
        7. *Thomas-Hunt*, b. September 6, 1875.

  v. Wallace (first), b. July 21, 1835; d. young.
  vi. Wallace, b. August 19, 1837; d. Feb. 9, 1891, at Harrisburg, Pa.; graduated at College of New Jersey in 1857; was

an attorney-at-law; m., September 10, 1885, Louisa Bliss, daughter of John H. Bliss, of Erie, Pa.

vii. Calvin, b. May 26, 1840; graduated at College of New Jersey, 1860; commissioned October 24, 1861, captain in Forty-ninth regiment, Pennsylvania Volunteer Infantry, army of Potomac; resigned January 18, 1863; studied medicine and graduated from Jefferson Medical College, Philadelphia, March, 1866; appointed first lieutenant and assistant surgeon United States army, May 14, 1867; captain, May 14, 1870; promoted to major and surgeon United States army, July 21, 1885; m., April 26, 1877, Josephine Lesesne, daughter of John F. Lesesne, M. D., of Georgetown, S. C.; and had issue (surname DeWitt):

1. *Wallace*, b. June 1, 1878.
2. *Lesesne*, b. January 9, 1880.
3. *Mary-Wallace*, b. February 15, 1884.

viii. John, b. October 10, 1842; graduated at College of New Jersey, 1861; studied theology at Princeton and Union Theological Seminaries of Presbyterian Church; ordained June, 1865; pastor at Irvington, N. Y., 1865-69; pastor Central church, Boston, 1869-76; pastor Tenth Presbyterian church, Philadelphia, 1876-82; professor of Church History Lane Theological Seminary, 1882; received degree of D. D. from the College of New Jersey, 1877; published "Sermons on Christian Life," 1885; m., August 20, 1874, Laura Aubrey Beaver, daughter of Thomas Beaver, of Danville, Pa.; who d. 1892.

ix. Mary, b. November 25, 1846; d. April 8, 1870.

XXVII. BENJAMIN JOHN WALLACE,[6] (Eleanor,[5] William, Charles,[3] John,[2] Charles,[1]) b. August 10, 1810, at Harrisburg, Pa.; d. July 25, 1862, at Philadelphia. His father dying when he was only six years of age, he was left to the care of an amiable and excellent mother, whose early training fitted him for the position he occupied with so much success in his maturity. When of suitable age he became a pupil of the Harrisburg Academy, that institution being in charge of the ablest instructors. The culture he received at the school fitted him for admission to the United States Military Academy at West Point, to which he was appointed, where he was rapidly gaining a foremost place, when his heart convinced him that a higher vocation was to be his calling. He left West Point, was prepared for Princeton College and the ministry of the

Presbyterian Church, under the care of Rev. John Hutchinson, of Mifflintown, a former tutor in the Harrisburg Academy. After graduating with high honor he was licensed to preach, and was called at once to a western charge. The degree of Doctor of Divinity was conferred upon him by his *alma mater*. His elegance as a writer and eloquence as a speaker soon brought him into great prominence in his denomination and in all religious circles, so that when the *Presbyterian Quarterly*, the organ of the "New School," was projected, he was at once selected as its editor. His brilliance of style gave character to this publication, and as long as he lived it was a prosperous and popular publication. Mr. Wallace was pastor of churches in Pittsburgh, York, and at other points; president and professor of Delaware College, at Newark, in that State. Unfortunately for his fame as an author, his literary productions are scattered throughout the ephemeral publications of his time. It need not be repeated that both as speaker and writer he was captivating and graceful, of fine stature and polished address, in society one of the most entertaining of a long roll of able men, whose cultivated minds directed the thoughts of the generation of which he was so distinguished an ornament. Dr. Wallace m., at Pittsburgh, November 5, 1832, SARAH COCHRAN, daughter of George Cochran, b. 1812; d. 1869, in Pittsburgh, Pa. They had issue (surname Wallace):

    i. Ernest-Cochran, b. 1833; d. 1867; m. Emma Deihl; no issue.
    ii. Irwin-Maclay, b. 1835; d. 1862, at Pittsburgh; was a lieutenant United States army.
    iii. Ellen, b. 1838; d. 1865; m. Preston Forster; no issue.
    iv. Mary, b. 1840; d. 1845.
    v. Florence, b. 1843; d. 1880; m. Hugh Hamilton, M. D., of Harrisburg, (*see Hamilton record*).
    vi. Alfred-Cochran, b. 1845; d. 1847.
    vii. Sarah-Cochran, b. 1849; d. 1854.
    viii. Marion, b. 1850; d. 1883; m. Rev. John K. McKallip, of Bellaire, Ohio.
    ix. Arthur Harris, b. 1853; d. 1887.

XXVIII. IRWIN MACLAY WALLACE,[6] (Eleanor,[5] William,[4] Charles,[3] John,[2] Charles,[1]) b. October 10, 1813; m. ELIZABETH REED, of Erie. They had issue:

  i. William-Maclay, b. 1847.
  ii. Mary, b. 1849; d. young.
  iii. Robert-Reed, b. 1851.
  iv. Eleanor-Maclay, b. 1853; m. Lieut. Samuel K. Allen, United States navy, grandson of Col. Ethan Allen, of the Revolution.
  v. Elizabeth Harris, b. 1855.
  vi. Jane-Maclay, b. 1857; d. inf.
  vii. Anna, b. 1859; d. inf.

XXIX. WILLIAM MACLAY HALL,[6] (Esther,[5] William,[4] Charles,[3] John,[2] Charles,[1]) b. February 16, 1801, in Harrisburg, Pa.; d. August 28, 1851, in Bedford, Pa., where he was interred, but, in 1878, his remains were removed to the cemetery at Harrisburg, Pa. He was educated at the Harrisburg Academy and Princeton College; studied law with Francis R. Shunk, and admitted to the Dauphin county bar at the April term, 1822. He began the practice of law at Lewistown, and became one of the most brilliant advocates in the Juniata Valley. Subsequently, imbued with the conviction that it was his duty to enter the ministry, he abandoned the law, studied theology at the Allegheny Seminary, and was licensed to preach by the Pittsburgh Presbytery. He was stationed at Milroy, Mifflin county, Pa., but, owing to partial failure of health, was appointed agent of the American Board of Commissioners for Foreign Missions at Philadelphia. At this period he was connected with the New School Assembly, but afterwards transferred his relations to the Old School, and joined the Presbytery of Carlisle. After acting some years as agent of the General Assembly Board of Foreign Missions, he accepted a call to the Presbyterian church at Bedford, Pa., where he labored until declining health compelled him to relinquish his charge. The Rev. Mr. Hall married ELLEN CAMPBELL WILLIAMS, daughter of Benjamin Williams and his wife Nancy Fisher, and niece of Rev. Joshua Williams, of Centre county, Pa.; d. January 23, 1878, at Harrisburg, Pa. They had issue (surname Hall):

   i. Henry-Williams, b. Dec. 12, 1826, at Lewistown, Pa.; d. s. p.
32. *ii. William-Maclay*, b. November 3, 1828; m. Ellen Rowan Cramer.
33. *iii. George-Duffield*, b. February 19, 1831; m., first, Louisa Miller; secondly, Lucretia Allen.

34. iv. *Louis-Williams*, b. July 4, 1833 ; m. Eliza Warford.
   v. *Catharine-Julia*, b. November 10, 1835, at Perryville, Pa.; m., October 22, 1857, Nathaniel Breading Hogg, b. 1818, in Uniontown, Pa.; son of George H. Hogg, and through his mother, a grandson of Rev. Dr. Ewing ; he graduated at Kenyon College, and read law with his uncle, Judge Ewing, at Uniontown, Pa.; settled at Newark, O., where he managed for several years the stores and farms belonging to his father's estate ; is a partner in the foundry of Totten & Co.; resides in Allegheny city, Pa.
   vi. *Mary*, b. March 7, 1838, at Philadelphia, Pa.; m. Francis Jordan, b. February 5, 1820, in Bedford county, Pa.; he was educated at Augusta College, Kentucky, and at Franklin and Marshall College, Pennsylvania ; studied law; was admitted to the Bedford county bar; soon after appointed district attorney, and subsequently elected to the same position; in 1855 was elected to the State Senate ; was appointed by President Lincoln paymaster in the army, which, at the close of two and a half years of active service, he resigned ; under Gov. Geary he held the office of Secretary of the Commonwealth, and and in 1882 filled the same position for a brief period ; resides at Harrisburg in the active practice of his profession.
   vii. *Ellen*, b. January 30, 1846, in Bedford, Pa.; m., April, 1872, James Heron Crosman ; and had issue (surname Crosman):
      1. *John-Heron*, b. 1873.
      2. *Mary-Hall*, b. 1874.
      3. *Louis-Hall*, b. 1877.
      4. *George-Hampden*, b. 1880.
      5. *Hall-Maclay*, b. 1884.

XXX. CATHARINE JULIA HALL,[6] Esther,[5] William,[4] Charles,[3] John,[2] Charles,[1]) b. August 14, 1804, in Harrisburg, Pa.; d. July 17, 1832, at Reading, Pa.; m., June 30, 1830, GARRICK MALLERY, b. April, 17, 1784, in Middlebury, Conn.; d. July 6, 1866, in Philadelphia, Pa. He was of unmixed English descent; being in direct male line from Peter Mallery, who arrived in Boston in 1638, and went to New Haven settlements with Rev. Theophilus Eaton's company, March 7, 1644. Through his mother, Hannah Minor, he was in direct male line from Thomas Minor, who came to Pequot with John Winthrop's company and settled there in 1646. Several of his ancestors were military officers in the colonial service, and in the Revolutionary war. Garrick Mallery graduated at Yale College in 1808, and after a term at Litchfield Law School went to Wilkes-Barré, Pa.; the same year read law with Judge Wells, and was admitted to the bar in 1811; He served in the Pennsylvania House of Representatives from 1827 to 1830, in which he was distinguished for promoting the internal-improvement system of the State. In 1831 he was appointed president judge of the Third Judicial District, composed of the counties of Berks, Northampton and Lehigh. He resigned his commission in 1836; removed to the city of Philadelphia, where he practiced law until his death, for several years before that time being master in chancery of the Supreme Court. In 1840 he received the degree of LL. D. from Lafayette College. Judge Mallery was thrice married; m. first, in 1811, Sylvina Pierce Butler, daughter of Lord Butler, of Wilkes-Barré; secondly, Catharine Julia Hall; thirdly, in 1838, Jeanette Otto, daughter of Dr. John C. Otto, of Philadelphia. By the first wife there were five children, and by his third wife four children; by the second wife, Catharine Julia Hall, there was issue (surname Mallery):

    i. Garrick, b. April 23, 1831, in Wilkes-Barre, Pa.; d. October 24, 1894, at Washington city; was educated at the preparatory department of the University of Pennsylvania, and graduated at Yale College in 1850; in 1853 received the degree of LL. B. from the University of Pennsylvania, and the same year admitted to the bar of Philadelphia, where he practiced law and engaged in literary pursuits until the war of the Rebellion, when he entered the service; rose to the rank of lieutenant colonel, and brevet colonel; on the re-organization of the regular army he was appointed captain first infantry; was twice severely wounded, and received twice brevets for gallantry in action; in the reconstruction period in 1869 and 1870, being on military duty in Virginia as judge advocate on the staff of the commanding general, he was also Secretary of State, and adjutant general with the rank of brigadier general; in 1870 was placed on duty with the chief signal officer of the army at Washington, remaining in that office until 1877, when he was ordered to report to the Secretary of the Interior for duty connected with the ethnology of the North America Indians, in which work he continued until his death; edited several works issued officially by the Government. He was retired July 1, 1879, for wounds received in line of duty. Mr. Mallery m., April 14, 1870, in Richmond, Va., Helen Marlan Wyckoff, daughter of Rev. A. V. Wyckoff, of New Brunswick, N. Y.

XXXI. WILLIAM IRWIN MACLAY,[7] (John,[6] William,[5] John,[4] Charles,[3] John,[2] Charles,[1]) b. March 27, 1820; d. June 20, 1825; m., November 16, 1841, at Pittsburgh, Pa., SARAH H. STACKHOUSE. They had issue:

   i. Jane-Anne, b. August 16, 1842, in Pittsburgh; m. John S. Tittle; reside at Johnstown, Pa.; and had issue (surname Tittle):
     1. *Elizabeth-Findlay*, b. March 3, 1864.
     2. *William-Maclay*, b. November 19, 1867; d. May 8, 1885.
   ii. Emma-S., b. November 11, 1845, in Pittsburgh, Pa.; m., November 29, 1877, William H. Bynon, of Tipton, Mo.
   iii. Ellen Maclay, b. October 18, 1847, in Johnstown, Pa.; m., first, December 23, 1870, George Fritz; d. August 5, 1873; m., secondly, December 8, 1880, Robert Murphy.
   iv. William-Stackhouse, b. December 13, 1849, in Johnstown, Pa.; d. September 30, 1853.
   v. Elizabeth-Findlay, b. February 17, 1852; d. August 31, 1853.
   vi. Mary-Torrence, b. December 15, 1854; d. May 25, 1860.

XXXII. WILLIAM MACLAY HALL[7] (William-Maclay[6] [Hall,] Esther,[5] William,[4] Charles,[3] John,[2] Charles,[1]) b. November 3, 1828, in Lewistown, Pa. He received a thorough preparatory education, and graduated from Marshall College, Mercersburg, in 1846, being the valedictorian of his class. He read law with William Lyon, of Bedford, and was admitted to the bar in August, 1849. Began practice at Bedford, and soon achieved honorable distinction in his profession. In January, 1865, he was appointed by President Lincoln judge advocate with the rank of major, and served one year. In 1868 he served on a commission to revise the statutes of the State of Pennsylvania, with Judge Derrickson and Wayne MacVeagh. Upon the death of Judge King in January, 1871, Gov. Geary appointed him president judge of the Sixteenth Judicial District, then comprising the counties of Bedford, Somerset, Franklin, and Fulton, and at the October election elected to the same position for the term of ten years. After declining a re-nomination, Judge Hall quitted the bench on the 1st of January, 1882, the judicial term having been extended one month by the Constitution of 1874. Throughout the entire term of Judge Hall, the business of the district was great, and an unusually large number of cases of importance was adjudicated. During his administration very few reversals of his decisions were made by the Supreme Court. Since leaving the bench he has not been actively engaged in his profession. He resides near the borough of Bedford, Pa. Judge Hall m., September 9, 1859, by Rev. J. H. Symonds, ELLEN ROWAN CRAMER, of Cumberland, Md., b. January 4, 1849. They had issue (surname Hall):

 i. Catharine-Julia, b. February 12, 1862.
 ii. William-Maclay, b. September 6, 1864.
 iii. George-Louis, b. February 25, 1867.
 iv. John-Cramer (twin), b. February 25, 1867 ; d. September 19, 1867, at Cumberland, Md.
 v. Emily-Rowan, b. October 15, 1870 ; m. Charles Gibson Brown.
 vi. Nathaniel-Breading, b. August 25, 1872; d. July 28, 1888, in Bedford, Pa.
 vii. Eleanor-Maclay, b. August 4, 1874.
 viii. Richard Cecil, b. May 27, 1882.

XXXIII. GEORGE DUFFIELD HALL,[7] (William-Maclay[6] [Hall], Esther,[5] William,[4] Charles,[3] John,[2] Charles,[1]) b. February 19, 1831, at Lewistown, Pa.; d. December 6, 1883, at St. Louis, Mo. He graduated in 1849 from Marshall College, Mercersburg, Pa. Began the study of law, but afterwards entered the banking house of William Russell, at Lewistown. In 1852 went to Pittsburgh as a clerk in the firm of Lyon, Shorb & Co., iron manufacturers; from thence, in 1854, to St. Louis, where he took charge of the branch store of the Sligo Iron Company, which he managed with great energy and success. About 1860 he became part owner, and afterwards sole owner. He was very hospitable and generous, of fine belles-lettres attainments, and of great conversational powers; an active member of the Presbyterian Church, with high character and standing in the community for integrity and honor. He left twenty-five thousand dollars to the different boards and benevolent enterprises of the Presbyterian Church, and about the same sum in legacies to his aunts and sisters, with an estate of about half a million of dollars to his children. Mr. Hall was twice married; m., first, LOUISA MILLER; no issue; m., secondly, LUCRETIA ALLEN. They had issue (surname Hall):

 i. Allen.
 ii. Louis-Maclay.
 iii. Mabel-Harlekenden.
 iv. George-Duffield.

XXXIV. LOUIS WILLIAMS HALL,[7] (William-Maclay[6] [Hall], Esther,[5] William,[4] Charles,[3] John,[2] Charles,[1]) b. July 4, 1833, at Allegheny, Pa. He received a good education; studied law, and was admitted to the bar in 1854. He was soon after appointed solicitor for the Pennsylvania Railroad company at Altoona. That road was just opened over the Allegheny mountains, and Altoona was the location of the chief offices of the transportation of the company. Herman J. Lombaert was general superintendent with all the powers of the now general manager. The office of the chief engineer was also at that point, and the location was being made there for the principal shops of the company. It being the headquarters of these officers, the position of solicitor there was an important and delicate one, and the attorney had many questions before him of immense importance to the company and its interests. Mr. Hall's practice soon became large and lucrative, not only in Blair, but the contiguous counties. In 1859, when little more than eligible, he was elected to the State Senate as the Republican candidate from the strong Democratic district of Cambria, Blair, and Clearfield counties. He was appointed chairman of the Judiciary Committee on his first advent in the Senate, of a body composed of such legal minds as Penny, of Allegheny; Clymer, of Berks; Ketchum, of Luzerne; Welsh, of York; Palmer, of Schuylkill; Finney, of Crawford; McClure, of Franklin, and others prominent in the profession of the State. The war of the Rebellion breaking out, Gov. Curtin called an extra session of the Assembly in April, 1861, when Mr. Hall was chosen Speaker of the Senate. It was at that extra session that the famous Three-million-dollar-loan bill to arm the State, and other important war measures were passed. Mr. Hall was again chosen Speaker at the beginning of the regular session in January, 1862. He was elected for a new term, and for another district, in which Blair county was placed in October, 1864, running largely ahead of his ticket. He was again chosen Speaker of the Senate at the end of the session of 1866, and also at the commencement of the regular session in 1867, having been chosen three times presiding officer of that body, an honor never before accorded to any one. At the close of his term he declined a re-nomination, and since then has devoted himself exclusively to the practice of his profession. Having been appointed solicitor and counsel of the Pennsylvania railroad, at Harrisburg, on the 1st of October, 1868, he took up his residence in that city. To-day he occupies the same position, being connected with them for over thirty years. He is yet in the mental vigor and prime of life, although sixty years of age, and has probably been connected with as many matters of importance in his profession as any man of his age. Among the numerous leading cases in the courts he has argued within the last few years may be mentioned those of the "Commonwealth *vs.* Credit Mobilier of America," twice tried before Judge Pearson and twice in the Supreme Court; "Commonwealth *vs.* George O. Evans," the claim of the State for a very large amount; Mr. Evans being defended by Mr. Hall and the late Judge Black; "The Commonwealth *vs.* Pennsylvania Canal company," being an attempt of the State by statute to compel the canal company to alter their dams, feeders, and works, without compensation, so as to allow the passage of fish, the case involved probably half a million of dollars, and was decided by the Supreme Court in favor of the canal company; "James Freeland *vs.* Pennsylvania Railroad company," an attempt to hold the company responsible for consequential damages caused by the raising the great Clark's Ferry dam; decided by the Supreme Court in favor of the railroad company. Mr. Hall m., November 26, 1867, ELIZA WARFORD. They had issue (surname Hall):

 i. Eliza, d. s. p.
 ii. Ellen, b. November 19, 1869.
 iii. Mary-Grace, b. November 4, 1871.
 iv. Louis-Williams, b. December 2, 1873.
 v. Francis-Jordan, b. April 1, 1878.

McCORMICK FAMILY.

I. One of the signers of " the humble address of the Governor, officers, clergy, and other gentlemen in the city and garrison of Londonderry," to William and Mary, of the date of July 29, 1689, shortly after the famous siege of that noted stronghold of Protestantism, was JAMES McCORMICK.[1] Further than that we have little knowledge of him, save that he was the ancestor of the family of whom we have this record. Among other children he had issue:

2.   i. *Hugh*, b. about 1695; m., and had issue.
3.   ii. *Thomas*, b. 1702; m. Elizabeth Carruth.

II. HUGH McCORMICK,[2] (James,[1]) b. about 1695, in the Province of Ulster, Ireland; emigrated with his family to Pennsylvania prior to 1735, and located in Paxtang township, Lancaster, now Dauphin county, Pa. He married, and had issue:

4.   i. *John*, b. 1718; m. Jean Cathay.
     ii. *James*, b. 1721; m., and had issue, but probably went into the valley of Virginia.
5.   iii. *Samuel*, b. 1723; m., and had issue.
6.   iv. *Hugh*, b. 1725; m. Sarah Alcorn.

III. THOMAS McCORMICK,[2] (James,[1]) b. about 1702, in the Province of Ulster, Ireland; d. about 1762, in East Pennsboro' township, Cumberland county, Pa. He accompanied his brother Hugh to America, in 1735. In 1745 he and his wife each took out a warrant for one hundred acres of land in Hanover township, then Lancaster county, Pa. About that time, or shortly after, he removed with his family west of the Susquehanna, locating in East Pennsboro' township, Cumberland county, Pa. He married in Ireland, about 1726, ELIZABETH CARRUTH, b. about 1705 in Ireland; d. January, 1767, in East Pennsboro' township, Cumberland county, Pa. She was the daughter of Adam Carruth, and sister of Walter Carruth, both early settlers in Hanover township, Lancaster county, Pa. They had issue:

7. i. *Thomas*, b. 1727; m. Jean Oliver.
8. ii. *James*, b. 1729; m. Mary Oliver.
9. iii. *William*, b. 1732; m. Mary Wiggin.
10. iv. *Hugh*, b. 1735; m. Catharine Sanderson.
11. v. *Robert*, b. 1738; m. Martha Sanderson.
12. vi. *Elizabeth*, b. 1740; m. Matthew Loudon.

IV. JOHN MCCORMICK,[3] (Hugh,[2] James,[1]) b. about 1718, in or near Londonderry, Ireland; d. in October, 1782; and buried in Silvers Spring churchyard, of which church he was a member. He located in East Pennsboro' township as early as 1745; and upon the formation of the county of Cumberland in 1750, was named in the act as one of the trustees for the purchasing of land on which to build a court-house and prison. During the French and Indian war his dwelling was stockaded and the refuge of the frontier settlers, and hence designated as "McCormick's Fort at Conedoguinet." He m. JEAN CATHAY, who deceased the latter part of January, 1788. They had issue:

 i. *John*, m., and had issue: *Thomas*, and *Hudson*.
 ii. *Margaret*, m. Hugh Quigley; and had issue (surname Quigley): *Elizabeth, John, William, Samuel, Esther, Jane,* and *Sarah*.
 iii. [*Jane*], m. David McClure; and had issue (surname McClure): *Samuel, Thomas, John, James, William, Wilson,* and *David*.
 iv. *Elizabeth*, m. James Sharon; and had issue (surname Sharon): *Elizabeth, Sarah, Mary, Isabella, William,* and *James*.
 v. [*Ann*], m. David Adams; and had issue (surname Adams): *William,* and *Ann*.

V. SAMUEL MCCORMICK,[3] (Hugh,[2] James,[1]) b. about 1723, in the Province of Ulster, Ireland; d. in July, 1765, in the township of East Pennsboro', Cumberland county, Pa. He took up a tract of land in that section, the warrant for which was issued the 14th day of August, 1745. The land adjoined that of his brother, John McCormick, and the Conedoguinet creek. His wife, whose name is unknown, died prior to her husband. They had issue:

 i. *James*, b. 1747.
 ii. *Elizabeth*, b. 1749; m. William McNitt [McKnight].
 iii. *Jane*, b. 1751; m. Archibald McGuire.
 iv. *Mary*, b. 1754; m. James Chambers.

v. *Sarah,* b. 1756 ; m. Arthur Chambers.
vi. *Agnes,* b. 1758 ; m. Henry McElroy.
vii. *Margaret,* b. 1761.
viii. *Ann,* b. 1763.

VI. HUGH MCCORMICK,³ (Hugh,² James,¹) b. about 1725, in the Province of Ulster, Ireland; d. September, 1777, in Middleton township, Cumberland county, Pa. About 1758, he removed from Paxtang to the homestead of his father-in-law, on Conedoguinet creek, which was deeded to him, October 30, 1758, by James Alcorn, Sr., and Mary, his wife, of Middleton township, being 136 acres of land in said Middleton township, together with the houses, barns, and out-houses on same. About the year 1770, he purchased 1,300 acres of land in the White Deer Valley, now within the boundary of Lycoming county, Pa., and his two sons, Seth and Thomas, settled there. He was a prominent man on the frontiers, and, at the outset of the Revolution, rendered much aid, by his counsel and his purse, to raise troops for the Continental service. In the Provincial Conference, of June, 1776, he served as a member, but, owing to ill health, declined further official honors. He m., about 1749, SARAH ALCORN, youngest daughter of James and Mary Alcorn.* They had issue :

13.   i. *James,* b. 1750 ; m. Isabella Dixon.
      ii. *Mary,* b. 1752 ; m. Capt. Robert Peebles, a wealthy farmer, who resided near Shippensburg, Pa.; and had issue, four sons, all of whom married and settled in the same neighborhood.
      iii. *Thomas,* b. 1754 ; d. October 6, 1826 ; located, about 1775, on South creek, a branch of White Deer Hole creek, in Lycoming county, Pa., about three miles from its mouth ; was a justice of the peace for some years ; m. Elizabeth Crockett ; their remains lie buried in the old Presbyterian, now Lutheran, graveyard, on the southwest side of Penny Hill, in Buffalo Valley ; left no issue, he had adopted his great-nephew, to whom he bequeathed his estate.

---

*JAMES ALCORN d. July, 1761 ; his wife, MARY ALCORN, d. February, 1763. Their children were :
   i. *James,* m., and had *Robert, Mary,* and *Jean.*
   ii. *Katharine,* m. David Steel.
   iii. *Victoria,* m. William Rankin.
   iv *Sarah,* m. Hugh McCormick.

14. iv. *Seth*, b. 1756; m. Margaret Simmons.
   v. *Sarah*, b. 1758; m. —— Woodrow, and removed to Ohio, when it was so new and so far away that frequent intercourse with its inhabitants was impossible, and nothing more is known of them.
   vi. *Eleanor*, b. 1760; d. unm.; lived with her mother and younger sister, whom she survived several years.
15. vii. *Hugh*, b. 1762; m. Elizabeth Fullerton.
16. viii. *John*, b. 1765; m. Mary Curtis.
   ix. *Amelia*, b. 1767; m. William Gabby, a prominent farmer, who resided near Hagerstown, Md.; no issue.

VII. THOMAS MCCORMICK,³ (Thomas,² James,¹) b. about 1727, in the north of Ireland; d. in 1778, in East Pennsboro' township, Cumberland county, Pa.; was a member of the Presbyterian church at Silvers Spring, his name appearing as one of the guarantors of the salary of the Rev. John Steel, pastor of that congregation, June 26, 1768. He m. in 1756, JEAN OLIVER,* b. 1728; d. December 7, 1804, in East Pennsboro' township, Cumberland county, Pa.; daughter of John Oliver and Mary Patterson. They had issue:

17. i. *John*, b. March 26, 1757; m. Ann Sample.
   ii. *William* (twin), b. March 26, 1757; m. Mary Williamson, daughter of James and Prudence Williamson; no issue.
   iii. *Isabella*, b. December 29, 1759; d. September 7, 1823; m., May 15, 1783, John Walker, and had issue, nine children.
   iv. *Elizabeth*, b. December 15, 1761; d. December 15, 1831; m., in 1786, John Buchanan.
   v. *Mary*, b. March 18, 1763; d. May 22, 1842; m., January 9, 1790, John Sample, and had issue, nine children.
   vi. *Jane*, b. February 19, 1765; d. November 6, 1790; m. George Hammond; no issue.
   vii. *Sarah*, b. March 1, 1767; d. 1844; m. William Lytle Brown; no issue.
   viii. *Grizzle* [*Griselda*], b. April 7, 1769; m., June, 1818, Ezra Wright; no issue.

---

* James, Jane, and Mary Oliver, were the children of John Oliver and Mary Patterson. They were all born in Ireland. Their father, John Oliver, died in Ireland, and his widow married Joseph Clark, and they with her three children emigrated to America in 1737, settling eventually in East Pennsboro' township, adjoining the farm of Elizabeth McCormick.

VIII. JAMES MCCORMICK,² (Thomas,² James,¹) b. about 1729, in the Province of Ulster, Ireland; d. in January, 1802, in East Pennsboro' township, Cumberland county, Pa.; buried in Silvers Spring churchyard; resided his entire lifetime on the old homestead. He m., in 1760, MARY OLIVER, b. 1728, in Ireland; d. November 29, 1804, in East Pennsboro', Cumberland county, Pa. They had issue:

18.   *i. James*, b. 1761; m. Margaret Oliver.
      ii. Robert, b. 1764; d. 1809; unm.
19.   *iii. William*, b. 1766; m. Margery Bines.
      iv. Elizabeth, d. s. p.
      v. Isabella, d. s. p.

IX. WILLIAM MCCORMICK,³ (Thomas,² James,¹) b. 1732, in or near Londonderry, Ireland; d. 1812, in Perry county, Ohio. As early as 1755, he and his brothers, Hugh and Robert McCormick, are supposed to have settled in what was then the far west or frontier, on the Juniata river, in Fermanagh township, now within the boundaries of Juniata county, Pa., near "The Narrows." His property was described as on the north side of Juniata, joining the said Juniata, Hugh McCormick, John McClure, and John Riddle." Thomas and William took out warrants for this land in 1755. Previous to 1780, he moved across the river to Milford township, in the same county. Among the records of Silvers Spring church we find his name signed to a guarantee of the pastor's (Rev. John Steel) salary, dated June 27, 1768. He sold his farm in 1803, and removed to Perry county, Ohio, where he died. He m., in 1756, MARY WIGGIN, b. 1735; d. 1814; daughter of Ennion Wiggin. They had issue:

    i. Elizabeth, b. 1757; m. William Bowland; and had issue (surname Bowland): *Catharine, William, Robert, Alexander, Hugh, John, Sarah,* and *Mary.*
    ii. Margaret, b. 1759; m. Thomas Black; and had isssue (surname Black): *James, William, John, Samuel, Mary, Elizabeth,* and *Anna.*
    iii. Thomas, b. 1761; m. Ann Morrison; and had issue:
        1. *Flora*, b. 1798; m., 1835, Christopher Neil.
        2. *William*, b. 1800, in Juniata county, Pa.; d. 1837, in Hancock county, O.; m., in 1827, Elizabeth Hamilton; and had issue, *Sarah-Ann.*

McCormick Family.

3. *James*, b. 1802; removed to Paulding county, O.; m., in 1830, Margaret Black; and had issue, beside two others: *Josiah, Mary-Ann*, and *Thomas*.
4. *Mary*, b. 1805; d. 1835.
5. *Anna*, b. 1808.
6. *Elizabeth*, b. 1810; m., 1836, Henry Dishong.
7. *John-Morrison*, b. 1815; removed to Michigan; m., 1840, Martha Guyter; and had issue, beside two others: *Rebecca*, and *Thomas*.

iv. *Anna*, b. 1764; m., 1793, David Hardy; and had issue (surname Hardy): *Thomas, Eleanor, Mary, Jane, Elizabeth, Margaret*, and *Anna*.

v. *William*, b. 1766; d. 1832, in Logan county, O.; was twice married; m., first, in 1796, Elizabeth Black; d. 1801; and had issue:
    1. *James*, b. 1797; d. 1845, in Washington county, Ia.; unm.
    2. *William*, b. 1799; resided in Seneca county, O.; m. Elizabeth Heck; and had issue: *George*, and *John*.
    3. *Elizabeth*, b. 1801; d. 1840; m. Nathaniel Swartz.

William McCormick m., secondly, in 1802, Isabella Shaw; and had issue:
    4. *Nancy*, b. 1803; m. John Gilmore.
    5. *Mary*, b. 1804; m., first, James Meehan; secondly, James Collins.
    6. *Margaret*, b. 1806; m. her cousin, William McCormick.
    7. *John*, b. 1808; resided in Logan county, O.; m. Miss Stewart.
    8. *Jane*, b. 1809; m. —— Hemphill.
    9. *Sarah*, b. 1811; m. Allan Gilmore.
    10. *Kizia*, b. 1812.
    11. *Isabella*, b. 1814.

20. vi. *James*, b. 1769; m. Rebecca Cunningham.

vii. *John*, b. 1771; resided in Fayette county, O.; m., in 1800, Elizabeth Hardy; and had issue:
    1. *Elizabeth*, b. 1801; d. 1835.
    2. *William*, b. 1802; resided in Indiana; m., in 1832, his cousin, Margaret McCormick, daughter of William McCormick.
    3. *Lois*, b. 1811; d. 1835.
    4. *John*, b. about 1812; resided in Fayette county, Ohio.
    5. *Calvin*, b. about 1814; resided in Fayette county, Ohio.

viii. Hugh, b. 1775; resided in Perry county, Ohio; m., in 1802, Martha Martin; and had issue:
1. *Mary*, b. 1803; m. Samuel Martyr.
2. *Sarah*, b. 1805; m. William T. Daily.
3. *Samuel*, b. 1807; resided in Seneca county, Ohio; m., in 1826, Lavenia Pevee; and had issue: *Joseph, Margaret,* and *Henry.*
4. *Absolem*, b. 1809; resided in Perry county, Ohio; m., in 1832, Elizabeth Ashbaugh; and had issue: *John-T., Samuel, David, Mary, Catharine, Margaret,* and *Martha.*

X. HUGH MCCORMICK,³ (Thomas,² James,¹) b. about the year 1735; d. in September, 1799, in Stott county, Kentucky. William, Hugh, and Robert McCormick were among the first settlers and land-owners within the present limits of Juniata county, Pa. They, and their brother Thomas, took out warrants in 1755 for a tract of land located two miles north of Mifflintown, along the Juniata river, in Fermanagh township, and the three first-named settled thereon about that time. On several occasions they were driven out by the Indians, the last being in 1786, when they fled for refuge to Huntingdon county. They returned home in 1787, and immediately thereafter Hugh McCormick erected a large stone house on his property, which it is said was built partly with the view of using it as a fort in case of another Indian raid, the windows being made high and narrow. This house is yet standing, apparently, without a flaw or seam in its walls. The brothers are described as being very large and robust men, fond of frontier life, and in every way suited to its dangers and excitements. Hugh served in the war for Independence, and Mrs. Catharine Laird, a granddaughter, says of him: "Grandfather Hugh McCormick lived at the beginning of the Revolutionary war on the Juniata river. Grandmother said that when he came home from the war he was covered with rags. In his knapsack he had only a conch shell, which she kept until her death, and gave to our mother to be handed down as a memento of his service." That shell is now in possession of his grandson, Col. George M. Chambers, of Jacksonville, Ill. By deed dated October 19, 1798, Hugh McCormick and Catharine, his wife, disposed of the farm in Fermanagh township, and soon thereafter removed with their family to Scott county, Ky. Mr. McCormick m., in 1767, CATHARINE SANDERSON, b. 1742; d. in 1810, in Scott county, Ky.; daughter of George Sanderson,* of Middleton township, Cumberland county, Pa. They had issue:

21.   i. *Martha*, b. 1768; m. Rowland Chambers.
      ii. *Elizabeth*, b. 1770; d. 1824; m. David Logan; and had issue (surname Logan): *David-M.*, and *Hugh-McCormick*.
      iii. *George*, b. 1772; d. September, 1816, unm., from disease contracted in the war of 1812.
      iv. *William*, b. 1774; d. 1839, unm.; he was in the quartermaster's department under General Harrison at the time of the battle of Tippecanoe.
22.   v. *Mary*, b. 1776; m. Samuel Glass.
      vi. *Hugh*, b. 1779; d. 1795.

XI. ROBERT MCCORMICK,³ ('Thomas,² James,¹) b. in 1738, in Hanover township, then Lancaster county, Pa.; d. October 12, 1818, in Augusta county, Va. He, with his brothers, William and Hugh McCormick, settled in Fermanagh township, now in Juniata county, about 1755. He sold his property in Fermanagh township on the 22d of July, 1779, and from thence he removed to the valley of Virginia, where he purchased four hundred and fifty-one acres of land near the town of Midway, situated on both sides of the line between the counties of Augusta and Rockbridge. He was a Revolutionary soldier, and fought in the battle of the Cowpens. By

---

*GEORGE SANDERSON was the eldest son of Alexander and Jean Sanderson, who emigrated from Scotland prior to 1750, and settled in Middleton township, Cumberland county, Pa. His father was one of the first elders in the Monaghan Presbyterian Church. He died about the first of February, 1760, and had issue (surname Sanderson): *George, Alexander, Barbara, Martha, William, John, James*, and *Margaret*. The son, George Sanderson, b. about the year 1712; d. about 1787. He was twice married, his first wife a Ross, the second, Jane Aitken. There was issue only by first wife (surname Sanderson):

    i. *Robert*, b. 1738; m. Mary ———, and had *George*, and *Robert*.
    ii. *John*, b. 1740; d. 1799; m. Sarah McMichael; no issue.
    iii. *Catharine*, b. 1742; d. 1810; m. Hugh McCormick.
    iv. *Margaret*, b. 1743; m. James Elliott, and had a son *George*.
    v. *Mary*, b. 1745; m. David Elliott, and had sons, *George*, and *Robert*.
    vi. *Martha*, b. 1747; d. prior to 1808; m. Robert McCormick.

occupation he was a farmer and weaver, and his family, until a recent date, have had in their possession some beautiful linen table cloths which he wove himself. He was an elder in the Presbyterian church, and a man who was well versed in the Scriptures, and, in conversation on religious subjects, is said to have been very able and entertaining. He m., about 1770, MARTHA SANDERSON, daughter of George Sanderson, and sister of the wife of his brother Hugh. She died in Augusta county, Virginia, prior to 1808, and is buried by the side of her husband, in the Old Providence Presbyterian burying ground, about two miles from the homestead. They had issue :

23. i. *George-Elliot*, b. 1771 ; m. Jane Steel.
 ii. *Martha*, b. 1773; m. Richard Brient ; resided in Rockbridge county, Va.; no issue.
 iii. *Elizabeth*, b. 1774 ; m. Hugh Gibson ; removed from Rockbridge county, Va., to Henderson, Kentucky ; and had issue (surname Gibson):
   1. *John-B.*, d. 1872, in Dayton, O.; was raised by his uncle, Robert McCormick, and took his name; was, at one time, Attorney General of the State of Tennessee; a man of very bright intellect, and of a most cheerful and genial disposition ; he m. Miss Raley ; no issue.
   2. *Ellen*, m. Mr. Prewett.
24. iv. *William*, b. April 12, 1776 ; m., first, Mary Steel ; secondly, Sarah McClelland.
25. v. *James*, b. January 7, 1778 ; m., first, Irene Rogers ; secondly, Rachel Nisonger ; thirdly, Rachel Clark.
26. vi. *Robert*, b. June 8, 1780 ; m. Mary Anna Hall.

XII. ELIZABETH MCCORMICK,³ (Thomas,² James,¹) b. about 1740, in Hanover township, then Lancaster county, Pa.; d. 1767, at Carlisle, Pa.; m., 1760, MATTHEW LOUDON, b. about 1737, in the north of Ireland; d. about the year 1790 ; in Carlisle, Pa. They had issue (surname Loudon):

 i. *Mary*, b. 1761 ; d. 1822 ; m., 1782, James Macfarlane ; and had issue (surname Macfarlane):
   1. *Elizabeth*, b. June, 1783 ; m., 1805, Gen. John Thompson, of Centre county, Pa.; and had issue (surname Thompson): *Nancy*, m. William Cooper ; *Mary*, m. George Jack ; *Matthew-Loudon*, m. Maria Spear ; *Moses*, m. Mary Irvine ; *John*, m. Mary

Kyle; Dr. *James*, of Washington, D. C.; and *William*, m., first, Priscilla Taylor; secondly, Eliza Allen.
2. *Rosanna*, m. Henry Taylor.
3. *Janet*, m. Joseph Kyle; and had nine children.
4. *James*, d. at seventy-eight years; m. —— Henry, and had *William*, and *Robert*.
5. *William*, d. 1853; m. Hannah Means; and had issue (surname Macfarlane): *Rosanna, Elmira, James*, and *William*.
6. *Margaret*, d. 1840; m. William Thompson; and had issue (surname Thompson): *Nancy-Rosanna, Sarah-Jane*, m. John Sterrett, *Emma, Elizabeth-Loudon*, m. Joseph Mitchell, *William-Joseph*, and *James-Macfarlane*.
7. *Robert*, b. 1801; d. 1825.
8. *Andrew*, b. 1803; m. Mary Smith.
9. *Nancy*, d. 1842; m. William Smith; no issue.

ii. *Archibald*, b. March 18, 1762; d. March 22, 1832, at Carlisle, Pa.; buried at Middle Ridge churchyard; but in 1883, his remains, with those of his wife, were removed to Silvers Spring graveyard; was a farmer and owned a farm adjoining his father's, where he resided from 1788 to 1820, when he removed to Perry county, Pa., where he died; he m., October 24, 1788, Margaret Bines, b. October 24, 1769; d. March 27, 1832; daughter of Thomas Bines and Margaret Vance; and had issue (surname Loudon):

 1. *Elizabeth-McCormick*, b. October 24, 1789; d. December 21, 1856; m., January 29, 1818, James Bell.
 2. *John*, b. September 15, 1792; m. Nancy Giffen.
 3. *Matthew*, b. 1794; d. 1855; m., 1839, Sarah Fulton.
 4. *Margaret*, b. September 18, 1796; m., 1826, Henry Ewalt.
 5. *Thomas-Bines*, b. 1799; d. 1849; m., 1830, Sarah Irvine.
 6. *James*, b. February, 1802; d. December 29, 1878; m., 1855, Mrs. Ann Engleheart.
 7. *Mary-Ann*, b. May 1, 1805; d. October 25, 1848.
 8. *Margery-Bines*, b. 1808; m , December 6, 1832, Dr. Isaac Wayne Snowden; and had issue (surname Snowden):
  a. Nathaniel-Randolph, b. Oct. 7, 1833; d. s. p.
  b. Archibald-Loudon, b. August 9, 1835; m. Lizzie R. Smith; and had issue: *Caroline, Mary*, and *Charles-Randolph*.

   c. *Margaret*, b. January 10, 1838; d. 1853.
   d. *Sarah-G.*, b. April 5, 1841; m. Dr. Thomas H. Stewart.
   e. *Mary-A.*, b. March 31, 1848.
  9. *William-McCormick*, b. 1811; m., 1837, Elizabeth Patterson; and had, beside four children d. in infancy, residing in Hannibal, Mo. (surname Loudon):
   a. *Elizabeth*, b. 1838.
   b. *Thomas*, b. 1840.
   c. *Margaret*, b. 1852.
 iii. *Catharine*, d. s. p.

XIII. JAMES MCCORMICK,[4] (Hugh,[3] Hugh,[2] James,[1]) b. about 1750, in East Pennsboro' township, Cumberland county, Pa. He m., March 15, 1774, ISABELLA DIXON, daughter of John and Arabella Dixon, of Dixon's Ford, Swatara creek, Penn'a, (*see Dixon record*), and with his brothers, Seth and Thomas, emigrated to White Deer Valley, Lycoming county, in the same State, where his father, in 1770, had bought a large tract of land. In 1777 he represented White Deer township in the committee of Northumberland county, and his name appears among a list of the inhabitants of White Deer, with that of his brother Thomas, in 1778. He is believed to have gone to the Revolutionary war, but this is not certain, and nothing more is definitely known about him except that, in 1782, he was a resident of Augusta county, Va., as shown by a deed bearing date May 25, of that year. His wife, Isabella, was a woman of strong character, and, during the "Great Runaway" of 1778, escaped from the valley by fleeing on horseback with her eldest child in her arms. She lived until May 10, 1824, spending the latter years of her life with her daughter, Mrs. Robert Sloan, in Harrisburg. On her mother's side, she was descended from the Murrays, and was herself first cousin to Lindley Murray, the grammarian, and to John Murray, one of the earliest presidents of the Chamber of Commerce, of New York. They had issue:
 27. i. *Hugh*, b. February 14, 1777; m. Esther Barbara Kumbel.
   ii. *Sarah*, b. 1779; m. Robert Sloan.

XIV. SETH MCCORMICK,[4] (Hugh,[3] Hugh,[2] James,[1]) b. in 1756, in Paxtang township, then Lancaster county, Pa.; d.

January 17, 1835. About the year 1775, in company with his brother Thomas, he settled on South creek, a branch of White Deer Hole creek, three miles from its mouth, in now Lycoming county, Pa. His remains, with those of his wife, lie buried in the old Presbyterian, now Lutheran graveyard, at the stone church on the southwest side of Penny Hill in Buffalo Valley. He m. MARGARET SIMMONS. They had issue:

 i. *Robert,* b. 1785; d. 1857; m. Nancy Foresman.
 ii. *Samuel-S.,* b. 1787; d. 1864; m. Elizabeth Piatt.
 iii. *Thomas,* b. 1790; d. 1820; m. Maria Hammond.
 iv. *Seth,* b. 1793; d. December, 1821; m. Hannah Hammond; d. 1869; and had issue:
  1. *James-H.*
  2. *Mary.*
  3. *Margaret,* m. D. Watson Foresman.
  4. *Seth-T.,* b. January 17, 1817; d. December 1, 1878; entered life as a farmer and lumberman, but subsequently studied law, and was admitted to the Lycoming bar, where he soon attained the front rank in his profession; he was largely interested in the welfare of the city of Williamsport, where he spent the best years of his useful and busy life. Mr. McCormick m., in 1837, Ellen Miller, dau. of William Miller; and had issue:
   a. *Sarah-E.,* m. William D. Oakes, of Ogle county, Ill.
   b. *Henry-Clay,* b. June 30, 1844; studied law and was admitted to the bar in 1866; was elected to the Fiftieth and Fifty-first Congresses, where he served with ability; in January, 1895, Governor Hastings appointed him Attorney General of Pennsylvania; he m. Ida Hays (*see Forster record*).
   c. *William-M.*
   d. *Horace-G.,* a physician of Williamsport.
   e. *Hannah,* m. Thomas L. Painter, of Allentown.
   f. *Frank-H.*
   g. *Seth-T.*
 v. *Hugh,* b. 1795; d. 1830; unm.
 vi. *John,* b. 1797; d. 1850; m. Sarah Coryell.
 vii. *Joseph,* b. 1799; d. 1877; m. Margaret Schooley.
 viii. *Sarah,* b. 1802; d. 1870; m. Robert J. Foresman.
 ix. *Cynthia,* b. 1805; resides at Tipton, Ia.; m. Samuel Eason.
 x. *Susan,* d. 1807; m. Matthew B. Hammond; resides near South Bend, Ind.

XV. HUGH MCCORMICK,[4] (Hugh,[3] Hugh,[2] James,[1]) b. about 1762. He resided on his father's homestead, two miles from Carlisle, until 1815 or '16, when he moved to Fauquier county, Va., where he died. He m. ELIZABETH FULLERTON, of Greencastle, Pa., sister of David, Humphrey, and Thomas Fullerton, who removed to Ohio at an early day. They had issue:

28.   i. *Charles-N.*, b. 1787; m., and had issue.
     ii. *Hugh*, b. 1789; m., but no issue.
     iii. *Mary-E.*, b. 1791; m. Charles Kemper, of Warrenton, Va.; and had issue (surname Kemper):
        1. *Leigh-R.*
        2. *Charles-H.*, m., and resides near Warrenton, Va.
        3. *Ellen.*
     iv. *Joseph*, b. 1793; m., and removed to Linn county, Mo.
     v. *Elvina*, b. 1796; d. s. p.
     vi. *Fullerton*, b. 1798; d. s. p.
     vii. *Martha*, b. 1800; d. at the age of seventeen years.

XVI. JOHN MCCORMICK,[4] (Hugh,[3] Hugh,[2] James,[1]) b. about 1765, in Middleton township, Cumberland county, Pa.; was given a liberal education, and removed, when a young man, to Leesburg, Fauquier county, Va., where he engaged in teaching. He m. MARY CURTIS, only child of Mrs. Helen Curtis.* They had issue:

     i. *Emily*, m., and left one son.
     ii. *Helen*, b. about 1806; m. Roberdeau Annan, b. March 31, 1804; d. December 15, 1852, son of Dr. Daniel Annan and Jane, daughter of Gen. Daniel Roberdeau, of the Revolution; removed to St. Louis, Mo., where he was a merchant. On being left a widow, Mrs. Annan had means sufficient for a comfortable support, but was deprived of it by mismanagement and fraud combined, and in her declining years found a quiet and comfortable home in an institution which, in her more prosperous days, she aided in establishing.

---

* Mrs. Helen Curtis was a Scotch lady of rare excellence of character, and was widowed before the birth of her daughter, at Alexandria, Va., and took refuge during the Revolutionary war, in Leesburg, purchasing there a home, where she spent the remainder of her life in great comfort, dying at the age of seventy-three, having lived to see her two daughters arrive at maturity, and both filling important positions at the head of a large and flourishing female seminary.

XVII. JOHN MCCORMICK,⁴ ('Thomas,³ Thomas,² James,¹) b. March 26, 1757, near Silvers Spring, East Pennsboro' township, Cumberland county, Pa.; d. September 22, 1815, in Northumberland county, Pa. In 1794 he disposed of his property and removed to Northumberland county. He m., about 1791, ANN SAMPLE, daughter of John Sample. They had issue:

  i. Elizabeth, b. Nov. 28, 1792; d. 1814; m., in 1812, John Cook.
29. *ii. Robert*, b. January 25, 1796; m. Elizabeth Montgomery.
  iii. Jane, b. May 27, 1798; d. Jan. 14, 1872; m. John Sample, Jr.
  iv. Maria, b. July 30, 1800; d. December 21, 1854; unm.
30. *v. John*, b. December 20, 1802; m. Martha Giffen.
31. *vi. William*, b. March 13, 1805; m. Rachel Slote.
  vii. Sarah, b. July 28, 1807; d. April 22, 1888; m. David Davis.

XVIII. JAMES MCCORMICK,⁴ (James,³ Thomas,² James,¹) b. in 1761, in East Pennsboro' township, Cumberland county, Pa.; d. April 17, 1814, at Carlisle, Pa. At the time of his decease the *Carlisle Herald* gave these facts relating to him, which we herewith incorporate: "He studied mathematics with Mr. Oliver, and was, afterwards, two years teacher in the academy at York. In 1787 he was elected a teacher in Dickinson College. In 1792 he was made a professor, and continued, for twenty-seven years, to instruct with ability. During this period he was associated with the Reverend Doctors Nisbet and Davidson, and has been instrumental in imbuing with mathematical and philosophical science many who have sustained respectable characters in church and in state. In 1792 he received the honorable degree of A. B., and, in 1810, that of A. M. For some years he acted as a magistrate, and, for many years, sustained the office of ruling elder in the Presbyterian church. In all relations he supported an unblemished character—highly respected by his fellow-citizens—by the trustees of the college, and has ever had the warm attachment of his pupils. It may be said that he was a laborious instructor and an upright magistrate. In his integrity, all men had confidence. His heart was open to the distresses of the unfortunate, and his hand was ever ready to afford relief. As a man, he was peculiarly inoffensive, and had scarcely a personal enemy in the world. In the endearments of domestic life he sustained the relations of son, husband, parent, and friend much beloved. He was a believer in Jesus Christ and in the doctrines of the reformation. Having dismissed all concern for the world, he felt interested only for the concerns of religion, and manifested a deep concern for the congregation with which he was connected. He delighted to speak of his own hopes and prospects, manifesting an experimental acquaintance with religion, and giving to those around him ample testimony of his unshaken trust in the Redeemer. He met death without fear, calmly and cheerfully resigning up his soul into the hands of his Creator. By his lamented death Dickinson College has lost one of its earliest and ablest instructors; learning and religion, a friend; and society, an upright citizen. He has left behind him a bereaved widow and fatherless children, whose loss is very great, but his friends may confidently trust that his soul has ascended to the regions of eternal day, 'to the joys of his Lord.'" "Mark the perfect man, and behold the upright, for the end of that man is peace!"

" The sweet remembrance of the just
Shall flourish when they sleep in dust."

In addition to the foregoing, it may be stated that his relative, Isabella Oliver, published a monody on his death. Besides his position as professor of mathematics in Dickinson College, he held, as alluded to in the obituary quoted, the office of justice of the peace of Carlisle several years, to which he was appointed by Governor Mifflin, April 16, 1795. Prof. McCormick m., in 1790, his cousin, MARGARET OLIVER, daughter of James Oliver. They had issue:

  i. James, b. 1791; d. 1807.
  ii. Oliver, b. 1793; d. 1810.
  iii. William, b. 1797; d. 1835, unm.
  iv. Maria, b. November 27, 1802; d. October 1, 1827; m., March 18, 1823, John McCandlish; and had issue (surname McCandlish): *Margaret.*
  v. Margaret, b. 1803; d. 1831.
32. *vi. Robert*, b. February 6, 1805; m. Susan Ulp.

XIX. WILLIAM MCCORMICK,[4] (James,[3] Thomas,[2] James,[1]) b. 1766, near Silvers Spring, Cumberland county, Pa.; d. June 13, 1805; his tombstone in Silvers Spring church graveyard bears this testimony, "endeared to all who knew him by his benevolence and integrity." He m., in 1800, MARGERY BINES, b. August 22, 1767; d. April 23, 1849; buried by the side of her husband in Silvers Spring churchyard. They had issue:

  i. Margaret, b. February 24, 1801; d. November 29, 1853; unm.
33. *ii. James* (twin), b. February 24, 1801; m. Eliza Buehler.

XX. JAMES MCCORMICK,⁴ (William,³ Thomas,² James,¹) b. 1769, in Milford township, now Juniata county, Pa.; served in the war of 1812; resided in Perry county, Ohio; m., 1801, REBECCA CUNNINGHAM. They had issue:

  i. William, b. about 1802; d. 1857, in Perry county, O.; m., 1832, Elizabeth Johnson; and had issue:
   1. *James-T.*
   2. *Shadrack-J.*
   3. *Sarah.*
   4. *Amos-G.*
   5. *Francis-M.*
   6. *David-L.*
   7. *Mary-E.*
  ii. Robert, b. 1804; d. 1848; resided in Seneca county, O.; m., 1830, Nancy Hitt; and had issue:
   1. *William-Jackson.*
   2. *James-T.*
   3. *Robert-W.*
   4. *Lydia-Ann.*
   5. *Rebecca.*
  iii. James, b. February 8, 1807; resided in Perry county, O.; m., 1838, Elizabeth A. Tucker; and had issue:
   1. *Rebecca E.*
   2. *George-J.*
   3. *Eliza-J.*
   4. *Nancy-A.*
  iv. Johnson, b. April 28, 1809; d. August, 1885, near Blakesburg, Monroe county, Iowa; unm.
  v. Hugh, b. July 11, 1811; d. March 22, 1871; served as a soldier in the war for the Union; resided in Hardin county, O.; m., in 1847, Nancy Parmer; no issue.
  vi. Mary-A., b. April 28, 1814; d. 1869; resided in Marion county, Iowa; m., 1837, Samuel Coen.
  vii. Rebecca-J., b. June 10, 1819; d. 1876; unm.

XXI. MARTHA MCCORMICK,⁴ (Hugh,³ Thomas,² James,¹) b. in the spring of 1768; d. in 1830, in Woodford county, Ky.; m. ROWLAND CHAMBERS, son of Arthur and Jean Chambers.

They had issue, beside six children died in infancy (surname Chambers):

  i. Catharine, b. 1796; m., first, William Logan; secondly, Mr. Laird.
  ii. George-M., b. June 28, 1800; resided [1885] in Jacksonville, Ill.; one of the earliest residents, and a highly esteemed citizen; m., January 15, 1829, Eleanor E. Irwin; d. April 21, 1888; and had issue (surname Chambers):
    1. *Catharine-L.*, b. January 30, 1830; m. Dr. G. R. Henry, of Burlington, Iowa.
    2. *Rowland-Ross*, b. January 16, 1832; m. Georgianna Trabue.
    3. *Nancy-Maclay*, b. January 19, 1834; m. George W. Moore.
    4. *John-Irwin*, b. May 15, 1836; m. Alice E. Askew.
    5. *Anna-Elizabeth*, b. September 15, 1838; m. Joseph H. Taylor, of Columbus, Neb.
    6. *George-Maxwell*, b. September 3, 1841.
    7. *Leonard-Wheeler*, b. November 10, 1844; m. P. McCartney.
    8. *Martha*, b. December 13, 1847; d. April, 1850.
    9. *Ellen*, b. August 2, 1850; m. Charles E. Bradish, of Springfield, Ill.

XXII. MARY McCORMICK,[4] (Hugh,[3] Thomas,[2] James,[1]) b. 1776; d. April 8, 1816; m., January 14, 1800, SAMUEL GLASS; d. February 1, 1837, in Scott county, Ky. They had issue (surname Glass):

  i. Catharine, b. November 26, 1800; d. April 30, 1833; m. Samuel E. Shaw.
  ii. Joseph, b. November 6, 1802; d. June 21, 1804.
  iii. Samuel, b. October 16, 1804; resided in Shelby county, Ky.; m., March 18, 1834, Sarah E. White; and had issue (surname Glass):
    1. *Thomas-W.*, b. January 13, 1835; d. s. p.
    2. *Mary-C.*, b. March 29, 1837; d. s. p.
    3. *Samuel D.*, b. April 28, 1840.
    4. *Sarah-M.*, b. July 1, 1843.
    5. *J.-Edwin*, b. August 17, 1847.
    6. *Emma-M.*, b. March 10, 1853.
  iv. Paulina, b. April 19, 1807; d. August 10, 1859; m. Dr. D. N. Sharp, of Shelby county, Ky.; and had issue (surname Sharp):
    1. *Mary*, b. December 6, 1840; m. W. B. Allen.
    2. *David*, b. June 1, 1842; m. Virginia McKenny.
    3. *Samuel-G.*, d. in inf.

 4. *Mildred*, b. December 2, 1845 ; d. October 31, 1862 ; m. Cyrus Reid.
 5. *Kate-R.*, b. May 12, 1847 ; m. John S. Shannon.
 6. *Robert*, d. in inf.
v. *Hugh-McCormick*, b. April 24, 1809 ; d. April 15, 1852, in Shelby county, Ky.; m. Martha J. Venable ; and had issue (surname Glass):
 1. *Lizzie-C.*, b. October 30, 1842 ; m. James Venable.
 2. *Samuel*, b. September 5, 1844; d. June 14, 1871.
 3. *James-V.*, b. October 25, 1846.
 4. *Mary-M.*, b. August 19, 1849 ; m. William L. Crooks.
vi. *Mary-M.*, b. March 8, 1811 ; d. February 10, 1840 ; m. Alexander Robinson ; and had issue (surname Robinson):
 1. *Mary-P.*, b. May 20, 1831 ; m. William S. Harbison.
 2. *Kate-G.*, b. May 9, 1833 ; d. March, 1855 ; m. William R. Jarvis.
 3. *Samuel-G.*, b. December 30, 1834 ; d. 1836.
 4. *Paulina*, b. December 16, 1836.

XXIII. GEORGE ELLIOT MCCORMICK,[4] (Robert,[3] Thomas,[2] James,[1]) b. in 1771, in Fermanagh township, now Juniata county, Pa.; d. April 25, 1849, in Henderson county, Ky.; was raised in Rockbridge county, Va., where his father removed when he was eight years old ; removed to Henderson county, Ky., where he bought a large farm, and at which place he died. He m., in 1797, JANE STEEL, d. in 1843; daughter of David Steel, of Rockbridge county, Va. They had issue :
 i. *Robert*, b. 1798 ; d. March, 1842 ; resided on a farm on the banks of the Ohio river ; m. Nancy Griffen, of Henderson county, Ky.; and had issue :
  1. *Carmal;* resides in Newburg, Ind.
 ii. *Hugh*, b. 1800 ; d. November, 1835, in Henderson county, Ky.; m. Sarah Wright ; and had issue:
  1. *George-W.;* resides in Forest City, Ark.
 iii. *Mary*, d. 1856 ; m. Albert G. Hill ; and had two children.
 iv. *Milton*, b. 1806 ; d. 1870 ; m. Susan Warren, of Warwick county, Ind.; resided in Newburg, Ind.; and had issue :
  1. *Charles-Milton;* resides in Henderson county, Ky.
  2. *Dora*, m. N. G. Stanley ; resides in Davis county, Ky.
  3. *Cyrus-H.*
  4. *John-S.*
 v. *Elizabeth*, d. 1859 ; m. William Shelby ; resided in Owensboro', Ky.; and had three children.
 vi. *John-Steel;* resided on a large farm near Henderson, Ky ; m. Martha Elam ; and had issue :

1. *Sidney*, m. Julia Walker.
2. *Nancy*.
3. *George*.
4. *Martha*.
5. *Lee*.

vii. Jane, b. 1820; d. 1862; unm.

viii. Nancy, d. 1875; m. W. T. Shelby; resided in Memphis, Tenn., and had three children.

XXIV. WILLIAM MCCORMICK,⁴ (Robert,³ Thomas,² James,¹) b. April 12, 1776, in Fermanagh township, now in Juniata county, Pa.; d. in the spring of 1838, in Augusta county, Va.; was raised in Rockbridge county, Va., whither his father removed when the son was three years of age. He was twice married; m., first, February 3, 1801, MARY STEEL. They had issue:

34. *i. Robert*, b. July 13, 1802; m. Sarah Steel.

ii. William-Steel, b. May 29, 1804; d., 1884, at Patterson, Mo.; m., January 25, 1838, Rebecca Crow.

William McCormick m., secondly, in 1807, SARAH MCCLELLAND. They had issue:

iii. Mary-Steel, b. August 6, 1808.

iv. Thomas, b. September 2, 1809; m. —— Campbell.

v. James-Stevenson, b. February 7, 1819.

vi. George-Brown, b. December 18, 1822.

vii. Sarah-Sanderson, b. 1824.

viii. Joseph-I., b. May 12, 1830.

XXV. JAMES MCCORMICK,⁴ (Robert,³ Thomas,² James,¹) b. January 7, 1778, in Fermanagh township, now in Juniata county, Pa.; and was raised in Rockbridge county, Va.; removed to Ohio about 1805 or 1806, and settled at Gallipolis, Gallia county, afterwards at West Mill Grove, Wood county, that State; where he died August 30, 1839. He was thrice married; m., first, February 9, 1804, IRENE ROGERS. They had issue:

i. Martha, b. November 14, 1804; m., July, 1824, Joseph Waddell; resided in Mason city, W. Va.; and had one child.

35. *ii. John-R.*, b. August 5, 1806; m. Sarah R. Waddell.

James McCormick m., secondly, December 29, 1807, RACHEL NISONGER, b. September 11, 1785; d. November 2, 1826. They had issue:

iii. *Harvey*, b. March 80, 1809; d. September 8, 1889; resided
in Gallia county, O.; m., January, 1836, Cordelia Morton; and had issue:
  1. *Thomas*, b. 1838.
iv. *Robert*, b. April 4, 1811; resided in Wood county, O.; m.,
October 20, 1836, Mary Ann Shesser, b. November 10,
1818; and had issue:
  1. *Mary-E.*, b. July 29, 1835; d. September 4, 1836.
  2. *Martha*, b. August 28, 1837.
  3. *Sarah-A.*, b. July 16, 1840; d. December 26, 1842.
  4. *Rachel-A.*, b. June 20, 1844; d. May 29, 1848.
v. *James*, b. February 1, 1813; m., 'first, December 5, 1838,
Margaret Waddell; and had issue:
  1. *James-H.*, b. March 16, 1843.
  2. *George-H.*, b. February 14, 1845.
  3. *Samuel-R.*, b. Sept. 17, 1847; d. Dec. 7, 1877.
  4. *Elizabeth*, b. November 8, 1849.
  5. *Ephraim*, b. February 16, 1852.
James McCormick m., secondly, Mary Cherrington; and
had issue:
  6. *Marion*, b. February 21, 1856.
  7. *Margaret*, b. October 17, 1857.
  8. *Mary*, b. February 12, 1864; d. October 22, 1874.
James McCormick m., thirdly, Vesta Trowbridge; fourthly,
Deborah Ray; resided in Gallipolis, O.
vi. *George*, b. January 10, 1815; d. June 8, 1878; resided in
Wood county, O.; m., April 16, 1848, Mary Bradner; b.
May 27, 1828; d. December 16, 1871; and had issue:
  1. *James*, b. July 28, 1852.
  2. *Sarah*, b. August 2, 1854.
  3. *George*, b. October 16, 1856.
  4. *Mary-E.*, b. December 2, 1860.
  5. *Charles*, b. 1864; d. 1865.
  6. *William-H.*, b. February 2, 1866.
vii. *Margaret*, b. February 9, 1818; d. August 28, 1856; m.,
October 4, 1836, David Adams; resided in Wood
county, O.
viii. *Christine*, b. March 30, 1820; d. May, 1866; m. John A.
Rogers; resided in Gallia county, O.; and had five children.
ix. *Elizabeth*, b. July 7, 1822; d. April 15, 1872; m., 1841, Alexander Adams; resided in Wood county, O.
x. *Sarah*, b. November 14, 1824; d. January 2, 1852; m. ——
Brubaker; resided in Wood county, O.

James McCormick m., thirdly, June 5, 1827, RACHEL CLARK;
no issue.

XXVI. ROBERT McCORMICK,[4] (Robert,[3] Thomas,[2] James,[1]) b. June 8, 1780, on Walnut Grove farm, Rockbridge county, Va.; d. July 4, 1846, on the paternal homestead, and buried in the old Providence graveyard. He received an ordinary education acquired at a private school of his neighborhood, and was instructed in the strictest tenets of the Seceder branch of the Presbyterian Church. Throughout his life he took great pleasure in the acquirement of historical and scientific knowledge, and was very fond of astronomy. He was a man of remarkable mechanical genius, and seldom failed to accomplish what he undertook. Having blacksmith and carpenter shops, and being himself naturally a good workman, with almost any kind of tools, it was no difficulty for him to make whatever he desired of either wood or iron. The first record we have of his endeavors in the line of invention was in the construction of a reaping machine, on which he worked and experimented from and after 1809. From the nature of the testimony concerning his early inventions in this line, it would appear that he constructed more than one device between the years 1809 and 1825. At all events there is evidence to show that he was engaged at various times, during those years, experimenting on his reaper, and that he used various devices for cutting, and in all probability he made several attempts at making a machine during all those sixteen or seventeen years. This would seem to be corroborated by the statements, first, of his two nephews (Robert, son of William, and Robert, son of James McCormick), who stated that their fathers told them that Robert McCormick had invented a reaper in 1809; second, of his son Cyrus, who stated that his father had invented a reaper in 1816; thirdly, by Robert McCormick, above referred to, who stated that his uncle Robert showed him in the year 1825 or 1826 a machine he had just invented. One of the cutting devices he used on one of his machines was a system of rotary saws about eight or ten inches in diameter, which revolved, shear fashion, past the edge of a stationary knife. The saws were driven by bands from a cylinder which was turned by the revolution of the main wheel of the machine. This machine had vertical reels to sweep the grain across the cutters, and when cut delivered it on a platform in the rear of the cutters, while an endless apron carried it across the platform and delivered it on one side of the machine. Another cutting device which he used consisted of stationary curved sickles against which the grain was forced and cut by vertical reels with pins in their peripheries. Parts of this early machine were, for many years, stored away in the loft of the old malthouse, on the home farm, and were familiar objects to those about the farm. The reaping machine was not the only mechanical problem that commanded the thought and inventive genius of Robert McCormick. He found time to exercise his ingenuity in other directions as well, and reaped harvests of success in several mechanical inventions, briefly described as follows: In the winter of 1830–31 there was a great deal of talk, and much in the newspapers on the subject of raising hemp. Only one thing seemed to be in the way of its becoming a very profitable product, and that was the difficulty of cheaply and profitably reducing the fibre to its required marketable shape. Acting on this seeming demand Robert McCormick invented a very ingenious and perfect working hemp-brake, and in connection with it a horse power by which it was driven, and in the fall of 1831 he operated it successfully. He also invented a machine for cleaning the hemp when broken. The excitement over hemp raising, however, dying out, the demand for the machines never amounted to much, although a number of them were built and sold. At another time he invented and manufactured a very ingenious threshing machine, in connection with which he made a horse power of peculiar construction. He also built a clover sheller of stone, resembling an ordinary mill somewhat, but never did anything with it, except for his own use. He also invented and made a blacksmith's bellows, which was of a tub form, and of which he built and sold a large number. He invented a water power that worked by confined pressure, somewhat on the principle of the steam engine; and also a hillside plow. As it was Mr. McCormick's ambition that his sons should follow husbandry as a profession, he purchased a farm of three hundred acres, situated a mile and a half from his own homestead, and another of seven hundred acres on the South river, nine miles west of his home. On each of these places he had a saw mill, and on the South river farm and his home place he had flour mills, which he operated successfully. Prior to 1837 Mr. McCormick gave the South river farm to his son, Cyrus H., who, on account of the losses sustained in the furnace business, deeded back that property to his father, in part payment of his share of said losses. Mr. McCormick afterwards gave the same property to his son, Leander J. He gave the home farm, at his death, to his son, William S. When we consider the extensive operations he constantly had on hand, it will be seen that Robert McCormick was a man of great business and executive ability, as well as inventive genius. For many years he carried on farming on four farms, aggregating in all 1,800 acres, and at the same time operated two flour mills and two saw mills, besides which he kept carpenter and blacksmith shops busy, manufacturing various kinds of machinery of his own invention. In 1834, in connection with his son Cyrus, he built what is known as "Cotopaxi furnace," but through the mismanagement of their partner, followed by the financial panic of 1837, he was compelled to sell the Old Providence farm, which belonged to his wife, as well as the furnace property. Cyrus soon after left home with the intention of seeing what he could do towards establishing and introducing a reaper of his own invention into the vast wheat fields of the west. Leander J. left school and went into the shop, William S. took entire management of the farming operations and finance, while Mr. McCormick and Leander manufactured the reapers, horse powers, blacksmith's bellows, other machinery and tools. Thus, through the combined efforts of all, in due time the family were extricated from their financial embarassments. Just as he was beginning to feel the freedom of being out of debt Mr. McCormick was overtaken by a heavy snow storm in returning home from his South river farm, where he had been attending the shipment of reaping machines to Lynchburg. He became chilled, took a severe cold, from the effects of which he never recovered. Robert McCormick m., February 11, 1808, MARY ANNA HALL, b. June 24, 1780; d. June 1, 1853; daughter of Patrick Hall.* Mrs. McCormick was a woman of

---

*Patrick Hall was born in county Armagh, Ireland, in 1751, emigrated to America in 1770, and settled in Augusta county, Va., where he married Susanna McChesney about the year 1775.

bright and cheerful disposition, a devout Christian, and very ambitious for the future welfare of her children. She had a fine constitution, of fair complexion, with dark eyes and hair. They had issue:

- 36.   *i. Cyrus-Hall*, b. February 15, 1809; m. Nettie Fowler.
-       *ii. Robert-Hall*, b. May 24, 1810; d. June 28, 1826, at his father's home in Rockbridge county, Va.
-       *iii. Susan-Jane*, b. August 1, 1813; d. June 27, 1826, at her father's home in Rockbridge county, Va.
- 37.   *iv. William-Sanderson*, b. November 2, 1815; m. Mary Ann Grigsby.
- 38.   *v. Mary-Caroline*, b. April 18, 1817; m. Rev. James Shields.
- 39.   *vi. Leander-James*, b. February 8, 1819; m. Henrietta M. Hamilton.
-       *vii. John-Priestly*, b. November 8, 1820; d. September 4, 1849, at his father's home in Rockbridge county, Va.
- 40. *viii. Amanda*, b. September 17, 1822; m. Hugh Adams.

XXVII. HUGH McCORMICK,[5] (James,[4] Hugh,[3] Hugh,[2] James,[1]) b. February 14, 1777, in White Deer Valley, now Lycoming county, Pa.; d. March 28, 1828, in the city of New York. He went to New York about the year 1798, and with his cousin, Richard Cunningham, engaged in the leather business under the firm name of Cunningham & McCormick. He was a prominent member of the Mechanics and Tradesmen's society, and the Manumission society, and died at the early age of fifty-one years. Mr. McCormick married, in 1801, ESTHER BARBARA KUMBEL, daughter of William Kumbel, of New York. She died there September 1, 1854. They had issue:

-      *i. Isabella-Frances*, b. Feb. 9, 1802; d. July 11, 1882; unm.
- 41. *ii. Richard-Cunningham*, b. December 5, 1803; m. Sarah Matilda Decker.
-      *iii. Amanda*, b. August 29, 1805; d. January 25, 1885; unm.
-      *iv. Mary-Ann*, b. February 3, 1807; d. March 27, 1876, in Newark, N. J.; m., October 22, 1844, Charles Augusta Carter, d. August 23, 1884, in Newark, N. J.; and had issue (surname Carter):
  - 1. *William-Dexter*, b. July 8, 1845; m., October 9, 1867, Kate Brigden Badger, of Newark, N. J.; and had issue (surname Carter):
    - *a. Richard-Mortimer*, b. July 21, 1868; d. February 28, 1871.
    - *b. William-Eliot*, b. July 22, 1870; d. March 12, 1874.

   c. Kate-Frances, b. August 17, 1872 ; d. February 9, 1874.
   d. Raymond Dexter, b. January 5, 1876.
   e. Edith-Badger, b. October 21, 1878.
   f. Helen-Rhoda, b. November 16, 1883.
  2. *John-Richard*, b. April 22, 1848.
 v. Emeline, b. 1809 ; d. March 30, 1871 ; unm.
 vi. William, b. 1811 ; d. 1868.
 vii. Louisa, b. September 4, 1813 ; d. January 20, 1876 ; m., November 17, 1840, William A. Cummings ; resided in New York until 1860, when they removed to Darien, Conn., afterwards to Brooklyn, where they both died, the latter in the year 1878 ; and had issue (surname Cummings):
  1. *William-McCormick*, b. September 6, 1841 ; m., 1863, Kate Downer, of Darien, Conn.; and had issue (surname Cummings):
   a. Louise, b. 1864 ; d. in inf.
   b. Josephine-H., b. 1866.
   c. William, b. 1870.
  2. *Charles Curtis*, b. April 6, 1846 ; m., December 24, 1874, Anna Haviland, of Hudson, N. Y.
  3. *Hettie-Louisa*, b. November 21, 1851 ; m., May 28, 1872, Isaac Downer Weed; and had issue (surname Weed): *Louise*, b. 1873; d. s. p.
  4. *Isabella-Frances*, b. August 4, 1853.
42. *viii. John*, b. January 15, 1818 ; m. Caroline Pilsbury.

XXVIII. CHARLES N. McCORMICK,[5] (Hugh,[4] Hugh,[3] Hugh,[2] James,[1]) b. in Middleton township, Cumberland county, Pa.; m., and had issue :

 i. Robert-B., settled in Dover, Loudoun county, Va., as teacher ; m. Kate Reynolds, of Clark county, Va.; and had issue : *Roberdeau, Hugh-Pendleton, Charles, Mary-E., Rose, Carrie, Kate,* and *William.*

XXIX. ROBERT McCORMICK,[5] (John,[4] Thomas,[3] Thomas,[2] James,[1]) b. January 25, 1796; d. September 10, 1874, in Milton, Pa.; m., May 19, 1830, ELIZA WOOD, *nee* Montgomery, dau. of David and Agnes (Shaw) Montgomery. They had issue :

 i. David-Montgomery, d. inf.
 ii. John, d. unm.
 iii. Robert, k. at Bardstown, Ky., December 26, 1864, while serving in Seventh Pennsylvania Cavalry.
 iv. Charles-C., b. February 18, 1838 ; d. January 31, 1884, at Milton, Pa.; received a collegiate education ; entered

the Union service as a private in 1861 ; promoted to captain Seventh Pennsylvania Cavalry November 18, 1861 ; to colonel January 10, 1865 ; and brevet-brigadier general, March 13, 1865, for long, faithful and gallant service ; at the close of the war returned to Milton. Gen. McCormick m., June 80, 1868, Charlotte A. Wright, dau. of L. M. Wright, and his wife, Sarah Blake, of Troy, N. Y.; and had issue : *Robert-C.*, *Helen-C.*, and *Walter-Wright.*

v. *Agnes*, m. William P. Dougal, b. December 28, 1823 ; d. July 8, 1890 ; served in the war of the Rebellion as captain 150th Regt., Pa. Vols., and severely wounded at the battle of Gettysburg ; and had issue (surname Dougal) : *James, Robert, William, Eliza, Charles, Agnes,* and *Margaret.*

vi. *William-C.*, resides in McPherson county, Kansas.

XXX. JOHN MCCORMICK,[5] (John,[4] Thomas,[3] Thomas,[2] James,[1]) b. December 20, 1802 ; d. August 6, 1869, at Milton, Pa.; m., April 23, 1825, MARTHA GIFFEN. They had issue:

i. *Robert*, b. September, 1826 ; d. December, 1828.
ii. *Ann-Elizabeth*, b. June, 1828 ; m. John L. Watson.
iii. *John*, b. April, 1831 ; m., 1855, Rebecca Vincent.
iv. *Mary-G.*, b. April, 1833.
v. *James-S.*, b. February, 1835 ; d. February, 1837.
vi. *Margaret*, b. 1840 ; m. Dr. James P. McCleary.
vii. *William*, b. December, 1845 ; killed at the battle of Murfreesboro', January 1, 1863.

XXXI. WILLIAM MCCORMICK,[5] (John,[4] Thomas,[3] Thomas,[2] James,[1]) b. March 13, 1805 ; d. in 1884, at Centreville, Mich.; m., October 6, 1828, RACHEL SLOTE. They had issue:

i. *William-Edwin*, b. February 19, 1830; d. Dec. 20, 1843.
ii. *Sarah-J.*, b. March 21, 1831 ; m., B. F. Dressler.
iii. *Clara-Ann*, b. September 18, 1833 ; d. October 14, 1838.
iv. *James-Slote*, b. October 12, 1835 ; m., March 28, 1865, Mary F. Emery ; reside at Knoxville, Tenn.
v. *John*, b. January 4, 1841 ; d. February 17, 1841.
vi. *Martha E.* (twin), b. January 4, 1841.
vii. *Hannah-G.*, b. June 4, 1843 ; m., January 29, 1867, Rev. William H. Blair, a Presbyterian clergyman.

XXXII. ROBERT MCCORMICK,[5] (James,[4] James,[3] Thomas,[2] James,[1]) b. February 6, 1805, in Cumberland county, Pa.; d. January 24, 1877, in Chariton, Iowa ; studied medicine, and, at the age of twenty-two, or twenty-three, located in Sharon,

Mercer county, Pa.; after the death of his wife, he removed to Chariton. He m., in 1829, SUSAN ULP, who d. in 1847. They had issue :

    i. James-Oliver, b. October 3, 1830 ; d. s. p.
    ii. Elizabeth, b. November, 1832 ; d. March, 1876.
    iii. William-Laughlin, b. November, 1834 ; d. March, 1884.
    iv. Albert-Ulp, b. May 4, 1837 ; m., and had issue.
    v. Margaret, b. April 24, 1840.
    vi. Robert-Bryson, b. 1843 ; d. in infancy.
    vii. Emily, b. June, 1846.

XXXIII. JAMES MCCORMICK,[5] (William,[4] James,[3] Thomas,[2] James,[1]) b. February 24, 1801, near Silvers Spring, Cumberland county, Pa.; d. January 19, 1870, at Harrisburg, Pa. When less than five years of age, he lost his father by a fatal accident. Paternal care thus devolved upon his mother, a bright, determined woman, and by her his preparatory studies were carefully made, fitting him at an early age for Princeton College, where he graduated with reputation, and began the study of law with Andrew Carothers, Esq., of Carlisle. He was admitted to the bar of Cumberland county in 1823, and to that of Dauphin county at the August term, 1825. His most successful career never faltered as long as he was able to give his professional duties any attention, and, indeed, followed him after his retirement from all active pursuits. He served in the borough council a long time, and was president of that body, also of the Dauphin Deposit bank, of the Harrisburg cemetery, of the Harrisburg Bridge company, and one of the trustees of the Pine Street Presbyterian church. In all these positions he was a cautious and able adviser. He uniformly declined candidature for office, as also offers of the highest honors of his profession. Upon his retirement he gave the powers of his active mind to the management of a large estate, consisting of furnaces, rolling-mills, grist-mills and farms. All these interests were successful, and, notwithstanding his physical disability, conducted in a masterly and systematic manner. Mr. McCormick m., in 1830, ELIZA BUEHLER, b. November 11, 1806, at Erie, Pa.; d. December 25, 1877, at Harrisburg, Pa.; only daughter of George Buehler and Maria Nagle. She was, indeed, a most estimable woman. To each noble charity, benevolent enterprise, philanthropic movement, Christian endeavor, hospital or home in the city of Harrisburg she was a friend, promoter and benefactor. From no good cause or charitable work or needy poor did she withhold her hand or deny her bounty. They had issue:

43.   *i. Henry*, b. March 10, 1831 ; m. Annie Criswell.
44.   *ii. James*, b. October 31, 1832; m. Mary Wilson Alricks.
45.   *iii. Mary*, b. October 10, 1834; m. James Donald Cameron.

XXXIV. ROBERT MCCORMICK,[5] (William,[4] Robert,[3] Thomas,[2] James,[1]) b. July 13, 1802, in Augusta county, Va.; d. December 4, 1879; resided on a farm near Old Providence Presbyterian church in the county named. He m., March 4, 1824, SARAH STEEL, b. December 4, 1804, and is yet [1885] living. They had issue:

  i. William-Steel, b. January 17, 1825.
  ii. Nathaniel-Davis, b. December 3, 1826.
  iii. Mary-Jane, b. December 22, 1828.
  iv. Robert-Alexander, b. July 23, 1831.
  v. Sarah-Martha, b. December 22, 1833.
  vi. John-Addison, b. February 4, 1837.
  vii. Rebecca-Jane, b. November 17, 1840.
  viii. Virginia, b. August 15, 1843.
  ix. Phoebe-Ann, b. September 12, 1845.

XXXV. JOHN R. MCCORMICK,[6] (James,[5] William,[4] Robert,[3] Thomas,[2] James,[1]) b. August 5, 1806, in Virginia; d. September 7, 1854, in Gallia county, O.: m., in 1827, SARAH WADDELL, b. August 19, 1810. They had issue:

  i. William, b. October 22, 1828; m., first, Catharine Hanson; secondly, Hannah Blake.
  ii. James-A., b. July 23, 1830; d. February 3, 1831.
  iii. John-W., b. December 20, 1831; m., first, Caroline Mills; secondly, Sarah Mills.
  iv. Mary-W., b. August 17, 1833 ; m. John T. Halliday.
  v. Samuel-R., b. January 6, 1836; d. September 13, 1836.
  vi. Sarah-E., b. September 12, 1837 ; m. John S. Mills.
  vii. Irene-E., b. November 24, 1839; m. William G. Mills.
  viii. Martha-Ellen, b. June 16, 1843 ; d. May 15, 1871 ; m. William Graham.
  ix. Charles-H., b. April 13, 1847; m. Augusta Halliday.
  x. Caroline-Isabella, b. March 11, 1850 ; d. November 24, 1850.
  xi. Romaine-E., b. June 25, 1852; m. Dr. Edwin S. Rickets; reside in Portsmouth, O.
  xii. [A son, twin,] b. June 25, 1852 ; d. 1852.

XXXVI. CYRUS HALL MCCORMICK,[5] (Robert,[4] Robert,[3] Thomas,[2] James,[1]) b. February 15, 1809, on the old homestead, Walnut Grove Farm, Rockbridge county, Va.; d. Tuesday, May 13, 1884, at his residence on Rush street, Chicago, Ill. The minute story of his life is a story of inspiration and encouragement to the American youth of to-day. This is a story of humble beginnings, high aims, earnestness of purpose, and integrity of character. And it is the story of a life crowned with fruition. In addition to his extensive farming interests Robert McCormick, the father of Cyrus, operated saw and grist mills of considerable proportions for those early days, and to facilitate the work of keeping his agricultural implements in repair, a blacksmith and carpenter shop were accessories of the farm. Much of the work done in these shops by Robert McCormick was in connection with his experiments in the construction of a reaping machine. Tests in the field to determine the merits of this machine were held in the early part of the summer of 1831, but the results were not dissimilar to those of preceding years. Repeated experiments had ended only in disappointment, and Robert McCormick's machine was laid aside, his ideas abandoned and his hopes destroyed. But while these field tests of 1831 failed to justify the expectations of the father, they were sufficient to arouse the native ingenuity of the son, Cyrus, and start him on that career of success which made him famous and placed his name among those of the foremost inventors of the age. Cyrus Hall McCormick was the eldest of a family of eight children; the son of a farmer, his educational advantages were not superior to those of the average farmer boy of the day. For him the "college year" began and ended with the winter months, and the "Old Field School" was his Alma Mater. There he learned the rudiments of a common school education, and upon that foundation built a superstructure of knowledge gleaned from the maps and charts that hang upon the walls of the universe. With keen observation and retentive memory, and with a judgment that most unerringly separated the wheat from the chaff, he may be rightly classed with that nobility of self-made men whose names have added luster to their times, and to whose benefactions mankind will ever be indebted. Cyrus, while still a boy, spent much time in the farm shops, and early evinced the inheritance of his father's inventive traits, by fashioning from wood or iron such tools or small implements as he needed in his work. At the age of fifteen he swung the scythe in line with his father's workmen in the harvest field, making for this purpose a grain cradle which lightened his toil and made it possible for him to keep his work abreast of the older and more sinewy laborers. In the same year he constructed a hillside plow, which threw alternate furrows on the lower side, being thus either a right hand or a left hand plow. It was patented in 1831, but a few months later the young inventor supplanted it with something better, called the self-sharpening, horizontal plow, the first perfect self-sharpening plow ever invented. After the signal failure of his father's grain cutting machine in the early summer of 1831, Cyrus, then twenty-two years old, gave serious thought to the subject which had so long engrossed the parent's attention, and, as thought and action went hand in hand with him, he promptly began the construction of his reaper upon new and widely different principles from those employed in the abandoned machine of his father, which he had carefully studied. This machine consisted of a great framework, having a number of fixed sickle hooks on the front, with perpendicular cylinders to press the stems of the grain against and across the edges of the hooks, and then carry it to the stubble side and cast it out to the binders in swaths. His father's crude mechanism possessed no ideas that he could utilize, and he was left to the resources of his own intellect for ways and means. As a prime essential he felt that the grain should be operated upon in a mass by a horizontal reciprocating blade. Without being more specific, it is sufficient to say that with his own hands the young man toiled on during the summer until he had constructed and combined the four cardinal principles found to-day in every successful harvesting machine, principles which "if dispensed with," says so eminent an authority as Edward H. Knight, A. M., LL. D. (in his New Mechanical Dictionary), would wipe every reaper out of existence." These underlying requisites of the reaper, invented, combined, and constructed by Cyrus Hall McCormick in 1831, are the reciprocating blade in projecting fingers; the platform for receiving the falling grain; the revolving reel for drawing the grain back to the knife and laying it upon the platform; and the divider, to separate the grain to be cut from that left standing. This machine, drawn by one horse, was put to a practical test late in the harvest of 1831, in a six acre field of oats grown by John Steele, near Walnut Grove. Here it was that the reaper achieved its first success; here it was that Robert McCormick, whose repeated failures had prompted him to discourage his son's ambition, acknowledged the superior genius of that son; here was ushered in an era marked by the elevation of one great branch of farm labor from out of its slavery, an epoch in which the material prosperity of the world has been augmented many hundred fold, the lines of civilization widened, and the progress of humanity significantly advanced. Not at once were the great possibilities of the reaper appreciated by the inventor, but gradually its value became known to an ever widening circle, and its distinguishing features were the subject of many a discussion. This description of Mr. McCormick's first reaper is found in the second volume of the *Mechanics' Magazine* of 1833:

"We have omitted until now to furnish our agricultural friends with an account of a machine for cutting grain, invented by one of our ingenious and respectable countrymen, Mr. Cyrus H. McCormick, and which we witnessed in operation in a field of grain during the late harvest in the neighborhood of this place. A large crowd of citizens were present at the trial of it, and although the machine was not as perfectly made as the plan is susceptible of, yet we believe it gave general satisfaction. We have been furnished with some certificates from several of our intelligent farmers, one of which we have appended to the following description of the invention :

"This machine is so constructed as to leave a long or a short stubble, to operate alike well on tall or short grain. It is drawn by one horse walking by the side of the grain in shafts; just behind is a wheel about two feet three inches in diameter, which runs on the ground, by which the machinery is operated, having a cog-wheel with forty cogs screwed to it. There is a small wheel (with nine cogs) working in that, having another one on the same shaft with twenty-eight, which works another small one, turning a small crank, behind the wheel, and from this crank the knife receives a vibratory motion. It is about four and a half feet long, with an edge somewhat like that of a sickle (having teeth) straight and projecting into the grain at right angles to the horse. Behind the knife is an apron five or six feet long of thin plank; and this frame connects with and is made fast to the frame which supports the main wheel, having a slide or small wheel under it, to support it, say about five feet from the main wheel. Alongside the apron, by the point of the knife, and extending some distance before the knife, is raised a partition of cloth, for the purpose of dividing and keeping separate the cut grain from that which is left standing. There is a reel, as it is termed, which is about six or seven feet in diameter, and the same length of the knife. This is made by framing arms in each end of a shaft, say eight, the points of which are joined together by pieces, called ribs, parallel to the shafts. The reel is revolved as the machine advances by a band from the main wheel to one on its shaft, the object of which is to draw the grain back to the knife, which will be done whether straight or tangled, upright or leaning, unless below an angle of forty-five degrees, and to throw it on the apron. When a sufficient quantity shall have been collected for a sheaf, the hand who attends it draws it off the apron with a rake. The grain is prevented from slipping with the edge of the knife by pieces of wire projecting before it within one or two inches of each other.

" June 18, 1833.

"I certify that Mr. C. H. McCormick's reaping machine, with a horse, was employed by me in the late harvest, and though I did not work it much, I was satisfied with its work. I tried it for an hour, and calculated what it would do for a day, and found that it would cut in a day about twelve acres. I done so more than once. The present year was unfavorable for the trial, as the wheat was lodged in the field. I was so satisfied that I bought one. This preparation was necessary—the ground must be clean, free from stumps and large stones. JAMES McDOWELL."

On the 31st day of December, 1833, Obed Hussey obtained letters patent on a grain cutting machine possessing two of the features found in the McCormick. To guard against further attempts at piracy, on the 20th of May, 1834, Mr. McCormick wrote the following letter to the editor of the *Mechanics' Magazine and Register of Inventions and Improvements*, and applied for his patent, which he shortly obtained. The letter is as follows:

"TO THE EDITOR OF THE MECHANICS' MAGAZINE:

"*Dear Sir:*—Having seen in the April number of your magazine a cut and description of the reaping machine said to have been invented by Obed Hussey, of Ohio, last summer, I would ask a favor of you to inform Mr. Hussey and the public, through your columns, that the principle, namely, cutting grain by means of a toothed instrument, receiving the rotary motion from a crank, with the iron teeth projecting above the edge of the cutter, for the purpose of preventing the grain from partaking of its motion, is a part of the principle of my machine, and was invented by me, and operated on wheat and oats in July, 1831. This can be attested to the entire satisfaction of the public and Mr. Hussey, as it was witnessed by many persons. Consequently, I would warn all persons against the use of the aforesaid principle, as I regard and treat the use of it, in any way, as an infringement of my rights.

"Since the first experiment was made of the performance of my machine, I have, for the mutual interests of the public and myself, been laboring to bring it to as much perfection as the principle admitted of before offering it to the public. I now expect to be able in a very short time to give such an account of its simplicity, utility, and durability as will give general, if not universal, satisfaction.

"The revolving reel, as I conceive, constitutes a very important, in fact, indispensible part of my machine, which has the effect, in all cases, whether the grain be tangled or leaning, unless below an angle of forty-five degrees to the ground, to bring it back to the cutter and deliver it on the apron when cut.

"Very respectfully yours, etc.,

"CYRUS H. MCCORMICK."

In 1834 he purchased an interest in a smelter and devoted his energies to the management of the iron works until the panic tidal wave of 1837 swept over the country, when the growing young industry was stranded and its promoters all but hopelessly involved in the general wreck. In a ruin in which hundreds of men lost everything Cyrus H. McCormick saved his honor. He took the stand that every dollar of the firm's obligations should be met, and to this end he sacrificed all his possessions including the farm which his father had given him. Starting again with no capital but energy and determination, and an inborn sense of integrity, his efforts were thenceforth devoted to the improvement and introduction of the reaper. Its manufacture began in a small way in the shops on the old Virginia farm. The swath cut by the McCormick in those first years was small indeed, but it was wide enough to warrant a branching out. The fame of the reaper and the demand for it far outran the facilities for its manufacture, and in 1845 larger shops were established at Cincinnati, O., while arrangements were also made for the building of the machine by a firm at Brockport, N. Y., in order that the east and west could be thus supplied from these respective centers. But even these plans soon proved inadequate for the best service to the trans-Mississippi regions, and Mr. McCormick believing Chicago to be the predestined center of the country's agricultural interests, decided to make that city the permanent home of his industry, and thither the reaper plant was removed in 1847. The next year marked the decided impetus in the manufacture of reapers and that seven hundred machines should have been turned out seemed almost incredible—as wondrous even as to-day seems the magic city herself, still the home of the McCormick grain and grass cutting machines, of which more than one hundred thousand are now annually built and sold. To incur the jealousy of contemporaries is one of the penalties which genius must ever pay for the promotion of her subjects, and, as may be fancied, the case of Cyrus Hall McCormick affords no exception to the rule. In 1848 a most unjust decision emanated from the United States Patent Department, the true construction of which decision is, that because the reaper was so valuable an implement and so desirable to all the world the inventor's patent should not be renewed, but that all should have an opportunity to engage in its manufacture. By reason of this unprecedented edict the bars were let down that those who chose to follow might enter in and appropriate the fruits of the pioneer's work. As a result, reaper manufactories sprung up in various parts of the country, and in due time many of these users of appropriated ideas, noting with deep solicitation the still further advancement and continued success of Mr. McCormick's machines, either openly proclaimed themselves the original inventors, or sought to give the credit to some other individual who might possibly have experimented in this branch of invention; and whose very obscurity made the advocacy of his cause easy for them. For Cyrus Hall McCormick, it is sufficient to say that his claim has been upheld by the highest judicial tribunals, and that International Juries of Award in invariably bestowing the grand prizes upon the McCormick machine have deemed it simple justice to assert, as a personal tribute to the sagacity and perseverance of Mr. McCormick that such honors as they did thus bestow were not more for the practical utility of the machine itself than for their recognition of the originality and genius of the inventor. In proof of this it should be remembered that in 1849 the United States Commissioner of Patents said of the McCormick reaper: "It is one of those great and valuable inventions which will commence a new era in the progress of improvement and whose beneficial influence is felt in all coming time." In 1851, in London, was held the first World's Fair, and from the records of that Exposition we quote: "The McCormick reaper is the most valuable article contributed to this exhibition, and for its originality and value, and its perfect work in the field it is awarded the Council Medal." Another international exhibit was held in Paris in 1855. The McCormick reaper was there and was awarded the grand gold medal, and in the jury's report may be found these significant statements: "The McCormick reaper is the type after which all others are made, ... not one of the imitations equals the original." Again at Paris in 1867 the question of the invention of the reaper was under discussion, and in a report written by M. Eugene Tisserand, Director General of the Imperial Domains, it was said: "The man who has labored most in the general distribution, perfection and discovery of the first practical reaper is assuredly Mr. McCormick, of Illinois. Equally as a benefactor of humanity, and as a skillful mechanician, Mr. McCormick has been adjudged worthy of the highest distinction of the Exposition." A report was also made upon the same occasion by M. Aureliano, who said: "It is Mr. McCormick who invented the first reaper . . . . . the details of which are, it may be said, the type after which all others have been constructed." Reference has been made to the refusal of the United States Patent Commissioner to renew the McCormick patent in 1848. In 1859 his patent of 1845 was also refused extension. The Commissioner at this time was the Hon. D. P. Holloway, than whom no man more fully recognized the fact that Mr. McCormick was alone entitled to the credit of having invented the reaper, as witness these words :

"Cyrus Hall McCormick is an inventor whose fame, while he is yet living, has spread throughout the world. His genius has done honor to his own country, and has been the admiration of foreign nations, and he will live in the grateful recollections of mankind as long as the reaping machine is employed in gathering the harvest."

In addition to the long list of trophies won by Mr. McCormick's machine, the inventor himself was the recipient of many enviable marks of personal recognition. Among these may be mentioned the degree of the Cross of the Legion of Honor, conferred upon him by Emperor Napoleon III., in 1868, a distinction then bestowed upon but few, and reserved in recognition of great services to the world. Again in 1878, while at Paris, Mr. McCormick was elected corresponding member of the French Academy of Sciences, on the ground of his "having done more for the cause of agriculture than any other living man." As may be presumed, the inventor of the reaper was liberally rewarded for his work, but this reward was not poured into his lap while he waited in idleness. He never waited. His entire life was one continuous workday. In him were combined to a rare degree the qualities of the genius, and the man of business. He was sagacious, far-seeing, energetic. "In Chicago's memorable baptism of fire, in 1871, the great McCormick Reaper Works went down in the general destruction. Promptly the work of rebuilding was commenced on a scale more elaborate, resulting in a plant which far outranked the old in equipment, facility and capacity, the immense business of which was conducted under the personal supervision of its originator until his death in 1884. An outline of the life of Cyrus Hall McCormick which should consider only his career as a great inventor and successful manufacturer would lack much completeness. His home, social and religious ties were of the strongest nature. That such a man should be deeply religious is the natural corollary, and his religion manifested itself in a thousand ways remembered by men, while perpetual monuments to his generosity and philanthropy will tell the story to generations yet to come.

The McCormick Theological Seminary of the Presbyterian Church is one of these. In 1859 Mr. McCormick laid a proposition before the General Assembly of the Presbyterian Church, then convened at Indianapolis, offering to endow the professorships of the Presbyterian Theological Seminary of the Northwest on condition that it be located in Chicago. The Assembly readily acquiesced, and from Mr. McCormick this great and influential religious school has received magnificent donations and benefactions. Of a similar nature was his purchase of the *Interior*, a newspaper established in Chicago to represent the Presbyterian Church. The waves of financial disaster were beating about it, when, at the solicitation of the friends of the cause it represented, he purchased it and placed it upon a sound basis. In 1858, Mr. McCormick m. NETTIE FOWLER, daughter of Melzar Fowler, of Jefferson county, New York. They had issue :

- *i. Cyrus-Hall, Jr.*, b. May 16, 1859 ; educated at Chicago High School and Princeton College ; mastering the affairs of business which his father had built up, he was made president of the McCormick Harvesting Machine Company in 1884 ; represented its interests at the Paris Exposition in 1889, and decorated by the President of the French Republic as an officer of " *Le Merite Agricole ;*" is largely interested in church and educational interests ; he m., March 5, 1889, Harriet Bradley Hammond ; and they had issue :
    1. *Cyrus*, b. September 22, 1890.
    2. *Elizabeth*, b. July 12, 1892.
    3. *Gordon*, b. June 21, 1894.
- *ii. Mary-Virginia*, b. May 5, 1861.
- *iii. Robert*, b. October 27, 1864 ; d. December, 1865.
- *iv. Anita-Eugenie*, b. July 4, 1866 ; m., September 26, 1889, Emmons Blaine ; d. June 18, 1892, son of Hon. James G. Blaine ; passing away in his early manhood, his noble and beautiful personality was a great loss to a host of friends and especially to his revered and honored father. Mrs. Blaine resides in Chicago ; and they had issue (surname Blaine):
    1. *Emmons*, b. August 30, 1890.
- *v. Alice*, b. May 15, 1870 ; d. January, 1871.
- *vi. Harold-Fowler*, b. May 2, 1872 ; m., November 26, 1895, Edith Rockefeller.
- *vii. Stanley-Robert*, b. November 2, 1874.

XXXVII. WILLIAM SANDERSON MCCORMICK,[5] (Robert,[4] Robert,[3] Thomas,[2] James,[1]) b. November 2, 1815, in Rockbridge county, Va.; d. September 27, 1865, at Jacksonville, Ill.; buried in Graceland cemetery, near Chicago. He acquired a good education in the ordinary branches through private teachers and at a neighboring school. He was a bright scholar, and, at an early age, became an important and valuable assistant to his father, taking charge of the farming operations and accounts, thus relieving him from much care and enabling him to devote most of his time to mechanical and manufacturing pursuits. To him the renewed prosperity of the family was largely due after the financial reverses of his father in 1837. He was a progressive man in whatever he did, and in his early farming operations he adopted the best and latest improvements. Upon the death of his father in 1846, he inherited the home farm. However, in 1850, at the solicitation of his brother, Cyrus, he removed to Chicago, where he assumed the management of the reaper business already established. In 1859, he acquired one fourth interest, and much of its great and continued success is owing to his untiring skill, energy, and executive ability. Soon after the breaking out of the war of the Rebellion, he anticipated a great rise in property and values, and taking advantage of the situation, he bought for the firm a large amount of Chicago real estate in what is now the heart of the city. The wisdom of this action was soon apparent, and the firm realized a very large profit from this investment. From the effects of close and unremitting application to business and great nervous strain, Mr. McCormick finally broke down, and, in the spring of 1865 was compelled to give up all business, but to no purpose. Personally, he was of a cheerful disposition, quick spoken, and, although diffident, was among his friends a most interesting and agreeable man. Mr. McCormick m., in June, 1846, MARY ANN GRIGSBY, daughter of Reuben Grigsby, a prominent farmer who resided on his handsome estate called Hickory Hill, between Lexington and the Natural Bridge, in Rockbridge county, Va., where Mrs. McCormick was born. They had issue:

i. Robert-Sanderson, b. July 26, 1849; resides in Chicago, Ill.;
m., June 8, 1876, Katharine Medill, daughter of Joseph
Medill, of Chicago, and had issue:
  1. *Joseph-Medill*, b. May 16, 1877.
  2. *Katrina*, b. Jan. 16, 1879; d. July 9, 1879.
  3. *Robert-Rutherford*, b. July 30, 1880.

ii. William-Grigsby, b. June 3, 1851; resides in Chicago, Ill.;
m., October, 1873, Eleanor Brooks, daughter of Walter
Brooks, of Baltimore, and had issue:
  1. *Carrie*, b. July 24, 1874.
  2. *William-S.*, b. November 22, 1875; d. Jan. 1, 1880.
  3. *Mary-Grigsby*, b. July 18, 1878.
  4. *Walter-Brooks*, b. September 10, 1880.
  5. *Eleanor-Harryman*, b. November 7, 1882.
  6. *Chauncey-Brooks*, b. December 7, 1884.
  7. *Ruby*, b. Dec., 1891.

iii. Emma-Louise, b. Oct. 14, 1854; d. March 4, 1893; m.,
June 18, 1878, Perry H. Smith, Jr., son of Hon. Perry
H. Smith, Sr., of Chicago; and had issue (surname
Smith):
  1. *Perry-H.*, b. March 18, 1879; d. March 27, 1879.
  2. *Ruby-McCormick*, b. September 11, 1880.
  3. *Perry-Herbert*, b. March 29, 1885.
  4. *Robert-McCormick*, b. Nov., 1889.

iv. Anna-Reubenia, b. May 22, 1860; m., May 29, 1882, Edward
Blair, son of William Blair, of Chicago; and had issue
(surname Blair):
  1. *Edith*, b. May 5, 1883.
  2. *William-McCormick*, b. May 2, 1884.
  3. *Seymour*, b. May, 1889.

v. Lucy-Virginia, b. April 11, 1864; m. Oct. 9, 1888, Samuel
Rountree Jewett; reside in Chicago; and had issue
(surname Jewett):
  1. *McCormick*, b. Nov. 15, 1890.
  2. *Ellen-Rountree*, b. Feb. 9, 1892.
  3. *Emma-McCormick*, b. May 4, 1893.

XXXVIII. MARY CAROLINE MCCORMICK,[5] (Robert,[4] Robert,[3] Thomas,[2] James,[1]) b. April 18, 1817, in Rockbridge county, Va.; d. March 18, 1888, at Chicago, Ill. She received a good early education through private teachers, and completed her course of studies at Staunton. She m., May 11, 1847, Rev. JAMES SHIELDS, b. December 11, 1812, in Pittsburgh, Pa.; d. August 19, 1862, in Prairie du Chien, Wis.; son of

James Shields and Frances Perry. His parents came to America from County Tyrone, Ireland, in 1811. His father was a contractor and builder by occupation, and, in religion, a strict Presbyterian. Mr. Shields received a collegiate education at Western University, Pittsburgh, where he graduated in 1830. After completing a full term at the Theological Seminary of the United Presbyterian Church, he was licensed to preach April 2, 1834. In the spring of 1835 he was ordained pastor of the congregations of Fermanagh and Tuscarora, in Juniata county, Pa., and continued to preach to the first-named church until his death. He never enjoyed robust health, and, in July, 1862, at the solicitation of his brother-in-law, William S. McCormick, he left home for a season of recreation among the streams and lakes of Minnesota, but, on reaching Prairie du Chien, he was taken seriously ill, and died there. Mr. Shields had been previously married; first, January 30, 1839, Hannah McKinstry, who died a year after; he m., secondly, Mary R. Gracy, who left one child, *Mary-Gracy*, now married to William J. Wallace, of Newville, Pa. James Shields and Mary Caroline McCormick had issue (surname Shields):

    i. James-Hall. b. June 1, 1849; resides in Chicago, Ill.; m., October 17, 1878, Nellia Manville Culver, of Chicago, and had issue (surname Shields):
        1. *Irene,* b. November 1, 1879.
        2. *Nellia-Carolyn,* b. February 9, 1881.
        3. *James-Culver,* b. July 31, 1882.
        4. *Viola,* b. February 27, 1884.
        5. *Charles-Culver,* b. December 31, 1885.
        6. *Amanda,* b. October 19, 1887.
        7. *Grace,* b. June 24, 1889.
        8. *Robert-McCormick,* b. June 18, 1891.
        9. *Constance,* b. April 15, 1893.
    ii. Amanda-McCormick, b. December 25, 1850; m., November 23, 1880, Harry C. Tillman, of Detroit, Mich.; and had issue (surname Tillman):
        1. *Caroline-Hogarth,* b. August 22, 1881; d. March 22, 1882.
    iii. Cyrus-Sanderson, b. September 30, 1852; d. December 14, 1854.

XXXIX. LEANDER JAMES MCCORMICK,[5] (Robert,[4] Robert,[3] Thomas,[2] James,[1]) b. February 8, 1819, at the family homestead, Walnut Grove, Rockbridge county, Va. He received an education in the ordinary branches of study through private teachers. As a young man his time was mostly employed in his father's shop, where he developed considerable mechanical talent. A number of valuable improvements were made by him to the McCormick reaper at an early day. In 1847 he went to Cincinnati, O., where, in partnership with his brother, Cyrus, he built one hundred reapers for the harvest of that year. In the spring of 1849 he removed with his family to Chicago, where he took charge of the manufacturing department of the reaper business, acquiring one sixth interest in the same. From 1850 to 1859 he held the same position on a salary. In 1859 he and his brother, William S., became interested in the business to the extent of one fourth each, the firm becoming C. H. McCormick & Bros. After William S. McCormick's death he acquired a full one third interest. In 1879 the McCormick Harvesting Machine Company was organized, of which he became vice-president and held one-quarter of the capital stock. In 1889 he sold out this interest and retired from the business. By the Chicago fire of 1871 he lost his home and other valuable property, but, by energy and activity, soon rebuilt nearly all his buildings, personally planning and superintending the construction of the new McCormick reaper works. A few years since he decided to make a contribution to the cause of science in his native State. The result was the donation by him of a magnificent refractor telescope, the second largest of its kind in the world, to the University of Virginia, at Charlottesville. He resides in the city of Chicago. Mr. McCormick m., October 22, 1845, HENRIETTA HAMILTON, b. May 25, 1822, daughter of John Hamilton, of Rockbridge county, Va. They had issue:

  i. Robert-Hall, b. September 6, 1847 ; m., June 1, 1871, Sarah Lord Day, of New York; and had issue:
   1. *Henrietta-Hamilton*, b. February 22, 1872.
   2. *Eliza-Day*, b. July 11, 1873.
   3. *Robert-Hall, Jr.*, b. July 10, 1878.
   4. *Phoebe-Lord*, b. October 6, 1879.
   5. *Mildred*.
  ii. Maria.
  iii. Henrietta-L., b. April 22, 1857; m., November 14, 1883,

Frederick E. Goodhart, of London, England; and had issue (surname Goodhart):
  1. *Leander-McCormick*, b. August 10, 1884.
  2. *Frederick*.
iv. *Leander-Hamilton*, b. May 27, 1859; m., January, 1888, Constance Plummer, of Canterbury, England; and had issue:
  1. *Leander-J.*, b. January 6, 1889.
  2. *Edward-Hamilton*, b. August 3, 1890.
  3. *Allister-Hamilton*, b. August 3, 1891.

XL. AMANDA J. McCORMICK,[5] (Robert,[4] Robert,[3] Thomas,[2] James,[1]) b. September 17, 1822, in Rockbridge county, Va.; d. October 12, 1891, at Chicago, Ill. She was a woman remarkable for her beautiful Christian character and unselfish devotion to her family, whose example and influence were felt by all who surrounded her, and her rare qualities acknowledged by a large circle of warm friends and relatives. She m., May 8, 1845, HUGH ADAMS, b. February 10, 1820, in Rockbridge county, Va.; d. March 10, 1880, in Chicago, Ill., son of James Adams. His father was a man of fine mind, intelligent and highly respected, a brother of Senator Robert Adams from Tennessee. His mother was a most industrious, practical woman, and a devoted Christian. While a resident of Virginia Hugh Adams was a successful merchant, and one of the most popular business men of that State. Soon after his marriage he removed to Keer's Creek, Rockbridge county, where he engaged in merchandising. In 1857 he went to Chicago, where he became interested in the grain commission business, and known as the principal of the firm McCormick, Adams & Co. For twenty-three years he was prominently identified with the commercial prosperity of Chicago. His reputation in commercial circles was of the very best, and his name was looked upon as the synonym of all that was honorable and upright in business transactions. He was a consistent member of the Fourth Presbyterian church of Chicago, and a regular attendant upon its meetings, entering heartily into all its work for the Master— a man of simple, unostentatious tastes and habits, and of tender sympathy for the poor. They had issue (surname Adams):
  i. *Mary-Caroline*, b. April 21, 1846, in Rockbridge county, Va.; m., June 8, 1869, in Chicago, Ill., John E. Chapman, of

Warehouse Point, Conn., b. September 1, 1836. and d. January 4, 1882, in New York City; and had issue (surname Chapman):
    1. *Anna*, b. June 21, 1870, in Chicago, Ill.
    2. *John-Adams*, b. June 29, 1873, in Chicago, Ill.
ii. *Robert-McCormick*, b. October 21, 1847, in Rockbridge county, Va.; m., October 21, 1874, in St. Louis, Mo., Virginia Claiborne; and had issue (surname Adams):
    1. *Hugh-Claiborne*, b. Sept. 6, 1875, at St. Louis, Mo.
    2. *Mildred-Kyle*, b. Oct. 20, 1877, at St. Louis, Mo.
    3. *Amanda-McC.*, b. August 26, 1880, at Old Sweet Springs, Va.
    4. *Natalie*, b. Oct. 19, 1882, at Webster Groves, Mo.
    5. *Virginia-Claiborne*, b. August 3, 1885, at Webster Groves, Mo.
    6. *Robert-McCormick*, b. April, 1890.
    7. *Marion Kyle* (twin), b. April, 1890.
iii. *Cyrus-Hall*, b. February 21, 1849, in Rockbridge county, Va.; m., September 26, 1878, in Chicago, Ill., Emma J. Blair, daughter of Lyman Blair; and had issue (surname Adams):
    1. *Cyrus-Hall*, b. July 30, 1881, in Chicago, Ill.
iv. *James-W.*, b. January 2, 1853, in Rockbridge county, Va.
v. *Sarah-Ella*, b. March 10, 1855, in Rockbridge county, Va.; d. May 10, 1893; m., June 9, 1886, Willis E. Lewis, of St. Louis; and had issue (surname Lewis):
    1. *Genevieve*, b. July 17, 1888.
vi. *Hugh-L.*, b. May 5, 1857, in Rockbridge county, Va.; d. June 4, 1891; m., November 1, 1881, in Milwaukee, Wis., Susan Kirby; and had issue (surname Adams):
    1. *Hugh*, b. August 2, 1882, in Chicago, Ill.
    2. *Lita*, b. September 21, 1883, in Milwaukee, Wis.
vii. *Edward-Shields*, b. December 12, 1859, in Chicago, Ill.; m., April 15, 1895, Amie Irwin.
viii. *Amanda-Virginia*, b. March 3, 1862, in Chicago, Ill.; m., October 12, 1886, Wallace Farwell Campbell; and had issue (surname Campbell):
    1. *Mary-Virginia*, b. March 24, 1888.

XLI. RICHARD CUNNINGHAM McCORMICK,[6] (Hugh,[5] James,[4] Hugh,[3] Hugh,[2] James,[1]), b. December 5, 1803, in the city of New York; d. October 28, 1857; was actively engaged in business, and secretary of the Merchants' Exchange. He m., June 16, 1831, SARAH MATILDA DECKER, of New York; d., January 11, 1878, in Jamaica, L. I. They had issue:

46. i. *Richard-Cunningham*, b. May 23, 1832; m., first, Margaret G. Hunt; secondly, Elizabeth Thurman.
  ii. *Alfred-Decker*, b. November 27, 1834; m., November 27, 1865, Sarah Elizabeth Van Wicklen, of Woodhaven, L. I., who d. October 1, 1874; and had issue:
     1. *Richard-Cunningham*, b. December 4, 1866.
  iii. *Isabella-Frances*, b. January 6, 1836; d. July 6, 1841.
  iv. *Sarah-Matilda*, b. December 12, 1838; m., June 23, 1864, Dexter H. Walker; and had issue (surname Walker):
     1. *Edith May*, b. May 29, 1874.
  v. *Mary-Louisa*, b. July 22, 1841.
  vi. *William-Henry*, b. October 8, 1846; d. June 8, 1850.
  vii. *Florence-Nightingale*, b. September 3, 1855.

XLII. JOHN MCCORMICK,[6] (Hugh,[5] James,[4] Hugh,[3] Hugh,[2] James,[1]) b. January 15, 1818, in the city of New York; in 1845 became secretary of the Atlantic Dock company, Brooklyn, an office he filled for forty years. He m., February 17, 1845, CAROLINE PILSBURY, daughter of John and Abigail Eliot Pilsbury, of Newburyport, Mass. They had issue:

  i. *Eliot*, b. May 5, 1849; d. 1891; entered Columbia College, N. Y., in 1866; editor of the *Christian Union*, 1877–1882, and of the *New York Observer*, 1883.
  ii. *Isabella-Esther*, b. August 29, 1853; m., January 16, 1883, Edgar Wade Abbott, of Brooklyn, N. Y.; and had issue (surname Abbot):
     1. *Helen-Barbara*, b. September 13, 1884.
     2. *Caroline Isabel*, b. May 28, 1886.

XLIII. HENRY MCCORMICK,[6] (James,[5] William,[4] James,[3] Thomas,[2] James,[1]) b. March 10, 1831, in Harrisburg, Pa. He received his education at the Harrisburg Academy, Partridge's Military Institute, and graduated from Yale College in 1852. He commenced the study of the law with his father, but his taste being for a more stirring pursuit, he gave it up and learned the iron business at Reading furnace, now Robesonia, at the first opportunity purchasing an interest in the Henry Clay and Eagle furnaces, near Marietta, Lancaster county. In 1857 Paxtang furnace came under his management, and, in 1866, the nail-works at Fairview, Cumberland county, at the mouth of the Conedoguinet creek, which he conducted for twenty-five years. In 1865, before a railway spanned the continent, he crossed the great plain and mountain range to the

Pacific coast, returning by the Isthmus of Panama. In 1877 he visited Europe. Long before these journeys he had shown his devotion to his country. At the opening of the Rebellion, he offered his life and services to the cause of patriotism, gathering a company of volunteers, company F, Lochiel Grays, of the Twenty-fifth regiment, Pennsylvania volunteers, in the three months' service. In 1862 he was chosen colonel of the First regiment, Pennsylvania militia, under Major Gen. John F. Reynolds and assigned to the command of the First brigade. The object of forming this division being accomplished by the contest at Antietam, it was mustered out of service. Under the act relative to a new geological survey of Pennsylvania, he was appointed by Governor Hartranft a commissioner, and by his colleagues its treasurer, filling these positions until the work was done. As a co-trustee of his father's estate, he has shown tact and judgment, and, in the pursuit of all the business in which he is engaged, great energy and success. To all benevolent objects he is a most generous giver, without ostentation or publicity. As an evidence of the esteem in which he is held, it may be stated that when a candidate for Congress in 1882, his majority in his native county was one hundred and fifty-nine, while his party was in a minority of nearly fifteen hundred on the vote for other offices. Col. McCormick m.. June 29, 1867, ANNIE CRISWELL, daughter of John Vance Criswell and Hannah Dull. They had issue:

  i. Henry-Buehler, b. June 12, 1869; m., June 13, 1895, Mary Laetitia Boyd, dau. of James Boyd and Louisa Yeomans.
  ii. Vance-Criswell, b. June 19, 1872.
  iii. Mary-Cameron, b. December 18, 1873; d. June 3, 1883.
  iv. Isabel, b. January 9, 1876; d. November 29, 1876.
  v. Hugh, b. March 1, 1878; d. June 11, 1879.
  vi. Annie, b. March 2 1879.

XLIV. JAMES MCCORMICK,[6] (James,[5] William,[4] James,[3] Thomas,[2] James,[1]) b. October 31, 1832, in Harrisburg, Pa. He was educated in the common schools, Capt. Partridge's Military Institute, the Harrisburg Academy, graduating from Yale College in 1853; studied law under his father; was admitted to the bars of Dauphin and Cumberland counties, and practiced for several years. Upon the death of his father, he ecame one of the trustees of his estate, a charge that absorbed his time and attention to such a degree that he abandoned his profession. The magnitude of this estate and the enterprises conducted under it require caution, prudence and judgment in its management. Mr. McCormick has shown all these qualities in the successful performance of his duties. He has never held political office, but, in the religious and charitable work of the day, occupies a conspicuous position. He had been an elder in the Pine Street Presbyterian church from 1858 to 1894, a successful Sunday-school tutor, president and trustee of the Young Men's Christian Association; in all the active work of his denomination, a most efficient and liberal agent; a large contributor to the Home for the Friendless, Harrisburg; to all charitable objects, and, from its opening, president of the Harrisburg hospital—one of its most active, attentive and competent advisers. He m., May 26, 1859, at Harrisburg, Pa., MARY WILSON ALRICKS, b. November 24, 1833; d. August 5, 1891, at Harrisburg, Pa.; daughter of Herman Alricks and Mary Wilson Kerr (*see Alricks record*). They had issue:

 i. Herman, b. June 8, 1860; d. January 25, 1867.
 ii. Henry, b. October 15, 1862.
 iii. James, b. December 12, 1863.
 iv. William, b. April 24, 1866.
 v. Donald, b. October 29, 1868.
 vi. Eliza, b. August 6, 1871.
 vii. Mary-Kerr, b. March 11, 1874; d. May 7, 1877.
 viii. Robert, b. April 18, 1878.

XLV. MARY MCCORMICK,[6] (James,[5] William,[4] James,[3] Thomas,[2] James,[1]) b. October 10, 1834; d. March 23, 1874, at Harrisburg, Pa. She m. JAMES DONALD CAMERON, b. 1833, in Middletown, Pa.; son of Gen. Simon Cameron and Margaret Brua. He received a classical education and studied at Princeton College. Upon leaving college he entered the Middletown bank as clerk, of which he subsequently became cashier. From 1866 to 1874 he was president of the Northern Central railroad, in which latter year the road was leased to the Pennsylvania Railroad company. General Grant appointed him Secretary of War, May 22, 1876, which office he held until the close of that administration. In 1876 he was a delegate to the National

Republican Convention at Cincinnati, and, upon the resignation of his father, General Cameron, as United States Senator, was elected by the Legislature to fill the vacancy, subsequently re-elected for the full term ending March 3, 1885, and again for the terms ending March 3, 1891, and March 3, 1897. They had issue (surname Cameron):

 i. Eliza-McCormick, m. William H. Bradley, of Newark, N. J.;
  d. ———; and had issue (surname Bradley):
   1. *Joseph-Gardiner.*
   2. *James-Donald-Cameron.*
 ii. Virginia-Rolette, m. Alexander Rogers, of New Jersey; appointed second lieutenant Fourth cavalry, U. S. A., June 16, 1875; first lieutenant, July 6, 1879; now (1895) captain Fourth cavalry; they had issue :
   1. *C.-R.-Perry.*
   2. *James-Donald-Cameron.*
   3. *Alexander.*
 iii. James-McCormick, resides at Harrisburg, Pa.
 iv. Mary.
 v. Margaretta-Brua, m. J. William Clark, of Newark, N. J.; and had issue (surname Clark):
   1. *William.*
   2. *James-Cameron.*
 vi. Rachel-Burnside.

Mr. Cameron m., secondly, May 9, 1878, ELIZABETH SHERMAN, daughter of Judge Sherman, of Cleveland, O.

XLVI. RICHARD CUNNINGHAM McCORMICK,[7] (Richard-Cunningham,[6] Hugh,[5] James,[4] Hugh,[3] Hugh,[2] James,[1]) b. May 23, 1832. He was educated in New York, and went, in 1854, to the Crimean war as a correspondent of one of the New York journals. On his return he published two volumes of travels, "A Visit to the Camp before Sebastopol" and "St. Paul's to St. Sophia." In 1858 and 1859 he edited the *Young Men's Magazine*, and was instrumental in founding the Young Men's Christian Association in this country, being for some time corresponding secretary of the New York organization. During the early months of the war of the Rebellion he was with the Federal army in the field as correspondent for the New York *Evening Post*. In 1861 President Lincoln appointed him chief clerk of the Department of Agriculture, and, in 1863, secretary of the Territory of Arizona. In 1866 he became Governor of the same Territory, from which he was elected, in the year 1869, delegate to Congress. In this capacity he served the Territory six years, while he also represented the Territory in the Republican National Convention of 1876, and in the Centennial Exhibition of the same year. During the presidential campaign which immediately followed, he acted as secretary of the Republican National Committee, and, on the election of Rutherford B. Hayes, was appointed Assistant Secretary of the Treasury, which ill health subsequently obliged him to resign. In 1878 he became American Commissioner to the Paris Exposition, and on the successful completion of that service retired from public life. He m., first, MARGARET G. HUNT, who d. April 30, 1867; and secondly, ELIZABETH THURMAN, daughter of Senator Allen G. Thurman, of Ohio.

McNAIR OF DERRY.

I. DAVID MCNAIR,[2] b. in the parish of Donaghmore, county Donegal, Ireland, emigrated to America in 1733, and took up 200 acres of land in then Derry township, Lancaster county, Province of Pennsylvania. He was the son of ALEXANDER MCNAIR,[1] a Scotch settler in the north of Ireland. Of his children we have no record. A brother, ROBERT MCNAIR,[2] came to Pennsylvania about 1737. He died prior to 1752, leaving a wife and children as follows:

2.   i. *Alexander*, b. 1730; m., and had issue.
    ii. *Samuel*, b. 1732.
   iii. *Mary*, b. 1734.
    iv. *Robert*, b. 1737.

II. ALEXANDER MCNAIR,[3] (Robert,[2] Alexander,[1]) b. in 1730, in parish of Donaghmore, county Donegal, Ireland; d. about the close of the 18th century near Pittsburgh; m. a daughter of Robert Dunning. They had issue:

3.   i. *Alexander*, b. 1774; m. Susanne Marguerite de Reilhe.
    ii. *Dunning*, m., and had *Dunning*, of Washington City, m. Kitty Steele; *Anna-Maria*, m. Mr. Anderson, of Louisville, Ky.; and *Margaret*, m. Mr. Steele, of the same place.
   iii. *David*, m., and had *David*, m. Miss Florettry, and *Ella*.
    iv. *Robert*, m., and had *Mary*, m. Mr. Minton; *Eliza*, m. Mr. Baldwin, of New Orleans; and *Robert*, of same place.
     v. *Ezekiel*, located in or near Erie, Pa.

III. ALEXANDER MCNAIR,[4] (Alexander,[3] Robert,[2] Alexander,[1]) b. in 1774, in Derry township, Lancaster county, Pa. He received a fair English and classical education under Joseph Hutchinson, whose remains are interred in old Derry graveyard, and who was a superior teacher. He subsequently attended a term at the Philadelphia College, now University of Pennsylvania, but his father dying, he was called home to the paternal farm in Derry. The mother shortly after deceased, and the sons, Dunning and Alexander, agreed to settle their parent's estate in a novel manner—that whosoever would be the victor in a fair encounter should be the owner of the homestead. Alexander received a severe whipping at the hands of his brother, to which he afterwards acknowledged he owed the honor of being Governor of Missouri. In 1799, through the influence of Senator William Maclay, of Harrisburg, he received the appointment of lieutenant of infantry in the U. S. army, having formerly served as lieutenant in command of a company from Dauphin county in the Whiskey Insurrection of 1794. In 1804 he went to the Missouri Territory, then recently acquired, where he served a number of years as U. S. Commissary, stationed at St. Louis. In a St. Louis tax list for 1811 he appears taxed for one of the nineteen "carriages of pleasure" then held in that city.* In 1812 he was appointed adjutant and inspector general, and during the war with England was a colonel of Missouri militia in the United States service. The name of Alexander McNair appears among a list of merchants and traders in 1817, doing business in St. Louis. He was the first Governor of Missouri, holding office from 1820, when the State government was formed, to 1824. At the expiration of his term of office he filled an important position in the Indian department. He died in St. Louis, March 18, 1826, aged fifty-two years, and his remains rest in Calvary cemetery, that city. He was a man of great popularity, and strict integrity, and left to his family an honored name. Governor McNair married, in 1805, SUSANNE MARGUERITE DE REILHE, a native of St. Louis. She was the daughter of Antoine and Stella (Camp) de Reilhe,

---

* We learn that Gov. McNair resided at one time on the corner of Main and Spruce streets, St. Louis, in a double house, two rooms deep, with servants' quarters outside. This house was built of logs set upright, as the French custom was. It was surrounded by a wide veranda, supported by cedar posts, with a neat railing around it. This house was daguerrotyped by Easterly when in a state of extreme dilapidation, and about to be pulled down, and often appears in the public prints as "the residence of Gov. McNair, the first Governor of Missouri." At the time he held office, and prior, he lived in a house west of Broadway, in what was then the northern suburbs; with improved grounds and an avenue bordered with roses, leading to the front entrance. It was at a later date locally known as the "Biddle Mansion."

and granddaughter of the Rev. Dr. Camp, formerly of Amherst county and parish, Virginia, and the first Episcopalian minister to move as far west as the Mississippi of whom there is any record. Dr. Camp went with George Rogers Clarke's expedition in 1778, as far as Louisville, where Clarke abandoned his boats and crossed the country to Kaskaskia. Dr. Camp-descended the river to Natchez, and the next year returned and settled at Kaskaskia, where he died April 20, 1786. The same year his widow, Mrs. Ann (Olivier) Camp and her four daughters, one of whom had just married Antoine de Reilhe, moved to St. Louis, where the future Mrs. McNair was born January, 1787. The father of Mrs. McNair was a French gentleman of position, with very polished manners, and his wife dying early, he devoted himself to the education of his three children. Mrs. McNair, the eldest, was highly educated for that time, and possessed manners of extreme elegance. She married Mr. McNair when eighteen years of age, and her bridal trip was to accompany her husband on horseback to Pittsburgh, where he went on business and to visit some relatives. After some months they returned in boats, which were taking government supplies to western posts. She survived her husband thirty-seven years, and left but four of her large family living. She died in St. Louis, June 17, 1863, and rests in Calvary cemetery by the side of her husband. They had issue:

    i. [*A dau.*], d. at the age of seventeen.
    ii. [*A son*], d. at the age of fifteen.
    iii. Dunning, killed by lightning, June 3, 1831.
    iv. Alexander-W., d. 1849, at Santa Fé, New Mexico; served in the Mexican war.
    v. Frederick, d. in August, 1833, in New Orleans, of yellow fever.
    vi. Antoine-Reilhe, m. three times; of the first marriage, there was one son, Dr. McNair, who d. in 1880; of the second marriage, is Commander McNair, U. S. Navy, residing at Saratoga, N. Y.; the last wife and children reside in St. Louis.
    vii. Margaret-Caroline, m., first, Charles D. Ward, a surveyor and civil engineer, of Maryland; m., secondly, John Garrison, of Philadelphia, and resided there until his death; resides in St. Louis with two children, and has one daughter, a nun in the Convent of the Sacred Heart.

- viii. *Louise*, m. Judge Samuel Jones, of Pittsburgh, Pa., where she resides.
- ix. *Lafayette*, served in the Mexican war; d. in 1854, at New Orleans, of yellow fever.
- x. *Stella*, m. Jules Cabanne, of St. Louis, a grandson of Charles Gratiot, on whose porch the transfer of the Western country was made to Captain Stoddard for the United States; Mr. Cabanne died about 1873, and his widow and three children reside in St. Paul, Minn.

McNAIR OF HANOVER.

I. THOMAS McNAIR,[1] probably a relative of David McNair referred to in the preceding record, b. in 1737, in the parish of Donaghmore, county Donegal, Ireland; d. July 25, 1830, in Hanover township, Dauphin county, Pa.; emigrated to America about the year 1762, and took up land in Hanover township. From some documents in possession of his descendants he left brothers, William and Robert, in Ireland. A certificate of character and church membership, signed by Benjamin Holmes and dated Donaghmore, 20th August, 1762, states that "Thomas McNair was born and educated in this parish; a descendant of an ancient Protestant family, deservedly esteemed in their country, has industriously followed his business, and always maintained an unexceptional moral character, and was admitted to church privileges with us." He was a soldier of the Revolution and a leading man in Hanover for half a century. He was twice married, first, ANN WALLACE, b. March 15, 1748; d. September 22, 1793, in Hanover; daughter of Robert Wallace and Mary Clyde, (*see Wallace of Hanover*). They had issue:

  i. Mary. b. 1772; d. December 2, 1774.
  ii. Martha, b. August 12, 1774; d. January 11, 1808, at Shippensburg, Pa.; m. Samuel Sturgeon.
  iii. Robert, b. May 13, 1777; d. in 1800 or 1801, in St. Domingo, of yellow fever; unm.
2. *iv. William,* b. May 24, 1780; m. Edith Bartles.
  v. James, b. January 13, 1783; d. October 1, 1799.
3. *vi. Moses,* b. June 11, 1785; m. Martha Williamson.
  vii. Ann, b. August 17, 1787; d. May 28, 1841, near Berwick, Pa.; unm.
4. *viii. Thomas,* b. March 10, 1790; m. Agnes Ferguson.

Thomas McNair m., secondly, MARY STRAIN, b. 1758, in Hanover; d. October 22, 1821, in Hanover; buried beside her husband, his first wife, and children, in old Derry church graveyard. They had issue:

ix. *John-Andrew*, b. May 13, 1797; d. June 12, 1846, at the residence of his brother William, near Dayton, O., and buried in Bath church graveyard.

x. *Mary*, b. September 1, 1798; d. October 18, 1864, in Indiana; m. William Baird, of Hanover; left no issue.

xi. *Robert-Wallace*, b. August 19, 1800; d. in Boston, Mass., a few years after his marriage; m. Eliza ———; and had *Ann*, who, with her mother, resided in Boston.

II. WILLIAM MCNAIR,[2] (Thomas,[1]) b. May 24, 1780, in Hanover township, Lancaster, now Dauphin county, Pa.; d. October 23, 1842, near Dayton, O.; m., June 16, 1829, EDITH BARTLES; d. September 2, 1872. They had issue:

i. *Margaret*, b. April 8, 1830; m. William H. Kendall; and had issue (surname Kendall): *Charles-A., James, George-F.,* and *Alverdie*.

ii. *Thomas*, b. October 23, 1832; resides in Marion, Ind.; m. Miss Overmier, of Columbus, O.; and had issue.

iii. *John*, b. August 25, 1835; d. July 15, 1877; unm.

iv. *William*, b. May 17, 1838; m. Anna Landon, of Piqua, O.; and had *Robert*.

v. *Anna-Mary* (twin), b. May 17, 1838; d. November 5, 1855.

vi. *James*, b. May 27, 1841; killed October 19, 1864, at battle of Cedar Creek; buried in Bath graveyard beside his parents.

III. MOSES MCNAIR,[2] (Thomas,[1]) b. June 11, 1785, in Hanover township, Lancaster, now Dauphin county, Pa.; removed, in 1811, to the Mad River country, O., where he died; m. MARTHA WILLIAMSON. They had issue:

i. *Thomas*, d. February 6, 1885; a physician, who settled in St. Louis; m., and had issue.

ii. *Ann*, m., in October, 1836, George Mossier, a merchant of Fairfield, O.; and had issue (surname Mossier): *Buena, Ella,* and a son, d. in childhood.

iii. *Edith*, was twice married; her second husband, ——— Webster; and had issue.

iv. *Margaret*, m. James McCord, of St. Louis; and had issue (surname McCord): *Edna*.

IV. THOMAS MCNAIR,[2] (Thomas,[1]) b. March 10, 1790, in Hanover township, Dauphin county, Pa.; d. July 23, 1847, at Berwick, Pa., of cholera, contracted while on a visit to Tennessee just previous; m., December 7, 1819, AGNES FERGUSON, b. March 14, 1795, in Hanover; d. July 20, 1848, at Berwick,

Pa., daughter of David Ferguson and Jean (Henderson) Rogers, (*see Ferguson record*). They had issue:

    i. Jane-Ferguson, b. October 5, 1820; d. May 26, 1891, at Hazleton, Pa.; bur. at Mauch Chunk, Pa.; m., May 5, 1841, William Wilson Righter, M. D., d. at Beaver Meadows, Pa; and had issue among others (surname Righter):
        1. *Annie-M.*, d. at Mauch Chunk; m. W. W. Weaver.
        2. *Euphemia*, m. Arthur P. Wood, of Omaha, Neb.; and had issue (surname Wood): *William-Righter, Jane-McNair*, d., and *Mary-Lewis.*
        3. *Thomas-McNair*, m. Gertrude Leisenring, of Upper Lehigh, Pa.; and had issue (surname Righter): *Walter-Leisenring*, and *Jane*.
        4. *John McFee*, Union Pacific R. R.
    ii. Ann-Wallace, d. s. p.
5.   *iii. Thomas-Speer*, b. October, 1824; m. Mary Stevens.
    iv. Anna-Mary, resides in Omaha, Neb.; unm.
    v. David-Henderson, b. July 8, 1831; d. July 18, 1881, at Bowie Station, Arizona: m., Sept. 22, 1860, Mary Elizabeth Setzer; and left *Thomas-Righter*, and *David-Ferguson.*
    vi. William-Edwards, d. August 6, 1857; unm.
    vii. James-Sharon, b. October 5, 1838, in Foundryville, Pa., a civil and mining engineer; was first lieutenant, company G, Thirty-second regiment, Pa. Vols., in 1863; m. Rebecca E. Vincent, of Hazleton, Pa.

V. THOMAS SPEER MCNAIR,[3] (Thomas,[2] Thomas,[1]) b. October, 1824, in Hanover township, Dauphin county, Pa. He is a civil and mining engineer, Lehigh Valley Railroad company, residing at Hazleton, Pa., of which borough he has been chief burgess, president of council, and prominently identified with its leading enterprises. Mr. McNair m., August 14, 1866, MARY STEVENS, a native of England. They had issue:

    i. Annie-Agnes.
    ii. Thomas-Ferguson.
    iii. Robert-Stevens, d. s. p.
    iv. William-Righter.
    v. Jane-Ferguson.
    vi. John-Calvin, d. s. p.
    vii. Donald Wallace.
    viii. Mary-Stevens.
    ix. Rebecca-Sharon.
    x. James-Bertley.

MÜLLER [MILLER] AND LOBINGIER.

I. JOHN GEORGE MÜLLER,[2] son of Rudolph Müller,[1] (more frequently written Miller), b. September 21, 1715, in the Canton of Zurich, Switzerland; emigrated with his family to America in 1752, and settled in Lebanon township, Lancaster county, Province of Pennsylvania. He took the oath of allegiance, October 23, 1752. He had been an officer in the Swiss service, and when the French and Indian war broke out he was commissioned a lieutenant in Col. James Burd's regiment of Provincial forces, May 8, 1760 (*see Penn'a Arch.*, 2d ser., vol. ii., p. 605), promoted to a captaincy on the northern frontiers, October 2, 1764 (*ib. p. 615*). Captain Müller d. April 19, 1765, in Lebanon township, leaving a wife, BARBARA GLONINGER, who survived her husband several years, dying in 1783. They had issue :*

    i. John, b. 1740; d. prior to 1785; was first lieutenant of Seventh company, Ninth battalion, Lancaster county associators, in 1777; m. Juliana [Baker], d. prior to 1785; and had a son *Rudolph.*

    ii. Ursula, b. 1742; m. Martin Thomas, (*see Thomas record*).

2.   *iii. Anna*, b. 1744; m. Matthias Reigard.

3.   *iv. Rudolph*, b. 1746; m., first, Catharine [Lick], secondly, Susanna [Weiss].

4.   *v. Elizabeth*, b. 1748; m. Christopher Lobingier.

    vi. Barbara, b. 1750; m. John Wolf, of Cumberland county, Pa.; nothing further learned of them.

    vii. Mary, b. 1752; m. Henry Felger, of Westmoreland county, Pa.; no further information.

---

*Subsequently, after the death of his father, followed HENRY MÜLLER [Moeller], nephew of the foregoing, and concerning whom we have the following record: He was born in 1749, in Hamburg, Germany, and on the occasion referred to, at the age of eighteen years, came to America, having received a classical education in the University of Göttingen. Henry had a good instructor. He was brought to the notice of the Rev. Dr. Muhlenberg, who secured him the appointment as assistant in a school in which he was himself at that time giving instruction, in the meantime devoting all his leisure

II. ANNA MÜLLER,³ (John-George,² Rudolph,¹) b. 1744, in the Palatinate, Germany; d. February, 1810, in Lebanon township, Lebanon county, Pa.; m. MATTHIAS REIGARD, b. 1740; d. in 1790, in Lebanon township. They had issue (surname Reigard):

to the study of theology under the direction of his patron. In the year 1774 he was licensed to preach by the Lutheran Synod of Pennsylvania. Mr. Müller's first regular pastoral charge was at Reading, where he remained from August, 1775, to August, 1777, when he removed to Philadelphia. Having consecrated himself to the work of the ministry, he evinced much of a self-denying spirit in preaching the gospel to the poor, and laboring to collect and build up congregations in the most obscure places, and under the most unfavorable circumstances. He served for some time as chaplain to an associated battalion in the war of the Revolution. Mr. Müller, about 1783, became the settled pastor of the church at Albany, N. Y., and it was under his ministry that the first Lutheran church edifice in that city was built. In 1789 he received and accepted a call to New Holland, Lancaster county, Pa., where he continued very laboriously engaged until 1795, when he took charge of the Lutheran interests in Harrisburg and in the neighborhood. He was the first pastor after the separation of the Lutheran from the Reformed congregation. Here he remained seven years, and although his duties were laborious, his ministry was a successful one. In the year 1802, much to the regret of the congregation, he relinquished this charge, returned to his former field of work in the State of New York, where he continued about six years (the period he usually allowed himself for continuance in one place), when he accepted a call to the united churches of Sharon and New Rhinebeck, Schoharie county, N. Y., where he officiated until physical infirmity rendered him incapable of attending to his pastoral duties. He died at Sharon, on the 16th of September, 1829, in the eightieth year of his age. Mr. Müller in person was rather thick set, somewhat below the medium height, and very agreeable in manners and appearance. As a preacher he was not brilliant, but instructive and practical, while in the more private duties of the pastoral office was eminently felicitious and faithful. He was a bright example of the Christian spirit, and an eminently devoted minister. The Rev. Mr. Müller was twice married. He married, first, on September 19, 1775, ESTHER OTT, sister of John Nicholas Ott. She probably died at Harrisburg, Pa. He married, secondly, the widow of Baron Zedwick, who lost his life in the French war. This latter connection proved every way a happy one, for his wife was a woman of sweet manners and amiable disposition. She died in 1827. We have no knowledge if they left any descendants.

i. Jacob, m., and left issue.
ii. Elizabeth, m. Henry Kleber, of Mt. Pleasant township, Westmoreland county, Pa.
iii. Barbara, m. Jacob Steinman, son of Conrad Steinman,* of Bethel.
iv. Henry, m. Barbara Henner, daughter of John Henner.†
v. Christopher.
vi. John, m., and left issue.
vii. Anna.
viii. David.
ix. Matthias.
x. Anna-Mary.
xi. Catharine.

III. RUDOLPH MÜLLER,² (John-George,² Rudolph,¹) b. about 1746, in the city of Hamburg, Germany; d. November, 1806, in Annville township, Dauphin, now Lebanon county, Pa.; came with his parents to America to then Lancaster county, and brought up as a farmer; m., first, CATHARINE ———; and had issue; secondly, SUSANNA ———, who survived her husband several years. They had issue:

  i. John, b. 1766.
  ii. Henry, b. 1768.
  iii. David, b. 1770.
  iv. Catharine, b. 1772; m. Henry Williams.
5. *v. Elizabeth*, b. October 6, 1774; m. John Philip Imboden.
  vi. Anna-Maria, b. October 9, 1776; d. December 6, 1849; m. Peter Killinger, b. October 27, 1776; d. Nov. 6, 1848.
  vii. Mary, m. John Seegrist.
  viii. Christiana.

---

*CONRAD STEINMAN, of Bethel township, Lebanon county, Pa., d. prior to 1788, leaving a wife Anna Maria, and children, *Jacob, Philopena, Magdalena, Anna, John, Catharine,* and *Barbara,* m. George Sheaffer.

† JOHN HENNER, of Lebanon township, now Lebanon county, Pa., d. May, 1797. His first wife, and mother of his children, was Magdalena Steinman, of Switzerland, granddaughter of Ulrick Steinman, from whose estate there was an inheritance for his children. His second wife, Elizabeth, survived him. His children were:
  i. Emanuel.
  ii. John, d. prior to 1797, leaving a wife Barbara, and a son *John*; to the latter his grandfather left his musket, bayonet, and sword, used in the Revolution.
  iii. Magdalena, d. prior to 1797.
  iv. Barbara, m. Henry Reigard.

IV. ELIZABETH MÜLLER,³ (John-George,² Rudolph,¹) b. 1748, in the city of Hamburg, Germany; d. September 5, 1815, in Stoystown, Somerset county, Pa.; m., in 1766, CHRISTOPHER LOBINGIER, b. 1744, in Paxtang township, Lancaster, now Dauphin county, Pa.; son of Christopher Lobingier, a native of Wittenberg, Germany, who settled in then Lancaster county, Pa., prior to 1735. The son removed to Mount Pleasant township, Westmoreland county, Pa., in 1772; was a delegate to the first Constitutional convention of the State, which convened at Philadelphia, July 15, 1776; an influential member of the Committee of Correspondence for the county of Westmoreland, 1775-76; and under the Constitution of 1790 a representative to the General Assembly from 1791 to 1793. He died at his residence in Mount Pleasant township, July 4, 1798. They had issue (surname Lobingier):

6.   *i. John*, b. April 5, 1767; m., first, Sophia Moyer; secondly, Elizabeth Cross.
      ii. Christopher, b. circa, 1769; m., and left issue, four daughters, who m. respectively, Matthew, Henry, and Peter Graff, and Mary Welty; one of the latter's daughters marrying Jacob Newmyer, whose son was John C. Newmyer, a distinguished State Senator of Pennsylvania.
7.   *iii. Catharine*, b. 1771; m. Jacob Painter.
      iv. Barbara, b. 1773; m. a Mr. Leassure, and left issue.
      v. Mary, b. 1775; m. Mr. Kimmel, of Somerset county, Pa.; removed to Michigan.
      vi. Elizabeth, b. 1777.
      vii. Rudolph, b. 1780.
      viii. Susanna, b. 1782; m. Mr. Kimmel, of Somerset county, Pa.
      ix. George, b. 1784; m., and left three children.

V. ELIZABETH MÜLLER,⁴ (Rudolph,³ John-George,² Rudolph,¹) b. October 6, 1774; d. March 1, 1862, near Annville, Lebanon county, Pa.; m. JOHN PHILIP IMBODEN, b. March 26, 1774; d. May 25, 1849, near Annville, Pa.; son of Johannes Sweigart Imboden, b. October 22, 1733; d. July 20, 1819, and his wife Elenora, b. July 29, 1741; d. July 16, 1813. They had issue (surname Imboden):

      i. Philip, m., and had *Henry*, who resided in East Greenville, Stark county, O.
      ii. Solomon, m., and had *Mary, John,* and *George.*
      iii. Jacob, b. July 6, 1805; d. February 16, 1886; unm.

iv. *Samuel*, b. June 24, 1807; d. August 15, 1875; m., first, ———— Kreider; and had issue:
   1. *Mary*.
   2. *Elizabeth*.
   3. *Nancy*.
He m., secondly, the widow of his brother William; and had issue:
   4. *Moses*, d. s. p.
   5. *Lydia*, d. s. p.
   6. *Lavinia*, d. s. p.
   7. *Samuel*, resided near Annville, Pa.
   8. *Susan*, m. Michael Moyer; resides in Campbellstown, Pa.

v. *William*, m. ———— Kreider; and had issue:
   1. *William*, m. a daughter of Daniel Heilman; and had two children.
   2. *Mary-Ann*, m. John Hotz; reside near Annville, Pa.

vi. *Daniel*, m., first, ———— Imboden; and had issue:
   1. *Daniel*.
He m., secondly, Elizabeth Ellenberger.

vii. *John*.

viii. *George*, b. November 8, 1814; d. October 4, 1854; m. Sarah Heilig; resided in Annville, Pa.; and had issue:
   1. *Emma*, m. Joseph Ehrman.
   2. *Philip*, m. Catharine Smith.
   3. *George*, m. Amanda Killian.
   4. *Jacob*, m. Emma Black.
   5. *Adam*, m. Sarah Herr.
   6. *Clara-Anna*, m. Abraham Herr.

ix. *Nellie*, m. Philip Carmony; resided in Annville, Pa.

x. *Elizabeth*.

VI. JOHN LOBINGIER,[4] (Elizabeth,[3] John-George,[2] Rudolph,[1]) b. April 5, 1767, in Paxtang township, Lancaster, now Dauphin county, Pa.; d. February 26, 1859, in Mount Pleasant township, Westmoreland county, Pa. In 1797 he built the old home at Laurelville, and shortly after removed there from the Ligonier Valley; he was a member of the Legislature, and an associate judge of the county; was engaged in the iron business, controlling several furnaces, and also sank a number of oil wells. He was twice married; m., first, July 7, 1789, SOPHIA MOYER, b. July 26, 1770; d. May 18, 1838. They had issue (surname Lobingier):

  i. Elizabeth, b. September 11, 1790; m. John Connell.
  ii. Mary, b. September 25, 1792; d. 1880; m. Casper Markle, brother of Gen. Joseph Markle.
8. *iii. Jacob,* b. February 21, 1795; m. Mary Stauffer.
  vi. Sarah, b. May 14, 1797; m. Christian Fetter.
9. *v. John,* b. August 21, 1799; m. Elizabeth Smith.
  vi. Susanna, b. March 12, 1802; d. s. p.
  vii. Christopher, b. August 12, 1803; d. December 3, 1836, at Rodney, Miss.
  viii. Hannah, b. August 20, 1806; m. Shepard Markle, of West Newton, Westmoreland county, Pa.
  ix. Sophia, b. February 2, 1809; m. Dr. Philip G. Young, of Washington county, Pa.; resides at Chicago.
  x. George, b. February 7, 1811; d. February 11, 1829.
  xi. Catharine, b. August 8, 1813; d. March, 1860, in Fayette county, Pa.; m. Rev. James Darsie.

Judge Lobinger m., secondly, ELIZABETH CROSS, b. 1792; d. October 3, 1861; no issue.

VII. CATHARINE LOBINGIER,[4] (Elizabeth,[3] John-George,[2] Rudolph,[1]) b. 1771, in Westmoreland county, Pa.; d. at the age of eighty-four, and buried in Markle cemetery; m., in 1793, JACOB PAINTER, b. in Berks county, Pa.; d. at the age of fifty-nine years; son of Jacob Painter, a native of Mecklenberg, Germany. The son settled on a farm in Hempfield township, Westmoreland county, Pa., prior to 1790, and built a stone grist mill. He was an energetic, active business man, a member of the Legislature several terms, and a justice of the peace for a long period. He was the Whig candidate for member of Congress, and came within seventeen votes of being elected over William Findley. Afterwards served as an associate judge of the county, a position he filled at the time of his death. He was a man of commanding presence, being almost six feet in height, and heavy set. He had been previously married, his first wife being a MISS RAPIERE, by whom he had *Elizabeth,* who became the wife of Gen. Joseph Markle, *Rebecca, Catharine, Tobias, George,* and *Elias.* By his second wife, CATHARINE LOBINGIER, there was issue (surname Painter):

  i. Mary, b. 1794.
  ii. John, b. 1796.
  iii. Jacob, b. 1798.

    iv. Christopher, b. 1800.
    v. George, b. 1802.
    vi. Joseph, b. 1804.
    vii. Benjamin, b. 1806.
    viii. Susanna, b. 1808.
    ix. Israel, b. November 11, 1810; d. July 4, 1880, in Westmoreland county, Pa.; remained on his father's farm until the age of seventeen; taught the district school two terms, and afterwards attended several sessions at Jefferson College, Canonsburg; from 1832 to 1835 he became interested in salt wells, and during his whole life was an active and enterprising citizen, greatly assisting in the development of the vast industries of his native county; from 1846 to 1848 he represented his district in the State Legislature, and was canal commissioner from 1849 to 1852; was a delegate to the Democratic National Convention at Charleston, S. C., in 1860, identifying himself with the Douglas wing of his party.
    x. Sophia, b. 1812.

VIII. JACOB LOBINGIER,[5] (John,[4] [*Lobingier*,] Elizabeth,[3] John-George,[2] Rudolph,[1]) b. February 21, 1795, in Mount Pleasant township, Westmoreland county, Pa., where he d. October 11, 1855. He was for many years a justice of the peace, served as captain and major of the militia, and was president of the Somerset and West Newton turnpike company. He married MARY STAUFFER, b. April 21, 1801; d. October 8, 1879. They had issue (surname Lobingier):

    i. John-Stauffer, b. October 31, 1820; d. February 20, 1821.
    ii. Elizabeth, b. April 13, 1822; d. in Greensburg, Pa.; m., March 18, 1845, David K. Marchand, b. December 3, 1816; editor of the *Register* from 1841 to 1861.
    iii. Jacob, b. March 20, 1824; d. June, 1887; educated at Bethany College, and since 1847 resided on the old estate at Laurelville; served as a justice of the peace, and for twenty-five years held the office of postmaster; he m., March 18, 1847, Lillias F. Stewart, b. October 25, 1827, daughter of Andrew Stewart, Esq., and had issue (surname Lobingier):
        1. *Quincy-Adams*, b. January 8, 1848; m. Anna E. Wells, of Steubenville, O.
        2. *Henry-Schell*, b. October 22, 1849; d. March, 1887; graduated at Bethany College, 1873; was a minister in the Disciples Church; m. Annie H. St. Clair.

3. *Ada-Bonnette*, b. April 15, 1855.
4. *J.-Frank*, b. July 13, 1859.
5. *Andrew-Stewart*, b. December 22, 1862.
6. *Paul*, b. February 20, 1868 ; d. September 5, 1870.

iv. *Franklin-B.*, b. May 17, 1826; d. April 5, 1857, at Laurelville, Pa.; educated at Bethany College, and was a noted minister of the Disciples Church, preaching in Maryland, Virginia, and Pennsylvania.

v. *Maria*, b. January 30, 1829 ; m., February 24, 1848, Jonathan N. Shallenberger ; reside at Braddocks, Pa.

vi. *George*, b. December 9, 1832; educated at Washington and Jefferson College, Washington, Pa.: read law with Henry F. Schell, Esq., of Somerset, Pa., and was admitted to the bar and practiced in Illinois ; subsequently entered the ministry of the Church of Christ (Disciples) in 1867 ; resided in Hebron, Thayer county, Neb., a number of years, where he was nominated for the office of judge of the county court of said county, without his knowledge, and while he was scores of miles distant engaged in preaching the gospel, and elected in November, 1881, to that position, without any personal solicitation on his part ; was re-elected twice after that, and served three terms in said office ; he m., September 23, 1857, Ada B. Stewart, daughter of Andrew Stewart, Esq., of Somerset, Pa.; and had issue (surname Lobingier):

1. *Milton-Stewart*, b. April 30, 1860; educated at Salem Academy, New York ; now residing on a fruit farm in Colorado ; m. Della M. Allen.
2. *Charles-Sumner*, b. April 30, 1866, at Lanark, Ill.; spent his early boyhood in New York and Vermont ; removed with his parents to Hebron, Neb., in 1878 ; graduated at the State University of Nebraska with the degree of B. A., 1888, and at Law School of same institution ; received degree of M. A., 1892, and LL. M., 1894 ; was Assistant State Librarian and Supreme Court Reporter of Nebraska, 1888-92, editing vols. 26-84, inc., Nebraska Law Reports ; Associate Compiler Nebraska Consolidated Statutes, 1891 ; regular contributor to Am. & Eng. Encyclopædia of Law since 1890, writing therefor up to date (1895) nine articles, including those on corporate "Stock" and "Stockholders;" since 1892 has been engaged in active practice of law in Omaha, Neb., in addition to legal literary pursuits.

vii. Christopher-C., b. June 7, 1840 ; served in Gen. Burnside's corps in the Rebellion ; m., January 10, 1865, Helena Mills, of Braddocks, Pa.; where he resides.

IX. JOHN LOBINGIER,[5] (John,[4] [*Lobingier,*] Elizabeth,[3] John-George,[2] Rudolph,[1]) b. August 21, 1799, at Laurelville, Westmoreland county, Pa.; d. May 16, 1885, at Mount Pleasant, that county. After his farm life, his business was teaming, and many years were spent in transportation service, the turnpike filling the place for commercial purposes then, which is now occupied by the railroad. After his marriage, he became the owner of a large farm east of Mount Pleasant, which he operated in conjunction with his other enterprises. He continued to reside on his farm until the increasing infirmities of an honorable old age admonished him that the heat and burden of the day should be borne by younger shoulders. He accordingly built a handsome residence in the town and in 1882 removed into it. From that time he spent the evening of his life in well-earned leisure. In 1840 he became a member of the Middle Presbyterian church, and continued an active supporter there until the Memorial Presbyterian church was formed, when he, with his family, transferred their membership to the new congregation. He had a large circle of acquaintances by whom he was highly respected for his sterling qualities of mind and heart. Mr. Lobingier was one of the most active and enterprising men of the county; and served in most of the local offices of his locality. He m., November 25, 1824, ELIZABETH SMITH, b. August 22, 1805 ; d. July 8, 1856, in Mount Pleasant township. They had issue (surname Lobingier):

    i. Sophia-Amanda, b. April 29, 1826 ; m., June 25, 1846, Dr. Francis M. McConaughy ; reside in Nebraska.
    ii. Jacob-Smith, b. July 24, 1828; m., December 25, 1860, Mary Jane Cochran, b. November, 17, 1837 ; and had issue (surname Lobingier):
        1. *Edward*, b. September 6, 1861 ; d. February 6, 1865.
        2. *John*, b. August 2, 1863.
        3. *Alice-Iona*, b. January 10, 1865.
        4. *Walter Smith*, b. June 11, 1869.
        5. *Hettie-L.*, b. May 1, 1871.
        6. *Chauncey*, b. July 30, 1873.

   7. *Charles-D.*, b. March 16, 1875.
   8. *Martha-McMillan*, b. December 14, 1878.
 iii. *Mary-Elizabeth*, b. April 22, 1831 ; d. February 21, 1854 ; m., January 27, 1853, Henry Freed ; and had issue (surname Freed):
   1. *Mary-Elizabeth*, b. February 8, 1854 ; m., first, September 4, 1879, L. F. Wenner ; d. April, 1883 ; m., secondly, February 3, 1885, G. W. Bailey.
 iv. *Lavinia-Emily*, b. March 3, 1835.
 v. *Eliza-Catharine*, b. November 7, 1837 ; m., first, October 16, 1860, O. P. Griffin ; m., secondly, J. B. Evans, of Topeka, Kan.
 vi. *John-Markle*, b. November 29, 1840 ; d. November 20, 1844.
 vii. *Anna-Malinda*, b. July 27, 1843.
 viii. *William-Henry*, b. May 1, 1846 ; d. July 29, 1877.
 ix. *Josephine*, b. May 31, 1849 ; m., May 8, 1879, G. F. P. Griffin.

MURRAY OF HARRIS' FERRY.

I. PATRICK MURRAY,[1] b. March 17, 1755, in county Donegal, Ireland; d. July 23, 1854, in Orange township, Ashland county, O. He came to America at the outset of the struggle for Independence, and we find that on the 3d of June, 1776, he enlisted in Captain James Parr's company, of the First regiment, of the Pennsylvania Line, for three years or during the war. He was discharged in 1782, and shortly after settled at Harris' Ferry, on the Susquehanna, and when, two years after, the town of Harrisburg was laid out, established himself in business as a "clothier and fashioner." In the year 1800 he removed with his family to Greensburg, Westmoreland county, Pa., remaining there until 1809, when he located in Stark county, O. In 1812 he and his son James volunteered in the brigade of Gen. Reasin Beall, organized for the defence of the border settlers in the Northwest. While quartered at Fort Meigs the army became much distressed for want of provisions; the roads to the settlements were long, rough, and in poor condition, passing mostly through dense forests, and across marshes and bogs. The quantity of forage consumed by the cavalry as well as the supply of the quartermaster's department for the troops made it difficult to furnish the necessary rations at the proper time. On more than one occasion the troops were on the point of starvation, and this, with the inclemency of the weather, made their sufferings almost unbearable. Several reminiscences of this period, in Mr. Murray's history, have been preserved to us which show that under the most adverse circumstances his mother wit and his indomitable energy never forsook him, while his patriotism was none the less enthusiastic by his many deprivations. After General Beall returned, the father and son served a second enlistment, and were at the battle of Fort Meigs. In that contest the elder Murray was separated from his company, and the grass being very tall it was presumed by his comrades that he had been killed and scalped by the Indians. After a few hours he appeared in the camp amid the cheers of his companions at his safe return. Upon the expiration of his term of service he returned to his home in Stark county, where he remained until 1812, when he removed to what is now Orange township, then Richland county, O. It is said of him that, although his education was defective, he had a very retentive memory, and enjoyed at the close of his long life the relation of the exploits and border achievements of himself and other early pioneers in that section of Ohio. In many respects he was a remarkable man, and was all his life-time active, energetic, and industrious. On the 4th of July the year he was ninety-nine years of age he rode to Ashland in a buggy, walked about one mile during the day and returned home, some three miles, in the evening. He voted for ten different Presidents of the United States. Mr. Murray m., September 2, 1786, at Harrisburg, Pa., by Rev. John Elder, of Paxtang, MARY BRERETON BEATTY, b. 1769, in county Down, Ireland; d. March 2, 1853, in Ashland county, O.; with her husband buried in Orange graveyard; daughter of James Beatty and Alice Ann Irwin, (*see Beatty record*). They had issue:

2.   *i. James*, b. August 14, 1787; m. Jane Hansell.
3.   *ii. Edward*, b. November 4, 1789; m. Rebecca Christina Youngblood.
     iii. Catharine, b. October 4, 1791; d. s. p., at Harrisburg, Pa.
     iv. Patrick, b. September 1, 1793; d. s. p., at Harrisburg, Pa.
4.   *v. Susannah*, b. December 25, 1795; m., first, William Cazier; secondly, John Barber.
5.   *vi. William*, b. March 18, 1797; m. Mary Chalcoat.
6.   *vii. John*, b. April 5, 1799; m. Elizabeth Urie.
7.   *viii. Mary*, b. April 13, 1801; m. James Ralston.
8.   *ix. Elizabeth*, b. July 13, 1803; m. George W. Urie.
9.   *x. Alice-Ann*, b. August 14, 1805; m. George Thompson.
     xi. Sarah, b. 1807.
     xii. Rebecca (twin), b. 1807, d. s. p.
10. *xiii. George*, b. December, 1809; m. Jane A. Urie.
11. *xiv. Anne-Hill*, b. January 1, 1813; m. Jacob Brandeberry.
12. *xv. Hugh*, b. March 4, 1816; m. Elizabeth Nazor.

II. JAMES MURRAY,[2] (Patrick,[1]) b. August 14, 1787, in Harrisburg, Pa.; d. May 28, 1858, near Versailles, Ripley county, Ind.; was a soldier in the war of 1812, serving in the Northwest with his father; studied medicine and resided for a time in the city of Cincinnati, afterwards removing to the State of Indiana, where he died. He m., in 1824, near Lawrenceburg, Ind., JANE HANSELL, b. August, 1801, at Thirsk, England; d. July 21, 1883, at Guilford, Ind.; daughter of Thomas Hansell and Ann Collier. They had issue, all b. in Dearborn county, Ind.:

  i. Thomas-Hansell, b. June 27, 1825; d. October 16, 1858, in New Orleans, La.; m., at Cincinnati, O., December 16, 1852, Catharine Salvage; d. in Cincinnati, O.; and had issue:
    1. *Albert-Hansell*, b. November 5, 1853, in Cincinnati, O.; d. at Guilford, Ind.
  ii. John-Collier, b. Mar. 24, 1827; d. 1862, in New Orleans, La.
13. *iii. Francis-Harrison*, b. February 2, 1829; m. Martha Jane Cooper.
  iv. George-Thompson, b. January 12, 1831; d. October 4, 1839, at Dillsborough, Ind.
  v. Jacob-Beatty, b. September 9, 1832; d. November 23, 1839, at Dillsborough, Ind.
  vi. Mary-Ann, b. September 23, 1834; d. December 8, 1839, at Dillsborough, Ind.

III. EDWARD MURRAY,[2] (Patrick,[1]) b. November 4, 1789, in Harrisburg, Pa.; d. November 14, 1862, in Ashland county, O.; served in the war of 1812–14; m., March 4, 1813, in Harrisburg, Pa., by Rev. Philip Gloninger, REBECCA CHRISTINA YOUNGBLOOD, b. August 26, 1788, in Lebanon, Pa.; d. December 23, 1871, in Ashland county, O.; daughter of John Casper and Catharine Youngblood. They had issue:

14. *i. Catharine-Elizabeth*, b. December 4, 1814; m. Henry Gerkey.
  ii. Mary-Ann, b. February 23, 1818, in Ashland county, O.; d. February 26, 1884; m., February 24, 1870, by Rev. William Saddler, William Peters (see XVIII); no issue.
15. *iii. John-W.*, b. February 1, 1820; m. Christina Reese.
16. *iv. Campbell*, b. March 28, 1822; m. Matilda Fast.
17. *v. Edward,*b. Nov. 27, 1824; m. Mary Elizabeth Coleman.
18. *vi. Rebecca-Christina*, b. April 21, 1827; m. William Peters.

IV. SUSANNAH MURRAY,[2] (Patrick,[1]) b. December 25, 1795, in Harrisburg, Pa.; d. May 10, 1876, in De Kalb county, Ind.; m., first, December, 1811, WILLIAM CAZIER, b. about 1788, in Pennsylvania; d. in 1822, in Canton, Stark county, O.; son of Abraham Cazier and Mary Jenkins. They had issue (surname Cazier):

  i. James, b. September 12, 1812, in Stark county, O.; supposed to have been lost on the lakes in 1837.
  ii. Abraham, b. March 29, 1815, in Stark county, O.; d. July 2, 1841, in Hancock county, O.
  iii. Mary, b. March 14, 1817, in Stark county, O.; d. January 8, 1843, in Sandusky, O.; m., September 23, 1841, Harmon R. Foster; no issue.
19. *iv. Murray*, b. February 6, 1819; m. Sarah Colhoun.
20. *v. Elizabeth*, b. March 14, 1821; m. Eli Fast.

Susannah Murray Cazier m., secondly, in Montgomery, Richland county, O., June 5, 1824, JOHN BARBER, b. April 30, 1798, in the Province of Lower Canada; d. July 9, 1863, in De Kalb county, Ind.; son of Augustus Barber* and Elizabeth Smith. They had issue (surname Barber):

  i. Alice-Ann, b. January 26, 1825, in Ashland county, O.; d. July, 1846, in De Kalb county, Ind.; m., November 10, 1842, Jonas H. Roe, of De Kalb county, Ind.
  ii. Levisa, b. December 30, 1826, in Sandusky, O.; d. July, 1846, in De Kalb county, Ind.; m., October 10, 1844, in De Kalb county, Ind., William Webster; and had issue (surname Webster):
    1. *George*, b. July 13, 1846, in De Kalb county, Ind.; resides near Newville, Ind.
21. *iii. John-Wesley*, b. April 30, 1828; m. Jane Norris.
  iv. Julia, b. May 30, 1830, in Sandusky, O.; m. Norman Smith.
  v. Levina-Murray, b. August 26, 1835, in Sandusky, O.; d. in infancy.
  vi. Sarah-Ellen, b. April 17, 1838, in Sandusky, O.; resides at Fort Wayne, Ind.

V. WILLIAM MURRAY,[2] (Patrick),[1] b. March 18, 1797, in Harrisburg, Pa.; d. 1852, in Ashland county, O.; m. MARY CHALCOAT, b. in Washington county, Pa. They had issue:
  i. George.
  ii. James.
  iii. Rachel.
  iv. Mary.
  v. Hugh; resides at Nova, Ashland county, O.
  vi. Samuel.
  vii. William.
  viii. Agnes.
  ix. Jane-Ann.

---

*Augustus Barber, b. in 1758, in the State of New York; d. December 10, 1854, in Stafford township, DeKalb county, Ind.; m. Elizabeth Smith, daughter of Benjamin Smith, of New York.

VI. JOHN MURRAY,² (Patrick,¹) b. April 5, 1799, in Harrisburg, Pa.; d. August 4, 1850, in Morgan county, Mo.; studied surveying; afterwards became treasurer of Richland county, O., two terms, and then removed to Missouri; m., December 25, 1823, in Richland county, O., ELIZABETH URIE, b. February 22, 1804, in Richland county, O.; d. August 5, 1854, in Morgan county, Mo. They had issue:

22.   i. *George-Washington*, b. September 27, 1824; m. Nancy Warring Fuqua.
      ii. *William*, b. July 15, 1826, in Richland county, O.; d. July 27, 1844.
23.   iii. *Mary-Ann*, b. May 5, 1828; m., first, Robert Urie; secondly, Alfred John Leary.
24.   iv. *Elizabeth*, b. June 17, 1830; m. John Pardee.
      v. *John*, b. September 27, 1832, in Richland county, O.; d. September, 1863, by assassination, in Georgetown, Ill.
25.   vi. *Susanna*, b. May 28, 1835; m. Andrew Jackson Hunter.
      vii. *Rebecca-Jane*, b. March 27, 1838, in Richland county, O.; d. of cholera August 6, 1854, in Morgan county, Mo.
      viii. *Thomas-McGuire*, b. April 20, 1840, in Richmond county, O.; resides near Mexico, Audrain county, Mo.
26.   ix. *Alverda*, b. August 8, 1843; m. Samuel Brandenburgh.
      x. *Hiram*, b. January 18, 1846, in Morgan county, Mo.; d. August 22, 1849.
27.   xi. *Commodore-Perry*, b. March 13, 1848; m. Elizabeth T. Ridgway.

VII. MARY MURRAY,² (Patrick,¹) b. April 13, 1801, in Westmoreland county, Pa.; d. April 4, 1827, in Montgomery township, Ashland county, O.; m., March 18, 1824, by Josiah Gallup, J. P., JAMES RALSTON, b. January 20, 1799, in Washington county, Pa.; son of Robert Ralston and Jane Woodburn. They had issue (surname Ralston):

28.   i. *William*, b. December 31, 1824; m. Agnes Finney.
29.   ii. *Alexander*, b. February 6, 1826; m. Salome Trauger.

VIII. ELIZABETH MURRAY,² (Patrick,¹) b. July 13, 1803, in Westmoreland county, Pa.; d. October 13, 1861, at Ashland, O.; m., January 5, 1832, at Ashland, O., by Daniel Campbell, J. P., GEORGE W. URIE, b. February 22, 1806, in Washington county, Pa.; son of Solomon and Elizabeth Urie, and grandson of Col. Thomas Urie, of the Revolution. In 1815 he accompanied his father's family to Ohio, locating in Orange township, in the present county of Ashland. He learned the trade of millwright, and also that of carpenter. Possessing strong military tastes, he was a prominent character at drill and general muster, passing through all the offices from captain to colonel. In the fall of 1845 he was elected treasurer of Richland county, and upon the erection of Ashland county, in 1846, resigned and was elected the first treasurer of the new county, which office he held two terms. In 1853 he was elected a member of the State Board of Equalization from the district comprising Richland and Ashland counties, and in 1857 appointed deputy U. S. Marshal for the northern district of Ohio, and aided in taking the census of 1860. In 1865 he was elected recorder of Ashland county, serving until 1874, when he was elected mayor of Ashland, which office he filled acceptably two years. He resided in Ashland, where he enjoyed the continued confidence and esteem of his fellow citizens. Had been twice married. By his first wife, Elizabeth Murray, there was issue (surname Urie):

30. i. *Mary-Jane*, b. October 9, 1834; m. Giles Porter.
31. ii. *Alice-Ann*, b. January 24, 1836; m. Thomas Milton Beer.
32. iii. *Elizabeth-Helen*, b. April 30, 1837; m. William Wiley Anderson.
   iv. *Wilson-Shannon*, b. February 17, 1839; d. July 17, 1844.
   v. *Sarah-Annie*, b. February 18, 1841, at Ashland, O.; m., April 29, 1873, by Rev. John Robinson, D. D., Sherman Ward Beer; b. May 6, 1839, near Ashland, O.; son of Judge William Beer and his wife Mary Mann; reside at Ashland, O.
   vi. *Adeline-Murray*, b. June 9, 1844; d. September 9, 1852.

IX. ALICE ANN MURRAY,[2] (Patrick,[1]) b. August 14, 1805, in Westmoreland county, Pa.; resided near Guilford, Ind.; m., in Dearborn county, Ind., October 15, 1828, by Rev. George Randall, GEORGE THOMPSON, b. January 22, 1792, in Yorkshire, England; d. August 5, 1873, in Dearborn county, Ind. They had issue (surname Thompson):

   i. *James-Murray*, b. August 12, 1829, in Cincinnati, O.; d. September 26, 1848, in Dearborn county, Ind.
   ii. *William*, b. April 2, 1832, in Cincinnati, O.; d. July 14, 1866, in Dearborn county, Ind.; m., August 24, 1865, by Rev. Benjamin Plummer, Eliza Ann Smith, b. November 3, 1833, in Dearborn county, Ind.; daughter of John Smith

and Catharine Tucker (she subsequently m. Robert Haddock), and had issue (surname Thompson):
1. *William*, b. May 24, 1866 ; d. December 8, 1868, in Dearborn county, Ind.

 iii. Mary-Ann, b. March 20, 1834, in Cincinnati, O.; d. March 19, 1835.

33. *iv. George-Wilson*, b. September 7, 1836 ; m. Catharine Cordelia Lockridge.
34. *v. Jane-Ann*, b. September 3, 1838 ; m. Luke Firth.

 vi. John, b. September 2, 1841 ; resides in Cincinnati, O.; m., May 2, 1867, by Rev. Maxwell P. Gaddis, Ella Lowe, of Cincinnati, O.; they had issue (surname Thompson):
1. *Claude*, b. February 23, 1868.

35. *vii. Jacob-Beatty*, b. October 10, 1843 ; m Jenny Jumper.
36. *viii. Mary-Elizabeth*, b. October 31, 1847 ; m. Melancthon Eleazer Washburn.

X. GEORGE MURRAY,² (Patrick,¹) b. December, 1809, in Stark county, O.; d. August 23, 1854, in Ashland county, O.; m., January 1, 1835, by John Snurr, J. P., JANE A. URIE, b. August 30, 1815, in Hopewell township, Washington county, Pa.; d. August 26, 1879, in Ashland, O.; daughter of Thomas Urie and Rebecca Crosby. They had issue :

37. *i. Adeline-A.*, b. February 14, 1838 ; m. Ohio Pancoast.
38. *ii. Addison*, b. January 10, 1840 ; m. Agnes Jourdan.

XI. ANNE HILL MURRAY,² (Patrick,¹) b. January 1, 1813, in Stark county, O.; resides at Paradise Hill, Ashland county, O.; m., in Ashland, O., October 17, 1836, by David Campbell, J. P., JACOB BRANDEBERRY, b. December 25, 1812, in New Lisbon, Columbiana county, O.; d. November 9, 1884, in California ; son of Rudolph Brandeberry and Susan Reifsnyder. They had issue (surname Brandeberry):

 i. Milton-Murray, b. September 6, 1837, in Ashland county, O.; d. March 22, 1840.

39. *ii. Mary-Jane*, b. February 12, 1841 ; m. Nehemiah S. Carl.
40. *iii. Annette*, b. April 16, 1843 ; m. David Huff.

 iv. Elizabeth. b. February 23, 1845 ; resides at Savannah, Ashland county, O ; m., December 20, 1871, by Rev. William Saddler, Newton A. Craft ; and had issue (surname Craft):
1. *Mary Anna*, b. May 11, 1873.

 v. Irwin-Rudolph, b. January 17, 1847, in Eaton county, Mich.; when last heard from was in Montana

    vi. Adaline, b. October 17, 1850; resides in Orange, Ashland county, O.; m., October 17, 1872, by Rev. George Z. Coekel, Clark Kendig, b. 1854, in Orange township, Ashland county, O.; son of Jacob Kendig and Magdalena Workman; and had issue (surname Kendig):
      1. *Mary-Annette*, b. April 25, 1873.

XII. HUGH MURRAY,² (Patrick,¹) b. March 4, 1816, in Ashland county, O.; d. June 12, 1850, in Orange township, Ashland county, O.; m., in Richland county, O., October 6, 1843, by Rev. George Liller, ELIZABETH NAZOR, b. March 20, 1820, in Lancaster county, Pa.; daughter of Jacob Nazor and Susan Sherk; resides near Nankin P. O., Ashland county, O. They had issue:

      i. Elzy, b. July 13, 1844; resides at Bannock City, Mont.
41.   *ii. Frances*, b. November 11, 1845; m. Samuel Beeghly.
      iii. Alexander, b. February 22, 1847.
42.   *iv. Mary*, b. January 29, 1848; m. Joseph Beeghly.
      v. James-Patrick, b. August 8, 1849; resides at Bannock City, Mont.

XIII. FRANCIS HARRISON MURRAY,³ (James,² Patrick,¹) b. February 2, 1829, in Dearborn county, Ind.; resides at Dayton, Campbell county, Ky.; m., at Cincinnati, O., December 12, 1852, by Rev. Mr. Thornburg, MARTHA JANE COOPER, b. January 22, 1832, in Boone county, Ky.; daughter of James Cooper and Mary Bradley. They had issue:

    i. Eva-Jane, b. December 9, 1853, in Cincinnati, O.; m., May 16, 1878, by Rev. Mr. Thomas, George Dallas Stroman, b. February 10, 1847, at Lebanon, Warren county, O.; son of James Stroman and Phoebe Thaker; reside at Dayton, Ky.; and had issue (surname Stroman):
      1. *Harrison-Dallas*, b. June 22, 1880.
      2. *Anna-Blanche*, b. January 19, 1882.
      3. *Harley*, b. April 21, 1884.
    ii. James-Edgar, b. July 27, 1855, in Cincinnati, O.; a physician; resides at Middletown, O.; m., September 20, 1881, by Rev. R. R. Thompson, Alice E. Hunter, of Richland county, O.; and had issue:
      1. *Carl*, b. July 3, 1882.
      2. *Bernice*, b. June 23, 1884.
      3. *Sylvia-Tennessee*, b. December 19, 1885; d. August, 30, 1891.
      4. *Martha-Grace*, b. October 10, 1890.

iii. Anna-Mary, b. October 28, 1857, in Versailles, Ind.; m. Joseph Murray (*see* XLVI).

iv Macy-B., b. November 18, 1859, in Versailles, Ind.; m., September 22, 1881, James I. Hunter, of Richland county, O.; and had issue (surname Hunter):
   1. *Leona-A.*, b. May 16, 1883.
   2. *B.-Arbie*, b. November 19, 1884.

v. John-Hansell, b. September 27, 1862, in Versailles, Ind.; d. May 13, 1864, at Morris Hill, Ind.

vi. Martha-Effie, b. November 10, 1864, at Morris Hill, Ind.; d. September 6, 1888, in Guilford, Ind.; buried in Dayton, Ky.

vii. Harrison-Wilber, b. September 28, 1867, in Dayton, Ky.

XIV. CATHARINE ELIZABETH MURRAY,[3] (Edward,[2] Patrick,[1]) b. December 4, 1814, in Harrisburg, Pa.; d. January 31, 1829, near Nankin P. O., Ashland county, Pa.; m., in Ashland county, O., by David Campbell, J. P., November 24, 1840, HENRY GERKEY, b. August 8, 1818, in Dauphin county, Pa.; son of George Gerkey and Regina Martin. They had issue, all born in Liberty, Hardin county, O., (surname Gerkey):

   i. George, b. August 12, 1844, in Liberty, Hardin county, O.; resides at Hastings, Barry county, Mich.; m., January 17, 1867, in Van Buren, Hancock county, O., by Eliba Hasson, J. P., Hannah Snyder, b. at Pickington, Fairfield county, O.; and had issue, all born in Carlton, Barry county, Mich. (surname Gerkey):
      1. *Marquibell*, b. November 30, 1873.
      2. *Henrietta*, b. May 9, 1875.
      3. *Belladonna*, b. November 30, 1877.

   ii. John-Henry, b. September 25, 1849, in Liberty, Hardin county, O.; resides at Hastings, Barry county, Mich.; m., January 12, 1871, by Rev. Marshall Chandler, Minerva Garlinger, b. February 8, 1850, in Liberty, Hardin county, O.; and had issue (surname Gerkey):
      1. *Mary-Catharine*, b. Februa,y 13, 1877, in Carlton, Barry county, Mich.

XV. JOHN W. MURRAY,[3] (Edward,[2] Patrick,[1]) b. February 1, 1820, in Ashland county, O.; resides near Lima, Allen county, O.; m. October 27, 1840, in Ashland county, O., by David Campbell, J. P., CHRISTINA REESE, b. May 8, 1824, in Stark county, O.; daughter of Daniel Reese. They had issue:
   i. Daniel.
   ii. Melissa-Ann.

 iii. Lorenzo-Dow, b. September 4, 1849, in Ashland county, O.
 iv. Roxilla.
 v. Mary-Bell, b. April 10, 1854, in Ashland county, O.
 vi. Charles, b. July 18, 1860, in Allen county, O.

XVI. CAMPBELL MURRAY,³ (Edward,² Patrick,¹) b. March 28, 1822, in Ashland county, O.; d. February 8, 1850, in Ashland county, O.; m. October 12, 1843, by David Campbell, J. P., MATILDA FAST, b. January 7, 1823, in Ashland county, O.; d. February 7, 1850, in Ashland county, O.; daughter of Jacob Fast, and granddaughter of Christian Fast, a soldier of the Virginia Line in the Revolution. They had issue :

 43. *i. Wilson-Shannon*, b. Dec. 9, 1845 ; m. Isabel Fulks Stough.

XVII. EDWARD MURRAY,³ (Edward,² Patrick,¹) b. November 27, 1824, in Ashland county, O.; resides near Adario, Richland county, O.; m., December 23, 1847, in Ashland county, O., by Rev. Charles Demming, MARY ELIZABETH COLEMAN, b. January 5, 1830, in Columbia county, Pa.; daughter of Joseph Coleman and Diadem Kinney. They had issue :

 44. *i. John*, b. October 20, 1849 ; m. Ellen Cline.
 45. *ii. Diadem*, b. May 26, 1851 ; m. Louis Milton Viers.
 46. *iii. Joseph*, b. October 21, 1853 ; m. Anna Mary Murray.
   iv. William, b. May 9, 1866, in Richland county, O.

XVIII. REBECCA CHRISTINA MURRAY,³ (Edward,² Patrick,¹) b. April 21, 1827 ; d. July 20, 1869, in Ashland county, O.; m., November 2, 1845, in Orange township, Ashland county, O., by David Campbell, J. P., WILLIAM PETERS, b. December 8, 1823, in Lebanon county, Pa.; son of Edward Peters and Mary Trosell; resides near Nankin P. O., Ashland county, O. They had issue (surname Peters):

 i. John, b. December 29, 1846 ; d. July 6, 1871, in Ashland county, O.; m., April 23, 1868, by Rev. William Saddler, Virginia Nunemaker, b. January 28, 1850, in Brooke county, W. Va.; daughter of Andrew Nunemaker and Rachel Phillips ; and had issue (surname Peters):
  1. *William-Edward*, b. April 12, 1869, in Ashland county, O.
  2. *Eva-May*, b. September 30, 1870, in Ashland county, O.

Murray of Harris' Ferry. 515

 ii. William, b. April 27, 1853; resides near Nankin P. O., Ashland county, O.; m. January 13, 1876, by Rev. John Cyrens, Rosella Fast, b. May 9, 1858, in Ashland county, O.; daughter of Eli Fast and Lydia Berry.

 iii. Mary-Jane, b. December 5, 1856; d. October 5, 1878, in Orange township, Ashland county, O.; m., November 12, 1876, by Rev. George Worst, George William Pixley, b. April 22, 1851, in Lorain county, O.; son of Willard Pixley and Lydia Smith; and had issue (surname Pixley):

  1. *Leon*, b. January 29, 1878, in Ashland county, O.

 iv. Catharine, b. October 30, 1859; m., November 1, 1877, by Rev. George Worst, William Franks, b. November 11, 1853, in Centre county, Pa.; son of Michael Franks and Anna Homan; reside near Nankin P. O., Ashland county, O.

XIX. MURRAY CAZIER,[3] (Susannah,[2] Patrick,[1]) b. February 6, 1819, in Stark county, O.; resides at Brimfield, Noble county, Ind.; m., April 6, 1843, in Seneca county, O., by Rev. Mr. Turner, SARAH COLHOUN, b. September 11, 1818, in Schuylkill county, Pa.; d. September 24, 1874, in Noble county, Ind.; daughter of Frederick Colhoun and Elizabeth Baker. They had issue (surname Cazier):

 i. Oliva, b. January 12, 1844, in Seneca county, O.; d. February 20, 1844.

 ii. William, b. May 14, 1847, in De Kalb county, Ind.; resides at Melvern, Mills county, Ia.; m., November 22, 1872, in Mills county, Ia., Martha Williams, b. September 9, 1856, in Mills county, Ia.; daughter of Amos Williams and Caroline McIntire; and had issue (surname Cazier):

  1. *Ray*, b. May 22, 1875.

  2. *Bertha-May*, b. February 13, 1877.

 iii. Elizabeth, b. August 22, 1848, in De Kalb county, Ind.; resides at Brimfield, Noble county, Ind.; m., January 9, 1873, by Rev. William Wilson, Wesley Barnes, b. November 8, 1845, in Morrow connty, O.; d. March, 1875, in Jewell county, Kans.; son of Ashman Barnes and Sarah Imes; and had issue (surname Barnes):

  1. *Clyde*, b. November 3, 1874, in Holt county, Mo.

 iv. Marion-Howard, b. November 29, 1850, in DeKalb county, Ind.; resides at Albion, Ind.

 v. Mary, b. September 5, 1853, in DeKalb county, Ind.; resides at Bellevue, O.; m., September 5, 1877, in Noble county, O., by Rev. Preston McKinney, Charles Frederick Murray, b. July 20, 1844, in Oberlin, O.; son of John Russell Murray and Abigail Hopkins.

vi. George, b. December 10, 1855, in Williams county, O.

vii. Alice, b. April 7, 1858, in Noble county, Ind.

XX. ELIZABETH CAZIER,[3] (Susannah,[2] Patrick,[1]) b. March 14, 1821, in Ashland county, O.; resides near Brimfield, Noble county, Ind.; m., first, November 8, 1842, in DeKalb county, Ind., ELI FAST, b. March 4, 1816, in Pennsylvania; d. March 16, 1861, in Ashland county, O.; son of Jacob Fast and Catharine Rex. They had issue (surname Fast):

    i. Julia-Ann, b. August 22, 1843, in Ashland county, O.; resides near Nova P. O., Ashland county, O.; m., March 4, 1876, by Henry Summers, J. P., George Phelps, b. April 2, 1834, in Benton, Yates county, N. Y.; son of Elisha P. Phelps and Jane E. Kniffin; and had issue (surname Phelps):

        1. *Ada-Frances*, b. January 24, 1864.
        2. *Edward-Bernard*, b. March 1, 1873.

    ii. Elzina-Alice, b. July 11, 1846, in Ashland county, O.; resides near Nova P. O., Ashland county, O.; m., March 31, 1875, by Rev. Christian Weaver, Emmett Eddy, b. September 30, 1853, in Avilla, Noble county, Ind.; son of Ithamar Eddy and Elizabeth Hite.

    iii. James-Lafayette, b. November 17, 1854; resides at Troy, Ashland county, O.

Mrs. Elizabeth Cazier Fast m., secondly, March 12, 1876, BENJAMIN FRANKLIN BOOTS, b. May 12, 1823, in Penn Yan, N. Y.; son of Benjamin Boots and Susan Basum.

XXI. JOHN WESLEY BARBER,[3] (Susannah,[2] Patrick,[1]) b. April 30, 1828, in Sandusky county, O.; resides at Butler, DeKalb county, Ind.; m., September 20, 1846, JANE NORRIS, b. June 14, 1827, in Tuscarawas county, O. They had issue (surname Barber):

    i. Alice-Ann, b. July 19, 1848, in De Kalb county, Ind.; resides near Albion, Noble county, Ind.; m., August 28, 1874, by Elder Ward, James Gaby; b. July 7, 1848, in Noble county, Ind.; son of Timothy Gaby and Amanda Edmonds.

    ii. Levisa-Ann (twin), b. July 19, 1848; resides near Albion, Noble county, Ind.; m., March 10, 1870, by Elder James Hadsell, William Henry Wickard; b. June 25, 1843, in

Stark county, O.; son of David Wickard and Elizabeth Shoe; and had issue (surname Wickard):
1. *Charles-Edwin*, b. January 16, 1872.
2. *Mary-Elizabeth*, b. January 7, 1876.

iii. *Jeremiah-Augustus*, b. December 10, 1851.
iv. *Catharine*, b. July 12, 1854.
v. *Susannah*, b. December 15, 1856.
vi. *Edwin-Eugene*, b. March 20, 1859.
vii. *George-Ellsworth*, b. June 26, 1861.
viii. *John-Charles*, b. July 1, 1863.

XXII. GEORGE WASHINGTON MURRAY,³ (John,² Patrick,¹) b. September 27, 1824, in Richland county, O., resides near Shawnee Mound, Henry county, Mo.; m., in Benton county, Mo., June 18, 1846, by Hosea Powers, J. P., NANCY WARRING FUQUA, b. December 4, 1826, in Greenup county, Ky.; d. February 12, 1879, in Henry county, Mo.; daughter of William Fuqua* and Lydia Warring. They had issue:

i. *Virginia-Ann*, b. May 18, 1847, in Morgan county, Mo.; m., December 24, 1868, John B. Simpson; and had issue (surname Simpson):
1. *Eddie*, b. November 14, 1869, in Clinton county, Mo.; d. August, 1876, in Memphis, Tenn.
2. *Elizabeth*, b. March 12, 1871, in Henry county, Mo.
3. *Albert*, b. February, 1877, in Memphis, Tenn.

ii. *Gaylord-Canada*, b. Aug. 20, 1848, in Morgan county, Mo.
iii. *Dorcas-Elizabeth*, b. April 28, 1850, in Morgan county, Mo.; d. May 11, 1865, in Henry county, Mo.
iv. *Mary-Urie*, b. April 21, 1852; d. November 14, 1855, in Morgan county, Mo.
v. *Thomas-Calvin*, b. Dec. 14, 1853, in Morgan county, Mo.
vi. *Cynthia-Caroline*, b. August 8, 1855, in Morgan county, Mo.; resides near Shawnee Mound, Henry county, Mo.; m., July 18, 1877, by Rev. W. L. King, James Willis Wiley; b. September 14, 1853, in Henry county, Mo., son of John and Eliza Jane Wiley.
vii. *Joseph-Wiliary*, b. May 24, 1857, in Henry county, Mo.
viii. *Samuel*, b. November 10, 1859.
ix. *Luella*, b. April 19, 1861.

XXIII. MARY ANN MURRAY,³ (John,² Patrick,¹) b. May 5, 1828, in Richland county, O.; resides near Brownsville, Saline

---
*WILLIAM FUQUA, b. March 8, 1800, in Virginia; d. January 4, 1853, in Jackson county, Mo.; m. Lydia Warring; b. February 16, 1802, in Mason county, Ky.; d. May 6, 1877, in Henry county, Mo.

county, Mo.; m., first, in Morgan county, Mo., May 7, 1847, ROBERT URIE, b. October 1, 1823, in Orange township, Ashland county, O.; d. October 1, 1848, in Bates county, Mo.; son of Thomas Urie and Margaret Culbertson. They had issue (surname Urie):

    i. Julia-Ann-Robert, b. August 27, 1848, near Versailles, Mo.

Mrs. Urie m., secondly, in Morgan county, Mo., January 20, 1860, ALFRED JOHN LEARY; b. June 14, 1830, at Kingston, Canada West; son of Benjamin Leary and Mary Kendall. They had issue (surname Leary):

    ii. John-George, b. November 4, 1860, in Florence, Mo.
    iii. Pleasant-Alfred, b. March 17, 1863, in Henry county, Mo.; d. July 27, 1864, in Sedalia, Pettis county, Mo.
    iv. Mary-Susan, b. August 18, 1865, in Sedalia, Mo.
    v. William-Frank, b. June 19, 1867, in Sedalia, Mo.; d. September 11, 1869.
    vi. Alice-Belle, b. August 4, 1869, in Sedalia, Mo.

XXIV. ELIZABETH MURRAY,[3] (John,[2] Patrick,[1]) b. June 17, 1830, in Richland county, O.; d. September 10, 1864, in Bates county, Mo.; m., in Morgan county, Mo., February 14, 1861, by 'Squire Mulholland, JOHN PARDEE, b. May 27, 1820, in Wytheville, Wythe county, Va.; son of Philo Pardee and Rachel Montgomery; resides near Crescent Hill, Bates county, Mo. They had issue (surname Pardee):

    i. William, b. July 23, 1863, in Harrisonville, Cass county, Mo.

XXV. SUSANNAH MURRAY,[3] (John,[2] Patrick,[1]) b. May 28, 1835, in Richland county, O.; resides at Hunter's Warm Springs, Montana; m., in Benton county, Mo., October 12, 1858, by 'Squire Hindsworth, ANDREW JACKSON HUNTER, b. March 18, 1816, in Franklin county, Va.; son of John Hunter* and Sarah Price; is a physician of prominence; a graduate of Transylvania University, Ky., and the owner of the celebrated Hot Springs of Montana. They had issue (surname Hunter):

    i. Mary-Lee, b. July 7, 1859, in Georgetown, Randolph county, Ill.

---

*JOHN HUNTER, b. 1760, in Franklin county, Va.; d. 1819, in Cumberland county, Ky.; m. SARAH PRICE, b. 1766, in Franklin county, Va.; d. 1854 in Cumberland county Ky.

ii. Davis-Beauregard, b. February 25, 1861, in Shamrock, Callaway county, Mo.
iii. Lizzie-Kate, b. January 25, 1863, in Downeyville, Jackson county, Ill.
iv. Thomas-Stonewall-Jackson, b. November 25, 1864, in Virginia City, Montana; d. at Benson's Landing, on the Yellowstone.
v. Montana-Queen, b. November 4, 1866, in New York City, Montana; d. s. p.
vi. Sallie-Price, b. November 27, 1867, in New York City, Montana.
vii. Emma-Sidney-Johnson, b. October 24, 1869, at Confederate Gulch, Montana; d. at Hot Springs, Montana.

XXVI. ALVERDA MURRAY,³ (John,² Patrick,¹) b. August 8, 1843, in Richland county, O.; resides near Batchelor, Callaway county, Mo.; m., in Benton county, Mo., October 16, 1861, by Elder William B. Douglass, SAMUEL BRANDENBURGH b. October 17, 1836, in Montgomery county, Mo.; son of Jonathan Brandenburgh and Mary Smith. They had issue, all b. in Callaway county, Mo., (surname Brandenburgh):

i. Jackson-Davis, b. January 27, 1863.
ii. Mary-Susan, b. April 7, 1865.
iii. Nancy-Jane, b. June 30, 1867.
iv. Carrie-Jerusha, b. August 4, 1869.
v. Algie-Mason, b. April 4, 1872.
vi. Emma-Thomas, b. September 28, 1874.
vii. Samuel-Edward, b. April 27, 1877.

XXVII. COMMODORE PERRY MURRAY,³ (John,² Patrick,¹) b. March 13, 1848, in Morgan county, Mo.; resides near Benton City, Audrain county, Mo.; m., in Callaway county, Mo., March 20, 1873, by Elder William C. Ridgway, ELIZABETH FRANCES RIDGWAY, b. June 11, 1855, in Callaway county, Mo.; daughter of Ambrose Dudley Ridgway and Ann America Vest. They had issue, all b. in Audrain county, Mo.:

i. Clara-Leelie, b. February 2, 1874.
ii. Annie-Eliza, b. February 4, 1876.
iii. Thomas-Pinkney, b. June 23, 1878.

XXVIII. WILLIAM RALSTON,³ (Mary,² Patrick,¹) b. December 31, 1824; resides at Fayetteville, Tenn.; m., in Mansfield, O., May 15, 1860, by the Rev. David Paul, AGNES FINNEY, b. April 20, 1830, in Mansfield, O.; daughter of Thomas

Finney and Nancy Culbertson. They had issue (surname Ralston):

    i. William, b. July 10, 1861, at Ashland, O.
    ii. J.-Huss, b. September 1, 1862, at Ashland, O.
    iii. Thomas-Franklin, b. November 24, 1863, at Ashland, O.
    iv. Mary, b. September 11, 1865, at Ashland, O.
    v. James, b. August 8, 1867, at Ashland, O.
    vi. Joseph-Guy, b. February 10, 1869, at Ashland, O.; d. August 16, 1877, at Fayetteville, Tenn.
    vii. Agnes, b. July 16, 1871, at Ashland, O.
    viii. Columbia, b. July 4, 1873, at Mansfield, O.; d. September 15, 1877, at Fayetteville, Tenn.
    ix. Oscar, b. October 24, 1875, at Mansfield, O.
    x. McNeil, b. December 30, 1878, at Fayetteville, Tenn.

XXIX. ALEXANDER RALSTON,[3] (Mary,[2] Patrick,[1]) b. February 6, 1826, at Ashland, O.; resides at Calhoun, Richland county, Ill.; m., at Plymouth, O., November 24, 1855, by Rev. George N. H. Peters, SALOME TRAUGER, b. February 12, 1834, in Bucks county, Pa.; daughter of Samuel Harpel Trauger and Susanna Maust. They had issue (surname Ralston):

    i. Mary-Lura, b. June 10, 1859, at Plymouth, Richland county, O.
    ii. Mack-Trauger, b. April 5, 1865, at Auburn, De Kalb county, Indiana.

XXX. MARY JANE URIE,[3] (Elizabeth,[2] Patrick,[1]) b. October 9, 1834, in Ashland, O.; d. September 10, 1875, in Ashland, O.; m., November 9, 1865, by Rev. John Robinson, D. D., GILES PORTER, b. January 1, 1832, in Huron county, O.; son of Ira Porter and Lucy Smith; resides at Geneseo, Ill. They had issue (surname Porter):

    i. Ella, b. December 2, 1867.
    ii. Bertha, b. February 14, 1870.

XXXI. ALICE ANN URIE,[3] (Elizabeth,[2] Patrick,[1]) b. January 24, 1836, in Ashland, O.; m., May 8, 1852, by Rev. Thomas Beer, THOMAS MILTON BEER, b. March 2, 1837, near Ashland, O.; son of Richard Beer and Jane Anderson; reside in Ashland, O. They had issue (surname Beer):

    i. Lizzie-Janette, b. December 24, 1863.
    ii. Frank, b. December 24, 1868.
    iii. Harry-Caleb, b. February 12, 1876.

XXXII. ELIZABETH HELEN URIE,³ (Elizabeth,² Patrick,¹) b. April 30, 1837, in Ashland, O.; resides at Belleville, Richland county, O.; m., June 29, 1865, by Rev. John Robinson, D. D., WILLIAM WILEY ANDERSON, b. November 6, 1839, in West Rushville, Fairfield county, O.; son of Rev. James Anderson and Lawrence Marvin; is a minister of the Presbyterian Church. They had issue (surname Anderson):

 i. Clara, b. June 2, 1868.
 ii. Dora, b. November 4, 1872.

XXXIII. GEORGE WILLIAM THOMPSON,³ (Alice-Ann,² Patrick,¹) b. September 7, 1836, in Dearborn county, Ind.; resides at Centreville, Iowa; m., January 1, 1867, by Rev. Benjamin Plummer, CATHARINE CORDELIA LOCKRIDGE, b. October 18, 1846, in Yorkville, Dearborn county, Ind.; daughter of Hollis Stuart Lockridge* and Hannah E. Perrine. They had issue (surname Thompson):

 i. Eddie-Stuart, b. Sept. 14, 1867, at Cameron, Mo.; d. s. p.
 ii. Willie-Lockridge, b. Mar. 20, 1869, at Cameron, Mo.; d. s. p.
 iii. Truman-Wilson, b. March 8, 1871; d. February 4, 1872, at Cameron, Mo.
 iv. Jenny-Bell, b. September 14, 1873, at Cameron, Mo.; d. September 5, 1876, at Centreville, Ia.
 v. John-Murray, b. Feb. 27, 1876, at Centreville, Iowa; d. s. p.
 vi. Frederick, b. December 19, 1878, at Centreville, Iowa; d. February 28, 1879.

XXXIV. JANE ANN THOMPSON,³ (Alice-Ann,² Patrick,¹) b. September 3, 1838, in Dearborn county, Ind.; resides at Mirabile, Caldwell county, Mo.; m., August 30, 1866, by Rev. Benjamin Plummer, LUKE FIRTH, b. July 5, 1836, in Boone county, Ky.; son of William Firth and Ann Stubs, both natives of England. They had issue (surname Firth):

 i. Alice-Ann, b. July 2, 1867.
 ii. Mary-Elizabeth, b. September 13, 1869; d. January 15, 1879, in Caldwell county, Mo.
 iii. Viola-Eliza, b. August 6, 1871.
 iv. William-Thompson, b. February 5, 1873.

---

*HOLLIS STUART LOCKRIDGE, b. June 2, 1815, at Madison, Ind.; m. Hannah E. Perrine, b. March 25, 1820, at Yorkville, Dearborn county, Ind.

v. *Luella*, b. June 24, 1874.
vi. *Oliver-Francis*, b. March 11, 1877.

XXXV. JACOB BEATTY THOMPSON,³ (Alice-Ann,² Patrick,¹) b. October 10, 1843, in Dearborn county, Ind.; resides at Melvern, Osage county, Kan.; m., in Ripley county, Ind., December 1, 1867, by Allen Campbell, J. P., JENNY JUMPER, b. August 31, 1846, in Dearborn county, Ind.; daughter of Alden H. Jumper and Amanda F. Noyes.* They had issue (surname Thompson):

 i. *Albert-Clyde*, b. December 13, 1868, in Dearborn county, Ind.; d. s. p.
 ii. *Willana*, b. February 11, 1870, in Oswego county, Kans.
 iii. *Alice-Ann*, b. June 20, 1872, in Osage county, Kans.
 iv. *Ethel-M.*, b. May 1, 1875, in Caldwell county, Mo.

XXXVI. MARY ELIZABETH THOMPSON,³ (Alice-Ann,² Patrick,¹) b. October 31, 1847, in Dearborn county, Ind.; resides near Guilford, Dearborn county, Ind.; m., October 31, 1866, by Rev. Benjamin Plummer, MELANCTHON ELEAZER WASHBURN, b. April 20, 1836, in Coolville, Athens county, O.; son of Roswell Washburn† and Lura Cleveland. They had issue (surname Washburn):

 i. *Willie-Gordon*, b. November 3, 1868.
 ii. *Charles-Thompson*, b. Sept. 25, 1873; d. Nov. 18, 1874.
 iii. *Cora-Pearl*, b. October 4, 1876.
 iv. *John*, b. August 22, 1878.

XXXVII. ADALINE A. MURRAY,³ (George,² Patrick,¹) b. February 14, 1838, in Orange township, Ashland county, O.; resides in Ashland, O.; m., June 6, 1867, by Rev. John Robinson, D. D., OHIO PANCOAST, b. March 6, 1839, in Wooster, O.; son of Hezekiah B. and Rebecca Pancoast. They had issue (surname Pancoast):

 i. *Duff*, b. March 1, 1868.
 ii. *Anna*, b. January 12, 1870.
 iii. *Ray*, b. October 23, 1872.

---

*ALDEN H. JUMPER, b. February 16, 1819, in Lincoln county, Me.; m. Amanda F. Noyes, b. September 1, 1825, in Dearborn county, Ind.; resides in Osage county, Kans.

†ROSWELL WASHBURN, b. 1792, in Deerfield, Conn.; d. May 17, 1873, in Athens county, O.; m., in 1827, Lura Cleveland, b. 1803, in Athens county, O.; d. July 9, 1839.

XXXVIII. ADDISON MURRAY,³ (George,² Patrick,¹) b. January 10, 1840, in Orange township, Ashland county, Pa.; resides at Galion, O.; m., May 25, 1869, by Rev. Mr. Miller, AGNES JOURDAN, b. in Galion, O.; daughter of Joseph and Catharine Jourdan. They had issue:

 i. Alfaretta, b. November 30, 1870, in Galion, O.
 ii. Addie, b. November 23, 1879.

XXXIX. MARY JANE BRANDEBERRY,³ (Anne-Hill,² Patrick,¹) b. February 12, 1841, in Ashland, O.; resides at Dresden, Powshick county, Ia.; m., April 26, 1866, NEHEMIAH S. CARL. They had issue (surname Carl):

 i. Albert-A., b. February 1, 1867.
 ii. Anne-Hill, b. February 27, 1869.
 iii. David-J., b. September 4, 1870; d. March 11, 1871.
 iv. Elias-N., b. March 9, 1872.
 v. Matthew, b. January 18, 1874; d. August 14, 1874.
 vi. Martha (twin), b. January 18, 1874.
 vii. Isaac, b. July 31, 1876; d. August 9, 1876.

XL. ANNETTE BRANDEBERRY,³ (Anne-Hill,² Patrick,¹) b. April 16, 1842, in Ashland, O., where she now resides; m., December 6, 1860, by Thomas Hayes, J. P., DAVID HUFF, b. March 3, 1839, in Hancock county, O.; son of Andrew Huff and Grace Reeves. They had issue (surname Huff):

 i. William-Irwin, b. October 2, 1861, in Hancock county, O.
 ii. Eliza-Murray, b. July 23, 1864, in Ashland, O.
 iii. Mary-Ellen, b. July 21, 1866, in Ashland, O.
 iv. Arthur-Evington, b. March 27, 1871, in Ashland, O.

XLI. FRANCES MURRAY,³ (Hugh,² Patrick,¹) b. November 11, 1845, in Ashland, O., where she now resides; m., September 5, 1865, by Rev. P. J. Brown, SAMUEL BEEGHLY, b. February 1, 1839, in Somerset county, Pa.; son of John Beeghly and Catharine Peek. They had issue (surname Beeghly):

 i. Elzy-Murray, b. April 17, 1867.
 ii. Cora-Alice, b. May 27, 1869; d. September 14, 1871.
 iii. Tullius-Cicero, b. April 26, 1873.
 iv. Calvin-Murray, b. July 26, 1876.

XLII. MARY MURRAY,³ (Hugh,² Patrick,¹) b. January 29, 1845, in Ashland county, O., where she now resides; m., September 24, 1868, by Rev. William Saddler, JOSEPH BEEGHLY, b. March 31, 1837, in Somerset county, Pa.; son of

John Beeghly and Catharine Peek. They had issue (surname Beeghly):

 i. James-Urbana, b. March 12, 1870.
 ii. Clark-Edmund, b. November 18, 1874.

XLIII. WILSON SHANNON MURRAY,⁴ (Campbell,³ Edward,² Patrick,¹) b. December 9, 1845, in Orange county, O.; resides near Adario, Richland county, O.; m., October 8, 1868, by James Alberson, J. P., ISABEL FULKS STOUGH, b. May 29, 1849, in Montgomery township, Ashland county, O.; daughter of Jonas Stough and Mary Ann Gerhart. They had issue:

 i. Sarah-Matilda, b. August 10, 1869, in Ruggles township, Ashland county, O.; m., March 4, 1891, John A. Creveling; and had issue (surname Creveling):
  1. *Connor-Murray*, b. January 3, 1892.
  2. *Rutha*, b. December 20, 1893; d. June 15, 1894.
 ii. Mabel-B., b. February 10, 1871, in Orange township, Ashland county, O.; m., December 25, 1892, John M. Bright; and had issue (surname Bright):
  1. *Byron-Wilson*, b. September 10, 1894.
 iii. Edward-A., b. December 16, 1872, in Butler township, Richland county, O.; m., October 25, 1894, Amanda E. Harnly.
 iv. Mittie-Blanchy, b. March 8, 1875.
 v. Lizzie-Artimisa, b. March 15, 1877.
 vi. Alvin-C., b. February 1, 1887.

XLIV. JOHN MURRAY,⁴ (Edward,³ Edward,² Patrick,¹) b. October 20, 1849, in Orange township, Ashland county, O.; resides near Adario, Richland county, O.; m., March 2, 1876, by Rev. Mr. Lawrence, ELLEN CLINE, b. July 15, 1852, in Butler township, Richland county, O.; daughter of Samuel Cline and Elizabeth Baird. They had issue:

 i. Roy, b. October 31, 1876.
 ii. Ray (twin), b. October 31, 1876.
 iii. Edward, b. March 13, 1884.

XLV. DIADEM MURRAY,⁴ (Edward,³ Edward,² Patrick,¹) b. May 26, 1851, in Orange township, Ashland county, O.; resides near Adario, Richland county, O.; m., February 19, 1874, by Rev. S. T. Boyd, LOUIS MILTON VIERS, b. February 14, 1851, in Richland county, O.; son of Liverton Viers and Jane Parker. They had issue (surname Viers):

 i. Lottie, b. December 19, 1874; d. July 13, 1887.
 ii. Edward, b. May 16, 1876; d. July 7, 1887.
 iii. Nettie, b. June 9, 1878; d. July 12, 1887.
 iv. Mary-Jane, b. February 16, 1882.
 v. Bertha-Grace, b. September 80, 1883; d. July 20, 1887.
 vi. Clark, b. March 26, 1885; d. July 21, 1887.
 vii. Mattie-Bell, b. October 7, 1886.
 viii. Elzy, b. October 14, 1888; d. February 18, 1892.
 ix. William, b. February 18, 1891.

XLVI. JOSEPH MURRAY,[4] (Edward,[3] Edward,[2] Patrick,[1]) b. October 21, 1853, in Ashland county, O.; resides near Adario, Richland county, O.; m., October 9, 1879, by the Rev. E. L. Sanders, at Dayton, Ky., ANNA MARY MURRAY, b. October 23, 1857, in Versailles, Ind.; daughter of Francis Harrison Murray[2] (James,[2] Patrick[1]). They had issue:

 i. Martha-Blanche, b. January 1, 1881.
 ii. Edna-Lee, b. December 27, 1883.
 iii. Joseph-Hansel, b. March 20, 1886.
 iv. Mary-Florence, b. November 17, 1889; d. November 2, 1894.

MURRAY OF SWATARA.

I. JOHN MURRAY,[1] a native of Scotland, came to America late in life with his two sons and their families. He probably died a few years afterwards. The only members of his family of whom we have record are the following :

2. i. *William*, b. February 24, 1690; m. [Isabella] Lindley.
3. ii. *John*, b. 1691 ; m., and had issue.

II. WILLIAM MURRAY,[2] (John,[1]) b. February 24, 1690, in Scotland, emigrated to America in 1732. His father and brother John accompanied him. They settled on the Swatara, in the Province of Pennsylvania. He m. [ISABELLA] LINDLEY, sister of Thomas Lindley, of Scotland, who also emigrated to Pennsylvania about the same time, and located in the neighborhood of the Murrays. It is not definitely known whether either the Murrays or Lindleys came direct from Scotland or had sojourned in Ireland for some time. William Murray d. on his farm July 24, 1773, his wife probably preceding him. They had issue, among others, five sons :

    i. *Samuel*, went to Carolina, and died there about 1817.
    ii. *William*, went to Carolina, and died there many years before 1818.
4. iii. *James*, b. 1729 ; m. Rebecca McLean.
5. iv. *John*, b. 1731 ; m. Margaret Mayes.
6. v. *Thomas*, b. about 1737 ; m. Eleanor Collier.

III. JOHN MURRAY,[2] (JOHN,[1]) b. about 1691, in Scotland; emigrated to the Province of Pennsylvania in 1732 in company with his brother and other friends. On the 10th of January, 1737, he obtained a land warrant from the Proprietaries of Pennsylvania, and on the " 14th of ye 9th month," 1739, had the same located upon two hundred acres and twelve perches of land adjoining the northwest side of "Swahatawro" (Swatara) creek, then in Hanover township, Lancaster county, Pa. Adam Read, an early settler and prominent in frontier times, held an adjoining tract on the north by improvement. On the first of March, 1744, John Murray obtained another warrant, which was located, about a year afterward, east of the other tract, and between it and land of James Stewart. This latter tract is now within the limits of Lebanon county, the former, the homestead, being within the present bounds of Dauphin county, a short distance from Dixon's Ford on the Swatara. The date of death or name of John Murray's wife we have been unable to gather. Of their children, however, we have the following:

    i. William, b. 1714; m., and had issue, among others:

        1. *John*, b. 1737; known as "Presbyterian John" to distinguish him from his cousin, John Murray, son of Robert (*see* VI). In early life he went to New York and entered the store of his uncle, Robert Murray, with whom he became associated in 1771 in business under the firm name of Robert & John Murray; subsequently he withdrew from the co-partnership and with his sons formed that of John Murray & Sons; in his church relations he was a Presbyterian, and for many years an elder in Rev. Dr. John Rodgers' church; in politics, a Federalist, enjoying the intimate acquaintance of such men as Rufus King and Alexander Hamilton. He was greatly esteemed in the mercantile community, and presided over the New York Chamber of Commerce from 1798 to 1806; died at his country seat, on Murray Hill, October 17, 1808; his children were *John-R., Hamilton, Hannah*, and *Mary*.

    ii. Samuel, b. 1717; about the year 1755 went to the Carolinas; nothing further known of him.

7.   *iii. Robert*, b. 1721; m. Mary Lindley.

    iv. Arabella, b. 1725; d. 1775; m. John Dixon, (*see Dixon of Dixon's Ford.*)

IV. JAMES MURRAY,³ (William,² John,¹) b. about 1729, in Scotland; d. February 15, 1804, on his farm adjoining the borough of Dauphin, Dauphin county, Pa. For this farm he entered an application in the Land Office in 1768. In 1775 he was chosen to represent Upper Paxtang township in the Committee of Safety for Lancaster county and attended the meetings of the Committee in Lancaster on the 8th, 9th and 10th of November. At this time he was a captain of "a company of foot in the Fourth battalion of Associators in the county of Lancaster." On the fourth of July, 1776, at a military convention representing the fifty-three battalions of Associators of Pennsylvania, he was present as a captain. With John Rogers and John Harris, on the 8th of July, 1776, by appointment of the Provincial Conference, he superintended the election at Garber's Mill for the Sixth district of Lancaster county, to choose delegates to the convention that assembled on the 15th of the month, and which framed the first Constitution of the Commonwealth. During the remainder of that and the following year he was almost in constant active military service with his company. His company, a roll of which appears in Dr. Egle's *Notes and Queries*, First Series, p. 7, and in Pennsylvania Archives, Second Series, vol. xiii., p. 310, went into the Continental service in July or early in August, 1776. In a return of the troops quartered in and near Philadelphia, made August 27th, of that year, it is reported sixty strong. It participated in the battles of Trenton and Princeton. He commanded one of the companies of the Tenth battalion, Lancaster county militia, and was with the expedition up the West Branch in 1779. The exposures to which Captain Murray was subjected during the Revolutionary struggle brought on an attack of rheumatism, from which for many years prior to his death he was a constant sufferer. He m. REBECCA MCLEAN, a native of Scotland, who d. August 7, 1795. The remains of both rest, side by side, in the old Dauphin cemetery. They had issue:

8.   i. *Margaret*, b. 1756; m. John Simpson.
    ii. *William*, b. 1759; settled in Tennessee.
    iii. *Annie*, b. 1761; m. Samuel Davidson.
    iv. *Rebecca*, b. 1763; m. Samuel Brown, of Hanover.
    v. *Isabella*, b. 1765; m. Robert Chambers.
    vi. *John*, b. 1768; settled on Chillisquaque creek, Northumberland county; he was a member of the House of Representatives from 1807 to 1810, and served as a member of Congress, 1817 to 1821; he married Margaret Murray, a daughter of Col. John Murray, (*see* v).

V. JOHN MURRAY,[3] (William,[2] John,[1]) b. about 1731, in Scotland; d. February 3, 1798, in Dauphin county, Pa. In 1766 he took up a tract of land called the "Indian Burying

Ground," lying on the Susquehanna, immediately above his brother James' farm, which adjoined the present town of Dauphin. He commanded a rifle company, which in March, 1776, was attached to Col. Samuel Miles' battalion, and participated in the battles of Long Island, White Plains, Trenton, and Princeton. He was promoted to major April 18, 1777, and lieutenant colonel of the Second Pennsylvania regiment in 1780, serving until the disbanding of the army in 1783. He then returned to his family and farm. Governor Mifflin appointed him a justice of the peace August 29, 1791, the only political office he ever held. He was an ardent Whig of the Revolution, and a brave officer. Colonel Murray m., December 29, 1762, by Rev. John Elder, MARGARET MAYES, b. 1733, in the north of Ireland; d. June 22, 1807, in Upper Paxtang township, Dauphin county, Pa.; buried by the side of her husband in the old cemetery near Dauphin borough; daughter of Andrew and Rebecca Mayes. They had issue, among others:

    i. William, b. September 6, 1764; d. March 18, 1840; in 1805 removed to Ohio; m., March 17, 1796, Deborah Latta, and had issue: Two sons and two daughters.

    ii. Margaret, b. February 5, 1770; m. John Murray, son of Capt. James Murray, of Paxtang; both buried in the Chillisquaque cemetery, Northumberland county, Pa.

    iii. Rebecca, b. October 19, 1774; d. January 6, 1837; m., April 19, 1804, Innis Green, b. March 25, 1776; d. August 4, 1830; son of Col. Timothy Green and Mary Innis; received a tolerably fair English education, an essential in the Scotch-Irish settlements; his father who built a mill at the mouth of Stony Creek, on the Susquehanna, about 1790, dying in 1812, Innis took charge of it; he was appointed by Governor Findlay one of the associate judges of the county of Dauphin, August 10, 1818, resigning, however, October 23, 1827, having been elected to the National House of Representatives; he served during the Twentieth and Twenty-first Congresses; Governor Wolf re-appointed him, January 26, 1832, associate judge, a position he held at the time of his death.

VI. THOMAS MURRAY,[3] (William,[2] John,[1]) b. in Scotland about 1737; d. November 18, 1799. He m. ELLEN or ELEANOR COLLIER, b. about 1739; d. December 17, 1800. He settled in Northumberland county. They had issue:

i. *William*, d. July 24, 1773.

ii. *Mary*, b. 1770; d. September 14, 1843; she m. Capt. John Gaston, who died in the war of 1812; in 1814 Mrs. Gaston moved to Ohio.

iii. *Anna*, b. May, 1772; d. February 1, 1821, in Highland county, O.; she m., in 1802, William Boyd; this family removed to Ohio in 1814; and they had issue (surname Boyd):
1. *Thomas Murray*, b. January 5, 1803.
2. *Sarah*, b. 1805.
3. *William*, b. 1807; lived in Illinois.
4. *Jane*, b. 1809; d. in inf.

iv. *James*, b. July 13, 1776; d. December 24, 1834; removed a short time before the war of 1812 to Highland county, O.; m. Mary Mitchell, in Dauphin county; and they had issue:
1. *Ellen*, m. William Collier.
2. *Mitchell-H.*, m., and had two children.
3. *Samuel*, m., and had issue.
4. *Thomas*, m., and had issue.
5. *Mary-Mitchell*. m. F. Lavery.
6. *James*, m., and had issue; resided in Greenfield, O.
7. *John*, m., and had issue; resided in Greenfield, O.
8. *Jane*, d. young.

v. *Susannah*, b. March, 1777; m., in 1802, Samuel Russell; and had issue (surname Russell):
1. *Andrew*, b. January 3, 1803; decd.; resided near Pottsville, Pa.
2. *Eleanor*, b. 1804; unm.; lived on old farm near Muncy.
3. *Thomas*, b. 1807; lived at Pottsville.
4. *Isabel*, b. 1809; d. 1813.
5. *Mary*, b. 1811; d. 1813.
6. *Isabel-K*, b. 1813; unm.; lived on old farm.
7. *James*, b. 1816; d. 1816.
8. *Susan*, b. 1818; unm.; lived on old farm.
9. *Samuel*, b. July 28, 1820; m. Miss Blair; and had issue.

VII. ROBERT MURRAY,[3] (John,[2] John,[1]) b. about 1721, in Scotland; d. July 22, 1786, in the city of New York. He came to America with his parents and remained on the Swatara until about the year 1750, when he removed to North Carolina when the immigration thither was in full tide. Two or three years sufficed, however, when he turned his face northward and settled in the city of New York, where he entered into mercantile pursuits; subsequently purchasing the tract of land known as "Murray Hill," now in the heart of the metropolis. This became historical as the spot where Mrs. Murray, during the Revolution, entertained Lord Howe and his officers long enough to enable the American troops under Putnam to escape. Although brought up in the Westminster Confession, and members of Old Derry church, whatever may have been the cause we know not, Robert Murray and his wife joined the Society of Friends in New York, and it was therefore in the tenets of this persuasion that his large family of children were instructed. Of his parents, the son, in his autobiography, thus writes: "My parents were of respectable character, and in the middle station of life. My father possessed a good flour mill at Swatara, but being of an enterprising spirit and anxious to provide handsomely for his family, he made several voyages to the West Indies, in the way of trade, by which he considerably augmented his property. Pursuing his inclinations, he in time acquired large possessions, and became one of the most respectable merchants in America. . . . . My mother was a woman of an amiable disposition, and remarkable for mildness, humanity, and liberality of sentiment. She was, indeed, a faithful and affectionate wife, a tender mother, and a kind mistress." Robert Murray m., in 1744, MARY LINDLEY, daughter of Thomas Lindley. They had issue, twelve children, of whom we have the names of only four:

9.   i. *Lindley*, b. 1745 ; m. Hannah Dobson.
10. ii. *John*, m. Catharine Bowne.
11. iii. *Beulah*, m. Martin Hoffman.
     iv. *Susan*, d. 1808; m. Gilbert Colden Willett.

VIII. MARGARET MURRAY,[4] (James,[3] William,[2] John,[1]) b. 1756, in Paxtang township, Lancaster county, Pa.; d. April 27, 1826, at Huntingdon, Pa.; m., May 7, 1776, by Rev. John Elder, JOHN SIMPSON, b. about 1744, in Buckingham township, Bucks county, Pa.; d. February 3, 1807, in Huntingdon, Pa. His parents, John and Mary Simpson, went south and were residing in North Carolina in 1783 and in Georgia in 1791. The son learned blacksmithing, and, in 1763, settled on the

Susquehanna, in what was then Upper Paxtang township, Lancaster, now Dauphin county. On the 15th of August, 1775, he was commissioned second lieutenant of Capt. James Murray's company in the Fourth battalion of Associators, of Lancaster county. On the 28th of January, 1777, Lieut. Col. Cornelius Cox, of the battalion, ordered him to remain in the "Continental smith-shop" at Bristol. He served during the greater part of the Revolution, towards its close in command of a company of militia, when he returned to his farm. In the spring of 1793 he removed to Huntingdon, where he passed the remainder of his days. They had issue, save the last two, all born in Paxtang (surname Simpson):

'12.   i. *Rebecca*, b. April 8, 1777; m. John Patton.
      ii. *Margaret*, b. January 30, 1779; d. March 3, 1829; unm.
      iii. *James*, b. June 20, 1781; d. January 31, 1851, in Huntingdon, Pa.; was a surveyor, and elected commissioner of Huntingdon county, in 1819; was, in his younger days, an officer of the militia, and passed through all the grades from lieutenant to colonel.
      iv. *Martha*, b. February 15, 1786; m., May 6, 1806, George Anshutz, Jr., who removed to Pittsburgh, where they both died; and had issue (surname Anshutz): *George-S.*, *Margaretta*-S., m. Thomas Linford, *Oliver-R.*, *Edmund-Murray*, and *Theodore*.
      v. *Anna*, b. July 9, 1788; d. May 26, 1856, in Franklin township, Huntingdon county, Pa.; m. William Curry.
      vi. *Sarah*, b. September 10, 1791; d. s. p.
13.   vii. *Elizabeth-Isabella*, b. August 22, 1794; m. Daniel Africa.
14.   viii. *John*, b. June 21, 1798; d. July 19, 1872; m., first, Mrs. Elizabeth Ramsey; secondly, Mrs. Mary McAllister.

IX. LINDLEY MURRAY,[4] (Robert,[3] John,[2] John,[1]) b. in 1745 on the banks of the Swatara, in Lancaster, now Dauphin county, Pa.; d. February 16, 1826, at his residence near York, England. He received a good education, but having a dislike to mercantile pursuits, studied law, and was admitted to the bar at the age of twenty-one. The year after he married. His limited practice was temporarily interrupted by a visit to England, whither his father had preceded him in hope of benefitting his health. He returned to New York in 1771, and renewed the practice of law with marked success; tiring of it, however, when the Revolution broke out and New York was occupied by the British army, or having no sympathy with the cause of Independence, he removed to Islip, on Long Island, and entered a mercantile life. We have always given Lindley Murray credit for his religious principles as having precluded him from taking part in the struggle between the Colonies and the mother country, but in a letter in our possession, written by William Darby to his friend, Mrs. Anna Dixon, the true incentive is, perhaps, given. Mr. Darby was well acquainted with the men of his time—he was intimate with the patriots of the Revolution, and learned much of the inward history of the people, concerning whom, it is to be regretted, he did not give his reminiscences. William Darby was born in the same neighborhood, and was intimate with the Dixons and Roans, to the former of whom Murray was related, and through them learned more of him than biographers choose to tell. In the success and greatness of a man, we too often lose sight of the grave errors into which he may have fallen. But we are loath to dispel the bright halo which glimmers around the life of the celebrated grammarian. Sabine classes him among the Loyalists of the Revolution, and Darby, in contrasting him with his cousin, Robert Dixon, whose blood was the first Pennsylvania offering to the cause of Independence, speaks of Murray's taking sides with the enemies of his country. This we can easily understand. Surrounded by his religious friends whose peace principles would not allow them to take up arms—although many hundreds did, who were subsequently disowned for it—and in a city occupied by the king's troops, he himself says he had little faith in the successful resistance of the Colonies. It was thus he became a loyalist. His father's business and his own thrived, and the rule of England was sufficient for him. We venture the opinion that there were really few instances where religious principles made men Tories. Mercenary motives were generally at the bottom of it. It is to be regretted that Lindley Murray's silent influence should have been on the side of British oppression and tyranny. At the close of the war he had amassed a fortune, and, when peace had dawned, he sailed away from the land of his nativity and the home of liberty. His attachment to the home of his fathers, he said, "was founded on many pleasing associations. In particular, I had strong prepossessions in favor of a residence in England, because I was ever partial to its political constitution and the mildness and wisdom of its general laws. . . . . Only leaving my native country, there was not, therefore, any land in which I could cast my eyes with so much pleasure, nor is there any which could have afforded me so much real satisfaction as I have found in Great Britain. May its political fabric, which has stood the test of ages and long attracted the admiration of the world, be supported and perpetuated by Divine Providence." In 1784 he went to England, and, after visiting several localities, purchased a small estate at Holdgate, about a mile from York, upon which he resided until his death. Living in ease and retirement, he entered upon a literary life which proved a successful one, and has inscribed his name high upon fame's portals. In 1787 he published a small work entitled "The Power of Religion on the Mind," which passed through seventeen editions. His next work, and that by which he is principally known, was his "English Grammar," first published in 1795, and such was the unexpected demand for it that several editions were published during the same year. Following this, appeared "English Exercises," and a "Key," an abridgement of which treatises were published in one volume in 1797. His other writings are "The English Reader," with an "Introduction and Sequel," "The English Spelling Book," a new edition of his Grammar, "Exercises and Key," in two octavo volumes, a selection from Horne's "Commentary on the Psalms," and "The Duty and Benefit of Reading the Scriptures." Lindley Murray's educational publications were not alone confined to his mother tongue. He prepared two French works, "Introduction au Lecteur Francois" and "Lecteur Francois," which soon came into general use, were highly commended, and passed through a large number of editions. His life in England was a busy one, as it was an eventful one. No American who made a European tour failed to visit Holdgate. His personal appearance, his unassuming demeanor and his conversational powers excited in the minds of all visitors great admiration. Lindley Murray m., June 22, 1767, HANNAH DOBSON, d. in England and buried by the side of her husband at Holdgate. They had no children.

X. JOHN MURRAY,[4] (Robert,[3] John,[2] John,[1]) b. August 3, 1758; d. August 4, 1819, in the city of New York. He was known as "Quaker John;" was a member of the Manumission Society; a director of the New York hospital, and in 1811 vice-president of the New York Free School Society. He was deeply interested in the cause of education, and the meeting of prominent citizens of New York, which led to the organization of the old Public School Society, was held at his residence in Franklin Square. He m. CATHARINE BOWNE, sister of Walter Bowne, who was one time mayor of New York. They had issue:

 i. Robert-J., m. Elizabeth Colden; and had issue: *D.-Colden, Robert, Caroline, Mary*, and *Gertrude*.
 ii. Lindley, m. Elizabeth Cheeseman; and had *Lindley, Jr., John, Ann-Eliza, Catharine, Margaretta, Jane, Hannah, Joseph-K., William, Edward*, and *Mary-K.*; Lindley, Jr., m., and had *Lindley, Frank-T., John, Georgianna-T., Catharine-B., Grace, Louisa-T., Bertha*, and *Emily*; while John had a son *John*.
 iii. Mary, m. Dr. Perkins; and had issue (surname Perkins): *Benjamin*.
 iv. Susan, m. William Ogden; and had issue (surname Ogden): *Susan-Lindley*, m. Lindley Murray Hoffman.

XI. BEULAH MURRAY,[4] (Robert,[3] John,[2] John,[1]) b. in the city of New York; lived and died there; m. MARTIN HOFFMAN, of that city; one of New York's prominent early citizens. They had issue (surname Hoffman):

 i. Murray, b. 1792; d. 1878; m., first, Frances Burrall; secondly, Mary Ogden; and had issue: *Julia, Murray, William, Frances, Burrall*, and *Susan-Ogden*.
 ii. Lindley-Murray, b. 1794; m. Susan Lindley Ogden; and had issue: *Susan-Ogden, William-Ogden, Edward, Katharine*, and *Elizabeth*; Elizabeth Hoffman m. George M. Miller; and had issue (surname Miller): *Hoffman*, m. Edith McKeever, *Mary-L., Leverett-S., Elizabeth-H.*, and *Edith-M.*
 iii. Martin, b. 1796; m. Elizabeth Hale Gilman; and had issue: *Lindley-Murray, Emily, Martin, Arthur, Matilda, Leighton*, and *Serena*; Lindley Murray Hoffman m. Margaret

L. Ring (nee Mott); and had issue: *Louisa G., Emily, Virginia-Colden*, and *Martin*.

iv. *Anna-Maria*, b. 1797; m. Anthony R. Livingston.

XII. REBECCA SIMPSON,[5] (Margaret,[4] James,[3] William,[2] John,[1]) b. April 8, 1777, in Paxtang township, Lancaster county, Pa.; d. October 15, 1845, in Huntingdon, Huntingdon county, Pa.; m., April 16, 1801, JOHN PATTON, b. December 25, 1757, in Franklin county, Pa.; d. May 23, 1836, on his farm in Woodcock valley, Walker township, Huntingdon county, Pa. In his earlier years he resided in the town of Huntingdon, and was six times elected sheriff, and his term of service as principal and deputy extended over a period of twenty years; he was an efficient public officer. They had issue (surname Patton):

 i. *William-Moore*, b. February 16, 1803; d. August 9, 1871; m., in 1842, Rebecca Boal, of Ohio, and settled in Kentucky; and had issue (surname Patton): *George-Boal, William*, d. s. p., *William-A.*, and *Clara Bell*.

 ii. *John-Simpson*, b. June 15, 1806; d. August 30, 1850; resided a few years on the homestead farm; appointed collector of tolls on the canal, removed to Huntingdon; afterwards settling in Kentucky, where he died; m., September 1, 1836, Catharine Huyett; and had issue (surname Patton): *Elizabeth, Margaret-Murray, Caroline*, and *William-Penn*.

 iii. *Elizabeth*, b. June 30, 1808; d. March 31, 1811.

 iv. *James* (twin), b. June 30, 1808; d. September 16, 1836; m., March, 1832, Elizabeth Vandevander, daughter of Isaac Vandevander; and had issue (surname Patton): *Rebecca, Annie*, and *John*.

 v. *Joseph*, b. October 6, 1810; resides in Kentucky; was thrice married; m., first, January 9, 1840, Nancy Givin, daughter of John Givin; and had issue (surname Patton): *Ellen, John, James*, and *Silas*; by a second marriage there was issue: *William*, and *Joseph*; his second wife dying about 1857, he married again in 1864.

 vi. *Benjamin-F.*, b. November 26, 1812; resided in Altoona, Pa., and died there July 6, 1885; for many years in the mercantile business at Warrior's Mark, Pa., and served two terms as associate judge of Huntingdon county; m., January 23, 1836, Eliza Addleman; and had issue (surname Patton): *Rebecca, Ettie, Sarah, Emma, John-T., George-A., William*, and *Harry*.

vii. Rebecca-Simpson, b. March 14, 1815; d. December 13, 1862; m., December 24, 1840, James Campbell, of McConnellstown, Pa.; and had issue (surname Campbell): *Margaretta*, m. Dr. G. L. Robb, of Huntingdon, *Mary*, and *Caroline*.

viii. George-W., b. September 6, 1817; d. March 7, 1882, in the city of Philadelphia; buried at Altoona, Pa.; for several years was one of the lessees of Union Furnace, and manager at Blair Furnace, but removed to Altoona at an early day; in 1854 he was chosen the first chief burgess of that borough, and re-elected in 1855; in 1861 appointed postmaster, serving eight years, and in 1870 elected an associate judge; subsequently removing to Philadelphia; he was twice married; m., first, June 10, 1845, Mary B. Burket, d. March 28, 1856, and had issue (surname Patton):

1. *Thomas-Blair*, b. May 6, 1847; at Altoona.
2. *William-A*, b. October 21, 1849; assistant to the President of the Pennsylvania Railroad; m., December 13, 1876, Katharine Linn, dau. of John Linn, formerly of Perry county, Pa.; and had issue:
    a. *John-Linn*, b. October 13, 1883.
3. *John-Howard*, b. July 29, 1851; Pennsylvania railroad office, Altoona.

Mr. Patton m., secondly, December 19, 1861, Emma J. Hawksworth; and had issue:

5. *Mary-V.*, b. November 3, 1865.
6. *Margaret-Murray*, b. July 3, 1870; d. Dec. 15, 1889.

XIII. ELIZABETH ISABELLA SIMPSON,[5] (Margaret,[4] James,[3] William,[2] John,[1]) b. August 22, 1794, in the borough of Huntingdon; d. February 14, 1867, at Atsion, N. J.; buried in the cemetery at Huntingdon, Pa.; m., August 19, 1830, DANIEL AFRICA, b. 1794, at Huntingdon, Pa.; d. December 13, 1865, in his native town and there buried. His grandfather, Christopher Africa, emigrated from near Hanover, Germany, and at first settled at Germantown, Pa., subsequently removing to Hanover, York county, that State. He had two sons, Michael and Jacob. Michael Africa m. Catharine Graffius, of York, and in 1791 removed to Huntingdon. They were the parents of Daniel Africa. The latter was a man of prominence and influence in the community; was deputy surveyor for that county from 1824 until 1830, and for twenty-two years a justice of the peace. His knowledge of the law was much more thorough than that usually possessed by magistrates. He was familiar with many of the English and American decisions, especially with those of the Pennsylvania courts, and kept a book in which he noted a great number of important cases, many of these relating to the land laws. Daniel Africa and his wife had issue (surname Africa):

  i. Margaret-Murray, b. July 4, 1831; d. s. p.
14. *ii. John-Simpson*, b. Sept. 15, 1832; m. Dorothea C. Greenland

XIV. JOHN SIMPSON,[5] (Margaret,[4] James,[3] William,[2] John,[1]) b. June 21, 1798, in the borough of Huntingdon, Pa.; d. July 19, 1872. He was twice married; m., first, Mrs. ELIZABETH RAMSEY, d. April 14, 1852. They had issue (surname Simpson):

  i. John-Murray, a farmer; resides in Oneida township, Huntingdon county, Pa.
  ii. Anna-M.
  iii. Lydia-M.
  iv. George-A., was color-bearer of the 125th regiment, Pennsylvania volunteers, and killed at the battle of Antietam, September 17, 1862.
  v. James-Randolph, seriously wounded at Antietam; in 1866 elected prothonotary of Huntingdon county; now practicing law in the borough of Huntingdon, Pa.

John Simpson m., secondly, Mrs. MARY MCALLISTER. They had issue (surname Simpson):

  vi. Fannie, m. 1882.

XV. JOHN SIMPSON AFRICA,[6] (Elizabeth-Isabella,[5] [*Simpson*], Margaret,[4] James,[3] William,[2] John,[1]) b. September 15, 1832, in Huntingdon, Pa., where he resides. He was educated in the public schools and Huntingdon Academy. After leaving school he learned the practice of surveying and civil engineering with his father and uncle, James Simpson. His first work after completing his studies was with Samuel W. Mifflin, chief engineer in the locating of the Huntingdon and Broad Top railroad. In 1853 he was elected county surveyor. During the sessions of 1858 and 1859 he was one of the clerks of the State Senate, and in 1859 elected to the Legislature. In 1854 and 1855 he served as burgess of the borough, and in 1871 elected to the same office for three years. Under the Constitution of 1873, the department of Internal Affairs was organized, and Mr. Africa was appointed deputy secretary under Gen. William McCandless. "His knowledge and experience peculiarly qualified him for putting the new department into successful operation. The entire labor and responsibility of doing so devolved upon him, and it is well known to the people of the State how faithfully the duty was performed, and how creditably and honorably he acquitted himself in the important trust." In 1878 he was nominated by the Democratic State Convention for the head of that department, and although his vote was highly flattering, he failed of an election. Four years afterwards, in 1882, however, he was again nominated for the same position, and was elected for the term of four years. In 1880 President Hayes appointed him supervisor of the census for the Seventh district of Pennsylvania, comprising fourteen counties in the central part of the State. He was elected cashier of the First National Bank, of Huntingdon, in 1881, and served until he was sworn in as Secretary of Internal Affairs in 1883. In addition to these public and official duties, he has been identified with the leading business enterprises of his native town. Soon after the expiration of his term as Secretary of Internal Affairs in 1886, he was chosen president of the Union Trust Company, of Philadelphia, which position he still occupies. He is also a director in the First National Bank, of Huntingdon, Pa. From 1885 to 1890 he served as an officer in the Grand Lodge of Masons, of Pennsylvania, and in 1891 and 1892 was Grand Master. Mr. Africa m., January 1, 1856, DOROTHEA C. GREENLAND, d. November 15, 1889, daughter of Joshua Greenland, of Huntingdon. They had issue (surname Africa):

   i. Benjamin-Franklin, b. 1856; d. 1857.
   ii. Benjamin-Franklin (second), b. August 15, 1858; is treasurer and superintendent of the Gas and Electric Light Works, at Huntingdon, Pa.; m., November 5, 1885, by Rev. Robert J. Keeling, D. D., Susan I. Meyers, dau. of Benjamin F. Meyers, of Harrisburg, Pa.; and had issue:
      1. *John-Simpson*, b. September 18, 1886, in Harrisburg, Pa.

2. *Benjamin-Meyers*, b. July 11, 1888.

iii. *James-Murray*, b. April 11, 1863; a civil engineer, and chief engineer of the Pennsylvania Midland Railroad company; m., in Reading, Pa., June 1, 1893, Eleanor McKnight, dau. of Charles C. McKnight; and had issue:
  1. [*A dau.*), b. April 20, 1894; d. inf.
  2. *James-Murray*, b. May 21, 1895.

iv. *Walter-Greenland*, b. April 11, 1863; became a resident of Manchester, N. H., in June, 1887, where he is treasurer and superintendent of the People's Gas Light Company, treasurer and agent of the Manchester Electric Light Company, director of the Merchants' National bank, and chairman of the finance committee of the Board of Trade; m., in Huntingdon, Pa., November 17, 1887, Maud Cunningham, b. April 11, 1865, dau. of Robert M. Cunningham; and had issue:
  1. *Dorothea-C.*, b. November 18, 1888.
  2. *Esther-Bessie*, b. January 21, 1890.
  3. *Walter-Murray*, b. April 22, 1892.

v. *Bessie*, d. February, 1867, at Atsion, N. J.

NEVILLE AND CRAIG.

I. JOHN NEVILLE,[2] son of GEORGE NEVILLE,[1] and Ann Burroughs, who was a cousin of Lord Fairfax, was b. July 26, 1731, on the head waters of Occoquan river, Virginia. His father's residence is laid down on Governor Pownall's, and Fry and Jefferson's maps, also on map in Spark's "Life and Writings of Washington." On the map in Jefferson's Notes on Virginia," edition of 1787, it is laid down near the head of Bull Run, a branch of the Occoquan. He was an early acquaintance of Washington, and served with him in Braddock's expedition. He subsequently settled near Winchester, Frederick county, where he held the office of sheriff. He was in Dunmore's expedition of 1774. Prior to this he had made large entries and purchases of land on Chartier's creek, and built a house, now owned and occupied by Mrs. Mary Wrenshall, and was about to remove there when the Revolutionary troubles began. He was elected a delegate from Augusta county to the Provincial Convention of Virginia, which appointed George Washington, Peyton Randolph, and others to the first Continental Congress, but was prevented by sickness from attending. On the 7th of August 1775, the Provincial Convention of Virginia ordered him to march with his company and take possession of Fort Pitt. December 23, 1776, he was appointed a justice of Yohogania county court, but considering the distracted state of the country, occasioned by the boundary dispute, and his position as commandant at Fort Pitt, he prudently declined the appointment. He was colonel of the Fourth Virginia regiment in the Revolutionary war. Subsequent to the Revolution he was a member of the Board of Property, and of the Supreme Executive Council of Pennsylvania, and of the Pennsylvania Convention which ratified the Federal Constitution; he was also a member of the Convention which formed the Constitution of Pennsylvania in 1789-90. In 1791, at the urgent solicitation of the President and the Secretary of the Treasury, he accepted the appointment of Inspector of the Revenue in the Fourth Survey of the District of Pennsylvania, which he held until after the suppression of the Whiskey Insurrection and establishment of the supremacy of the laws of the United States. He was appointed agent, at Pittsburgh, for the sale of lands, under the act of Congress, passed May 18, 1796, entitled "an act for the sale of the lands of the United States in the Territory northwest of the Ohio, &c." He died on Montour's Island, now Neville township, Allegheny county, Pa., July 29, 1803, and was buried in the First Presbyterian churchyard, Pittsburgh. The inscription on his tombstone, now almost illegible, is as follows:

In memory of | GENERAL JOHN NEVILLE, | *who departed this life* | *July 29, 1803;* | *Aged 72 years and 3 days.* | *During his long life* | *he filled many important offices,* | *both* | *Civil and Military;* | *in the former, he was virtuous and disinterested;* | *in the latter, he was patriotic and brave.* | *He enjoyed* | *the friendship and confidence of the* | *illustrious Washington.* | *The day of his death witnessed the* | *most pleasing Tribute* | *that can be paid to the* | *memory* | *of a mortal,* | *The sincere regrets of his* | *friends* | *and the* | *tears* | *of the neighboring poor.*

General Neville was a consistent member of the Protestant Episcopal Church; and the first Episcopal church west of the Allegheny mountains was built at his expense, on the site of the present stone church at Woodville, Allegheny county, Pa. He m., August 24, 1754, WINIFRED OLDHAM, b. 1736, in Virginia; d. 1797, in Pittsburgh, Pa. She was descended from John Oldham, who emigrated to Virginia from England, in March, 1635. His son, Thomas Oldham, was the father of Col. Samuel Oldham, of Westmoreland county, Va., b. 1680; d. 1762; m. Elizabeth Newton, b. 1687; d. 1759. Their son, John Oldham, b. 1705, m. Anne Conway, and had *Winifred*, m. John Neville; *Mary-Ann*, m. Maj. Abraham Kirkpatrick, and Col. *William*, m. Penelope Pope. Maj. Abraham Kirkpatrick had three daughters; one of whom *Mary-Ann*, m. Dr. Joel Lewis, and had A. Kirk Lewis, and Mrs. Maria L. Bigham; *Eliza*, m. Christopher Cowan, and was the mother of Mrs. Mary Wrenshall, Mrs. Ebbs, and Mrs. Swartzwelder; *Amelia-Louisa*, m. Judge Shaler, and was the mother of Conway, Clarence,

Louisa-Amelia, and Augusta. Louisa A. Shaler was killed by a fall from a horse. Col. William Oldham, killed at St. Clair's defeat in 1791, m., in 1783, Penelope Pope, had *Abby*, who m. Samuel Churchill, and had Samuel B. Churchill, of Louisville, Ken. The children of General Neville were:

2.   *i. Presley*, b. September 6, 1755; m. Nancy Morgan,
3.   *ii. Amelia*, b. 1763; m. Major Isaac Craig.

II. PRESLEY NEVILLE,³ (John,² George,¹) b. September 6, 1755, at Winchester, Va.; d. December 1, 1818, at his residence near Neville, Clermont county, Ohio, thirty miles above Cincinnati. After graduating at the University of Philadelphia, with distinguished reputation for classical attainments, he entered the army in 1775, in the twentieth year of his age, as a lieutenant in the company commanded by his father, Gen. John Neville. He quickly rose to the rank of major, and, as such, became aid-de-camp to the Marquis de Lafayette. Similarity of feeling and manners created an ardent friendship between these accomplished, and, at that time, young officers, which continued uninterrupted, and retained Major Neville in the family of the Marquis two years. In January, 1780, the Fourth Virginia regiment, commanded by his father, Gen. John Neville, was ordered to Charleston, S. C., with Presley Neville as lieutenant-colonel. He was made prisoner at the surrender of Charleston, and returned thence to Virginia on parole, but was exchanged before the close of the war. Presley Neville took part in the battles of Trenton, Princeton, Brandywine, Germantown, and Monmouth. At Monmouth he had a horse killed under him. After his marriage, he moved to a property he owned on Chartier's creek, called Woodville. In 1792 he removed to Pittsburgh, where he resided until 1816. Presley Neville was always honored with the friendship of General Washington, and held many of the most confidential offices under the general and State governments. An obituary notice of him by Mr. Ormsby in the *Pittsburgh Gazette*, of December 18, 1818, says: "It falls to the lot of but few men to enjoy so great a degree of personal popularity, as has attended the subject of this notice through life. He was favored by Providence with the possession of an ample fortune, which enabled him to indulge to excess a benevolence as warm and as expansive as ever glowed in a mortal breast. It had a fault; it was too lavish for prudential maxims to mingle in its council, and too honorable to doubt the rectitude of its ardent impulses. Like most generous men, he suffered dearly for his liberality; but he repined not at this dispensation of Providence, nor repented of those acts which he performed with pleasure and reflected on with pride. He was admired by his equals, respected by his inferiors, and loved by all who knew him; the oppressed clung to him for support, and the prayers of the needy ascended to heaven in his favor. . . . . He breathed his last on the banks of the Ohio, not surrounded by all the comforts of life, for this would have been too great a happiness for an old soldier, but he drew his last sigh surrounded by his children, on the soil granted to him for his Revolutionary services. At the present day the remembrance of those services are of little value, except as a theme of pride to his descendants; but the future historian will rank him among those heroes to whom his country owes her independence." There are some incidents in the life of Louis Phillipe, connected with the Nevilles, so creditable to him, that they are here introduced: "About the year 1796 the Duke of Orleans, afterwards Louis Phillipe, King of France, accompanied by his two brothers, Montpensier and Beaujolais, came to the western country. On arriving at Pittsburgh, then a small village, they found one or two *emigres*, who had formerly filled prominent stations under the *ancienne regime*, but who were now earning a scanty subsistence in carrying on some little business of merchandise. One of them, the Chevalier Du Bac, proposed to General Neville, whose house was always the temple of hospitality, where he was in the habit of dining every Sunday, and at whose table and fireside the unfortunate *emigre* was sure to find a hearty welcome, to introduce the travelers. The general at first received the proposition with coldness. He said he had been a soldier of the Revolution, the intimate of Rochambeau and Lafayette, and, of course, entertained a feeling of the deepest respect for the memory of the unfortunate Louis, not as a monarch, but as a most amiable and virtuous man. He insisted that no good could spring from the infamous exciter of the Jacobins, the profligate Egalité. But, "mon Général," (said the chevalier, with a shrug of the shoulders, and most melancholy contortion of his wrinkled features,) "ils sont dans les grande misère, et 'ils out été chassé, comme nous autres, par ces vilains sans culottes." The chevalier knew his man, and the *bon hommie* of the general prevailed. "Eh, bien! chevalier, alez, rendre nos devoirs aux voyageurs, et qu'ils dinent chez nous demain." The strangers accepted his courtesy, and became intimate with and attached to the family of the kind-hearted American; the charms of the conversation of the Duke of Orleans, and his various literary attainments, soon obliterated for the moment the horrible career of his father from the minds of the hearers. The brothers, on quitting Pittsburgh, left a most favorable impression on the minds of the little circle in which they were received so kindly. The recollection of the amiable Beaujolais was particularly cherished; and when the news of his death in Sicily, a few years after, reached the West, the family of General Neville expressed the sincerest sorrow." Many years later the *Cincinnati Republican* says: "Immediately upon the landing of the Prince De Joinville in this city he inquired for Morgan Neville, expressed a desire to see him, and regretted to hear of his death. Louis Phillipe, the father of the young Prince, when an exile in this country, became acquainted with Morgan Neville, then a lad residing at Pittsburgh, and with the late General Neville, his father, into whose house the exile was hospitably received. Louis Phillipe had remembered this little kindness amid the varied and embarrassing scenes of his life, and gave in charge of his son, when coming to this country, to find out Morgan Neville and renew his acquaintance." A few years later, another son of the general, "Captain Frederick Neville, of the United States navy, happened to enter the port of Marseilles; Louis Phillipe hearing of it, sent for him and received him, with utmost kindness and attention, into his family." General Neville m., October 15, 1782, NANCY MORGAN, of whom Breckinridge, in his *Recollections of Persons and Places of the*

West, writing of Presley Neville, says: "He married the daughter of the celebrated General Morgan, an elegant and accomplished lady, who blessed him with an offspring as numerous and beautiful as the children of Niobe." They had issue (surname Neville):

 i. Morgan, b. December 25, 1783; d. March 1, 1840; attorney-at-law, author and editor of the *Pittsburgh Gazette;* about 1824 removed to Cincinnati and became secretary of an insurance company; m., March 6, 1811, Nancy Barker; and had issue:
  1. *Morgan-LaFayette*, m. a sister of Governor Dennison, of Ohio.
  2. *Julian*, d. July, 1882; a wealthy merchant of New Orleans before the Rebellion; an outspoken Union man, who was stripped of everything, and died poor.
  3. *John*, d. in New York.
  4. *Eugene*, d. s. p.
  5. *Cornelia*, m. Hon. James Graham, of New Orleans, member of Congress and historian; author of "Life of General Morgan."
 ii. Emily, b. February 15, 1786; d. February 5, 1821; m., November 5, 1807, Col. W. D. Simms, of Alexandria, Va.; and had issue (surname Simms):
  1. *Virginia*, m. Frank Taylor, of Washington, D. C.
  2. *Neville*, m. Miss McGuire.
 iii. Fayette, b. February 25, 1788; d. unm.
 iv. Elizabeth, b. November 18, 1789; m., January 24, 1810, James O'Hara, Jr.; no issue.
 v. Nancy, m. Maj. John Read, U. S. A.; and had issue (surname Read):
  1. Dr. *Robert*, d. in California.
  2. *Nancy*, m. Jesse Farmer.
  3. *Emily*, m., in 1863, Richard Oldham.
  4. *Winifred-Neville*, m. William L. Kidwell, of Missouri.
 vi. Fanny, m., first, Charles Simms, of Alexandria, Va.; secondly, Charles Wilkins, of Pittsburgh; and had issue (surname Wilkins): *Presley-Neville;* m., thirdly, Captain Forster; and had issue (surname Forster): *Rhoda.*
 vii. Presley, Jr., m. Olivia Kerr; and had issue:
  1. *Sarah*, m. Hugh Wilson, of Washington, Pa.
  2. *Frederick*, went to Texas.
viii. Edgar.
ix. Clarence.

x. Winifred, m., first, March 22, 1822, Major Matthew Magee, U. S. A.; secondly, Dr. Nathan Kouns, M. D.; and had issue (surname Kouns):
   1. Dr. *Jacob-Neville*, the great traveler.
   2. *Presley-Morgan*, d. in California.
   3. *Nathan-C.*, author, &c.
   4. Dr. *Ivan-Wisner*, deceased.
xi. Francis, lost on the United States sloop "*Hornet*" September, 1829.
xii. Ellen, d. 1842; m., 1831, James Burns; and had issue, with others (surname Burns):
   1. *Olivia*, m. Walter Brown, of Fort Leavenworth.
   2. *Winifred*.
xiii. Frederick. captain in U. S. navy; d. in Philadelphia, October 21, 1877.
xiv. Montimore, d. s. p.

III. AMELIA NEVILLE,[3] (John,[2] George,[1]) b. April 4, 1763, at Winchester, Va.; d. February, 1849, on Montour's Island, near Pittsburgh, Pa.; m., February 1, 1785, ISAAC CRAIG,[1] b. 1741, near Hillsborough, county Down, Ireland; d. May 14, 1826, on Montour's Island, and is buried in the graveyard of the First Presbyterian church, Pittsburgh. He emigrated to America in 1765, and settled in Philadelphia, where he became a master-builder. In November, 1775, he received an appointment as ranking lieutenant of marines in the navy then being fitted out, and in that capacity served ten months on board the Andrew Doria, commanded by the gallant and unfortunate Nicholas Biddle. While on the Doria, that vessel formed one of the squadron of Commodore Hopkins, which captured the two forts, Nassau and Montague, upon the island of New Providence, in the West Indies, capturing the governor and a large number of cannon and military stores, then much needed by the Americans, and subsequently used in the forts in Rhode Island and on the Delaware. On his return he received a captain's commission dated October 22, 1776. In the latter part of November the marines were ordered to join the army and do duty as infantry, and in that capacity, Captain Craig was present at the crossing of the Delaware, the capture of the Hessians at Trenton, and at the battle of Princeton. On the 3d of March, 1777, he was appointed a captain in a regiment of artillery then formed, under the command of Col. Thomas Proctor, in which he continued to serve until it was disbanded at the close of the Revolution. On the 11th of September, 1777, he was engaged in the battle of Brandywine, where he was severely wounded. The ensuing month he was at the battle of Germantown, and his company was one of those which cannonaded Chew's house, which was so gallantly defended by Major Musgrave. Having passed the ordeal of Valley Forge, early in the spring of 1778 Captain Craig and several other officers were ordered to Carlisle to learn the laboratory art, under the instruction of Capt. Isaac Coren, an officer of skill and experience. On the 29th of March, 1779, he was ordered to the command of the fort at Billingsport, on the Delaware, below Philadelphia. May 20th the regiment was ordered to Easton, and joined Sullivan in his expedition against the Six Nations, returning to Easton on the 18th of October following. The severe winter of 1779-80 he was with |the army at Morristown, N. J. On the 20th of April, 1780, Captain Craig was ordered to Fort Pitt with a detachment of artillery and military stores, where he arrived on the 25th of June. Here he continued in command of the artillery until the 29th of July, 1781, when he left his detachment for the Falls of Ohio (Louisville) to join General Clark in his intended expedition against Detroit. He returned to Fort Pitt the 26th of November. During his absence down the river, he had been promoted to the rank of major, from the 7th of October, 1781. In November, 1782, General Irvine received intelligence that the British had established a military post at Sandusky, and were about to establish one either at Cuyahoga or Grand river. He, therefore, ordered Major Craig to take with him the General's aid, Lieutenant Rose, and six active men, and proceed to Cuyahoga and Grand river, to ascertain whether the enemy were making such attempts. This order was eloquent in urging Major Craig to be cautious, and not be stimulated by his zeal for the service to venture too far, and concludes by saying: "One man falling into the hands of the enemy may not only ruin your whole present business, but also prevent future discovery." The major and his party started on their expedition on the 13th of November, taking with them one horse, with a supply of provisions. They crossed the Big Beaver river at its mouth. Thence they proceeded in a direction south of west, as if bound to the Indian town at the forks of Muskingum, pursuing that course until night, and then turned directly north, and traveled all night in that direction. This was done to mislead and elude the pursuit of Indians who may have followed them. When they arrived, as they supposed, within a day's march of the mouth of the Cuyahoga, they left one man with the extra provisions. It was the intention, upon rejoining this man, to have taken a fresh supply of provisions, and then proceed to examine the mouth of Grand river. General Irvine had in his instructions treated this as a point of less importance than the Cuyahoga, but yet worthy of attention. The weather proved very unfavorable after the separation, and the Major, with his party, was detained beyond the appointed time, and the soldier, with the horse, had disappeared; so that when they reached the designated place, weary and half-famished, they found no relief, and had before them a journey of more than one hundred miles through a hostile wilderness. The examination of Grand river had to be abandoned, and the party was compelled to hasten back to Fort Pitt. Variable and tempestuous weather made the return journey laborious and painful. Pursuing the most direct course homeward, before they reached the Conoquenessing, the weather became extremely cold, and they found the stream frozen over, but the ice not firm enough to bear the weight of a man. They resorted to the following expedient as the best the circumstances allowed: A large fire was kindled on the northern bank, and when it was burning freely, the party stripped off their clothes; one man took a heavy bludgeon to break the ice, while each of the others followed with portions of the clothes and arms in one hand and a fire-brand in the other. Upon reaching the southern bank of the stream, these brands were placed together and a brisk fire soon raised, by which the party dressed themselves. Upon reaching the Cranberry plains, they were delighted to find there a hunting party, consisting of Capt. Uriah Springer and other officers, and some soldiers from Fort Pitt. Here, of course, they were welcomed and kindly treated. They reached the fort on the 2d of December, and Major Craig reported that there was no sign of occupancy at the mouth of the Cuyahoga. At the very time the party were crossing the Conoquenessing, November the 30th, 1782, the Treaty of Peace between the United States and Great Britain was signed at Paris. The treaty was ratified by Congress on the 19th of April, 1783, and the disbandment of the army soon followed. Major Craig and Col. Stephen Bayard formed a partnership to carry on the mercantile business in Pittsburgh, and to deal in lands. On the 22d of January, 1784, by articles of agreement, they purchased from the Penns *the first ground that was sold within the limits of Pittsburgh*. In September, 1787, an act was passed by the Legislature incorporating the Presbyterian congregation of the town of Pittsburgh; eleven trustees were named, of whom six were officers of the Revolutionary army, Major Craig being one. In the spring of 1788, Major Craig retired from business to Farm Hill, adjoining the farms of his father-in-law, and brother-in-law Col. Presley Neville. He remained there but a short time. When the National Government was organized, his old commander and true friend, Gen. Henry Knox, was appointed the first Secretary of War, and in February, 1791, offered him the situation of quartermaster and military storekeeper at Pittsburgh, then a frontier town; this he accepted and held until after the election of Jefferson. Major Craig, like the great majority of the officers of the Revolution, belonged to the party of which Washington and Hamilton were the leaders, and not very long after Jefferson came into power he was removed from office. After the declaration of war in 1812, his services were again sought for, when the knowledge acquired from Captain Coren at Carlisle was found valuable in preparing munitions of war for the northwestern army. After this war he removed to Montour's Island, where he died. Major Isaac Craig had two brothers, JAMES CRAIG, who resided in Philadelphia, and died there of yellow fever, August 20, 1798; had a daughter Eliza, who m. Edward Gray; their daughter, *Elizabeth Gray*, m. Hon. John P. Kennedy, Secretary of the Navy, under Fillmore; JOHN CRAIG, the other brother, was a

Loyalist; he resided in New York; his daughter, Ann Craig, who was very wealthy, died in Jersey City in 1875. Major Craig had a sister, JANE, who never married; she died in New York. His father was agent for the earl of Hillsborough, and died at Hillsborough. Major Craig and his wife, Amelia Neville, had issue, beside three children d. in infancy, (surname Craig):

    i. *Harriet*, b. December 26, 1785; d. May 29, 1867; m., July 5, 1809, John H. Chaplin; and had issue (surname Chaplin):
        1. *William-Craig*, b. April 10, 1810; d. April 25, 1856; lieutenant commander U. S. navy; m., July 31, 1839, Sarah J. Crossan.
        2. *Amelia*, b. December 1, 1812; m. Thomas L. Shields.

4. ii. *Neville-B.*, b. March 29, 1787; m. Jane Ann Fulton.
    iii. *Matilda*, b. March 12, 1788; d. ——— —; m., December, 1811, Reese E. Fleeson; and had issue (surname Fleeson):
        1. *Reese-C.*, d. 1863; owner and editor of *Pittsburgh Dispatch*.
        2. *Isaac-Craig*, d. s. p.
        3. *William*, d. s. p.
        4. *Thomas-Plunket*.
        5. *Eugene*, d.
    iv. *Presley-Hamilton*, b. May 28, 1789; d. August 8, 1848; surgeon U. S. A.; medical director of the army under General Taylor in Mexico.
    v. *Henry-Knox*, b. March 7, 1791; d. December 7, 1869; general and chief of ordnance, U. S. A.; m. Maria Bethune Hunt, d. July 13, 1888; daughter of Major Hunt, of the Massachusetts Line in the Revolutionary war, and a descendant of Peter Faneuil, who, in 1742, presented Faneuil Hall to the city of Boston; and had issue (surname Craig):
        1. *Benjamin-Faneuil*, M. D., deceased, of the Smithsonian Institution.
        2. *John-Neville*, captain, U. S. A.; d. 1885.
        3. *Jane-Bethune*, m. General Hawkins, U. S. A.
        4. *Presley-Oldham*, lieutenant, U. S. artillery; volunteered in Hunt's battery at first battle of Bull Run, and killed in that action.
        5. *Mary*, deceased; m. General Hunt.
        6. *Amelia-Neville*.
        7. *Belle*, m. ——— Berlin, U. S. A.

 vi. John-Neville, b. February 7, 1793; d. July 21, 1870; unm.
 vii. William, b. November 26, 1794; d. young.
 viii. Isaac-Eugene, b. March 3, 1797; a lieutenant in U. S. engineer corps; fell in a duel with Lieutenant Maul, at Bay St. Louis, July 25, 1819; the duel was caused by remarks of Lieutenant Maul regarding a lady of Carlisle, Pa.; both fell at the first fire. The *Pittsburgh Gazette* of September 28, 1819, says: "in a farewell letter addressed to his brother the minute before he met his antagonist, he expressed his repugnance to the practice, but, like the lamented Hamilton, he submitted, because otherwise he feared his usefulness would be destroyed."
 ix. Oldham-G., b. March 14, 1800; d. suddenly of heart disease at Cologne, Germany, October 4, 1874, when on his way to visit his eldest son; he was for many years teller in the bank of Pittsburgh; m. Matilda Roberts, daughter of Hon. Samuel Roberts, and had issue (surname Craig):

  1. *Isaac-Eugene,* an artist, residing at Florence, Italy.
  2. *Samuel-Roberts,* d.
  3. *Caroline-Roberts,* deceased; m. Rev. William Ely, of Germantown, Pa.
  4. *Morgan,* d.

 x. Amelia-Neville, b. July 7, 1801; d. October 22, 1877; unm.

IV. NEVILLE B. CRAIG,[2] (Isaac,[1]) b. March 29, 1787, in Colonel Bouquet's redoubt; d. March 3, 1863. He was educated at the famous Pittsburgh Academy and Princeton College; admitted to the bar August 13, 1810; was city solicitor from 1821 to 1830; owner and editor of the *Pittsburgh Gazette* (which he converted to the first daily in Pittsburgh) from 1829 to 1841. About this time he was elected to the Legislature; subsequently, an investigation was made in regard to members supplying themselves with merchandise at the expense of the State, showing that "every member, except Mr. Craig, of Allegheny, had received a share." "The Centennial volume of the First Presbyterian church of Pittsburgh" styles him "the historian *par excellence* of the city he adorned." His publications are authorities; they are "The Olden Time," two volumes, 1846-7; "History of Pittsburgh," 1851; "Memoir of Major Robert Stobo," 1854; "Life and Services of Major Isaac Craig," 1854, and "An Exposure of a few of the many Misstatements in H. M. Brackenridge's History of the Whiskey Insurrection," 1859.

He was a member of the First Presbyterian church, and of the American Antiquarian and other societies. Mr. Craig m., May 1, 1811, JANE ANN FULTON, b. August 11, 1789, in Harrisburg, Pa.; d. January 14, 1852, in Pittsburgh, Pa.; daughter of Henry and Isabel Fulton, (*see Fulton record*). They had issue (surname Craig):

5. i. *Isabel-Wilson*, b. September 25, 1812; m. Rev. Henry G. Comingo.
6. ii. *Emily-Neville*, b. June 29, 1814; m. Lieut. Alfred Beckley, U. S. A.
    iii. *Mary-Jane*, b. March 23, 1816; d. April 22, 1834, at Washington, Pa.; m. Rev. William Orr.
    iv. *Harriet-Matilda*, b. Sept. 26, 1817; d. Jan. 14, 1850.
    v. *Margaret-Fulton*, b. July 16, 1820; d. August 22, 1821.
7. vi. *Isaac*, b. July 18, 1822; m. Rebecca McKibbin.
    vii. *Henry-Fulton*, b. August 5, 1824; d. December 12, 1824.
8. viii. *Eliza-Gray*, b. August 27, 1828; m. Alexander M. Wallingford.
9. ix. *Annie-Neville*, b. July 11, 1830; m. John S. Davison.
    x. *Presley-Neville*, b. July 12, 1833; d. April 22, 1834.

V. ISABEL WILSON CRAIG,[3] (Neville-B.,[2] Isaac,[1]) b. September 25, 1812; m., April 10, 1838, Rev. HENRY C. COMINGO, D. D., b. February 2, 1809, near Harrodsburg, Ky.; d. December 1, 1861, at Steubenville, O. His family were a part of a Dutch colony coming from Adams county, Pa., and before that from New York. He graduated at Centre College, Ky., in 1832, being chosen valedictorian of his class. After graduation he became a tutor in the college. In 1834 he entered Princeton Theological Seminary, and was licensed to preach by the Presbytery of New Brunswick, February 3, 1836. Stopping to preach in Steubenville, O., on his way home to Kentucky, he was detained by the ice in the river, and called to the pastorate of the First Presbyterian church, and ordained May 24, 1837. Here he continued twenty-five years. In 1855 his health being seriously impaired, he went abroad for nearly a year. On the 17th of November, 1861, he preached a sermon on the twenty-fifth anniversary of his coming to the church; preached again the next Sabbath, and the next, the 1st of December, died. He was a member of the Boards of Directors of Washington College, Pa., and the Western Theological Seminary, in Allegheny City, Pa. He was a man of deep piety, broad sympathies, eminently genial disposition, and great usefulness. A memorial of Dr. Comingo was published by his church, and a more extended one afterwards privately printed by his widow ; also, a sketch of him is given in Nevin's Cyclopedia of the Presbyterian Church. They had issue (surname Comingo) :

 i. Henry, b. February 25, 1839 ; d. April 25, 1839.
 ii. Edward-Gray, b. June 22, 1848; d. March 22, 1884.
 iii. Neville-B.-Criag, b. March 8, 1850.

VI. EMILY NEVILLE CRAIG,³ (Neville-B.,² ISAAC,¹) b. June 29, 1814 ; d. March 9, 1845, at Fayette C. H., Va.; m.; December 13, 1831, ALFRED BECKLEY, a native of Lexington, Ky.; appointed second lieutenant Fourth artillery, July 1, 1823 ; first lieutenant, July 31, 1831 ; resigned October 24, 1836. They had issue (surname Beckley) :

 i. John, b. March 26, 1833 ; m. Margaret Price; and had issue: *Mary-Emily*, d. s. p, *Bettie-Dixon, John*, and several who died in infancy.
 ii. Neville-Craig, b. December 5, 1834 ; d. October 16, 1885 ; m. Elizabeth O. Love ; and had issue : *Emily, Robert-Whitton, Annie Davison, Neville*, and *Mary Alice*.
 iii. Henry-Martyn, b. November 28, 1836 ; m. Mary Johnson ; and had issue : *Annie-Isabel*, d. s. p., *Gilbert-Lee*, and *Clarence*.
 iv. William-Gregory. b. July 29, 1839 ; m. Margaret Esther Duncan ; and had issue : *Emily-Virginia, Laura Steel, Walter-Lee, Emily-Neville*, and *John-Duncan*.
 v. Isaac-Craig, b. March 2, 1841 ; m. Mary Duncan ; and had issue : *Clinton-Theodore, Robina, Edward-Gray-Comingo*, and *Sarah*.
 vi. Alfred, b. March 5, 1843 ; m. Emma Virginia Carper ; and had issue : *Annie-Davison, Eliza-Wallingford*, and one child d. in inf.
 vii. Emily-Neville, b. January 12, 1845 ; d. May 12, 1848.

VII. ISAAC CRAIG,³ (Neville-B.,² Isaac,¹) b. July 18, 1822. Few men in Pennsylvania are deserving of more grateful recognition than Mr. Craig. As author and historian he is an authority on the history of Western Pennsylvania, and the Ohio Valley ; and the historical societies of Pennsylvania, Chicago, Buffalo, Virginia, and the Aztec Club have testified their appreciation of his services by electing him a member of their organizations. Mr. Craig is a vice-president of the Pennsylvania Historical Society, member of Pennsylvania State Society of the Cincinnati, and the Pennsylvania Society of the Sons of the Revolution. His life has been devoted to study and research. He resides in Allegheny City. Mr. Craig m., January 12, 1847, REBECCA MCKIBBIN, daughter of Hon. Chambers McKibbin. They had issue (surname Craig):

    i. Neville-B., b. December 1, 1847; m. Margaret Sullivan.
    ii. Jane, b. July 14, 1849; d. July 24, 1857.
    iii. Emily-Neville, b. May 11, 1851; d. August 28, 1851.
    iv. Winifred-Oldham, b. November 10, 1852.
    v. Chambers-McKibbin, b. December 26, 1854.
    vi. Henry-Fulton, b. November 21, 1858; d. July 29, 1861.
    vii. Isaac, b. December, 27, 1860.
    viii. Rebecca, b. May 1, 1863.
    ix. Presley-Neville, b. April 2, 1865; d. December 17, 1870.
    x. Oldham-Gray, b. September 3, 1869.

VIII. ELIZA GRAY CRAIG,³ (Neville-B.,² Isaac,¹) b. August 27, 1828; d. March 12, 1881; m., December 30, 1851, ALEXANDER M. WALLINGFORD, b. at Harrodsburg, Ky. They had issue (surname Wallingford):

    i. Annie-Craig, b. October 20, 1852; d. July 25, 1853.
    ii. Presley-Neville, b. July 8, 1854; d. July 19, 1854.
    iii. John, b. April 17, 1856; d. September 15, 1856.
    iv. Neville [twin], b. April 17, 1856; d. September 17, 1856.
    v. Emily-Neville, b. May, 1864; d. August 19, 1867.

IX. ANNIE NEVILLE CRAIG,³ (Neville-B.,² Isaac,¹) b. July 11, 1830; m., May 1, 1855, JOHN S. DAVISON, b. in New York City. They had issue (surname Davison):

    i. John-Roberts, b. September 25, 1856; d. July 2, 1868.
    ii. Neville-Craig, b. January 3, 1860.
    iii. Frederick, b. June 11, 1862.
    iv. Mary-Louisa, b. April 6, 1864.

ORTH OF LEBANON.

I. BALZER or BALTHASER ORTH,[1] b. May 5, 1703; emigrated from the Palatinate, Germany, to Lebanon township, Lancaster, now Lebanon county, Pa., about the year 1725. On the right bank of the Danube, about fifteen miles east of Vienna, is the village of Orth, containing about three thousand inhabitants. In the year 1170 Hartneid von Orthe purchased the village and estate surrounding it, founded a church, and erected a castle. It remained in the family for several successive generations, when the proprietor, about the close of the seventeenth century, sold out and removed to Moravia, one of the northern provinces of Austria. The family cannot be traced from Moravia to the Rhine. Balzer Orth had warranted to him, on the 25th of November, 1735, three hundred acres of land in Lebanon township, "whereon he has been long settled." He d. October 20, 1788, at the extreme age of eighty-five years. He m., in 1729, ANNA CATHARINA ROEHMER, who d. October 19, 1789, in Lebanon county, Pa. They had issue, all born in now Lebanon county:

      i. Jacob, b. September 3, 1730; d. 1731.
2.   *ii. Adam*, b. March 9, 1733; m. Anna Catharina Kucher.
3.   *iii. Balthaser*, b. June 14, 1736; m. Rosina Kucher.
4.   *iv. Elizabeth*, b. August 14, 1739; m. Andrew Albright.

II. ADAM ORTH,[2] (Balzer,[1]) b. March 9, 1733, in Lebanon township, Lancaster, now Lebanon county, Pa.; d. November 15, 1794, in Lebanon township; buried in Hebron Moravian graveyard, near Lebanon, Pa. He was brought up amid the dangers and struggles of Pennsylvania pioneer life; received the limited education of the "back settlements," and yet, by self-culture and reading, became a man well-informed and of more than ordinary intelligence. During the French and Indian war he commanded the Lebanon township company in Rev. John Elder's ranging battalion. In 1769 he was one of the commissioners of the county of Lancaster. During the

Revolution he was early identified with the movement, and, although well advanced in years, assisted in the organization of the associated battalions, and was appointed sub-lieutenant of the county March 12, 1777. Upon the formation of the county of Dauphin he served as a representative in the General Assembly in 1789 and 1790. He was opposed to the adoption of the Federal Constitution, and took an active part in the Harrisburg Conference of 1788. For a long period he operated and owned New Market forge, which, at his death, he bequeathed to his son, Henry. One of the pioneers in the manufacture of iron in Lebanon county, a man of energy and indomitable perseverance, we are glad to preserve this record of him and his services. Colonel Orth m., May 24, 1757, by Rev. George Weiser, ANNA CATHARINA KUCHER, b. January 12, 1738; d. September 17, 1794; daughter of Peter and Barbara Kucher,* of Lebanon township, Lancaster county, Pa. They had issue:

    i. Elizabeth, b. June 3, 1758; d. 1764.
    ii. John, b. March 9, 1760; d. July 9, 1764.
    iii. Rosina, b. March 19, 1762; m. —— Smith.
    iv. Joseph, b. April 3, 1764; d. January 29, 1769.
    v. Maria-Elizabeth, b. April 5, 1766; m., first, John Keller; secondly, —— Shaffner.
5.   *vi. Catharine*, b. October 31, 1767; m. John Gloninger.
6.   *vii. Regina*, b. October 9, 1770; m. David Krause.
7.   *viii. Christian-Henry*, b. March 24, 1773; m. Rebecca Rahm.
    ix. Johanna, b. January 25, 1777.

III. BALZER ORTH,² (Balzer,¹) b. June 14, 1736, in Lebanon township, Lancaster, now Lebanon county, Pa.; d. October 6, 1794, in Lebanon township. He served in the war of

---

*PETER KUCHER, of Lebanon township, d. January, 1775, leaving a wife Barbara, and children as follows:

    i. Christopher, m. Mary —— ——.
    ii. Anna-Catharina, b. January 12, 1738; m. Adam Orth.
    iii. Rosina, b. March 19, 1741; m. Balthaser Orth.
    iv. Peter.
    v. George-Michael, b. February 10, 1747; d. March 18, 1748.
    vi. Gottleib, b. April 8, 1753; d. October 3, 1776; unm.
    vii. Barbara, m. John Stone; and had issue (surname Stone): *Joseph*, and *Margaret*.

the Revolution, and was very prominent, as is to be learned from the diary of the Moravian church at Hebron, now Lebanon, recently published. He m., April 26, 1763, in Hebron church, near Lebanon, by Rev. Zahm, ROSINA KUCHER; b. March 19, 1741; d. April 3, 1814, in Lebanon township, and buried beside her husband in Hebron churchyard. They had issue:

8.   i. *Gottleib*, b. February 23, 1764; m. Sarah Steiner.
    ii. *Andreas*, b. February 11, 1765; d. October 16, 1788; buried at Hebron.
   iii. *Johann-Jacob*, b. October 11, 1766; d. November 6, 1790; m., and left issue.
9. iv. *Maria-Barbara*, b. November 9, 1768; m., first, Matthias Morrett; secondly, Martin Light.
     v. *Joseph*, b. December 19, 1770; d. April 18, 1848; m. Elizabeth Giesman.
    vi. *Justina-Elizabeth*, b. March 3, 1773; d. December 2, 1775.
   vii. *Christina-Julianna*, b. April 22, 1775; m., and left issue.
  viii. *Johanna-Catharine*, b. December 21, 1777; m., October 8, 1797, Jacob Widener, of Chambersburg, Pa.

IV. ELIZABETH ORTH,[2] (Balzer,[1]) b. August 14, 1739, in Lebanon township, Lancaster, now Lebanon county, Pa.; d. June 4, 1830, at Lititz, Lancaster county, Pa. She m., November 19, 1766, ANDREW ALBRIGHT (Albrecht), b. April 2, 1718, at Zella, near Sahl, in Thuringia, Germany. He was a gunmaker by trade, and after practicing his business in Halberstadt, Prussia, in 1741, became armorer to a regiment from that town, which served in Silesia and Bohemia during the war of the Austrian succession. In 1750, after hearing Count Zinzendorf preach at Halle, he came to America with a band of young Moravians, and commenced his trade at Christian's Spring in Northampton county. Here his guns became famous, and they were among the first manufactured in the Province. Later, in the service of the Moravian Church he became instructor of music at Nazareth Hall, and in 1766, presided over the Sun Inn at Bethlehem. In 1771 he removed to Lititz, where he resumed the making of guns. During the war of the Revolution, Lancaster county became the center of a brisk production of arms; and it is a fact that more guns were manufactured there than in all the Colonies together. Others engaged in the business were Judge William Henry, the Lefevres, Vondersmiths, etc., of Lancaster town. Mr. Albright d. April 19, 1802, at Lititz, Pa. He left issue (surname Albright):

    i. Andrew, b. February 28, 1770, at Bethlehem, Pa.; d. November 24, 1822, at Sunbury, Pa.; went to Lewisburg, Pa., where he resided until elected sheriff of Northumberland county, when he removed to Sunbury; was elected a member of the Assembly in 1808, and in 1813 appointed by Governor Snyder an associate judge of the county; in October preceding his death he had been elected a State Senator; was noted for his integrity and very popular throughout Buffalo Valley; was twice married, first, to Catharine Rahm; b. July 20, 1769; d. March 9, 1810; daughter of Conrad Rahm and Catharine Weiser; m., secondly, the widow of Jacob Youngman and mother of John G. Youngman, of Sunbury; they had no issue.

    ii. John-Henry, b. August 5, 1772, at Lititz, Pa.; d. January 27, 1845, at Nazareth, Pa.; he was educated at the parochial school at Lititz, and learned gunsmithing with his father; subsequently sent to the workshop of William Henry (who had been an apprentice of his father), at Nazareth, where he completed his trade; after his marriage settled at Lancaster, but in 1796 removed to Chambersburg, and in 1798 to Shippensburg, where he was successful in business; desiring to live among the Moravian brethren, he removed to Gnadenhütten, O., but his health failing him, he returned to Pennsylvania, residing for a time in Warwick township, near Lititz, and finally, in 1816, to Nazareth, where he died; was twice married; he m., first, March 27, 1795, Barbara Hubley; d. at Nazareth, Pa.; dau. of Bernard Hubley, of Lancaster, Pa.; and had issue (surname Albright):

        1. *Maria-Eliza*, b. February 27, 1796, at Lancaster; d. September 6, 1842, at Bethlehem; m. Rev. John Peter Kluge, a Moravian missionary to the West Indies; and left issue.

        2. *Susan*, b. August 28, 1797, at Chambersburg; d. March 18, 1887, at Chester, Pa.; m. John Deemer; and left issue.

        3. *Maria-Barbara*, b. June 21, 1799, at Shippensburg; d. March 5, 1842, at Hyde Park, Pa.; m., March 23, 1817, William Henry, grandson of Judge William Henry, of Revolutionary fame, and son of

William Henry, founder of the Boulton gun works in Northampton county; formed the first company to develop the iron and coal beds of the Lackawanna Valley; and was one of the founders of the city of Scranton; and left issue.

4. *Andrew*, b. March 28, 1802; d. February 23, 1837, at Moontown, near Nazareth; unm.
5. *Bernard-Hubley*, b. November 8, 1804; d. August 28, 1806.
6. *James*, b. August 29, 1806; d. September 13, 1827, at Nazareth.
7. *Thomas-John*, b. July 5, 1808, at Gnadenhütten, O.; d. February 9, 1890, at St. Louis, where he carried on an extensive gun trade; m. Elizabeth Brodhead; and they left issue.
8. *Anna-Sophia*, b. June 25, 1810, at Lititz; d. September 2, 1873, at Nazareth; m. Rev. John C. Brickenstein, a Moravian minister, and noted educator who came to America about 1824; his ancestors originally came from Holland to East Friesland in the Sixteenth century, under the name of Bruysteen; this was translated into Brückenstein when the family removed to the city of Magdeburg, Prussia—in defence of which against Count Tilly, an ancestor distinguished himself during the "Thirty Years' War;" they left issue.
9. *Joseph-Jacob*, b. September, 23, 1811, at Warwick, Lancaster county; d. January 12, 1888, at Scranton; was an early iron-master in Northampton county, Pa., and Botetourt county, Va.; afterwards removing to Scranton, Pa., where he was sales agent for the Delaware and Hudson Canal Company, president of a national bank, and a pioneer in the anthracite coal trade to the West; he m. Elizabeth Sellers; his children, *Joseph-J.*, of Buffalo; *Henry*, of Utica; *Mrs. Raymond Bennell*, and *Mrs. James W. Archbald*, of Scranton, in his memory, erected the Albright Memorial Library Building, and presented the same to the city of Scranton.
10. *Aquila-Ernest*, b. July 6, 1813, at Warwick, Pa.; d. January 28, 1871, at Livonia, N. Y.; m., and left issue.

John Henry Albright m., secondly, January 11, 1831, at Nazareth, Pa., Catharine Louisa Beck; and they had issue, all b. at Nazareth.

11. *Oliver Benjamin*, b. December 10, 1831; d. April 24, 1862, at Nazareth.
12. *Augustus-Alexander*, b. March 31, 1834; d. January 14, 1842.
13. *Jacob-Theodore*, b. May 3, 1836; resides at Bethlehem, Pa.
14. *Caroline-Amelia*, b. May 8, 1839; resides at Bethlehem, Pa.

iii. *Jacob*, b. 1774, at Lititz, Pa.; emigrated to the West at an early period.

iv. *Susan-Elizabeth*, b. 1778, at Lititz; m. John Philip Bachman, a pioneer organ builder.

v. *Gottfried*, b. 1782, at Lititz, Pa.; served in the war of 1812; m., and left descendants.

V. CATHARINE ORTH,[3] (Adam,[2] Balzer,[1]) b. October 31, 1767, in Lebanon township, Lancaster, now Lebanon county, Pa.; d. June 17, 1848, in Lebanon, Pa.; m. JOHN GLONINGER, b. September 19, 1758, in Lebanon township, then Lancaster county, Pa.; d. January 22, 1836, in Lebanon, Pa.; with his wife buried in the Reformed church graveyard; son of Philip and Anna Barbara Gloninger. His ancestors were among the earliest settlers in that locality. His father, born in 1719, died December 11, 1796; his mother, born March 12, 1831, died September 23, 1810, and are both buried in the old Reformed church cemetery at Lebanon. John Gloninger received most of his instruction from the pastor of the Reformed church, who was also teacher of the school. When the Revolution broke out he served as a subaltern officer in the Associators. Towards the close of the war he was in command of a battalion of militia. Upon the organization of the county of Dauphin he was appointed by the Supreme Executive Council, county lieutenant, May 6, 1785. He was delegate to the Constitutional Convention of 1790, a representative to the General Assembly in 1790, resigning to accept the position of State Senator, which office he also in time resigned, preferring the quiet of home life to the vexations of legislative experience. He was appointed by Governor Mifflin—a warm personal friend—one of the associate judges of the county of Dauphin, August 17, 1791. This position, owing to the distance and the inconvenience of travel, he afterwards resigned. However, upon the erection of the new county of Lebanon, in 1813, he was commissioned one of the associate judges, an office he filled many years. Few men had more extended influence, and were more highly respected and beloved than Judge Gloninger. They had issue (surname Gloninger):

 i. *Philip*, b. February 17, 1788, in Lebanon, Pa; d. there September 10, 1816. Having acquired the necessary preparatory education in the schools of his native town, he entered Dickinson College, where he early completed his literary course. Subsequently he studied divinity under the Rev. C. L. Becker, D. D., of Baltimore, one of the most distinguished theologians and pulpit orators of the age. At a meeting of the Reformed Synod, held at Germantown, in the autumn of 1808, Mr. Gloninger was present, and presented a call from the Reformed church at Harrisburg, with the request that he be "placed over them as their pastor." At the same synod he was ordained. Beside the congregation at Harrisburg there were four others in his charge—Shoop's, Wenrick's, Middletown, and Hummelstown. He soon became prominent in his church, and was appointed by the Synod one of the first two delegates sent by that body to the Synod of the Dutch Reformed church. Owing to "bodily infirmities," he resigned his charge in June, 1814. He returned to Lebanon, where he died. He was a man of superior pulpit talents, naturally gifted, and reared under circumstances highly favorable to the development of his moral and intellectual endowments, became distinguished as a preacher, and early attained a prominent position among his ministerial brethren. He was a faithful pastor, and our paternal grandmother, who was one of his parishioners, in her four score years, spoke very tenderly of the youthful preacher, Gloninger, so dearly beloved and highly esteemed. He m., in 1810, Eliza Clark. The widow afterwards married Lieut. Robert H. Hammond.

10. ii. *John-W.*, b. September 23, 1798; m., first, Mary Ann Hassinger; secondly, Catbarine Arndt.
 iii. *Cyrus*, b. 1804; d. December 22, 1821.

VI. REGINA ORTH,[3] (Adam,[2] Balzer,[1]) b. October 9, 1770, in Lebanon township, then Lancaster county, Pa.; d. November 3, 1847, in Lebanon, Pa.; m. DAVID KRAUSE, b. August 30, 1752, in Lebanon township, Lancaster, now Lebanon county,

Pa.; d. December 22, 1820, in Lebanon, Pa.; son of Andrew Krause, a native of Prussia, a physician and an early settler in Lebanon township, and his wife Barbara. David Krause was a farmer by occupation. During the Revolutionary war he was an active participant, commanded a company of Associators in the Jersey campaign of 1776, and the campaign around Philadelphia in 1777; subsequently commissary of Colonel Greenawalt's battalion. He was elected a member of the Assembly from Dauphin county in 1785, and under the Constitution of 1790 served in the House of Representatives from 1797 to 1799. From 1795 to 1797 he was one of the commissioners of Dauphin county. He was afterwards appointed by Governor Snyder one of the associate judges of the county of Lebanon, holding the position at his death. They had issue (surname Krause):

  i. Catharine, b. March 20, 1788; d. June 3, 1864; m. Jacob Greenawalt, (*see Greenawalt record*).
  ii. Elizabeth, b. September 23, 1796; d. April 23, 1847; m. Frederick Boas, (*see Boas record*).
11. *iii. John*, b. December 17, 1798; m. Elizabeth G. Lineaweaver.
12. *iv. David*, b. November 2, 1800; m. Catharine Orr.

VII. CHRISTIAN HENRY ORTH,[3] (Adam,[2] Balzer,[1]) b. March 24, 1773, in Lebanon township, Lancaster, now Lebanon county, Pa.; d. 1816, in the city of Baltimore, Md.; in life went by the name of Henry, dropping Christian. He received a good English education, and was brought up in the iron business. Upon the death of his father he became the owner of New Market forge, but, being elected sheriff of the county of Dauphin, commissioned October 17, 1797, like the vast majority who have followed him in that office, he became financially shipwrecked. In 1801 he was elected State Senator, serving until 1804, when he positively declined further continuance in office. Governor Snyder appointed him flour inspector of the port of Philadelphia in January, 1809, but he resigned this office in April following, when he entered mercantile pursuits in Philadelphia. He remained in that city until about the commencement of the late war with England, when he removed to Baltimore, and had there established a successful business as a merchant, when he suddenly died, at the age of forty-three. Mr. Orth m., in 1794, REBECCA RAHM, b. November 22, 1773; d.

December 31, 1843, at Harrisburg, Pa.; daughter of Conrad Rahm and Catharine Weiser. They had issue:

 18. *i. Catharine*, b. January 1, 1795; m., first, John Whitehill; secondly, Col. William Piper.

  ii. Adam-Henry, b. 1798; d. October 15, 1833, in Harrisburg, Pa.; studied law, and was admitted to the Dauphin county bar at the November term, 1822; he held the office of district attorney for Dauphin county in 1827 and 1828, and, for several years, in addition to the duties of his profession, he was transcribing clerk of the House of Representatives; he m., May 3, 1832, Elizabeth Cox, b. 1813; d. January 13, 1836; daughter of John B. Cox, of Estherton, and had one son, *Adam*, who died young.

 14. *iii. Rebecca*, b. 1800; m. Luther Reily.

  iv. Henry, b. 1803; d. 1821.

  v. William, b. 1806; d. 1824.

 15. *vi. Caroline*, b. 1810; m. John O. Witman.

 16. *vii. Edward-Lawrence*, b. 1814; m. Martha Cummins Kerr.

VIII. GOTTLEIB [GODLOVE] ORTH,[3] (Balzer,[2] Balzer,[1]) b. February 23, 1764, in Lebanon township, then Lancaster, now Lebanon county, Pa.; d. 1831, in Lebanon, Pa.; m., November 3, 1795, SARAH STEINER, b. 1773; d. 1834. They had issue:

  i. Balzer, b. August 10, 1796; m., and left issue.

  ii. Rosina, b. September 30, 1798; m. John Behm.

  iii. Andrew, b. February 1, 1801; d. June 20, 1825.

  iv. Henry, b. May 20, 1803; m., first, Sarah Fox, of Harrisburg, Pa.; secondly, Maria Stein; no further knowledge.

  v. Rebecca, b. 1805; d. June 18, 1805.

  vi. Adam, b. May 8, 1808; m. Frances Seibert; nothing further is known of him.

 17. *vii. Gottleib (Godlove) Steiner*, b. April 22, 1817; m., first, Sarah E. Miller; secondly, Mary A. Ayres.

IX. MARIA BARBARA ORTH,[3] (Balzer,[2] Balzer,[1]) b. November 9, 1768, in Lebanon township, Pa.; d. May 14, 1851, at the residence of John Egle, near Decatur, Ill.; was twice married; first, to MATTHIAS MORRETT, a Huguenot, who died in November, 1795, leaving issue (surname Morrett):

  i. Elizabeth, b. November 13, 1791; d. March 15, 1879; m., October 25, 1812, John Egle, b. March 19, 1788; d. February 6, 1863, near Decatur, Ill.; and had issue (*see* Egle record).

Mrs. Morrett m., secondly, MARTIN LIGHT, of Lebanon, Pa. They had issue (surname Light):
   ii. *Orth*, d. at Lebanon, Pa.
   iii. *Sarah*, m. Samuel Rice.

X. JOHN W. GLONINGER,[4] (Catharine,[3] Adam,[2] Balzer,[1]) b. September 23, 1798, at Lebanon, Pa.; d. March 10, 1874, in his native town. He received his education at the principal schools of Lebanon and Harrisburg, completing it in the city of Baltimore. In 1815 he returned home, and commenced the study of medicine with Dr. King. Early in 1816 he went to Philadelphia, and became a private pupil of Professor Dorsey, then in the height of his fame, at the same time attending lectures in the medical department of the University of Pennsylvania and at Blockley Hospital. In 1817 he was elected a member of the Philadelphia Medical Society. He continued his studies in Philadelphia until the death of Professor Dorsey, which occurred in 1818, when he went with the majority of Doctor Dorsey's private pupils to New York. Here he entered the office of the distinguished Professor Hosack, at the same time attending lectures in the College of Physicians and Surgeons, where he graduated April 1, 1819. He continued his studies in the hospitals of New York and Philadelphia, and early in 1820 returned to Lebanon, where he commenced the practice of medicine. There he soon took a leading position as a physician and surgeon, and maintained it for thirty years. As a general practitioner he was careful, attentive, and distinguished for his accuracy of diagnosis; as a surgeon he was eminent, but his specialty was diseases of the eye, and as an oculist he ranked among the best in the country, being particularly successful in operations for cataract. For the first twenty years of his professional career he was a frequent contributor to the medical journals. Many of the articles show that he was not only a careful observer but a close student, and that he was keeping pace with the progress of medical science. In 1823 he was elected a member of the Pittsburgh Medical Society; in 1826 made a Fellow of the University of New York, and Jefferson Medical College, the same year, conferred upon him the honorary degree of M. D. In 1838 he was elected an honorary member of the New York State Medical Society, and in 1841 the University of Maryland conferred the honorary degree of M. D. upon him, the University of Pennsylvania doing the same in 1848. In March, 1841, he was elected president of the Lebanon bank, a position which he held until January 14, 1867, when he declined a re-election. He always took a deep interest in the church of his fathers, and was mainly instrumental in remodeling the First Reformed church, at Lebanon, about 1844, and later in the founding and building of St. John's church. He freely contributed of his means to all church enterprises, and for many years was a trustee of Marshall College, and also one of the founders and trustees of the Lebanon Academy. Dr. Gloninger was twice married ; m., first, December 25, 1820, MARY ANN HASSINGER, of Philadelphia, who died in February, 1846. She was a woman of much culture and refinement, and the mother of all his children. They had issue (surname Gloninger) :

 i. Eliza-H., b. August 10, 1825 : m., May 14, 1848, David B. Marshall, b. October 30, 1823, at Annville, Lebanon county, Pa.; d. June 29, 1861, at Lebanon, Pa., son of Dr. John Marshall and Elizabeth Behm. He received an excellent education at Mount Airy Academy, and in early manhood entered the office of his father as a student of medicine, attended lectures in the medical department of the University of Pennsylvania, from which institution he graduated in the spring of 1844. After graduation he began the practice of his profession in connection with his father at Annville, where he remained three years, subsequently practicing at Reading one year, when he permanently located at Lebanon. He soon acquired an extensive and lucrative practice, and took high rank in the profession. Endowed with strong natural talent, good judgment, and strong powers of observation and application, he needed only the opportunities which a large practice gave him to enable him to prove his ability as a practitioner, and to maintain a firm hold upon the affections of the people with whom he came in contact, and among whom he labored. He died in the prime of life. Possessed of a generous nature, he was greatly esteemed and respected by all, and his loss deeply lamented in the community as that of a valuable and upright citizen. They

had five children, only one of whom survives (surname Marshall):
  1. *Robert-L.*, resides at Lebanon, Pa.
18. ii. *Cyrus-Dorsey*, b. March 13, 1824; m. Julia A. Beaumont.
    iii. *Matilda*, b. December 12, 1825; m. John Wetherill, Jr., of Philadelphia.
    iv. *David-Stanley*, b. March 28, 1828; graduated in medicine in 1849 from University of Pennsylvania; m. Mrs. Abigail Smith; and had issue (surname Gloninger): Dr. *Ellwood, John-P.*, an attorney-at-law, and *Lizzie-Mar*, all of Philadelphia.
    v. *Catharine-Alice*, b. April 15, 1832; m. Dr. A. H. Light, of Lebanon; and had issue (surname Light):
        1. *Ralph-Hutchinson.*
        2. *Matilda-Gloninger.*
        3. *Warren-Gloninger.*
        4. *Helen-Mar.*

Dr. Gloninger m., secondly, June 15, 1847, CATHARINE ARNDT; d. August 8, 1885, at Lebanon, Pa.

XI. JOHN KRAUSE,[4] (Regina,[3] Adam,[2] Balzer,[1]) b. December 17, 1798, in Lebanon, Pa.; d. December 27, 1866, in Lebanon, Pa. He received a good English education, and at different periods was intrusted with official positions in the State. He was chief clerk of the Auditor General's office under the administration of Governor Shulze; chief clerk of the Treasury under Governor Porter, and was held in high esteem by the heads of departments for his integrity and capability. He served as a member of the State Legislature from 1834 to 1836, and discharged his duty with signal ability. In social life he was genial and attractive, and always a high-toned Christian gentleman. Mr. Krause m., June 2, 1825, ELIZABETH GILBERT LINEAWEAVER, b. September 5, 1804; d. August 26, 1862, in Lebanon, Pa.; daughter of Peter Lineaweaver and Susanna Gilbert. They had issue (surname Krause):
    i. *Amelia-E.*, b. February 18, 1826; m., January 13, 1848, John Weidman Mish, b. April 22, 1822, in Lebanon, Pa.; son of John Bickel Mish* and Maria Weidman. He read

---

* JOHN BICKEL MISH, son of Jacob Mish and Catharine Bickel, was b. January 12, 1791, at Harrisburg, Pa.; d. December 15, 1837, at Lebanon, Pa. He was educated at the Harrisburg private schools and the academy, and studied medicine with Dr. Samuel Agnew, then one of the leading physicians in the State. He attended lectures at

law with his uncle, Jacob Barge Weidman, and was admitted to the Lebanon bar at the August term, 1845. In 1850 he was elected district attorney of Lebanon county. In 1856, at the organization of the Lebanon Gas Light Company, was chosen secretary and treasurer, and continues to hold that position. Served as vice-president of the Lebanon National Bank; afterwards president of the Lebanon Dime Saving's Bank, and subsequently vice-president and cashier of the First National Bank, from which he retired June 5, 1885. He served as borough treasurer several years, and during his term of office succeeded in refunding two hundred thousand dollars of seven per cent. loan at four per cent. He resides at Lebanon, Pa.; they had issue (surname Mish):

1. *John-Krause*, b. August 3, 1849; d. Sept. 7, 1850.
2. *Matilda-Kline*, b. December 17, 1852; m. Charles H. Killinger; and had issue (surname Killinger):
    a. *Amelia-Krause*, b. February 22, 1880; d. October 18, 1884.
    b. *Catharine-Hittel*, b. December 11, 1883.
3. *Mason-Physick*, b. July 20, 1854; m. Carrie Stackhouse.
4. *William-Weidman*, b. March 18, 1858.
5. *Elizabeth-Krause*, b. July 7, 1861; d. April 17, 1862.
6. *Robert-Coleman*, b. June 11, 1863.
7. *John-Weidman*, b. April 11, 1867.

the University of Pennsylvania, and graduated therefrom in 1816. He began the practice of his profession at Jonestown, where he remained some four or five years. About the year 1821 he located in the town of Lebanon, where he continued the practice of medicine until the close of his life. He was prothonotary of the county in 1837, and at the same time serving as chief burgess of the borough during the "shin-plaster" era. As a physician he devoted his life to the work, and was exceedingly humane and philanthropic in his profession—highly respected and appreciated in the community. Dr. Mish m., about 1816, Maria Weidman, daughter of Capt. John Weidman, of the Revolution, b. May 10, 1793; d. in 1866, in Lebanon; they had issue (surname Mish):

i. *John-Weidman*, m. Amelia E. Krause.
ii. *Physick-Bickel*, m. Catharine Hammond, sister of Col. David Hammond.
iii. *Catharine-Elizabeth*.
iv. *Charles-Carroll;* studied medicine and graduated from the University of Pennsylvania in 1848; is in the active practice of his profession at Lebanon, Pa.; he m. Martha Lower, daughter of William Lower, of Philadelphia.

XII. DAVID KRAUSE,⁴ (Regina,³ Adam,² Balzer,¹) b. November 2, 1800, in Lebanon, Pa.; d. June 13, 1871, in Norristown, Pa. He was educated under Rev. Mr. Ernst, of the Lutheran church at Lebanon, and subsequently studied law with Hon. Jonathan Walker, of Pittsburgh, and there admitted to the bar. He returned to Lebanon and began practice. He went to Harrisburg as the private secretary of Governor Shulze, and was admitted to the Dauphin courts, August 15, 1825. He was appointed Deputy Attorney General in August, 1826, and re-appointed in 1829. From 1825 to 1826, with Gen. Simon Cameron, he published and edited the *Pennsylvania Intelligencer*. He was elected a member of the House of Representatives in 1835 and 1836. On the election of Governor Porter, in 1839, he took editorial charge of the *State Journal*, which he conducted with much ability. In January, 1845, a vacancy occurring in the Montgomery and Bucks county judicial district, Mr. Krause was appointed to that bench. He filled the position acceptably and honorably, but, in 1851, when the judiciary became elective, he positively declined the office. He then retired to private life. In 1862, and again in 1863, upon the invasion of Pennsylvania by the Confederates, he volunteered as a private soldier in the Pennsylvania militia, although then in the sixty-third year of his age. Judge Krause m., in September, 1826, CATHARINE ORR, of Philadelphia; b. September, 1800; d. December, 1875, at Norristown, Pa. They had issue (surname Krause):

    i. Emily-Regina, b. 1827; d. in infancy.
    ii. Annie, b. 1829; d. in infancy.
    iii. Annie-E., b. February 16, 1830.
    iv. Emily-C., b. March, 1833; d. September 24, 1854.
    v. Mary, b. February 7, 1835; m., October, 1867, Mahlon Preston; b. January, 1839, in Caln, Chester county, Pa.; son of Isaac C. Preston and Mary Price; he was educated at Greenwood Dell Academy; studied medicine with Dr. J. B. Wood, of West Chester, and graduated in 1861 from the Homeopathic Medical College of Pennsylvania, located at Philadelphia; in 1862 located at Norristown, where he continues in the practice of his profession; and had issue (surname Preston):
        1. *Frederick-Hahnemann*, b. September 7, 1868.

2. *Catharine-Krause*, b. April 7, 1872.
3. *Emily-Krause*, b. March 18, 1875.

vi. *Frederica*, b. March 3, 1837; m. Henry Orth Witman, (see XIV).

vii. *David*, b. December, 1840; appointed first lieutenant, Fourteenth infantry, May 14, 1861; captain, July 31, 1863; brevet major, March 13, 1865, for gallant and meritorious service in the battle of Gettysburg; subsequently promoted major; d. September 12, 1885, at his post, Fort Sully, Dakota; was unm.

viii. *William*, b. April, 1844; graduated from West Point; appointed second lieutenant; and first lieutenant, Nineteenth infantry, June 23, 1865; transferred to Thirty-seventh infantry, September 21, 1866; transferred to Third infantry, August 11, 1869; subsequently promoted to captain; m., October 1, 1879, Alice Higgins, of Montana.

XIII. CATHARINE ORTH,[4] (Henry,[3] Adam,[2] Balzer,[1]) b. January 1, 1795, in now Lebanon county, Pa.; d. July 25, 1844. She was twice married; m., first, November 30, 1820, JOHN SANDERSON WHITEHILL; b. November 12, 1793, in the Pequa settlement, Lancaster county, Pa.; d. August 18, 1829; son of George and Abigail Whitehill.* They had issue (surname Whitehill):

i. *George*, b. July 4, 1822; resided at Hopewell, Bedford county, Pa.; m. Mary Roberts; and had issue, *Emma, Edward, Luther*, and *Ella*.

ii. *Henry*, b. August 18, 1825; d. October 31, 1856.

iii. *Rebecca*, b. August 14, 1829; m., March 2, 1854, James Elder, (see *Elder* record).

Mrs. Whitehill m., secondly, in October, 1834, WILLIAM PIPER, of Bedford county, Pa., b. 1784; d. February, 1853; son of Col. John Piper, of the Revolution, and his wife Elizabeth Lusk. He represented Bedford county in the Legislature

---

*GEORGE WHITEHILL (1760–1821) and ABIGAIL (1762–1825), his wife; they had issue (surname Whitehill):

i. *John*, b. April 26, 1788; d. September 30, 1790.

ii. *James-Scull*, b. December 27, 1789; d. 1799.

iii. *Nancy*, b. November 4, 1791; d. 1794.

iv. *John-Sanderson*, b. November 12, 1793; d. August 18, 1829; m. Catharine Orth.

v. *Nancy* (second), b. March 21, 1797; d. 1801.

vi. *Eleanor*, b. October 8, 1800; m. Philip Frazer.

of Pennsylvania ; commanded a regiment of militia during the war of 1812-14, and was Adjutant General of the State during the administration of Governor Ritner. He was a remarkable athlete. They had issue (surname Piper):

 iv. Luther-Reily, b. October, 1835 ; severely wounded in the battle of Fredericksburg, December 13, 1862, from the effects of which he died January 1, 1863.
 v. William (twin), b. October, 1835 ; d. in infancy.

XIV. REBECCA ORTH,[4] (Henry,[3] Adam,[2] Balzer,[1]) b. about 1800, in Harrisburg, Pa.; d. October 15, 1854; m., in 1820, LUTHER REILY, b. 1794, in Myerstown, Pa.; d. February 20, 1854, in Harrisburg, Pa.; son of Capt. John Reily,* of the army of the Revolution, and his wife, Elizabeth Myer. He studied medicine with Dr. Martin Luther, a prominent physician of that period, and located at Harrisburg; served as a medical officer in the war of 1812-14 ; became quite popular in political affairs, and was elected to the Twenty-fifth Congress of the United States. Preferring his professional life to that

---

*JOHN REILY was born at Leeds, England, on the 12th of April, 1752. His father, Benjamin Reily, emigrated soon after, and was a gentleman of some note in the Province of Pennsylvania. Receiving a classical education, the former began the study of law, and was admitted to the bar on the eve of the Revolution. Accepting a commission as captain in the Twelfth regiment of the Pennsylvania Line, subsequently (1778) transferred to the Third regiment, he served with valor and distinction, and was severely wounded at Bonhamton, N. J., being shot through the body. Returning home he slowly recovered, when he resumed the practice of his profession. He was present and took part in the first term of the Dauphin county court, in May, 1785. In 1795 he published at Harrisburg "A Compendium for Pennsylvania Justices of the Peace," the first work of that character printed in America. Captain Reily d. at Myerstown, May 2, 1810. He m., at Lancaster, on May 20, 1773, by Rev. Thomas Barton, of the Episcopal Church, Elizabeth Myer, the daughter of Isaac Myer, the founder of Myerstown, Lebanon county, b. April 2, 1755 ; d. April 2, 1800. They had a large family. Captain Reily was not a brilliant orator, but was perfectly reliable as a lawyer, and had an extensive practice at the Lancaster, Berks, and Dauphin courts. He was a tall, courtly gentleman, and an ardent Whig of the Revolutionary era ; was a polished writer, and a manuscript book of literary excerpts in the possession of his descendants shows a refined and cultivated taste.

of a public one, he positively declined further honors, and devoted the remainder of his days to that calling in which he was so successful, and on which he shed a bright lustre. They had issue (surname Reily):

 i. Catharine, b. September, 1822; d. July, 1823.
 ii. Rebecca-Elizabeth, b. 1824; d. August 2, 1882.
 iii. Mary-Emily, b. 1827; d. September 1, 1889, at Spring Lake Beach, N. J.; buried at Harrisburg, Pa.; m., December 28, 1854, George W. Porter, M. D., of Harrisburg, Pa.; son of David R. Porter, Governor of Pennsylvania; he studied medicine, and graduated from the medical department of the University of Pennsylvania in 1851; located at Harrisburg, and was engaged in the active practice of his profession up to the time of his appointment by President Buchanan, in 1857, as postmaster—a position which he filled until 1861; resides at Harrisburg, Pa.; and had issue (surname Porter):

  1. *Rebecca-Reily*, b. October 10, 1855; m., October 18, 1892, William Wesley Trout, of Spring Lake, N. J.; and had issue (surname Trout):
   a. Elsie-Porter, b. September 20, 1895.
  2. *George-W.*
  3. *Caroline-Reily*, m. Melancthon S. Shotwell; and had issue (surname Shotwell):
   a. George-Porter, b. June 9, 1889.
   b. David-Rittenhouse, b. June 1, 1895.
  4. *Josephine*, m., June 7, 1883, William Buehler Hammand, son of Charles Elliot Hammond; and had issue (surname Hammond):
   a. George-Porter, b. October 28, 1885.
   b. Emily-Elizabeth, b. September 27, 1888.
   c. Helen-Goodwin, b. December 20, 1893.
  5. *Emma-Wagner*, m. John M. Poyer.
  6. *Elizabeth-Reily*, m. Thomas G. Hunter.
 iv. John-Whitehill, b. 1830; d. March 20, 1860; m., April 30, 1858, Catharine Elder Doll (*see Elder record*); and had issue (surname Reily):
  1. *Rebecca-Elizabeth*, m. Walter J. Bradshaw.
  2. *John-Whitehill*, m. Helen Margaret Boas.
 v. George-Wolf, b. 1834; d. February 8, 1892, at Harrisburg, Pa.; educated at Yale College; studied medicine, and graduated from the medical department, University of Pennsylvania, 1857; in 1870 elected president of the Harrisburg National Bank, and relinquished the practice of his profession, holding the position until his

death; he m., February 5, 1861, Elizabeth H. Kerr, daughter of William M. Kerr; and had issue (surname Reily):
1. *Luther*, b. November, 1861; d. 1862.
2. *William-Kerr*, b. 1862; d. 1863.
3. *Elizabeth-H.*, m. Edward Bailey.
4. *George-Wolf*.
5. *Caroline*, m., November 6, 1895, James Bradshaw Bailey.
6. *Mary-Emily*.
vi. *Caroline-Matilda*, b. 1836; resides at Harrisburg.

XV. CAROLINE ORTH,[4] (Henry,[3] Adam,[2] Balzer,[1]) b. ———, 1810, in Harrisburg, Pa.; d. January 10, 1848, in Harrisburg, Pa.; m., April 17, 1828, JOHN OTTO WITMAN, b. January 11, 1802, in Reading, Pa.; d. April 12, 1884, in Halifax, Dauphin county, Pa., son of Benjamin Witman and Margaret Otto. He was educated at private schools and the Reading Academy. He was a clerk in the Surveyor General's office under Gabriel Hiester, during Governor Shulze's administration; studied medicine under Dr. Luther Reily, attended lectures at University of Pennsylvania in 1826-27; was physician to the Dauphin county almshouse in 1827-28; received the honorary degree of M. D. from the University of Maryland in 1843; commenced the practice of medicine in Harrisburg in 1827, and continued till 1832, when he removed to Gratz, Dauphin county, Pa., where he practiced till 1837, when he returned to Harrisburg and associated himself with Doctors Luther Reily and E. L. Orth, which continued until 1840; then removed to Halifax, Dauphin county, Pa., where he continued in an active and extensive practice till the fall of 1870, when bodily infirmity compelled him to relinquish all except office-work. They had issue (surname Witman):

i. *Henry-Orth*, b. January 22, 1830; d. February 13, 1892, at Washington, D. C.; educated in the public schools, and at Capt. Alden Partridge's Military and Scientific Institute, Harrisburg; studied medicine with his father and graduated from Jefferson Medical College, Philadelphia, in 1851; for a number of years practiced his profession at Halifax; subsequently removing to Harrisburg, Pa.; in 1891 appointed medical examiner to the Pension Bureau at Washington City; during the war

for the Union served as lieutenant of Company E, Sixth regiment, P. V. M., and captain of Company C, Thirty-sixth regiment, P. V. M.; he m., October 11, 1866, Frederica Krause, b. March 3, 1837; daughter of Judge Krause, of Norristown, Pa., (see XI); and had issue (surname Witman):
1. *Bertha*, b. August 8, 1867; m. George V. Nash.
2. *Caroline*, b. October 23, 1869.
3. *Ralph*, b. June 6, 1872.
4. *Alice*, b. February 7, 1875.

ii. *Luther-Reily*, b. 1836; d. August 6, 1864, at Chattanooga, from wounds received at Peach Tree Creek, near Atlanta, Ga., July 20, 1864; appointed sergeant major of Forty-sixth regiment, Pa. Vols., May 1, 1862; promoted adjutant February 12, 1863.

iii. *Edward-Lawrence*, b. 1838; entered the service during the Rebellion as first lieutenant of Company D, Forty-sixth regiment, Pa. Vols., September 2, 1861; promoted captain in September, 1862; promoted lieutenant colonel Two Hundred and Tenth regiment, P. V., September 26, 1864; commissioned colonel April 12, 1865; mustered out with regiment May 30, 1865.

iv. *Rebecca-Catharine*, b. 1844; m., April 26, 1871, Robert H. Moffitt, D. D. S.; reside at Harrisburg, Pa.; and had issue (surname Moffitt):
1. *Luther-Reily*, b. December 28, 1872; graduated from Princeton College, 1893.
2. *John-Jordan*, b. August 13, 1874.
3. *Robert-Hopkins*, b. March 22, 1876.
4. *Caroline-Reily*, b. January 13, 1878.
5. *George-Reily*, b. November 15, 1879.
6. *Rebecca-Charlotte*, b. February 8, 1881.
7. *Thomas-Robinson*. b. February 26, 1884.

Dr. John O. Witman m., secondly, February 14, 1851, MARGARET S. REED.

XVI. EDWARD LAWRENCE ORTH,[4] (Henry,[3] Adam,[2] Balzer,[1]) b. January 4, 1814, in the city of Baltimore, Md.; d. April 15, 1861, in Harrisburg, Pa. His father dying while the son was in early life, the mother removed to her former home, Harrisburg, where the boy was carefully brought up. He received the education of the borough schools and entered the Harrisburg Academy where he pursued the higher branches. He subsequently began the study of medicine with his brother-in-law, Dr. Luther Reily, afterwards attending the lectures at Jefferson Medical College, Philadelphia, from which institution he graduated March 12, 1834. Locating at Harrisburg, he began the practice of his profession in partnership with Doctor Reily, which continued until the death of the latter. Few practitioners became as successful as these noted physicians were, and none at the Capital were ever so deservedly popular. For seven years after the death of his life-long friend, Doctor Orth continued his professional life, enjoying not only a large practice, but the confidence and love of his numerous patients. As a physician, he was learned, skillful, self-sacrificing, sympathetic, and faithful. In the community he was greatly beloved for his unassuming, gentle, and gentlemanly demeanor. In the language of a contemporary, "he was a man of fine culture, a careful, attentive, and conscientious physician, quiet and unobtrusive in manner." For many years he was one of the the trustees of the Presbyterian church; was a director of the Harrisburg bank, and served in the borough council. Doctor Orth m. MARTHA CUMMINS KERR, daughter of the Rev. William Kerr, of Donegal, and Mary Wilson, (*see note to Alricks record, p. 22*). They had issue:

    i. Mary-Wilson, m., September 3, 1860, Jacob Fridley Seiler, son of Jacob Seiler and Susan Fridley; b. at Harrisburg, Pa.; he graduated from Yale College in 1854; conducted a private school several years, and since 1860 has been principal of the old Harrisburg Academy; they had issue (surname Seiler):
        1. *Martha-Orth*.
        2. *Susan*.

   ii. Henry-Luther, studied medicine with Dr. George W. Reily; served some time as a medical cadet in the army; graduated from medical department, University of Pennsylvania, in 1866; in 1866 was appointed surgeon of the Northern Central Railroad Company, and in 1873 surgeon of the Pennsylvania Railroad Company, positions which he filled until 1891; from 1873 to 1884 he was president of the Board of U. S. Pension Surgeons at Harrisburg; in 1889 was appointed a trustee of the Pennsylvania State Lunatic Hospital; and August 28, 1891, elected superintendent and physician of the same institution; elected president of the State Medical Society in 1892; Dr. Orth m., June 30, 1868, Elizabeth Bridgeman Dixon, daughter of Joseph Shipley Dixon and his wife Sarah Edwards Bridgeman; and had issue:

1. *Edward-Lawrence.*
2. *Anna-Shipley-Dixon.*
3. *Roberta-Elizabeth.*

 iii. James-Wilson, m. Bertha E. Ross, d. s. p.
 iv. Rebecca-Reily.

XVII. GODLOVE STEINER ORTH,[4] (Godlove,[3] Balzer,[2] Balzer,[1]) b. April 22, 1817, in Lebanon township, Lebanon county, Pa.; baptized June 1, 1817, by Rev. Abram Reinke, of the Moravian Church; d. December 16, 1882, in Lafayette, Ind. He was educated at Pennsylvania College, Gettysburg; studied law, and upon his admission to the bar in 1839, removed to Lafayette, Ind. From 1843 to 1850, continuously, he served as a member of the State Senate of Indiana; elected president of that body in 1845, and thus became acting lieutenant governor of the State. He was presidential elector on the Taylor and Fillmore ticket, 1848, and a member of the Peace Conference in 1861. In 1862 he entered the service as captain in the Seventy-sixth regiment, Indiana volunteers, being placed in charge of the United States ram "Horner," and assigned to duty on the Ohio river. He was elected to the Thirty-eighth, Thirty-ninth, Fortieth, and Forty-first Congresses from his district, and to the Forty-third Congress from the State at large. Upon the adjournment of the latter Congress, he was appointed and accepted the position of United States Minister to Vienna, having previously declined the mission to Brazil, tendered him by President Grant, filling the duties of that position with remarkable ability. It is stated that upon his first presentation to the emperor, the conversation, agreeably to Mr. Orth, was conducted in German. After a short conversation, the emperor asked, "Tell me, in what part of Germany were you born?" Mr. Orth replied, "Not in Germany, but in Pennsylvania, in the United States." "But," said the emperor, "you speak the pleasing accent of the Rhine." This shows that the so-called Pennsylvania German is a dialect of the great German language of Europe, from whence it was brought, and where, to this day, it is living in all its freshness and vigor as it did centuries ago. On his return from Vienna, Mr. Orth was elected to the Forty-sixth Congress, and in 1879 received the complimentary vote of his party for United States Senator against Hon. Daniel W. Voorhees, and was re-elected to the Forty-seventh Congress as a Republican. In August, 1882, he was unanimously nominated by his party for representative in the Forty-eighth Congress. He was a man of warm and sincere friendship, of sturdy honor, and of clear and vigorous intellect. Few men had a wider and more steadfast acquaintance and friendships, none more honest in his duties to man and to his country. He was devotedly and tenderly attached to his family and fireside, caring more for those than the honors of success and the applause of the world. He left a name honorable to his memory, dear to his family, and a part of the history of his State and Nation. Upon the death of Matthew Carpenter, he used language in his eulogy fitly applicable to his own life, career, and character: "Strong in the conviction of a well-matured and equally well-balanced mind, he stood firm in the conscious rectitude of his position, and hence he was a safe legislator, a wise counsellor, and a true friend. He stood erect as God created him, and dared to do right for the sake of the right." Mr. Orth was twice married; m., first, in 1840, SARAH ELIZABETH MILLER, of Gettysburg, Pa., who d. in 1849. They had issue:

 i. Dr. William-M., b. 1842.
 ii. Julia, b. 1844; d. 1849.

Godlove S. Orth m., secondly, August 28, 1850, MARY A. AYERS, only daughter of one of the earliest settlers of Lafayette, Ind., who survives. They had issue:

 iii. Mary-R., b. September 29, 1851.
 iv. Harry-Ayers, b. September 27, 1856; attorney-at-law, resides at Lafayette, Ind.

XVIII. CYRUS DORSEY GLONINGER,[5] (John W.[4] [*Gloninger*], Catharine,[3] Adam,[2] Balzer,[1]) b. March 13, 1824; d. August 23, 1872, at Lebanon, Pa. His preliminary studies were pursued at the Lebanon Academy, after which he entered Marshall College, then at Mercersburg, graduating in 1843. He began the study of medicine with his father; attended lectures at the University of Pennsylvania, graduating in 1846. The two following years were spent in the medical universities and hospitals of Europe, his accurate and familiar acquaintance with the French and German languages greatly facilitating his studies in the scientific centers of the Old World. Returning home, he commenced the practice of medicine, and shortly acquired a marked reputation for ability and skill in every department of his profession. Like his father, he devoted much of his attention to diseases of the eye, and, in the course of twenty-six years, attained a high rank in this important specialty. He was strictly scientific and regular, faithful to his patients, and honorable to his professional brethren. Aside from the science of medicine, Dr. Gloninger's literary studies were extensive. He was especially well informed in all that relates to the collateral sciences, and his knowledge of sacred and profane history, strengthened by travel and observation, made him an agreeable and entertaining companion. His contributions to various journals and periodicals showed a highly-cultivated mind. As a public man he was greatly esteemed; was twice nominated by the Democratic party, of which he was an adherent, a candidate for Congress, in 1866 and in 1870, but defeated, owing to the strength of the opposition in his district. In the industrial enterprises of his native town he took a warm interest. He was one of the founders of the Lebanon Manufacturing Company, of which he was president; he was president of the Lebanon National Bank, and in his church, St. John's Reformed, was an active and zealous member. His private charities were numerous, and he gave a willing support to the various evangelical and christianizing enterprises of the day. The poor found in him a friend, and his professional life was a philanthropic mission. Dr. Cyrus D. Gloninger m., December, 1851, JULIA A. BEAUMONT, b. at Wilks-Barré, Pa., daughter of Hon. Andrew Beaumont and Julia Colt. They had issue (surname Gloninger):

  i. Mary-A., m. Harry E. Gilroy, member of the Philadelphia bar; and had issue (surname Gilroy): *Julia.*
  ii. Nellie-B., m. Rev. Walter Jorden, of Philadelphia; and had issue (surname Jorden): *Walter-B.*
  iii. Dr. *Andrew-B.*, studied medicine under Dr. D. Stanley Gloninger, and graduated from the medical department of the University of Pennsylvania, April 13, 1883; is in the active practice of his profession at Lebanon, Pa.
  iv. Cyrus-Dorsey.

PARKER AND DENNY.

I. RICHARD PARKER[1] and JANET, his wife, emigrated from the Province of Ulster, Ireland, in 1725, and settled three miles from Carlisle, acquiring land by patent near the Presbyterian Glebe Meeting-house, on the Conedoguinet creek, in Cumberland county, Province of Pennsylvania, in 1734. His application, made at that date, was for the land on which he had "resided ye ten years past." We have no record of their death, save that Richard Parker died prior to 1750, his wife surviving fifteen years. They had, among other children, issue as follows:

2.   *i. John*, b. 1716; m. Margaret McClure.
3.   *ii. Thomas*, b. 1720; m. Eleanor Ferguson.
4.   *iii. Richard*, b. 1725; m. Martha ———.
      iv. William, b. 1727; m., and had issue, Dr. *Thomas*, of Pittsburgh, Pa., who m. Lydia McDowell, and left two sons.
      v. Martha, d. unm., at the age of eighty-four years.
      vi. Susannah, m. ——— Dunning, and left issue.
5.   *vii. James*, m. Mary [Eleanor] Boyd.

II. JOHN PARKER,[2] (Richard,[1]) b. about the year 1716; d. prior to 1785; m. MARGARET MCCLURE, who d. May, 1792. They had issue:

6.   *i. Agnes*, b. 1741; m. William Denny.
      ii. Richard, b. 1743; served in the war of the Revolution; m. and removed to Kentucky, where he died; his daughter m. Thomas Crittenden, brother of Hon. John J. Crittenden.
7.   *iii. Elizabeth*, b. 1746; m. Francis Campbell.
8.   *iv. Mary*, b. 1748; m. William Fleming.
      v. Margaret, b. 1751; m. John Calhoun; removed to Georgetown, D. C.; no further information.
9.   *vi. Alexander*, b. 1753; m. Rebecca Blair.
      vii. Andrew,* served in the war of the Revolution, and accompanied his brother Richard to Kentucky.

---

* So stated in the Memoir of Major Ebenezer Denny, by his son, as published in the "Publications of the Historical Society of Pennsylvania," vol. vii, p. 208.

580   *Pennsylvania Genealogies.*

III. THOMAS PARKER,[2] (Richard,[1]) b. about 1720, in the north of Ireland; d. April 23, 1776, in Cumberland county, Pa. He was a prominent man on the frontiers during the French and Indian wars, and was an officer in the Provincial service. He m. ELEANOR FERGUSON, b. 1727, in Ireland; d. July 23, 1775, at Carlisle, Pa. They had issue:

    i. William, b. 1749; d. December 24, 1812; m. Elizabeth Templeton, b. 1752; d. 1829; and had issue:
        1. *David*, d. May 28, 1829; unm.
        2. *Eleanor*, d. s. p.
    ii. John, b. 1751; served in the war of the Revolution; m. —— Graham; no further record of him, save that his descendants intermarried with the Ankeneys and Tillsons, of Somerset county, Pa.

10.   *iii. Jane*, b. February 14, 1753; m. John Dunbar.
    iv. Susanna, m. Robert Forbes; and had issue (surname Forbes): *Elizabeth, Thomas, Andrew,* and *Robert.*
    v. Martha, d. February 11, 1837; unm.
    vi. Richard, b. September 8, 1763; d. April 26, 1814; unm.; he was a major in the U. S. army, and at the time of his death military storekeeper at Carlisle, Pa.
    vii. Matthew, probably d. s. p.

IV. RICHARD PARKER,[2] (Richard,[1]) b. about 1725, in Ireland; d. August, 1774, in West Pennsboro' township, Cumberland county, Pa.; m. MARTHA ——. Of this branch of the family we have nothing definite, save that the older members went into the Virginia Valley about the beginning of the Revolution; of the younger children, Dr. Lemuel Gustine was the guardian—he was their relative by marriage. They had issue:

    i. John, b. 1749.
    ii. Alexander, b. 1751.
    iii. Mary, b. 1753.
    iv. James, b. 1755.
    v. Margaret, b. 1758.
    vi. William, b. 1761.
    vii. Henry, b. 1763.
    viii. Richard, b. 1765.

V. JAMES PARKER,[2] (Richard,[1]) b. about 1731; d. about the close of the Revolutionary war; m. MARY [ELEANOR] BOYD. They had issue:

i. Richard, b. 1753; d. February, 1778; m. Rebecca Boyd; d. September, 1781; and had issue: *James*.
11. *ii. Jane*, b. 1755; m. John Forbes.
12. *iii. Rebecca*, b. 1758; m. Dr. Lemuel Gustine.
13. *iv. Andrew*, b. 1763; m. Margaret Williams.

VI. AGNES PARKER,³ (John,² Richard,¹) b. 1741, near Carlisle, Pa., m., in 1760, WILLIAM DENNY, b. 1737, in Chester county, Pa.; d. about the year 1800, in Carlisle, Pa.; removed to the Cumberland Valley in 1745; was the first coroner of Cumberland county, and, during the Revolution, was commissary of issues; he was the contractor for the erection of the court house at Carlisle in 1765, and which was destroyed by fire in 1845; was a gentleman of the old school, high-minded and dignified in manner and conversation. They had issue (surname Denny):

14.   *i. Ebenezer*, b. March 11, 1761; m. Nancy Wilkins, of Pittsburgh.
    ii. Priscilla, b. May 28, 1763; d. February 22, 1849, at Carlisle, Pa.; m. Simon Boyd, of Carlisle, an officer in the Second battalion of Associators of Cumberland county, in the Revolution; left no issue.
    iii. William, b. March 24, 1765; d. in infancy.
    iv. Nancy [Agnes], b. August 31, 1768; d. January 11, 1845, unm., at Carlisle.
15.   *v. Margaret*, b. June 25, 1771; m. Samuel Simison.
    vi. Mary (1st), b. February 13, 1775; d. in her third year.
16.   *vii. Mary [Polly]*, (2d), b. March 5, 1778; m. George Murray, of Carlisle.
    viii. Elizabeth, b. April 22, 1781; d. March 27, 1848, unm., at Carlisle.
    ix. Boyd, b. February 20, 1783; d. at Pittsburgh, Pa.

VII. ELIZABETH PARKER,³ (John,² Richard,¹) b. about 1746; d. prior to 1792; m. FRANCIS CAMPBELL,* b. 1737; d. in 1790; was a man of prominence in the public affairs of his day. They had issue (surname Campbell):

---

* It may be interesting in this connection to give the following reference to the ancestry of Francis Campbell:

I. DUNCAN CAMPBELL,¹ of the noble house of Breadalbane, born in Scotland; married there in 1612, MARY MCCOY, and removed with his wife, in the same year, to Ireland. They had issue, among other children whose names have not been preserved by the descendants in

17.   *i. Parker*, b. 1768; m. Elizabeth Calhoun.
18.   *ii. Agnes*, b. 1770 ; m. Robert Tate.
     iii. Francis, b. 1772; m., and had issue.
     iv. James, b. 1774; was a lawyer of brilliant talents; m. Cassandana Miller, daughter of Gen. Henry Miller, of the Revolution, and had issue.
     v. George, b. 1777 ; m., and had issue.
     vi. Elizabeth, b. 1779.
     vii. Ebenezer, b. 1781 ; m. Catharine Miller ; and had issue (surname Campbell) : *Henry, Ellen*, and *Mary-Ann*.

VIII. MARY PARKER,³ (John,² Richard,¹) b. 1748, in Cumberland county, Pa.; m. WILLIAM FLEMING, b. in Cumberland county, Pa. They had issue (surname Fleming) :

America, a son JOHN CAMPBELL,² b. in 1621; m., in 1655, GRACE HAY, daughter of Peter Hay, and had issue :
     i. Dugald, his descendants settled in Rockbridge county, Va.
2.   *ii. John*, b. 1656 ; m., and had issue.
     iii. Robert, b. 1665; m. in 1696; his descendants settled in Orange, now Augusta county, Va., in 1740.

II. JOHN CAMPBELL,² (John,² Duncan,¹) b. 1656, in the north of Ireland ; d. February 20, 1734, in Derry township, then Lancaster county, Pa.; buried in the graveyard of old Derry church ; in 1726 came to Pennsylvania, with his family, his wife probably dying before emigrating. They had issue :
     i. Robert, removed to Virginia : m., and had issue five children, four daughters and one son, the last dying young ; the name of one daughter, *Rebecca*, has been transmitted.
     ii. David, in 1741 removed from Pennsylvania to Augusta county. Va.; m. Margaret Hamilton, and left issue.
     iii. James, b. 1689; d. May 31, 1771 ; buried in Derry church graveyard ; was twice married, his second wife, Agnes, b. 1707 ; d. April 3, 1757, and is buried by the side of her husband ; they left issue.
     iv. Patrick, b. 1690; "a strong churchman ;" removed from Pennsylvania to Virginia about 1740.
3.   *v. John*, b. 1692; m., and had issue.

III. JOHN CAMPBELL,⁴ (John,³ John,² Duncan,¹) b. in 1692, in Ireland ; d. 1764, at York, Pa.; a minister of the Episcopal Church ; m., and had issue :
     i. James, b. 1731; in 1760 removed to Virginia.
     ii. Eleanor, b. 1733 ; d. 1735.
     iii. Francis, b. 1737 ; m. Elizabeth Parker.
     iv. John, b. 1740 ; d. 1797 ; was one of the most eminent lawyers in Western Pennsylvania.

i. Ann, m. [William] Lyon, (*see Lyon record*).
ii. Nancy, m., first, Charles Gregg; and had issue (surname Gregg): *Alexander*, m. Mary Miller; she m., secondly, Robert Clarke.
iii. James, m., first, Frances Randolph; and had issue (surname Fleming):
    1. *William*, m. Rachel Moore.
    2. *Ann*, m., first, Ichabod Randolph; secondly, Joseph Shrom.
James Fleming m., secondly, Margaret Clark; and had issue (surname Fleming):
    3. *John*, m. Martha Coyle.
    4. *Margaret-Parker*, m. William B. Murray.
iv. John, m. Margaret Fleming.
v. Mary, m. —— Denny.
vi. Rebecca, m. Robert Elliott.
vii. Susanna, m. Paul Randolph.
viii. Sarah, m. Richard Crain, (*see Crain record, p. 150*).
ix. Margaret, m. George Crain.
x. Elizabeth, m. William Crain.

IX. ALEXANDER PARKER,³ (John,² Richard,¹) b. about 1753, in Cumberland county, Pa.; d. about 1792, at Carlisle, Pa. He was an early associator at the outset of the war of the Revolution; was commissioned second lieutenant of the Sixth Pennsylvania battalion, Col. William Irvine, January 9, 1776; promoted first lieutenant, October 25, 1776; served as captain of the Pennsylvania Line in the Seventh regiment, March 21, 1777; transferred to Fourth Pennsylvania, January 17, 1781, and subsequently to Second Pennsylvania, January 1, 1783, serving until the close of the war. He was one of the original members of the Society of the Cincinnati. He laid out the town of Parkersburg, at the mouth of the Little Kanawha, where he had extensive land possessions. In the old graveyard at the Meeting House springs, two miles northwest of Carlisle, there is a large slab covering the remains of Major Parker and two of his children, bearing this inscription: *Sacred | to the memory of | Major Alexander Parker | and his two children | Margaret and John.* Strange to say there are no dates given of birth or death. Major Parker married, in 1783, REBECCA BLAIR, daughter of William Blair, b. 1753; d. suddenly, April 23, 1826, while in attendance at service in the Associate, or Seceder church, Carlisle, Pa. They had issue:

  i. Margaret, b. 1784; d. s. p.
  ii. John, b. 1786; d. s. p.
19. *iii. Mary*, b. 1789; m. William Robinson.
  iv. Anne-Alexander, b. 1791; d. April, 1809; buried in the old graveyard at Carlisle, Pa.

Mrs. Rebecca Blair Parker afterwards married CHARLES McCLURE, b. 1739; d. February 8, 1811, at Letort Springs, near Carlisle, Pa. Mr. McClure had previously married, first, Anna Blair, who died young; he then married, secondly, Amelia Blair, b. 1765; d. February 1, 1793; and had issue. Mrs. Rebecca Blair Parker and Charles McClure had issue (surname McClure):

 i. Charlotte, b. January 7, 1800; d. June 25, 1880, in Chicago, Ill.; m., in 1817, Adam Hays, b. 1792; d. August, 1857; was educated at Dickinson College; studied medicine with Doctor McCoskry, and graduated from the medical department, University of Pennsylvania, in 1811; entered the army as an assistant surgeon and resigned at the close of the war; practiced medicine in Chillicothe, O., and Carlisle; in 1829 removed to Pittsburgh; then to Madison, Ind., where he died; and had issue (surname Hays):
  1. *Joseph*, d. s. p.
  2. *Rebecca-McClure*, m. Jesse Whitehead; and had issue.
  3. *Charles*, d. s. p.
  4. *William*, d. s. p.
  5. *Mary-Robinson*.
 ii. Charles, represented Cumberland county in the Legislature in 1835; was Secretary of the Commonwealth under Governor Porter; and a man of much prominence in public affairs; m. Margaretta Gibson, daughter of Chief Justice Gibson; and had issue (surname McClure):
  1. *Charles*, appointed captain commissary subsistence volunteers, April 28, 1862; brevet major volunteers, brevet lieutenant-colonel volunteers, and brevet colonel volunteers, October 21, 1865, for faithful and meritorious service; captain commissary subsistence U. S. A., August 17, 1866; brevet major, August 17, 1866, for faithful service in the subsistence department; m., and had issue.
  2. *William*.
  3. *George*.
 iii. William-Blair, an attorney-at-law, and was president judge

of the courts at Pittsburgh, Pa.; m. Lydia S. Collins; and had issue.

    iv. Rebecca, m. Elisha White; and had issue (surname White): *Charlotte*, m. Rev. F. T. Brown, D. D.

X. JANE PARKER,³ (Thomas,² Richard,¹) b. February 14, 1753; d. March 8, 1833; m. JOHN DUNDAR, b. 1737; d. June 2, 1810; son of William and Catharine Dunbar.* He was a man of mark in the decade preceding the war for Independence, and during that struggle took a prominent and decided part. He served his country well and faithfully. Mr. Dunbar had been previously married to Mary Mitchel, their children being *William*, m. Elizabeth Forbes, and *Margaret*, m. Thomas Urie. Both left descendants. Jane Parker and John Dunbar had issue (surname Dunbar):

20.   *i. Eleanor*, b. April 4, 1775; m. John Creigh.

XI. JANE PARKER,³ (James,² Richard,¹) b. about 1755, in Cumberland county, Pa.; m. JOHN FORBES, also a native of that county, where they both lived and died. They had issue (surname Forbes):

    i. Jane.
    ii. Elizabeth, m. William Dunbar; and had issue (surname Dunbar):
        1. *Mary*, d. s. p.
        2. *Jane*, m. James Lindsey; and had issue (surname Lindsey):
            a. Jane-Elizabeth, m. Andrew Ralston.
        3. *John*, m. Agnes Grayson; and had issue (surname

---

*WILLIAM DUNBAR and Catharine, his wife, were natives of the north of Ireland, emigrating to America about the year 1730. They settled near Meeting-House springs, on the Conedoguinet, Cumberland county, Pa., and were near neighbors of the Parkers and Creighs. They had issue (surname Dunbar):

    i. Jane, m. Andrew Mitchel; removed to Washington, Pa.
    ii. Elizabeth, m. John McConnell; resided in Tuscarora Valley.
    iii. John, m. Jane Parker.
    iv. Sarah, m. John Young; removed to Virginia.
    v. Thomas, m. Ann Keys; settled in Tennessee.
    vi. Martha, m., first, James Keys; secondly, James Watson.
    vii. Mary, m. John Quinn; removed to Tennessee.
    viii. William.
    ix. Samuel (twin), m. Jane Clark; removed to Kentucky.
    x. Margaret.

Dunbar): *James-Grayson, John, William-Mitchell, James-Alfred, Andrew-Forbes, Mary-Elizabeth, Margaret-Jane,* and *Alice.*

iii. *James,* d. s. p.
iv. *Andrew,* d. s. p.
v. *Rebecca,* m. Matthew Agnew, and had issue (surname Agnew):
    1. *John.*
    2. *Andrew,* m. Rebecca Carothers.
    3. *Nancy,* d. s. p.
    4. *Jane.*
    5. *Samuel,* m. —— Eberly.
vi. *John-P.,* d. s. p.
vii. *Mary,* m. William Lindsey; and had issue (surname Lindsey): *John,* m. Rachel Davidson, and *William,* d. s. p.
viii. *Margaret.*
ix. *Richard,* d. August 30, 1823.

XII. REBECCA PARKER,[3] (James,[2] Richard,[1]) b. about 1758, near Carlisle, Pa.; m. LEMUEL GUSTINE, b. 1749, in Saybrook, Conn.; d. October 7, 1805, at Carlisle, Pa.; studied medicine in the Wyoming settlement, probably with Dr. William Hooker Smith, whose daughter became his first wife; she died in 1778, and their daughter, Sarah, in 1792, became the wife of the Rev. Nathaniel Snowden. At the surrender of the Wyoming troops, in July, 1778, Dr. Gustine signed the terms of capitulation, and succeeded in making his escape with his daughter, reaching Fort Augusta in a boat; afterwards Harris' Ferry, and subsequently Carlisle, where he became distinguished as a practitioner of medicine. They had issue (surname Gustine):

    i. *James,* b. 1780; educated at Dickinson College; studied medicine with his father, and graduated M. D. from the University of Pennsylvania; located in Natchez, Miss., but afterwards returned to Carlisle to assist his father. Several years after his father's death he returned to Mississippi, where he spent the remainder of his life as a planter and a practitioner of medicine.
    ii. *Samuel,* educated at Dickinson College; studied medicine, and after practicing several years in Carlisle, went South with his brother James.
    iii. *Richard,* was a physician, and d. October 1, 1814, at Natchez, Miss.
    iv. *Lemuel.*
    v. *Maria.*
    vi. *Jane.*

XIII. ANDREW PARKER,³ (James,² Richard,¹) b. about 1763; m. MARGARET WILLIAMS. They had issue :

21.   *i. Mary*, b. about 1789 ; m. Robert Urie Jacob.
      ii. Richard, b. 1791 ; m. Hadassa Graham ; and had issue :
         Andrew-Henderson, Mary, and *Richard-McCue*.
22. *iii. James*, b. 1793 ; m. Hannah C. Doty.
     iv. Rebecca, b. 1795 ; d. s. p.
23.   *v. Elizabeth*, b. April 3, 1797 ; m. William M. Henderson.
     vi. Williams, m. Sarah Chambers, dau. of John Chambers and Jane Urie ; and had issue :
        1. *John-Chambers.*
        2. *William-Henderson.*
        3. *Davidson-Urie.*
        4. *George-Sharswood.*
        5. *Lizzie-Boyd.*
        6. *Thomas-Urie.*
24. *vii. Andrew*, b. May 21, 1805 ; m. Ann Eliza Doty.

XIV. EBENEZER DENNY,⁴ (Agnes,³ John,² Richard,¹) b. March 11, 1761, at Carlisle, Pa.; d. July 21, 1822, at Pittsburgh, Pa., and was interred in the First Presbyterian churchyard. At the beginning of the Revolution, Ebenezer Denny, although in his fifteenth year, was the bearer of dispatches to Fort Pitt, and subsequently entered on board a privateer which cruised in the West Indies. He was commissioned an ensign in the First Pennsylvania regiment of the Line in 1778, or 1779; transferred to Seventh Pennsylvania in August, 1780 ; promoted lieutenant in Fourth Pennsylvania, May 23, 1781, and, shortly afterwards, to captain. At the surrender of Cornwallis, at Yorktown, October 19, 1781, Captain Denny was selected and detailed to plant the American flag on the British parapet. He served in the Carolinas to the close of the war, and subsequently became adjutant to General Harmar, and aid-de-camp to General St. Clair. Major Denny was one of the original members of the Society of the Cincinnati. His "journal" is printed in the *Collections of the Historical Society of Pennsylvania*, and is edited, with a concise memoir, by his son, William H. Denny. At the close of the Indian campaign in the Northwest, he removed to Pittsburgh. In 1794 he was appointed commander-in-chief of the expedition to Le Bœuf. In the war of 1812 he was commissary of purchases to supply the Pennsylvania volunteers on the Erie and Niagara frontier. He was one of the commissioners of Allegheny county, and also its first treasurer, and, when Pittsburgh became a city, he was its first mayor. July 1, 1793, Major Denny m. NANCY WILKINS, a native of Carlisle, and a daughter of Capt. John Wilkins, Sr.,* b. 1775: d. May 1, 1806. They had issue who survived (surname Denny):

 i. Harmar, b. May 13, 1794, in Pittsburgh, Pa., where he d. January 29, 1852; graduated at Dickinson College; was a member of the Pennsylvania Legislature; and a representative in Congress from 1829 to 1837; was a member of the Constitutional Convention of 1837-8, and honorably distinguished as a lawyer, statesman and Christian gentleman; m. Elizabeth F. O'Hara, daughter of Gen. James O'Hara, of Pittsburgh; and had issue (surname Denny):

  1. *Mary-O'Hara*, m. J. W. Spring; and had issue.

---

*JOHN WILKINS, the son of John Wilkins, was born in Donegal township, Lancaster county, June 1, 1733. The elder John, the son of Robert Wilkins, an early settler on Chiques creek, was an Indian trader and took an active part against the Marylanders during the boundary difficulties, who offered £50 for his arrest. He was captured and taken to Annapolis jail, but subsequently released. He died in 1741. John, the younger, removed to Carlisle, in 1763, and ten years later to Bedford, engaging in mercantile pursuits. At the outbreak of the Revolution he organized a company of associators and in 1776 was commissioned a captain in the Continental service, and was at Brandywine and Germantown. He was a member of the Convention of July 15, 1776, from Bedford county. In November, 1783, he removed to Pittsburgh, opened a store at the northeast corner of Fourth and Wood streets, and, upon the organization of Allegheny county, was appointed one of the associate judges of the court. He served as member of the Supreme Executive Council in 1790; was chief burgess of the borough of Pittsburgh; commissioner of public buildings, and was county treasurer from 1794 to 1808. He died at Pittsburgh, December 11, 1809. His son, *John*, born in 1761, an officer of the Revolution, brigadier-general during the Whiskey Insurrection, and prominent in the history of Western Pennsylvania, d. April 30, 1816. William Wilkins, b. in 1779; d. June 23, 1865, member of the Legislature; U. S. Senator, 1831-4; Minister to Russia, 1835; member of Congress, 1843-4; Secretary of War, 1844-5, and judge of the U. S. District Court for Western Pennsylvania, was a grandson.

2. *James-O'Hara*, m., first, Catharine Dallas; secondly, Margaret Stevenson, and had issue by the latter.
3. *William-Croghan*, m., first, Elizabeth Denny; secondly, Nancy (Tripp) Stevenson; and had issue by both.
4. *Elizabeth-O'Hara*, m. Hon. Robert McKnight; and had issue.
5. *Catharine*, d. s. p.
6. *Agnes*, d. s. p.
7. *Caroline*, m. Rev. William M. Paxton, D. D., (his second wife); and had issue.
8. *Amelia-Mellizena*, m. Thomas J. Brereton, captain U. S. A.; and had issue.
9. *Harmar*.
10. *Matilda-Wilkins*.
11. *Henry-Baldwin*, d. s. p.

ii. *William-H.*, deceased; a physician; m., first, Sophia DuBarry; secondly, Maria Poe; and had issue by both (surname Denny):
1. *Ebenezer*, U. S. N.
2. *Duplessis*.
3. *Sophia*, m. Brady Wilkins; d. September 25, 1892.
4. *Rebecca*, m. Dr. T. S. Verdi; and had issue.
5. *Juliette*, m. Thomas Gibson; and had issue.
6. *Georgianna*.
7. *Tolma*.
8. *Henry*.

iii. *St. Clair*, a major in the U. S. A.; b. at Pittsburgh, Pa.; d. August 18, 1858; appointed second lieutenant, Fifth infantry, July 1, 1832; first lieutenant November 30, 1835; captain April 12, 1836; transferred to Eighth infantry July 7, 1838; resigned April 30, 1839; appointed major and paymaster October 15, 1841; m. Caroline Hamilton; and had issue (surname Denny):
1. *Morgan-Willoughby*.
2. *Elizabeth*, m. William Croghan Denny.
3. *Annie-H.*, m. William Mathias Corcoran.
4. *Caroline*, m. Joseph N. DuBarry, b. November 19, 1830; d. December 16, 1892.
5. *William-Morgan*, m. Elizabeth Wellendorf.
6. *J.-M.-Brooke*.

iv. *Agnes* [*Nancy*], m. Edward Harding, of the U. S. A.; b. in Maryland; d. February 15, 1855; appointed second lieutenant, artillery corps, July 24, 1818; transferred to Second artillery June 1, 1821; commissioned first lieu-

tenant May 10, 1826; captain of ordnance May 30, 1832; major July 10, 1851; and had issue (surname Harding):
1. *Ebenezer-Denny*, appointed second lieutenant, Eighteenth infantry, June 9, 1862; first lieutenant January 15, 1863; transferred to Twenty-seventh infantry September 21, 1866; captain January 7, 1867; retired October 19, 1867; m. Venie Morgan, daughter of Gen. George W. Morgan.
2. *Elizabeth*, m. Oliver W. Barnes.
3. *William*.
4. *Van Buren*.

XV. MARGARET DENNY,[4] (Agnes,[3] John,[2] Richard,[1]) b. June 25, 1771; d. December 8, 1847, at Carlisle, Pa.; m. SAMUEL SIMISON. They had issue (surname Simison):
 i. *Parker*, b. February 10, 1794; d. October 8, 1868, at Carlisle, Pa.; m. Maria Humrich; and had issue.
 ii. *Elder*, b. March 13, 1796; d. in Ohio; m., and had issue.
 iii. *Nancy*, b. March 10, 1798; d. April 30, 1825, at Carlisle, Pa.; m. Elisha Doyle; and had issue.
 iv. *John*, b. September 30, 1800; d. January 31, 1855, in Alabama; m., and had issue.
 v. *Isabella*, b. March, 1803; d. in infancy.
 vi. *Boyd-Denny*, b. September, 1805; d. October 11, 1871, in Alabama; m., and had issue.
 vii. *Eliza*, b. August 2, 1810; resides at Mt. Vernon, Ala; m. Mr. Roper; and had issue.

XVI. MARY DENNY,[4] (Agnes,[3] John,[2] Richard,[1]) b. March 5, 1778; d. April 10, 1845, in Carlisle, Pa.; m., June 21, 1804, at Carlisle, Pa., by Rev. Robert Davidson, D. D., GEORGE MURRAY, b. March 17, 1762, at Fort Pitt, now Pittsburgh, Pa.; d. May 6, 1855, at Carlisle. He was the only child of William and Susanna (Sly) Murray. In the list of persons at Fort Pitt, not belonging to the army, in July of 1760, is her name, also the name of her younger sister, Rachel, and the names of her parents, George and Margaret Sly. (*Pennsylvania Magazine*, vol. ii, pp. 303-305.) The mother died, leaving George an orphan. He was brought to Carlisle, where his father engaged in real estate and mercantile business, but died, leaving the lad "an orphan, in the care of James Pollock, Thomas Alexander, and George Stevenson," all leading men of the county, and by whom he was afterwards apprenticed to Simon Boyd, of Carlisle. In due time he became the partner of his master in an extensive business, and subsequently succeeded him in it. He also married the youngest sister, but one, of Mr. Boyd's wife. He was a model artisan of the kind, and a man whose life was characterized by strict probity and a high sense of honor, regulated and controlled by the precepts and spirit of Christianity. With a mind rational, and with the bright hope of a blissful immortality, he departed this life in his ninety-fourth year. They had issue (surname Murray):

    i. Priscilla-Boyd, b. July 8, 1805; d. October 28, 1877, at Carlisle, Pa.; m. Andrew Comfort, b. October, 1800; d. April 3, 1845; and had issue (surname Comfort):
        1. *Ann-Parker.*
        2. *Mary-Murray.*
        3. *George-Andrew.*
        4. *William-Murray*, b. June 10, 1834; d. April 12, 1855, s. p.
        5. *Boyd-Simison*, died in infancy.
        6. *Catharine-Elizabeth*, died in infancy.
        7. *Henry-Duffield.*
        8. *Alexander-Gregg.*
    ii. William, b. August 5, 1807; died in infancy.
    iii. William-Boyd, b. September 4, 1808; m. Margaret Parker Fleming; and had issue (surname Murray):
        1. *Margaret-Fleming.*
        2. *Harmar-Denny.*
        3. *Mary-Denny.*
        4. *Mellizena*, d. s. p.
    iv. Charles-Gregg, b. October 14, 1810; d. March 31, 1891; m. Margaret Blair; b. October 31, 1819; and had issue (surname Murray):
        1. *Charles-Samuel*, m., and had issue.
        2. *Talbot-Chambers*, m., and had issue.
    v. George, b. December 27, 1812; d. December 8, 1884; m. Elizabeth Baker, b. February 22, 1818; d. August 6, 1865; and had issue; all died in infancy.

25.   *vi. Joseph-Alexander*, b. October 2, 1815; m., first, Ann Hays Blair; secondly, Lydia Steele Foster.
    vii. Nancy-Denny, b. September 26, 1817; d. August 26, 1818.

XVII. PARKER CAMPBELL,[4] (Elizabeth,[3] John,[2] Richard,[1]) b. 1768, at Carlisle Pa.; d. July 30, 1824, at Washington, Pa.

He studied law at Carlisle, where he was admitted to practice, and in 1794, removed to Washington, Pa., being admitted to that bar at the December term of court. He was considered the most brilliant lawyer of his day, and the old records of the courts of Western Pennsylvania show that he was extensively engaged in the trial of most of the causes instituted. He was particularly eloquent. He served as a volunteer aid to Gen. Adamson Tannehill in the war of 1812, on the Niagara frontier. Parker Campbell m. ELIZABETH CALHOUN, of Chambersburg, Pa., who d. in 1846, at New Orleans, La. They had issue (surname Campbell):

> i. *Nancy*, d. 1871; m. Samuel Lyon, (*see Lyon record*).
> ii. *Elizabeth*, d. 1828; m., first, William Chambers, of Chambersburg, Pa.; secondly, John S. Brady, of Washington, Pa.
> iii. *Eleanor*, d. 1872; m. John Ritchie, of Washington, Pa.; d. at the age of seventy, in Texas.
> iv. *Francis*, d. 1844; unm.; an attorney-at-law.
> v. *John*.
> vi. *Parker*, b. in 1815; d. 1880, at Richmond, Va.; a civil engineer and banker, m. Isabella Sprigg; b. 1823; d. 1876; daughter of Samuel and Amelia Sprigg; and had issue (surname Campbell):
>> 1. *Samuel-Sprigg*, b. 1846; broker, of Richmond, Va.
>> 2. *Elizabeth-Calhoun*, b. 1848; m. Maj. Channing M. Bolton, late C. S. A., a civil engineer.
>> 3. *Ida-Mallom*, b. 1854; m., April 10, 1878, John Lawrence Schoolcraft, broker, of Richmond, Va.
>> 4. *Parker*, b. 1860; d. 1864.

XVIII. NANCY CAMPBELL,[4] (Elizabeth,[3] John,[2] Richard,[1]) b. about 1770; m. ROBERT TATE, b. about 1768. They had issue (surname Tate):

> i. *Elizabeth*, b. 1792; m. Thomas Larrimer.
> ii. *Mary*, b. 1794; m. John Wishart, of Washington, Pa.; b. 1780, in Thornhill Parish, Perthshire, Scotland; d. June 19, 1864; the son of Dr. David Wishart, who emigrated to America in 1796; studied medicine with his father, and graduated from the University of Pennsylvania in 1808, shortly after locating at Washington, Pa.; he was twice married; by first wife, Mary Tate, there was issue (surname Wishart):
>> 1. *Henrietta*, d. s. p.

2. *Jane*, m. Alexander W. Acheson, judge of Washington county courts.
3. *David*, is a physician; served in the Rebellion as a lieutenant, Twenty-second regiment, Pennsylvania cavalry; m. Sarah Hastings.
4. *Nancy*, d. s. p.
5. *Robert-Tate*, m. Ellen Oliver.
6. *Mary*, m. Rev. David Lowrie, of Beaver county, Pa.
7. *Margaretta*, m. Alfred G. W. Carter, a lawyer of Cincinnati, O.

iii. *Julianna*, m. John Uncles; and had issue (surname Uncles): *John*, *James*, and *Ann-Eliza*.
iv. *Henrietta*, d. August 19, 1859; m. Thomas Gregg; and had issue (surname Gregg): *Robert*, *John*, *Mary*, and *Thomas*.
v. *Sarah*, m. Charles Reemer; and had issue (surname Reemer): *James*, *William-Francis*, *Henry*, *Catharine*, *Nancy*, *Sarah*, and *Elizabeth*.
vi. *Samuel*, accidentally killed at Bloody Run by falling from a horse.
vii. *Lucinda*, m. John McAlister; and had issue (surname McAlister): *Henrietta*, *Elizabeth*, *Corridon*, *Jesse*, *Sarah*, *Mary-Jane*, and *Lucinda*.
viii. *Nancy*, m. William Dennison; and had issue (surname Dennison): *Mary*, *Elizabeth*, *Ann*, *Catharine*, *William*, and *Ellen*.
ix. *Jane*, d. s. p.
x. *Margaret*, m. Rev. William D. Smith, D. D.; and had issue (surname Smith): *James*, and *Mary*.

XIX. MARY PARKER,[4] (Alexander,[3] John,[2] Richard,[1]) b. 1789, at Carlisle, Pa.; d. at Pittsburgh, Pa.; m. Gen. WILLIAM ROBINSON, of Allegheny City; a very prominent man in Western Pennsylvania, and the first mayor of Allegheny City. They had issue (surname Robinson):

i. *James*, d. unm.
ii. *William-O'Hara*, m., and had issue.
iii. *Alexander-Parker*, m., and had issue.
iv. *Charles-McClure*, d. unm.
v. *John*, m., and had issue.
vi. *Francis-Pringle*, m., and had issue:
vii. *Annie*, m., first, Mr. Blair; secondly, Mr. Speer.
viii. *Mary-Parker*, m., and had issue.
ix. *Henry*, drowned in the Allegheny river whilst skating, in his twelfth year.

XX. ELEANOR DUNBAR,⁴ (Jane,³ Thomas,² Richard,¹) b. April 4, 1775; d. August 4, 1861; m., May 22, 1796, JOHN CREIGH, b. September 13, 1773; d. November 7, 1848, at Carlisle, Pa., and there buried; son of John Creigh and Jane Houston, of Silvers Spring.* He was educated at Dickinson

*I. JOHN CREIGH, b. about 1680, at Temple Patrick, near Carrickfergus, Ireland; m. MARY ―― in 1708. They transferred their church membership from Temple Patrick church to Carnmoney in 1710. He was ordained a ruling elder in Carnmoney church, May 21, 1718, as the records of the church now in existence show. His name is entered regularly as attending meetings of the session until 1731, after which date the session minutes are badly kept, and from 1748 to 1761 no minutes of session are in existence. There is no record of the date of death of either John or Mary Creigh. John Creigh had five children, as shown by the baptismal record, viz.:

   i. Elizabeth, b. December 23, 1712.
   ii. Mary, b. February 3, 1715.
 2. *iii. Thomas*, b. April 23, 1717.
   iv. John, b. December 17, 1718.
   v. Sarah, b. January 31, 1720.

II. THOMAS CREIGH, the son of John and Mary Creigh, was b. at White House, near Carnmoney, Ireland, April 23, 1717; he m., September 22, 1740, JANET MCCREERIE, b. June 15, 1719. He died in Ireland; but his widow, with her two unmarried daughters, followed her sons, John and Thomas, to America, arriving in Carlisle June 19, 1790, where she died January 10, 1797. Thomas Creigh and Janet, his wife, had issue (surname Creigh):

 3. *i. John*, bap. August 30, 1741; m., first, August 25, 1766, Jane Huston; m., secondly, June 11, 1812, Isabella Mateer.
   ii. Agnes, bap. March 13, 1743; d. in Virginia, July 10, 1799; unm.
   iii. Mary, bap. February 24, 1745; m., June 18, 1786, Hugh Kirkpatrick; this family never left Ireland, and her descendants are still living near Carmoney.
   iv. Catherine, m. John Tomb (or Tomm), in Ireland; came to America prior to 1790; took up land in Westmoreland county in October, 1790, where she d. September 16 1792, leaving an infant child, *Janet-Creigh-Tomb*, b. May, 1792.
   v. Janet, bap. August 23, 1748; d. November 15, 1833, in Lewisburg, Va., unm.
   vi. Elizabeth, bap. February 10, 1751; d. in Ireland; unm.
   vii. Thomas, bap. May 13, 1753; d in inf.
   viii. David, bap. December 11, 1755; d. in inf.

College, graduating in 1792, studied medicine with Dr. Samuel McCoskry, of Carlisle, and graduated an M. D. from the University of Pennsylvania. In 1795 he located at Pittsburgh, but in 1799 removed to Landisburg, Perry county, Pa., where he continued until 1819, when he returned to Carlisle, where he passed the remainder of his life. In the war of 1812–14 he enrolled a company which was accepted by the Governor. From 1827 to 1833 he was a trustee of Dickinson College and for many years was a trustee of the Presbyterian church. As a physician he ranked among the first in his profession, and

ix. Thomas (second), bap. January 15, 1757; d. December 2, 1847, in Lewisburg, Va.; m. Margaret Lynn Williams.

x. Jane, m. Hugh McCleary in Ireland; came to America in 1790, and settled near Carlisle; in 1798 they removed to Greenbriar county, Va., where he d. in 1808; she d. December 8, 1846, in Lewisburg, Va.

xi. Nancy, came to America with her sister, Catherine Tomb (Tomm), and lived with her in Westmoreland county until Catherine's death, after which she made her home with her brothers until her death.

III. JOHN CREIGH, bap. August 30, 1741, in Ireland; d. February 13, 1813, at Carlisle, Pa.; emigrating to America in 1761, he settled, at first, in East Pennsboro', Cumberland county, Pa., afterwards locating at Carlisle. The Revolutionary war coming on he took a decided and active part in the patriot cause, and during that struggle was quite prominent in public affairs. He was in the Jersey campaign of 1776, and, as an officer of the State, administered the oath of allegiance to all persons within his district. He m., first, August 25, 1766, JANE HUSTON, d. October 31, 1808; daughter of Samuel Huston, of East Pennsboro', Cumberland county, Pa. They had issue:

i. Isabella, b. October 10, 1767; d. June 28, 1848; m., first, Samuel Alexander; secondly, Robert Evans.

ii. Thomas, b. August 16, 1769; d. October 29, 1809; unm.; studied law under Thomas Duncan, and admitted to practice July 2, 1791.

iii. Samuel, b. October 2, 1771; d. August 21, 1836; m., first, Martha Hunter; secondly, Jane Mahon.

iv. John, b. September 13, 1773, (*see Parker record*).

v. Mary, b. December 10, 1775; d. September 24, 1830; m. John Kennedy, judge of the Supreme Court.

vi. Elizabeth, b. February 3, 1779; d. December 3, 1829; m. Samuel Duncan, d. 1819.

John Creigh m., secondly, June 11, 1812, ISABELLA MATEER.

had a large and laborious practice. Throughout his medical life he regarded the honor and virtue of the medical profession as of the highest character, and, as far as his influence went, he condemned every attempt to lower the status of that profession. They had issue (surname Creigh):

26.   i. *John-Dunbar*, b. April 26, 1797 ; m. Caroline R. Williamson.
     ii. *Richard-Parker*, b. December 8, 1798; d. September 23, 1826 ; unm ; studied law with his brother, and was admitted to the bar in 1825.
     iii. *Jane-Eliza*, b. November 22, 1800; d. April 17, 1803.
     iv. *Samuel*, b. September 23, 1802; d. September 10, 1872, in Miami county, Kan.; buried in the Quaker burying ground near Ossawatomie ; studied law and was admitted to the Carlisle bar ; in 1871 removed to Kansas.
     v. *Mary*, b. July 30, 1804 ; d. March 4, 1837 ; m., December 15, 1831, Thomas B. Jacobs, and had issue (surname Jacobs):
        1. *John-Creigh*, b. March 13, 1833 ; d. August 21, 1835.
        2. *James-Cyrus*, b. June 15, 1834 ; d. July 24, 1834.
     vi. *Eleanor-Jane*, b. October 2, 1806.
27.   vii. *Thomas*, b. September 9, 1808 ; m., first, Ann Hunter Jacobs ; secondly, Jane McClelland Grubb.
28.   viii. *Alfred*, b. December 16, 1810; m., first, Sarah Jane Cooke ; secondly, Julia Ann Stephenson.
     ix. *William-Linn*, b. June 21, 1813; d. April 15, 1866, in Waynesburg, Greene county, Pa.; learned printing, and subsequently studied medicine under his father; and settled in Waynesburg, Pa.; m., October 15, 1846, Rachel Edwards, b. April 14, 1822; d. March 13, 1870; and had issue (surname Creigh):
        1. *Richard-Parker*, b. July 31, 1847 ; d. May 12, 1892.
     x. *Isabella-Mateer*, b. May 15, 1814 ; d. August 9, 1815.

XXI. MARY PARKER,[4] (Andrew,[3] James,[2] Richard,[1]) b. about 1789; d. in Philadelphia, Pa.; m. ROBERT URIE JACOB. They had issue (surname Jacob):

     i. *Jerman*, m., first, Anna Chapman ; no issue; secondly, Elizabeth Wilson, and had issue : *Robert*, m. Mary Long, of Huntingdon, *Mary*, and *Alexander-Wilson*.
     ii. *Margaret*, m. Dr. Robert Martin ; and had issue (surname Martin):
        1. *Andrew-Parker*, m. Mary Stansberry, of Philadelphia, and had *Bessie*, d. s. p., and *May*.
        2. *Samuel*.
     iii. *Andrew-Parker*, m. M. Elizabeth Vanvalzah ; and had issue : *Harriet*.

iv. *Ellen-Doty*, m. Dr. John I. Marks ; and had issue (surname Marks): *Catharine-J.*, m. John McClure, *Jane*, and *Robert-Urie.*

v. *Catharine* (twin), m. Lewis T. Watson ; and had issue (surname Watson); *Charles-Parker, Edwin*, d. s. p., *Thomas-Urie, Arthur-Wellesley, Jerman*, d. s. p., and *Gouvernour-Kemble.*

XXII. JAMES PARKER,[4] (Andrew,[3] James,[2] Richard,[1]) b. about 1793; m. HANNAH C. DOTY. They had issue :

  i. *Andrew*, d. in infancy.
  ii. *Joseph-Williams*, unm.
  iii. *James-Gustine*, d. unm.
  iv. *Ellen-Doty*, m. F. G. Franciscus ; and had issue (surname Franciscus):
    1. *Ellen-Parker*, d. s. p.
    2. *James-Parker.*
    3. *John-Thompson.*
    4. *Kate Parker.*
    5. *William-Mortimer*, d. s. p.
    6. *Lewis-Pascault*, d. s. p.
    7. *Harry-Doty*, d. s. p.
    8. *Joseph-Ormsby*, d. s. p.
    9. *Francis-Carson*, d. s. p.
  v. *Robert Urie*, d. unm.
  vi. *Richard-C.*, m. Ellen Morgan, of Washington, D. C.; and had issue : *Caroline* and *James.*
  vii. *Roswell-Southard*, d. unm.
  viii. *Margaret-Urie*, m. Homer Benedict, deceased,; and had issue (surname Benedict):
    1. *Margaret*, m. S. Charles Knight, of Glenlock, Pa.
  ix. *Catharine-Jacob*, m. Dr. George Hoover, deceased ; and had issue (surname Hoover):
    1. *Hannah-Parker.*
  x. *Alvin-Boyd.*
  xi. *Thomas-Davidson*, m. Margaret Lawrence ; no issue.
  xii. *Henry-Wilson*, d. in infancy.
  xiii. *Jerman-Jacob*, m. Annie McCoy ; and had issue :
    1. *Charles-McCoy.*

XXIII. ELIZABETH PARKER,[4] (Andrew,[3] James,[2] Richard,[1]) b. April 3, 1797 ; d. February 2, 1860 ; m. WILLIAM MILLER HENDERSON,* b. May 28, 1795. They had issue (surname Henderson):

---

* His father, Matthew Henderson, died July 19, 1886, aged about seventy years ; and his mother, Margaret Henderson, d. April 16, 1841, aged eighty-two years.

i. *James-Wilson*, m. James B. Alexander ; and had issue (surname Henderson):
   1. *Samuel-Alexander.*
   2. *William-Miller.*
ii. *Andrew-Parker.*
iii. *Robert-Miller*, b. March 11, 1827 ; graduated from Dickinson College ; studied law, and was admitted to the Carlisle bar ; served in the Legislature, 1851-52 ; in the war of the Rebellion, was a captain in the Seventh Pennsylvania reserves ; promoted lieutenant colonel ; after the second Bull Run battle, being then severely wounded, he resigned ; was breveted brigadier general for meritorious conduct ; subsequently accepted the office of provost marshal of the Fifteenth district of Pennsylvania ; was appointed president judge of the judicial district of Dauphin and Lebanon, which position he filled several years with distinguished ability, and then resigned ; resides at Carlisle, Pa., engaged in his profession ; he m. Margaret Webster, of Baltimore, Md.; and had issue (surname Henderson):
   1. *William-M.*
   2. *John-Webster.*
   3. *Margaret-Thornbury.*
   4. *Elizabeth-Parker.*
   5. *Robert-Miller.*
   6. *Rebecca.*
   7. *Robert-M.*, d. in infancy.
iv. *Sarah-Ellen.*
v. *Margaret*, m. John C. Hager ; and had issue (surname Hager):
   1. *Elizabeth-Henderson.*
   2. *Catharine.*
   3. *Cecilia-Ellmaker.*
   4. *Margaret-H.*
   5. *John-C.*
   6. *Sarah-E.*
   7. *William-Henderson.*
   8. *Edward-Townsend.*
vi. *Rebecca.*
vii. *Harriet-Seeley*, d. s. p.
viii. *William-Matthew*, d. s. p.
ix. *Richard-Parker.*

XXIV. ANDREW PARKER,[4] (Andrew,[3] James,[2] Richard,[1]) b. May 21, 1805, in Cumberland county, Pa.; d. January 15, 1864, in Mifflintown, Pa. He was educated at Dickinson College, Carlisle, graduating in 1824; studied law under Andrew Carothers, and admitted to the bar in 1826. He soon after commenced the practice of his profession at Lewistown, Pa., and subsequently appointed Deputy Attorney General for Mifflin county, removing to Mifflintown, the then county seat, where he resided until his death. He served as a representative in Congress from 1851 to 1853. He was an able lawyer, and his practice and reputation extended to all the neighboring counties. Mr. Parker m., April 26, 1831, ANN ELIZA DOTY. They had issue:

 i. Ezra-Doty, b. April 15, 1833; resides at Mifflintown, Pa.; m., February 12, 1863, Mary McDowell Hamilton, b. August 19, 1841; d. November 25, 1864; and had issue:
  1. *Andrew*, b. November 19, 1863.
  2. *James-Frow*, b. November 20, 1864; d. in inf.
 Mr. Parker m., secondly, October 18, 1866, Jennie Howard Vanvalzah; and had issue:
  3. *Harriet-Howard*, b. November 10, 1867.
  4. *Rebecca-Cloyd*, b. November 10, 1869.
  5. *Thomas-Vanvalzah*, b. September 29, 1871.
  6. *Edmund-Southard*, b. February 28, 1874.

 ii. James-Williams, b. January 29, 1835; d. November 13, 1838.

 iii. Rebecca-Cloyd, b. August 12, 1837; resides at Ridley Park, Pa.; m., November 10, 1869, David R. B. Nevin; and had issue (surname Nevin):
  1. *May-Pierce*, b. November 19, 1871.
  2. *Andrew-Parker*, b. April 6, 1873.

 iv. Edmund-Southard, b. October 25, 1839; resides in Mifflintown, Pa.; m., February 23, 1865, Mary Isabella Wilson; and had issue:
  1. *Mary-Wilson*, b. Nov. 23, 1865; d. August 4, 1866.
  2. *Anna-Eliza*, b. January 12, 1867.
  3. *William-Wilson*, b. August 18, 1868.
  4. *Edmund-Southard*, b. November 13, 1869.
  5. *Isabella-Jane*, b. November 19, 1870.
  6. *Ezra-Doty*, b. August 15, 1872.
  7. *Helen-Wilson*, b. November 21, 1873.
  8. *Brainard-Warner*, b. January 26, 1875.
  9. *Lucy-Wilson*, b. May 8, 1876.
  10. *Ruth-Evelyn*, b. March 4, 1879; d. December 3, 1882.
  11. *Andrew*, b. February 1, 1883.

 v. Margaret-Williams, b. October 25, 1841; d. Dec. 22, 1842.

 vi. Thomas-Urie, b. December 4, 1843; resides at Mifflintown, Pa.; m., December 3, 1865, Mary Charlotte Martin; and had issue:

1. *Catharine-Martin*, b. August 1, 1868.
2. *Thomas-Urie*, b. June 29, 1870.

vii. *Mary-Jacob*, b. May 16, 1846 ; m., February 29, 1873, Brainard H. Warner ; reside in Washington, D. C.; and had issue (surname Warner) :
   1. *Julia*, b. November 23, 1873 ; d. in inf.
   2. *Bessie* (twin), b. November 23, 1873.
   3. *Brainard-H.*, b. June, 1875.
   4. *Anna-Parker*, b. September, 1876.
   5. *Mary-Jacob*, b. July, 1879.

viii. *Ann-Eliza*, b. August 25, 1848; m., March 14, 1878, Robert McMeen, of Mifflintown, Pa.; and had issue (surname McMeen) :
   1. *Andrew-Parker*, b. December 9, 1883.

ix. *Andrew*, b. November 19, 1850 ; d. May 27, 1852.
x. *James Andrew*, b. November 15, 1852 ; d. February 24, 1853.
xi. *Ellen-Elizabeth*, b. December 11, 1854 ; d. January 26, 1859.

XXV. JOSEPH ALEXANDER MURRAY,[5] (Mary[4] [*Denny*], Agnes,[3] John,[2] Richard,[1]) b. October 2, 1815, at Carlisle, Pa., where he d. November 27, 1889. His preparatory education had been acquired in his native place and elsewhere, and in August, of 1837, he graduated from the Western University of Pennsylvania, at Pittsburgh. In the autumn of the same year he entered the Western Theological Seminary, in Allegheny, Pa., and from it he graduated in the autumn of 1840. In October, of the same year, he was licensed to preach the gospel by the Presbytery of Ohio, which then embraced the churches in and about Pittsburgh. Soon afterwards, he received invitations to visit vacant churches, and accepted one to preach at Marion, Ohio. This church he supplied for six months, from December, of 1840, to May, of 1841, inclusive, but finally declined a unanimous call to become its pastor. He then visited his native place, and in October, of 1841, he received and accepted a call to the united congregations of Monaghan (Dillsburg) and Petersburg, and was ordained and installed pastor of the same by the Carlisle Presbytery in April, of 1842. This relation happily and usefully subsisted for about eighteen years. During his pastorate the present church edifice was erected at Dillsburg. For years he served there also as school director, and president of the board. During the same period several invitations had been received to churches in other places, but declined. Finally, however, in consequence of impaired health, he resigned the charge; the pastoral relation was dissolved in October, of 1858, and he then retired to Carlisle. His health never afterwards permitted him to undertake the active work and assume the responsibilities of a settled pastor, but he supplied several churches, often filled vacant pulpits, and assisted his clerical friends. On four different occasions he was sent by his Presbytery as a commissioner to the General Assembly—in 1844, 1861, 1865, and 1875. On the last occasion he was also chosen by his Synod, with Hon. H. W. Williams, to defend, if necessary, a decision of said body before the General Assembly, and in this highest church court he was appointed one of the Judicial Committee. In 1876 he was chosen, by acclamation, moderator of the Synod of Harrisburg. In 1869 his *alma mater* conferred on him the honorary degree of Doctor of Divinity. In 1870 he was elected a corresponding member of the Numismatic and Antiquarian Society of Philadelphia. In 1873 he was elected a member of the Historical Society of Pennsylvania. In 1880 he was elected a member of the American Philosophical Society at Philadelphia. He was president of the Cumberland County Bible Society, secretary of the Historical Association of Carlisle, &c. Several of his discourses and addresses have been published. He frequently contributed to some of the periodicals of our country—literary, historical and religious. But, in no instance, would he ever consent to accept of any work or position that would interfere with his high calling and character as a minister of the Gospel of Jesus Christ. Rev. Dr. Murray was twice married; m., first, April 25, 1843, ANN HAYS BLAIR, daughter of Andrew Blair, b. May 6, 1819; d. September 14, 1875, at Carlisle, Pa. They had issue (surname Murray):

> i. *Mary-Elizabeth*, b. February 11, 1848; m., January 2, 1868, Charles F. Himes, Ph. D.; b. June 2, 1838, in Lancaster county, Pa.; he graduated at Dickinson College in 1855; a teacher until 1860; professor of mathematics in Troy University from 1860 to 1863; from 1863 to 1865 engaged in scientific studies at the University of Giessen, Germany, and in the latter year entered upon the position

occupied until recently—professor of natural science in his *alma mater*, but now that of physics, and the senior professor in the college. As a scientist he deservedly holds a front and honorable rank, and has made frequent contributions of a scientific and educational character, among them, "Leaf Prints," "The Steroscope," "Wills' Table for Qualitative Chemical Analysis, Translated and Enlarged," "Bunsen's Flame Reactions," "Methods and Results of the Observation of the Total Solar Eclipse of 1869," "Photographic Investigations, including Improved Photographic Toning Process," "Preparation of Photographic Plates by Daylight," "Actinism," and articles in the *Annual Record of Science and Industry*, from 1873 to 1877, &c.; in 1879 published "Historical Sketch of Dickinson College;" and had issue, besides two children died in infancy, (surname Himes):

1. *Mary-Murray.*
2. *Anna-Magdalene.*

Rev. Dr. Murray m., secondly, October 2, 1879, LYDIA STEELE FOSTER, of Philadelphia, b. March 9, 1836, in Carlisle; daughter of Crawford Foster.

XXVI. JOHN DUNBAR CREIGH,[5] (Eleanor[4] [*Dunbar*], Jane,[3] Thomas,[2] Richard,[1]) b. April 26, 1797; d. June 4, 1882, at San Francisco, Cal. He received an academical, collegiate, and legal education at Carlisle, Pa.; studied law with Andrew Carothers, and was admitted to the bar in 1819. Shortly after he located at Landisburg, Perry county, Pa. He continued in the law several years, but subsequently entered the iron business, and for a long time managed Stewart's and Dunbar's furnaces in Fayette county, and Caroline Furnace in Perry county. However, he returned to the bar and practiced in St. Louis and Pittsburgh, eventually locating in San Francisco. He had the honor of filling the office of judge of the different courts in that city, but at the end of his term declined a re-election, preferring to return to his profession, in which he continued until his death—one of the most brilliant minds at the California bar. Judge Creigh was twice married; m., first, September 5, 1826, CAROLINE RAMSEY WILLIAMSON; d. May 9, 1856. They had issue (surname Creigh):

 i. John, b. October 30, 1828 ; d. November 28, 1881 ; m. Mrs. Mary Smith ; uo issue.
 ii. Samuel-Williamson, b. January 13, 1831 ; d. September 28, 1880 ; m. Mary L. Stackpole.
 iii. Thomas, b. March 30, 1833 ; d. unm.
 iv. Alfred-H.-W., b. March, 1838 ; unm.
 v. Isabella-Mary, b. 1842 ; m., first, Col. J. Blanchard Miles, killed in the battle of the Wilderness, May, 1864 ; secondly, Thomas C. Fisher.
 vi. Ellen-Dunbar, b. April 17, 1845 ; m. Wilson Miller.
 vii. Jane-Parker, b. 1847 ; d. s. p.
 viii. Caroline-Williamson (twin), b. 1847 ; d. s. p.

Judge Creigh m., secondly, November 1, 1865, CATHARINE J. PHILLIPS, of Philadelphia.

XXVII. THOMAS CREIGH,[5] (Eleanor[4] [*Dunbar*], Jane,[3] Thomas,[2] Richard,[1]) b. September 9, 1808, in Landisburg, Perry county, Pa.; d. April 21, 1880, at Mercersburg, Pa. After passing through the grammar school connected with Dickinson College, he entered that institution, from which he graduated in 1828. Studied theology under the Rev. George Duffield, D. D., of Carlisle, and completed his theological course at the seminary at Princeton. He was licensed to preach by the Presbytery of Carlisle, April 12, 1831. On the 27th of September following he was installed pastor of the Presbyterian church at Mercersburg, Franklin county, Pa., and, for almost half a century, that was the field of his ministerial labors. He filled that office acceptably to the people of his charge, and was beloved by the citizens of every denomination. He was a faithful messenger of the gospel of Christ. Rev. Dr. Creigh was twice married; m., first, February 14, 1833, ANN HUNTER JACOBS, b. July 3, 1809 ; d. October 16, 1836. They had issue (surname Creigh):

 i. John, b. December 1, 1533 ; d. April 17, 1861.
 ii. James-Jacobs, b. November 25, 1835 ; is an Episcopalian minister ; m., June 6, 1865, Emma Colton Barber ; and had issue, *Mary-Dunbar*.

Rev. Dr. Creigh m., secondly, November 29, 1837, JANE MCCLELLAND GRUBB, b. May 21, 1809; d. June 11, 1891. They had issue (surname Creigh):

 iii. Joseph-Brainerd, b. December 19, 1838 ; d. May 28, 1862.

vi. Thomas-Alfred, b. October 6, 1840; m. Mary McClelland Irwin; and had issue: *Thomas*, and *Alfred-Irwin*; reside in Omaha, Neb.

v. William, b. April 4, 1842; d. April 5, 1847.

vi. Ellen-Dunbar, b. April 13, 1845.

XXVIII. ALFRED CREIGH,[5] (Eleanor[4] [*Dunbar*], Jane,[3] Thomas,[2] Richard,[1]) b. December 16, 1810, at Landisburg, Perry county, Pa.; d. May 2, 1889, at Washington, Pa. He received an academical and classical education at Dickinson College, Carlisle, where he graduated in 1830, receiving the degree of A. B., and, in 1833, that of A. M. He began the study of medicine with his father, and assisted him for several years in his profession. Turning his attention to literary pursuits, he published several historical works of value, "Masonry and Anti-Masonry," "History of Knights Templar in Pennsyluania," two volumes, "History of Washington county, Pa.," and, also, a "History of Greene county, Pa." In 1850 the University of Kentucky, at La Grange, conferred upon him the degree of LL. D. For almost fifty years he had been prominently identified with the masonic fraternity. Alfred Creigh was twice married; m., first, August 5, 1841, SARAH JANE COOKE, b. September 11, 1814; d. October 8, 1842; daughter of John Cooke, of Berkeley county, Va., and Sarah Swearingen, daughter of Andrew Swearingen, of Washington, Pa. They had issue (surname Creigh):

i. Ellen-Dunbar, b. September 30, 1842; d. s. p.

Dr. Creigh m., secondly, September 10, 1844, JULIA ANN STEPHENSON, b. August 23, 1813; d. March 9, 1891; daughter of William Stephenson and Margaret Crawford. They had issue (surname Creigh):

ii. Ellen-Dunbar (2d), b. September 8, 1845.

iii. William-Thomas, b. September 21, 1848.

iv. John-Wishart, b. July 30, 1850; d. July 10, 1894.

v. Mary-Margaret-Stephenson, b. August 3, 1853; d. January 14, 1854.

vi. James-Stephenson, b. February 28, 1855.

vii. Alfred-Richard, b. October 30, 1858; d. January 1, 1860.

ROAN OF DERRY.

I. ARCHIBALD ROAN,[1] a native of Scotland, settled in Grenshaw, Ireland, about the year 1690. He was a weaver by trade, of good education, and a Covenanter. Of his children, two came to America, of whom we have record :
2.   *i. Andrew*, b. 1713 ; m. Margaret Walker.
3.   *ii. John*, b. April 30, 1717 ; m. Anne (Cochran) Leckey.

II. ANDREW ROAN,[2] (Archibald,[1]) b. 1713, in Grenshaw, Ireland ; d. 1768, in Derry township, Lancaster, now Dauphin county, Pa.; emigrated to America in the year 1739, in company with his brother, Rev. John Roan. He was a weaver by trade, and it is probable from this fact that Webster and Sprague in their Annals of the Presbyterian Church in America state that the Rev. John Roan was a weaver, when such was not the case. It is a well-known fact, however, that among the Scotch-Irish settlers, every man had some trade or occupation. Andrew Roan, at his death, left a wife MARGARET WALKER, who did not survive him long, and children as follows :

    i. Margaret, b. 1737 ; m., 1755, James Barnett, (*see Barnett record*).
    ii. William, b. 1740; removed to Tennessee, there married and died.
    iii. Sally, b. 1743.
    iv. Hugh, b. 1747.
    v. Jennett, b. 1753 ; m. Thomas Foot.
4.   *vi. Archibald*, b. 1755.

III. Rev. JOHN ROAN,[2] (Archibald,[1]) b. April 30, 1717, (O. S.,) in Grenshaw, Ireland ; d. October 3, 1775, in Derry township, Lancaster, now Dauphin county, Pa. He received a good education, and emigrated to Pennsylvania about 1740. He entered the "Log College," and taught school on the Neshaminy and in Chester county while pursuing his theological studies. He was licensed by the "Newside" Presbytery of New Castle, and, in the winter of 1744, sent to Hanover, Va.

The following year (1745), he was settled over the united congregations of Derry, Paxtang, and Conewago, the latter having one-fifth of his time. The minutes of the Synod placed Roan in Donegal Presbytery, and "points of difficulty," says Webster, "continually arose." Towards the latter days of his ministry, Mr. Roan missionated frequently on the south branch of the Potomac. He lies interred in Derry church graveyard. On his tombstone is this inscription :

Beneath this stone | are deposited the Remains | of an able, faithful | courageous & successful | minister of Jesus Christ | The Rev'd John Roan | Pastor of Paxton, Derry & Mount Joy | Congregations | from the year 1745 | till Oct. 3, 1775 | when he exchanged | a Militant for a triumphant Life | in the 59 year of his Age.

The Rev. John Roan m., August 21, 1750, Mrs. ANNE (COCHRAN) LECKEY, b. March 25, 1724; d. April 22, 1788, in Chester county, Pa.; daughter of James Cochran and Anne Rowan. They had issue :

    i. Isabella, b. July 8, 1751 ; d. November 27, 1758.
5. *ii. Jane*, b. May 3, 1753 ; m. William Clingan.
    iii. Anne, b. May 13, 1755 ; d. September 1, 1763.
    iv. Alexander, b. April 7, 1757 ; d. September 10, 1757.
6. *v. Elizabeth*, b. August 14, 1758; m. William Clark.
7. *vi. Flavel*, b. July 3, 1760.
8. *vii. Mary*, b. March 24, 1764; m. Nathan Stockman.

IV. ARCHIBALD ROAN,³ (Andrew,² Archibald,¹) b. 1755, in Derry township, Lancaster, now Dauphin county, Pa. Upon the death of his father, in 1768, he was placed in the care of his uncle, the Rev. John Roan. In the will of the latter this mention is made of him : "I also allow to my nephew, Archibald Roan (in case the above persons, the Rev. George Duffield and my executors, apprehend him religiously disposed), twenty pounds towards his college expenses." He studied law, and removed to Tennessee, where he obtained a license to practice that profession. He was shortly afterwards appointed district attorney general, and, in 1795, honored with the position of judge of the Supreme Court of Tennessee. From 1801 to 1804 he was Governor of that State, and held a number of important offices. He was a gentleman of education, a leading jurist, and an honorable citizen of the State of his adoption. He d. at his residence, near Jonesboro', but we have not the date. In honor of him Tennessee named one of its counties. Dr. Ramsey, the venerable historian of Tennessee, and president of the State Historical Society, gives us the following: "In person he was about six feet high, tall and erect, slender, graceful and dignified, exceedingly modest, rather taciturn, always retiring and unpretending—a well-bred, old-fashioned Virginia gentleman of the last century. The color of his eyes is not now recollected. A little scholarly in his conversation, his voice, and his mien and general manner—unostentatious in his charities and his benefactions. He belonged to the Presbyterian Church, and, if the writer mistakes not, was an elder in Pleasant Forest church, near Campbell's Station, in Knox county. Like Cincinnatus, he went from his farm to his seat on the bench; from the plow to the executive office at Knoxville, Tenn., where the scepter of Judah then was. He was the second Governor of the State of Tennessee, and the immediate successor of Governor Sevier, who was the first. But, unlike Sevier, Governor Roan was without ambition. He had no aspirations to office or political preferment; he preferred the quiet of home and of domestic life. He m. a Miss CAMPBELL, of the Virginia Campbells. He had three sons. *James* became a physician and was a successful practitioner in Nashville, Tenn. *Andrew*, it is supposed, settled there too; while the third son, the writer believes, went west and died. A daughter became the first wife of Col. Reynolds A. Ramsey. * * * * Much more might be said for Governor Roan. He left no stain upon his high and honorable character. The King's English is too feeble, not sufficiently expressive, to describe it or portray his genuine worth. Another has used another language to describe him truthfully—*Integer vitae e scelerisque purus.*"

V. JANE ROAN,[3] (John,[2] Archibald,[1]) b. May 3, 1753, in Derry township, Lancaster, now Dauphin county, Pa.; m., June 11, 1778, WILLIAM CLINGAN, of Chester county, b. in 1756, son of Thomas Clingan [1722–1788], and Margaret, his wife. In Dunlap's *Pennsylvania Packet* for June 17, 1778, then published at Lancaster, during the occupation of Philadelphia by the British, we find the following reference to the marriage of Jane Roan, daughter of the Rev. John Roan and William Clingan: "Was married last Thursday (June 11, 1778), Mr. William Clingan, Jr., of Donegal, to Miss Jenny Roan, of Londonderry, both of this county of Lancaster—a sober, sensible, agreeable, young couple, and very sincere Whigs. This marriage promises as much happiness as the state of things in this, our sinful world, will admit. This was truly a Whig wedding, as there were present many young gentlemen and ladies, and not one of the gentlemen but had been out when called on in the service of his country, and it was well-known that the groom in particular had proved his heroism, as well as Whigism, in several battles and skirmishes. After the marriage was ended, a motion was made, and heartily agreed to by all present, that the young unmarried ladies should form themselves into an association by the name of the Whig Association of the Unmarried Young Ladies of America, in which they should pledge their honor that they would never give their hand in marriage to any gentleman until he had first proved himself a patriot, in readily turning out when called to defend his country from slavery, by a spirited and brave conduct, as they would not wish to be the mothers of a race of slaves and cowards." They removed to Buffalo Valley, where they resided until their death. Mr. Clingan was a prominent and influential personage on the frontiers, during and subsequent to the war of the Revolution. He d. May 24, 1822, his wife surviving until May 7, 1838. They had issue (surname Clingan):

  i. Margaret, b. October 18, 1779; m., November 15, 1798, John Scott.
  ii. John, b. April 26, 1781; d. September, 1841; unm.
  iii. Annie, b. January 23, 1783; d. April 19, 1867; m., March 19, 1812, Joseph Lawson.
  iv. Thomas, b. May 19, 1785; d. April 24, 1858; m., in 1813, Margaret Lewis.
  v. Elizabeth, b. January 13, 1787; d. April 5, 1872; m., March 26, 1812, Thomas Barber.

vi. George, b. October 26, 1788; d. January 14, 1860; m., in 1817, Eliza Scott.

vii. Flavel, b. March 18, 1795; d. October 17, 1876; m., May 25, 1819, Mary Scott.

VI. ELIZABETH ROAN,[3] (John,[2] Archibald,[1]) b. August 14, 1758, in Derry township, Lancaster, now Dauphin county, Pa.; m. WILLIAM CLARK, a native of Hanover; an early settler in Buffalo Valley, where he died in 1813. She was his second wife. They had issue (surname Clark):

i. Roan, b. June 9, 1788; m., and left issue.
ii. Sarah, b. November 19, 1789; d. May 9, 1857; unm.
iii. William, b. May 5, 1791; d. unm.
iv. Flavel, b. February 9, 1793; d. March 6, 1858; unm.
v. Margaret, b. November 18, 1794; d. unm.
vi. Walter, b. January 27, 1797; m., and left issue.
vii. James, b. September 18, 1799; was thrice married; d. suddenly, at Lewisburg, Union county, Pa., October 22, 1864; two of his sons, *James-C.* and *Asbury*, are distinguished ministers, the former a Methodist, the latter a representative of the Presbyterian faith and stock.

VII. FLAVEL ROAN,[3] (John,[2] Archibald,[1]) b. July 31, 1760, in Derry township, Lancaster, now Dauphin county, Pa. After his mother's death he removed to Buffalo Valley, where two of his sisters who were married had settled. He was a man of education, but quite erratic, and never married. As he says in a letter to his cousin, Sankey Dixon, he "served three years as sheriff of Northumberland county, two years a member of the Assembly, three years a county commissioner, and, for a considerable time, captain of a rifle company." He further says, "the sheriff business embarrassed me considerably," as was really the case. He subsequently taught school and died in 1817, at the age of fifty-seven. A diary or journal kept by him, and freely quoted from by Hon. John Blair Linn in his admirable *History of the Buffalo Valley*, is entertaining reading.

VIII. MARY ROAN,[3] (John,[2] Archibald,[1]) b. March 26, 1764, in Derry township, Lancaster, now Dauphin county, Pa.; d. December 24, 1847, at the residence of her son-in-law, James Sharpe, at Sharpesburg, Allegheny county, Pa. She m.,

October 10, 1789, NATHAN STOCKMAN, b. September, 1763, in the north of Ireland; came with his parents to Chester county, Province of Pennsylvania, in 1765. After his marriage he located in Buffalo Valley, from whence he removed to Beaver Falls, Beaver county, Pa., about 1801, where he died, very suddenly, on the 5th of April, 1812. They had issue (surname Stockman):

    i. *James*, b. November 4, 1791; d. May 10, 1844, at San Antonio, Texas; he left one daughter, who married Reeve Lewis, and resides on Lake Providence, La.

    ii. *Annie*, b. January 28, 1793; d. 1878; m. Mark Clark, of Beaver county, Pa.; they had twelve children.

    iii. *John-Roan*, b. November 9, 1796; d. April 24, 1842; married in Pittsburgh, but subsequently removed to Natchez, Miss., where he died; left eight children, five of whom survive, the daughters in Natchez; a son, *S.-Dryden* Stockman, in New Orleans, and *John-R.* Stockman, in San Francisco.

    iv. *Isabella*, b. September 2, 1798; d. August, 1873; m. James Sharpe, Pittsburgh, d. March, 1861; of their children (surname Sharpe), *James-Stockman*, an unusually bright young man, died while a student at Jefferson College, Canonsburg, *Mary-Roan-Stockman*, *Jane-Beltzhoover*, *John-Roan-Stockman*, *Eliza L.*, m. Clarke; the latter alone survives.

    v. *Joseph*, b. July 2, 1800; d. unm. at New Orleans, in March, 1835.

    vi. *Samuel*, b. January 18, 1802; went South, and for many years was never heard of.

    vii. *Laird-Harris*, b. 1804; d. s. p.

    viii. *Jane-Harris*, b. April 5, 1807; m., in 1823, Daniel Beltzhoover, of Pittsburgh; in 1832 removed to Natchez, Miss.; they had five children; Mrs. Beltzhoover afterward resided in Pittsburgh.

FAMILY OF ROBINSON.

I. Among the earliest Scotch-Irish settlers in Pennsylvania was the family of THOMAS ROBINSON,[1] who came to America prior to the year 1730. The sons, Andrew, William, and Richard located in Derry township, then Lancaster county, Pa.; the others in the adjoining township of Hanover. Thomas Robinson d. prior to 1740. He had issue, among others:

2. i. *Philip*, b. 1698; m., and had issue.
3. ii. *Andrew*, b. 1700; m. Agnes Boal.
    iii. *William*, b. 1703; little known of him or his family, and it is more than probable that they went southward about the year 1750.
    iv. *Richard*, b. about 1710; d. in February, 1768, leaving a wife Isabel, and children *Richard, James, John, Thomas,* and *Eleanor*; the latter probably followed the tide of emigration into Virginia and the Carolinas.
    v. *Samuel*, b. about 1715; took up a tract of land in Hanover township in 1743.
    vi. *Thomas*, b. about 1720; m., and had a son *John*, to whom he deeded, in 1767, his plantation called Newry, in Hanover township, which he had warranted to him in 1752. Nothing further is known of either.

II. PHILIP ROBINSON,[2] (Thomas,[1]) b. about the year 1698, in the north of Ireland, came to the Province of Pennsylvania with his father's family, prior to 1730. His name appears on the first tax list of Hanover township, Lancaster county. He settled with his family on Manada creek, near the Gap. During the Indian war, 1755–1763, there was a fort on his farm for defence against the Indians and the safety of the settlers. His sons were already grown men, for in 1755, Governor Morris addressed a letter to Samuel Robinson, sending with it one hundred pounds of gunpowder to be used by the inhabitants of Hanover in "defence of themselves and their country." Beside their farm, the Robinsons were millers, owning a mill on the Manada at the Gap, and furnishing supplies to the government during that war. Philip Robinson d. in May, 1770; his wife's name is unknown, and her death preceded her husband's. They had issue:

4.   *i. Samuel*, b. 1723 ; m. Jean Snoddy.
  ii. Thomas, b. 1725 ; d. December, 1780, leaving a wife, *Jean*, but no issue. He left his property to *four nephews*, who were named for him—sons of Samuel, George, Agnes, and Sarah, his brothers and sisters.
5. *iii. George*, b. 1727 ; m., first, Mary Martin ; secondly, Ann Wylie.
  iv. Agnes, b. 1730 ; m. Robert Robinson, (see VI).
  v. Sarah, b. 1732 ; m. Robert Thompson ; and had issue (surname Thompson): *Thomas*, and *Alexander*.

III. ANDREW ROBINSON,[2] (Thomas,[1]) b. about 1700, in the north of Ireland ; d. February 16, 1797, in Londonderry township, Dauphin county, Pa.; m. AGNES BOAL, b. 1702 ; d. December 28, 1792.   They had issue :
  i. Thomas, b. 1729 ; d. August, 1758 ; m. Effy Finney, who subsequently became the wife of Col. Timothy Green. Thomas Robinson left issue :
    1. *Jane*, b. 1751 ; m. Robert Sturgeon.
    2. *Mary*, b. 1753.
    3. *Elizabeth*, b. 1756.
6. *ii. Robert*, b. 1732 ; m. Agnes Robinson.
  iii. John.
  iv. Mary, m. [Robert] McCleary.
  v. Elizabeth, m. —— Henderson.

IV. SAMUEL ROBINSON,[3] (Philip,[2] Thomas,[1]) b. 1723 ; d. ———— ; m. JEAN SNODDY, daughter of William Snoddy,* of Hanover ; b. 1730 ; d. 1769.   They had issue :
  i. Mary [Polly], m. Benjamin Clarke.
  ii. Joseph.
  iii. John, m. Jean Thompson, daughter of John Thompson, of Hanover ; and had *John*.
  iv. Thomas, was living in August, 1789 ; m. Jean Hay, daughter of John Hay, Esq.; and had issue : *John, Andrew, Agnes, Mary, Sarah, Elizabeth*, and *Juliann*.
  v. Samuel.

V. GEORGE ROBINSON,[3] (Philip,[2] Thomas,[1]) b. 1727; d. March 5, 1814. He settled in Cumberland, now Perry county, Pa., about the year 1755, at the head of Shearman's creek. He was commissioned a justice of the peace by the Proprietary Government, and, during the Indian wars, had a fort on his

---

* William Snoddy, son of John Snoddy, d. May, 1785, in Hanover, leaving a wife and several children.

farm, into which, in 1756, it is stated, the whole of the inhabitants of Shearman's Valley were gathered. He served in the army of the Revolution, though nearly fifty years of age when the war opened. He removed to Kentucky in 1797, whither, also, eight of his children, with their families, settled. Here he died at the age of eighty-seven. He was twice married; m., first, MARY MARTIN; secondly, ANN WYLIE; and had issue:

7. i. *Mary*, m. John Black.
8. ii. *John*, m. Margaret Logan.
9. iii. *Margaret*, m. Samuel Logan.
10. iv. *Jonathan*, b. June 15, 1752; m. Jean Black.
11. v. *Agnes*, m. James Fisher.
    vi. *Sarah*, d. 1801; m. James Fergus; and had issue (surname Fergus): *James*, and *George*.
    vii. *Esther*, m. James Logan; and had issue (surname Logan): *George*.
    viii. *Martha*, m. John Crawford; and had issue (surname Crawford): *George*, and four daughters.
12. ix. *George*, m. Mary Thorn.
13. x. *Thomas*, m. Mary McCord.

VI. ROBERT ROBINSON,[3] (Andrew,[2] Thomas,[1]) b. 1732; d. July 6, 1819; m. AGNES ROBINSON, b. 1730; d. ———; daughter of Philip Robinson, of Hanover. They had issue:

14. i. *Andrew*, b. 1760; m. Jean Crain.
    ii. *Mary*, b. 1763; d. January 11, 1797; m. John Gray.
15. iii. *Thomas*, b. 1765; m., first, Letitia Moorhead; secondly, [Mary] Clark.
    iv. *Elizabeth*, b. 1770; m. Charles Clark; and had issue (surname Clark): *Robert, Mary, Thomas, John*, and *Sarah*.
    v. *Robert*, b. 1774; d. January 5, 1814; m., May 23, 1809, by Rev. Clarkson, Rachel Skyles, b. March 14, 1789; d. March 28, 1857; and had issue:
        1. *Harriet-Ann*, b. August 7, 1811; m., 1829, by Rev. Groh, John Logan, b. April 22, 1800; no issue.

VII. MARY ROBINSON,[4] (George,[3] Philip,[2] Thomas,[1]) m. JOHN BLACK, of Shearman's Valley, where they both lived and died. They had issue (surname Black):

i. *Mary*, m. ——— Ramsey.
ii. *Jane*, m. ——— Meredith.
iii. *Abigail*, m. ——— Carson.
iv. *Hetty*, m. ——— Wiseman.
v. *Rebecca*, m. ——— Matteer.

vi. John.
vii. Jonathan.
viii. Robinson, m. Eliza Noble.
ix. James, m. Mary Noble.
x. Samuel, m. Mary Nelson.
xi. George.
xii. William.
xiii. Thomas.

VIII. JOHN ROBINSON,[4] (George,[3] Philip,[2] Thomas,[1]) m. MARGARET LOGAN. They had issue:
i. John.
ii. George, m. ——— Logan, and had two daughters.

IX. MARGARET ROBINSON,[4] (George,[3] Philip,[2] Thomas,[1]) m. SAMUEL LOGAN. They had issue (surname Logan):
i. James.
ii. Samuel.
iii. Hetty.
iv. Nancy.
v. Martin, m., and had *Catharine.*
vi. Alexander, m., and had three or four children.
vii. Mary, m., first, William Anderson; secondly, Rev. Benjamin L. Baldridge.
viii. Esther, m. Adam Rankin.

X. JONATHAN ROBINSON,[4] (George,[3] Philip,[2] Thomas,[1]) b. June 15, 1752; d. July 11, 1834, near Georgetown, Ky., whither he removed from now Perry county, Pa., in 1785. During the war of the Revolution he served as a captain in the Fourth battalion of militia, in the county of Cumberland, and was in service about six years. He m. JEAN BLACK, of Perry county, Pa. They had issue:
i. John, d. s. p.
16. *ii. Mary,* m. John Robinson.
iii. Abigail.
17. *iv. George,* m. Martha McConnell.
v. Hetty, d. unm.
vi. Jonathan, d. unm.
vii. Thomas, m. Mary McConnell; no issue.
viii. Jane, m. James Dougherty; and had issue (surname Dougherty): *Sidney-Jane.*
ix. Margaret, d. unm.
x. John-McCracken, b. 1793; d. April 26, 1843; m. Mary Ratcliffe; and had *James,* and *Margaret.*

xi. Anne-Wylie, m. Francis R. Palmer; and had issue (surname Palmer): *Jonathan, Jane-Black, William,* and *Charles.*

18. *xii. James-Fisher,* b. 1800; m., first, Susan Mansell; secondly, Willina S. Herndon.

XI. AGNES ROBINSON,⁴ (George,³ Philip,² Thomas,¹) m. JAMES FISHER. They had issue (surname Fisher):
  i. *Margaret,* m. Rev. William Rainey.
  ii. *Hetty,* m. James Logan, and had nine children.
  iii. *Mary [Molly],* m. William Logan, and had seven children.

XII. GEORGE ROBINSON,⁴ (George,³ Philip,² Thomas,¹) m. MARY THORN. They had issue:
  i. *Thomas.*
  ii. *Mary [Polly],* m. Francis Leech, and had a son and daughter.
  iii. *George,* m., and had two sons.
  iv. *James,* d. s. p.
  v. *James* (2d).
  vi. *John.*
  vii. *Hetty.*
  viii. *Oliver,* d. 1819.

XIII. THOMAS ROBINSON,⁴ (George,³ Philip,² Thomas,¹) b. 1773; d. July 12, 1830; m. MARY McCORD, daughter of William McCord* and Mary McKinney. He resided in Perry

---

*WILLIAM McCORD was a native of Hanover township, Lancaster, now Dauphin county, Pa., where he was b. about the year 1742. He d. in Erie county, Pa., whither he removed in the early days of that county, on the 9th of September, 1806. He was thrice married; m., first, in 1765, MARY McKINNEY, who d. April 9, 1783. They had issue (surname McCord):
  i. *Joseph,* b. January 9, 1766; d. February 7, 1813; m. Elizabeth McCord.
  ii. *John,* b. December 5, 1767; d. February 13, 1839; m., 1795, Mary Harkness, b. 1775; d. 1852; daughter of William Harkness, of Cumberland county, Pa.
  iii. *William,* b. March 15, 1769; d. January 5, 1796.
  iv. *Samuel,* b. October 16, 1770; d. September 20, 1825; m., April 19, 1798, Mary [Polly] Blaine, b. September 30, 1773; d. January 4, 1837; daughter of William Blaine.
  v. *Grizelda,* b. September 27, 1772; d. October 31, 1795; m. John Morrison.
  vi. *Mary,* b. July 28, 1777; d. April 23, 1843; m. Thomas Robinson.

county, Pa., until 1798, when he removed to Erie county, Pa. His family, with some families of the McCords, Blaines, and Moorheads, were among the first settlers of that region. They were all from Central Pennsylvania, and settled east of Erie, Pa., where their descendants formed a large community of thrifty and intelligent farmers, organizing two Presbyterian churches. They had issue:

19.   *i. William-Andrew*, b. July 20, 1795 ; m. Nancy Cochran.
20.   *ii. Hetty*, b. March 15, 1797 ; m. Alvah Barr.
21.   *iii. Nancy*, b. April 8, 1799 ; m. William Doty.
22.   *iv. George-Washington*, b. June 12, 1801 ; m., first, Matilda Willis; secondly, Pamela Hubbard.
      v. John, b. August 17, 1803 ; d. August 25, 1823.
     vi. Mary-Ann, b. October 11, 1805 ; d. July 31, 1839 ; m. Benjamin Royce Tuttle ; and had issue (surname Tuttle):
        1. *Edwin-Rush*, b. 1830 ; d. December 27, 1863 ; m., June 15, 1855, Mary Sherwood ; and had issue (surname Tuttle):
          a. Edith-Sherwood, b. November 17, 1858 ; d. June 16, 1881.
          b. Annie-Robinson, b. September 5, 1860 ; m., April 30, 1885, William H. Jeffers, D. D., LL. D., Prof. of Old Testament Literature, Ecclesiastical History, and History of Doctrines, Western Theological Seminary. Allegheny, Pa.
          c. Mary-Georgiana, b. May 19, 1863.
        2. *Thomas*.

---

     vii. Rosanna, b. May 23, 1779 ; d. November 1, 1830 ; m. Alexander T. Blaine, b. 1776 ; d. February 18, 1817 ; son of William Blaine.
    viii. Andrew, b. July 27, 1781 ; m. Rosanna Bell.
     ix. James, b. March 20, 1783 ; d. October 18, 1865 ; m., first, Susan Davidson ; secondly, Jane Sturgis.

William McCord m., secondly, RACHEL SCUDDER. They had issue (surname McCord):

      x. David, b. July 22, 1786.
     xi. Alexander, b. September 17, 1787 ; m. Elizabeth Shrom.
    xii. Robert, b. October 17, 1792 ; d. March 6, 1826 ; m., first, Lucy Davidson, d. September 3, 1824 ; secondly, Margaret Woodburn, d. September 19, 1839.
   xiii. Isaac, b. March 3, 1795 ; d. 1849 ; m., first, Mary Leman ; secondly, Hannah McClellan.

William McCord m., thirdly, —— PATTERSON.

vii. Joseph-McKinney, b. December 26, 1808; d. December 28, 1843; m. Sarah Crosby; and had issue:
    1. *Franklin-Case.*
    2. *Francis-Mary,* m. Alexander F. Williams; and had issue (surname Williams): *Ella-Ophelia,* and *Annie-Sarah.*

viii. Alexander-Hamilton, b. May 3, 1811; m., May, 1833, Lomira Willis; and had issue:
    1. *Mary.*
    2. *Lydia,* m. James L. Angell; and had issue (surname Angell): *Harriet-Robinson.*
    3. *Willis.*
    4. *Hamilton.*

ix. Eliza-McCord, b. August 13, 1813; m., April 28, 1839, Dyer Loomis; and had issue (surname Loomis):
    1. *Mary-Eliza.*
    2. *Joseph-Warren.*
    3. *George-Lamartine.*

x. Samuel-McCord, b. January 26, 1816; m., August 14, 1838, Nancy Townsend; and had issue:
    1. *Mary-Louise,* b. July 12, 1839.

XIV. ANDREW ROBINSON,⁴ (Robert,³ Andrew,² Thomas,¹) b. 1760; d. June 8, 1846; m. JEAN CRAIN, b. 1765; daughter of George Crain and Jean Sturgeon, (*see Crain record*). They had issue:

    i. Nancy, b. April 4, 1791; d. December 15, 1876; unm.
    ii. George, b. March 23, 1793.
    iii. Robert-B., b. December 15, 1794; d. February 26, 1834; unm.
    iv. Joshua, b. January 20, 1796; d. December 27, 1874; m. Nancy Youtz; and had issue:
        1. *William-Crain,* m., first, Catharine Sturtz, b. September 15, 1842; d. January 15, 1876; and had issue; he m., secondly, Eliza Grunden, b. January 23, 1846.
        2. *Rachel-Mary.*
23.   *v. William-Crain,* b. June 29, 1797; m. Jennette Lytle.
    vi. Mary, b. July 23, 1799; d. January 16, 1876; m., March, 1829, John Lemon, b. April 26, 1806; d. ———; no issue.

XV. THOMAS ROBINSON,⁴ (Robert,³ Andrew,² Thomas,¹ b. 1765; d. ———; m., first, LETITIA MOORHEAD. They had issue:
    i. Robert.
    ii. James.
    iii. Eliza.
    iv. Matilda.

Thomas Robinson m., secondly, [MARY] CLARK. They had issue:
   v. *Thomas-C.*
   vi. *Charles-C.*
   vii. *Sarah-Ann.*
   viii. *John.*
   ix. *Agnes.*
   x. *Mary.*
   xi. *Andrew.*

XVI. MARY ROBINSON,[5] (Jonathan,[4] George,[3] Philip,[2] Thomas,[1]) m. JOHN ROBINSON,[5] (John,[4] Samuel,[3] Philip,[2] Thomas.[1]) They had issue:
   i. *Jonathan.*
   ii. *Newton.*
   iii. *Harvey.*
   iv. *Jane,* m. —— Silvers.
   v. *Ann.*

XVII. GEORGE ROBINSON,[5] (Jonathan,[4] George,[3] Philip,[2] Thomas,[1]) m. MARTHA MCCONNELL. They had issue:
   i. *Eliza-Jane,* m. Thomas Price, of New Orleans; and had issue (surname Price): *Eleanor,* m. Dr. Morse, and *Harry.*
   ii. *William.*
   iii. *Jonathan-Beach.*
   iv. *Fielding.*
   v. *George.*

XVIII. JAMES FISHER ROBINSON,[5] (Jonathan,[4] George,[3] Philip,[2] Thomas,[1]) b. 1800. He and his brother, John McCracken Robinson, graduated in the same class, Transylvania University, Lexington, Ky., and both chose the profession of the law. John removed to Illinois; became distinguished as a lawyer; served two terms as United States Senator, 1830–1842; was a judge of the Supreme Court of that State, and died while on the bench at the early age of about forty-seven. James F. became equally distinguished at the bar in Kentucky; refused political honors repeatedly, being offered the seat that had been filled by Henry Clay. Upon the opening of the Rebellion he was chosen to the Kentucky Senate; made speaker to meet the emergency of the resignation of Governor Magoffin, who sympathized with the secession movement. On his resignation

Family of Robinson.

Mr. Robinson became governor, and held the office with great ability and patriotism during the most trying year of the war. After the war he resumed again the duties of his profession. He married twice; m., first, December 26, 1821, SUSAN D. MANSELL, d. September 27, 1835. They had issue:

24. i. *Emilia-Jane*, b. July 14, 1827; m., first, John B. Burbridge; secondly, W. S. Downey.
25. ii. *James-Fisher*, b. November 25, 1832; m. Molly Wheeler.

James F. Robinson m., secondly, March 21, 1839, WILLINA S. HERNDON. They had issue:

iii. *Scott-Herndon*, b. May 30, 1842.
iv. *John-McCracken*, b. May 80, 1844; m. Elizabeth Pope.
v. *George-Sidney*, b. February 11, 1846; m. Florida Johnson.
vi. *Madison-Johnson*, b. August 30, 1847.
vii. *Stephen-Gano*, b. 1849; d. May 22, 1849.
viii. *Willa-Ewing*, b. March 11, 1851.
ix. *Philip-Eldon*, b. October 26, 1853.
x. *Stephen-Gano*, b. December 29, 1859.

XIX. WILLIAM ANDREW ROBINSON,[5] (Thomas,[4] George,[3] Philip,[2] Thomas,[1]) b. July 20, 1795, in Cumberland, now Perry county, Pa.; was taken by his parents to Erie county, Pa., in 1798, where he d. March 10, 1871, greatly respected and beloved in the church and in the community where he passed his life. He m., March 9, 1820, NANCY COCHRAN, b. December 22, 1797; d. March 22, 1884; daughter of Alexander Cochran and Nancy Martin. Of the six sons from this marriage, five became bankers in Pittsburgh, Pa. They had issue:

i. *Rosanna-Blaine*, b. August 14, 1821; m. John Davidson McCord; and had issue (surname McCord):
   1. *Charles-Clifford.*
   2. *Ella.*
   3. *Mary-Robinson*, m., October 10, 1878, Joseph De-Forest Junkin, of Philadelphia; and had issue (surname Junkin):
      a. *Joseph-DeForest, Jr.*, b. November 9, 1879.
      b. *Rosamond*, b. August 15, 1886.
      c. *George*, b. June 25, 1891.
ii. *Alexander-Cochrane*, b. November 6, 1822; d. December 31, 1875; with his brothers, John F., David, William, and Samuel, went to the city of Pittsburgh about the year

620   *Pennsylvania Genealogies.*

1850, and in a few years united in forming the banking firm of Robinson Bros., now for many years a well-known, honored and successful house; he m., October 28, 1868, Katharine Mather Ely, b. May 7, 1835; and had issue:
    1. *Alexander-Cochrane*, b. October 19, 1864; graduated from Western University, Pittsburgh, 1882; m., October 2, 1890, Emma Payne Jones; and they have issue:
        a. Alexander-Cochrane, b. November 2, 1891.
        b. John-Noel, b. December 25, 1892.
        c. David, b. August 18, 1894.
    2. *Selden-Marvin*, b. November 20, 1866.
    3. *Rose-Lena*, b. Nov. 19, 1871; d. March 12, 1876.
    4. *Philip-Ely*, b. May 18, 1875.
  iii. John-F., b. March 19, 1824; a banker of Pittsburgh, Pa.; resides at Sewickley, Pa.; m. Philena Alice Livingston.
  iv. Nancy-Martin, b. March 30, 1826; d. July 21, 1875; m. Dr. Alexander Cochran; and had issue (surname Cochran):
    1. *William-Robinson*, b. April 6, 1864; graduated from Western University, Pittsburgh, 1882; graduated from medical department, University of Pennsylvania, 1885.

26. *v. Thomas-Hastings*, b. Jan. 30, 1828; m. Mary Wolf Buehler.
  vi. David (twin), b. January 30, 1828; d. January 7, 1895; was for many years especially prominent not only in his business as a banker, but in the benevolent and religious movements of Pittsburgh; he was a generous and large contributor to these agencies; was a director, trustee, and treasurer of the Western Theological Seminary, one of the oldest and largest institutions of its kind in the State; for thirty years a ruling elder of the First Presbyterian church of Pittsburgh, and was connected with various other trusts; was unmarried.
27. *vii. William-Andrew*, b. June 17, 1830; m. Alice Blaine.
  viii. Samuel-Martin, b. July 9, 1833; banker, Pittsburgh, Pa.; resides at Allegheny.

XX. HETTY ROBINSON,[5] (Thomas,[4] George,[3] Philip,[2] Thomas,[1]) b. March 15, 1797, d. February 27, 1844; m., October 19, 1819, ALVAH BARR, d. March 10, 1861. They had issue (surname Barr):
    i. Mary-Ann, b. December 8, 1820; d. December 10, 1846; m. William Hilton; and had issue (surname Hilton): *Ella M.*

Family of Robinson. 621

ii. *Julia-S.*, b. September 11, 1823; d. February 1, 1846; m. James H. Hubbard.
iii. *Martha*, b. September 25, 1825; m. Wright Murphy; and had issue (surname Murphy): *Robinson-Barr, Martha-Charlotte*, and *Fannie-Ella*.
iv. *Milton-F.*, b. November 13, 1829; m. Catharine Johnson; and had issue: *Margaret-Lovina, William-Milton, Robinson-Lincoln, Hettie-Martha*, and *Oliver-Edwin*.
v. *Edwin-Thomas*, b. December 22, 1832; d. July 15, 1853.
vi. *Robinson-A.*, b. July 6, 1838; m. Nancy Slocum; and had issue: *Hetty-Ann, Edward-Robinson, George-Slocum*, and *William-M.*

XXI. NANCY ROBINSON,[5] ('Thomas,[4] George,[3] Philip,[2] Thomas,[1]) b. April 8, 1799; d. January 18, 1845; m., December 13, 1820, WILLIAM DOTY, b. 1795; d. May 19, 1864. They had issue (surname Doty):

i. *Calvin-Robinson*, b. October 1, 1821; d. September 22, 1860; m. Sarah A. Townsend; and had issue: *Kate-Carroll, William-Henry-Calvin, Sarah*, and *Emma-Frank*.
ii. *Cordelia-Robinson*, b. April 10, 1825; m. John S. Annise.
iii. *William*, b. June 12, 1834; d. November 9, 1834.

XXII. GEORGE WASHINGTON ROBINSON,[5] ('Thomas,[4] George,[3] Philip,[2] Thomas,[1]) b. June 12, 1801; d. January 4, 1877; was twice married; m., first, March 16, 1825, MATILDA WILLIS. They had issue:

i. *Sarah-Matilda*, b. November 29, 1826; d. 1863; m. Newton Truesdale; and had issue (surname Truesdale):
   1. *George-Henry*, m., April 4, 1894, Laura A. Graves.
ii. *Joseph-Willis*, b. May 25, 1829; m. America Robertson.
iii. *Josiah-Whitney* (twin), b. May 25, 1829; m. Nancy J. Ferguson; and had issue:
   1. *Mary-Matilda*, m., June 2, 1892, Edward H. Lichtenwalter.
   2. *Jane-America*.
iv. *Edwin-Evans*, b. December 8, 1833; m. Rosetta J. Bailey; and had issue: *William-E.*

George W. Robinson m., secondly, December 25, 1838, PAMELIA HUBBARD, d. December 19, 1876. No issue.

XXIII. WILLIAM CRAIN ROBINSON,[5] (Andrew,[4] Robert,[3] Andrew,[2] Thomas,[1]) b. June 29, 1797; d. December 11, 1879; m., March 18, 1829, JENNETTE LYTLE, b. June 3, 1802; d. April 25, 1881. They had issue:

28. i. *Martha-Jean*, b. May 24, 1830; m. George Ross.
   ii. *William-Crain*, b. March 16, 1832; d. Nov. 28, 1859; unm.
   iii. *Christiana-Lytle*, b. May 23, 1834; m., January 19, 1865, by Rev. Andrew D. Mitchell, Adam Detweiler; b. February 5, 1839; no issue.
   iv. *Grace-Lytle*, b. September 28, 1836; m., February 22, 1866, by Rev. Andrew D. Mitchell, John B. Bomberger; b. March 10, 1833; and had issue (surname Bomberger):
     1. *William-Robinson*, b. November 21, 1866.
     2. *Jennette-Robinson*, b. August 1, 1868.
     3. *Martin-Eby*, b. April 19, 1870.
     4. *Grace-Bennett*, b. August 16, 1874; d. Dec., 1880.
   v. *Sanford-B.*, b. December 1, 1838; m., October 26, 1872, Louisa Catharine Maulfair, b. March 2, 1850; and had issue:
     1. *Mary-Jennette*, b. April 7, 1873.
     2. *Grace-Ann*, b. Dec. 2, 1875; d. February 2, 1877.

XXIV. EMILIA JANE ROBINSON,[6] (James,[5] Jonathan,[4] George,[3] Philip,[2] Thomas,[1]) m., first, JOHN B. BURBRIDGE; and had issue (surname Burbridge):

   i. *John.*
   ii. *Susan-Robinson*, m. Lewis B. Grigsby.
   iii. *Willina Barnes*, m. James Barclay.
   iv. *Mary-Shrever.*

Mrs. Burbridge m., secondly, WILLIAM S. DOWNEY; no issue.

XXV. JAMES FISHER ROBINSON,[6] (James,[5] Jonathan,[4] George,[3] Philip,[2] Thomas,[1]) m. MOLLY WHEELER. They had issue:

   i. *James-Wheeler.*
   ii. *Abigail.*
   iii. *Willie-Braxton.*
   iv. *Thomas-Mansell.*

XXVI. THOMAS HASTINGS ROBINSON,[6] (William-Andrew,[5] Thomas,[4] George,[3] Philip,[2] Thomas,[1]) b. January 30, 1828, in North-East township, Erie county, Pa. He entered Oberlin College, Lorain county, O., in 1846, having prepared in the preparatory department of the same institution, and graduated in 1850, pursuing the full course. During his college vacations he taught in public and select schools, and, for a year or more after his graduation, he was principal of the academy at Ashtabula, O., and, for six months, principal of the Normal School at Farmington, in that State. He entered the Western Theological Seminary, Allegheny, Pa., in 1851, graduating in April, 1854. He was licensed to preach by the Presbytery of Ohio, June 13, 1854, and, in July following, was called to the colleague pastorate of what is now known as the Market Square Presbyterian church, at Harrisburg, Pa., as an associate with the Rev. William R. DeWitt, D. D. He began his ministration in October, 1854, and was ordained and installed on the 21st of January, 1855, by the Presbytery of Harrisburg. After the withdrawal of the Rev. Dr. DeWitt, in 1864, and his decease, in 1867, he continued in sole charge of the church until his resignation, in 1884. He was moderator of the Synod of Pennsylvania (N. S.), in 1861; stated clerk of the Synod of Harrisburg, 1870-1882, and stated clerk of the Synod of Pennsylvania, 1882-1883, when he resigned, as also his thirty years' pastorate of the Market Square church, Harrisburg, to accept the professorship of Sacred Rhetoric, Church Government, and Pastoral Theology, in the Western Theological Seminary, at Allegheny, into which office he was inducted April 16, 1884. He was a director of the seminary from 1874 to 1884, and was a trustee of Princeton College from 1875 to 1885. Resides in Allegheny City. Rev. Dr. Robinson m., in 1856, MARY WOLF BUEHLER, daughter of Henry Buehler and Anna Margaretta, only daughter of Governor Wolf, of Pennsylvania. They had issue:

    i. Henry-Buehler, b. December 27, 1857; d. December 30, 1857.
    ii. Anna-Margaretta, b. July 21, 1859; d. December 23, 1881.
    iii. William-Andrew, b. September 26, 1861, at Harrisburg, Pa.; he graduated from Princeton College in the highest rank in 1881; two years were then spent in Europe at the Universities of Leipsic and Heidelberg, and in traveling; after serving as a tutor at Allegheny, and as a professor at Marietta, O., and at Lewisburg University, Pennsylvania, he was called to the Professorship of Greek in Lehigh University, South Bethlehem, Pa., entering on its duties in September, 1888; this place he still holds; he m., November 26, 1888, Anna Greer MacLaren, daughter of Rev. Donald MacLaren, D. D., and Elizabeth Stockton Green; and had issue:
        1. *Elizabeth-MacLaren*, b. February 8, 1890.
        2. *Thomas-Hastings*, b. January 18, 1893.

iv. Eliza-McCormick, b. August 5, 1863; m., October 9, 1890, George Richmond Fleming; and had issue (surname Fleming):
 1. *Anna-Margaretta*, b. July 30, 1891.
 2. *Susan-Mowry*, b. April 23, 1895.
v. Edward-Orth, b. May 20, 1865; graduated from Princeton College, 1886; engaged in the real estate business, Pittsburgh.
vi. Thomas-Hastings, b. February 6, 1871; graduated from Princeton College, 1891; in the banking business, Pittsburgh.
vii. Mary-Buehler, b. January 26, 1874.

XXVII. WILLIAM ANDREW ROBINSON,[6] (William-Andrew,[5] Thomas,[4] George,[3] Philip,[2] Thomas,[1]) b. June 17, 1830, in Erie county, Pa. He entered the army, May 1, 1861, as sergeant of company A, Ninth Reserves, P. V.; promoted first lieutenant company E, Seventy-seventh regiment, P. V., November 30, 1861; promoted captain April 22, 1862; commanded as major (not mustered); campaigned in the several States of Virginia, Kentucky, Tennessee, Alabama, Louisiana, and Texas, fighting on many a field—Stone River, Corinth, Liberty Gap, and Chickamauga, where he was wounded and taken prisoner in a night engagement, September 19, 1863. For the subsequent fifteen months he shared, with fellow-soldiers, imprisonment at Libby prison, Macon, Camp Sorghum (Columbia), and Charleston, where he was one of six hundred Union officers placed by Confederate authority under the fire of Union guns from ships in Charleston harbor. After his release he rejoined his regiment, was promoted to lieutenant colonel in command of the regiment, and was breveted brigadier general for distinguished service March 13, 1865; and was mustered out of service, with regiment, after a closing campaign in Texas, December 6, 1865. He is now a member of the banking house of Robinson Bros., Pittsburgh, Pa. He m. ALICE BLAINE, daughter of Alexander Blaine and Sarah A. Platt. They had issue:
 i. Alice, b. March 29, 1876.
 ii. Alexander-Blaine, b. April 7, 1878.
 iii. William-Andrew, b. August 22, 1880.

XXVIII. MARTHA JEAN ROBINSON,[6] (William-Crain,[5] Andrew,[4] Robert,[3] Andrew,[2] Thomas,[1]) b. May 24, 1830; m.,

March 16, 1852, by Rev. John Winebrenner, V. D. M., GEORGE ROSS, b. November 22, 1821 ; d. November 30, 1880, in Lebanon, Pa. His grandfather, Dr. Joseph Ross, was a native of Montgomery county, Pa., and married Mary Maria McClintock, of Pottstown. After his marriage he removed to Hummelstown, Dauphin county, where, on November 8, 1792, his son, Robert May Ross, was born. Shortly after the birth of Robert May, his mother died, when Dr. Joseph Ross removed to Elizabethtown. His son, Robert, was sent to Montgomery county among his mother's relatives, where he was raised and educated. When grown to manhood he returned to Elizabethtown, and about the year 1815 married Barbara Redsecker, a daughter of George Redsecker. They had six children, of whom George was the third, and the eldest son. His ancestors on his father's side were of Quaker origin, his mother's of Swiss descent, and were known as Pennsylvania-German. His father engaged in mercantile pursuits, and at an early age, between school-hours, young George assisted him. At the age of ten he was sent to a select school at Reading, from thence to Lititz, where he remained two years. In May, 1838, he commenced to learn the drug business at Lancaster, afterwards continuing in the same occupation at Harrisburg. When quite a small boy he took great interest in the study of botany, a science which he pursued with great delight throughout life, and this fact becoming known to Col. John Roberts, a botanist of some reputation, a warm friendship sprang up between them, and young Ross was encouraged and assisted in his studies. At the same time he began the study of Latin at a select school in Harrisburg. At the close of his apprenticeship, he was offered special inducements by his uncle, Abraham Redsecker, who had purchased a drug store in Elizabethtown, which he accepted, and returned to his native place in December, 1842. After several years he purchased the store from his uncle and engaged in business for himself. He shortly after began the study of medicine with Dr. Nathaniel Watson, of Donegal, and graduated from Jefferson Medical College, Philadelphia, in 1849. He immediately began the practice of his profession in Elizabethtown, continuing at the same time the drug business, and soon acquired a large practice. In the spring of 1852 he purchased a property in Lebanon, to which place he removed in October following. He however quit the practice of medicine and devoted his entire time to the drug trade, and soon succeeded in building up a large and successful business. Dr. Ross took an active interest in the development of Lebanon, and was associated in various enterprises which tended to promote its prosperity. Having, in the year 1842, united with the Church of God, a body of Christians organized under the labors of Rev. John Winebrenner, he became conspicuous for his disinterested labors and great liberality. In 1857 the General Eldership elected him a member of the Board of Publication, and he was re-elected at each subsequent meeting; was a member of the committee which published the "Church Hymn Book," and subsequently elected general book agent, in which capacity he issued a number of books and pamphlets, conducting the publishing interests with such judgment and business tact that what was a cumbersome debt when he assumed its management soon became a source of revenue, a large fund having been accumulated during the almost twenty years of his management. In addition to these general church interests, he was, in 1868, elected treasurer of the East Pennsylvania Eldership, in which position he was continued eleven years, when increasing business cares demanding his attention obliged him to resign. They had issue (surname Ross):

 i. Mary-Jennette, b. December 23, 1852; d. November 19, 1871, at Bethlehem, Pa., where she was attending school.
 ii. George-Redsecker, b. October 17, 1854; m., April 12, 1894, at Harrisburg, by Rev. Dr. George B. Stewart, Sarah Lavinia Raymond, b. October 23, 1856.
 iii. William-Robinson, b. July 8, 1856; m., October 3, 1882, by the Rev. Samuel A. Martin, at Lebanon, Valeria Rhinehart Smith, b. October 2, 1861; and had issue:
  1. *William-Robinson*, b. November 30, 1884; d. January 9, 1886.
  2. *George*, b. January 5, 1887.
 iv. Robert-May, b. November 6, 1861; d. October 24, 1863.
 v. Martha-Elizabeth, b. January 6, 1866; d. February 5, 1876.

RUTHERFORD OF PAXTANG.

[In the year 1689, several brothers, of the Scotch family of Rutherford, joined the army of William III when he invaded Ireland—were present and fought at the battle of the Boyne. Two of them were company officers, and the third was a Presbyterian clergyman. They all remained on the island, one settling in the county Tyrone, another in the county Down, and the minister in the county Monaghan. Several of the sons of these men emigrated to America during the decade between 1720 and 1730; among them was Thomas Rutherford, the progenitor of the family in Paxtang. As an instance of how family likeness is preserved through ages, it may be here stated that the portrait of David Rutherford, grandfather of Sir Walter Scott, which hangs in the dining-hall facing the Tweed at Abbotsford, would answer equally well as a portrait of the late Dr. Rutherford, of Harrisburg, although the Doctor's ancestor left Scotland two centuries ago. No likeness of Thomas Rutherford is in existence, and the only description of him is a traditionary one, which represents him as a dark-haired, well-built man, about five feet ten inches in height, full of energy and of such business habits as led to financial success. There is a spice of romance connected with his early manhood which may not be uninteresting to the reader. His attachment to Jean Mordah, whom he afterwards married, was reciprocated. The Mordahs were about to sail for America, and Thomas, fearing he might lose his Jean, proposed and was accepted, but poor Jean was scarcely sixteen and her parents said "no," and took her with them across the sea. On the cover of his memorandum book, preserved in the family, Thomas inscribed the legend, "*Enquire for Dennygall.*" This was the location of the Mordahs in Pennsylvania, and, in the following year, 1729, he appeared in person at their door and claimed his Jean. Mr. Mordah, doubtless, still thought the pair too young, and, in order that more time might be gained, required his prospective son-in-law to be the possessor of a certain sum of money, with which to begin the world, before he would entrust the young lady to his keeping. Thomas, like Jacob of old, was obliged to acquiesce, and took his departure for Philadelphia. When he returned he was mounted on a good horse and had with him the documents which satisfied the old gentleman's requirements. They were married in 1730, and lived in Donegal until after the death of John Mordah, in 1744, when they removed to Derry, and, in 1755, to Paxtang, where they spent the remainder of their days. Their house, a two-story log, stood on the site of the present residence of Silas B. Rutherford, at Paxtang station, and was burned down in 1840. The old house standing directly opposite the station was built after Thomas Rutherford's death, about 1783, and the old stone house over the spring was, probably, built before Mr. Rutherford bought the property.]

I. THOMAS RUTHERFORD,[1] b. June 24, 1707, in parish Derrylouran, county Tyrone, Ireland; d. April 18, 1777, in Paxtang; m., by Rev. James Anderson, September 7, 1730, JEAN MORDAH, daughter of John and Agnes Mordah, b. April 5, 1712, in the parish of Gorty-Lowery, county Tyrone, Ireland; d. August 10, 1789. They had issue, all born in Donegal, Lancaster county, Pa:*

---

*From the old memorandum book referred to, we have the following record, wonderfully complete and satisfactory of its kind:

Thomas Rutherford, born the 24th day of June, A. D. 1707; and baptized by the Rev. John McClave, in the parish of Derrylouran, county Tyrone, living in Cookstown.

Jean Mordah, my wife, born the 5th day of April, A. D. 1712; and baptized by the Rev. John McClave in Gorty-Lowry.

Me and my wife was married the 7th day of September, A. D. 1730, by the Rev. James Anderson, in Donney Gall, America.

Our eldest daughter, Agnes, the 9th day of July, 1731; and baptized by the Rev. James Anderson. Died when four years old.

Our second daughter, Ellenor, was born the 16th day of January, 1733; and baptized by Rev. James Anderson.

Our third daughter, Jean, was born the 22d day of June, A. D. 1734; baptized by the Rev. Mr. Anderson.

Our son John was born the 16th day of February, A. D. 1737; baptized by Rev. Mr. Anderson.

Our son Thomas was born the 14th day of August, 1788. Died when about one year old.

i. Agnes, b. July 9, 1731; d. 1735.
2. *ii. Eleanor,* b. January 16, 1733; m., first, William Wilson; secondly, John Davison.
3. *iii. Jean,* b. June 22, 1734; m. Thomas Mayes.
4. *iv. John,* b. February 16, 1737; m. Margaret Parke.
  v. Thomas, b. August 14, 1738; d. 1739; buried in Donegal churchyard.
  vi. Agnes, b. September 14, 1740; m. William Gray.
  vii. Thomas, b. February 12, 1743; d. January 8, 1760; buried in Paxtang graveyard.
5. *viii. Mary,* b. February 18, 1745; m. Andrew Mayes.
  ix. Elizabeth, (twin), b. February 18, 1745; d. s. p.
  x. James, b. August 27, 1747; d. March 6, 1809; m. Margaret Brisban, b. 1753; d. March, 1825; they had no issue, and are both interred in Paxtang church burial ground.
6. *xi. Samuel,* b. December 13, 1749; m. Susan Collier.
7. *xii. Elizabeth,* b. February 27, 1752; m., first, Patrick Gallaway; secondly, Patrick Harbison; thirdly, Thomas Archibald.

II. ELEANOR RUTHERFORD,[2] (Thomas,[1]) b. January 16, 1733, in Donegal, Lancaster county, Pa.; d. December, 1799, in Paxtang, and there buried; was twice married; m., first, WILLIAM WILSON, and had issue; she m., secondly, JOHN DAVISON; d. 1772. They had issue (surname Davison):

  i. Elizabeth, b. 1766.
  ii. Agnes, b. 1768; m. John Young, son of James Young, of Hanover, and removed to Susquehanna county, Pa.
  iii. Robert, b. 1772; d. about 1855, in Stone Valley; m., and had issue: *John,* who is still (1885) living; *Powel, Eleanor, Jane,* m. David Irwin, and removed to Illinois, and *Isabella,* unm.

Our fourth daughter, Agnes, was born the 14th day of September, 1740; baptized by the Rev. Mr. Richard Sankey.

Our son Thomas was born the 12th day of February, 1743; baptized by the Rev. Samuel Black.

Our two daughters, Mary and Elizabeth, born the 18th day of February, 1745. Elizabeth died when about eight months old, baptized by Rev. Samuel Black.

Our son James was born the 28th day of August, 1747; and baptized by the Rev. John Elder.

Our son Samuel was born 13th day of December, 1749; and baptized by the Rev. Richard Sankey.

Our daughter Elizabeth was born on the 27th of February, 1752 and baptized by the Rev. Richard Sankey.

III. JEAN RUTHERFORD,² (Thomas¹) b. June 22, 1734, in Donegal township, Lancaster county, Pa.; d. in South Carolina at an advanced age; m. THOMAS MAYES.* They had issue (surname Mayes):

    i. Jean.
    ii. John, d. in 1827.
    iii. Edward, was an elder in the Presbyterian church, living in 1833, in Union district, South Carolina.
    iv. Margaret, living in 1833, in Alabama.
    v. Elizabeth, m. William Davidson; removed to Illinois; and had issue (surname Davidson): *John, Andrew, William,* and three daughters.
    vi. Thomas.

IV. Captain JOHN RUTHERFORD,² (Thomas,¹) b. February 16, 1737, in Donegal, Lancaster county, Pa. He accompanied his father to Paxtang in 1755. In the year 1760, in connection with the latter, he purchased the plantation, containing nearly four hundred acres, on which Rutherford station, on the P. & R. railroad, is now (1895) located. This property, although divided into three tracts, is still owned by his descendants; and his mansion house, built before the Revolution, is used as a dwelling by his great-grandchildren. When the troubles with England arose, which led to the struggle for independence, he was active in his opposition to British tyranny. He was a

---

*THOMAS MAYES was the eldest son of Thomas and Margaret Mayes, of Paxtang. Thomas, Sr., died in August, 1764; and had issue:

    i. Thomas.
    ii. Margaret.
    iii. Rebeckah.
    iv. Andrew, d. June, 1754; m. Rebecca ———, and left *James, Mary, Rachael, Rebecca, Margaret,* and *Susanna.*
    v. James.
    vi. Mary.
    vii. Samuel.
    viii. Elizabeth.
    ix. Martha.
    x. Jean, m. ——— Hilton.
    xi. William.
    xii. John.
    xiii. Dorcas.
    xiv. Matthew.

member and officer, throughout the war, of the "Liberty Association of Pennsylvania," and served as captain of a company in the campaigns of 1776 and 1777 in the Jerseys and in Eastern Pennsylvania. He afterwards commanded a detachment from several companies against the Indians. Throughout his life, we find Mr. Rutherford's name connected with many enterprises, both civil and ecclesiastical, which show him to have been a representative man and trusted citizen. He d. at his home in Paxtang, October 2, 1804. Captain Rutherford m., February 4, 1762, MARGARET PARKE, b. 1737 ; d. January 18, 1810. They had issue :

    i. Jane, b. August 26, 1763 ; d. February 28, 1807 ; m., June 29, 1780, Samuel Hutchinson ; removed to Montour county, where they lived and died.

    ii. Martha, b. February 22, 1765 ; d. August 27, 1849 ; m. Capt. James Collier ; removed to Greenfield, Ohio, and there buried.

    iii. Thomas, b. November 28, 1767 ; d. October 15, 1793 ; buried at Paxtang.

8.   *iv. Samuel*, b. July 16, 1769 ; m. Elizabeth Brisban, daughter of Capt. John Brisban.

    v. Mary, b. September 13, 1771 ; m. Robert Gray.

9.   *vi. John*, b. January 15, 1774 ; m., first, Jean Meader ; secondly, Priscilla (Espy) Barrett.

10. *vii. William*, b. August 4, 1776 ; m. Sarah Swan.

V. MARY RUTHERFORD,² (Thomas,¹) b. February 18, 1745 ; m. ANDREW MAYES. They removed to South Carolina ; and had issue (surname Mayes):

    i. John, b. April 30, 1768.

    ii. Jean, b. December 25, 1769.

11. *iii. James*, b. September 21, 1771 ; m., and had issue.

12. *iv. Thomas*, b. June 18, 1773 ; m. Nancy McCormick.

    v. Samuel, b. April 10, 1775.

    vi. Elizabeth, b. January 22, 1777 ; m. ——— Davidson ; emigrated to Decatur county, Ill., and d. there. They had ten children—seven daughters and three sons ; the latter (surname Davidson), *John, Andrew*, and *Baxter*. Baxter Davidson remained on the old homestead in Decatur county.

13. *vii. Andrew*, b. February 8, 1780 ; m., and had issue.

    viii. Mary, b. March 5, 1782.

    ix. Robert, b. June 3, 1784.

    x. Susannah, b. October 9, 1787.

 xi. Eleanor, b. September 20, 1789.
 xii. Rutherford, b. May 31, 1792; removed to Georgia.

 VI. SAMUEL RUTHERFORD,[2] (Thomas,[1]) b. December 13, 1749; d. May 2, 1785. He held a commission as second lieutenant in Captain Joseph Sherer's company; served in the Jerseys and the neighborhood of New York in 1776; was taken prisoner at the battle of Long Island, and confined for a time in one of the celebrated prison-ships, to the great injury of his health. He m., March 14, 1776, SUSANNA COLLIER, b. September 17, 1750; d. May 8, 1813. They had issue:

 i. Jean, b. February 11, 1779; d. s. p.
 ii. Susanna, b. January 20, 1780; d. s. p.
14. *iii. Thomas*, b. September 27, 1782; m. Mary Shultz.
 iv. James, b. February 24, 1785; d. August 9, 1786.

 VII. ELIZABETH RUTHERFORD,[2] (Thomas,[1]) b. February 27, 1752. She was thrice married; m., first, PATRICK GALLAWAY, who joined Captain Matthew Smith's company, of Paxtang, and was on the expedition to Quebec in 1775, but never returned. She m., secondly, PATRICK HARBISON, and removed with him to the home of the Mayes, in Spartansburg district, S. C. Mr. Harbison was, soon after, killed by the Tories, and Andrew Mayes removed with his family, together with Mrs. Harbison, to the settlement of the Mordahs, in Iredell county, N. C. Here Mrs. Harbison m. THOMAS ARCHIBALD. Some of the descendants of these families reside in the South and West, but we have no knowledge of their whereabouts.

 VIII. SAMUEL RUTHERFORD,[3] (John,[2] Thomas,[1]) b. July 16, 1769; d. November 26, 1833; m. ELIZABETH BRISBAN, b. September 29, 1770; d. April 24, 1843; daughter of Captain John Brisban.* They had issue:

---

 * CAPTAIN JOHN BRISBAN, a native of county Tyrone, Ireland, b. December 25, 1730. With an elder brother he came to America at the outset of the French and Indian war. He was a soldier in that sanguinary struggle for French supremacy in America, and held a lieutenant's commission in the English army. He was a part of the time in Canada, and with General Wolfe on the celebrated Plains of Abraham. For his services he received a grant from George III of two thousand acres of land in Virginia. He subsequently settled in Lan-

i. Margaret-Parke, b. April 6, 1795; d. May 18, 1879; m. John R. Collier, of Ohio, and had issue.
ii. Isabella-Simmons, b. August 18, 1797; d. March 10, 1852.
iii. Jane-Hutchinson, b. September 13, 1799; d. August 18, 1851; buried in Stephenson county, Ill.; m. Robert Foster, and had issue.
iv. Eliza, b. October 30, 1801; m. John P. Rutherford, and had issue.
v. Martha-Brisban, b. January 16, 1804; d. October 12, 1884; buried at Springfield, O.; m. Hugh Wilson, and had issue.

15. *vi. John-Brisban*, b. November 28, 1805; m. Keziah Parke.
vii. James, b. February 14, 1808; d. April 7, 1809.
viii. Mary-Ann, b. June 14, 1810; d. December 14, 1884; m. Samuel S. Rutherford.

IX. JOHN RUTHERFORD,³ (John,² Thomas,¹) b. January 15, 1774, at Paxtang; d. May 1, 1832. He received a good education; was a surveyor, and for a time in the employ of the Presqu' Isle Land company, and, in 1817, was member of the Legislature from Dauphin county. After the death of his uncle, James Rutherford, in 1809, he purchased the moiety of his grandfather's farm, which had fallen to James upon the death of Thomas, in 1777, and now (1885) owned by John A. Rutherford. There he spent the remainder of his life. He

caster county. He early espoused the cause of the Colonies, and, receiving a commission as captain in the Second (Colonel St. Clair's) Pennsylvania battalion, January 5, 1776, raised a company mostly in the upper part of then Lancaster county, now Dauphin and Lebanon, which was in active service in Canada. At the close of that arduous campaign he was transferred to the Third regiment of the Pennsylvania Line, resigning in July, 1777. He subsequently returned to the service, and at the close of the war to his farm near "Bird-in-Hand," Lancaster county, when he was appointed collector of military fines. He was, however, too kind-hearted to oppress the delinquents, consequently he became responsible to the government for the amount, which resulted in Captain Brisban becoming poor and penniless. All the papers pertaining to his military services were sent to Washington for the purpose of securing a pension, but, unfortunately, lost. Captain Brisban was married twice, and left issue by both. He died at the residence of his son-in-law, Samuel Rutherford, near Harrisburg, Pa., March 13, 1822, aged ninety-one years. He lies buried in Paxtang church graveyard.

m., first, JEAN MEADER, b. 1808; d. September, 1827. They had issue:

    i. Levi, b. 1825, in Paxtang; d. February 8, 1851, at Harrisburg, Pa. After the death of his father, in 1832, he was taken by his uncle, William Rutherford, in whose family he remained until he attained his majority. He received a liberal education, and read medicine under Dr. W. W. Rutherford, of Harrisburg, graduating at the University of Pennsylvania in March. 1849. He at once began the practice of medicine at New Cumberland, which promised bright, but, his health failing, he was compelled to relinquish the duties of his profession. He returned home, and undertook the superintendence of the farm, hoping thereby to reëstablish his health. This proved futile, for he gradually failed. Intelligent, amiable, and upright, Dr. Levi Rutherford's young life left a rose-tinted memory in many households.

    ii. Jackson-Gray, b. August 31, 1827; resides at Dry Run, Franklin county, Pa.; m. Sarah S. Rutherford,[5] (Samuel,[4] William,[3] John,[2] Thomas,[1]) b. January 10, 1841; and had issue:
        1. *Jackson*, b. May 29, 1868.
        2. *Elizabeth-Beulah*, b. June 7, 1870.

John Rutherford m., secondly, PRISCILLA [ESPY] BARRETT, b. August 25, 1791; d. August 23, 1873. They had issue:

    iii. William, b. February 24, 1830; d. February 2, 1892, at Cedarville, Stephenson county, Ill.; m. Mary Calvin Hutchinson, b. April 15, 1837; daughter of Thomas Hutchinson; and had issue:
        1. *Vernettie-Bell*, b. April 9, 1862; m., September 17, 1885, A. Orville Clingman.
        2. *Alice-Priscilla*, b. October 2, 1864.
        3. *John-Parke*, b. May 2, 1868; d. August 15, 1887.
        4. *Thomas-Hutchinson*, b. July 10, 1872.

    iv. Samuel, b. September 5, 1832; d. March 1, 1892, at Cedarville, Ill.

X. WILLIAM RUTHERFORD,[3] (John,[2] Thomas,[1]) b. August 4, 1776, in Paxtang; d. there, January 17, 1850. He received a fair education, and was brought up as a farmer. Born amid the thunders of the Revolution, he inherited the military spirit of his father, and became quite prominent as an officer, serving in all grades from lieutenant up to that of a commission of colonel, which office he declined. In 1816 he was elected a director of the poor, and served as a member of the House of Representatives from 1819 to 1821, and again from 1829 to 1831. He was one of the most influential men of his day in the county of Dauphin, and a representative man thereof. Colonel Rutherford m., March 17, 1801, SARAH SWAN, daughter of William Swan, who d. June 18, 1852, aged seventy-three years. They are both buried in old Paxtang church graveyard. They had issue:

16.   *i. John-Parke*, b. February 14, 1802; m. Eliza Rutherford.
      ii. Martha, b. November 10, 1803; unm.; d. October 20, 1851.
17.   *iii. William-Wilson*, b. November 23, 1805; m. Eleanor Crain.
      iv. Margaret, b. September 6, 1808; d. June 7, 1889; unm.
18.   *v. Samuel*, b. October 8, 1810; m. Elizabeth Pawling.
      vi. Sarah, b. May 25, 1812; d. March 28, 1873; buried at Middletown; m. Daniel Kendig.
19.   *vii. Abner*, b. March 31, 1814; m. Ann Espy.
20.   *viii. Hiram*, b. December 27, 1815; m., first, Lucinda Bowman; secondly, Harriet Hutchinson.
      ix. Mary, b. June 4, 1817; d. April 14, 1818.
      x. Cyrus-Green, b. July 7, 1819; d. March 30, 1850; unm.

XI. JAMES MAYES,³ (Mary,² Thomas,¹) b. September 21, 1771; removed to Coles county, Ill., and accidentally killed, about 1830, by the falling of a tree. He m., and had issue (surname Mayes):

    i. George-W., d. in 1858.
    ii. William-J., d. in 1863, in the army.
    iii. Benjamin-F., resided in State of Washington.
    iv. Thomas-H., resided in Kentucky.
    v. Alexander.
    vi. Nancy-J., d. s. p.
    vii. Eleanor.
    viii. Sarah-J.
    ix. Dorcas.

XII. THOMAS MAYES,³ (Mary,² Thomas,¹) b. June 18, 1773; removed to Illinois and d. there, October 15, 1850; m. NANCY MCCORMICK, daughter of James McCormick and Mary Carson, of Hanover. They had issue (surname Mayes):

    i. Andrew, b. October 1, 1799; d. in 1859, in Wayne county, Ill.
    ii. James, b. April 15, 1806; was killed at the battle of Shiloh.
    iii. Nancy [twin], b. April 15, 1806.
    iv. Jane, b. May 10, 1810; m. —— Leach; and had a son, Rutherford.

v. Elizabeth [twin], b. May 10, 1810.
vi. Sarah, b. 1813.
viii. Gillico, b. August 18, 1816; resided in Adams county, Ill.; was twice married; m., first, Jacob Veach, who d. July July 13, 1851; and had issue (surname Veach):
    1. *John-F.*, b. October 4, 1839; served in the civil war four years; resides in Barton county, Kansas.
    2. *Andrew-A.*, b. December 10, 1840; was killed at the battle of Shiloh.
    3. *Mary*, b. January 17, 1844.
    4. *Ellen*, b. March 13, 1847.
    5. *James-W.*, b. October 21, 1850.
She m., secondly, November 6, 1856, Jacob Buffington, b. February 25, 1809, in Hardin county, Va.

XIII. ANDREW MAYES,³ (Mary,² Thomas,¹) removed to Illinois, where he married and died. They had issue (surname Mayes):
    i. Thomas-J., b. in 1842; resided twenty-five miles southwest of Oakland, Ill.
    ii. William-C.
    iii. James-C., d. in 1864, from disease contracted in the war for the Union.
    iv. John-M.
    v. Nancy-Jane.

XIV. THOMAS RUTHERFORD,³ (Samuel,² Thomas,¹) b. Septemper 27, 1782; d. August 4, 1805; m. MARY SHULTZ, b. March 5, 1786; d. April 1, 1839. They had issue:
21.   *i. Samuel-Shultz*, b. December 17, 1803; m. Mary A. Rutherford.
    ii. Mary-Collier, b. February 8, 1805; d. August 13, 1872; unm.; buried at Paxtang.

XV. JOHN BRISBAN RUTHERFORD,⁴ (Samuel,³ John,² Thomas,¹) b. November 28, 1805, in Swatara township, Dauphin county, Pa.; d. October 10, 1892, on the farm where he was born. Being the only surviving son, he succeeded to the farm property of his father upon his death, November 26, 1833, and made farming his main business through life. In early manhood, Mr. Rutherford was elected captain of the Dauphin cavalry, hence his military title. He was active in politics, and was elected member of the Legislature on the Whig ticket in 1848, and reëlected in 1849. In 1857 he was elected to the State Senate for three years, on the Republican ticket. He was treasurer of the Pennsylvania State Agricultural Society for a long time—elected in 1864 and served twenty-five years. Mr. Rutherford was identified with the various offices in his township, and, in old Paxtang church was a ruling elder. He m., March 19, 1833, KEZIAH PARKE, d. July 2, 1885; daughter of Col. James Parke, of Parkesburg, Chester county, Pa. They had issue:

    i. Samuel, d. in infancy.
    ii. Mary-Lucinda, b. March 10, 1835; m. James McClure; resides at Glen Moore, Chester county, Pa.; and had issue (surname McClure):
        1. *Margaret-Moore.*
        2. *Florence.*
        3. *Jennie-Rutherford.*
        4. *John-B.-Rutherford.*
        5. *Mary-Parke.*
        6. *Gertrude.*
    iii. Eliza-Jane, b. May 8, 1837; m. Rev. Samuel Dickey, of Oxford, Chester county, who d. January 14, 1884; and had issue (surname Dickey):
        1. *Samuel.*
        2. *Irvine-Rutherford.*
    iv. Adaline-Margaret, m. W. Franklin Rutherford.
    v. Samuel-Parke, b. September 18, 1841; resides at Gum Tree, Chester county, Pa.; m. Elizabeth R. Bunn, of Lancaster county, Pa.; and had issue:
        1. *Frank-Parke.*
        2. *John-Marshall.*
        3. *John-Brisban.*
    vi. John-Quincy-Adams, b. November 9, 1843; m. Margaret Brown Elder, (see *Elder record*,) and had issue:
        1. *Howard-Ainsworth.*
        2. *Ralph-Brisban.*
        3. *Nancy*, d. s. p.
        4. *Eleanor-Virginia.*
        5. *Isabella-Parke.*
        6. *John-Quincy.*
        7. *Margaret-Brown.*
        8. *Matthew-Robinson.*
        9. *Arthur-Parke.*
    vii. Francis-Wilson, b. December 4, 1845; m. Eleanor Sherer Elder, (see *Elder record*,) and had issue:
        1. *Joshua-Elder.*
        2. *Thomas-Mordah.*

3. *Norman-Parke.*
4. *Francis-Wilson.*
5. *Marion-Gertrude,* d. inf.
6. *Samuel.*

viii. Keziah-Virginia.

ix. Marion-Gertrude, m. S. Ralston Dickey, of Oxford, Chester county, Pa.; and had issue (surname Dickey):
1. *Frances-Rutherford.*
2. *John-B.-Rutherford.*

XVI. JOHN PARKE RUTHERFORD,[4] (William,[3] John,[2] Thomas,[1]) b. February 14, 1802, in Swatara township, Dauphin county, Pa.; d. May 12, 1871. He was a farmer, and brought up in that pursuit. He held many places of public trust in his life; was superintendent of the Wiconisco canal as early as 1837, an auditor of the county, a jury commissioner, and was vice-president and treasurer of the Pennsylvania State Agricultural Society. He was a strong anti-slavery advocate, as all his family were, and many a weary pilgrim, in the days of the fugitive slave act, sore of foot and heart, found in Captain Rutherford hospitable assistance, material aid, and manly encouragement. He hated slavery because he considered it a moral sin and a political blight upon the free institutions of America. During the late Rebellion he served as quartermaster in the United States army, ranking fourth on the list. While stationed at Harper's Ferry he was captured in one of the raids on that stronghold, but released on parole. He was then ordered to Camp Douglas, and subsequently to Charleston, S. C. In the latter city, about the close of the war, he contracted a disease from the effects of which he never fully recovered. Captain Rutherford m. ELIZA RUTHERFORD, b. October 30, 1801 ; d. January 30, 1860; daughter of Samuel Rutherford. They had issue:

i. Samuel-Silas-Brisban, b. April 28, 1825; m., first, Mary Caroline Walker, d. September 26, 1874; daughter of James Walker, and had issue:
1. *James-Walker,* m., 1887, Annie Gill.
2. *John-Percy,* m. Alice Hosier.
3. *Bessie,* m., Feb. 27, 1889, James A. Rutherford.
4. *Ramsay.*
5. *Thomas-Wilson.*

Mr. Rutherford m., secondly, October, 1888, Ann E. Walker.

ii. William-Swan, b. August 19, 1827 ; d. January 24, 1895 ; m. Jane Eliza Rutherford,[5] (Samuel,[4] Thomas,[3] Samuel,[2] Thomas,[1]) b. August 29, 1840; and had issue:
  1. *Mary-Brisban*,
  2. *Allan*.
  3. *Eliza-Edna*.
  4. *William-Sumner*.
  5. *Edmund-Foster*.
  6. *Margaretta-Simmons*.
iii. John-Alexander, b. November 23, 1830; d. December 17, 1891 ; m. Lydia A. Galt, d. February 14, 1880; daughter of Alexander Galt, of Lancaster county ; and had issue:
  1. *Alexander-Galt*.
  2. *John-Parke*.
  3. *Frances-Jane*, m. Matthew Brown Elder.
  4. *Andrew-Mitchell*.
  5. *Eliza-Wilson*, m., June 5, 1895, Arthur Hamilton Bailey.
  6. *Lydia-Bertha*.
iv. Elizabeth-Martha, b. June, 1833.
v. Sarah-Margaret, b. August 21, 1835 ; m. Rev. Job D. Randolph ; and had issue (surname Randolph):
  1. *Eliza-Rutherford*, m. Rev. William Voorhees.
  2. *Myrvin-Paul*.
vi. Mary-Jane, b. December 9, 1837 ; m. John Elder, (*see Elder record*).
vii. Eleanor-Gilchrist, b. April 15, 1841.

XVII. WILLIAM WILSON RUTHERFORD,[4] (William,[3] John,[2] Thomas,[1]) b. November 23, 1805, in Paxtang, now Swatara township, Dauphin county, Pa.; d. March 13, 1873, at Harrisburg, Pa. He commenced the study of medicine with Dr. Whiteside, of Harrisburg, then a prominent physician, in 1830; and after the removal of Dr. Whiteside, continued under the instruction of Dr. Dean. He attended the lectures of Jefferson Medical College, 1830–32, graduating from that institution on the 7th of March the latter year. He located first at Mechanicsburg, where he remained nearly a year, when, entering into partnership with his preceptor, Dr. Dean, he removed to Harrisburg, where, for forty years, he practiced his profession, winning for himself an honorable name not only at home but abroad. Dr. Rutherford had what few physicians possessed—a most perfect knowledge of diseases in general ; and it mattered little what the case, his diagnosis, when called in consultation, was final as it was accurate. An extensive practice of over forty years in every department of medicine and surgery gave him such a perfect knowledge of his profession that the loss of his advice and assistance in difficult cases was severely felt by his surviving brethren. For eight years prior to his death he had been the regularly appointed surgeon to the Pennsylvania Railroad company, although he served it some ten years previously when called upon. From the organization of the old Harrisburg Gas company he was one of its directors, and, at his death, president of the company. In numerous other enterprises he took an active part, and was always one of Harrisburg's public-spirited citizens. His life was an eventful one, and one fraught with many incidents of interest. In season and out of season, in life and in death, his good-natured face appeared upon the stage, gladly, even tearfully, welcome. Dr. Rutherford married ELEANOR CRAIN, daughter of Col. Richard M. Crain, (see Crain record). They had issue:

  i. Dr. *Alexander-Dean,* d. June 27, 1877; m. Annie E. Huntsberger; no issue.
  ii. *Sarah-Swan,* d. February 10, 1865; m. W. Harvey Brown, captain U. S. A.
  iii. *Elizabeth-Crain,* m. John C. Kunkel, (see *Kunkel record*).
  iv. *Alice-Agnes,* d. s. p.

XVIII. SAMUEL RUTHERFORD,[4] (William,[3] John,[2] Thomas,[1]) b. October 8, 1810; d. March 26, 1872; buried at Paxtang. He m. ELIZABETH PAWLING, b. October 18, 1816; d. April 24, 1881. They had issue:

  i. *Sarah-Susannah,* b. January 10, 1841: m. Jackson G. Rutherford.
  ii. *John-Harding,* b. Oct. 11, 1842; d., Dec. 26, 1892, unm.
  iii. *Mary-Martha,* b. November 9, 1845; d. June 24, 1884; m. Samuel Beattie, of Shippensburg, Pa.
  iv. *Margaret-Swan,* b. Sept. 2, 1847; d., March 17, 1890, unm.
  v. *Keziah-Ann,* b. March 3, 1849; m. Jacob L. Walker, of Kansas City, Mo.
  vi. *Horace-Greely,* b. Oct. 14, 1852; d. Jan. 10, 1863.
  vii. *Alice-Elizabeth,* b. March 11, 1855; d. Jan. 1, 1863.
  viii. *Samuel-Wilson,* b. December 26, 1857; m. Matilda Rhoads, daughter of Simeon Rhoads, of Hummelstown, Pa.

XIX. ABNER RUTHERFORD,[4] (William,[3] John,[2] Thomas,[1]) b. March 31, 1814, on the Rutherford homestead in Swatara township, Dauphin county, Penn'a; d. September 2, 1891; buried in Paxtang. He received the education afforded by the select schools of Paxtang Valley, and was a farmer by occupation. The last fifteen years of his life he was president of the first National Bank of Hummelstown; was identified with other corporations, and active in various local enterprises of his day. He was one of the early members of the Pennsylvania Anti-Slavery Society, and in 1835 was captain of the tenth company, Ninety-eighth regiment, Pennsylvania militia. For many years he was one of the vice-presidents of the Pennsylvania State Agricultural Society, in the founding of which he took a prominent part. His energy and ability, combined with his business habits, produced that success which genererally follows. Mr. Rutherford married, February 28, 1839, ANN ESPY, youngest daughter of William Espy, of Swatara. They had issue:

22.   i. *William-Franklin*, b. December 7, 1839; m. Adaline M. Rutherford.
    ii. *John-Marshall*, b. September 4, 1841; d. May 24, 1869; served as a soldier in the company raised at Oberlin College, Ohio, for the emergency of 1862, marching to Kentucky; in 1863 enlisted in the Nineteenth Pennsylvania cavalry, Colonel Wynkoop, and was employed on detached service along the Baltimore and Ohio railroad and as commissary sergeant of the regiment; mustered out with regiment
    iii. *Susanna-Espy*, b. September 17, 1843; d. May 5, 1846.
    iv. *Sarah-Ann*, b. August 31, 1845; d. December 21, 1883; m. Dr. A. C. Renninger; d. December 8, 1877; and had issue (surname Renninger): *Abner-Rutherford*.
    v. *Abner*, b. December 22, 1847; d. January 10, 1855.
    vi. *Alice-Agnes*, b. May 16, 1849; d. August 26, 1850.
    vii. *Susanna-Elizabeth*, b. September 21, 1850.
    viii. *Ada-Byron*, b. November 29, 1852; m. Spencer F. Barber; and had issue (surname Barber):
        1. *Ann-Espy.*
        2. *William-Byron.*
        3. *James-Rezner.*
        4. *Nelson-Rutherford.*

XX. HIRAM RUTHERFORD,[4] (William,[3] John,[2] Thomas,[1]) was the eighth member of his father's family, and was born at the old Rutherford homestead, in Swatara township, Dauphin county, Pa., on the 27th of December, 1815. He was raised, as were all his brothers, to a thorough practical acquaintance with the labors of the farm, and received such education as the schools of Paxtang afforded. At the age of eighteen, he commenced the study of medicine with his brother, Dr. W. W. Rutherford, of Harrisburg, and graduated from Jefferson Medical College, at Philadelphia, in the spring of 1838. With ten dollars in his pocket and a few drugs in his saddle-bags, he set out on horse-back to seek his fortune. He located at Millersburg, on the Susquehanna, at that time a village of five hundred inhabitants. After a sojourn of two and a half years, the Doctor concluded that the road to fortune did not lie, for him, in Lykens Valley, and, in the latter days of the year 1840, he again packed his saddle-bags, and, with three hundred dollars in his pocket, mounted his horse and set his face towards Illinois—the "*E-le-noy*" of the emigrants of those days—"the home of the wild deer, the gopher and the prairie-wolf." At the end of an eighteen days' journey, he halted at a little hamlet in Coles county, now the flourishing town of Oakland, where he has ever since resided. The practice of medicine in the Western States, is, even now, very laborious, but when Dr. Rutherford began, it was much more so; the roads were mostly deer-paths, and the deep, sluggish streems flowed on to the sea unvexed by either bridges or ferries. His practice was large, extending over half a degree of latitude and longitude. But increasing years and failing strength warned him, at length, that it was time to retire from the active duties of a profession so exacting, and, for the last decade, he has devoted his time and energies principally to the management of his large agricultural interests. As a physician, a business man, and a trusted citizen, his life has been a success. The people of his adopted county have shown their confidence in his integrity and business qualifications by repeatedly calling him to serve on the county board (similar to that of county commissioners in Pennsylvania), and to various other public trusts in the town and township of Oakland; likewise their appreciation of his intelligence by keeping him in the school board continuously since 1843. And, although he has almost filled out the measure of four score years, he is still marching in the front rank with the active men of Coles county. The Doctor has been

twice married. He m., first, LUCINDA BOWMAN, of Millersburg, Pa., b. April 19, 1821; d. September 12, 1845. They had issue:
    i. *John*, b. April 21, 1844; resides in Oakland, Coles county, Ill.; m. Kate (Nash) Ashmore, b. September 2, 1844; and had issue:
        1. *Eva-Lucinda*, b. June 16, 1883.
        2. *Hiram-John*, b. January 27, 1887.

Dr. Rutherford m., secondly, HARRIET HUTCHINSON, of Springfield, Ill.; b. August 26, 1826. They had issue:
    ii. *Robert*, b. April 16, 1849; resides in Newman, Douglass county, Ill.; m. Mary Fletcher Valodin, b. December 6, 1851; and had issue:
        1. *Bertha*, b. May 25, 1872.
        2. *John-Marshall*, b. November 16, 1873.
        3. *Harriet-Agnes*, b. July 24, 1875.
        4. *Burt-Wilson*, b. April 13, 1877.
        5. *Ada*, b. July 23, 1879; d. Sept. 28, 1881.
        6. *Robert*, b. June 19, 1883.
        7. *Paul-Valodin*, b. February 14, 1886.
        8. *Marie*, b. March 27, 1889.
        9. *Jean*, b. December 20, 1890.
        10. *Charles-Valodin*, b. November 8, 1893.
    iii. *Cyrus*. b. November 14, 1850; m., September 22, 1885, Mary McIntyre, b. December 16, 1851; and had issue:
        1. *Wistar*, b. August 3, 1889, d. s. p.
        2. *Eugenia*, b. June 29, 1892.
    iv. *Thomas*, b. January 16, 1853; resides at Newman, Douglas county, Ill.; m. Rose Zimmerman, b. August 16, 1855; and had issue:
        1. *Cyrus-Wilson*, b. May 24, 1875.
        2. *Bessie*, b. February 15, 1884; d. August 20, 1885.
        3. *Hiram-Brown*, b. August 26, 1886.
        4. *Katie*, b. May 23, 1890.
    v. *Abner*, d. s. p.
    vi. *Abner-Wilson*, d. s. p.
    vii. *Kate*, b. January 16, 1858; m. John Menauh.
    viii. *Wilson*, b. March 2, 1860.
    ix. *Anna-Espy*, b. June 14, 1864.
    x. *Martin-Luther*, b. October 21, 1866; m. Lucy Reed, b. August, 1865; and had issue:
        1. *Anna*, b. August 20, 1889.
        2. *Leo-Martin*, b. December 14, 1891.

XXI. SAMUEL SHULTZ RUTHERFORD,[4] ('Thomas,[3] Samuel,[2] Thomas,[1]) b. December 17, 1803; d. January 23, 1872. In early life Mr. Rutherford was one of the masters of the school at Paxtang, and a member of the troop of horse, known as the Dauphin cavalry. He m. MARY A. RUTHERFORD,[4] (Samuel,[3] John,[2] Thomas,[1]) b. June 14, 1810; d. December 14, 1884. They had issue:

    i. *Mary-Lucretia.*
    ii. *John-Edmund,* b. December 17, 1838; m., first, Annie Hammond McPherson, b. December 19, 1844, in Frederick, Md.; d. April, 3, 1882; and had issue:
        1. *Samuel-McPherson,* b. September 5, 1869; graduated from West Point Military Academy, June 11, 1892; commissioned second lieutenant of cavalry same date, and assigned to the Fourth U. S. cavalry August 31, 1892.
        2. *Robert-Mordah,* b. November 21, 1871.
        3. *Nannie-Hammond.*
        4. *Mary-Agnes,* d. inf.
        Mr. Rutherford m., secondly, March 23, 1887, Delia McCullough, of Elkton, Md.
    iii. *Jane-Eliza,* b. August 29, 1840; d. May 20, 1891; m. William Swan Rutherford (see XVI).
    iv. *Samuel-Harvey,* b. March 3, 1843; m. Fanny E. Scholl, of Frederick, Md.; d. December 14, 1884; and had issue:
        1. *Samuel-Scholl,* b. October 23, 1873.
        2. *Jessie-Sanderson,* d. inf.
    v. *Martha-Keziah.*
    vi. *James-Addison,* b. April 8, 1847; m., February 27, 1889, Bessie Rutherford.
    vii. *Margaret-Susanna.*
    viii. *William-Brisban,* d. s. p.
    ix. *Albert-Collier.*

XXII. WILLIAM FRANKLIN RUTHERFORD,[5] (Abner,[4] William,[3] John,[2] Thomas,[1]) b. December 7, 1839; resides in Paxtang Valley, Swatara township, Dauphin county, Pa.; m. ADALINE MARGARET RUTHERFORD,[5] (John,[4] Samuel[3] John,[2] Thomas,[1]) b. March 22, 1839. They had issue:

    i. *Anna-Espy.*
    ii. *Helen-Parke,* b. May 13, 1866; d. August 29, 1889.
    iii. *Richard.*
    iv. *Jane-Dickey.*
    v. *Adaline-Margaret.*
    vi. *Marshall.*
    vii. *Keziah-Parke.*
    viii. *Donald-Irving.*

STEWART OF DRUMORE.

I. JOHN STEWART,[1] a Scotch covenanter of the seventeenth century, fled from Scotland to the county Down, in the north of Ireland. It is traditional that he had incurred penalties for non-compliance with royal edicts respecting religious worship and enforcing attendance at the Parish church. It was at the period when the government of Charles II, (1660-1685), the most disreputable of the English kings, was engaged in its fruitless attempts to force Episcopacy upon the Scottish nation. The north of Ireland had become a refuge for proscribed Presbyterians and condemned covenanters, and thither he went, preferring to abandon his native hills rather than go back on the solemn league and covenant entered into by the Scottish people in 1643, who recognized as their only standard the Westminster confession of faith as ratified by the General Assembly of the church of Scotland, in 1647. The persecution of the covenanters and harassment of the adherents to Presbyterianism, which King Charles pronounced "a religion not fit for a gentleman," continued until the establishment of freedom of conscience by the revolution of 1688. John Stewart d. in 1720, and of his family, we have record of one son only:

   2. *i. Robert*, b. 1665.

II. ROBERT STEWART,[2] (John,[1]) b. near Glasgow, Scotland, A. D. 1665, in the reign of Charles II; d. 1730. Upon the death of his father, he also moved into Ireland, locating in Drumore township, county Down, twelve miles from Belfast. The people of this county, as a whole, are of Scottish origin. The Ayrshire dialect was commonly spoken till towards the end of the eighteenth century. This county is remarkable for its inequality of surface and number of hills, from which its name originated. The lives of father and son, John and Robert Stewart, therefore, embraced that most remarkable period in the history of England commencing in the reign of Charles I, through the Commonwealth under Cromwell, Charles II, James II, William and Mary, Queen Anne, George I, and into the reign of George II. Robert Stewart had a large family, of whom we have record only of

3.   i. *Samuel*, b. 1698; m. Mary McClay.
4.   ii. *Hugh*, b. June 11, 1719; m. first, Hannah Dallas; secondly, Nancy Moore.

III. SAMUEL STEWART,[3] (Robert,[2] John,[1]) b. in 1698, near Glasgow, Scotland; d. 1770, in Lancaster county, Pa. He emigrated to the north of Ireland with his father's family in 1720. In 1735, accompanied by his youngest brother, Hugh, he crossed the ocean, landing in Philadelphia, and settled in Drumore township, Lancaster county, Province of Pennsylvania, near Chestnut Level, a Scotch-Irish settlement, where had been established a Presbyterian meeting-house, ministered to by the Rev. John Thompson, of Donegal Presbytery. In person, Samuel Stewart was large and well proportioned, six feet in height, Roman nose, bluish-grey eyes, brown hair, and ruddy complexion. He m., in Ireland, MARY McCLAY, who was noted for her very dark complexion and large person. They had issue:

    i. *John*, b. in Ireland; removed to the Marsh Creek settlement, now Adams county, Pa.; killed in the battle of Germantown, in 1777.

5.   ii. *Samuel*, m., first, Nancy Templeton; secondly, Agnes Calhoun.

    iii. *Elijah*, b. in Lancaster county, Pa.; d. in 1807, in Lower Paxtang township, Dauphin county, Pa.; after his death his widow removed to Ohio with her family, where his descendants now live, principally in Butler, Clark and Trumbull counties. They had issue: *Sarah*, m. James Finney, *John, Samuel, Margaret*, m. William Finney: *Mary*, m. William Stewart, *Nancy, James*, and *Jane*.

    iv. *Mary*, b. in Lancaster county, Pa.; m., 1764, Robert Patterson; in 1792 removed to Westmoreland county, Pa., and had seven sons and two daughters.

    v. *Andrew*, b. in Lancaster county, Pa.; settled in Hanover township; killed in an Indian raid.

    vi. *James*, b. in Lancaster county, and finally settled in Allegheny county, Pa.

    vii. *Hugh*, b. in Lancaster county, Pa.; settled in Kentucky; his descendants settled in Indiana.

    viii. *Joseph*.
    ix. *Robert*.
    x. *Anthony*.

IV. HUGH STEWART,³ (Robert,² John,¹) b. near Glasgow, Scotland, June 11, 1719; d. October 8, 1798; buried in the graveyard of the old Covenanter church, three miles east of Harrisburg, Pa., of which church he was the main supporter. At the age of sixteen years he accompanied his elder brother, Samuel, and family, in their migration to the Province of Pennsylvania, in 1735. He landed with a capital in coin equivalent to one dollar and twenty-five cents, and having learned the trade of weaving, followed it for many years ; settled finally in Paxtang township, about six miles from Harris' Ferry, where he acquired a large estate, for the times. His name first appears on the tax list of 1750. In 1780 he was assessed for four hundred and five acres. He was considered a very handsome man, of more than ordinary height, and retained through life his Scotch accent. Hugh Stewart was twice married; m., first, in 1750–1, HANNAH DALLAS, b. 1727, in Ireland; d. 1760, and buried with her husband. They had issue, all born in Paxtang:

    i. Jane, b. November 1, 1751 ; d. in 1824, near Monroe, Butler county, O., where they settled at a very early day; m., in 1772, John Robinson; and had issue (surname Robinson): *Sarah* and *Hannah* (twins), *Jane, William, Hugh, John-D., James-B.,* and *Mary-R.*

    ii. John, b. July 2, 1753 ; m. a sister of John Robinson, his brother-in-law, and moved to the Redstone settlement in Fayette county, Pa., where they lived half a century ; and had issue: *William, John, James, Samuel, Hugh, Hannah,* and *Mary.*

    iii. William, b. October 21, 1757 ; m., 1780, Martha Walker, and removed to Allegheny county, Pa.; and had issue: *Margaret, Hannah, Jane, Rebecca, Elizabeth, Martha, James, William, Samuel,* and *John.*

    iv. Hugh, b. October 1, 1759 ; in consequence of a deformity in his feet, unfitting him for active life, he became a teacher; settled in the Redstone country, Fayette county, Pa.; thence he removed to Rush county, Indiana, near Flat Rock creek; m., in 1793, Mary Wilson; and had issue: *Wilson,* and *Hugh.*

Hugh Stewart, Sr., m., secondly, in 1764, NANCY MOORE, b. 1735 ; d. March 22, 1790. They had issue :

6.   *v. Robert,* b. March 8, 1765; m. Sarah Finney.

vi. *Samuel*, b. March 5, 1767; m., in 1796, Jane Patterson, and settled in Allegheny county, Pa., north-west of Pittsburgh; and had issue: *James, Robert, Hugh, Nancy, Flora, John-W., Margaret, Samuel, Jane, William, Joseph,* and *Uriah-P.*
7. vii. *Joseph*, b. July 10, 1769; m. Sarah Stewart.
8. viii. *James*, b. February 28, 1774; m., first, Mary Sherer; secondly, Mary Maclay Stewart; thirdly, Margaret Reed.
ix. *Mary*, b. November 27, 1778, in Paxtang township; d. in 1853, and buried in the Monroe cemetery, Butler county, O.; m. Charles Stewart, (see XII).

V. SAMUEL STEWART,⁴ (Samuel,³ Robert,² John,¹) b. in the county Down, Ireland; was brought to Pennsylvania in the emigration of his father's family, in 1735, and, on coming of age settled as a farmer in Hanover township, Lancaster county, now West Hanover, Dauphin county, Pa., about 1750. His warrant for one hundred acres of land was dated May 17, 1754, and, in an "assessment for the King's use, 1759, *Samuel Stuart*" is taxed five shillings. This township, established in 1737, and named in honor of the reigning family of Great Britain, almost exclusively settled by Scotch-Irish Presbyterians, was on the then frontier and contiguous to the Kittatinny mountains. From the date of his settlement therein, in 1750, until 1764, on account of its proximity to the wilderness, it was subject to Indian raids and depredations from which the inhabitants suffered fearfully in their persons and property, often being compelled to abandon their homes and fly for safety. This state of affairs continued until the massacre in Lancaster of the Conestoga Indians, who were the aiders and abettors of these outrages. A public meeting of the citizens of Hanover township, June 4, 1774, has gone into history, showing the earliest recorded movement towards independence, and, when the Revolutionary war began, the liberty loving and patriotic Scotch-Irish of Hanover were found faithful and active participants. Samuel Stewart entered as a private, serving in Col. Timothy Green's battalion for the defence of the frontier, and, in June 6, 1776, in Capt. James Rodgers' company of Lancaster county associators, "destined for the camp in the Jerseys." On the erection and organization of the county of Dauphin, in 1785, we find him upon the first grand jury, composed of prominent citizens. A Presbyterian by birth and a supporter of the old Hanover church, founded in 1735, and situated eleven miles east of Harrisburg, the records show that on "November 2, 1788, Samuel Stewart and Nancy Stewart, his wife, were admitted to the Lord's table." Samuel Stewart d. September 16, 1803, and was buried in Hanover church graveyard. He was a large man, weighing two hundred and thirty pounds, six feet in height, eyes blue and complexion fair. His surviving wife, Agnes Calhoun, and his son, Samuel Elder Stewart, were the executors named in his will. He m., first, NANCY TEMPLETON, daughter of Robert and Agnes Templeton, of Hanover; d. 1788, and buried in old Hanover church graveyard. They had issue, all born in Hanover township:

  i. Sarah, b. 1771 ; d. February 3, 1835, in Butler county, O.; m. Joseph Stewart, (see VII).
9. *ii. Robert-Templeton*, b. June 15, 1773 ; m., first, Mary Dunlop; secondly, Mrs. Mary E. Hamilton.
10. *iii. Samuel-Elder*, b. January 8, 1775; m. Elizabeth Elder.
11. *iv. James-B.*, b. 1777 ; m. Ann Beatty.
12. *v. Charles*, b. 1778 ; m. Mary Stewart.
13. *vi. John-Templeton*, b. 1781 ; m. Ann Elder.
  vii. Mary-Maclay, b. 1784; d. 1816, in Butler county, O.; m. James Stewart, (see VIII).
  viii. Agnes (Nancy), b. 1786 ; d. February 25, 1827; buried in Monroe cemetery, Butler county, O.; m., in 1806, John R. Beatty, of Butler county, O., who died in 1870; all were members of the U. P. Church. They had issue (surname Beatty): *Nancy, Sarah, Mary, John, Jane, Samuel, Amanda Elizabeth, Lavinia*, and *David-Charles*.

Samuel Stewart m., secondly, in 1789, AGNES (Nancy) CALHOUN, b. 1763; d. August 29, 1823; buried in the cemetery at Graysville, Huntingdon county, Pa.; daughter of William and Hannah Calhoun, of Paxtang township, Dauphin county, Pa. On the death of her husband in 1803, she purchased a farm in West Hanover township, Dauphin county, Pa., adjoining the farm of Robert Stewart, ten miles east of Harrisburg, on the Jonestown road, where she remained until the spring of 1813, when she removed to Spruce Creek, Centre county, Pa. They had issue, all born in Hanover:

14. *ix. William-Calhoun*, b. 1790 ; m., first, Jane Dunlop; secondly, Mrs. Miltenberger.

15.   *x. David*, b. October 30, 1792; m. Sarah Walker.
16.   *xi. Thomas-Finney*, b. August 11, 1794; m. Mary Bailey, of Spruce Creek.
     xii. Margaret-Agnes, b. April 8, 1796; d. May 26, 1835, in Pittsburgh, Pa.; early in life she joined the Presbyterian Church; was at Mrs. Leah Maguire's school, in Harrisburg, in 1812; in person, was rather tall, with dark hair, dark complexion, hazel eyes, prominent forehead, rather full face. and fine expression; she m. John Lyon, (*see Lyon record*).

VI. ROBERT STEWART,[4] (Hugh,[3] Robert,[2] John,[1]) b. March 8, 1765, in Paxtang township, Lancaster county, Pa.; d. in 1854; buried in old Paxtang church graveyard. He m., March 10, 1789, SARAH FINNEY, b. August 10, 1768; d. 1811. They had issue, all born in Hanover township, Dauphin county, Pa:

17.   *i. Agnes-(Nancy)-Crain*, b. January 19, 1790; m. James B. Robinson.
    ii. Susanna, b. 1791.
18. *iii. Thomas-P.*, b. May 31, 1794; m. Martha B. Stewart.
19. *iv. Robert*, b. September 17, 1795; m. Sarah Barnett.
     v. Sarah, b. May 22, 1797, in Hanover township, Dauphin county, Pa.; m. John Cleeland, of Clark county, O.; and had issue (surname Cleeland): *Sylvester, Frank, Robert, John-William, Ann-Elizabeth, Sarah-Caroline, Charlotte-M.*, and *Margaret-R.*
    vi. Mary, b. November 30, 1798; m. John Rice, of Middletown, Butler county, O.; and had issue (surname Rice): *Sarah*, and *Mary*.
   vii. Jane, b. April 7, 1800.
  viii. Samuel, b. April 22, 1802.
    ix. John, b. September 30, 1803; d. of cholera, 1849; buried in Monroe cemetery, Butler county, O.; m., July 24, 1831, his cousin, Nancy T. Beatty, daughter of John R. Beatty, (*see* v); and had issue: *Robert-Sylvanus, Sarah-Agnes, Angelina, Mary*, and *John-Milton*.
     x. Margaret, b. October 10, 1806; m. Henry Cramer, of Wooster, O.; and had issue (surname Cramer): *Henry, Michael, Margaret, Caroline, Elizabeth, Ann*, and *Mary*.
    xi. William-Crawford, b. August 22, 1810.

VII. JOSEPH STEWART,[4] (Hugh,[3] Robert,[2] John,[1]) b. July 10, 1769; d. October 13, 1855; buried in Monroe cemetery; m., December 20, 1792, by Rev. James Snodgrass, SARAH STEWART, daughter of his cousin Samuel Stewart, of Hanover township, (*see* v). In conjunction with his brother, James Stewart, administered on his father's estate and became the owners of the homestead which they sold in 1805. In the spring of that year, Joseph and James Stewart with their respective families removed to Ohio, making the trip to Pittsburgh by wagon, and down the Ohio river by flat boat, and settled in Butler county, near the present town of Monroe. Became an elder in the United Presbyterian Church. They had issue:

> *i. James*, b. 1793, in Paxtang township, Dauphin county, Pa.; d. 1864, in Illinois; m. Susan Finney.
> *ii. Samuel-B.*, b. 1795; d. 1871; m., 1824, Sarah Barnett.
> *iii. Jane*, m. her cousin, Robert Stewart, of Indiana.
> *iv. Nancy*, b. 1799; m., 1819, her cousin, Elijah Finney.
> *v. Joseph-F.*, b. 1801; m., 1832, Prudence Ammons, of Butler county, Ohio.
> *vi. Sarah*, b. 1803; d. 1870; m., 1824, David Reynolds, of Piqua, Ohio.
> *vii. Mary*, b. 1805, in Butler county, Ohio; m., 1825, Samuel Holmes, of Bellbrook, Ohio.
> *viii. John*, died young.
> *ix. Charles.*
> *x. Eliza*, died young.

VIII. JAMES STEWART,[4] (Hugh,[3] Robert,[2] John,[1]) b. in Paxtang township, February 28, 1774; m., November 17, 1803, MARY SHERER, daughter of Samuel Sherer and Elizabeth Barnett, of Swatara township, Dauphin county, Penn'a. Moved to Ohio in company with his brother Joseph, in 1805, and settled near Monroe, Butler county. They had issue:

> *i. Joseph-Crain*, b. August 18, 1804, in Paxtang township; m., 1826, Nancy Templeton Stewart, daughter of Samuel Elder Stewart, of Clark county, Ohio, (see x).
> *ii. Samuel-Sherer*, M. D., b. October 20, 1807, in Butler county, Ohio; d. in 1872; studied medicine, and practiced at Jones Station, Dearborn county, Indiana; was twice married; first wife unknown; m., secondly, in 1852, Mary Ann Churchill, of New York.
> *iii. James-Barnett* (twin), b. October 20, 1807; d. 1851.

Mary Sherer Stewart died October 21, 1807, after the birth of her twin sons, and was the first adult buried in Monroe cemetery, then open woods, and her grave was protected by a pen of logs. James Stewart married, secondly, in 1808, MARY MACLAY STEWART, daughter of his cousin, Samuel Stewart, of Hanover, (*see* v). They had issue:

    iv. Nancy-M., b. May 15, 1812, and m., in 1833, John Patterson, of Monroe.

Mary Maclay Stewart died in 1816, and was buried in Monroe cemetery. James Stewart married a third wife, MARGARET REED, of Lewistown, Pa. They had issue:

    v. Mary-Jane, b. April 20, 1823; m., in 1840, Edward Kimball, of Cincinnati, O.; she fell heir to the homestead on which her father settled in 1805; and resides thereon.

James Stewart was a *United Presbyterian* of the strictest sect. He met death in an extraordinary manner, May 4, 1835, as he was driving in a spring wagon, on the public road near Monroe, with his wife, and niece, Nancy Stewart, daughter of Charles Stewart, a hugh tree standing by the road side fell upon the party, killing all instantly.

IX. ROBERT TEMPLETON STEWART,[5] (Samuel,[4] Samuel,[3] Robert,[2] John,[1]) b. June 15, 1773; d. October, 1835, at Hollidaysburg, Pa., while *en route* to Pittsburgh; buried at Saltsburg, Indiana county, Pa. He settled in Bellefonte in the year 1800, and was admitted to the bar of Centre county at the November term. He was retained in the famous slander suit of McKee *vs.* Gallagher, August term, 1801, in which there were fourteen lawyers for the plaintiff and twenty-two for defendant. In 1810 he was appointed postmaster, and continued in office until 1819. In 1810 engaged in mercantile pursuits with his brother, William C., and in 1819, entered into partnership with John Lyon in the manufacture of iron; residence at Coleraine Forges, Huntingdon county. In 1828 Lyon and Stewart sold Coleraine Forges to Joseph and James Barnett and Anthony Shorb. He moved to Pittsburgh in 1823, and built Sligo Rolling Mill. Represented Allegheny county in the Pennsylvania Legislature in 1831-32. Disposing of his interests in the iron business, Mr. Stewart went to manufacturing salt on the Kiskiminetas. He was a man of genial disposition and social habits, and of great practical humor. In person, above the ordinary size, and of very dark complexion, which he inherited from his grandmother Stewart. He m., in 1809, by Rev'd Henry Wilson, MARY DUNLOP, daughter of James Dunlop, and Jean, dau. of Andrew Boggs, of Donegal township, Lancaster county, Pa., who, in connection with James Harris, in 1795, laid out the town of Bellefonte. Mary Dunlop Stewart died in 1827, aged forty-five years, and was buried in the First Presbyterian churchyard, Pittsburgh. They had issue, nine children, among whom were :

    i. Harriet, b. 1816; d. July 16, 1895, s. p.; m., 1843, by Rev. Samuel Cooper, James Harris Linn, of Bellefonte, ironmaster, who died April 6, 1876.

20.   *ii. Jane-Ann*, b. 1820; m. John M. McCoy, M. D.

Robert T. Stewart married, secondly, in 1831, Mrs. MARY E. HAMILTON,* of Middlesex, Cumberland county, Pa., who died in Pittsburgh in 1842.

---

* DANIEL ELLIOTT, the father of Mrs. Mary E. Hamilton, was an Indian trader as early as 1765 at the forks of the Ohio. In 1772 he moved to Donegal township, and in 1774 married Elizabeth Lowrey, b. October 31, 1757, one of the daughters of Col. Alexander Lowrey, of Lancaster county, Pa., one of its prominent citizens of Revolutionary times. Daniel Elliott afterwards, in 1777, returned to the west and established a trading post at Saw Mill run, on the Ohio river, opposite Allegheny, where he purchased a large tract of land. The issue of this marriage was John, West, and Mary Elliott, who, in 1804, married James Hamilton, of Leacock township, Lancaster county, (b. 1778). They moved to Middletown, Dauphin county, in 1806, where Mr. Hamilton entered into large business operations. About the year 1825 he purchased an estate called Middlesex, near Carlisle, Pa., (the estate of the late Col. Ephraim Blaine, of Revolutionary fame,) to which he moved and where he died about 1829, and was interred in the old Carlisle cemetery. They had issue, all born in Middletown :

    i. Alexander-Lowrey, b. 1806.
    ii. Sarah, d. in youth ; buried at Carlisle.
    iii. James, d. in the Texan war.
    iv. William, b. October 5, 1811.
    v. George-Plumer, b. May 14, 1818; d. 1882; he became eminent as a lawyer and member of the Pittsburgh bar ; he married Hadessa, daughter of Major Irons, P. M., of Washington, Pa.; he left a son *George-Porter-Hamilton*, also an attorney-at-law.

Colonel Lowrey's youngest daughter, *Frances*, married Samuel Evans, from whom descends grandsons, Amos Slaymaker, an attorney-at-law of Lancaster city, and Samuel Evans, Esq., of Columbia, Pa.,

X. SAMUEL ELDER STEWART,[5] (Samuel,[4] Samuel,[3] Robert,[2] John,[1]) b. January 8, 1775, in Hanover township; d. July 2, 1857. He removed to Clark county, O., near Clifton; was an elder in the Presbyterian Church; in the war of 1812 a captain in the Third Ohio regiment, Col. James Findlay, and was at Hull's surrender. Captain Stewart m., October 11, 1808, by Rev. James Snodgrass, ELIZABETH ELDER, eldest daughter of Robert Elder, merchant, of Hanover, who d. in 1869; both buried in Clifton cemetery. They had issue:

    i. Robert-Elder, b. 1811; m., 1846, Mary Jane McClung, of Butler county, O.; resides in Clark county, O.
    ii. Ann-Jane, b. 1813; m., 1840, William Cowan.
    iii. Nancy-T., m. Joseph Crain Stewart, of Springfield, O., the son of James Stewart, (see VIII).
    iv. Samuel-Templeton, b. in 1817.
    v. Sarah-M.
    vi. Elizabeth-Elder, b. in 1824; m., 1848, David Cowan, of Bloomington, Ill.
    vii. Maria, b. 1830; m., 1860, George Cornelius, of Bloomington, Ill.
    viii. Cyrus, b. 1833; m., 1862, Amanda R. Wilmoth; reside in Logan county, Ill.

XI. JAMES B. STEWART,[5] (Samuel,[4] Samuel,[3] Robert,[2] John,[1]) b. 1777; d. 1828; one of the pioneers of Clark county, Ohio, whither he removed in 1806, having purchased his land from the Government only four years after the organization of the State. He m., in 1807, ANN BEATTY, b. 1787; d. 1856. They had issue:

    i. Martha-Beatty, m. Thomas P. Stewart, grandson of Hugh Stewart, (see XVIII).
    ii. Nancy-Templeton, b. 1810; d. February 27, 1845.
    iii. Samuel, b. November 4, 1812; d. October 10, 1871, in Clark county, O.; m. Caroline Nelson, b. August 30, 1813; d. December 14, 1894; and had issue:

---

the historian of Lancaster county and a veteran of the war of the Rebellion, who, for meritorious services was promoted to a captaincy. The Hon. George Plumer Smith, of Philadelphia, formerly of Pittsburgh, son of James Smith from county Tyrone, Ireland, who married Mary Plumer, daughter of George Plumer and Margaret, another daughter of Colonel Lowrey, is also in the same connection, and of a family prominent in the early annals and settlement of Western Pennsylvania.

1. *Jennie-A.*, b. March 25, 1838; m., April 11, 1876, Samuel Watson, d. September 28, 1893.
2. *Sarah-A.*, b. May 14, 1841; d. March 8, 1895; m., September 6, 1866, George M. Cox.
3. *Susan-N.*, b. April 18, 1843; m., January 20, 1880, William Wilson.
4. *Mellie-Templeton*, b. September 29, 1845; m., December 25, 1866, James T. Lott.
5. *Clara-M.*, b. October 21, 1848; d. March 3, 1871.
6. *James-H.*, b. April 15, 1851; d. October 23, 1868.
7. *Frank-T.*, b. March 31, 1858.
8. *Ella-M.*, b. June 2, 1859; m., December 21, 1876, J. S. Hurless.

iv. *John-Beatty*, b. November 8, 1814; m., February 28, 1837, Eliza McKinney, b. 1813.
v. *Susan-Elder*, b. 1820; d. July 24, 1895; m., Henry Crozier.
vi. *Sarah-Margaret*, b. October 30, 1822; m., April 3, 1845, Amos B. Casey, b. August 15, 1819; d. July 22, 1890.

XII. CHARLES STEWART,[5] (Samuel,[4] Samuel,[3] Robert,[2] John,[1]) b. 1778; d. 1846; m., March 30, 1802, by Rev. James Snodgrass, of the Hanover Presbyterian church, MARY STEWART, daughter of Hugh Stewart, (*see* IV). In 1802 he moved to Ohio, and settled near Monroe, Butler county. In this year Ohio was organized into a State, which made him one of her earliest citizens. He was in the Government service in the war of 1812, and had the reputation of being an impetuous, brave and daring soldier. He became a member of the United Presbyterian Church, in 1806, and, in connection with his cousin, Samuel Stewart, and his brothers-in-law, Joseph and James Stewart, founded the United Presbyterian church of Monroe. He and his wife were both buried in Monroe cemetery. They had issue, all born in Butler county, O.:

i. *Nancy*, b. January 12, 1805; accidently killed by the falling of a tree, May 4, 1835. (*see* VIII).
ii. *Jane*, b. 1806; m., 1834, Robert Griffen, of Middle Fork, Ind.
iii. *Samuel-Logan*, b. 1809; m., first, 1829, Elizabeth G. Bryson, d. 1842, and had issue, four sons; he m., secondly, Mrs. C. Stryker, and had issue, *David-M.*
iv. *Mary*, m., 1836, John W. Stewart, son of Samuel Stewart, her mother's brother; reside in Peoria county, Ill.
v. *Margaret*, b. 1814; m., 1848, Elijah Patterson, a great grandson of Samuel Stewart, (III).

vi. *Elizabeth*, b. 1815; m. Robert Stewart Robinson, great grandson of Hugh Stewart, (IV).
vii. *John-W.-D.*, b. 1818; m., 1848, Martha Mallory.
viii. *James-R.*, b. 1821; m., 1845, Ann E. Cleeland, great granddaughter of Hugh Stewart, (VI).

XIII. JOHN TEMPLETON STEWART,[5] (Samuel,[4] Samuel,[3] Robert,[2] John,[1]) b. 1781; d. April 16, 1850; b. in Hanover township, Dauphin county, Pa., and with his elder brother, James B. Stewart, removed to Ohio in 1806 and settled in Clark county, on the Little Miami river. He was elected justice of the peace in 1813, serving until 1838; was the first clerk of Green township, Clark county; appointed associate judge of the Common Pleas Court of same county, serving one term, from 1837 to 1840. He m., March 2, 1815, ANN ELDER, daughter of Robert Elder, of Hanover, Dauphin county, Pa., and sister of his brother Samuel's wife; both interred in Clifton cemetery. They had issue:

21. i. *Juliana*, b. December 26, 1815; m. David Anderson.
22. ii. *Perry*, b. 1818; m. Rhoda Ann Wheeler.
23. iii. *Elder-Robert*, b. January 20, 1821; m. Rachel E. Jacoby.
24. iv. *Samuel*, b. March 26, 1823; m. Mary Ann Marshall.
25. v. *Charles*, b. July 17, 1825; m., first, Isabel Nicholson.
26. vi. *James-M.*, b. March 30, 1828; m. Rebecca C. Jacoby.
27. vii. *Thomas-Elder*, b. Sept. 29, 1830; m. Delilah A. Marshall.
28. viii. *Oscar-Nesbitt*, b. February 5, 1833; m. Rachel Nicholson.
    ix. *William-Calhoun*, b. 1835; m., 1880, Elizabeth Theodosia Sellers; and have issue: *Hazel*, b. September 27, 1887; reside on the old homestead.
    x. *Harriet*, b. June 22, 1838; d. September 8, 1839.

XIV. WILLIAM CALHOUN STEWART,[5] (Samuel,[4] Samuel,[3] Robert,[2] John,[1]) b. 1790, in Hanover township, Dauphin county; d. May 31, 1850, in Cincinnati, O.; engaged in general merchandizing in Centre and Huntingdon counties, Pa.; he subsequently became a member of the iron manufacturing firm of Lyon, Shorb & Co., of Pittsburgh, and represented his company in Cincinnati. He m., first, JANE DUNLOP, of Bellefonte, b. 1801; d. in Cincinnati, April 27, 1841; she was a niece of his brother, Robert T. Stewart's wife. They had issue:

i. *Laura*, b. in Bellefonte, Pa.; m. Col. Charles Jones, planter, of Red River, Catahoula Parish, La.; Colonel Jones

was shot in a feud with General Liddell, of Mississippi; and had issue (surname Jones):
1. *Ella*, m. in Switzerland and d. abroad.
2. *William*, shot in the jail in which he and his father had taken refuge.
3. *Rosa*; resides at Jonesville, La.
4. *Cuthbert-Bullett.*
5. *Francois.*

ii. Rev. *John-Dunlop*, b. February 23, 1824; m. Margaret Schell, b. September 26, 1827; daughter of John and Margaret Schell, of Birmingham, Pa.; and had issue a numerous family, of whom the survivors [1895] are:
1. *Alice*, b. February 25, 1849; m., November 26, 1867, Samuel Berlin.
2. *John-Anderton-Collins*, b. January 19, 1856; m. Bertha K. Martin, of Hollidaysburg, Pa.; b. October 3, 1859.
3. *Laura*, b. December 12, 1857, in Tyrone, Pa.; m., December 12, 1876, Wilbur Fisk Meminger, evangelist, b. 1851, in Green Briar county, West Virginia; and had issue (surname Meminger): *Willie-Stewart, Paul-Jones,* and *Charles-Richard.*
4. *Jesse-Smith*, civil engineer, b. May 16, 1866, in Tyrone, Pa.
5. *Charles-Bertie*, merchant, b. December 31, 1868; m. Carrie E. Gray, daughter of Z. B. and Amanda Gray.
6. *Harry-Lawrence*, b. August 13, 1873, in Tyrone, Pa.

iii. Rev. *William-Calhoun*, b. June 17, 1829; d. in New York City April 10, 1894; m., first, Mary Forgey Conklin (widow), and had issue:
1. *William-Calhoun*; residence, California.

Rev. William Calhoun, m., secondly, Laura Forgey, sister of Mary; he m., thirdly, Agnes; and had *Deborah, Agnes, Anna,* and *Nemeha.*

iv. *Jesse-Smith*, b. in Cincinnati, April 24, 1832; in the war of the Rebellion was first lieutenant of Company A, 125th regiment, Pennsylvania volunteers; was killed in the battle of Chancellorsville, 1863; m. Mary M. Clarke, daughter of James and Sarah C. Clarke, of Birmingham. Pa., b. 1841; d. 1859; and had *Jesse,* and *William,* both d. in infancy.

v. *Ella*, m. Robert G. Bushnell, of Pittsburgh; d. December 28, 1894.

Mr. Stewart, m., secondly, Mrs. MILTENBERGER, *nee* Oliver, of Pittsburgh, who survived her husband.

XV. DAVID STEWART,⁵ (Samuel,⁴ Samuel,³ Robert,² John,¹) b. October 30, 1792, in Hanover township, Dauphin county; d. May 29, 1869, at Coleraine Forges, Huntingdon county, Pa.; buried in the Spruce Creek cemetery at Graysville. He was twenty-one years of age at the time of the exodus of the family from Hanover to Centre county in 1813. He became the general manager at Pennsylvania Furnace, and subsequently entered the firm under the title of Shorb, Stewart & Co., which was synonymous with that of Lyon, Shorb & Co., Pittsburgh, manufacturers of the famed Juniata iron. Mr. Stewart was, undoubtedly, the most prominent and wealthy member of this large family; resided at Coleraine Forges, Huntingdon county, from 1831 until his death. His house was noted for its elegant and liberal hospitality. In person he was large and imposing, showing traits of his Scotch ancestry, and was the last of his father's family, a long lived race, and it may be noted that from the birth of his eldest brother, Robert, to the date of his own death, embraced a period of nearly one hundred years. He m., May 22, 1822, SARAH WALKER, daughter of John Walker and Ann, his wife, of Alexandria, Huntingdon county, Pa., originally from county Strabane in the north of Ireland. She was born September 23, 1799, and died at Coleraine Forges, April 24, 1874, having survived her husband, by whose side she now lies buried. They had issue:

29. i. *Ann-Caroline*, b. March 8, 1823; m. James Rowland Hughes.
30. ii. *Samuel-Calhoun*, b. Sept. 6, 1824; m. Margaret Sample.
31. iii. *William-Walker*, b. April 4, 1826; m. Mary McGuffy.
    iv. *Catharine-Walker*, b. 1827, at Pennsylvania Furnace.
    v. *Frances*, b. August 30, 1829, at Pine Grove Mills; m., November 8, 1859, Lewis M. Speer, of Bellevernon, Fayette county, Pa.; d. September 15, 1883; and had issue (surname Speer): *David-Stewart, Samuel-Calhoun, Frank-Marchand*, and *John Stogdel*; reside in Wooster, O.
    vi. *Margaretta*, b. December 30, 1831, at Coleraine Forges.
    vii. *David-Walker*, b. at Coleraine Forges; m., June 5, 1862, Sarah Spinning, of Springfield, O.; and had issue: *Emily McAlpine*, and *Margaret*; reside at Dayton, O.
    viii. *Thomas*, d. July 31, 1837.

XVI. THOMAS FINNEY STEWART,⁵ (Samuel,⁴ Samuel,³ Robert,² John,¹) b. August 11, 1794, in Hanover township,

Dauphin county, Pa.; d. August 8, 1864, and buried in Cedar Grove cemetery at Petersburg, Pa. He left Dauphin county with his mother in 1813, settling in Ferguson township, Centre county, where he pursued the occupation of farming until his latter years, when he removed to Petersburg, Huntingdon county, Pa. In 1851 he was elected an associate judge of the several courts of Huntingdon county. He married, in 1818, MARY BAILEY, daughter of John Bailey; b. in 1798; d. in 1866, and buried beside her husband. John Bailey, her father, was born in Chester county, and settled on Spruce Creek in 1790. He was the son of Richard Bailey and Mary Wilson, both of Ireland, who settled in Chester county at a very early day. Judge Stewart had a large family, seven of whom died in infancy. The survivors were:

 i. Samuel, b. 1819; d. 1868; m., 1845, Jane Kelly; removed to Iowa in 1855.
 ii. John-Bailey, d. 1894.
 iii. Nancy.
 iv. Margaret, b. 1824; m., 1847, David Byers, of Smicksburgh, Pa
 v. Jane-Ann.
 vi. James-G., b. 1829; m., 1851, Matilda Frew.
 vii. David, d. 1863.
 viii. Harriet, d. 1865; buried in Cedar Grove Cemetery.

XVII. AGNES CRAIN STEWART,[5] (Robert,[4] Hugh,[3] Robert,[2] John,[1]) b. in Hanover township, Dauphin county, Pa., January 19, 1790; d. April 20, 1872. She m., November 12, 1812, her cousin, JAMES B. ROBINSON, farmer, son of John Robinson and Jane Stewart (*see* IV), b. October 16, 1783; d. November 25, 1865; both buried in Monroe cemetery. They had issue (surname Robinson):

 i. John-Finney, b. March 9, 1816; d. March 4, 1817.
 ii. Robert-Stewart, b. May 13, 1818; d. March 4, 1865; m., September 26, 1844, his cousin, Elizabeth Stewart, (*see* X).
 iii. Sarah-Marjorie, b. August 3, 1820; d. December 30, 1883; m., September 14, 1848, John W. Fitzgerald.
 iv. Nancy-Maria, b. April 11, 1824; d. April, 1884; m., August 11, 1845, Alexander P. Robinson.
 v. Hannah-Susanna, b. September 11, 1828; d. October 9, 1856; m., May 21, 1846, William Gustine.
 vi. James-Wilson, b. August 19, 1829; m., October 22, 1850, Caroline Kimball.

vii. Thomas-Crain, b. October 28, 1831; m., March 11, 1856, his cousin, Nancy Melvina, daughter of Thomas P. and Martha B. Stewart (XVIII), b. October 14, 1833; d. October 1, 1884; Mr. Stewart is a farmer and stock raiser of Piqua, O.: and had issue:
  1. *Kate-May*, b. May 19, 1858.
  2. *Isadora-Norwood*, b. July 17, 1860.
  3. *Dana*, b. January, 1865; d. in inf.
  4. *Minnie B.*, b. March 22, 1870; d. in inf.

XVIII. THOMAS P. STEWART,[5] (Robert,[4] Hugh,[3] Robert,[2] John,[1]) b. May 31, 1794; d. April 16, 1880; was a farmer and resided near Springfield, O. He m., May 27, 1828, MARTHA B. STEWART (*see* XII), b. February 16, 1809; d. May 17, 1881. They had issue:

  i. Sarah-Ann, b. March 14, 1829; d. in inf.
  ii. James-C., b. November 30, 1831; d. January 2, 1833.
  iii. Nancy-Melvina, b. October 14, 1833; d. October 1, 1884; m., March 11, 1856, Thomas Crain Robinson, (*see* XVII).
  iv. Margaret-S., b. March 24, 1836; d. January 12, 1862; m., September 6, 1855, Jacob N. Lott.
  v. Mary-Ann, b. March 3, 1838; d. August 19, 1878; m., February 11, 1868, Martin Anderson.
  vi. Martha-Rebecca, b. September 27, 1840; m., July 25, 1865, Michael Shocknessy.
  vii. Benjamin-F., b. October 20, 1843; d. December 25, 1858.

XIX. ROBERT STEWART,[5] (Robert,[4] Hugh,[3] Robert,[2] John,[1]) b. September 17, 1795, in Hanover township, Dauphin county, on the farm bequeathed to his father by Hugh Stewart, where he died June 25, 1878; buried in the East Harrisburg cemetery. This farm remained in the family one hundred and eighteen years, until 1881, when the last of Hugh Stewart's descendants remaining in Dauphin county left Pennsylvania to settle in Ohio. Robert Stewart was many years a trustee of the old Hanover Presbyterian church, and the custodian of the church records, which the Dauphin County Historical Society now possesses. He m., May 5, 1829, SARAH BARNETT, daughter of Thomas Barnett, b. March 13, 1806, in Hanover township, Dauphin county, Pa.; d. July 12, 1878, and buried with her husband. They had issue:

  i. Rev. *Robert-Crain*, b. March 14, 1830; m., first, October 27, 1864, Mary Fulqham, b. March 5, 1844; d. September 16, 1889; and had issue:

Stewart of Drumore. 661

    1. *Robert-A.*, b. January 4, 1866; m., May 1, 1895, Maggie C. Jennings.
    2. *William-W.*, b. July 18, 1868; m., June 4, 1892, Ella M. Jennings, b. October 12, 1869; and had issue: *Helen*, b. September 21, 1894.
    3. *Merle-M.*, b. November 2, 1872.
    4. *Edith-F.*, b. September 24, 1876.
  Mr. Stewart m., secondly, May 21, 1891, Mrs. Margaret Parsons; reside at Tupper's Plains, Meigs county, O.
ii. Sarah-Jane,
iii. Margaret-Elizabeth.
iv. Nancy-Rebecca.
v. Susan-Mary; d. May 13, 1858.
vi. Thomas-Barnett, b. September 23, 1840, at Piqua, Miami county, O.; m., December 31, 1872, Matilda McIlhenny, b. October 29, 1847; and they had issue: *Robert-Earl, John-Joseph, Sarah-Elizabeth, Thomas Robinson, Leonora, Arthur, Charles-Gilbert,* and *Pearl.*
vii. John-Joseph.
viii. Harriet-Caroline.
ix. William-Calvin, of Monroe, O.; m., 1882, Ella Stewart.

XX. JANE ANN STEWART,[6] (Robert-Templeton,[5] Samuel,[4] Samuel,[3] Robert,[2] John,[1]) b. in 1820; m., in 1843, by Rev. Dr. Linn, JOHN M. MCCOY, M. D., of Bellefonte. He was b. February 4, 1816, in Belleville, Mifflin county, Pa.; d. January 19, 1879. Dr. McCoy and James Harris Linn, brothers-in-law, were associated in the iron business under the firm name of McCoy & Linn, their works being on Spring creek near Bellefonte. They had issue (surname McCoy):

    i. Frank, b. in Bellefonte, Pa.; m., October 30, 1879, Esther Ellen Allison, daughter of William Allison and Sarah McNitt, of Potter's Mills, Centre county, Pa.; iron manufacturer, residing at Bellefonte.
    ii. Mary-Stewart, b. July 9, 1849; d. September 29, 1883; m., J. Dunlop Shugart, banker of Bellefonte; and had issue (surname Shugart): *John, Jane-Ann, Frank,* and *Kate.*

XXI. JULIANA STEWART,[6] (John-Templeton,[5] Samuel,[4] Samuel,[3] Robert,[2] John,[1]) the only daughter of John Templeton Stewart and Ann Elder, b. December 26, 1815; m., in 1833, DAVID ANDERSON, b. June 22, 1808, in the Parish of Aylyth, Scotland. He came to America in 1821; d. December 26, 1886. They had issue (surname Anderson):

i. *Ann-Stewart*, b. September 22, 1834; m. James Cowan, farmer, Clifton, Clark county, O.
ii. *John-Stewart*, b. October 12, 1836; a Union soldier in the war of the Rebellion; m. Elizabeth Tindall; d. February 22, 1888.
iii. *James-Edwin*, b. October 30, 1838; d. October 27, 1840.
iv. *Moses-Russell*, b. December 31, 1841; d. August 14, 1849.
v. *Agnes*, b. September 27, 1843; d. August 8, 1874.
vi. *Oliver-H.*, b. October 18, 1845; a Union soldier in the war of the Rebellion; m. Jeannette Dallas; resides at Springfield, O.
vii. *Emma*, b. December 2, 1850; m. C. C. Collins, of Santa Ana, Cal.
viii. *Mary*, b. November 16, 1852; resides at Springfield, O.
ix. *Ella-J.*, b. November 8, 1854; m., first, Wesley Walton; d. January 20, 1884; m., secondly, John E. Bunker, of Santa Ana, Cal.
x. *William-Wallace*, b. November 23, 1856; m. Agnes M. Kator, Santa Ana, Cal.
xi. *David-Livingston*, b. February 8, 1859; m. Sara E. McCulloch, Santa Ana, Cal.
xii. *Robert-Sumpter*, b. August 21, 1861; farmer, Clifton, O.; m. Alice F. Barber.

XXII. PERRY STEWART,[6] (John-Templeton,[5] Samuel,[4] Samuel,[3] Robert,[2] John,[1]) b. 1818, in Green township, Clark county, Ohio. Mr. Stewart was in person, a man of large proportions, and having military aspirations, served as captain of a volunteer rifle company from 1840 to 1849. Captain Stewart was township trustee in 1848, and justice of the peace in 1860. In 1862 he raised Company A of the 96th O. V. I., of which he served as captain until after the battle of Chickamaugua, 1863. He was county commissioner 1866-67, and represented Clark county in the House of Representatives of the Fifty-eighth General Assembly, 1868-9. Captain Stewart m., October 15, 1844, RHODA A. WHEELER, b. 1824, in Clark county, O. They had issue:

i. *Harriet-J*, b. 1845; m., 1866, James Hatfield; served in the war of the Rebellion in Company B, O. V. I., and in Company D, 8th Ohio cavalry, until the close of the war, 1865.
ii. *Julia-Ann*, b. 1847; m., 1869, Robert N. Elder; in the war of the Rebellion served three years until the close of the war, as a private and corporal in Company A, 94th O. V. I.

iii. David-Wilmot, b. 1848; m., 1874, Amanda McClintock; he served, 1864, as a private in Company D, 146th O. V. I.

iv. John-Templeton, b. 1850; m., 1877, Anna M. Keiffer: residence, Greencastle, Ind.

v. Mary-E., b. 1852; m., 1874, Samuel K. Kerr; reside in Washington city.

vi. Charles-Fremont, b. 1856; m., 1880, Clara Garlough; he is clerk of Green township, Clark county, O.

vii. Ellen-Jane, b. 1859; m., 1880, George Nicholson.

viii. Jessie-Isabel, b. 1861; d. in 1865.

ix. Perry-Morton, b. 1866.

x. Ebenezer-Wheeler, b. 1868; m., 1893, Annetta Shobe.

XXIII. ELDER ROBERT STEWART,[6] (John-Templeton,[5] Samuel,[4] Samuel,[3] Robert,[2] John,[1]) b. January 20, 1821; m., October 1, 1846, RACHEL E. JACOBY, b. March 20, 1823; d. April 5, 1885; bur. in Ferncliff cemetery, Springfield, O.; resides at Salt Lake City, Utah. They had issue:

i. Laura-Ann, b. October 8, 1847; m., October 1, 1868, Francis Tiernan, of Illinois; a contractor.

ii. Rebecca-Ann, b. May 7, 1849; m., October 12, 1871, Dr. Edwin Isaac Thorn, of Salt Lake City, Utah.

iii. Henry-Jacoby, b. November 11, 1830; d. December 1, 1851.

iv. Una-B., b. November 20, 1852; m., September 20, 1876, Joseph G. Jacobs, of Salt Lake City, Utah.

v. Nancy-Jane, b. March 20, 1855; m., September 24, 1879, Leander Brown Corry, of Springfield, O.

vi. John-Jacoby, b. May 29, 1857; m., June 7, 1883. Flora R. Dickson; reside at Salt Lake City, Utah.

XXIV. SAMUEL STEWART,[6] (John-Templeton,[5] Samuel,[4] Samuel,[3] Robert,[2] John,[1]) b. March 26, 1823; d. March 23, 1888; Mr. Stewart resided in Hardin county, O., twenty-eight years and was an extensive and successful farmer and live stock dealer. He was county commissioner of Hardin county for several years. He m., 1848, MARY ANN MARSHALL, b. June 9, 1825, in Selma, Clark county, O.; d. July 13, 1890; both interred in Kenton, O. They had issue:

i. Marshall, b. November 12, 1850; farmer and stock dealer, Hardin county, O.; m., Feb. 20, 1886, Olive Stevenson.

ii. Ella, b. 1852; m., October 15, 1872, I. Walker Lewis, wool dealer of Rushsylvania, O.

iii. Chase, b. October 26, 1856; educated at the Wesleyan University, Delaware, O., and at the University of Chicago, from which he graduated in 1880; and also graduated from the law school in Washington City in 1882; elected to a second term as prosecuting attorney for Clark county, and takes an active part in the politics of the State; resides at Springfield, O.

 iv. Mary, b. December 3, 1861; m., October 8, 1885, Charles B. Corry, of Bellefontaine, O.
 v. Elizabeth, b. February 23, 1863; m., October 6, 1887, J. J. Boone, M. D., of Mount Victory, O.
 vi. Katie, b. May 13, 1871.

XXV. CHARLES STEWART,[6] (John-Templeton,[5] Samuel,[4] Samuel,[3] Robert,[2] John,[1]) b. July 17, 1825. He was colonel of a home military organization in 1863; president and director of an agricultural society; land appraiser for Springfield township in 1890, and also a large wool grower. He m., first, February 16, 1854, ISABEL JANE NICHOLSON, d. March 29, 1859. They had issue:

 i. John-Andrew, b. May 11, 1855; d. July 6, 1881; m. Angeline Spencer, of Ill.

Mr. Stewart m., secondly, March 29, 1865, JESSIE MATTHEWSON, of Eson, Scotland. They had issue:

 ii. Annetta, b. April 21, 1866; d. February 22, 1884.
 iii. Katharine-Ann, b. April 16, 1868; m., May 26, 1892, Caleb J. Tuttle.
 iv. William-Matthewson, b. July 20, 1870.
 v. Mabel, b. September 16, 1872.
 vi. James-Bruce, b. September 3, 1875; d. May 3, 1880.
 vii. Jessie-Isabel, b. November 13, 1878.

XXVI. JAMES M. STEWART,[6] (John-Templeton,[5] Samuel,[4] Samuel,[3] Robert,[2] John,[1]) b. March 30, 1828. Probate judge of Greene county, Ohio; m., October 19, 1854, REBECCA Jacoby, sister of Rachel E., his brother Elder Robert's wife. They had issue, living in Xenia, O.:

 i. Ida-May, b. Aug. 5, 1855; m., March 30, 1876, S. B. LaSourd.
 ii. Leila-Ada, b. April 24, 1858; m., March 4, 1881, William D. Cooly, of Green county, O.
 iii. Cora-Ann, b. June 19, 1860; d. December 12, 1891; m. Charles C. Jackson.
 iv. Flora-Belle, b. March 13, 1863; d. February 1, 1873.

XXVII. THOMAS ELDER STEWART,[6] (John-Templeton,[5] Samuel,[4] Samuel,[3] Robert,[2] John,[1]) b. September 29, 1830. He was first lieutenant of Company D, 146th regiment, O. V. I., in the Civil war, and wagonmaster of the 94th regiment, a justice of the peace for Green township, Clark county, O. He m., November 16, 1858, DELILAH ANN MARSHALL. They had issue:

 i. Sarah-Ethel, b. August 18, 1859; m., December 22, 1881, Robert F. Corry, of Springfield, O.
 ii. Anna-May, b. August 14, 1861.
 iii. Lucy-Marshall, b. June 30, 1865.
 iv. Edwin-Earl, b. August 12, 1870.
 v. Bertha-Belle, b. May 8, 1874.

XXVIII. OSCAR NESBITT STEWART,⁶ (John-Templeton,⁵ Samuel,⁴ Samuel,³ Robert,² John,¹) b. February 5, 1833. He served in the first call for volunteers in the war of the Rebellion, 1861, in the 16th O. V. I. He m., January 28, 1862, RACHEL NICHOLSON, sister of Isabel J., his brother Charles' wife. They had issue:

 i. Perry-Herbert, b. December 12, 1862; m., January 28, 1888, Remina Tuttle.
 ii. Ralph-Nicholson, b. April 12, 1868.
 iii. Frank-Ernest, b. April 15, 1870.

XXIX. ANN CAROLINE STEWART,⁶ (David,⁵ Samuel,⁴ Samuel,³ Robert,² John,¹) b. March 8, 1823, at Pennsylvania Furnace; d. May 16, 1869, at Blairsville, Pa.; buried in Blairsville cemetery. She m., at her father's residence, Coleraine Forges, October 16, 1861, the Rev. JAMES ROWLAND HUGHES, of the Presbyterian Church, who was b. March 17, 1819, in Butler county, Pa.; graduated at Washington College, Pennsylvania, 1845; studied theology, and licensed to preach by the Presbytery of Steubenville, O., October 16, 1847; was pastor of Rehoboth church, Redstone Presbytery, fifteen years; principal of Blairsville Seminary three years, and then, in 1870, accepted a pastorate in Dayton, O., where he now resides. They had issue (surname Hughes), all b. in Rostraver township, Westmoreland county, Pa.:

 i. Mary-Wilson, b. November 20, 1852; m., by Rev. James Rowland Hughes, October 15, 1878, James M. Colwell, b. July 16, 1853; a pharmacist, of Urbana, O., son of William H. and Eliza J. Colwell; their ancestors emigrated from Ireland in 1732 and settled in New Jer-

sey, whence Judge A. R. Colwell and Electa J., his wife, removed to Urbana, Champaign county, O., in 1816; and had issue (surname Colwell), all b. in Urbana, O.
1. *Caroline-Ward*, b. May 9, 1880.
2. *Helen-Hughes*, b. August 21, 1882.
3. *Donald-Stewart*, b. February 2, 1888.
4. *Elizabeth*, b. November 22, 1890.

ii. *Elizabeth-Walker*, b. April 15, 1856.
iii. *Sarah-Stewart*. b. September 30, 1860; m., April 23, 1889, Charles Judson McKee, attorney-at-law, Dayton, O., b. January 23, 1856, at Hillsboro, O.; and had issue (surname McKee):
1. *Rowland-Hughes*, b. August 21, 1891.
2. *Philip-Judson*, b. October 19, 1892.
3. *Janet* (twin), b. October 19, 1892.

iv. *Fanny-Stewart*, b. April 6, 1863; d. 1866.
v. *James-Rowland*, b. August 9, 1865; general business operator; m., June 23, 1892, by Rev. James R. Hughes, of Dayton, O., Evelyn Kenaga, b. February 18, 1869; daughter of Joseph E. Kenaga and Melissa Fuller, all now of Urbana, O.

XXX. SAMUEL CALHOUN STEWART,[6] (David,[5] Samuel,[4] Samuel,[3] Robert,[2] John,[1]) b. September 6, 1824, at Pennsylvania Furnace, Huntingdon county, Pa. He was educated at Jefferson College; became general manager of Coleraine and Tyrone forges under the operations of Lyon, Shorb & Co., of Pittsburgh, of which firm he was a member. He is a man of prominence in his county—a director of the Lewisburg and Tyrone Railroad company, and an elder in the Presbyterian church; resides at Tyrone Forges, Blair county, Pa. He m., June 15, 1865, MARGARET SAMPLE, daughter of Dr. N. W. Sample (who d. 1849) and Sarah Steele, of Leacock township, Lancaster county, Pa., and granddaughter of Gen. John Steele, of Revolutionary fame; she d. April 13, 1893, at Tyrone Forges, the residence of her daughter. They had issue:

i. *Roberts-Lowrie*. b. March 22, 1866; m. Grace Sylvester, and have *Robert;* master mechanic, San Bernardino, Cal.
ii. *Jeanette-Steele*, b. June 10, 1867.
iii. *Carrie-Hughes*, b. February 17, 1869; m., February 21, 1895, by the Rev. H. H. Henry, Charles Richard McMillen, of Princeton, N. J., civil engineer, Pennsylvania railroad.
iv. *Betty-Walker*, b. October 7, 1871.

v. Samuel-Calhoun, b. October 31, 1874.
vi. Margaret-Hamilton, b. January 25, 1879.
vii. Nathaniel-Sample, b. May 8, 1882.

XXXI. WILLIAM WALKER STEWART,[6] M. D., (David,[5] Samuel,[4] Samuel,[3] Robert,[2] John,[1]) b. April 4, 1826, at Pennsylvania Furnace; d. September 26, 1872, at the Monongahela House, Pittsburgh; buried in Dayton, O., the place of his residence. Dr. Stewart was educated at Jefferson College, Pa., and at the University of Virginia, and received his diploma from Jefferson Medical College, of Philadelphia. He m., June 15, 1854, MARY McGUFFY, daughter of Prof. William McGuffy, of the University of Virginia. They had issue:

 i. William-McGuffy, b. April 21, 1855, in Dayton, O.; d. February 12, 1859.
 ii. Sallie-Walker, b. June 9, 1857, in Virginia; d. February 21, 1876, in London, England; buried in Dayton, O.
 iii. Mary-McGuffy, b. February 24, 1863; d. in infancy.
 iv. Kate-Walker, b. June 1, 1865, in Dayton, O.

SWAN FAMILY.

I. The family of Swan is of English origin, but the ancestors of the Swans who settled in Hanover and Paxtang townships, Lancaster county, Pa., belonged to one of the one hundred English families whom King James of England placed in possession of an equal number of Irish confiscated estates. At what time RICHARD SWAN,[1] emigrated with his family to America we have no account, nor of all his children, save the names of six sons. Upon an examination of the records of the Land Department of the State, we have the following data, relating to early surveys in Lancaster county : " Alexander Swan had surveyed to him on the 23d of January, 1743, one hundred and fifty acres in Hanover township, adjoining land of Andrew Lachin and others." * * * "On the 25th of August, 1767, there was surveyed to Hugh Swan two hundred and eighty-three acres of land, adjoining land of James Wallace, John Carson and the Blue Mountain, in Paxtang township." * * * "To Moses Swan there was surveyed, on the 8th of November, 1774, one hundred and fifty acres, adjoining William McRoberts on the north, Andrew Carson on the east, John Jameson on the south and Alexander Johnson on the west, in Paxtang township." We have no knowledge of the name of Richard Swan's wife. They had, among others, issue :

2. i. *James,* b. 1711 ; m. Mary ———.
3. ii. *Moses,* b. 1718 ; m. Jean Barnett.
  iii. *Joseph,* b. 1715; resided in Letterkenny township, Franklin county, in 1786.
4. iv. *William,* b. 1719 ; m. Jennett Shields.
  v. *Richard,* b. 1725 ; settled in Philadelphia ; a merchant, and was one of the signers of the non-importation resolutions of 1765.
5. vi. *Alexander,* b. 1727 : m. Martha Gilchrist.

II. JAMES SWAN,[2] (Richard,[1]) b. 1711 ; d. December, 1741 ; settled in Hanover township, Lancaster, now Dauphin, county, Pa.; m. MARY ———; d. 1767. They had issue:

i. *James.*
ii. *Alexander.*
iii. *Margaret.*
iv. *Mary.*
v. *Jean.*
vi. *Sarah*, m. Robert Bell, of Hanover, and had a son *James.*

III. MOSES SWAN,[2] (Richard,[1]) b. 1713, in the north of Ireland; came to America with his parents about 1730, and settled in Paxtang township. He d. about 1785. He m., in 1737, JEAN BARNETT, b. 1715; daughter of John and Jennett Barnett. They had issue:

    i. *Hugh*, b. 1738; m., April 4, 1782, by Rev. John Elder, Martha ———.
    ii. *John*, b. 1740; m. and removed to now Washington county, Pa., prior to 1771; and had issue, among others, *John*, and *Thomas.*
    iii. *Isaac*, b. 1742; d. unm.
    iv. *Catharine*, b. 1743; m. Thomas Porter.
6.   v. *William*, b. 1745; m. Martha Renick.
    vi. *Joseph*, b. 1747; resided in Hamilton township, now Franklin county, Pa., in 1785.
    vii. *Moses*, b. 1749; m., and had a son *Moses.*
    viii. *Jean*, b. 1751.
    ix. *Margaret*, b. 1753; m. John Thompson.
7.   x. *Richard*, b. 1755; m. Catharine Boggs.*

IV. WILLIAM SWAN,[2] (Richard,[1]) b. 1719, in Ireland; settled in Hamilton township, Franklin county, Pa., and there d. in January, 1773; m. JENNETT SHIELDS. They had issue:

---

*JAMES BOGGS, of Paxtang, d. July, 1753. In his will he speaks of his wife MARY, and also his children Thomas and Elizabeth, then residing in Ireland, and, "if they came with his wife to this country" were to have a share in his estate. They did not come, and William Boggs, who emigrated with his father, remained in possession of the homestead. He died in April, 1782, in Paxtang, leaving a wife Lydia, who subsequently married Joseph White, and issue as follows:

    i. *James.*
    ii. *Catharine*, m. Richard Swan.
    iii. *Annie*, m. Andrew Wiley.
    iv. *Margaret.*
    v. *Elizabeth.*
    vi. *William.*
    vii. *Lydia.*
    viii. *John.*

i. William.
ii. Margaret.
iii. Jennett.
iv. Robert.

V. ALEXANDER SWAN,[2] (Richard,[1]) b. 1727, in Ireland, settled in Hanover township, Dauphin county; d. March, 1778; m. MARTHA GILCHRIST, daughter of James and Jean Gilchrist, of Paxtang. They had issue:

i. Samuel.
ii. Alexander.
iii. Jean, m. James Taylor.
iv. Mary, m. William Owens.
v. Margaret, m. Thomas Finney.
vi. Agnes, m. Andrew Armstrong; in 1795, resided at Harrisburg.

VI. WILLIAM SWAN,[3] (Moses,[2] Richard,[1]) b. 1745, in Paxtang township; d. prior to 1787; m., in 1775, MARTHA RENICK, b. November 30, 1755, daughter of Henry Renick and Martha Wilson. They had issue:

8.   *i. Margaret,* b. 1776; m. James Ingram.
ii. Sarah, b. January 1, 1779; d. June 17, 1852; m. William Rutherford, (see *Rutherford* record).
iii. Moses, b. 1781; d. at Harrisburg, September 11, 1822.
iv. William, b. 1783.

VII. RICHARD SWAN,[3] (Moses,[2] Richard,[1]) b. 1755, in Paxtang township, Dauphin county, Pa.; d. April, 1808, in Erie county, Pa. He was a soldier in Capt. James Cowden's company, during the Revolutionary war, and was in actual service during the campaign in New Jersey, and around Philadelphia. In the Whiskey Insurrection of 1794, he commanded a company of volunteers. In 1797 he went to Erie county, Pa., purchased a tract of land, but did not remove thither until 1802, when he located at the mouth of Walnut creek, as the manager of the Harrisburg and Presqu' Isle Land Company's mills at that point. He was one of the earliest pioneers in that section of Pennsylvania. Captain Swan m. CATHARINE BOGGS, b. February 8, 1759, in Paxtang township, Dauphin county, Pa.; d. April, 1843, in Erie county, Pa., daughter of William and Lydia Boggs. They had issue, all of whom, except the youngest, were born in Paxtang township:

Swan Family. 671

9.   i. *Lydia*, b. September 15, 1789 ; m. Joseph McCreary.
     ii. *William-Boggs*, b. February 27, 1791 ; d. February 10, 1792.
10. iii. *John-Joseph*, b. March 14, 1793 ; m. Eunice Ann White.
     iv. *William*, b. November 25, 1794 ; went west and died there about 1833 ; unm.
11. v. *Richard*, b. December 4, 1796 ; m. Margaret Boal Sturgeon.
12. vi. *Moses*, b. December 9, 1798; m. Virginia Bates.
13. vii. *Andrew-Cavet*, b. July 29, 1802 ; m. Angeline Mitchell.

VIII. MARGARET SWAN,⁴ (William,³ Moses,² Richard,¹) b. 1776, in Paxtang; d. at Harrisburg; m., November 26, 1799, by Rev. Nathaniel Snowden, Major JAMES INGRAM, b. 1761 ; d. August 12, 1811, at Harrisburg, and is buried in Paxtang church graveyard. They had issue (surname Ingram):

   i. *William*.
   ii. *Martha-Smith*, m. William Dick Boas, (*see Boas record*).
   iii. *Sarah*, d. unm.
   iv. *Maria*, m. Nathaniel Henry.
   v. *James*.

IX. LYDIA SWAN,⁴ (Richard,³ Moses,² Richard,¹) b. September 15, 1789, in Paxtang township, Dauphin county, Pa.; d. April, 1866, in Erie county, Pa.; m., September 12, 1811, JOSEPH F. MCCREARY. They had issue (surname McCreary):

   i. *Samuel-Slater*, b. September 12, 1812 ; m. Joanna O. Brooks, and had issue.
   ii. *Richard-Swan*, m. Louisa Barr, and had issue.
   iii. *Selina-C*.
   iv. *John-J.*, d. s. p.
   v. *Mary E*.
   vi. *Jackson*, b. August 29, 1823 ; m., first, Mary Ann Love ; secondly, Rebecca Josephine Love ; and had issue.
   vii. *David-B.*, b. Feb. 27, 1826 ; was educated at the Erie Academy and Washington College ; afterwards taught school at Erie, and was principal of the Winchester, Ky., Seminary from 1851 to 1853 ; read law with Judge Galbraith, and in 1858 was admitted to the Erie bar ; in the war of the Rebellion entered the service as first lieutenant company B of the Erie regiment; assisted in the organization of the 145th regiment P. V., and was appointed lieutenant colonel, subsequently promoted colonel, and later breveted brigadier general ; in 1866 elected to the legislature, serving two terms ; in 1868 was Adjutant General of the State, filling the office with distinction three years ; resides in Erie ; m., in 1851, Annette Gun-

nison, dau. of E. D. Gunnison; and had issue (surname McCreary):
1. *Sophia*, m. Henry A. Clark.
2. *Wirt*, graduated in 1884 from the U. S. Naval Academy.

viii. Lydia-Ann, m. William Love ; and had issue.

ix. Martha-Swan, m. Thomas Love ; and had issue.

X. JOHN JOSEPH SWAN,[4] (Richard,[3] Moses,[2] Richard,[1]) b. March 14, 1793, in Paxtang township, Dauphin county, Pa.; d. July 22, 1878, at Swanville, Erie county, Pa. At the age of sixteen he taught school in Girard borough, and afterwards at Mill Creek and Erie. In 1812 he assisted in the survey of the "Triangle," and also responded to the call of service in the war of that year. In 1818 and 1819 he was in the mercantile business at Conneaut, O.; from 1821 to 1822 at Green Bay, Mich. In 1823 he returned to Erie county, took up land, established a homestead and followed farming. He served as county auditor from 1831 to 1833. Mr. Swan m., June, 1825, EUNICE ANN WHITE, b. May 15, 1805; d. October 22, 1855. They had issue:

i. Lucinda.

ii. Eliza-Catharine.

iii. Charles-John, d. June 18,1877.

iv. Andrew-Francis, b. October 16, 1832 ; d. April 18, 1876 ; enlisted as a private in the 6th regiment, United States cavalry, July 19, 1861; was promoted to first sergeant company G of that regiment; subsequently, in the volunteer service, to major and lieutenant colonel ; had his horse shot under him at Shepherdstown, Va., and was wounded in a charge on Fort Magruder, Williamsburg, Va.; wounded at Cold Harbor, and, at last, was compelled to resign towards the close of the war. In 1867 was elected sheriff of Erie county, Pa.

v. Harriet.

vi. Adelaide-Mary, d. April 13, 1867.

vii. Henry-Harrison.

viii. Lavinia, m. William Hoskinson, Jr ; and had issue.

ix. Henry-Clay, m. Virginia S. Rogers ; and had issue.

x. Josephine.

xi. Eugene-Barnett, served in the war of the Rebellion ; m. Mary Jennings.

xii. Clayton-Kleber.

XI. RICHARD SWAN,⁴ (Richard,³ Moses,² Richard,¹) b. December 4, 1796, in Paxtang township, Dauphin county, Pa.; m., January 26, 1826, MARGARET BOAL STURGEON, b. September 3, 1805; daughter of Jeremiah Sturgeon and Jane Moorhead. They had issue:

 i. William-Boggs.
 ii. Jane-Sturgeon, m. John C. Perkins; and had issue.
 iii. Edwin, m. Anna Rumbaugh.
 iv. Emily, m. George Perkins.
 v. Sophia, m. Edwin Heron; and had issue.
 vi. Rosannah, b. August 21, 1840; d. January 25, 1846.
 vii. Mary, m. William Brewster.
 viii. Byron-Wallace.

XII. MOSES SWAN,⁴ (Richard,³ Moses,² Richard,¹) b. December 9, 1798, in Paxtang township, Dauphin county, Pa.; d. June 30, 1833, at Galena, Ill.; m. VIRGINIA BATES, b. February 9, 1809, in Henry county, Ky.; d. September 2, 1865, at Galena, Ill. They had issue:

 i. David-Bates, d. s. p.
 ii. Emily, m., June 15, 1858, William Bell, of Lexington, Ky.; and had issue.

XIII. ANDREW CAVET SWAN,⁴ (Richard,³ Moses,² Richard,¹) b. July 29, 1802, in Erie county, Pa.; d. July, 1867, at Galena, Ill.; m. ANGELINE MITCHELL. They had issue:

 i. George, d. s. p.
 ii. Emily C., m. ——— Chilson; and had issue.
 iii. John-Mitchell.

THOMAS OF HEIDELBERG.

I. THEODORUS THOMAS,[1] a native of Switzerland, and a refugee from the Palatinate, Germany, with his wife and a portion of his family, emigrated to America in 1736, landing at Philadelphia on the 16th of September that year from the "ship, ' Princess Augusta,' Samuel Merchant, master, from Rotterdam, last from Cowes." He settled in what is now Heidelberg township, Lebanon county, Pa., then in Lancaster county, in the neighborhood of Scheafferstown. He died a few years afterwards, leaving a wife, ANNA [SCHEAFFER], and children as follows:

2.   i. *Martin*, b. 1702 ; m., and had issue.
      ii. *Theodorus*, b. 1708 ; m., and left issue, but no record of the family.
      iii. *Jacob*, b. 1715 ; no information.
      iv. *Anna*, b. 1718 ; m. Henry Weiss, of Heidelberg.

II. MARTIN THOMAS,[2] (Theodorus,[1]) b. about 1702, in the Palatinate, Germany ; d. circ. 1768, in Lebanon township, then Lancaster county, Pa. He emigrated with his family to America in the year 1749, landing at Philadelphia on the 30th of August that year, his father having preceded him several years. The ship, "Crown," Michael James, master, in which they embarked, was heavily laden, having no less than five hundred souls on board on its arrival, out of over six hundred at leaving Rotterdam. The mortality on that crowded vessel was fearful, and it is hardly probable that the family of Martin Thomas entirely escaped. He became quite prominent in the early history of Heidelberg township, where he settled ; was lieutenant of a ranging company on the frontiers during the French and Indian wars, 1756–7, and overseer of roads in 1761. He left a wife BARBARA, and children, as follows:

      i. *Philip*, b. 1725 ; nothing further is known of him, save that he married and went southward.
3.   ii. *Theodorus*, b. 1727 ; m. Catharine [Bomberger].
4.   iii. *Jacob*, b. 1729 ; m. Ursula ———.
      iv. *Henry*, b. 1731 ; it is supposed accompanied his brother to the valley of Virginia.

5.   v. *Adam*, b. 1733 ; m., and left issue.
    vi. *Anna*, b. 1735.
6. vii. *Martin*, b. March 15, 1737 ; m. Ursula Müller.

III. THEODORUS THOMAS,³ (Martin,² Theodorus,¹) b. about 1727, in the Palatinate, Germany; d. in May, 1790, in Lebanon township, Dauphin, now Lebanon county, Pa. He served in the Indian and Revolutionary wars ; was overseer of the poor in Heidelberg township in 1761, and served in other official positions. He m. CATHARINE [BOMBERGER]. They had issue:

    i. Theodorus [*Durst*], b. 1759 ; m. Mrs. Regina Spycker, widow of John Spycker, (by whom she had issue, surname Spycker, *Benjamin* and *John-Peter*,) ; and had issue :
        1. *Barbara*, m. Christopher Uhler.
7.   *ii. Martin*, b. 1761 ; m. Elizabeth Strohm.
8.   *iii. John*, b. 1763 ; m. Anna Wolfersberger.
    iv. Jacob, b. 1765 ; resided in Londonderry township, where he died in 1785 ; m. Catharine Hostetter, daughter of John and Barbara Hostetter.
    v. Catharine, b. 1767 ; m. John Becker, d. December, 1789; and had issue (surname Becker):
        1. *Matthias*.
        2. *Henry*.
        3. *Catharine*, d. prior to 1789 ; m. Martin Miller.
        4. *Elizabeth*, m. —— Good.
        5. *Frederick*.
9.   *vi. Margaret*, b. November 11, 1769 ; m. Johannes Wolfersberger.
  vii. Maria, b. 1771 ; m. Abraham Smith.

IV. JACOB THOMAS,³ (Martin,² Theodorus,¹) b. 1729, in the Palatinate, Germany ; d. November, 1771, in Lebanon township, Lancaster, now Lebanon county, Pa.; he left a wife URSULA (who after remaining a widow a few years, married George Shrombaugh, of Lebanon township,) and children, as follows :

    i. Barbara, b. 1754.
   ii. Jacob, b. 1756 ; enlisted February 7, 1776, in Capt. Rudolph Brunner's company, Col. Arthur St. Clair's battalion of Pennsylvania, in the war of the Revolution, of which he was promoted corporal, June 13, 1776.
  iii. Ursula, b. 1760.
  iv. John, b. 1762 ; m. Anne ——.

V. ADAM THOMAS,³ (Martin,² Theodorus,¹) b. about 1733, in the Palatinate, Germany; d. September, 1762; leaving among other children :
    i. Veronica, m. Peter Lehr, of Dauphin county, Pa.
    ii. Elizabeth, m. Jacob Miller, of Cumberland county, Pa.

VI. MARTIN THOMAS,³ (Martin,² Theodorus,¹) b. March 15, 1737, in Heidelberg township, then Lancaster county, Pa.; d. July 15, 1802, in East Pennsboro' township, Cumberland county, Pa. He served, as a private, in the French and Indian war in his father's company, and, prior to the Revolution, established a furnace in the neighborhood of Shamokin, Northumberland county, Pa. He served in the struggle for Independence as sergeant of Capt. John Simpson's company, First battalion, Northumberland county associators, March 25, 1776, and subsequently sergeant in Third regiment, Pennsylvania Line. During the "Great Runaway" of 1778, his family fled from the locality, and settled on the Yellow Breeches, in Cumberland county, where he built a stone mill, yet standing, and where he remained until his death. He disposed of his Northumberland county property, receiving a large sum in Continental currency therefor, which, before he had the opportunity to re-invest, became worthless. He was one of the founders of Friedens Kirche, near the present Shiremanstown. He m., in 1767, URSULA MÜLLER, b. 1740, in Lebanon township, now Lebanon county, Pa.; d. 1807, in East Pennsboro' township, Cumberland county, Pa.; daughter of John and Barbara Müller (*see Müller and Lobingier.*) They had issue:

    i. Martin, b. 1768 ; d. 1824, at Shippensburg, Pa.; unm.
10. *ii. John*, b. 1770; m. Mary Renninger.
    iii. Elizabeth, b. May 2, 1772 ; d. August 5, 1867 ; m. Valentine Egle. (*see Egle record*).
    iv. Catharine, b. January, 1777 ; d. July 2, 1860, near Newville, Pa.; m. Frederick Mentzer, b. 1776 ; d. 1860; and had issue beside a daughter (surname Mentzer):
        1. *Frederick*, d. September 4, 1864 ; m., and had issue.
    v. Adam, b. 1779 ; d. unm.
    vi. George, b. 1781 ; m., and removed to the West.
11. *vii. Jacob*, b. February 2, 1783 ; m. Mary Bear.
12. *viii. Anna-Margaret*, b. September 12, 1785 ; m. Jacob Gheer.
13. *ix. Mary*, b. 1787 ; m. Gilbert Burnett.

VII. MARTIN THOMAS,⁴ (Theodorus,³ Martin,² Theodorus,¹) b. about 1761, in Lebanon township, then Lancaster county, Pa.; d. August, 1822, in Londonderry township, Dauphin county, Pa. He served in the war of the Revolution at the age of eighteen; was a miller by occupation, and a substantial farmer. He m. ELIZABETH STROHM; d. prior to 1820; daughter of George Strohm, Sr., of Lebanon township, Lebanon county, Pa. They had issue:
    i. Jacob.
    ii. Magdalena, m. ——— Hawk.
    iii. Susannah, m. ——— Wolfersberger.

VIII. JOHN THOMAS,⁴ (Theodorus,³ Martin,² Theodorus,¹) b. about 1763; d. January, 1795, in Lebanon township, Dauphin, now Lebanon county, Pa. It is probable most of his family went West, and thus have been lost trace of. He m. ANNA WOLFERSBERGER. They had issue:
    i. John.
    ii. Jacob.
    iii. Margaret.
    iv. Barbara.
    v. Elizabeth.
    vi. Anna.

IX. MARGARET THOMAS,⁴ (Theodorus,³ Martin,² Theodorus,¹) b. November 11, 1769, in Lebanon township, Lancaster, now Lebanon county, Pa.; d. November 28, 1832, at Campbellstown, and there buried; m. JOHANNES WOLFERSBERGER, b. April 11, 1767; d. September 8, 1818, at Campbellstown, and there interred; son of Philip and Susanna Wolfersberger. They had issue (surname Wolfersberger):
    i. John, b. October 6, 1789; d. November 29, 1864; m. Elizabeth ———, b. December 15, 1790; d. February 25, 1852.
    ii. Elizabeth, b. September 16, 1792; d. December 2, 1867; unm.

X. JOHN THOMAS,⁴ (Martin,³ Martin,² Theodorus,¹) b. about 1770, in Lebanon township, now Lebanon county, Pa.; d. about 1834, at Paris, Stark county, O., and there buried. He went to Western Pennsylvania a few years after his marriage, locating at Beaver Falls; about 1809, removing to Columbiana county, O. He was thrice married; m., first, MARY RENNINGER, b. in Cumberland county, Pa.; d. 1804, at

Beaver Falls, Pa.; daughter of Conrad and Mary Renninger. They had issue :

14. *i. Sarah*, b. 1794 ; m. Daniel Hammond.
15. *ii. Sybilla*, b. 1796 ; m. John Hammond.
    iii. Mary. b. 1798; d. 1828, at Paris, O.; m. William Lutz; d. in 1847, at Paris. O.; and had issue (surname Lutz¹:
        1. *Elizabeth*, d. 1830, at Paris, O.
    iv. George, b. 1800 ; d. 1821, at Paris, O.
    v. Rebecca, b. 1802 ; d. 1824, at Paris, O.

John Thomas m., secondly, about 1807, at Beaver Falls, ELIZABETH HENNING, b. 1786, in Pennsylvania ; d. 1819, at Paris, O. They had issue :

   vi. Lena, b. 1808 ; d. 1820, at Paris, O.
16. *vii. Martha*, b. September 1, 1810 ; m. George Pore.
17. *viii. Elizabeth*, b. December 23, 1812 ; m. Josiah W. Chapman.
    ix. John, b. 1815 ; m. Minerva Taylor ; reside at Horse Neck, W. Va.
18. *x. Catharine*, b. March 15, 1818; m. David Bowman.

John Thomas m., thirdly, Mrs. SARAH MONTGOMERY. They had issue:

19. *xi. Amanda*, b. December 15, 1821; m. Mortimer F. Reed.
    xii. [A son]; d. in infancy, and buried at Paris, O.

XI. JACOB THOMAS,[4] (Martin,[3] Martin,[2] Theodorus,[1]) b. February 2, 1783, in East Pennsboro' township, Cumberland county, Pa.; d. May 29, 1822, in Adams county, Pa.; buried in Bender's church graveyard. He m., in 1811, in Perry county, Pa., MARY BEAR, b. January 15, 1790, in Perry county, Pa.; d. March 20, 1872, in Adams county, Pa.; buried by the side of her husband ; daughter of Jacob Bear and Catharine Zimmerman. They had issue :

20. *i. George-Bear*, b. October 7, 1812 ; m. Catharine Ebert.
    ii. [A dau.], b. January 17, 1814 ; d. in infancy.
21. *iii. Martin*, b. January 2, 1815 ; m. Susan Eicholtz.
22. *iv. Mary*, b. June 19, 1817 ; m. Joseph Hartzel.
    v. Catharine, b. September 15, 1819; d. Nov. 4, 1888; unm.
23. *vi. Margaret*, b. August 19, 1821 ; m. John Landis Latshaw.

XII. ANNA MARGARET THOMAS,[4] (Martin,[3] Martin,[2] Theodorus,[1]) b. September 12, 1785, in East Pennsboro' township, Cumberland county, Pa.; baptized by Rev. Anthony Hautz; d. August 20, 1824; buried in Friedens Kirche graveyard,

Thomas of Heidelberg. 679

near Shiremanstown, Pa. She was a devoted Christian, and a most amiable woman. She m., January, 1808, JACOB GHEER, b. November 5, 1784, near Lisburn, Cumberland county, Pa.; d. February 14, 1859, near Elliottsville, in Shearman's Valley, Perry county, Pa., and there buried. He was a farmer. They had issue (surname Gheer), all born at the old homestead in Cumberland county, Pa., six miles west of Harrisburg, on the State road to Gettysburg:

    i. Eliza, b. January 25, 1809; d. May 31, 1823; buried at Frieden's Kirche.
    ii. Mary, b. June 15, 1810; d. May 9, 1822; buried at Frieden's Kirche.
    iii. Matilda, b. June 20, 1812; d. November 10, 1860; buried in Bellwood cemetery, near Bellwood, Blair county, Pa.; she was a noble Christian woman, and among the first members of the Rev. John Winebrenner's church.
24. *iv. John*, b. November 7, 1814; m. Amelia A. Patterson.
    v. Martin, b. April 14, 1817; d. July 14, 1818; buried at Frieden's Kirche.
25. *vi. Margaret*, b. September 28, 1820; m. John S. Lobaugh.
    vii. Jacob, b. March 3, 1822; d. August 21, 1824; buried at Frieden's Kirche.
    viii. Thomas, b. July 14, 1823; d. about 1850; buried near Petersburg, Perry county, Pa.

XIII. MARY THOMAS,[4] (Martin,[3] Martin,[2] Theodrus,[1]) b. 1787, in East Pennsboro' township, Cumberland county, Pa.; d. March 18, 1858, at Harrisburg, Pa. She was a woman of intelligence, kind and benevolent, and a strict Presbyterian. She m., in 1818, by Rev. Henry Wilson, of Silvers Spring church, GILBERT BURNETT, b. July 13, 1778, in Concord township, Delaware county, Pa.; d. December 14, 1855, at Harrisburg, Pa., and there buried; son of John Burnett* and Rebecca Key. They had issue (surname Burnett):

---

*JOHN BURNETT m. in Philadelphia, September 21, 1759, by the Rev. William Sturgeon, of the Church of England, REBECCA KEY. They both died well advanced in years, in Washington county, Pa. They had issue, all born in Concord township, now Delaware county, Pa. (surname Burnett):

    i. Elias, b. Easter Sunday, March 22, 1761, at 5 P. M.; baptized August 26, 1764, by Rev. George Craig.
    ii. John, b. Whit Sunday, June 10, 1764, at 5 P. M.; baptized August 26, 1764, by Rev. George Craig; d. s. p.

i. Augustus, b. June 20, 1820; d. December 16, 1884, at Harrisburg, Pa.; he was educated at the private schools of the town and at the Harrisburg academy; early in life learned merchandizing; and followed that pursuit many years; in a quiet, unobtrusive way he accomplished much good, and the deeds which he effected will live after him; he was a good citizen, and an earnest Christian; Mr. Burnett, m., October 20, 1858, Rebecca J. Pugh, daughter of James Pugh; she resides at Centreville, Del.

XIV. SARAH THOMAS,[5] (John,[4] Martin,[3] Martin,[2] Theodorus,[1]) b. 1794, in East Pennsboro' township, Cumberland county, Pa.; d. about 1858, in DeKalb county, Ind.; buried at Hamilton, Steuben county, Ind.; m., at Paris, Ohio, DANIEL HAMMOND, b. about 1792; d. about 1862; buried at Hamilton, Ind. They had issue (surname Hammond):

i. George, d. in DeKalb county, Ind.; m. Christina Hood.
ii. Lena, m. John Clark; reside in DeKalb county, Ind.

---

iii. Elizabeth, b. January 3, 1767, at 7 P. M.; baptized June 8, 1767, by Rev. George Craig; d. April 30, 1855, in Washington co., Pa.; m. William Brimner, d. April 26, 1850.
iv. Thomas, b. August 25, 1769, "It being as great a Druth as ever was known in this part;" baptized November 26, 1769, by Rev. George Craig; d. 1836, in Chester county, Pa.; buried at Birmingham Meeting-House; m. Susan Seal.
v. James, b. August 10, 1773, at 1 A. M.; baptized October 26, 1773, by Rev. George Craig; m., and had issue.
vi. Gilbert, b. July 27, 1776, at 12 o'clock, midnight; d. September 1, 1777.
vii. Gilbert, (2nd) b. July 13, 1778, in the afternoon; baptized in Middletown, Pa.; was twice married; m., first, April 21, 1804, by Rev. N. R. Snowden, Elizabeth Wallace, b. 1782; d. at Harrisburg, Pa.; daughter of Samuel Wallace (see *Wallace and Weir*); and had issue:
   1. *Caroline*, b. 1804, at Baltimore, Md.; m. James Denning.
   2. *Henrietta*, b. 1807, at Baltimore, Md.; d. 1827, in Chester county, Pa.

Gilbert Burnett m., secondly, Mary Thomas, (see *record*).
viii. Rebecca, b. June 12, 1782, at Middletown, Pa.; deceased at Frankfort Springs, Pa.; m. Andrew Knox.
ix. Ann, b. April 29, 1787, at Middletown, Pa.; d. s. p.

iii. Elizabeth, d. 1870, in DeKalb co., Ind.; m. Jacob Weaver.
iv. Anna, m. John Musser ; reside in Hamilton, Steuben county, O.
v. Mary, m. Philip Mann ; reside in DeKalb county, Ind.
vi. Martha, m. ―― Rorabaugh.

XV. SYBILLA THOMAS,[5] (John,[4] Martin,[3] Martin,[2] Theodorus,[1]) b. 1796, in East Pennsboro' township, Cumberland county, Pa.; d. about 1829, at Paris, O.; m., in 1818, at Paris, O., JOHN HAMMOND ; d. about 1839, at Paris, O. They had issue (surname Hammond) :

    i. Jacob, b. December, 1819 ; m. Amanda Clark ; resided in DeKalb county, Ind.
    ii. Mary, b. 1821 ; d.; m. Michael McEnderfer.
    iii. Elizabeth, b. 1823 ; d. s. p.
    iv. Thomas, b. 1825 ; m. Elizabeth Hood ; reside at Summit, DeKalb county, Ind.

XVI. MARTHA THOMAS,[5] (John,[4] Martin,[3] Martin,[2] Theodorus,[1]) b. September 1, 1810, in Columbiana county, O.; d. January 20, 1893, in Dunkirk, Hardin county, O.; m., January 15, 1828, GEORGE PORE, b. April 15, 1802, in Westmoreland county, Pa.; d. December 13, 1882, in Hancock county, O. They had issue (surname Pore) :

    i. John-T., b. May 19, 1829, in Stark county, O.; d. January 12, 1876, in Hancock county, O.; m., October 7, 1869, Matilda Ann Carman, b. September 18, 1838 ; d. Octo- 25, 1870 ; and had issue :
        1. *Louis-Marshall*, b. October 16, 1870.
    ii. George-A., b. June 30, 1831 ; d. April 13, 1885; m., first, August 21, 1858, Hannah L. Zeagly, b. 1838 ; d. April 4, 1866 : and had issue :
        1. *William-Milton*, b. December 23, 1859.
        2. *Martha-Frances*, b. December 7, 1861 ; d. September 18, 1882 ; m., June 28, 1881, Noah Blosser ; and had issue (surname Blosser):
            a. William-Franklin, b. April 11, 1882.
        3. *Peter-Franklin*, b. Sept. 10, 1863 ; d. in infancy.
    George A. Pore m., secondly, August 16, 1870, Susan Ream, b. June 20, 1847, in Hancock county, O., and had issue :
        4. *Eva-Eldice*, b. May 29, 1871.
        5. [*A son*], b. November 10, 1873 ; d. Dec. 15, 1873.
        6. *Sarah-Charlotte*, b. March 21, 1878.
        7. *Flossie-Gertrude*, b. October 12, 1879.
        8. *Lydia-May*, b. Sept. 22, 1881 ; d. Sept. 22, 1883.

iii. *Philip*, b. December 4, 1832; d. December 29, 1874; m., July 23, 1859, Lydia Ann Clark, b. August 12, 1837, in Delaware county, O.; and had issue:
1. *Alva-Franklin*, b. June 15, 1860; d. Sept. 11, 1874.
2. *James-Edward*, b. October 19, 1862; m., October 20, 1883, Clara Montgomery.
3. *Clark*, b. March 4, 1864.
4. *John-Wesley*, b. December 11, 1867.
5. *Mary-Luella*, b. April 4, 1869.
6. *Ruth-Lucilla*, b. December 15, 1871.
7. *Laura-May*, b. August 6, 1873.
8. *Lucy-P.*, b. April 22, 1876; d. March 19, 1877.

iv. *Elizabeth*, b. March 4, 1836; resides at Ada, Hardin county, O.; m., October 19, 1869, John Wright Nelson, b. May 19, 1838, at Huntersville, Hardin county, O.; d. January 6, 1895; and had issue (surname Nelson):
1. *John-Ross*, b. April 12, 1874; d. May 28, 1877.
2. *Flora-Olive*, b. April 5, 1880; d. January 26, 1895.

v. *Sarah-Catharine*, b. May 9, 1839; d. January 4, 1865; m., January 24, 1863, George A. Richert, b. in Stark county, O.; d. 1884, and had issue (surname Richert):
1. *George-Clifford*, b. Nov. 22, 1864; d. Oct. 22, 1865.

vi. *Josiah-H.*, b. June 6, 1841; d. May 1, 1879; m., September 14, 1869, Lucy Ann Newson, b. October 19, 1851, in Monroe county, O.; no children.

vii. *Margaret-Ann*, b. May 14, 1843; d. August 14, 1844.

viii. *Franklin-C.*, b. November 23, 1845; resides on the old homestead in Hancock county, O.; m., September 12, 1872, Sarah Ann Crist; and had issue:
1. *Flora-Alberta*, b. August 29, 1874.
2. *Charles-Clifford*, b. Sept. 18, 1876; d. Sept. 21, 1880.
3. *Martha-Mary*, b. February 17, 1879.
4. *Laura-Mabel*, b. March 22, 1881.

ix. *Levi-Thomas*, b. April 13, 1849; m., October 25, 1870, Ella Gertrude Hermes, b. April 19, 1853, in Wyandot county, O.; and had issue:
1. *Oliver-Elba*, b. May 18, 1872.
2. *Clarence-Clyde*, b. June 21, 1873; d. Jan. 5, 1874.
3. *George-Glenn*, b. October 31, 1876.
4. *Lillie-Grace*, b. May 3, 1880.
5. *Nellie-Blanche*, b. March 28, 1883.

x. *Martha-Caroline*, b. January 31, 1852; m., October 27, 1870, William Pifer, b. October 25, 1850, in Hancock county, O., and had issue (surname Pifer):
1. *Lucy-Dell*, b. October 19, 1872.
2. *Nellie-Elida*, b. January 9, 1877.

XVII. ELIZABETH THOMAS,[5] (John,[4] Martin,[3] Martin,[2] Theodorus,[1]) b. December 23, 1812, in Columbiana county, O.; resides in Edinburgh, O. She m., December 21, 1837, JOSIAH WHITNEY CHAPMAN, b. July 8, 1808, in Rootstone, Portage county, O.; d. February 13, 1884, in Edinburgh, O., son of Beman Chapman and Sarah Whitney. His parents came from Toland, Conn., and he was next to the eldest of a family of ten children. The youngest brother was Professor I. O. Chapman, many years connected with Mt. Union College. Josiah W. Chapman was a farmer, owned a fine farm in Edinburgh where all his married life was spent. They had issue (surname Chapman):

    i. Sarah-Elizabeth, b. September 29, 1840 ; m., August 15, 1861, Hugh J. Caldwell, b. June 7, 1835, in Trumbull county, O.; attended college at Delaware and Mt. Union, O., graduating from the latter institution in 1860 ; in 1862 was elected superintendent of the schools at Warren, O.; in 1866 resigned and accepted the superintendency of the schools at Gallipolis ; in the meantime, studied law, graduating from Cleveland Law College under General Crowell, in 1871, and the same year entered upon the practice of that profession at Lawrence, Kan.; in 1875 he removed to Cleveland, O., where he now resides, practicing his profession. Mr. and Mrs. Caldwell had issue (surname Caldwell):*

---

*HUGH J. CALDWELL was the son of David Caldwell and Elizabeth Christy. His grandfather, Hugh Caldwell, with his wife, Jane Anderson, natives of county Derry, Ireland, emigrated to America in 1804, and settled in West Chester, Pa. In 1810 they removed to Trumbull county, O.; there they lived and died. Their children were :

    i. David, b. October 4, 1804.
    ii. Jane, m. John Hoover ; removed to Minnesota.
    iii. James, resides in Trumbull county, O.
    iv. John, bought the old homestead, and died there.
    v. Nancy, m. William H. Bard.
    vi. Hugh, a minister of the M. E. Church ; removed to Oregon.
    vii. William, resides in Trumbull county, O.
    viii. Eliza, m. Benjamin Cranage, a merchant of Warren, O.

The eldest son, David Caldwell, was thrice married ; m., first Emeline M. Hart, who d. May 27, 1828 ; no issue. He m., secondly, February 9, 1832, Elizabeth Christy ; d. January, 1867 ; daughter of William Christy and Mary Snook, of Essex, N. J. They had issue :

1. *William-Ernest*, b. July 5, 1862, in Edinburgh, Portage county, O.; m., April 27, 1892, Anna Louise Stranahan ; and had issue :
   a. *Hugh-Ebenezer*, b. January 20, 1893.
2. *Alfred-Percy*, b. October 17, 1864, in Warren, Trumbull county, O.; d. June 14, 1889.
3. *Francis-Asbury*, b. March 26, 1867, in Gallipolis, Gallia county, O.; m., June 12, 1889, Minnie A. Newberry, b. October 31, 1866 ; and had issue :
   a. *Frances-Lilian*, b. May 26, 1890.
   b. *Blanche-Elizabeth*, b. January 12. 1892.
   c. *Alice-Mary*, b. June 5, 1893.
4. *Florence*, b. August 31, 1868, in Gallipolis, O.
5. *Halliday-Miles*, b. Jan. 18, 1873 ; d. August 16, 1873.
6. *Hugh-Whitney*, b. November 15, 1874, in Lawrence, Kan.; d. July 16, 1889.

ii. *Amanda-Loama*, b. May 31, 1843.
iii. *Rhoda-Lodema*, b. June 27, 1846.

XVIII. CATHARINE THOMAS,[5] (John,[4] Martin,[3] Martin,[2] Theodorus,[1]) b. March 15, 1818, near Paris, Stark county, O.; d. November 19, 1884, at Osnaburg, Stark county, O.; m., February 27, 1842, by Peter Stimmel, Esq., DAVID BOWMAN, b. October 14, 1819, in Stark county, O.; d. November 4, 1874; buried in Roland cemetery, Canton, O. They had issue (surname Bowman):

i. *Emanuel-Thomas*, b. July 14, 1843 ; m., April 23, 1867, Elizabeth Simmers ; and had issue.
ii. *Joanna*, b. March 6, 1845; d. April 21, 1847; buried at Paris, O.
iii. *Winfield-Scott*, b. April 5, 1847; d. August 19, 1874; buried in Roland cemetery, Canton, O.; m., March 21, 1871, Susan Hammond ; resides in DeKalb county, Ind.; and had issue :
   1. *Herbert*, b. September 23, 1872.
iv. *William-Franklin*, b. June 3, 1849 ; resides in Stark county, O.

---

i. *Mary-Jane*, d. 1854, in her twenty-second year.
ii. *Hugh-J.*, b. June 7, 1835 ; m. Sarah Elizabeth Chapman.
iii. *John-O.*, b. January 5, 1839 ; member of the Second Ohio cavalry ; killed June 1, 1864, in the battle of the Wilderness near Ashland station.
iv. *Calvin*, b. August 2, 1842; member of the One Hundred and Fifth Ohio volunteers ; killed September 23, 1863, in the battle of Chickamauga.

Thomas of Heidelberg. 685

v. *George-Washington*, b. March 25, 1851 ; d. September 8, 1874 ; buried in Roland cemetery, Canton, O.
vi. *Albert-Byron*, b. January 10, 1853 ; d. September 9, 1874.
vii. *Charles-Cassius*, b. July 10, !1855; m., January 17, 1878, Margaret J. Troutner, b. July 19, 1854 ; and had issue :
   1. *Slata-Vindella*, b. Oct. 17, 1878 ; d. Aug. 15, 1879.
   2. *Lucy-May*, b. August 21, 1880.
   3. *Grace-Alice*, b. June 20, 1882.
   4. *Laura-Leona*, b. February 15, 1885.
   5. *Oscar-Benton*, b. April 28, 1888.
viii. *Emma-Augusta*, b. October 24, 1857 ; d. December 31, 1889.
ix. *Mary-Alice*, d. May 12, 1888.

XIX. AMANDA THOMAS,[5] (John,[4] Martin,[3] Martin,[2] Theodorus,[1]) b. December 15, 1821, near Paris, Stark county, O.; resides at Marshall, Clark county, Ill.; m., December 11, 1842, MORTIMER FRANCIS REED, b. May 30, 1816, in Canton, Stark county, O.; d. July 2, 1864, in Marshall, Ill.; son of Timothy Herbert Reed and Elizabeth Franklin. They had issue (surname Reed):

i. *Sarah*, b. November 17, 1843 ; m., December 22, 1867, Ira W. Center ; and had issue (surname Center):
   1. *William-Franklin*, b. October 20, 1868.
ii. *Timothy-Herbert*, b. September 29, 1845 ; m., February 20, 1876, Hannah Gross, b. Dec. 9, 1848; and had issue :
   1. *Mortimer-Franklin*, b. February 4, 1877.
   2. *Jacob-Herbert*, b. August 30, 1878.
   3. *Robert-Burns*, b. February 14, 1881.
   4. *Frank-E.*, b. March 24, 1882.
   5. *Flora-Bell*, b. March 17, 1883.
   6. *Kate Irene*, b. October 10, 1885.
iii. *Walter-Burdock*, b. February 22, 1847 ; d. October 15, 1848.
iv. *Elizabeth-Franklin*, b. February 2, 1849 ; m., June 10, 1869, Reese P. English ; and had issue (surname English):
   1. *Edmund-Reed*, b. July 18, 1869.
   2. *Mary*, b. July 29, 1871.
v. *Diora*, b. March 21, 1851 ; m., November 15, 1871, Francis E. Janney, b. February 28, 1849; d. December 4, 1880 ; and had issue (surname Janney):
   1. *Bessie Amanda*, b. Jan. 21, 1873 ; d. June 19, 1878.
   2. *Mortimer-Francis*, b. October 28, 1874 ; d. December 31, 1879.
   3. *Susanna-Dora*, b. May 13, 1878.
   4. *Milo-Reed*, b. July 3, 1880.
vi. *Thomas-P.*, b. February 26, 1853 ; d. March 21, 1854.

vii. Charles-Fremont, b. April 12, 1858.
viii. Jacob, b. June 11, 1860; d. April 2, 1882.

XX. GEORGE BEAR THOMAS,[5] (Jacob,[4] Martin,[3] Martin,[2] Theodorus,[1]) b. October 7, 1812, near New Cumberland, Cumberland county, Pa.; removed to York county, and became quite prominent in local affairs; for many years, he served as postmaster of the office named for him, Thomasville, where he resides. He m., June 10, 1834, by Rev. Daniel Gotwalt, CATHARINE EBERT, b. July 23, 1812, in Adams county, Pa.; d. February 11, 1879, in York county, Pa.; daughter of John Ebert and Catharine Smyser. They had issue:

 i. John, b. May 10, 1835; m., December 8, 1859, by Rev. Hoffheins, Lovina Mummert, b. April 26, 1839, in Hamilton township, Adams county, Pa.; daughter of George Mummert and Magdalena Chronister; and had issue:
  1. *Emma-Estella*, b. July 29, 1861; m., December 25, 1891, Emory Fidler.
  2. *George-Franklin*, b. June 7, 1863.
  3. *Martin-Henry*, b. October 5, 1865.
  4. *Willis-Edwin*, b. April 16, 1872.
 ii. Jacob, b. December 3, 1836, in Newton township, Cumberland county, Pa.; m., October 31, 1865, by Rev. C. J. Deininger, Elizabeth Hubley, b. December 22, 1836, in West Manchester township, York county, Pa.; daughter of John Hubley and Mary Slagle; and had issue:
  1. *John-Henry*, b. December 22, 1866; m., December 25, 1891, Ida Kate Gross, b. December 8, 1868; and had issue:
   a. *Bayard-Gross*, b. December 8, 1890.
   b. *Estella-May*, b. July 21, 1893.
  2. *George-William*, b. February 28, 1869; m., June 29, 1890, Catharine Anna Stauffer, b. August 20, 1870; and had issue:
   a. *Emory-Pattison*, b. September 22, 1890; d. August 25, 1892.
   b. *Venus-Daniel*, b. December 29, 1892.
   c. *Kate-Elizabeth*, b. February 24, 1895.
  3. *Edward-Allen*, b. September 14, 1875.
 iii. Martin, b. December 29, 1838, in Dickinson township, Cumberland county, Pa.; m., August 26, 1866, by Rev. C. J. Deininger, Mary Ann Yesler, b. May 3, 1834, in Dover township, York county, Pa.; daughter of Jacob Yesler and Susanna Harbaugh; and had issue:

Thomas of Heidelberg. 687

1. *Isabella*, b. October 8, 1867.
2. *Sarah-Ann*, b. August 2, 1872 ; d. March 13, 1873.

iv. *Henry-Kyle*, b. April 8, 1844 ; in Menallen township, Adams county, Pa.; m., June 1, 1868, by Rev. Jacob Ziegler, Leah Spangler, b. August 10, 1847, in Paradise township, York county, Pa.; daughter of George Spangler and Sarah Koch.

v. *Mary-Catharine*, b. April 30, 1843, in Menallen township, Adams county, Pa.

vi. *George-William*, b. January 20, 1846; d. September 7, 1849.

vii. *Hannah-Elizabeth*, b. February 17, 1848, in Menallen township, Adams county, Pa.; m., April 10, 1870, by Rev. C. J. Deininger, Henry Stauffer, b. February 3, 1842, in Jackson township, York county, Pa.; son of Henry Stauffer and Margaret Gladfelter ; and had issue (surname Stauffer):

   1. *Luther-Grant*, b. November 7, 1870.
   2. *Charles-Milton*, b. January 28, 1872.
   3. *Mazie-Kate*, b. August 11, 1873.
   4. *Henry-Thomas*, b. February 13, 1875.
   5. *Lizzie-Day*, b. Nov. 25, 1876 ; d. January 6, 1883.
   6. *Paul-Hays*, b. April 25, 1878.
   7. *Elsie-Margaret*, b. January 27, 1880.
   8. *Howard-Arthur*, b. August 6, 1881.
   9. *John-Franklin*, b. May 15, 1883.
   10. *Elmer-Clayton*, b. January 2, 1885.
   11. *Willis-Edmund*, b. July 25, 1886.
   12. *Annie-Grace*, b. March 12, 1888.
   13. *George-Washington*, b. August 11, 1890.
   14. *Jacob-Mervin*, b. October 17, 1894.

viii. *Nathaniel-Augustus*, b. September 5, 1850, in Tyrone township, Adams county, Pa.; d. November 9, 1852.

ix. *Margaret-Lovina*, b. January 23, 1854, in Reading township, Adams county, Pa.; m., October 17, 1875, by Rev. C. J. Deininger, Lewis Schriver, b. September 17, 1839, in West Manchester township, York county, Pa.; son of Frederick Schriver and Sarah Weigle ; and had issue (surname Schriver):

   1. *Isabella-Jane*, b. April 17, 1876.
   2. *Howard-Lewis*, b. June 4, 1878 ; d. May 29, 1879.
   3. *Elizabeth*, b. August 18, 1880.
   4. *Clara-May*, b. February 10, 1882.

XXI. MARTIN THOMAS,[5] (Jacob,[4] Martin,[3] Martin,[2] Theodorus,[1]) b. January 2, 1815, in Menallen, now Butler township, Adams county, Pa. He is a substantial farmer, and has been more or less prominent in church and local affairs. He m., February 26, 1836, by Rev. Daniel Gotwalt, SUSAN EICHOLTZ, b. July 16, 1806, in Menallen, now Butler township, Adams county, Pa.; d. January 26, 1879, in Adams county, Pa.; daughter of Jacob Eicholtz and Catharine Rife. They had issue:

 i. George-William, b. December 8, 1840; m., September 21, 1865, by Rev. J. K. Miller, Ann May Bushey, b. September 12, 1841, in Latimore township, Adams county, Pa.; daughter of Jacob Y. Bushey and Elizabeth Brough; and had issue:
  1. *Lettie-Alice*, b. March 17, 1867; m., October 11, 1894, John C. Walter.
  2. *Kemphor-Edward*, b. March 8, 1869.
 ii. Martin-Henry, b. August 18, 1847; d. January 9, 1882; accidentally killed near Indianapolis, Ind.; m., January, 1879, Elsie Louise Deitrick; d. May 22, 1881, at Abbottstown, Pa.; and had issue:
  1. *Elsie-Louise*, b. May 15, 1881.

XXII. MARY THOMAS,[5] (Jacob,[4] Martin,[3] Martin,[2] Theodorus,[1]) b. June 19, 1817, in Menallen, now Butler township, Adams county, Pa.; d. March 5, 1886, near Goldenville, Adams county, Pa.; m., March 24, 1836, by Rev. Daniel Gotwalt, JOSEPH HARTZEL, b. May 31, 1813, in Menallen, now Butler township, Adams county, Pa.; d. October 25, 1863; son of George Hartzel and Mary Bream. They had issue (surname Hartzel):

 i. Margaret-Elizabeth, b. April 14, 1837; m., February 6, 1873, by Rev. David W. Wolf, Jacob Sherk Boyer, b. September 27, 1841; son of John Boyer and Elizabeth Sherk; resides in Guthrie county, Iowa; and had issue (surname Boyer):
  1. *John-Clayton*, b. August 19, 1874.
  2. *Harvey-Hartzel*, b. November 17, 1877.
 ii. Hannah-Mary, b. September 7, 1838; resides at Mummasburgh, Adams county, Pa.; m., December 13, 1860, by Rev. Jacob Ziegler, Abraham Hart, b. September 25, 1835, at Mummasburgh, Adams county, Pa.; son of Abraham Hart and Elizabeth Comfort; and had issue (surname Hart):
  1. *Augustus-Burnett*, b. February 2, 1862; m., April 8, 1889, Lucy Iro Sidener, b. December 81, 1860; re-

side near Penora, Guthrie county, Iowa; and had issue:
- a. *Carroll-Ernest*, b. March 2, 1891.
- b. *Leona-Ruth*, b. November 1, 1892.
- c. *Bessie-Anna*, b. October 27, 1894.

2. *Florence-May*, b. June 10, 1864; m., December 4, 1883, Oscar H. Diehl; and had issue (surname Diehl):
- a. *Ruth-Ethel*, b. April 7, 1884.
- b. *Lawrence-Hart*, b. October 16, 1885.
- c. *John-Roy*, b. September 12, 1888.
- d. *Esther-Alberta*, b. January 16, 1891.
- e. *Paul-Oliver*, b. November 2, 1892.

3. *Emma-Kate*, b. September 1, 1865; m., January 1, 1885, Milton F. Hoover; and had issue (surname Hoover):
- a. *Bertha-Jane*, b. March 1, 1886.
- b. *Stella-May*, b. June 3, 1887.
- c. *Mary-Elizabeth*, b. March 26, 1889.
- d. *Harry-Herman*, b. May 23, 1891.
- e. *Blanche-Alice*, b. April 19, 1893.
- f. [*A dau.*], b. March 12, 1895.

4. *Anna-Margaret*, b. January 20, 1867.
5. *Mary-Ellen*, b. August 10, 1868.
6. *Alice-Rebecca*, b. June 16, 1870.
7. *Oliver-Peter*, b. January 27, 1872.
8. *Henry-Whitmore*, b. January 16, 1874.
9. *John-Franklin*, b. November 13, 1877.
10. *Maria-Alberta*, b. July 29, 1879; d. March 1, 1881.
11. *Susan-Gertrude* (twin), b. July 29, 1879.
12. *Ursula-Grace*, b. February 13, 1882.

iii. *Oliver-Thomas*, b. November 23, 1840; d. December, 1881, in Florida.

iv. *Amanda-Catharine*, b. December 16, 1844; resides near Goldenville, Adams county, Pa.

v. *Florence-Matilda*, b. May 4, 1850; resides near Goldenville, Adams county, Pa.

XXIII. MARGARET THOMAS,[5] (Jacob,[4] Martin,[3] Martin,[2] Theodorus,[1]) b. August 14, 1821, in Menallen township, Adams county, Pa.; resides at Marion, Franklin county, Pa.; m., November 26, 1846, by Rev. C. F. Hoffmeier, JOHN LANDIS LATSHAW, b. November 5, 1821, in East Berlin, Adams county, Pa.; d. April 2, 1895, at Marion, Franklin county, Pa., son of Peter Latshaw and Susanna Landis. He was quite prominent in public affairs, serving in some of the important offices of the county of Franklin, and during life identified with several prominent local industries. They had issue (surname Latshaw):

> i. *Mary-Elizabeth*, b. April 6, 1848, in Antrim township, Franklin county, Pa.; resides near Savoy, Ill.; m., December 21, 1871, by Rev. Moses Kieffer, D. D., John Thomas Maxwell, b. September 14, 1846, in Antrim township, Franklin county, Pa., son of William James Maxwell, M. D., and Anna Barbara Stenger; and had issue (surname Maxwell):
>> 1. *William-Irwin*, b. July 17, 1873.
>> 2. *Clinton-L.*, b. June 23, 1881.
>
> ii. *William-Peter*, b. April 14, 1849; m., first, November 13, 1873, by Rev. B. G. Huber, Catharine Grove, b. October 1, 1848; d. July 25, 1877; daughter of John Grove and Magdalena Strock; and had issue (surname Latshaw):
>> 1. *John-Grove*, b. August 16, 1874.
>> 2. *William-Harvie*, b. Sept. 1, 1876; d. Feb. 4, 1877.
>
> William P. Latshaw m., secondly, January 27, 1880, Malinda Whitmore.
>
> iii. *Catharine-Thomas*, b. October 19, 1853; resides near Waynesboro, Pa.; m., December 21, 1876, by Rev. H. S. Comfort, George Boonebrake Foltz, b. August 25, 1849, at Waynesboro, Franklin county, Pa.; son of George W. Foltz and Anne Boonebrake; and had issue (surname Foltz):
>> 1. *Lillie-Margaret*, b. March 13, 1879.
>> 2. *Anna-May*, b. August 29, 1880.
>> 3. *Mary-Elizabeth*, b. July 24, 1882.
>> 4. *Beverly-Augustus* (twin), b. July 24, 1882.
>> 5. *Emma-Catharine*, b. August 2, 1887.
>
> iv. *Sarah*, b. January 26, 1856; d. February 10, 1856.
>
> v. *John-Edward*, b. October 2, 1860; resides at Marion, Pa.

XXIV. JOHN GHEER,[5] (Anna-Margaret,[4] Martin,[3] Martin,[2] Theodorus,[1]) b. November 7, 1814, in Cumberland county, Pa.; he was brought up on a farm, but subsequently learned cabinet-making, which business he has carried on forty-two years. Resides at Bellwood, Blair county, Pa. He was twice married; m., first, May 1, 1840, at Williamsburg, Pa., AMELIA AMANDA PATTERSON, b. April 20, 1816; d. October 5, 1851, daughter of Thomas Patterson and Jane Slack. They had issue (surname Gheer):

i. Jane-Margaret, b. November 13, 1846. By profession a teacher ; in the fall of 1879 she was sent by the Woman's Foreign Missionary Society of the M. E. Church to Japan, arriving at Yokohama on the 15th of November. She opened a school at Nagasaki, where she met with remarkable success, remaining until May, 1885, when she was sent to Fukuoha, a city of between sixty and seventy thousand inhabitants, where she established another school.

ii. Anna-Matilda, b. July 5, 1848 ; resides at Altoona, Pa.; m., June 21, 1877, Daniel Hicks, b. October 7, 1845, twelve miles from Pittsburgh Landing, Lawrence county, Tenn.; and had issue (surname Hicks):
   1. *Mary-D.*, b. August 19, 1878.
   2. *John-Gheer*, b. May 2, 1881 ; d. May 26, 1882.
   3. *Amelia-Patterson*, b. Dec. 11, 1883 ; d. Sept. 2, 1884.

iii. Thomas-Patterson, b. September 4, 1851, at Bellwood, Blair county, Pa.; where he resides ; m., May 27, 1875, Addie Renner, b. May 27, 1848, at Petersburg, Huntingdon county, Pa.; daughter of Abram Renner and Martha Jones ; and had issue (surname Gheer):
   1. *Mary-Martha*, b. March 8, 1876, at Osceola, Clearfield county, Pa.
   2. *John-Renner*, b. July 2, 1877, at Bellwood, Blair county, Pa.
   3. *Charles-Wesley*, b. January 18, 1879.
   4. *Amelia-Jane*, b. January 17, 1885.

John Gheer m., secondly, at Carlisle, Pa., March 24, 1853, MARY ANN BELL, b. August 27, 1817, at Carlisle, Pa.; dau. of Isaac Burrows Bell and Catharine Hoffer.

XXV. MARGARET GHEER,[5] (Anna-Margaret,[4] Martin,[3] Martin,[2] Theodorus,[1]) b. September 28, 1820, in Cumberland county, Pa.; d. March 18, 1866, in Woodson county, Kan.; buried in Le Roy cemetery. She m., at Mechanicsburg, Pa., February 25, 1840, by Rev. Stowe, JOHN SHULTZ LOBAUGH, b. July 28, 1814, in Adams county, Pa.; d. June 2, 1883 ; buried by the side of his wife ; son of Abraham Lobaugh and Catharine Shultz. He removed from Pennsylvania in the spring of 1856 to Henry county, Ia., where he farmed four years ; subsequently to now Woodson county, Kan., where he took up a fine tract of land, and became one of the pioneers in that section, on which he resided up to the time of his death.

During the Rebellion he served one year in the 9th regiment of Kansas cavalry. They had issue (surname Lobaugh):

 i. Matilda, b. April 28, 1841, near Mechanicsburg, Cumberland county, Pa.; resides near Lay P. O., Montgomery county, Kan.; m., at Geneva, Allen county, Kan., January 28, 1868, by Rev. S. M. Irwin, Samuel Walker, b. September 30, 1841, at Athensville, Ill.; son of John Anderson Walker and Elizabeth Sears; and had issue (surname Walker):

  1. *Rosaline-Alberta*, b. October 19, 1868; m. Charles Furnas; resides at Denver, Col.; and have issue (surname Furnas):
   a. David-S., b. October 12, 1891.
   b. Nellie, b. September 10, 1893.
  2. *Herbert-Raymond*, b. April 30, 1870; d. July 1, 1878, killed in a tornado.
  3. *Minnie-Rebecca*, b. January 27, 1872.
  4. *John-Gilbert*, b. March 29, 1873; m. Myrtle Reeve.
  5. *Harry-Ellsworth*, b. September 6, 1875.
  6. *Lucena-Belle*, b. August 15, 1877.
  7. *Hugh-Donald*, b. March 15, 1879.
  8. *Lotta-Estella*, b. March 23, 1881.
  9. *Ada*, b. June 22, 1883.

 ii. Joseph-Shultz, b. March 4, 1843; resided near Sedan, Chatauqua county, Kan.; suddenly disappeared February 18, 1887, supposed to be murdered; served during the Rebellion in the Ninth regiment, Kansas cavalry; m., September 12, 1576, by Rev. Mr. Tobias, Mary Adelaide Faber, b. September 12, 1847, in the State of Indiana; daughter of Christopher Faber and Elizabeth Parkison; and had issue (surname Lobaugh):

  1. *Clara-Winona*, b. March 26, 1867; m., July 3, 1884, William Ramsey.
  2. *Nannie*, b. April 24, 1869; d. November 4, 1873.
  3. *George-Ellis*, b. May 18, 1871.
  4. *Lillie*, b, November 17, 1873.
  5. *John-Leonard*, b. December 25, 1875.
  6. *William-Frederick*, b. February 1, 1878.
  7. *Guy*, b. 1880.
  8. *Vincent*, b. May 18, 1885.

 iii. Jacob-Gheer, b. November 2, 1845; served in the Rebellion in the Ninth Kansas cavalry; resides near Montrose, Henry county, Mo.; m., November 23, 1867, Rachel Melissa Thompson, b. February 29, 1844, near Liberty, Clay county, Mo.; daughter of Robert Thompson and Margaret Birney; and had issue (surname Lobaugh):

1. *Mary-Margaret*, b. Oct. 26, 1868 ; d. May 25, 1870.
2. *John-Robert*, b. June 27, 1871.
3. *Sarah-Isabel*, b. February 25, 1874 ; d. s. p.

iv. *John-Thomas*, b. January 18, 1847 ; resides near Pullman, Whitman county, State of Washington ; m., October 7, 1868, by Rev. Enoch Ely, Sarah Hershey, b. September 14, 1850, in Ogle county, Mo.; daughter of Isaac Hershey and Susan Long ; and had issue (surname Lobaugh):

1. *Isaac Elmer*, b. July 22, 1870 ; m. Florence Williams.
2. *Mary Annette*, b. June 2, 1872.
3. *Albert-Monroe*, b April 10, 1875.
4. *Ernest-Allen* [twin], b. April 10, 1875 ; d. s. p.
5. *Dora-Oleta*, b. June 15, 1877.
6. *Alice*, b. April, 1880.
7. *Ira*, b. 1882.
8. *Claude*, b. 1885.

v. *Mary*, b. July 8, 1849, at Newport, Pa.; d. s. p.

vi. *Margaret-Jane*, b. October 27, 1851, at Newport, Pa.; d. January 13, 1879, in Montgomery county, Kan.; m., June 4, 1865, in Woodson county, Kan., by Rev. S. M. Irwin, DeWitt Clinton Krone, b. April 17, 1844, in Macon county. Ill.; son of Daniel Krone and Sarah Ann Kister ; and had issue (surname Krone):

1. *Naomi*, b. June 11, 1869 ; the first white child born on Sycamore creek, Kansas, and while the land was yet in possession of the Indians.
2. *Jesse-Linn*, b. Nov. 29, 1870; d. Dec. 23, 1870.
3. *Myrtus-Catharine*, b. March 23, 1872.
4. *Mabel-May*, b. December 10, 1874.
5. *Walter-Wallace*, b. November 7. 1877.

vii. *Ira-Day*, b. March 1, 1857, in Washington county, Iowa ; resides at Neosha Falls, Kan.

viii. *William-Augustus*, b. April, 1859, in Washington county, Iowa ; resides in State of Washington.

ix. *Sarah-Catharine*, b. June 22, 1861 ; m , November 30, 1885, Charles Lewis Krone, son of Daniel Krone and Sarah Ann Kister ; reside near Radical City, Kan.

WALLACE OF HANOVER.

I. ROBERT WALLACE,[1] b. 1712, in Londonderry, Ireland ; d. April 10, 1783, in Hanover, Lancaster county, Pa. He came to America about 1735, locating on the Swatara, Lancaster county, Pa. He served as coroner of Lancaster county from October 4, 1746, to October 8, 1749. Mr. Wallace m., *circa* 1740, Mary Clyde, of the "Irish Settlement," b. 1721 ; d. April 12, 1784. They had issue :

2. i. *Moses*, b. April 22, 1741 ; m. Jean Fulton.
  ii. *Isabel*, b. March 15, 1744 ; d. Aug. 28, 1755.
  iii. *Elizabeth*, b. May 10, 1746 ; m. Joseph Boyd, (*see Boyd of Derry*).
  iv. *Ann-Maria*, b. March 15, 1748 ; m. Thomas McNair, (*see McNair record*).
3. v. *James*, b. August 18, 1751 ; m. Sarah Elder.
  vi. *Andrew*, b. March 24, 1755 ; d. s. p.
4. vii. *Isabel*, b. February 23, 1757 ; m. Moses Gillmor.
5. viii. *Mary*, b. December 19, 1766 ; m. Hugh Graham.

II. MOSES WALLACE,[2] (Robert,[1]) b. April 22, 1741 ; d. November 11, 1803, in Paxtang, Dauphin county, Pa. He served as private in the Sixth battalion of York county associators in 1778. Mr. Wallace m. JEAN FULTON, b. 1748 ; d. May, 1786 ; daughter of Richard Fulton and Isabel McChesney (*see Fulton record*). Moses Wallace and his wife are buried in old Paxtang church graveyard. They had issue :

  i. *Robert*, b. 1770 ; d. s. p.
  ii. *Richard*, b. 1772 ; d. December 23, 1803 ; unm.
  iii. *Elizabeth*, b. 1776 ; d. January 12, 1802 ; unm.
6. iv. *Isabel*, b. 1776 ; m. Alexander Wills.

III. JAMES WALLACE,[2] (Robert,[1]) b. August 18, 1751 ; d. December 15, 1823. He received a good English and classical education at Philadelphia ; but at the death of his father remained upon the ancestral farm in Hanover, where he resided until the close of his active and busy life. In the war for Independence he was a member of Capt. William Brown's company, in active service during the vigorous campaigns in and around Philadelphia and in the Jerseys. In 1779 he commanded a company of rangers for frontier service, and at the close of the war was major of a battalion of associators. In the subsequent military organizations, as directed by the State and National governments, he rose to be brigadier general of the militia, and is thus distinguished. He served as one of the commissioners of the county from 1799 to 1801; was elected to the House of Representatives of the State Assembly, serving from 1806 to 1810. He was chosen to the Fourteenth, Fifteenth, and Sixteenth Congresses of the United States, and was distinguished in that body, not so much for his eloquence in debate, but for his practical common sense and remarkable executive ability. Having served six years faithfully, to the regret of his constituents he declined a re-nomination, and retired to the quiet of farm life, where he spent the evening of his days. General Wallace m., June 19, 1787, SARAH ELDER, b. October 19, 1752; d. February 14, 1822; daughter of Rev. John Elder and Mary Simpson, (*see Elder record*). They had issue:

    i. Mary, b. 1790; m. Matthew B. Cowden, (*see Cowden record*).
7.   *ii. John*, b. 1792; m. Jane McEwen.
8.   *iii. Elizabeth*, b. 1794; m. Robert Clark.

IV. ISABEL WALLACE,[2] (Robert,[1]) b. February 23, 1757; d. September 16, 1828; m., November 9, 1784, MOSES GILLMOR, b. 1750, in the townland of Burt, parish of Templemore, county Donegal, Ireland; d. June 10, 1825, at Harrisburg, Pa.; buried in Paxtang graveyard. Until his seventeenth year he remained in Ireland, when he came with an uncle to America, settling in Hanover township, Lancaster, now Dauphin, county, Pa. Prior to the Revolution, he returned to Ireland on business connected with his father's estate, but the breaking out of the war delayed his return until near its close. Upon the laying out of the town of Harrisburg, in 1785, Mr. Gillmor erected a house and established himself in the mercantile business, which he successfully carried on a quarter of a century. He was quite prominent in local political affairs, and in the First Presbyterian church, of which he was one of the founders, he was an elder thirty-four years. They had issue (surname Gillmor):

i. Thomas, b. 1785 ; d. September 25, 1792.
ii. Mary, b. 1786 ; d. July 30, 1793.
9. *iii. William,* b. 1788 ; m. Isabella Cowden.
iv. Robert, b. 1790 ; d. November 13, 1867 ; unm.
v. Margaret, b. 1792 ; d. February 10, 1839 ; unm.

V. MARY WALLACE,[2] (Robert,[1]) b. December 19, 1766 ; d. May 8, 1822, in Hanover township, Dauphin county, Pa.; m., October 11, 1787, HUGH GRAHAM, b. February 15, 1762 ; d. May 23, 1834, in Hanover township, Dauphin county, Pa., and buried in the old churchyard there. They had issue (surname Graham):

10. *i. John,* b. February 28, 1789 ; m. Jane Ferguson.
11. *ii. Robert,* b. May 4, 1791 ; m. Roxana Winchel.
iii. Ann, b. August 31, 1793 ; m. William Barnett (*see Barnett record*).
12. *iv. Mary,* b. December 16, 1795 ; m. Andrew McClure.
13. *v. Hugh,* b. June 16, 1798 ; m. Sarah Cathcart.
14. *vi. James-Wallace,* b. November 12, 1801 ; m. Mary Crandle.
vii. Moses, b. January 24, 1805 ; m., 1834, Mary Ryan.
15. *viii. William,* b. November 12, 1807 ; m. Hester Christopher.

VI. ISABEL WALLACE,[3] (Moses,[2] Robert,[1]) b. 1776 ; d. January 27, 1826 ; m., May 8, 1806, ALEXANDER WILLS, b. April 8, 1783 ; d. April 18, 1853 ; son of James Wills* and Mary Lawson. He served as a justice of the peace of Cumberland county for many years ; and was a gentleman of prominence and influence. They had issue (surname Wills):

---

*JAMES WILLS, b. in March, 1739, in the township of Kilcomly, parish of Argyle, county Managhan, Ireland ; d. March 14, 1822, at McKeesport, Pa. He came to America in 1793. Mr. Wills m., 1778, Mary Lawson, b. 1757 ; d. January 2, 1820. They had issue (surname Wills):

i. Rebecca, b. 1779 ; d. June 15, 1834 ; m. James Gibson, of Pittsburgh ; and had issue (surname Gibson):
1. *Alexander,* b. 1807 ; d. October 19, 1839.
2. *Mary,* d. 1836 ; m. Andrew Wolf.
3. *James Madison,* d. 1836.
ii. John, d. October 22, 1822 ; m. Eliza Emerson ; and had issue : *Lawson, John,* and *William.*
iii. James, d. October 12, 1822 ; m., and had issue : *David,* and *Isabella.*
iv. Alexander, b. April 8, 1788 ; m. Isabel Wallace.
v. Isaac, merchant at Harrisburg.

16. i. *Jane-Maria*, b. June 8, 1808; m. William Audenreid.
    ii. *Rebecca-Gibson*, b. January 23, 1811; m. Dr. Joseph Crain, (*see Crain record*).
17. iii. *Caroline*, b. April 21, 1817; m. Matthew Semple.

VII. JOHN WALLACE,³ (James,² Robert,¹) b. 1792; d. 1843, in Indiana; m. JANE McEWEN, of Cumberland county, Pa. They had issue:

   i. *John*, m., and resided in Missouri.
   ii. *Sarah-Elder*, m. James Robertson, of Knoxville, Ill.
   iii. *Mary-Simpson*, m. John Robertson.
   iv. *Elizabeth*, d. s. p.
   v. *Ellen*, m. John Beatty, of Shippensburg, Pa.
   vi. *Caroline*, m. William Morrow, of Shippensburg.

VIII. ELIZABETH WALLACE,³ (James,² Robert,¹) b. 1796; d. 1842; m. ROBERT CLARK, of Montour county, Pa.; son of Charles Clark and grandson of Col. Robert Clark,* of Hanover, and with his wife, buried in Derry churchyard, Montour county. They had issue (surname Clark):

   i. *Charles-Brownfield*, d. s. p.
   ii. *Sarah-Elder*, resides in Harrisburg, Pa.
   iii. *James-Wallace*, d. s. p.
   iv. *Annie-Eliza*, d. 1883, in Harrisburg, Pa.

---

*From the family Bible of Col. Robert Clark, we have the following record:

   These are some of the particulars that hath happened from my birth to this present time.
   I, Robert Clark, of Londonderry township, Lancaster county, was born January 2, 1740.
   My mother, Ann Brownfield Clark, died April 12, 1765.
   I was married to Sarah Hutchison, August 20, 1765.
   Sarah Hutchison Clark was born June 7, 1745, and my father-in-law, John Hutchison, died September 6, 1765.
   Charles Clark, our first born, was born August 9, 1766.
   Our twin children, were born July 6, 1768, one died when 22 hours old, and the other, Margaret, died September 4, 1768.
   Our daughter, Ann, was born October 3, 1769.
   Our daughter, Mary, was born October 17, 1772, and died February 4, 1773.
   Our daughter, Margaret, was born December 26, 1773.
   Our son, John, was born June 6, 1776.
   Our son, Robert, was born September 28, 1778.

IX. WILLIAM GILLMOR,³ (Isabel,² Robert,¹) b. 1788; d. August 28, 1856; m., March 24, 1812, ELIZABETH COWDEN, b. March 27, 1784; d. October 17, 1857; daughter of James Cowden and Mary Crouch. They had issue (surname Gillmor):
    i. *Wallace-Moses*, b. 1816; d. December 28, 1840.
    ii. *Mary*, b. 1818; d. February 26, 1844; m. Joshua Elder, (*see Elder record*).
    iii. *James-Cowden*, b. 1820; d. April 4, 1837.
    iv. *Isabel-M.*, b. 1822; d March 10, 1854.
    v. *William*, b. January 2, 1826; d. January 29, 1855.

X. JOHN GRAHAM,³ (Mary,² Robert,¹) b. February 28, 1789; d. May 13, 1871; m., March 14, 1816, JANE FERGUSON, b. December 27, 1787; d. January 2, 1819; daughter of David Ferguson and Jane (Henderson) Rogers, of Hanover. They had issue (surname Graham):
    i. *David-Ferguson*, m., October 31, 1844, Eliza Krumbach, and had issue.
    ii. *Fannie*, m., January 31, 1856, David G. Miller, of Hardin county, Ky.

XI. ROBERT GRAHAM,³ (Mary,² Robert,¹) b. May 4, 1791; d. August 20, 1862; m., 1819, ROXANA WINCHEL. They had issue (surname Graham):
    i. *Robert*, m. Miss Morman, and had issue.
    ii. *Mary*.

XII. MARY GRAHAM,³ (Mary,² Robert,¹) b. December 16, 1795; d. 1857; m., 1817, ANDREW McCLURE, removed to near Franklin, O., in 1825. They had issue (surname McClure):

Our daughter, Mary, was born Sunday, March 25, 1781.
Our daughter, Sarah, was born February 9, 1786.
On a tombstone in Derry graveyard, Montour county, is the following inscription:

In memory of | Robert Clark, | who departed this life | on the 23d day of Jan., 1821, | aged 81 years and 21 days, | and of his wife | Sarah Clark, | who departed this life | on the 19th day of Aug., 1820, | aged 75 years, 2 months, and 12 days. | They lived as man and wife | 55 years, | in the full enjoyment | of domestic bliss. |

    Thrice happy they in pure delights,
    Whom love in mutual bonds unites,
    Unbroken by complaints or strife,
    E'en to the latest hours of life.

i. *James.*
ii. *Hugh.*
iii. *Dr. Alexander-W.*
iv. *Mary-Ann*, m. Robert H. Todd, of Middletown, O.

XIII. HUGH GRAHAM,[3] (Mary,[2] Robert,[1]) b. June 16, 1798; d. 1866; in 1831 removed to near Middletown, O.; m., 1824, SARAH CATHCART, of Hanover. They had issue (surname Graham):

i. *Isabel*, d. 1852; m. John C. Smith.
ii. *Hugh*, m. Miss Murray, and had issue.

XIV. JAMES WALLACE GRAHAM,[3] (Mary,[2] Robert,[1]) b. November 12, 1801; d. ———; m. MARY CRANDLE. They had issue (surname Graham):

i. *Wallace.*
ii. *Helen*, m. ——— Haddocks.
iii. *Alonzo.*

XV. WILLIAM GRAHAM,[3] (Mary,[2] Robert,[1]) b. November 12, 1807; m., 1834, HESTER CHRISTOPHER. They had issue (surname Graham):

i. *Mary.*
ii. *Elizabeth.*
iii. *Theodore*, of Louisville Ky.
iv. *James*, of Frankfort, Ky.
v. *Alice*, m. Mr. Beidleman, of Chicago.
vi. ———, m. Mr. Thomas, of Louisville, Ky.; and had issue.
vii. *Edwin.*
viii. *Gustavus.*

XVI. JANE MARIA WILLS,[4] (Isabel,[3] Moses,[2] Robert,[1]) b. June 8, 1808, at Walton Farm, Cumberland county, Pa.; d. ——— in Philadelphia. She m., April 23, 1826, WILLIAM AUDENREID, b. March 14, 1793; d. December 2, 1850; son of Lewis and Anna C. Audenreid. His parents came from Switzerland in 1793; and his grandfather, John Casper Audenreid, was an officer under Marshal Saxe at the battle of Fontenay. Mr. Audenreid was a State Senator from the Schuylkill district, an earnest advocate of the public school system, and a gentleman of strict integrity. They had issue (surname Audenreid):

i. *Isabel-Wallace.*
ii. *Alexander-Wills*, d. young.

iii. *Lewis-Lawson*, d. young.
iv. *William-Gratton*, is a retired merchant; director of the Trust Company of North America; resides at Chestnut Hill, Pa.; m. Emma Martin, dau. of Dr. Martin, of Bethlehem, Pa.; and had issue:
    1. *Emma*, b. October 5, 1867; m. William Mitchell, of Philadelphia.
    2. *William*, b. December 13, 1870; m., 1893, Ethel Grier, of Pittsburgh.
    3. *Mary-Wallace.*
    4. *Louise.*
v. *James-Wallace*, d. young.
vi. *John-Thomas*, coal merchant of Philadelphia; m. Emma Young, dau. of Charles Young, of Philadelphia; and had issue:
    1. *Charles-Young*, b. December 9, 1863; a lawyer.
    2. *Jane-Wills*, b. September 20, 1865; m. William W. Fitler, of Philadelphia.
    3. *William-Francis*, b. February 22, 1867.
    4. *Lewis*, b. March 23, 1870.
    5. *Marion*, b. April, 1873.
    6. *Helen*, b. December 14, 1874.
vii. *Joseph-Crain*, b. November 6, 1859, in Pottsville, Schuylkill county, Pa.; d. June 3, 1880, in the city of Washington, D. C. After receiving a preliminary education at Dickinson College, he was appointed to West Point in 1857, from which institution he graduated June 24, 1861, and shortly after sent into the field as second lieutenant of the Fourth, now the First, cavalry; afterwards commissioned as first lieutenant and adjutant of the Sixth cavalry, with rank from date of graduating. He immediately entered upon active duty and served in various capacities during the rebellion of the seceding States, 1861–1865. He was successively on the staffs of Generals D. Tyler, E. V. Sumner, John E. Wool, U. S. Grant and W. T. Sherman. He was promoted, in 1866, to the rank of captain of the Sixth United States cavalry, and in 1869, was breveted colonel and aid-de-camp to General Sherman. From 1869 Colonel Audenreid had been stationed at Washington City, being chief of the staff of the Lieutenant General. During these years of relaxation from active military service, he became much interested in historical and genealogical research. Besides preparing material for a biography of his father, he had almost completed a genealogical record of his own and allied families. He had a high veneration for

the last resting places of his ancestry, and several years prior to his death, the time-defaced tombstones which marked the spot of his honored dead in old Paxtang Church graveyard were, by his direction, chiseled anew and reset. As an officer he was brave and chivalric ; as a citizen, honorable and upright, and, as a friend, sincere and faithful. Colonel Audenreid m. Mary J. Colkit, daughter of Coffin Colkit, of Philadelphia; and had issue (surname Audenreid):

    1. *Florence*, m. Ludwig, Count de la Forest Divonne, of Paris, France, where they reside.

viii. *Anna-Christiana*, m. James S. Coates, of Philadelphia; and had issue (surname Coates): *Helen*.

ix. *Jane-Maria*, m. Albert Groff, merchant, of Philadelphia ; and had issue (surname Groff):

    1. *Isabella-Audenreid*, b. May 6, 1870.
    2. *Rebecca*.
    3. *Annie*.

x. *George-Albert*, m. Mary Gray, of Boston, Mass.

xi. *Louise-Catharine*, b. August 21, 1841; m., June 18, 1880, Pierce Crosby, rear admiral, U. S. N., retired; appointed from Pennsylvania, Jan. 5, 1838, midshipman; passed midshipman, May 20, 1844; master, Nov. 4, 1852; lieutenant, Sept. 3, 1853; commander, Sept. 2, 1862, of Steamer Pinola, W. G. B. Squadron, and afterwards Iron clad Steamer Sangamon; commanded Steamer Florida 1863-4, N. A. B. Squadron ; commanded Shamokin, South Atlantic Squadron, 1866-8; commissioned captain, May 27, 1868; member of examining board, 1869 ; commander, Oct. 3, 1874.

XVII. CAROLINE WILLS,[4] (Isabel,[3] Moses,[2] Robert,[1]) b. April 21, 1817; d. August 7, 1883, at Mayence, Germany. She m., May 24, 1842, MATTHEW SEMPLE, b. May 21, 1813, in Philadelphia ; d. May 17, 1867. He and his wife are buried in Laurel Hill cemetery, Philadelphia. He was the son of Matthew Semple and Hannah Jackson. He graduated from the University of Pennsylvania in 1839. Becoming interested in homeopathy, he was one of the founders of the Homeopathic Medical College in 1848, filling the chair of chemistry and toxicology for eight years, and for three years was dean of the faculty. In 1860 he became one of the founders of the New York Homeopathic College, occupying the chair of chemistry and toxicology of that institution at the time of his death.

Interested as he was in medical science, and believing in the higher education of women, he also filled the same chair for three terms in the Woman's Medical College of Philadelphia. He was possessed with a remarkable memory. It was no uncommon thing for him to read a book and six months afterward quote from it, and correctly refer to the page and line from which his quotation was given. He could read a poem of several pages once and repeat it almost word for word. Passionately fond of chemistry, study was his delight. In fact he was a man of deep learning, and possessing in a remarkable degree such a gift in the use of language, his conversational powers made him a most delightful companion. They had issue (surname Semple):

 i. Annie, b. February 28, 1843; m. William E. Littleton, lawyer of Philadelphia; member of the Constitutional Convention of 1873-74; president of Select Council of Philadelphia, and for three terms clerk of quarter sessions; and had issue (surname Littleton):
  1. *Grace*, b. March 29, 1873.
  2. *Alice*, b. March 9, 1876.
 ii. Isabel-Wallace, b. 1845.
 iii. Matthew, b. 1847; m. Lydia Roberts Clapp, daughter of N. T. Clapp, Esq.; and had issue:
  1. *Walter-M.*, b.   ; d. December 21, 1887.
  2. *Helen*, b. September 15, 1889.
 iv. Robert-Alexander, b. 1849; m. Mary Wattson, daughter of Thomas B. Wattson.
 v. Caroline-Eliza, b. January 1, 1851; d. April 11, 1886; m. Jordan Stabler, of Baltimore, Maryland; and had issue surname Stabler):
  1. *Edith*, b. May 31, 1878.
  2. *Florence*, b. March 16, 1880.
  3. *J-Herbert*, b. October 16, 1885.
 vi. Samuel-P.

WALLACE AND WEIR.

I. JOHN WALLACE,[1] a native of Scotland, fled to Ireland during the persecution of the Scottish Covenanters, where he lived and died. He m. MARTHA HAYS, daughter of William Hays (*see Hays record*), also a fugitive from religious persecution, locating in county Tyrone, Province of Ulster, Ireland. John Wallace and Martha Hays had, among other children :

2.   i. *Samuel*, b. 1730 ; m. Margaret Patton.

II. SAMUEL WALLACE,[2] (John,[1]) b. about 1730, in county Tyrone, Ireland; d. October 3, 1798, in Allen township, Cumberland county, Pa.; came to America about 1756 ; resided some time near Philadelphia, but subsequently settled in Allen township, Cumberland county, Pa. During the struggle for Independence he was in active service; as captain in Col. William Chambers' battalion of Cumberland county associators, July, 1787, and again on the frontiers of Bedford county in July, 1778. He m., in 1762, MARGARET PATTON, b. 1741, in Ireland; d. September 10, 1782, in Allen township, Cumberland county, Pa.; youngest daughter of Andrew Patton, who, with her father and two sisters, came to America in 1760. Samuel Wallace and his wife are buried in Silvers Spring church graveyard. They had issue (surname Wallace):

    i. *John*, b. November 14, 1763 ; d. 1843, near Columbus, O.; removed to Ohio in 1813 ; left four children.
3.   ii. *Mary*, b. September 8, 1765 ; m. Samuel Weir.
4.   iii. *Sarah*, b. October 8, 1767 ; m. Samuel Brooks.
5.   iv. *Joseph*, b. June 30, 1769 ; m. Margaret King.
6.   v. *Samuel*, b. June 20, 1771 ; m. Sarah ———.
    vi. *Martha*, b. April 23, 1773 ; d. September 25, 1843 ; m. John Hays, (*see Hays record*).
7.   vii. *William*, b. August 31, 1775 ; m., and left issue.
    viii. *Elizabeth*, b. October 17, 1777 ; d. March 13, 1815 ; m. Gilbert Burnett, (*see Thomas record*).
    ix. *Margaret*, b. October 15, 1780 ; d. March 19, 1788.

III. MARY WALLACE,[3] (Samuel,[2] John,[1]) b. September 8, 1765, in Allen township, Cumberland county, Pa.; d. November 18, 1836, at Harrisburg, Pa.; m., May 4, 1797, SAMUEL WEIR, b. September 29, 1744, near Ballymony, county Antrim, Ireland; d. August 15, 1820, at Harrisburg, Pa. He was the eldest son of James Weir, and came to America in 1775, locating in the township of Derry, Dauphin county, Pa. A year subsequently we find him in the army of the Revolution as lieutenant of infantry, rendering important service at Trenton, Princeton, Brandywine, and Germantown. At the close of the war he removed to a farm he purchased near Harrisburg, but shortly after, in 1787, began merchandizing in that town, and became one of the most prominent business men of the borough. He assisted in organizing the Presbyterian church at Harrisburg, and was one of the first ruling elders. It is stated that he was three times married; by his first wife, name unknown, there was issue (surname Weir):

 i. Dr. James, b. April 11, 1779; d. March 20, 1803.

By his third wife, MARY WALLACE, there was issue (surname Weir):

 ii. Samuel, b. February 15, 1798; d. June 9, 1847, at Columbia, S. C.; resided for many years at Columbia, S. C., editing and publishing a newspaper there and enjoying the friendship and esteem of the foremost men of the time, and wielding a strong influence; he lost by death several children; a daughter, Mary Catharine Weir m., December 11, 1851, James H. Rion, a lawyer, of Winneboro', S. C., who d. December 12, 1886.

8. *iii. John-Andrew*, b. January 19, 1802; m., first, Catharine E. Wiestling; secondly, Mary Matilda Fahnestock.

9. *iv. James-Wallace*, b. August 9, 1805; m. Hanna A. (Fahnestock) Mahany.

IV. SARAH WALLACE,³ (Samuel,² John,¹) b. October 8, 1767, in Allen township, Cumberland county, Pa.; d. May 3, 1827; m. SAMUEL BROOKS. They had issue (surname Brooks):

 i. William.
 ii. Margaret.
 iii. Susan.
 iv. Mary.
 v. Sarah.
 vi. Elizabeth.
 vii. Samuel.
 viii. Joseph.
 ix. John.

V. JOSEPH WALLACE,³ (Samuel,² John,¹) b. June 30, 1769, in Allen township, Cumberland county, Pa.; d. February 5, 1821, at Baltimore, Md.; m. MARGARET KING. They had issue (surname Wallace):

 i. William-King.

VI. SAMUEL WALLACE,³ (Samuel,² John,¹) b. June 20, 1771, in Allen township, Cumberland county, Pa.; d. October 10, 1831, at Chillicothe, O., whither he had removed in 1813; m. SARAH ———. They had issue, among others, (surname Wallace):

 i. Edward.
 ii. William.
 iii. Samuel.
 iv. John.
 v. Margaret.

VII. WILLIAM WALLACE,³ (Samuel,² John,¹) b. August 31, 1775, in Allen township, Cumberland county, Pa.; d. June 11, 1856, at Harrisburg, Pa.; went to Ohio early in this century, and, subsequently, to the vicinity of Paris, Ill. He m., and had issue (surname Wallace):

 i. John.
 ii. Margaret-Patton.
 iii. Thomas.
 iv. Rebecca.
 v. William.
 vi. Samuel.

VIII. JOHN ANDREW WEIR,⁴ (Mary,³ Samuel,² John,¹) b. January 19, 1802, at Harrisburg, Pa.; d. October 10, 1881. He was educated in the private schools of the town and at the Harrisburg Academy. He learned coach-making, and, subsequently, went into the hardware business, which he continued a number of years, afterwards connecting with it the drug trade, taking into partnership his nephew, D. W. Gross. During the administration of Governor Ritner he served as a clerk in the office of the Secretary of the Commonwealth. In 1840 he was elected prothonotary of Dauphin county, a position he filled two terms (six years). While serving in this office he was chosen a director of the Harrisburg Bank, and afterwards became teller in that institution, in which capacity he continued until 1880. While performing these duties he was treasurer of the State Lunatic Hospital, at Harrisburg, from its first establishment in 1850 to 1880. For nearly fifty years he was an elder in the first Presbyterian church of Harrisburg, and took a warm interest in the promotion of the Sunday-school system. He was one of the first, firmest, and influential friends of the anti-slavery cause in Dauphin county. Mr. Weir m. twice; first, CATHARINE E. WIESTLING, b. February 21, 1810; d. May 18, 1845; daughter of John S. Wiestling. They had issue, all born in Harrisburg, Pa. (surname Weir):

 i. Mary-E., b. February 7, 1835; d. April 7, 1835.
 ii. Catharine-E., b. July 7, 1836; d. December 13, 1841.
 iii. Anna-C., resides at Harrisburg, Pa.
 iv. James-Wallace, b. June 8, 1841; d. May 18, 1883; served as an officer in the army during the Civil War of 1861-5.
 v. Ellen-J., b. December 11, 1843; d. August 11, 1863.

Mr. Weir m., secondly, MARIA MATILDA FAHNESTOCK, b. December 15, 1808; d. August 28, 1883, in Harrisburg, Pa.; daughter of Obed Fahnestock and his wife, Anna Maria Gessell. They had issue (surname Weir):

 vi. J.-Howard, b. August 21, 1852; d. July 29, 1853.
 vii. Sibyl-M., resides at Harrisburg, Pa.

IX. JAMES WALLACE WEIR,[4] (Mary,[3] Samuel,[2] John,[1]) b. August 9, 1805, at Harrisburg, Pa.; d. March 14, 1878. He received a good education, excelled as a scholar, and his taste for study and reading drew him towards the printing office. He learned the art with John S. Wiestling, and, after his apprenticeship, spent some time in the printing house of the Messrs. Johnson, of Philadelphia. On the 26th of November, 1833, having been chosen teller of the Harrisburg Bank, he accepted that position, holding it until October 30, 1844, when he was chosen cashier of the bank. When the institution became a national bank in 1874, he was unanimously elected its cashier, which office he held until his death, a period of over forty-four years. As a bank officer and a financier he gained an enviable distinction for his uniform courtesy, for unimpeachable integrity, and for ability of the highest order. Few bankers in the Commonwealth can present a record equal to his in years of service, in successful administration of affairs through financial trouble, and for such rigid honesty. But not alone as a banker was he distinguished. He was gifted with rare social qualities and a graceful wit, which made him one of the most companionable of men. In movements for the reformation of society, he was always foremost not only giving his time and labor, but contributing freely of his means to the accomplishment of what he thought a philanthropic purpose. To the poor and lowly he was always a kind and true friend, and his charities, though not ostentatious, were made with a free and open hand. His literary taste and ability were of high order, and he frequently wrote for the press; was the author of several religious tracts, published by the American Sunday-school Union. In 1838 appeared a small volume, "Manual of Prayer," which was published with an introduction by Rev. Albert Barnes, of Philadelphia. In 1854 "The Closet Companion" appeared, and passed through several editions. After his death "Home Worship," a book of prayer for the family circle was published. In the Presbyterian church, of which he was nearly forty-four years an elder,—as superintendent of the Sabbath-school for a similar period,—and in every walk and pursuit in life he was active, energetic, consistent, pure in character, and lofty in purpose. Mr. Weir m. Mrs. HANNA A. (FAHNESTOCK) MAHANY; d. February, 1872. No issue.

WALLACE AND HOGE.

I. WILLIAM HOGE,[1] a native of Musselburgh, Scotland, came to America shortly after 1682. On the same ship came a family consisting of a Mr. Hume, his wife, and daughter, from Paisley. On the passage the father and mother both died, and young Hoge took charge of the daughter and landed at New York, where he left the girl with a relative, and settled himself at Perth Amboy, N. J. He subsequently married the daughter, BARBARA HUME, removed to Penn's Three Lower Counties, now the State of Delaware; from thence to Lancaster county, Pa.; and finally to the Valley of Virginia, about three miles south of Winchester, where he died about 1750. They had a large family, many of whose descendants became distinguished in church and State. Their oldest son was :

  2.   *i. John*, b. 1699 ; m. Gwenthleen Bowen Davis.

II. JOHN HOGE,[2] (William,[1]) b. about 1699 at Perth Amboy, New Jersey ; d. October, 1754, in East Pennsboro' township, Cumberland county, Pa. He went with his father to the Three Lower Counties, and there married. About the year 1729 removed to East Pennsboro' township, then Lancaster, now Cumberland county, Pa., where he afterwards purchased a large tract of land from the Proprietaries, portions of which remained in possession of some of his descendants until recent date. Mr. Hoge m., about 1722, GWENTHLEEN BOWEN DAVIS, who survived her husband some years. They had issue (surname Hoge):

     i. John, b. about 1723 ; d. February 11, 1807 ; he graduated at Nassau Hall (Princeton, N. J.,) in 1748 ; a Presbyterian minister ; was ordained in 1755, and became quite distinguished in the church. He was one of the first members of the Huntingdon Presbytery. He married and left issue, but we have no information concerning them.

    ii. Jonathan, b. July 23, 1725 ; d. April 19, 1800, of paralysis. He received a liberal education, and was brought up a farmer. He was a justice of the peace from 1764 to the Revolution; was a member of the Constitutional Convention of July 15, 1776; member of the Assembly in 1776, and again from 1778 to 1783; member of the Supreme Executive Council from March 4, 1777, to November 9, 1778, and from November 3, 1784, to October 20, 1787; member of the Council of Safety from October to December, 1777; one of the commissioners to remove the public loan offices in September, 1777; one of the committee to superintend the drawing of the Donation Land Lottery, October 2, 1786; member of the Board of Property in 1785-6; and by Governor Mifflin, appointed one of the associate judges of Cumberland county, August 17, 1791. Judge Hoge was a prominent and influential man—his entire life was an active and busy one. He married and left issue. One of his daughters married **David Redick**, who was quite conspicuous in the early history of Western Pennsylvania, and Vice-President of the State in 1788.

3. *iii. David*, m., and left issue.
  iv. Mary.
4. *v. Elizabeth*, m. William Walker.
  vi. Sarah.
  vii. Rebecca.
5. *viii. Abigail*, m. Joseph Wallace.
  ix. Benjamin, the youngest child died in early life.

III. DAVID HOGE,[3] (John,[2] William,[1]) b. about 1735; d. December 5, 1804. He received a good education; took a very active part in the Revolutionary contest, and was sheriff of the county of Cumberland. About the year 1771, he purchased the Hunter tract of land in the Chartiers Valley, embracing what is now the town of Washington, Pa. In 1781 he laid out the town, and, in 1785, sold the most of it to his sons, John and William, who removed to Washington, and lived and died there. David Hoge m. and had issue (surname Hoge):

  i. John, b. September 12, 1760; d. August 5, 1824; entered the Revolutionary army at the age of sixteen; became second lieutenant in Colonel William Irvine's (Sixth) battalion, and captured in the Canada campaign at Three Rivers, June 8, 1776. He was not exchanged until 1779. In 1783 he was chosen a member of the Council of Censors, under the Constitution of 1776, and was one of the members of the Constitutional Convention of 1789-90. He was chosen to the State Senate in 1791, and again in 1794, and served in Congress in 1804 and 1805. He was a Federalist. He married a daughter of William Quail.

ii. *David,* Jr., located in Washington, Pa., for a time, but, being appointed agent for the United States Land Office he removed to Steubenville, O., where he died; he m. Jane Scott, daughter of Thomas Scott; and they had a large family.

iii. *Eliza,* m., April 14, 1783, Rev. Samuel Waugh, b. 1749; d. January 3, 1807; he was pastor of the united congregations of Monaghan and Silvers Spring from 1782 to the date of his death; he was a sound divine, a very acceptable preacher, and highly esteemed by his people; they left issue.

iv. *Jonathan,* settled near Morgantown, W. Va., where he lived and died, leaving two children.

v. *William,* d. 1813; settled in Washington, Pa., and owned a half interest in the property; he was elected on the Republican or Democratic ticket member of Congress, and served from 1801 to 1803, but resigned in 1804, when his brother was elected to the vacancy; and again chosen in 1806, serving from 1807 to 1809; from 1798 to 1802 he filled the office of associate judge of the county; he m. Isabella Lyon, daughter of Samuel Lyon and Eleanor Blaine, (*see Lyon record*).

IV. ELIZABETH HOGE,³ (John,² William,¹) b. about 1730; d. at an advanced life in East Pennsboro' township, Cumberland county, Pa. She m. WILLIAM WALKER, a few years her senior. His father, of the same name, of English birth, was a lieutenant under the Duke of Marlborough, fought in Queen Anne's army in Germany, and was at the battle of Blenheim. He came to America in 1710, and settled in Philadelphia, where the son was born. William Walker served as a subaltern officer and on the frontiers during the French and Indian war. He resided in East Pennsboro' township, Cumberland county, and was a substantial farmer. Of their children we have the names of only two (surname Walker):

6. i. *John,* b. July 20, 1754; m. Isabella McCormick.
7. ii. *Jonathan-Hoge,* b. 1756; m. Lucretia Duncan.

V. ABIGAIL HOGE,³ (John,² William,¹) m. JOSEPH WALLACE. But little has come down to us concerning them. They had issue (surname Wallace):

8.   i. *James*, m. Rachel Elder.
     ii. *Jonathan-Hoge*, m. Mary Hoge, daughter of Jonathan Hoge ; and had issue (surname Wallace) : *Joseph, Jonathan-H., James*, and *Isabella*, some of whom settled near Springfield, Ohio.
     iii. *Joseph*, m., and removed to the Genesee country, State of New York.
     iv. *Mary*, probably d. s. p.
     v. *Abigail*, m. Mr. Fetter ; no issue.
9.   vi. *Gwenthleen*, m. Samuel Criswell.

VI. JOHN WALKER,[4] (Elizabeth,[3] John,[2] William,[1]) b. July 20, 1754, in East Pennsboro' township, Cumberland county, Pa.; d. July 26, 1825. He served in the war of the Revolution, and, about the commencement of the century, settled in Erie county, Pa., where he died. He m., May 15, 1783, ISABELLA MCCORMICK, b. December 29, 1758, in East Pennsboro' township, Cumberland county, Pa.; d. September 7, 1823, in Erie county, Pa.; daughter of Thomas McCormick and Jean Oliver, (*see McCormick record*). They had issue (surname Walker) :

   i. *William*, b. February 12, 1784 ; d. January 23, 1855 ; m., September 18, 1800, Isabella Blaine, b. 1781 ; d. May 29, 1815 ; and had issue :
      1. *Mary-Isabella*, b. August 22, 1811 ; m., January 3, 1855, James McKay ; no issue.
      2. *Grizzle*, b. 1814 ; d. April 28, 1815.
   ii. *Jane*, b. November 23, 1785 ; d. February 25, 1836 ; unm.
   iii. *Thomas*, b. September 27, 1787 ; d. January 2, 1819 ; unm.
   iv. *Margaret*, b. November 23, 1789 ; deceased ; m., March 8, 1821, David Quail ; d. May 4, 1860; and had issue (surname Quail) :
      1. *William*, b. Sept. 26, 1822 ; m. Susan Alexander.
      2. *Isabella*, b. October, 1824 ; m., in 1854, W. Ewing ; and had issue (surname Ewing) : *Margaret*, d. s. p., *John-W.*, and *David-Quail*.
      3. *John-Walker*, b. August, 1826 ; d. December, 1826.
      4. *Huston*, b. October, 1827 ; d. January, 1835.
      5. *Sarah-Ann*, b. November, 1829 ; d. 1857 ; m. William McKeenan.
      6. *Grizzle*, b. March, 1832 ; d. 1851.
   v. *Elizabeth-Grizzle*, b. September 27, 1792 ; m., June 8, 1824, John Rankin, b. May, 1787 ; and had issue (surname Rankin):

1. *Isabella-Walker*, b. April 27, 1825; d. January 22, 1859, in Kansas.
2. *Samuel-Edmeston*, b. April 14, 1827; m. Nancy Maria Crawford.
3. *Mary-Ann*, b. October 26, 1830; m., March 4, 1851, her cousin, John H. Walker.
4. *Catharine-Maderville*, b. October 25, 1832; m., November 16, 1853, her cousin, John D. Walker.
5. *John-Walker*, b. April 4, 1835; m., March 30, 1859, Mrs. Harriet Harper.

vi. *James-Oliver*, b. January 16, 1795; d. January 2, 1819; unm.
vii. *Jonathan*, b. March 27, 1797; deceased; m., May 22, 1827, Rebecca ———, b. July 20, 1810; and had issue (surname Walker):

1. *John-H.*, b. March 7, 1828; m., March 4, 1851, Mary Ann Rankin.
2. *Grizzle*, b. December 11, 1829.
3. *Rebecca*, b. June 19, 1832; d. August 11, 1846.
4. *Thomas*, b. April 6, 1834.
5. *James-Oliver*, b. May 7, 1837.
6. *William*, b. May 30, 1839.
7. *Isabella*, b. July 23, 1841; d. May 22, 1842.
8. *Isabella-McCormick*, b. September 2, 1843.
9. *Jane*, b. November 28, 1845.
10. *Henrietta*, b. June 15, 1850.
11. *Margaret*, b. November 26, 1853.

10. viii. *John-Hoge*, b. Feb. 9, 1800; m. Catharine Dudley Kelly.
ix. *David-Oliver*, b. October 27, 1802; d. August, 1841; m., January 3, 1826, his cousin, Maria Morton; and had issue :

1. *John-David*, b. April 28, 1828; m., November 16, 1853, his cousin, Catharine Dudley Rankin.
2. *George-Morton*, b. September 16, 1830; in 1858 removed to the West.
3. *Elizabeth*, dec.; m., in 1858, Dr. Miles.
4. *William-Thomas*, b. August 2, 1839.

VII. JONATHAN HOGE WALKER,[4] (Elizabeth,[3] John,[2] William,[1]) b. 1756, in East Pensboro' township, Cumberland county, Pa.; d. in January, 1818, in Natchez, Miss., while on a visit to his son Duncan. During the struggle for independence he was in active service, especially in the Canada campaign of 1776, in the company of which his cousin, John Hoge, was lieutenant, as also in the Sullivan expedition against the Indians in 1779. He studied law under Stephen Duncan, of Carlisle, and soon after his admission to the bar removed to Northumberland, Pa. On March 1, 1806, he was appointed by Governor McKean president judge of the Fourth Judicial district, removed to Bellefonte, and in 1810 to Bedford. On being appointed United States district judge in 1818 he removed to Pittsburgh. Judge Walker was a fine scholar, an able lawyer, and an eminent judge. He m., about 1790, LUCRETIA DUNCAN, daughter of Stephen Duncan, of Carlisle, Pa. They had issue (surname Walker):

 i. Stephen-Decatur, b. March 13, 1791; d. July 13, 1797.
 ii. Duncan-S., d. unm. at Natchez, Miss.
 iii. Mary-Ann, m. ―――― Pourtell.
 iv. Robert-John, b. July 23, 1801, at Northumberland, Pa.; d. November 11, 1869, in Washington City; educated at the University of Pennsylvania; admitted to the bar at Pittsburgh in 1822; in 1826 removed to Mississippi, where he entered vigorously into law and politics, taking an active part in 1832 and 1833 against nullification and secession; was elected to the United States Senate in 1836, and again in 1840; was appointed by President Polk Secretary of the Treasury; he was the first to propose the annexation of Texas; after leaving the Treasury he was tendered by President Pierce commissioner to China, which he declined; in 1857 he accepted the governorship of Kansas on the pledge of the President that the State constitution should be submitted to the vote of the people; but after rejecting the fraudulent returns in Kansas and opposing the Lecompton constitution, he resigned, and going before Congress, defeated the attempt to force the corrupt measure in the Territory; after Mr. Lincoln's election he took ground earnestly and immediately in favor of reinforcing the southern forts and of sustaining the Union by force, if necessary; in 1863 was appointed financial agent of the United States in Europe, and succeeded in negotiating two hundred and fifty million of the five-twenty bonds; during his public life of forty years Mr. Walker exercised a strong and often controlling influence in affairs; he had a broad and comprehensive mind and a patriotism that embraced the whole country; as a financier he takes high rank.
 v. Charlotte-Corday, m., in Mississippi.
 vi. Martha-Elizabeth-Duncan, b. July 23, 1806, in Northumberland, Pa.; d. September 15, 1874, in Hoboken, N. Y.; was educated by her father; for nearly two years editor

of the "Continental Monthly," and contributed poems, sketches, and tales; was a good linguist, and translated several works from the German and French; she m., in 1824, lieutenant, afterwards Gen. William Cook, of New Jersey.

VIII. JAMES WALLACE,[4] (Abigail,[3] John,[2] William,[1]) b. about 1744; d. towards the close of the century. He served in the war of the Revolution, and became quite prominent in the affairs of Dauphin county upon its organization. He is generally confounded with General James Wallace, (*see Wallace of Hanover*). He m. RACHEL ELDER, b. 1746; d. June 30, 1832. They had issue (surname Wallace):

    i. *Elizabeth*, d. s. p.
11. ii. *Joseph*, b. March 29, 1786; m. Sarah Evans Cummins.

IX. GWENTHLEEN WALLACE,[4] (Abigail,[3] John,[2] William.[1]) She m. SAMUEL CRISWELL. They had issue (surname Criswell):

    i. *Robert*, went west or south about 1815.
    ii. *Mary*, m. Captain Clark, of the U. S. A., and died early, leaving one child, *Gwenthleen*, who married Captain McCrea, U. S. A.; and they had two sons, and daughters *Virginia*, and *Gwenthleen*.
    iii. *Hannah*, d. unm.
    iv. *Hetta*, d. in January, 1846; m. Isaac Addams, of Cumberland county, Pa.; left no issue.
    v. *Elizabeth*, m. James Quigley, of Cumberland county, Pa.; she died early, leaving children *Mary* and *Hetty*. Mary m., first, Harkness Addams, and had *James* and *Samuel*; m., secondly, James Maguire, and had *Thomas*.
    vi. *Gwenthleen*, d. 1837, at Prairie du Chien; m. Col. John Greene, U. S. A., d. September 21, 1840, in Florida; and had issue (surname Greene):
        1. *Hugh-Brady*, d. in Florida, shortly after his father.
        2. *Gwenthleen*, m. Capt. William McKissack, U. S. A.; d. January 27, 1849.
        3. *Rose*, m. Col. John C. McFerran, U. S. A.; d. April 25, 1872; and had issue (surname McFerran): *Gwenthleen*.
        4. *Fanny*.
        5. *Henrietta*.
    vii. *Wilhelmina*, m. Captain Dawson, U. S. A.; both died young, leaving one son, A. H. H. Dawson, who became a lawyer at the New York City bar.

X. JOHN HOGE WALKER,⁵ (John [*Walker*],⁴ Elizabeth,³ John,² William,¹) b. February 9, 1800, in East Pennsboro' township, Cumberland county, Pa.; d. January 25, 1875, in Erie, Pa. He graduated at Washington College; studied law, and in 1824 began the practice of his profession at Erie, Pa. He was elected to the Pennsylvania Legislature on the anti-Masonic ticket in 1833, 1834 and 1835, and was made chairman of the Committee on Ways and Means, and leader of his party in the House. In 1849 he was elected State Senator. His last service was in the Constitutional Convention of 1873, to which he was chosen as a delegate-at-large, and of which body he was chosen president. Though prominently identified with public affairs and always a man of strong and unconcealed political opinions, his greatest prominence was, undoubtedly, as a lawyer. He was the leader of the Erie bar for more than a generation, and his legal fame was commensurate with the State limits. Mr. Walker m., May 3, 1831, CATHARINE DUDLEY KELLY, b. April 14, 1811; d. November 8, 1860, at Erie, Pa. They had issue (surname Walker):

    i. *John-William*, b. April 19, 1832; m., June 18, 1861, Annie Virginia Harrison, of Kittanning, Pa.
    ii. *Thomas-McCormick*, b. February 4, 1834; m., March 15, 1866, Agnes Caughey, of Erie, Pa.
    iii. [*A son*], b. February 4, 1836; d. in infancy.
    iv. *Catharine-D.*, b. January 4, 1885; m., December 30, 1862, Samuel A. Davenport, of Erie, Pa.; and had issue.
    v. *George-W.*, b. April 26, 1840; d. August 7, 1871; a young man of unusual promise.
    vi. *James-Oliver*, b. June 18, 1842; d. April 19, 1844.
    vii. *Isabella-McCormick*, b. February 11, 1845; m., April 25, 1867, H. N. Armstrong; reside in Brookfield, Mo.; and had issue.
    viii. *Quincy-Adams*, b. March 15, 1847; d. February 2, 1865.
    ix. *Mary Jane*, b. October 30, 1849; m., February 24, 1878, Dilman F. Beemer; reside at Brookfield, Mo.
    x. *Harry*, b. August 15, 1852; d. April 6, 1879, at Brookfield, Mo.

XI. JOSEPH WALLACE,⁵ (James [*Wallace*],⁴ Abigail,³ John,² William,¹) b. March 29, 1786; d. February 22, 1867, at Harrisburg, Pa. He received a good English education, and about the year 1809 or 1810, we find him the manager of New Market

Forge, Lebanon county, for John Elder; subsequently employed at Hope Furnace, in Lancaster county. He removed to Harrisburg prior to 1812, and with Joshua Elder entered into mercantile life; afterwards in business alone for many years. In the war of 1812-14 he volunteered with the Harrisburg artillerists, and marched as far as York. He served in the Harrisburg borough council, and was treasurer a long term of years. He was quite prominent as an anti-Mason, having been chairman of the State committee during the Ritner campaign, and afterwards appointed Deputy Secretary of the Commonwealth under that administration. For many years he was secretary and treasurer of the Harrisburg Bridge company, of the Middletown Turnpike company, and Peter's Mountain Turnpike company. He was a gentleman of high moral character and worth, greatly esteemed in the community, and ever enjoyed their confidence and respect. Mr. Wallace m., May 28, 1816, SARAH EVANS CUMMINS, b. January 16, 1787, in Chester county, Pa.; d. August 21, 1858, at Harrisburg, Pa., and with her husband there buried. They had issue (surname Wallace):

 i. Henrietta-Hannah, b. February 23, 1817; d. March 7, 1817.
 ii. Elizabeth, b. February 1, 1818; d. January 30, 1857; m., June 1, 1843, William C. McPherson, M. D., a prominent and influential physician at Harrisburg, Pa.; son of John Bayard McPherson,* of Gettysburg, Pa.; and had issue (surname McPherson):

---

*John Bayard McPherson was the grandson of Robert and Janet McPherson, who settled in the "Marsh Creek Settlement," now Adams county, Pa., in the autumn of 1735. Robert McPherson died there December 25, 1749, and his wife, Janet, September 23, 1767. Their son, Robert McPherson, b. in 1730, came to be a man of prominence in the early history of the State, and, in connection with the brief sketch of his great-grandson, Judge McPherson, the following reference to him will be appropriate: Robert McPherson was educated at Rev. Dr. Alison's school at New London. His father died December 25, 1749, and his mother on the 23d of September, 1767. In 1751 he married Agnes, the daughter of Robert Miller, of the Cumberland Valley. In 1755 he was appointed treasurer of York county, and commissioner in 1756. The latter office he resigned on accepting a commission as captain in the Third battalion of the Provincial forces, May 10, 1758, serving under General Forbes on his expedition against Fort Duquesne. From 1762 to 1765 he was sheriff of the

1. *Sarah.*
2. *John-Bayard,* b. November 5, 1846, at Harrisburg, Pa. He received his early education at the Harrisburg Academy and in the schools of Sidney, O., where he resided from 1858 to 1862; he entered Princeton College in August, 1862, from which institution he graduated in 1866. He studied law with John Hanna Briggs, in Harrisburg, and with Scammon, McCagg & Fuller, in Chicago, and was admitted to the Dauphin county bar in January, 1870; he was elected district attorney in 1874 and served during the years 1875, '76, '77. A portion of the time he was in law partnership with Hon. Wayne MacVeagh, and afterwards with Lyman D. Gilbert. In February, 1882, he was appointed by Governor Hoyt to fill a vacancy in the office of additional law judge of the Twelfth Judicial district, caused by the resignation of Judge Henderson, and the consequent promotion of Judge Simonton to the president judgeship, and, in November, 1882, he was elected without opposition

---

county, and from 1764 to the beginning of the Revolution, was a justice of the peace under the Proprietary, and was recommissioned under the first Constitution. From 1765 to 1767 he was a member of the Provincial Assembly, and, in 1768, was appointed county treasurer to fill a vacancy. At the outset of the war of Independence, he was commissioned a colonel of one of the York county battalions of associators; was a member of the Provincial Conference which met at Carpenter's Hall, June 18, 1776, and represented the county in the convention of July 15th following. During that and the following year he was in active duty in the Jerseys and in the subsequent campaign around Philadelphia. After his return from the field he was employed as the purchasing commissary for the western end of York county. From 1781 to 1785 he served as a member of the Assembly. Colonel McPherson was one of the charter members of the corporation of Dickinson College, and continued to act as a trustee until his death. He was an elder in the Upper Marsh Creek Presbyterian church, which was organized in 1740, or within two years of the beginning of the settlement. His death, from paralysis, occured on the 19th of February, 1789, his wife surviving him until September 12, 1802. He had a large family. Two of his sons, *William* and *Robert*, were officers in the service of the Revolution. Some of his descendants remain in Adams county, but the great majority are scattered over the various States of the Union. Another son was *John-Bayard*, father of William C. McPherson.

to the same place. Judge McPherson m., December 30, 1879, Annie Cochran Patterson, daughter of Judge David W. Patterson and Mary Slaymaker, of Lancaster, Pa.; and had issue (surname McPherson):
    a. Mary-Slaymaker, b. October 16, 1880.
    b. Elizabeth-Wallace, b. October 13, 1882.
  3. *Joseph-Wallace*, d. s. p.
iii. Lucilla-Stanley, b. December 4, 1819; d. July 5, 1837.
iv. Joseph-Cummins, b. September 16, 1821; d. October 6, 1847, at Matamoras, Mexico, of yellow fever.
v. Sarah-Ann, b. May 16, 1825; d. May 30, 1826.
vi. James, b. June 13, 1827; d. May 30, 1832.

WIESTLING FAMILY.

I. SAMUEL CHRISTOPHER WIESTLING,[1] b. June 4, 1760, at Oschatz, in the Canton or district of Meisischen, Germany, during a visit of his mother to her parents. The home of his parents was Colba, on the river Saale, in Lower Saxony. Inasmuch as the military law of Prussia required all Prussian officers and citizens to have the name of every child recorded in the church book of the town wherein it was born, this was done in his case. The record was also made in the military canton book or soldiers' roll of Oschatz. He was baptized shortly after, his sponsors being Samuel Ludwig Goldman, Christopher Henry Ahren, and Mrs. Catharine Elizabeth Wiestling, all residents of Colba. His parents were CHRISTOPHER MARTIN WIESTLING[1] and Dorothea Elizabeth Goldman. His father, who held the office of secretary of Colba, and was widely known, died in 1769. The widow afterwards married Michael Horst, a justice of the peace of Acken, on the river Elbe, in whom Samuel found a kind parent; was sent to school, and carefully educated. Subsequently, being influenced and guided by the counsel of his preceptors, Herr Ruprecht and his brother-in-law, the Honorable Inspector Gehring, his step-father persuaded him to study theology, and through the recommendation of those mentioned, he was received into the Hallische Weisenhaus. But this life was irksome to him, and unsuited to the natural bent of his mind, and, becoming discontented, he returned to his home at Colba. In April, 1774, he was placed under the instruction of the State Surgeon and "Land Physician," Dr. Unger, but the doctor having died on the 1st of May, 1776, he, with a good recommendation, went to Halle, and put himself under the care and tuition of Field-Surgeon Ollenroth, with whom he remained until 1778. This gentleman very kindly secured for him regular college privileges, under Professors Mäkel, Nestsky, Dr. Younghaus, and others. As war broke out about this time between the Emperor Joseph and King Frederick II.—the bone of contention being Bayern, and a part of the Prussian army being stationed in Alsace, under Prince Henry—he was recommended by his principal for the position of Lazar-Surgeon, and was accordingly examined and appointed on June 3, 1778. On July the 1st the army marched to Dresden, and the field hospital was removed to Thorgan. In the beginning of October he was taken sick, in consequence of which he obtained leave to return home. On recovering his health, in November, he went to Halle and resumed his studies under the professors already named, until the year 1779, when he went to Dresden for the purpose of continuing his studies in anatomy in the then existing preparatory institute, under the care of the Elector's counselor, Pietrochen. Here the branches of anatomy, physiology, physics, materia medica, chemistry, pathology, and therapeutics were as thoroughly taught by Dr. Hoffrath and Professors Meiden and Thomrianie as they were in Halle. But botany was neglected, though chirurgery was also thoroughly taught by the general surgeon, Wilde. In the spring of 1780 he went to Berlin to prosecute, under the Berlin State Accouchour, Dr. Hagan, his studies in obstetrics, which he had already commenced at Halle, under Catenius, Loesicke, Schmucker and Thedus. He remained during the summer in a private college of medicine, chirurgery and anatomy. In October of the same year he returned to Dresden, to visit the preparatory school of anatomy. In April of the following year he went to Amsterdam to visit John Herman Osterdyke, who had been his intimate friend in Halle, and who was now a doctor of medicine in Amsterdam. This afforded him an opportunity to visit the Land and Sea Hospital located there, and also the Amsterdam College of Medicine and Surgery, of which Dr. Herman Gerhard Osterdyke, the father of his friend, was the president. Through the kindness of the general surgeon of the hospital, the Hon. B. Hasson, he had free access to the Gast-Huys. His friend going to Halle to hold his "Inaugural Disputations," in order to the promoting, under the supervision of Dr. Leopold Osterdyke, and at his earnest persuasion he gladly accompanied him. He remained in Halle, until April, 1782, when he returned to Amsterdam, where he attended the Hospital and College of Medicine and Surgery until June of 1782, when he was appointed to a position as navy doctor and surgeon, he having passed a creditable examination before the Committee of the Honorable Board of Admiralty. At this time an expedition started out from the Netherlands to America, under the embassador from Holland, with two ships laden with linen, a frigate, and a cutter. He was ordered to duty on this expedition as navy surgeon. He set sail on June 4, 1783, with a favoring wind. His record says, "We left Texel, and on October 4, 1783, we reached the port of Chester on the Delaware, in Delaware county, and State of Pennsylvania. The voyage was not all smooth sailing, as we encountered winds and rough seas. Indeed, on one occasion one of the vessels came very near swamping and emptying us all out into the sea. However, with hard work, good management, and the interposition of a kind Providence we kept above water and arrived safely on *terra firma*." As it was obligatory upon all students and artisans in Germany to travel and see the world before they could pursue the practice of their chosen profession or trade, our young doctor concluded to see something of the New World before returning. He accordingly left the vessel in company with a friend named Godfrey Fritchey, and started on foot on a tour of observation. They traversed middle Pennsylvania which was not then as now, "the garden spot of the world," but was sparsely settled, and the whole country deeply impressed with the desolation and devastation consequent upon the Revolutionary war. Visions of the "home beyond the sea," however, beckoned them to return, and they turned their footsteps towards Philadelphia with a view of finding a vessel to carry them home. At the Trappe, in Montgomery county, in Pennsylvania, they fell in with a gentleman by the name of Messemer or Minsker, who was proprietor of an inn at that place, who, learning that the subject of this sketch was a thoroughly-educated German physician, succeeded in persuading him to tarry with him, as he had a sick wife, who had been bedridden for a long time, and upon whom he had expended quite a sum of money to physicians, to little or no purpose.

This was an episode in his life that shaped his destiny for the future. This man offered to pay him twenty dollars in hand, with his boarding for self and friend, and find the medicine. He regarded this as a good and advantageous offer, under the peculiar circumstances, and accepted it. The case was a serious and obstinate one, and although it baffled others, he was entirely successful, and this fortunate turn of affairs afterwards proved to be the foundation of a large and paying practice at the Trappe. About the year 1792 or 1793 he, with his family and that of his father-in-law, removed to Dauphin county, locating on farms along the Blue mountain, on the road leading from the Susquehanna river to Linglestown. His new home was about two miles from the river and five miles from the city of Harrisburg, in now Susquehanna township. Here he continued in pursuit of his profession until the spring of 1811, when they removed to the town of Harrisburg, where his practice greatly increased, until the year 1817, when he was stricken with paralysis, which terminated his medical career. He died April 28, 1823, in the sixty-third year of his age, thus ending a life of active usefulness, respected by all who knew him. Dr. Wiestling m., May 10, 1785, ANNA MARIA BUCHER, b. September 7, 1765, in Montgomery county, Pa.; d. May 10, 1836, in Harrisburg, Pa.; daughter of Casper and Catharine Bucher, of Paxtang.* They had issue:

2.   *i. John-Solomon*, b. September 18, 1787 ; m. Salome Youse.
3.   *ii. Anna-Maria*, b. June 29, 1789 ; m. Abraham Gross.
4.   *iii. Samuel-Christopher*, b. April 24, 1791 ; m. Henrietta Doll.
    iv. Jacob-Henry, b. January 22, 1783, in Vincent township, Montgomery county, Pa.; d. 1826, at Hanover, York county, Pa. He was educated at Harrisburg, studied

---

* CASPER BUCHER, of Paxtang, Dauphin county, Pa.; d. September, 1800, leaving a wife, Catharine, and children as follows :
    i. Rev. *John-Casper.*
    ii. Elizabeth, m. Jacob Engle.
    iii. Catharine, m. Henry Goetz.
    iv. Anna-Maria, m. Dr. Samuel C. Wiestling.
    v. Dorothea, m. Godfrey Fritchey.
    vi. Magdalena, m. Henry Shiley.
    vii. Jacob.

The executors of his estate were his wife and Jacob Bucher, Esq.

theology under the Rev. Philip Gloninger there, and was licensed by the Reformed Synod to preach the gospel in 1812, and about the same time received and accepted a call to Hanover, York county, Pa., which included three congregations in his charge. Owing to some difficulty with reference to the Manchester congregation, he stood disconnected from the Synod for some years. In 1821 application to that body was made in his behalf, and in the following year he was received. Several other congregations were added to his charge, and his field of labor consisted of five congregations, in which he continued to preach to the end of his life. He died at the age of thirty-three years, and is buried in the graveyard connected with the Reformed church at that place. Mr. Wiestling was a man of talent, and more than ordinary pulpit abilities. He was conscientious and faithful in the discharge of all his public and private duties, and his piety and moral deportment were of an undoubted and unexceptionable character. Respected and esteemed by the community generally, he was especially beloved by the people of his own charge, among whom he labored with much acceptance. He m. Rachel Wagner; and they had issue: *J.-Quincy*, d. s. p., and *Maria-K*.

    v. *Elizabeth-Dorothea*, b. June 3, 1795; m. Norman Callender; they lived and died in Meadville, Pa.; and had issue (surname Callender):
        1. *Samuel-N.*, m. Eliza Harbine.
        2. *Cornelius-W.*, d. 1885, in Tennessee.
        3. *Joshua*, d. in infancy.
        4. *Joseph*, d. in infancy.
        5. *Elizabeth*.
        6. *Maria*.
        7. *Ellen*, m. Philip Laufer.

5. vi. *Joshua-Martin*, b. February 28, 1797; m. Catharine Youse.
    vii. *Frederick-C.*, b. June 12, 1799; d. February 27, 1834.
    viii. *Sarah-Magdalena*, b. May 29, 1802; d. February 6, 1840; m. Rev. Henry Wagner; and had issue (surname Wagner):
        1. *Theophilus-Wiestling*, b. September 4, 1829; m. Mary A. Stilz.
        2. *Samuel-Gross*, b. October 4, 1831; m. Rebecca Ernst.
        3. *Maria-Catharine*, b. Jan. 28, 1833; d. July 9, 1834.
        4. *Catharine-Elizabeth*, b. October 22, 1834; d. September 24, 1836.

5. *John-Henry*, b. January 28, 1887; m. A. Josephine Withers.
6. *Caroline-Sarah*, b. March 28, 1888; d. March 28, 1861.
7. *Sarah-Magdalena*, b. January 30, 1840; d. March 27, 1840.

6. ix. *Benjamin-Joseph*, b. September 16, 1805; m. Matilda Eveline Ross.
7. x. *George-P.*, b. May 4, 1808; m. Margaret Berryhill.
xi. *Catharine-E.*, b. February 21, 1810; m. John A. Weir, (*see Wallace and Weir*).

II. JOHN SOLOMON WIESTLING,[3] (Samuel-Christopher,[2] Christopher-Martin,[1]) b. September 18, 1787, in Vincent township, Montgomery county, Pa.; was baptized by Rev. Mr. Foght, and confirmed to the Reformed church by the Rev. J. Helfenstein, of Harrisburg. Mr. Wiestling learned the art of printing, and for many years carried on a newspaper at Harrisburg, subsequently removing to Columbus, O., where he died February 27, 1842. He m., December 24, 1811, by Rev. Philip Gloninger, SALOME YOUSE, b. January 16, 1791, at Harrisburg; d. April 7, 1872, at Huntingdon, Pa., daughter of George and Mary Youse. They had issue, all born, save the youngest, at Harrisburg, Pa.:

i. *Samuel-Zebulon*, b. November 7, 1812; d. April 80, 1882, at Harrisburg.
ii. *Mary*, b. December 27, 1814; d. June 9, 1882, at Harrisburg.
iii. *Juliana-Salome*, b. October 14, 1816; d. September 21, 1842, at Orbisonia, Pa.; m. August 18, 1835, Thomas E. Orbison, of Orbisonia, Pa.
iv. *Albert-Youse*, b. August 19, 1818; d. May 29, 1836, at Hollidaysburg, Pa.
v. *Adaline-Elizabeth*, b. March 12, 1821; m., October 20, 1841, at Columbus, O., Rev. Abraham Bartholomew, of Carroll county, O.; reside at Chartiers, Allegheny county, Pa.
vi. *Amanda-Catharine*, b. March 10, 1823; d. October, 1875, at Huntingdon, Pa.; m , October 14, 1841, at Orbisonia, Pa., Brice X. Blair, of Shade Gap, Pa.
vii. *Henrietta-Louisa*, b. May 4, 1825; m., October, 1850, Jonathan Mureamer, of Columbus, O., where they reside.
viii. *Cornelia-Rachel*, b. November 12, 1827; resides at Huntingdon, Pa.

ix. John-Henry, b. February 7, 1831; m., October 14, 1858, Martha L. Johnson ; reside at Philadelphia.
x. Franklin-Livingston, b. December 26, 1836, at Hollidaysburg, Pa.; d. October 31, 1839, at Columbus, O.

III. ANNA MARIA WIESTLING,[3] (Samuel-Christopher,[2] Christopher-Martin,[1]) b. June 29, 1789, in Vincent township, Montgomery county, Pa.; d. August 3, 1855, at Harrisburg, Pa.; m., June 13, 1809, ABRAHAM GROSS, b. December 24, 1781, in Montgomery county, Pa.; d. August 25, 1834, in Middle Paxtang township, Dauphin county, Pa.; son of John Gross and Rachel Sahler. His father, John Gross, was born in November, 1749, in Western Massachusetts, not far from the Hudson river, where his parents were early settlers from the Palatinate, being of Huguenot descent. On the eve of the Revolution John Gross removed to now Montgomery county, Pa. He entered into the spirit of that contest at the outset, and was commissioned first lieutenant January 5, 1776, in Col. Arthur St. Clair's (Second Pennsylvania) battalion ; subsequently promoted a captain in the Third Pennsylvania at its organization, which was formed on the basis of the former, but with several of his colleagues in St. Clair's battalion, seem never to have accepted the position, or, if they did, declined it shortly after, especially upon the resignation of Col. Joseph Wood in July, 1777. After the close of the war he removed with his family to now Middle Paxtang township, Dauphin county, Pa., where he lived the remainder of his days, dying January 2, 1823. Mr. Gross m., about 1778, Rachel Sahler, b. in 1756, in Ulster county, New York ; daughter of Abraham Sahler and Elizabeth Du Bois, of Huguenot extraction. She d. August 16, 1828, and with her husband buried in the old cemetery at Dauphin.* Abraham Gross and his wife had issue (surname Gross):

---

*The children of JOHN GROSS[1] and his wife, RACHEL SAHLER, were:

i. Elizabeth, b. 1779 ; d. in Montgomery county, Pa.
ii. Abraham, b. December 24, 1781 ; m. Anna Maria Wiestling (*see above*).
iii. Catharine, b. 1784 ; d. January 13, 1807.
iv. Daniel, b. 1786 ; d. December, 1806.

8.   i. *Daniel-Wiestling,* b. March 11, 1810 ; m. Elizabeth Kunkel.
   ii. *Catharine-Eleanor,* b. January 17, 1812.
   iii. *Anna-Maria,* b. May 27, 1814 ; d. October 20, 1838.
   iv. *Rachel-Amelia,* b. January 18, 1817 ; d. March 25, 1836.
   v. *Elizabeth-Caroline,* b. March 28, 1821 ; d. March 13, 1824.
   vi. *Samuel-Christian,* b. March 8, 1826 ; d. August 11, 1826.
   vii. *Sarah-Adaline,* b. April 14, 1830 ; resides in Bridgewater, Rockingham county, Va.; m., March 1, 1853, Rev. Joseph S. Loose, d. 1894 ; was a minister of the Reformed Church ; and had issue (surname Loose):
      1. *Otho-Benjamin.*
      2. *Elizabeth-Henrietta.*

IV. SAMUEL CHRISTOPHER WIESTLING,[3] (Samuel-Christopher,[2] Christopher-Martin,[1]) b. April 24, 1791, at the Trappe, Montgomery county, Pa.; d. July 24, 1830, at Harrisburg, Pa.; was a physician of prominence, having studied medicine under his father ; during the war of 1812-14, was assistant surgeon of the regiment of Colonel Ritscher. Dr. Wiestling m., April 10, 1817, by Rev. Frederick Rauhauser, HENRIETTA DOLL, b. in York, Pa.; d. in Lebanon, Pa.; daughter of Joseph Doll and Esther Welsh. They had issue:

2.   v. *Christian,* b. March 1, 1788 ; m. Ann Custer.
   vi. *George,* b. 1790 ; d. s. p.
   vii. *Rachel,* b. 1793 ; d. April 14, 1802.

II. CHRISTIAN GROSS,[2] (John,[1]) b. March 1, 1788, in Montgomery county, Pa.; d. March 23, 1843, in Middle Paxtang township, Dauphin county, Pa.; m. ANN CUSTER, b. September 5, 1796 ; d. March 30, 1879 ; daughter of Peter and Rebecca Custer, of Montgomery county, Pa.; both buried in the old cemetery at Dauphin. They had issue (surname Gross):
   i. *John-Christian,* m. Elizabeth Everly ; removed to Illinois.
   ii. *Rebecca,* m. Robert Branyan ; settled in Mansfield, O.
   iii. *Rachel,* d. s. p.
   iv. *Ann,* m. Leonard Poffenberger, of Dauphin.
   v. *Jacob-H.,* m. Kate Ryan ; removed to Illinois.
   vi. *Samuel,* d. s. p.
   vii. *Mary-Ellen,* d. s. p.

It may be here stated that Henry Gross, brother of John Gross first named, d. in Middle Paxtang township, Dauphin county, Pa., January, 1815. His estate was devised to his wife, Susanna, and his nephews, Abraham Gross, "son of my brother John," Henry Gross and Samuel Cline.

i. *Caroline-E.*, m. Thomas M. Bibighaus, of Lebanon, and had *Henry, Harriet, Alvin, Caroline, Thomas*, and *Maria*.
ii. *Joseph-Callender*, m. Martha Armstrong, and had *Samuel-C., Jane, Valentine, Cornelius*, and *William*.
iii. *Maria*, d. s. p.
iv. *Samuel-Christopher*, m. Eliza Weaver, and had *Washington-W.*, and *Hannah-M.*; both d. in inf.
v. *Jacob*, d. s. p.

V. JOSHUA MARTIN WIESTLING,[3] (Samuel-Christopher,[2] Christopher-Martin,[1]) b. February 28, 1797, in now Susquehanna township, Dauphin county, Pa.; baptized at Shoop's church by Rev. Christian H. Kurtz; d. January 15, 1854, at Harrisburg, Pa. In the year 1811, being then of the age of fourteen years, he moved with his parents into the town of Harrisburg, where he continued to reside until his death. Although afforded but limited facilities of acquiring an education by attending the schools of that period, yet, having the advantage of the instructions of his father, who was a man of thorough education and culture, and being himself an indefatigable student, reading and studying whenever and however the oppotunity presented, he grew to manhood with his naturally fine mental endowments admirably cultivated and liberally developed. Of studious habits and love of knowledge, these characteristics adhered to him throughout his life. A man of original thinking powers, and possessed of mental capacity of a high order, he gave, notwithstanding an extensive and laborious medical practice, diligent investigation to all the leading questions of the day, and careful study in the wide and diversified field of general knowledge. He was, consequently, upon all the leading subjects of information, a natural scholar, and, throughout his whole life, was recognized by his fellow-townsmen as in the front rank of generous knowledge, and a man of very general powers. His special field of usefulness, however, was that of medicine. In his preparation for his profession, his preceptors were his father, Dr. Samuel C. Wiestling, Sr., and an elder brother, Dr. Samuel C. Wiestling, Jr., both thoroughly educated physicians of skill and wide experience. He attended the course of medical lectures of the University of Pennsylvania. His father becoming disabled to continue in active practice by reason of a paralytic stroke in the year 1817, he succeeded him in his profession, first in partnership with his brother, Dr. Samuel C. Wiestling, Jr., which continued for a few years, and subsequently alone. This was about the year 1821 or 1822. Acquiring a large and extensive practice, both in town and country, he prosecuted the duties of his profession with a degree of faithful devotion and judicious skill which won for him the admiration and high regard of the medical fraternity and the unlimited confidence of the whole community until his death. In stature, he was about six feet in height, broad shouldered, of large head, erect in carriege, full chested, rather stout in figure and person, and dignified in appearance. He was of a cheerful disposition, affable in his manners, generous in his impulses, of sympathetic and benevolent habits, unselfish and forbearing, and, as a consequence, he was popular throughout his life. Dr. Wiestling m., January 22, 1824, CATHARINE YOUSE, b. March 24, 1800; d. March 4, 1854, at Harrisburg, Pa.; daughter of George and Mary Youse. They had issue:

  i. Mary-Ellen, resides at Lebanon, Pa.; m. T. T. Worth; until his death, in 1884, was for many years editor of the *Lebanon Courier;* no issue.

  ii. Jacob-G., d. January 10, 1884; a physician of prominence; m., December 22, 1852, Susanna Herr; and had issue:
   1. *Joshua-Martin.*
   2. *Alice-H.*
   3. *Guy-Stewart.*
   4. *Ralph-Gilbert.*

  iii. Catharine, d. June 1, 1894, in Philadelphia; m., first, James D. Bartholomew, d. s. p.; secondly, S. G. Lewis; d.; and had issue.

  iv. Annie-E.

  v. Joshua-Martin, b. October 5, 1837. He was educated in the private and select schools of Harrisburg, the Harrisburg Academy and the Cumberland Valley Institute. He entered Franklin and Marshall College in 1855, graduating therefrom in 1857. Began the study of law with A. J. Herr, Esq., and admitted to the Dauphin county bar, September 4, 1860. During the Rebellion he served as second lieutenant, company D, One Hundred and Twenty-seventh regiment, Pa. Volunteers, and was promoted, September 1, 1862, to first lieutenant. On the

19th of March, 1868, he was appointed by Surgeon General King, of Pennsylvania, one of the commissioners to visit the general hospitals in the West, to look after and care for the sick and wounded Pennsylvania soldiers. He was the first register in bankruptcy under the National bankrupt act of 1867 for the Fourteenth Pennsylvania Congressional district, on the nomination of Chief Justice S. P. Chase, United States Supreme Court, May 29, 1867. He discharged the duties of that office until early in the fall of 1868, when, being nominated for district attorney for the county of Dauphin, he resigned. He was elected district attorney, October 13, 1868, and re-elected October 10, 1871, serving two full terms. In 1890 removed to Seattle, State of Washington, where he is in the practice of his profession. Mr. Wiestling m., June 2, 1864, GEORGIANNA HOOVER, daughter of John and Sophia Hoover, of Gettysburg, Pa. They had issue:
1. *Frank-Beecher*, b. April 5, 1865.
2. *Walter-Scott*, b. June 8, 1867; d. in infancy.
3. *Mary-Ellen*, b. September 9, 1869; d. in infancy.
4. *Paul-Gilbert*, b. June 19, 1871; d. in infancy.
5. *Georgianna-Elouise*, b. November 8, 1872.
6. *Sophia-Margaretta*, b. Aug. 21, 1874; d. in infancy.
7. *Joshua-Bucher*, b. August 17, 1878; d. s. p.
8. *Virginia*, b. June 4, 1882.

vi. Julia-A., m. C. Penrose Sherk, of Lebanon, Pa.

VI. BENJAMIN JOSEPH WIESTLING,[3] (Samuel-Christopher,[2] Christopher-Martin,[1]) b. September 16, 1805, in Middle Paxtang township, Dauphin county, Pa.; d. July 30, 1883, in Middletown, Pa. He was educated in the public schools of Harrisburg, whither his father removed in 1811, and also at the Harrisburg Academy. He began the study of medicine with his father, and subsequently continued under the instructions of his elder brothers, Drs. Samuel C. and Joshua M. He attended lectures at the University of Pennsylvania, graduating from the medical department of that institution in 1827. He located at Middletown, Pa., where, for over a period of fifty years, he was in the active practice of his profession; and down almost to the last hour of his life, his superior medical knowledge was brought into requisition. Dr. Wiestling m., June 23, 1831, MATILDA EVELINE ROSS; d. October 31, 1884, daughter of Andrew Ross and Hannah Templin. They had issue:

 i. Mary Fisher, d. June 9, 1883 ; m. Rev. Andrew D. Mitchell, b. February 2, 1824, in York county, Pa.; d. March 20, 1882, at Fort Grant, Arizona. He graduated at Jefferson College in 1841, and afterwards spent some time in teaching. In 1844 he matriculated at Princeton Theological Seminary, where he prepared for the ministry. He came under the care of the Carlisle Presbytery, in 1849, as a licentiate from the Donegal Presbytery, and at the same time calls were placed in his hands from the united charge of Paxtang and Derry. These he accepted, and in 1858 was ordained and installed pastor of that people, whom he acceptably served until 1874, when, at his own request, the pastoral relation was dissolved. Subsequently he declined certain positions that were in his offer, but in 1876 he accepted the appointment of post chaplain in the United States army by his friend, the Hon. J. D. Cameron, then Secretary of War. He spent five years at the military prison of Fort Leavenworth, Kansas, and was transferred, in the fall of 1881, to Fort Grant, Arizona, where he died. Mr. Mitchell has also been the very acceptable stated clerk of the Carlisle Presbytery from 1857 to the year of his appointment as chaplain, 1876, when he resigned, and received the special commendation of the Presbytery for his very faithful services. They had one child.

 ii. Anna, d. s. p.
 iii. Eveline-Ross.
 iv. Benjamin-Joseph, m. Carrie Augusta Etter.
 v. Dr. *Robert-Ross*, m. Katharine Hirst.
 vi. Anna-Catharine, d. August 14, 1842.
 vii. Elizabeth-Louisa, m. Rev. Henry L. Rex.
 viii. Hannah-Ray.
 ix. Dr. *John-Weir*, m. Emma Elizabeth Smith.
 x. Catharine-Rebecca.

VII. GEORGE P. WIESTLING,[3] (Samuel-Christopher,[2] Christopher-Martin,[1]) b. May 4, 1808, in Paxtang, now Susquehanna township, Dauphin county, Pa.; d. May 31, 1883, at Harrisburg, Pa. He was educated in the schools of the borough and the Harrisburg Academy. He learned the art of printing with his brother, John S. Wiestling, who edited and published the *Pennsylvania Intelligencer*. He afterwards worked as a compositor in the different newspaper offices at the State capital. About the year 1842 he established himself in the wood and coal trade, in which he continued down through life, being one of the first to engage in it. For a period of fifty years he was leader of the Reformed church choir. Having a love for music, and being endowed with fine talents in that direction, he took special delight in their cultivation. He was an active member of the church with which he so long identified himself as its musical leader, and for forty-four years an elder. He was faithful to every trust, honest and upright in all his dealings with the world, earnest and sincere in every good work, and his memory will remain green in the hearts of those who honor him. Mr. Wiestling m. MARGARET BERRYHILL, daughter of Samuel Berryhill. They had issue:

  i. Col. *George-Berryhill*, b. January 28, 1835; d. June 17, 1891; an iron manufacturer and a man of mark in the Cumberland Valley.
  ii. *Anna-Mary*, resides at Mont Alto, Pa.
  iii. *John*, d. s. p.
  iv. *Ellen*, resides at Mont Alto, Pa.
  v. *Edward*, m., and resides at Chambersburg, Pa.

VIII. DANIEL WIESTLING GROSS,[4] (Anna-Maria,[3] Samuel-Christopher,[2] Christopher-Martin,[1]) b. March 11, 1810, in Middle Paxtang township, Dauphin county, Pa. He was educated in the schools of the borough of Harrisburg, and at the academy there. He learned the profession of druggist and apothecary, commenced business in 1830, and continued therein until the year 1894. He served in the municipal offices of member of the town council and school director for a long period. He was for many years one of the trustees of the State Lunatic Hospital at Harrisburg, and afterwards its treasurer. He was president of the board of trustees of the Theological Seminary of the Reformed Church, vice-president of the board of trustees of Franklin and Marshall College, and was president of the board of publication of the Reformed Church for many years. Mr. Gross m., November 18, 1841, ELIZABETH KUNKEL, b. March 1, 1823; d. June 18, 1882, at Harrisburg, Pa.; daughter of George Kunkel and Catharine Ziegler, (*see Kunkel record*). They had issue (surname Gross):

 i. George-Abraham, b. May 6, 1843; resides at Harrisburg, Pa.; m., October 30, 1866, Mary A. Wingerd; and had issue (surname Gross):
  1. *Mary-Elizabeth*, m. Dr. John Miller Turpin Finney; and had issue (surname Finney):
   a. John-Miller-Turpin, b. July 26, 1894.
  2. *Helen.*
  3. *Daniel-Wingerd.*
  4. *Katharine-Kunkel.*
 ii. John-Kunkel, b. June 15, 1845; resides at York, Pa.; m., April, 1874, Anna M. Mesick, daughter of the Rev. John F. Mesick, D. D., of Somerville, N. J.; and had issue (surname Gross):
  1. *Elizabeth-Kunkel.*
  2. *John-Hendricks-Mesick.*
  3. *Jeanette-Le Rue-Perrine* (twin).
  4. *Margaret-Allison.*
 iii. Joshua-Wiestling, b. August 11, 1847; m., May 11, 1880, Almeda N. Grove.
 vi. Daniel-Wiestling, b. July 18, 1849; d. March 9, 1850.
 v. Edward-Ziegler, b. November 6, 1851; m., May 18, 1876, Nancy C. Criswell, daughter of Vance Criswell and Hannah Dull; and had issue (surname Gross):
  1. *Hannah-Criswell*, b. January 28, 1878.
  2. *Henry-McCormick*, b. May 21, 1885.
 vi. Henry-Sahler, b. February 6, 1854; m., December 7, 1881, Laura B. Cornman.
 vii. Robert, b. July 20, 1862; d. September 21, 1862.
 viii. Mary-Elizabeth, b. June 19, 1865; d. July 17, 1866.

WIGGINS AND SIMONTON.

I. JOHN WIGGINS,[2] son of JAMES WIGGINS[1] and JEAN, his wife, was b. about 1680, in the north of Ireland. He came to America and settled on Beaver Creek, in Paxtang township, Lancaster county, Province of Pennsylvania, prior to August, 1732. His name appears on the first assessment list of the north end of Paxtang for 1749. He d. in February, 1762, his will being probated the month following. He left a wife MARY [BARNETT], and children as follows:

2. i. *John*, b. 1712; m. Elizabeth ———.
    ii. *James*, b. 1714.
    iii. *Jean*, b. 1716.
    iv. *Martha*, b. 1718.
    v. *Margaret*, b. 1720.
    vi. *Agnes*, b. 1723; m. Thomas Maguire, and had a daughter Sarah.

At this time it seems as if his youngest children, John and Agnes, with his wife, were the only members of his family in America, for, in the disposition of his estate, he directs that the other children were to have their share, "if they came to this country." It is probable they came, and afterwards went with the tide of Scotch-Irish immigration southward, as the name appears in Virginia and the Carolinas.

II. JOHN WIGGINS,[3] (John,[2] James,[1]) b. 1712, in Ireland; came to America with his parents, and remained on the paternal farm; he d. June 12, 1794. He was one of the early pioneers in Paxtang, and, during the Indian forays of 1755-1763, was more or less prominent as an officer in the ranging companies. He m. ELIZABETH ———, b. 1716; d. June 5, 1784. They are both interred in Paxtang graveyard. They had issue:

   i. *Thomas*, b. 1746; d. August, 1798. He studied medicine, and served in the war of the Revolution; was surgeon of the New Eleventh Pennsylvania Line, Col. Thomas Hartley, commissioned July 1, 1778. Owing to ill health, due to the previous exposures in the service, he resigned January 23, 1780.

 ii. *John*, b. 1748; d. October 21, 1830, in Northumberland county, although his will is probated as of Lower Paxtang; left a wife, but no issue. It is said that, when a young man, he was attacked by a panther on his way home from Paxtang church, and killed the animal with his fists, although he bore the marks of its claws all his life.

 iii. *Elizabeth*, b. 1751; d. October, 1830.

 iv. *James*, b. 1754; d. June, 1805; unm., bequeathing his estate to his surviving brother and sisters

3. v. *Jean*, b. 1756; m. Dr. William Simonton.
4. vi. *Margaret*, b. 1758; m. James Henderson.
5. vii. *Mary*, b. 1760; m. John Simonton.
6. viii. *Agnes*, b. 1762; m. William Brandon.

III. JEAN WIGGINS,[4] (John,[3] John,[2] James,[1]) b. 1756, in Paxtang; d. October, 1824; she m., November 17, 1777, WILLIAM SIMONTON, b. 1755, in county Antrim, Ireland; d. April 24, 1800, in Hanover township, Dauphin county, Pa. He was brought to this country at the age of ten by his uncle, the Rev. John Simonton, pastor of the Great Valley Presbyterian church, in Chester county, Pa. Under the direction of this uncle he received his academic and professional education. Soon after completing his medical course he entered upon the practice of his profession, but at what place is unknown. In 1784 he purchased a tract of land called "Antigua," containing one hundred and eighty-two acres, situated in West Hanover township, from Joseph Hutchison. Upon this farm he resided all his life. All the traditions which have reached us concerning his standard as a physician, a man, and a Christian, are highly favorable. A fitting testimonial to his life, labors, and character was prepared by the Rev. James Snodgrass, pastor of Hanover church, and delivered on the occasion of his funeral. His remains, with those of his wife, are interred in old Hanover graveyard. They had issue (surname Simonton):

 i. *Jean*, m. [James] Clark.

 ii. *Thomas*, m. Elizabeth ———; removed to Greene county, Pa.

 iii. *James*, m. Ann Bell.

7. *iv*. Dr. *William*, b. 1788 ; m. Martha Davis Snodgrass.
   v. *John-Wiggins*, b. 1790; d. November, 1833.
   vi. *Elizabeth-Wiggins*, b. 1792; d. September, 1834.

IV. MARGARET WIGGINS,⁴ (John,³ John,² James,¹) b. 1758, in Paxtang; m., March 20, 1787, JAMES HENDERSON, son of John Henderson. They had issue (surname Henderson):
   i. *John*, b. 1788.
   ii. *Thomas*, b. 1790.
   iii. Dr. *William*, b. 1792; d. 1849; m., and had issue.
   iv. *Elizabeth*, b. 1795.
   v. *Margaret*, b. 1797.
   vi. *James*, b. 1800.

V. MARY WIGGINS,⁴ (John,³ John,² James,¹) b. 1760 in Paxtang; d. prior to 1805 ; m. JOHN SIMONTON, brother of Dr. William Simonton, Sr., d. in October, 1824. They had issue (surname Simonton) :
   i. *John-Wiggins*, d. prior to 1830 ; m., and had *John-Wiggins*.
   ii. *Thomas*, d. prior to 1830.

VI. AGNES WIGGINS,⁴ (John,³ John,² James,¹) b. 1762, in Paxtang; m. WILLIAM BRANDON, son of William and Isabella Brandon,* of Hanover ; removed from Hanover about 1792. They had issue (surname Brandon):
   i. *Thomas*.
   ii. *James*.
   iii *Ann*, m. James Pettigrew, son of David Pettigrew.

VII. WILLIAM SIMONTON,⁵ (Jean,⁴ John,³ John,² James,¹) b. in 1788, in Hanover township, Dauphin county, Pa.; d. May 17, 1846, in Hanover. At the death of his father he was only twelve years of age. His early education was received under the direction of his mother, and consisted of the branches usually taught in the country schools of that period. As he was inclined to the medical profession, he studied Latin under the tuition of the Rev. James R. Sharon, pastor of Derry and Paxtang churches. After the usual preliminary instruction under a private preceptor, he studied medicine with Dr. Samuel Meyrick, of Middletown, afterwards attending lectures of the Medical Department, University of Pennsylvania, in Philadel-

---

* WILLIAM BRANDON, of Hanover, died in April, 1753, leaving a wife, Isabella, and children: *James, Catharine, Ann*, and *William*.

phia, from which he received the degree of M. D. In the distribution of property resulting from his father's death, the farm "Antigua" was equally divided between him and his brother, John W. Simonton. The latter occupied the homestead until his death in 1824, which occurred a few days previous to the death of his mother. After the erection of the necessary buildings in 1818, he took possession of his new home, where the remainder of his life was spent. While his time was devoted to the practice of medicine, the farming operations were carried on under his superintendence. He always took an interest in political affairs, and was accustomed to act with the Whigs in opposition to the Democrats, who had retained possession of the National Government from the election of Andrew Jackson in 1824. He was elected county auditor in 1823, serving three years, and in 1838 he was nominated as a candidate for Congress from the district then composed of the counties of Dauphin and Lebanon, and was elected by a large majority. He was re-elected in 1840. During the extra session of Congress, held in the summer of 1841, Dr. Simonton's health gave way. Having been accustomed to an active life and to exercise on horseback, strict attention to public business, with confinement to the atmosphere of Washington during the heated term, so prostrated him physically that he was unable to attend regularly upon the sessions of 1842 and 1843. He never fully recovered his health, though he resumed his medical practice, which was continued nearly three years after the close of his congressional career. In person Dr. Simonton was five feet eleven inches in height, of good presence and proportions, with regular features and very black hair, which retained its color to the last. He was a modest, diffident man, but of a genial and friendly disposition. For some years previous to his death he was an elder of old Derry church, and while in Washington a member of the Congressional prayer-meeting. He was a decided Presbyterian in his faith, and ever took a deep interest in the affairs of the denomination to which he belonged. He was a strict observer of the Sabbath, and of the services of the sanctuary. He maintained family worship, and was careful to give his children a religious training. He acquired a good reputation as a physician, and for many years had an extensive country practice. Dr. Simonton m. MARTHA DAVIS SNODGRASS, b. 1790; d. April, 1862, daughter of Rev. James Snodgrass,* of Hanover. They had issue (surname Simonton):

    i. Martha-Davis, m. Rev. Thomas D. Bell, b. 1815; d. July 4, 1848, in Harrisonburg, Va.; and had issue, two sons died in childhood, and Rev. William D. Bell, of Iowa.

   ii. Jane; residing in St. Paul, Minn.; m. Rev. John H. Rittenhouse, who d. some thirty years ago in Columbia county, Pa.; and had issue (surname Rittenhouse):
      1. *Charles-R.*, vice-president bank in St. Paul.
      2. *Martha*, m. John Williams, Minneapolis.
      3. *Mary*, m. David Lambe; residing at St. Paul.

  iii. Rev. *William*, D. D.; graduated at Delaware College and Princeton Theological Seminary; was settled at Sunbury, Pa., Williamsport, Pa., and now at Emmittsburg, Md.; m. Anna Grier, niece of Justice Grier, of the Supreme Court, United States : and had issue : *Alice, Elizabeth, Sarah, Martha*, and *Grier*, all living.

  iv. Elizabeth, m., in 1860, Rev. A. L. Blackford, went with him as missionary to Rio Janeiro, Brazil, where she died, and where he remained as a missionary of the Board of Missions of Presbyterian Church, until his death in 1890.

---

*James Snodgrass, the son of Benjamin Snodgrass, was born near Doylestown, Bucks county, Pa., July 23, 1763. His grandfather came from the north of Ireland about the year 1700, locating in Bucks county, Pa. He graduated at the University of Pennsylvania in 1783, and was for a brief time a tutor therein. He studied theology under direction of the Rev. Nathaniel Irwin, then pastor of the church at Neshaminy, and was licensed to preach the gospel by the Presbytery of Philadelphia in December, 1785. After preaching about a year and a half in destitute places in the central and northern part of New York, on the 16th of October, 1787, he accepted the call of the Hanover congregation of May previous, and until his ordination on the 13th of May, 1788, he gave his attention to that church. At his installation there were present of the Presbytery of Carlisle the revered and honored ministers Revs. John Elder, John Hoge, John Linn, John Craighead, Robert Cooper, and Samuel Waugh. His pastorate extended over a period of fifty-eight years, and he was the last who ministered at Hanover. His death occurred July 2, 1846, and he lies interred in old Hanover church graveyard. The Rev. Snodgrass was twice married. His first wife, Martha, b. November 12, 1760; d. December 20, 1828; his second wife, Nancy, b. in 1770; d. January 24, 1839, and are both interred in the same graveyard.

v. Anna-Mary, b. 1824; d. 1851.

vi. John-Wiggins, received his preparatory education at the country school near old Hanover church, continued at the Strasburg Academy, Lancaster county, Pa., then at Lafayette Collège, Easton, graduating at the College of New Jersey in 1850; studied law with Hamilton Alricks, and admitted to the Dauphin county bar at the April term, 1853; in 1866 he was elected district attorney; and, in 1881, president judge of the Twelfth Judicial district of Pennsylvania. It may be here recorded of him that every opinion handed down since he has held this important position has shown an intimate knowledge of the laws of his native State, much literary ability, and acute perception of such facts as are necessary in considering cases, and in nearly every instance have been sustained by the higher court. In 1895 the honorary degree of L. L. D. was conferred upon him by the trustees of Franklin and Marshall College. Judge Simonton m., July 8, 1856, Sarah H. Kunkel, daughter of George Kunkel and Catharine Ziegler. They have living:

1. *Anne-M.*, b. 1869; resides at Harrisburg, Pa.

vii. James-Snodgrass, graduate Princeton College and Theological Seminary: tutor, Princeton College; professor, College of Vassouras, Brazil, S. A.; and now professor of Modern Languages, Washington and Jefferson College, Washington, Pa.

viii. Thomas-Davis, doctor of dental surgery, St. Paul, Minn.

ix. Ashbel-Green, d. December 9, 1867, at São Paulo, Brazil, South America. His classical education began in the Harrisburg Academy, under the tuition of the Rev. Mahlon Long. After two years preparatory study, he entered the College of New Jersey, from which he graduated in 1852, his scholarship and acquirements being of the first rank. In the autumn of the same year he went to the South, with his brother James, and took charge of an academy for boys in Starkville, Miss., where he taught with much success for eighteen months. In July, 1854, he returned to Harrisburg and entered upon the study of the law. In the spring of 1855 he decided upon a theological course, and for this purpose prepared himself for entering the theological seminary at Princeton, which he did in September of that year. He was licensed to preach by Carlisle Presbytery, which met at Greencastle on the 14th of April, 1858. He had decided upon a missionary life, and after consultation and appli cation to the Presbyterian Board of Foreign Missions, was ordered to Brazil. He was ordained by the Presbytery of Carlisle, at Harrisburg, April 14, 1859, and, on the 19th of June following, sailed from Baltimore in the merchant ship " Banshee " for Rio Janeiro. He arrived at the latter place on the 12th of August, and at once entered upon his field of labor. In the spring of 1862 he returned to the United States, married Helen Murdock, daughter of William Murdock, of Baltimore, Md., on the 19th of March, 1863, and sailed for Brazil, May 23, 1863, reaching the harbor of Rio on the 16th of July. His wife died, after a short illness, on the 28th of July, 1864, which, to a missionary in a foreign land, was an incalculable loss. Towards the close of March, 1865, he made a missionary tour into the province of São Paulo, returning to his post in Rio early in May. Near the close of 1865, the Presbytery of Rio de Janeiro was organized at São Paulo, that being the mission station of his brother-in-law, Rev. A. L. Blackford. It was soon perceived that his overtaxed energies began to give way under the gradual approaches of the disease which forever ended his earthly activities. Unable to continue his labors, he left Rio for the home of his sister, at São Paulo, the last week in November, 1867. No relief came, and, after a brief illness, he died the month following. He was buried on the same day from the little church of São Paulo, two Englishmen and two Americans officiating as pall-bearers, addresses being made in Portuguese by Rev. Mr. Blackford and Rev. Emanuel Pires.

WILSON, IRISH SETTLEMENT.

I. THOMAS WILSON,[1] ancestor of Hugh, was an officer in King William's army, among the first to cross the river Boyne, on horseback, on the morning of the 1st of July, 1690. He was specially rewarded for this bravery, with a grant of land. He resided in county Cavan, Ireland, having an extensive bleach-green within a mile of Coote Hill, not far from the county town. His ancestors had emigrated from Scotland to Ireland. Thomas had but one son :

  2. *i. Hugh*, b. 1689 ; m. Sarah Craig.

II. HUGH WILSON,[2] (Thomas,[1]) b. 1689, in county Cavan, Ireland; m. SARAH CRAIG, in Ireland; emigrated to America, and settled in "the Irish Settlement" as early as 1736. His home lay northwest of what is now known as Howertown, in Allen township, Northampton county, Pa. His land comprised seven hundred and thirty acres, to which he obtained title March 7, 1737, and June 29, 1738. He erected a flouring mill which was only torn down in the spring of 1857. Upon the erection of Northampton county, March 11, 1752, he was one of the commissioners named in the act to purchase land at Easton for the court house and prison, and was commissioned one of the justices of the peace for the county, June 9, 1752, and as such assisted in holding the first courts in Northampton county. His last commission as justice was issued March 15, 1766. He died in the autumn of 1773, and is buried in the old graveyard at the Settlement. He was a brother-in-law of Thomas Craig, the elder, who went to the Irish Settlement as early as 1728. They had issue :

      i. William, b. in Ireland; removed from the Settlement to Philadelphia, where he followed merchandizing for some time; thence he removed to the West Indies, where he died.
3. *ii. Mary-Ann*, b. May 21, 1719 ; m. Rev. Francis McHenry
4. *iii. Elizabeth*, b. 1721; m. Capt. William Craig.
5. *iv. Thomas*, b. 1724 ; m. Elizabeth Hays.
6. *v. Charles*, b. January 30, 1726; m. Margaret McNair.

vi. *Samuel*, m., and had issue :
  1. *Hugh*, b. 1761 ; d. November 30, 1830 ; m. Elizabeth Osman.
  2. *Abram*, b. April 13, 1765 ; d. January 30, 1840; m. Mary Young ; and had issue : *Samuel, Hugh-Osman, John,* and *Eliza-Ann.*
  3. *Thomas*, d. uum.
  4. *Samuel*, d. unm.
  5. *Sarah*, m. —— Mulhallon.
  6. *Abigail*, m. —— Duel.
  7. *Mary*, m —— Sharp.
  8. *Elizabeth*, m. —— Winter.
vii. *James*, (no record).
7. viii. *Margaret*, b. 1734 ; m. William McNair.
  ix. *Francis*, was the youngest son of the emigrant ; he returned to Ireland, studied divinity, and was admitted to orders in the Episcopal Church ; he settled in Virginia, was a tutor in the family of General Lee, and died about the year 1812.

III. MARY ANN WILSON,³ (Hugh,² Thomas,¹) b. May 21, 1719, in county Cavan, Ireland ; d. October 19, 1793. Webster, in his "History of the Presbyterian Church," says, " Rev. Francis McHenry married, before leaving Ireland, Mary, eldest daughter of Hugh Wilson, of Coote Hill, in county Cavan." Rev. Francis McHenry, b. October 18, 1710 ; d. January 23, 1757. According to Alexander R. Henry's statement, "the McHenrys lived on a small island between Scotland and Ireland, called Rothlin, whence they were driven to the glens of Antrim, in the north of Ireland, near Bally Castle, by the Clan McDonald, of Scotland. Rev. Francis came to America with his two brothers, who were Roman Catholics. One settled in Baltimore. Fort McHenry, named for a member of this family. (*Quaere*, Hon. James McHenry, Secretary of War under President Washington, January 27, 1796.) The other settled at or near Pittsburgh. Mr. McHenry was licensed November 10, 1738 ; ordained at Neshaminy, July 12, 1739. In 1743 he was installed pastor over the Presbyterian church at Deep Run, seven and one-half miles northwest of Doylestown, Bucks county, where he was pastor for fourteen years. The late Dr. Andrews, one of Mr. McHenry's successors at Deep Run, speaks of him (*Centennial History, 1876,*) thus: "He was a pure scholar, able preacher, and a man whose godly life gave influence where he was known. His learning and natural gifts were adapted to make him a shining light in the history of Presbyterianism," etc. They had issue :

 i. Dr. *Matthew*, b. 1743; d. December 13, 1783; was surgeon of the ship Montgomery, of the Pennsylvania Navy, appointed April 13, 1776; discharged March 29, 1777. (*Pa. Archives, 2d ser., vol. i, page 318*); m. Margaret Gregg, daughter of Robert Gregg; d. March 17, 1796, aged 43; and had issue (surname McHenry):
  1. *Ann*, d. October 18, 1818, aged 41.
  2. *Elizabeth*, d. June 8, 1831, aged 57.
  3. *Matthew*, d. at Mt. Holly, N. J.
8. *ii. William*, b. May 6, 1744; m. Mary Stewart.

IV. ELIZABETH WILSON,³ (Hugh,² Thomas,¹) b. about 1721; and survived her husband several years. She m. WILLIAM CRAIG. He was a captain in the Associated Regiment of Bucks county in 1747–48 (*Pa. Archives, 2d ser., Vol. ii., p. 505.*) He was a son of Thomas Craig, the elder, and died before 1772, as the former in his will of date November 25, 1772, proved June 6, 1779, bequeaths his estate to his daughter-in-law, Elizabeth, and his son William's children by name, except a special legacy of £17 10 s. to Thomas Craig, "son of my brother, Daniel Craig." A pretty clear indication that Thomas Craig, the elder, had no living children, and no other descendants than William's children. He appoints "his brother-in-law, Richard Walker, Esq.," in connection with Arthur Lattimore and John Ralston, his executors. They had issue (surname Craig):

 i. General *Thomas*; he was a captain in Col. Arthur St. Clair's battalion in the campaign in Canada, 1776; promoted lieutenant colonel Sept. 7, 1776, and colonel of Third Pennsylvania, Continental Line, August 1, 1777; serving all through the Revolutionary war. He was selected as one of the major generals of the Provisional army in 1798, and was still major general of the militia for Northampton county in 1812–1814. He died at Allentown, January 20, 1832, aged ninety-two years (*see Biddle's Autobiography*, p. 353, for an account of an interview with him in 1815, and anecdote—and note to page 354, *ibid*).

ii. Hugh; we have no other information, except that he is named next after Thomas in his grandfather's will.

iii. Charles; was first lieutenant of Captain Miller's company, Col. William Thompson's battalion of rifle men in the campaign before Boston in 1775, and was promoted captain in November, 1775. He was captain in the First Pennsylvania, Continental Line; and wounded in the battle of Brandywine, September 11, 1777. He married a daughter of Marks Bird, of Reading, and shot himself in the summer of 1782, leaving a widow and one child (see an account of his deliberate suicide in *Biddle's Autobiography*, note to page 172).

iv. William; was a captain in the Third Pennsylvania, Continental Line, July 4, 1777; resigned June 1, 1779; was living in May, 1787, "but soon fell a sacrifice to his intemperance" (*Biddle's Autobiography*, p. 216).

v. Mary, m. George Palmer, coroner of Northampton county in 1781; deputy surveyor, and a man of prominence in his day; and had issue (surname Palmer), all buried in the old "Settlement" burying-ground :
1. *John*, b. 1778; d. June 14, 1813; unm.
2. *Eliza*, b. 1780; d. February 13, 1808; m. James Ralston, Esq., who d. January 20, 1836, aged sixty-nine years.

vi. Sarah, m. Hugh Wilson, son of Charles Wilson, (*see* XI).

vii. Nancy, m. Dr. Taylor.

viii. Elizabeth, m. Capt. John Craig, who was not a relative; and had issue (surname Craig):
1. *William*, m. Miss Mowry, of New Jersey.
2. *Charles*, m. Miss Mowry, sister of above.

V. THOMAS WILSON,³ (Hugh,² Thomas,¹) b. in 1724. According to the tradition among his descendants, he was about twelve years old when his father, Hugh, emigrated from Ireland. He married, in 1760, ELIZABETH HAYS, daughter of John Hays and Jane (Love), his wife, who emigrated from Londonderry, Ireland, and after a short stay in Chester county removed to the "Irish Settlement." Thomas Wilson was, during the Revolution, largely engaged in supplying the Continental army with flour. He was paid in Continental currency, and suffered heavily by its depreciation. In consequence he sold his land in Allen township, and removed to Buffalo Valley, now Union county in 1792. He purchased the farm on which the Union county, fair buildings are located, about one mile west of Lewisburg on the turnpike, where he died, February 25, 1799, according to the inscription on his tombstone in the Lewisburg cemetery, aged seventy-four years. His widow removed, in 1803, with her sons, William and Thomas, to Beaver county, Pa., where she died in December, 1812. They had issue :

9. i. *Hugh*, b. October 21, 1761 ; m. Catharine Irvine.
   ii. *Sarah*, d. 1844 ; m. Richard Fruit, removed to Mercer county, Pa.; and had issue (surname Fruit) :
       1. *Robert*, d. in 1880, leaving twelve children, all residing in Mercer county, Pa.
       2. *Thomas*, d. in 1850 ; and had issue : two sons and two daughters, residing in Mercer county.
       3. *William*, d. 1877 ; one child living, *Sarah*, m. to James Trimble, of Philadelphia, grandson of James Trimble, Esq., who was Deputy Secretary of the Commonwealth from 1791 to 1836.
       4. *John*, d. 1838 ; leaving issue, three children, in Mercer county.
       5. *Elizabeth-A.*, m. Thomas Williamson ; and left eight children.
       6. *Catherine-W.*, m. Alva Morris ; d. leaving four sons.
   iii. *Elizabeth*, b. 1769 ; d. February 8, 1797 ; m. James Duncan, b. 1758 in Scotland ; d. October 14, 1843 ; he was the first sheriff of Centre county in 1801 ; and had issue (surname Duncan) :
       1. *Thomas*,, b. 1794 ; d. October 5, 1825 ; m. Susan Irvin (*see Linn's History of Centre county, Pa., p. 204, for notice of Irvin Family*) ; and had issue :
           a. *Elizabeth-I.*, d. June 23, 1880, at Reading, Pa.; m. John M. Hale ; and had issue (surname Hale) :
               a. *James-P.*. d. December 24, 1881, at Philipsburg, Pa.
               b. *Elias-W.*, d. June 13, 1881, at Philipsburg, Pa.; m., and had issue : *James-P.*, *Richard-A.*, *Mary-E.*, and *Susan-C.*
               c. *Susan-M.*, d. December 4, 1880 ; m. Thomas G. Welles ; and had issue (surname Welles): *Hubert-Gideon*.
               d. *Carrie*, m. A. J. Steinman, Esq., of Lancaster, Pa., and had issue (surname Steinman): *Elizabeth-D.*

  e. Reuben-C., d. March 8, 1869 ; m. granddaughter of Dr. Diller Luther ; and had issue : *Ruby-Caroline.*
 b. James, d. at New Orleans, La.; an attorney-at-law ; left issue, *Maud.*
 c. John, d. at Bellefonte, Pa.; s. p.
2. *David,* b. 1797; d. September 6, 1855, at Spring Mills, Pa.; m. Susan Hayes, of New Berlin, Pa.; d. September 8, 1865 ; and had issue (surname Duncan):
 a. Robert-H., of Milton, Pa.; m. Louisa, daughter of Dr. James Douglass; and had issue : *D.-Wallace, Louisa-Dougal,* and *Alexander-H.*
 b. Dr. *Thomas,* surgeon United States army, 1861–5 ; d. July 27, 1867, in Mo.; s. p.
 c. Mary, of Spring Mills, Pa.

 iv. William, b. 1772; d. November 6, 1840, in Beaver county, Pa.; m., 1810, Anne White ; d. December, 1865 ; and had issue :
  1. *Francis-Thomas,* b. November 23, 1822; resides at Pleasant Hill, Lawrence county, Pa.; m., June 16, 1846, Mary A. Morrison ; and had issue :
   a. William-C., teacher in the State Normal School, Providence, R. I.
   b. Anne-E., a missionary in India.
   c. Harriet, m. J. Leibendorfer, of Wurtemberg, Lawrence county, Pa.
   d. Charles-C.
   e. Mary-C.
   f. Matilda-B.

10. *v. Thomas,* b. June 17, 1775 ; m. Agnes Hemphill.
 vi. Mary, m. Jonathan Coulter, Esq.; and had issue (surname Coulter): *Thomas,* of Perrysburg, Ohio, now deceased, and two daughters.
 vii. Jane; drowned when a child in the mill race in Northampton county.
 viii. James, Esq.; educated at Canonsburg, Pa.; studied law and located in New Orleans, his commission to practice dated June 28, 1804, signed by Gov. W. C. C. Claiborne, of Louisiana.
 ix. Margaret, m. John Thomas, of Buffalo Valley ; removed to Darlington, Beaver county, Pa.; and had issue (surname Thomas):
  1. *Eliza,* b. 1805; d. September, 1861 ; m., September 27, 1826, John Courtney ; d. September, 1862.

2. *Sarah*, b. 1807; d. March 26, 1884; unm.
3. *Mary*, b. ———; d. April 24, 1882, at Wellsville, Ohio; m. George Imbrie, b. 1795; d. Aug., 1879.
4. *Electa*, m. Moses Louthan; reside at New Waterford, Ohio.
5. *Caroline*, m. David Harvey; reside in Allegheny City, Pa.
6. *John*, d. 1859, at Beaver C. H.; m. Elizabeth Mace, d. at Beaver C. H., November 25, 1884.
7. *Jane*, m. John Pierce; living at Darlington, Pa.
8. *Enoch*, b. December 25, 1823; m., March 31, 1850, Elizabeth E. Hall; reside at West Bridgewater, Beaver county, Pa.

VI. CHARLES WILSON,[3] (Hugh,[2] Thomas,[1]) b. January 30, 1726; d. August 20, 1768; m. MARGARET MCNAIR, b. March 2, 1728; d. November 25, 1823. They had issue:

   i. Sarah, b. January 3, 1757; d. December, 1778; unm.
   ii. Christiana, b. January 13, 1759; d. 1839, in Groveland, N. Y.; m. William Latimer; and had issue (surname Latimer):
      1. *John*, whose children are Mrs. *Adaline* Logan and *Cortland* Latimer, of Dansville, N. Y.

11. *iii. Hugh*, b. June 15, 1761; m. Sarah Craig.
   iv. Anne, b. December 14, 1762; d. March 15, 1763.
   v. John, b. August ?, 1765; d. January 1, 1857, in Allen township, Northampton county, Pa.; he was a ruling elder in the Presbyterian church for fifty years; m. Ann Hayes, b. August 9, 1772; d. January 8, 1851; and left issue:
      1. *Charles*, m. Catharine Miller; removed to Highland county, Ohio.
      2. *Jane*, d. October 18, 1826; unm.
      3. *William-McNair*, b. July 18, 1806; d. January 18, 1851; m. Jane Brittam.
      4. *Margaret*, b. June 10, 1809; d. near Bath, Pa., April 23, 1887, in the Settlement; m. Joseph Horner, d. July 27, 1866, aged seventy-five; and had issue (surname Horner):
         a. Sarah-A., m. Baxter B. McClure.
         b. Jennie, residing on the homestead.
      5. *John-H.*, of Jersey Shore, Pa.; m. Mary A. Hays, a descendant of John Hays; she d. March 29, 1885, aged seventy years.

6. *Mary-H.*, d. September 13, 1877, at Quincy, Ill.; m. Rev. Leslie Irwin; d. November 16, 1878 (*see sketch in Clyde's Irish Settlement* ").

vi. *Margaret*, b. May 15, 1767; m., October 18, 1792, James Rosebrugh; removed to Groveland, N. Y., in 1795.—See genealogy in Clyde, page 127; also sketches of the family by James R. Leaming, M. D., a grandson (*ibid. page 313, &c.*)

vii. *Samuel*, m., and had issue: *Hugh, Abram, Thomas, Samuel, Sarah, Abigail, Mary*, and *Elizabeth*.

viii. *Jane*; no record.

VII. MARGARET WILSON,[3] (Hugh,[2] Thomas,[1]) b. 1734, in the Irish Settlement; d. July 20, 1783; m. WILLIAM MCNAIR, b. 1727, in Ireland; d. 1823, near Mt. Morris, N. Y.; son of John McNair and Christiana Walker. In 1798 William McNair and his sons left the Irish Settlement for the valley of the Genesee and settled in Sonyea, near Mt. Morris, Livingston county, N. Y. They had issue (surname McNair):

i. *John*, b. 1760; d. 1813; m. Mrs. Deborah Isabella Page; and had issue: *William-Penn, Mary-Ann, Hugh-Wilson*, and *Charles-Williamson*.

ii. *Hugh*, b. 1765; d. 1844; m., first, Phœbe Torbert; secondly, Mrs. Eliza Tate Dungan; and had issue: *Margaret-Tate, William-Wilson, Mary, John-C., Charles-Wilson, Susan, Henrietta, Hugh, Samuel-Torbert, Phœbe, Ann-Eliza, David-Anthony*, and *Clement-Dungan*.

iii. *Charles*, b. 1767; d. about 1853, unm., at Brokenstraw, Pa.

iv. *Christiana*, b. 1769; d. 1808; m. William Parkinson; and had issue (surname Parkinson): *Charles, James, Richard*, and *Thomas*.

v. *Sarah*, b. 1772; d. 1783.

vi. *William*, b. 1774; d. 1813.

vii. *Margaret*, b. 1778; d. 1831; m. her cousin, David McNair; and had issue (surname McNair): *John-L., William, Margaret-Wilson, David-Denny*, and *Phœbe-Torbert*.

William McNair afterwards m. SARAH HORNER, of the Settlement, and had four children.

VIII. WILLIAM MCHENRY,[4] (Mary-Ann,[3] Hugh,[2] Thomas,[1]) b. May 6, 1744; d. November 25, 1808. He was a mill-wright by trade, and remarkable for muscular strength. He was born at the parsonage at Deep Run, lived there all his days, and was buried from the old homestead. He m., December 4, 1770,

MARY STEWART, b. November 13, 1753; d. November 27, 1832. They had issue (surname McHenry):

  i. *Francis*, b. October 19, 1771; d. October 11, 1776.
 ii. *Ann*, b. December 16, 1773; d. October 6, 1775.
iii. *Elizabeth*, b. March 7, 1776; d. December 16, 1818; m., May 17, 1798, Evan James, b. January 19, 1773; d. August 4, 1830; and had issue (surname James):
  1. *Josiah*, b. 1798.
  2. *William-McHenry*, b. September, 1800; d. July 20, 1861, at Plumsteadville, Bucks county, Pa.; physician; m. January 13, 1835, Huldah Jones; no issue.
  3. *Robert-Evan*, b. September 26, 1802; d. August 13, 1860, at Centreville, Northumberland county, Pa.; a physician; m., June 2, 1836, Caroline Dietterich; and had issue (surname James):
    a. *Frances-M.*, b. August 20, 1839; m. Hiram Long, M. D., of Sunbury, Pa.
    b. *Mary-E.*, b. August 31, 1841; m. Truman H. Purdy, of Sunbury, Pa.; member of Legislature, 1884-5; and had issue (surname Purdy): *Carrie, Truman*, and *Hiram*.
    c. *William-McH.*, b. April 15, 1844; m. Caroline Criswell; and had issue (surname James): *Carrie*, d. February 15, 1886, at Steelton, Pa., aged sixteen years, and *Edith*.
    d. *Jacob-D.*, b. April 12, 1846; m. Laura Clement, of Sunbury, Pa.; and had issue (surname James): *Clement*, and *Robert-E.*
    e. *Robert-E.*, b. August 9, 1848; was a member of the Legislature from Northampton county, 1877-8; at present, bank examiner; resides at Easton, Pa.; m., April 4, 1877, Anna Heller; and had issue (surname James): *Robert-E.*
 iv. *Samuel*, b. June 22, 1778; m. Margaret Piatt, of Belvidere, N. J.; removed to junction of the White Water and Miami, Ohio; and had issue, seven daughters.
  v. *Anna*, b. May 22, 1780; d. February 10, 1839, in New York.
 vi. *Sarah*, b. July 9, 1782; d. May 27, 1814, at Deep Run.
vii. *Mary*, b. April 3, 1789; d. November 6, 1816, at Deep Run.
viii. *Rebecca*, b. January 2, 1791; d. 1880, near McSherrysville, York county, Pa.; m. Isaac Michener; and had issue (surname Michener): *Samuel, Nelson, Elizabeth, Mary-Ann*, and *Sarah*.

ix. William, of Scott, Wayne county, Pa., b. September 23, 1794 ; d. October 22, 1880, at Deposit, Broome county, N. Y.; m., March 6, 1817, Margaret Fell, b. July 20, 1794; d. November 13, 1868 ; daughter of Joseph and Hannah Fell; and had issue (surname McHenry):
1. *Wilhelmina*, b. April 6, 1818 ; m., June 2, 1842, Robert Johnston.
2. *Charles-S.*, b. February 18, 1820; m., December 22, 1852, Margaret E. Latta, b. June 9, 1824; d. November 13, 1889; daughter of Rev. John E. Latta; and had issue (surname McHenry):
    a. Mary-DuB., b. October 23, 1853 ; d. May 15, 1884, in Doylestown, Pa.
    b. Kate-L., b. Nov. 9, 1859 ; d. March 14, 1877.
    c. William-E., b. February 9, 1868.
3. *Mary-F.*, b. October 24, 1822.
4. *Sarah*, b. June 28, 1825 ; d. December 29, 1852.
5. *Louisa*, b. December 15, 1827 ; d. June 22, 1856.
6. *Amanda*, b. October 5, 1830 ; m., November 15, 1870, Herman Smith.
7. *Francis*, b. January 17, 1833 ; m., December 24, 1856, Julia Fuller.
8. *Caroline*, b. February 11, 1836.
9. *Emeline*, b. Oct. 26, 1838 ; d. Nov. 11, 1855.

IX. HUGH WILSON,[4] ('Thomas,[3] Hugh,[2] Thomas,[1]) b. October 21, 1761, in Allen township, Northampton county ; d. October 9, 1845, on his farm, near Lewisburg, Pa. He served a number of tours during the Revolution, as a militiaman, under Col. Nicholas Kern. Removed to Buffalo Valley, now Union county, Pa.; and kept store at Lewisburg, 1798–1804. He m., February 17, 1790, CATHARINE IRVINE, b. November 16, 1758; d. August 21, 1835 ; daughter of Capt. William Irvine, who was a cousin of Gen. William Irvine, of the Revolution. They had issue :

12.   *i.* Dr. *William-Irvine*, b. November 10, 1793 ; m. Mary Potter.
    ii. Elizabeth, b. August 10, 1796 ; d. November 24, 1882 ; m., December 16, 1824, William Cooke Steedman, b. April 25, 1797; d. December 17, 1840; grandson of Col. William Cooke, of the Twelfth Pennsylvania, Continental Line ; and had issue (surname Steedman):
    1. *Catharine-H.*, b. October 23, 1825 ; m., September 24, 1850 ; U. Q. Davis, M. D., of Milton, Pa.; accidentally killed on the railroad October 5, 1887 ;

and had issue (surname Davis): *Sidney*, M. D., of Petersburg, Pa., m., October 3, 1883, Bertha Cresswell, daughter of George Cresswell, of Petersburg, Pa.; *Miriam*, *Edward*, of U. S. Navy, *Jessie*, *Myron*, and *Catharine*.

2. *Francis-W.*, b. April 20, 1828 ; resides in Louisville, Ky.; m., October 18, 1853, Catharine Radford, of Shelby county, Ky., b. December 23, 1834 ; and had issue (surname Steedman):
    a. *James-B.*, M. D., b. May 26, 1856; m., July 11, 1876, Adda R. Davies ; and had issue: *Leila-R.*, b. August 5, 1877 ; *Laura-R.*, b. November 9, 1880.
    b. *Sarah-M.*, b. April 14, 1858.
    c. *Kate-W.*, b. September 16, 1860.
    d. *William-C.*, b. February 11, 1863.
    e. *Elizabeth-W.*, b. September 13, 1865.

3. *Harry-C.*, M. D., b. July 12, 1832 ; wounded in U. S. service, 1861-64 ; d. May 23, 1876, at Mifflinburg ; m., March 24, 1863, Julia Bound, of Milton, Pa.; and had issue : *William*.

iii. *Francis*, b. November 26, 1801 ; d., February 15, 1874 ; resided in Buffalo township, Union county, Pa.; m., July 14, 1832, Mary Chamberlin, b. 1813 ; d. July 23, 1891 ; daughter of Col. Aaron Chamberlin ; and bad issue :

1. *Catharine-I.*, b. 1838 ; m., March 27, 1861, B. F. Hursh ; and had issue (surname Hursh): *Frank*, and *Guy*, residing in Lancaster, Kan.

2. *Francis*, M. D., of Toledo, O., b. December 5, 1841; m., December 2, 1868, Nannie Haines; and had issue : *Dale W.*, and *Mary*.

3. *Mary-P.*, b. April 1, 1844 ; d. January 9, 1866 ; m., December 23, 1863, Jacob M. Moyer, Esq., and had issue (surname Moyer): *Mayne*, of Philadelphia.

4. *William-L.*, of Jefferson county, Kan.; m. Anne Schrack ; and had issue : *Harry-T.*, and *Emily*.

5. *Elizabeth*, of Lewisburg, Pa.; unm.

iv. *Margaret-Irvine*, b. October 12, 1804 ; m., July 20, 1826, James F. Linn, Esq., of Lewisburg, (*see Linn, of Lurgan, record*).

X. THOMAS WILSON,[4] (Thomas,[3] Hugh,[2] Thomas,[1]) b. June 17, 1775; d. July 7, 1860; m. October 7, 1806, AGNES HEMPHILL, b. February 19, 1783; d. January 29, 1867. They had issue :

i. James, b. September 19, 1807; residing at Clinton, Lawrence county, Pa.; m. Margaret Morton; d. July 25, 1873; and had issue:
   1. *Nancy*, b. May 14, 1838; d. December 26, 1883; m. Thompson Warnock.
   2. *Thomas-D.*, b. July 3, 1840; m. Christina Mehara.
   3. *Hannah*, b. October 2, 1842; m. John McCandless.
   4. *William-H.*, b. December 4, 1844; attorney-at-law, Davenport, Iowa.
   5. *Albert-H.*, b. August 27, 1849; druggist, East End, Pittsburgh.
   6. *Emma-O.*, b. Sept. 24, 1851; m. James Davidson.
   7. *Mary-F.*, b. June 25, 1855; m. Dr. J. Rhodes, of Chewton, Lawrence county, Pa.
   8. *Jessie*, b. June 18, 1857; m. William Hamilton.

ii. Nancy-B., b. December 25, 1808; m., November 26, 1830, David Frew, b. 1803; reside at Princeton, Lawrence county, Pa.; and had issue (surname Frew):
   1. *James-K.*, b. October 2, 1831; resides at New Lisbon, O.; m. Eliza A. Gardner.
   2. *Thomas-W.*, b. October 16, 1832, of Princeton, Pa.
   3. *Nancy-J.*, b. May 28, 1834; m. James B. Aiken, Rose Point, Pa.
   4. *Joseph-H.*, b. September 10, 1836; merchant at Princeton; m. Kate Willar.
   5. *David-W.*, b. December 25, 1838; resides at Winfield, Kan.; m. Margaret Hawkins.
   6. *P. H.*, of Princeton, Pa., b. February 26, 1843.
   7. *Mary-E.*, b. May 28, 1844; m. James A. Gardner; attorney-at law, New Castle, Pa.
   8. *William-M.*, of Grove City, Pa., b. February 9, 1847; m. Margaret Aiken.
   9. *Melissa*, b. March 10, 1849; m. James Wilson, of Princeton, Pa.
   10. *Albert-F.*, b. December 25, 1851; m. Mary Willar, Princeton, Pa.

iii. Jane, b. March 31, 1810; unm; resides at Zelienople, Butler county, Pa.

iv. Eliza, b. January 5, 1812; m., January, 1838, Robert Fullerton, of Mt. Jackson, Lawrence county, Pa., who d. January 9, 1884; and had issue (surname Fullerton):
   1. *Margaret*, b. October 23, 1838; m. Robert M. Davidson, of Enon Valley, Lawrence county, Pa.
   2. *John*, b. August 10, 1840, of Enon Valley; m. M. J. Gilmour.
   3. *Thomas-W.*, b. Dec. 3, 1841, of Mt. Jackson, Pa.

4. *James*, b. April 27, 1843; resides at Alliance, O.;
   m. Margaret E. Swisher.
5. *Nancy-J.*, b. November 7, 1844; m. William P.
   Kelso, of Mt. Jackson.
6. *Albert*, b. December 5, 1846; m. Mary J. Miller, of
   Mt. Jackson,
7. *Mary*, b. July 8, 1848.
8. *Robert-S.*, b. August 9, 1851; m. Mary B. Nesbit,
   d. June 10, 1881.
9. *William*, b. July 13, 1853; of Mt. Jackson.

v. *Thomas*, b. November 26, 1813; resides at Slippery Rock, Butler county, Pa.; m., June 28, 1842, Mary Davidson; d. October 10, 1865, aged forty-seven years; and had issue:
   1. *Margaret-M.*, b. July 21, 1843; resides at Eaton Rapids, Mich.
   2. *Nancy-E.*, b. July 12, 1845; m., September 9, 1868, Dr. S. Davis, of Denver, and had *Blanche*.
   3. *William-H.*, b. February 22, 1848; m., October 24, 1882, Augusta L. Leason, and had issue:
       a. *Mary-E.*, b. July 28, 1883.
       b. *Ray-P.*, b. October 26, 1884.
   4. *Clement*, b. May 4, 1851; d. December 25, 1856.
   5. *Caroline*, b. October 31, 1854.
   6. *Robert-C.*, b. December 22, 1858; resides at Toledo, Ohio.

vi. *Mary-A.*, b. Feb. 6, 1816; unm.; resides at Zelienople, Pa.

vii. Col. *Joseph-H.*, b. May 16, 1820; graduated at Jefferson College; district attorney of Beaver county for three years; member of the House of Representatives of Pennsylvania from Beaver county, 1859-1861; commissioned colonel of One Hundred and First regiment, Pennsylvania Volunteers, October 4, 1861; d. in service near Roper's church, Va., May 30, 1862, of disease contracted in the trenches before Yorktown, Va. His remains rest in the cemetery at Zelienople, Butler county, Pa.

viii. *John-Hays*, b. May 22, 1822; resides at North Sewickley, Beaver county; m., March 8, 1849, Mary E. Mehard; and had issue:
   1. *Agnes-I.*, b. December 26, 1849; m. Dr. J. M. Withrow, of North Sewickley, Pa.
   2. *Christiana*, b. February 17, 1852; m. J. C. McCandless, of New Galilee, Beaver county, Pa.
   3. *William-L.*, b. May 2, 1854; m., October, 1880, Anne Hillman; reside at Clinton, Beaver county, Pa.

4. *Osmar-T.*, b. March 4, 1857 ; m., October 30, 1882, Virginia West; resides at North Sewickley, Pa.
5. *James S.*, b. Nov. 10, 1862 ; of Beaver Falls, Pa.
6. *Loyal-W.*, b. March 25, 1866.

ix. *Francis-S.*, b. July 2, 1824 ; resides in Franklin township, Beaver county, Pa.; m , February 2, 1860, Catharine Wallace; and had issue:
1. *Jane*, b. December 3, 1860.
2. *Mary*, b. October, 1862.
3. *Adaline*, b. November, 1864.
4. *Frank-W.*, b. September, 1866.
5. *William-T.*, b. October, 1868.
6. *Agnes-H.*, b. September, 1870.
7. *Belle-V.*, b. September, 1872.
8. *Catharine-E.*, b. June, 1875.
9. *James-S.*, b. March, 1882.

x. *Craig-B.*, b. December 14, 1827; resides in Petersburg, Ohio; m., May 11, 1853, Elizabeth Pontius; and had issue:
1. *Alice-E.*, b. April 23, 1855; m. Robert D. Brewster, of Mt. Jackson.
2. *Mary-L.*, b. February 21, 1857.
3. *John-P.*, b. October 20, 1858.
4. *Nannie-H.*, b. November 7, 1860.
5. *Joseph-H.*, b. March 21, 1863.
6. *William*, b. January 2, 1865.
7. *Robert-T.*, b. May 15, 1867.
8. *Edith-M.*, b. September 28, 1869.
9. *Frank-S.*, b. September 18, 1871.

XI. HUGH WILSON,[4] (Thomas,[3] Hugh,[2] Thomas,[1]) b. June 15, 1761, in the Settlement; d. August 13, 1845. He removed to Buffalo Valley, now in Union county, Pa., in 1792; was associate judge of Union county from October 11, 1813, to March 26, 1840. He m. SARAH CRAIG. They had issue:

i. *William-Craig*, b. November 25, 1788; d. December 9, 1841; m., at Salona, Clinton county, Pa., January 17, 1829, Ruth Waddle (in 1855 living in Bellefonte, Pa.); and had issue:
1. *Charles T.*, b. September 1, 1832; depot master, Pennsylvania railroad, Altoona, Pa.
2. *Macada-D.*, b. May 23, 1838; m. William S. Tripple, of Bellefonte, Pa.

 ii. Hugh, d. at Freeport, Ill., July 3, 1873, aged eighty-one; m. Jane Forster; and had issue: *Hugh*, of Freeport; *Robert*, of Mifflinburg; *Jane*, m. Samuel Young, of Mifflinburg; *Sarah-A.*, *Mary*, and *Martha*, of Freeport, Ill.
 iii. John, d. January 24, 1842; m. —— Stevenson.
 iv. Eliza, m., January 20, 1829, Walter Devling, of Clinton county, Pa.
 v. Craig, d., and had issue: *William*, and Mrs. Thomas R. Lewis, of Lewisburg, Pa.

XII. WILLIAM IRVINE WILSON,⁵ (Hugh,⁴ Thomas,³ Hugh,² Thomas,¹) b. November 10, 1793, near Hartleton, now Union county; d. September 22, 1883, at Bellefonte, Pa. He studied medicine under Dr. James Dougal, Sr., of Milton, and, in 1818, removed to Centre county, locating at Earlytown, whence he removed to Potter's Mills. He m., February 23, 1819, MARY POTTER, b. April 8, 1798; d. January 19, 1861; daughter of Judge James Potter and granddaughter of General James Potter, of the Revolution. They had issue:

 i. Catharine-Irvine, b. January 17, 1821; m., May 30, 1844, Hon. Andrew G. Curtin. (*see Gregg record*).
 ii. James-P., M. D., b. July 24, 1825; d. July 5, 1864; surgeon of U. S. volunteers, 1861–1864; m., September 13, 1854, Sarah I. Kinney (*see Gregg and Curtin record*); and had issue:
  1. *Julia-I.*, d. s. p.
 iii. Mary-A., b. September 25, 1828, in Bellefonte; unm.
 iv. Lucy-P., b. October 19, 1830; m., June 5, 1856, Frederick Moyer, M. D.; and had issue (surname Moyer):
  1. *Andrew-G.-C.*, b. March 2, 1857; resides at Sandy Ridge, Pa.
  2. *William-W.*, b. October 12. 1858; resides at Bellefonte, Pa.
 v. Elizabeth, b. March 23, 1833; m., June 15, 1859, Rev. John Elliot, b. April 13, 1829; and had issue (surname Elliot):
  1. *Mary-A.*, b December 3, 1861; m., June 20, 1882, Robert P. Carpenter.
  2. *Christiana*, b. May 5, 1865; resides in Oswego, Kan.
 vi. Laura, b. November 3, 1835; m., May 12, 1857, Rev. George Elliot, of Newton Hamilton, Pa., brother of above; and had issue (surname Elliot): *William-W.*, *James*, *Bessie*, d. December 20, 1889, *Kate*, d. July 19, 1889, m. Charles O. Vandevanter, of Leesburg, Va., and *John*.

vii. Col. *William-P.*, b. December 30, 1837; d. August 6, 1886; Col. Wilson served in war of 1861-5, on Gen. Hancock's staff; m., April 22, 1869, Ellen Dickson, daughter of Rev. Hugh Dickson, D. D., Philadelphia; and had issue:
    1. *Allen-D.*, b. March 7, 1870.
    2. *Wayne-McV.*, b. January 5, 1876.
    3. *Hugh-Irvine.*
viii. Capt. *Frank*, U. S. A., b. January 15, 1840; d. s. p.
ix. *Alice*, b. January 31, 1842; resides in Bellefonte, Pa.

WYETH FAMILY.

I. NICHOLAS WYETH,[1] b. in 1595, in England; d. July 19, 1680, at Cambridge, Mass. He emigrated to America prior to 1645, when he purchased a property in Cambridge, which, for more than two centuries, remained in possession of his descendants in the male line. He was twice married; first, prior to his coming to America, and had issue:

    i. Sarah, b. in England; m., December 11, 1651, John Fiske, of Watertown, Mass.

Mr. Wyeth m., secondly, REBECCA ANDREW, widow of Thomas Andrew; he d. in May, 1698, his widow subsequently became the wife of Thomas Fox. By this marriage Mr. Wyeth had issue:

    ii. Mary, b. January 26, 1649; d. in May or June, 1698; unm.
    iii. Nicholas, b. August 10, 1651; d. prior to 1723; m., first, September 6, 1681, Lydia Fiske, d. March 10, 1697-8, without issue; secondly, June 30, 1698, Deborah Parker, and had *Mary,* d. s. p.
    iv. Martha, b. July 10, 1653: d. prior to 1680; m. —— Ives.
2.   *v. John,* b. July 15, 1655; m. Deborah Ward.
3.   *vi. William,* b. January 1, 1657; m. Ruth Shepard.

II. JOHN WYETH,[2] (Nicholas,[1]) b. July 15, 1655; d. December 13, 1706; m., January 2, 1682, DEBORAH WARD, daughter of John Ward. They had issue:

    i. Elizabeth, b. October 6, 1684; d. s. p.
    ii. Deborah, b. November 20, 1686; d. above the age of ninety; m., in 1714, Samuel Bowman, d. 1716; and had issue.
    iii. John, b. December 21, 1688; d. s. p.
4.   *iv. Jonathan,* b. March 3, 1689-90; m. Hepzibah Champney.
    v. Hannah, b. 1693; baptized April 18, 1697; d. December 12, 1756; m., first, in 1712, Nathaniel Prentice, d. October 24, 1722; secondly, in 1724, Jason Winship.
    vi. Thankful, b. 1696; baptized April 18, 1697; m., December 6, 1716, William Winship, b. 1691.; d. January 26, 1774, and left issue.
5.   *vii. Ebenezer,* b. 1698; m. Susanna Hancock.

viii. Elizabeth, b. 1701; baptized May 25, 1701; d. October 8, 1759; m., October 2, 1718, John Winship, b. 1697; d. November 7, 1659, and had issue.

6.   *ix. John*, b. December 27, 1705; m. Elizabeth Hancock.

III. WILLIAM WYETH,² (Nicholas,¹) b. January 1, 1657; killed by the Indians about 1st October, 1703; m., October 16, 1683, RUTH SHEPARD. They had issue:

  i. Ruth, b. November 29, 1685.
  ii. William, b. January 31, 1687-8.
  iii. Deborah, b. 1690; m., June 22, 1710, Joshua Gamage.
  iv. Martha, b. 1693; baptized 1696-7; m., October 12, 1716, William Fessenden, b. 1694; d. May 26, 1756, leaving issue.

IV. JONATHAN WYETH,² (John,² Nicholas,¹) b. March 3, 1689-90; d. September 24, 1743; m. HEPZIBAH CHAMPNEY, daughter of Daniel and Hepzibah Champney. They had issue:

  i. Jonathan, b. October 12, 1714; d. s. p.
7.   *ii. Jonathan* (2d), b. July 27, 1716; m. Sarah Wilson.
  iii. Sarah, bap. August 17, 1718; d. September 23, 1743; unm.
  iv. Deborah, bap. August 24, 1720; m., December 29, 1743, Daniel Prentice, b. May 17, 1717; d. about 1776, leaving issue.
  v. Noah, bap. October 28, 1722; d. prior to 1743.

V. EBENEZER WYETH,³ (John,² Nicholas,¹) b. 1698; d. April 3, 1754; m., about 1726, SUSANNAH HANCOCK, b. 1707; d. July 29, 1789. They had issue:

8.   *i. Ebenezer*, b. April 8, 1727; m. Mary Winship.
9.   *ii. Jonas*, b. February 19, 1730; m. Hepzibah Tidd.
  iii. Susanna, b. March 2, 1734; m., October 1, 1760, Mansfield Tapley.
10.   *iv. Noah*, b. July 7, 1742; m. Elizabeth Fitch.
  v. Sarah, b. 1746; d. March 31, 1815; m., first, Torry Hancock, b. 1746; bap. April 6, 1746; d. July 17, 1778; and had issue; secondly, James Munroe, Sr.

VI. JOHN WYETH,³ (John,² Nicholas,¹) b. December 27, 1705; d. October 23, 1756; was a selectman of Cambridge, from 1750 to 1756. He m., December 20, 1733, ELIZABETH HANCOCK, b. 1705; d. February 23, 1793; daughter of Nathaniel Hancock. They had issue:

  i. John, bap. December 29, 1734; d. s. p.
  ii. Elizabeth, bap. July 4, 1736; d. s. p.

iii. Martha, bap. July 23, 1738.
iv. Elizabeth, bap. Nov. 30, 1740; d. September 17, 1804; unm.
v. John, bap. March 6, 1743; d. February 2, 1811; graduated at Harvard in 1760; was a clergyman at Gloucester, Mass., from February 5, 1766, to 1768; and subsequently practiced law there; never married.
vi. Prudence, bap. April 28, 1745.
vii. Jonathan, bap. Nov. 13, 1748; d. September 29, 1756.

VII. JONATHAN WYETH,⁴ (Jonathan,³ John,² Nicholas,¹) b. July 27, 1716; d. April 26, 1767; m., November 14, 1750, SARAH WILSON, b. 1723; d. April, 1785; daughter of Andrew Wilson. They had issue:

i. Jonathan, bap. July 28, 1751; d. May 16, 1796.
ii. Joseph (twin), bap. July 28, 1751; m., and left issue.
iii. Sarah, bap. February 22, 1761; m. Ebenezer Smith.
iv. Hepzibah (twin), bap. February 22, 1761; m. Samuel Brooks, of Plymouth, Mass.

VIII. EBENEZER WYETH,⁴ (Ebenezer,³ John,² Nicholas,¹) b. April 8, 1727; d. August 4, 1799; was a farmer, and selectman from 1781 to 1790 in Cambridge; m., November 5, 1751, MARY WINSHIP, b. April 19, 1730; d. September 9, 1798; daughter of Joseph and Anna Winship. They had issue:

11.   *i. Ebenezer*, b. December 17, 1752; m. Elizabeth W. Green.
    ii. Mary, b. September 17, 1755; d. October 7, 1790; unm.
12.   *iii. Jonas*, b. May 17, 1757; m. Elizabeth Smith.
    iv. Joshua, b. October, 1758; d. February, 1832; removed to Ohio, where his descendants reside. Joshua Wyeth was one of the celebrated Boston tea party in 1773, at the time of the destruction of the British tea in Boston harbor; he was a journeyman blacksmith in Boston, living with a Tory master, and owing to his being a young man, not much known in town, and not liable to be easily recognized, it was proposed that he and other young men, similarly unknown, should lead in the business; therefore, he and his companions were dressed to resemble Indians, and their faces were smeared with soot or lamp-black. Their most intimate acquaintances among the spectators "had not the least knowledge of them." "We surely resembled," said he in a narration of the affair, "devils from the bottomless pit, rather than men."
    v. William, b. May 22, 1760; d. June 8, 1776.
    vi. Susanna, b. May 14, 1762; d. December 29, 1788; m., December 6, 1779, William Watson.

Wyeth Family.   759

13. vii. *Jacob*, b. April 29, 1764; m. Elizabeth Jarvis.
   viii. *Anna*, b. February, 1766; d. April 15, 1842; m., March 6, 1785, Benjamin Cutter, b. November 7, 1761; d. March 7, 1824; no issue.
   ix. *Gad*, b. July 27, 1768; m., December 1, 1793, Polly Kendall, and removed to Ohio, where they left descendants.
14. x. *John*, b. March 31, 1770; m., first, Louisa Weiss; secondly, Lydia Allen.
   xi. *Elizabeth*, b. February 12, 1772; d. February 23, 1793.

IX. JONAS WYETH,[4] (Ebenezer,[3] John,[2] Nicholas,[1]) b. February 19, 1730; d. February 15, 1813; resided on the old homestead, and was a selectman in 1777 and 1778; m., March 29, 1753, HEPZIBAH TIDD, b. August 22, 1730; d. May 25, 1801; daughter of David Tidd and Hepzibah Reed, of Lexington, Mass. They had issue:

   i. *Lucy*, b. February 7, 1754; d. October 16, 1850; m. Thomas Coolidge, of Watson, who, in 1790 removed with his family to Livermore, Maine, where they both died.

X. NOAH WYETH,[4] (Ebenezer,[3] John,[2] Nicholas,[1]) b. July 7, 1742; d. September 10, 1811; m., March 12, 1763, ELIZABETH FITCH, of Bedford, Mass.; b. 1739; d. May 5, 1823. They had issue:

   i. *Noah*, b. June 24, 1763; d. prior to Aug., 1807, leaving issue.
   ii. *Elizabeth*, b. March 4, 1765; m., February 14, 1785, Andrew Newell.
   iii. *Lydia*, b. February 3, 1766.
   iv. *Rhoda*, b. May 18, 1768.
   v. *Dorcas*, b. November 21, 1770; d. prior to August, 1804; m. Samuel Hill.
   vi. *Isaac*, b. February 10, 1773; d. September 6, 1779.
   vii. *Job*, b. June 14, 1776; d. June 5, 1840; m. Lydia Convers Francis, b. 1779; d. January 4, 1850; daughter of Benjamin Francis and Lydia Convers.

XI. EBENEZER WYETH,[5] (Ebenezer,[4] Ebenezer,[3] John,[2] Nicholas,[1]) b. December 17, 1752; m., first, Mrs. ELIZABETH (WINSHIP) GREEN, of Norwich, Conn.; daughter of Capt. Joseph Winship. They had issue:

   i. *Ebenezer*, bap. May 17, 1778; m. Naomi Cook; and left issue.
   ii. *William*, baptized January 23, 1780.
   iii. *Joseph*, baptized July 29, 1781.
   iv. *Elizabeth*, b. March, 1783.

v. Stephen, b. 1785 ; m., December 10, 1815 Sarah Wright, b. 1794 ; d. July 17, 1831.

XII. JONAS WYETH,[5] (Ebenezer,[4] Ebenezer,[3] John,[2] Nicholas,[1]) b. May 17, 1757 ; d. October 3, 1817 ; m., April 8, 1792, ELIZABETH SMITH, b. 1771 ; d. September 16, 1853. They had issue:

 i. Elizabeth, b. July 22, 1792.
 ii. Jonas, b. September 3, 1794 ; d. June 14, 1867 ; m., February 8, 1820, Elizabeth N. Flagg ; and there was issue.
 iii. Nancy, b. September 9, 1796 ; m. Richard C Hastings, of Boston, Mass.
 iv. Susan, b. May 6, 1798 ; m. Oren Willard
 v. Harriet, b. September 30, 1800 ; m. Reuben Winslow, of Roxbury, Mass.
 vi. Mary, b. December 2, 1802.
 vii. John, b. February 17, 1805 ; d. September 25, 1871, at Roxbury, Mass.; was engaged in the West India trade ; m. Mary Ann Newman
 viii. Francis, b. May 14, 1807 ; d. May 27, 1862.
 ix. Sarah, b. October 29, 1809 ; d August 19, 1817.
 x. Joseph, b. January 20, 1813 ; d. April 10, 1846, at Guadaloupe.

XIII. JACOB WYETH,[5] (Ebenezer,[4] Ebenezer,[3] John,[2] Nicholas,[1]) b. April 29, 1764 ; d. January 14, 1857 ; graduated at Harvard in 1792 ; m. ELIZABETH JARVIS, b. 1768 ; d. January 20, 1858 ; daughter of Nathaniel Jarvis. They had issue :

 i. Jacob, b. February 10, 1797 ; graduated at Harvard in 1820 ; was a physician, and removed to Illinois, where he died.
 ii. Leonard, b. 1797 ; d. January, 1855, in New York.
 iii. Charles, b. 1800 ; settled in Baltimore, Md.
 iv. Nathaniel-Jarvis, b. 1802; d. August 29, 1865 ; m. Elizabeth Jarvis Stone, b. January 29, 1824; d. August 31, 1856 ; no issue. "Nathaniel Jarvis Wyeth was one of the most active and energetic men ever born in Cambridge. About 1830 he led a band of adventurers across the Rocky Mountains to Oregon; after his return he engaged in the ice business at Fresh Pond, Mass.; was one of the first shippers of that article to foreign or coastwise ports, and through life conducted that business with great skill and efficiency."

XIV. JOHN WYETH,[5] (Ebenezer,[4] Ebenezer,[3] John,[2] Nicholas,[1]) b. March 31, 1770, at Cambridge, Mass.; d. January 23, 1858, at Philadelphia, Pa. He was, at an early age, apprenticed to the printing business, and, on reaching his majority, was induced to go to San Domingo, to superintend a large printing establishment. While there, the insurrection of the blacks occurred, and all that he had acquired was lost. It was with great difficulty that he even succeeded in escaping from the island, and then only by the connivance of a friend, one of the officers who assisted in searching the vessels about leaving the port. Dressed as a common sailor and working among them, he eluded their vigilance, and subsequently reached Philadelphia. Arriving at Philadelphia, he worked some time in the different printing establishments there, and, in 1792, went to Harrisburg, Pa., where, in connection with John Allen, he purchased the paper started the previous year by Major Eli Lewis, and commenced the publication of the *Oracle of Dauphin*, a newspaper he successfully carried on until November, 1827. Mr. Wyeth's paper supported the Federal views of that great party during the whole course of its existence. Its columns were open, nevertheless, to the communications of all. In those days, before the principles of Republican rule were fully digested, many a nervous essay was put forth on either side of the question by able men of both parties. He was appointed postmaster of Harrisburg in October, 1793, under the administration of President Washington, of which he was a strenuous advocate and admirer. He was removed in July, 1798, by Mr. Adams' Postmaster General, on account of "the incompatibility of the office of postmaster and the editor of a newspaper." In connection with his newspaper, Mr. Wyeth established a bookstore and a publishing house, from which he issued a large number of books, the most notable of which were: Judge Henry's "Narrative of the Quebec Expedition," Graydon's "Memoirs," and a music book compiled by himself. The circulation of the latter, for that early day, was wonderful, its several editions aggregating one hundred and twenty thousand copies. To this he supplemented a second part, intended especially for the Methodist church, of which there were published about twenty-five thousand. He was one of Harrisburg's most energetic citizens, and was deeply interested in its prosperity and welfare. He caused the construction of several valuable improvements, which remain as evidence of his enterprising spirit and good judgment. He was one of the earliest friends of the Harrisburg Academy, and served as a trustee, of which body he was also president. Upon his retirement from publisher, he removed to Philadelphia, where he died at the advanced age of eighty-eight years. His life, thus prolonged, was marked by affability and cheerfulness, and his philosophy was of practical character. He was exceedingly industrious, and, whilst in business, could always find something for his hands to do, and in later life, when the concerns of his printing office were transferred to younger hands, he knew how to divide his time between his reading and his social pleasures. Mr. Wyeth was twice married; m., first June 6, 1793, LOUISA WEISS, b. April 29, 1775; d. June 1, 1822, at Harrisburg, Pa.; daughter of Lewis and Mary Weiss, of Philadelphia.* They had issue, all born in Harrisburg, Pa.:

  i. Louisa, b. August 6, 1796; d. November 10, 1875; m., April 22, 1817, Samuel Douglas, b. 1781, near the town of Newton-Limavady, county Derry, Ireland; d. July 8, 1833, at Harrisburg, Pa.; son of Henry Douglas and Jane Blair. He received a classical education in Scotland, but came to America about the age of seventeen, and located at Pittsburgh with a brother, the Rev. Joseph Douglas, who had preceded him. Here he studied law, and was admitted to the bar in 1804, and began his profession there. In 1812 he volunteered as aid to General Adamson Tannehill, and was with him in the expedition to Black Rock. In 1817 Mr. Douglas was nominated for Congress against Judge Henry Baldwin, but was defeated by a small majority. The same year he went to Harrisburg in the interests of securing

---

*LEWIS WEISS, b. December 28, 1717, in Berlin, Prussia; studied conveyancing, and emigrated to America, landing at Philadelphia on the 13th of December, 1755, where he opened an office on Arch street, between Fourth and Fifth. He was one of the founders of the German Society of Philadelphia, of which he was president. He was a Moravian, and acted as an attorney for that denomination prior to 1782, and was a judge of the Court of Common Pleas in 1786. He d. October 22, 1786, at Philadelphia. One of his daughters m. George Kline, of Carlisle; another, John Wyeth, of Harrisburg, both printers and editors.

proper legislation for a bridge across the Allegheny; and, subsequently, was induced to locate there. He was appointed Deputy Attorney General for Dauphin county, July 17, 1819, under Governor Findlay. Governor Wolf commissioned him February 10, 1830, Attorney General of the State, a position he held three years. He was a gentleman of fine classical attainments, of refined tastes, a good criminal lawyer, and highly esteemed by the members of his profession. They had issue.

ii. *John*, b. June 6, 1799; d. May 11, 1876, at Chambersburg, Pa.; m. Elmira Canfield, b. February 18, 1811; d. August 16, 1878. They had a large family of children.

iii. *Mary*, b. September 25, 1800; resided in Chambersburg, Pa.; m., in 1827, Rev. Daniel McKinley; d. Dec. 7, 1855.

iv. *Francis*, b. April 5, 1806; d. July 2, 1893. He was educated at the Harrisburg Academy, and learned the art of printing in his father's office, subsequently entering Jefferson College, Canonsburg, from which institution he graduated in November, 1827. On his return home his father, who had conducted the *Oracle of Dauphin* thirty-five years, transferred that paper to his son, which he edited and published several years. He also entered into the business of bookseller and publisher. At the time Mr. Wyeth took charge of the *Oracle* the Whig party had just come into existence, of whose principles and policy he was an enthusiastic supporter. Becoming, however, tired of an editor's life, he sold out the newspaper establishment about 1831, continuing his other business until 1859, when he disposed of that. In April, 1861, at the outbreak of the Rebellion, he was placed in charge of the quartermaster's department at Camp Curtin, where he continued until the general government assumed control over all the military organizations of the State. On the 20th of July, 1862, Governor Curtin appointed him one of the commissioners from Pennsylvania to visit all the hospitals in the Army of the Potomac, in the interest of the volunteer soldiers of the State who were sick or wounded, and, as his commission reads, "to supply the wants of the suffering and needy as far as lies in your power, without infringing on any of the regulations or rights of the army, and assure each and all that their condition awakens the liveliest interest and sympathy of the people and Governor of Pennsylvania." Returning home, he reported the condition of the wounded soldiers, with this recommendation, that where it is possible "those from Pennsylvania be transferred to hospitals in their own State, that they might be near to their friends and acquaintances." This was, subsequently, carried out during the continuance of the war. On November 28, 1863, he was again directed to visit the various hospitals. For a long term of years he was one of the trustees of the Harrisburg Academy, and president of the same. Mr. Wyeth was twice married; m., first, May 29, 1829, Susan Huston Maxwell, d. December 24, 1841, daughter of William and Ann Maxwell, of Franklin county, Pa.; and had issue:

1. *William-Maxwell*, merchant; m., and residing in St. Joseph, Mo.
2. *John*, senior member of the prominent drug firm, Wyeth Bros., of Philadelphia.
3. *Francis-H.*, resides in Philadelphia.

Mr. Wyeth m., secondly, Sarah C. Carson, daughter of Charles Carson, of Harrisburg, Pa.; and had issue:

4. *Charles-Carson*, d. s. p.
5. *Parker-C.*

v. Rev. *Charles-Augustus*, d.; a Presbyterian minister.
vi. *Louis*, b. August 30, 1812; m. Euphemia Allen, of Alabama.
vii. *Samuel-Douglas*, b. May 16, 1817; d. January, 1881, at Washington, D. C.; learned the trade of printing and established a stereotype foundry in Philadelphia, subsequently entered journalism and went to Washington City, where he published a book, "Ins and Outs of Washington." He wrote a pamphlet on the bronze doors of the National Capitol, and was, in many respects, "a human directory and encyclopedia," At the time of his death he had in press a book entitled, "The Federal City," but it has remained unissued. He was a gentleman of culture, but of eccentric habits. He m. Carrie Wardwell.

Mr. Wyeth m., secondly, May 2, 1826, LYDIA ALLEN, of Philadelphia; no issue.

GENEALOGICAL NOTES.

BYERS OF DERRY.

I. JOHN BYERS,[1] a native of Germany, came to Pennsylvania prior to 1740, with his children herein named. He settled in what was then Derry township, Lancaster county, Pa., where he died prior to 1750. Of his children we have the names of—
  2. *i. John*, m., and left issue.
  3. *ii. Frederick*, m., and left issue.
  4. *iii. Casimir*, m., and left issue.

II. JOHN BYERS,[2] (John,[1]) located in what subsequently became Hanover township, Dauphin county, Pa., where he took up a large tract of land. He died about the year 1760, leaving a wife LETITIA (who subsequently married Thomas Sharp, of Hanover,) and children:
    i. William.
    ii. Mary, m. Henry Cowan.
    iii. Catharine.
    iv. John, m., and died prior to his father, leaving a son, *Robert.*
    v. Ann.
    vi. George.

III. FREDERICK BYERS,[2] (John,[1]) a native of Germany, from whence he emigrated with his father, died prior to the war for Independence, in Derry township, then Lancaster county, Pa. He was a substantial farmer, and a man of prominence in frontier times. He had six or seven daughters, and one son:
  5. *i. John*, b. March 9, 1759; m. Margaret Rahm.

IV. CASIMIR or CASTLE BYERS,[2] (John,[1]) d. prior to 1786, leaving a farm in Derry township, Dauphin county, Pa., which he had purchased in 1761, to his children. He was a soldier of the Revolution, and served on the committee of observation for the county of Lancaster. He was very prominent during that struggle for Independence, and highly honored and respected by his neighbors. His children were:

i. John, d. in 1805, leaving, among other children, *Robert,* and Sarah.
ii. Elizabeth, m. Jacob Kaufman.
iii. Mary, m. Ludwig Brandt.
iv. Eve, m. Peter Landis.
v. Catharine, m. John Bair.
vi. Barbara, m. Jacob Rahm.
vii. Mary.
viii. Margaret.

V. JOHN BYERS,³ (Frederick,² John,¹) b. March 9, 1759; d. August 6, 1834; m. MARGARET RAHM; removed to Franklin county, Pa., where they both lived and died. They had issue:

6.   *i. Frederick,* b. May, 1780; m. Anna Eby.
ii. Castle, m. Mary [Polly] Koons.
iii. Margaret, m. Peter Cook.
iv. John, d. unm.
v. Melchoir, d. unm.
vi. Jacob, d. unm.
vii. William, m. Mary [Polly] Small.
viii. Samuel, m. Maria Wingerd.
iv. Mary, m. Martin Wingerd.

VI. FREDERICK BYERS,⁴ (John,³ Frederick,² John,¹) b. May, 1780, in Dauphin county; d. October 17, 1854; m., April, 1802, ANNA EBY, d. May 23, 1823. They had issue:

i. John, b. March 11, 1803; m., in 1827, Fanny Detweiler.
ii. Margaret, b. August 11, 1804; m., 1824, Peter Cook.
iii. Catharine, b. October 15, 1805; m., 1826, James Crawford.
7. *iv. Eby,* b. July 17, 1807; m., and left issue.
v. Jacob, b. July 22, 1809; m., first, Miss Kerr; secondly, Ann Kennedy; thirdly, Mrs. Grier.
vi. Annie, b. September 19, 1811; m. Samuel Shively.
vii. Elizabeth, b. July, 1813; m. John Logan.
viii. Frederick, b. April 7, 1815.
ix. William, b. November 14, 1816; m. Marsh Jeffrey.
x. Mary, b. August 15, 1818; m. David Clugston.
xi. Levi, b. May 17, 1823; unm.

Frederick Byers m., secondly, in 1826, Mrs. BENEDICT. They had issue:

xii. Amanda, b. November 27, 1827; m. Michael Immel.

VII. EBY BYERS,⁵ (Frederick,⁴ John,³ Frederick,² John,¹) b. July 17, 1807, in Derry township, Dauphin county; d. June 18, 1880, at Harrisburg, Pa. Mr. Byers was an enterprising citizen of Harrisburg, where he lived half a century. He was upright in business, and was greatly esteemed by his fellow citizens. He was thrice married ; m., first, in 1830, CATHARINE TENNET, d. s. p.; m., secondly, in 1834, MARGARET MCARTHUR. They had issue :

 i. Frederick-Eby, d. 1894, at Harrisburg, Pa.; unm.
 ii. Margaret.

Eby Byers m., thirdly, in 1854, JULIA UPDEGRAFF, who survived her husband.

EAGLEY FAMILY.

I. ABRAHAM EGLI,[1] as he wrote the name, located in Paxtang about 1770, where he took up a tract of land on Beaver creek. He was a soldier of the Revolution, and a farmer in comfortable circumstances. His descendants in the male line followed the oldest son Abraham, who removed to Erie county, Pa., in 1803, under the auspices of the Harrisburg and Presqu' Isle Land company. Although he wrote his name Eagly, the present generation have added another letter by writing it Eagley. The progenitor of this family b. in 1735 ; d. August 17, 1785, in Paxtang ; his wife Susanna, b. in 1737; d. October 12, 1807, in Paxtang. They had issue:

2. *i. Abraham*, b. April 4, 1773 ; m. Katharine Boehm.
 ii. Susanna, b. September 30, 1774 ; d. March 31, 1854 ; m. Jacob Stauffer, son of Christian and Veronica Stauffer, b. February 5, 1765 ; d. about 1850. Their descendants reside in Columbiana county, Ohio.
 iii. Jacob, b. August 13, 1776 ; d. May 21, 1852; removed to Erie county, Pa., in 1812, where he died; m. Mary Roop, b. March 24, 1783 ; d. December 25, 1824 ; and had *John, Susanna, Jacob, Catharine,* and *Abraham.*
 iv. Catharine, b. September 18, 1777 ; d. January 7, 1829 ; m. Jacob Nisley ; and had issue.

II. ABRAHAM EAGLEY,[2] (Abraham,[1]) b. April 4, 1773 ; d. June 8, 1851 ; removed to Erie county, Pa., and settled in Springfield township in 1803, where most of the descendants of this branch of the family reside. He m., in 1794, CATHARINE BOEHM, b. December 5, 1772 ; d. December 26, 1843. They had issue :

i. Mary, b. January 17, 1795 ; d. April 5, 1853 ; m., October 26, 1813, John Stough, b. March 19, 1784 ; d. March 14, 1858 ; and had issue (surname Stough), *George, Barbara, Peter, Mary, Susannah, John, Rebecca, Catharine, William, Margaret, Sophia, Lydia,* and *Nancy*.

ii. Barbara, b. November 24, 1796 ; d. March 11, 1875 ; m., August 9, 1827, David Russell, b. February 24, 1788 ; d. September 28, 1859; and had issue (surname Russell). *John,* and *Mary-Ann.*

iii. Catharine, b. February 18, 1801 ; d. February 11, 1859 ; m., June 19, 1834, Benjamin Bond, b. August 6, 1797; d. May 28, 1839 ; and had issue (surname Bond), *Miriam,* and *Simeon.*

iv. Christian, b. October 26, 1803 ; d. February 12, 1848 ; m., first, March 12, 1835, Eliza Bond, b. August 25, 1812 ; d. February 17, 1840 ; and had *Catharine, Lindamine* and *Eliza* ; m., secondly, January 4, 1843, Eliza (Smith) Markwell, b. March 24, 1811 ; d. November 16, 1868, without issue.

v. John, b. December 7, 1805 ; d. 1894 ; m., first, May 3, 1842, Tabitha May, b. November 24, 1819 ; d. June 21, 1851, without issue; m., secondly, March 2, 1852, Nancy Anderson, b. October 12, 1820 ; and had *John.*

vi. Abraham, b. April 2, 1809 ; m., first, November 14, 1843, Sarah Gerred, b. June 14, 1823 ; d. November 4, 1850 ; and had *Henry, Catharine* and *Eunice* ; m., secondly, January 9, 1853, Sophia C. Smith, b. March 15, 1828 ; d. May 14, 1879 ; and had *Casper, George, Millard, Frank, Jessie, Mary, Charles,* and *Smith.*

vii. Daniel, b. November 5, 1815 ; m., January 9, 1842, Jane Guthrie, b. May 18, 1817; and had *Lawrence.*

viii. Joseph, b. December 2, 1819; m., January 3, 1841, Caroline Lybarger, b. November 9, 1821 ; and had *Frank,* and *James.*

GRAY OF PAXTANG.

I. JOHN GRAY,[1] b. in county Antrim, Province of Ulster, Ireland, in 1698; emigrated to America about 1730, locating at first in Chester county, Pa.; subsequently, in Paxtang township, Dauphin county. He was one of the early pioneers in that section of the Province, and, during the French and Indian war (1755–1764), was captain of a rifle company in Col.

Gray of Paxtang. 769

Elder's battalion, subsequently Col. Asher Clayton's. He d. in February, 1785, and is buried in Paxtang church graveyard. Captain Gray was twice married; first, in 1730, to SUSANNA ARMSTRONG, b. 1700; d. October, 1750; and there was issue:

    i. George, b. 1732; d. February 25, 1798; unm.
    ii. Joseph, b. 1734; d. October 13, 1794; m., November 11, 1779, Elizabeth Forster, b. 1744: d. April 18, 1816; their only child, *Susan*, m. William Espy, (*see Espy record*).
2. *iii. William*, b. 1738; m. Agnes Rutherford.

He m., secondly, in 1753, HANNAH (STEVENSON) SEMPLE,* b. 1711; d. November, 1781; and there was issue:

3. *iv. John*, b. 1754; m., first, Mary Robinson; secondly, Mary Falls.
4. *v. Robert*, b. 1757; m. Mary Rutherford.
    vi. Hannah, b. 1759; m., December 4, 1777, George Dixon, and had *William*, and *John;* William was killed at the battle of Lundy's Lane; John m., and left descendants, one of whom was William Dixon, of Philadelphia.

The original farm owned by John Gray was, upon his death, divided into four tracts, and remains in that shape to the present. These tracts were severally inherited by Joseph, George, Robert, and John. George dying unmarried, his farm passed out of the family. Joseph's is owned by his grandson, Josiah Espy; John's, by his grandson, the late J. Newton Gray, and Robert's, by his granddaughter, Mrs. Mary Jane Bigham.

II. WILLIAM GRAY,² (John,¹) b. 1738, in Paxtang; d., 1815, near Lewisburg, Union county, Pa.; was an early settler in Buffalo Valley, and a captain in the war of the Revolution; m. AGNES RUTHERFORD, b. September 14, 1740, in Paxtang; d. about 1813 in Buffalo Valley; daughter of Thomas Rutherford and Jean Mordah, (*see Rutherford record*). They had issue:
    i. Jane, b. 1770; d. at the residence of her son, Robert Hutchison, at Mill Hall, Pa.; m., first, William Wallace; sec-

---

*She was the widow of George Semple, and by him had three children (surname Semple): *Sarah* m., October 19, 1769, William Brown; *Mary* m. —— Coulter, and with the Browns removed to Greenbriar county, Va.: and *George*.

ondly, December 18, 1810, Samuel Hutchison.
ii. Susanna, b. 1772 ; d. in Columbia county about 1810 ; m., first, William Hudson ; secondly, Andrew Foster.
iii. Mary, b. 1774 ; d. September 8, 1837, in Buffalo Valley ; m. John Dunlap, d. September 26, 1842.
iv. Margaret, b. 1776 ; d. March, 1856, at Hartleton, Union county, Pa.; m. John Hays.
v. Nancy, b. 1778 ; d. at the residence of her son, Hudson, about 1849; m. Hudson Williams.
vi. Sarah, b. 1780 ; d. unm.
vii. Eleanor, b. 1782 ; d. at Lewisburg ; m. John Robinson.

III. JOHN GRAY,[1] (John,[1]) b. 1754, in Paxtang; d. May 30, 1819, buried in Paxtang churchyard; m., first, in 1789, MARY ROBINSON, b. 1767 ; d. in Paxtang, and interred in Derry church burial ground. They had issue :

i. Nancy, b. 1790; d. February 16, 1845 ; m. William B. McBay, b. 1792 ; d. September 27, 1837 ; both buried in Hanover church graveyard; and had issue (surname McBay): *Mary,* and *Jane.*
ii. Joseph, b. June, 1792 ; d. September 13, 1861 ; m., June 1, 1830, Jane H. Gray, daughter of Robert Gray and Mary Rutherford ; and had issue :
  1. *John-Newton,* b. April 28, 1831 ; d. January 30, 1895.
  2. *Mary-Louisa,* b. January 1, 1833.
  3. *Ellen-Jane,* b. Nov. 22, 1836 ; m. Harry Nesbit.

John Gray m., secondly, MARY FALLS, b. 1860; d. July 17, 1822; buried in Paxtang church graveyard. No issue:

IV. ROBERT GRAY,[2] (John,[1]) b. 1757, in Paxtang; d. April 27, 1848, and buried in Paxtang church graveyard. He served in the war of the Revolution, and was with the half-starved and illy-clad army of Washington during the cantonment at Valley Forge. His stories of the hardships endured during the struggle for Independence were sadly interesting. He lived a long and honorable life, and was the last of that gallant band of the heroes of "Seventy-Six," in his locality. He m. MARY RUTHERFORD, daughter of Capt. John Rutherford and Margaret Parke ; b. September 13, 1771 ; d. August 16, 1863. They had issue :

i. Margaret-Park, b. July 22, 1792 ; d. Feb. 11, 1873 ; unm.
ii. Sarah-Stevenson, b. October, 1793 ; d. July, 1864, near Springfield, O.; m. Matthew Humes, and left issue.

Gross Family.

iii. *John-Rutherford*, b. March, 1795; d. March, 1877, in Indiana; m. Miss Lefevre, and left issue.
iv. *Jane-Hutchison*, b. July 8, 1796; d. December 6, 1870, on the old homestead in Paxtang; m. Joseph Gray, and left three children.
v. *Thomas-Morehead*, b. March 17, 1798; d. January 28, 1857.
vi. *Martha-Collier*, b. December 13, 1801; d. February 19, 1895, in Paxtang.
vii. *William*, b. May, 1803; d. 1895; settled in Indiana; m. Margaret Hays, d. January, 1865.
viii. *Eliza*, b. November 4, 1804; d. November 10, 1841; m., June 19, 1837, Robert Wilson, of Highspire (his second wife) left two children, both dead.
ix. *Samuel*, b. April, 1806; d. October 19, 1881, in Paxtang.
x. *Joshua*, b. 1808; d. unm. in 1839, at New Orleans.
xi. *Mary*, b. July 10, 1810; d. January 17, 1881; m. James Hays, of Hummelstown; buried in Paxtang.
xii. *Eleanor*, b. 1812; d. June 28, 1832.
xiii. *Esther*, b. 1817; d. 1842, near Gettysburg, Adams county, Pa.; m., September 11, 1838, James McGaughey, and left a daughter, the wife of John Bigham.

GROSS FAMILY.

I. JACOB GROSS,[1] from Mayence on the Rhine, emigrated to the United States, then the British Colonies, towards the close of the year 1759. He had several sons, of whom we have the following:

    i. *Isaac.*
    ii. *Abraham.*
    iii. *Daniel.*
2.   iv. *Jacob*, b. December 22, 1780; m. Anna Moyer.

II. JACOB GROSS,[2] (Jacob,[1]) b. December 22, 1780, in Bucks county, Pa.; d. November 26, 1865, in Beamsville, C. W.; a minister of the gospel; removed to Beamsville, Canada West, now Ontario, in 1817; m., first, December 18, 1817, ANNA MOYER, b. July 17, 1799, in Bucks county, Pa.; d. January 22, 1827, in Beamsville, C. W. They had issue, all b. at Beamsville, C. W.:
3.   i. *Samuel*, b. October 15, 1818; m. Mary Ann Roades.
    ii. *Mary*, b. September 30, 1820; m., June 17, 1842, Christian Bushey; reside in Landisville, N. J.

4. iii. *Anna*, b. September 26, 1822; m. David Housser.
5. iv. *John*, b. January 14, 1825; m. Elizabeth Barber.
6. v. *Elizabeth*, b. May 15, 1827; m. George C. Eggert.

Rev. Jacob Gross m., secondly, August 23, 1831, SALOME MOYER, b. September 19, 1796, in Lancaster county, Pa.; d. April 10, 1878, in Beamsville, C. W. They had issue:

 vi. *Susannah*, b. Jan. 21, 1834; resides in Lansdale, Pa.; unm.
7. vii. *Salome*, b. October 24, 1836; m. Rev. H. F. Seiple.
 viii. *Jacob*, b. November 26, 1838; d. May 20, 1841, at Beamsville, C. W.

III. SAMUEL GROSS,[3] (Jacob,[2] Jacob,[1]) b. October 15, 1818, at Beamsville, C. W.; resides at Landisville, Atlantic county, N. J.; m., December 7, 1843, MARY ANN ROADES, b. January 26, 1826. They had issue:

 i. *William-H.*, b. September 15, 1844, in South Cayuga, C. W.; removed to Erie, in 1865, where he resides; m., January 17, 1882, Effie M. Laurie, b. September 24, 1851, in Buffalo, N. Y.; daughter of Rev. Alexander G. Laurie.
 ii. *John-Roades*, b. June 14, 1846, in South Cayuga, C. W.; resides in Galveston, Texas.

IV. ANNA GROSS,[3] (Jacob,[2] Jacob,[1]) b. September 30, 1820; m., October 17, 1843, DAVID HOUSSER, b. June 8, 1818, in the township of Clinton, county Lincoln, Ontario. They had issue (surname Housser):

 i. *Israel-Gross*, b. July 23, 1845.
 ii. *Salome*, b. June 26, 1847.
 iii. *John-H.*, b. May 11, 1849; m., June 10, 1874; resides at Winnipeg, Manitoba
 iv. *Gideon-B.*, b. June 23, 1851: m., August 29, 1882, Ellen G. Elliott, of Brantford, Ontario.
 v. *Susie*, b. March 29, 1854; m., October 13, 1880, George H· Williams, of Thorold, Ontario.
 vi. *J.-Wesley*, b. June 3, 1856.
 vii. *D.-Franklin*, b. August 27, 1858; d. September 4, 1860.
 viii. *Annie*, b. July 10, 1864.

V. JOHN GROSS,[3] (Jacob,[2] Jacob,[1]) b. January 14, 1825, in Beamsville, C. W.; now resides in Welland, Ontario; m., September 22, 1852, at Saltfleet, C. W., ELIZABETH BARBER. They had issue:

 i. *Lucetta-Jane*, b. February 17, 1854, at Beamsville, C. W.; resides in St. Catharine, C. W.

Gross Family. 773

ii. Mary-Lorinda, b. October 28, 1855, at Beamsville, C. W.; m. Dr. W. E. Burgar; reside in Welland, Ontario; and had issue (surname Burgar):
  1. *Donna*, b. July 18, 1877.
  2. *Della*, b. December 15, 1878.
  3. *Oliver*, b. October 24, 1880.
  4. *Frederick*, b. September 19, 1882.
iii. Salome-Amelia, b. July 4, 1857, in Clinton, C. W.; m., at Welland, Ontario, Herbert E. Ryan; reside in Dunkirk, N. Y.; and had issue (surname Ryan):
  1. *Irene*, b. June 2, 1877.
  2. *Maude*, b. July 1, 1879.
  3. *Nellie*, b. February 22, 1881.
  4. *Burton*, b. September 20, 1883.
iv. John-Franklin, b. July 19, 1859, in Clinton, C. W.; m. Clara A. Casper, b. February 8, 1865, in Thorold, Ontario; and had issue:
  1. *Frank-Leroy*, b. February, 1885; d. in inf.
v. William, b. March 29, 1862, in Clinton, C. W.; resides in Welland, Ontario.

VI. ELIZABETH GROSS,[3] (Jacob,[2] Jacob,[1]) b. May 15, 1827; m., May 24, 1853, GEORGE C. EGGERT, b. October 22, 1826, in the city of Berne, Canton of Berne, Switzerland; emigrated to America in 1831. They had issue (surname Eggert):

i. Samuel, b. February 7, 1854, in Buffalo, N. Y.; d. November 15, 1854.
ii. George-Ezra, b. October 15, 1855, in Buffalo, N. Y.
iii. Lystra, b. September 3, 1858, in Berne, Huron county, Ontario; m., June 20, 1877, John Birney Gretter, of Greensboro', N. C.; and had issue (surname Gretter):
  1. *Jean-Birney*, b. December 28, 1882.
iv. Ida-May, b. May 27, 1863, in Berne, Huron county, Ontario.

VII. SALOME GROSS,[3] (Jacob,[2] Jacob,[1]) b. October 24, 1836; m., April 16, 1868, Rev. H. F. SEIPLE, b. February 17, 1843, near Catasauqua, Pa.; graduated from Amherst College in 1866; reside at Lansdale, Pa. They had issue (surname Seiple):

i. Arthur-W.-H., b. June 13, 1869, at Tiffin, Ohio.
ii. Lucretia-H.-B., b. June 9, 1871, at Weaversville, Northampton county, Pa.
iii. Lillian-T.-S., b. November 5, 1874, at Landisville, N. J.; d. December 15, 1881, at Lansdale, Pa.
iv. Beatrice-W.-C., b. July 14, 1878, at Weaversville, Pa.

INDEX OF SURNAMES.

Abbott, 483.
Abel, 344.
Abercrombie, 276.
Acheson, 593.
Ackerman, 305, 310.
Adams, 248, 413, 441, 459, 463, 481, 482, 761.
Addams, 31, 32, 56, 714.
Addison, 415.
Addleman, 536.
Adkins, 14.
Africa, 532, 537-540.
Agnew, 567, 586.
Ahren, 719.
Aiken, 751.
Ainley, 155.
AINSWORTH, 1-6, 8, 148.
Aitken, 447.
Alberson, 524.
Albert, 109.
Alcorn, 440, 442.
Albright, 9, 12, 345, 556, 558-561.
Alder, 253.
Aldrich, 92.
Alger, 208.
Alexander, 21, 170, 171, 280, 317, 318, 319, 322, 329, 391, 398, 426, 590, 598, 711.
Alfree, 329.
Alison, 279, 316, 317, 415, 716.
ALLEN, 1, 7-14, 40, 64, 65, 68, 69, 125, 157, 172, 219, 224, 297, 316, 317, 350, 355, 374, 433, 438, 449, 456, 502, 759, 761, 764.
Allison, 30, 270, 390, 661.
ALRICKS, 15-26, 156, 254, 319, 467, 485.
Alward, 194.
Amesbury, 235.
Ammons, 651.
Amon, 292.
ANDERSON, 2, 4, 27-36, 56, 87, 89, 154, 187, 191, 218, 286, 383, 388, 488, 510, 520, 521, 614, 628, 656, 660, 661, 768.
ANDREWS, 1-6, 139, 756.
Andross, 16.
Angell, 177, 617.
Angle, 380.
Annan, 452.
Annise, 621.
Ankeney, 580.
Anshutz, 532.
Antes, 252.
Arago, 217.
Archibald, 629, 632.
Armatt, 46.
Armstrong, 52, 232, 320, 383, 384, 385, 386, 403, 426, 670, 715, 727, 769.
Arnaud, 328.
Arndt, 562, 567.
Arnold, 142, 389.
Ashbaugh, 446.
Ashmore, 643.
Ashton, 167, 178.
Askew, 456.
Atkinson, 178, 256.
Atwood, 267.
Aughenbaugh, 364.
Austin, 173.
Aul, Auld, 37.
Audenreid, 697, 699, 701.
AWL, 37-46, 191, 194, 252.
Ayers, 577.
AYRES, 33, 34, 47-61, 125, 235, 247, 257, 262, 276, 284, 396, 564.

Babb, 360.
Bachman, 561.
Backenstose, 161, 163.
Bacon, 152.
Badger, 463.
Baer, 350.
Bailey, 46, 101, 145, 207, 208, 249, 369, 372, 504, 573, 621, 639, 650, 659.
Baillie, 407.
Bain, 75.
Bair, 766.
Baird, 115, 116, 250, 256, 339, 493, 524.
Baker, 28, 181, 187, 191, 495, 515, 591.
Baldridge, 614.

Pennsylvania Genealogies.

Baldwin, 93, 390, 397, 488, 762.
Ball, 94, 376.
Ballantyne, 136.
Bane, 166.
Banks, 133.
Barber, 506, 508, 516, 608, 641, 662, 772.
Barclay, 622.
Bard, 683.
Barker, 34, 36, 74, 546.
Barlett, 163.
Barnes, 235, 515, 590, 707.
BARNETT, 8, 62–77, 146, 149, 200, 210, 211, 605, 650, 651, 652, 660, 668, 669, 696, 733.
Barnhart, 296, 299.
Barnitz, 117, 357, 360, 361.
Barnsley, 183.
Barr, 22, 404, 426, 616, 620, 671.
Barrett, 345, 351, 631, 634.
Barrow, 142.
Barton, 571.
Bartles, 492, 493.
Bartholomew, 724, 728.
Bartley, 221.
Baskin, 340.
Bastedo, 355.
Basum, 516.
Bates, 100, 103, 671, 673.
Bauder, 137.
Baugher, 309, 320.
Baughman, 168.
Bausman, 107.
Baxter, 292, 425.
Bay, 189.
Bayard, 550.
Bayley, 28, 30, 31, 141, 275.

Baymiller, 168.
Beach, 57, 60.
Beader, 312.
Beall, 505.
Beane, 355, 363.
Bear, 676, 678.
Beard, 183.
Beates, 343.
Beattie, 640.
BEATTY, 78–97, 167, 176, 197, 202, 506, 649, 650, 654, 697.
Beaujolais, 545.
Beaumont, 567, 578.
Beaver, 175, 431.
Beck, 146, 560.
Becker, 675.
Becket, 232, 234.
Beckley, 553, 554.
Beecher, 877.
Beeghly, 512, 523, 524.
Beemer, 715.
Beer, 510, 520.
Beetle, 2.
Beggs, 374.
Behm, 564, 566.
Beidleman, 699.
Belcher, 235.
Bellar, 121.
Bell, 13, 64, 87, 90, 130, 143, 214, 247, 249, 250, 258, 261, 275, 282, 449, 616, 669, 673, 691, 734, 737.
Beilman, 102
Beltzhoover, 610.
Bemus, 257.
Ben, 82.
Bender, 201.
Benedict, 249, 394, 597, 766.
Benezet, 39.
Benham, 45.
Benner, 382.
Bennett, 133, 165, 171, 220, 261.

Bent, 255.
Bently, 263.
Benton, 382.
Berger, 93.
Berlin, 347, 551, 657.
Berry, 515.
Berryhill, 724, 731.
Bertram, 27, 188, 270, 272, 273.
Best, 353.
Betts, 336, 339.
Bibighaus, 727.
Bickel, 101, 567.
Biddle, 547, 742, 743.
Bidwell, 136, 137.
Biers, 370, 377.
Bigelow, 207.
Bigham, 542, 769, 771.
Bigler, 86, 121, 341, 429.
Billmyer, 380.
Bills, 210.
Bines, 444, 449, 455.
Bingham, 82.
Bintling, 160, 161.
Bird, 165, 171, 743.
Birdsall, 350.
Birney, 692.
Bishop, 154, 163.
Bissel, 260.
Black, 4, 188, 439, 444, 445, 613, 614, 629.
Blackburn, 35, 79.
Blackford, 737, 739.
Blackiston, 329.
Blackman, 239, 240.
Blaine, 272, 279–281, 383, 387, 476, 615, 616, 620, 624, 653, 710, 711.
Blair, 13, 281, 321, 367, 368, 411, 465, 478, 482, 579, 583, 591, 593, 601, 724, 762.
Blake, 53, 465, 467.
Blank, 120.

Index of Surnames.

Blattenberger, 108, 109.
Bleeker, 369.
Bliss, 431.
Blocher, 309.
Blosser, 681.
Boal, 76, 150, 265, 536, 611, 612.
BOAS, 41, 98-106, 160, 222, 572, 671.
Bobo, 373.
Bodine, 165, 169.
Boehm, 767.
Boggs, 18, 20, 296, 653, 669, 670.
Bolton, 345, 381, 592.
Bombaugh, 174, 358.
BOMBERGER, 107-112, 358, 364, 622, 674, 675.
Bomgardner, 163.
Bond, 768.
Boonebrake, 690.
Boots, 516.
Bottorff, 59.
Botts, 120.
Boude, 197.
Bound, 750.
Bouquet, 107.
Bousch, 263.
Bower, 44.
Bowers, 226, 320.
Bowman, 345, 362, 635, 643, 678, 684, 685, 756.
Bowland, 444.
Bowlby, 165.
Bowne, 531, 535.
Bowyer, 402.
Boyce, 250.
BOYD, 69, 73, 113-119, 146, 173, 185, 319, 322-324, 342, 361, 363, 484, 524, 530, 579, 580, 581, 591, 694.

Boyer, 100, 102, 370, 371, 688.
Brackenridge, 286.
Braddock, 367.
Bradley, 512.
Bradish, 456.
Bradner, 459.
Bradshaw, 205, 207, 572.
Brady, 111, 592.
Brainard, 328.
Brandeberry, 506, 511, 523.
Brandenburg, 509, 519.
Brandon, 320, 734, 735.
Bransford, 173.
Brandt, 766.
Branyan, 726.
Bratton, 117, 118.
Brazee, 341.
Breaden, 187.
Bream, 688.
Breathitt, 221.
Breckenridge, 545.
Breden, 157.
Breed, 96.
Breeze, 28, 300.
Brehler, 253.
Brenneman, 350.
Brereton, 80, 589.
Brewer, 172, 200, 236.
Brewster, 217, 403, 753.
Brickenstein, 560.
Bridgeman, 575.
Brient, 448.
Bright, 524.
Briggs, 717.
Brimner, 680.
Brinton, 424.
Brisban, 629, 631, 632, 633.
Brisben, 113, 114.
Brisbin, 134, 135, 174, 402.
Briscoe, 426.
Brittam, 746.

Brodhead, 560.
Brodnax, 221.
Brooks, 240, 305, 307, 308, 478, 671, 703, 704, 758.
Brotherline, 296.
Brough, 688.
Brown, 1, 3, 9, 11, 20, 145, 148, 154, 173, 178, 222, 231, 287, 304, 373, 376, 379, 385, 390, 404, 416, 418, 425, 437, 443, 523, 528, 547, 585, 640, 694, 769.
Browne, 46.
Brownfield, 697.
Brownson, 422.
Brownlee, 87, 88.
Brua, 485.
Brubaker, 459.
Brumbaugh, 344.
Brunner, 675.
Bruner, 242.
Bryan, 253, 406.
Bryson, 125, 131, 132, 424, 655.
Bubb, 262.
Buchanan, 84, 265, 272, 274, 318, 324, 345, 399, 443.
Buckman, 56.
Buehler, 455, 466, 620, 623.
BUCHER, 5, 10, 52, 120-142, 722.
Buell, 96, 261.
Buffington, 264-268.
Bull, 21, 24.
Bunker, 662.
Bunn, 345, 363, 637.
Bunstine, 99.
Buoy, 364.
Burbridge, 391, 421, 619, 622.
Burgauer, 122, 123.

Burd, 48, 51, 71, 144, 247, 250, 495.
Burgar, 773.
Burke, 137, 397.
Burket, 537.
Burling, 376.
Burnett, 301, 361, 676, 679, 680, 703.
Burns, 547.
Burnside, 503.
Burrall, 535.
Burrough, 153, 541.
Burt, 120.
Bushby, 95.
Bushey, 688, 771.
Bushman, 361.
Bushnell, 590.
Bust, 237.
Butler, 24, 352, 435.
Butt, 137.
Byerly, 331.
Byers, 272, 659, 765, 767.
Bynon, 436.

Cabanné, 491.
Cadwell, 212, 397.
Calahan, 166.
Calder, 105, 307, 313, 314, 343.
Caldwell, 133, 212, 231, 292, 683, 684.
Calhoun, 215, 229, 387, 579, 582, 592, 646, 649.
Callender, 284, 723.
Camblin, 336, 337.
Cameron, 130, 132, 243, 352, 467, 485, 486, 569, 730.
Camp, 490.
Campbell, 14, 75, 157, 188, 199, 206, 330, 386, 388, 390, 394, 418, 458, 482, 511, 513, 514, 537, 579,

581, 582, 591, 592, 607.
Candee, 426.
Candler, 128.
Canfield, 763.
Cann, 255.
Cannarow, 349.
Cannon, 209.
Carl, 511, 523.
Cargin, 82.
Carman, 681.
Carmony, 499.
Carothers, 75, 82, 90, 466, 586, 602.
Carpenter, 197, 201, 275, 332, 577.
Carper, 305, 554.
Carr, 4, 16, 224.
Carroll, 172, 258.
Carruth, 440.
Carson, 82, 90, 118, 157, 196, 255, 338, 350, 358, 363, 613, 635, 668.
Carter, 49, 221, 463, 593.
Carver, 93.
Casey, 655.
Casper, 773.
Cassels, 128.
Catenius, 720.
Cathay, 440, 441.
Cathcart, 234, 696, 699.
Caughey, 715.
Cauffman, 108, 109.
Cavet, 247.
Cazier, 506, 507, 508, 515, 516.
Center, 685.
Chalcoat, 506, 508.
Chamberlin, 373, 378, 750.
Chamberlain, 280.
Chambers, 31, 54, 57, 81, 89, 146, 151, 154, 246, 247, 258, 269,

315, 316, 385, 390, 391, 441, 442, 446, 455, 456, 528, 587, 592, 703.
Champney, 756, 757.
Chandler, 513.
Chapman, 348, 481, 482, 596, 678, 683, 384.
Chaplin, 551.
Charlton, 133, 134, 140.
Chase, 236, 729.
Chayne, 265, 267, 359.
Cheeseman, 535.
Cherrington, 459.
Chestnut, 399.
Chevalier, 28.
Childs, 206.
Chilson, 673.
Christopher, 696, 699.
Christy, 683.
Chronister, 686.
Church, 262, 404.
Churchill, 543, 651.
Claiborne, 199, 482, 745.
Clapp, 702.
Clarie, 45.
Clark, 35, 76, 215, 237, 265, 267, 297, 390, 443, 448, 459, 486, 548, 562, 583, 585, 606, 609, 610, 613, 618, 672, 681, 682, 695, 697, 714, 734.
Clarke, 371, 403, 583, 610, 612, 657.
Clarkson, 613.
Clay, 299, 365, 387.
Clayton, 189, 329, 769.
Cleaver, 374.
Cleeland, 650, 656.
Clemens, 262.
Clement, 748.
Clendenin, 417.
Cleveland, 522.
Clever, 425.

Index of Surnames.

Cline, 514, 524, 726.
Clingan, 606–608.
Clingman, 634.
Clinton, 290, 827.
Cloke, 832.
Clokey, 78.
Clopper, 278.
Clows, 127.
Clugston, 766.
Clunie, 820.
Clyde, 492, 694, 747.
Clymer, 39, 438.
Coates, 373, 701.
Coburn, 91.
Cockfield, 223.
Cochran, 6, 19, 71, 146, 148, 158, 215, 229, 257, 333, 341, 343, 375, 423, 432, 503, 605, 606, 616, 619, 620.
Coekel, 512.
Coen, 455.
Coffee, 380.
Colden, 535.
Cole, 160, 191, 253.
Coleman, 200, 211, 308, 507, 514.
Colhoun, 508, 515.
Colkit, 701.
Collier, 507, 526, 529, 530, 629, 631, 632, 633.
Collins, 585, 662.
Colt, 578.
Colwell, 277, 665, 666.
Comerer, 380.
Comfort, 591, 688.
Comingo, 553, 554.
Comly, 50, 53.
Compton, 343.
Conklin, 657.
Connell, 500.
Conner, 278.
Conrad, 423.
Consor, 288.

Convers, 759.
Conway, 140, 171, 542.
Conyngham, 25.
Cook, 3, 6, 20, 173, 212, 239, 270, 275, 453, 714, 759, 766.
Cooke, 596, 604, 749.
Coolbaugh, 356.
Cooly, 664.
Coolidge, 759.
Cooper, 128, 276, 368, 373, 448, 507, 512, 653, 737.
Coover, 359.
Copeland, 101, 160.
Corbet, 9.
Corbit, 329.
Corcoran, 589.
Cordner, 82.
Coren, 548.
Cornman, 732.
Cornelius, 654.
Cornwallis, 318.
Corry, 663, 664, 665.
Coryell, 451.
Coulter, 368, 375, 385, 745, 769.
Countryman, 171.
Courtney, 745.
Cowan, 89, 654, 662, 765.
COWDEN, 115, 117, 143–147, 211, 695, 696, 698.
Cowdrey, 277.
Cowgill, 329.
Cox, 2, 57, 60, 166, 191, 196, 239, 247, 420, 426, 564, 655.
Coyle, 207, 583.
Cozzens, 203.
Crabb, 350–353.
Craft, 511.
CRAIN, 1, 2, 11, 34, 63, 148–155, 214, 365, 583, 613, 617, 635, 640, 697.

CRAIG, 66, 114, 149, 265, 328, 541–555, 679, 680, 740, 742, 748, 746, 753.
Craighead, 204, 210, 238, 420, 737.
Cramer, 433, 437, 650.
Cranage, 683.
Crandle, 696, 699.
Crane, 235.
Crangle, 84.
Craven, 171, 182.
Craver, 346.
Crawford, 28, 373, 613, 712, 766.
Creigh, 585, 594–604.
Cresap, 117.
Cresswell, 128, 750.
Creveling, 524.
Crist, 682.
Criswell, 56, 58, 467, 484, 711, 714, 732, 748.
Crittenden, 221, 579.
Crockett, 442.
Croll, 348, 350, 355.
Crolby, 397.
Cromwell, 348.
Crooks, 457.
Crosby, 63, 66, 511, 617, 701.
Crosman, 434.
Cross, 498, 500.
Crossan, 551.
Crouch, 143, 145.
Crow, 458.
Crowell, 611.
Crozier, 152, 655.
Crull, 182.
Cruse, 276.
Cryder, 136.
Culbertson, 281, 380, 409, 410, 420, 421, 423, 518, 520.
Cullen, 96.
Culp, 306.

Culver, 479.
Cummings, 146, 464.
Cummins, 714, 716.
Cunningham, 386, 445, 455, 463, 540.
Curll, 425.
CURTIN, 289-302, 338, 367, 377, 394, 438, 754, 763.
Curtis, 443, 452.
Curry, 63, 532.
Curwen, 244.
Custer, 726.
Cutter, 759.
Cuvier, 217.
Cyrens, 515.

Daily, 446.
Dale, 417, 426.
Dallas, 117, 588, 646, 647, 662.
Dangler, 241.
Darby, 156, 533.
Darsie, 500.
Davenport, 284, 287, 715.
Davidson, 83, 92, 212, 218, 380, 453, 528, 586, 590, 616, 630, 631, 751, 752.
Davies, 750.
Davis, 102, 154, 181, 282, 331, 453, 708, 749, 750, 752.
Davison, 553, 555, 629.
Davy, 347.
Dawson, 79, 81, 714.
Day, 338, 480.
Deacon, 94.
Dean, 151, 154, 155, 639.
Deaton, 173.
Decker, 275, 463, 482.
Deemer, 559.
Defrees, 205.
D'Hinayossa, 15, 16.

Deihl, 432.
Deininger, 686, 687.
Deitrick, 197, 310, 688.
De Joinville, 545.
De Lisle, 308.
Demming, 514.
Demuth, 344.
Denning, 361, 680.
Dennison, 25, 546, 593.
Denniston, 141, 390, 397.
DENNY, 385, 579-604.
Dentzel, 195.
Derby, 236, 256.
Derabery, 172.
De Reilhe, 489, 490.
Derrickson, 77, 397, 436.
Deshler, 99.
Detweiler, 621, 766.
De Villemont, 387.
Devling, 754.
Devoe, 169.
DeWitt, 56, 206, 225, 326, 369, 423, 429-431, 623.
Deyarmond, 231.
Dick, 99, 100, 160.
Dickey, 53, 246, 247, 637, 638.
Dickson, 65, 69, 409, 410, 663, 755.
Diehl, 689.
Dietterich, 748.
Dill, 150.
Diller, 120, 344.
Dinkle, 326.
Dishong, 445.
Dismukis, 173.
Disney, 96.
Divonne, 701.
DIXON, 7, 156-158, 224, 442, 450, 527, 533, 575, 769.
Dobson, 531, 535.
Dock, 352.

Doll, 199, 206, 207, 572, 722, 726.
Donald, 244.
Donaldson, 49, 73.
Donehower, 376.
Dorsey, 565.
Dorrance, 197.
Donovan, 152.
Doty, 371, 587, 597, 599, 616, 621.
Dougal, 465.
Dougherty, 184, 614.
Douglas, 23, 745, 762.
Douglass, 136, 201, 397, 519.
Dougleman, 388.
Downer, 96, 464.
Downey, 80, 84, 85, 619, 622.
Doyle, 590.
Drake, 369.
Dreisbach, 428.
Dressler, 465.
Driscol, 166.
Dry, 183.
Duane, 351.
Du Bac, 544.
DuBarry, 589.
DuBois, 11, 725.
Duchat, 397.
Duel, 741.
Duff, 74.
Duffield, 124, 189, 603, 606.
Dull, 484, 782.
Dumars, 9.
Dunardy, 172.
Dunawdry, 172.
Dunbar, 580, 585, 594.
Duncan, 44, 254, 280, 284, 285, 380, 554, 595, 710, 712, 713, 744.
Duncanson, 252.
Dungan, 747.
Dunlap, 770.

Index of Surnames. 781

Dunlop, 47, 320, 649, 653, 656.
Dunmore, 541.
Dunn, 5, 72, 340, 421.
Dunning, 488, 579.
Dunott, 311.
DuPlante, 389.
Durgan, 50.
Durkee, 285.
Dussinger, 107, 108.
Duvall, 207.
Duyckinck, 370.
Dye, 173.

Eager, 164.
Eagle, 159, 166.
EAGLEY, 767, 768.
Early, 348.
Eason, 451.
Easton, 68.
Eaton, 434.
Ebersole, 379.
Ebbs, 542.
Eberly, 586.
Ebert, 678, 686.
Eby, 766.
Eckels, 312.
Eddy, 516.
Eden, 90.
Edge, 50.
Edgar, 178, 417.
Edmeston, 319, 321, 424.
Edmonds, 516.
Edmonston, 40.
Edwards, 33, 35, 386, 596.
Ege, 276.
Eggert. 772, 773.
EGLE, 87, 159-186, 528, 564, 676.
Egli, 159, 767.
Ehrman, 499.
Eicholtz, 678, 688.
Eicke, 220.
Elam, 457.

ELDER, 21, 22, 37, 38, 70-73, 146, 147, 187-213, 247, 252, 257, 265, 275, 321, 322, 325, 506, 529, 531, 570, 629, 637, 639, 649, 654, 656, 662, 669, 694, 695, 698, 737, 769.
Eldridge, 236.
Eliot, 483.
Ellenberger, 499.
Elliott, 19, 113, 114, 299, 326, 395, 400, 447, 583, 653, 754, 772.
Ellis, 246, 329.
Ellmaker, 196.
Elson, 168.
Elton, 319.
Ely, 552, 620, 693.
Emerson, 115, 117, 164, 696.
Emery, 465.
Emmert, 93, 97.
Emminger, 112.
Engle, 722.
Engleheart, 449.
English, 684.
Ensley, 399.
Entriken. 58.
Eppler, 99.
Erb, 108, 110.
Ernst, 569, 723.
Eshercombe, 65, 67.
ESPY, 9. 103, 148, 191, 198, 214-227, 229, 246, 388, 635, 641, 769.
Etter, 109, 730.
Ettley, 108, 110.
Evans, 18, 19, 46, 293, 359, 360, 385, 489, 504, 595, 653.
Everhart, 298.
Everly, 726.

Ewalt, 449.
Ewing, 2, 4, 200, 214, 220, 374, 387, 421, 434, 711.
Eyre, 385, 390.
Eyster, 351, 352.

Faber, 692.
Fackler, 356.
Fager, 265-267.
Fahnestock, 704, 706, 707.
Faneuil, 551.
Fairfax, 541.
Falls, 769.
Faries, 403.
Farmer, 546.
Farragut, 180.
Fast, 507, 508, 514, 515, 516.
Fassett, 421.
Featherbee, 47.
Fechtig, 84, 93, 96.
Fell, 397, 749.
Felger, 495.
Felton, 172.
Fendrich, 138.
Fenwick, 154.
Fergus, 613.
FERGUSON, 170, 173, 212, 228-231, 331, 492, 493, 579, 580, 621, 696, 698.
Fetter, 500, 711.
Fessenden, 757.
Fickes, 420.
Fitchorn, 306.
Fields, 170.
Filbert, 283.
Fillmore, 550.
Finch, 164.
Finckle, 347, 349.
Findlay, 125, 243, 326, 420, 428, 529, 763.
Findley, 86.
Finlay, 79, 80.

Finney, 39, 65, 70, 230, 231, 402, 438, 509, 519, 520, 612, 646, 647, 650, 651, 670, 732.
Firth, 511, 521.
Fish, 179.
Fishburn, 347.
Fiske, 756.
Fisher, 25, 94, 168, 307, 393, 394, 433, 603, 613, 615.
Fitch, 757, 759.
Fitler, 700.
Fitzgerald, 659.
Fitzhugh, 370.
Flagg, 760.
Fleeson, 551.
FLEMING, 232 - 245, 321, 367, 372, 385, 579, 582, 583, 591, 624.
Fletcher, 185.
Flora, 107, 108.
Florettry, 488.
Flournoy, 276.
Foeser, 304.
Fought, 724.
Fogle, 121.
Folk, 93.
Foltz, 690.
Foot, 252.
Forbes, 107, 217, 411, 580, 581, 585, 605, 716.
Fordney, 344.
Foresman, 451.
Forgey, 657.
Forman, 390, 396.
Forney, 306, 311, 328.
Forrest, 423.
FORSTER, 24, 48, 52, 101, 149, 194, 209, 214, 222, 246 - 263, 290, 432, 451, 546, 754, 769.

Forsythe, 386.
Foster, 173, 230, 356, 372, 508, 591, 602, 633, 770.
Fournet, 216.
Foust, 419.
Fowler, 463, 476.
Fox, 167, 179, 564.
Francis, 759.
Francisco, 169.
Franciscus, 597.
Franklin, 685.
Franks, 67, 515.
Frantz, 304.
Frazer, 81, 88, 114, 327, 420, 570.
Frederick, 375.
Freed, 504.
Freeland, 439.
French, 45.
Frew, 659, 751.
Frick, 343.
Fritchey, 722.
Fritz, 436.
Frow, 322.
Fruit, 744.
Fry, 164, 224, 541.
Fulford, 278.
Fuller, 29, 666, 717, 749.
Fullerton, 443, 452, 751.
Fulqham, 660.
FULTON, 264-268, 449, 551, 553, 694.
Fuqua, 509, 517.
Furlow, 166, 172.
Furnas, 692.
Furr, 166, 172.

Gaby, 516.
Gabby, 443.
Gaddis, 511.
Gage, 235.
GALBRAITH, 5, 191, 197, 269-288, 374, 380, 671.
Gallagher, 652.
Gallaway, 629, 632.
Gallup, 509.
Galt, 639.
Galulia, 239.
Gamage, 757.
Gamble, 335.
Gans, 176.
Garrard, 315.
Gardiner, 116.
Gardner, 231, 235, 237, 751.
Garland, 27, 212.
Garlinger, 513.
Garlough, 663.
Garrigan, 348.
Garringer, 226.
Garrison, 490.
Gaston, 580.
Gates, 308.
Gause, 176.
Gearhart, 43.
Geary, 181, 434.
Geddes, 421.
Gehring, 719.
Geisey, 208.
Gemmill, 29.
Geissinger, 349.
George, 806.
Gerhard, 223.
Gerhart, 524.
Gerkey, 507, 513.
Gerred, 768.
Gerrett, 397.
Gerry, 266.
Gessell, 706.
Getz, 100.
Gheer, 676, 679.
Giberson, 199.
Gibson, 66, 81, 88, 89, 158, 276, 285, 286, 318, 335 - 337, 448, 584, 589, 696.
Giddings, 235.

Index of Surnames.

Giesman, 558.
Giffen, 449, 453, 465.
Gilbert, 235, 366, 405, 567, 717.
Gilchrist, 143, 145, 234, 240, 246, 668, 670.
Gill, 638.
Gillespie, 244, 272, 387.
Gilliard, 342, 358, 363.
Gilliland, 235, 400.
Gillmor, 146, 147, 211, 322, 694, 695, 698.
Gilmour, 751.
Gillum, 305.
Gilman, 535.
Gilmore, 84, 287, 415.
Gilroy, 578.
Gilson, 73.
Girard, 60.
Givin, 536.
Gladfelter, 687.
Glass, 447, 456, 457.
Glen, 232, 233.
Gleim, 428.
Gloninger, 84, 206, 495, 507–578, 723.
Glover, 164, 172.
Goble, 12.
Godshal, 322.
Goetz, 722.
Goldman, 719
Goldsborough, 180.
Good, 135, 675.
Goodhart, 327, 481.
Goodman, 181.
Goodrich, 170, 412.
Goodwin, 205.
Gordon, 92, 212, 276, 339, 417.
Gore, 73, 225, 428.
Gorgas, 313, 359.
Gotwalt, 686, 688.
Graffius, 537.
Graham, 40, 61, 63, 64, 68, 71, 228–231, 332, 371, 383, 386, 391,
393, 421, 467, 546, 580, 587, 694, 696, 698, 699.
Grant, 302, 485, 576, 700.
Gratiot, 491.
Graves, 621.
Gray, 218, 222, 550, 613, 629, 631, 657, 768–771.
Graybill, 75.
Graydon, 761.
Grayson, 585.
Green, 7, 8, 38, 39, 40, 131, 197, 276, 299, 529, 612, 623, 748, 758.
Greene, 714.
GREENAWALT, 303–314, 563.
Greenland, 538, 539.
Greenleaf, 287.
Greenlee, 410.
Greer, 80, 81, 84, 88, 152, 409.
GREGG, 38, 44, 45, 289–302, 367, 583, 593, 742.
Gregory, 339.
Gretter, 773.
Gridley, 170.
Grier, 700, 737, 766.
Griffen, 457, 655.
Griffin, 504.
Griffith, 189.
Grigsby, 463, 477, 622.
Griswold, 259.
Groff, 701.
Groh, 547.
GROSS, 181, 357, 358, 361, 685, 686, 705, 722–732, 771–773.
Grosman, 43.
Grossman, 305.
Grove, 75, 690, 732.
Grouf, 183.
Grubb, 596, 603.
Grunden, 617.
Guest, 161.
Guilford, 205, 206.
Gunnison, 672.
Gustine, 322, 580, 581, 586, 659.
Gutelius, 304.
Guthrie, 3, 768.
Gwin, 425.
Guyter, 445.

Haart, 306.
Hackenburg, 231.
Hackett, 364.
Haddock, 511, 699.
Hadsell, 516.
Hagenbach, 5.
Hager, 196, 598.
Hagan, 720.
Haight, 95.
Haines, 5, 750.
Hale, 744.
Halfman, 345.
Haldeman, 165, 172.
Hall, 253, 263, 277, 414, 423, 424, 433–439, 448, 462, 746.
Haller, 104.
Halliburton, 167.
Halliday, 80, 87, 467.
Halloday, 173.
Halsey, 220.
Hamill, 4, 396, 402, 403.
Hamlin, 234, 244.
HAMILTON, 18, 21, 66, 114, 150, 253, 315–333, 337, 368, 408, 432, 444, 463, 480, 527, 550, 552, 582, 589, 599, 649, 653, 751.
Hammond, 443, 451, 476, 562, 568, 572, 678, 680, 681, 684.

Hancock, 132, 756, 757.
Hand, 389.
Handshue, 344.
Hanna, 81, 89, 195, 247, 251.
Hannis, 94.
Hansell, 506, 507.
Hanson, 371, 467.
Harbaugh, 379, 686.
Harbert, 330, 332.
Harbine, 723.
Harbison, 457, 629,632.
Harding, 226, 300, 589, 590.
Hardy, 445.
Harkness, 56, 131, 132, 204, 615.
Harkley, 344.
Harlan, 58.
Harmar, 587.
Harnly, 524.
Harper, 344, 712.
Harrington, 119.
Harris, 29, 43, 196, 207, 249, 300, 383, 388, 395, 409, 413, 414, 416, 424, 528.
Harrison, 69, 74, 149, 230, 299, 446, 715.
Hart, 182, 332, 688.
Hartley, 733.
Hartman, 363.
Harton, 232, 234.
Hartranft, 314.
Hartzel, 678, 688.
Harvey, 134, 746.
Harwood, 192.
Hassal, 346.
Hassinger, 562, 566.
Hasson, 513, 720.
Hastings, 378, 451, 593, 760.
Hatch, 152.
Hatfield, 48, 126, 136, 662.
Hatton, 67, 146.

Hauer, 307.
Haupt, 346, 348, 349.
Hautz, 162, 678.
Haviland, 464.
Hawk, 322, 677.
Hawkins, 551, 751.
Hawksworth, 537.
HAYS, 19, 191, 250, 259, 262, 275, 280, 324, 330, 334 – 340, 347, 451, 584, 703, 740, 743, 746, 770, 771.
HAY, 168, 582,· 612.
Hayes, 57, 59, 245, 394, 487, 539, 745, 746.
Header, 136.
Heaton, 49.
Heck, 445.
Heilig, 162, 165.
Heilman, 499.
Heinitsh, 343.
Heisely, 341, 344.
Helfenstein, 724.
Heller, 748.
Hemphill, 420, 445, 745, 750.
Henderson, 24, 119, 230, 416, 427, 587, 597, 598, 612, 717, 734, 735.
Hendricks, 389.
Hendrickson, 356.
Henner, 497.
Henning, 678.
Henricle, 381.
Henry, 158, 322, 389, 449, 456, 559, 671, 741, 761.
Hensel, 346.
Heppich, 108, 109.
Herbein, 99.
Herman, 59.
Hermes, 682.
Herron, 249, 410, 419.
Heron, 251, 673.

Herr, 358, 366, 499, 728.
Herndon, 615, 619.
Hershey, 118, 693.
Herschel, 217.
Hetrick, 304, 306.
Heymer, 71.
Hicks, 54, 691.
Hiester, 55, 195, 257, 294, 295, 302, 353.
Higgins, 570.
Hildreth, 412.
Hill, 80, 83, 85, 91, 92, 96, 225, 280, 350, 457, 759.
Hillman, 752.
Hilton, 620, 630.
Himes, 601, 602.
Hindsworth, 518.
Hines, 164, 168.
Hinny, 356.
Hipsley, 239.
Hirst, 730.
Hiser, 8.
Hite, 516.
Hitt, 455.
Hitner, 390.
Hoch, 123, 124.
Hodgson, 96, 176.
Hoff, 283, 344.
Hoffer, 310, 691.
Hoffheins, 686.
Hoffman, 531, 535.
Hoffmeier, 689.
Hoffrath, 720.
HOGE, 320, 387, 708–718, 737.
Hogg, 82, 434.
Holcombe, 141.
Holden, 299.
Holihan, 164.
Holland, 56.
Hollenback, 197, 227.
Holliday, 19, 281.
Hollingshead, 6.
Hollingsworth, 67.

Index of Surnames.   785

Hollock, 387.
Hollister, 2, 4.
Holloway, 474.
Holmes, 177, 205, 391, 416, 425, 492, 651.
Holzworth, 845.
Homan, 515.
Hood, 87, 680, 681.
Hooker, 288.
Hoover, 597, 683, 689, 729.
Hopkins, 134, 516.
Horner, 129, 236, 746, 747.
Horst, 719.
Horning, 41, 52.
Hortter, 124, 125.
Hosack, 565.
Hosier, 638.
Hoskinson, 77, 672.
Hosmer, 252.
Hostetter, 675.
Hotz, 499.
Hough, 125, 127.
Householder, 326.
Houseman, 80, 84.
Houser, 257, 351, 352.
Housser, 772.
Houston, 594.
Houtz, 126, 134.
Howard, 324.
Howe, 318.
Hoyer, 357.
Hoyt, 208.
Hubbard, 331, 616, 621.
Hubbell, 309, 369.
Huber, 690.
Hubley, 345, 396, 559, 686.
Huddlestone, 168.
Hudson, 770.
Huff, 511, 523.
Hughes, 57, 67, 658, 665, 666.
Huggins, 235, 236.

Huling, 2, 3, 218, 222, 272, 275.
Humbert, 45.
Hume, 69, 708.
Humes, 770.
Hummel, 70, 126, 137, 138, 267, 306, 347, 357, 358.
Humrich, 590.
Hunt, 4, 75, 231, 281, 286, 344, 350, 363, 483, 487, 551.
Hunter, 49, 91, 96, 509, 512, 513, 518, 572, 595.
Huntsberger, 640.
Hurley, 203.
Hursh, 750.
Hussey, 471, 472.
Huston, 23, 57, 594, 764.
Hutchinson, 631, 634, 635, 643, 697, 734, 769, 770.
Huyett, 536.
Hyndman, 32.

Imboden, 497, 498, 499.
Imbrie, 746.
Imes, 515.
Immel, 766.
Ingraham, 237.
Ingram, 100, 101, 200, 670, 671.
Inman, 220, 224.
Innis, 40, 529.
Irons, 653.
Irvin, 135, 142, 295, 296, 297, 298, 301, 744.
Irvine, 24, 88, 276, 284, 285, 379, 448, 449, 548, 549, 583, 709, 744, 749.
Irwin, 54, 79, 80, 131, 132, 263, 409, 410,
414, 417, 419, 422, 424, 456, 482, 506, 604, 629, 692, 693, 737, 747.
Isenberg, 416.
Isett, 125, 126, 130.
Ives, 170, 756.
Ivory, 286.

Jack, 448.
Jackson, 174, 224, 232, 248, 262, 345, 386, 664, 701.
Jacob, 587, 596.
Jacobs, 104, 663.
Jacobus, 233, 236, 596, 603.
Jacoby, 126, 137, 656, 663, 664.
Jeager, 356.
James, 748.
Jameson, 668.
Janney, 685.
Jarrett, 132, 209.
Jarvis, 457, 759, 760.
Jefferis, 20.
Jeffers, 616.
Jefferson, 81, 89, 248, 377, 412, 413, 541, 550.
Jeffrey, 766.
Jenkins, 2, 259, 421, 507.
Jennings, 100, 103–106, 661, 672.
Jewett, 478.
John, 56.
Johnson, 21, 25, 26, 67, 72, 125, 131, 148, 256, 355, 408, 455, 554, 619, 621, 668, 706, 725.
Johnston, 57, 58, 63, 66, 67, 267, 373, 394, 400, 417, 426, 427, 749.

Jones, 33, 36, 56, 176, 179–182, 185, 191, 197, 266, 620, 656, 691, 748.
Jordan, 145, 146, 434.
Jorden, 578.
Jourdan. 511, 523.
Jumper, 511, 522.
Junkin, 151, 154, 337, 619.

Kane, 75.
Karg, 241.
Kator, 662.
Kauffman, 341, 344, 345, 766.
Kays, 345.
Kean, 47, 48, 257, 320.
Kearney, 418.
Kearsley, 218.
Keeling, 177, 539.
Keen, 253.
Keene, 192, 216.
Keeso, 369, 370.
Keet, 359.
Keifer, 152.
Keiffer, 663.
Keim, 353, 354.
Keith, 290.
Kelker, 86, 176, 304, 305.
KELLER, 115, 117, 336, 337, 341–349, 358, 557.
Kellog, 262.
Kellogg, 405.
Kelly, 29, 30, 246, 247, 393, 404, 659, 712, 715.
Kelso, 276, 381, 752.
Kelsey, 256.
Kelton, 265.
Kemp, 82.
Kemper. 452.
Kenaga, 666.
Kendall, 493, 518, 759.

KENDIG, 110, 350–356, 512, 635.
Kennedy, 33, 36, 90, 390, 403, 550, 595, 766.
Kenner, 273.
Kepler, 136.
Kern, 749.
Kerr, 21, 22, 167, 178, 331, 485, 546, 564, 573, 575, 663, 766.
Ketchum, 438.
Kettlehume, 96.
Key, 679.
Keys, 143, 585.
Kibby, 215.
Kidd, 260.
Kidner, 169.
Kidwell, 546.
Kieffer, 268, 375, 690.
Kilgore, 83, 85, 92.
Killian, 499.
Killinger, 497, 568.
Killough, 345.
Kimball, 262, 652, 659.
Kimmell, 236, 379, 498.
Kincaid. 4, 31.
King, 111, 173, 359, 366, 394, 420, 436, 517, 527, 565, 703, 705, 729.
Kinney, 296, 514, 754.
Kinsloe, 30.
Kirby. 6, 482.
Kirk, 257.
Kirkpatrick, 166, 198, 214, 218, 299, 542, 594.
Kirkwood, 313, 418.
Kissel, 305.
Kister, 693.
Kleber, 497.
Kline, 762.
Kling, 341, 345.
Kloss, 322, 327.
Kluge, 559.

Klump, 343.
Knapp, 205.
Knauff, 346.
Knisely, 268.
Kniffin, 516.
Knight, 469, 597.
Knox, 149, 680.
Koch, 687.
Kochler, 374.
Kolbmar, 121.
Kolp, 111.
Kohrbaus, 120.
Koons, 766.
Kouns, 547.
Krause, 99, 100, 102–104, 304, 307, 557, 562–570.
Kreider, 344, 499.
Kremer, 422.
Krider, 10, 12.
Kring, 167.
Krone, 693.
Krumbach, 698.
Kucher, 556–558.
Kuhn, 275.
Kuhne, 84.
Kumbel, 157, 450, 463.
KUNKEL, 96, 110, 119, 130, 133, 140, 224, 267, 342, 347, 357–366, 640, 726, 731, 738.
Kurtz, 341, 345, 727.
Kyle, 449.

Lacey, 84.
Lachin, 668.
Lafayette, 543.
Laird, 67, 86, 200, 250, 257, 446, 447, 456.
Lamb, 418.
Lamberson, 205.
Lamberton, 338.
Lambe, 737.
Lancaster, 311.

Index of Surnames. 787

Landis, 133, 141, 355, 689, 766.
Landon, 493.
Lane, 283, 284.
Lang, 293.
Langworthy, 400.
Lape, 226.
LaPorte, 404.
Larimer, 299, 592.
Larner, 347.
Larrobee, 350, 354.
Lashells, 262, 340, 417, 425, 428.
LaSourd, 664.
Latimer, 746.
Lattimore, 742.
Latta, 529, 749.
Latshaw, 678, 689, 690.
Laub, 307, 312.
Lauer, 160.
Lauman, 348, 353, 361.
Laurie, 772.
Laverty, 363.
Law, 247, 251, 252, 254, 262.
Lawrence, 125, 128, 131, 253, 281, 597.
Lawson, 608, 696.
Lawton, 56.
Lazear, 390, 398.
Lazenby, 183.
Leach, 334, 335, 635.
Leachman, 119.
Leacock, 177.
Leaming, 747.
Leary, 509, 518.
Leason, 752.
Leasure, 498.
Leckey, 605, 606.
Leddick, 235.
Lee, 239, 260, 268.
Leech, 348, 615.
Leeper, 274.
Leet, 77.
Lefevre, 771.
Lehman, 275.

Lehr, 676.
Leib, 295.
Leiby, 348.
Leisenring, 494.
Leitch, 334.
Leman, 616.
Lemon, 13, 617.
Lemmon, 305.
Leonard, 235.
LeRoux, 328.
Lesesne, 431.
Lesher, 60.
Lester, 5, 354.
Levan, 99, 101.
Lewis, 327, 362, 482, 608, 610, 663, 728, 754, 761.
Lichtenwalter, 621.
Lick, 495.
Liddell, 657.
Liebendorfer, 745.
Light, 3, 558, 565, 567.
Liller, 512.
Lincoln, 174, 261, 393, 403, 430, 436, 486.
Lindsey, 335, 585, 586.
Line, 199, 204, 207, 224, 226.
Lindley, 526, 527, 531.
Lineaweaver, 563, 567.
Linford, 532.
LINN, 367–382, 410, 418, 537, 609, 653, 661, 737, 750.
List, 258.
Little, 335.
Littleton, 702.
Livingston, 536, 620.
Lloyd, 332.
Lobaugh, 679, 691, 692, 693.
Lobdell, 138.
LOBINGIER, 495, 498–504.
Lochman, 86, 167, 342.
Lochrane, 386.

Lockhart, 257.
Lockridge, 511, 521.
Lockwood, 843.
Loesicke, 720.
Logan, 127, 400, 447, 456, 613, 614, 615, 746, 766.
Loire, 239.
Lombaert, 438.
Long, 162, 166, 172, 260, 596, 698, 748.
Loomis, 296, 617.
Loose, 726.
Lossing, 290.
Loster, 172.
Lott, 655, 660.
Loucks, 360.
Loudon, 441, 448–450.
Loughey, 43.
Louthan, 746.
Love, 256, 554, 671, 672, 743.
Lowden, 299.
Lowdermilch, 156.
Lowe, 511.
Lower, 568.
Lowrey, 18, 19, 653, 654.
Lowrie, 135, 396, 401, 402, 594.
Lowry, 397.
Ludlow, 11, 315, 331.
Lueder, 226.
Lucas, 2.
Lukens, 49.
Lusk, 570.
Luther, 266, 744.
Lutz, 70, 120, 166, 678.
Lybarger, 768.
LYON, 56, 58, 133, 280, 318, 383–407, 414, 423, 424, 436, 437, 583, 592, 650, 652, 658, 710.
Lytle, 40, 51, 262, 617, 621.

Mace, 746.
Mackey, 63, 64, 65.
Madison, 248.
Magee, 547.
Magoffin, 618.
Magraw, 101.
Maguire, 650, 714, 733.
Mahany, 704, 707.
Mahargue, 9.
Mahon, 420, 595.
Mains, 381.
Mäkel, 719.
Mallery, 424, 434, 435, 436.
Mallory, 656.
Maltby, 226.
Maloney, 396, 405.
Mankin, 158.
Mann, 7, 681.
Manning, 51, 95.
Mannon, 305.
Mansell, 615, 619.
Mansfield, 346.
Manus, 102.
Marchand, 501.
March, 212.
Marks, 375, 597.
Maris, 132, 139, 140.
Markle, 500.
Markwell, 768.
Marquis, 66.
Marr, 49, 298.
Marshall, 12, 192, 201, 566, 567, 656, 663, 665.
Martin, 140, 158, 165, 183, 383, 385, 446, 513, 596, 599, 612, 613, 619, 626, 657, 700.
Martyr, 446.
Marvin, 521.
Mason, 303, 312, 387.
Matlack, 111.
Mateer, 594, 595, 613.
Matthews, 81, 89, 231, 236.

Matthewson, 664.
Maul, 552.
Maulfair, 622.
Maust, 520.
Mawhiney, 89.
Maxwell, 244, 690, 764.
May, 768.
Mayee, 418.
Mayes, 1, 9, 526, 529, 629, 630, 631, 635, 636.
Mazurie, 60.
Mead, 339, 419.
Meader, 631, 634.
Means, 393.
Mears, 168.
Medill, 478.
Meehan, 445.
Mehara, 751.
Mehard, 752.
Meister, 305.
Meiden, 720.
Meminger, 657.
Menauh, 643.
Mentges, 160, 161.
Mentrenger, 121, 122.
Mentzer, 676.
Mercer, 237, 411.
Merchant, 674.
Meredith, 39, 613.
Merriman, 72.
Mesick, 94, 732.
Messemer, 721.
Metcalf, 77.
Meteer, 291.
Metzgar, 280.
Mewer, 186.
Meyers, 224, 539.
Meyer, 283.
Meyrick, 735.
Michener, 748.
Middlecoff, 351, 352.
Middleton, 111.
Mifflin, 39, 84, 384, 529, 538, 561.
Miles, 148, 375, 529, 603, 712.

Miller, 152, 224, 225, 276, 305, 306, 312, 345, 428, 433, 437, 451, 523, 535, 564, 577, 582, 583, 603, 675, 676, 688, 698, 716, 743, 746, 752.
Milligan, 394.
Milliken, 133, 141.
Millman, 12.
Mills, 467, 503.
Miltenberger, 649, 657.
Miner, 25, 190.
Minor, 434.
Mish, 115, 118, 567, 568.
Minsker, 721.
Minster, 366.
Minton, 488.
Mitchel, 319, 585.
Mitchell, 69, 74, 96, 216, 217, 295, 298, 299, 314, 317, 353, 449, 530, 622, 671, 673, 700, 730.
Mitchelson, 399.
Mitten, 2.
Moffitt, 574.
Monahan, 223.
Monroe, 184.
Montgomery, 48, 51, 127, 133, 215, 247, 291, 294, 342, 364, 453, 464, 518, 678, 682.
Moody, 278.
Moon, 253.
Moorbach, 122.
Moore, 60, 90, 114, 133, 142, 148, 149, 207, 246, 247-250, 307, 330, 336, 337, 371, 456, 583, 646, 647.
Moorhead, 8, 63, 66, 72, 76, 77, 89, 613, 617, 673.
Mordah, 627, 628.

Index of Surnames. 789

More, 235, 237.
Morehead, 221.
Morford, 370.
Morgan, 378, 396, 543, 545, 546, 590, 597.
Morman, 698.
Morrett, 163, 168, 558, 564.
Morris, 275, 346, 406, 412, 744.
Morrison, 40, 67, 73, 210, 444, 745.
Morrow, 373, 697.
Morse, 618.
Morsell, 389.
Morton, 72, 152, 459, 712, 751.
Mosher, 120.
Mossgrove, 92.
Mossier, 493.
Mott, 536.
Motter, 110, 364.
Mount, 350.
Mowry, 201, 234, 243, 748.
Moyer, 227, 498, 499, 750, 754, 771.
Muhlenberg, 45, 302, 306, 495.
Mulford, 155.
Mulhallon, 741.
Mulholland, 152, 390, 397.
Mullen, 359.
Mullet, 258.
MÜLLER, 120, 162, 310, 495–504, 675, 676.
Mullikin, 281.
Mummert, 686.
Munroe, 757.
Murdoch, 401.
Murdock, 215, 221.
Mureamer, 724.
Murphy, 118, 239, 372, 428, 436, 621.
MURRAY, 40, 80, 200, 251, 275, 281, 282, 354, 372, 450, 505–540, 581, 583, 590, 591, 600, 601, 602, 699.
Musgrave, 485.
Musselman, 127.
Musser, 681.
Muzio, 253.
Myer, 571.
Myers, 97, 163, 204, 353, 359.
Mytinger, 124, 125, 134.

McAllen, 31, 33.
McAlister, 318, 324, 398, 593.
McAllister, 191, 193, 215, 229, 532, 538.
McArthur, 766.
McAteer, 135.
McBay, 770.
McBeth, 372.
McCain, 286, 287.
McCallum, 163.
McCalmont, 372, 373.
McCammon, 194.
McCandless, 539, 751, 752.
McCandlish, 454.
McCarrell, 234, 245, 275.
McCartney, 456.
McCauley, 91, 208.
McCherry, 353.
McChesney, 264, 694.
McClain, 245, 272.
McClave, 628.
McClay, 646.
McCleary, 465, 595, 612.
McClellan, 24, 273, 281, 616.
McClelland, 271, 378, 424, 448, 458.
McClenaghan, 215, 229.
McClintock, 8, 625.
McClone, 345.
McCloy, 79, 82, 90.
McClung, 286, 654.
McClure, 67, 69, 71, 79, 80, 145, 148, 200, 214, 218, 219, 222, 243, 286, 309, 393, 414, 438, 441, 444, 579, 584, 597, 637, 696, 698, 746.
McClurg, 233, 237.
McCombs, 82, 233, 238.
McConaughey, 503.
McConnell, 48, 199, 209, 232, 234, 236, 244, 585, 614, 618.
McCook, 351.
McCord, 493, 613, 615, 616, 619.
MCCORMICK, 8, 22, 33, 35, 81, 89, 118, 156, 157, 220, 262, 272, 279, 334, 365, 368, 418, 440–487, 631,635, 710, 711.
McCosh, 113.
McCoskry, 584, 594.
McCoy, 221, 338, 581, 597, 653, 661.
McCracken, 71.
McCrea, 714.
McCreary, 671.
McCreerie, 594.
McCue, 345.
McCullogh, 399.
McCullough, 271, 273, 644, 662.
McCune, 409, 420.
McDonald, 115, 168, 250, 378, 408, 425.
McDonough, 429.
McDowell, 281, 322, 327, 471, 579.

McElfatrick, 109.
McElroy, 442.
McEnderfer, 681.
McEwen, 1, 2, 9, 10, 65, 67, 695, 697.
McFadden, 10, 178.
McFarlane, 323, 324, 448.
McFarland, 198, 255, 256, 350, 354.
McFarquhar, 22.
McFerran, 714.
McGaughey, 771.
McGiffin, 387.
McGinley, 419.
McGrath, 101.
McGrew, 179.
McGuire, 230, 441, 546.
McGuffy, 638, 667.
McHenry, 740, 741, 742, 747, 748, 749.
McIlhenny, 66, 661.
McIntire, 515.
McIntyre, 260, 643.
McKallip, 332, 432.
McKay, 244, 711.
McKean, 193, 321, 384.
McKeehan, 222.
McKee, 12, 78, 80, 81, 82, 88, 90, 200, 210, 286, 294, 652, 666.
McKeenan, 711.
McKeever, 535.
McKeig, 36.
McKelvy, 398.
McKenny, 456.
McKibbin, 553, 555.
McKinley, 192, 270, 763.
McKinney, 191, 199, 231, 515, 615, 655.
McKinstry, 479.
McKissack, 714.
McKnight, 264, 299, 401, 410, 421, 422, 441, 540, 589.

McLanahan, 295.
McLane, 329.
McLean, 260, 315, 319, 526, 528.
MacLaren, 623.
MACLAY, 38, 42, 323, 368, 390, 395, 408–439.
Maclean, 45, 325.
McMahon, 379.
McMath, 233, 236.
McMeen, 600.
McMichael, 447.
McMicken, 252.
McMillan, 66, 270.
McMillen, 666.
McMinn, 299.
McMordie, 32, 33.
McMullin, 84, 94.
McMurray, 117, 295.
McMurtrie, 296, 299, 354, 355.
MCNAIR, 117, 171, 182, 231, 488–494, 694, 740, 746, 747.
McNamara, 9, 11.
McNaughton, 379, 421.
McNealy, 172.
McNeill, 47, 48, 49, 269.
McNitt, 661.
McPherson, 393, 644, 716, 717, 718.
McReily, 310.
McRoberts, 668.
McQueen, 32.
McTeer, 265.
MacVeagh, 9, 169, 436.
McVey, 386.

Nagle, 466.
Nash, 574.
Naudain, 324, 327–329.
Nazor, 506, 512.
Neal, 4, 328.
Neely, 383.

Neil, 154, 444.
Nelson, 79, 81, 247, 614, 654, 682.
Nesbit, 192, 200, 201, 752, 770.
Nestsky, 719.
NEVILLE, 55, 541–555.
Nevin, 19, 422.
Newberry, 684.
Newell, 234, 239, 759.
Newman, 760.
Newmyer, 498.
Newson, 682.
Newton, 217, 542.
Nicholas, 331.
Nichols, 164, 240, 394, 419.
Nicholson, 656, 663, 664, 665.
Nicolls, 401, 407.
Neiwiler, 122.
Nimmo, 158.
Nintker, 168.
Nisbet, 453.
Nisley, 366, 767.
Nisonger, 448, 458.
Nixon, 355.
Noble, 200, 614.
Nolen, 100, 104.
Norris, 508, 516.
North, 252.
Norton, 346.
Noxon, 396.
Noyes, 522.
Nunemacher, 360.
Nunemaker, 514.
Nye, 341, 344.

Oakes, 451.
Oden, 93.
Ogden, 394, 535.
O'Hara, 548, 588.
Ohr, 204.
Older, 237.
Oldham, 185, 542, 543, 546.

Index of Surnames.

Oliver, 10, 386, 441, 443, 414, 454, 593, 711.
Olivier, 490.
Ollenroth, 719.
O'Neal, 94.
Onslow, 223.
Orbison, 724.
Ormsby, 543.
Orr, 114, 153, 398, 563, 569.
Orrick, 423.
ORTH, 22, 100, 168, 276, 556–578.
Orvis, 401, 407.
Orwig, 320.
Osman, 741.
Osterdyke, 720.
Oswald, 121.
Ott, 12, 123, 496.
Otto, 435, 573.
Overholt, 287.
Overmier, 493.
Owens, 261, 670.

Page, 35, 747.
Painter, 10, 451, 498, 500.
Palmer, 49, 170, 421, 438, 615, 743.
Pancoast, 46, 301, 511, 522.
Pardee, 405, 509, 518.
Pardon, 308.
Parham, 46.
Park, 282.
Parke, 629, 631, 633, 637, 770.
PARKER, 34, 172, 236, 327, 524, 579–604, 756.
Parkinson, 747.
Parkison, 692.
Parmentier, 60.
Parmer, 455.
Parr, 505.

Parry, 328.
Parsons, 363, 405, 661.
Parks, 18, 20, 238, 238.
Parthemore, 110.
Partridge, 174, 573.
Patterson, 62, 72, 101, 164, 187, 191, 233, 270, 278, 328, 335, 343, 368, 374, 378, 381, 386, 391, 392, 399, 417, 423, 424, 443, 450, 616, 646, 648, 652, 655, 679, 690, 718.
Patheal, 165.
Pattison, 128, 141, 175, 404.
Patton, 142, 212, 214, 229, 247, 321, 395, 425, 532, 536, 537, 703.
Paul, 519.
Paulding, 74, 75.
Pauli, 312.
Pawling, 635, 640.
Paxson, 53.
Paxton, 589.
Payne, 220.
Peacock, 104.
Pearson, 6.
Peebles, 442.
Peek, 523, 524.
Peeples, 31, 33.
Peifer, 307.
Peiper, 231.
Penn, 16, 411.
Penny, 438.
Percels, 236.
Percy, 70.
Perkins, 33, 35, 535, 673.
Perrine, 350, 521.
Perry, 133, 479.
Peters, 53, 54, 370, 371, 507, 514.
Pettigrew, 735.

Pevee, 446.
Phelps, 516.
Philips, 230.
Phillips, 544.
Phillipe, 136, 137, 142, 404, 514, 603.
Piatt, 451, 748.
Pierce, 746.
Pierepont, 297.
Pietrochen, 720.
Pifer, 682.
Pilsbury, 464, 483.
Piper, 199, 202, 564, 570, 571.
Pires, 739.
Pitt, 25.
Pixley, 515.
Platt, 624.
Plitt, 342, 347.
Plumer, 19, 654.
Plummer, 481, 510, 521, 522.
Plunket, 409, 416.
Poe, 589.
Poffenberger, 726.
Polk, 329.
Pollard, 217, 223.
Pollock, 5, 66, 73, 139, 281, 299, 378, 379, 380, 382, 429, 590.
Pomeroy, 419.
Pontius, 753.
Pool, 125, 127, 304, 306.
Poor, 234, 241.
Poorman, 305.
Pope, 542, 619.
Porcher, 142.
Pore, 678, 681, 682.
Porter, 44, 104, 126, 133, 140, 141, 346, 358, 396, 402, 403, 404, 510, 520, 567, 572, 669.
Posey, 94.
Postlethwaite, 280.
Potter, 145, 294, 295, 316, 749.

Potts, 94, 115, 116.
Pouillet, 217.
Pourtell, 713.
Powell, 94, 216.
Power, 321.
Powers, 517.
Pownall, 541.
Poyer, 572.
Pratt, 169.
Prentice, 756, 757.
Pressler, 11.
Preston, 205, 220, 332, 569.
Prewett, 448.
Price, 5, 518, 554, 569, 618.
Prince, 32.
Proctor, 359, 548.
Proud, 376.
Proudfit, 381, 429.
Prudden, 236.
Pugh, 398, 680.
Purdy, 748.
Pursel, 44.
Purviance, 54, 424.
Pusey, 378.
Putnam, 531.
Pyre, 123.

Quail, 710, 711.
Query, 408, 417.
Quigley. 441, 714.
Quinn, 585.

Radford, 750.
Rainey, 615.
Rahm, 557, 559, 563, 564, 765, 766.
Raley, 448.
Ralston, 50, 54, 237, 286, 506, 509, 519, 520, 585, 742, 748.
Ramsey, 3, 5, 228, 281, 309, 532, 538, 607, 613, 692.
Randall, 510.

Randolph, 541, 583, 639.
Rankin, 442, 614, 711, 712.
Rapiere, 500.
Rapp, 99.
Ratcliffe, 614.
Rathbone, 249.
Rauhauser, 726.
Raush, 168.
Ray, 126, 459.
Raymond, 626.
Rea, 409.
Read, 151, 364, 546.
Ream, 681.
Record, 295.
Redfield, 217.
Redick, 709.
Redsecker, 347, 363, 625.
Reece, 5.
Reed, 39, 48, 50, 129, 164, 245, 248, 250, 251, 387, 397, 423, 432, 574, 643, 648, 652, 759.
Reeder, 152.
Reel, 102, 361, 678, 685.
Reehm, 303.
Reemer, 593.
Reese, 283, 507, 513.
Reeves, 196, 523, 692.
Regenaus, 344.
Reid, 457.
Reifsnyder, 511.
Reigard, 495–497.
Reigart, 275.
Reily, 103, 164, 207, 208, 355, 564, 571–573.
Reimsnyder, 360.
Reinhart, 400.
Reinke, 576.
Reist, 108, 109.
Reitzell, 83.
Remington, 314.

Renick, 273, 669, 670.
Renner, 691.
Renninger, 641, 676, 677.
Rex, 53, 516, 730.
Reyburn, 152.
Reynders, 141.
Reynolds, 93, 116, 195, 242, 256, 262, 297, 390, 397, 410, 417, 422, 464, 651.
Rhoads, 640.
Rhodes, 751.
Rice, 355, 429, 565, 650.
Richards, 4, 199, 208, 209, 295.
Richardson, 425.
Richert, 682.
Richie, 405.
Richmond, 47, 243.
Ricketts, 203, 467.
Ridgway, 170, 509, 519.
Riddle, 7, 9, 75, 444.
Rife, 110, 111, 362, 688.
Righter, 494.
Ring, 536.
Ringland. 109–111, 355.
Ringwalt, 325.
Rion, 704.
Riston, 130.
Ritchey, 148, 150, 151, 199, 204, 230.
Ritchie, 592.
Ritner, 44, 427, 571, 705.
Ritscher, 726.
Rittenhouse, 737.
Roades, 771, 772.
ROAN, 7, 62, 118, 189, 605–610.
Robb, 537.
Roberdeau, 452.
Roberts, 241, 249, 286, 326, 393, 399, 552, 570, 625.
Robertson, 378, 621, 697.

Index of Surnames.

ROBINSON, 19, 39, 53, 70, 76, 86, 148, 158, 165, 184, 185, 187, 192, 199, 244, 375, 429, 457, 520, 584, 593, 611-626, 647, 650, 656, 659, 660, 769, 770.
Robison, 137.
Rochambeau, 544.
Rock, 34.
Rockefeller, 287, 476.
Rockwell, 251.
Rodenberger, 108.
Rodgers, 375, 648.
Roe, 508.
Roehmer, 556.
Rogers, 4, 8, 68, 114, 229, 230, 235, 312, 448, 458, 459, 486, 528, 672, 698.
Rohrbach, 44.
Roland, 288.
Roller, 13.
Roop, 767.
Roper, 590, 752.
Rorabaugh, 681.
Rose, 53, 548.
Rosebrugh, 747.
Rosecranz, 339.
Ross, 111, 138, 208, 358, 362, 393, 399, 447, 576, 622, 625, 626, 724, 729.
Rossiter, 346.
Rotharmel, 306.
Roumfort, 361.
Rowan, 180, 606.
Rowe, 169.
Rowland, 188.
Rowson, 118.
Royse, 226.
Rudy, 94.
Rumbaugh, 673.
Runck, 350.
Rundle, 256.

Ruprecht, 719.
Rush, 250, 295.
Russell, 200, 210, 388, 393, 530, 768.
RUTHERFORD, 79, 81, 151, 211, 222, 223, 350, 356, 358, 365, 627-644, 670, 769, 770.
Ryan, 696, 726, 773.
Ryenearson, 245.
Ryschacker, 121.

Sage, 165, 300, 367, 377.
Saddler, 507, 514, 523.
Sadtler, 347.
Sahler, 725.
Salvage, 507.
Sample, 443, 453, 658, 666.
Sanders, 184, 525.
Sanderson, 441, 447, 448.
Sanford, 131.
Sankey, 629.
Saurman, 59.
Sausser, 241.
Savage, 385, 391.
Sawyer, 7, 9, 10, 148, 150.
Scheaffer, 337, 341-347.
Schee, 328, 329.
Scheffer, 103.
Schell, 502, 657.
Schindel, 179.
Schmidt, 167.
Schmucker, 720.
Schneider, 282.
Schofield, 380.
Scholl, 644.
Schoolcraft, 592.
Schooley, 451.
Schoonover, 226.
Schrack, 750.
Schram, 345.

Schreiner, 109.
Schriver, 687.
Schroover, 201.
Scott, 56, 59, 82, 96, 126, 127, 128, 135, 136, 197, 272, 274, 291, 294, 608, 609, 627, 710.
Scriven, 370.
Scudder, 616.
Sebaugh, 350, 355.
Seal, 680.
Seaman, 173.
Sears, 692.
Searles, 2.
Seegrist, 497.
Seibert, 346, 358, 564.
Seiler, 100, 101, 176, 208.
Seiple, 772, 773.
Sellers, 560, 656.
Selzer, 342.
Semple, 91, 387, 697, 701, 702, 769.
Sergeant, 223.
Serviss, 152, 379.
Sener, 848.
Setzer, 494.
Sevier, 607.
Sewalt, 362.
Seymour, 369.
Shaeffer, 117.
Shaffer, 69.
Shaffner, 304, 557.
Shaler, 542.
Shallenberger, 502.
Shandy, 172, 183.
Shank, 256.
Shannon, 457.
Sharon, 204, 318, 395, 441.
Sharp, 222, 456, 741, 765.
Sharpe, 244, 343, 420, 610.
Shatzer, 305.

Pennsylvania Genealogies.

Shaw, 3, 4, 129, 445, 456, 464.
Sheaff, 299, 302,
Sheaffer, 109, 497.
Sheetz, 52.
Shelby, 457, 458.
Sheldon, 168, 297, 320.
Shelly, 34, 111, 350, 355.
Shelmire, 50.
Shepard, 756, 757.
Sherer, 65, 68, 70, 71, 199, 200, 209, 210, 212, 370, 632, 648, 651.
Sherk, 512, 688, 729.
Sherman, 220, 486, 700.
Shesser, 459.
Sherwood, 616.
Shields, 72, 83, 91, 463, 478, 479, 551, 668, 669.
Shiley, 722.
Shippen, 197.
Shipley, 234, 244.
Shipps, 52.
Shira, 69, 75.
Shively, 756.
Shocknessy.
Shoát, 166.
Shobe, 663.
Shoe, 517.
Shoemaker, 361.
Shoop, 288.
Shorb, 402, 437, 652, 658.
Shotwell, 572.
Shrom, 80, 86, 176, 583, 616.
Shrombaugh, 675.
Shuart, 236.
Shugert, 26, 661.
Shultz, 326, 632, 636.
Shultze, 122.
Shulze, 55, 243, 294, 326, 352, 567, 569.

Shunk, 285, 297, 433.
Shupe, 73.
Sidener, 688.
Sidney-Taylor, 46.
Sidesinger, 418.
Sigler, 178.
Sigmund, 263.
Silvers, 74.
Simcox, 109.
Simison, 581, 590.
Simms, 546.
Simmers, 684.
Simmons, 155, 443, 451.
Simons, 170, 252.
Simpson, 187, 191, 216, 320, 517, 528, 531, 532 – 539, 676, 695.
SIMONTON, 358, 366, 717, 733–739.
Sinclair, 92.
Siney, 379.
Sisson, 374.
Skerrett, 45.
Skyles, 613.
Slack, 690.
Slagle, 351, 352, 686.
Slaughter, 33.
Slauson, 235.
Slaymaker, 265, 268, 333, 553, 718.
Sloan, 118, 450.
Slocum, 621.
Slote, 453, 465.
Sly, 590.
Small, 326, 358, 766.
Smallwood, 128, 249.
Smaltz, 310.
Smead, 281.
Smethers, 94.
Smith, 7, 12, 20, 51, 56, 58, 59, 102, 110, 112, 119, 156, 157, 163, 167, 169, 178, 189, 192, 200, 209, 211, 232, 234, 235, 270,

294, 298, 312, 322, 332, 348, 361, 368, 378, 400, 406, 417, 421, 449, 478, 499, 500, 503, 508, 510, 515, 519, 557, 567, 586, 593, 603, 626, 654, 675, 699, 730, 749, 759, 768.
Smock, 171.
Smyser, 276, 686.
Smythe, 226, 331.
Snethen, 95.
Snoddy, 612.
Snodgrass, 1, 2, 7, 9, 65, 71, 72, 76, 322, 410, 421, 650, 734, 735–739.
Snook, 683.
Snow, 328.
Snowden, 21, 29, 57, 84, 423, 449, 586, 680.
Snurr, 511.
Snyder, 59, 100, 125, 135, 196, 284, 286, 343, 344, 352, 372, 406, 424, 513, 563.
Sober, 102.
Somerville, 130.
Sordis, 207.
Soule, 235.
Southwick, 350.
Spahr, 118.
Spalding, 170.
Spangler, 319, 326, 360, 430, 687.
Spayd, 321.
Spear, 270, 448.
Speed, 370.
Speer, 3, 208, 387, 593, 658.
Spencer, 161, 164, 664.
Spinning, 658.
Sponsler, 153, 352.
Sprigg, 592.
Spring, 588.
Springer, 549.

Index of Surnames.

Spycker, 160, 675.
St. Clair, 501, 587, 633, 675, 725, 742.
Stabin, 122.
Stabler, 702.
Stacy, 115.
Stackhouse, 428, 436, 568.
Stackpole, 347, 603.
Stahl, 341, 344.
Stanley, 457.
Stansberry, 596.
Stark, 73.
Stauffer, 57, 500, 501, 686, 687, 767.
Steedman, 339, 749, 750.
Steel or Steele, 44, 48, 189, 233, 237, 244, 294, 327, 442, 443, 448, 457, 458, 467, 470, 666.
Stees, 305, 320.
Stehley, 306.
Stein, 564.
Steiner, 121, 122, 558, 564.
Steinman, 497, 744.
Stelling, 363.
Stem, 100.
Stenger, 690.
Stephen, 3, 5, 191, 193.
Stephens, 170.
Stephenson, 166, 596, 604.
Sterling, 197, 198.
Sterrett, 40, 388, 390, 397, 449.
Sterry, 430.
Stevens, 236, 237, 256, 494.
Stevenson, 134, 216, 373, 589, 590, 663, 754, 769.
STEWART, 1, 2, 28, 29, 70, 71, 73, 214, 219, 256, 270, 340, 878, 395, 445, 450, 501, 502, 527, 626, 645–667, 742.
Stidham, 17.
Stilz, 723.
Stimmel, 684.
Stine, 357, 359.
Stinson, 230.
Stirling, 27.
Stobo, 552.
Stockman, 606, 610.
Stockton, 223.
Stoddard, 237.
Stoehr, 304, 505.
Stoek, 203.
Stone, 76, 347, 557.
Story, 287.
Stouch, 348.
Stough, 513, 524, 768.
Stout, 329.
Stover, 306.
Stowe, 691.
Strain, 3, 157, 492.
Stranahan, 684.
Straughan, 328.
Strasser, 263.
Strawbridge, 114.
Streeper, 47.
Street, 234, 242.
Strine, 178, 344.
Strock, 690.
Strode, 386.
Stroh, 38, 41.
Strohm, 3, 675, 677.
Stroman, 512.
Stroud, 45.
Stroup, 341, 346.
Strumpf, 396.
Stryker, 655.
Stuart, 236, 254.
Stubs, 521.
Studebaker, 360.
Sturgeon, 38, 75, 76, 148, 224, 492, 612, 617, 671, 673.
Sturges, 344.
Sturgis, 616.
Sturtz, 617.
Stuveysant, 15, 16.
Sullivan, 548.
Summers, 212, 516.
Sumner, 249, 254, 255, 259, 700.
Sutherland, 381.
Suydam, 398.
Swaim, 172, 173, 184.
SWAN, 62, 78, 79, 631, 635, 668–673.
Swartz, 34, 305, 310, 312, 362, 445.
Swartzwelder, 542.
Swearingen, 538.
Sweeny, 305.
Swenck, 122.
Swift, 125.
Swingley, 4.
Swisher, 752.
Swoope, 126, 135, 142.
Sylvester, 666.
Symonds, 437.

Tabret, 344.
Taggart, 228.
Tannehill, 592, 762.
Tapley, 757.
Tash, 380.
Tate, 30, 31, 582, 592.
Taylor, 67, 153, 154, 187, 192, 214, 354, 390, 449, 456, 546, 670, 678, 743.
Teall, 260.
Templeton, 201, 409, 415, 580, 646, 649.
Templin, 730.
Tennet, 767.
Tennent, 118.
Terry, 363, 396.
Tewksbury, 251.
Thaker, 512.
Thaw, 69, 397.

Thedus, 720.
Thielmann, 167.
Thom, 292.
THOMAS, 161, 162, 213, 267, 339, 345, 390, 495, 512, 674 – 693, 699, 745.
Thomason, 324, 330, 340.
Thompson, 21, 29, 39, 42, 126, 156, 162, 168, 191, 193, 194, 210, 266, 268, 327, 372, 381, 418, 448, 449, 506, 510, 512, 521, 522, 612, 646, 669, 692, 743.
Thomrianie, 720.
Thorn, 161, 165, 370, 613, 615, 663.
Thornburg, 512.
Thurman, 483, 487.
Tice, 200, 212.
Tidd, 757, 759.
Tiernan, 663.
Tilghman, 286.
Till, 263.
Tillman, 479.
Tillson, 580.
Tilly, 219.
Timberlake, 249.
Tindall, 662.
Tisserand, 474.
Tittle, 436.
Tobias, 692.
Todd, 9, 43, 70, 90, 117, 118, 155, 224, 402, 699.
Tomb, 594, 595.
Torbert, 171, 747.
Torbut, 262.
Torrance, 272, 277.
Torrence, 75.
Totten, 154, 434.
Towles, 84, 94, 363.
Townsend, 237, 350, 397, 617, 621.

Trabue, 456.
Tracy, 396, 405.
Trauger, 509, 520.
Tressler, 343, 348.
Tripp, 589.
Tripple, 753.
Trimble, 367, 744.
Tritt, 880.
Trosell, 514.
Trout, 572.
Troutner, 685.
Trowbridge, 459.
Truesdale, 621.
Truman, 117.
Tryon, 45.
Turbett, 391.
Tucker, 296, 511.
Tugard, 239.
Turley, 95.
Turner, 139, 220, 288, 314, 515.
Tuttle, 616, 664, 665.
Tyler, 53, 700.

Uhland, 304.
Uhler, 267, 675.
Ulmer, 120.
Ulp, 454, 466.
Uncles, 593.
Unger, 268, 719.
Updegraff, 767.
Urie, 506, 509, 510, 511, 518, 520, 521, 585, 587.

Vail, 2.
Valentine, 396, 401.
Valodin, 643.
Van Campen, 219.
Van Cleve, 3, 5.
Vance, 361, 449.
Vandevander, 345, 536.
Vandevanter, 754.
Van Doren, 4.
Van Dyke, 139.
Van Dwyn, 235.
Van Eman, 129.

Van Gundy, 86.
Van Horn, 103, 106, 150, 151.
Van Hook, 321.
Van Riper, 2.
Vanvalzah, 596, 599.
VanValkenburgh, 142.
Van Vliet, 429.
Van Wicklen, 483.
Vaughan, 220.
Vaughn, 326.
Veach, 636.
Veith, 120, 122.
Venable, 457.
Verdi, 589.
Vest, 519.
Vickers, 11.
Viers, 514, 524.
Vincent, 397, 465, 494.
Vogelsang, 168.
Von Buskirk, 327.
Vondersmith, 344.
Von Treupel, 163, 167, 236, 237.
Voorhees, 577, 639.

Waddell, 458, 459, 467.
Waddle, 753.
Wade, 134, 174, 233, 235.
Wagner, 163, 723.
Wainwright, 139.
Waldschmid, 99.
Walker, 20, 85, 134, 290, 293, 375, 443, 458, 483, 569, 605, 638, 640, 647, 650, 658, 692, 709 – 713, 742, 747.
Wall, 202.
WALLACE, 69, 72, 75, 89, 113, 114, 146, 153, 191, 209, 245, 264, 330, 332, 333, 334– 336, 414, 423, 430– 432, 479, 492, 680, 694 – 718, 753, 769.

Index of Surnames. 797

Wallingford, 553, 555.
Walsh, 87.
Walter, 688.
Walters, 173.
Walton, 662.
Wanner. 99.
Ward, 29, 756.
Wardwell, 764.
Waream, 263.
Warford, 434, 439.
Warner, 600.
Warnock, 751.
Warren, 418, 457.
Warring, 517.
Washburn, 330, 511, 522.
Washington, 268, 303, 389, 541, 550, 741, 761.
Waters, 19.
Watson, 20, 58, 84, 91, 130, 139, 179, 262, 286, 297, 298, 359, 388, 465, 585, 597, 625, 655, 757.
Watts, 149, 276.
Wattson, 702.
Waugh, 32, 87, 94, 95, 96, 167, 364, 710, 737.
Weakley, 31.
Weatherly, 54.
Weaver, 304, 494, 516, 681, 727.
Webb, 165, 171.
Webber, 170.
Webster, 188, 189, 387, 493, 508. 598.
Weed, 464.
Weems, 183.
Weidler, 310.
Weidman, 567, 568.
Weigle, 687.
WEIR, 703–707, 724.
Weiser, 558, 559, 564.
Weiss, 495, 674, 759, 762.

Weizgarver, 252.
Welker, 44.
Wellendorf, 589.
Welles, 252.
Wells, 92, 227, 343, 501.
Welsh, 129, 254, 726.
Welshofer, 357.
Welty, 498.
Wenner, 504.
Wesley, 282.
West, 17, 19, 106, 753.
Westbrook, 267.
Westcott, 216.
Wetherill, 567.
Wheat, 184.
Wheaton, 280.
Wheeler, 619, 622, 656, 662.
White, 80, 86, 192. 200, 203, 281, 286, 456, 585, 669, 671, 672, 745.
Whitehead, 584.
Whitehill, 149, 151, 209, 321, 422, 564, 570.
Whitely, 253.
Whiteside, 91, 191, 199, 209, 219, 319, 639.
Whitfield, 188.
Whitlock, 164.
Whitmore, 690.
Whitney, 220, 683.
Whittlesey, 396.
Wickard, 516, 517.
Wickersham, 312.
Wickivere, 418.
Widener, 558.
WIESTLING, 112, 704, 706, 719–732.
Wiggin, 441, 444.
WIGGINS, 733–739.
Wikoff, 151.
Wilcox, 376.
Wilde, 720.

Willar, 751.
Willard, 760.
Willets, 370.
Wiley, 517.
Willis, 421.
Wilmoth, 654.
Wilhelm, 355, 363, 364.
Wilkins, 218, 546, 581, 588, 589.
Willett, 53, 531.
Williams, 59, 114, 115, 168, 236, 251, 252, 281, 331, 332, 424, 433, 497, 515, 581, 587, 601, 617, 693, 737, 770, 772.
Williamson, 31, 56, 179, 419, 427, 443, 492, 493, 596, 602, 743.
Willis, 150, 153, 616, 617, 621.
Wills, 694, 699–702.
Willson, 264.
WILSON, 2, 13, 22, 64, 79, 82, 114, 152, 165, 191, 197, 201, 214, 223, 264, 265, 295, 296, 297, 300, 318, 350, 367, 374, 379, 380, 382, 398, 399, 515, 546, 575, 596, 599, 629, 633, 647, 652, 655, 659, 670, 679, 740 – 755, 757, 758, 771.
Winchel, 696, 698.
Winebrenner, 282, 362, 626, 679.
Wing, 204.
Wingerd, 732, 766.
Winn, 128.
Winship, 756–759.
Winslow, 760.
Winter, 163, 741.
Winters, 4.

Winthrop, 434.
Wiseman, 613.
Wishart. 592.
Wistar, 253.
Wister, 103.
Witte, 349.
Witman, 564, 570, 573, 574.
Withers, 724.
Witherspoon, 250.
Withrow, 752.
Wolcott, 242.
Wolf, 54, 57, 130, 495, 529, 623, 688, 763.
Wolfe, 632.
Wolfersberger, 307, 675, 677.
Wonderly, 69.
Wood, 103, 129, 225, 226, 464, 494, 569.
Woodburn, 509, 616.
Woodhull. 429.
Woodle, 177.
Woodrow, 443.
Woolverton, 29.
Woods, 214, 215, 218, 228, 229, 387.

Wool, 700.
Work, 270, 275.
Workman, 512.
Worrall, 197, 324, 424.
Worst, 515.
Worth, 728.
Wray, 143, 281.
Wrenshall, 542.
Wright, 38, 82, 149, 165, 169, 170, 173, 222, 232, 233, 249, 258, 261, 271, 396, 404, 443, 457, 465, 760.
Wyckoff, 436.
WYETH, 756–764.
Wylie, 229, 612, 613.
Wynkoop, 641.

Yalden, 401.
Yale, 77.
Yeomans, 484.
Yerkes, 48, 50, 51.
Yesler, 686.
Yetter, 110.

Yingling, 97.
Young, 1, 128, 137, 185, 243, 250, 252, 346, 500, 585, 629, 700, 741, 754.
Youngblood, 506, 507.
Younghaus, 719.
Youngman, 559.
Youse, 722–728.
Youtz, 617.
Yüng, 167.
Yunker, 120.

Zacharias, 311.
Zahm, 344.
Zeagly, 681.
Zedwick, 496.
Zeller, 120, 134.
Ziegler, 348, 357, 358, 687, 688, 731, 738.
Zimmerman, 307, 643, 678.
Zinn, 304, 306, 311, 312.
Zoll, 92.
Zollinger, 361.

www.ingramcontent.com/pod-product-compliance
Lightning Source LLC
Chambersburg PA
CBHW052106010526
44111CB00036B/1487